12-12-98

THE

JG 26

WAR DIARY

VOLUME 2: 1943-1945

DONALD L. CALDWELL

GRUB STREET · LONDON

Published by
Grub Street
The Basement
10 Chivalry Road
London SW11 1HT

Copyright © 1998 Grub Street, London
Text copyright © Donald Caldwell

Maps by Graeme Andrew

British Library Cataloguing in Publication Data
Caldwell, Donald L.
The JG 26 war diary
Vol. 2: 1943–1945
1. Germany. Luftwaffe. Jagdgeschwader 26 ""Schlageter" – History
2. World War, 1943–1945 – Aerials operations, German
I. Title
940.5'44'943

ISBN 1-898697-86-8

Typeset by Pearl Graphics, Hemel Hempstead

Printed and bound in Great Britain by
Biddles Ltd, Guildford and King's Lynn

**Dedicated to the memory of
Adolf Galland,
the guiding force of Jagdgeschwader 26
and the German fighter arm**

CONTENTS

PREFACE iv

ACKNOWLEDGEMENTS v

1. THE LAST PAUSE (January-May 1943) 7
2. THE EASTERN FRONT (January-July 1943) 65
3. BLOCKING THE TIDE (June-August 1943) 97
4. THE WAR OF ATTRITION (September-December 1943) 147
5. THE AIR WAR IS LOST (January-May 1944) 195
6. THE INVASION FRONT (June-August 1944) 265
7. DEFENSE OF THE GERMAN BORDER (September-December 1944) 339
8. GOTTERDÄMMERUNG (January-8 May 1945) 403

GLOSSARIES 481
   1. ABBREVIATIONS
   2. AVIATION TERMS
   3. GERMAN TERMS

APPENDICES

I. ORGANIZATION AND STRENGTH 1943-1945 483
II. UNIT COMMANDERS 1943-1945 485
III. BASES 1943-1945 488
IV. VICTORY CLAIMS: 1939-1945 491
V. CASUALTIES: 1939-1945 531

SOURCES 551

BIBLIOGRAPHY 557

MAPS

   THE PAS DE CALAIS 561
   THE EASTERN FRONT 562
   MISSION MAPS: 5 APR 1943; 30 JULY 1943; 17 AUG 1943 (REGENSBURG); 563–9
   17 AUG 1943 (SCHWEINFURT); 11 FEB 1944; 6 MAR 1944; 13 APR 1944
   OPERATION BODENPLATTE (1 JAN 1945) 570

INDEX 571

PREFACE

This volume completes this author's comprehensive history of Jagdgeschwader 26 (JG 26). The book takes JG 26 from the beginning of 1943, when the American 8th Air Force first began to make its presence felt over occupied Europe, until the end of the war, which found the remnants of the Jagdgeschwader flying daily missions from bases near the German-Danish border. Although always outnumbered, JG 26 had managed to dominate the airspace over northern France in 1941 and 1942 by skillfully choosing the time and place for its battles with the Royal Air Force. But in 1943 the destructive potential of the American B-17s and B-24s took away that option; they had to be attacked under all circumstances. The American fighter escorts, which JG 26 defeated easily in their early encounters, grew rapidly in numbers and experience. Trapped in a war of attrition that it could not win, the Luftwaffe, and with it JG 26, began an inexorable decline. The men of JG 26 fought on, scoring some spectacular, if isolated, successes over Normandy, Arnhem, and the Ardennes. The unit's replacement pilots were so poorly trained and badly outnumbered that most were killed before their fifth mission, but the survivors continued their struggle until the bitter end. My interviews with these men, who describe their secrets of survival in the bluntest of terms and struggle to explain why they continued to fight for a lost, and evil, cause, are among the unique aspects of the book. All of the quotations from German pilots are being published here for the first time.

The main body of the book is a daily account of the wing's activities—similar in format to a war diary, but one which takes full advantage of Allied records and post-war research to give an accurate, well-balanced presentation. As only two of the ca. forty volumes of the unit's official diary survived the war, the creation of a daily combat log was not simply a matter of copying records, but required careful comparison of Allied documents, especially those derived from radio intelligence, with the limited material available from Germany. This book is based largely on primary documentation obtained from the unit's veterans and on archival material from Germany, the UK, and the USA. The first results of my thirteen years of research on the Luftwaffe were a general history and a photographic history of JG 26 which were so popular with that unit's veterans that they gave me unprecedented access to their personal documents and photo collections. The present book is thus new in every respect. In common with my previous works, great care has been taken to place each event in its historical context, to maximize readability and understanding. The war of wits between the 8th Air Force mission planners and the Luftwaffe fighter controllers is presented here in greater detail than ever before, and should be of interest to all students of the European air war.

I take full responsibility for the book's errors of commission and omission, and welcome correspondence with anyone who has corrections or other information to share concerning JG 26 or any other aspect of Second World War aviation. My next project is a jointly-authored general study of the German air defenses, which will fill the last major gap in the published history of the air war over Western Europe.

Donald Caldwell
Lake Jackson, Texas
May, 1998

ACKNOWLEDGEMENTS

This book could not have been written without the help of the Luftwaffe veterans, whose numbers are unfortunately but inevitably growing fewer by the year. Those who provided material for this volume during the thirteen years of its preparation were: Hermann Ayerle, Hans Backhaus, Herr Balloff, Ernst Battmer, F. W. Bauerhenne, Günther Blömertz, Erich Burmeister, Peter Crump, Gottfried Dietze, Helmut Dölling, Georg Eder, Günther Egli, Xaver Ellenrieder, Adolf Galland, Heinz Gehrke, Georg Genth, Adolf Glunz, Heinz Gomann, Hans Hartigs, Karl-Heinz Hartmann, Lieselotte Hays, Alfred Heckmann, Heinrich Heuser, Jörg Kiefner, Gerhard Kroll, Heinrich Kirch, Walter Krupinski, Ottomar Kruse, Hans Kukla, Erwin Leykauf, Werner Molge, Johannes Naumann, Josef Niesmak, Karl-Heinz Ossenkop, Dietrich Peltz, Wolfgang Polster, Hans Prager, Günther Rey, Jan Schild, Gottfried Schmidt, Walter Schmidt, Hans Schöndorf, Gerhard Schöpfel, Rolf Schrödter, Waldemar Söffing, Georg Spies, Otto Stammberger, Gerhard Strasen, Walter Stumpf, Siegfried Sy, Walter Tepperis, Erhard Tippe, Fritz Ungar, and Gerd Wiegand.

Families of the following deceased veterans also provided photographs and/or information: Artur Beese, Joachim Günther, Erich Jauer, Heinz Kemethmüller, Josef Priller, Herr Reimers, and Bernhard Wollnitz.

Information from the "other side" is a necessary component of any balanced military history. My thanks go to the following American airmen for their cooperation: William Beyer, William Binnebose, George Brooks, Gerald Brown, Bill Bryan, Ed Burford, William Capron, George Carpenter, H. H. Christensen, Elmer Clarey, McCauley Clark, Darrell Cramer, Jack Curtis, Bernard Dennehy, James Doyle, Frank Klibbe, Walker Mahurin, Joe Matte, Merle Olmsted, Bob O'Neill, Chet Patterson, Steve Pisanos, Herman Schonenberg, Robert Seelos, Luther Smith, John Truluck, George Vanden Heuvel, Chuck Yeager, and Hubert Zemke.

Of equal help were the following Allied pilots: Ray Danzey (RNZAF), Tony Gaze (RAAF), Ted Hall (RAAF), Johnnie Johnson (RAF), Dan Nowosielski (RAF), Rod Smith (RCAF), and Jack Stafford (RNZAF).

The fraternity of airwar historians and enthusiasts has continued to help me with generous gifts of time, information, leads, photographs, and/or photographic assistance; the list of their names keeps growing from book to book. I wish to acknowledge: Arno Abendroth, Eric-Jan Bakker, Charlotte Baldridge, Bernd Barbas, Rémi Baudru, John Beaman, Christer Bergström, Steve Blake, Winfried Bock, Johan Breugelmans, David Brown, N. P. Buswell, Steve Coates, Philippe Couderchon, A. J. Cranston, Jim Crow, Curt Deatrick, Cynrick De Decker, Arie De Jong, Ivo De Jong, Wim de Meester, Joachim Eickhoff, Pat Eriksson, Russ Fahey, Stephen Fochuk, John Foreman, Robert Forsyth, Norman Franks, Garry Fry, Steve Gotts, John Gray, Peter Grimm, Russell Guest, J. A. Hey, Carl Hildebrandt, Janet Howard, Jim Kitchens, Pierre Koreman, Malcolm Laing, Joss Leclercq, Richard Lutz, John Manrho, Wojtek Matusiak, Lex McAulay, Ian McLachlan, Michael Meyer, Andrey Mikhailov, Kees Mol, Eric Mombeek, George Morrison, Michal Mucha, Henk Nootenboom, Werner Oeltjebruns, Frank Olynk, Leslie Owen, Jim Perry, Peter Petrick, Gert Poelchau, Jochen Prien, Ron Pütz, W. G. Ramsey, Lorenz Rasse, Jean-Louis Roba, Maurice Rowe, Brown Ryle, Dilip Sarkar, Chris Shores, Hugh Smallwood, Barry Smith, Paul Sortehaug, Sam Sox, Klaes Sundin, Günter Sunderman, Helmut Terbeck, Chris Thomas, Richard Tiedeman, Etienne Vanackere, Dominique van den Broucke, Rob van den Nieuwendijk, Frans van Humbeek, Erwin van Loo, Lothair Vanoverbeke, Luc Vervoort, Dave Wadman, Pierre Watteeuw, and Tony Wood.

The Bundesarchiv-Bildarchiv (Koblenz), the Bundesarchiv-Militärarchiv (Freiburg), and the Canadian Public Archives have granted permission to reprint photographs from their collections.

I wish to acknowledge the help given me by the professional staffs of the British Public Records Office, the Bundesarchiv-Militärarchiv (Freiburg), the Lake Jackson Public Library, the Auburn University Library, and the United States Air Force Historical Research Agency.

To any helpers whose names I have left out, please accept my apologies and my implied thanks. And as always, my gratitude goes to my wife Jackie for her constant patience and support.

Chapter One

THE LAST PAUSE

January - May 1943

1 January

The winter of 1942-1943 was proving to be a quiet one along the English Channel. These next several months would be the last period of relative inactivity experienced by Jagdgeschwader 26 "Schlageter", JG 26, for the rest of the war. Major Gerhard Schöpfel's Geschwader Stab was packing up at St. Omer-Wizernes and preparing to move to Lille-Vendeville. Major Johannes Seifert's First Gruppe (I/JG 26) and its three Staffeln, the 1st, 2nd, and 3rd, were at Wizernes, as was the 10th (Jagdbomber) Staffel, the Jabostaffel (fighter-bomber squadron), which reported administratively to Seifert. Hptm. Conny Meyer's Second Gruppe, the famous "Abbeville Boys", was at Abbeville-Drucat with the 5th and 6th Staffeln. Hptm. Josef "Pips" Priller's Third Gruppe was at Wevelgem, on the outskirts of Courtrai in western Belgium, with the 7th and 8th Staffeln. The newly-authorized 11th Staffel, which Major Schöpfel apparently planned to use as an operational training unit, was organizing at Wevelgem. The 4th Staffel, from the Second Gruppe, and the 9th Staffel, from the Third, were based south of Rouen at Beaumont-le-Roger. This was in the area of operations of JG 2; the two Staffeln were substituting for II/JG 2, which was in Tunisia, and reported to Jafü 3 (Jagdfliegerführer 3, or Fighter Control Unit 3). The rest of JG 26 formed the day fighter component of Jafü 2.

Both the Allies and the Luftwaffe had transferred units to North Africa, and were lower in operational strength than the previous autumn. The American 8th Bomber Command could muster only four inexperienced groups of B-17s and two low-strength groups of B-24s. The 8th Fighter Command had only one unit on strength – the Spitfire-equipped 4th Fighter Group, which had been formed from the RAF's three Eagle Squadrons. The RAF had sent many of its fighter squadrons abroad, but its tactical bomber command, No. 2 Group, had replaced its obsolete Blenheims with more modern Bostons, Venturas, and Mosquitoes, and was prepared to resume flying missions to the Continent. The RAF's Fighter Command was available to escort both American and British bombers, but was limited to the coastal regions by the short range of its Spitfires. The newest British fighter, the Hawker Typhoon, was unsuitable for escort work, but could be valuable at low level, as JG 26 would soon learn.

The Luftwaffe units based in the westernmost part of the Third Reich were part of Generalfeldmarschall Hugo von Sperrle's Luftflotte 3, headquartered in Paris. The western day fighters, and a few night fighters, were administered by Jagddivision 3, commanded by Genmaj. Junck in Metz. Tactical control was exercised by the Jagdfliegerführer (fighter control unit or units), abbreviated as Jafü. JG 26 was usually under the control of Jafü 2, commanded by Obst. Vieck in St. Pol, which was responsible for defending the Pas de Calais and the industrial areas of northeastern France and western Belgium. JG 2, the "Richthofen" Geschwader, was the only other day fighter unit in France. It was split between Jafü 3, which defended northern France and the approaches to Paris, and Jafü Brittany, which watched over that peninsula's submarine bases. Jafü command and control procedures had been developed and perfected versus the RAF's day offensives in 1941-1942. The German fighter aircraft and pilots were at this time fully the equal of their opponents. The defenses were stretched very thin, but morale was high. They were outnumbered nearly every time they took to the air, but until the arrival of the Americans they had been required to attack only when conditions were in their favor, and they had scored a large number of victories over the RAF in 1941-1942 at low cost to themselves.

Today, bad weather kept the Allies on their side of the Channel, allowing most of the pilots to sleep off their New Year's hangovers. During the previous summer and autumn each Staffel had flown to a dispersal field every morning, returning to their home field and quarters at nightfall. This practice was not carried out during the winter months owing to the short period of daylight and the prevalent poor weather, and formation flights to other airfields were only made in response to direct, or perceived, threats. One Staffel from each Gruppe was kept at readiness; the pilots of one Schwarm from each had to sit in their aircraft at *Stizbereitschaft*, or cockpit readiness, while the other duty pilots waited out the day in the Gruppe ready rooms. The pilots of the other Staffeln lounged in their quarters or in the *Casinos* (pilots' messes.) The ground staffs went about their daily routines. The *Schwarzemänner* (black men) of the ground crews tinkered with the aircraft. The Geschwader was equipped primarily with Fw 190s, and was almost up to its authorized strength. The Stab had five Fw 190A-4s on hand, with all five operational – abbreviated on the strength returns as 5 (5) aircraft. The First Gruppe reported a strength of 33 (26) Fw 190A-4s. The Second Gruppe had 33 (26) Fw 190A-4s and 11 (7) Bf 109G-4s; the Third Gruppe, 35 (29) Fw 190A-4s and 3 (2) Bf 109G-1s and G-4s. The Jabostaffel reported a strength of 14 (13) bomb-carrying Fw 190A-4/U3s; the 11th Staffel had 12 (8) Bf 109G-4s and G-1s.

2 January

Genmaj. Adolf Galland, the *General der Jagdflieger* (General of the Fighter Arm) in Berlin, had celebrated Christmas with JG 26, his former unit. The visit, ostensibly a pleasure trip, had unforeseen consequences for several Geschwader officers. Galland had complained for months about the poor results obtained by the Geschwader against the American heavy bombers, and spent Christmas day quietly sizing up the formation leaders. Orders arrived today for the Second Gruppe Kommandeur, Hptm. Meyer, transferring him to a training unit. His replacement was Oblt. Wilhelm-Ferdinand "Wutz" Galland of the 6th Staffel, the general's younger brother. Wutz was only nineteen months out of flight school, and his meteoric rise within the Geschwader would certainly have led to complaints of favoritism had he not been a popular commander as well as a gifted combat pilot, already claiming twenty-one victories.

The only combat flights made by the Geschwader were put up by the two Staffeln west of the Seine, the 4th and the 9th, in response to reports of two small Allied formations above the Channel. No contact was made. The Second and Third Gruppen took the opportunity to train. Several of the Second Gruppe pilots made flights in brand-new Bf 109G-4s, which were supposed to replace their Fw 190s over the next month. Hptm. Priller took his Third Gruppe aloft for formation practice.

3 January

The 8th Bomber Command bombed the submarine pens at St. Nazaire, and lost seven B-17s shot down and 44 B-17s plus three B-24s damaged by fighters and ground fire. The fighter opposition was provided by III/JG 2, which claimed fifteen victories, all confirmed. The two JG 26 Staffeln took off as a reserve force, but did not make contact. They did, however, succeed in attracting the attention of the Spitfire wing tasked with escorting the bombers home, and the RAF fighters failed to contact the bombers. The JG 26 Staffeln on the Pas de Calais were held on the ground, while the 8th Staffel was scrambled from Wevelgem, probably against a diversion, but did not make contact.

I/JG 27 had been rested briefly at Krefeld after its long service in North Africa. Today the Gruppe began transferring to Évreux, where it would constitute a third

A Fw 190A-4/U3 of 10(Jabo)/JG 26, photographed at St. Omer-Wizernes on 8 January. *(Meyer)*

Gruppe for JG 2 and eventually release the two JG 26 Staffeln to return to their home Gruppen.

Lt. Horst Sternberg replaced Oblt. Galland in command of 5/JG 26. Sternberg, a professional officer, had joined the 5th Staffel in March 1941, right out of flight training. He was made a *Staffelführer*, or Staffel leader, which was a probationary or temporary appointment, rather than a full-fledged *Staffelkapitän*. This was becoming the standard procedure in the *Jagdwaffe* (German Fighter Arm). The Luftwaffe still had no training course for Staffel commanders; the skills had to be picked up on the job. Successful Staffelführer were eventually promoted to Staffelkapitäne, with the appropriate ceremony.

4 January
The only Geschwader combat flight was made by the Jabostaffel, which sent a single Schwarm to bomb Winchelsea in Sussex. The wing of Fw. Herbert Müller's Focke-Wulf hit an overhead cable, and he crashed to his death in England.

5 January
Hptm. Walter Hoeckner and Obfw. Alfred Heckmann, both experienced fighters from the Eastern Front, joined the 1st Staffel after tours as instructors. Hoeckner was named Staffelkapitän, displacing Oblt. Franz Nels, who transferred to the Third Gruppe.

8 January
At a conference for fighter leaders in Berlin, Genmaj. Galland presented Major Schöpfel and Major Priller with three startling pieces of information. First, in the next few weeks JG 26 was to begin transferring to Russia, trading bases with the "Green Heart" Geschwader, JG 54, on the northern sector of the Eastern Front. Second, Schöpfel was to leave the Geschwader effective 10 January to become Ia (Operations Officer) at Jafü Brittany, the fighter control unit defending the submarine bases. Third, Priller would replace Schöpfel as JG 26 Kommodore. Pips Priller was the most successful pilot then in the Geschwader, with eighty-one air victories, and was thus, by the simplistic criteria followed by the Luftwaffe, ready for a higher command. Priller's other qualifications were more important to General Galland, however. In addition to being a proven combat leader, he was energetic, quick-witted, outspoken, and innovative – all qualities shared by Galland himself. Priller's effervescent and good-natured public persona was totally unlike Galland's, but it masked a thorough-going professionalism. Galland felt that Priller was the perfect choice to jolt his favorite Geschwader back onto the course he had charted for it in 1940 and 1941.

The Third Gruppe flew the only Geschwader combat mission for the day. It was scrambled from Wevelgem at 1207 to intercept an Allied formation plotted between Calais and Dunkirk, but failed to make contact.

The Second Gruppe began transferring in stages from Abbeville-Drucat, its base for all of 1942, east to Vitry-en-Artois, in the Douai industrial district. The two airfields were of equivalent size and facilities; each had three concrete runways. But Abbeville, fifteen miles from the mouth of the Somme, was now too exposed. Its location was known to every pilot in England, and it was a favorite alternate target for Allied medium bombers and fighter-bombers. Vitry was farther inland, beneath the direct route between England and the Ruhr. It was closer to the bases of the rest of the Geschwader, and it was hoped that the Jafü 2 controllers would thus be able to assemble larger formations to oppose the American heavy bombers when they began bombing Germany, which now seemed inevitable.

The 9th Staffel also changed bases today, leaving Beaumont-le-Roger in mid-afternoon. But instead of rejoining the Third Gruppe at Wevelgem, it was sent farther west, to Vannes on the southern coast of Brittany, as reinforcement for III/JG 2, the principal fighter force defending the submarine bases on the peninsula.

9 January

The RAF's first Circus of the year targeted Abbeville-Drucat, punctuating the Luftwaffe's decision to leave it. (A Circus was a large-scale fighter sweep containing a small number of light bombers as bait to attract the German fighters.) All three Gruppen scrambled between 1324 and 1327. The Second Gruppe, still flying from Abbeville, met the Spitfire IX Wing over the Somme Estuary, and claimed two Spitfires for the loss of Uffz. Ludwig Roth of the 5th Staffel. Only one Spitfire went down; it was piloted by S/L Moreau of No. 340 Sqd. (Free French). Moreau's Spitfire was seen to crash in the sea, and the Germans sent out rescue boats, but without success. The First Gruppe tangled with another formation of Spitfires farther north, over Marquise. Lt. Wolfgang Neu of the 3rd Staffel bailed out of his Focke-Wulf with injuries; the Gruppe claimed no victories. Part of the Third Gruppe also made contact with the RAF force, but without result. The dozen Bostons with the Circus turned back without bombing, as the weather had turned bad.

As rapidly as possible, the RAF was replacing the remaining Spitfire Vs in its front-line fighter squadrons with Spitfire IXs. The latest variant, the Spitfire IXB, had a 1400 HP Merlin 61 engine with a two-stage, two-speed supercharger that automatically provided this power at 20,000 feet (6100 meters). The RAF had tested their new fighter against a captured Fw 190A-3 the previous autumn. The head-to-head flyoff was conducted at RAF Farnborough by two noted pilots, W/C Jamie Rankin and P/O Hugh Godefroy. Godefroy described the test in his autobiography, *Lucky 13:*

> "The things that I discovered about the comparative performance of the Spitfire IXB proved invaluable to me in the next two years. In level flight and high speed, the 190 flew slightly nose down. With a higher wing loading than the Spitfire, the 190's maximum rate of climb was attained at an air speed of about 240 mph [386 km/h]. The Spitfire IXB's maximum rate of climb was attained at 160 mph [257 km/h]. Thus, if you were foolish enough to try to follow the 190 in full throttle climb at the same angle, you would soon find out that he was above you. On the other hand, if you pulled away and held the Spitfire at an airspeed of 160, you would climb at a much steeper angle and end up with a height advantage. Below 20,000 feet in speed runs there wasn't much in it either way. But above 20,000 feet, the Spitfire IXB's second blower kicked in, giving it the advantage. The Spitfire could not compete with the rate of roll of a Fw 190. If Jamie followed the favourite German technique of flicking over on his back and going down, he would pull away from me in the first 2-3000 feet [6-900 meters]. After that, the Spitfire IXB could gradually catch him. Jamie never bothered trying to turn inside me in my Spitfire. Both of us knew that it wasn't possible. That was one advantage that all British fighters enjoyed. At the end of the trials, when I added up the pluses and minuses, I came to the conclusion that I would still prefer a Spitfire IXB."

The *Kanalgeschwader* (Jagdgeschwader based on the English Channel) had by now replaced their Fw 190A-3s with Fw 190A-4s, which had water-methanol injection that increased its top speed by 20 mph up to 5700 meters (18,700 feet), the rated altitude of its BMW 801D radial engine. The Fw 190A-4 thus had the edge in speed over the Spitfire IX up to that altitude. Godefroy's observation that the Spitfire was better above 20,000 feet was true for the rest of the war with respect to the radial-engine Fw 190A, owing to the Merlin engine's superior supercharger.

10 January

Major Priller's first day as Kommodore was spent finalizing plans for the movement of the Geschwader to Russia. The exchange with JG 54 was to take place by Gruppen and Staffeln, staged to ensure continuity of the defensive coverage in the West. Only the pilots, key staff members, and certain items of critical equipment were to move. The maintenance crews, aircraft, and other equipment were to remain on their original bases. Major Seifert's First Gruppe would move first, in exchange for III/JG 54. Probably not coincidentally, the First Gruppe had recently acquired two experienced Eastern Front pilots, Hptm. Hoeckner and Obfw. Heckmann, the latter a Knight's Cross holder. The next unit to leave would be Oblt. Klaus Mietusch's 7th Staffel, in exchange for 4/JG 54. Mietusch's unit had picked up its own Eastern Front veteran in late December, when Obfw. Heinz Kemethmüller joined the Staffel. Kemethmüller had earned the Knight's Cross in Russia while a member of JG 3.

11 January

Routine patrols were flown, without contacting the few Allied aircraft that ventured across the Channel. The 4th Staffel Focke-Wulf of Uffz. Friedrich Rybosch overturned while landing on Beaumont-le-Roger, injuring Rybosch.

In a letter dated today, Adolf Galland offered some advice to his brother, the new Second Gruppe Kommandeur:

> "Succeeding a leader who did nothing, it is easy to get by, just doing a little. I put it to you again – fight like a lion for your Gruppe. The lowest enlisted men must feel that now they have a real leader; they will then go through fire for you. You can have no interests other than your Gruppe. You must have things in hand, for

Hptm. Wutz Galland in the cockpit of his Fw 190A, soon after he became Kommandeur of the Second Gruppe in January. *(Naumann via Roba)*

you face tasks that are totally new and very difficult. Nothing is obvious and nothing happens by itself. Everything must be talked through a hundred times and each success must be achieved by hard work – you have no suspicion of how much work one man can endure. No failure can be permitted that could have been avoided through more thorough planning, clearer orders, and crisper execution.

It is not wise to become too familiar with the Kapitäne and other officers. Nevertheless, one can be their best comrade. Your care and concern for the 'Cavaliers' need not cease. Uppermost in their minds must be – 'Our Kommandeur knows the cares and worries of even the lowest man; he is approachable by anyone; he only demands what is necessary, and never asks anything that he himself is not prepared to do...'"

Wutz Galland took most of his brother's admonitions to heart, and became a highly successful Gruppenkommandeur. His warm and open personality did not permit him to remain aloof from his men, however, and the few surviving "Cavaliers" have fond memories of his late-night drinking parties with them in the Casino.

Major Priller's replacement as Third Gruppe Kommandeur arrived at Wevelgem. He was Hptm. Fritz Geisshardt, who had received the Knight's Cross with Oak Leaves for his victories in Russia and had then been successful in the Mediterranean theater with I/JG 77 and II/JG 27. His arrogance grated on some Third Gruppe pilots, who felt that he treated his bare-necked brethren of the Kanalgeschwader with too much disdain – Knight's Crosses, the popular neckwear of the Jagdflieger, were not easy to earn in the West. But he was an extremely competent combat pilot, and it was apparent that the friend of JG 26 in Berlin was doing all he could to keep the quality of the unit's replacement pilots high.

13 January

A clear morning portended a very active day over the Pas de Calais. Uffz. Wilhelm Mayer of the 6th Staffel was up from Abbeville at 0835 on a reception flight for a morning recon mission to the English coast. Shortly after noon, RAF formations began crossing into France. The Third Gruppe was the first defensive unit up, at 1230, and made contact, but without result. At about this time a raider destroyed a First Gruppe Focke-Wulf on St. Omer-Arques. A Circus containing 18 Ventura bombers hit Abbeville just after the Second Gruppe had cleared the field at 1320. Several escorting Spitfires were holed by fighters of 11/JG 2, which had crossed the Somme Estuary to help out, and which lost one of their number to the Spits. The Second Gruppe had only one claim, and one casualty – and it was the same aircraft. Uffz. Johann Irlinger of the 6th Staffel, flying a Bf 109G-4, was shot down over the field and crashed in his airplane. According to Peter Crump, who was an eyewitness, Irlinger was shot down by his own Gruppenkommandeur, Hptm. Galland, who mistakenly identified the Messerschmitt as a Spitfire. The incident was of course cleaned up for the official records.

The major raid of the day was carried out by sixty-four 8th Bomber Command B-17s. Their target was the Fives locomotive factory in Lille. The First and Third Gruppen were scrambled well before the bombers crossed over Calais at 1413, and were able to form up in time to attack the lead bomber group, the 305th, before it reached the target. Fifteen B-17s were damaged, but only one went down, claimed by Uffz. Scheyda (3rd Staffel) and Obfw. Kemethmüller (7th Staffel). The fighters flew in line astern; each flight contained five or six aircraft. All attacks were made from dead ahead and on the same level as the bombers. Most fighters attacked singly, half-rolling into a split-S upon reaching the bomber formation. Only the 305th Group was attacked. Ten of its twenty-two Fortresses were damaged, some severely, but only one bomber failed to return to its base, a fact that caused considerable discussion in headquarters from Lille to Berlin. The bomber gunners claimed twenty-nine Fw 190s. This was later reduced to six, but in fact no Focke-Wulf suffered reportable damage.

The Spitfire escorts of the American 4th Fighter Group did not appear until the bombers had turned for home.

14 January

Three 4th Fighter Group Spitfires flew a Rhubarb, a low-level sweep by a small formation of fighters, along the coast west of Ostend. According to the American records, two Fw 190s appeared out of driving rain and were shot down into the sea. The victories were duly confirmed. There is no evidence from the German side of any flight activity at all on this day.

15 January

The day's only combat mission was a *Störangriff* (nuisance raid) on England by a Schwarm of Jabostaffel Focke-Wulfs. These raids specifically targeted civilians, and were not popular with the pilots of the Geschwader, one of whom, Peter Crump, called them a miserable waste of men and resources. Orders for these attacks, sometimes called *Vergeltungsangriffe* or vengeance raids, came directly from Berlin, usually soon after a damaging raid on Germany by RAF night bombers. A report of this mission has survived as part of the RAF interrogation report of Lt. Hermann Hoch, who was shot down and taken prisoner on 20 January. One must always be suspicious of such sources, but apparently Lt. Erwin Busch's Schwarm of Jabos was ordered to attack the town of Rye early in the morning. Before they reached England, they encountered a Royal Navy patrol boat and bombed it. As this was a violation of the mission orders, they were bombed up at Arques and sent out again. This time Lt. Busch was unable to retract his landing gear, so all four aircraft jettisoned their bombs and returned to base. Bombs were reloaded and the four took off once more, this time with a "close escort" of four 3rd Staffel Focke-Wulfs. By now it was mid-afternoon, and the British defenses were wide awake. The Jabos carried out their bombing mission, with unrecorded results. Uffz. Herbert Bremer, one of the escorts, was hit by antiaircraft fire before he crossed the coast at Rye, and crashed to his death in the Channel.

16 January

The 4th Staffel was scrambled from Beaumont in response to Allied air traffic over the Channel, but failed to make contact. Over the next three days the Staffel left Beaumont and returned to the Second Gruppe, which was still flying from Abbeville-Drucat. Routine patrols and training flights were flown by the rest of the Geschwader. During the week Lt. Paul Schauder left the 11th Staffel to join the Geschwader Stab; he was replaced as 11th Staffel Kapitän by Hptm. Werner Patz. Obfw. Hermann Schmeinl reported to the Geschwader and joined the Stab. Lt. Manfred Draheim and Uffz. Anton Kratzel reported for duty from flight training and were assigned to the First Gruppe. Obfw. Leopold Eichinger and Fw. Karl Willius left the 3rd Staffel for tours as instructors.

17 January

RAF Fighter Command Rhubarbs provoked Jafü 3, to the west of the Pas de Calais, and Jafü Holland-Ruhr, to the east of it, to send up small flights of interceptors, but the Jafü 2 controllers kept JG 26 on the ground.

RAF Bomber Command attacked Berlin for the first time in fourteen months. The German defenses were taken by surprise, and only the inability of most of the bombers to find the city prevented major damage. The Deutschlandhalle, the largest covered hall in Europe, was totally destroyed mere minutes after it was evacuated by a circus troupe and its audience of about ten thousand. The Luftwaffe was ordered to retaliate on London with the largest vengeance raid to date. It would take place on the 20th.

18 January

Patrols sent up by the First and Second Gruppen had no results, with one exception.

Fw. Hermann Meyer's 4th Staffel Schwarm was vectored to a pair of No. 4 Sqd. Mustang Is on a tactical reconnaissance mission over the Somme, and Meyer was able to shoot one down near Rue. Its pilot did not survive.

Lt. Walter Meyer of the 7th Staffel died in the Lille military hospital. Meyer had been a JG 26 NCO pilot since early 1940, and had claimed at least eighteen air victories before colliding with his wingman while taking off from Wevelgem on 11 October, 1942. Meyer entered the hospital with severe injuries, and never left it. The cause of his death was listed as tuberculosis.

19 January

Obfw. Glunz of the 4th Staffel was assigned the morning reconnaissance mission to England from Abbeville. He swept the English coast from Hastings to Dover in his Fw 190A-4 without incident. His Second Gruppe comrades continued training in their new Bf 109Gs. Uffz. Leo Müller wrecked one while attempting to take off from Abbeville; Müller was slightly injured.

The two tables below list the Geschwader's victory claims and casualties for the first through the nineteenth of January. The same format will be followed throughout the book. In the claims lists, "Claim #" is the sequential number of the pilot's claim as documented in the unit at the time or by later research, which has required adjustments in a few instances owing to delays by the German Air Ministry (RLM) in confirming or rejecting claims. Not all Third Gruppe claims can be assigned claim numbers, owing to the lack of a comprehensive list for the Gruppe. A blank in this column together with a "no" in the "Conf" column means that the claim was never filed by the unit, but has been established by contemporary evidence such as logbook entries, news releases, or eyewitness testimony. The "Place" column includes the Jagdwaffe map coordinates, where available. The unit of the "Opponent" is the author's best estimate. It should not be inferred that this opposing aircraft was actually destroyed; that judgment is made in most cases in the text. The notations in the Confirmation ("Conf") column are conservative: a "yes" means that the number of the confirmation document issued by the RLM is known; a "no" means that either the claim was not filed or is known to have been rejected by the Geschwader or the RLM; cases whose dispositions are unknown are noted as "unk". A fourth category, "i.O.", is taken directly from the newly-located RLM claims microfilms. The exact meaning of these initials is not known, but it was marked on claims with a good chance of ultimate confirmation, and probably means either in Ordnung (in order) or im Ordner (with the supervisor).

The emphasis in the casualty lists is on pilot losses; aircraft losses in which the pilot escaped injury will be listed in only a few special cases. Abbreviations used in the "Cas" column are: KIA = killed in action; KIFA = killed in a flying accident; KAC = killed in a non-flying accident; WIA = wounded in action; WIFA = wounded in a flying accident; WAC = wounded in a non-flying accident; POW = prisoner of war; MIA = missing in action. The date is written in European style: i.e., day first, month second, year third. The time is 24-hour military time.

JG 26 Victory Claims: 1 - 19 January 1943

Date	Rank	Name	Unit	Cl #	Aircraft	Place	Time	Opponent	Conf
09-01-43	Hptm.	Galland W-F.	II CO	22	Spitfire	W of Somme Estuary	1345	340 Sqd	yes
09-01-43	Lt.	Hoppe	6	3	Spitfire	W of Cayeux	1345	340 Sqd	yes
13-01-43	Uffz.	Scheyda	3	3	B-17	Lo (N of Lille)	1430	305 BG	yes
13-01-43	Obfw.	Kemethmüller	7	61	B-17	Ypres-Lille	1415	305 BG	yes
13-01-43	Hptm.	Mietusch	7		B-17	Lille	1435	305 BG	no
18-01-43	Fw.	Meyer H.	4	3	Mustang	near Rue	1057	4 Sqd	yes

JG 26 Casualties: 1 - 19 January 1943

Date	Rank	Name	Cas	Unit	Aircraft	WNr	Mkgs	Place	Time	Cause	Allied Unit
03-01-43	Uffz.	Jenner, Anton	no	1	Fw 190A-4			Arques		landing	non-op

03-01-43	Uffz.	Glaser, Otto	WIFA 2	Fw 190A-4	648		Arques		engine	non-op
04-01-43	Fw.	Müller, Herbert	KIA 10J	Fw 190A-4	2439	bk 4 + bomb	Winchelsea	1400	hit cable	n/a
09-01-43	Oblt.	Neu, Wolfgang	WIA 3	Fw 190A-4	5642		nr Marquise		Spitfire	
09-01-43	Uffz.	Roth, Ludwig	KIA 5	Fw 190A-4	2406	< bk 3	nr Abbeville-Drucat a/f		Spitfire	
11-01-43	Uffz.	Rybosch, Friedrich	WIFA 4	Fw 190A-4	2301	wh 7	Beaumont le Roger a/f		crashed	non-op
13-01-43	Uffz.	Irlinger, Johann	KIA 5	Bf 109G-4	16119	bk 4	nr Abbeville		Fw 190	n/a
15-01-43	Uffz.	Bremer, Herbert	KIA 3	Fw 190A-4	2382	yl 5	off Rye	1710	flak	n/a
19-01-43	Uffz.	Müller, Leo	no 4	Bf 109G-4	16125		Abbeville-Drucat a/f		aborted	n/a t/o

20 January

England was hit today by its largest daylight bombing attack since 1940. A maximum strength *Vergeltungsangriff* had been ordered; unfortunately for the Luftflotte 3 planners, the trained bomber force available was minuscule – fewer than two dozen fighter-bombers from the two Jabostaffeln, 10(Jabo)/JG 2 and 10(Jabo)/JG 26. They were to be supplemented by a few aircraft from JG 2 and the fighter school in Paris, carrying fragmentation bombs, and would be escorted by fighters from JG 2 and JG 26. The reinforcements arrived at JG 26's airfields on the Pas de Calais on the 19th. The raid would be carried out in three waves. The first, containing the two Jabostaffeln and escorts from the Stab and First Gruppe of JG 26, would cross the Channel at minimum altitude and drop their 500 kg bombs on London. The second wave, ten minutes behind, would contain JG 2 fighters carrying fragmentation bombs, escorted by the Fw 190s of the Second Gruppe Stab and the 4th and 5th Staffeln, and the new Bf 109s of the 6th Staffel. It would cross the English coast at medium altitude and attempt to reach London. III/JG 26 made up the third wave, which would climb to operational altitude and loiter off the English coast to intercept any pursuing RAF fighters. A total of ninety fighters and fighter-bombers was scheduled to take part.

The morning reconnaissance mission to the English coast was attempted by a pair of 8th Staffel Focke-Wulfs. Two No. 609 Sqd. Typhoons on standing patrol intercepted the Germans off the coast. One shot Lt. Hans Kümmerling into the sea, while the other chased the surviving Fw 190 back to France.

The raid was scheduled to get under way at noon. One of the escort pilots, Gefr. Heinrich Heuser of the 2nd Staffel, rated this mission, his sixth, as his most noteworthy of the war. He recalls:

> ''School aircraft and their pilots had moved to the coast, some to my base at St. Omer-Arques. The combat-experienced instructors bragged of the mission in the local bars; the rest of us were afraid that the Resistance would get word of the raid back to England. The first weather forecast for the 20th was bad; solid clouds over London at 400 meters [1300 feet], making the balloon cables especially dangerous. After much alcohol in the morning and with great queasiness in our stomachs, we took off from Arques at 1202 and proceeded across the Channel under the forecast clouds and in complete radio silence. As we neared the English coast, the cloud cover ripped away, and we saw only scattered clouds and bright sun – there was not a single English fighter in the sky, and there were no balloons over London. After the bombs were dropped, we separated from the bomb carriers and climbed back toward the coast to get above the English fighters and protect our returning Jabos. Over the Channel, we contacted the enemy, and fought them in and out of the clouds. We landed at Arques after eighty-three minutes in the air. Obfw. Paul Kierstein of our Staffel did not return.''

The thirty-four Fw 190s in the first wave attained complete surprise. The barrage balloons were down, and were attacked by the escort as soon as they were raised; seven were claimed destroyed. Bombs were dropped on the London dock area, but most hit the streets of Greenwich, which were filled with noon-hour crowds. Civilian casualties were heavy. Bombs hit the Sandhurst Road School, killing thirty-eight children and six teachers. As this was a low-level raid in good visibility, the British publicized the attack widely, accusing the Germans of deliberately targeting the school. The Jabos almost escaped unscathed. According to the after-action report, one pilot lost a hand to an anti-aircraft shell, but his identity has unfortunately not been traced. Lt. Hermann Hoch's Focke-Wulf was hit by light antiaircraft fire as he re-crossed the coast, and he turned back to force-land in a Sussex field. He was able to ignite his emergency detonator and destroy his airplane before he was taken prisoner.

Few RAF fighters were able to reach the withdrawing Germans. The duty pilots of the Biggin Hill Wing had been lunching outside their ready room when the Focke-Wulfs roared past *en route* to London. W/C Richard Milne and No. 611 Squadron's S/L Hugo Armstrong took off and headed south, where they were able to catch the end of the formation as it retreated over the coast. Milne shot down Obfw. Kierstein. Oblt. Fülbert Zink, Kierstein's Staffelkapitän, claimed a Spitfire over the Channel, but none are known to have gone down at this time.

The two dozen Fw 190s and Bf 109s of the second wave had no luck at all. Every available No. 11 Group fighter had been ordered to the Sussex coast, where they were well-positioned to meet the new raiders as they arrived. Few if any of this group reached London. Most of the bomb-carriers dropped their loads on Brighton, and all aircraft attempted to turn back for France as quickly as possible. The 5th Staffel encountered the Spitfires of No. 340 Sqd. (Free French), and lost Fw. Alfred Barthel, who was seen to bail out into the Channel. Two 6th Staffel Schwärme were routed by a lone pair of No. 609 Sqd. Typhoons that had scrambled from Manston on word of the initial wave. The Messerschmitts attempted a crossing maneuver in the clouds, and two of them collided. Lt. Kurt-Erich Wenzel was killed; Uffz. Heinz Marquardt bailed out into the Thames Estuary, from which he was rescued by the British ASR service. Debris from Wenzel's aircraft struck Lt. Hans Mayer, blinding him in one eye. He was able to force-land on Abbeville-Drucat. Uffz. Heinz Budde was shot down by one of the Typhoons. He bailed out, and floated in the Thames Estuary for three days before he was picked up by an ASR boat. F/O J. R. Baldwin, the Typhoon pilot, visited Budde in the hospital; Budde gave him his clasp knife in gratitude for prolonging the search. Spitfires and Typhoons pursued the surviving German aircraft back to France, where a sixth 6th Staffel pilot, Uffz. Helmut Peters, was shot down and killed by S/L Don Kingaby of No. 122 Squadron. The beleaguered Second Gruppe claimed no victories.

The third wave, consisting of the Geschwader Stabsschwarm and the Third Gruppe, took off from Wevelgem at 1211, crossed the Belgian coast at 10,000 feet, and climbed to 18,000 feet over the Channel. Major Priller then led the three dozen Focke-Wulfs west, paralleling the English coast. Priller claimed a Spitfire north of Canterbury at 1235, but apparently the only two RAF fighters shot down this day were the victims of Oblt. Klaus Mietusch of the 7th Staffel, who downed a No. 91 Sqd. Spitfire into the Channel south of Margate at 1242, and, after returning to France, destroyed a No. 332 Sqd. Spitfire over Ardres at 1312. The only Third Gruppe casualties resulted from forced-landings on Calais-Marck owing to low fuel; at least two Focke-Wulfs were damaged, and Uffz. Robert Hager was injured.

Air traffic over the Channel remained heavy until nightfall, as German formations searched for missing comrades and RAF fighters attempted to thwart them. No. 609 Squadron scored at least one more victory, sending one JG 2 Fw 190 into the Channel, while a second crash-landed on St. Valery. The Typhoon squadron was thus responsible for five of the nine German fighters destroyed this day. According to the No. 609 Squadron historian, today's combats "put the Typhoon on the map." Broad exposure in the Allied media had not yet brought the type to the attention of Luftwaffe Intelligence, however; neither of the 6th Staffel pilots taken prisoner this day had even heard of the Typhoon, which had been in service on the Channel coast for eight months.

The six tons of bombs dropped on London and the four claims for air victories cost the Geschwader its heaviest single-day toll to date; eight aircraft were lost with their pilots, and two pilots returned with serious injuries. In addition, JG 2 lost one pilot killed and one injured. General Galland issued an after-action report praising the Jabos and blaming the Second Gruppe losses on "operational mistakes." It is worth noting that the careers of neither the Second Gruppe Kommandeur, Hptm. Wutz Galland, nor the 6th Staffel Kapitän, Hptm. Johannes Naumann, suffered any noticeable damage from this failure.

This Great London Raid was not repeated. The Germans were too few in numbers, and the British defenders were too strong – Fighter Command flew 214 sorties today against the ninety attackers. Never again would the fighter Staffeln of the Schlageter Geschwader appear in strength over England.

Fw. Fred Barthel, photographed at Abbeville-Drucat. On 20 January he bailed out into the Channel off Calais after being hit by a No. 340 Sqd. (Free French) Spitfire. Searches were unsuccessful. In May his body washed ashore in the German Bight near Cuxhaven. *(Crump)*

JG 26 Casualties: 20 January 1943

Date	Rank	Name	Cas	Unit	Aircraft	WNr	Mkgs	Place	Time	Cause	Allied Unit
20-01-43	Fw.	Barthel, Alfred	KIA	5	Fw 190A-4	2460	bk 5	Channel	1245	Spitfire	340 Sqd
20-01-43	Uffz.	Budde, Heinz	POW	6	Bf 109G-4	16102	br 7	E of Dover	1300	Typhoon	609 Sqd
20-01-43	Uffz.	Hager, Robert	WIA	8	Fw 190A-4	7102	bk 4	Calais-Marck a/f	1328	landing	n/a
20-01-43	Lt.	Hoch, Hermann	POW	10J	Fw 190A-4	2409	bk 2	Seaford-Surrey + bomb	1345	light flak	
20-01-43	Obfw.	Kierstein, Paul	KIA	2	Fw 190A-4	2375	bk 7	Dungeness	1245	Spitfire	B Hill Wing
20-01-43	Lt.	Kümmerling, Hans	KIA	8	Fw 190A-4	7037	bk 8	3km W of Cap Gris Nez	0915	Typhoon	609 Sqd
20-01-43	Uffz.	Marquardt, Heinz	POW	6	Bf 109G-4	16113	br 12	E of Ramsgate	1300	Typhoon	609 Sqd
20-01-43	Lt.	Mayer, Hans	WIA	6	Bf 109G-4	16121	br 6	Ramsgate	1300	Typhoon	609 Sqd
20-01-43	Uffz.	Peters, Helmut	KIA	6	Bf 109G-4	16094	br 14	f/l Ardres	1330	Spitfire	122 Sqd
20-01-43	Lt.	Wenzel, Kurt-Erich	KIA	6	Bf 109G-4	16141	br 11	Thames Est	1300	Typhoon	609 Sqd

JG 26 Victory Claims: 20 January 1943

Date	Rank	Name	Unit	Cl #	Aircraft	Place	Time	Opponent	Conf
20-01-43	Major	Priller	Ge CO	82	Spitfire	N of Canterbury	1235	332 Sqd	unk
20-01-43	Oblt.	Zink	2 CO	31	Spitfire	25km NW of Boulogne	1312	332 Sqd	unk
20-01-43	Hptm.	Mietusch	7 CO	27	Spitfire	4-5km S of Margate	1242	91 Sqd	unk
20-01-43	Hptm.	Mietusch	7 CO	28	Spitfire	Ardres	1312	91 Sqd	unk

21 January

Luftwaffe air activity over the Channel remained brisk, as the Geschwader, and especially the Second Gruppe, continued the fruitless search for missing pilots. The RAF responded to the large number of radar plots and radio intercepts by sending fighter sweeps across the Channel. Only one combat resulted.

Hptm. Galland selected twelve pilots, the men with the best eyesight in his command, to fly a search mission for Fw. Barthel, who had been seen to bail out over the Channel on the 20th. A pair of No. 609 Sqd. Typhoons swept through the Focke-Wulf formation, shot down Uffz. Wolfgang Taufmann, a new pilot who was bringing up the rear, and disappeared into the clouds. The German search was not successful – Barthel's body was to wash up on the German coast in May – and at the debriefing only Uffz. Peter Crump and Uffz. Heinz Gomann correctly identified the British fighters, Crump because he had recently seen an article on the new type in the Swiss magazine *Interavia*. According to Peter Crump,

> "Our identification was dismissed by our Kommandeur with the comment, 'What you two saw were Vultee Vanguards'. The discussion continued in a nervous atmosphere. The stronger and those in authority had the 'right'. The surprise attack was only possible because these Vultee Vanguards were easily confused with Focke-Wulfs – so said Galland. But in defense of his honor I must add that a few days later the Kommandeur sought out his old Staffel and told Gomann and me, 'You two were right; they were Typhoons. This morning the First Gruppe fought a battle with these new aircraft.' This was typical of the man."

The First Gruppe began packing today for its move to the Leningrad Front.

22 January

The morning was spent on routine patrols. All three Gruppen were scrambled at 1450 on a report of heavy bombers crossing the coast. The "heavies" proved to be an RAF Circus containing a dozen Boston light bombers, escorted by the usual beehive of Spitfires. The target, one of the St. Omer airfields, was reached before the German fighters could form up for an attack, but the departing formation was pursued over the Channel and three Spitfires were claimed. Two claims were confirmed, but apparently only one Spitfire, from No. 350 Sqd. (Belgian), was lost. RAF claims are unknown, but the Spitfire pilots of the American 4th Fighter Group claimed three Fw 190s and one Bf 109. No German aircraft sustained reportable damage.

Hptm. Galland flew his first combat mission in a Bf 109. It did not go well, even though he shot down a Spitfire. Vision from the cockpit was extremely poor in comparison to that from the Fw 190, and he was bounced by another fighter formation – fortunately, these were Luftwaffe Fw 190s, which he was able to evade. After landing, he told his crew chief to repack his parachute in a "proper fighter" – his Fw 190. Galland had always defended the planned re-equipment of his Gruppe with Bf 109s in front of his men, but personal experience changed his mind. He pulled some strings, and the few Bf 109s left in the Gruppe after the 20 January mission were taken away and given to the Third Gruppe, whose new Kommandeur, an experienced Messerschmitt pilot, preferred them. The Second Gruppe would continue to fly Fw 190s until the end of the war.

Uffz. Wolfgang Polster transferred from the 8th Staffel to the new 11th Staffel, both at Wevelgem, and made his first flight in a Bf 109G-1 high-altitude fighter. According to Polster, the 11th Staffel was intended to be a specialized Höhenstaffel, or high-altitude Staffel, thus filling the same role as its predecessor, also designated the 11th Staffel, which had been destroyed in Tunisia at the end of 1942. Some records refer to the 11th as an *Endausbildungsstaffel*, or operational training Staffel; Polster says that this is not true, although the Staffel seemed to receive more than its share of inexperienced pilots direct from flight training. The Bf 109G-1 had been in service since the previous July, but had not been successful. According to Polster, the aircraft, lacking the engine for which it was designed, was deficient in maximum altitude, climb rate, and maneuverability. Its pressurized cabin required thick canopy panes, further restricting the Messerschmitt's always marginal vision. Another feature was a real killer. Methanol-water injection was used to boost engine performance up to its rated altitude. The methanol tank was narrow and was positioned longitudinally, leading to stability and center-of-gravity problems as the liquid flowed back and forth; the fighter had a tendency to flip on its back unexpectedly.

23 January

The 8th Air Force returned to action today with an attack on the Lorient submarine base. The only JG 26 unit active in the defense was Lt. Stammberger's 9th Staffel, flying from Vannes with III/JG 2. The target was obvious, and the Jafü 3 controller patiently kept his fighters away from the RAF diversions and escorts until all of the Spitfires had turned back. The Vannes aircraft then attacked, followed by others flying from Brest. To the Americans, the German attacks seemed better coordinated than before, and were made by formations of six aircraft instead of in pairs or singly. Attacks persisted until the bombers were again over the Channel, even after the arrival of the return escort. Five B-17s went down, all from the 303rd Bomb Group; two more crash-landed in England. Stammberger's Staffel did well, receiving credit for two B-17s. 7/JG 2 claimed four, accounting for the other American losses.

Lt. Stammberger was proving to be a successful formation leader against the heavy bombers. Stotto Stammberger recalls the missions of this period:

> "My tactics always depended on the situation – where was the enemy, where was I? We could easily see a large formation at a distance of 5-7 km [3-4 miles]; much sooner, if there were condensation trails. Let's assume there is no escort and I am to one side of the formation. I am flying at 420 km/h [260 mph], the bombers at 360 km/h [220 mph]. I estimate that I am five minutes from the formation. If I am beneath the formation, it will take longer; if I am above it, I can approach it more rapidly. As Staffelkapitän I fly at only 420 km/h, so that my ten aircraft can stay with me easily. The bomber armada has seen us already; indeed, we have been seen on radar and reported to the bombers. A glance at the gauges; fuel enough for two or three attacks. I decide to attack from behind and beneath and sideslip toward the bombers. I have previously ordered my Staffel to close up the formation, so that each Schwarm will hit a bomber from the same side. The bombers open fire on us while we are 1500 meters [5000 feet] away, when they determine our direction of attack. We fly through the defensive fire for about a minute before we open fire. Imagine that you are standing under a shower-bath, but don't want to get wet! At 400 meters [1300 feet] we first fire our machine guns; our targets are the gun turrets of the bombers under attack. At 200 meters [650 feet] we fire our cannon; our targets are the engines, if possible the outer ones, which cause the bomber to go unstable. If the engines are hit, the bomber sheers out of formation, and the uninjured crew members bail out. The pilot either attempts a forced landing or bails out himself. When the pilotless, damaged aircraft nears the ground, the Flak opens fire and reports a victory! But we don't see that; we can't think about the fate of the bomber, because we have broken away downward after the attack and are climbing back up to begin the game a second time. Perhaps three or four of my planes are still with me; the others are nowhere to be seen. My pilots have scattered to the winds, landed at other fields, bailed out, or been killed. We won't know their fates until several hours of anxious waiting. Our aircraft are all unserviceable; all have been damaged. But we have sufficient reserves; we have plenty of aircraft, but no pilots. When I am able to take the most favorable position, I attack from the front; there the bombers are the weakest. I go after the pilots, the bombardier, the radioman, or whoever else is in the cockpit. I have only a few seconds for a burst of fire, while they must sit there. I shot down three bombers from the front and two from behind. Reichsmarschall Göring later forbade us to attack from the front, saying successes were too few. The defensive fire of the bombers was just as strong from the front, but we were through it more quickly."

The rest of JG 26 was kept busy over the Pas de Calais by a new type of Allied mission. Whirlwinds and Mustang Is of the RAF Army Cooperation Command were released from their usual reconnaissance tasks and flew a large number of Rhubarbs, making what were described by the RAF as "very successful" attacks on railroads, trucks, and high-voltage pylons. The only defensive strategy with a chance of success against such hit-and-run raids was a system of overlapping coastal patrols, but contact remained a matter of luck. At noon Oblt. Sternberg walked into the Abbeville ready room and ordered two of his 5th Staffel Unteroffiziere, Peter Crump and Hans Meyer, to fly the next patrol in a pair of Bf 109s that happened to be operational; Crump was to lead. The weather on this day favored RAF raids. There was high cloud cover, with scattered clouds at low altitude; visibility otherwise was good. After a short period at cockpit readiness, the pair were ordered to relieve a pair of 6th Staffel aircraft in the air. While preparing to take off, the pilots heard the Jafü report a flight of four *Indianer* (enemy fighters) south of Boulogne. Since they were taking off in that direction, Crump ordered his wingman to head for the stated area at minimum altitude, without any appreciable change in course. Shortly after takeoff, Crump spotted two dots at ten o'clock; these quickly became visible as two Mustangs, coming directly at him. Crump had already grasped his firing lever, and had the enemy leader in his sights before he was seen in turn. Startled, the leader broke away, presenting his underside as a target. After taking a short burst of fire, the Mustang fell away over its left wing.

Crump next turned his attention to the other Mustang. It had banked toward his fighter, and was firing behind him. Crump pulled his aircraft into a tighter bank. After several turns, the Messerschmitt gained on the Mustang, and Crump put some short bursts of fire into its left rear fuselage and tail. At this, the Allied pilot gave up, turned toward a large field, and made a forced landing.

After this engagement, Crump resumed his surveillance flight, since four Mustangs had been reported. Toward the end of the patrol, Crump spotted another Mustang over the Somme Estuary, coming from the direction of Dieppe. Its pilot saw the Germans, banked toward the northwest, and flew off. Crump chased after the Mustang at full throttle, but could not close to less than 450 meters (500 yards). He cursed not being in his Focke-Wulf, while peppering the enemy fighter with short bursts of cannon fire. The Mustang rocked back and forth at each burst and then barreled away, right on the water. Crump gave up the chase when his Messerschmitt's cannon ran out of ammunition. The two Mustangs he had downed were from No. 168 Squadron, and were the only RAF fighters lost over the Continent this day.

Although the Jabostaffeln had come through the 20 January mission with only one loss, attacks on that scale were not repeated. They resumed the type of mission that had become standard the previous year – attacks by unescorted Schwärme on shipping and on military targets such as railroads, electrical relay stations, and gasoline tanks near the coast. Today's targets were missed, and several houses in Hailsham were destroyed. Uffz. Alfred Immervoll's Fw 190 was hit by Canadian Army anti-aircraft fire as he retraced his course, and he crashed to his death 450 meters (500 yards) out in the Channel.

25 January

Most of the Second Gruppe aircraft left Abbeville today for Vitry-en-Artois. Part of the 5th Staffel was left behind. Several Staffeln were scrambled over the course of the day, but no contacts were made.

26 January

From his new base at Vitry, Uffz. Gomann flew the morning recon mission along the English coast from Hastings to Dungeness. A large Circus crossed the Channel shortly after noon, and all three Gruppen were scrambled in response. No. 64 and No. 306 Squadron each lost a Spitfire, one to Hptm. Galland and the other to Uffz. Crump, although the latter's claim was never filed. I/JG 2 crossed the Somme Estuary in support, and lost two Focke-Wulfs north of Le Touquet to Spitfires. The Kapitän of 2/JG 2, Oblt. Christian Eickhoff, who had previously commanded 2/JG 26, was shot down into the Channel. The Second Gruppe flew several missions in search of Eickhoff, but these were unsuccessful. JG 26 lost no aircraft or pilots this day, but two of its Focke-Wulfs force-landed with combat damage.

JG 26 Victory Claims: 22 - 26 January 1943

Date	Rank	Name	Unit	Cl #	Aircraft	Place	Time	Opponent	Conf
22-01-43	Hptm.	Galland W-F.	II CO	23	Spitfire	WNW of Gravelines	1530	350 Sqd	yes
22-01-43	Lt.	Hoppe	5	4	Spitfire	NW of Gravelines	1515	350 Sqd	unk
22-01-43	Hptm.	Mietusch	7 CO	29	Spitfire	10-15km N of Gravelines	1515		unk
23-01-43	Uffz.	Crump	5	3	Mustang	S of Montreuil	1345	168 Sqd	yes
23-01-43	Uffz.	Crump	5	4	Mustang	S of Montreuil	1346	168 Sqd	yes
23-01-43	Uffz.	Dörre	9	4	B-17	unknown	1420	303 BG	unk
23-01-43	Lt.	Kestel	9	1	B-17	unknown	1417	303 BG	unk
26-01-43	Hptm.	Galland W-F.	II CO	24	Spitfire	Watten	1252	64 or 306 Sqd	yes
26-01-43	Uffz.	Crump	5		Spitfire	5km N of Dunkirk	1245	64 or 306 Sqd	no

27 January

Uffz. Gomann flew the recon mission again today; this time, to vary the routine, from Dungeness to Hastings. The rest of the Geschwader flew patrols, and scrambled at least one Staffel in response to reported Allied activity, but failed to make contact. The principal Allied effort was the 8th Air Force's first raid on Germany, to Wilhelmshaven. The bombers crossed the North Sea far out of JG 26's range.

28 January

Low clouds restricted flying. The Third Gruppe was scrambled from Wevelgem shortly after 1100 as several enemy aircraft were reported headed toward the base. The base was indeed attacked – by a single No. 137 Sqd. Whirlwind, piloted by an Australian, F/O B. L. Musgrave. Only one pair of Fw 190s was in a possible position to intercept. Uffz. Heinrich Wälter had to attack from beneath, but overshot, and passed in front of the Whirlwind. Reacting by instinct, Musgrave fired a quick burst from the Whirlwind's four 20-mm nose cannon; the Focke-Wulf was hit and dived straight into the ground. The Australian pilot made good his escape in the clouds, but had no idea that he had hit the German aircraft, and filed no claim. The outcome of his combat, and the identification of his victim, only became known as a result of recent research.

Hptm. Galland was awarded the German Cross in Gold, a gaudy chest decoration known throughout the Luftwaffe as the *Spiegelei*, or Fried Egg. His victory total stood at twenty-four.

JG 26 Casualties: 21 - 28 January 1943

Date	Rank	Name	Cas	Unit	Aircraft	WNr	Mkgs	Place	Time	Cause	Allied Unit
21-01-43	Uffz.	Taufmann, Wolfgang	KIA	4	Fw 190A-4	692	wh 4	SW of Calais		Typhoon	609 Sqd
23-01-43	Uffz.	Immervoll, Alfred	KIA	10J	Fw 190A-4	5636	-+-	Beachy Head-Hailsham	1050	light flak	n/a
28-01-43	Uffz.	Wälter, Heinrich	KIA	8	Fw 190A-4	5622	bk 2	Dadizeele-Beselaere	1108	Whirlwind	137 Sqd

29 January

The Geschwader was required to send up patrols to oppose the irritating RAF Rhubarbs. Only one combat resulted, and it had no recorded result.

31 January

The Geschwader was grounded for two days by the weather. Personnel moves during the last half of the month found Hptm. Gerhard Philipp joining the Stab as Geschwader operations officer; Obfw. Walter Grünlinger transferring from the Third Gruppe to the Stab to continue flying as Major Priller's wingman; Obfw. Friedrich Lindelaub returning to duty with 1/JG 26 after five months in the hospital; Obfw. Franz Hiller leaving the First Gruppe for instructor duty; and Uffz. Anton Jenner transferring from the 1st to the 11th Staffel. Several new pilots reported for duty from flight training, and were assigned as follows: Uffz. Michael Hecker, Uffz. Anton Kratzel, Fw. Hans Ruppert – First Gruppe; Uffz. Gerhard Falkner – Second Gruppe; Uffz. Karl Gathof – Third Gruppe; Uffz. Karl Seebeck, Uffz. Rudolf Stutt – 11th Staffel. It should be pointed out that personnel lists exist for only a few Staffeln, and all of these are for 1945. The best sources of arrival dates for new pilots are their casualty reports and brief biographies in the Geschwader *Ehrenbuch*, or Honors Book. Pilots could transfer into and out of the Geschwader without leaving a trace in the surviving records. The available data are presented here, in the belief that some information is better than none.

1 February

Uffz. Gomann was again picked to fly the morning recon mission, and he flew down the English coast from Eastbourne to Dungeness without incident. A few patrols were flown by the rest of the Geschwader, following one of which a Second Gruppe Fw 190 crash-landed on Vitry-en-Artois owing to pilot error.

2 February

Despite heavy cloud cover, a large RAF formation crossed the French coast at 0945. All three Gruppen were scrambled in response. None of the German formations located the enemy, but one German plane was found and destroyed by an Allied unit. The Spitfires of No. 331 Sqd. (Norwegian) were flying south over St. Omer at 7000 meters (23,000 feet) when one flight leader spotted a lone Bf 109 600 meters (2000 feet) below on an opposite course. The German pilot was Uffz. Gerhard Vogt, in a 6th Staffel Bf 109G-4. The Norwegian pilot dived on the Messerschmitt, followed by the two members of his flight. All three hit the German fighter, which dived vertically into the clouds below, trailing heavy flames and smoke. Vogt managed to bail out, but was wounded severely in one shoulder and foot, and spent four months in the Arras hospital.

3 February

Although the weather continued poor, air activity picked up. Four Fw 190s of the Jabostaffel made an early-morning attack on Ashford and escaped unscathed. At 1045 a large enemy force approaching the Belgian coast brought all three Gruppen into the air. The formation was Circus 258. Twelve No. 21 Sqd. Venturas were to bomb the Third Gruppe base at Wevelgem. Escort was provided by six Spitfire squadrons of the Northolt and Hornchurch Wings. The multiple diversionary sweeps and relays of escorts that had characterized the massive 1942 Circuses were absent today, and the six Spitfire squadrons proved to be inadequate. The Venturas turned back short of the target owing to heavy cloud, and were attacked by three waves of Focke-Wulfs as they retreated across the Channel. One Ventura crashed off Calais, while two others were written off after crash-landing in England. The three bombers were credited to Hptm. Galland, who claimed a "Hudson" – aircraft identification was never one of Wutz's strengths – and Hptm. Kelch and Obfw. Kemethmüller of the 7th Staffel. The escort apparently lost contact in the clouds, and only No. 308 Sqd. (Polish) had the bombers in sight when the Focke-Wulfs arrived. The Poles, still flying obsolescent Spitfire Vbs, were overwhelmed, and were chased back to the English coast, losing four planes while claiming two probable Fw 190s. The Geschwader claimed seven Spitfires; five of these claims were confirmed. Oblt. Fülbert Zink, the 2nd Staffel Kapitän, had one confirmed and one unconfirmed victory; these were the final claims on the Channel Front for the First Gruppe before the last of its pilots departed for Russia. Another victorious pilot was Fw. Erich Jauer of the 7th Staffel, who had worked his way back up to a position of *Rottenführer* (element leader) after being banished to an aircraft factory in 1941. Kemethmüller, Jauer's *Schwarmführer* (flight leader), attacked a Spitfire off Dunkirk at an altitude of 2500 meters (8200 feet). Kemethmüller turned away when the fighter began to smoke, leaving it for Jauer to finish off. After one burst of fire, the Spitfire rolled on its back and its Polish pilot bailed out into the sea – unfortunately, he was never found. This was Jauer's first victory, after a long and tortuous journey; an enthusiastic victory celebration awaited him back at Wevelgem.

In mid-afternoon, another RAF formation was sent to France on a similar mission. Circus 259 contained twelve No. 464 Sqd. Venturas; their target was the St. Omer railroad yard. Their escort comprised three Spitfire wings; one of these, the Northolt Wing, was sent ahead on an advance sweep. The Second and Third Gruppen attacked after the Venturas had successfully dropped their bombs. One bomber, which had been hit by Flak, was finished off by Lt. Aistleitner of the 8th Staffel, who claimed a Hudson; the rest escaped. The Kenley Wing's No. 416 Sqd. (RCAF) bore the brunt of the German attack. Three of its Spitfires were shot down over the coast by Hptm. Karl Borris and his 8th Staffel; the survivors were pursued out to sea by part of the Second Gruppe, whose Hptm. Galland shot down a fourth Spitfire in mid-Channel. One of the Canadians was rescued by the British; two, by the Germans. The Spitfire squadrons claimed a total of three Fw 190s destroyed, four probably destroyed, and three damaged (abbreviated 3-4-3 Fw 190s) on this mission, but in fact, none were destroyed, and only two were damaged. Uffz. Karl Weiss of the 8th Staffel was seriously wounded in his battle with No. 416 Squadron, and force-landed his damaged aircraft southwest of Bergues. A I/JG 2 Focke-Wulf landed on Abbeville with moderate damage; any victory claims by the Richthofen Geschwader remain unknown.

An hour after the RAF force reached England, Uffz. Mayer of the 6th Staffel led a Rotte of Bf 109s across the Channel on an evening recon mission. Their sweep from Eastbourne to Folkestone was uneventful.

Major Priller (2nd from right) congratulates Fw. Erich Jauer (3rd from right) on his first victory, a No. 308 Sqd. (Polish) Spitfire. Jauer's Schwarmführer, Obfw. Kemethmüller, is on his right – Wevelgem, 3 February. (*Jauer*)

Date	Rank	Name	Unit	Cl #	Aircraft	Place	Time	Opponent	Conf
03-02-43	Oblt.	Zink	2 CO	32	Spitfire	7km SW of Gravelines	1105	308 Sqd	yes
03-02-43	Oblt.	Zink	2 CO	33	Spitfire	N of Cassel	1057	308 Sqd	unk
03-02-43	Hptm.	Galland W-F.	II CO	25	Hudson	10km from Fort Philip	1105	21 Sqd Ventura	yes
03-02-43	Hptm.	Galland W-F.	II CO	26	Spitfire	12-15km N of Fort Philip	1112	308 Sqd	yes
03-02-43	Hptm.	Galland W-F.	II CO	27	Spitfire	12-15km N of Dunkirk	1528	416 Sqd	yes
03-02-43	Fw.	Glunz	4		Spitfire	N France	1530	416 Sqd	no
03-02-43	Lt.	Sternberg	5 CO	11	Spitfire	7km NE of Calais	1110	308 Sqd	yes
03-02-43	Uffz.	Crump	5		Spitfire	5km N of Calais	1100	308 Sqd	no
03-02-43	Obfw.	Mackenstedt	6	5	Spitfire	10-12km NW of Gravelines	1108	308 Sqd	yes
03-02-43	Fw.	Jauer	7	1	Spitfire	5-7km W of Dunkirk	1112	308 Sqd	i.O.
03-02-43	Hptm.	Kelch	7	1	Ventura	10-15km NW of Dunkirk	1115	21 Sqd	i.O.
03-02-43	Obfw.	Kemethmüller	7	62	Ventura	NW of Dunkirk	1112	21 Sqd	i.O.
03-02-43	Hptm.	Borris	8 CO		Spitfire	N of Poperinghe	1521	416 Sqd	yes
03-02-43	Hptm.	Borris	8 CO		Spitfire	Poperinghe-Bergues	1521	416 Sqd	yes
03-02-43	Lt.	Aistleitner	8	11	Hudson	NW of Gravelines	1527	464 Sqd Ventura	yes
03-02-43	Obfw.	Heitmann	8		Spitfire	Dunkirk-Calais	1108	308 Sqd	unk
03-02-43	Obfw.	Kalitzki	8	1	Spitfire	N of Gravelines	1535	416 Sqd	yes

4 February

Obfw. Glunz led the morning recon mission to the English coast. Nothing worth noting was seen. At noon the North Weald Wing and its two Norwegian Spitfire squadrons crossed the French coast on a Rodeo, which was a sweep by fighters only. The two dozen Spitfires brought a massive response by the Geschwader. The Second and Third Gruppen scrambled in strength from Vitry and Wevelgem, and Major Priller led the remaining First Gruppe pilots up from Vendeville. All made contact, but the combats of the First and Second Gruppen were inconclusive. Hptm. Geisshardt led his Third Gruppe Stabsschwarm in what should have been a perfect bounce of No. 331 Squadron, out of the sun. But the Norwegian squadron leader broke into the attack and followed the Schwarm in its dive away. He closed on the German fighters and fired on the aircraft flying in the left rear position; the Fw 190 burst into flames and dived vertically into the ground, killing Lt. Gerhard Seifert, the Gruppe adjutant and the brother of the First Gruppe Kommandeur. The 7th Staffel was also bested in its encounter with the Norwegians. Obfw. Kemethmüller was hit, and his engine was damaged. He force-landed north of Merville with injuries severe enough to keep him in the hospital until mid-May, when he was able to join the 7th Staffel in Russia. The North Weald Wing sustained no losses in these combats, and filed a modest 1-1-1 claims for Fw 190s.

5 February

A morning attack on Hailsham by a Schwarm of Jabostaffel Fw 190s precipitated all of the action on this miserably wet day. The Jabos were met off the English coast by a pair of No. 609 Sqd. Typhoons – this time identified by the Germans as Tomahawks – and Uffz. Herbert Büttner was hit and bailed out into the Channel. The Second Gruppe was ordered to search for him and cover the German ASR launches. The German air activity in turn prompted the No. 11 Group controllers to send up several Spitfire squadrons. No. 611 Squadron made contact with the two 5th Staffel Schwärme. Heinz Gomann recalls:

"I was over the Channel, very low. Behind me were two Spitfires, almost in firing position. I pulled up into the broken cloud deck, and when I dropped out, the two Spitfires were right in front of me. I opened fire on the lead aircraft, and it immediately crashed in the water. I then fired on the second aircraft, but with no apparent effect. I remember this combat exactly – mine was the only victory over the Channel this day, and it prompted an extensive sea search. We learned from the radio intercepts that my victim was the Biggin Hill wing commander."

Gomann's recollection is very close to perfect. His victim was, in fact, S/L Hugo Armstrong, the Australian leader of No. 611 Squadron and a prominent member of the Biggin Hill Wing, with more than ten air victories at the time of his death. The squadron's report matches Gomann's account in every detail.

Gefr. Heuser was one of the few First Gruppe pilots who had not yet left for Russia. He was assigned to fly the evening recon mission to the English coast, and was permitted to fly it in Hptm. Seifert's old aircraft, which was marked with a Kommandeur's "double chevron".

JG 26 Casualties: 2 - 5 February 1943

Date	Rank	Name	Cas	Unit	Aircraft	WNr	Mkgs	Place	Time	Cause	Allied Unit
02-02-43	Uffz.	Vogt, Gerhard	WIA	6	Bf 109G-4	16129	br 10	W of Ypres		Spitfire	331 Sqd
03-02-43	Uffz.	Weiss, Karl	WIA	8	Fw 190A-4	785	bk 9	SW of Bergues	1535	Spitfire	416 Sqd
04-02-43	Lt.	Seifert, Gerhard	KIA	III St	Fw 190A-4	5725	<gr2+I	2km W of Bailleul	1230	Spitfire	331 Sqd
04-02-43	Obfw.	Kemethmüller, Heinz	WIA	7	Fw 190A-4	2438	wh 5	N of Merville	1302	Spitfire	331 Sqd
05-02-43	Uffz.	Büttner, Herbert	KIA	10J	Fw 190A-4	2435	bk 1+ bomb	SE of Hastings		Typhoon	609 Sqd

7 February

Bad weather kept both sides on the ground on the 6th, but the clouds lifted enough on the 7th to permit some training and test flights. Hptm. Galland's Second Gruppe made practice attacks on a Do 217. Some sources say that the 4th Staffel Kapitän, Oblt. Kurt Ebersberger, crashed and injured himself today while landing on Ligescourt. Hptm. Borris, the 8th Staffel Kapitän, was up in mid-afternoon on a test flight and was vectored to intercept a pair of Typhoons that were strafing a railroad train. He caught the British fighters at low altitude near Staden and shot down F/L P. Nankivell, who had shot down Uffz. Büttner two days previously. Nankivell died in the crash of his Typhoon.

JG 26 Victory Claims: 5 - 7 February 1943

Date	Rank	Name	Unit	Cl #	Aircraft	Place	Time	Opponent	Conf
05-02-43	Uffz.	Gomann	5	2	Spitfire	8km NNW of Boulogne	1211	611 Sqd	yes
07-02-43	Hptm.	Borris	8 CO		Typhoon	Staden	1446	609 Sqd	yes

8 February

Uffz. Crump, still flying from Abbeville, flew the morning recon mission to England. It was delayed until 1000 by the weather, but was uneventful. RAF fighters swept the Pas de Calais at noon above heavy cloud cover. Major Priller and his Stab flight took off, as did the Second and Third Gruppen, but neither side could locate the other. Two Third Gruppe Focke-Wulfs made forced landings with technical problems, and sustained damage in hard landings.

10 February

After a day on the ground, the two opponents sparred once again over the Pas de Calais. Small flights from the First and Second Gruppen contacted RAF fighters, but without result. Fighter Command's major effort was made to the west, and a fair-sized battle was fought with I/JG 2 over the Orne Estuary. Major Priller made two escort flights, probably for an inspection trip by an unidentified higher commander, and obtained credit for a combat sortie after the first one.

The 11th Staffel was not truly operational, but was ordered to fly a rare combat mission today, on the smallest possible scale – it was given the responsibility for the evening recon mission to England. Off the English coast the pair of Messerschmitts

The pilots of the 7th Staffel pose for a photograph while at readiness. From left: unknown, Obfw. Heinz Kemethmüller, unknown, unknown, Uffz. Wöge, Uffz. Günther Patzke (KIA 21 Sep 44), Hptm. Günther Kelch (KIFA 31 Jul 43), Oblt. Klaus Mietusch (KIA 17 Sep 44), Uffz. Hans Pritze (KIA 7 Jul 43), unknown, unknown, Fw. Erich Jauer (POW 18 Jun 43) – Wevelgem, early 1943. *(Jauer)*

encountered two No. 609 Sqd. Typhoons on standing patrol from Manston. The British fighters chased the Germans back toward France in a driving rain. The RAF element leader fired a few rounds at the trailing Messerschmitt, and, as hoped, the German fighter started jinking, allowing the Typhoon to close the range to 70 meters (80 yards). At this distance a brief burst of 20 mm fire set the Bf 109 ablaze. It crashed two kilometers off Cap Blanc Nez. Fw. Karl Friedrich apparently got out of his aircraft, but drowned. That same afternoon, the 11th Staffel left the Wevelgem base of the Third Gruppe and transferred to Merville. It saw no further combat until June. Although 11th Staffel stalwart Wolfgang Polster denies it today, the Staffel was, in fact, treated as a training unit.

11 February
The weather improved enough that Jafü 2 could expect a resumption of RAF raids, in at least Rhubarb strength, and the Second Gruppe was ordered to resume coastal patrols. No Geschwader fighter contacted the enemy, and the only battle over its defensive zone was fought, and won, by a flight from III/JG 2, whose Kommandeur, Oblt. Egon Mayer, shot down a Spitfire off Boulogne at 1210. The Stab of III/JG 2 and 7/JG 2 had left Brittany and were now flying from a base near the Channel coast. The Stab soon returned to Vannes, but 7/JG 2 remained in northern France for several months, and several times joined the Geschwader in its battles over the Channel. 9/JG 26 remained at Vannes, leaving Jafü Brittany with the equivalent of one full Gruppe with which to defend the submarine bases.

13 February
After a day's pause, the RAF was up in strength. Three Rodeos and one Circus targeted the west coast of the Pas de Calais. The Geschwader pilots available for duty sortied at least three times during the day; some pilots made four flights. The Second Gruppe moved back to Abbeville for the day, and this Gruppe and the III/JG 2 detachment were in the best positions to meet these raids. The clouds were so thick that many German flights, especially those made from bases to the east, failed to find the enemy, but those that did inflicted heavy punishment on the Spitfires. The twelve Bostons of

the morning Circus bombed Boulogne harbor; results were poor, but the Second Gruppe hastened to the area in full force. This was apparently the intention of the Fighter Command planners, who sent a large force of Spitfires on a Rodeo which reached Boulogne ten minutes after the Bostons had left. But the Jafü 2 radar operators had detected this new force as it left the English coast, and Galland's Gruppe was able to ambush it. Galland himself shot down Cdt. Schloesing, the leader of No. 340 Sqd. (Free French), who was able to evade capture and return to England. A second Spitfire was shot down into the sea, and a third crash-landed in England. The Second Gruppe filed two more claims; 7/JG 2, which was also involved in this battle, claimed one Spitfire.

Shortly after noon, the Second Gruppe and 7/JG 2 were scrambled again on reports of another RAF formation heading in the same direction. Its target proved to be Boulogne, and Galland was able to set up yet another successful ambush. Galland and two of his pilots shot down three Spitfires of No. 485 Sqd. (RNZAF) off Le Touquet, while 7/JG 2 downed a Spitfire from S/L J. E. Johnson's No. 610 Squadron. In mid-afternoon Galland's Gruppe was scrambled for a third time. Radio intercepts indicate that an air battle took place, but neither side sustained any losses. The day's action petered out near darkness when a small force of fighters was ordered to find and destroy several loose barrage balloons off Cap Gris Nez. Gefr. Heuser, who was among the few First Gruppe pilots remaining at Arques, probably flew on this mission, which was unsuccessful; this was his fourth mission of the day without enemy contact.

The successes of the Second Gruppe brought back memories of the Abbeville Boys and the "Focke-Wulf summer" of 1942. The Gruppe and 7/JG 2 claimed eight Spitfires off Boulogne – Fighter Command's actual losses totaled six shot down, and one damaged. No German pilots were injured, and no aircraft were lost, although two Fw 190s force-landed with combat damage at various times during the day – Fighter Command claimed 3-1-5 Fw 190s.

A III/JG 54 Bf 109 force-landed near Dunkirk during the day after its engine failed on a transfer or training flight. This is the first mention in the available records of III/JG 54, which had now arrived on the Channel Front. Major "Seppl" Seiler's Gruppe, containing the 7th, 8th, and 9th Staffeln of the Green Heart Geschwader, was to share Lille-Vendeville with Major Priller and the JG 26 Stab until it was declared fully operational, at which time it would gain its own base and operate independently. For now it would come under Priller's command as the "Lille Gruppe."

JG 26 Victory Claims: 13 February 1943

Date	Rank	Name	Unit	Cl #	Aircraft	Place	Time	Opponent	Conf
13-02-43	Hptm.	Galland W-F.	II CO	28	Spitfire	6km W of Hardelot	1017	340 Sqd	yes
13-02-43	Hptm.	Galland W-F.	II CO	29	Spitfire	SE of Le Touquet	1220	485 Sqd	yes
13-02-43	Lt.	Donner v.	II St	2	Spitfire	8-10km W of Boulogne	1018		yes
13-02-43	Lt.	Sternberg	5 CO	12	Spitfire	NE of Watten	1025		yes
13-02-43	Uffz.	Crump	5		Spitfire	near Watten	1030		no
13-02-43	Lt.	Hoppe	5	5	Spitfire	5km E of Étaples	1230	485 Sqd	yes
13-02-43	Oblt.	Naumann	6 CO	10	Spitfire	NE of Rue	1224	485 Sqd	yes
13-02-43	Hptm.	Ruppert K.	9 CO	20	Spitfire	5-10km S of Mer de Glinau	1106		i.O.

14 February

Today's air activity over the Channel was apparently a carry over from an engagement between torpedo boats the previous night. German radar operators detected several Royal Navy motor torpedo boats circling off Cap Gris Nez early in the morning. They had no business being there in daylight, but were apparently assisting a boat that was trying to get underway. Surprisingly, only a few German aircraft were sent to investigate this choice target; all of these were from Egon Mayer's III/JG 2 detachment. The Second Gruppe, which would certainly have received the call had it still been at Abbeville, had returned to Vitry. The RAF radio intercept service picked up the Jafü 2 orders to Mayer's unit, and No. 609 Squadron was quickly scrambled from Manston. The two flights met over the damaged MTB. The Typhoons shot down three Fw 190s of Mayer's Stabsschwarm in the subsequent battle, killing all three pilots; two Typhoons were also lost with their pilots.

15 February

The Germans successfully passed convoys of small ships through the Channel for much of the war. The Allies, uncertain of their nationality, usually let them pass. From time to time a blockade runner or an armed merchant raider attempted the passage. The presence of a large ship in the Channel always prompted a brisk response from the RAF, which still smarted from the embarrassment of the previous February's Channel Dash. The German armed merchant ship *Coronel* was now berthed at Dunkirk. Three Circuses were mounted today, beginning at 1300, in an attempt to sink it. The Jafü 2 controllers were slow to recognize the target, and failed to position their fighters for an interception. The second Circus was a repeat of the first; again, no contact was made. When a third attack force was detected, the defenders were directed not to the coast, but to mid-Channel, to intercept it on its return flight. This third Circus was the largest of the day; its bomber component comprised twenty-two B-24s from the 44th Bomb Group. One B-24 was shot down by the Dunkirk Flak. A second was shot down east of Dover by Oblt. Hohagen, the Kapitän of 7/JG 2, but the attempted interception was otherwise unsuccessful. Hptm. Galland and a 7/JG 2 pilot claimed Spitfires off Ramsgate, but no RAF loss has been traced. Uffz. Johannes Kemper and Uffz. Karl Bruhn, both of the 7th Staffel, were shot down in mid-Channel, and two more Third Gruppe Focke-Wulfs crash-landed on Wevelgem after this mission. Fighter Command claimed 11-2-5 Focke-Wulfs during the day, and the 7th Staffel suffered the only two losses; these match up best with the claims made by the Norwegians of the North Weald Wing, which sustained no losses.

Gefr. Heuser flew a last nonproductive sortie from Vendeville in mid-afternoon, and then boarded a train for East Prussia with the last group of First Gruppe pilots to leave for the Eastern Front.

JG 26 Casualties: 10 - 15 February 1943

Date	Rank	Name	Cas	Unit	Aircraft	WNr	Mkgs	Place	Time	Cause	Allied Unit
10-02-43	Fw.	Friedrich, Karl	KIA	11/54	Bf 109G-4	16103	rd 10	N of Cap Blanc Nez	1715	Typhoon	609 Sqd
15-02-43	Uffz.	Bruhn, Karl	KIA	7	Fw 190A-4	5728	wh 6	15km NW of Dunkirk	1546	Spitfire	331 or 332 Sqd
15-02-43	Uffz.	Kemper, Johannes	KIA	7	Fw 190A-4	2434	wh 8	15km NW of Dunkirk	1550	Spitfire	331 or 332 Sqd

16 February

Improved weather brought a resumption of the Second Gruppe coastal patrols, which on this day found nothing. A noon scramble by Major Priller's Stabsschwarm and the Second Gruppe was also unsuccessful, and it was not until late evening, when another Circus was sent to bomb the *Coronel* at Dunkirk, that contact was made. Claims for two downed Spitfires were confirmed; the day's only three Spitfire losses were attributed by the RAF to oxygen failure, but one could have resulted from Oblt. Naumann's attack, which was made at an altitude of 8000 meters (26,000 feet).

The major Allied attack of the day was on the St. Nazaire submarine pens by seventy-one B-17s and eighteen B-24s of the understrength 8th Bomber Command. Once again the Jafü 3 controller held his fighters away until the eleven escorting fighter squadrons turned back. Lt. Stammberger's 9th Staffel, termed the "Vannes Staffel" in the 8th Bomber Command operations research summary, was the first to attack the bombers, just as they left the target. The Staffel attacked continuously for the next forty-five minutes, in head-on passes to very close range by one or two aircraft. The bombers claimed 16-11-2 of the dozen Focke-Wulfs, but only Lt.

Stammberger's aircraft was hit hard enough to be entered in the German records. One shell smashed his canopy, and fragments hit his left hand. He and Fw. Dörre teamed up to shoot down one B-17, and Uffz. Schwarz downed another. Stammberger's injuries were slight. The next day he and his Staffel were ordered to rejoin its parent Gruppe in Belgium, after receiving a commendation from the JG 2 Kommodore, Obstlt. Oesau.

The III/JG 2 Staffeln flying from Brest apparently failed to score, but the three Staffeln of I/JG 2, flying a second sortie from St. Brieuc, attacked in groups of four to six until the bombers were halfway back across the Channel, before turning back at the approach of the Spitfire withdrawal escort, which was apparently running very late. I/JG 2 filed six victory claims, of which five were confirmed. Some Bf 109s from a reconnaissance Staffel, 2/NAGr 13, put in a late appearance and claimed two B-17s over the Channel, but these claims were not confirmed. Six B-17s failed to return from the mission, two each from the 303rd, 305th, and 306th Bomb Groups.

JG 26 Victory Claims: 15 - 16 February 1943

Date	Rank	Name	Unit	Cl #	Aircraftd	Place	Time	Opponent	Conf
15-02-43	Hptm.	Galland W-F.	II CO	30	Spitfire	6-8km SE of Ramsgate	1604		yes
16-02-43		II. Stab	II St	4	Spitfire	8km NW of Abbeville	1735	402 Sqd	yes
16-02-43	Oblt.	Naumann	6 CO	11	Spitfire	Bourseville	1728	402 Sqd	yes
16-02-43	Fw.	Dörre	9	5	B-17	2.5km SW of Pleuradeur	1120		i.O.
16-02-43	Uffz.	Schwarz E.	9	2	B-17	6-10km W of Ploermal	1125		i.O.
16-02-43	Lt.	Stammberger	9		B-17-HSS	St Nazaire	1120		no

17 February

The day's major Allied operation was another attack on the *Coronel*, which was still at Dunkirk and was still undamaged by the week's attacks. Twelve No. 21 Sqd. Venturas made the attempt, but were turned back by clouds. No. 124 Squadron, flying high cover in its high-altitude Spitfire VIs, was blown all the way to St. Omer by a strong tailwind. The isolated squadron was easy pickings for the thirty Fw 190s of the Second Gruppe, which downed four of the Spitfires without loss. Uffz. Gomann took part in this mission and was then assigned to escort a VIP's Ju 52 from Vitry to Calais-Marck and back.

The JG 26 Jabostaffel was redesignated 10 (Jabo)/JG 54 today; this Staffel would be staying in France when the rest of JG 26 moved to the Eastern Front. A change-of-command ceremony was held at St. Omer-Wizernes. It was attended by the Green Heart Kommodore, Obstlt. Hannes Trautloft, who flew over from his command post near Leningrad. The Jabo pilots removed their Schlageter armbands, but little else changed; they remained under JG 26 for administration, while tactically they operated independently, as before. During its twelve months as 10(Jabo)/JG 26, the Staffel had lost eighteen pilots killed and two POWs, by far the highest losses of any JG 26 Staffel.

The 7th Staffel pilots left today by train from Courtrai. Their ultimate destination was Krasnogvardeisk, on the Leningrad Front; advance detachments from the Third Gruppe Stab and the 7th, 8th, and 9th Staffeln were already there. The 9th Staffel had returned from Vannes to Wevelgem to replace the 7th Staffel in Jafü 2. A Green Heart Staffel, 4/JG 54, was *en route* from Russia, and would be assigned to III/JG 26 until the remainder of its own Gruppe, II/JG 54, arrived from the Eastern Front.

In all probability 11/JG 26 was officially redesignated 11/JG 54 on this date. (The designations 11/JG 26 and 11/JG 54 are used almost interchangeably in documents dated from January to June, 1943.) General Galland intended to raise the establishment strength of each of the Jagdgruppen based in the West to four Staffeln. Thus the 11th Staffel was a convenient "extra", available to augment any Gruppe of JG 54 upon its arrival in the West. There was apparently no plan to send this Staffel to Russia.

A Fw 190A-5/U3 fighter-bomber of 10(Jabo)/JG 54, redesignated from 10(Jabo)/JG 26 on 17 February. *(Bundesarchiv-Bildarchiv)*

A Fw 190A-5/U3 fighter bomber takes off from St. Omer-Wizernes carrying a 500kg bomb. This aircraft belongs to 10(Jabo)/JG 54, the former 10(Jabo)/JG 26. *(Bundesarchiv-Bildarchiv)*

JG 26 Victory Claims: 17 February 1943

Date	Rank	Name	Unit	Cl #	Aircraft	Place	Time	Opponent	Conf
17-02-43	Obfw.	Glunz	4	24	Spitfire	Ardres	1045	124 Sqd	yes
17-02-43	Fw.	Meyer H.	4	4	Spitfire	NW of St. Omer	1046	124 Sqd	yes
17-02-43	Uffz.	Crump	5	5	Spitfire	1km W of Guines	1049	124 Sqd	yes
17-02-43	Lt.	Hoppe	5	6	Spitfire	6km SE of Calais	1102	124 Sqd	yes

25 February

The Geschwader made no combat flights for an eight-day period, only training and test flights, patrols, and scrambles with no contact. Perhaps the most noteworthy event during this period was the declaration by Luftflotte 3 that I/JG 27 was at last operational. Although it was flying from Bernay and Beaumont-le-Roger and thus came under the control of Jafü 3, it could assist Jafü 2 when called upon, which might happen fairly often until III/JG 54 became operational in place of the departed I/JG 26.

Two Jabostaffel pilots, Lt. Otto-August Backhaus (KIA 9 Apr 43) and Lt. Siegfried Stosberg, relax at St. Omer-Wizernes in early 1943. *(Hays)*

26 February

The morning recon mission was flown by an 8th Staffel Rotte. They flew west from Wevelgem before turning north near Boulogne, but never came close to England. They were attacked southwest of Cap Gris Nez by four Typhoons from the Geschwader nemesis, No. 609 Squadron. One Focke-Wulf made it back to France, but Lt. Hermann Thiessen crashed into the Channel.

The RAF continued its attacks on the *Coronel*; to date these had been totally without success. Beginning at 1100, five attacks were made, each by a dozen Venturas. These operations were called Roadsteads, which was the code term for attacks on shipping. Only the first and fourth were intercepted, and only the first lost any aircraft; Hptm. Galland and Obfw. Glunz each shot down a No. 122 Sqd. Spitfire. According to the Allied records, the fourth wave of bombers was hit by "more than seventy-one" German aircraft, which had to be every airplane reporting to Jafü 2. No RAF airplane went down. During these two combats one Second Gruppe pilot bailed out without injury, and one 7/JG 54 Bf 109 crashed near Boulogne, killing its pilot. This was the first III/JG 54 combat loss on the Channel Front.

27 February

The day's only flying activity centered on Dunkirk. The RAF sent yet another Roadstead to attack the *Coronel*. The bomber component comprised twenty-four Venturas. Hptm. Galland led the Second Gruppe up from Vitry at 1407. Galland climbed toward a large Spitfire formation over the French-Belgian coast. It turned away as the Germans approached. Galland saw an opportunity to cut off part of the formation, and flew out to sea. Oblt. Sternberg's 5th Staffel was at the right rear of the formation, with Uffz. Crump and his wingman flying at the extreme right. The Spitfires belonged to the all-Canadian Kenley Wing, whose leader was surprised to see the Focke-Wulfs approaching them so far out to sea. The leading flight, from No. 403 Squadron, broke up and came back around to the right. They were ignored by Sternberg, who maintained his position in the Gruppe formation despite Crump's shouted warnings. According to Peter Crump, "Sternberg possessed little tactical sensitivity and a great herd instinct, and was somewhat immovable and clumsy in his thinking."

Peter Crump's crew chief, "Sepp", paints the sixth victory bar, for a No. 403 Sqd. (RCAF) Spitfire, on Crump's Fw 190A-4 "black 10," W.Nr. 5658 – Vitry-en-Artois, 27 February. *(Crump)*
\

The Spitfires' attack downed two Focke-Wulfs. Lt. Karl Müller-Göbs, a newly-arrived pilot on his first mission, was killed when a wing of his fighter collapsed. The Focke-Wulf of Müller-Göbs' element leader, Uffz. Heinz Gomann, was hit in the cockpit and engine, and Gomann himself was hit in the hand. He turned for the coast, streaming fuel. He reached Calais and prepared for a forced-landing. Neglecting to first shut off the ignition, he closed the throttle, and a backfire immediately ignited the leaking fuel. Gomann had to jump from 100 meters (330 feet). He hit the ground just as his parachute opened, suffering further injuries. Gomann was seriously burned on his wrists and face, "Everywhere I wasn't wearing leather." He was picked up by an ambulance and regained consciousness in the Calais hospital, which fortunately was highly proficient at treating burns. He remained sedated on morphine for fourteen days, until the pain became bearable.

Meanwhile, Crump had followed his *Schwarmführer* (flight leader), Obfw. Paul Fritsch, in a climbing turn toward the rest of the Spitfires. The fighter closest to Crump presented him with a target at a deflection of 40-50 degrees. At 275 meters (300 yards) range, Crump fired a short burst from all six guns. The Spitfire tipped over its left wing, leveled off, and toppled over again, its controls obviously damaged. A fascinated Peter Crump watched the enemy pilot repeat this falling-leaf maneuver until he had used up most of his altitude of 7500 meters (25,000 feet); at this point the Allied pilot gave up and bailed out. The Canadian pilot did not survive. Crump received credit for one Spitfire. Fritsch was credited with a second Spitfire, from 8000 meters (26,000 feet), but only one was lost, and Crump's target had probably already been hit by Fritsch.

JG 26 Victory Claims: 26 - 27 February 1943

Date	Rank	Name	Unit	Cl #	Aircraft	Place	Time	Opponent	Conf
26-02-43	Hptm.	Galland W-F.	II CO	31	Spitfire	10-15km W of St. Omer	1035	122 Sqd	yes
26-02-43	Obfw.	Glunz	4	25	Spitfire	W of St. Omer	1037	122 Sqd	yes
27-02-43	Uffz.	Crump	5	6	Spitfire	50-60km NNW of Dunkirk	1432	403 Sqd	yes
27-02-43	Obfw.	Fritsch P.	5	2	Spitfire	50-60km NNW of Dunkirk	1434	403 Sqd	yes

JG 26 Casualties: 24 - 27 February 1943

Date	Rank	Name	Cas	Unit	Aircraft	WNr	Mkgs	Place	Time	Cause	Allied Unit
24-02-43	Ogfr.	Stahl, Berthold	WIFA	11/54	Bf 109G-1	14087		Merville		engine	non-op
26-02-43	Lt.	Thiessen, Hermann	KIA	8	Fw 190A-4	674	bk 6	SW of Cap Gris Nez	0855	Typhoon	609 Sqd
26-02-43	Uffz.	Wilkemeier, Erich	KIA	III/54	Bf 109G-4	16153		near Boulogne		combat	
27-02-43	Uffz.	Gomann, Heinz	WIA	5	Fw 190A-4	2455	bk 12	Calais	1430	Spitfire	402 or 403 Sqd
27-02-43	Lt.	Müller-Göbs, Karl	KIA	5	Fw 190A-4	7063	bk 9	60km NW of Dunkirk	1430	Spitfire	402 or 403 Sqd

28 February

There was little flying today, and no contact with Allied aircraft. In the month's principal personnel moves, Hptm. Kurt Ruppert resumed his position as 9th Staffel Kapitän after an extended absence from the Geschwader. Hptm. Kurt Ebersberger left the 4th Staffel for a tour as a Staffelkapitän and instructor in Jagdgruppe Ost. Oblt. Stotto Stammberger left the 9th Staffel and took over the 4th as Staffelführer. Major Werner Lederer joined the Geschwader to take charge of the ground staff. Fw. Wilhelm Freuwörth, a Knight's Cross holder with fifty-six victories in 2/JG 52, joined the 6th Staffel. Lt. Walter Matoni, who had served in the Geschwader briefly in 1941 and had then gone to JG 2, arrived after a tour as an instructor and was also assigned to the 6th Staffel. Hptm. Paul Steindl rejoined JG 26 from JG 54 and was assigned to the Third Gruppe Stab. Fw. Gottfried Dietze left the First Gruppe for instructor duty, thus missing his chance for a tour on the Eastern Front. Lt. Waldemar Radener joined the Geschwader, apparently from training, and was assigned to the 6th Staffel. Only a handful of replacements are known to have arrived from the training schools; one was Obfw. Alfred Günther, who was assigned to the Second Gruppe.

3 March

The RAF did not make an appearance on the 1st, but sent a few flights of fighters across the Channel on the 2nd. These were not large enough to justify scrambling entire Staffeln, but the standing patrols failed to make contact, and these patrols were strengthened on the 3rd – Major Priller pulled a shift, as did Uffz. Polster, flying from the new 11th Staffel base at Merville. Obfw. Glunz was sent across the Channel in mid-afternoon to search out any activity, but found nothing. The Allied air forces stayed on the ground.

4 March

Despite bad weather, the 8th Bomber Command ordered the first American attack on the Ruhr. Only one of the four B-17 groups found Germany. Five B-17s were shot down, four by Fw 190s of II/JG 1, flying from Woensdrecht. All of JG 26 was ordered into the air, but no B-17s flew far enough west for Jafü 2 to direct an interception, and no contacts were made. The next day the 4th Staffel transferred to Bonn to guard against a return trip to the Ruhr by the Americans, but when this did not take place in several days, the Staffel returned to Vitry.

6 March

The B-17 force bombed the submarine pens at Lorient, losing three bombers to III/JG 2. Jafü 2 did not order its aircraft up.

7 March

The two Jabostaffeln were ordered to fly a combined full-strength mission to England. Eighteen unescorted Fw 190A-5/U3s crossed the Channel at minimum altitude and at 1352 dropped their bombs on Eastbourne, killing fourteen civilians and seven servicemen. The Jabos had not been detected by radar, and the few RAF fighters up on patrol were unable to catch them. A number of Geschwader fighters took off and escorted the Jabos back to Wizernes, but no contact was made with the Allies. Other Staffeln scrambled during the day to oppose RAF fighter sweeps, but these too failed to make contact.

8 March

The 8th Bomber Command split its small force, sending fifty-four B-17s to Rennes in Brittany while sixteen B-24s targeted the Rouen railroad yards. The B-24s were escorted by sixteen RAF Spitfire squadrons, and supported by a sweep by 4th Fighter Group Spitfires. Jafü 2 and Jafü 3 combined their forces against the Rouen raid, and were able to get the JG 26 Stabsschwarm and Second Gruppe, as well as 12/JG 2 and part of I/JG 27 into position for a perfectly coordinated attack. Major Priller's force and the Jafü 3 Messerschmitts held off the escorts, allowing Hptm. Galland to lead his two dozen Focke-Wulfs in a tight right bank into a head-on attack on the B-24s – *von Schnauze auf Schnauze*, or "snout to snout", in the German phrase. Their attack was devastating. The lead bomber burst into flames, followed by the No. 2 aircraft in the leading vee. The bomber formation fell apart completely; bombs were scattered over the French countryside as the aircraft sought to evade the German fighters. The two lead B-24s, from the 44th Bomb Group, crashed in France, while a 93rd Bomb Group aircraft crashed after reaching England. Major Priller shot down one of the escorting Spitfires, as did Lt. Eder of 12/JG 2. The Allied escorts shot down two 12/JG 2 aircraft, whose pilots bailed out, and one from 3/JG 27, whose pilot was killed. The Schlageter fighters suffered no damage or loss. They were proudest, however, of having forced the bombers to turn back before reaching their target. This proved to be the only such triumph ever gained over the 8th Air Force.

JG 26 Victory Claims: 8 March 1943

Date	Rank	Name	Unit	Cl #	Aircraft	Place	Time	Opponent	Conf
08-03-43	Major	Priller	Ge CO	83	Spitfire	8km NW of St Valery en Caux	1415	340 Sqd	unk
08-03-43	Hptm.	Galland W-F.	II CO	32	B-24	Totes?	1404	44 BG	yes
08-03-43	Obfw.	Glunz	4	26	Spitfire	Rouen	1406	340 Sqd	unk
08-03-43	Obfw.	Roth	4	18	B-24	Barentin?	1405	44 BG	yes
08-03-43	Uffz.	Crump	5		B-24-HSS	N of Rouen	1400	44 BG	no
08-03-43	Oblt.	Naumann	6 CO	12	B-24	15km SE of Hastings	1408	44 BG	yes

9 March

Shortly after noon several Geschwader fighters flew a sweep over Canterbury, of which the RAF radio intercepts provide the only surviving record. There was no RAF interception, and, if ground targets were attacked, no British casualties. In mid-afternoon the Lille and Vitry Gruppen scrambled after word was received of several Allied formations crossing the French coast. No contact was made.

10 March

A large Rodeo swept across the Pas de Calais in mid-afternoon. The Lille and Vitry Gruppen were scrambled, but were held back from attacking when no bombers were found. The only casualty was one III/JG 54 Bf 109, which was slightly damaged in a passing encounter. This was the first combat mission for the Americans' new fighter, the P-47 Thunderbolt. The American pilots found radio communications impossible owing to interference from their ignition systems, and the P-47s were withdrawn from combat for a month for electrical modifications.

A late-evening Rodeo brought the Schlageter fighters into the air. There were no bombers present, and no attack was ordered. W/C Milne, leading the high cover with the Biggin Hill Wing, saw fifteen Fw 190s beneath him, dived behind the formation, and "exploded" one of the Focke-Wulfs; the others immediately half-rolled and dived away. Milne's target was piloted by Lt. Hans Mayer of the 6th Staffel. The injured Mayer was able to crash-land his badly damaged plane at Arras.

11 March

In mid-afternoon the two Jabostaffeln flew a full-strength combined mission to the English coast. Twenty-seven Focke-Wulfs crossed the Channel at minimum altitude, dropped their bombs on Hastings, and reversed course for France. No German aircraft were lost, and no serious damage was done. The Lille and Vitry Gruppen provided return escort, but the RAF did not pursue the Jabos across the Channel. Two III/JG 54 Messerschmitts collided northwest of Lille while airborne on this reception flight, and one pilot was killed.

12 March

The Jabostaffeln flew their second combined mission in two days. Twenty-four Jabos crossed the English coast at 0730; apparently some penetrated as far as London. Only No. 609 Squadron's standing patrol was able to make contact. Two Typhoons followed Fw. Emil Bösch of 10(Jabo)/JG 54 back across the Channel and shot him down off Dunkirk. A 10(Jabo)/JG 2 Focke-Wulf crashed on Coxyde with combat damage, killing the pilot. The Second Gruppe, patrolling the Thames Estuary, and Priller and III/JG 54, patrolling the French coast, failed to make contact; two Green Heart Messerschmitts force-landed with engine problems.

The four B-17 groups bombed the Rouen railroad yards shortly after noon. Jafü 2 had its fighters up from Lille and Vitry in ample time to make an interception, but no contact was made. It is possible that there was a problem passing the control to Jafü 3, in whose area the target lay.

The American 8th Fighter Command, which had only one fighter group, the 4th, operational at this time, seemed to be fighting an independent war. It rarely took part in escort missions, but instead flew small-scale sweeps which the Germans usually ignored. In late afternoon two squadrons from the 4th swept St. Omer. The two formations were fifteen miles apart, and two airborne 9th Staffel pilots saw the opportunity to make a clean bounce. Fw. Dörre shot down one American Spitfire, and the two Focke-Wulfs then escaped untouched.

13 March

The Second Gruppe scrambled from Vitry at 1345 after a formation was reported over the Channel; the Allied aircraft apparently never crossed the French coast, and the Germans landed forty-five minutes later, only to take off again in twenty minutes when a large formation which included heavy bombers was plotted east of Dieppe. At this time Major Priller led III/JG 54 up from Vendeville, and 12/JG 2 and I/JG 27 took off from their bases west of the Somme. The bomber force comprised eighty B-17s *en*

The Geschwader Stabsschwarm catch up on their reading while at readiness. Major Priller is second from left; Hptm. Gäth, third. The Fw 190A-4 is Priller's W.Nr. 2386 – Vendeville, early 1943. *(Cranston)*

A "black man" of the ground crew poses beside a Geschwaderstab Fw 190A-4 – Vendeville, early 1943. (*Cranston*)

route to the Amiens railroad yards. The bombers were late in forming up, and both bombers and escort were badly scattered. Enough Allied fighters stayed within sight of the B-17s to break up most of the German attacks, however, and no B-17s were shot down, although eleven were damaged. The all-Canadian Kenley Wing, flying high cover for the rear box of bombers, broke up the Second Gruppe attack, damaging Obfw. Hermann Meyer's Focke-Wulf sufficiently that his attacker was able to catch Meyer in his dive and destroy the aircraft, killing Meyer. Hptm. Galland and part of his Gruppe pulled up and dived on the rear of the Spitfire formation, beginning a savage dogfight in which three Spitfires were lost, one from No. 402 Squadron and two from No. 403. Three Spitfires from the other escort squadrons were lost, all apparently the victims of Hptm. Heinrich Setz, the Kommandeur of I/JG 27, which was flying its first full-strength combat mission from France. Setz, who had 138 air victories to his credit, was then shot down and killed. A second I/JG 27 pilot was shot down, but survived, and a third was killed on takeoff from Bernay. A 12/JG 2 pilot was killed by Spitfires, and two III/JG 54 Bf 109s had to force-land with engine damage. The B-17s scattered their bombs on several targets of opportunity. Neither side could claim victory in this day's air battles.

JG 26 Victory Claims: 12 - 13 March 1943

Date	Rank	Name	Unit	Cl #	Aircraft	Place	Time	Opponent	Conf
12-03-43	Fw.	Dörre	9	6	Spitfire	unknown	1630	4 FG	unk
13-03-43	Hptm.	Galland W-F.	II CO	33	Spitfire	Étaples	1535	402 or 403 Sqd	yes
13-03-43	Lt.	Radener	4		Spitfire	E of Étaples	1533	402 or 403 Sqd	no
13-03-43	Lt.	Wiegmann	6	1	Spitfire	5km E of Berck-sur-Mer	1531	402 or 403 Sqd	yes

14 March

A Rodeo to Le Touquet by the Biggin Hill Wing precipitated the day's only major combats. Hptm. Galland led his men up from Vitry at 1720, in ample time to reach position before the Spitfires turned south to parallel the French coast. Galland ordered one Staffel to drop below and act as bait. W/C Milne saw these eight Focke-Wulfs and radioed, "Anyone who wishes may dive and attack." This ambiguous order caused some confusion, especially among the French pilots of No. 340 Squadron, which made up half the wing. Galland and the rest of his Gruppe waited upsun to pounce on the diving Spitfires. In the resulting combats W/C Milne, a supernumerary wing commander, and a sergeant pilot from No. 611 Squadron were shot down; the only German loss was Lt. Ernst Hahne of the 4th Staffel, who apparently collided with the leader of No. 340 Squadron, who then crashed. Of these five pilots, only W/C Milne survived; he was pulled from the Channel by the crew of a German patrol boat.

JG 26 Victory Claims: 14 March 1943

Date	Rank	Name	Unit	Cl #	Aircraft d	Place	Time	Opponent	Conf
14-03-43	Hptm.	Galland W-F.	II CO	34	Spitfire	10km SW of Boulogne	1755	B Hill Wing	yes
14-03-43	Obfw.	Glunz	4	27	Spitfire	2-3km SW of Boulogne	1759	B Hill Wing	yes
14-03-43	Lt.	Hahne	4	2	Spitfire	St. Cécile Plage	1758	340 Sqd	yes
14-03-43	Obfw.	Kruska	6	3	Spitfire	5km W of Camiers	1754	B Hill Wing	yes
14-03-43	Uffz.	Mayer	6	1	Spitfire	Somme Estuary	1757	B Hill Wing	yes

JG 26 Casualties: 10 - 14 March 1943

Date	Rank	Name	Cas	Unit	Aircraft	WNr	Mkgs	Place	Time	Cause	Allied Unit
10-03-43	Lt.	Mayer, Hans	WIA	6	Fw 190A-4	7059	br 6	Arras		Spitfire	B Hill Wing
11-03-43	Fw.	Stern, Artur	KIA	III/54	Bf 109G-4	14886		nr Lille		air collision	n/a
12-03-43	Fw.	Bösch, Emil	KIA	10J	Fw 190A-5	829	bk 12	10km N of Dunkirk	0829	Typhoon	609 Sqd
								+bomb			
13-03-43	Obfw.	Meyer, Hermann	KIA	4	Fw 190A-4	5615	wh 12	SE of Le Tréport		Spitfire	403 Sqd
14-03-43	Lt.	Hahne, Ernst	KIA	4	Fw 190A-4	653	wh 4	nr Boulogne-St. Cécile	1758	Spitfire	340 Sqd

15 March

The Geschwader pilots spent the day on routine defensive patrols. No contact was made with Allied aircraft. On about this date 2/JG 27 left Jafü 3 and the rest of I/JG 27 and transferred to Amsterdam-Schipol, under the jurisdiction of Jafü Holland-Ruhr. Here it reinforced JG 1, which was responsible for the daylight air defense of all of Germany and The Netherlands. This front was still quiet, and the probable reason for the transfer was to give the Staffel some additional training.

Personnel moves during the first half of March saw Lt. Ernst Janda transfer from the 4th Staffel to 3/JGr Ost as a Staffelführer and instructor; Lt. Otto Hummel, a former Flak officer, join the Second Gruppe Stab from flight training; Lt. Dietrich Kehl join the 5th Staffel from flight training; Uffz. Karl Seebeck join the 7th Staffel from 11/JG 54; Uffz. Rudolf Stutt join the Third Gruppe Stab from 11/JG 54; and Uffz. Helmut Bäumener, Uffz. Werner Schwan, Lt. Otto Triebnig and Uffz. Walter Ullrich join the First Gruppe in Russia from flight training.

16 March

There was no flying. Hptm. Wilhelm Gäth was named 2nd Staffel Kapitän and left the Geschwader Stab for Russia to replace Hptm. Fülbert Zink, who was missing in action.

23 March

Some sad news was received from North Africa. The Kommodore of JG 77, Major Joachim Müncheberg, a pre-war member of JG 26 and one of its most successful, best-known, and popular officers in 1940-1942, was killed when debris from a Spitfire he

had just attacked struck his Messerschmitt, causing it to crash.

24 March

For a full week flying activity was restricted to test flights, training, and patrols. This morning the weather was just good enough to support a mission across the Channel, and the two Jabostaffeln were ordered up. At 0945, the Kapitän of 10 (Jabo)/JG 54, Oblt. Paul Keller, led fifteen Fw 190s on a low-altitude approach to Ashford. The formation split up near the town; one flight bombed the railroad station with good results, while most of the remaining aircraft scattered their bombs in the town. Keller himself strafed a gasoline truck standing in a factory yard and blew it up. His aircraft, which was still carrying its

Oblt. Paul Keller, the Kapitän of 10 (Jabo)/JG 54. He was killed over England on 24 March in the explosion of his bomb. *(Vanoverbeke)*

bomb, then exploded. Its bomb had been hit, either by fragments from the truck or by a light antiaircraft shell. The double explosion caused serious damage to the factory. The raid was the heaviest blow to the county of Kent in the entire war. Fifty civilians were killed, and seventy-seven were seriously injured. The popular Oblt. Keller was succeeded by Oblt. Erwin Busch, an amazingly lucky pilot who retained command of the fighter-bomber unit for the rest of the war.

The Second Gruppe provided the forward escort for the Jabos, while the Lille and Wevelgem forces patrolled the coast. The only RAF fighters to make contact were two No. 91 Sqd. Spitfires already airborne on standing patrol. A 5th Staffel Schwarm attacked the pair off Dungeness. Fw. Crump shot one into the sea, while Fw. Freuwörth's target was able to crash-land on Lympne.

25 March

Small flights of fighters from Fighter Command and the Second Gruppe sparred over the Channel all afternoon. First blood went to the RAF. No. 64 Squadron was sweeping south of Abbeville at 11,900 meters (39,000 feet) when twenty Fw 190s were spotted below. The Spitfires turned into the sun and dived to the attack. Only one German aircraft was hit, that of Lt. Hans-Günther Lörzer. The injured Lörzer was able to belly-land his aircraft near Arras, but it was a total write-off. Late in the afternoon Fw. Freuwörth led several 5th Staffel Focke-Wulfs across the Channel and engaged two patrolling No. 609 Sqd. Typhoons. One British pilot bailed out into the Channel, from which he was rescued with injuries. One Fw 190 was claimed by the Typhoon pilots, but all returned to France safely.

JG 26 Victory Claims: 24 - 25 March 1943

Date	Rank	Name	Unit	Cl #	Aircraft	Place	Time	Opponent	Conf
24-03-43	Uffz.	Crump	5	7	Spitfire	10km NNW of Cap Gris Nez	1015	91 Sqd	yes
24-03-43	Fw.	Freuwörth	5	57	Spitfire	8km E of Dungeness	1017	91 Sqd	unk
25-03-43	Fw.	Freuwörth	5	58	Spitfire	5km S of Dover	1814	609 Sqd Typhoon	yes

27 March

A smooth merger of III/JG 54 into the Western order of battle had proved difficult. Too large to merge into the flying organizations already present, the unit had had to undergo a crash course in the rigorous conditions of the Channel Front. Everything was more difficult than in the East, beginning with the burdensome personal equipment – oxygen mask, life jacket, flare gun, etc. – and continuing with the need to maintain close formation in high altitude flight. All of this had to be mastered before the pilots could be pitted against the western Allies. The Gruppe trained for six weeks, closely watched by Major Priller, who took his responsibility for the new unit very seriously. He monitored their formation flights from the air, and several times bounced them from behind without being spotted by a single pilot. Disgusted, Priller stubbornly refused to declare the Gruppe operational. III/JG 54 was detached from JG 26 on this date and ordered to Oldenburg, near Bremen. From this location, it could assist JG 1 in defending northern Germany against the infrequent raids by the American heavy bombers, while remaining outside the range of Allied fighters.

In contrast to the problems of III/JG 54, Graf Matuschka's 4/JG 54 had replaced 7/JG 26 smoothly and without incident. It did not operate independently, but functioned as a third III/JG 26 Staffel under Hptm. Geisshardt at Wevelgem.

Major Priller's pessimistic reports to Berlin caused Gen. Galland to reconsider his decision to bring the rest of JG 54 to the *Kanalfront* (Channel Front); the skills possessed by the pilots of JG 2 and JG 26 were apparently unique. The Geschwader exchange was first postponed, and then canceled; at the appropriate time the First Gruppe and the 7th Staffel would return to their Geschwader in the west.

28 March

Shortly after noon seventy B-17s were dispatched to bomb the Rouen railroad yards. The Spitfire escort missed the rendezvous and the small force of bombers flew a triangular course in mid-Channel, allowing the defenders ample time to get airborne. Shortly after finding the bombers, the Spitfires had to turn back because of low fuel, giving the Second Gruppe and 12/JG 2 a clear shot at the B-17s. Nine were damaged, but only one went down, the victim of Lt. Eder of 12/JG 2. Eder himself was injured by the bombers' fire, but was able to force-land his badly-damaged Messerschmitt on Beaumont-le-Roger.

Two squadrons of De Havilland Mosquitoes had been allotted to No. 2 Group, the organization commanding the RAF's light day bombers. These exceptional aircraft were fast enough to outrun any German fighter in level flight, and thus flew their missions without fighter escort, even though the bombers lacked any form of defensive armament. This evening, while returning from a reconnaissance of the English coast, Uffz. Wilhelm Mayer's 6th Staffel Rotte spotted six Mosquitoes headed toward Dunkirk at low level. Fw. Adolf "Addi" Glunz's Schwarm scrambled from Vitry immediately to defend their airfield, and found themselves in a position to intercept the bombers, which were approaching Liège. Addi Glunz downed two of the bombers within one minute, and was back on the ground ten minutes after taking off.

29 March

The weather took a turn for the worse, and the Pas de Calais fighters flew only routine patrols and a few training flights for the next two days. 10(Jabo)/JG 54 attempted a small *Störungsangriff* on Eastbourne, but were met by a patrol of No. 610 Sqd. Spitfires which shot down two of the Focke-Wulfs. Ogfr. Joachim Koch was killed, but the second pilot survived his bailout into the Channel and was rescued by a German patrol boat.

JG 26 Casualties: 24 - 29 March 1943

Date	Rank	Name	Cas	Unit	Aircraft	WNr	Mkgs	Place	Time	Cause	Allied Unit
24-03-43	Oblt.	Keller, Paul	KIA	10J CO	Fw 190A-5	2787	bk 7 + bomb	Ashford		own bomb	n/a

| 25-03-43 | Lt. | Lörzer, Hans-Günther | WIA | 6 | Fw 190A-4 | 7077 | br 7 | Arras | | Spitfire | 64 Sqd |
| 29-03-43 | Uffz. | Koch, Joachim | KIA | 10J | Fw 190A-5 | 2576 | bk 4+ bomb | Brighton | 1215 | Spitfire | 610 Sqd |

Fw. Crump sits out ten-minute readiness on his airplane's tire – Vitry-en-Artois, spring 1943. *(Crump)*

31 March

Today's target for the 8th Bomber Command was Rotterdam, but the entire formation of 103 B-17s was blown off course by unanticipated high winds, resulting in numerous course changes above the Channel. Four of the six bomber groups aborted the mission, and the Second Gruppe did not catch the other two groups until they were half-way back across the Channel. Galland was concerned about the state of his fuel, and ordered his pilots to make no more than one pass from the rear before turning for France. Fw. Crump glanced at his fuel gauge, decided that an attack was possible, and confirmed the decision with his wingman, Lt. Otto Hummel. Crump picked out a target, from the trailing 305th Bomb Group. It caught fire between its No. 1 and No. 2 engines, and its pilot pulled it from formation, streaming flames and black, oil-fed smoke. Crump turned back after his one attack, and having seen no crash did not bother to file a victory claim; the bomber crew all bailed out safely over England.

The only other German formation to reach the bombers was Oblt. Stammberger's 4th Staffel, which was split from the Second Gruppe and sent after what proved to be a diversionary formation of B-24s. Stammberger made one attack from the front and a second from the rear, after which one B-24 dropped from the formation in flames. Stammberger saw it crash into the Channel, but the rest of his Staffel were on their way home, and he could find no witness to the crash. That evening, the Wissant radio listening service reported that a B-24 had radioed at 1245 that it was no longer controllable due to enemy action, and that its crew was going to bail out. The time and the bomber's location, sixty miles north of Ostend, matched Stammberger's encounter report perfectly, giving him the basis to file a claim, which was, however, rejected by the RLM. The B-24 was from the 93rd Bomb Group; no-one survived its crash. Crump's and Stammberger's victims were the only two bombers lost to enemy action on this date. Ironically, neither loss resulted in a victory credit on the German books.

Personnel moves during the last half of March saw Oblt. Konrad von Donner leave the Second Gruppe Stab to become the adjutant of the Third Gruppe; Fw. Walter Scholz join the 5th Staffel from 10/JG 5; Lt. Günther Blömertz, Lt. Wolfgang Grimm, and Uffz. Erwin Hanke join the Second Gruppe from training; and Lt. Ernst Todt join the 7th Staffel in Russia from training.

JG 26 Victory Claims: 28 - 31 March 1943

Date	Rank	Name	Unit	Cl #	Aircraft	Place	Time	Opponent	Conf
28-03-43	Obfw.	Glunz	4	29	Mosquito	S of Lille	1841	105 Sqd	yes
28-03-43	Obfw.	Glunz	4	28	Mosquito	S of Lille	1842	105 Sqd	yes
31-03-43	Oblt.	Stammberger	4 CO	4	B-24	100km NW of Ostend	1248	93 BG	unk
31-03-43	Uffz.	Crump	5		B-17-HSS	Thames Estuary	1245	305 BG	no

2 April

Flights for the first two days of April were restricted to defensive patrols. Major Priller revived the concept of the *Führungsverband* or "leader's unit" used by Adolf Galland in 1941 and ordered Oblt. Borris's 8th Staffel to join him at Lille-Vendeville. To the east, the air defenses of Germany were doubled, on paper, by dividing JG 1 in two. A new Geschwader, JG 11, was formed from two its four Gruppen.

3 April

A morning raid on Eastbourne by 10(Jabo)/JG 54 cost the British twenty-six civilian dead and the Germans one pilot, Uffz. Fritz Ebert, who was shot down and killed by light antiaircraft fire.

In mid-afternoon eight Typhoons were dispatched to attack Abbeville-Drucat. The Kenley Wing swept from Le Touquet to St. Omer in advance of the fighter-bombers, and caught the Second Gruppe still climbing from Vitry. W/C J. E. "Johnnie" Johnson, flying his first mission in command of the all-Canadian Kenley Wing, gives full credit to his controller in England for putting the wing upsun of the Germans, in perfect position for an attack. Johnson led No. 416 Squadron to the left, while No. 403 Squadron dived on the right side of the Focke-Wulf formation, whose leader had by now seen the Spitfires and was climbing toward them. In the initial attack the two Canadian squadron leaders each flamed a trailing Fw 190, killing Uffz. Heinrich Damm and. Uffz. Albert Meyer. In the subsequent dogfights, W/C Johnson shot down Uffz. Hans Hiess, who had lost his Schwarm; Hiess bailed out, but his parachute did not open. Obfw. Glunz shot down a No. 416 Sqd. Spitfire, the only Allied loss. After returning to Kenley the jubilant Canadians were credited with six victories, but the other three Focke-Wulfs that had been hit succeeded in landing on Vitry and Merville.

At 2012 several small Mosquito formations were reported crossing the French and Belgian coasts at low altitude. A 6th Staffel patrol was in a position to intercept, and Obfw. Mackenstedt shot down one of the RAF bombers south of Beauvais. The base at Vitry then had to turn on its recognition lights in order for the late patrols to find the field.

JG 26 Victory Claims: 3 April 1943

Date	Rank	Name	Unit	Cl #	Aircraft	Place	Time	Opponent	Conf
03-04-43	Obfw.	Glunz	4	30	Spitfire	Le Touquet	1608	416 Sqd	yes
03-04-43	Obfw.	Mackenstedt	6	6	Mosquito	3km S of Beauvais	2030	139 Sqd	yes

JG 26 Casualties: 3 April 1943

Date	Rank	Name	Cas	Unit	Aircraft	WNr	Mkgs	Place	Time	Cause	Allied Unit
03-04-43	Uffz.	Damm, Heinrich	KIA	4	Fw 190A-4	732	wh 11	St. Omer-Le Touquet	1630	Spitfire	403 or 416 Sqd
03-04-43	Uffz.	Meyer, Albert	KIA	5	Fw 190A-5	1159	bk 5	Channel Narrows	1630	Spitfire	403 or 416 Sqd
03-04-43	Uffz.	Hiess, Hans	KIA	6	Fw 190A-4	2440	br 5	Neuville near Montreuil	1630	Spitfire	Kenley Wing
03-04-43	Uffz.	Ebert, Fritz	KIA	10J	Fw 190A-5	835	bk 11 +bomb	Eastbourne		Spitfire	Northolt Wing
03-04-43	Lt.	Heinemeyer, H.-Joachim	WIFA	11/54	Fw 190A-4	5606		Merville		engine	non-op

4 April

The Allied target today was the Renault motor vehicle factory southeast of Paris. Several feints and diversions were flown in an attempt to disperse the German defenses. At 1304 Jafü 2 detected the heavy bombers half-way across the North Sea from Harwich. The Second Gruppe was scrambled and ordered to patrol the coast until the direction of the attack was known. The bombers turned east, but then back to the southwest, and the Gruppe was quickly landed and refueled. At 1324 the Caen airfield was bombed by No. 2 Group Venturas. I/JG 2 intercepted this force, and then had to land. At 1352 the 8th Staffel was ordered up from Vendeville, and the Third Gruppe from Wevelgem. The fighters joined up, probably under Hptm. Geisshardt, and proceeded toward the Somme Estuary. At 1410 Hptm. Galland led the Second Gruppe up from Vitry toward Beauvais, where Jafü 3 was assembling all available fighters in order to attack the returning bombers in strength. In the meantime the bombers had made their southern turn, proceeded to the Paris area unmolested, and at 1415 made a good bombing run.

Major Oesau, the JG 2 Kommodore, led I/JG 2 and the operational Staffel of JG 105, a training unit, in the first attack on the eighty-five unescorted B-17s north of Paris. They made several passes before the formation reached the Rouen area. At this point the JG 26 Gruppen began making concentrated head-on attacks to close range. Most attacks were made from eleven, twelve, and one o'clock high, by one or two Schwärme simultaneously. Spacing between the German attacking units was much closer than previously, only 900-1400 meters (1000-1500 yards), catching bombers out of position when they jinked to evade the previous fighters. The bombers' withdrawal cover, the Spitfires of the Northolt and Kenley Wings, arrived shortly thereafter, but their orders called for them to be at 30,000 feet (9100 meters), well above the bombers, and Galland and Geisshardt were able to fend them off for a while with only part of their units. The battle eventually degenerated into a general fighter melee over the Channel, from which the bombers escaped after losing four of their number; sixteen others were damaged.

JG 26 lost Fw. Karl Fackler (6th Staffel) killed, and Uffz. Robert Hager (8th Staffel) injured, and the associated 4/JG 54 lost Ogfr. Jürgen Birn in this battle. Two Second Gruppe and two Third Gruppe Fw 190s, plus one 4/JG 54 Bf 109, returned to base with combat damage. Hptm. Galland claimed two B-17s, the second of which was unconfirmed, the 8th Staffel's Oblt. Borris claimed a third, and Major Oesau was awarded the fourth. The Northolt and Kenley Wings lost eight Spitfires; four of the Second Gruppe claims were confirmed, as was one by the 8th Staffel, one by the 9th, and two by I/JG 2.

The day's combats were not yet finished. At 1900 Priller's Stabsschwarm and part of the Second Gruppe were scrambled in response to an Allied bomber force proceeding east from the Channel into the North Sea. This was another Ventura formation, flying toward The Netherlands. The interception was left to II/JG 1 at Woensdrecht; this unit claimed three Venturas and four Spitfires, without loss.

JG 26 Victory Claims: 4 April 1943

Date	Rank	Name	Unit	Cl #	Aircraft	Place	Time	Opponent	Conf
04-04-43	Hptm.	Galland W-F.	II CO	35	Spitfire	SE of Fécamp	1440	315, 316 or 403 Sqd	yes
04-04-43	Hptm.	Galland W-F.	II CO	36	B-17	8km E of Fécamp	1445	303 or 305 BG	yes
04-04-43	Hptm.	Galland W-F.	II CO	37	B-17	20-30 km N of Fécamp	1455	303 or 305 BG	unk
04-04-43	Obfw.	Glunz	4	31	Spitfire	SW of Dieppe	1442	315, 316 or 403 Sqd	unk
04-04-43	Oblt.	Sternberg	5 CO	13	Spitfire	NW of Rouen	1442	315, 316 or 403 Sqd	yes
04-04-43	Lt.	Hoppe	5	7	Spitfire	30km S of Beachy Head	1455	315, 316 or 403 Sqd	yes
04-04-43	Oblt.	Naumann	6 CO	13	Spitfire	10km SW of Dieppe	1442	315, 316 or 403 Sqd	yes
04-04-43	Uffz.	Mayer	6		Spitfire	25km NW of Dieppe	1500		no
04-04-43	Hptm.	Borris	8 CO		B-17	Rouen-Dieppe	1440	303 or 305 BG	yes
04-04-43	Uffz.	Hager R.	8		Spitfire	E of Rouen near Blauville	1437	315, 316 or 403 Sqd	yes
04-04-43	Uffz.	Holl	9		Spitfire	Rouen	1440	315, 316 or 403 Sqd	yes

Date	Rank	Name	Cas	Unit	Aircraft	WNr	Mkgs	Place	Time	Cause	Allied Unit
04-04-43	Ogfr.	Birn, Jürgen	KIA	4/54	Bf 109G-4	19369	wh 16	St Denis-Rouen	1440	B-17	
04-04-43	Fw.	Fackler, Karl	KIA	6	Fw 190A-4	2392	br 12	Channel Narrows		missing	
04-04-43	Uffz.	Hager, Robert	WIA	8	Fw 190A-4	2391	bk 11	2km SE of Rouen	1350	B-17	

5 April

The Allied target for today was the ERLA aircraft repair facility at Antwerp. The 104 B-17s and B-24s feinted toward Abbeville before reversing course. They then turned east before finally turning southeast toward Antwerp. The Second Gruppe pilots matched these moves and had burned half their fuel before turning for Antwerp. Major Priller led the 8th Staffel and the Third Gruppe directly to Antwerp and was able to form up for head-on attacks before the escort turned back at Ghent; the British fighters were too far above and behind the formation to intervene. The first concentrated attack broke the cohesiveness of the bomber formation. Only eighty-two B-17s managed to bomb their target; most of the 306th Bomb Group overshot and hit the small city of Mortsel, killing many women and children and bringing the Americans a rebuke from the Belgian ambassador in Washington. This group, which was in the lead, was split up by the Germans' initial pass, and thus bore the brunt of the rest of the attacks. Major Priller and Hptm. Ruppert of the 9th Staffel received credit for downing B-17s on this first pass, but only one went down at this time. Hptm. Geisshardt, who was flying in Priller's Schwarm, was hit by return fire from the bombers. Bleeding profusely from a wound in the abdomen, Geisshardt dived away from the battle and made a smooth landing on the airfield at St Denis-Westrem. His blood loss proved fatal; the medical personnel at the Ghent hospital could not save him, and he died early the next morning.

Hptm. Galland's Second Gruppe raced to Antwerp at full throttle, and found itself in position to make a head-on attack just as the 306th turned off the target. They tore through the scattered bombers, causing several to fall away. Three crashed in Belgium and were credited to Second Gruppe pilots; duplicate credits were awarded to II/JG 1. The Second Gruppe aircraft were low on fuel and had turned back for Vitry when the four Spitfire squadrons of the withdrawal escort arrived. II/JG 1 Focke-Wulfs engaged the Spitfires off the coast, as did I/JG 2, which had flown all the way from Triqueville

The remains of Lt. Robert Seelos' 306th Bomber Group B-17F after being shot down by Adolf Glunz north of Antwerp on 5 April. *(Seelos)*

and had to turn back for the coastal field at Coxyde after a few minutes of inconclusive combat. One JG 2 pilot force-landed near Ostend with severe injuries. He was the only German casualty attributable to the escorts, which were for the most part ineffective. Four B-17s were lost, all from the 306th. Thirteen more bombers returned with damage. The American bomber commanders skirted around the issue at their evening conference, but their displeasure with their Allies was made clear. In a sense, the presence of the Spitfires simplified the German defenders' job. The fighter controllers had learned to recognize the Spitfire escorts, which typically flew at 9100 meters (30,000 feet), at least 1500 meters (5000 feet) above the bombers. Formations that high always gave away the presence of heavy bombers beneath them. The Luftwaffe fighter leaders had the option to attack the escort, wait until it turned back, or, as today, ignore them and attack the bombers before the escort could react.

The German commanders had reason to be pleased; today was the first time that fighters from three different commands had combined forces for an interception. Fritz Geisshardt was the day's only fatality, and only three Geschwader aircraft sustained reportable damage. Hptm. Kurt Ruppert replaced Geisshardt as Third Gruppe Kommandeur; Hptm. Paul Steindl took over the 9th Staffel.

JG 26 Victory Claims: 5 April 1943

Date	Rank	Name	Unit	Cl #	Aircraft	Place	Time	Opponent	Conf
05-04-43	Major	Priller	Ge CO	84	B-17	20km W of Ostend	1512	306 BG	yes
05-04-43	Hptm.	Galland W.-F.	II CO	38	B-17	S of Antwerp	1525	306 BG	yes
05-04-43	Oblt.	Stammberger	4 CO	5	B-17	N Antwerp-Dintelnoord	1535	306 BG	yes
05-04-43	Obfw.	Glunz	4	32	B-17	N of Scheldt Estuary	1538	306 BG	unk
05-04-43	Hptm.	Ruppert K.	9 CO	21	B-17	N of Ghent	1522	306 BG	yes

6 April

Small flights of Geschwader aircraft patrolled the Pas de Calais from dawn until after sunset without contacting the few RAF formations that crossed the Channel.

A newly-organized Staffel, 12/JG 54, arrived at Lille-Vendeville and was attached to JG 26. The Staffel was commanded by Oblt. Erwin Leykauf, a member of the Green Heart Geschwader since before the war. The Staffel flew Bf 109s, and soon left Vendeville for Wevelgem to join the Third Gruppe, which was to be the Geschwader Messerschmitt Gruppe. The 6th Staffel left Vitry and joined Priller at Lille. Priller now had two Staffeln, the 6th and 8th, under his direct operational control; they became known as the *Geschwadergruppe*.

12/JG 54 had been formed as part of Gen. Galland's master plan for the expansion of his day fighter force. Galland's battles with Hitler and the Luftwaffe High Command over the strength of Germany's fighter forces were never-ending. Pleas for defensive forces were guaranteed to send Hitler into a tirade. Not until 1943 was fighter production allowed to increase. Galland did not immediately create new Geschwader to absorb these aircraft, since he lacked sufficient commanders and specialists to staff them. Instead, the existing Jagdstaffeln were first increased in size, from twelve aircraft and pilots to sixteen. The next step would be to increase all Gruppen to four Staffeln, and finally, all Jagdgeschwader to four Gruppen. The first of the new Staffeln to be formed were sent west, where the need was greatest. It had been anticipated that JG 54 would soon replace JG 26 in the west and would add the Staffeln to its three Gruppen; thus the new Staffeln were given JG 54 designations. 11/JG 54 was already here; a new 10/JG 54 would arrive in May.

8 April

After a day of inactivity, the Geschwader flew a few uneventful patrols, and one successful mission. The Second Gruppe scrambled from Vitry at 1816, led by Oblt. Stotto Stammberger of the 4th Staffel, and headed west. A small Allied formation was

Hptm. Fritz Geisshardt, Kommandeur of III/JG 26, who died on 6 April of wounds received from B-17 gunners the previous day. *(Meyer)*

reported headed across the Somme Estuary at high altitude. This proved to be the all-Norwegian North Weald Wing, flying a Rodeo. The Germans engaged the surprised Norwegians at 9400 meters (31,000 feet) over Dieppe. Stammberger out-turned his target and hit it in the wings with a high-deflection shot. The Spitfire burst into flames and spun out, crashing south of Dieppe. There were no other casualties in this engagement.

The leaders of two new American fighter groups, the 56th and the 78th, crossed the French coast for the first time, under the tutelage of veterans from the 4th Fighter Group. The flight by a dozen P-47s was uneventful, which was good news for the Americans – their aircraft had performed well, and the electrical problems that had kept the type out of combat had apparently been solved.

9 April

In late afternoon 10(Jabo)/JG 54 attempted another raid on Folkestone in poor weather, beginning what proved to be a very bad few hours for the Geschwader. Uffz. Karl Heck was shot down into the Channel by a patrolling No. 609 Sqd. Typhoon. After refueling at Wizernes, his Jabostaffel comrades immediately returned to the area to search for him, as was standard procedure; a patrol boat was also sent out from Calais, escorted by several fighter formations. Unfortunately for the Germans, the RAF knew this procedure well, and fighters from three squadrons were waiting for them. Three Focke-Wulfs were shot down by the Spitfires and Typhoons. They were piloted by Lt. Otto-August Backhaus (Jabostaffel), Obfw. Kurt Kruska (6th Staffel), and Lt. Eugen Spieler (8th Staffel); all were killed, as was Heck. One Typhoon was claimed shot down, but the aircraft, actually a Spitfire, reached England with moderate damage.

This proved to be the last daylight mission to England by 10(Jabo)/JG 54. During its year in combat on the Channel, the Staffel had lost twenty pilots, well over 100% of its assigned strength, but was now to switch to slightly less hazardous work. Oberst Dietrich Peltz, a young bomber commander and a personal favorite of the Führer, had recently been named to the new position of *Angriffsführer* (Attack Leader) England. Peltz was under orders to rebuild the German bomber forces in France and resume the Blitz on England. As part of the subsequent reorganization, the two Jabostaffeln became part of a new *Schnellkampfgeschwader*, or fast bomber wing, and switched to night bombing. 10(Jabo)/JG 54, the former 10(Jabo)/JG 26, was redesignated 14/SKG 10. It later moved to Italy, and from there to the Eastern Front, where it served until the end of the war.

JG 26 Casualties: 5 - 9 April 1943

Date	Rank	Name	Cas	Unit	Aircraft	WNr	Mkgs	Place	Time	Cause	Allied Unit
05-04-43	Hptm.	Geisshardt, Fritz	KIA	III CO	Fw 190A-4	7051	-P	St D-Westrem	1515	B-17	
09-04-43	Uffz.	Winter, Horst-Günther	KIFA	5	Fw 190A-4	7042	bk 4	nr Arras		crashed	non-op
09-04-43	Obfw.	Kruska, Kurt	KIA	6	Fw 190A-4	5668	br 11	NW of Boulogne		Spitfire	611 Sqd

09-04-43	Lt.	Spieler, Eugen	KIA	8	Fw 190A-4	5612	bk 3	15km W of Boulogne	1815	Typhoon	1 Sqd
09-04-43	Lt.	Backhaus, Otto-August	KIA	10J	Fw 190A-5	7290	bk 12	NW of +bomb Cap Gris Nez		Spitfire	611 Sqd
09-04-43	Uffz.	Heck, Karl	KIA	10J	Fw 190A-5	831	bk 14	Channel-S of +bomb Folkestone		Typhoon	609 Sqd

10 April

Several Fighter Command Rodeos brought no response from the Jafü 2 controller, who refused to order an *Alarmstart* (scramble) unless heavy bombers were in the air or there was a good possibility that an isolated fighter force could be intercepted. No. 611 Squadron's Sgt. Dick Due expressed the attitude of many frustrated RAF pilots when he wrote in his logbook today, "Attempted to lure the crafty Hun up – but no go!"

11 April

Four No. 2 Group Mosquitoes bombed Malines at low altitude. One was damaged by flak, slowing it enough to permit two patrols to reach it and shoot it down. Hptm. Steindl, the new 9th Staffel Kapitän, was awarded a victory credit, as was a pilot from 2/JG 1.

JG 26 Victory Claims: 8 - 11 April 1943

Date	Rank	Name	Unit	Cl #	Aircraft	Place	Time	Opponent	Conf
08-04-43	Oblt.	Stammberger	4 CO	6	Spitfire	5km S of Dieppe	1855	332 Sqd	yes
09-04-43	Fw.	Grünlinger	Ge St		Typhoon	15km NW of Cap Gris Nez	1845	611 Sqd Spitfire	unk
11-04-43	Hptm.	Steindl	9		Mosquito	Destelbergen near Ghent	2036	139 Sqd	yes

13 April

The RAF sent a Circus containing Ventura light bombers to bomb the Abbeville railroad yards. The Second Gruppe was scrambled from Vitry, and made contact with the Spitfire escort, but could not obtain a good attacking position, and was recalled. The small standing patrols failed to contact any of the several sweeps sent across the Channel by the Allies, including one by the American 8th Fighter Command. Twelve fighters from each of the three P-47 groups swept St. Omer and returned to England, minus one P-47 which crashed into the Channel after its engine failed. The Americans flew the mission in one of several formations used by RAF Fighter Command, the "javelin". Each flight of four fighters was in trail, stepped down behind the leader. The number two and three flights in the squadron were at the same altitude as the leader's, but somewhat behind them. The trailers edged forward during the course of the mission, and each flight crossed the French coast as an unwieldy vertical string. The Americans lost no time scrapping the javelin formation, and when they next appeared over France it was in the Luftwaffe's finger-four.

14 April

An RAF Circus to Le Havre prompted a response from JG 2 that cost the Richthofen Geschwader seven pilots for no loss to the Allies. JG 26 was scrambled, but was held in position over the Pas de Calais.

I/JG 27 transferred today from Bernay to Poix, southwest of Amiens. The Gruppe had been totally ineffective since its disastrous mission on 13 March, and its 2nd Staffel had already been separated from the Gruppe and sent to The Netherlands. The rest of the Gruppe was now moved to the border between Jafü 2 and Jafü 3, in the hope that it could reinforce either JG 26 or JG 2 as needed – each Jagdgeschwader was at this time missing one of its three organic Gruppen.

15 April

In mid-afternoon Oblt. Graf von Matuschka, the Kapitän of 4/JG 54, was shot down and killed by Spitfires that were sweeping Marquise. He was succeeded as Kapitän by Oblt. Deterra. This was the day's only combat involving the Geschwader or its associated units. A sweep by sixty P-47s from the three American fighter groups brought most of the Geschwader into the air at 1730, but the Thunderbolts turned east when they reached the coast at Ostend, and the airborne fighters were held where they were. The interception was left to II/JG 1 at Woensdrecht. The 4th Fighter Group component of the mixed American formation dived on the climbing Focke-Wulfs and claimed three destroyed, but none sustained reportable damage. After escaping in an *Abschwung* (split-S), one 5/JG 1 Schwarm was able to zoom up, fall in behind the diving P-47s, and shoot two down.

There were few personnel changes in the Geschwader during the first half of April. Lt. Karl-Heinz Schmidt joined the Second Gruppe Stab. Reporting from ferry units were Gefr. Hans-Walter Sander, who was assigned to the Second Gruppe, and Fw. Wilhelm Würtz, who was assigned to the new 12/JG 54; reporting for duty from training were Fw. Hans Fischer, who was assigned to the Second Gruppe; Fhj.-Fw. Gottfried Otto, who joined the 7th Staffel in Russia; and Uffz. Fritz Fritzlehner, who was assigned to 12/JG 54.

16 April

There was action today to the east and the west of the Pas de Calais, but no Allied aircraft entered the JG 26 operational zone. The Second Gruppe pushed their patrols out to mid-Channel, without contact. The Americans attacked the U-boat bases at Brest and Lorient, and lost four heavy bombers to JG 2. RAF Spitfires swept Vlissingen, and for the loss of two of their own, shot down and killed the II/JG 1 Kommandeur and his wingman.

17 April

Today's Allied feints and diversions did an excellent job of keeping the Geschwader out of the action. The Vitry and Wevelgem Gruppen scrambled early, as the American heavy bombers crossed the English coast, but the bombers eventually headed due east across the North Sea, far out of range. Their target was Bremen. III/JG 54, in its first operation in its new theater, teamed up with JG 11 and the Flak to shoot down sixteen of the unescorted B-17s. In the meantime, several Allied formations patrolled in the Channel; the JG 26 fighters chased back and forth in response, but were not ordered to intercept, and no contact was made. The principal mission for the RAF was a raid on Abbeville by No. 2 Group Venturas. Their escorting fighters were concentrated on the eastern side of the formation, and screened off the Focke-Wulfs of the approaching Second Gruppe so well that Wutz Galland was heard by the British Y-Service (radio intercept) operators to order his fighters to remain in formation, as there were too many RAF fighters about. Although Stotto Stammberger claimed to have damaged a Spitfire, Galland was the only JG 26 member to claim a victory, a Mustang. There were no Mustangs present; it is possible that Wutz attacked a No. 56 Sqd. Typhoon that crashed after its engine failed. Most of the RAF escort's battles were with I/JG 2, I/JG 27, and II/JG 2; the last-named unit had recently returned to the Channel Front from Tunisia. Eight Messerschmitts and Focke-Wulfs were lost for a cost of three Spitfires. The vulnerable Venturas were not touched.

18 April

Wevelgem was strafed and bombed by Typhoons, which were being tried out in a new role as fighter-bombers. One groundcrewman was killed. Attempts at interception were unsuccessful. The JG 26 patrols failed to contact Allied aircraft during the day.

19 April

No contact was made. Wutz Galland expressed his frustration, and was allowed to push the Second Gruppe patrols almost to the English coast, without success. While

returning from patrol, Uffz. Gerhard Falkner of the 4th Staffel collided with a hangar, damaging his Focke-Wulf and injuring himself.

20 April

The morning patrols failed to make contact. Late in the afternoon, an "unfortunate series of conflicting orders from the Jafü" (in the words of survivor Peter Crump), left six 5th Staffel Focke-Wulfs off Dieppe facing a head-on attack by a large formation of Spitfires out of the setting sun. After the attack by No. 315 Sqd. (Polish), one Focke-Wulf spun out and hit the water, killing Uffz. Erich Kleffner. The Germans scattered in all directions. Crump, newly promoted to Feldwebel, tried a favorite escape maneuver – he spun out of a tight turn and dived, apparently out of control, until just enough altitude remained for recovery. He then pulled out and headed for the coast, skimming the Channel. He joined his four surviving comrades at Vitry.

Major Priller visits his former Third Gruppe command at Wevelgem in April or May, flying a Geschwaderstab aircraft assigned to Hptm. Gäth. *(Bundesarchiv-Bildarchiv)*

Fw. Xaver Ellenrieder, who had left the 7th Staffel in Russia on the 10th, reported to the 8th Staffel at Vendeville. His first assignment was an escort mission for Generalfeldmarschall Sperrle's Ju 52. Sperrle, the Luftflotte 3 commander, had come over from Paris to inspect the JG 26 fighter bases.

21 April

Generalfeldmarschall Sperrle's visit to Vitry was sufficient reason for the Second Gruppe to parade in honor of the promotion of the leaders of all three of its Staffeln, Oblt. Otto Stammberger, Oblt. Horst Sternberg, and Oblt. Johannes Naumann, to the formal command positions of Staffelkapitäne. All had previously been serving as Staffelführer, a probationary position not found in the Luftwaffe tables of organization. Sperrle's speech was interrupted at noon by the loudspeaker's urgent squawk – a large enemy force was approaching the Somme Estuary at an altitude of only 3000 meters (9,800 feet). The pilots broke ranks and ran for their aircraft, leaving Sperrle standing in the square. No. 2 Group was paying a return visit to the Abbeville railroad yards. Galland's three Staffeln caught up to the Allied formation as it wheeled north after the bombing run, and quickly avenged their failure of the 17th. Galland led his Stab flight and one Staffel in an attack on the bombers, eleven Venturas of No. 21 Squadron, while the other fighters took on the Spitfire escort. The Fw 190s made simultaneous passes from the front, the front quarter, and beneath the bombers, slashing through the fighter screen and breaking off their attacks only fifty meters from the Venturas. Three bombers burst into flames and crashed, two from the attacks of the Kommandeur himself; the third was eventually credited to Oblt. Sternberg, after he won a coin toss with Oblt. Stammberger.

Both fighter formations now broke apart, Spitfire and Focke-Wulf tumbling in and out of towering clouds in a deadly game of cat-and-mouse. Lt. Hans Fischer of the 4th Staffel shot down a Spitfire over the coast. After the furious action had nearly spent itself, Fw. Crump spotted a lone Spitfire flying away from him, silhouetted against a cloud. After a quick look in all directions – more Spitfires could break out of the clouds at any time – he attacked, damaging it in the engine and the underside of the fuselage. The Spitfire broke to the left, emitting a cloud of black smoke. It dived away in a flat curve, and crashed south of Boismont. Both downed Spitfires were from No. 610 Squadron. The Gruppe suffered no casualties or damage. Peter Crump was the last pilot to land, and recalls:

> "I had totally forgotten the representative of the Reichsmarschall. During our absence, Sperrle had made a whirlwind tour of the individual Staffeln and the Flak units surrounding the field. He had, for example, ordered one of the pilots of my Staffel put under fourteen days close arrest. The reason – he had let important military equipment fall unguarded into enemy hands. The guilty party had had the misfortune to suffer a flat tire while taxiing to the edge of the field. He had naturally climbed out of the aircraft and returned to the dispersal on foot. The Feldmarschall had met him when he arrived at our dispersal. The chief armorer advised the speechless, flabbergasted pilot to tell the 'old man' that he had returned to the dispersal to get a replacement aircraft in order to rejoin the Gruppe on the mission. So said – so done! And then the unexpected happened. With the words 'Well done, my son!', and a clap on the shoulder, the punishment was withdrawn as quickly as it had been imposed. That was an out-of-bounds play, even for the Wehrmacht!"

JG 26 Victory Claims: 17 - 21 April 1943

Date	Rank	Name	Unit	Cl #	Aircraft	Place	Time	Opponent	Conf
17-04-43	Hptm.	Galland W-F.	II CO	39	Mustang	20km WNW of Somme Estuary	1506	56 Sqd Typhoon	yes
21-04-43	Hptm.	Galland W-F.	II CO	40	Ventura	NE of Somme Est-NW of Abbeville	1214	21 Sqd	yes
21-04-43	Hptm.	Galland W-F.	II CO	41	Ventura	10-20km W of Somme Est	1220	21 Sqd	yes
21-04-43	Oblt.	Stammberger	4 CO		Ventura	N of Abbeville	1220	21 Sqd	no
21-04-43	Lt.	Fischer H.	4	1	Spitfire	N of Port le Grand	1213	610 Sqd	yes
21-04-43	Oblt.	Sternberg	5 CO	14	Ventura	Acheux	1216	21 Sqd	yes
21-04-43	Uffz.	Crump	5	8	Spitfire	2km S of Boismont	1217	610 Sqd	yes

22 April
The Geschwader continued its routine of defensive patrols, without result. The Second Gruppe pushed the envelope once more, flying to within five miles of Hastings, but found nothing.

23 April
The coastal patrols were, as usual, unsuccessful, but Obfw. Fritsch of the 5th Staffel led his "offensive-defensive" patrol all the way across the Somme Estuary to Dieppe, where he shot down a No. 41 Sqd. Spitfire that was on a shipping reconnaissance mission. Fritsch received credit for one Mustang destroyed.

28 April
After four more days of patrols, Oblt. Stammberger assigned the early-morning reconnaissance mission to himself, in hopes of stirring up some activity. He took off at 0626 and patrolled the English coast from Dover to Dungeness without seeing anything worth reporting. The Second Gruppe kept up its patrols until after nightfall, but the Allies stayed on their side of the Channel.

29 April
At noon the 8th Fighter Command mounted their largest mission of the war. One hundred and twelve P-47s from the three groups swept the coast from Ostend to Woensdrecht. Major Priller's Geschwadergruppe, which at this period comprised the

Oblt. Otto Stammberger, Kapitän of the 4th Staffel in the spring of 1943. He was severely wounded by Spitfires on 13 May. *(Stammberger)*

6th and the 8th Staffeln, was given the honor of making the interception. By the time the unit reached the coast from Lille it had reached 7000 meters (24,000 feet). Continuing their climb, the Focke-Wulfs made an attack on the middle squadron from dead ahead, sweeping in by pairs, firing short, well-aimed bursts, and diving away. Two Thunderbolts and pilots were lost, one to Uffz. Mayer of the 6th Staffel, and the other to Obfw. Heitmann of the 8th Staffel.

The American group leader's radio was not functioning, and by the time the high squadron noticed what was going on below them, three more P-47s had suffered serious damage in turning combats, in which the Fw 190s had the edge. Both sides soon broke for their bases; the Germans sustained no damage, although Fw. Ellenrieder had to make a forced landing on Ghent-Denis with a broken connecting rod.

As one result of this battle, the Americans began flying at ever-increasing altitudes. For the next several months they approached the coast at 30,000 feet (9100 meters), well above the Fw 190's optimum altitude. Their presence was quite obvious, and they could usually be ignored. They were rarely released to dive on the German fighters, even when the latter were engaged with Spitfires or bombers at the typical combat altitudes of 20-25,000 feet (6100-7600 meters). Wutz Galland developed an open contempt of the P-47s, calling them *Nicht-Einmischer* (non-intervenors); this attitude would later cost him his life.

The rest of the day brought no more successes. The Second Gruppe flew west after its scramble, to the west coast of the Pas de Calais, but found nothing. One 5th Staffel pilot lost control of his aircraft and had to bail out north of Poix; the crash was attributed to pilot error.

JG 26 Victory Claims: 23 - 29 April 1943

Date	Rank	Name	Unit	Cl #	Aircraft	Place	Time	Opponent	Conf
23-04-43	Obfw.	Fritsch P.	5	3	Mustang	25km W of Somme Estuary	1128	41 Sqd Spitfire	yes
29-04-43	Uffz.	Mayer	6	2	P-47	30km N of Ostend	1332	56 FG	yes
29-04-43	Obfw.	Edmann	8		Spitfire	5-10km N of Zeebrugge	1324	56 FG P-47	yes
29-04-43	Obfw.	Heitmann	8	7	P-47	Knokke	1320	56 FG	unk

JG 26 Casualties: 15 - 29 April 1943

Date	Rank	Name	Cas	Unit	Aircraft	WNr	Mkgs	Place	Time	Cause	Allied Unit
15-04-43	Oblt.	Matuschka, Siegfried	KIA	4/54 CO	Bf 109G-4	19222		near St Inglevert		Spitfire	
19-04-43	Uffz.	Falkner, Gerhard	WIFA	4	Fw 190A-4	5694	wh 5	Vitry-en-Artois a/f		landing	n/a
20-04-43	Uffz.	Kleffner, Erich	KIA	5	Fw 190A-4	7108	bk 4	NNW of Dieppe	1930	Spitfire	315 Sqd
29-04-43	Fw.	Zens, Franz	WIFA	5	Fw 190A-4	5663	bk 12	SW of Amiens N of Poix		lost control	n/a

30 April

The month ended on somewhat of a low note. There was no contact with the enemy, and three Second Gruppe Fw 190s were damaged in taxi accidents while attempting to scramble from Vitry-en-Artois.

By month's end the 9th Staffel had re-equipped with Bf 109G-6s, and the Third Gruppe at Wevelgem, commanding 9/JG 26, 4/JG 54, and 12/JG 54, was now an all-Messerschmitt outfit. Whether from lack of leadership, equipment problems, or some other reason, the Gruppe was very quiet during this period; battle honors usually went to the Focke-Wulf units at Vitry and Lille-Vendeville.

The Third Gruppe would fly various modifications of the Bf 109G-6 for the next eighteen months. A wide variety of engine boost systems and armament combinations were employed, and published performance figures vary widely. These numbers are meaningless unless the *Rüstsätze* (armament modifications) and the *Umrüst-Bausätze* (factory modifications) of the aircraft under test are noted. An accepted top speed and critical altitude for a Bf 109G-6 with MW 50 (methanol-water injection) and standard armament was 621 km/h (386 mph) at 6900 meters (22,640 feet). The airplane was noticeably slower than the P-47C at all altitudes; this performance disparity increased when newer American fighters entered service later in 1943.

There were few personnel changes during the last half of April. Hptm. Werner Patz, the Kapitän of 11/JG 54, which was still serving as an operational training unit at Merville, transferred from the Geschwader and was replaced by Oblt. Walter Otte. Lt. Ernst Heinemann transferred from 11/JG 54 to 4/JG 26. Only two pilots are known to have joined the Geschwader from training units: Uffz. Peter Bürger was ordered to the Second Gruppe, while Uffz. Hans Hein was sent to 11/JG 54, apparently for more training.

1 May

Today's battles took place far to the west, as 8th Bomber Command once again

The rations carriage arrives at Vitry-en-Artois in the spring of 1943, bringing the mid-day meal for the Second Gruppe readiness pilots and the groundcrew-men. *(Crump)*

targeted the St. Nazaire submarine pens. As before, Jafü Brittany held his fighters off until the escorting Spitfires had turned back, and then unleashed them; JG 2 and the Flak shot down seven of the seventy-eight B-17s dispatched, damaged another two beyond repair, and damaged a further twenty.

Uffz. Gomann and his wingman flew the evening recon mission to England. Gomann sighted a flight of four Spitfires. Outnumbered, the Germans slipped back to France; this was as close to combat as any member of the Geschwader came today.

A new Staffel, 10/JG 54, was established in the Second Gruppe. Hptm. Rudolf Leuschel was named its leader. Rudi Leuschel was apparently an eager advocate of new weaponry, and his Staffel did much of the testing of aerial bombs for the Geschwader. He and Gefr. Sander developed a special skill in dropping 250 kg aerial mines on bomber formations; an accuracy of ± 5 meters was claimed.

For practice, a model of a B-17 was constructed at Vitry, and suspended above the ground on poles; cement bombs were then dropped on it. After a small modification to the fighters' Revi gunsight, practice missions were flown. There were plans to replace the original timed fuses with acoustic ones, which would be activated by the sounds of the engines of the heavy bombers. Later the 10th Staffel was the first to be equipped to fire 21 cm rocket mortar shells. The *Kanaljäger* (Channel fighters) rejected these weapons as too detrimental to their fighters' performance. They were used with some success by the fighters of the *Reichsluftverteidigung* (RLV), the German air defense organization, up until the range of the American fighter escorts increased sufficiently to reach their zone of operations.

Other innovations were evaluated in the Geschwader during this period. Obstlt. Priller tested, and rejected, a true gyroscopic gunsight. The sight did not reappear at the front until the final weeks of the war. Uffz. Heinz Backeberg of the 5th Staffel persuaded the Second Gruppe technical officer to modify a Fw 190 to test one of his ideas. A 250 kg bomb was attached beneath the fuselage with a 5 mm-thick cable, which was rolled up on a drum inside the fuselage. The pilot was to drop the bomb above a bomber formation. It would hang suspended from the cable until it contacted a bomber and exploded. The bomb jerked loose from the cable on every test. Backeberg was still tinkering with the idea when he was killed on 14 May; his invention died with him.

The units of the Geschwader that were in Luftflotte 3 were now disposed as follows:

Lille-Vendeville: Geschwadergruppe – Stab/JG 26, 6/JG 26 and 8/JG 26
Vitry-en-Artois: Second Gruppe – 4/JG 26, 5/JG 26, and 10/JG 54
Wevelgem: Third Gruppe – 9/JG 26, 4/JG 54, and 12/JG 54
Merville: 11/JG 54

The last-named Staffel, which some documents have listed as part of the First Gruppe for administration, was apparently declared operational in the coming week and transferred to Wevelgem, where it joined the Third Gruppe.

3 May

Much of the Geschwader was in the air from dawn to dusk – Fw. Crump sortied five times – with little to show for the effort. The day started with a victory. Lt. Radener led his 4th Staffel Schwarm across the Somme Estuary and attacked a pair of No. 41 Sqd. Spitfire XIIs that were on a coastal recon mission off Dieppe. One Spitfire was shot down; the other outran the Fw 190s.

11/JG 54 was flying from Wevelgem today. On one scramble the Messerschmitt of Uffz. Ludwig Lentz was caught by a crosswind and crashed into a hangar, killing Lentz and destroying two 11th Staffel Fw 190s. Several mid-day scrambles resulted in a single contact, during which Lt. Blömertz of the 4th Staffel shot down a Mosquito. His claim was not confirmed, although a No. 540 Sqd. Mosquito was lost at this time. In mid-afternoon several of the Staffeln were ordered to dispersal fields, a practice that had been abandoned the previous autumn. The movement may have been part of a drill; Ligescourt and Audembert saw their first fighters in many months. The Geschwadergruppe was split up; part of the 6th Staffel flew to Audembert, while Hptm. Naumann led the rest of his 6th Staffel and at least part of the 8th to Schipol. Here they were well positioned to back up II/JG 1 and 2/JG 27 as they defended against the major raid of the day, a Circus directed at the Amsterdam power station. This raid had been planned by No. 12 Group and contained a dozen No. 487 Sqd. Venturas. The direction of the raid was revealed by a fighter sweep of Flushing that was a half hour too early. The Venturas' escorts were inadequate in number and lagged behind the bombers as they crossed the Dutch coast. The Germans were up in force, and II/JG 1 fell on the unwieldy bombers as 2/JG 27 attacked the escort and cut it off from the bomber formation. The leader of the close escort, W/C Peter "Cowboy" Blatchford, was shot down and killed. Ten of the Venturas crashed in the target area or

A pilot of the 8th Staffel, the Adamsonstaffel, relaxes beside his Fw 190A-4 – Wevelgem, early 1943. *(Matthiesen via Petrick)*

off the coast; there were few survivors among their crews. The Spitfires of the rear cover wing shot down three of the pursuing Focke-Wulfs, but the damage had already been done. The JG 26 reinforcements scrambled and took part in the latter stages of this battle. Hptm. Naumann claimed a Spitfire off Zandvoort, but the claim was not confirmed, and the RAF fighter apparently escaped.

Late in the evening the Kenley Wing swept across the Pas de Calais from Nieuport to Boulogne. Several small flights of defenders reached the Spitfires as they re-crossed the coast. Two Focke-Wulfs were claimed by the Canadians. Uffz. Gomann was able to force-land on Étaples; Fw. Karl Ehret was injured when his airplane exploded after he crash-landed it.

JG 26 Victory Claims: 3 May 1943

Date	Rank	Name	Unit	Cl #	Aircraft	Place	Time	Opponent	Conf
03-05-43	Lt.	Blömertz	4	1	Mosquito	80km NNW of Fécamp	1345	540 Sqd	unk
03-05-43	Lt.	Radener	4	1	Spitfire	20km W of Somme Estuary	0650	41 Sqd	yes
03-05-43	Hptm.	Naumann	6 CO	14	Spitfire	W of Zandvoort	1815		unk

JG 26 Casualties: 3 May 1943

Date	Rank	Name	Cas	Unit	Aircraft	WNr	Mkgs	Place	Time	Cause	Allied Unit
03-05-43	Fw.	Ehret, Karl	WIA	6	Fw 190A-4	717	br 9	Rue		Spitfire	416 Sqd
03-05-43	Uffz.	Lentz, Ludwig	KIFA	11/54	Bf 109G-3	16275	rd 7	NW Wevelgem a/f	1347	takeoff	n/a

4 May

The day's major raid came in late afternoon, and was an attack on Antwerp industrial areas by seventy-nine B-17s. At 1920 Major Priller led his Geschwadergruppe up from Vendeville, formed up with the Second Gruppe from Vitry, and headed east. They sighted the Allied formation near Vlissingen. Although the American P-47s flew well above the bombers and never made contact, today's close escort wings, Spitfires from Biggin Hill and Northolt, were well positioned, and succeeded in keeping the Schlageter fighters away from the bombers until the formation was back over the Scheldt Estuary. Oblt. von Donner of the Second Gruppe Stab claimed a B-17 at this

The Wulf-Hund visits Vendeville in early 1943. This 303rd Bomb Group B-17F was shot down by the 9th Staffel while led by Lt. Stammberger on 12 December 1942, and was the first Flying Fortress restored to flying condition by the Luftwaffe. *(G. Schmidt)*

time, but none were lost, and his claim was not confirmed. II/JG 1 arrived from Woensdrecht, but had apparently been given too low an altitude by the controller. They were pounced on by the Spitfires and had to dive away. Major Priller claimed a Spitfire, as did two II/JG 1 pilots and a Bf 109 pilot from the ERLA factory defense flight; three Spitfires were in fact lost. The Germans lost no fighters, but this was a dramatic Allied victory, and Göring's message that evening accused his fighter pilots of being "cowardly dogs."

JG 26 Victory Claims: 4 May 1943

Date	Rank	Name	Unit	Cl #	Aircraft	Place	Time	Opponent	Conf
04-05-43	Major	Priller	Ge CO	85	Spitfire	Westerschelde-NW of Antwerp	1842		unk
04-05-43	Oblt.	Donner v.	II	3	B-17	Scheldt Estuary	1548		unk

11 May

On the 10th, Obfw. Willi Roth of the 4th Staffel was awarded the German Cross in Gold, for eighteen air victories. The next enemy contact came today, on a noon scramble by Priller and his Geschwadergruppe. They had a brush with the Kenley Wing off Gravelines. Neither side scored, but the six Mitchells that the Spitfires were escorting turned back without bombing their target, the Boulogne railroad yards.

12 May

II/JG 1, which had been complaining that its Woensdrecht base was too small and too far forward to permit effective interceptions, transferred to Schipol. It was replaced at Woensdrecht by the nine Bf 109s of 2/JG 3; part of JG 3 had been withdrawn from the Eastern Front, and was being incorporated in stages into the defenses of Jafü Holland-Ruhr.

13 May

Priller's Geschwadergruppe and Galland's Second Gruppe were ordered to scramble shortly before noon in response to a large formation approaching the Belgian coast. Suddenly the Allied formation turned to the south, toward northern France. The Focke-Wulf pilots were therefore summoned back to Lille and then could see above them, to

Maj. Priller's Fw 190A-5, W.Nr. 7298, in flight in May or June 1943. *(Bundesarchiv-Bildarchiv)*

Priller cleans his sunglasses in preparation for a flight made for the benefit of a Propaganda Company photographer – Lille-Vendeville, mid-1943. *(Bundesarchiv-Bildarchiv)*

the north toward Dunkirk, condensation trails on a southerly course, which proved to belong to a tight formation of Spitfires. At this time Jafü 2 ordered its pilots to land immediately. There were fifteen squadrons of Spitfires in the area, escorting a mere six Mitchells to Boulogne. All of the Focke-Wulfs dived away except Stotto Stammberger's flight. His radio was defective, and he failed to notice the departure of the rest of his own 4th Staffel. He waited for the Spitfires to attack, as called for by the standard German tactics. The other Staffeln should have been to one side and above him, in order to fall on the attackers from above, while Stotto let the Spitfires approach to firing distance before breaking into the attack and beginning the dogfight. But his Schwarm was alone. His second element disappeared on the break, leaving only his wingman, who left the scene when Stammberger's airplane was hit by a diving No. 331 Sqd.

Spitfire and caught fire. Stammberger was at 7500 meters (25,000 feet) when his fuel tank exploded; he bailed out, but his chute didn't open fully. A third of it was burned through, and his fall was slowed only by a bubble of trapped air. He was whirled in circles, and was knocked out when he landed. He regained consciousness ten days

Obfw. Glunz, seated in one of his "white 9s" in early 1943. This is probably W.Nr. 0739, in which Otto Stammberger was shot down on 13 May. *(Glunz)*

later in the St. Omer hospital, having suffered, in his words, "a severe brain concussion, and second and third degree burns, but fortunately, nothing broken!" Oblt. Stammberger returned to the front in October, but was not restored to combat status. Lt. Helmut Hoppe of the 5th Staffel took his place as leader of the 4th Staffel.

In mid-afternoon the four B-17 groups of the 8th Bomber Command's 1st Bomb Wing made the day's major attack, on the Potez repair facility at Meaulte. The four B-17 groups of the new 4th Bomb Wing provided the principal diversion by bombing St. Omer, covered by the three P-47 groups. The well-practiced Schlageter fighters rose from all three of their airfields. The 4th Bomb Wing attack was ignored by the Jafü, which kept close watch on the larger 1st Bomb Wing formation as it reversed course several times in the Channel. When it finally turned for France, the Geschwader was able to attack it in strength before the Spitfires, which were again too high, could intervene. The 91st Bomb Group, in the low box, caught much of the attack. The yellow-nosed Focke-Wulfs attacked in Rotten or Schwärme from twelve o'clock low, thus avoiding the supporting fire of the higher bomber boxes. The first attack came as the lead group crossed the French coast, and the frontal attacks continued until the formation reached the coast on its way back to England. The 91st lost B-17s to Major Priller and Lt. Hoppe; one B-17 was lost to flak, and eleven others were hit by fighters and/or flak – one was severely damaged by a bomb dropped by a Second Gruppe Fw 190, but reached its home base.

Much of the escorting Spitfires' effort was expended against I/JG 27, up from Poix, and several JG 2 Staffeln that were flying from Abbeville as well as their regular bases west of the Somme. Uffz. Werner Lonsdorfer of the 6th Staffel was the only Geschwader pilot lost to the escorts; he was shot down in flames near St. Omer. An 11/JG 54 Bf 109G-3 was shot down near St. Pol, but its pilot bailed out safely. Four JG 2 pilots were lost during the day, as were seven Spitfire pilots.

JG 26 Victory Claims: 13 May 1943

Date	Rank	Name	Unit	Cl #	Aircraft	Place	Time	Opponent	Conf
13-05-43	Major	Priller	Ge CO	86	B-17	nr Amplier-5km E of Boulogne	1624	91 BG	unk

13-05-43	Major	Priller	Ge CO	87	Spitfire	8km NW of Étaples	1646	416 Sqd	unk
13-05-43	Lt.	Hoppe	5	8	B-17	S of Amiens	1627	91 BG	yes
13-05-43	Hptm.	Naumann	6 CO	15	Spitfire	20km NW of Albert	1635	416 Sqd	yes
13-05-43	Lt.	Leuschel	10 CO	2	Spitfire	E of Bray (BE)	1632	416 Sqd	unk

JG 26 Casualties: 13 May 1943

Date	Rank	Name	Cas	Unit	Aircraft	WNr	Mkgs	Place	Time	Cause	Allied Unit
13-05-43	Oblt.	Stammberger, Otto	WIA	4 CO	Fw 190A-4	739	wh 9	near St. Omer	1230	Spitfire	331 Sqd
13-05-43	Uffz.	Lonsdorfer, Werner	KIA	6	Fw 190A-4	2433	br 13	near St. Omer		Spitfire	

14 May

The Americans attacked four separate targets with their small bomber force. The experienced 1st Bomb Wing and one B-24 group made a very successful attack on the Kiel shipyards, losing eight bombers. III/JG 54 lost five Bf 109s and two pilots; a third pilot, Lt. Rudolf Klemm, lost an eye. The first operational B-26 Marauder group in the new 3rd Bomb Wing made a low-level attack on the Ijmuiden power station outside Amsterdam. The bombers were not intercepted, but the attack was ineffective.

The Schlageter fighters were called upon to attack the other two forces. The 4th Bomb Wing sent two groups against each of two targets, the automotive plants in Antwerp and the Wevelgem base of the Third Gruppe. The bomb groups assigned to take out Wevelgem did an effective job, killing and wounding a number of ground personnel and pilots, destroying and damaging aircraft, and carpeting the landing ground with craters. For the first time, a Geschwader airfield was left unserviceable by an air raid. The Third Gruppe was forced to move to the small Lille-Nord field. Lt. Paul Schauder of the 9th Staffel collided with a No. 611 Sqd. Spitfire immediately after takeoff, causing the crash of both aircraft. The two pilots bailed out successfully; Schauder suffered an eye injury that put him out of action for months. Oblt. Erwin Leykauf, Kapitän of 12/JG 54 and a newcomer to the western theater, decided to take off during the attack, but wrecked his Messerschmitt by shearing its landing gear off in a bomb crater.

The two Gruppen of JG 1 formed the main defensive force against the Antwerp bombers, but Galland was ordered to break off his pursuit of the withdrawing Wevelgem force and fly to Antwerp at full speed. The Y-Service heard him order two attacks on the bombers, one from the front and one from the rear, before his fuel state forced Galland to return to Vitry, which was ordered to keep the landing ground clear for his arrival. The air combats associated with the two raids were widespread and bitterly fought. Oblt. Hans Naumann, Kapitän of the 6th Staffel, shot down a 351st Bomb Group B-17 near Wevelgem with only twenty rounds of ammunition. A burst in the cockpit persuaded the bomber crew to bail out; nine reached ground safely. A second B-17 was credited to Oblt. Sternberg of the 5th Staffel. Hptm. Rudolf Leuschel, Kapitän of the new 10th Staffel, shot down a 78th Fighter Group P-47 over Antwerp, while Fw. Gomann of the 5th Staffel claimed a Spitfire of the supporting force.

Fw. Peter Crump was one of the last Second Gruppe pilots in the air. While heading for the emergency field at Vlissingen, on Walcheren Island, he spotted a B-17 over the coast, about five miles away and at an altitude of only 750 meters (2500 feet). It was coming right at Crump. Although flying on empty, Crump took up a pursuit curve. He attacked from the low left rear. A thin flame shot from the bomber's left wing tanks, at the same time as something hit Crump's cockpit. After a last backward glance at the Fortress, which was descending in a steep left bank, trailing flames, Crump headed for Vlissingen as quickly as possible. The B-17 gunner had shot out his electrical system. Crump lowered his landing gear mechanically, but had to land on the very short field without his flaps and trim tabs. He received no credit for his shootdown, which was probably a 95th Bomb Group machine already hit by Oblt. Sternberg and/or a JG 1 pilot. The B-17 crashed on North Beveland Island; there were no survivors.

Lt. Erwin Leykauf's 12th Staffel Bf 109G-6 after he attempted to take off from Lille-Vendeville during a carpet bombing attack on 14 May; Leykauf was uninjured. *(Leykauf)*

German fighter losses to the gunners in the new B-17 groups were unusually high. Two 5th Staffel pilots, Lt. Hans-Jürgen Rüskamp and Uffz. Heinz Backeberg, were killed by bomber fire, and Hptm. Karl Borris, Kapitän of the 8th Staffel, was forced to bail out from his damaged Focke-Wulf. He opened his parachute too soon, and it partially collapsed. Borris was extremely fortunate to survive a fall from 7000 meters (22,000 feet). He suffered numerous broken bones, and required a long stay in the hospital. Another pilot of his Staffel, Obfw. Willi Kalitzki, was seriously injured by B-17 fire, while a 6th Staffel pilot, Obfw. Siegfried Beyer, was injured by Spitfires but survived his parachute jump.

JG 26 Victory Claims: 14 May 1943

Date	Rank	Name	Unit	Cl #	Aircraft	Place	Time	Opponent	Conf
14-05-43	Lt.	Radener	4		B-17-HSS	NW of Antwerp	1300	351 BG	unk
14-05-43	Oblt.	Sternberg	5 CO	15	B-17	Scheldt Estuary	1315	95 BG	yes
14-05-43	Uffz.	Crump	5		B-17	10km NW of Vlissingen	1330	95 BG	no
14-05-43	Uffz.	Gomann	5	3	Spitfire	W of Schouwen	1326		yes
14-05-43	Hptm.	Naumann	6 CO	16	B-17	Dadizeele	1240	351 BG	yes
14-05-43	Oblt.	Schauder	9 CO	12	Spitfire V	Bruges-W of Stalhille	1245	611 Sqd	unk
14-05-43	Oblt.	Leuschel	10 CO	3	P-47	6km N of Ath	1325	78 FG	unk

JG 26 Casualties:14 May 1943

Date	Rank	Name	Cas	Unit	Aircraft	WNr	Mkgs	Place	Time	Cause	Allied Unit
14-05-43	Uffz.	Backeberg, Heinz	KIA	5	Fw 190A-4	677	bk 30	E Ghent-Scheldt Est	1315	B-17	
14-05-43	Lt.	Rüskamp, H-Jürgen	KIA	5	Fw 190A-5	7320	bk 6	SW Antwerp	1315	P-47	4 FG
14-05-43	Obfw.	Beyer, Siegfried	WIA	6	Fw 190A-4	7038	br 17	Wevelgem a/f	1230	P-47	4 or 78 FG
14-05-43	Hptm.	Borris, Karl	WIA	8 CO	Fw 190A-5	7326	bk 19	Wevelgem	1235	B-17	
14-05-43	Obfw.	Kalitzki, Willi	WIA	8	Fw 190A-5	7297	wh 12	Woensdrecht	1235	B-17	
14-05-43	Lt.	Schauder, Paul	WIA	9	Bf 109G-6	16448	yl 8	near Stalhille	1245	Spitfire	611 Sqd
14-05-43	Oblt.	Leykauf, Erwin	no	12/54	Bf 109G-6	outline 11+		Wevelgem a/f	1230	taxi	n/a
14-05-43	Lt.	Ostrowitski, Gerhard	WIA	12/54	none			Wevelgem	1230	bomb	n/a

15 May

The B-17s all headed east across the North Sea to bomb Helgoland and Emden,

9th Staffel Bf 109Gs taxi out for takeoff. This series of photographs has often been misidentified, but the Bissegem church confirms the unit and date – Wevelgem, April-May 1943. *(Bundesarchiv-Bildarchiv)*

staying well out of range of the fighters on the Pas de Calais, but punishing III/JG 54 again. One RAF Circus targeted Caen, drawing the attention of Jafü 3 to the west, where it sent most of I/JG 2, while a second Circus bombed the I/JG 27 base at Poix. The Second Gruppe scrambled to intercept the latter formation, but only a few pilots made contact. The Gruppe made no claims, and sustained no losses; I/JG 2 claimed six victories and lost four pilots, some over Caen and the rest around Poix.

The first half of May saw Hptm. Paul Steindl transfer to 11/JG 54, giving up command of the 9th Staffel to Lt. Paul Schauder, who came over from the Geschwader Stab. Fw. Xaver Ellenrieder transferred from the 8th to the 4th Staffel. Fw. Peter Bürger and Fw. Karl Laub joined 11/JG 54 from 5/JG 26 and 9/JG 54 respectively. Lt. Hans Heitmann, Obfw. Willi Roth, and Obfw. Erich Schwarz left for an instrument flying course. Joining the Geschwader from flight training were Uffz. Gerhard Schulwitz, who reported to the new 10th Staffel in the Second Gruppe, and Uffz. Karl Trapp, who joined the 12th Staffel in the Third Gruppe.

16 May

The 8th Bomber Command stood down today, but the three P-47 groups flew two sweeps of the Dutch and Belgian coasts. The Geschwader scrambled at 1230 and Major Priller led the Geschwadergruppe and the Third Gruppe east, while the Second Gruppe patrolled the French coast. At 1255 II/JG 1 scrambled late from Woensdrecht, led by the JG 1 Kommodore, Major Hans Philipp. They were unable to reach the approaching 78th Fighter Group formation before the latter dived on them and shot down the II/JG 1 Kommandeur. Priller's force arrived at this time, and Priller quickly gained firing position on a Thunderbolt. One crashed into the Scheldt Estuary at this time; its pilot was taken prisoner. Major Philipp and a II/JG 1 pilot also claimed Thunderbolts; only one was lost, although a 78th FG pilot returned to England with injuries. A P-47 pilot shot down Uffz. Friedrich Kaiser of the 6th Staffel north of Ghent; Kaiser died in his plane. The Bf 109 of Uffz. Hermann Leicht of 4/JG 54 was hit in this same combat. Leicht attempted an emergency landing in a grain field. His aircraft hit an embankment, bringing it to a sudden stop. Leicht's skull was crushed by his gun sight.

The 8th Fighter Command flew its second sweep to the same area late in the after-noon. Jafü 2 scrambled its fighters, but held them over France, and no contact was made.

A scramble of 9th Staffel Bf 109G-6s from Wevelgem in April or May 1943. *(Bundesarchiv-Bildarchiv)*

17 May

The 8th Bomber Command returned to Brittany and bombed the Lorient U-boat base. III/JG 2 made a successful interception from Vannes, downing five B-17s, while the RAF kept the rest of JG 2 busy with Rodeos along the western Channel coast. Jafü 2 held its fighters back, although I/JG 27 was up from Poix, losing one Bf 109. At 2030 Fw. Glunz's 4th Staffel Schwarm prepared to take off from Vitry to make practice interceptions on a Do 17F. Lt. Ernst Heinemann taxied into Uffz. Gerhard Birke's aircraft, killing Birke. The practice flight was called off, but ten minutes later Fw. Ellenrieder had to taxi around the wreckage and take off on a reconnaissance of the English coast from Dover to Ramsgate; his mission was uneventful.

JG 26 Casualties: 16 - 17 May 1943

Date	Rank	Name	Cas	Unit	Aircraft	WNr	Mkgs	Place	Time	Cause	Allied Unit
16-05-43	Uffz.	Kaiser, Friedrich	KIA	6	Fw 190A-4	2399	br 4	Zaffelaere-N of Ghent	1300	bomber	
16-05-43	Uffz.	Leicht, Hermann	KIA	4/54	Bf 109G-4	19210	wh 11	N Philipine		combat	
17-05-43	Uffz.	Birke, Gerhard	KIFA	4	Fw 190A-5	2636	wh 3	Vitry a/f	2030	ground collision	non-op
17-05-43	Lt.	Heinemann, Ernst	WIFA	4	Fw 190A-4	2394		Vitry a/f	2030	ground collision	non-op

18 May

Obfw. Addi Glunz was the first Geschwader pilot off the ground today. He was assigned the morning recon mission, although he was quite senior for such tasks, and flew along the coast from Dover to Folkestone without incident. At noon Jafü 2 scrambled a few fighters on the report of an Allied formation approaching the Dutch coast at low altitude. The Geschwader fighters landed shortly thereafter; of the bombers, eleven B-26s of the 322nd Bomb Group, only one early return survived the attentions of the light Flak and II/JG 1, and the surviving B-26 crews were grounded for retraining in medium-altitude bombing.

An RAF Circus to the western coast of the Pas de Calais brought the Geschwadergruppe and the Second Gruppe into the area in mid-afternoon. The Second Gruppe became entangled with the withdrawal escort near Le Touquet, but neither side scored. Fw. Crump's logbook records a victory over a Spitfire southeast of Dieppe on this mission. The claim was not filed. No Spitfires were lost, the location was far from the known site of the combat, and the date in the logbook may be incorrect. As the logbooks were kept by the Staffel clerks and not the pilots themselves, this was unfortunately not an unknown occurrence.

Another Allied formation approached an hour later, but the Second Gruppe was kept on the ground. Generalfeldmarschall Sperrle was visiting Vitry once again; the occasion this time was the presentation of the German Cross in Gold to Hptm. Wutz Galland, after thirty-four victories. Late that evening Uffz. Wilhelm Mayer was among the pilots assigned to escort Sperrle's Ju 52 back to Paris.

The second Allied formation turned west along the Dutch coast. It proved to be another high-altitude sweep by the three American P-47 groups, escorting nothing. JG 1 left the honors to the JG 26 Geschwadergruppe and Third Gruppe. The latter's Bf 109s out-climbed the Fw 190s and made the first contact, approaching the 4th Fighter Group at 9100 meters (30,000 feet) after the latter had turned for England at Ostend. The 334th Fighter Squadron broke around and dived on the Bf 109s, which dived away, according to the standard procedure of the Jagdwaffe. But this was suicide against P-47s. Lt. Duane Beeson chased Obfw. Heinz Wefes of 4/JG 54 until the latter bailed out at one hundred feet; unfortunately, Wefes' parachute did not open. Lt. Kestel of the 9th Staffel shot down a 4th Group Thunderbolt; the combats had ended and the P-47s had regained altitude before the arrival of Major Priller and his Fw 190s.

JG 26 Victory Claims: 16 - 18 May 1943

Date	Rank	Name	Unit	Cl #	Aircraft	Place	Time	Opponent	Conf
16-05-43	Major	Priller	Ge CO	88	P-47	Scheldt Estuary	1312	78 FG	unk
18-05-43	Uffz.	Crump	5		Spitfire	6km SE of Dieppe	1500		no
18-05-43	Lt.	Kestel	9	2	P-47	unknown	1705	4 FG	unk

19 May

The Allied heavy bombers headed east today to bomb Kiel and Flensberg. The three P-47 groups swept the Dutch coast in distant support, but Jafü Holland-Ruhr did not respond. Jafü 2 ordered the Third Gruppe up from Wevelgem and had them patrol in mid-Channel, in case the P-47s took the same homeward route as the previous day, but no contact was made. Late in the evening the Second Gruppe was scrambled in response to some RAF activity off the west coast of the Pas de Calais, but, again, no enemy aircraft were seen.

20 May

With good weather and longer days, the Geschwader resumed its defensive patrols, today pushing them out over the Channel. No enemy activity was found. Uffz. Karl Trapp of the 12th Staffel ran out of fuel before reaching his base, and destroyed his Messerschmitt while attempting a forced landing near Étaples.

21 May

Again the 8th Bomber Command turned east, today hitting Wilhelmshaven and Emden. An abortive RAF Circus to Abbeville brought the Second Gruppe over from Vitry, but no contact was made. The three P-47 groups made their usual "bus run" along the Belgian and Dutch coasts, and today the Third Gruppe was released to chase them. Once again they were caught below the P-47s of the 4th Fighter Group, and once again the 334th Squadron was assigned the bounce. This time the honors went to the Germans. Three Thunderbolts crashed after a "tremendous dogfight over the North Sea and Ostend", in the words of the 4th FG historian. No German aircraft sustained reportable damage. Unfortunately, this month is missing from the

Luftwaffe claims microfilms, and the identities of the victorious German pilots are not known.

Obfw. Glunz was once again assigned the evening recon mission to England, which was once again uneventful.

22 May

Fw. Ellenrieder left Vitry at 0802 on the morning recon mission to England. He returned early with a bad engine and had to make a wheels-up landing on the field. The weather closed in shortly afterward, ending flying for the day.

23 May

The growing 8th Bomber Command had begun to strike cities along the north German coast with some frequency. Today the Third Gruppe, comprising the Gruppenstab, 9/JG 26, 4/JG 54, and 12/JG 54, moved to Cuxhaven-Nordholz in northern Germany, to lend support to JG 1, III/JG 54, and the newly-formed JG 11, the principal day fighter units within the borders of Germany. 11/JG 54 remained in France, and after joining the Geschwadergruppe at Lille-Vendeville was made fully operational. When 7/JG 26 returned from Russia and rejoined the Third Gruppe, 4/JG 54 left JG 26, and served as the nucleus for a new Gruppe, IV/JG 54, and three new Staffeln – which re-used the designations 10/JG 54, 11/JG 54, and 12/JG 54. IV/JG 54 went to the Eastern Front to provide JG 54 with a third Gruppe, since III/JG 54 stayed in the Reich defense force in Germany as an independent Gruppe.

The weather remained bad, and there was little flying along the Channel coast. Obfw. Glunz was once more assigned the evening recon mission to England, which was carried out without incident.

24 May

The only Geschwader flight recorded today was Fw. Ellenrieder's morning recon mission to England, from which he had to return early owing to bad weather and poor visibility.

25 May

The weather improved enough for 8th Fighter Command to send another high-altitude sweep along the Belgian coast. With no operational Bf 109s remaining in the theater, the job of chasing the P-47s was given to the Second Gruppe and its Fw 190s. Some of the Focke-Wulf pilots got near enough to the Thunderbolts to be given credit for combat sorties, but they could not close on them. The Americans did not see them, and no combats resulted.

26 May

Jafü 2 ordered its fighters to resume their coastal patrols, despite somewhat questionable weather. The high-flying P-47s were plotted, as were several small RAF sweeps, but no contacts were made. Uffz. Leo Müller of the 4th Staffel suffered a serious head injury when his Fw 190 overturned while he was making a forced landing on Merville.

27 May

According to the German records, the P-47s were accompanied today by a few Spitfires. II/JG 1 made the interception over Eecloo, and damaged two Spitfires for the loss of two Focke-Wulfs and their pilots. The JG 26 Geschwadergruppe was scrambled, but was recalled and landed after the Jafü got a report of another Allied formation leaving England. This proved to be a small RAF Circus that was not intercepted.

28 May

The first reports of Allied activity were received late in the afternoon. Both the Geschwadergruppe and the Second Gruppe were scrambled at 1725, but only the latter made contact. The Northolt Wing (Polish) was caught near Bergues while escorting some Venturas, and Oblt. Sternberg of the 5th Staffel shot one of the Spitfires down. This activity caught the attention of the American P-47s approaching Dunkirk from the east at 30,000 feet (9100 meters), and some came down to do combat, but neither side sustained any more losses.

29 May

The 8th Bomber Command attacked Rennes, La Pallice and Lorient in Brittany. All available fighters of JG 2 were employed by Jafü 3 and Jafü Brittany, but no assistance was requested of Jafü 2, and JG 26 stayed on the ground.

30 May

At noon Major Priller took off in the Stab Bf 108 Taiphun for Rechlin, the principal Luftwaffe flight test center, to attend a fighter leaders' conference called to discuss new equipment and tactics. The rest of the Geschwader pilots busied themselves with patrols and training flights. At 1930 Uffz. Mayer and other Geschwadergruppe pilots took off to provide a reception for SKG 10 Jabos which were returning from England. Seven of the fighter-bombers failed to return; the Schnellkampfgeschwader lost twenty-one pilots in May, and switched wholly to night bombing.

31 May

American air activity was restricted to another ineffective high-altitude coastal sweep by the three P-47 groups. In response, the Geschwader was scrambled at noon, but was soon ordered to return to base. A more tempting target appeared in late afternoon, in the form of a dozen No. 2 Group Venturas, which bombed the Zeebrugge coke ovens on the Belgian coast and then wheeled for England. Their principal escort was provided by the aggressive Canadians of W/C Johnnie Johnson's Kenley Wing, which positioned itself on the landward side of the bombers and attacked the Second Gruppe as it approached. A full-scale dogfight ensued, in which Fw. Hans Danneberg (4th Staffel) and the very experienced Lt. Rolf-Georg Mondry (5th Staffel) were shot down and killed. Both Oblt. Sternberg and Lt. Hoppe claimed Spitfires, but while Sternberg's target, from No. 403 Squadron, crashed just off the coast, Hoppe's regained England with damage. The Second Gruppe was up until dark searching for the three pilots off Ostend, but none of them were found.

In the last half of May, Lt. Karl-Heinz Kempf joined 11/JG 54 from a tour in a training unit. Kempf had won the Knight's Cross in 7/JG 54, but had a real interest in training, and was a welcomed addition to the unofficial operational training Staffel. In other moves, Gefr. Hans-Walter Sander transferred from the 4th Staffel to the 8th, and Lt. Hans Fischer left the 4th Staffel for training duty.

JG 26 Victory Claims: 28 - 31 May 1943

Date	Rank	Name	Unit	Cl #	Aircraft	Place	Time	Opponent	Conf
28-05-43	Oblt.	Sternberg	5 CO	16	Spitfire	Bergues	1752	315 Sqd	yes
31-05-43	Lt.	Hoppe	4 CO	9	Spitfire	10km N of Dunkirk	1753	403 Sqd	yes
31-05-43	Oblt.	Sternberg	5 CO	17	Spitfire	1km N of Ostend	1750	403 Sqd	yes

JG 26 Casualties: 18 - 31 May 1943

Date	Rank	Name	Cas	Unit	Aircraft	WNr	Mkgs	Place	Time	Cause	Allied Unit
18-05-43	Obfw.	Wefes, Heinrich	KIA	4/54	Bf 109G-4	19246	wh 6	Ghistelles near Ostend	1705	P-47	4 FG
20-05-43	Uffz.	Trapp, Karl	no	12	Bf 109G-6	19657		Étaples		no fuel	n/a
26-05-43	Uffz.	Müller, Leo	WIFA	4	Fw 190A-4	2395	wh 7	Merville a/f		engine	n/a
31-05-43	Fw.	Danneberg, Hans	KIA	4	Fw 190A-5	7305	wh 10	in sea 10km N of Ostend	1640	Spitfire	403 Sqd
31-05-43	Lt.	Mondry, Georg	KIA	5	Fw 190A-5	7303	bk 14	in sea SE of Mariakerke	1640	Spitfire	403 or 421 Sqd

Chapter Two

THE EASTERN FRONT

January - July 1943

By all accounts, the January announcement that JG 26 was to move to the Eastern Front was popular with the Geschwader pilots – the quality of the Soviet opposition remained low, and aerial victories, the prerequisite for honors and promotions in the Jagdwaffe, were still easy to obtain. The unit was to trade places with the Green Heart Geschwader, JG 54. The exchange was to take place by Gruppen and Staffeln, staged to permit continuity of defensive coverage. Only the pilots, key staff members, and certain items of critical equipment were to move. Maintenance crews, aircraft, and all other equipment were to remain on their original bases.

JG 54 was the only single-engine fighter Geschwader in Luftflotte 1, which was responsible for supporting Army Group North, whose front lines had stabilised after the investiture of Leningrad in the early months of the eastern campaign. JG 54 had occupied its four principal airfields continuously since September, 1941. After a mostly uneventful 1942, both the northern and southern ends of Army Group North's front had recently become active.

In early January, the Red Army began an offensive to relieve besieged Leningrad. Two army groups succeeded in linking up at the town of Schluesselburg, on the southern shore of Lake Ladoga, thus relieving the siege. The Germans sealed off the penetration by 18 January, but could not throw the Russians out of the corridor they had won. Only six miles wide, every square foot of it was within range of German field artillery. Soviet attempts to widen the corridor continued until 1 April, without further success.

To the south, the Russians had begun an offensive to eliminate the Demyansk salient. This was a German-occupied bulge in the Soviet lines just south of the III/JG 54 base at Rielbitzi on Lake Ilmen. It had been formed during the Soviet winter offensive of 1941. The Russian attacks had persisted since the previous November, in decreasing strength. The decision was made to replace III/JG 54 with I/JG 26 in one step, as this part of the front was moderately quiet; the 7th Staffel would join I/JG 54 outside Leningrad. As the two components of JG 26 fought entirely separate campaigns, they will be discussed separately in this account. In the absence of unit or Allied records, the reconstructed daily reports are very dependent on the few available logbooks.

I/JG 26 on the Demyansk and Moscow Fronts

21 January

The first trainload of First Gruppe pilots and ground staff left France.

27 January

First Gruppe personnel began assembling at Heiligenbeil, a major Luftwaffe servicing base in East Prussia. Here they obtained brand-new Fw 190A-5 fighters, plus some Fw 190A-4s. The next few days were spent installing and testing the planes' radios and armament. Hptm. Schrödter commanded a small test unit at Heiligenbeil, and asked that Uffz. Jan Schild of the 2nd Staffel stay on to help test fly newly-arriving aircraft. Schild did not rejoin the First Gruppe until March. While at Heiligenbeil the Gruppe was reinforced by two pilots just out of flight school, Uffz. Michael Hecker and Uffz. Hans Ruppert.

31 January

Major Seifert took off with the Stabsschwarm to fly to Riga, but was forced to turn back to Heiligenbeil owing to bad weather. Hptm. Rolf Hermichen of the 3rd Staffel, who knew this part of the front well from duty here as a Bf 110 pilot in 1941, then led the Gruppe to Riga without incident, and two days later led the Gruppe in formation to Rielbitzi, on Lake Ilmen.

2 February

Rielbitzi was a typical Feldflugplatz, or front-line airfield, but the Green Heart personnel had done their best to make it comfortable in the sixteen months they had been there. It was now mid-winter, and the temperature averaged -40°C. The Schlageter pilots moved into their quarters in the village adjacent to the field and were briefed on their new assignments. Combat in Russia was far different from anything they had experienced in the West. Aircraft seldom flew above 3000 meters (10,000 feet), and most combats took place well below that altitude. Luftwaffe fighters never flew in greater than Staffel strength; the Schwarm was the most common tactical formation, and many patrols were flown by Rotten of two aircraft. Dead reckoning navigation, or pilotage, was extremely important. German pilots tried to keep a sense of the location of their own lines from the moment of takeoff, and if possible remained within gliding distance of friendly territory. Few pilots survived a crash-landing behind the Russian lines. Finally, whenever beyond the lines they had to be concerned with Soviet antiaircraft fire, which was usually far more dangerous than Soviet fighters.

The *freie Jagd*, the "free hunt" or uncontrolled fighter sweep, was the preferred mission. On the Eastern Front, these were most often flown by Schwärme against reported formations of Soviet bombers and attack aircraft. The German patrols usually remained well behind their own lines, and their losses were very light. The Luftwaffe had originated the tactics of the Schwarm, and the skilled teamwork of the German pilots made them almost invulnerable to Soviet fighters at this stage of the war.

The newcomers sat through their lessons impatiently, while their aircraft were made ready for combat. Fw 190s were new to the holdover ground crews from III/JG 54, who took a few days to adapt the fighter's maintenance procedures for the subfreezing temperatures. The pilots studied their maps, compared them against the frozen wasteland surrounding them, and waited to be declared operational. In the meantime, II/JG 54 at nearby Staraya Russa maintained the pressure on the Soviets around Demyansk.

14 February

The first assignment for the Gruppe was ground attack, a new task for the Schlageter pilots. Seifert's men were ordered to strafe the hordes of Russian infantry that were massed along the shores of Lake Ilmen, and attack the motorised sleds and horse-drawn supply trains in the Russians' rear. After several hard days, in each of which the pilots flew between eight and ten missions, the Russians pulled back.

16 February

Major Seifert's Stabsschwarm and the 1st Staffel intercepted a large formation of Il-2 *Shturmoviki* ground-attack aircraft, and shot down eleven without loss. The scoring was spread among seven pilots, including Major Seifert; his adjutant, Lt. Heinrich Jessen; the 1st Staffel Kapitän, Hptm. Höckner; and Obfw. Heckmann.

Date	Rank	Name	Unit	Cl #	Aircraft	Place	Time	Opponent	Conf
16-02-43	Maj.	Seifert	I CO	43	Il-2	8km SE of Adler 7			yes
16-02-43	Lt.	Jessen	I	1	Il-2	15km S of Adler 7			yes
16-02-43	Hptm.	Höckner	1 CO	40	Il-2	USSR (PQ 18453)			yes
16-02-43	Hptm.	Höckner	1 CO	41	Il-2	USSR (PQ 18422)			yes
16-02-43	Ogfr.	Gauss	1	1	Il-2	USSR (PQ 18454)			yes
16-02-43	Obfw.	Heckmann	1	54	Il-2	USSR (PQ 28142)			yes
16-02-43	Obfw.	Heckmann	1	55	Il-2	USSR (PQ 18423)			yes
16-02-43	Gefr.	Kaiser	1	1	Il-2	USSR (PQ 18454)			yes
16-02-43	Gefr.	Kaiser	1	2	Il-2	USSR (PQ 18452)			yes
16-02-43	Fw.	Söffing	1	1	Il-2	USSR (PQ 18464)			yes
16-02-43	Fw.	Söffing	1	2	Il-2	USSR (PQ 18461)			yes

17 February

The Gruppe encountered its first formation of skilled Soviet fighter pilots, and sustained its first losses in the new theater. Uffz. Heinrich Schnell of the 3rd Staffel took a direct hit from Russian antiaircraft fire while over Demyansk, and was killed. Uffz. Friedrich Kneiss of the same Staffel contacted the ground accidentally while maneuvering to attack Il-2s or evade their escorts, lost control of his Focke-Wulf, and crashed to his death. Gefr. Helmut Kaiser of the 1st Staffel lost a dogfight with Yak-3s and was forced to land, fortunately within the German lines. The Yaks then destroyed his Fw 190 with gunfire, while Kaiser ran for his life. He survived, with slight injuries. Four additional Gruppe aircraft force-landed with combat damage; one was so badly hit that it had to be written off. The Soviet fighters, new Yak-3s and some lend-lease P-40C Tomahawks, had succeeded in protecting the Il-2s, and at the cost of only three of their number.

Uffz. Heinrich Schnell of the 3rd Staffel. He was killed by Soviet antiaircraft fire on 17 February. (*Vanoverbeke*)

I/JG 26 Victory Claims: 17 February 1943

Date	Rank	Name	Unit	Cl #	Aircraft	Place	Time	Opponent	Conf
17-02-43	Lt.	Beese	1	7	P-40	USSR (PQ 18463)			yes
17-02-43	Fw.	Söffing	1	3	P-40	USSR (PQ 10461)			yes
17-02-43	Lt.	Dippel	2	10	P-40	USSR (PQ 18433)			yes

18 February

Pilots of the 1st and 3rd Staffeln destroyed LaGG-3 fighters and five Il-2s, without loss. Their heavily-armed Focke-Wulf fighters gave promise of solving the vexing problem of the *Shturmovik*, which had proved resistant to the attacks of the three-gunned Bf 109Fs and Bf 109Gs of JG 54.

19 February

The Gruppe continued its campaign against the *Shturmoviki*, downing three today and one the following day. One 1st Staffel Fw 190A-4 had to belly-land south of Staraya Russa with a bad engine.

I/JG 26 Victory Claims: 18 - 19 February 1943

Date	Rank	Name	Unit	Cl #	Aircraft	Place	Time	Opponent	Conf
18-02-43	Hptm.	Höckner	1 CO	42	Il-2	USSR (PQ 28454)			yes
18-02-43	Obfw.	Heckmann	1	56	Il-2	USSR (PQ 28351)			yes
18-02-43	Obfw.	Heckmann	1	57	Il-2	USSR (PQ 28311)			yes
18-02-43	Obfw.	Lindelaub	1	1	Il-2	USSR (PQ 28173)			yes
18-02-43	Hptm.	Hermichen	3 CO	22	LaGG-3	USSR (PQ 28321)			yes
18-02-43	Uffz.	Scheyda	3	4	Il-2	USSR (PQ 28354)			yes
19-02-43	Hptm.	Hermichen	3 CO	23	Il-2	USSR (PQ 18293)			yes
19-02-43	Hptm.	Hermichen	3 CO	24	Il-2	USSR (PQ 18462)			yes
19-02-43	Uffz.	Münch	3	1	Il-2	USSR (PQ 18463)			yes

20 February

The commander of Army Group North, Generalfeldmarschall von Küchler, requested permission to begin a staged withdrawal from the Demyansk salient, which lengthened his lines to no strategic or tactical purpose. Sobered by the ongoing catastrophe at Stalingrad, Hitler uncharacteristically gave his permission. The new assignment of the First Gruppe was to cover II Corps as it prepared to withdraw from the salient.

For the next month, II Corps fought to pull back in an orderly fashion, while the Soviets attempted to catch them on open ground and destroy them from the air. The few air histories published in the USSR after the war tend to be so one-sided and filled with propaganda that they are of little use to anyone looking for a balanced presentation. The memoirs of Gen.-Maj. Kostenko, the Soviet fighter commander at Demyansk, may be an exception. He wrote that this campaign saw the first serious Soviet challenge to German fighter supremacy. In his view, the Soviet pilots, many in new Yak-7bs and La-5s, were successful in both offensive and defensive roles. They frequently fought through the fighter sweeps that preceded German bomber attacks – the Germans lacked sufficient fighters for orthodox escort formations – in order to fall on the bombers. The Soviet fighters were so successful in their own escort role that Kostenko began calling upon the Il-2s to bait the Focke-Wulfs and Messerschmitts into combat. The performance of Gen. Kostenko's force was so impressive that the Soviet High Command awarded it the coveted Guards designation, and it became the 1st Guards Fighter Air Corps, strong evidence that Kostenko's claims have some substance.

The pilots of the two Luftwaffe fighter Gruppen on the scene, I/JG 26 and II/JG 54, were unaware that their supremacy was under serious challenge, but a major failing of the Jagdwaffe was an unwillingness to take a broad view of its responsibilities. Although its fighter pilots won many individual battles after 1942, the German armed forces that the fighters were ostensibly supporting never won another campaign. Many of the Jagdflieger were happy as long as there were easy targets to shoot down, and there were medals to be earned; the fact that the *harder* targets pressed on with their missions and attacked the German ground forces or the rapidly-shrinking Luftwaffe bomber arm without interference was not of primary importance to these men.

21 February

The 1st Staffel pilots shot down four fighters over Demyansk, with no loss to themselves. Major "Assi" Hahn, the II/JG 54 Kommandeur, was shot down by a Soviet fighter in the Demyansk area and taken prisoner.

I/JG 26 Victory Claims: 20 - 21 February 1943

Date	Rank	Name	Unit	Cl #	Aircraft	Place	Time	Opponent	Conf
20-02-43	Fw.	Söffing	1	4	Il-2	USSR (PQ 18214)			yes
21-02-43	Hptm.	Höckner	1 CO	43	LaGG-3	USSR (PQ 18294)			yes
21-02-43	Hptm.	Höckner	1 CO	44	P-40	USSR (PQ 18264)			yes

| 21-02-43 | Lt. | Beese | 1 | 8 | P-40 | USSR (PQ 18264) | | | yes |
| 21-02-43 | Obfw. | Lindelaub | 1 | 2 | LaGG-3 | USSR (PQ 18291) | | | yes |

22 February

Part of the 2nd Staffel had left France late, and just now joined the Gruppe at Rielbitzi. Gefr. Heinrich Heuser, one of these newcomers, was taken from the Staffel and assigned to the Stabsschwarm. The four pilots – Major Seifert, Lt. Heinrich Jessen, Uffz. Heinz-Günther Klems, and Heuser – would fly together for the next several months. Heuser recalls that most of the flight's missions were freie Jagden at 4-6000 meters (13-20,000 feet). This was usually above the Red Air Force formations, which could be attacked or not as Seifert saw fit. Other tasks were bomber escort, interceptions, and ground support.

An exuberant Lt. Hans Dippel (KIFA 8 May 44) (2nd from left) describes an air battle to some of his 2nd Staffel comrades. *(Heuser)*

23 February

Gefr. Heuser's first mission on the Eastern Front was a success. Soviet troops were attempting to cross Lake Ilmen by boat. The Stabsschwarm was ordered to strafe the boats and any troops caught massing on the shore. Several boats were sunk; Heuser was credited with one of these. His second mission, a freie Jagd, was also successful. Major Seifert and Lt. Jessen each shot down an Il-2, while two others were claimed by 2nd Staffel pilots. Two 1st Staffel pilots claimed LaGG-3s during the day, but on a separate mission, according to the map coordinates. (Unfortunately, the times and exact locations of most of the First Gruppe victory claims in Russia remain unknown.)

I/JG 26 Victory Claims: 23 February 1943

Date	Rank	Name	Unit	Cl #	Aircraft	Place	Time	Opponent	Conf
23-02-43	Maj.	Seifert	I CO	44	Il-2	USSR (PQ 1843)			yes
23-02-43	Lt.	Jessen	1	2	Il-2	USSR (PQ 1843)			yes
23-02-43	Ogfr.	Gauss	1	2	LaGG-3	USSR (PQ 29773)			yes
23-02-43	Fw.	Söffing	1	5	LaGG-3	USSR (PQ 29772)			yes
23-02-43	Lt.	Dippel	2	11	Il-2	USSR (PQ 18272)			yes
23-02-43	Uffz.	Glaser	2	1	Il-2	USSR (PQ 18261)			yes

27 February

First Gruppe pilots shot down six aircraft during the day: one Pe-2, one P-39, two P-40s, and two LaGG-3s.

Date	Rank	Name	Unit	Cl #	Aircraft	Place	Time	Opponent	Conf
27-02-43	Hptm.	Höckner	1 CO	45	P-40	USSR (PQ 28122)			yes
27-02-43	Hptm.	Höckner	1 CO	46	P-40	USSR (PQ 28311)			yes
27-02-43	Obfw.	Lindelaub	1	3	LaGG-3	USSR (PQ 18391)			yes
27-02-43	Fw.	Söffing	1	6	P-39	USSR (PQ 18382)			yes
27-02-43	Oblt.	Zink	2 CO	34	LaGG-3	USSR (PQ 1846)			yes
27-02-43	Lt.	Dippel	2	12	Pe-2	USSR (PQ 18394)			yes

28 February

The Stabsschwarm scored again; Major Seifert claimed a P-39 and a new La-5, while Lt. Jessen downed a Pe-2 and a MiG-3. The 2nd Staffel Kapitän, Oblt. Fülbert Zink, a recent arrival from France, began his Eastern Front scoring by downing a P-39.

Obfw. Alfred Heckmann, with fifty-seven victories the most successful pilot in the Gruppe, left the front for a tour as an instructor with Jagdgruppe Ost.

I/JG 26 Victory Claims: 28 February 1943

Date	Rank	Name	Unit	Cl #	Aircraft	Place	Time	Opponent	Conf
28-02-43	Maj.	Seifert	I CO	45	P-39	USSR (PQ 18412)			yes
28-02-43	Maj.	Seifert	I CO	46	LaGG-3	USSR (PQ 1835)			yes
28-02-43	Lt.	Jessen	I	3	Pe-2	USSR (PQ 18354)			yes
28-02-43	Lt.	Jessen	I	4	MiG-3	USSR (PQ 1835)			yes
28-02-43	Oblt.	Zink	2 CO	35	P-39	USSR (PQ 2834)			yes

1 March

While the Demyansk withdrawal was still underway, Army Group Center began a line-straightening move of its own, on a scale large enough to be given a code name, Operation *Büffel* (Buffalo). The army pulled back from the Rzhev-Vyazma salient to a new, fortified line east of Smolensk and Yelnya. II/JG 54 moved south to assist JG 51, the only German fighter wing covering the central part of the front.

2 March

The First Gruppe continued its routine of freie Jagden from Rielbitzi. The Stabsschwarm patrol engaged the enemy, and gained mission credit, but made no victory claims.

Uffz. Walter Ullrich reported to the Gruppe from training, and was assigned to the 3rd Staffel.

3 March

The newly-promoted Hauptmann Zink was the day's only scorer, claiming a Pe-2. A 1st Staffel aircraft had to make an emergency landing on Rielbitzi owing to an equipment failure, and sustained moderate damage.

4 March

Small Gruppe formations were up all day on freie Jagden. The Red fighters were avoided, and three bombers, two Pe-2s and one Il-2, were shot down.

I/JG 26 Victory Claims: 3 - 4 March 1943

Date	Rank	Name	Unit	Cl #	Aircraft	Place	Time	Opponent	Conf
03-03-43	Hptm.	Zink	2 CO	36	Pe-2	USSR (PQ 1865)			yes
04-03-43	Lt.	Beese	1	9	Il-2	USSR (PQ 18217)			yes
04-03-43	Uffz.	Fast	2	5	Pe-2	USSR (PQ 1986)			yes
04-03-43	Hptm.	Hermichen	3 CO	25	Pe-2	USSR (PQ 18242)			yes

5 March

Gefr. Heuser was given credit for three combat missions today. In the morning he flew escort for Ju 87s. A noon freie Jagd was drawn 50 kilometers south of Lake Ilmen by

Fw. Pleese and Uffz. Fast, photographed at Rielbitzi in late February or early March. *(Heuser)*

reports of many enemy aircraft, which proved to be true; the Stabsschwarm wound up in combat with twenty Red fighters, and Fw. Karl Preeg, a recent transfer from the 8th Staffel who was apparently flying with the Stab while Seifert evaluated his abilities, was shot down and killed. Heuser also contacted the enemy on a late-afternoon freie Jagd, during which Major Seifert shot down one Pe-2 and two Il-2s. Over the course of the day the three Staffeln claimed three fighters and eight bombers, and suffered no casualties, although Hptm. Zink's Focke-Wulf sustained such severe combat damage that it had to be written off.

I/JG 26 Victory Claims: 5 March 1943

Date	Rank	Name	Unit	Cl #	Aircraft	Place	Time	Opponent	Conf
05-03-43	Maj.	Seifert	I CO	47	Pe-2	USSR (PQ 1822)			yes
05-03-43	Maj.	Seifert	I CO	48	Il-2	USSR (PQ 1816)			yes
05-03-43	Maj.	Seifert	I CO	49	Il-2	USSR (PQ 1824)			yes
05-03-43	Hptm.	Höckner	1 CO	47	P-40	USSR (PQ 18214)			yes
05-03-43	Obfw.	Söffing	1	7	LaGG-3	USSR (PQ 18251)			yes
05-03-43	Lt.	Dippel	2	13	Il-2	USSR (PQ 18484)			yes
05-03-43	Lt.	Kunze	2	1	Il-2	USSR (PQ 18352)	1236		yes
05-03-43	Hptm.	Hermichen	3 CO	26	P-40	USSR (PQ 18443)			yes
05-03-43	Lt.	Boer	3	1	Pe-2	USSR (PQ 1836)			yes
05-03-43	Lt.	Grimm	3	1	Il-2	USSR (PQ 1864)			yes
05-03-43	Fw.	Scheyda	3	5	Il-2	USSR (PQ 1864)			yes
05-03-43	Fw.	Scheyda	3	6	Il-2	USSR (PQ 1838)			yes
05-03-43	Fw.	Scheyda	3	7	Il-2	USSR (PQ 1837/38)			yes
05-03-43	Fw.	Scheyda	3	8	Pe-2	USSR (PQ 1836)			yes

6 March

A 2nd Staffel aircraft was forced to crash-land on Rielbitzi after being hit by Soviet antiaircraft fire. Damage was assessed as moderate.

7 March

The 2nd Staffel Fw 190 of Uffz. Hans-Joachim Fast overturned while he was attempting to take off from Rielbitzi to escort He 111s. The aircraft caught fire, and Fast, who was trapped in the cockpit, burned to death.

The 1st and 3rd Staffeln claimed nine victories. Hptm. Hoeckner had the most successful day of any First Gruppe pilot to date, claiming four Il-2s and two P-40s.

Uffz. Jan Schild, having finally been released by Hptm. Schrödter, arrived at Rielbitzi today from Heiligenbeil *via* Riga.

I/JG 26 Victory Claims: 7 March 1943

Date	Rank	Name	Unit	Cl #	Aircraft	Place	Time	Opponent	Conf
07-03-43	Hptm.	Höckner	1 CO	48	Il-2	USSR (PQ 18352)			yes
07-03-43	Hptm.	Höckner	1 CO	49	Il-2	USSR (PQ 18322)			yes
07-03-43	Hptm.	Höckner	1 CO	50	Il-2	USSR (PQ 18193)			yes
07-03-43	Hptm.	Höckner	1 CO	51	Il-2	USSR (PQ 19573)			yes
07-03-43	Hptm.	Höckner	1 CO	52	P-40	USSR (PQ 19673)			yes
07-03-43	Hptm.	Höckner	1 CO	53	P-40	USSR (PQ 18382)			yes
07-03-43	Hptm.	Hermichen	3 CO	27	Pe-2	USSR (PQ 18551)			yes
07-03-43	Hptm.	Hermichen	3 CO	28	Pe-2	USSR (PQ 18254)			yes
07-03-43	Lt.	Grimm	3	2	LaGG-3	USSR (PQ 18543)			yes

Uffz. Hans-Joachim Fast of the 2nd Staffel. He was killed in a takeoff accident from Rielbitzi on 7 March, a few days after this photo was taken. *(Heuser)*

Major Johannes Seifert (KIA 25 Nov 43), First Gruppe Kommandeur for most of its tour of duty on the Eastern Front. *(Heuser)*

9 March
The day's freie Jagden resulted in claims for two Lavochkin fighters.

10 March
Freie Jagden were flown, but were unsuccessful. Obfw. Waldemar Söffing of the 1st Staffel broke his nose in a forced landing south of Staraya Russa. The records conflict as to whether the landing was necessitated by combat damage or routine engine failure.

13 March
One 3rd Staffel aircraft was written off after sustaining serious damage from Soviet antiaircraft fire; a second sustained moderate damage while aborting a takeoff from Rielbitzi.

14 March

While on a freie Jagd, Hptm. Fülbert Zink was shot down in a noon-hour combat that had drifted across the lines, and did not make it back; he had to be listed as missing in action. Hptm. Wilhelm Gäth, a supernumerary pilot with the Geschwader Stab, was summoned from France to replace Zink as 2nd Staffel Kapitän.

During the day the Gruppe began moving to Dno, which was southwest of Rielbitzi and due west of Staraya Russa. The reason for the move is unknown, but was probably necessitated by the condition of the Rielbitzi landing ground. The first mission from Dno resulted in the destruction of a 3rd Staffel Focke-Wulf during an aborted takeoff. Another 3rd Staffel plane sustained serious damage from antiaircraft fire and crash-landed on Dno. On the positive side of the ledger, six air victories were claimed

Hptm. Fülbert Zink, Kapitän of the 2nd Staffel – KIA 14 March 1943. *(Molge)*

during the day.

Fw. Helmut Bäumener reported to the 3rd Staffel from flight training. Bäumener was a Wehrmacht veteran who had previously earned the Iron Cross First Class and

Wreckage of Hptm. Zink's Fw 190A-4 "black 13" (W.Nr. 7176) in which he was killed on 14 March. *(Heuser)*

the Narvik campaign medal.

I/JG 26 Victory Claims: 9 - 14 March 1943

Date	Rank	Name	Unit	Cl #	Aircraft	Place	Time	Opponent	Conf
09-03-43	Lt.	Draheim	I	1	LaGG-3	USSR (PQ 18346)			yes
09-03-43	Hptm.	Höckner	1 CO	54	LaGG-3	USSR (PQ 18471)			yes
14-03-43	Maj.	Seifert	I CO	50	Pe-2	USSR (PQ 18282)			yes
14-03-43	Lt.	Jessen	I	5	LaGG-3	USSR (PQ 1827)			yes
14-03-43	Lt.	Beese	1	10	Il-2	USSR (PQ 19848)			yes
14-03-43	Lt.	Wilms	1	1	Il-2	USSR (PQ 19849)			yes
14-03-43	Lt.	Wilms	1	2	Il-2	USSR (PQ 19867)			yes
14-03-43	Fw.	Zirngibl	3	2	Il-2	USSR (PQ 1988)			yes

15 March

Gefr. Heuser flew three freie Jagden with the Stabsschwarm; these were its first missions from Dno. The first two contacted the enemy, but without result. The third reached firing position above and behind a group of LaGG-3s. Major Seifert let his wingman Heuser lead the attack, and Heuser downed a LaGG, for his first victory. Lt. Jessen also scored during the day, as did Fw. Zirngibl of the 3rd Staffel. A 1st Staffel Fw 190 was damaged while landing on Dno; the cause was attributed to the weather.

16 March

Gefr. Heuser flew two freie Jagden, both of which contacted enemy aircraft. Major Seifert shot down an Il-2 during one of them. Uffz. Adam of the 3rd Staffel claimed a LaGG-3. Two 2nd Staffel aircraft sustained damage, one from antiaircraft fire and the other in a weather-hindered landing on Dno.

17 March

The day's freie Jagden resulted in one victory; Fw. Scheyda of the 3rd Staffel claimed a Yak-1.

18 March

Fw. Günther Rau of the 3rd Staffel took off from Rielbitzi to intercept Soviet attack planes, and failed to return. He was shot down in combat east of Staraya Russa, and

Two First Gruppe pilots, Uffz. Kaase and Uffz. Adam, shortly after their return from a combat flight – note the damaged aileron. *(Heuser)*

was initially carried as missing in action. Obfw. Söffing returned to action and claimed an Il-2, and Fw. Scheyda, who was rapidly building up his score, claimed an Il-2 and a Yak-7. Yet another Gruppe aircraft was destroyed while aborting a takeoff from Dno, and Gefr. Heuser destroyed his Fw 190A-5 while force-landing on the field at Tuleblya with a bad engine.

Army Group North completed its successful withdrawal from Demyansk. The northern sector now fell quiet until the Russian spring, with its mud and swollen rivers, had ended, and the large Red Air Force formations seen the previous month left for other parts of the front. Weather and ground fire became the most dangerous opponents.

Lt. Heinrich Jessen (KIFA 10 Jan 44) of the First Gruppe Stab.*(Heuser)*

19 March

One Gruppe aircraft was destroyed, and a second was damaged, in a night bombing attack on Dno by an R-2 biplane flying a harassing mission. Swift revenge was exacted by Uffz. Glaser of the 2nd Staffel, who took off and shot the attacker down.

I/JG 26 Victory Claims: 15 - 19 March 1943

Date	Rank	Name	Unit	Cl #	Aircraft	Place	Time	Opponent	Conf
15-03-43	Lt.	Jessen	I	6	MiG-3	USSR (PQ 19733)			yes
15-03-43	Gefr.	Heuser, Hein	2	1	LaGG-3	USSR (PQ 1827)	1600		yes
15-03-43	Fw.	Zirngibl	3	3	LaGG-3	USSR (PQ 18274)			yes
16-03-43	Maj.	Seifert	I CO	51	Il-2	USSR (PQ 18211)			yes
16-03-43	Uffz.	Adam III	3	1	LaGG-3	USSR (PQ 18872)			yes
17-03-43	Fw.	Scheyda	3	9	Yak-1	USSR (PQ 1844)			yes
18-03-43	Obfw.	Söffing	1	8	Il-2	USSR (PQ 19763)			yes
18-03-43	Fw.	Scheyda	3	10	Yak-7	USSR (PQ 18275)			yes
18-03-43	Fw.	Scheyda	3	11	Il-2	USSR (PQ 19847)			yes
19-03-43	Uffz.	Glaser	2	2	R-2	USSR (PQ 19883)			yes

22 March

Gefr. Heuser was given a break from the week's routine of unsuccessful freie Jagden and ordered to escort an Hs 126 on a reconnaissance mission. Heuser was credited with a combat sortie, which meant only that he had crossed the lines. Another Gruppe aircraft was destroyed while crash-landing on Dno with a bad engine; the primitive servicing conditions were obviously taking their toll on the aircraft.

23 March

To the immediate south of the Gruppe operational area, Operation Büffel came to an end. It succeeded in shortening the affected part of Army Group Center's front lines from 550 to 175 kilometers (from 340 to 110 miles). In isolated combats during the this day and the next, Gruppe pilots claimed four victories, without loss.

I/JG 26 Victory Claims: 23 - 24 March 1943

Date	Rank	Name	Unit	Cl #	Aircraft	Place	Time	Opponent	Conf
23-03-43	Hptm.	Hermichen	3 CO	29	Yak	USSR (PQ 00412)			yes

24-03-43	Hptm.	Höckner	1 CO	55	Pe-2	USSR (PQ 00261)		yes
24-03-43	Lt.	Beese	1	11	Pe-2	USSR (PQ 18574)	0728	yes
24-03-43	Obfw.	Söffing	1	9	Pe-2	USSR (PQ 00412)		yes

31 March

In its quarterly strength return to Berlin the Gruppe reported a total of thirty-five Fw 190A-4s and Fw 190A-5s on hand, of which twenty-four were operational. Forty-eight pilots were present, of whom thirty-five were available for duty. The authorized strength of the Gruppe was forty aircraft and pilots.

Fw. Karl Willius returned to the 3rd Staffel after his tour as an instructor, and Fw. Wilhelm Hofmann returned to the 1st Staffel from four months in hospital. Both pilots were welcomed with enthusiasm. Willius was one of the best NCO pilots in the Gruppe, and Hofmann, who had only one victory, was considered an excellent, dedicated pilot whose success was overdue.

1 April

Uffz. Jan Schild flew his first combat sortie since arriving in Russia – a weather reconnaissance flight at dawn.

3 April

The Stabsschwarm flew a freie Jagd that took them north. After contacting the enemy they landed on Gatschina, the I/JG 54 base west of Leningrad. They flew a second freie Jagd from Gatschina, and returned to Dno after their third. Uffz. Schild remained at Dno and was credited with a combat sortie after escorting an Hs 126 recon aircraft to Staraya Russa. Lt. Artur Beese of the 1st Staffel claimed an Il-2 during the day, but the claim was not confirmed.

4 April

Uffz. Schild was once more assigned the dawn weather recon mission, and carried it out without incident. An hour after landing he was scrambled to intercept an enemy formation. Gefr. Heuser, who had by now apparently left the Stab and rejoined the 2nd Staffel, took part in a mid-morning freie Jagd, and in mid-afternoon was scrambled to

Mealtime in the Russian spring, showing a very personalized use of mosquito netting. Uffz. Jan Schild is on the far right. *(Heuser)*

A photograph of 2nd Staffel pilots at readiness, possibly taken at Dno in April. From left, standing: Fw. Pleese, Lt. Staschen, Uffz. Kaase, Uffz. Ecker; seated: Uffz. Schild, Lt. Dippel, Lt. Kunz, Fw. Schwentick. *(Heuser)*

intercept some Soviet aircraft. The day's only victory was a "Yak-4" credited to Fw. Scheyda. A 3rd Staffel aircraft sustained combat damage, but landed on Dno safely.

I/JG 26 Victory Claims: 3 - 4 April 1943

Date	Rank	Name	Unit	Cl #	Aircraft	Place	Time	Opponent	Conf
03-04-43	Lt.	Beese	1	12	Il-2	USSR (PQ 18251)			unk
04-04-43	Fw.	Scheyda	3	12	Yak-4	USSR (PQ 08624)			yes

One of the Fw 190A-4s flown in the USSR by Uffz. Heinrich Heuser of the 2nd Staffel. *(Heuser)*

A First Gruppe Fw 190A-4 in the USSR. *(Heuser)*

6 April

Ogfr. Karl-Heinz Janning of the 2nd Staffel crashed for unknown reasons immediately after taking off from Dno, and was killed. His aircraft's propeller tore off and careened into the servicing area, where it hit and killed a groundcrewman. Uffz. Werner Schwan of the 1st Staffel crash-landed his Focke-Wulf while returning from a sortie, sustaining injuries serious enough that in May he was sent to hospital in Germany.

10 April

The 2nd Staffel escorted a Ju 88 formation to Cholm in the morning. Gefr. Heuser took part in a freie Jagd in mid-afternoon, while in the evening Uffz. Schild was assigned to escort an Hs 126 to the Novgorod-Volchov bridgehead.

11 April

Two 3rd Staffel pilots were credited with downing fighters: Fw. Ahrens shot down a LaGG-3, while Fw. Willius downed a "LaGG-4", a non-existent type that probably indicated an early La-5; this was Willius's first victory since returning to the Gruppe.

I/JG 26 Victory Claims: 11 April 1943

Date	Rank	Name	Unit	Cl #	Aircraft	Place	Time	Opponent	Conf
11-04-43	Fw.	Ahrens	3	2	LaGG-3	USSR (PQ 18241)			yes
11-04-43	Fw.	Willius	3	25	LaGG-4	USSR (PQ 1835)			yes

20 April

The 2nd Staffel was occupied with daily scrambles, escort missions, and freie Jagden without result. Although documentation is lacking, it may be assumed that the daily routine of the rest of the Gruppe was similar. The first aircraft accident since the 6th was recorded today. A 1st Staffel Fw 190A-4 sustained moderate damage in a belly-landing on Dno necessitated by engine failure. Three days later a Stab Fw 190A-5 was damaged to the same extent, and for the same reason.

The 2nd Staffel dispersal, probably at Dno. Uffz. Heuser made three combat flights in "black 8." *(Heuser)*

Fw 190A "black 2", probably photographed at Dno in May, at which time it was Uffz. Heuser's regular aircraft. *(Heuser)*

24 April
Gefr. Heuser took part in an early morning escort mission, accompanying Ju 87s which bombed some bridges. Heuser received the heaviest antiaircraft fire in his life, recalling later that, "It was most impressive to see massive numbers of antiaircraft shells in various colors rising glowing from the ground and exploding – a mystical and dangerous fireworks."

25 April
Uffz. Schild left Dno in a Fw 190 this morning for home leave. He made it as far as Heiligenbeil today, with an intermediate stop in Riga.

1 May
Gefr. Heuser flew a new type of mission – railroad patrol. The partisans had become

2nd Staffel personnel on a base with hard-surfaced taxi strips and earthen dispersals – possibly Dno in April. From left: Uffz. Schild, two mechanics, Fw. Pleese, mechanic, the Oberwerkmeister (line chief), Lt. Dippel, Fw. Horst Schwentick (KIA 5 May 44). *(Heuser)*

Gefr. Heinrich Heuser of the 2nd Staffel, probably photographed at Dno in May. He obviously did not remind the person who borrowed his camera to keep his finger from in front of the lens. *(Heuser)*

such a threat to the German supply lines that front-line air units had to be diverted to defend against them. Heuser received combat mission credit for each of these patrols, which were repeated over the next several days.

One of the Gruppe utility aircraft, a Fw 58, was damaged in a forced landing. The cause was given as engine failure.

5 May
Hptm. Höckner claimed the first victory for the Gruppe since 11 April, a Pe-2.

6 May
The Gruppe moved back to Rielbitzi from Dno.

7 May
Gefr. Heuser flew two freie Jagden today, taking off for the first at the unusual time of 0355. One or both of the 2nd Staffel missions was successful; Lt. Staschen and Fw. Schwentick each shot down Il-2s, the first victories for each.

I/JG 26 Victory Claims: 5 - 7 May 1943

Date	Rank	Name	Unit	Cl #	Aircraft	Place	Time	Opponent	Conf
05-05-43	Hptm.	Höckner	1 CO	56	Pe-2	USSR (PQ 53124)			yes
07-05-43	Fw.	Schwentick	2	1	Il-2	USSR (PQ 1981)			yes
07-05-43	Lt.	Staschen	2	1	Il-2	USSR (PQ 1976)			yes

One of the Fw 190A-4s flown in the USSR by Uffz. Heinrich Heuser of the 2nd Staffel. *(Heuser)*

Hptm. Wilhelm Gäth, Zink's successor as 2nd Staffel Kapitän, receives a telephone message at the Staffel dispersal. *(Heuser)*

9 May

The Gruppe transferred today to Smolensk, in the central sector of the Eastern Front, and thus joined Luftflotte 6, which was responsible for supporting Army Group Center. The move was part of the buildup for Operation Zitadelle, the Kursk offensive, which was scheduled to begin on 12 June.

12 May

The Gruppe moved farther south from Smolensk to Shatalovka, and then fifty kilometers east to Ossinovka. The transfer took several days. On today's flight, the Stabsschwarm encountered ten MiG-3s escorting four Il-2s; Major Seifert was able to shoot down one of the *Shturmoviki*.

13 May

Lt. Arno Staschen's first mission from Ossinovka ended tragically. He became lost while flying near Yelnya, east of Smolensk. At 2130, out of fuel, he made a forced landing in a field. He hid himself overnight in some nearby woods, as the area was known to contain partisans. The next day, nearby villagers reported a suspicious person in the woods. The Army sent *Hilfswilligen* (Russian volunteers) to flush out the suspected Russian agent. Staschen, hearing the troops call out in Russian, assumed that he was under attack by partisans and opened fire with his pistol. At this, he was shot and killed by the Hilfswilligen.

Freie Jagden from the new base proved profitable. Fw. Willius shot down three

Pe-2s and one MiG-3 during the day, for his 26th-29th victories. Fw. Ahrens also downed a Pe-2, for his third victory, and Maj. Seifert claimed a MiG-3, for his 53rd.

I/JG 26 Victory Claims: 12 - 13 May 1943

Date	Rank	Name	Unit	Cl #	Aircraft	Place	Time	Opponent	Conf
12-05-43	Maj.	Seifert	I CO	52	Il-2	USSR (PQ 36612)			yes
13-05-43	Maj.	Seifert	I CO	53	MiG-3	USSR (PQ 4556/64)			yes
13-05-43	Fw.	Ahrens	3	3	Pe-2	USSR (PQ 35481)			yes
13-05-43	Fw.	Willius	3	26	Pe-2	USSR (PQ 35431)			yes
13-05-43	Fw.	Willius	3	27	Pe-2	USSR (PQ 35431)			yes
13-05-43	Fw.	Willius	3	28	Pe-2	USSR (PQ 35462)			yes
13-05-43	Fw.	Willius	3	29	MiG-3	USSR (PQ 4555)			yes

14 May

Scrambles and freie Jagden resulted in successes for the 1st Staffel; four Staffel pilots claimed victories during the day. Fw. Heinz-Günther Klems of the Stabsschwarm overturned while landing on Ossinovka after a reconnaissance flight. He was pulled from his airplane by his element leader, Lt. Jessen, who was credited with saving his life. The extent of Klems' injuries is unknown, but when he returned to the Geschwader it was to join the ground staff. In late 1943, he was commissioned and transferred to the office of the General of the Fighter Arm.

I/JG 26 Victory Claims: 14 May 1943

Date	Rank	Name	Unit	Cl #	Aircraft	Place	Time	Opponent	Conf
14-05-43	Oblt.	Beese	1	13	Pe-2	USSR (PQ 54242)			yes
14-05-43	Uffz.	Christof	1	6	LaGG-3	USSR (PQ 54331)			yes
14-05-43	Fw.	Hofmann W.	1	2	LaGG-3	USSR (PQ 41484)			yes
14-05-43	Obfw.	Söffing	1	10	LaGG-3	USSR (PQ 54312)			yes

Uffz. Michael Hecker (KIA 27 May 44) of the 2nd Staffel, probably photographed at Dno in May. *(Heuser)*

15 May

Enlisted men from the Gruppe Stab, and groundcrewmen from the 3rd Staffel, were formed into anti-partisan teams and sent on ground patrols from Ossinovka. Today two men of the Stabskompanie drowned when their boat capsized as they were patrolling a nearby swamp. The sweeps and escort missions flown on this and the next few days resulted in no encounters with enemy aircraft, and at least three Focke-Wulfs were damaged in landing accidents.

20 May

The Gruppe transferred two hundred kilometers farther southwest, to Orel. It was now based in the middle of the salient that the German Army was planning to use as the jumping-off point for the forthcoming Kursk offensive. On about this date Major Seifert was informed that he was to give up command of the First Gruppe.

A relaxed Hptm. Gäth, probably photographed at Dno in May. *(Heuser)*

Unknown to Seifert, his mother had invoked a little-used law and requested his removal from combat duty. His younger brother Gerhard had been a pilot in the Third Gruppe, and had died on the Kanalfront in February. Johannes was now the sole remaining male in the family, and was thus exempted by law from front-line service. Hptm. Fritz Losigkeit, a prewar member of the First Gruppe, was designated as Seifert's replacement. Losigkeit had requested a transfer from I/JG 1 after quarreling with the 1st Jagddivision staff, and was thus available for immediate transfer.

Uffz. Werner Kaiser reported to the 3rd Staffel today, the last replacement pilot to reach the Gruppe while it was in the East.

22 May

On a pre-dawn escort mission to Kursk, Hptm. Gäth, the Kapitän of the 2nd Staffel, shot down a P-39.

24 May

Uffz. Schild returned to the 2nd Staffel today, reaching Smolensk from Warsaw in a new Fw 190.

27 May

Air activity increased on both sides of the lines. Several scrambles were flown against intruding Red Air Force formations. Uffz. Schild took part in one of these from Smolensk, and was credited with a combat sortie. Escorts were also flown for Bf 110 Jabos. Oblt. Neu and Fw. Willius of the 3rd Staffel were credited with shooting down MiG-3 fighters.

28 May

Fw. Willius claimed another MiG-3 today, but one of the more unusual claims of the tour was filed by Fw. Bernhard Schellknecht of the 3rd Staffel, who shot down a Curtiss O-52 Owl, one of only nineteen of the tubby observation planes to reach the Soviet Union *via* Lend-Lease. Scrambles and sweeps were flown from Orel, Smolensk, and Ossinovka for the next several days.

31 May

The 3rd Staffel claimed three bombers today, an SB-2 and two Il-2s.

I/JG 26 Victory Claims: 22 - 31 May 1943

Date	Rank	Name	Unit	Cl #	Aircraft	Place	Time	Opponent	Conf
22-05-43	Hptm.	Gäth	2 CO	7	P-39	USSR(PQ 6218/19)			yes
27-05-43	Oblt.	Neu	3	1	LaGG-3	USSR (PQ 5366)			yes
27-05-43	Fw.	Willius	3	30	LaGG-3	USSR (PQ 5362)			yes
28-05-43	Fw.	Schellknecht	3	1	Curtiss O-52	USSR (PQ 07583)			yes
28-05-43	Fw.	Willius	3	31	LaGG-3	USSR (PQ 63253)			yes
31-05-43	Fw.	Ahrens	3	4	Il-2	USSR (PQ 16362)			yes
31-05-43	Uffz.	Münch	3	2	Il-2	USSR (PQ 16334)			yes
31-05-43	Fw.	Zirngibl	3	4	SP-2?	USSR (PQ 26854)			yes

Wreckage of the Red Air Force photo-reconnaissance A-20 shot down by Uffz. Heinrich Heuser on 1June. *(Heuser)*

Lt. Heinrich Sprinz of the 2nd Staffel. He was killed by an American B-26 gunner on 30 July 1943, shortly after the unit's return to the Western Front. *(Heuser)*

1 June

The 2nd Staffel had a busy day today from Ossinovka. After an early-morning scramble Hptm. Gäth shot down a Pe-2; his victory was witnessed by his wingman, Jan Schild. Heinrich Heuser scrambled in mid-afternoon on what proved to be his last mission in the East, and one of his most memorable. He and his wingman were vectored toward Smolensk, and as they reached 4000 meters Heuser saw a single Boston approaching from the west, right over the Smolensk runway. It was apparently returning from a reconnaissance flight. The pair of Focke-Wulfs made two attacks from the rear. The Boston did not deviate from its course as its gunner returned fire. The light bomber force-landed near the runway in flames, and was found to contain a one-meter camera, a novelty that was quickly sent to the RLM. Heuser gained brief acclaim for downing the first Boston seen in the sector, and four days later left for home leave.

Major Seifert received word of his new posting, and left Orel to take a position on the staff of the German mission to Bulgaria.

2 June

Luftflotte 6 executed Operation Carmen, one of its largest air raids of 1943. Several waves of escorted bombers attacked the Kursk rail station and other transportation targets in preparation for Operation Zitadelle. The Red Air Force scrambled 386 fighters in defense of their salient, and claimed to have shot down 104 Luftwaffe aircraft by fighters and forty-one by antiaircraft fire, for the loss of twenty-seven of their own fighters. The official Soviet history notes that this massed air raid was the "last major daytime raid by fascist aviation against Soviet rear facilities."

The full extent of the participation by the First Gruppe in this raid is unknown. Uffz. Schild escorted two separate missions containing mixed flights of Bf 110s and Ju 88s. Four Soviet fighters were shot down during the day; one 2nd Staffel Focke-Wulf crash-landed on Orel with moderate combat damage.

Fw. Schellknecht became the last casualty for the Gruppe in the Soviet Union. His engine quit while on a reconnaissance sortie over the Kursk salient, and he was forced to land behind the Russian lines; he was never heard from again.

3 June

The ground staff began packing for the return to France. Uffz. Christof shot down a Pe-2, the last Eastern Front victory for the First Gruppe. Operation Zitadelle, the reason the Gruppe had moved to the Central Front, was postponed repeatedly and did not get underway until 5 July.

I/JG 26 Victory Claims: 1 - 3 June 1943

Date	Rank	Name	Unit	Cl #	Aircraft	Place	Time	Opponent	Conf
01-06-43	Hptm.	Gäth	2 CO	8	Pe-2	USSR (PQ 35652)			yes
01-06-43	Uffz.	Heuser Hein.	2	2	A-20	USSR (PQ 35793)	1445		yes
02-06-43	Lt.	Dippel	2	14	P-40	USSR (PQ 62195)			yes
02-06-43	Oblt.	Neu	3	2	LaGG-3	USSR (PQ 62159)			yes
02-06-43	Fw.	Willius	3	32	LaGG-3	USSR (PQ 62189)			yes
02-06-43	Fw.	Willius	3	33	LaGG-3	USSR (PQ 62194)			yes
03-06-43	Uffz.	Christof	1	7	Pe-2	USSR (PQ 44289)			yes

Lt. Arno Staschen (2/JG 26) – KIA 13 May 1943. *(Vanoverbeke)*

4 June

Before dawn part of the Gruppe flew to Shatalovka, a small field right behind the front lines. In the afternoon they flew a *Jagdvorstoss,* or fighter strike, which penetrated sixty kilometers (forty miles) beyond the front. This unusual mission served both as a farewell to Russia and as a perverse kind of orientation flight for Major Losigkeit, who had been ordered to stay in the East and report to JG 51. When the First Gruppe returned to the Reich, it was thus temporarily without a Kommandeur.

6 June

The Gruppe began the flight to Germany in their Fw 190s; after a brief stopover at Rheine in western Germany to exchange their aircraft, most pilots had reached Poix by the 10th. The unit had claimed 126 aerial victories during its tour, for the loss of nine pilots and three members of the ground staff.

I/JG 26 Casualties in the USSR

Date	Rank	Name	Cas	Unit	Aircraft	WNr	Mkgs	Place	Time	Cause	Allied Unit
17-02-43	Gefr.	Kaiser, Helmut	WIA	1	Fw 190A-5	1098	wh 4	nr Salutsche		Yak-3	
17-02-43	Uffz.	Kniess, Friedrich	KIA	3	Fw 190A-5	2546	yl 5	near Lake Ilmen (PQ 19713)		hit ground	n/a
17-02-43	Uffz.	Schnell, Heinrich	KIA	3	Fw 190A-5	1099	yl 11	SE of Lake Ilmen (PQ 1823)		flak	n/a
05-03-43	Fw.	Preeg, Karl	KIA	1	Fw 190A-4	7141	<llgr 3	S Staraya Russa (PQ 1836)	1302	fighter	
05-03-43	Hptm.	Zink, Fülbert	no	2 CO	Fw 190A-4	7173		S of Shvinochovo		combat	
07-03-43	Uffz.	Fast, Hans-Joachim	KIFA	2	Fw 190A-5	2550	bk 7	Rielbitzi a/f		takeoff	n/a
10-03-43	Obfw.	Söffing, Waldemar	WIFA	1	Fw 190A-4	840	wh 7	S of Staraya Russa		engine	n/a
14-03-43	Hptm.	Zink, Fülbert	KIA	2 CO	Fw 190A-4	7176	bk 13	E of Werschinskojec	1130	missing	
18-03-43	Fw.	Rau, Günther	KIA	3	Fw 190A-5	2589	yl 10	near Rielbitzi a/f	1630	missing	
06-04-43	Ogfr.	Janning, Karl-Heinz	KIFA	3	Fw 190A-4	2485	yl 4	Dno a/f		crashed	non-op
06-04-43	Uffz.	Schwan, Werner	WIA	1	Fw 190A-4	7146		Dno a/f		landing	n/a
13-05-43	Lt.	Staschen, Arno	KIA	2	Fw 190A-5	1100	bk 7	E of Smolensk		shot after f/l	n/a

The 7th Staffel on the Leningrad Front

25 January
The principal sources for the story of the 7th Staffel Eastern Front tour are the few surviving logbooks and Erich Jauer's *Abschussmeldungen* (victory reports), which were made available by his son. According to Xaver Ellenrieder's logbook, his last flight from Wevelgem with the 8th Staffel was on 9 January. His next flight was from Heiligenbeil to Riga, on 25 January. The same route would be taken by the First Gruppe six days later. Ellenrieder flew on from Riga to Gatschina, west of Leningrad. This would become the 7th Staffel's base – but Ellenrieder had arrived a month too soon. It is possible that he was part of the advance detachment from the 7th or 8th Staffel, or he may have been under orders to join I/JG 54, possibly to assist the Green Heart pilots in their transition to Fw 190s, which they had just received. His task and even his Staffel assignment during this period is unknown. Over the next six weeks he made only four flights, to Riga, Heiligenbeil, and the First Gruppe base at Rielbitzi, all identified in his logbook as transfers rather than the more plausible ferry flights, before settling down with the 7th Staffel at Gatschina.

17 February
The 7th Staffel left Courtrai by rail. The Staffel was commanded by the highly-experienced Hptm. Klaus Mietusch; his deputy was Hptm. Günther Kelch.

28 February
After a stop at Heiligenbeil to receive and test-fly their aircraft, the Staffel reached Krasnogvardeisk-Gatschina, which had been the base of I/JG 54 as well as several bomber and Stuka units since September, 1941. It had previously been a Red Air Force base, and was the best-equipped airfield in the northern sector. Gatschina was also the location of one of the former Czar's summer castles, which had been appropriated by the Luftwaffe for pilots' quarters. The headquarters of JG 54 was at another fully-equipped airfield, nearby Siverskaya. The Soviet opposition in this area comprised the 13th Air Army, which was based in Leningrad, and the 14th Air Army, which covered the Volkhov Front to the east of Leningrad. No 1943 strength returns have been located, but in early 1944 these two organizations commanded a total of 1200 aircraft. The Luftwaffe fighter opposition in the area consisted of the forty fighters of I/JG 54; to these would now be added the dozen Fw 190s of 7/JG 26.

3 March
The 7th Staffel was subordinated to Hptm. Hans Philipp's I/JG 54, which had just converted from Bf 109s to Fw 190s. Apparently the theater orientation of the 7th Staffel proceeded in parallel with the familiarization flights of the Green Heart Gruppe in their new fighters. Today Lt. Alois Westermair became the first Eastern Front casualty of the Staffel when he was killed in one of the 2/JG 54 Fw 190A-4s. His element leader, a JG 54 pilot, reported that Westermair climbed through a cloud and dived back out in inverted position. His aircraft then began making erratic movements; Westermair never regained control, and was killed when the aircraft dived into the ground.

7 March
Fw. Erich Jauer of the 7th Staffel took off from Gatschina at 1150 as wingman to Oblt. Götz of 2/JG 54 in a two-man freie Jagd to Oranienbaum. After an hour of patrolling at an altitude of 1000 meters (3200 feet) the pair saw four Il-2s, escorted by three LaGG-3s. The pair climbed to the attack, and shot down two Il-2s before the escorts could intervene. Jauer got on a MiG-3's tail at 500 meters (550 yards), and a quick burst of cannon fire set the Soviet fighter ablaze; its landing gear dropped, and it crashed into a snowy field. Götz ran out of ammunition while attacking another MiG;

Jauer took over the attack, and fired on the fighter down to a distance of fifty meters, at an elevation of twenty meters. The MiG crashed into a snowbank on the edge of the village.

Erich Jauer's three scores put him in the early lead among the pilots of the Staffel, which gave him no small amount of satisfaction. Jauer had first served in JG 26 in 1941, but his inability to get along with his Staffelkapitän resulted in his banishment to a factory test squadron. It took him a year to get back to the Kanalfront, and to the Geschwader, where Mietusch accepted him into the 7th Staffel. From all indications, Mietusch cared little for his men as individuals – he rarely spoke to the NCO pilots at all – and judged them solely by their accomplishments in the air. That was fine with Jauer; he had been given a second chance, and was prepared to make the most of it.

Fw. Xaver Ellenrieder reported to the Staffel at Gatschina today, as did Uffz. Karl Seebeck, the first replacement pilot to reach the unit in Russia. Seebeck had just finished his operational training in 11/JG 54 at Merville.

7/JG 26 Partial Victory Claims: 7 March 1943

Date	Rank	Name	Unit	Cl #	Aircraft	Place	Time	Opponent	Conf
07-03-43	Fw.	Jauer	7	3	Il-2	6km SSW Peterhof (PQ 90254)	1249		yes
07-03-43	Fw.	Jauer	7	4	LaGG-3	4km SSW Peterhof (PQ 90263)	1250		yes
07-03-43	Fw.	Jauer	7	5	LaGG-3	8km SW Peterhof (PQ 90253)	1252		yes

12 March
Fw. Ellenrieder made his first flight with the 7th Staffel, a routine frontal familiarization flight. The only Staffel documentation available for the next week are the entries in Ellenrieder's logbook. These are probably typical of the experiences of the rest of the Staffel. There were no casualties or aircraft damage; this information is available elsewhere, and is almost complete. However, there is no comprehensive list of the Staffel victory claims. Complete claims data exist for its three top scorers in Russia, Mietusch, Kemethmüller, and Jauer. Günther Kelch and/or some of the "lesser lights" could well have scored during this week.

13 March
Fw. Ellenrieder flew a freie Jagd in early afternoon, for which he received combat sortie credit.

14 March
Fw. Ellenrieder was assigned to escort a reconnaissance Bf 110. The mission was completed satisfactorily, and Ellenrieder was credited with a combat sortie.

15 March
Fw. Ellenrieder flew a dawn weather recon mission, and a mid-morning freie Jagd to the "north zone", meaning in all probability to the Oranienburg pocket, west of Leningrad on the Gulf of Finland.

17 March
Before daybreak Ellenrieder flew to the small field at Gorodyetz. During the day he escorted Ju 87s on a bombing mission south of Staraya Russa, and escorted a Hs 126 recon aircraft on a mission to Novgorod.

The host for the Staffel at Gatschina, Major Hans Philipp, scored his 200-203rd victories today; he was the second pilot in the Luftwaffe to reach 200.

19 March
Again flying from Gatschina, Ellenrieder took part in a freie Jagd that resulted in a battle with three LaGG-3s near Kolyimo.

20 March

The engine of Hptm. Mietusch's Fw 190A-4 failed while he was taking off from Gatschina. The aircraft turned over and was totally destroyed. The extent of Mietusch's injuries are unknown – the original notation in the equipment loss returns was changed from "injury" to "no injury" – but Mietusch was apparently out of action for the next two months.

21 March

Hptm. Kelch and Fw. Jauer took off in mid-afternoon for a freie Jagd to Kolpino. While flying at 4700 meters (15,500 feet) the pair saw six LaGG-3s 500 meters (1600 feet) beneath them on a reverse course. Kelch reversed direction and dived on them. The Red fighters turned toward the Germans, but Jauer saw a straggler and opened fire on it from the rear at one hundred meters distance. The LaGG dived vertically and crashed in a field on the northeast bank of the Neva River. Kelch's successes in this battle, if any, are unknown.

Lt. Ernst Todt reported for duty with the Staffel after completing flight training.

22 March

Fw. Ellenrieder took off at noon and completed an escort mission for Ju 87s without incident. Fw. Jauer was given a similar assignment in mid-afternoon. He again flew as Hptm. Kelch's wingman, and took position as detached escort for thirteen Ju 87s to Krasny-Bor. After the bombing run, the escorts split up into elements to fly independent freie Jagden. Kelch and Jauer saw several Il-2s coming south from Leningrad at 500 meters, escorted by I-16 Ratas. The pair dived on the *Shturmoviki* as they bombed and strafed. Jauer's target began to smoke, but he was then attacked by the Ratas and left the area. The crash of the Il-2 was confirmed by an artillery unit. Again, it is not known if Kelch scored in this engagement.

24 March

Fw. Ellenrieder flew an escort mission for Ju 88s, without incident.

25 March

Fw. Ellenrieder flew three escort missions from Gatschina during the day; three for Ju 88 bombers, and one for an Hs 126 reconnaissance aircraft.

26 March

Fw. Ellenrieder flew a dawn escort mission for Ju 88 bombers attacking Soviet troops that were continuing to enlarge the Schluesselburg corridor. He next flew as Fw. Jauer's wingman; the two made up the close-escort Rotte for a single Bf 110 which flew to Kolpino on Lake Ladoga on a photo-reconnaissance mission. The pair were then directed by the local controller to an enemy formation, which proved to be several LaGG-3s at 100 meters altitude. Jauer dived, and as the LaGGs banked away he got on the tail of one of a pair of fighters. Jauer shot his target down, and Ellenrieder dispatched the other. Both LaGGs crashed in a field two kilometers northwest of Krasny-Bor. In his *Abschussmeldung* (victory report), Jauer identifies his wingman Ellenrieder as a member of the 8th Staffel. This is strong evidence that Ellenrieder was never officially on the roster of the 7th Staffel, but only on loan until the expected arrival of his own Staffel in the theater. It is worth noting that his information cannot be gleaned from Ellenrieder's own logbook.

7/JG 26 Partial Victory Claims: 21 - 26 March 1943

Date	Rank	Name	Unit	Cl #	Aircraft	Place	Time	Opponent	Conf
21-03-43	Fw.	Jauer	7	6	LaGG-3	SSW of Ovzino (PQ 00272)	1445		yes
22-03-43	Fw.	Jauer	7	7	Il-2	Krasny-Bor (PQ 00414)	1515		yes

26-03-43	Fw.	Ellenrieder	7	1	LaGG-3	USSR	0915	unk
26-03-43	Fw.	Jauer	7	8	LaGG-3	2km NW of Krasny-Bor (PQ 0041)	0955	yes

30 March

Fw. Ellenrieder flew two escort missions this afternoon: the first for Ju 87 Stukas, and the second for a Hs 126 recon aircraft.

3 April

Fw. Ellenrieder's routine of escort missions continued; for fifteen Ju 87s in the morning, and for a single Bf 110 recon aircraft in the afternoon.

4 April

Fw. Ellenrieder escorted a single Bf 110 on a morning mission. During the day a Staffel Fw 190A-5 belly-landed on Gatschina after sustaining moderate damage from antiaircraft fire.

5 April

Fhj.-Fw. Gottfried Otto reported to the Staffel for duty after completing flight training.

6 April

Fw. Ellenrieder's assignment today was the dawn weather reconnaissance mission.

10 April

In mid-afternoon Fw. Ellenrieder flew an uneventful freie Jagd, following which he was released from duty with the Staffel and sent home. On or before 20 April he reported to the 8th Staffel Kapitän, Oblt. Borris, at Lille-Vendeville.

13 April

Soviet air reconnaissance had detected seventy fighters on Gatschina, and the 13th Air Army sent a large formation of Pe-2s and Il-2s to knock them out. They were intercepted over the front lines by I/JG 54 Fw 190s, which according to Soviet records shot down two Pe-2s for the loss of one Fw 190. The formation succeeded in reaching the field and bombed the landing ground and parked aircraft. The role that the 7th Staffel played in the defense is unknown. A Staffel Fw 190A-4 was destroyed in a forced-landing on Gatschina after its engine failed.

7 May

An Fw 190A-4 sustained medium damage in a crash-landing on Gatschina. The cause was listed as equipment failure. This is the only piece of data available on the activities of the Staffel between 13 April and 14 May.

14 May

Obfw. Heinz Kemethmüller had arrived in the theater and flew five touch-and-goes today. These were his first flights since being wounded over Calais on 4 February. The Staffel was now flying from Siverskaya, the long-time headquarters of JG 54. Kemethmüller's logbook is the only one available with coverage of this part of the Staffel's Russian sojourn; his missions were probably typical of those of the rest of the Staffel.

15 May

Obfw. Kemethmüller made two familiarization flights, and was declared ready for duty. His first operational flight in this Russian tour followed quickly thereafter; he was given credit for a combat sortie, but his logbook does not give any more details.

Heinz Kemethmüller, photographed in the winter of 1944-45 and added to Jauer's collection post-war. *(Jauer)*

16 May
Obfw. Kemethmüller took part in an early-morning freie Jagd to the "north zone", and was given sortie credit. Shortly after noon he flew to the small field at Vitino. Late that evening he made a combat sortie from Vitino, and then returned to Siverskaya.

17 May
Obfw. Kemethmüller took off at 0255 and flew to Vitino, made two combat sorties before 1100, and returned to Siverskaya.

18 May
Obfw. Kemethmüller scrambled from Siverskaya at 1230 after receiving a report of Red Air Force aircraft in the area, but his Rotte was unable to find them.

19 May
Obfw. Kemethmüller took off at 0311 for Vitino, landing there at 0345. He scrambled on an intercept mission at 0520, but failed to make contact. He returned to Siverskaya at 1320.

21 May
The Staffel varied their routine and moved west to Kotly in search of targets. Again they got started early; Kemethmüller's transfer was made between 0245 and 0306. His first combat flight from Kotly was flown from 0521 to 0607, and flushed some game. Hptm. Mietusch shot down two LaGG-3s and one Pe-2 near Cape Ustinski, for his first three victories in Russia, and his 30th-32nd total; Kemethmüller downed one LaGG-3 and one Pe-2, for his 63rd and 64th victories. These two pilots scored in a second mission that morning. The Staffel flew a third mission from Kotly that afternoon, with unknown results, and returned to Siverskaya later the same day.

7/JG 26 Partial Victory Claims: 21 May 1943

Date	Rank	Name	Unit	Cl #	Aircraft	Place	Time	Opponent	Conf
21-05-43	Hptm.	Mietusch	7 CO	31	LaGG-3	Koporski Bight near Dolgovo	0535		unk
21-05-43	Hptm.	Mietusch	7 CO	30	LaGG-3	N part of Lake Chapolovo	0547		unk
21-05-43	Hptm.	Mietusch	7 CO	32	Pe-2	Cape Ustinski	0555		unk
21-05-43	Hptm.	Mietusch	7 CO	33	I-153	3-4km S of Lavansaari	1020		unk
21-05-43	Obfw.	Kemethmüller	7	63	Pe-2	Glubkoye Osero	0546		yes
21-05-43	Obfw.	Kemethmüller	7	64	LaGG-3	USSR	0551		yes
21-05-43	Obfw.	Kemethmüller	7	65	I-16	USSR	1021		yes

24 May
The Staffel again tested the air around Kotly, but its successes are unknown. Kemethmüller took off at 0925 to make the move, flew one combat sortie from Kotly, and returned to Siverskaya that evening.

25 May
Kemethmüller flew one early afternoon mission, an escort flight for a Bf 110 recon aircraft.

26 May

This afternoon the Staffel escorted twenty-nine He 111s, in all probability a full Geschwader, on their bombing mission. Any claims by the Staffel remain unknown.

27 May

In the afternoon Luftflotte 1 sent a formation of thirty-three He 111s escorted by twelve Fw 190s to bomb Novaya Ladoga, north of Volkhov. They were detected by Soviet radar in time to scramble twelve 86th GIAP Yak-7Bs and nine 156th Fighter Regiment (156th IAP) LaGG-3s. The 86th GIAP claimed six He 111s and two Fw 190s, for the loss of two Yak-7Bs and one pilot. The 156th IAP interception resulted in no claims or losses. Hptm. Mietusch claimed a LaGG-3 on this mission. Its pilot bailed out, a comment that Mietusch was always careful to make in his logbook, which was available to historians at one point after the war, but unfortunately can no longer be located. As no LaGG-3s were lost, Mietusch's victim was probably the 86th GIAP Yak-7B whose pilot bailed out safely.

Obfw. Kemethmüller flew two escort missions for single Bf 110s. The first was identified as an artillery ranging flight; Kemethmüller engaged two La-5s and four LaGG-3s in combat, but without result. The purpose of the second Bf 110's mission was not stated, but was probably battlefield reconnaissance.

28 May

Kemethmüller flew one mission in the morning, an escort flight for a Hs 126 recon aircraft.

30 May

At 0450 Hptm. Günther Kelch and Lt. Horst Reck scrambled from Siverskaya to intercept a reported Soviet formation. They flew over the Oranienburg pocket and contacted four Il-2s and three LaGG-3s over the Gulf of Finland. After an inconclusive combat they headed back to land, only to be taken under attack by two Finnish I-153s. Kelch evaded the biplanes easily and returned to base; Reck, however, did not return. No trace of him was ever located. Upon investigation it was found that the Finnish pilots claimed the destruction of two LaGG-3s and one La-5 that morning. As the Fw 190 was very similar in appearance to the La-5, it became apparent that Reck's death had resulted from a tragic error in identification.

Obfw. Kemethmüller flew a shipping reconnaissance mission to Lake Ladoga in the morning, and shortly after noon joined the Staffel in escorting thirty-nine He 111s in an attack on Kopena. Kemethmüller engaged a lone LaGG-3, and shot it down.

The day's major mission did not get underway until late in the evening. According to Soviet sources, forty-seven He 111s and Ju 88s attacked targets on Osinovets Island in Lake Ladoga in several waves, escorted by a total of twenty Fw 190s and Bf 109s. Yak-1s, Yak-7Bs, Lagg-3s, and P-40s from a number of Red Air Force units took part in the interception, and claimed seven He 111s and eleven Fw 190s for the loss of three fighters. Sub-Lt. A. P. Khoroshkov cut the tail off of an He 111 with his propeller. Both aircraft crashed into Lake Ladoga; Khoroshkov bailed out safely. The 7th Staffel escorted a formation of thirty-seven He 111s on this mission; Hptm. Mietusch shot down a LaGG-3 which crashed into Lake Ladoga.

31 May

Kemethmüller took off at 0432 for a freie Jagd to the "north zone". No contact was made, and no sortie credit was given. He next took off at 1115 to escort a Hs 126 on an artillery ranging mission. Hptm. Mietusch downed a LaGG-3 in mid-afternoon on a sortie whose purpose was not recorded; the Soviet pilot bailed out. And in late afternoon Kemethmüller flew another freie Jagd without enemy contact. He was credited with a combat sortie for this mission, probably because he had crossed the battle lines.

Date	Rank	Name	Unit	Cl #	Aircraft	Place	Time	Opponent	Conf
27-05-43	Hptm.	Mietusch	7 CO	34	LaGG-3	USSR (PQ 00264)	1331	86th GIAP Yak-7B	unk
30-05-43	Hptm.	Mietusch	7 CO	35	LaGG-3	Lake Ladoga (PQ 11782)	1955		unk
30-05-43	Obfw.	Kemethmüller	7	66	LaGG-3	Kopena	1355		yes
31-05-43	Hptm.	Mietusch	7 CO	36	LaGG-3	USSR (PQ 00243)	1615		unk

1 June

Luftflotte 1 mounted two large raids on a railroad bridge in Volkhov. There is no evidence that the 7th Staffel took part in the early morning mission, but Obfw. Kemethmüller took off from Siverskaya in mid-afternoon to escort forty-five He 111s to Volkhov. A large group of LaGG-3s, perhaps fifteen to twenty aircraft, attempted to intercept, but were driven off, according to the comments in Kemethmüller's logbook. According to Soviet sources, a total of eighty Luftwaffe bombers and thirty escorts took part in this raid. Eight Yak-7Bs from the crack 86th GIAP took on most of the escort and shot down four Fw 190s without loss. LaGG-3s and La-5s from two other air regiments then attacked the bombers, and claimed four Ju 87s and one He 111 without loss.

Late in the evening Fw. Jauer took off with his wingman, Uffz. Wöge, as close escort for a Bf 110 spotting artillery fire on the Schluesselburg corridor. Wöge spotted a single banking LaGG-3 across the Neva River at an altitude of 2000 meters (6600 feet). Jauer ordered Wöge to stay with the Bf 110, dived behind the LaGG, pulled up, and fired one burst. The Soviet fighter dived immediately, and crashed in a field.

2 June

Part of the Staffel flew to Kotly early in the morning. No large-scale missions were ordered, but in mid-afternoon Kemethmüller and Jauer were scrambled to intercept six Pe-2s reported over Lavessari Island. While flying west of the island at 3000 meters (9800 feet), the pair saw six Pe-2s, trailed by one Yak-1 and five La-5 escorts, on a crossing course east of the island at 1000 meters (3300 feet). The Focke-Wulfs dived on the bombers. Jauer made three attacks on the Pe-2 on the left of the formation. Kemethmüller turned to face the escorts, and shot one La-5 into the sea west of Lipovo. One minute later Jauer's target burst into flames, and its right wing broke off. The bomber's gunner managed to get out, jumping just before the plane hit the water. The pair returned to Kotly, and flew back to Siverskaya that evening.

5 June

At noon, Luftflotte 1 dispatched eighty He 111s and Ju 88s and twenty escorts to bomb Novaya Ladoga, a major Soviet base north of Volkhov. Interceptors from both the Leningrad and the Volkhov districts met the raid. According to Soviet sources, Yak-7Bs from the 86th GIAP drew off most of the escort, allowing the other units to make head-on attacks on the bombers. The Red Air Force claimed three Fw 190s, one Bf 109, and seven He 111s. No Soviet fighters were shot down; two damaged fighters from the 240th Fighter Division (240th IAD) force-landed safely on their own bases. According to Heinz Kemethmüller's logbook, the 7th Staffel escorted forty-five He 111s on this mission. Kemethmüller engaged a single P-40 Warhawk in combat, and claimed its destruction.

7/JG 26 Partial Victory Claims: 1 - 5 June 1943

Date	Rank	Name	Unit	Cl #	Aircraft	Place	Time	Opponent	Conf
01-06-43	Fw.	Jauer	7	9	LaGG-3	5km N of Ostrovky (PQ 00254)	2109		yes
02-06-43	Fw.	Jauer	7	10	Pe-2	2km W of Lipovo (PQ 90113)	1456		yes

02-06-43	Obfw.	Kemethmüller	7	67	La-5	2km W of Lipovo (PQ 90113)	1455	yes
05-06-43	Obfw.	Kemethmüller	7	68	P-40	Lake Ladoga	1210	240th IAD yes

8 June

A reconnaissance Pe-2 had reported seventy aircraft on Siverskaya; seventeen Pe-2s, eighteen Il-2s, and sixty-four escorts were dispatched in the morning to destroy them. The 7th Staffel had already transferred to Vitino; while taxiing for the takeoff at 0215, one Fw 190A-5 collided with something and sustained moderate damage. Kemethmüller scrambled twice from Vitino to intercept the marauding Soviet aircraft, but failed to make contact. According to Soviet sources, twenty Luftwaffe aircraft were destroyed on Siverskaya, and another fifteen were damaged.

Kemethmüller returned to Siverskaya at noon, and was ordered to escort forty He 111s to Volkhov. He picked Fw. Jauer as his wingman and took off at 1515. They flew detached escort in front of the bombers. While over Volkhov at 5700 meters they saw what they reported to be several I-180s at 5000 meters (16,000 feet), climbing from the west to attack. The Focke-Wulfs dived immediately, and attacked the fighters head-on. Each downed an I-180 on his first pass, breaking up the attack on the bombers. (The I-180 was an experimental radial-engine Polikarpov fighter that was pictured in the Luftwaffe recognition handbooks, but was never placed in production. These fighters were probably La-5s.) According to Soviet sources, this raid on Volkhov by forty-five bombers and fifteen fighters was successfully repulsed.

Late in the evening Fw. Jauer scrambled from Siverskaya to intercept four LaGG-3s reported in the area; Lt. Todt flew as his wingman. While 35 kilometers (22 miles) northwest of Mga at 1600 meters (5200 feet), and after a long search, Jauer saw four LaGG fighters flying in two formations. He attacked one pair from above, and shot one aircraft down in flames.

7/JG 26 Partial Victory Claims: 8 June 1943

Date	Rank	Name	Unit	Cl #	Aircraft	Place	Time	Opponent	Conf
08-06-43	Fw.	Jauer	7	11	I-180	2-3km NW Volkhov (PQ 20124)	1558		yes
08-06-43	Fw.	Jauer	7	12	Yak-7	N of Yaksolovo (PQ 00252)	2029		yes
08-06-43	Obfw.	Kemethmüller	7	69	Yak-7	10km NW of Volkhov (PQ 20123)	1557		yes

9 June

Obfw. Kemethmüller flew three escort missions during the day: the first for a single reconnaissance Bf 110; the second for nine Jabos of unspecified type, but probably also Bf 110s; and the third for three Ju 88s and thirty Do 217s, which made a low-level attack on a village. There were no enemy fighters about, so Kemethmüller aided the mission objective by strafing houses.

10 June

One Staffel Fw 190A-5 crash-landed on Siverskaya during the day with moderate combat damage.

11 June

Obfw. Kemethmüller flew escort for a Bf 110 and engaged in combat with five La-5s, without result.

12 June

Kemethmüller took off late in the evening to intercept enemy aircraft, but nothing was found, and no credit was received for a combat sortie.

The 7th Staffel in Russia. On left, Fw. Erich Jauer (POW 18 Jun 43); with dog, Uffz. Wöge; behind him, Hptm. Klaus Mietusch (KIA 17 Sep 44); behind him, Hptm. Günther Kelch (KIFA 31 Jul 43); third from right, Lt. Erich Burkert (KIA 21 Jan 44) – Gatschina, 16 June. *(Jauer)*

17 June

The Staffel took off at 0430 on a full-strength escort mission for forty Ju 87s attacking targets south of Schluesselburg. Ten LaGG-3s from the 29th Guards Fighter Aviation Regiment (29th GIAP) were engaged south of the target. Hptm. Mietusch shot one of these down; it is not known if any other pilot scored. Capt. Aleksander Gorbachevsky was shot down after claiming one Bf 109 and one Ju 87, and bailed out safely. Gorbachevsky would be named a Hero of the Soviet Union in February, 1944.

18 June

The Staffel took off at 0545 to escort forty Ju 87s to Volkhovstroi. After the bombs were dropped, the fighters split up into Rotten and flew independent freie Jagden on their return to Siverskaya. Many found targets among the Soviet fighter formations in the area. Obfw. Kemethmüller fought with a LaGG-3, a P-40, and a Yak-1, and shot down the last-named; he noted in his logbook that Staffel claims for the mission totaled one LaGG-3, three P-40s, and two Yak-1s. Hptm. Mietusch received credit for shooting down two LaGG-3s on this mission.

Fw. Jauer's wingman, Uffz. Pritze, lost Jauer on the return. Jauer was attacked by P-40s southeast of Volkhovstroi. He shot one down, but overshot a second, and when he throttled back sharply, his synchronization gear failed and he shot off his own propeller. He jumped out of his plane, opened his parachute two hundred meters above the ground, and landed safely, 125 kilometers (75 miles) behind the lines. He evaded capture for two days, but could not find a way to get across the Volkhov River – it was too cold to swim – and had to surrender. He was one of the few Luftwaffe aircrewmen to survive Soviet POW camp. Pritze claimed two victories on Jauer's behalf, apparently based on the latter's radio messages, although Jauer himself never felt that he had hit the second fighter. Both victories were claimed as P-39s, although Jauer's loss report states that they were P-40 Warhawks. P-40s were common on the northern part of the front, and less so elsewhere; they entered the Soviet Union at Murmansk, as cargo on the northern convoys.

Date	Rank	Name	Unit	Cl #	Aircraft	Place	Time	Opponent	Conf
17-06-43	Hptm.	Mietusch	7 CO	37	LaGG-3	5km NE of Volkhovstroi	0513	29th GIAP	unk
18-06-43	Hptm.	Mietusch	7 CO	38	LaGG-3	forest near Kinderovo	0612		unk
18-06-43	Hptm.	Mietusch	7 CO	39	LaGG-3	swamp N of Podborovye	0619		unk
18-06-43	Hptm.	Mietusch	7 CO	40	LaGG-3	USSR (PQ 00264)	1715		unk
18-06-43	Hptm.	Mietusch	7 CO	41	LaGG-3	USSR (PQ 00292)	1718		unk
18-06-43	Hptm.	Mietusch	7 CO	42	Yak-7	Lake Ladoga (PQ 10131)	2020		unk
18-06-43	Fw.	Jauer	7		P-39	USSR (PQ 20161)	0600		unk
18-06-43	Fw.	Jauer	7		P-39	USSR (PQ 20161)	0605		unk
18-06-43	Obfw.	Kemethmüller	7	70	Yak-1	Ladoga region USSR	0612		yes
18-06-43	Obfw.	Kemethmüller	7	71	LaGG-3	Volkhovstroi	1222		yes

19 June

Kemethmüller flew one mission in the late afternoon, an escort flight for four He 111s bombing Volkhovstroi. No enemy aircraft were sighted. This was Heinz Kemethmüller's 400th combat sortie; on his return he was awarded the traditional garland of oak leaves.

21 June

Again today Obfw. Kemethmüller participated in an escort mission for He 111s to Volkhovstroi; today there were twelve bombers.

22 June

Obfw. Kemethmüller had the early watch, and was scrambled at 0225 to intercept Il-2s and Yak-1 escorts that were approaching the airfield. Kemethmüller shot down one of the *Shturmoviki* directly over Siverskaya. The Soviet bomber was probably from the 9th Ground-Attack Aviation Division (9th ShAD), eighteen of which bombed the field as part of a three-wave attack that claimed a total of twenty Luftwaffe aircraft on the ground.

Kemethmüller took part in two combat missions in the afternoon. The first was flown as Hptm. Mietusch's wingman. They attacked six LaGG-3s, and Kemethmüller had to hold position on his leader's wing as Mietusch shot down two of them, for his 43rd and 44th victories. The late mission was an escort for two Ju 88s and three Do 217s; no enemy aircraft were seen.

7/JG 26 Partial Victory Claims: 22 June 1943

Date	Rank	Name	Unit	Cl #	Aircraft	Place	Time	Opponent	Conf
22-06-43	Hptm.	Mietusch	7 CO	43	LaGG-3	USSR (PQ 90134)	1530		unk
22-06-43	Hptm.	Mietusch	7 CO	44	LaGG-3	USSR (PQ 90164)	1533		unk
22-06-43	Obfw.	Kemethmüller	7	72	Il-2	Siverskaya a/f USSR	0233	9th ShAD	yes

24 June

Obfw. Kemethmüller took part in an early-morning escort for forty-five Ju 87s. The Focke-Wulfs had a battle with LaGG-3s and La-5s, but Kemethmüller made no claims; any successes for the Staffel remain unknown. He escorted a single Bf 110 over the lines in the evening, and then left for a brief home leave; he rejoined the Staffel on 5 July, at Nordholz.

29 June

Major Priller notified Hptm. Mietusch that Hptm. Ruppert had been killed in action, and that Mietusch had been promoted to the command of the Third Gruppe.

30 June

Hptm. Günther Kelch took command of the 7th Staffel; Hptm. Mietusch left for Germany. On 5 July he took over the Third Gruppe from Hptm. Hermichen, who had been filling in temporarily. In its quarterly strength return to Berlin today, the Staffel reported a total of eleven Fw 190A-4s and Fw 190A-5s on hand, of which eight were operational. Twelve pilots were present, of whom seven were available for duty. The authorized strength of the Staffel was sixteen aircraft and pilots.

9 July

Uffz. Hans Pritze became the last 7th Staffel casualty in the East, failing to return from a mission over Schluesselburg. Flying as wingman to Uffz. Grollius, he had escorted He 111s in an attack on a railroad station near Schum. The pair were attacked by four P-39 Airacobras, and Pritze was never seen again.

10 July

The last Staffel pilot left for Germany on about this date. They were to join the Third Gruppe at Cuxhaven-Nordholz; the Gruppe had at this time been separated from the rest of the Geschwader to reinforce the defenses of northern Germany. The Third Gruppe was now equipped solely with Messerschmitt fighters, and the 7th Staffel pilots would have to learn the idiosyncrasies of the Bf 109G very quickly.

The 7th Staffel lost three pilots killed and one prisoner in its four months in the East. According to Josef Priller's unit history, the Staffel was credited with sixty-three air victories during their tour. Subtracting the known claims of Mietusch, Jauer, Kemethmüller, and Ellenrieder leaves twenty-three without attribution. Subtracting Günther Kelch's claims total before leaving Luftflotte 3 from his total at his death, soon after his return to the West, gives a maximum of twelve claims for Kelch in Russia. The remaining 10-12 claims were spread among the 12-15 other pilots who served in the Staffel in Russia.

The record of 7th Staffel in Russia was excellent – comparable to its performance in the Mediterranean theater in 1941 – but this time it had made no impression on the enemy, and its departure went unnoticed. The same can be said for the tour of the First Gruppe; it too had had no effect on the course of the war.

7/JG 26 Casualties in the USSR

Date	Rank	Name	Cas	Unit	Aircraft	WNr	Mkgs	Place	Time	Cause	Allied Unit
03-03-43	Lt.	Westermair, Alois	KIFA	7	Fw 190A-4	5750	bk 10	Tossno	1100	crashed	non-op
20-03-43	Hptm.	Mietusch, Klaus	WIA	7 CO	Fw 190A-4	7147		Krasnogvardeisk a/f		engine	n/a
30-05-43	Lt.	Reck, Horst	KIA	7	Fw 190A-4	5802	wh 8	W of Cape Ustje		Finn I-153	
18-06-43	Fw.	Jauer, Erich	POW	7	Fw 190A-5	2551	wh 6	nr Schluesselburg a/f	0600	P-39	
09-07-43	Uffz.	Pritze, Hans	KIA	7	Fw 190A-5	1308	wh 5	nr Schluesselburg a/f	1626	P-39	

Chapter Three

BLOCKING THE TIDE

June - August 1943

1 June

The Third Gruppe was now at Cuxhaven, leaving only five JG 26 Staffeln on duty on the Kanalfront – two in the Geschwadergruppe (excluding 11/JG 54, which was not fully operational), and three in the Second Gruppe. Until the return of the First Gruppe from Russia, the two I/JG 27 Staffeln now at Poix would be called on to play a greater role in the defense of the Pas de Calais. At noon Jafü 2 ordered all available I/JG 27 and JG 26 fighters to take off and intercept a small formation of Spitfires. This was the two-squadron Kenley Wing, whose Canadians were glad to see the Luftwaffe in the air. The Jafü attempted to sandwich the Spitfires between the two approaching German formations, but the Spitfires turned into each attack as it came in, and a massive dogfight involving about eighty fighters was soon underway in the area between Abbeville, Doullens, and St. Pol. The Canadians had the better of it, claiming three Bf 109s and losing no-one. I/JG 27 claimed one Spitfire, but lost three Bf 109s, including that of their Kommandeur, Hptm. Erich Hohagen, who bailed out with injuries. The JG 26 Focke-Wulf pilots claimed nothing and lost nothing, which was often the case in prolonged battles between evenly-matched opponents. Uffz. Gomann was surprised by the tactics of his confident Kommandeur, and wrote in his logbook, "Galland attacked from below and engaged in a turning battle, even though Spitfires are better in turns."

Although some contemporary documents refer to the 10th, 11th, and 12th Staffeln as units of JG 54 throughout June, and no specific date for their official redesignations as JG 26 Staffeln has been found, it is obvious that by this date these Staffeln were part of JG 26 in fact if not yet in name, and they will be referred to as 10/JG 26, 11/JG 26, and 12/JG 26 from this point forward in the book. The 11th Staffel had an especially difficult time establishing its identity. Within the space of six months it was 11/JG 26, 11/JG 54, and again 11/JG 26. To further complicate matters, it was considered the successor to an earlier 11th Staffel, which had been part of the First Gruppe until it was disbanded in late 1942. Some documents indicate that the new 11th was a "First Gruppe" Staffel for administrative purposes, even though it never based with that Gruppe and did not go with it to the Eastern Front. Other records call it a "Third Gruppe" Staffel, which it later became. But it did not serve with the Third Gruppe during the latter's detached service at Nordholz. During the summer of 1943, the 11th remained in limbo as a lonely, semi-independent, semi-operational Staffel.

2 June

Seventeen SKG 10 Fw 190A-5 Jabos bombed Ipswich at dawn. The Second Gruppe took off from Vitry to escort the fighter-bombers back to Arques. Fw. Crump and Uffz. Gomann reported contacting Spitfires and Typhoons, no real combats took place, and neither side sustained any casualties over the Channel. One SKG 10 Focke-Wulf was shot down over England.

3 June

The Channel pilots spent the day on routine patrols; the only excitement came when several loose barrage balloons arrived from England. No information is available on Third Gruppe activities at Cuxhaven-Nordholz prior to 11 June.

4 June

The Second Gruppe was scrambled at noon, but failed to contact any of the sweeping Spitfires. Part of II/JG 2 was now flying from Abbeville; the Richthofen fighters did engage the RAF, and lost one Bf 109 destroyed and one damaged. The rest of the day's flights by the Schlageter fighters were limited to patrols and the evening recon mission.

5 June

The Channel pilots flew uneventful defensive patrols. Uffz. Wilhelm Mayer of the 6th Staffel was ordered to patrol some railroad lines, which he did without incident. The French *Maquis* were nowhere near as numerous or as dangerous as the Russian partisans, but were attracted to the same types of targets. Railroad sabotage was as yet uncommon in France, but the Wehrmacht found it prudent to make periodic shows of force.

6 June

Small formations of Allied aircraft were reported over the Channel, none apparently crossed the French coast, and no interceptions were ordered. Uffz. Mayer flew escort for a convoy off Boulogne, without incident, and was then sent on two railroad patrols; the Germans apparently had reason to believe that the Allies were planning a sabotage operation.

Obfw. Ellenrieder transferred from the 4th Staffel at Vitry to his former unit, the 8th or "Adamson" Staffel, now in the Geschwadergruppe at Vendeville, and flew one training mission. This was apparently under the tutelage of Major Priller, who had returned from a conference in Rechlin.

7 June

Numerous patrols were flown today in poor weather; no Allied aircraft were encountered. The engine of Ogfr. Norbert Holtz's Fw 190A-4 failed while he was on patrol from Vendeville and he crash-landed in a marsh between Courtrai and Ghent, sustaining injuries. The aircraft could not be recovered, and was still buried in the swamp in 1998.

The First Gruppe began arriving at Rheine from Russia. Here they received replacement aircraft and, it is hoped, short leaves before returning to the western air front.

10 June

The First Gruppe began arriving at Poix, replacing I/JG 27, which was packing up to move to Marseille-Marignan in southern France for more training. 3/JG 27 remained at Poix for several more weeks. One First Gruppe Fw 190A-4 was destroyed in a crash-landing on Poix-Nord; the cause was listed as pilot error.

The 8th Air Force was still grounded by bad weather at their English bases, but No. 2 Group sent small Ramrods to bomb three power stations. Major Priller led the 6th and 8th Staffeln in an attack on a dozen Venturas bombing Zeebrugge. Priller was the only German pilot to score; he was credited with downing a Ventura, but apparently all returned to England. I/JG 1 attacked the six Mitchells approaching Langerbrugge, broke up the formation, and shot one bomber down, but were then engaged by the Spitfire escort and lost three Focke-Wulfs and one pilot, while shooting down two Spitfires.

11 June

Fighter Command Spitfires were active, flying four Rodeos over the Pas de Calais between noon and 1730. The 3/JG 27 pilots remaining at Poix-Nord scrambled and lost one of their number killed and two Bf 109s damaged, for no known claims. A II/JG 2 Messerschmitt was also lost. The two JG 26 Gruppen scrambled twice. The first mission failed to make contact; during the second, No. 611 Squadron lost a

Spitfire north of Amiens to Obfw. Glunz. This squadron claimed a Fw 190 destroyed, but none sustained reportable damage.

8th Bomber Command chose the U-boat yards in Wilhelmshaven as its first target in June. The 252 B-17s were attacked by a succession of Luftwaffe fighter units for over an hour. The first was a new Gruppe, III/JG 1, flying from Leeuwarden in northern Holland. III/JG 26, flying new Bf 109G-4/R6 and Bf 109G-6/R6 "gunboats" with MG 151/20 cannon in bulky underwing gondolas, took part from Nordholz, and claimed two B-17s. Uffz. Anton Meissner of 4/JG 54, which was still flying with the Third Gruppe, was hit by B-17 gunners and bailed out of his Bf 109 with severe injuries. A total of eight B-17s went down; sixty-two more were damaged. The German pilots claimed a total of twenty-two B-17s destroyed; only one fighter pilot other than Meissner was injured, and only seven fighters were destroyed or damaged. The bombers failed to damage their target. The Third Gruppe played a full role in this defensive success, which was widely publicized in Germany. Unfortunately for the Germans, overclaiming and its consequent over optimism would remain a serious problem whenever several units attacked the same bomber formations.

JG 26 Victory Claims: 10 - 11 June 1943

Date	Rank	Name	Unit	Cl #	Aircraft	Place	Time	Opponent	Conf
10-06-43	Maj.	Priller	Ge CO	89	Ventura	W of Coxyde	1855		yes
11-06-43	Obfw.	Glunz	4	33	Spitfire	N of Doullens	1642	611 Sqd	yes
11-06-43	Uffz.	Stutt	III St		B-17	N of Wilhelmshaven	1752		yes
11-06-43	Fw.	Niese	9	3	B-17	Grossheide-Norden	1757		yes

12 June

The Second Gruppe busied itself with more railroad patrols. The 8th Bomber Command stayed on the ground while its planners determined its next mission; the 8th Fighter Command dispatched a single group, the 56th, on a late-evening sweep of Ostend. Both JG 26 Gruppen were scrambled. A 56th Fighter Group pilot claimed to have surprised and shot down a Fw 190 for the P-47 unit's first confirmed victory, but no German aircraft sustained reportable damage, and there is no indication in the available records that any JG 26 aircraft contacted the P-47s.

13 June

On a morning sweep of the coast at 27,000 feet (8000 meters), the 56th Group spotted a Staffel of Fw 190s climbing in their direction. Col. Hubert "Hub" Zemke, the Group commander, led two flights of Thunderbolts down onto the German fighters. The Focke-Wulf pilots, from the new Second Gruppe Staffel, 10/JG 26, were taken by surprise. Zemke claimed two, while Lt. Robert S. Johnson exploded a third. The 10th Staffel lost Ogfr. Heinrich Zenker killed and Obfw. Karl-Heinz Böcher wounded in this combat. The Staffeln had apparently gotten separated from the rest of the Second Gruppe, some of whose pilots later contacted the P-47s and fought them without result.

The Spitfire wings were also active this morning. The Geschwadergruppe was vectored to a Spitfire formation, and Ogfr. Schöhl of the 8th Staffel shot down a No. 65 Sqd. Spitfire into the Channel, although his claim was never confirmed. The Focke-Wulf of Obfw. Willi Grams overturned when he attempted to land on Vendeville; Grams broke his back and died.

The Thunderbolt and Spitfire sweeps were in support of unescorted 8th Bomber Command raids on Kiel and Bremen. Hptm. Kurt Ruppert led thirty-two Third Gruppe Bf 109Gs up from Nordholz to intercept the Kiel attackers. As the Messerschmitts made a rear pass on the lead group, Ruppert was hit, and bailed out. He attempted to open his parachute before his speed had dropped sufficiently in free-fall, and his harness ripped, throwing Ruppert free and to his death. German parachutes had caused the death of many pilots; within a year, the old hemp harnesses would be replaced by a synthetic material similar to nylon. Ruppert was the only JG 26 casualty in this

Uffz. Heinz Gomann's Fw 190A-5 "black 22" (W.Nr. 1243), awaits repairs outside the Second Gruppe workshop at Vitry-en-Artois after surviving its 13 June collision with a 78th Fighter Group P-47, which crashed. Gomann was shot down in this aircraft by a 56th Group P-47 on 17 August, surviving with injuries. *(Crump)*

Hptm. Ruppert, the Third Gruppe Kommandeur from 7 April until his death on 13 June. After his Messerschmitt was hit by B-17 fire, he attempted to open his parachute at too great a speed, and his harness ripped. *(Molge)*

battle, which cost the lead group eight Flying Fortresses. The 4th Bomb Wing lost a total of twenty-two B-17s out of seventy-six dispatched; the 1st Bomb Wing's attack on Bremen was lightly opposed, and only four of its bombers were lost. The Luftwaffe victory claims were reasonably accurate today; thirty-five victory credits were awarded, five to pilots of the Third Gruppe. Their attacks were concentrated on the hapless 95th Bomb Group, which was flying an experimental, ineffective formation and lost ten B-17s.

The day's activities were not yet over. In the late afternoon, forty-four P-47s of the 78th Fighter Group flew a sweep over Ypres and St. Pol. The Second Gruppe was up in good time. They were not spotted by the Thunderbolt formation until they were diving to the attack from ten o'clock high. Uffz. Gomann expected the P-47s to break up and away, as the Spitfires did, but his target stayed in formation, and Gomann rammed it, clipping off part of its wing. The P-47 went out of control and crashed, killing its pilot; Gomann returned to Vitry, landed smoothly with only slight damage, and was congratulated by Hptm. Galland, who also reminded him to fire his guns next time.

Gomann's wingman, Lt. Lange, claimed a P-47, as did the newly-promoted Fw. Wilhelm Mayer. A second P-47 crashed near Ypres, its location matching Lange's claim; Mayer's target was probably one of the two damaged P-47s that made it back to England. No German fighters were lost, although three probables were awarded to American pilots.

JG 26 Victory Claims: 13 June 1943

Date	Rank	Name	Unit	Cl #	Aircraft	Place	Time	Opponent	Conf
13-06-43	Uffz.	Gomann	5	4	P-47	Armentières	1448	78 FG	yes
13-06-43	Lt.	Lange F.	5	1	P-47	St. Jean-Ypres	1450	78 FG	yes
13-06-43	Fw.	Mayer	6	3	P-47	40-50km NNW of Dunkirk	1454	78 FG	yes
13-06-43	Ogfr.	Schöhl	8		Spitfire	20km N of Dunkirk	0955	65 Sqd	unk
13-06-43	Obfw.	Erbskorn	9	1	B-17	18km N of Lütjenburg	0938	95 BG	unk
13-06-43	Uffz.	Holl	9		B-17	Königsforde	0924	95 BG	yes
13-06-43	Lt.	Kestel	9	3	B-17	Schönberg	0931	95 BG	yes
13-06-43	Fw.	Niese	9	4	B-17	9km SSE of Kiel	0928	95 BG	yes
13-06-43	Uffz.	Steinberg	9	1	B-17	12km NNE of Lake Selenter	0936	95 BG	yes

JG 26 Casualties: 7 - 13 June 1943

Date	Rank	Name	Cas	Unit	Aircraft	WNr	Mkgs	Place	Time	Cause	Allied Unit
07-06-43	Ogfr.	Holtz, Norbert	WIFA	8	Fw 190A-4	5730	bk 4	Deinze-Nazareth	1100	engine	n/a
11-06-43	Uffz.	Meissner, Anton	WIA	4/54	Bf 109G-4	19368	wh 14-	Wilhelmshaven		B-17	
13-06-43	Obfw.	Böcher,Karl-Heinz	WIA	10/54	Fw 190A-4	2415	wh 15	nr Furnes	0930	P-47	56 FG
13-06-43	Ogfr.	Zenker, Heinrich	KIA	10/54	Fw 190A-4	795	wh 4	SE of Furnes	0930	P-47	56 FG
13-06-43	Hptm.	Ruppert, Kurt	KIA	III CO	Bf 109G-6	16425	<<+I	Neumünster	0930	B-17	
13-06-43	Obfw.	Grams, Willi	KIFA	8	Fw 190A-5	1222	bk 1	Vendeville a/f		landing	n/a

15 June

The Schlageter fighters at Vendeville and Vitry continued their routine of coastal and railroad patrols in mediocre weather. A B-17 raid on Bernay was recalled, and Jafü 2 left the interception of the Kenley Wing's supporting sweep of Rouen to Jafü 3, which sent up I/JG 2. The Gruppe lost two Focke-Wulfs to the Canadians, and made no claims.

Hptm. Rolf Hermichen was named interim Kommandeur of the Third Gruppe, and left Poix for Nordholz. Lt. Wolfgang Neu replaced Hermichen as interim leader of the 3rd Staffel.

The 11th Staffel was declared ready for operations, and the last of its pilots left Mönchen-Gladbach to join the Geschwadergruppe at Vendeville.

16 June

Two No. 1 Sqd. Typhoons attacked the Bethune railroad yards at dawn, damaging nine locomotives. Part of the 4th Staffel, which had the duty at Vitry, scrambled to intercept the Typhoons on their return flight to England. They were caught over the Channel. Lt. Kehl forced one Typhoon back toward France, where it crashed. Lt. Hoppe thought that his target crashed in the Channel, but it reached the English coast and crash-landed on the Lympne emergency field.

A Walrus ASR seaplane and four No. 91 Sqd. Spitfires were immediately dispatched from England to look for the missing Typhoon pilot. Hptm. Galland led the rest of his Gruppe off from Vitry and soon found the Spitfires. All four were claimed. Two did in fact crash in the Channel; one pilot was killed, while the second was rescued by the ASR aircraft. Hptm. Galland, Oblt. Sternberg, and Obfw. Glunz received victory credits; Fw. Crump, who was badly outranked, did not bother to file his claim.

JG 26 Victory Claims: 16 June 1943

Date	Rank	Name	Unit	Cl #	Aircraft	Place	Time	Opponent	Conf
16-06-43	Hptm.	Galland W.-F.	II CO	42	Spitfire	between Calais & Dover	0710	91 Sqd	yes

16-06-43	Lt.	Hoppe	4 CO	10	Typhoon	mid-Channel	0530	1 Sqd	yes
16-06-43	Lt.	Kehl	4	1	Typhoon	6km SE of Arras	0534	1 Sqd	yes
16-06-43	Obfw.	Glunz	4	34	Spitfire	20km NW of Cap Gris Nez	0707	91 Sqd	yes
16-06-43	Oblt.	Sternberg	5 CO	18	Spitfire	10km SE of Dover	0706	91 Sqd	yes
16-06-43	Uffz.	Crump	5		Spitfire	mid-Channel	0700	91 Sqd	no

The 8th Staffel's Ogfr. Horst-Günther Schöhl. He accidentally killed a comrade while cleaning a weapon and was demoted from Unteroffizier to Gefreiter, but regained his rank within a few months. *(Wiegand via Mombeek)*

17 June

In the morning, No. 2 Group sent a dozen Bostons to bomb Vlissingen. The Second Gruppe scrambled from Vitry, but was quickly landed when the direction of the attacking formation became clear. Part of the Geschwadergruppe caught the rear cover off Zeebrugge, and Lt. Matoni of the 6th Staffel shot down a No. 316 Sqd. Spitfire. The bombers proceeded to the target unmolested. II/JG 1 took off in strength from Woensdrecht, but was bounced by the Spitfires of North Weald Wing, whose Norwegian pilots shot down five of the Focke-Wulfs without loss to themselves.

In mid-afternoon, Fighter Command conducted a large, multi-stage Rodeo, or sweep, of the Pas de Calais. The Jafü was expecting bombers, and only when these failed to materialize were the two JG 26 Gruppe formations vectored toward the last formation in the sweep – the Kenley Wing. The two Gruppen followed a well-practiced tactic. The Geschwadergruppe stayed below the Spitfires as targets for a bounce, while Hptm. Galland climbed with his Second Gruppe to catch the Spitfires in their dive. W/C Johnson hit a trailing Fw 190 during his dive, and Uffz. Günther Freitag crashed to his death. The two Kenley squadrons then split up and began climbing to deal with the Second Gruppe Focke-Wulfs coming down on their rear. The 5th Staffel Kapitän, Oblt. Horst Sternberg, damaged a Spitfire sufficiently to be given credit for its destruction, but was then rammed by a Spitfire, according to the Luftwaffe records, and had to bail out with injuries. One of these two Spitfires made it back to England; the second disappeared during the course of the mission. The No. 421 Squadron commander, S/L P.L.I. Archer, who had just taken over the post that morning, was split from his formation and was then shot down by Uffz. Paul Schwarz of the 6th Staffel, for his first victory. Archer did not get out of his aircraft, which crashed into soft ground near St. Omer. Schwarz visited the site that evening with a comrade. Neither Archer nor his aircraft were disturbed until 1996, when a team of aviation archaeologists partially excavated the airplane in the mistaken belief that it was the Spitfire in which W/C Douglas Bader had been shot down in 1941. The Spitfire's Merlin engine was buried seventeen feet deep. It is not surprising that hundreds of aircrewmen remain missing in the soft soil of northwestern Europe more than fifty years after the end of World War II.

Part of the Second Gruppe engaged P-47s as the latter were crossing the Pas de Calais on one of their high-altitude sweeps, but without result. The 8th Fighter Command flew 1011 sorties between 1-17 June, claiming 4-1-2 Fw 190s for the loss of two P-47s.

JG 26 Victory Claims: 17 June 1943

Date	Rank	Name	Unit	Cl #	Aircraft	Place	Time	Opponent	Conf
17-06-43	Oblt.	Sternberg	5 CO	19	Spitfire	5km SW of Hazebrouck	1545	421 Sqd	yes
17-06-43	Lt.	Matoni	6	5	Spitfire	10km NW of Zeebrugge	0950	316 Sqd	yes
17-06-43	Uffz.	Schwarz P.	6	1	Spitfire	10km SW of St. Omer	1556	421 Sqd	yes

18 June

The enemy stayed north of the Channel, and the weather did not permit much flying. The First Gruppe, not yet operational from Poix, was able to fly a practice intercept mission with a captured B-17.

19 June

Today's flying was restricted to training, coastal patrols, and railroad patrols. One First Gruppe Fw 190A-4 force-landed on Poix after its engine failed on a non-operational flight.

Hptm. Walter Höckner gave up the 1st Staffel and took command of II/JG 1 at Woensdrecht. Lt. Artur Beese was named Führer of the 1st Staffel.

Oblt. Walter Otte was transferred from the Geschwader. Hptm. Paul Steindl replaced Otte as Kapitän of the 11th Staffel.

20 June

The 8th Bomber Command remained grounded. In the morning, Allied fighters swept the French coast without opposition. The only bombers to cross the Channel were a dozen Bostons of No. 2 Group, which bombed the non-operational First Gruppe at Poix in early afternoon, escorted by thirteen Spitfire squadrons. The Geschwadergruppe and the Second Gruppe scrambled at 1300 and flew southwest. The first-named unit apparently encountered the Hornchurch Wing, without result. Hptm. Galland split his Gruppe, climbing with two Staffeln to get in the sun. Part of the Kenley Wing saw the lower Fw 190s, but as No. 421 Squadron dived to attack them, Galland's Staffeln hit both No. 421 and No. 403 Squadrons, which had remained above. S/L "Buck" McNair of No. 421 Squadron shot down Uffz. Erwin Hanke of the 4th Staffel, who crash-landed near Douai with injuries. No. 403 Squadron lost three Spitfires, to Hptm. Galland, Obfw. Glunz, and Fw. Crump.

JG 26 Victory Claims: 20 June 1943

Date	Rank	Name	Unit	Cl #	Aircraft	Place	Time	Opponent	Conf
20-06-43	Hptm.	Galland W.-F.	II CO	43	Spitfire	NE of Hesdin	1330	403 Sqd	i.O.
20-06-43	Obfw.	Glunz	4	35	Spitfire	NE of Étaples	1335	403 Sqd	yes
20-06-43	Uffz.	Crump	5	9	Spitfire	near Vielles les Blequin	1334	403 Sqd	yes

21 June

Small formations of RAF fighters crossed the coast, enticing up equally small formations from the Pas de Calais. No contact was made. Aircraft from the First Gruppe were airborne; the RAF Y-intercept service picked up their radio transmissions for the first time since their return from the East.

22 June

The 8th Bomber Command scheduled its first mission to the Ruhr. Two hundred and thirty-five B-17s were dispatched to the synthetic rubber plant at Hüls. The JG 26 units in France and Belgium were fully occupied by the various feints and diversions flown by the RAF and part of the 8th Air Force. RAF Mitchells bombed Rotterdam, which occupied II/JG 1 for a while but did not keep them away from the main raid. The extensive Ruhr flak belt and the Jafü Holland-Ruhr day fighters, the three Gruppen of JG 1 plus I/JG 3 and III/JG 54, shot down sixteen B-17s and damaged seventy-five, but could not prevent extensive damage at Hüls.

The major Allied diversion was an attack on the Antwerp automobile plants by two new B-17 groups, the 381st and 384th. The target was specifically chosen to keep the Schlageter fighters away from the main force, and that plan worked successfully, even though the bombers were thirty minutes late owing to difficulty in forming up. The three American fighter groups were even later, owing to confusing orders, and did not meet the bombers until they reached Walcheren on their return flight. The Jafü was able to tell Major Priller, leading the Geschwadergruppe, and Hptm. Galland, leading the Second Gruppe, that the bombers were unescorted. The two formation leaders planned their attacks accordingly. Priller, who was airborne slightly earlier, was able to swing to the east and attack the bombers from the front before they reached the target. The Focke-Wulfs made one pass through the formation in flights of six to eight; three B-17s fell away. Obfw. Johann Edmann, a wingman in the Stabsschwarm, was hit by bomber fire and crash-landed on Woensdrecht with severe injuries. The Second Gruppe caught up with the bombers as they were leaving the target and attacked them from the rear. Galland urged his men to make repeated attacks, and many had run out of ammunition before the belated arrival of the Thunderbolts forced them to break off. The Second Gruppe claimed four B-17s, and was given victory credit for three; Galland got credit for the *endgültige Vernichtung* (final destruction) of his second B-17, which was undoubtedly one of those which dropped from formation as a result of Priller's attack, and was also credited to Fw. Mayer as a *Herausschuss*, or separation. The two B-17 groups lost four B-17s over the Continent and into the sea, and a fifth that crashed in England. The Second Gruppe pilots pulled away from the P-47s with some urgency; Lt. Radener was credited with shooting one down, but no P-47s were lost this day. The American fighter pilots claimed seven Fw 190s and one Bf 109; the Bf 109s in the area were from III/JG 1 and the ERLA factory protection Staffel. The Fw 190s were all from Galland's Gruppe; three of these force-landed on Vlissingen, one crash-landed at Antwerp, and a fifth crash-landed on its return to Vitry. Hptm. Naumann and Fw. Crump were wounded; the other three pilots were uninjured.

The return course of the Hüls force was due west toward Rotterdam; this was barely within range of the First Gruppe at Poix, but they were the only uncommitted fighter force in the area, and were scrambled at 0946 to try their luck. They were unable to penetrate the Spitfire escort, but Fw. Christof of the 1st Staffel shot down a No. 453 Sqd. Spitfire west of Rotterdam. This was the first victory for the First Gruppe since its return to the western theater.

Fw. Vogt led his 6th Staffel Schwarm up from Vendeville at 1023 for a second sortie. They freelanced in search of any straggling bombers, and at 1126 were vectored toward St. Omer, where a single B-17 was reported flying at low altitude. After repeated attacks, Vogt was able to shoot the crippled bomber into the Channel off Dunkirk.

Late in the afternoon No. 2 Group sent a Circus containing a dozen Venturas to bomb Abbeville-Drucat. The entire Geschwader was scrambled, but as soon as the

Adamsonstaffel aircraft mechanic Gödecker sits in the cockpit of Fw 190A-5 "black 16" (W.Nr. 7313). Uffz. Gerd Wiegand is on the ground. Obfw. Johann Edmann was severely injured in this aircraft on 22 June when hit by B-17 fire. *(G. Schmidt)*

enemy force was correctly identified, "all fighters not in contact with the enemy" – which meant all of them – were ordered to land.

The new categories assigned to the claims of Hptm. Galland and Fw. Mayer were the result of an attempt by the RLM to increase the morale and effectiveness of the pilots assigned to attack heavy bombers. The pilots of the western Geschwader were convinced that their eastern brethren received more than their fair share of battle honors. Promotions and awards in the German Air Force were based on success in combat. This basic principle could not be changed, but in recognition of the difficulty of the struggle against the heavy bombers, the Luftwaffe instituted a point system for decorations. Points were awarded to fighter pilots as follows:

	POINTS AWARDED PER		
Aircraft Type	*Abschuss* (shoot-down)	*Herausschuss* (separation)	*endgültige Vernichtung* (final destruction)
Fighter	1	0	0
Twin-engine bomber	2	1	$^1/_2$
Four-engine bomber	3	2	1

The system recognized the fact that damaging a bomber sufficiently to force it from its combat box was a more difficult task than the final destruction of a damaged straggler, but tended to lead to double claiming. Decorations were awarded after the following point totals had been reached:

AWARD	POINTS REQUIRED
Iron Cross Second Class	1
Iron Cross First Class	3
Honor Cup	10
German Cross in Gold	20
Knight's Cross	40

The Knight's Cross, which the pilots wore on a ribbon around their neck, even in combat, was recognized in the Jagdwaffe as the sign of a true Experte. Glory-hungry pilots were said to have a "neck rash". If it was their luck to be assigned to JG 26, their necks in all likelihood continued to itch until their deaths. Only one Knight's Cross had been awarded to a JG 26 pilot in each of the years 1941 and 1942, while two pilots, Wutz Galland and Addi Glunz, were so rewarded in 1943. The higher grades of the Knight's Cross, which in ascending order were the Oak Leaves, Swords, and Diamonds, were awarded in some numbers in the east, but were very uncommon in JG 26. During the entire war, only five pilots received any of the higher decorations while with the Geschwader.

It has been pointed out in many postwar references that the point system existed for the purpose of award qualification only. "Victory claims" and "points" were two distinct statistics. The requirements for the verification of victory claims remained unchanged; only the RLM in Berlin could confirm a claim, and this procedure could take more than a year. The practice of claiming "separations" died out in JG 26 in 1944, but was quite common during the savage combats of 1943. The award point tabulations failed to survive the war, and award points will not be mentioned again in this book.

JG 26 Victory Claims: 22 June 1943

Date	Rank	Name	Unit	Cl #	Aircraft	Place	Time	Opponent	Conf
22-06-43	Maj.	Priller	Ge CO	90	B-17	near Terneuzen	0932	381 BG	yes
22-06-43	Fw.	Christof	1	8	Spitfire	Goeree Is.	1032	453 Sqd	yes
22-06-43	Hptm.	Galland W-F.	II CO	44	B-17	10km NW of Vlissingen	0922	381 or 384 BG	yes
22-06-43	Hptm.	Galland W-F.	II CO		B-17-eV	20km NW of Vlissingen	0925	381 or 384 BG	yes
22-06-43	Obfw.	Glunz	4	36	B-17	Katz - N ofBeveland Is.	0915	381 BG	yes
22-06-43	Lt.	Radener	4	2	P-47	10-15km NW of Domburg	0934		yes
22-06-43	Uffz.	Crump	5		B-17	5km NW of Vlissingen	0930	381 or 384 BG	no
22-06-43	Lt.	Lange F.	5	2	B-17	3km W of Goes	0920	384 BG	yes
22-06-43	Hptm.	Naumann	6 CO	17	B-17	W of Antwerp -in sea	0915	384 BG	i.O.
22-06-43	Fw.	Mayer	6	4	B-17-HSS	Antwerp	0916	381 or 384 BG	yes
22-06-43	Fw.	Vogt	6	12	B-17	10km W of Dunkirk	1141	381 or 384 BG	yes

JG 26 Casualties: 17 - 22 June 1943

Date	Rank	Name	Cas	Unit	Aircraft	WNr	Mkgs	Place	Time	Cause	Allied Unit
17-06-43	Oblt.	Sternberg, Horst	WIA	5 CO	Fw 190A-5	7359	bk 12	W of Hazebrouck	1545	Spitfire	Kenley Wing
17-06-43	Uffz.	Freitag, Günther	KIA	8	Fw 190A-5	7308	bk 9	Stennvoorde?, E of Cassel		Spitfire	Kenley Wing
20-06-43	Fw.	Bäumener, Helmut	WIA	3	Fw 190A			near Vendeville		Spitfire	421 Sqd
20-06-43	Uffz.	Hanke, Erwin	no	4	Fw 190A-4	2372	wh 14	Orchies, SE of Capelle	1330	Spitfire	421 Sqd
22-06-43	Fw.	Crump, Peter	WIA	5	Fw 190A-4	793	bk 6	Scheldt Est	0930	P-47	
22-06-43	Hptm.	Naumann, Hans	WIA	CO 6	Fw 190A-5	7300	br 3	near Antwerp	1000	P-47	
22-06-43	Obfw.	Edmann, Johann	WIA	8	Fw 190A-5	7313	bk 16	2km S of Woensdrecht	0930	B-17	

23 June

The commanders of the German air defenses were frequently guilty of "fighting the last battle." The Americans had targeted the Ruhr for the first time on 22 June. Today, I/JG 26 transferred to Rheine from Poix, and III/JG 54 moved to Deelen from Oldenburg; both moves were made to strengthen the Ruhr defenses. Not only was Major Priller losing the First Gruppe again, this time to Jafü Holland-Ruhr; he was obligated to provide it with a Kommandeur, now that Seifert had left. Priller called

A clear view of the side of the 8th Staffel's Fw 190A-5 "black 16", showing its unusual personal marking, a bloody bird. Unfortunately, Gottfried Schmidt, the mechanic who supplied the photo, does not recall the incident that prompted the painting. *(G. Schmidt)*

Karl Borris in the hospital and awarded the command to him; Oblt. Kurt Ebersberger took over Borris's 8th Staffel on his return from instructor duty on the 26th.

Today's scheduled B-17 raid to the Villacoublay airbase near Paris was canceled owing to bad weather. The RAF sent its Bostons over the Channel anyway, and flew their planned diversion. The Geschwadergruppe and the Second Gruppe scrambled, and both contacted the Bostons with their Spitfire escort and the ever-hovering P-47s, but no combats were pursued to a conclusion.

24 June

Again today the 8th Bomber Command stayed on the ground, but the RAF sent three light bomber missions to the Pas de Calais area. These were called Ramrods, meaning that they were intended to do damage to their targets (any damage done by Circuses was incidental); they and the accompanying fighter and fighter-bomber sweeps were carried out with such vigor that the pilots of the Geschwader were in the air for most of the day. Many flew four or five sorties.

The first raid was an attack on Vlissingen by twelve Venturas. The Poles of the Northolt Wing were the close escort, and just past the target spotted and dived on a dozen Focke-Wulfs at low altitude. These were some of Galland's men, playing their old mousetrap trick. The 10th Staffel got the honor of springing the trap. Oblt. Leuschel and Uffz. Schulwitz each downed a No. 303 Sqd. Spitfire. One 10th Staffel Focke-Wulf was shot down in the subsequent melee; its pilot bailed out without injury.

The commanders of two of the American P-47 groups, the 56th and 78th, had been arguing for some time for permission to engage the Fw 190s and Bf 109s where they were, typically at 20-25,000 feet (6100-7600 meters) with the bombers and Spitfires, rather than expect the Germans to climb to their own altitude of 30,000 feet (9100 meters). Today one squadron of the 78th was released to dive on a pair of unsuspecting Fw 190s flying south of Ostend at only 10,000 feet (3000 meters). The fuel tank of Lt. Günther Blömertz's Focke-Wulf was hit on the bounce and Blömertz bailed out with severe burns. He returned to the Geschwader, but was never restored to flight status, ending the war as the Second Gruppe adjutant. The day's other 127 P-47 sorties were unsuccessful.

The pilots and staff officers of No. 486 Sqd. (RNZAF) pose with one of their ugly mounts in the summer of 1943. P/O Ray Danzey is third from the right on the wing, wearing a Mae West. Twelve of these pilots were killed, taken prisoner, or suffered serious wounds. *(Danzey)*

The noon Ramrod was an attack by a dozen Bostons on the St. Omer locomotive factory. The Kenley Wing flew a supporting sweep, and was vectored to several small formations of German aircraft, all apparently from the Second Gruppe. No. 403 Squadron broke up into flights and pairs, while No. 416 stayed above as high cover. Uffz. Gomann saw a Fw 190 being pursued by a Spitfire; he opened fire from long range, and shot it down. The Fw 190 then dived away and made a normal landing on Vitry with light damage. Its pilot, Obfw. Alfred Günther, who had sustained some splinter injuries in the combat, claimed to have forced the crash of one of two pursuing

Uffz. Hans Meyer of the 5th Staffel, who crashed in the Channel while battling Typhoons of No. 486 Sqd. (RNZAF) on 24 June. *(Vanoverbeke)*

Spitfires by "maneuvering"; he had then outrun the second back to base. Gomann, who landed a little later, gleefully informed the gathered crowd that it was he who had shot down the first Spitfire, and that the 'second' one had been piloted by him, Gomann. The Canadians saw the battle somewhat differently. F/L MacDonald damaged a Focke-Wulf, saw it dive away doing lazy rolls, and then saw a parachute near the German fighter. He claimed, and was awarded, the victory. His wingman disappeared without a trace during this combat. It was the Canadian wingman whom Gomann had shot down and whose parachute MacDonald saw; he survived the war as a POW.

In mid-afternoon a squadron of "Bombphoons" (bomb-carrying Typhoons) attacked Abbeville-Drucat, escorted by the conventional Typhoons of No. 486 Sqd. (RNZAF). They were

The Third Gruppe celebrates its 500th victory of the war while based at Lille in mid-1943. Lt. Hans-Georg Dippel and Oblt. Kurt Ebersberger engage a pair of local French beauties in conversation after the presentation of the bouquet. *(Wiegand via Mombeek)*

chased back to sea by some Second Gruppe Focke-Wulfs. Lt. Fritsch's Schwarm had an altitude advantage, and he led them in a clumsy bounce that hit nothing and ended up with Fritsch and his wingman just above the Channel with the No. 486 Squadron commander, S/L Desmond Scott, and his wingman in pursuit. After a brief, tense turning battle, Uffz. Hans Meyer lost control of his Focke-Wulf and it hit the sea inverted. Scott had difficulty bringing his own unwieldy Typhoon under control, but succeeded, and claimed the victory after returning to England. Fritsch in turn was credited with downing Scott.

The day's last Ramrod, an attack on the Yainville power station, took the Venturas and the escorting sweeps over the territory of Jafü 3, and I/JG 2 saw most of the action for the Luftwaffe. JG 26 was scrambled, but was held in reserve, and did not make contact.

JG 26 Victory Claims: 24 June 1943

Date	Rank	Name	Unit	Cl #	Aircraft	Place	Time	Opponent	Conf
24-06-43	Lt.	Fritsch P.	5	4	Typhoon	NW of Somme Estuary	1445	486 Sqd	yes
24-06-43	Uffz.	Gomann	5	5	Spitfire	Calonne-sur-la-Lys	1215	403 Sqd	yes
24-06-43	Uffz.	Meyer H.	5		Typhoon	NW of Somme Estuary	1445	486 Sqd	no
24-06-43	Oblt.	Leuschel	10 CO	4	Spitfire	SW of Ostend	0904	303 Sqd	unk
24-06-43	Uffz.	Schulwitz	10	1	Spitfire	St. Pierre Capelle	0905	303 Sqd	yes

25 June

The weather was so bad over France and Belgium that the fighters of Jafü 2 did no flying. The 8th Bomber Command sent 275 B-17s to bomb targets in Hamburg and Bremen, but the weather caused considerable confusion, and only 167 bombers dropped their bombs over land. *Luftwaffen Befehlshaber Mitte*, (LBH Mitte), the command controlling the air defenses of Germany at this time, put up all its day fighters, which were able to make multiple attacks on the scattered bomber formations, eventually shooting down eighteen and damaging sixty-one. The B-17s defended themselves with vigor, destroying a record twelve German fighters and damaging six. The First Gruppe, flying its first mission from Rheine, intercepted the Bremen force south of Emden and received credit in that night's OKW communiqué for the destruction of four B-17s; three of these claims were later confirmed. One victorious pilot was an Uffz. Schönrock, who was on temporary loan to the Gruppe from II/JG 1. Uffz. Schild had to force-land his moderately-damaged Focke-Wulf after the battle. The Third Gruppe made its interception some miles out to sea from Cuxhaven, and was credited by the OKW that evening with three victories; the name of one of the successful pilots is not known. Three of the Messerschmitt pilots failed to return, and were presumed to have crashed at sea as a result of the bad weather, combat damage, or both. The 12th Staffel airplane piloted by Lt. Gerd Kirschenlohr was seen to strike the water during his return from the mission, taking him to his death.

That evening Generalfeldmarschall Sperrle sent his congratulations to all members of JG 26 for the unit's 1500th aerial victory.

JG 26 Victory Claims: 25 June 1943

Date	Rank	Name	Unit	Cl #	Aircraft	Place	Time	Opponent	Conf
25-06-43	Hptm.	Gäth	2 CO	9	B-17	10km W of Papenburg (DP8)	0908	306 BG	yes
25-06-43	Oblt.	Dippel	2	15	B-17	6km S of Emden (CP8-4)	0908		yes
25-06-43	Uffz.	Schild	2		B-17	Norden	0915		no
25-06-43	Fw.	Dörre	9	7	B-17	30-40km NW of Helgoland	0902		yes
25-06-43	Obfw.	Erbskorn	9	2	B-17	15-20km NNW of Wangerooge	0903		yes

26 June

The 8th Bomber Command targeted Villacoublay despite continued bad weather over the Continent. The first diversions did not cross the coast until late afternoon. Bostons bombed the RAF's favorite target, Abbeville-Drucat, while Typhoons bombed Bernay. Jafü 2 scrambled its fighters, but brought them down quickly in anticipation of a raid by the heavy bombers. The first of these raids contained only forty-two bombers from two of what now totaled thirteen B-17 groups. They bombed Triqueville airfield on the Seine Estuary, and were so closely escorted by Spitfires that the defending Jafü 3 fighters could not get near them. Most could not disengage in time to regroup and attack the main force before it had bombed Villacoublay. When they did arrive, they concentrated on one group, the 384th, which was in the vulnerable low position in the lead wing. Four bombers went down, and several others dropped from formation.

In the meantime, Jafü 2 had scrambled all its fighters once again – Priller's Geschwadergruppe, the Second Gruppe, and some fighters at Poix and Abbeville, probably 3/JG 27 and part of II/JG 2. They headed for the coast to intercept a new, large force off Le Touquet. When seen, the enemy planes proved to be forty-eight P-47s, flying at 25,000 feet instead of their more customary 30,000. Jafü 2 ordered the fighters to be left alone. Major Priller obeyed, continued west, and downed a 384th Bomb Group B-17 off the coast between Dieppe and Le Tréport. Some pilots of the 4th Fighter Group spotted the Bf 109s of Priller's 11th Staffel, and dived on them as they raced for the coast at Dieppe. One pilot, Lt. Götz Schmidt, was shot down, but survived with injuries; an 8th Staffel Focke-Wulf was shot down near Rouen, probably by the bombers, but its pilot bailed out without injury.

In the meantime, Hptm. Galland had also continued west with his Gruppe, but only long enough to get upsun of the inviting formation of P-47s. In Galland's words, taken from his combat report,

> "From out of the sun at 7-8000 meters [23-26,000 feet] I attacked a formation of Thunderbolts that had just reached the bombers, far out to sea. The Gruppe was able to approach to close distance without detection. I fired on one Thunderbolt to the left of the formation from behind and below and observed cannon strikes. The

second burst of fire, from the side and behind at about fifty meters distance, exploded the Thunderbolt. Parts of the wing, fuselage and tail flew off. The aircraft dived away, out of control, and burst into flames. I did not observe the crash because its destruction was certain, and I attacked a second Thunderbolt."

The Thunderbolt pilots, taken by surprise and without their usual advantages of height and speed, broke in all directions. Those forced to turn with the Focke-Wulfs soon found their aircraft taking hits; four were shot down into the Channel. A fifth P-47 crashed off the English coast, and seven returned with serious damage; two of these had to be scrapped. One of the latter was piloted by Lt. Robert Johnson, a lucky survivor. Johnson was flying in the rear of the 62nd Fighter Squadron formation. His aircraft was so badly damaged in the initial bounce that he attempted to bail out, only to find his canopy jammed.

The story of Johnson's flight back across the Channel, followed by a Fw 190 pilot who peppered his P-47 with machine gun fire until he ran out of ammunition, then flew alongside him and rocked his wings in salute before turning back for France, is well known. The identity of the German pilot is unfortunately not known. Several names have been proposed, including that of Major Egon Mayer, the Kommandeur of III/JG 2, who is said to have had a "three Thunderbolt day" today. Mayer's name does not appear on the most complete victory list in the German archives; that is no proof that he was not involved, but as far as is known, his Gruppe was still based in Brittany, and no III/JG 2 pilots show up in the day's records as either victors or casualties. If Mayer did participate, he was probably flying as part of the Geschwader Stabsschwarm; he was to be named JG 2 Kommodore on 1 July.

The other two Gruppen of JG 2 were busy; pilots of I/JG 2 and II/JG 2 claimed three B-17s, two Spitfires, and one P-47, and the last was downed off Le Tréport at 1903, in the right time and place to be a 56th Fighter Group aircraft. Known German claims for these P-47s total nine confirmed and three not filed or unconfirmed, in fair agreement with the actual 56th losses of five destroyed, two damaged beyond repair, and five seriously damaged.

The 8th Bomber Command's B-24s, which were too few in numbers to form self-defending boxes and could not be mixed with the B-17s owing to performance differences, had contributed little to the Allied war effort from England. Today they began flying to North Africa for detached operations, to culminate on 1 August with the famous Ploesti raid.

JG 26 Victory Claims: 26 June 1943

Date	Rank	Name	Unit	Cl #	Aircraft	Place	Time	Opponent	Conf
26-06-43	Maj.	Priller	Ge CO	91	B-17	Dieppe-Le Tréport	1852	384 BG	yes
26-06-43	Hptm.	Galland W-F.	II CO	45	P-47	N of Neufchatel	1852	56 FG	yes
26-06-43	Hptm.	Galland W-F.	II CO	46	P-47	10km NW of Dieppe	1904	56 FG	yes
26-06-43	Lt.	Hoppe	4 CO	11	P-47	Neufchatel	1853	56 FG	yes
26-06-43	Lt.	Hoppe	4 CO	12	P-47	10km NW of Somme Estuary	1910	56 FG	yes
26-06-43	Obfw.	Glunz	4	37	P-47	NW of Neufchatel	1854	56 FG	unk
26-06-43	Obfw.	Glunz	4		P-47	NW of Neufchatel	1855	56 FG	no
26-06-43	Lt.	Radener	4	3	P-47	10-12km NNW of Le Tréport	1904	56 FG	yes
26-06-43	Fw.	Crump	5	10	P-47	15-20km NW of Somme Estuary	1910	56 FG	yes
26-06-43	Fw.	Scholz	5	2	P-47	20km N of Neufchatel	1900	56 FG	yes
26-06-43	Fw.	Mayer	6		P-47	20-30km NW of Dieppe	1900	56 FG	no

JG 26 Casualties: 24 - 26 June 1943

Date	Rank	Name	Cas	Unit	Aircraft	WNr	Mkgs	Place	Time	Cause	Allied Unit
24-06-43	Lt.	Blömertz, Günther	WIA	4	Fw 190A-4	5640	wh 8	Ichtegem-NE of Torhout	1000	P-47	78 FG

24-06-43	Obfw.	Günther, Alfred	WIA	5	Fw 190A-4	598	bk 11	S of St Omer		Spitfire	403 Sqd
24-06-43	Uffz.	Meyer, Hans	KIA	5	Fw 190A-4	2404	bk 18	10km W of Somme Est	1450	Typhoon	486 Sqd
25-06-43	Lt.	Kestel, Melchior	KIA	9	Bf 109G-6	15423	yl 4	North Sea		missing	
25-06-43	Uffz.	Lühs, Walter	KIA	9	Bf 109G-6	15428	yl 13	North Sea		missing	
25-06-43	Fw.	Niese, Alfred	KIA	9	Bf 109G-6	15419	yl 3	North Sea		missing	
25-06-43	Lt.	Kirschenlohr, Gerd	KIA	12/54	Bf 109G-6	15459	bl 9	Weser Estuary	1025	hit sea	n/a
26-06-43	Lt.	Schmidt, Gottfried	WIA	11	Bf 109G-3	16253		nr Dieppe		P-47	4 FG

Lt. Melchior Kestel was one of three 9th Staffel pilots who failed to return from a 25 June bomber interception over the North Sea in bad weather. *(Vanoverbeke)*

27 June

Poor weather again restricted flying activities. In late morning the Kenley and Hornchurch Wings flew a combined freelance sweep of Hardelot and St. Omer. The Geschwadergruppe scrambled from Vendeville at 1030 to investigate the intruders. The Hornchurch Wing, flying high cover, engaged 11th Staffel Messerschmitts, while W/C Johnson led the Kenley Wing in an attack on some Focke-Wulfs at 27,000 feet (8200 meters). The engagements were inconclusive; the Schlageter pilots made no claims and sustained no losses, although the RAF pilots claimed one Fw 190 and two Bf 109s.

28 June

The 8th Bomber Command again targeted the naval base at St. Nazaire. The JG 26 units at Vendeville and Vitry were scrambled, but soon landed, as the Allied formations were passing out of range. Part of the Second Gruppe landed on Poix to be nearer any subsequent activity, but a later mission located nothing. Jafü Brittany ordered III/JG 2 not to make contact until the Spitfire escort had turned back, and then unleashed them. Mayer's Gruppe claimed nine B-17s for the loss of one Focke-Wulf and pilot; eight of the 191 attacking B-17s were in fact lost, and another 57 were damaged.

29 June

Part of the American B-17 force, the 4th Bomb Wing, was dispatched to bomb targets around Le Mans. The defense was left to the two JG 2 Gruppen in Jafü 3. Jafü 2 scrambled only the JG 27 Staffel at Poix. Its JG 26 Staffeln spent the day on routine defensive patrols, which included some railroad patrols.

The 2nd Staffel transferred today from Rheine to Woensdrecht, where it joined II/JG 1 on the crowded field.

30 June

Again today the Geschwader was shut out of any action. In mid-afternoon a large Allied formation was plotted over the Channel, but it never approached the Continent, and Jafü 2 never scrambled its fighters in force, merely maintaining the routine coastal patrols.

Josef Priller was promoted to Oberstleutnant and immediately flew to Jafü 2 headquarters at St. Pol. During this period he was required to act as commander of the fighter control unit whenever Obst. Vieck was absent. The extreme shortage of talent in the upper ranks of the Luftwaffe forced him to occupy two full-time posts in July. He commuted between Lille and St. Pol almost daily during this period, and had to curtail his combat flying entirely.

Known personnel moves affecting the Geschwader in June include the departure of Oblt. Johann Aistleitner from the Third Gruppe, and Oblt. Wolfgang Neu from the 3rd Staffel, for instructor tours, Neu after only three weeks in the Geschwader; the return of Obfw. Erich Schwarz to the 9th Staffel, and Obfw. Willi Roth to the 4th Staffel, from instrument training; the transfer of Lt. Hans Heitmann directly to instructor duty after completing his own instrument training; the transfer of Uffz. Hermann Butzmann from the 4th Staffel to a ferrying unit; and the arrival of the following new pilots from flight training: Uffz. Kurt Kuhnert, Lt. Johannes Matthiesen, Uffz. Rudolf Oltmanns, Uffz. Horst Richter, Lt. Heinrich Sprinz, Uffz. Hans Thielmann - to the First Gruppe; Uffz. Walter Bürger, Uffz. Franz Gasser, Uffz. Martin Günther, Uffz. Harry Kubon - to the Second Gruppe; Lt. Josef Menze, Uffz. Horst Kirschner, Uffz. Kurt Schmidtke - to the Third Gruppe. Of these thirteen pilots, only one left the Geschwader alive. Harry Kubon transferred out in early 1944, and no information on his later career is available.

1 July

In mid-afternoon RAF Fighter Command mounted a large operation to harass the defenders of the Pas de Calais. Typhoons bombed the airfields at Lille and Abbeville while two multiple-Wing formations of Spitfires swept over the area. Some JG 2 Focke-Wulfs managed to avoid the Spitfires and shot down two No. 3 Sqd. Typhoons. The JG 26 fighters were much less successful. The Second Gruppe failed to make contact. All three Staffeln of the Geschwadergruppe did, without success. Pilots of the North Weald Wing spotted one 6th Staffel Schwarm while it was still in its climb near Ypres. Major Mehre, the Norwegian wing commander, led his flight in a dive on the Focke-Wulfs, which were flying very slowly, and one pilot was able to put a burst of fire into the cockpit of Uffz. Arnulf Bock's aircraft, which fell away in a vertical dive. Bock did not get out. Major Mehre overshot his own target, and claimed only to have damaged it, but Uffz. Paul Vohwinkel crashed to his death in the airplane.

At this time the Kenley and Hornchurch Wings were sweeping to the southwest, over Abbeville and St. Pol. The high-cover flight, from No. 403 Squadron, attacked a Schwarm of 11th Staffel Messerschmitts flying in line abreast, and downed three of them. Lt. Hans-Joachim Heinemeyer and Uffz. Albert Westhauser were killed; the third pilot was able to crash-land his badly-damaged airplane on Vendeville.

The three Thunderbolt groups continued their regimen of high-altitude coastal sweeps. Two 78th Fighter Group squadrons flying south of The Hague spotted German fighters below them. The Americans' full-power dives resulted in claims for 3-1-2 Fw 190s, but their CO, Col. Arman Peterson, disappeared without a trace. He was in fact shot down by a pilot of I/JG 1 who claimed two P-47s; this Gruppe lost one pilot. The loss of the popular Peterson, and before the end of July, his successor, so demoralized his pilots that their performance dropped noticeably. The 78th soon lost its position as the top-scoring American fighter group in the ETO, never to regain it.

JG 26 Casualties: 1 July 1943

Date	Rank	Name	Cas	Unit	Aircraft	WNr	Mkgs	Place	Time	Cause	Allied Unit
01-07-43	Uffz.	Bock, Arnulf	KIA	5	Fw 190A-5	7299	br 2	Hazebrouck		Spitfire	331 Sqd
01-07-43	Uffz.	Vohwinkel, Paul	KIA	6	Fw 190A-5	7307	br 3	NE of Hazebrouck		Spitfire	331 Sqd
01-07-43	Lt.	Heinemeyer, H-Joachim	KIA	11	Bf 109G-3	16254	rd 18	5km NE of Hesdin		Spitfire	403 Sqd
01-07-43	Uffz.	Westhauser, Albert	KIA	11	Bf 109G-3	16290	rd 14	8km NE of Hesdin		Spitfire	403 Sqd

2 July

The two Pas de Calais Gruppen were scrambled on reports of small enemy formations, as was the 2nd Staffel at Woensdrecht, but as no large formations followed, the fighters were quickly landed. The rest of the day was spent on routine defensive patrols.

3 July

Uffz. Schild flew an early-morning sea reconnaissance mission from Woensdrecht. He next took off at noon, to escort a captured B-17 on a tour of the JG 26 bases. The Pas de Calais units flew their routine patrols and test flights; on one of the latter, Uffz. Bruno Knobloch of the 11th Staffel crashed for undetermined reasons and was killed.

4 July

The 8th Bomber Command marked the anniversary of its first mission by sending 237 B-17s to bomb three widely-separated French targets: aircraft factories at Nantes and Le Mans and the U-boat base at La Pallice. Jafü 2 did not scramble its fighters until 1242, when the Nantes and Le Mans forces had already reached Laval. They were vectored to Le Havre to await the bombers' return, but they encountered "150 Spitfires" (quoting Addi Glunz's logbook) and were unable to reach the bombers. They kept patrolling, looking for an opening in the screen, but were unable to find one, and finally had to break off owing to low fuel. Some of the Vendeville fighters landed at Abbeville; this number included Obstlt. Priller, making the last flight recorded in his only surviving logbook. The Jafü 3 and Jafü Brittany controllers were also late in scrambling their aircraft, but they were closer to the B-17s' courses, and attacked in full force. The ever-enthusiastic Richthofen pilots claimed, and were credited with, twenty-one B-17s; actual B-17 losses were eight shot down and fifty-five damaged. JG 2 lost one pilot killed and two injured; twenty of its fighters were destroyed or damaged, most by the bombers while on the unescorted legs of their missions.

In the evening a dozen RAF Mitchells bombed Amiens, giving the JG 26 pilots another chance at the Spitfires. Jafü 2 scrambled a sizable force; aircraft of the Geschwadergruppe took off from Vendeville, Abbeville, and Poix. Second Gruppe Focke-Wulfs and II/JG 2 Messerschmitts nibbled at the swarm of Spitfires, and shot down four. One II/JG 2 pilot was shot down and killed; one Second Gruppe Focke-Wulf was slightly damaged.

JG 26 Victory Claims: 4 July 1943

Date	Rank	Name	Unit	Cl #	Aircraft	Place	Time	Opponent	Conf
04-07-43	Maj.	Galland W-F.	II CO	47	Spitfire	near Amiens	1737	122 Sqd	yes
04-07-43	Obfw.	Glunz	4		Spitfire	unknown	1745		no
04-07-43	Lt.	Radener	4		Spitfire	Berck-sur-Mer	1740		no
04-07-43	Oblt.	Leuschel	10 CO	5	Spitfire	near Berck-sur-Mer	1734	122 Sqd	yes

5 July

The new Third Gruppe Kommandeur, Hptm. Mietusch, reported in at Cuxhaven-Nordholz, as did some of the 7th Staffel pilots and ground staff. The interim Kommandeur, Hptm. Hermichen, returned to the 3rd Staffel at Rheine. The 7th Staffel pilots reclaimed their ground crews and quarters from 4/JG 54, whose pilots were packing to transfer to Königsberg. There they formed the cadre of a new Gruppe, IV/JG 54, which then went to the Eastern Front to serve as a third Gruppe for JG 54 – III/JG 54 would remain on the Western Front for the rest of the war. The 7th Staffel pilots were told to familiarize themselves with the new equipment of Third Gruppe, the Bf 109G-6, as quickly as possible; Obfw. Kemethmüller made seven flights today.

Oblt. Erwin Leykauf, Kapitän of the 12th Staffel, had had problems fitting in with JG 26 ever since his arrival in April, and asked his new Kommandeur, a friend from before the war, to help him return to the Green Heart Geschwader. The request was granted, and Leykauf left to form a new 11th Staffel in IV/JG 54. He was replaced by

Lt. Paul Fritsch (second from right) and several "black men" (mechanics, armorer, radioman) beside Fritsch's Fw 190A-4 "black 7" (W.Nr. 2436), in which he was killed by No. 303 Sqd. (Polish) Spitfires on 6 July. *(Crump)*

Hptm. Hermann Staiger, who transferred into JG 26 after a long tour as an instructor. Staiger was a Knight's Cross holder, having won the award in JG 51 in 1941.

6 July

The Allied fighters made several sweeps over the Continent. The three American P-47 groups paraded past Rotterdam, but attracted no attention from the experienced German controllers. The RAF controllers were able by this stage of the war to carefully position their fighters to give them the best shot at the enemy. The Northolt and Kenley Wings made two joint sweeps over Abbeville and Amiens, and both times attracted German fighters from Vitry and Poix – the latter included 3/JG 27 and at least part of II/JG 2. The morning flight was first attacked by a large number of Messerschmitts. The Kenley Wing drew first blood, downing two. The Poles of No. 303 Squadron shot down three more; on withdrawal they were attacked by Second Gruppe Fw 190s. A turning combat developed, in which the Poles had the advantage. Lt. Paul Fritsch was hit, and crashed into the Somme Estuary; a second 5th Staffel aircraft was damaged, but succeeded in belly-landing on Vitry. The 5th Staffel flew search missions in mid-afternoon, but did not find Fritsch.

An evening sweep of the same area by the same two RAF wings brought up the same defenders; the Germans were a little more cautious this time, and lost only one airplane, a Bf 109. The day's two sweeps cost the RAF nothing, while the losses of the Luftwaffe were not trivial. The Second Gruppe lost one Fw 190 destroyed with pilot, and one Fw 190 damaged. 3/JG 27 lost two Bf 109s destroyed and a third damaged; one pilot was killed and another injured. II/JG 2 lost four Bf 109s destroyed and one pilot injured. The two RAF wings claimed 2-0-1 Fw 190s and 5-0-1 Bf 109s. It has been noted previously that RAF Fighter Command's victory claims were shockingly overstated for the first half of the war. They were now approaching the accuracy of JG 26 claims.

7 July

Flying on this day and the next was restricted to coastal patrols and non-operational activities. Uffz. Kurt Friedrich of the 5th Staffel lost control of his Fw 190A-4 while on a training flight south of Arras, and crashed to his death.

JG 26 Casualties: 3 - 7 July 1943

Date	Rank	Name	Cas	Unit	Aircraft	WNr	Mkgs	Place	Time	Cause	Allied Unit
03-07-43	Uffz.	Knobloch, Bruno	KIFA	11	Bf 109G-3	16264	rd 3	nr Lille-Vendeville		crashed	non-op
06-07-43	Lt.	Fritsch, Paul	KIA	5	Fw 190A-4	2436	bk 7	8km W of Somme Est	2000	Spitfire	303 Sqd
07-07-43	Uffz.	Friedrich, Kurt	KIFA	5	Fw 190A-4	2393	bk 2	S Arras-Grévillers		crashed	non-op

8 July

III/JG 54 left Oldenburg and transferred to Schipol. The defense of northern Germany was left to JG 11, now at full three-Gruppe strength, and III/JG 26. Jafü Holland-Ruhr now had the three Gruppen of JG 1 plus I/JG 3, I/JG 26, and III/JG 54 available to defend the Ruhr, always a concern of the Luftwaffe High Command, although the 8th Air Force planners, well aware of its strong defenses, had to date left it almost entirely alone.

9 July

Wutz Galland, newly promoted to Major, led an early-morning patrol up from Vitry, and was vectored to a small formation of bombers and fighters in the Arras area. This was Ramrod 127, an attack on St. Omer by a dozen Mitchells. Galland led an attack on the escort, and claimed one Spitfire off Boulogne. Based on a witness's report of an airplane crash (which was recorded by the RAF Y-Service), Galland was credited with a victory. No Spitfire was in fact lost, but the battle honors were even. No. 316 Squadron claimed 1-1-1 Fw 190s in this fight, but no German fighter sustained reportable damage.

10 July

The 8th Bomber Command dispatched 286 B-17s to bomb targets in northern France. Bad weather prevented most from bombing, but thirty-one aircraft dropped on Caen, and thirty-six bombed Abbeville with fair results. The bomber commanders considered that the escort provided by eighteen Spitfire squadrons and eight P-47 squadrons was, for the most part, "excellent." Despite strong fighter opposition, only three B-17s were shot down. The Jafü 2 and Jafü 3 controllers waited until the bombers had crossed the French coast before scrambling their fighters, and attacks were thus limited to the bombers' return flights. The Second Gruppe reached the Somme Estuary in time to sight the bombers withdrawing from Abbeville, but they were already out of range, and the Jafü directed the Focke-Wulfs west, against the Caen force. Major Galland sighted the B-17s near Rouen and ordered his men into attack formation. Lt. Hoppe downed a 95th Bomb Group B-17 on his first pass, and attacks continued for ten more minutes before low fuel forced the Gruppe to break off. Pilots landed at Rouen, Octeville, and Poix, in addition to their Vitry base. The Geschwadergruppe also made contact in the Rouen area, but made no claims. No JG 26 aircraft sustained reportable damage. JG 2 lost one pilot killed and one injured, and 1-3 (one destroyed and three damaged) fighters, while claiming six B-17s and one Spitfire.

11 July

Bad weather once again limited flying. Obfw. Ellenrieder, up on a defensive patrol, was vectored to a pair of No. 198 Sqd. Typhoons on a low-level Rhubarb to Ghent, and shot one of them down.

JG 26 Victory Claims: 9 - 11 July 1943

Date	Rank	Name	Unit	Cl #	Aircraft	Place	Time	Opponent	Conf
09-07-43	Maj.	Galland W.-F.	II CO	48	Spitfire	near Boulogne	0816		yes

10-07-43	Lt.	Hoppe	4 CO	13	B-17	nr Fécamp- W of Rouen	0810	95 BG	i.O.
11-07-43	Obfw.	Ellenrieder	8	2	Typhoon	E of Ghent	1550	198 Sqd	i.O.

12 July

According to one source, Uffz. Emil Leitz of the 7th Staffel scored a confirmed victory today, over an undetermined aircraft type and under unknown circumstances. No other Third Gruppe flying activity is known.

13 July

Uffz. Leitz is said to have scored his second confirmed victory today, under unknown circumstances. Again, no other Third Gruppe flying activity is known.

14 July

The 2nd Staffel was joined at Woensdrecht by the rest of the First Gruppe. II/JG 1 left that Dutch base and replaced the rest of the First Gruppe at Rheine. The Ruhr was not yet receiving much attention from the Allied day bombers, and Rheine was an excellent permanent base on which to rest and refit.

Today's B-17 targets were Villacoublay, Le Bourget, and Amiens. Two hundred and one of the 279 bombers dispatched dropped their bombs. The raid on Villacoublay was an outstanding success; the hangars containing the Fw 190 repair facility of Luftflotte 3 were destroyed, along with seventy Fw 190s. Fifteen of these were assigned to JG 26; the rest were from every other Fw 190 unit in the area. Fighter, bomber, reconnaissance, headquarters, and training units were represented on the material loss list.

The Amiens raiding force was smaller and somewhat earlier than the others, and served to shield the main force from the Jafü 2 fighters. The Amiens bombers were escorted by all three American P-47 groups; the target was well within their range. Jafü 2 scrambled the Geschwadergruppe, the Second Gruppe, and the Poix fighters at 0730, as the Amiens force was crossing the French coast. The Poix fighters, Messerschmitts from 3/JG 27 and II/JG 2, were closest to the bombers' course, and had sighted them by 0739. The Poix formation leader delayed his attack until Major Galland arrived and radioed sarcastically, "What are you waiting for?" The P-47s had met the bombers at 0730, but the three German formations were allowed to attack the bombers for twenty minutes before the P-47s were able to divert them. Only one B-17 went down, apparently the victim of a 3/JG 27 Messerschmitt, but two more crash-landed in England, and an additional thirty-four were damaged. Two of the Bf 109s were shot down; one pilot was killed and the other injured.

The Poix fighters were ordered to land as soon as the P-47s put in their appearance, and the Geschwadergruppe was ordered to put down soon thereafter, also on Poix. According to Allied Intelligence, the fighters were refueled and rearmed in the record time of twelve minutes and took off again to intercept the withdrawing Villacoublay force, but there is no evidence for a second sortie in the surviving logbooks. If the mission did take place, it was unsuccessful.

In the meantime, some newly-arriving I/JG 2 Focke-Wulfs and II/JG 2 Messerschmitts battled with the 4th Fighter Group to the west of the Somme, near Le Tréport, while Galland and his men took on the 78th Fighter Group off Hesdin. In Galland's words, from his combat report,

> "After shooting down a Thunderbolt over the north bank of the Somme Estuary, I followed Lt. Kehl as he trailed a lone Fortress that he had shot from formation. As I banked toward a Schwarm of Thunderbolts that were preparing to attack Lt. Kehl, I was myself attacked from above and the side by three Thunderbolts and broke toward them, at which the lead aircraft flew off to the northwest. I then attacked the widely-spaced Kette and hit the lead aircraft from a distance of about 300 meters [325 yards]. We were then at an altitude of about 3500 meters [11,500 feet].

I noticed several hits by explosive shells. The Thunderbolt dived away trailing black smoke, and went into a steep dive about one thousand meters below."

Galland's first Thunderbolt did not crash immediately, but staggered back toward England, its badly-injured pilot, Lt. August DeGenero, holding the stick between his forearms. He couldn't crash-land because he couldn't buckle his harness, and so bailed out off the English coast, where he was quickly rescued. Galland's second victim was a member of the 8th Air Force staff who had previously served in the 78th Fighter Group as its executive officer. He, too, was able to get close to England before bailing out into the Channel, and was rescued. The only 78th Fighter Group fatality today was in the third P-47 to go down; ironically, it was hit by a B-17 gunner. The P-47 pilots managed but a single victory. Uffz. Harry Kubon of the 5th Staffel, a new replacement pilot, was shot down and bailed out into the Somme Estuary with slight injuries; he, too, was soon rescued.

15 July

The Allies did not put in an appearance over the Continent until mid-afternoon. The 8th Air Force did not fly, but No. 2 Group sent No. 107 Squadron's dozen Bostons to bomb the Poix airfield, accompanied by a full panoply of Typhoon fighter-bombers, escorting Spitfires, and supporting sweeps. Jafü 2 had its fighters up from Poix and Vitry well before the arrival of the bombers, which was something of a novelty. The Poix fighters first took on the low-flying Typhoons, shooting down one and badly damaging a second. The Messerschmitts also downed one Spitfire from the escort, probably from No. 332 Squadron, while losing one pilot killed and one injured. The Second Gruppe arrived minutes after the airfield was bombed, and waded into the bombers' close escort. This was No. 602 Squadron, which was still flying obsolete Spitfire Vs, and No. 485 Sqd. (RNZAF), in Spitfire IXs. Five Spitfires fell, as did Uffz. Heinrich Krieg's Fw 190, which blew up just as Krieg bailed out into the Channel. The path to the bombers was clear. Galland damaged one Boston, and claimed its destruction, but the bomber crash-landed in England. Galland then claimed a P-47, but the type was not even present. Given Galland's lack of recognition skills, this could have been anything, but was possibly a No. 181 Sqd. Typhoon that was late leaving the area. Neither of Galland's claims was confirmed.

W/C Johnson's Kenley Wing reached the Abbeville area on its sweep just as the battle ended. Johnson spotted a pair of Bf 109s and promptly shot one of them down. This was the day's last Luftwaffe combat loss on the Kanalfront, but not its last casualty. As a Second Gruppe Schwarm was landing on Ligescourt after an unsuccessful search for Uffz. Krieg, the engine of Uffz. Paul Schwarz's Fw 190A-5 failed, and he crashed to his death. Krieg's dinghy was sighted by a later search flight, and he was rescued by a ship before nightfall.

JG 26 Victory Claims: 14 - 15 July 1943

Date	Rank	Name	Unit	Cl #	Aircraft	Place	Time	Opponent	Conf
14-07-43	Maj.	Galland W-F.	II CO	50	P-47	10-15km W of Étaples	0805	78 FG	yes
14-07-43	Maj.	Galland W-F.	II CO	49	P-47	NW of Hesdin	0750	78 FG	unk
15-07-43	Maj.	Galland W-F.	II CO	51	Boston	Somme Estuary	1650	107 Sqd	unk
15-07-43	Maj.	Galland W-F.	II CO	52	P-47	10km NW of Somme Estuary	1655	181 Sqd Typhoon	unk
15-07-43	Lt.	Hoppe	4 CO	14	Spitfire	7-8km S of Berck-sur-Mer	1702	602 Sqd	yes
15-07-43	Lt.	Heinemann E.	4	1	Spitfire	5km E of Hesdin	1655	602 Sqd	yes
15-07-43	Uffz.	Gomann	5	6	Spitfire	5km W of Berck - Somme	1700	602 Sqd	yes
15-07-43	Lt.	Lange F.	5	3	Spitfire	Somme Estuary	1657	602 Sqd	yes
15-07-43	Lt.	Matoni	5	6	Spitfire	5km SW of Rue	1655	602 Sqd	yes

16 July

The only Geschwader fighters to contact the enemy were from the First Gruppe at Woensdrecht. A late-evening scramble found an Allied fighter formation near Zeebrugge, but any combats were inconclusive. A small force then took off at 2115 and flew a sea reconnaissance off the Dutch coast. Oblt. Kurt Kranefeld of the Gruppe Stab suffered engine failure while returning from this mission and injured himself in a dead-stick landing near Haarlem. Lt. Georg Kiefner, a new replacement pilot in the 3rd Staffel, flew on both of these missions and received credit for his first two combat sorties.

17 July

The 8th Bomber Command dispatched 332 B-17s in the morning to bomb targets in north Germany and Holland. Poor weather prevented the combat wings from forming up properly, and the mission was eventually recalled at 0955. Twenty-one bombers attacked Amsterdam with poor results, and another thirty-four bombed scattered German targets. The dispersed formations presented such a large number of targets to the Jafü Holland-Ruhr and Jafü German Bight controllers that they were unable to concentrate their fighters in any one area, and the opportunity to score heavily against unescorted bombers flying in poor formations was wasted. Only two bombers were shot down; another fifty-two were damaged.

The German disorganization is apparent in their inflated victory claims – the evening OKW communiqué gave the total as thirteen – and the high number of Luftwaffe losses to bomber fire, bad weather, and poor navigation over the North Sea; twenty fighters were damaged or destroyed. The First Gruppe was among the Amsterdam defenders, but was scrambled late, apparently never made a concerted attack, and filed only one claim, which was later withdrawn. Two First Gruppe aircraft crash-landed in the Dutch polders with combat damage. The Third Gruppe had better luck; it was scrambled in time to meet the incoming bombers over the North Sea, and the pilots made several attacks before breaking off to find their way back to Nordholz. Hptm. Staiger, Uffz. Holl, and Uffz. David filed claims; only that of Uffz. David was confirmed. Uffz. Alfred Schrickel of the 12th Staffel failed to return. Two Messerschmitts crash-landed on the German coast with engine damage; one pilot, Uffz. Alex Meyer, was injured.

JG 26 Victory Claims: 17 July 1943

Date	Rank	Name	Unit	Cl #	Aircraft	Place	Time	Opponent	Conf
17-07-43	Uffz.	Schild	2		B-17-HSS	unknown	1100		no
17-07-43	Uffz.	Holl	9		B-17	W of Helgoland (UO2)	0940	351 BG	unk
17-07-43	Hptm.	Staiger	12 CO	27	B-17F	German Bight(SP 1)	0928	351 BG	unk
17-07-43	Uffz.	David	12		B-17F	W of Helgoland (SO7)	0932	351 BG	yes

JG 26 Casualties: 14 - 17 July 1943

Date	Rank	Name	Cas	Unit	Aircraft	WNr	Mkgs	Place	Time	Cause	Allied Unit
14-07-43	Uffz.	Kubon, Harry	WIA	5	Fw 190A-4	7046	bk 4	Somme Est- E of Amiens		P-47	78 FG
15-07-43	Uffz.	Krieg, Heinrich	WIA	5	Fw 190A-4	789	bk 8	NW of Abbeville	1700	Spitfire	602 Sqd
15-07-43	Uffz.	Schwarz, Paul	KIFA	6	Fw 190A-5	7310	br 5	Ligescourt a/f	1800	engine	n/a
16-07-43	Oblt.	Kranefeld, Kurt	WIA	I St	Fw 190A-5	410261	gr 2	Zandvoort, 3km W of Haarlem		engine	n/a
17-07-43	Uffz.	Meyer, Alex	WIA	12	Bf 109G-6	15450		Weser Estuary		engine	n/a
17-07-43	Uffz.	Schrickel, Alfred	KIA	12	Bf 109G-4	19367	bl 2	North Sea		missing	

18 July

The only Allied aircraft to cross the Channel today were RAF fighters, who flew several sweeps of Abbeville and St. Pol. No JG 26 aircraft made contact. The Poix

An 8th Staffel Fw 190A-4, photographed in mid-1943. *(Wiegand via Mombeek)*

Messerschmitts were heavily engaged; II/JG 2 claimed three Spitfires, and lost one pilot; 3/JG 27 lost 1-1 aircraft, and sustained one injury. After its scramble from Vitry, part or all of the Second Gruppe landed on Ligescourt, near Abbeville, and it was decided to keep the Focke-Wulfs there for a while.

19 July
None of the widely dispersed JG 26 units came into contact with enemy aircraft. Several Third Gruppe pilots were given an opportunity to practice flying over the ocean by escorting a North Sea convoy; this was carried out without incident.

22 July
Obfw. Heitmann was at cockpit readiness on Vendeville with the 8th Staffel when the loudspeaker announced the approach of two low-flying enemy aircraft. He scrambled with his Rotte at 1330, chased a pair of No. 239 Sqd. Mustangs across the coast, and shot them into the Channel at 1337 and 1345.

Hptm. Horst Sternberg, the 5th Staffel Kapitän, was awarded the German Cross in Gold for nineteen aerial victories.

24 July
This was the first day of the 8th Air Force's "Blitz Week", its first sustained campaign. Its objective was to extend and weaken the German fighter defenses by flying seven bombing missions in seven consecutive days. Today's target was in Norway, which affected JG 26 not at all.

The First Gruppe was now flying morning and evening recon missions from Woensdrecht all the way to the English coast. This evening Uffz. Jan Schild's wingman, Uffz. Kurt Grossler, allowed the wingtip of his Fw 190A-5 to hit the water, and he crashed to his death off Ipswich. The Second Gruppe was scrambled four times from Ligescourt, but the St. Pol controller did not put them into contact with any of the RAF sweeps, and the Gruppe flew back to Vitry in the evening. Obfw. Ellenrieder of the 8th Staffel, flying from Vendeville, reached some Typhoons flying a Rhubarb, and claimed damage to one of them.

25 July

The night of 24-25 July brought the first truly destructive RAF night bombing raid of the war. The first use of Window, radar-reflecting metalized strips, rendered the German night fighters impotent, and an unprecedented concentration of bombs produced a firestorm in the heart of Hamburg. As partners in the Combined Bombing Offensive, it was the task of the 8th Air Force to spread the destruction by bombing the city on the following day. Cloud cover and intense smoke from the previous night's fires caused problems in target recognition, and only 100 B-17s bombed Hamburg or the surrounding area. The German Bight Jafü deduced the correct target very early. The Third Gruppe made its interception as the lead bombers approached the Elbe Estuary, and shot down three B-17s; three of its Bf 109G-6s force-landed with combat damage. JG 11 attacked the bombers continuously over Hamburg and back out to sea, and III/JG 1, flying from Leeuwarden in northern Holland, continued the attacks over the North Sea. Fifteen B-17s from the Hamburg force failed to return; another sixty-seven were damaged.

Another 118 bombers dropped on targets of opportunity around Kiel. This area was short of defenders, and only four B-17s were lost, although fifty-one were damaged, two of which crashed on landing. The German fighters claimed a total of twenty-three B-17s for the day, in close agreement with the true losses. This is a telling sign that today's fighter attacks were well-organized, and carried out by concentrated formations.

To divert the fighters of Jafü Holland-Ruhr, No. 2 Group sent a dozen Mitchells to bomb the Fokker factory in Amsterdam, and a dozen Bostons to attack nearby Schipol airfield, while newly-arrived American B-26 Marauders bombed the Ghent coke ovens. In the middle of all this activity, Typhoons bombed the airfield at Woensdrecht. The three P-47 groups swept along the Dutch coast at high altitude, and saw nothing. The RAF fighters of the close escort squadrons, mainly Spitfire V outfits from No. 10 and No. 12 Groups, saw plenty of action. The Jafü Holland-Ruhr controller sent II/JG 1 to northern Germany, and kept the rest of his fighters on the ground as long as possible, awaiting developments. I/JG 26 was finally sent up from Woensdrecht to deal with the Ghent attackers, while III/JG 54 took off from Schipol to defend its own airfield. The Green Heart pilots lost three Bf 109s, one pilot being killed and the other two injured, while claiming three Spitfires and two Typhoons. The RAF apparently lost 1-1 Spitfires from the Amsterdam escort. The First Gruppe waded into the close escort for the Ghent bombers and shot down four Spitfire Vs while damaging a fifth, without loss to themselves. Jafü 2 kept its fighters over its own territory. Some 8th Staffel fighters made contact with one of the RAF sweeps, and sighted some P-47s, but no serious combat resulted.

JG 26 Victory Claims: 22 - 25 July 1943

Date	Rank	Name	Unit	Cl #	Aircraft	Place	Time	Opponent	Conf
22-07-43	Obfw.	Heitmann	8	6	Mustang	15-20km N of Coxyde	1337	239 Sqd	yes
22-07-43	Obfw.	Heitmann	8	7	Mustang	25-30km N of Dunkirk	1345	239 Sqd	yes
25-07-43	Hptm.	Borris	I CO	27	Spitfire	N of Ghent (LH9-8)	1504	165 Sqd	yes
25-07-43	Hptm.	Borris	I CO	28	Spitfire	N of Ghent (LH2-1)	1509	165 Sqd	yes
25-07-43	Oblt.	Beese	1 CO	14	Spitfire	N of Ghent	1511	165 Sqd	yes
25-07-43	Fw.	Ahrens	3	5	Spitfire	nr Vlissingen (KG9) (in sea)(LH5)	1515	122 Sqd	yes
25-07-43	Hptm.	Mietusch	III CO	45	B-17F	10km N of Hamburg	1702		yes
25-07-43	Oblt.	Nels	III		B-17	10km SW of Stade	1632		yes
25-07-43	Hptm.	Staiger	12 CO	28	B-17F	N of Weser Estuary (BB 4-2)	1650		yes

26 July

Today's "Blitz Week" targets were two synthetic rubber factories in Hannover and the U-boat yards in Hamburg. Bad weather over the Continent forced most of the 303 B-

17s to bomb targets of opportunity. Unlike the 17th, the fighter controllers in northern Germany managed to coordinate their responses today, and twenty-one bombers were shot down; four more crashed before reaching base. The north German fighter units claimed thirty-three. The Third Gruppe again met the incoming bombers off the German coast, and claimed three, without loss. Two of the claims were never confirmed, but Oblt. Staiger did receive credit for his, the second in his noteworthy string of victories against the *dicke Autos* (fat cars, the Luftwaffe code word for heavy bombers).

Owing to the range limitations of the Allied Spitfires and Thunderbolts, bomber missions to northern Germany received no fighter escort at all. They were supported indirectly today, as usual, by raids and sweeps over the areas that were within Allied fighter range – northern France, Belgium, and The Netherlands. The three P-47 groups made two full-strength sweeps over an area that was bustling with aerial activity below them – and failed to make contact. Their formations were easily identified by the Jafü 2 and Jafü Holland-Ruhr controllers, who chose to ignore them, as they presented no threat. The Allied medium bombers, light bombers, and fighter-bombers – Marauders, Bostons, and Typhoons – attacked three of the best-known Jafü 2 fighter bases, at St. Omer, Wevelgem, and Abbeville, and provoked the desired reaction. The Second Gruppe skirmished with the sweeping Spitfire IXs, and, on a later mission, contacted some P-47s, but without result. The Geschwadergruppe was vectored to the Bostons and their close escort of No. 10 Group Spitfire Vs, and reached them just after they crossed the coast. Hptm. Johannes Naumann, the 6th Staffel Kapitän, had a clear path to the bombers. Hans Naumann recalls:

"It was a beautiful summer day on the Channel coast. The word came over the loudspeakers, 'Battle alarm! Light bombers with strong fighter protection approaching our coastal sector on a southeast course.' The Geschwaderstab and the Staffeln scrambled in the sequence we had so often practiced, and the *Gefechtsverband* (battle formation) climbed toward the reported enemy. Contact was made north of Lille at 6000 meters (20,000 feet). We climbed above the bombers, who were headed directly toward us in a tight formation of *Ketten* (threes), reached the altitude of the escorts, and reversed course. With our considerable height advantage, we attacked the bombers immediately, ignoring the escorts.

"Owing to my high speed I could not get a Boston of the rear Kette in my sights. I leapt over these and took the right bomber of the lead Kette under fire. I fired a single burst, which hit the fuselage and left engine. As I broke away, I saw the bomber drop from the formation. I then engaged some of the escort, until I was ordered away from them, at which time I was able to see my bomber dropping on one engine toward my own field. The Boston's trip ended with a clean belly-landing on Vendeville; it came to a halt almost exactly in front of my own dispersal.

"After my own landing, I first examined the bomber for damage and then saw the crew, who were surrounded by groundcrewmen. None of the four were injured – that is called luck! When it became clear that I was the victorious pilot, the gunner protested strenuously. He was firmly convinced that he had shot my machine down, but quieted somewhat after examining my absolutely clean 'Focke.'

"We continued our conversation in the Geschwader *Gefechtsstand* (command post), over a cognac. I learned that they had already finished their thirty-mission tour, but had agreed to come on one more mission after their squadron leader had softened them up with whisky. We shook hands before they were taken away for interrogation.

"I learned forty-seven years later that all of the crew survived their captivity. A British air war historian tracked down the pilot in New Zealand and put him in contact with me. The pilot, Jack Wilson, and his navigator MacDonald, a

Top: A 6th Staffel Fw 190A-6, photographed at Vitry-en-Artois on 26 July. The pilot exiting the cockpit is the Staffelkapitän, Hptm. Hans Naumann. *(Bundesarchiv-Bildarchiv).* Middle: A 6th Staffel Fw 190A-5 taxies from its camouflaged revetment at Vitry-en-Artois on 26 July. *(Bundesarchiv-Bildarchiv)* . Bottom: A 6th Staffel Fw 190A-6 in its revetment at Vitry-en-Artois on 26 July. *(Bundesarchiv-Bildarchiv)*

Scotsman, visited me in my home, and we exchanged our second handshake. Wilson had retired from the Royal New Zealand Air Force in 1975 as a Group Captain. I asked him a question that had bothered me since 1943 – why had he not tried to reach England on one engine? He answered that my attack had not only shot out the left engine, but had damaged the hydraulic controls to the right one, so that it could no longer be given full power."

The escorts finally caught up to Naumann's men, who shot down three Spitfires before the Luftwaffe controller ordered his men to land. The Geschwadergruppe sustained no damage, but did suffer two casualties. The excited, not to say foolhardy, Boston gunner had continued to fire wildly even as his bomber was landing. He injured Uffz. Hans-Günther Schöhl, an 8th Staffel pilot on the ground – and killed Karl Borris's dog.

JG 26 Victory Claims: 26 July 1943

Date	Rank	Name	Unit	Cl #	Aircraft	Place	Time	Opponent	Conf
26-07-43	Hptm.	Naumann	6 CO	18	Boston	Vendeville a/f	1116	88 Sqd	yes
26-07-43	Lt.	Radener	6		Spitfire	15km SE of Lille	1125	317 Sqd	no
26-07-43	Fw.	Vogt	6	13	Spitfire	Mouscron	1126	504 Sqd	yes
26-07-43	Oblt.	Dippel	8	16	Spitfire	3km E of Roubaix	1134	317 Sqd	yes
26-07-43	Uffz.	Schwarz E.	8	3	Spitfire	Lille-Nord a/f	1130	317 Sqd	yes
26-07-43	Uffz.	Holl	9		B-17	N of Leeuwarden (UL5)	1340		unk
26-07-43	Uffz.	Steinberg	9	2	B-17	W of Helgoland (UP 5-2)	1340		unk
26-07-43	Hptm.	Staiger	12 CO	29	B-17F	Weser Estuary (CS 9-2)	1154		yes

27 July

The weather forced an interruption of Blitz Week. No. 2 Group flew two Ramrods – twelve Venturas bombed the Zeebrugge coke ovens once again, while a dozen Mitchells bombed the Schipol airbase. III/JG 54 defended against the Schipol attack. The First Gruppe failed to contact it, and a 2nd Staffel Fw 190A-5 sustained heavy damage in a taxi accident on Deelen. The Jafü 2 fighters were scrambled during the day, probably against the Zeebrugge force, but missed it.

28 July

Although the weather remained bad, the 8th Bomber Command resumed its series of maximum-strength attacks on German targets. One hundred and eighty-two 1st Bomb Wing B-17s targeted Kassel, while 120 4th Bomb Wing B-17s headed toward Ochsersleben. Few bombers attacked the briefed targets; twenty-five were lost or written off after their return, and 118 were damaged. The day was notable in that two innovations were unveiled, one for each side. The Luftwaffe made its first effective use of aerial rockets; these were converted from 21 cm mortar shells and carried in underwing "stovepipe" launchers. JG 1 and JG 11 used them today, and two Staffeln of III/JG 26 would have them within the week. While wildly inaccurate, they could be fired from well outside the range of the bombers' defensive fire, and were intended to break up the bombers' tight formations, for which purpose a near miss was as good as a hit. The unwieldy launchers markedly reduced the performance of the fighters carrying them, but this was not a great concern to the Luftwaffe fighter commanders, because the Allied escort fighters had lacked the range to reach Germany – until today. The 4th Fighter Group attached droppable ferry tanks to their P-47s, and were able to pick up the B-17s at Emmerich, on the Dutch-German border. The 4th FG then had its best day yet, claiming nine victories for one loss. Its surprise appearance broke up a promising attack on the withdrawing bombers by the First Gruppe and JG 1. Fw. Ahrens of the 3rd Staffel shot one B-17 from its formation before the arrival of the escorts. His claim was not confirmed, but the 92nd Bomb Group B-17 did, in fact, crash near Breda. Uffz. Jan Schild claimed a second, but the claim was not filed. The bombers shot down two First Gruppe Focke-Wulfs. Lt. Otto Triebnig bailed out with slight injuries. The second pilot, Obfw. Waldemar "Vladimir" Söffing, elected to ride his aircraft down; it hit one of the many water-filled ditches around Dordrecht and overturned, breaking Söffing's neck. He survived, and resumed his combat career with the Gruppe in 1944. The Thunderbolts shot down Uffz. Herbert Kind, who bailed out suffering burns but soon returned to duty, and damaged a second, which force-landed on Deelen. Hptm. Hermichen shot down the 4th FG P-47, but his claim was not confirmed, although he had witnesses. Perhaps his saying that it was a "Typhoon" that he had shot down from 6000 meters (20,000 feet) raised suspicions in the RLM.

The Geschwadergruppe and the Second Gruppe were scrambled and eventually flew east to intercept the returning B-17s. They ran low on fuel, however, and did not attack. Part of the 8th Staffel encountered some Spitfires over the Scheldt. They lost one Focke-Wulf in a brief encounter, and then landed on Schipol. Some of the rest returned to their bases; others were ordered to land on Rheine, Deelen, and Venlo. Their comrades joined them in The Netherlands that evening. The Second Gruppe assembled at Deelen; the Geschwadergruppe, Venlo.

The Third Gruppe at Nordholz was not yet concerned about escorts reaching their zone of operations. They scrambled at 0838 and headed northwest to intercept the incoming bombers. Uffz. Emil Leitz crashed on takeoff and was killed. The rest made one attack at the limit of their range and claimed three B-17s. One 7th Staffel pilot destroyed his aircraft while landing on Nordholz; the cause was listed as pilot error.

JG 26 Victory Claims: 28 July 1943

Date	Rank	Name	Unit	Cl #	Aircraft	Place	Time	Opponent	Conf
28-07-43	Uffz.	Schild	2		B-17	NW of Hertogenbosch	1015		no
28-07-43	Uffz.	Schild	2		P-47	NW of Hertogenbosch	1015		no
28-07-43	Hptm.	Hermichen	3 CO	31	Typhoon	W of Rotterdam (IH1-HH7)	1217	4 FG P-47	unk
28-07-43	Fw.	Ahrens	3	6	B-17-HSS	nr Dordrecht (IL8-KL2)	1207	92 BG	unk
28-07-43	Obfw.	Kemethmüller	7	73	B-17F	N of Sylt (RP 5)	0916		yes
28-07-43	Fw.	Dörre	9	8	B-17F	NW of Helgoland (RO1-2)	0915		unk
28-07-43	Uffz.	Holl	9		B-17F	NW of Helgoland (SO5)	0920		yes

29 July

This morning's targets for the heavy bombers were Kiel and Warnemunde. Both were on the Baltic Sea, and the B-17s' flight paths took them well out of range of any JG 26 units except the Third Gruppe at Nordholz. The radar stations on the islands off the north German coast typically gave the Jafü German Bight a good hour's advance warning of raids to northern Germany, and the controllers generally tried to position the fighters for an interception near Helgoland Island, which was large enough to house a squadron of Bf 109s and thus had an airfield suitable for emergency landings. The Third Gruppe contacted the bombers at Helgoland and then pursued them all the way across the peninsula of Schleswig-Holstein to Kiel. The Gruppe shot down four B-17s before landing on the base at Schleswig. Three of its Messerschmitts sustained damage, and Lt. Dieter Völmle, the Gruppe adjutant, was injured. JG 11 claimed eight bombers; eight of its fighters were destroyed or damaged. The 8th Bomber Command lost nine B-17s destroyed or written off; seventy others were damaged.

Radio tests on the 8th Air Force heavy bomber bases in the early morning were an unerring precursor of a heavy bomber raid later that day, and were usually overheard by the German radio intercept service at Wissant. On such days Jafü 2, Jafü 3, and Jafü Holland-Ruhr would keep most of their fighters on the ground until the heavy bombers' routes had become clear. The medium bomber raids and fighter sweeps were a secondary priority, to be dealt with only if there was no hazard to the main task.

The 8th Air Service Command, which controlled the American medium bomber units at this time, used its rapidly-growing B-26 force to supplement No. 2 Group's thankless campaign of diversionary raids to low priority targets in northern France and the Low Countries. Today was typical. There were four medium bomber raids and several supporting sweeps by the Spitfires; only one raid and one sweep were intercepted. The Geschwadergruppe and the Second Gruppe had spent the night on bases in The Netherlands, awaiting another raid on the Ruhr, which did not come. They were scrambled against a medium bomber force that approached Schipol but turned back without bombing. No JG 26 aircraft made more than brief contact with the raiders. III/JG 54 tangled with the 56th Fighter Group escort and shot one P-47 down; one of its Bf 109s was damaged by the P-47s, and a second was hit by the gunner of a departing B-26.

The Geschwadergruppe was finally released to return to Vendeville, but its composition had changed. The 10th Staffel flew to Vendeville, while the 6th Staffel rejoined its parent unit, the Second Gruppe, on Deelen. The newly-formed 10th was the least successful of Priller's Fw 190 Staffeln, and it can be speculated that he wanted it under his personal supervision at Vendeville. It is possible that the timing implies that Obst. Vieck was now back on duty at St. Pol, and Priller intended to resume flying combat missions; Hptm. Naumann, the 6th Staffel Kapitän, would no longer be needed at Vendeville to lead the Geschwadergruppe.

The little-used 11th Staffel was scrambled alone from Vendeville to oppose the late-evening sweeps. Uffz. Walter Müller was shot down and killed by a No. 331 Sqd. Spitfire shortly after taking off; the Staffel reported no successes.

JG 26 Victory Claims: 29 July 1943

Date	Rank	Name	Unit	Cl #	Aircraft	Place	Time	Opponent	Conf
29-07-43	Obfw.	Kemethmüller	7	74	B-17	15km NE of Schleswig	0930	306 BG	yes
29-07-43	Oblt.	Schauder	9 CO	13	B-17	Schleswig (UQ4)	0925	306 BG	yes
29-07-43	Hptm.	Staiger	12 CO	30	B-17	Kiel (TQ)	0940	306 BG	yes
29-07-43	Hptm.	Staiger	12 CO	31	B-17	Kiel	0940	306 BG	unk

JG 26 Casualties: 24 - 29 July 1943

Date	Rank	Name	Cas	Unit	Aircraft	WNr	Mkgs	Place	Time	Cause	Allied Unit
24-07-43	Uffz.	Grossler, Kurt	KIFA 2		Fw 190A-5	410248	bk 6	N Sea E of Ipswich	2036	hit water	n/a
26-07-43	Uffz.	Schöhl, Horst-Günther	WIA 8		none			Vendeville	1130	Boston	88 Sqd
28-07-43	Obfw.	Söffing, Waldemar	WIA 1		Fw 190A-5	7375	wh 3	10km W of Dordrecht	1210	B-17	
28-07-43	Uffz.	Kind, Herbert	WIA 2		Fw 190A-5	410008	bk 11	Asperen-N of Herwijnen		B-17	
28-07-43	Lt.	Triebnig, Otto	WIA 3		Fw 190A-5	410237	yl 9	NE of Breda	1230	P-47	4 FG
28-07-43	Uffz.	Leitz, Emil	KIFA 7		Bf 109G-4	19349	wh 4	Nordholz-Ostfriesland a/f	0838	takeoff	n/a
29-07-43	Lt.	Völmle, Dieter	WIA	III St	Bf 109G-6	13153	< bl 2	20km NE of Kiel	0915	B-17	
29-07-43	Uffz.	Müller, Walter	KIA	11	Bf 109G-6	20307	rd 3	Calonne-sur-la-Lys		Spitfire	331 Sqd

30 July

The final mission of Blitz Week was an attack on Kassel by all 186 operational B-17s. All three P-47 groups had now been equipped with drop tanks, and the 8th Fighter Command had been ordered to abandon its high-altitude sweeps. The mission of the American fighters was now the close defense of the American bombers. The bombers' route took them through the heart of the Holland-Ruhr air defenses, and the bombers were ordered to fly in a single, long formation for mutual self-defense and to assist the escorts. This formation was a two-edged sword. The German controllers, who could count, located the entire strength of the 8th Bomber Command soon enough to concentrate fighters from four Jafü to intercept them. The German fighters flew an

The crash site of Uffz. Walter Müller's 11th Staffel Bf 109G-6 in the center of the village of Calonne-sur-la-Lys. Müller was shot down and killed on 29 July by a No. 331 Sqd. Spitfire, shortly after taking off from Lille-Vendeville. *(Leclercq)*

unprecedented 285 defensive sorties, including forty second sorties. Only the closest units of Jafü 2 and Jafü Holland-Ruhr were ordered to attack the bombers before they reached Kassel. To increase the total weight of their attack, the controllers concentrated the defending fighters along the bombers' return route. By accident or design, the three P-47 groups were all assigned to withdrawal escort. The result was the largest battle to date between American and German fighters. The Americans lost seventeen B-17s destroyed or written off, plus eighty-two damaged; seven P-47s were lost.

The American armada was still forming up over England when the 2nd and 3rd Staffeln were ordered to scramble from Woensdrecht at 0650. A medium bomber formation was already over the Dutch coast, and headed directly for their field. The Focke-Wulfs climbed to the east, into the rising sun. They were unable to prevent the bombing, which did little damage, but reached the bombers just as they made their turn off the target. Lt. Karl "Charlie" Willius led two Schwärme in an immediate attack, while the 3rd Staffel headed for the Spitfire escorts, which were several miles away. Willius dived below, and then pulled up beneath a straggling B-26 and put a burst of cannon shells into it. The bomber fell away in a spin and crashed into the Scheldt. The American gunners hit the leader of Willius's second Schwarm, Lt. Heinrich Sprinz, who escaped his burning aircraft but was unable to open his parachute, apparently because of his serious wounds. The seven remaining Focke-Wulfs then dived away on the approach of the Spitfires. They had attacked the 386th Bomb Group on the latter's first mission, and Willius was responsible for the first Marauder to be shot down from medium altitude in the ETO, although he called it a "Boston." The green bomber gunners received credit for 6-5 German fighters, more than were present, but downing even one was a creditable achievement in an engagement that lasted less than a minute.

The escorts had been occupied just long enough by the 3rd Staffel, whose Uffz. Münch shot down one No. 66 Sqd. Spitfire. Uffz. Werner Kaiser was shot down in this combat; he bailed out without difficulty, but was injured on landing.

The B-17 formation was now approaching the Belgian coast at Zeebrugge. The Geschwadergruppe scrambled from Lille at 0750 and headed north. The "Poix Gruppe" (II/JG 2 and 3/JG 27) was also scrambled, but they did not reach the bombers, and landed on Woensdrecht. In their absence, Jafü 2 requested Jafü 3 to order I/JG 2 to transfer from Évreux and Beaumont-le-Roger to Poix, for use against the returning bombers; this was done, and the Gruppe later made a successful interception.

The Geschwadergruppe (now the Stabsschwarm, 8th, 10th and 11th Staffeln) reached the bomber formation with too little altitude and turned to trail the bombers on their eastward course. They attacked near Antwerp, after the Spitfires turned back, and were joined by the First Gruppe from Woensdrecht. The Schlageter fighters claimed six B-17s before they were ordered to land at Antwerp and elsewhere for servicing; they eventually received credit for only one full victory, two separations from formation, and one final destruction, but Belgian researchers have confirmed three crash sites. Only one JG 26 aircraft was shot down at this time; Uffz. Gerd Wiegand of the 8th Staffel was hit by the bomber he shot down and bailed out with injuries.

The Second Gruppe was held on the ground at Deelen to be used against the returning bombers. It sortied at 0930 and attacked the bomber stream near Appeldoorn at about 1000. B-17s fell to the fire of Maj. Galland and Hptm. Naumann. The bombers brought down three Fw 190s of Naumann's 6th Staffel. Obfw. Wilhelm Mackenstedt crash-landed his aircraft and died in hospital of his injuries. Fw. Wilhelm Mayer made a successful crash-landing, suffering only slight injuries. Fw. Gerhard Vogt attempted to ram his target after he was hit; he then bailed out with serious injuries.

Fw. Peter Crump made an interception which resulted in one of his most memorable victories, although it was not confirmed. His high-speed approach from directly beneath the bomber was undetected, and he was thus unmolested by defensive fire as he pumped cannon shells into the B-17, which caught fire and crashed on the flatlands of the Rhine delta near Arnhem. The plane appeared to be unusually well armed, and Crump's inquiries resulted in his conclusion that he had downed a "flak cruiser" or YB-40, an experimental B-17 variant which was armed with extra guns and ammunition rather than bombs. Several YB-40s were flying with the 92nd Bomb Group during July, but none is known to have been lost on this mission.

The Third Gruppe was ordered up from Nordholz, and after a 400-kilometer (240-mile) approach flight had only enough fuel for a four-minute attack before searching for Dutch bases. They filed no claims.

The Geschwadergruppe was apparently sent up late on its second sortie, and became entangled with some Spitfires over the Scheldt Estuary. Fw. Wolfgang Polster claimed his first victory, a Spitfire, but it was not confirmed.

The late sortie of the First Gruppe was more successful. B-17s were claimed in the Nijmegen area by Hptm. Rolf Hermichen and Fw. Ernst Christof. The day's battles with the B-17s were brought to an end by the arrival of the American escort. The American fighters – 107 P-47s from all three operational groups, the 4th, 56th, and 78th – found the bombers under attack by "150-200 German fighters", many of which turned their attention to the Thunderbolts after evading the Americans' initial attack. Lt. Waldemar "Waldi" Radener of the 6th Staffel downed two P-47s over Arnhem, while Hptm. Hermichen of the 3rd Staffel was credited with flaming another over Dordrecht. The 1st Staffel's Fw. Christof was bounced by a 4th FG P-47 and jumped out of his aircraft. He hung up on the tail, and when he broke free, it was without his parachute. His was the only JG 26 aircraft shot down by the P-47s, which nevertheless emerged the clear victors after their heaviest combat to date. For seven losses, the

Fw. Ernst Christof, a successful 1st Staffel pilot. Christof was shot down and killed by a 4th Fighter Group P-47 on 30 July, shortly after downing his ninth victim, a B-17. *(Vanoverbeke)*

Thunderbolt units claimed 24-1-8 German fighters; these were from JG 1, JG 2, and JG 11. The most serious American loss was sustained by the 78th FG, which lost its new commander on his first mission.

The Luftwaffe air defense commanders had to be bitterly disappointed at the day's results. The OKW communiqué claimed the destruction of thirty B-17s, but the true number was known to be much lower. The defending fighters had been brought together in greater numbers than ever before. Command and control procedures had worked perfectly, and everything was in order for a smashing victory – which did not occur, owing to the untimely arrival of the Thunderbolts, which fought more aggressively than ever before. The future suddenly looked less promising.

The American fighter pilots were learning to take advantage of the strengths of their seven-ton war machines. The P-47C's dive performance was better than that of any other fighter then in service, and its zoom climb from a dive was excellent. Its rate of climb from low altitude was poor, however, barely half that of a Bf 109. Above 15,000 feet (4500 meters) the P-47C was faster than either the Fw 190A-4 or the Bf 109G-4. By 30,000 feet (9000 meters) this advantage had increased to 20-30 mph (32-48 km/h). At this altitude the P-47 was better than the Fw 190A in all combat parameters, and superior to the Bf 109G in everything but rate of climb and acceleration. At altitude the P-47 could turn with either German fighter, as long as speeds were kept above 200 mph (320 km/h). Unfortunately for the Americans, few combats took place at 30,000 feet; it was rare that the Germans had a good reason to be there. The dive-and-recover became the favorite combat maneuver for the P-47 pilots. The key to survival in the combat zone was speed. While over enemy territory, P-47 formations would typically cruise at 300-325 mph (480-520 km/h). Skillful pilots developed maneuvers to help them gain an advantage if caught in an unfavorable situation. Robert Johnson of the 56th Fighter Group found that when being chased, a barrel roll in the direction opposite to the enemy's turn would force the German pilot to overrun the Thunderbolt, which on completion of its roll would be behind the opponent.

JG 26 Victory Claims: 30 July 1943

Date	Rank	Name	Unit	Cl #	Aircraft	Place	Time	Opponent	Conf
30-07-43	Lt.	Göhringer	I St		B-17-HSS	S of Antwerp (MK3)	0825		yes
30-07-43	Fw.	Christof	1	9	B-17-eV	E of Ghent (MI5-7)	0835	388 BG	yes
30-07-43	Fw.	Willius	2	34	Boston	NW of Antwerp (LI1)	0705	386 BG	yes
								B-26	
30-07-43	Hptm.	Hermichen	3 CO	32	B-17	near Nijmegen (IM3)	1012	379 BG	yes
30-07-43	Hptm.	Hermichen	3 CO	33	P-47	near Dordrecht (IL2-3)	1015	4 FG	unk
30-07-43	Lt.	Kiefner	3		Boston-eV	unknown	0715		no
30-07-43	Uffz.	Münch	3	3	Spitfire	N of Vlissingen (KH7)	0715	66 Sqd	yes
30-07-43	Maj.	Galland W-F.	II CO	53	B-17	near Appeldoorn	1005	381 BG	yes
30-07-43	Fw.	Crump	5		YB-40	near Arnhem	1030		no
30-07-43	Hptm.	Naumann	6 CO	19	B-17	5km SE of Est	1025	91 BG	yes
30-07-43	Uffz.	Gomann	6		B-17-HSS	unknown	1015		no

30-07-43	Lt.	Radener	6	4	P-47	near Arnhem	1020	78 FG	yes
30-07-43	Lt.	Radener	6	5	P-47	3km S Werkendam (NL)	1028	56 FG	yes
30-07-43	Hptm.	Ebersberger	8 CO	28	B-17	Liège	0828		yes
30-07-43	Obfw.	Heitmann	8		B-17-HSS	SE Antwerp	0820		unk
30-07-43	Uffz.	Wiegand	8		B-17	W of Eupen (BE)	0820	379 BG	no
30-07-43	Flg.	Sander	10	1	B-17-HSS	St. Trond (BE)	0930	96 BG	unk
30-07-43	Fw.	Polster	11		Spitfire	Scheldt Estuary	1030		no

31 July

The 8th Bomber Command stood down for twelve days after Blitz Week. The 8th Air Service Command attempted to keep up the pressure by sending its B-26s across the Channel. One of today's four medium bomber missions was intercepted by the Geschwadergruppe. Hptm. Ebersberger shot down an escorting Spitfire of No. 165 Squadron, and one 10th Staffel Focke-Wulf had to force-land on Vendeville with combat damage. Fighter-bombers, probably Typhoons, bombed Vendeville during the day, damaging an 11th Staffel Bf 109G-6 and an 8th Staffel Fw 190A-6.

The Third Gruppe at Nordholz suffered a serious loss on a non-operational flight. The 7th Staffel Kapitän, Hptm. Günther Kelch, took off late in the evening to practice firing 21 cm rockets. One exploded in its tube when fired, setting Kelch's wing ablaze; he was unable to escape his aircraft. Sabotage was suspected, but the subsequent investigation found nothing.

Geschwader personnel moves in July included the transfer of Lt. Todt from the 7th Staffel to the Third Gruppe Stab, where he resumed his position as Hptm. Mietusch's wingman; the transfer of Oblt. Kranefeld from the 8th Staffel to the First Gruppe, where he rejoined Hptm. Borris as his adjutant; the return of Lt. Gottfried Dietze, Fw. Hans Dirksen, Obfw. Leopold Eichinger, and Obfw. Alfred Heckmann from instructor duty; the departure of Obfw. Josef Zirngibl for an instructor tour; the transfer of Uffz. Karl Weiss from the 8th Staffel to a reconnaissance Gruppe; the transfer of Uffz. Wolf-Dieter Glahn from the 10th Staffel to the new IV/JG 54, and the transfer of Oblt. Hans Dippel from the 2nd Staffel to the 8th, and shortly thereafter to the 7th, to replace Hptm. Kelch as Staffelführer.

Hptm. Günther Kelch, Klaus Mietusch's successor as 7th Staffel Kapitän, was killed on a 31 July practice mission when a 21 cm rocket exploded in its tube, setting Kelch's wing on fire. *(Vanoverbeke)*

JG 26 and neighboring JG 2 were the first beneficiaries of Gen. Galland's plan to increase the strength of all of the Jagdgeschwader. The establishment strength of the Gruppen had been increased from forty pilots to sixty-eight, by raising the number of Staffeln from three to four and the number of pilots in each Staffel from twelve to sixteen. After adding in the four planes of the Geschwader Stabsschwarm, the total Geschwader establishment was 208 aircraft. The true strength approached this level during mid-1943, but then began dropping. On a typical day in late 1943, each Gruppe had in reality only forty-five airplanes, and of these only thirty were operational. By the end of 1943, Gruppe formations rarely contained more than thirty air-craft, and frequently had only twenty.

To fill partially the new openings, a large draft of new pilots reported to the Geschwader during the month. Those pilots known to have arrived from training, and their assignments, were: Uffz. Hans-Georg Becker, Uffz. Johann Gulecke, Lt. Hans Hartigs, Lt. Georg Kiefner, Uffz. Herbert Kind, Uffz. Helmut Pittmann, Gefr. Hans Sandoz, Uffz. Philipp Schmelzer - First Gruppe; Uffz. Walter Berger, Uffz. Rudolf Georgi, Ofhr. Gert Heck, Uffz. Werner Hoffmann, Uffz. Johannes Höhme, Uffz. Adolf Jörg, Lt. Peter Kipping, Uffz. Gerhard Maletz, Fw. Hans Pittmann, Uffz. Johann Scheu, Uffz. Franz Schilling, Uffz. Erwin Scholz, Fw. Rudolf Weyrich, Lt. Hans Wölfert - Second Gruppe; Uffz. Günther Broda, Uffz. Heinrich Hering, Oblt. Hans Meyer, Obfw. Klaus Reinhardt, Fhr. Burghardt Wölke, Uffz. Erich Zandanell - Third Gruppe.

JG 26 Casualties: 30 - 31 July 1943

Date	Rank	Name	Cas	Unit	Aircraft	WNr	Mkgs	Place	Time	Cause	Allied Unit
30-07-43	Fw.	Christof, Ernst	KIA	1	Fw 190A-4	5616	wh 9	W Burgh-Haamstede	0835	P-47	4 FG
30-07-43	Uffz.	Falkner, Gerhard	WIA	4	Fw 190A-5	410257	wh 10	16km N of Almelo		no fuel	n/a
30-07-43	Uffz.	Kaiser, Werner	WIA	3	Fw 190A-5	5895	yl 9	25km S of Breda	0706	B-26	
30-07-43	Obfw.	Mackenstedt, Wilhelm	KIA	6	Fw 190A-5	7311	br 6	Doerinchem		B-17	
30-07-43	Fw.	Mayer, Wilhelm	WIA	6	Fw 190A-5	7222	br 4	Netterden		B-17	
30-07-43	Lt.	Sprinz, Heinrich	KIA	2	Fw 190A-4	5578	bk 6	1km W of Woensdrecht	0710	B-26	386 BG
30-07-43	Fw.	Vogt, Gerhard	WIA	6	Fw 190A-5	410006	br 13	NE of Duisburg		B-17	
30-07-43	Uffz.	Wiegand, Gerd	WIA	8	Fw 190A-5	410252		nr Tongeren	0835	B-17	
31-07-43	Hptm.	Kelch, Günther	KIFA	7 CO	Bf 109G-4	19358	wh 15	Neuwerk-Knechtsiel	2140	crashed	non-op

6 August

The Geschwader took advantage of the inactivity on the other side of the Channel to get some rest. Sea reconnaissance and convoy escorts still had to be flown, but the standing patrols were cut back. Large enemy incursions could be detected sufficiently early by radar and radio intercepts that the Gruppen could be scrambled in time to intercept them, and the use of patrols to chase Rhubarbs and small enemy reconnaissance flights was now considered an uneconomical waste of resources. Medium bomber raids fell in between these categories, but the Jafü generally chose to ignore them; the staffs of the Pas de Calais airfields had learned to deal with the damage they caused. Looking to the future, and the resumption of attacks on Germany, the Second Gruppe, which had been flying from Deelen, began a permanent base transfer from Vitry to Volkel. With the exception of Obstlt. Priller and his Geschwadergruppe at Vendeville, which were still in Luftflotte 3, all of JG 26 was now part of the German defense organization Luftwaffen Befehlshaber Mitte, subordinated either to Jafü Holland-Ruhr or the Jafü German Bight.

9 August

3/JG 27 had left Poix and joined I/JG 27 in Germany. The air defense of the Pas de Calais was now left to the Geschwadergruppe at Vendeville and II/JG 2 at Poix. Both units were scrambled several times against the B-26 Ramrods, which were growing in number and size, and lost battles with the Spitfires. II/JG 2 lost 4-2 Bf 109Gs near their St. Pol base; the New Zealanders of No. 485 Squadron claimed 6-0-1. After one Ramrod, part of the 8th Staffel followed No. 331 Squadron out to sea, but the Norwegians turned into the attack, and in the resulting dogfight Uffz. Hans-Joachim Stoller was killed. No Spitfires were lost, or claimed, this day.

12 August

The 8th Bomber Command returned to the offensive with an early-morning attack on the Ruhr. The weather interfered with the mission, and most of the 330 B-17s bombed targets of opportunity, or none at all. The Luftwaffe modified the plan they had attempted on 30 July by concentrating their fighters farther inland, out of reach of the P-47s, and directing them toward the northernmost of the two bomb wings. The result was the most successful interception to date. Of the 133 1st Bomb Wing B-17s that did not turn back early, twenty-five were shot down or were written off, and 103 were damaged. The vulnerability of these bombers was enhanced by a strange return course, due south from Geilenkirchen all the way to Koblenz, which gave the German fighters an additional fifteen minutes to attack before the P-47s arrived. The 4th Bomb Wing, shielded from attack by the First, lost only three bombers.

The JG 26 units nearest the coast, the Geschwadergruppe at Vendeville and the First Gruppe at Woensdrecht, were scrambled early and sent northeast. They contacted the bombers near Arnhem. They were under orders to avoid the fighters and attempt to split up the bomber formations to assist their comrades farther inland. The Geschwadergruppe attack was broken up by the 56th Fighter Group, which shot down and killed Lt. Hans-Joachim Wermbter of the 8th Staffel for the Thunderbolt unit's only success of the day. The American pilot was, however, given credit only for damaging the fighter. The First Gruppe made a concentrated attack on the bombers, and was credited with downing four, while sustaining damage to two Focke-Wulfs. Uffz. Jan Schild of the 2nd Staffel claimed the separation of a bomber from its formation near Essen, and was awarded the victory; it was Schild's first confirmed victory in 115 combat sorties. Uffz. Heinrich Heuser claimed the final destruction of a bomber, which normally would not have resulted in a victory credit – but he was awarded a full victory, nonetheless. Such were the vagaries of the Luftwaffe victory confirmation system. Some of the German pilots returned to Vendeville and Woensdrecht, but most had to put down on strange bases, only some of which were equipped to service them. Those pilots who could do so, prepared for a second sortie.

The Second Gruppe took off from Volkel at 0830 in full force and headed east. They met the bombers while the latter were on the southbound leg of their course, and had thirty uninterrupted minutes in which to make their attacks. Galland's men claimed the destruction of four, the separation of one, and the final destruction of one B-17, and received credit for three victories and the separation. One 4th Staffel Focke-Wulf was damaged so severely by bomber fire that it had to be written off.

Borris's and Priller's men were ordered up on second sorties to attack the scattered bombers as they returned over Antwerp and the southern Netherlands. They complied, in small numbers which were not noticed by the P-47s. Uffz. Philipp Schmelzer was injured by bomber fire near Antwerp. Lt. Kiefner shot down a Fortress north of Ghent for his first victory claim. It was not credited to Kiefner, although the crash site is known. Fw. Scheyda pursued his B-17 out to sea from Walcheren and claimed its destruction, but his claim was not confirmed. The Bf 109s of the 11th Staffel were attacked over the Scheldt by W/C Johnson's Canadians – formerly the Kenley Wing, they were now called "No. 127 Airfield" – but sustained no damage.

13 August

The Third Gruppe transferred today from Nordholz to Amsterdam-Schipol, where it displaced III/JG 54; the Green Heart unit left for a rest at Schwerin, on the Baltic Sea. All of the Geschwader except its administrative headquarters, the Kommodore, and his Geschwadergruppe were now concentrated in The Netherlands. One 7th Staffel pilot didn't make the transfer flight, however; the engine of Uffz. Heinrich Hering's Bf 109G-4 caught fire shortly after takeoff, and Hering bailed out with injuries just before the fighter exploded. The new arrivals at Schipol were immediately sent back up on area familiarization and sea recon flights, which were uneventful.

15 August

The 8th Air Force and the RAF began Operation Starkey, an extended tactical exercise intended to convince the Wehrmacht that an invasion of the Pas de Calais was imminent. The 8th Bomber Command tried its luck with tactical targets, bombing fighter airfields that had proven immune to the medium bombers' attacks. The fields at Amiens-Glisy, Merville, Poix, Vendeville, Vitry, and Vlissingen were all targeted; results were mixed. Four groundcrewmen were injured on Vendeville, and two Geschwaderstab aircraft were damaged. Three II/JG 2s were destroyed on Vitry, at what was probably a new base for that Gruppe.

The day's targets were all within Spitfire range, and the RAF provided effective escort. The P-47s returned to their old pastime, flying sweeps along the coast at high altitude. The American pilots reported no encounters with the Luftwaffe. The First Gruppe intercepted the Vlissingen raiders off Walcheren, and claimed one Spitfire and one Thunderbolt, while losing Ogfr. Horst Gauss to a Thunderbolt. No P-47s were present, and this combat was in fact with No. 453 Sqd. (RAAF), which claimed one Fw 190 for the loss of 1-1 Spitfires. In the day's only other contact by the Geschwader the 8th and 11th Staffeln battled the Vendeville raiders south of Lille. Uffz. Erich Zandanell of the 8th Staffel was hit by a fighter and bailed out with injuries. The victor was reported to be a Thunderbolt, but it was almost certainly a No. 332 Sqd. Spitfire.

JG 26 Victory Claims: 31 July - 15 August 1943

Date	Rank	Name	Unit	Cl #	Aircraft	Place	Time	Opponent	Conf
31-07-43	Hptm.	Ebersberger	8 CO	29	Spitfire	Gravelines	1130	165 Sqd	yes
12-08-43	Uffz.	Heuser Hein.	2	3	B-17	E of Arnhem (HO3)	0900	92 BG	yes
12-08-43	Gefr.	Sandoz	2	1	B-17	Essen (KP2)			yes
12-08-43	Uffz.	Schild	2	1	B-17	Essen (KO8)	0900		yes
12-08-43	Hptm.	Hermichen	3 CO	34	B-17	Mönchen-Gladbach (KN3-6)			yes
12-08-43	Lt.	Kiefner	3	1	B-17	N of Ghent (LH5-6)	1030	92 BG	no
12-08-43	Fw.	Scheyda	3	13	B-17	N Sea - Walcheren (IH7)		91 BG	unk
12-08-43	Maj.	Galland W-F.	II CO	54	B-17	near Siegburg	0908		unk
12-08-43	Lt.	Hoppe	4 CO	15	B-17	S of Eindhoven	0930		unk
12-08-43	Obfw.	Glunz	4	38	B-17	near Hagen	0905		yes
12-08-43	Obfw.	Glunz	4	39	B-17	W of Mönchen-Gladbach	0928		yes
12-08-43	Obfw.	Roth	4	19	B-17	near Köln-Ostheim	0910		yes
12-08-43	Hptm.	Naumann	6 CO	20	B-17-HSS	near Hagen	0900		yes
15-08-43	Oblt.	Beese	1 CO	15	P-47	Vlissingen - N Sea (KG9)	1157	453 Sqd Spitfire	yes
15-08-43	Hptm.	Hermichen	3 CO	35	Spitfire	Vlissingen - N Sea (KG7)	1158	453 Sqd	yes

JG 26 Casualties: 9 - 15 August 1943

Date	Rank	Name	Cas	Unit	Aircraft	WNr	Mkgs	Place	Time	Cause	Allied Unit
09-08-43	Uffz.	Stoller, Hans-Joachim	KIA	8	Fw 190A-4	5613	bk 11	7km NE of Calais	1930	Spitfire	331 Sqd
12-08-43	Uffz.	Schmelzer, Philipp	WIA	1	Fw 190A-5	7367	bk 1	SE of Antwerp		B-17	
12-08-43	Lt.	Wermbter, Hans-Joachim	KIA	8	Fw 190A-5	1329	bk 2	27km NNE of Hasselt	0845	P-47	56 FG
13-08-43	Uffz.	Hering, Heinrich	WIA	9	Bf 109G-4	19213	wh 14	Nordholz	0638	engine	non-op
14-08-43	Fw.	Otto, Gottfried	WIA	9	Bf 109G-4	19790		Schipol		engine	non-op
15-08-43	Ogfr.	Gauss, Horst	KIA	1	Fw 190A-5	5977	wh 4	10km W of Vlissingen	1210	Spitfire	453 Sqd
15-08-43	Uffz.	Zandanell, Erich	WIA	8	Fw 190A-4	792	bk 4	16km SW of Lille		Spitfire	332 Sqd

16 August

The previous day's bomb damage rendered Lille-Vendeville non-operational, and the Geschwadergruppe dispersed to other airfields; the 11th Staffel went to the small field known as Lille-Nord. The 12th Staffel left Schipol for Moorsele; its twelve Bf 109s were accompanied on the flight by Obstlt. Priller in his Fw 190. The Staffel would remain on Moorsele, separated from the rest of the Third Gruppe, for more than a month. The reason is unknown; it continued to fly most of its missions with the Gruppe, and rendezvous must have been difficult. The Second Gruppe began leaving

The Netherlands for France. The 6th Staffel transferred today; its new field was Tillé, a satellite of the large Luftwaffe base at Beauvais. Obfw. Xaver Ellenrieder transferred from the 8th Staffel to Biarritz for instructor duty with Jagdgruppe West. He had been removed from combat because his two brothers were missing in Russia, but he returned to JG 26 in January, 1944.

The B-17s tested the defenses of Jafü 3 with a raid on Paris-Le Bourget Airport, preceded by a smaller one on Abbeville and Poix. The latter raid was intercepted by the 11th Staffel and II/JG 2. The 11th Staffel reported no successes; the JG 2 victories cannot be separated from those obtained later in the day.

The Le Bourget force was accompanied all the way to the target by 4th Fighter Group P-47s equipped with pressurized belly tanks. All three JG 2 Gruppen intercepted, but the support by the 4th was extremely effective, and only four B-17s went down. The American fighter pilots claimed 18-1-8 German fighters for the loss of three P-47s. Fourteen JG 2 pilots were killed or injured; the Richthofen fighters claimed sixteen victories during the day, all of which were confirmed.

17 August

At the top of the 8th Air Force target list was the ball bearing industry, much of which was concentrated in the central German city of Schweinfurt. Regensburg, the principal production site for Messerschmitt fighters, was of only slightly lower priority; the Bavarian factory was even farther away from England than was Schweinfurt. Plans were drawn up to bomb both targets on a single day. In the final version, the smaller, newer 4th Bomb Wing would take off first and head to Regensburg on the most direct route, escorted as far as the German border by most of the available P-47s. After bombing, it would continue south over the Alps and land in North Africa. The larger, more experienced 1st Bomb Wing would follow fifteen minutes later, bomb Schweinfurt, and return to England; these B-17s would be seen home by the entire escort force, flying its second sortie. It was expected that the novelty and complexity of the combined mission would confuse the German controllers and exhaust their pilots. The greatest flaw in the plan, apart from its dependence on perfect weather and exact timing, arose from the limited range of the bombers of the 1st Bomb Wing, which forced them to take the most direct route to the target and return; unfortunately, this was a near-duplicate of the route to Regensburg as far as Schweinfurt. The German controllers would have to deal with three bomber formations flying on the same route on the same day. This hardly stretched their capabilities. Plans to concentrate the defending fighters along any deep-penetration course had been drawn up in the previous months. German pilots were now given briefings and maps describing the airfields to seek out at the end of long one-way combat flights, and these airfields had been equipped to service them. This would facilitate second sorties by fighters arriving in the battle zone from the most distant bases.

The English weather turned what was already a questionable mission into a disaster. The weather over western Europe was perfect this morning – except over the B-17 bases, which were fogged in. Plans were hastily changed. The 4th Bomb Wing needed daylight to land on unfamiliar fields in North Africa, and could thus only wait an hour, but would take off then. The 1st Bomb Wing would then wait three and one-half hours for the Regensburg escorts to return, refuel and rearm. Unfortunately, the fighter commanders were not asked to comment on the revised plan, which gave them an hour less than they required for the turnaround. The fighter protection was thus badly diluted. Only two of the four P-47 groups managed to fly two missions, the 56th and the new 353rd, the latter on its fourth day in combat. The German defenders, in contrast, would have no difficulty flying two missions.

The pre-dawn radio testing at the B-17 bases gave the German fighter controllers ample warning of a full-strength deep-penetration raid. Oberst Walter Grabmann, the Jafü Holland-Ruhr and a prewar JG 26 Gruppenkommandeur, scrambled the First Gruppe from Woensdrecht at 1048, just as the Regensburg force had finished crossing the English coast. It has been reported elsewhere that II/JG 1, also at Woensdrecht, took off at this time, but an examination of the war diary of that Gruppe shows that this was not the case; the scramble of Borris's men was simply a routine preliminary move. Within five minutes it was apparent that the B-17s were headed directly for the Dutch coast, and the Third Gruppe was ordered up from Schipol, but II/JG 1 was kept on the ground while the B-17s passed directly overhead. Borris began climbing to the east to gain a good attack position; Mietusch's men would already have the morning sun at their backs when they reached the bomber formation from Schipol.

The oncoming group consisted of 146 B-17s in a long formation of three small combat wings, with a small escort comprising two 353rd Fighter Group squadrons. The First Gruppe was waiting upsun and slightly above the bombers as they approached, in perfect position for an immediate head-on bounce. The skimpy fighter escort was apparently concentrated around the first combat wing; no P-47 pilot saw the Focke-Wulfs as they swept around in a left turn and hurtled toward the second combat wing. After flying through it, they hit the trailing wing and then broke away in all directions. Borris's own target, the last aircraft in the middle formation, burst into flames, sheered from the formation, and dived to earth – the first loss of the day for either side. Several B-17s in the rear combat wing began to smoke from damaged engines. The Focke-Wulf of Uffz. Hans Becker was slightly damaged, and Becker himself was hit, and he dropped away to make a forced landing on Venlo. No other German fighter was seriously damaged during this attack. Borris did not attempt to re-form his Gruppe for a second pass, but was content to let his pilots search for stragglers while awaiting landing orders from the Jafü.

Next to attack was the Third Gruppe. Upon its arrival it bored in on the rear of the bomber stream, which was totally unprotected by fighters. The Messerschmitts formed up, turned, and attacked the rear wing head-on. Only one bomber, the target of Obfw. Heinz Kemethmüller, was forced from the formation by this initial attack, but the German pilots came back in repeatedly over the next fifteen minutes. Unlike the cautious Borris, Hptm. Mietusch was a wild man in the air; he paid no apparent heed to his own personal safety or that of his pilots, who were under his orders to keep up the attack until forced by damage, low fuel, or low ammunition to break off. They concentrated on the rear two combat wings. Three more damaged Fortresses dropped back, but bomber fire hit Uffz. Fritz Fritzlehner of the 12th Staffel; he became the day's first JG 26 fatality. Oblt. Hans-Georg Dippel, Kapitän of the 7th Staffel, attempted a rear attack on the lead group of the lead wing, which subjected his Messerschmitt to the fire of at least sixty bomber gunners. It was hit numerous times, and cartwheeled through the 385th Bomb Group's formation in a scene spectacular enough to stand out in the memories of the American survivors on a day that was filled with mind-numbing horrors. Dippel was able to bring his plane under control and bail out without injury. One of his Staffel members belly-landed near Asperen with wounds; his name has not been located.

After the 353rd Fighter Group had reversed course to return to England, its commander, Major Loren McCollom, saw a formation of Bf 109s 2000 feet below him, at 24,000 feet (7300 meters). He dived on them undetected and loosed a burst from his eight .50s at the tail-end aircraft, observing "many strikes and sheets of flame". The plane fell away out of control, and McCollom had scored his group's first victory. The Messerschmitt pilot, Heinz Kemethmüller, was saved by his armor plate; his only injuries were to his hands, when the control column was shot from them. He stayed with his disintegrating plane and bailed out at the approved low altitude, destined for a short hospital stay.

One of the three B-17s that had pulled away from the 4th Bomb Wing's rear box was shot down by Fw. Werner Kraft of the 9th Staffel, who pulled alongside the crippled bomber to look it over and was then shot down by the right waist gunner. The other two B-17s were shot down by the lurking First Gruppe Focke-Wulfs. Oblt. Beese was given full victory credit for one; Hptm. Rolf Hermichen claimed the other, but it was credited informally to his wingman, Lt. Georg Kiefner, when it was found that Hermichen's guns had not been fired. However, as this claim was for the final destruction of an already-separated aircraft it was never submitted to the RLM and was not added to Kiefner's claims total; in this case the system worked exactly as it was supposed to.

The 56th Fighter Group relieved the 353rd on schedule; its pilots saw only one German fighter. The Jafü had seen the new fighters coming, and whisked his fighters away and back to their bases. When the last P-47 turned back at Eupen, the way was clear for new German fighter units, I/JG 1, I/JG 3, and III/JG 3, to continue the attacks without hindrance. Twenty-four bombers were shot down. Fifty others were damaged; of this number, two force-landed in Switzerland and eight ditched in the Mediterranean. The interceptions by I/JG 26 and III/JG 26 are of interest because these units attacked entirely alone, and finished off all of their cripples. Their claims can thus be compared closely to the American losses. Eight B-17s went down before Eupen was reached. One of these can be attributed to flak, according to the surviving crewmen. Geschwader pilots received credit for five victories and one separation. A second separation claim, Kemethmüller's, was rejected. The seven downed B-17s are thus a perfect match for the submitted claims. At least three final destructions were recorded by the two units, but these did not count as victories, since in theory each would match up with another pilot's claim for a separation from formation.

The Jafü 2 and Jafü Holland-Ruhr controllers were puzzled by the non-arrival of the larger part of the B-17 force; the two American bombardment wings had always in the past coordinated their attacks to split the defenses, and the earlier radio tests indicated that the other bombers were coming today. But they couldn't worry about them now. The B-26 and RAF diversion raids, which ordinarily preceded the heavy bombers, were now reported in the Channel. The enemy was coming across at such widely-spaced intervals today that these secondary forces, which were usually ignored, could be attacked. All five raids headed for the Pas de Calais, where the Geschwadergruppe was waiting in full strength. The first medium bombers across the French coast were twenty-nine B-26s, which bombed the dispersal field at Bryas. The Messerschmitts of 11th Staffel were probably ordered to take on the high cover, while the 8th and 10th Staffel Focke-Wulfs tried to reach the bombers.

The 11th Staffel was led today by Obfw. Hermann Hoffmann, who had spent most of his career as an instructor. He was surprised by the Spitfire high cover before he could prepare his own attack, and responded with the maneuver that Jagdwaffe pilots had used to escape from Spitfires for the past three years – he broke for the deck. The New Zealanders of No. 485 Squadron were flying the newest model Spitfire, the Mark IXB, and one pilot was able to catch Hoffmann after a long chase and shoot him down. The surviving Messerschmitts did not re-form and were never seen by the Marauder formation.

The 10th Staffel had no better luck. Uffz. Karl Hadraba made a quick pass through the bombers, but a pilot of No. 341 Sqd. (Free French) then shot him down in flames; Hadraba died in his plane. The Fw 190s, heavily outnumbered by the Spitfires, quickly broke off their attack.

The 8th Staffel was probably returning to base from this unsuccessful attack on the B-26s when a pair of its Focke-Wulfs encountered a number of Typhoons returning from a fighter-bomber attack on Lille-Vendeville. The German pilots found themselves in a position to make a single, long-range pass on one of the escorting squadrons. One Typhoon was hit and fell away in a spin. Its pilot regained control, but it crashed into the sea on its return flight. The victor was an experienced pilot, Obfw. Hans Heitmann. In the absence of wreckage he was unable to make his case, and his claim was rejected by the RLM.

The Second Gruppe was now based on several fields around Beauvais. It is known that the 5th Staffel was at Nivillers, and the 6th Staffel was at Tillé. The Gruppe was scrambled, but not vectored to a target, and landed forty-five minutes later to prepare for any future action. The Gruppe was next ordered to fly from Beauvais to Lille-Nord, which was much closer to the presumed path of the next heavy bomber raid, still assembling over England. But the Jafü 2 controller apparently forgot that Lille-Nord was a tiny field which usually held only a single Staffel. The Gruppe landed at 1430, shortly after the B-17s began crossing the English coast, and could not be refueled in time to play a role in the interception of the outbound Schweinfurt force.

Even without the Second Gruppe, Oberst Grabmann could feel confident when his radar operators reported the approach of the second B-17 force – exactly in the track of the first. The German defenders had been both surprised and disappointed when the Regensburg bombers had continued to the south after bombing. Thirteen Gruppen of single-engine fighters had been assembled along the bombers' assumed return route; this was the largest defensive force yet seen over Europe. Now the effort would not go to waste.

The first radar report of the 230 B-17s of the Schweinfurt force reached the controllers at 1426. This formation had a much larger fighter escort than its predecessor. Eight squadrons of Spitfires would accompany the B-17s as far as Antwerp. There they were to be relieved by two groups of P-47s, which could stay with the bombers as far as Eupen, on the Belgian side of the German border. The Focke-Wulfs at Woensdrecht, once again on the bombers' path, began taking to the air from 1430; I/JG 26 and II/JG 1 were told to make an immediate attack.

The Woensdrecht force had been reinforced by the Messerschmitts of III/JG 3, which were the first to contact the bombers. The German controller's orders brought them directly beneath the Spitfires, which promptly attacked, downing three and dispersing the German formation beyond recovery. The German pilots blamed the Jafü, but their error was at least partly due to their own inexperience in the western cauldron – this had been their first mission since their recall from the Eastern Front.

The Spitfires also fended off the early attacks by the Woensdrecht Focke-Wulfs. Fw. Ahrens tried to lead his 3rd Staffel Schwarm through a small gap in the coverage for a quick shot at the bombers, but the close escorts from No. 303 Squadron saw him, and Ahrens had to escape with a split-S. His wingman, Georg Kiefner, was not quick enough, and was shot down; he bailed out with a bullet in his knee.

One of the two P-47 groups, the 4th, missed rendezvous, and never reached its assigned position over the leading combat wings. The other unit, the 78th Fighter Group, carried out its escort of the rear B-17 wings exactly as ordered. It saw little combat, as the German fighters sheered off upon sighting the Thunderbolts and headed for the less well-defended van of the bomber stream. Borris's men stayed with the bombers far longer than on their earlier mission, and claimed four bombers before breaking away with low fuel. Uffz. Günther Schmidtke, who was on his first combat mission, flew as far as Koblenz, where he tried to make a dead-stick landing; his fighter overturned, and Schmidtke was killed.

Oberst Grabmann timed the approach of most of his defenders so that they contacted the bombers immediately after the escort turned back, as expected, at Eupen. For the next two hours, the bombers were battered by as many as nine Jagdgruppen at one time – an intensity of attack far in excess of anything previously experienced. Mietusch's Third Gruppe had taken off from Schipol at 1439 under orders to head southeast, toward Germany. They reached the bomber stream near Aachen, and stayed in contact for thirty minutes, claiming four of the twenty-nine B-17s that went down at this time. One Gruppe Messerschmitt was shot down, and three sustained damage, but none of its pilots was injured.

The leading American combat wing suffered by far the heaviest losses; twenty-two of its fifty-seven B-17s failed to return to England. The absence of the 4th Fighter Group had permitted I/JG 26 and II/JG 1 to prepare well-coordinated attacks in the undisturbed air ahead of the formation. Once the cohesiveness of the leading wing had been broken, successive attacks sought them out as the least well-defended part of the formation, in accord with the usual German pattern.

The German attacks slacked off when the B-17s began their bomb run on Schweinfurt. Only a few fighters were seen by the bomber crews on their return flight over Germany. The Germans were as exhausted as the Americans; their controllers were counting heavily on the attack of the only fresh Gruppe left in the area – Wutz Galland's II/JG 26. At 1650 Galland led his three Staffeln up from Lille-Nord and southeast, along the reciprocal of the bombers' return course. Priller and the Stabsschwarm met them in the air, but Galland probably retained the tactical command. They met the bomber stream head-on, just east of the German border with Belgium, and attacked the third of the three combat wings. Priller's target began to burn. Galland then re-formed as much of his Gruppe as he could and led it toward the front of this half of the formation, for a second head-on attack.

At this moment the Germans were stunned by fighters attacking from their rear – from the direction of Germany. Colonel Hub Zemke had led his "Wolfpack", the P-47s of the 56th Fighter Group, farther east than they had ever flown before; fifteen miles over the German border. He had reached the rendezvous point exactly on time and course, but had then overflown the B-17 formation, unobserved by the German attackers, who were thus set up for a surprise attack. Wutz Galland disappeared after the initial Thunderbolt bounce; the screamed warning of his wingman, Uffz. Heinz Gomann, had been of no benefit. Gomann's fighter was also hit. He managed to jump out, but got hung up on the plane's tail; he broke free just above the ground and was knocked out when he landed. After regaining consciousness he found that he had suffered only "slight injuries". He was nevertheless granted three weeks' home leave to recover. A third member of Galland's Stabsschwarm, Oblt. Konrad von Donner, was damaged on the same pass, and put down on Brussels-Evere. Galland's remains were discovered two months later, buried with the wreckage of his aircraft twelve feet deep in the soft soil near Maastricht.

Zemke's sudden arrival broke up the attack formations of several German units, which were forced to turn on the Thunderbolts. The 56th claimed 7-0-1 Fw 190s, 4-1-1 Bf 109s, and 5-0-7 twin-engine fighters in the prolonged battle, while losing three P-47s and pilots. Claims for these P-47s were filed by five German pilots from three Geschwader; Hptm. Naumann's claim was one of those confirmed. Two more Second Gruppe pilots had to force-land with damage; one of these men, Lt. Friedrich Lange, was injured.

When the 56th Group was relieved by the 353rd, there were no large Luftwaffe formations in the area; the remaining German fighters were scattered far and wide, searching for stragglers. Obfw. Glunz was the only German pilot to make a successful attack on the bomber stream after the arrival of the escort. Calmly sticking to his orders despite the chaos around him, he maintained contact with the bombers, and finally shot down a 305th Bomb Group B-17 northwest of Diest, attacking "alone, head-on, and with a P-47 on his ass", in the words of Ed Burford, a crewman on a nearby B-17. One more Second Gruppe pilot filed a B-17 claim. Fw. Zeschke followed a struggling 381st BG aircraft over the Channel and apparently delivered the final blow. He received credit for a full victory.

The final leg of the bombers' homeward-bound flight was covered by Spitfires. It was so uneventful that some Spitfire squadrons pulled away to fly sweeps. No. 403 Squadron was flying near Dunkirk when one of its Canadian pilots called out a lone Fw 190 that was flying in loose formation with the Spitfires, on their right. It was piloted by Lt. Helmut Hoppe, the 4th Staffel Kapitän, who was probably trying to reach one of the many airfields in the area and had simply failed to see the Spitfires. In the wild scramble that followed, the propeller of one Spitfire cut the fuselage of another in two. Hoppe claimed the victory, as he was the German pilot responsible for the destruction of the Spitfire, but since he had no witness, the claim was denied.

The day's claims for the Schlageter fighters totaled eighteen B-17s, one Typhoon, one Spitfire, and one Thunderbolt. Their losses totaled five pilots killed and six injured. It was one of their best days of the war, and was a demonstration of the

A scene from the grave-side service for Maj. Wilhelm-Ferdinand Galland, who was killed by 56th Fighter Group P-47s on 17 August. His medals have been borne to his grave site on a pillow; a common aspect of the funerals of Luftwaffe notables. *(Glunz)*

Wilhelm-Ferdinand Galland's passbook portrait. His Knight's Cross has been painted onto the photograph. *(B. Smith)*

importance of leadership and experience. Several Gruppen from other Geschwader had been entirely shut out; Priller lodged a complaint calling the III/JG 1 pilots *Leichenfledderei* (corpse-looters), for failing to make a single concerted attack. After reaching the bomber stream, its pilots had immediately split up to look for stragglers.

The disappearance of the popular and gifted Wutz Galland was a serious blow to the Geschwader and the Jagdwaffe. In his eight months as Gruppenkommandeur he had gained a reputation in the Luftwaffe (and to the Allies) as one of the best formation leaders in the West. The surviving pilots of his Gruppe still speak of him in affectionate terms, and are convinced that under his leadership they had once again become the best unit on the Kanalfront.

JG 26 Victory Claims: 17 August 1943

Date	Rank	Name	Unit	Cl #	Aircraft	Place	Time	Opponent	Conf
17-08-43	Obstlt.	Priller	Ge CO	92	B-17	N of Liège (ML7)	1740		yes
17-08-43	Hptm.	Borris	I CO	29	B-17	10km E of Deest (NL2)	1130	94 BG	yes
17-08-43	Oblt.	Beese	1 CO	16	B-17	nr Berendrecht (LI8)	1135		yes
17-08-43	Oblt.	Beese	1 CO	17	B-17	N of Louvain (ML)	1450	385 BG	yes $^1/_2$
17-08-43	Obfw.	Lindelaub	1	4	B-17	NW of Maastricht (ML)	1446	92 BG	yes
17-08-43	Uffz.	Hecker	2	1	B-17	E of Lille (OH6-9)	1500	91 BG	unk
17-08-43	Fw.	Ahrens	3	7	B-17	NW of Antwerp (LJ8)	1131	385 BG	yes
17-08-43	Fw.	Ahrens	3	8	B-17	Oostmalle (N of Antwerp) (LK8)	1530	381 BG	unk
17-08-43	Lt.	Kiefner	3		B-17-eV	Woensdrecht	1130	385 BG	no
17-08-43	Lt.	Hoppe	4 CO	16	Spitfire	S of Antwerp	1800	403 Sqd	unk
17-08-43	Obfw.	Glunz	4	40	B-17	NW of Schouwen (Hasselt-Antwerp)	1745	305 BG	yes
17-08-43	Hptm.	Naumann	6 CO	21	P-47	10km W of Liège	1700	56 FG	yes
17-08-43	Fw.	Zeschke	6	1	B-17	St. Trond [in Channel?]	1735		yes
17-08-43	Hptm.	Mietusch	III CO	46	B-17	SE of Schleiden-Eifel	1520		yes

17-08-43	Hptm.	Mietusch	III CO	47	B-17	S of Lake Laacher (PP5)	1525		yes
17-08-43	Lt.	Burkert E.	7	1	B-17	Eindhoven (LL7)	1142		yes
17-08-43	Obfw.	Kemethmüller	7		B-17-eV	S of Woensdrecht	1120	385 BG	no
17-08-43	Obfw.	Kemethmüller	7		B-17	Holland	1120		no
17-08-43	Obfw.	Heitmann	8		Typhoon	Lille-Vendeville	1200	182 Sqd	no
17-08-43	Fw.	Dörre	9	9	B-17	Genk	1135		yes $^{1}/_{2}$
17-08-43	Fw.	Kraft	9		B-17-eV	SE of Turnhout	1145	95 BG	unk
17-08-43	Uffz.	Steinberg	9	3	B-17-HSS	500m W of Montzen	1144		yes $^{1}/_{2}$
17-08-43	Hptm.	Staiger	12 CO	32	B-17	W of Pesch (NW of Aachen)	1520		yes
17-08-43	Fw.	Würtz	12		B-17	Ridder [Ridderkerk NL?]	1545		yes

JG 26 Casualties: 17 August 1943

Date	Rank	Name	Cas	Unit	Aircraft	WNr	Mkgs	Place	Time	Cause	Allied Unit
17-08-43	Uffz.	Becker, Hans-Georg	WIA	1	Fw 190A-4	620	bk 11	Liège - b/l Venlo		B-17	
17-08-43	Uffz.	Schmidtke, Günther	KIA	1	Fw 190A-5	410002	wh 5	Koblenz a/f		landing	
17-08-43	Lt.	Kiefner, Georg	WIA	3	Fw 190A-4	2386	yl 2	30km S of Antwerp	1455	Spitfire	303 Sqd
17-08-43	Major	Galland, Wm.-Ferdinand	KIA	II CO	Fw 190A-5	530125	<<+-	near Liège-5km W of Maastricht	1700	P-47	56 FG
17-08-43	Uffz.	Gomann, Heinz	WIA	5	Fw 190A-5	1243	bk 22	10km NE Hasselt-c/l St Trond		P-47	56 FG
17-08-43	Lt.	Kehl, Dietrich	no	5	Bf 109G-6	15923		Antwerp		no fuel	n/a
17-08-43	Lt.	Lange, Friedrich	WIA	5	Fw 190A-5	710006	bk 11	Eindhoven-2km SW Oerle	1805	B-17	
17-08-43	Uffz.	Hadraba, Karl	KIA	10	Fw 190A-5	410001	bl 17	NW of Hesdin-Lille	1155	Spitfire	341 Sqd
17-08-43	Obfw.	Kemethmüller, Heinz	WIA	7	Bf 109G-4	19216	wh 6	Leopoldsburg	1128	P-47	353 FG
17-08-43	Oblt.	Dippel, Hans-Georg	no	9	Bf 109G-6	18833		Gerolstein, WSW of Koblenz	1200	B-17	96 BG
17-08-43	Fw.	Kraft, Werner	WIA	9	Bf 109G-6	19466	yl 11	near Waterloo-Hasselt	1130	B-17	385 or 100 BG
17-08-43	Obfw.	Hoffmann, Hermann	KIA	11	Bf 109G-3	20225	rd 7	10km NW of Fruges	1205	Spitfire	485 Sqd
17-08-43	Uffz.	Fritzlehner, Fritz	KIA	12	Bf 109G-6	16494	bl 16	near Hasselt	1210	B-17	385 or 100 BG

18 August

Both sides had to deal with the aftermath of the previous day's mission. In England, the 8th Air Force gave its exhausted and shaken aircrewmen a single day of rest, and asked Washington to accelerate the movement of fighter groups to the ETO. Although there were still a few "true believers" among the bomber generals, the day of the "self-defending bomber" was over. In Berlin, the repercussions were more dramatic. Generaloberst Hans Jeschonnek, the Luftwaffe Chief of Staff, depressed over the powerful attacks by the USAAF on targets in southern Germany, followed within hours by a devastating raid on the Peenemünde rocket research facility by the RAF night bombers, committed suicide.

Back on the Channel front, Hptm. Hans Naumann was appointed Kommandeur of the Second Gruppe; Oblt. Waldemar Radener replaced Naumann as leader of the 6th Staffel. A B-26 Ramrod to Amsterdam was met by the First Gruppe. One Spitfire crashed when its pilot failed to switch fuel tanks in time to prevent his engine from quitting; Uffz. Pittmann was credited with forcing it down. A mid-day Spitfire incursion was met by the 11th Staffel, now flying from Lille-Nord, but the combats were inconclusive. A late-evening mission by the 2nd Staffel resulted in claims by Lt. Willius and Uffz. Heuser for Spitfires shot down off Dunkirk; the Spitfire unit has not been traced, and the Allied aircraft may well have been another type.

19 August

Typhoons began crossing the French coast shortly before noon, in advance of B-26 and

Uffz. Karl Hadraba of the 10th Staffel was killed on 17 August by a No. 341 Sqd. (Free French) Spitfire while attempting to intercept a B-26 formation. *(Vanoverbeke)*

Uffz. Fritz Fritzlehner of the 12th Staffel was the first JG 26 casualty on 17 August, the victim of B-17 gunfire. *(Vanoverbeke)*

Mitchell raids on Amiens and Poix. The Geschwadergruppe and the Second Gruppe sortied at noon and sought a position from which to launch an attack. The Second Gruppe pilots counted ninety Allied aircraft in the air over Amiens. The Geschwadergruppe engaged Spitfires, without success; Oblt. Johannes Meyer of the 10th Staffel was pursued and brought down 50 kilometers (30 miles) southeast of Amiens. The Second Gruppe maintained contact, and finally Lt. Hoppe's 4th Staffel dived to the attack. Obfw. Glunz reached the bombers, and claimed an "effective damage". Uffz. Martin Günther was hit by Spitfires, and bailed out northeast of Amiens with slight injuries. Hoppe's Schwarm caught six No. 182 Sqd. Typhoons approaching on a rear cover sweep, and shot down three without loss to themselves.

The next wave of aircraft to cross the Channel contained RAF Mitchells headed for Abbeville. The Jafü 2 controllers scrambled all three of the Pas de Calais Gruppen, but gave the actual attack order only to II/JG 2, flying from Vitry. The JG 26 aircraft were landed after only ten to thirty minutes to prepare for later action.

The approach of a bomber formation over the Somme Estuary at 1800 brought a massive German response. Jafü 2 scrambled its three Gruppen once more, and requested aid from Jafü 3. The bombers were B-26s, which were unable to bomb Bryas owing to cloud cover; it is probable that they were mistaken for the vanguard of the heavy bombers, which were then forming up over England. The Second Gruppe was heavily engaged west of the Somme; Hptm. Naumann downed a Spitfire off Le Tréport.

The Allied plan to keep the Calais fighters away from the heavy bombers worked to perfection in the case of the Second Gruppe, which was unable to fly a fourth sortie. The weakened 8th Bomber Command returned to battle with a well-escorted raid on three Dutch airfields: Woensdrecht, Gilze-Rijen, and Soubourg, near Vlissingen. The Woensdrecht force did not drop its bombs, owing to the unbroken cloud cover; the other two formations did bomb, and killed a number of Dutch civilians without materially affecting Luftwaffe operations. Five B-17s were lost and fifty were damaged on the unsuccessful operation.

Uffz. Erich Schwarz of the 4th Staffel, photographed in the summer of 1943 in front of his Fw 190A-6. Schwarz scored a total of eleven victories, and survived the war. *(Niesmak)*

The B-17s were escorted by ten squadrons of Spitfires on the penetration phase, two groups of P-47s over the target, and two groups of P-47s on the withdrawal. Oberst Grabmann had two JG 26 Gruppen, I/JG 3, and all three JG 1 Gruppen at his immediate disposal. Because the raid was coming so late in the day he could assume that its targets were near the coast, and he put in an early request for assistance from the more distant Gruppen. But it was his own fighters, plus those of Priller's Geschwadergruppe, that made contact. III/JG 1, under severe pressure to obtain results, arrived before the Spitfires left, and was punished badly, losing three pilots killed, one injured, and several Messerschmitts destroyed, for one Spitfire claim. The First Gruppe attack was also foiled, first by the Spitfires, and then by the P-47s; Lt. Leberecht Altmann bailed out of his fighter with injuries, while another First Gruppe Focke-Wulf pilot had to make a crash-landing.

Hptm. Mietusch led part of his Gruppe past the P-47s and into the bomber stream, but he was the only successful Third Gruppe pilot; his target dived away and crashed near Gilze-Rijen. Fw. Wilhelm Mensing and Fw. Werner Mössner were hit by B-17 gunfire and bailed out; Mensing lost an arm, and Mössner suffered severe burns. Lt. Werner Grupe was shot down and killed by a P-47. A fourth Third Gruppe pilot was shot down over Breda, and bailed out uninjured.

Obstlt. Priller led part of the Geschwadergruppe – probably just his Stabsschwarm and the experienced 8th Staffel – in the most successful attack of the day. He was able to position his fighters between the leading 56th Fighter Group squadron and the first combat wing of B-17s, and made a devastating head-on attack which resulted in the destruction of two bombers. These were credited to Priller and his wingman, Obfw. Grünlinger. Uffz. Schwarz of the 8th Staffel then flew toward the North Sea and shot down a crippled bomber; credit for the final destruction was shared with two JG 1 pilots.

JG 26 Victory Claims: 18 - 19 August 1943

Date	Rank	Name	Unit	Cl #	Aircraft	Place	Time	Opponent	Conf
18-08-43	Uffz.	Pittmann	1	1	Spitfire	N of Walcheren (IJ2)		131 Sqd	yes
18-08-43	Lt.	Willius	2	35	Spitfire	Ipswich (N Sea) (HD8-1)	1907		yes
18-08-43	Uffz.	Heuser Hein.	2	4	Spitfire	Dunkirk (ME3)	1914		yes
19-08-43	Obstlt.	Priller	Ge CO	93	B-17	de Beer Is. (Gilze-Rijen a/f)	1900	305 BG	unk
19-08-43	Obfw.	Grünlinger	Ge		B-17	Gilze-Rijen a/f	1900	305 BG	unk
19-08-43	Hptm.	Naumann	II CO	22	Spitfire	5km NW of Le Tréport	1832		yes
19-08-43	Lt.	Hoppe	4 CO	17	Typhoon	15km N of Amiens	1225	182 Sqd	yes
19-08-43	Lt.	Hoppe	4 CO	18	Typhoon	3-5km NW of Blangy?	1231	182 Sqd	unk
19-08-43	Obfw.	Glunz	4		B-26	N France	1230	323 BG	no
19-08-43	Lt.	Heinemann E.	4	2	Typhoon	1km SE of Canaples?	1224	182 Sqd	unk
19-08-43	Hptm.	Mietusch	III CO	48	B-17	NW Breda	1923	303 BG	yes
19-08-43	Uffz.	Schwarz E.	8	4	B-17-eV	unknown		388 BG	no

Date	Rank	Name	Cas	Unit	Aircraft	WNr	Mkgs	Place	Time	Cause	Allied Unit
19-08-43	Lt.	Altmann, Leberecht	WIA	1	Fw 190A-5	1091	wh 4	Epen-W of Breda	1930	P-47	56 FG
19-08-43	Lt.	Grupe, Werner	WIA	12	Bf 109G-4	19373	bl 3	Breda	2000	P-47	56 or 78 FG
19-08-43	Uffz.	Günther, Martin	WIA	4	Fw 190A-5	2405	wh 2	2.5km NE of Amiens		Spitfire	
19-08-43	Fw.	Mensing, Wilhelm	WIA	7	Bf 109G-4	19783	wh 3	Hertogenbosch-near Waspik	1930	B-17	
19-08-43	Oblt.	Meyer, Johannes	KIA	10	Fw 190A-5	2620	bl 4	25km E of Amiens		fighter	
19-08-43	Fw.	Mössner, Werner	WIA	9	Bf 109G-6	16394	yl 12	Waalwijk-N of Breda	1900	B-17	
19-08-43	Uffz.	Salomon, Heinz	WIFA	10	Fw 190A-4	794	br 16	Melderslo near Horst	1530	no fuel	n/a

21 August

While on a training flight from Lille-Nord, the engine of Uffz. Wolfgang Polster's Bf 109G-3 caught fire. Polster bailed out southwest of Lille with minor burns and other injuries.

22 August

Jafü 2 scrambled fighters from Vendeville, Beauvais, and Vitry to defend against late-evening raids by Bostons and B-26s. No victories were claimed. The Second Gruppe engaged the escorting Spitfires in combat, but without result, while two Bf 109s from II/JG 2, which was now flying from Vitry, force-landed with combat damage.

23 August

The B-26s came over early to bomb Gosnay. Again the Jafü 2 controllers scrambled all three Pas de Calais Gruppen. The RAF Y-intercept operators heard the Jafü order his fighters to attack, but the bombers turned back early owing to heavy cloud, and the escorting Spitfires were too numerous to approach. W/C Johnson changed the mission of his fighters, now redesignated No. 127 Wing (RCAF), to a sweep, and caught the 10th Staffel off the coast. Johnson and his Canadians shot down Obfw. Erich Borounick and Gefr. Helmuth Ullmann. Both crashed in their airplanes, although the Spitfire pilots claimed only one destroyed and one damaged. The other German units did not make contact, although the RAF Y-Intercept operators heard the Jafü order Hptm. Naumann to "carry out your orders." The RAF intelligence officers were apparently pleased to report the problems of "Hans". His predecessor, Major Galland, had been their favorite German. Galland's career had been followed closely by the RAF ever since his promotion to Staffelkapitän in 1942. Luftwaffe formation leaders used their nicknames instead of code names on the radio, and Wutz (pronounced "Vootz") had the most distinctive "handle" on the Channel coast. "The dynamic leader of the Vitry Wing" had gotten more ink in the RAF intelligence reports than any other Luftwaffe personality, and now he was gone. The Y-intercept report for 17 August had reported the unanswered calls of Wutz's pilots with what can only be described as sympathy.

A mid-afternoon scramble from Schipol cost the Third Gruppe Lt. Gerhard Karl, who was shot down and killed northwest of Gorinchem. His loss report identifies his opponents as Spitfires, but no suitable RAF claim has been located.

JG 26 Casualties: 21 - 23 August 1943

Date	Rank	Name	Cas	Unit	Aircraft	WNr	Mkgs	Place	Time	Cause	Allied Unit
21-08-43	Uffz.	Polster, Wolfgang	WIFA	11	Bf 109G-3	16277	rd 16	SW Lille-Wavrin		engine	non-op
23-08-43	Lt.	Karl, Gerhard	KIA	9	Bf 109G-4	20442	yl 15	6km NW of Gorinchem	1650	Spitfire	
23-08-43	Obfw.	Borounick, Erich	KIA	10	Fw 190A-5	7223	bl 12	6km E of Frévent-Artois		Spitfire	Kenley Wing
23-08-43	Gefr.	Ullmann, Helmuth	KIA	10	Fw 190A-5	7380	bl 3	3km NE of Frévent-Artois		Spitfire	Kenley Wing

27 August

The 8th Bomber Command was ordered to make a full-strength attack on a construction site at Watten, which was located between St. Omer and Dunkirk. The target was described as an "aeronautical facilities station", but the Allies strongly suspected that it was associated with the German secret weapons program – it was, in fact, to become a V-1 base. As the target was small, the 224 B-17s were split into four task forces, and briefed to bomb in trail, as groups or even squadrons. The task forces were spaced widely apart and took more than an hour to cross the target. They crossed the coast at Berck-sur-Mer, flew east, and then turned north to provide an adequate run to the target. This increased their risk, but it was unavoidable. It was believed that the Pas de Calais fighter Gruppen would exhaust themselves against the first wave, and could not be up again until the fourth, which was the earliest that reinforcements from other Jafü could arrive. The escort of twenty-three Spitfire squadrons and the four P-47 groups was distributed accordingly. The plan proved to be a sound one; three B-17s were shot down by flak, and only one was lost to fighter attack.

Jafü 2 scrambled its three Gruppen at 1908, before the first wave of B-17s had left the coast at Dungeness. The radio tests had indicated a full-scale attack, and the lateness of the hour implied a short penetration, so Obst. Vieck quickly concluded that the target was on the Pas de Calais. He requested assistance from Jafü 3 at 1922, and I/JG 2 was scrambled immediately from Beaumont and Évreux and sent northeast. The Geschwadergruppe and II/JG 2, which was flying from both Poix and Vitry, arrived first, but were unable to penetrate the escort. Hptm. Ebersberger, the 8th Staffel Kapitän, shot down a Spitfire near Arras, but two of his men were shot down; both bailed out without injury. The 11th Staffel lost a Messerschmitt, but its pilot was uninjured.

The Second Gruppe arrived in force from Beauvais and was able to make an impact. It first tore into the Biggin Hill Wing, which was flying as close escort to the first task force. Oblt. Matoni reached the bombers, and shot down a 351st Bomb Group B-17. Battles between the Spitfires and Focke-Wulfs began over St. Omer and continued out to sea past Calais. Uffz. Heinrich Krieg of the 5th Staffel was shot down and killed, but he was the only Gruppe casualty. Fw. Wilhelm Mayer shot down a No. 341 Sqd. (Free French) Spitfire near Merville, and his Kapitän, Lt. Radener, shot down the squadron's commander, Cdt. René Mouchotte, just off the coast. Neither German pilot could find a witness to his victory in the general melee, and they did not file their claims.

The Jafü 2 and Jafü 3 fighters were breaking away to land by 2010, and the second and third B-17 task forces did not see a German aircraft. The help of Jafü Holland-Ruhr had been requested at 2000, and the First Gruppe was sent west from Woensdrecht. It reached the Pas de Calais just in time to confront the fourth task force with its enlarged escort, and the Focke-Wulfs were quickly scattered; their battles with the Spitfires and P-47s were without result.

29 August

Obfw. Adolf Glunz was awarded the Knight's Cross today. The 25-year-old Glunz had pursued his goal of becoming a fighter pilot since childhood. He had joined the Luftwaffe in 1939, was chosen for fighter training in July 1940, and reported to JG 52 in April 1941. By mid-July, he had scored five victories on the Eastern Front. Such success by a neophyte attracted attention in the small Jagdwaffe, and Adolf Galland was able to get him reassigned to JG 26. Glunz quickly became acclimatized to life on the Channel coast. His victory total climbed steadily; at forty it brought him the Knight's Cross. Addi was the only non-commissioned JG 26 pilot ever to receive this award; he and Wutz Galland were the only members of JG 26 to get it in 1943. The new point system was not much help – decorations remained much harder to earn in the West than in the East, despite recognition by the RLM that the western units faced much stiffer opposition.

The rudder of Obfw. Glunz's Fw 190A-5 "white 9" (W.Nr. 7321), showing thirty-nine victories – Beauvais, 31 August. *(Petrick)*

Major Priller chats with Obfw. Glunz shortly after the latter's receipt of the Knight's Cross on 29 August. *(Glunz)*

MGen. Frank "Monk" Hunter was relieved as head of the 8th Fighter Command and sent to a training command in the USA. Hunter had persisted with his ineffective fighter-sweep strategy even after his mentors in RAF Fighter Command had abandoned it. His replacement, MGen. William Kempner, was focused single-mindedly on winning the war, whatever the cost. His fighter pilots immediately rose to the challenge.

31 August

The 8th Bomber Command targeted a number of Luftflotte 3 bases, the most important of which was the depot at Romilly. In an effort to outwait the unpredictable weather, it was scheduled for late afternoon. As had become the custom, the B-26s and RAF bombers would attempt to wear down the Pas de Calais fighters and airfields before the B-17s took off. Only one of the four B-26 groups was able to bomb. It had more success than most such raids; Vendeville sustained such damage that the Geschwadergruppe had to spend the next four days at Wevelgem. The 10th Staffel's Lt. Gert Heck was shot down and killed by Spitfires near Bethune while trying to defend his base, and an 8th Staffel plane was damaged, but landed safely.

The heavy bombers were not reported until 1800. It appeared to be a shallow-penetration raid across a broad front; Jafü 2 and Jafü 3 scrambled all of their fighters, and the First Gruppe took off from Woensdrecht. The weather did not cooperate with either side; most of the bombers aborted or bombed secondary targets, and the German fighters had difficulty keeping in formation or even finding the bombers. Only the Second Gruppe attacked the bombers. Obfw. Glunz shot down the only B-17 lost for the day; the 303rd Bomb Group aircraft crashed near Le Tréport. Oblt. Walter Matoni was injured by bomber fire and had to force-land his Focke-Wulf.

Hptm. Johannes Naumann, one of the few prewar members of the Geschwader still flying in combat, was awarded the German Cross in Gold for his twenty-two air victories.

Late in the evening the First Gruppe made a permanent base move, from Woensdrecht to Brussels-Grimbergen. They were now closer to the rest of the Geschwader, but were still in Jagdkorps I, under the control of Jafü Holland-Ruhr. The Woensdrecht airbase diary has survived, and the clerk recorded that the transfer meant the departure of twenty-three officers, three *Beamten* (civilian functionaries), 169 NCOs, 357 enlisted men, twenty-eight Fw 190s, one Fw 58, one Fi 156, one Bf 108, and four airfield protection detachments.

Geschwader personnel moves in August included the transfer of Lt. Karl Willius from the 3rd Staffel to the 2nd; the return of Fw. Helmut Bäumener to the 3rd Staffel, and Uffz. Hermann Butzmann to the 4th, from duty as ferry pilots; the return of Oblt. Ernst Janda to the 8th Staffel from a tour as an instructor; and the departure of Fw. Horst Schwentick and Obfw. Xaver Ellenrieder for instructor duty.

The following men are known to have reported to the Geschwader in August after completion of pilot training: Gefr. Helmut Hüttig, Uffz. Horst Kretschmer, Uffz. Günther Schmidtke, Fhj.-Uffz. Friedrich Schneider, Uffz. Ewald Schnier, Fw. Herbert Seidl - First Gruppe; Uffz. Heinrich Berg, Uffz. Ludwig Pötter, Uffz. Leo Przybyl, Uffz. Werner Steinkühler - Second Gruppe; Uffz. Helmut Bannischka, Uffz. Karl Claar - Third Gruppe.

JG 26 Victory Claims: 27 - 31 August 1943

Date		Name	Unit	Cl #	Aircraft	Place	Time	Opponent	Conf
27-08-43	Oblt.	Matoni	5	7	B-17	3km NW of Dunkirk	1935	351 BG	yes
27-08-43	Lt.	Radener	6 CO		Spitfire	NW of Dunkirk	1940	341 Sqd	no
27-08-43	Fw.	Mayer	6		Spitfire	Lens-Bethune-Arras	2000	341 Sqd	no
27-08-43	Hptm.	Ebersberger	8 CO	30	Spitfire	Arras (PF5-6)			yes
31-08-43	Obfw.	Glunz	4	41	B-17	Le Tréport	1932	303 BG	yes

JG 26 Casualties: 27 - 31 August 1943

Date	Rank	Name	Cas	Unit	Aircraft	WNr	Mkgs	Place	Time	Cause	Allied Unit
27-08-43	Uffz.	Krieg, Heinrich	KIA	5	Fw 190A-4	2379	bk 5	nr Merville-2km S of St Venant		Spitfire	
31-08-43	Oblt.	Matoni, Walter	WIA	II St	Fw 190A-5	530118	bk 1	Montdidier (F)		B-17	
31-08-43	Lt.	Heck, Gert	KIA	10	Fw 190A-5	7213	bl 6	S of Lille		Spitfire	
31-08-43	Hptm.	Michel, Wilhelm	WIA	8	none			Lille-Nord a/f		strafed	

Chapter Four

THE WAR OF ATTRITION

September - December 1943

2 September

The 8th Air Force was not ready to resume deep penetration raids, and was scheduling many of its missions to France or the Low Countries for late in the evening, gambling on clear skies; visual target identification over occupied Europe was mandatory. The late-summer weather over the United Kingdom and western Europe had established a pattern. Heavy morning fog would gradually burn off, resulting in a brief period of clear skies before warm, moist air blowing in from the North Sea created thick clouds. The clouds would often disperse in the evening as the air cooled down. The German fighter controllers could deduce the probable target just from the time the bombers took off, and assembled their forces accordingly.

The Second Gruppe was up from 1800 to 1900 in an unsuccessful chase of an unseen target that took them almost to Paris. Low on fuel, the Gruppe Stabsschwarm and the 6th Staffel landed on Creil. The American B-17s started crossing the English coast at about 1915, bound for Luftwaffe fighter bases in France, and the response of Jafü 2 and Jafü 3 was immediate. Every Jagdgruppe in northern France was scrambled, as was the First Gruppe from Grimbergen. The cloud cover over France remained unbroken. Most bomber groups turned back without finding a target, and the escorting P-47s were released to fly a sweep. Most of the German fighters struggled in the clouds for a while and returned to their bases; one Second Gruppe and two First Gruppe Focke-Wulfs were damaged on landing.

Hptm. Naumann and his small force got lucky while returning from Creil. They were flying at 7500 meters (25,000 feet), in thick but broken clouds, and spotted two flights of P-47s in a clear layer below. Col. Zemke had decided to make one last turn and sweep the bombers' return course with part of his group. Naumann got behind the P-47s, dived, and pulled up in their blind spot beneath. The first burst of cannon fire caused both aircraft of Zemke's second element to fall away and crash. Zemke's aircraft was struck; its engine quit, and he dived away to a safer altitude. Just as he was preparing to bail out, his engine started again; his supercharger had been hit, causing the engine to die at the higher altitude for lack of air. The Colonel flew back to England without further incident. A pilot in the second flight got into a turning battle with his attacker; hits in the P-47's air ducts caused it to lose so much manifold pressure that the Focke-Wulf was able to keep up with it easily when it dived away. The German pilot, Lt. Dietrich Kehl, followed the American from Lille to the coast before exhausting his ammunition on the tough Thunderbolt and turning back. The P-47 returned to England fit only for scrap. Naumann and three of his pilots claimed victories after this engagement, in which no German plane was hit. Three of these claims were sent to Berlin. Only one pilot, Fw. Karl Ehret, received credit for a victory; the other crashes had not been witnessed because of the lower cloud deck.

JG 26 Victory Claims: 2 September 1943

Date	Rank	Name	Unit	Cl #	Aircraft	Place	Time	Opponent	Conf
02-09-43	Hptm.	Naumann	II CO	23	P-47	near Lens	2021	56 FG	unk
02-09-43	Lt.	Kehl	II St	2	P-47	near Berck-sur-Mer	2025	56 FG	unk

3 September

In the morning the 8th Bomber Command took advantage of the predicted clear hours to send 233 B-17s and the four P-47 groups to several targets in the Paris region. The P-47s flew all the way to Paris, and provided good protection. Nine B-17s were lost to the defenses.

Jafü 2 scrambled all three of its Gruppen at 0900 and sent them south, anticipating an attack on Romilly. At 0930 the controller predicted that the bombers were headed for the Paris area, and gave his pilots free rein to attack. Control was never relinquished to Jafü 3, the local controller, who was busy with his own fighters. The two JG 26 Gruppen converged on the 1st Bomb Wing, which had targeted Romilly, while the JG 2 fighters attacked the 4th Bomb Wing nearer Paris proper. Uffz. Werner Hoffmann of the 5th Staffel had to put down early with engine problems. He selected Creil for a belly landing, but he had not dropped his auxiliary tank. It ignited on landing, burning Hoffmann. The Second Gruppe arrived at the bomber stream in time to make a head-on attack prior to the initial point, and Lt. Hoppe's target, a 92nd Bomb Group aircraft, pulled away from the formation and crashed. The attacks of the Gruppe continued for a half hour, despite the P-47s, and two more B-17s eventually went down, although the German pilots' claims were not confirmed. Lt. Karl-Heinz Schmidt of the 4th Staffel was hit by bomber fire and jumped out of his aircraft, but his parachute did not open. The Geschwadergruppe arrived a few minutes later, and made one pass at the bombers before being fully engaged with the 56th Fighter Group escort. The P-47 group lost one fighter to Lt. Radener, but shot down Oblt. Ernst Janda, who crashed with his aircraft, and Uffz. Erwin Scholz, who was killed when his Focke-Wulf overturned on crash-landing. Janda had led the 8th Staffel south from Wevelgem while climbing to 11,000 meters (36,000 feet). This was far above the P-47s, which could be seen approaching from the north. Janda's unit made one diving pass before the Thunderbolts caught up to the bomber formation; Janda was never seen again. Uffz. Gerhard Guttmann of the 10th Staffel was injured by a B-17 gunner, and force-landed in a meadow near Melun. Fw. Gerhard Vogt's plane was also hit by defensive fire, and he was slightly injured in his crash-landing. At least two more Geschwader aircraft force-landed with combat damage; the rest landed at Villaroche, Rosières, Creil, and other Jafü 3 airfields for servicing.

Six formations of Marauders, Mitchells, and Venturas attacked Luftflotte 3 airfields in mid-afternoon in missions associated with Operation Starkey, which was still in progress. The Pas de Calais Gruppen had returned to their bases, but the units reported low strengths, and only a few fighters were scrambled. Uffz. Gerd Wiegand of the 8th Staffel was up from Lille-Nord on a test flight when he received word of a medium bomber formation approaching the coast at Dunkirk. He located the Venturas, and took advantage of the confusion and spreading of the Spitfire escort owing to a sudden bomber course change to approach the bombers closely, from beneath the fighters. He opened fire on his target from forty meters (fifty yards), and the Ventura exploded; its fuselage came to rest on the Gravelines mole, where it lay looking like a beached whale.

Wiegand's was the only Luftwaffe success against the afternoon raids. The young Unteroffizier, an unusually sensitive and dedicated fighter pilot, had claimed his first victory, on his thirty-ninth mission. "The curse was broken", in his words. In his next fifty-one missions, Wiegand would bring down twenty-four more aircraft – a rate approaching one victory for each two combat sorties.

The airfield raids resulted in one Geschwader fatality. A 5th Staffel crew chief was buried in his foxhole at Beauvais-Tillé by an exploding thousand-pound bomb, and died of internal bleeding before he could be extricated. Activity over the Channel calmed down in late afternoon. The First Gruppe was scrambled from Grimbergen

Oblt. Ernst Janda of the 8th Staffel, which became the 4th Staffel in the reorganization of 1 October. Janda was killed by 56th Fighter Group P-47s on 3 September. *(Vanoverbeke)*

against two P-47 groups which were sweeping the Belgian coast at high altitude, but was unable to reach them.

The General of the Fighter Arm, Genmaj. Adolf Galland, today issued a set of combat instructions to all fighter units involved in the *Reichsluftverteidigung*, or RLV, the general term applied to the Reich air defenses. The document is of as much interest for what it implies as for what it says directly. The low rate of success against the American heavy bombers was of extreme concern to the Luftwaffe High Command, as was the increasing damage the bombers were now doing to their targets. Pilots and controllers were told for the first time that their top priority was to break up the bomber formations prior to bombing, and that "all possible means" were to be used to prevent the bombers from dropping on their planned targets. Effective immediately, frontal attacks were to be restricted to "especially favorable conditions by Gruppen proven successful at carrying them out." All other units were to attack from the rear. The approach was to be monitored by the formation leader, and any pilot who failed to close to the ordered firing distance without sufficient reason was to be brought before a court martial for cowardice before the enemy. Effective now, only bombers in formations were to be attacked; only after the entire formation was split up were individual bombers to be brought under fire. The instructions stressed the importance of multiple attacks and second sorties, and codified command and control procedures for fighters operating from bases other than their own.

Of Galland's twenty-six points, not one addressed the growing problem posed by the Allied fighter escorts. The reason can be simply stated – the Luftwaffe had no answer for the fighter escorts. Galland wanted to make attacks on the fighter formations a high priority for the Kanalgeschwader. At a minimum, this would force the American fighters to drop their belly tanks and reduce their radius of action. The RLV units farther inland would be the beneficiaries; attacks against unescorted bomber formations could be devastating. The JG 2 and JG 26 formation leaders, all of whom except Major Mayer of JG 2 had gained their greatest successes in 1941 and 1942 against RAF fighters, were enthusiastic supporters of this idea, which worked well the few times it was tried. But Hitler, and thus Göring, were totally against it, and no coherent strategy evolved before the growing numbers of American fighters and bombers were able to overwhelm the defenses.

JG 26 Casualties: 2 - 3 September 1943

Date	Rank	Name	Cas	Unit	Aircraft	WNr	Mkgs	Place	Time	Cause	Allied Unit
02-09-43	Uffz.	Schilling, Franz	WIFA	6	Fw 190A-4	702		Crillon		no fuel	n/a
03-09-43	Lt.	Schmidt,Karl-Heinz	KIA	4	Fw 190A-4	667	wh 10	Champenoux		B-17	
03-09-43	Uffz.	Hoffmann, Werner	WIFA	5	Fw 190A-4	5658	bk 6	Creil		engine	n/a
03-09-43	Uffz.	Scholz, Erwin	KIFA	6	Fw 190A-4	684		Creil		landing	n/a
03-09-43	Fw.	Vogt, Gerhard	WIA	6	Fw 190A-4	2456	br 11	Romilly-sur-Seine		B-17+ P-47	56 FG

| 03-09-43 | Oblt. | Janda, Ernst | KIA | 8 | Fw 190A-5 | 7234 | bk 18 | SE of Paris | | P-47 | 56 FG |
| 03-09-43 | Uffz. | Guttmann, Gerhard | WIA | 10 | Fw 190A-5 | 410258 bl 18 | Melun-f/l Villaroche | | | B-17 | |

JG 26 Victory Claims: 3 September 1943

Date	Rank	Name	Unit	Cl #	Aircraft	Place	Time	Opponent	Conf
03-09-43	Lt.	Hoppe	4 CO	19	B-17	N of Paris	0930	92 BG	yes
03-09-43	Obfw.	Glunz	4	42	B-17	E of Paris	1035	381 or 384 BG	unk
03-09-43	Lt.	Radener	6 CO	6	P-47	3km N of Guyancourt	0958	56 FG	unk
03-09-43	Fw.	Mayer	6	5	B-17	near Melun a/f	0957	381 or 384 BG	unk
03-09-43	Fw.	Mayer	6		P-47	near Creil	1000	56 FG	no
03-09-43	Uffz.	Wiegand	8	1	Ventura	Gravelines	1430	21 Sqd	yes

4 September

The medium bombers kept the pressure on the Luftwaffe fighters in northern France; nine missions were flown by American Marauders and RAF Bostons, Venturas, and Mitchells. There was no sign of a heavy bomber raid, and so Obst. Vieck was free to use his fighters against the mediums. The Schlageter fighters were active from 1000 to 2000 hours; they found the bombers well-protected by their escorts, and were forced to limit their attacks to the Spitfires, against which they had a measure of success.

Oblt. Leuschel claimed a Spitfire near Roubaix at 0903; the claim was not confirmed, and cannot be identified. The first attack wave crossed the French coast at 1000 hours in five formations, spread from Calais to the Seine. The Beauvais Gruppe (II/JG 26) and the Vitry Gruppe (II/JG 2) were scrambled first, and headed for the Somme Estuary. One Staffel was spotted near Le Tréport by No. 66 Squadron's Australian F/L Tony Gaze, who recalls:

> "I was back on Spit Vs after a year on Spit IXs, and we had to be very quick to move into any enemy aircraft before the IXs cut us out. I spotted a group of 190s about 1000 feet [300 meters] below, and went straight down. I followed one, firing until it caught fire. Climbing back up, I was looking for my No. 2, when I realized the aircraft behind me wasn't him. I was hit in the tail. We started a turning competition, but six more 190s joined in. I went to ground level and called for assistance. Using the shadows on the ground to judge range, I kept making distance toward the coast, turning when they got close enough to fire. I realized that without help I was in a hopeless situation. One 190 turning to avoid me flicked inverted, and I thought it must crash. As the coast came near, I was hit again, and could now see the shadow of my glycol stream. I soon had to put it down. The 190s were flying around watching, and I stupidly waved at them instead of playing dead. I didn't set off the incendiary device, because a Spit V had no secrets, and it would have given my position away. I ran off and hid, but the Resistance soon found me, patched me up, and got me smuggled over the Pyrénées and home."

Tony Gaze reached England on 28 October, and returned to combat. He was claimed by Fw. Gerhard Vogt, a rising star in the 6th Staffel; Gaze was his fourteenth victory. The only other Spitfire shot down on the morning mission was claimed by a beginner, Gefr. Heinz Wyrich, who put a No. 165 Sqd. Spitfire into the water off Berck-sur-Mer.

Some bombers came over in mid-afternoon, but attacks on these formations proved inconclusive. The evening wave of four bomber formations approached on a broad front, and crossed the coast between Étaples and the Scheldt. Elements of the three Pas de Calais Gruppen were sent up, some pilots on their third sorties, and the First Gruppe was scrambled from Grimbergen in full force. Despite repeated radioed instructions by Jafü 2 to attack the bombers, these could not be reached; the Spitfires cut off every attack.

No. 127 Wing (RCAF), flying high cover for the B-26s bombing Lille, saw a small group of Fw 190s approaching the bombers and immediately dived to the attack. The German aircraft were a mixed formation from Lille-Nord, and contained pilots from the Geschwader Stab, the 8th, and the 10th Staffeln. W/C Johnson's target was apparently Obfw. Walter Grünlinger, Priller's long-time wingman, who flew away toward the west before crashing in flames. Grünlinger's promotion to Leutnant and assignment as a Staffelführer had just been announced, but he did not live to assume the post. No. 403 Squadron's S/L F. E. Grant shot down Uffz. Horst Schöhl of the 8th Staffel, who bailed out with injuries so severe that the Canadians could see blood on his parachute canopy; Schöhl lived, but did not return to the Geschwader. Grant was then shot down, and his aircraft crashed near Roubaix, very near Schöhl's. No-one claimed Grant's aircraft, unless Leuschel's "0903" claim was a clerical error for 1903; in that case, time, place, and circumstances are a perfect match for Grant's loss.

The First Gruppe reached this same bomber formation as it was crossing the coast on the way out, and Lt. Willius and Uffz. Heuser of the 2nd Staffel claimed Spitfires off Dunkirk; one in fact went down, piloted by an American pilot on temporary duty with No. 131 Squadron.

The Second Gruppe was vectored to a B-26 formation bombing St. Pol, but got tangled up with Spitfires near Berck-sur-Mer. Lt. Ernst Heinemann and Obfw. Alfred Günther were shot down. Only Günther survived; he was picked up by a rescue boat within a half hour. Four Spitfires were claimed, and three were confirmed, but apparently only one went down; its pilot, from No. 129 Squadron, was rescued by the British.

JG 26 Victory Claims: 4 September 1943

Date	Rank	Name	Unit	Cl #	Aircraft	Place	Time	Opponent	Conf
04-09-43	Uffz.	Heuser Hein.	2		Spitfire	Dunkirk (ME3)	1914	131 Sqd	unk
04-09-43	Lt.	Willius	2		Spitfire	nr Dunkirk (ME8-1)	1914	131 Sqd	no
04-09-43	Lt.	Hoppe	4 CO	20	Spitfire	near Berck sur Mer	1946		yes
04-09-43	Uffz.	Hanke	4	1	Spitfire	near Berck sur Mer	1948		yes
04-09-43	Fw.	Weyrich	4	1	Spitfire	mid-Channel	1950		unk
04-09-43	Gefr.	Wyrich	4	1	Spitfire	mid-Channel	1028	165 Sqd	yes
04-09-43	Fw.	Vogt	6	14	Spitfire	S of Le Tréport	1030	66 Sqd	yes
04-09-43	Fw.	Vogt	6	15	Spitfire	W of Berck sur Mer	1955	129 Sqd	yes
04-09-43	Oblt.	Leuschel	10 CO	6	Spitfire	SE of Roubaix	0903		unk

JG 26 Casualties: 4 September 1943

Date	Rank	Name	Cas	Unit	Aircraft	WNr	Mkgs	Place	Time	Cause	Allied Unit
04-09-43	Obfw.	Grünlinger, Walter	KIA	Ge St	Fw 190A-5	7287	bk B-	W of Norrent-Fontes		Spitfire	127 Wing
04-09-43	Lt.	Heinemann, Ernst	KIA	4	Fw 190A-5	530414	wh 11	near Berck sur Mer		Spitfire	
04-09-43	Obfw.	Günther, Alfred	WIA	5	Fw 190A-5	1234	bk 8	5km N of Berck		Spitfire	
04-09-43	Uffz.	Schöhl, Horst-Günther	WIA	8	Fw 190A-5	530440	bk 3	Rollegem, S of Courtrai		Spitfire	403 Sqd

5 September

The heavy bombers stayed on the ground, and the effort by the mediums was limited to one B-26 raid on the Ghent coke ovens at 0915. Bombs were dropped on a nearby town, killing an Obergefreiter on the First Gruppe kitchen staff who was in the town shopping for produce. The Geschwadergruppe reached this formation on its way out, and Uffz. Wiegand shot down a No. 129 Sqd. Spitfire off Dunkirk, for his second victory. A pilot of his Staffel force-landed on Mardyck; he was uninjured, but his aircraft was later scrapped. The Messerschmitt pilots of the 11th Staffel were involved in at least three combats with the Spitfires, but without result.

6 September

The 8th Bomber Command reorganized itself into three Bombardment Divisions. The First was the old 1st Bomb Wing; the Second contained the B-24 units that were returning from North Africa; and the Third was the redesignated 4th Bomb Wing. The largest force yet employed on a single mission, 338 B-17s, was dispatched against aircraft industry targets in Stuttgart. The mission, officially characterized by the Americans as a "costly fiasco", was flown despite heavy cloud cover over the Continent. The formations became split up, and forty-five B-17s were destroyed, either by enemy action or by ditching or crash-landing after their fuel ran out.

The B-17s began crossing the English coast at 0840, on the most direct route toward Stuttgart – straight up the course of the Somme river. Jafü 2 and Jafü 3 had very little time to get their fighters up, and no successful interceptions were made on this phase of the bomber mission. The fighters landed, refueled, and waited for the determination of the bombers' return course. The numerous medium bomber and fighter bomber formations crossing the area - there were eight such missions flown during the day - were ignored, but two No. 168 Sqd. Mustangs on a recon flight prompted a scramble by some 11th Staffel fighters that had moved to Cambrai-Süd. Two Messerschmitts were damaged by the Mustangs; Uffz. Polster took a hit in his auxiliary tank, which he was able to drop.

The B-17s' return route proved to be to the west of their outbound track, and the First Gruppe moved from Grimbergen to Creil. The Second Gruppe took off from Beauvais and intercepted the bombers west of Paris. The thick clouds made the bombers hard to find, and once attacked, they tended to disappear in the lower layers. The First Gruppe claimed three B-17s, and the Second Gruppe claimed another three, but only Fw. Erich Scheyda's claim was confirmed. Uffz. Erwin Hanke was injured by bomber fire, and force-landed on the field at Romilly. The rest of the Second Gruppe returned to Beauvais.

The Geschwadergruppe and the Second Gruppe were scrambled again in the evening to oppose the last B-26 Ramrod of the day, which targeted the railroad yards at Amiens and Abbeville. The Lille unit did not make contact; the Beauvais fighters were caught near Poix by Spitfires. Uffz. Walter Berger and Fw. Adolf Jörg were shot down and killed; claims for Focke-Wulfs were filed by pilots from four Allied squadrons.

JG 26 Victory Claims: 5 - 6 September 1943

Date	Rank	Name	Unit	Cl #	Aircraft	Place	Time	Opponent	Conf
05-09-43	Uffz.	Wiegand	8	2	Spitfire	nr Dunkirk	0930	129 Sqd	yes
06-09-43	Fw.	Scheyda	3	14	B-17	6km NE of Chamont (TE3)	1300		yes
06-09-43	Fw.	Scheyda	3	15	B-17	unknown			unk
06-09-43	Fw.	Ullrich	3	1	B-17	unknown			unk
06-09-43	Oblt.	Sternberg	5 CO	20	B-17-HSS	30km NW of Paris	1218		unk
06-09-43	Lt.	Radener	6 CO		B-17-HSS	S of Reims	1210		unk
06-09-43	Fw.	Mayer	6	6	B-17-HSS	20km WNW of Cormeilles	1208		unk

7 September

The weather cleared enough in the early morning for the 8th Bomber Command to send the two B-17 Bomb Divisions against two nearby targets, Brussels-Evere airfield and the V-1 site at Watten. The First Gruppe was scrambled from Grimbergen against the Brussels formation, but the P-47 escort kept them away from the bombers. A bounce by 4th Fighter Group aircraft on the 1st Staffel went awry, and the 1st Staffel leader, Oblt. Artur Beese, chased a P-47 through a flak belt, which shot it down. Beese claimed a share of the victory, which was awarded. The Watten bombers were not intercepted at all. The Second Gruppe stayed on the ground until late afternoon, when Lt. Dietrich Kehl took off with the duty Schwarm to chase a pair of No. 168 Sqd. Mustangs. Kehl caught one, and shot it down. This Gruppe suffered a casualty later in the day, when Lt. Peter Kipping crashed fatally on Beauvais while on a test flight.

Date	Rank	Name	Cas	Unit	Aircraft	WNr	Mkgs	Place	Time	Cause	Allied Unit
06-09-43	Uffz.	Hanke, Erwin	WIA	4	Fw 190A-5	7321	wh 9	Romilly-sur-Seine		no fuel	n/a
06-09-43	Uffz.	Berger, Walter	KIA	6	Fw 190A-5	7306	br 8	12km NE of Poix		Spitfire	
06-09-43	Fw.	Jörg, Adolf	KIA	6	Fw 190A-5	7300	br 3	Molins		Spitfire	
07-09-43	Lt.	Kipping, Peter	KIFA	5	Fw 190A-4	7054	bk 14	Beauvais a/f		crashed	non-op

8 September

Operation Starkey, the Allied invasion exercise which to date had gone completely unnoticed by the Germans, reached a crescendo today when the mediums targeted the long-range guns at Boulogne. The principal diversion was an attack by two B-26 groups on Lille-Nord and Lille-Vendeville. Most of the pilots of the First and Second Gruppen and the Geschwadergruppe made two sorties, but had very little luck. Fw. Erich Schwarz of the 8th Staffel scored the only success against the Lille raiders, shooting down a No. 302 Sqd. Spitfire near Menen. In mid-afternoon, Schwarz and Uffz. Wiegand took off from Moorsele to chase a pair of No. 414 Sqd. Mustangs; Wiegand caught his Mustang over Mardyck and shot it down, for his third victory.

Two First Gruppe pilots were shot down by Spitfires at unrecorded times. Oblt. Beese bailed out with slight injuries after his Focke-Wulf was hit west of Cambrai. Fw. Helmut Bäumener, who had just returned to the unit after a long convalescence, was hit and force-landed in a farmyard near Lille. He was again severely injured, and this time did not return to the Geschwader.

The Third Gruppe began transferring today from Schipol, where it had seen little action, to Lille-Vendeville. The aircraft of the 7th and 9th Staffeln landed on Vendeville just in time to be bombed by the B-26s, which destroyed two of its Messerschmitts. Fw. Edgar Dörre of the 9th Staffel, with five B-17 victories the best non-commissioned "bomber-killer" of the Gruppe, was hit by Spitfires and crashed north of Mons in his airplane. The Third Gruppe had been displaced from Schipol by II/JG 3, which had come from the Eastern Front and had been declared ready for operations after one month in training at Uetersen. The 11th Staffel left Lille-Nord and flew the few miles to Vendeville, where it joined the Third Gruppe for the first time. The fourth Staffel of the Third Gruppe, the 12th, remained in isolation on Moorsele.

The 10th Staffel also left Lille-Nord at some time this week and rejoined its parent Second Gruppe at Beauvais. The 8th Staffel left Vendeville and, after flying from Moorsele and Wevelgem for a few days, joined the Geschwaderstab at Lille-Nord. The three organic Gruppen of the Geschwader were now in close proximity, and Priller broke up his unofficial Geschwadergruppe. The 8th Staffel was to stay under Priller's direct command as the *Führungsstaffel* (leader's squadron), however, until the following June.

9 September

The 8th Bomber Command brought Operation Starkey to an end with fragmentation and high explosive bomb attacks on eight Luftwaffe airfields in France. Several members of the Geschwader ground staff were killed or injured in the raids, and six of its aircraft were destroyed or damaged on the ground. The four P-47 groups of the exclusively-American escort were extremely effective. A Luftwaffe report stated that the P-47s prevented any head-on attacks by turning aggressively into every German approach. No Geschwader pilot filed a claim; Fw. Peter Crump, who had just returned to the 5th Staffel after a long home leave, noted in his logbook that he had downed a B-17 near Beauvais, but no bomber of the Beauvais force was in fact lost.

The B-26s and RAF bombers kept up the attacks on airfields and coastal installations for the rest of the day, but the Spitfires kept the German fighters away. The Third Gruppe was still digging out of Vendeville and Moorsele, but the other Staffeln of the Geschwader were involved in combats, most of which were inconclusive. The Focke-Wulf of Uffz. Herbert Kind was hit near St. Omer, and he force-landed with injuries. The only success of the entire day was scored by Uffz. Wiegand, who shot down a No. 122 Sqd. Spitfire as it was exiting France near Berck-sur-Mer.

JG 26 Casualties: 8 - 9 September 1943

Date	Rank	Name	Cas	Unit	Aircraft	WNr	Mkgs	Place	Time	Cause	Allied Unit
08-09-43	Oblt.	Beese, Artur	WIA	1 CO	Fw 190A-5	550474	wh 2	W of Cambrai		Spitfire	
08-09-43	Fw.	Bäumener, Helmut	WIA	3	Fw 190A-5	2688		W of Cambrai- f/l Vendeville		Spitfire	
08-09-43	Fw.	Dörre, Edgar	KIA	9	Bf 109G-6	18829	yl 5	Lens	1600	Spitfire	
09-09-43	Uffz.	Kind, Herbert	WIA	2	Fw 190A-4	2366		Coyecques-- f/l St Omer		Spitfire	

11 September

There was so little air activity over the Channel in the morning that the Second Gruppe scheduled and flew a rare, full-strength training mission in mid-afternoon, probably as a way of introducing its new Kommandeur, Major Johannes Seifert, to his unit. Seifert had been reprieved from his exile to Bulgaria after an appeal to General Galland. Since Seifert's former First Gruppe command was now held by Hptm. Borris, Hptm. Naumann, the junior Gruppenkommandeur in the Geschwader, was bumped from his job to make room for Seifert. Naumann returned to the 6th Staffel, and Lt. Radener resumed his previous position as Hptm. Naumann's deputy.

Shortly after the Gruppe had landed at its Beauvais fields and refueled, it was scrambled in response to a large raid approaching the coast west of Dieppe at low altitude. Peter Crump recalls:

> "About half-way to the coast we struck the enemy formation with what I believe were thirty aircraft - I can no longer remember exactly. We attacked the 20-25 Typhoons from above; our altitude was about 2500 meters [8000 feet].
>
> I fired at one from the left rear – I remember clearly that it turned very poorly compared to a Spitfire – after which it trailed a thick light-gray smoke plume and dived away steeply. I immediately found a second opponent in the by-now general dogfight and, after a quick glance around for security, attacked from the right and below. It too smoked at once, but this time with a darker color. The pilot, by now right down at ground level, steered toward a meadow. To my astonishment, his landing gear was down; I couldn't tell if my fire had caused it to drop, or whether it was a sign of surrender. At any rate, the plane touched down in good shape, but while still at a high speed it hit a small group of trees which stood in the meadow and exploded in a fireball."

No Focke-Wulfs were hit in this encounter. The Typhoons were the three-squadron No. 124 Wing on a bombing mission to Poix. Crump's victim was a flight sergeant from No. 175 Squadron. Lt. Hoppe shot down the Typhoon of the wing commander, W/C Alex Ingle; Ingle survived as a prisoner. Hptm. Naumann filed a third claim, but this was rejected.

JG 26 Victory Claims: 7 - 11 September 1943

Date	Rank	Name	Unit	Cl #	Aircraft	Place	Time	Opponent	Conf
07-09-43	Oblt.	Beese	1 CO	18	P-47	W of Rotterdam (IJ9)	1003	4 FG	yes
07-09-43	Lt.	Kehl	4	3	Mustang	near Rosay ?	1627	168 Sqd	yes
08-09-43	Fw.	Schwarz E.	8	5	Spitfire	NW of Menin	1026	302 Sqd	unk
08-09-43	Uffz.	Wiegand	8	3	Mustang	nr Dunkirk	1500	414 Sqd	yes
09-09-43	Fw.	Crump	5		B-17	Beauvais-Somme	0930		no
09-09-43	Uffz.	Wiegand	8	4	Spitfire	St. Pol	1600	122 Sqd	yes
11-09-43	Lt.	Hoppe	4 CO	21	Typhoon	S of Aumale-Beauvais	1848	124 Wing	yes
11-09-43	Fw.	Crump	5	11	Typhoon	near Haudramont	1841	175 Sqd	yes
11-09-43	Hptm.	Naumann	6 CO	24	Typhoon	near Forges			unk

13 September

Uffz. Horst Kretschmer, a new pilot in the 1st Staffel, was killed before taking part in his first combat mission. His engine failed on a training flight, and he crashed and burned at Hazebrouck. He died a week later in the Hazebrouck hospital.

Most of the Allied bombers were grounded by the weather, but one B-26 group attempted a mission to Woensdrecht. The bombers could not identify the target, and turned back at 1830. The escorting North Weald Wing then flew a sweep along the Belgian coast. Part of the Third Gruppe had been scrambled from Vendeville at 1822. The Messerschmitts flew below the cloud deck at only 1500 meters altitude, attempting without success to find the bombers. Major Kaj Birksted led the Norwegian Spitfires in a bounce of eight of the Bf 109s from above, hitting two. One force-landed with moderate damage, but Uffz. Helmut Bannischka of the 7th Staffel, attempting to bail out from only 200 meters (650 feet), was trapped in his aircraft when its wing fell off, and crashed with it, an event noted in both the Luftwaffe casualty report and the RAF encounter report.

15 September

The 8th Bomber Command attacked several targets near Paris, including the Romilly air depot. When their direction of flight was determined at 1804, the Jafü 2 controllers, undeterred by a large B-26 force overhead, scrambled the Pas de Calais units and sent them southwest. The B-26s were headed for Lille-Nord, but turned back without bombing, leaving the Spitfires behind to sweep the area. Many of the German fighters quickly got involved with the Spitfires; Fw. Hans Pittmann's Focke-Wulf was damaged, and he turned back and force-landed on Nivillers, destroying his aircraft and breaking many of his bones. The pilots that reached the Jafü 3 area were too late to catch the B-17s before bombing, and they put down on Creil to refuel and await the bombers' return. The Second Gruppe then made its interception, but it was totally ineffective. Flg. Hans-Walter Sander of the 10th Staffel was hit by bomber gunfire. He bailed out, struck his fighter's tail, and was severely injured. The Geschwader reported no successes this day.

16 September

In the evening the B-17s bombed targets on the Atlantic coast of France; part of their flight was unescorted, and III/JG 2 and a nearby operational training unit did quite well against them. The Second Gruppe was sent to Évreux to intercept the bombers on their return flight. Its Focke-Wulfs were overwhelmed by the Spitfires providing return cover and never found the B-17s. The pilots of the 4th Staffel were forced to form a defensive circle, and watched helplessly as Uffz. Franz Gasser was cut out of the circle and shot down by Spitfires of No. 91 Squadron. The remaining pilots broke away in the gathering dusk and returned to Beauvais.

18 September

Jafü 2 had its aircraft up for much of the afternoon in response to several medium bomber formations reported over the Channel, but most of the Allied formations turned back, as did the Germans. The one B-26 formation to bomb attacked the Beauvais-Tillé airfield, and was not intercepted, not even by the Second Gruppe Staffeln which based there.

The one air battle found in the Luftwaffe records has some unusual aspects. According to his casualty report, Fw. Rudolf David and the 12th Staffel intercepted a Typhoon squadron near Pont Audemer, southeast of Le Havre and far from the usual zone of operations for the Staffel; it is not known if the 12th Staffel had changed bases temporarily. David was the only casualty in this combat. He was shot down by a Typhoon and bailed out with foot injuries severe enough to keep him from returning to the Geschwader. No claim by a Typhoon unit has been found.

The Third Gruppe Stabsschwarm in late-summer 1943. Hptm. Mietusch is second from left, and his adjutant, Lt. Ernst Todt, is second from right. Todt was killed by a No. 41 Sqd. Spitfire on 19 September. *(Genth)*

19 September

There was no radio traffic from the heavy bomber bases, and thus the Jafü could pay full attention to the medium bomber and fighter-bomber raids. The first to appear contained B-26s making a return visit to Lille-Nord. Jafü 2 scrambled the fighters at Lille-Nord and Lille-Vendeville, while Jafü Holland-Ruhr ordered the First Gruppe up from Grimbergen. Contact was not made until after the bombing run, which did no recorded harm to Geschwader aircraft or personnel. All three Geschwader formations contacted the Spitfire escort between Lille and the coast, but no-one could reach the bombers. A Luftwaffe report noted that all approaches were broken up by Allied fighters diving from above. The Third Gruppe engaged No. 41 Squadron over Poperinghe. The Gruppe adjutant, Lt. Ernst Todt, was hit, and crash-landed violently in his plane; he died in the ambulance. Hptm. Mietusch shot down a Spitfire one minute after Todt's crash; as no Spitfire pilot claimed a Bf 109, Todt was probably shot down by Mietusch's victim. The First Gruppe hit the Spitfires a few minutes later, and Hptm. Borris downed a No. 91 Squadron aircraft southeast of Dunkirk. Uffz. Wiegand and his element leader chased a No. 411 Sqd. Spitfire all the way to Bruges before Wiegand shot it down. No Fw 190 was lost or damaged; the RAF pilots claimed 2-0-1 of them.

A Mitchell formation crossed the French coast in late afternoon, headed for Lens. Jafü 2 scrambled its fighters from Lille, Beauvais, and Cambrai, but only the last-named force, II/JG 2, made contact. The target was well within the zone of Jafü 3, and other JG 2 aircraft were brought up, but none could penetrate the Spitfire screen.

JG 26 Victory Claims: 19 September 1943

Date	Rank	Name	Unit	Cl #	Aircraft	Place	Time	Opponent	Conf
19-09-43	Hptm.	Borris	I CO	30	Spitfire	E of Ipswich (N Sea) (HF1)	1252	91 Sqd	yes
19-09-43	Hptm.	Mietusch	III CO	49	Spitfire	nr Poperinghe	1246	41 Sqd	yes
19-09-43	Uffz.	Wiegand	8	5	Spitfire	nr Brugge	1300	411 Sqd	yes

Date	Rank	Name	Cas	Unit	Aircraft	WNr	Mkgs	Place	Time	Cause	Allied Unit
13-09-43	Uffz.	Kretschmer, Horst	KIFA	1	Fw 190A-5	410222		Hazebrouck		engine	non-op
14-09-43	Uffz.	Bannischka, Helmut	KIA	7	Bf 109G-6	18867	wh 6	Wijnendale	1835	Spitfire	N Weald Wing
15-09-43	Fw.	Püttmann, Hans	WIA	5	Fw 190A-5	410234	bk 15	Beauvais		engine	n/a
15-09-43	Flg.	Sander, Hans-Walter	WIA	10	Fw 190A-5	710009	bl 11	18km E of Beauvais		B-17	
16-09-43	Uffz.	Gasser, Franz	KIA	4	Fw 190A-5	530730	wh 13	Cormeilles		Spitfire	91 Sqd
18-09-43	Fw.	David, Rudolf	WIA	12	Bf 109G-4	19374	bl 4	Pont Audemer	1900	Typhoon	
19-09-43	Lt.	Todt, Ernst	KIA	III St	Bf 109G-6	16386	<- gr 1	Poperinghe	1245	Spitfire	41 Sqd

21 September

The day's two medium bomber raids both crossed the French coast at about 1000 hours. Jafü 2 scrambled all four of its fighter units, and ordered them to assemble at the "focal point." Forty-four B-26s dropped sixty-five tons of bombs on Beauvais Tillé airfield at 1037, according to American records. No damage to the field or its contents was reported by its occupants, the Second Gruppe. Some Geschwader fighters were attacked by Spitfires near Amiens, and Lt. Manfred Draheim and Fw. Hans Dirksen were shot down and killed. Uffz. Gomann claimed a Spitfire, but the claim was reduced to one for effective damage, and no Spitfires were in fact lost.

The fighters from Lille-Nord and Beauvais broke free from the Spitfires and flew northeast after the other bomber formation, which contained Mitchells returning from a typically critical target for No. 2 Group, the Lens paint factory. Over St. Pol, Obstlt. Priller spotted a gap in the escort and led an immediate attack on the Mitchells. His target, from No. 98 Squadron, crashed. The target of Hptm. Naumann made it half-way across the Channel before force-landing; its crew was rescued by a Dover ASR launch. A third Mitchell was badly damaged, in what was one of the best JG 26 efforts against the medium bomber raids.

22 September

The weather continued poor, and the heavy bombers stayed on the ground. Today's medium bomber raids hit targets in western France. The JG 26 Gruppen were scrambled several times against RAF formations that proved to contain only fighters; no attacks were ordered. The P-47s, which now numbered six groups, swept the coast. An unidentified Staffel attempted to engage one formation, but their combat was inconclusive.

23 September

The B-17s returned to action today with two separate missions, one early in the morning and the other late in the afternoon. Their targets were all in northwestern or far western France, as were those of the medium bombers, with the exception of one B-26 Group that paid a return visit to Beauvais-Tillé. The Second Gruppe was scrambled very early and flew southwest under Jafü 3 control. It had no luck against the morning raid, and after refueling at Rouen and elsewhere, returned to Beauvais.

The B-26 raid was detected at 1610, and achieved its purpose of tying down the Jafü 2 fighters, all of which were up by 1615. At 1641 the controller ordered II/JG 2 and the Third Gruppe to come to the aid of the Second Gruppe, now in combat near its own field. The Third Gruppe arrived. The Spitfires shot down or damaged four of its Messerschmitts, all of whose pilots escaped injury. Oblt. Paul Schauder, the 9th Staffel Kapitän, downed a Spitfire, as did Major Seifert, for his first victory since his Eastern tour. Both Spitfires were apparently from No. 308 Squadron (Polish).

The defense against the evening B-17 raid was left to I/JG 2 and III/JG 2. The Americans lost three B-17s and one P-47 on the day's raids; JG 2 lost five pilots killed, seven injured, and at least fifteen fighters.

24 September

The Allied medium bombers and fighter-bombers were active from 1200 to 1800 hours against a variety of targets in northern France. The noon raids were attacks by Mitchells on an unused St. Omer airfield and the Amiens railroad yards. The Lille fighters were not scrambled to defend nearby St. Omer, but the Second Gruppe was sent up to intercept the Amiens force. Uffz. Gomann shot down a No. 129 Sqd. Spitfire near Amiens; Lt. Hoppe was also credited with a Spitfire, probably from No. 303 Sqd. (Polish). Lt. Otto Hummel's Focke-Wulf was hit by a Spitfire, and he force-landed on Beauvais. His landing gear collapsed, destroying his aircraft and injuring Hummel.

There was yet another B-26 attack on Beauvais-Tillé in mid-afternoon, but the Second Gruppe fighters were not there, having been sent to Rouen to intercept a raid that did not materialize. JG 2 was called on to defend Beauvais, and lost four Focke-Wulfs and three pilots to the Canadians of No. 127 Wing, who sustained no damage. The engine of Obfw. Alfred Günther's Focke-Wulf failed while the Second Gruppe was returning from its unsuccessful mission. Günther was injured, and his fighter was seriously damaged, in the consequent belly landing.

JG 26 Victory Claims: 21 - 24 September 1943

Date	Rank	Name	Unit	Cl #	Aircraft	Place	Time	Opponent	Conf
21-09-43	Obstlt.	Priller	Ge CO	94	Mitchell	St. Pol	1045	98 Sqd	unk
21-09-43	Uffz.	Gomann	5	7	Spitfire	10-15km NW of Le Tréport	1110		no
21-09-43	Hptm.	Naumann	6 CO	25	Mitchell	between Arras & St. Pol	1040	98 Sqd	yes
23-09-43	Maj.	Seifert	II CO	54	Spitfire	Le Fresne	1710	308 Sqd	yes
23-09-43	Oblt.	Schauder	9 CO	14	Spitfire	unknown	1710	308 Sqd	no
24-09-43	Lt.	Hoppe	4 CO	22	Spitfire	NE of Poix	1217	303 Sqd	yes
24-09-43	Uffz.	Gomann	5	8	Spitfire	SW of Amiens	1215	129 Sqd	yes

JG 26 Casualties: 21 - 24 September 1943

Date	Rank	Name	Cas	Unit	Aircraft	WNr	Mkgs	Place	Time	Cause	Allied Unit
21-09-43	Lt.	Draheim, Manfred	KIA 1		Fw 190A-5	7315	bk 8	8km NW of Albert		Spitfire	331 Sqd
21-09-43	Fw.	Dirksen, Hans	KIA 8		Fw 190A-5	1345	bk 11	10km NW of Albert		Spitfire	331 Sqd
24-09-43	Obfw.	Günther, Alfred	WIFA 5		Fw 190A-5	530728	bk 4	17km W of Amiens		engine	n/a
24-09-43	Lt.	Hummel, Otto	WIA 5		Fw 190A-5	530729	bk 2	Beauvais		Spitfire	

27 September

The 8th Bomber Command sent 246 B-17s to Emden, a mission that saw two new developments in the air war. Several bombers carried British H2S radar, which aided in the recognition of targets through the pervasive Continental undercast and would soon permit a great increase in the number of bomber missions. The other was the use of fully-pressurized 108-gallon drop tanks by the P-47s, which allowed them to accompany the bombers all the way to a German target for the first time. The bombers' approach flight crossed the North Sea and took them out of range of the Luftwaffe fighters flying from France. To prevent the movement of these fighters east, the Allied mediums and fighter-bombers revisited three French airfields.

The B-26s once again targeted Beauvais-Tillé, an indication of the respect the Allies retained for the former "Abbeville Kids" of the Second Gruppe. Oddly, no effort by this Gruppe to defend its own airfield appears in any available record – the field was possibly unserviceable from the previous attacks – but the Jafü 2 controller concentrated fighters from Lille and Cambrai and ordered attacks on the bomber formation from its Beauvais target until it recrossed the coast at Dieppe. The JG 2 Messerschmitts probably arrived first, but were dispersed by the RAF fighters, which "again stationed Schwärme of *Experten* (aces) very high, to dive on fighters already engaged in combat below", according to a report written by the Jafü control organization. The Third Gruppe continued the job of clearing out the escort; Lt. Peter

Reischer downed a No. 313 Sqd. Spitfire, and Hptm. Mietusch severely damaged one from No. 222 Squadron, for the loss of Uffz. Alfred Bäder, who was shot down from low altitude near one of the Beauvais airfields. The Lille-Nord force, comprising the 8th Staffel and the 2nd, which had been flying from Nord since the 23rd of September, reached the bombers near the coast, and Oblt. Wolfgang Neu claimed a "Boston" northeast of Rouen. The 387th Bomb Group Marauder was able to reach England, but with damage severe enough to send it to the scrap pile. Uffz. Michael Hecker of the 2nd Staffel claimed a Spitfire off Dieppe; the claim was not confirmed, but the No. 306 Sqd. Spitfire did in fact crash. Gefr. Hans Sandoz of the 2nd Staffel crash-landed east of Rouen with injuries severe enough to put him in the hospital for an extended period.

Part of the Second Gruppe got off the ground in response to an evening raid on Rouen-Sotteville by No. 2 Group Mitchells. Fw. Vogt claimed a Spitfire near Fécamp. His claim was not confirmed, but the No. 402 Squadron aircraft was in fact lost. No casualties were sustained by the Gruppe in what was apparently a low-strength effort.

JG 26 Victory Claims: 27 September 1943

Date	Rank	Name	Unit	Cl #	Aircraft	Place	Time	Opponent	Conf
27-09-43	Uffz.	Hecker	2	2	Spitfire	Somme Est (RC1)	1206	306 Sqd	yes
27-09-43	Oblt.	Neu	4	3	Boston	NE of Rouen?(SD?)		387 BG	unk
								B-26	
27-09-43	Fw.	Vogt	6	16	Spitfire	15km SE of Fécamp	1852	129 Sqd	unk
27-09-43	Hptm.	Mietusch	III CO		Spitfire	10-15km SW of Poix	1246	222 Sqd	no
27-09-43	Lt.	Reischer	7		Spitfire	Poix-Le Tréport	1111	313 Sqd	unk

28 September

Bad weather curtailed most flying until 3 October. Uffz. Rudolf Oltmanns' Focke-Wulf was caught by a gust of wind and overturned as Oltmanns attempted to land on Grimbergen following a training mission. The airplane was moderately damaged, and Oltmanns suffered slight injuries.

Geschwader personnel moves in September included the return of Oblt. Otto Stammberger after a partial recovery from his May injury. He was not cleared for flying, and joined the Geschwader ground staff, where he managed to make a number of flights in the Bf 108 courier aircraft. Fhj.-Obfw. Emil Babenz rejoined the First Gruppe from a ferry unit. Babenz had gone to Tunisia with the (first) 11th Staffel in late 1942 and had joined JG 53 when his Staffel was disbanded. He had been injured and, after recovering, had been sent to the ferry unit to regain his touch for flying. Babenz was the only 11th Staffel veteran to make it back to JG 26; he was an outstanding fighter pilot, and was given an enthusiastic welcome on his arrival at Grimbergen.

Also, two pilots left for tours as instructors, Lt. Heinrich Beer (3rd Staffel) and Lt. Johann Aistleitner (Third Gruppe), while Obfw. Franz Hiller (1st Staffel) and Lt. Wolfgang Neu (8th Staffel) returned from instructor duty. In other moves, Uffz. Anton Kratzel returned to the 2nd Staffel from ferry pilot duty; Uffz. Gerhard Falkner left the 4th Staffel to serve as a ferry pilot; Uffz. Wolf-Dieter Glahn rejoined the 1st Staffel from IV/JG 54; Fw. Wilhelm Hofmann transferred from the 1st Staffel to the 10th; Obfw. Hermann Schmeinl left the 4th Staffel for more Fw 190 training in Jagdgruppe Ost; and Fw. Peter Burger was given a permanent transfer from the 11th Staffel to a ferry unit on the grounds of constant illness.

The following men are known to have reported to the Geschwader in September after completion of pilot training: Lt. Joachim Günther, Lt. Herbert Weide - First Gruppe; Lt. Helmut Bruns, Fhr. Werner Fischer, Uffz. Hermann Kühn, Uffz. Wolfgang Kühne, Uffz. Gerhard Lissack, Uffz. Gerhard Loschinski, Uffz. Robert Ney - Second Gruppe; Uffz. Julius Richter, Fw. Bruno Schwarz, Lt. Kurt Vavken, Fw. Karl-Heinz Zeschke - Third Gruppe; Obfw. Friedrich Falke, Uffz. Heinz Voigt - 8th Staffel.

Date	Rank	Name	Cas	Unit	Aircraft	WNr	Mkgs	Place	Time	Cause	Allied Unit
27-09-43	Gefr.	Sandoz, Hans	WIA	2	Fw 190A-5	550720	bk 4	E of Rouen		Spitfire	
27-09-43	Uffz.	Bäder, Alfred	KIA	9	Bf 109G-6	140019	yl 12	Beauvais	1155	Spitfire	
28-09-43	Uffz.	Oltmanns, Rudolf	WIFA	1	Fw 190A-5	470051		Grimbergen a/f		landing	non-op

1 October

JG 26 had been operating for months with twelve Staffeln, conforming in part to the new tables of organization for the Jagdgeschwader. The existence of Priller's Geschwadergruppe had caused the operational structure of the three Gruppen to fluctuate. Today this structure was regularized by moving the 8th Staffel from the Third Gruppe to the First, giving each Gruppe four Staffeln. Also, more than half of the Staffeln were renumbered, providing each Gruppe with four sequentially-numbered Staffeln. The 8th Staffel was redesignated the 4th, joining the 1st, 2nd, and 3rd Staffeln in the First Gruppe. The 8th had originated before the war as the 4th Staffel of the Second Gruppe, but had been renumbered and moved to the then-new Third Gruppe in September, 1939. Through all of these moves, it kept its own unofficial identity as the Adamson Staffel, after the cartoon character which had adorned its aircraft from 1939 to 1941.

All of the Second Gruppe Staffeln were renumbered. The 4th Staffel became the 5th; the 5th became the 6th; the 6th became the 7th; and the 10th became the 8th. In the Third Gruppe, the 7th Staffel became the 9th, and the 9th became the 10th. The 11th and 12th Staffeln retained their designations.

One benefit of this apparently gratuitous renumbering was that it allowed the Staffel recognition colors to be regularized with a minimum of repainting, which was required of only four Staffeln. From now until the rundown of the Geschwader in 1945, the aircraft tactical numerals and Gruppe identification bars were painted strictly by the following scheme. The first Staffel in each Gruppe (i.e., the 1st, 5th, and 9th Staffeln) used white markings; the second (the 2nd, 6th, and 10th Staffeln), black; the third (the 3rd and 11th Staffeln), yellow; and the fourth (4th, 8th, and 12th Staffeln), blue. The 7th Staffel was the only exception to these RLM stipulations. Early in the war the 6th Staffel had substituted brown markings for yellow, and after becoming the 7th Staffel remained loyal to this decidedly non-standard shade until V-E day. The markings of the Geschwader and Gruppe Stab flights varied, but the previously-required chevrons, when carried, remained black, and the most common color for Stab numerals was green.

At about this time, the *Reichsluftverteidigung* (RLV), the fighter and flak defenses of Germany proper, underwent their most significant organizational changes of the war. Genobst. Hans-Jürgen Stumpff was given a new command, the Luftflotte Reich, with total responsibility for the aerial defense of Germany, including command of the antiaircraft regiments as well as both the day and the night fighters. These fighters came under Genlt. Josef "Beppo" Schmid's Jagdkorps I, which contained four Jagddivisionen. Only now could the fighters in Germany conduct a true defense in depth; previously, coordination of effort among the various Jagdfliegerführer was strictly informal. Oberst Grabmann, the most consistently successful of the Jagdfliegerführer, was promoted to the command of Jagddivision 3, but remained at Deelen.

Feldmarschall Sperrle's Luftflotte 3 was not directly affected by this reorganization. It retained its responsibility for the defense of France and western Belgium, commanding for this purpose Jagdkorps II in Paris, which contained the 4th Jagddivision, headquartered in Metz, and the 5th Jagddivision, headquartered in Paris. The 4th Jagddivison had only one Jafü, Oberst Vieck's 2nd in St. Pol, and one Jagdgeschwader, JG 26, under its administrative command. For operations, the three Gruppen of JG 26 were shifted among Jafü 3 to the west, Jafü 2, and Jafü Holland-Ruhr to the east.

2 October

The Second Gruppe transferred from Beauvais to Cambrai-Epinoy, where it was closer to the rest of the Geschwader, simplifying command by Obstlt. Priller and control by Jafü 2. It can be imagined that conditions at Beauvais had become unpleasant as a result of the recent air raids. Three Focke-Wulfs were damaged, and Fw. Walter Scholz was injured, in accidents on Epinoy at the end of the transfer flight.

3 October

The American heavy bombers remained grounded owing to the weather, but the B-26s returned to battle with attacks on five airfields: Lille-Vendeville and Beauvais-Tillé in France, and Haamstede, Schipol, and Woensdrecht in The Netherlands. No. 2 Group's bombers attacked six utility plants, all in the Jafü 3 zone of operations. This mission marked the return of Mosquito day bombers to No. 2 Group's order of battle, where they were replacing the Venturas.

The raids came in three waves, starting with the attacks on Holland at noon. The primary defense was put up by II/JG 3 from Schipol, with some help from the Third Gruppe from Vendeville, but the escort was too strong to penetrate.

The power plant raiders started crossing the French coast at about 1500. The easternmost of the screening Spitfire squadrons, No. 341 and No. 485, were attacked near Abbeville by the Second Gruppe and II/JG 2. Lt. Hans-Günther Lörzer was shot down and killed, and one JG 2 pilot bailed out without injury, but the Spitfire squadrons lost four aircraft. One Allied pilot was rescued by an ASR Walrus. Second Gruppe pilots claimed three of the Spitfires, and a JG 2 pilot claimed the fourth, but only the JG 2 claim was confirmed.

The Marauder force targeting Beauvais-Tillé apparently made its approach without encountering the Luftwaffe, but the Lille fighters hit the escort just off the bomb run. F/L R. B. Hesselyn of No. 222 Squadron, an eighteen-victory ace, shot down and killed Uffz. Joachim Leder of the 12th Staffel at 1830, but was then shot down in flames by a Fw 190 and a Bf 109, bailing out with leg injuries severe enough to prevent any attempt to evade capture. Hptm. Staiger claimed a Spitfire destroyed, and Hptm. Mietusch a damaged, at this time and place. Neither of their claims was confirmed. Fw. Wiegand was probably the Fw 190 pilot sharing the victory over Hesselyn. His notes give the correct location, but the clerk in his new Gruppe, the First, assigned the data from this claim to his claim of 5 October, and failed to record this one at all.

The Second Gruppe scrambled from Epinoy and was vectored to the east of Beauvais to intercept a formation that proved to contain only Spitfires. This was No. 127 Wing (RCAF), on a diversion to the Roye airfield. A large air battle ensued in which Fw. Crump shot down a No. 421 Sqd. Spitfire; its pilot bailed out and evaded capture. Crump's victory was not confirmed. S/L Robert "Buck" McNair, whose sixteen victories made him one of the top-scoring RCAF pilots, ditched in the Channel. He was rescued, but suffered impaired vision that prevented him from returning to combat. The Spitfire pilots received credit for five Fw 190s shot down. No Second Gruppe fighter sustained reportable damage, and there is no evidence for the presence of any other Focke-Wulf combat unit in the area. Canadian pilots were scrupulously accurate in their victory claims, and the five Fw 190s were possibly from an operational training unit.

JG 26 Victory Claims: 3 October 1943

Date	Rank	Name	Unit	Cl #	Aircraft	Place	Time	Opponent	Conf
03-10-43	Fw.	Wiegand	4		Spitfire	nr Dieppe	1830	421 Sqd	no
03-10-43	Lt.	Hoppe	5 CO	23	Spitfire	unknown	1547	341 or 485 Sqd	unk
03-10-43	Lt.	Hoppe	5 CO	24	Spitfire	10-15km W of Cayeux	1550	341 or 485 Sqd	unk

03-10-43	Obfw.	Glunz	5		Spitfire	unknown	1600	341 or 485 Sqd	no
03-10-43	Fw.	Crump	6	12	Spitfire	near Noyon	1850	41 Sqd	unk
03-10-43	Hptm.	Mietusch	III CO		Spitfire	NE of Beauvais	1825	222 Sqd	cl dam
03-10-43	Hptm.	Staiger	12 CO	33	Spitfire	Beauvais		222 Sqd	unk

4 October

The American B-17 mission to targets in central Germany went astray in bad weather. The lead bomber missed its target by one hundred miles, and numerous targets of opportunity were bombed. Although the B-26s dispatched to bomb the Jafü 2 airfields were recalled, relieving the controllers of any distractions, the Jafü and the Schlageter fighters were totally ineffective in their attempts to find and attack the American heavy bombers.

The engine of Uffz. Günter Steinberg's Bf 109G-6 caught fire as the 10th Staffel pilot was attempting to take off from St. Trond and the fighter crashed upside down, trapping Steinberg; he died in the subsequent fire.

5 October

The weather was poor, but several Allied units scheduled low-altitude missions. The Typhoons of No. 3 and No. 198 Squadrons flew Rhubarb and dive-bombing missions to various Belgian targets. Three No. 3 Squadron aircraft did not return; two were shot down by flak, and the third was lost to a Focke-Wulf piloted by Fw. Gerd Wiegand. Wiegand had been assigned to take a brand-new pilot, Uffz. Heinz Voigt, on his first orientation flight from Lille-Nord. The pair took off at 1025, and while flying along the various railroad lines and canals, which were vital landmarks as aids to navigation, Wiegand received a message that two *Indianer* (enemy fighters) were in map quadrant MF8 heading southeast, toward Courtrai and its neighboring airfield, Wevelgem. Wiegand set course to intercept, and, using hand signals, ordered Voigt to charge his weapons. Seconds later the Typhoons came into view directly ahead, just below the undercast. The RAF wingman saw or sensed the Focke-Wulfs and pulled up into the clouds. Wiegand altered course only a few degrees and opened fire on the other Typhoon, which crashed immediately. According to Wiegand, his sixth victory had taken less than thirty seconds from radio message to shootdown. Oddly, this victory was never confirmed, and both the location and aircraft type were recorded incorrectly in the First Gruppe claims list.

7 October

After escorting a Bombphoon squadron to its targets, the Typhoons of No. 198 Squadron were released to sweep along the Dutch coast below the morning cloud cover. A pair of Focke-Wulfs was seen approaching from the sea, and the RAF pilots gave chase. One of the German fighters was hit and crashed on the Ghent-Courtrai highway. The unfortunate German pilot was Lt. Johannes Matthiesen of the 1st Staffel, who had been returning from a sea reconnaissance mission.

JG 26 Casualties: 2 - 7 October 1943

Date	Rank	Name	Cas	Unit	Aircraft	WNr	Mkgs	Place	Time	Cause	Allied Unit
02-10-43	Fw.	Scholz, Walter	WIFA	6	Fw 190A-5	550186	bk 6	Epinoy a/f		landing	non-op
03-10-43	Lt.	Lörzer, Hans-Günther	KIA	7	Fw 190A-5	530726	br 8	WNW of Abbeville		combat	222 Sqd
03-10-43	Uffz.	Leder,Hans-Joachim	WIA	12	Bf 109G-6	20783	bl 6	5km NW of Noyon	1835	Spitfire	341 or 485 Sqd
04-10-43	Uffz.	Steinberg, Günther	KIFA	10	Bf 109G-6	20457	bk 13	St. Trond a/f	1253	takeoff	non-op
07-10-43	Lt.	Matthiesen, Johannes	KIA	1	Fw 190A-4	617	wh 5	Wielsbeke	0741	Typhoon	198 Sqd
07-10-43	Lt.	Reinhardt, Klaus	WAC	11	none			Vendeville a/f	1030	accident	non-op

8 October

The American B-17s and B-24s left the English coast shortly after noon and headed

east across the North Sea toward Bremen and Vegesack. The diversionary raids that normally kept the Jafü 2 fighters close to their bases were abandoned owing to the bad weather conditions. The First Gruppe was scrambled on reports of Allied aircraft over the Channel, but did not make contact. The Second Gruppe was not called on to fly today; the Third Gruppe was ordered to move to Leeuwarden to oppose the returning heavy bombers, and left Vendeville at about 1415. The Gruppe sortied from Leeuwarden at 1615 and flew out to sea fifty kilometers west of den Helder, where they encountered B-17s and some P-47s of the return escort. After a battle which resulted in no claims, the Gruppe returned to Vendeville.

9 October

The 8th Bomber Command attacked targets in East Prussia and Poland in its longest mission to date. The bombers were unescorted, but the German defenses in the area were known to be light, and surprise was counted on to keep losses to an acceptable level. As the heavy bombers headed east across the North Sea, four P-47 groups swept across The Netherlands, and B-26s bombed Woensdrecht, but the Jafü 2 and Jafü Holland-Ruhr controllers kept their fighters well away from them. The entire Geschwader was sent north to await the bombers' return, the First and Second Gruppen to Leeuwarden and the Third Gruppe to Eelde, but the bombers' return route was apparently farther north than in the past, and the fighters were not ordered up. They spent the night in northern Holland.

10 October

A large high-pressure area brought cloudless skies to Germany, while France was covered in the customary morning fog. The large volume of radio traffic from the American bomber bases presaged a heavy raid. When the bombers did not take off in time for a deep penetration raid, the Jafü Holland-Ruhr at Deelen concluded that the bombers were coming to northwestern Germany, and began to deploy his forces accordingly. Today these forces included all of JG 26, which had overnighted in Holland. Before the bombers took off, the First and Second Gruppen had left Leeuwarden; the First Gruppe for Deelen, and the Second Gruppe for the large permanent Luftwaffe base at Rheine. The skilled or lucky controller placed the latter Gruppe within twenty-five miles of the 8th Bomber Command's target for the day, the center of the city of Münster. Furthermore, the move was conducted in strict radio silence, and Allied intelligence never located the two Gruppen; the 8th Bomber Command mission report makes no mention of them.

At 1348, the leading Third Bomb Division began crossing the English coast at Felixstowe. It was followed fifteen minutes later by the First Bomb Division, which was given most of the P-47 escort in the expectation that the Third Bomb Division would achieve surprise. A total of 274 B-17s and 216 P-47s was dispatched. At 1405, the Third Gruppe Bf 109s took off from Eelde in far northern Holland; they had a lot of ground to cover. II/JG 3 took off from Schipol three minutes later; it was still five minutes before the Third Bomb Division reached the Dutch coast. The direction of the attackers having been well established, the Fw 190s of I/JG 26 and I/JG 1 were ordered to take off from Deelen; a few minutes later II/JG 26 flew off the runway at Rheine. The three Focke-Wulf Gruppen joined up in a single *Gefechtsverband* (battle formation). According to Heinz Gomann, this was the first and only time that his Second Gruppe was part of a force strong enough to carry out the old military aphorism, *Klotzen nicht Kleckern* (Strike hard, don't mess around.)

The German fighters continued to concentrate along the track of the bombers, which was tracing a line due east across The Netherlands. At 1440, a diversionary flight over the North Sea by the Second Bomb Division's B-24s aborted, freeing up all of the remaining defenders. At least thirteen Jagdgruppen and *Zerstörergruppen* (heavy fighter groups), approximately 350 fighters, would ultimately engage the Americans.

A direct course to Münster had been ordered so that the escorting P-47s could stay with the bombers all the way to the target. II/JG 3 was the first Gruppe to reach the bombers. The pilots had been read Galland's new instructions to attack from the rear, and were apparently driven off easily by the trailing First Bomb Division's heavy escort. A rookie fighter group, the 352nd, kept the leading Third Bomb Division well covered until 1448, when its Thunderbolts turned back over Dorsten, Germany. Its relief, the equally-new 355th Fighter Group, was still fogbound in England. A careful American plan had once again been spoiled by the English weather. The patient Germans saw their opportunity, and instantly took advantage of it. The onslaught began. The bomber crewmen in the leading 14th Bomb Wing's 390th, 95th, and 100th Groups saw, in the clear air ahead, an estimated 200 German fighters – all of whose leaders apparently considered themselves "proven successful" at head-on attacks, and thus exempt from the new orders prohibiting them. At 1453, nine minutes away from Münster, Schwärme of Fw 190s began level attacks on the low 100th Group from dead ahead. The Focke-Wulfs closed to 50-75 yards before flicking over and diving away. Within seven minutes, the entire "Bloody Hundredth" formation had vanished. Six Fortresses had been destroyed; six others were turning back with smoking engines. All of these bombers were doomed; only one of the thirteen B-17s dispatched by the group returned to England.

Attacks alternated between head-on passes by Fw 190s and Bf 109s from a number of Jagdgruppen, and rocket barrages from Me 410s positioned behind the leading wing. Most of the fighters broke away briefly when the bombers came within range of the Münster Flak defenses, which allowed the bombardiers to line up on their aiming point for this Sunday mission, the Münster cathedral, without hindrance. But the ever-eager Fw. Gerd Wiegand and his wingman, Uffz. Raimund Rösner, found themselves beneath the leading 95th Bomb Group just as the bombs began falling from the Fortresses' bomb bays. Dodging these projectiles, the two young pilots pulled up into a vertical climb, straining to regain an attack position ahead of the bombers. As they leveled off, the Fortresses made their left turn off the target, necessitating a stern chase by the pair. Wiegand dived at full speed and pulled up directly behind the B-17 at the left rear of the leading combat box. His first attack hit the plane's No. 1 engine, which began losing large pieces of metal. Smoking and raining debris, the B-17 slowly pulled away from its formation. Wiegand attacked again, from the right side. This time he hit the fuel tanks, and the Fortress's right wing began trailing a white stream of liquid. Wiegand and Rösner watched as eight crewmen bailed out. Next, so that Wiegand was assured of his victory, they followed the bomber until they saw it crash twelve miles north of Münster. The two pilots then sought out the nearest field, Münster-Handorf, and landed to refuel. The 95th Group Fortress became Wiegand's seventh confirmed victory.

Rocket attacks by Bf 110s and Me 410s resumed, followed by more head-on attacks by single-engine fighters, many with the checkered cowls of JG 1. Four more B-17s were ultimately lost by the 95th Group. Finally, as it appeared that the entire lead wing would be annihilated, the P-47s of the 56th Group arrived to begin their withdrawal escort. They sailed into the middle of the melee, splitting up into flights of four to reach as many German attackers as possible. Lt. Robert Johnson's Thunderbolt was badly damaged by a Fw 190, but not until he had shot down two planes to become an ace. Maj. David Schilling, the deputy commander of the 56th, also downed his fifth German fighter on this mission, as did Capt. Walter Beckham of the 353rd Fighter Group. The Schlageter fighters were now tracking down the Third Bomb Division aircraft that had been shot from their formations. All but one German fighter managed to avoid the attention of the Thunderbolts. Lt. Hans Mayer of the 8th Staffel was hit by a P-47, and survived a spectacular, cartwheeling attempt at a crash-landing on Twente.

The Third Gruppe apparently reached the bomber stream just after it had turned for home. Hptm. Staiger and Uffz. Hans Oeckel of the 12th Staffel were credited with the destruction of B-17s. Both pilots were wounded by the bombers' return fire; Staiger suffered additional injuries in his crash landing. These two men were the only Third Gruppe casualties.

The German fighters finally broke away to seek out suitable landing grounds in Holland or Belgium. The pilots of the Geschwader received a commendation from Generalfeldmarschall Sperrle in Paris, crediting them with nineteen bombers shot down and another nineteen shot from formation. Ten victories were ultimately confirmed; set against a casualty list of three injured pilots and five damaged or destroyed aircraft, it was a notable victory. The units of only a few of these B-17s can be determined. The tough birds rarely went down after a single attack, they could rarely be followed all the way to the ground, and only Gerd Wiegand kept a notebook documenting the position in formation of his targets, as well as the angle of deflection of his gunfire.

The other German defenders also did well; for a total loss of twenty-five fighters and twelve crewmen, they had destroyed thirty B-17s and one P-47. Nine of the German losses were twin-engine Bf 110s and Me 410s; it was obvious that these effective bomber destroyers would have to be shielded from the attentions of the American escorts if they were to remain a viable defensive weapon.

JG 26 Victory Claims: 5 - 10 October 1943

Date	Rank	Name	Unit	Cl #	Aircraft	Place	Time	Opponent	Conf
05-10-43	Fw.	Wiegand	4	6	Typhoon	NW of Courtrai (MF)	1100	3 Sqd	no
10-10-43	Obfw.	Lindelaub	1		B-17	unknown			no
10-10-43	Uffz.	Heuser Hein.	2	5	B-17	S of Rheine (HQ)	1515		yes
10-10-43	Fw.	Wiegand	4	7	B-17	E of Arnhem (HO1)	1510	95 BG	yes
10-10-43	Maj.	Seifert	II CO	55	B-17	NE of Rheine	1530		yes
10-10-43	Lt.	Hoppe	5 CO		B-17	unknown			unk
10-10-43	Oblt.	Sternberg	5 CO	22	B-17	Haaksbergen-Almelo	1523	390 BG	yes
10-10-43	Obfw.	Glunz	5	43	B-17	N of Deelen	1541	100 BG	yes
10-10-43	Uffz.	Scheu	6		B-17	unknown			no
10-10-43	Lt.	Radener	7		B-17-HSS	NE of Münster	1535		unk
10-10-43	Fw.	Polster	11	2	B-17	NW of Münster	1500	385 BG	unk
10-10-43	Hptm.	Staiger	12 CO	34	B-17	W of Münster		385 BG	yes
10-10-43	Uffz.	Oeckel	12	1	B-17	Netherlands		385 BG	yes

JG 26 Casualties: 10 October 1943

Date	Rank	Name	Cas	Unit	Aircraft	WNr	Mkgs	Place	Time	Cause	Allied Unit
10-10-43	Lt.	Mayer, Hans	WIA	8	Fw 190A-6	530770	bl 7	Enschede-Twente a/f	1530	P-47	
10-10-43	Hptm.	Staiger, Hermann	WIA	12 CO	Bf 109G-6	15920	bl 2	near Dorsten	1530	B-17	
10-10-43	Uffz.	Oeckel, Hans	WIA	12	Bf 109G-6	19645		Woerendonk		B-17	

14 October

The most successful daylight operation for the twin-engine fighters came only four days later, on the 8th Air Force's "Black Thursday". The bomber commanders scheduled a return trip to Schweinfurt on short notice, based on favorable weather conditions over the Continent, despite the knowledge that the fighter escort would be no stronger or longer-legged than that on 17 August. The long-ranged P-38 Lightnings were not yet operational, and the P-47 units had run out of 108-gallon drop tanks, which were being manufactured (slowly) in England, and would have to revert to 75-gallon tanks. All three Bomb Divisions were scheduled to fly the mission; each would be escorted by a single P-47 group on penetration, and a single group on withdrawal. There would be no diversionary raids; the courses of the three bomber formations would diverge slightly, in a weak attempt at deception.

The American airfields were blanketed in chilly autumn fog, but when the morning weather reconnaissance reported clear air over the Continent, the crews were ordered to their planes. The first of 291 B-17s took off at 1012. In Deelen, Oberst Grabmann, expecting a full-strength deep-penetration raid from the volume of radio traffic and time of takeoff, put his own fighter units on alert, and by 1130, fifty minutes before the bombers began crossing the English coast, he was asking the neighboring Jafü to bring their own fighters to full readiness. The poor weather over England prevented the B-17s from forming up properly and left the First Bomb Division in a vulnerable formation. The B-24s couldn't form up at all, and were ordered to fly a diversion in the North Sea, thus wasting one of the three airborne P-47 groups, which went with them. The B-17s and their P-47s finally took up a course to the southeast – on a straight line toward Schweinfurt. The First Bomb Division was to the east of and slightly ahead of the Third, ensuring that it would receive most of the attacks from the fighters of Jafü Holland-Ruhr.

Oberst Grabmann tried two new tricks this morning. He apparently ordered the Messerschmitts of III/JG 1 and I/JG 3 to attack the P-47 escort between Woensdrecht and Antwerp. Targeting the escorts deliberately was strictly in violation of Berlin's standing orders, but Grabmann probably felt that his past successes gave him some leeway. The 353rd Fighter Group took to the challenge well, however, shooting down seven Bf 109s while remaining fairly close to the bombers.

Grabmann ordered the rest of his fighters to concentrate over Düren, near the limit of the escort fighters' range, rather than send them piecemeal at the bombers while they were still over The Netherlands. The First and Second Gruppen had remained at Deelen and Rheine after the Münster mission, and were under Grabmann's command for the entire day. The Second Gruppe was apparently the first unit to arrive at the First Bomb Division formation. Obfw. Glunz and Gefr. Wyrich teamed up to shoot down a 353rd Fighter Group P-47, the only Allied fighter to be lost this day.

The moment the escort turned back near Aachen, the Fw 190s and Bf 109s began closing in. The Focke-Wulfs of JG 1 and JG 26 made their attack first – at twelve o'clock high, by Schwärme. Rocket-firing twin-engine fighters joined the battle early, firing their missiles from the rear of the bomber boxes. Three Second Gruppe pilots claimed B-17s shot down between 1330 and 1400 hours. Major Seifert's and Obfw. Roth's targets are known to have been from the 305th Bomb Group. That group's formation began to disintegrate at this time; it had lost thirteen of its sixteen B-17s prior to the bomb run. A 4th Staffel Focke-Wulf was shot down by the bombers, but its pilot bailed out without injury.

The First Gruppe attack brought down two B-17s, which were credited to two of the senior NCOs of the Gruppe, Obfw. Heckmann and Obfw. Eichinger. Uffz. Horst Richter was hit by the bombers' fire and bailed out, but died soon after reaching the ground. Uffz. Jan Schild's attack left his target's left two engines on fire. He recalls that he was then chased away from the bombers by Spitfires – undoubtedly P-47s – which damaged his Focke-Wulf's right aileron during a dogfight at low altitude. Schild was forced to make a belly landing east of Antwerp, which destroyed his aircraft but brought no injury to the pilot.

The clouds that had so disrupted the Americans' formations over England in the morning grew thicker during the day. None of the USAAF or RAF return escorts could get off their bases. The B-17s were only saved from annihilation by the movement of the front across the Channel. None of the Jafü Holland-Ruhr units were able to fly a second mission, owing at least in part to the worsening weather, and the Third Gruppe, when it finally got the order to scramble from Lille-Vendeville, was apparently not given a vector from which it could locate the bombers. The bombers' return route took them down the course of the Somme River to the Channel. The numerous JG 2 fighters in the area should have had it easy against the unescorted, disorganized bomber formations, but could claim only seven B-17s; the rest managed to escape in the towering cumulus formations.

Although the role of the Schlageter Geschwader in "Black Thursday" proved to be a minor one, sixty B-17s were destroyed by the Luftwaffe in three hours and fourteen minutes of continuous attacks; seven more bombers were scrapped in England. The tactics found successful over Münster were repeated time and again. The twin-engine fighters first fired rockets from outside the range of the defensive gunners. The explosions of the rockets disrupted the bomber formations and facilitated the head-on attacks of the single-engine fighters. Every German fighter unit in western Europe was ultimately employed – 833 combat sorties were flown. The Germans lost only thirty-eight fighters. The OKW announced that 121 American aircraft had been brought down. The true losses were only half that, but it was obvious to both sides that the defenders had won a stunning victory. The American doctrine of unescorted daylight bombing was finally dead. No more deep penetration raids would be made into Germany until the bombers could be escorted all the way to the target. The operational training of the first two groups of truly long-ranged American fighters, P-38 Lightnings, was rushed to completion.

JG 26 Victory Claims: 14 October 1943

Date	Rank	Name	Unit	Cl #	Aircraft	Place	Time	Opponent	Conf
14-10-43	Obfw.	Heckmann	1	58	B-17	Sedan? (RK7?)	1400		yes
14-10-43	Uffz.	Schild	2		B-17-HSS	E of Antwerp	1400		unk
14-10-43	Obfw.	Eichinger	3	3	B-17	St. Omer (NE1)	1400		yes
14-10-43	Maj.	Seifert	II CO	56	B-17	edge of Maastricht	1332	305 BG	yes
14-10-43	Obfw.	Glunz	5		P-47	near Budel	1400	353 FG	no
14-10-43	Obfw.	Roth	5	20	B-17	SW of Bonn	1403	305 BG	yes
14-10-43	Gefr.	Wyrich	5	2	P-47	WNW of Weert	1337	353 FG	unk
14-10-43	Hptm.	Naumann	7 CO	26	B-17	Domburg	1330		yes
14-10-43	Lt.	Radener	7		B-17-HSS	N of Koblenz	1335		no

15 October

Major Rolf Hermichen left Grimbergen today to take command of I/JG 11 at Husum. He was replaced as leader of the 3rd Staffel by Oblt. Heinrich Jessen.

Uffz. Wolfgang Polster left Vendeville for a brief tour as a test pilot at Rechlin. The Messerschmitt engineers still had not found the proper location for the methanol tank mounted in the Bf 109G-6, and Polster was called on to make programmed flights with the tank at various orientations and levels. Wolfgang Polster was probably recommended for the job by the Third Gruppe technical officer, who remembered Polster's strong opinions on the Bf 109G-1, the first version of the fighter with methanol boost.

18 October

The American heavy bomber raid targeted Düren, but was recalled over the North Sea owing to bad weather. The escort force of thirty-three P-38s, 296 P-47s, and numerous Spitfires was released to sweep the German-occupied coast. The controllers believed that there were bombers among them, but the Allied fighters were so thick that no attack was ordered. Third Gruppe Messerschmitts and 8th Staffel Focke-Wulfs skirmished with the Spitfires of No. 132 Squadron near Bethune. Fw. Wilhelm Hofmann shot down a Spitfire, but Fhr. Burghardt Wölke had to bail out of his Messerschmitt with severe injuries. Uffz. Ernst Laub of the 11th Staffel apparently encountered a 78th Fighter Group P-47 that had dropped from formation with propeller problems, and shot it down. One Messerschmitt and one Focke-Wulf sustained combat damage, and a Focke-Wulf was damaged in a dead-stick landing on Ligescourt necessitated by fuel shortage.

JG 26 Casualties: 14 - 18 October 1943

Date	Rank	Name	Cas	Unit	Aircraft	WNr	Mkgs	Place	Time	Cause	Allied Unit
14-10-43	Uffz.	Richter, Horst	KIA	3	Fw 190A-4	5807	yl 9	Geilenkirchen		B-17	
14-10-43	Uffz.	Schild, Heinrich	WIA	2	Fw 190A-5	1348		near Antwerp	1430	P-47	353 FG
18-10-43	Fhr.	Wölke, Burghardt	WIA	11	Bf 109G-6	26063		Bethune		Spitfire	132 Sqd

20 October

The RAF resumed flying sweeps to the Continent, despite continuing bad weather. The Hornchurch Wing flew an early mission to Lille that provided the Geschwader with its biggest success of the day. Fw. Wiegand's Schwarm was scrambled from Lille-Nord at 0925 on the report of a large formation crossing the coast. Wiegand confirmed that it contained only Spitfires, and then led his small force in an attack from behind and below an isolated section. The surprise attack was completely successful. According to Gerd Wiegand's records, each of the four members of the Schwarm downed a Spitfire. In reality, two No. 485 Sqd. (RNZAF) Spitfires crashed immediately, and a third made it back to England before its engine seized; its pilot then bailed out safely. None of the 4th Staffel pilots received credit for their victories.

Meanwhile, the 8th Air Force mission orders of the 18th had been copied. The Düren raid was on again. The mission was to be flown despite reports of heavy cloud cover over the Continent. It was to be the first American use of the British Oboe blind-bombing aid. The shallow-penetration raid would be escorted all the way to the target by a force comprising one P-38 group and seven P-47 groups. Once airborne, the bombers found cirrus clouds as high as 30,000 feet, and their formations were quickly split up. Only 114 of the 212 bombers dispatched were able to drop their bombs, and they had little effect.

The bombers' track across the Channel was pointed at Berck-sur-Mer, and Priller's Führungsstaffel and all three Gruppen were scrambled at 1320 and ordered west. The Stab arrived first and made a quick attack on the Third Bomb Division formation. Obstlt. Priller shot a 96th Bomb Group B-17 out of its formation. The Third Gruppe reached the First Bomb Division just as the latter abandoned the mission plan and made a hard left turn to seek out targets of opportunity. The Spitfires had gone, and the Thunderbolts had not yet arrived. Mietusch took the time to form up his Gruppe and lead them in a head-on attack. Mietusch and Hptm. Steindl each shot down a 303rd Bomb Group B-17 on their first pass – but according to the American witnesses, they were followed through the bombers by only six of their comrades. Two 12th Staffel pilots, Uffz. Alex Meyer and Lt. Werner Grupe, were hit by the bomber gunners. Grupe was able to bail out with injuries, but Meyer crashed in his plane. Mietusch then gathered as many of his Messerschmitts as he could and followed the First Bomb Division north, toward Brussels. Lt. Burkert downed another B-17, but the P-47s then arrived in force, ending all thoughts of further bomber attacks. Oblt. Dippel claimed a P-47; his claim was confirmed, but none were in fact lost. 78th Fighter Group P-47s shot down Fw. Konrad Eckhardt and Uffz. Hermann Friedrich. Eckhardt was killed, and Friedrich bailed out with injuries. The First Gruppe, up from Grimbergen, had no successes, and lost Uffz. Anton Kratzel to the B-17 gunners. Uffz. Raimund Rösner of the 4th Staffel apparently encountered some 355th Fighter Group Thunderbolts, which promptly shot him down.

The Second Gruppe mission was a total fiasco. It took off from Epinoy through low-lying rain clouds. The Gruppe formation broke up completely while penetrating the cloud deck. Because the cloud tops were at widely different altitudes, the emerging pilots could see only a few of their own planes. Peter Crump recalls:

"Only my wingman remained with me. Our little force came face-to-face with the bomber formation in the area of Brussels. We flew to one side of it and tried to climb as high as possible. What a magnificent sight – the sun beaming down; the deep blue sky above; the clouds below like cotton. And in between, the bomber formation pressed on to the southeast at 18,000 feet. There was not another German plane in sight. It was two lonely fighter pilots against an armada. My plan was to surprise the formation and its fighter escort from the greatest possible altitude, attacking its lead aircraft from the sun. However, our climb was cut short by the intervention of two Thunderbolts. At this altitude, about 10,500 meters [34,000 feet] and in this combat situation, we had to concede the superiority of the *Donnerbolzen* (Thunderbolts) and their turbo-superchargers. Our short-winded Focke-Wulfs hung limp and bloated in the sky, like two little sausages. I broke into the fighters, firing off all of my guns. We avoided further attacks by using our 'emergency brakes'; that is, by spinning out. This maneuver was only used in desperate situations; in this case it was successful.

"My Focke-Wulf came out of its spin in a vertical dive. It began to shudder. The entire surface of the wings was covered in condensation. I did not dare load the wings further by pulling back on the stick to end the dive. Past the vertical, the aircraft began slowly to pull out by itself, and at three hundred meters [one thousand feet] I had it back in level flight.

"My next problem was right beneath me – the continuous cloud deck. No gap in the clouds was to be seen, and I had no idea where I was. I carefully leveled my aircraft and dived. I caught sight of the ground – a patch of woods. That was just enough to get my bearings; I was over the Ardennes, near the German border. I landed at an emergency field near Vogelsang castle, and learned upon inquiry that my wingman had landed safely at Bonn-Hangelar."

One 5th Staffel pilot, Uffz. Walter Bürger, was shot down and killed by a 78th Fighter Group P-47 over Elsenborn, near the Ardennes. Lt. Hans Wölfert fell near Monschau, dead in his parachute. He had bailed out in the clouds, possibly panicked and disoriented, and died of the cold and/or anoxia.

The day as a whole was a minor disaster for the German defenses. Only nine B-17s were shot down, for the loss of nineteen German pilots killed or injured. The losses of JG 2 were about equal to those of JG 26. The Richthofen fighters' approach flight to the incoming bomber stream was broken up completely by the Spitfire XIIs of the Hawkinge Wing, which shot down ten Messerschmitts and Focke-Wulfs without a loss. JG 26 lost six pilots killed and two injured, and nine of its aircraft were wrecked. All of the casualties of the Schlageter Geschwader were 1943 replacements, boding ill for the future; it is certain that none of the five pilots shot down by P-47s had the skill or experience Peter Crump needed to survive after being bounced at 10,500 meters (34,000 feet).

JG 26 Casualties: 20 October 1943

Date	Rank	Name	Cas	Unit	Aircraft	WNr	Mkgs	Place	Time	Cause	Allied Unit
20-10-43	Uffz.	Kratzel, Anton	KIA	2	Fw 190A-5	5894	bk 8	Chimay-NW of Cambrai	1400	B-17	
20-10-43	Uffz.	Rösner, Raimund	KIA	4	Fw 190A-6	530574	bl 3	NE of Chimay	1400	P-47	355 FG
20-10-43	Uffz.	Bürger, Walter	KIA	5	Fw 190A-6	530732	wh 10	Krinkelt near Elsenborn		P-47	78 FG
20-10-43	Lt.	Wölfert, Hans	KIA	7	Fw 190A-6	530927	br 12	Monschau-Eifel		combat	
20-10-43	Fw.	Eckhardt, Konrad	KIA	9	Bf 109G-6	20480	wh 4	Leuze near Ath	1410	P-47	78 FG
20-10-43	Uffz.	Friedrich, Hermann	WIA	11	Bf 109G-3	16300	yl 2	Harchies near Mons	1415	P-47	78 FG
20-10-43	Lt.	Grupe, Werner	WIA	12	Bf 109G-4	19791	bl 14	6km SW of Hirson	1350	B-17	
20-10-43	Uffz.	Meyer, Alex	KIA	12	Bf 109G-6	18837	bl 1	N Hirson-6km NE of Chimay	1350	B-17	

Uffz. Raimund Rösner of the 4th Staffel. Rösner was killed in combat with 355th Fighter Group P-47s on 20 October. *(Vanoverbeke)*

Lt. Hans Wölfert of the 7th Staffel. On 20 October Wölfert bailed out at high altitude after combat with 78th Fighter Group P-47s, and froze to death in his parachute. *(Vanoverbeke)*

JG 26 Victory Claims: 18 - 20 October 1943

Date	Rank	Name	Unit	Cl #	Aircraft	Place	Time	Opponent	Conf
18-10-43	Uffz.	Laub	11	3	P-47	St Pol (PE4-9)	1410	78 FG	yes
18-10-43	Fw.	Hofmann W.	8	3	Spitfire	near Ardres	1420	132 Sqd	yes
20-10-43	Obstlt.	Priller	Ge CO	95	B-17-HSS	SE of Arras-Cambrai	1345	96 BG	unk
20-10-43	Fw.	Hager R.	4		Spitfire	Dixmuiden	0945	485 Sqd	unk
20-10-43	Obfw.	Heitmann	4		Spitfire	Dixmuiden	0945	485 Sqd	unk
20-10-43	Uffz.	Voigt	4		Spitfire	Dixmuiden	0945	485 Sqd	unk
20-10-43	Fw.	Wiegand	4		Spitfire	Dixmuiden	0945	485 Sqd	unk
20-10-43	Hptm.	Mietusch	III CO	50	B-17	Cambrai (PG-QH)	1410	303 BG	yes
20-10-43	Oblt.	Dippel	9 CO	17	P-47	unknown			yes
20-10-43	Lt.	Burkert E.	9	2	B-17	unknown		96 BG	yes
20-10-43	Hptm.	Steindl	11	10	B-17	crashed Mons (PG-PH)	1411	303 BG	yes

21 October

Lt. Georg Kiefner returned to Grimbergen after hospitalization for his 17 August injury. He made one familiarization flight, and was then ordered to Biarritz to complete his recovery while serving limited duty as an instructor.

22 October

The B-26s were now part of the 9th Air Force, the headquarters of which had moved from the Mediterranean Theater to England to command the American tactical air units in the forthcoming invasion. The Second Gruppe airfield at Cambrai-Epinoy was still near the top of their target list, and they returned to it this morning. Defending the field were the Second Gruppe, II/JG 2 from Vitry, and III/JG 2, which had recently transferred to Beaumont-le-Roger from Brittany. Only the Second Gruppe was successful; Fw. Karl Ehret of the 7th Staffel shot down a No. 421 Sqd. Spitfire southwest of Beauvais at 1033. JG 2 lost four aircraft in this battle with No. 127 Wing (RCAF).

The First Gruppe was responsible for carrying out sea reconnaissance missions from Grimbergen every morning and evening. These were generally uneventful, but this evening Uffz. Helmut Pittmann ran into an Antwerp church steeple while searching for his airfield with the sun in his eyes, and crashed to his death.

The Third Gruppe left Lille-Vendeville, exchanging bases with I/JG 3 at Bönninghardt. The move was apparently intended to give the JG 26 unit something of a break from operations. Although both of these Gruppen had seen some heavy fighting lately, the pressure of serving on the Pas de Calais, where enemy aircraft could be expected every day, weather permitting, was unique in the Jagdwaffe.

23 October

The Allies sent only a few fighter sweeps across the Channel. The Second Gruppe was scrambled to oppose one of these, and engaged two squadrons of Spitfires near Beauvais, but without result.

24 October

The B-26s were very active today. Three missions were flown to airfields in northern France. Their escort comprised forty-eight P-38s, 205 P-47s, and a large number of Spitfires. At noon the Second Gruppe was scrambled from Epinoy, the 4th Staffel from Lille-Nord, and I/JG 3 from Lille-Vendeville to meet a wave of medium bombers heading for Amiens. Fw. Crump was able to penetrate the escort, and his attack on a B-26 left the bomber smoking. It was not seen to crash, and Crump did not file a claim; the bomber in fact made it back to England. The escorting Spitfires from No. 331 and No. 332 Sqds. (Norwegian) gave I/JG 3 a rude introduction to life on the Pas de Calais, shooting down four of its Messerschmitts. The Gruppe lost one pilot killed and two injured; the uninjured pilot was Major Klaus Quaet-Faslem, the Gruppenkommandeur. The unit claimed no victories. Obfw. Wilhelm Freuwörth of the 6th Staffel was shot down by one of the Norwegians and bailed out with serious wounds.

Hptm. Ebersberger landed on Ligescourt for servicing after this interception. When he took off again, he was attacked by two reconnaissance Mustangs from No. 400 Sqd. (RCAF). Ebersberger jumped from his plane, but was too low for his parachute to open. His victory total at the time of his death was twenty-eight. Oblt. Wolfgang Neu was named Ebersberger's successor as leader of the 4th Staffel. At thirty-five years of age, Neu was the oldest pilot in the Geschwader. Neu was a reservist, and a pilot of only modest skills. He soon volunteered to fly his missions as Fw. Wiegand's wingman. Gerd Wiegand, who now had the highest score in his Staffel, was permitted to lead the entire unit in the air.

JG 26 Casualties: 22 - 24 October 1943

Date	Rank	Name	Cas	Unit	Aircraft	WNr	Mkgs	Place	Time	Cause	Allied Unit
22-10-43	Uffz.	Pittmann, Helmut	KIFA	1	Fw 190A-	5555	wh 3	5km N of Antwerp		hit church	n/a
24-10-43	Hptm.	Ebersberger, Kurt	KIA	4 CO	Fw 190A-6	550440	bl 1	3km S of Hesdin		Spitfire	400 Sqd
24-10-43	Obfw.	Freuwörth, Wilhelm	WIA	6	Fw 190A-6	530733	bk 8	S of Montdidier		Spitfire	N Weald Wing

29 October

Three Geschwader Staffelkapitäne were awarded the German Cross in Gold: Oblt. Helmut Hoppe (5th Staffel) after twenty-five air victories; Oblt. Horst Sternberg (6th Staffel) after twenty-two, and Hptm. Hermann Staiger (12th Staffel) after thirty-four.

31 October

The inventory of Fw 190s in the Geschwader increased during the month. The Stab ended the month with four; the First Gruppe, fifty; and the Second Gruppe, fifty-two. Nearly all were the Fw 190A-6 variant; there were only a few earlier models left. The

Third Gruppe, on the other hand, saw its stock of Bf 109s decrease from fifty to thirty. Five were lost in combat, one was a non-operational loss, and twenty-seven were transferred to another unit. This recipient was undoubtedly I/JG 3; the Third Gruppe apparently had to leave half of its fighters on Lille-Vendeville for the unit that relieved it. Twenty-five of its remaining fighters were Bf 109G-6s; the rest were earlier models.

Geschwader personnel moves during October included: the departure of Major Werner Lederer from the Stab; the transfer of Obfw. Heinz-Günther Klems to the staff of the General der Jagdflieger; the return of Lt. Hans Fischer to the 5th Staffel from instructor duty; the transfer of Uffz. Fritz Rapsch into the 3rd Staffel from Erprobungskommando 25; the transfer of Lt. Herfried Kloimüller into the 3rd Staffel from Jagdgruppe 50; and the return of Obfw. Hermann Schmeinl to the 4th Staffel from Fw 190 training.

Pilots reporting to the Geschwader from pilot training included: Ofhr. Josef Burglechner, Gefr. Siegfried Machner, Lt. Bernhard Törpisch - First Gruppe; Uffz. Josef Baumann, Uffz. Karl Bierkamp, Lt. Holger Bruns, Uffz. Erwin Hell, Lt. Friedrich Lange, Uffz. Kurt Stahnke - Second Gruppe; Fw. Hans Fischer, Uffz. Franz Piplitz, Uffz. Heinz Schreiber - Third Gruppe.

1 November

The Third Gruppe detached five pilots under Fw. Wolfgang Polster for temporary duty with II/JG 3 at Schipol. The pilots of the latter Gruppe had suffered serious losses in their brief time in Holland, and the task of Polster and his men was to supplement their training and teach them some secrets of survival on the Western Front.

2 November

Fw. Peter Crump led a *Rotte* (pair or element) up from Epinoy at 1243 on a routine defensive patrol. Its main purpose was to give his wingman, Uffz. Robert Ney, some flying experience. Ney had taken part in only two Schwarm *Alarmstarten* (scrambles) since joining the 6th Staffel on 14 September. The sharp-eyed Crump spotted a pair of No. 414 Sqd. (RCAF) Mustang Is engaged in a Rhubarb, but the resulting battle went against the Germans. Uffz. Ney was shot down from an altitude of 2000 meters (6500 feet), and died in his plane. The Canadians continued their mission, returning to claim both Focke-Wulfs shot down, plus four trains and one barge destroyed. They were flying the early Allison-engined variant of the Mustang; the type was supposed to be limited to low-level reconnaissance. The increasing strength and experience of the Allied units resulted in ever more aggressive tactics. The new German pilots, on the other hand, endangered their lives every time they took to the air. Few lived long enough to develop more than the most rudimentary flying skills.

Uffz. Horst Kirschner of the 9th Staffel. *(Vanoverbeke)*

3 November

On its largest mission to date, the 8th Bomber Command dispatched 566 B-17s and B-24s to Wilhelmshaven. At 1210, Fw. Polster sortied from Schipol with II/JG 3 to attack the bombers, but encountered instead the P-47s of the 4th Fighter Group, which were still waiting for their bombers to show up. The Messerschmitts shot two Thunderbolts down into the Zuider Zee, apparently without loss to themselves.

The Third Gruppe scrambled from Bönninghardt at about 1330 and headed north to attack the returning bomber formations. P-47s from the 56th Fighter Group bounced them just as they reached the bombers, shooting down three Messerschmitts and damaging a fourth. Fw. Wilhelm Latka was never seen again; Hptm. Paul Steindl and Fw. Willi Fischer survived with injuries. These three pilots were all flying Bf 109G-6/U4s; these fighters had a potent MK 108 engine-mounted 3 cm cannon in place of the usual 2 cm MG 151/20 cannon.

To take some pressure off the returning heavy bombers, the 9th Air Force B-26 units attacked several airfields. Two groups bombed Amsterdam-Schipol at 1545. II/JG 3 had not mastered the art of the rapid scramble, and its fighters were still trying to get off the field when the bombs started dropping. The Spitfire escorts from the Digby Wing (RCAF) pounced on the climbing Messerschmitts, and shot down five of them for the loss of one Spitfire. The German pilots, who were all killed, included Major Kurt Brändle, the II/JG 3 Gruppenkommandeur, and Uffz. Horst Kirschner, one of the III/JG 26 pilots on temporary duty with II/JG 3.

JG 26 Casualties: 2 - 3 November 1943

Date	Rank	Name	Cas	Unit	Aircraft	WNr	Mkgs	Place	Time	Cause	Allied Unit
02-11-43	Uffz.	Ney, Robert	KIA	6	Fw 190A-6	530711	bk 5	Albert, SW of Bapaume	1250	Mustang	414 Sqd
03-11-43	Uffz.	Kirschner, Horst	KIA	9	Bf 109G			20km W of Haarlem	1605	Spitfire	132 Sqd
03-11-43	Hptm.	Steindl,Peter-Paul	WIA	11 CO	Bf 109G-6/U4	19421	yl 6	E of Friesland-Holtgast	1400	P-47	56 FG
03-11-43	Fw.	Fischer, Willi	WIA	12	Bf 109G-6/U4	19641	bk 1	Stevensbeek		P-47	56 FG
03-11-43	Fw.	Latka, Wilhelm	KIA	12	Bf 109G-6/U4	20706	bl 3	LBH Mitte	1450	P-47	56 FG

5 November

The heavy bombers targeted two cities. The B-17s attacked Gelsenkirchen, while the B-24s headed for Münster. Attacks on the Pas de Calais airfields were scheduled for 213 B-26s, forty-nine Mitchells, twenty-four Bostons, 651 Spitfires, and eighty-two Typhoons. Until plans for the invasion of France were finalized, the huge and still growing tactical air forces in England had only two valid functions: the destruction of the V-1 launch sites, and the neutralization of the Luftflotte 3 Jagdgruppen, which numbered only six – the same six that had been serving on the Kanalfront since 1941. The First Gruppe flew to Köln-Ostheim, refueled, and waited in their cockpits for the heavies. I/JG 3 got away from Vendeville early and flew north to intercept the B-17s, and the Third Gruppe was far away at Bönninghardt. This left the Second Gruppe to face the mediums alone. This Gruppe was scrambled at 1330 and vectored toward a large force of tactical aircraft headed for Marquise, but the Jafü then reconsidered, and redirected it toward Deelen to join the attack on the withdrawing heavy bombers.

The German fighters had little success against the well-escorted bomber formations. Near Gelsenkirchen the First Gruppe made a pass at the First Bomb Division formation, during which Fw. Ahrens shot down a 92nd Bomb Group B-17. His unit was then scattered by the P-47s, which shot one Focke-Wulf down and forced two others to crash-land.

The Third Gruppe reached the Third Bomb Division B-17s, but was then dispersed by the 353rd Fighter Group, which shot down Uffz. Rudolf Stutt of the Gruppenstab, who crashed in his plane, and Uffz. Robert Pautner of the 9th Staffel, who bailed out with a shoulder wound. Two Messerschmitts force-landed with combat damage. Uffz. Hans Hein of the 11th Staffel shot down a Thunderbolt, probably from the 353rd.

Hptm. Staiger claimed a B-17 from the Third Bomb Division formation; this was probably a 388th Bomb Group aircraft.

The Second Gruppe reached the area too late to attack, and most pilots landed at Antwerp. The engine of Ofhr. Holger Bruns's Fw 190 seized up over Ghent, and he made a hurried crash-landing which destroyed his aircraft and trapped Bruns inside the wreckage; he was pulled free with only slight injuries.

JG 26 Victory Claims: 22 October - 5 November 1943

Date	Rank	Name	Unit	Cl #	Aircraft	Place	Time	Opponent	Conf
22-10-43	Fw.	Ehret	7	2	Spitfire	SW of Beauvais	1033	421 Sqd	unk
24-10-43	Fw.	Crump	6		B-26	S of Montdidier	1230		no
05-11-43	Fw.	Ahrens	3	9	B-17	Vierlingsbeek (KN4)	1403	92 BG	yes
05-11-43	Uffz.	Hein H.	11	1	P-47	unknown		353 FG	yes
05-11-43	Hptm.	Staiger	12 CO	35	B-17	Dortmund		388 BG	unk

JG 26 Casualties: 5 November 1943

Date	Rank	Name	Cas	Unit	Aircraft	WNr	Mkgs	Place	Time	Cause	Allied Unit
05-11-43	Ofhr.	Bruns, Holger	WIA	FA 5	Fw 190A-6	530922	wh 14	Deinze-15km SW of Ghent	1445	engine	n/a
05-11-43	Uffz.	Stutt, Rudolf	KIA	III St	Bf 109G-6/R2	27148	<+ gr 3	near Wesel-Voerde	1325	P-47	353 FG
05-11-43	Uffz.	Pautner, Robert	WIA	9	Bf 109G-6	15408	wh 12	Gelsenkirchen-Buer	1415	P-47	353 FG

11 November

The autumn weather over the Continent made it ever more difficult for the 8th Air Force to carry out its planned missions. Today only fifty-eight of the 167 Third Bomb Division B-17s that were dispatched bombed their assigned target, Münster, while all 175 First Bomb Division B-17s turned back at the coast because of heavy cloud which extended up to 32,000 feet. Tactical aircraft totaling 540 crossed the French coast starting at 1230, prompting Jafü 2 to scramble the First and Second Gruppen, despite the knowledge that a heavy bomb raid would be coming later in the day. The First Gruppe attacked two Spitfire squadrons, No. 19 and No. 122, which were sweeping St. Pol. The 3rd Staffel lost two Focke-Wulfs; Uffz. Spiegel crashed in his aircraft, and

Uffz. Robert Pautner of the 9th Staffel under attack by Lt. Ista of the 353rd Fighter Group near Gelsenkirchen on 5 November. *(Roba)*

Fw. Peter Ahrens bailed out with severe burns. No Spitfires were claimed. After this combat the Gruppe was ordered to land on Wevelgem. While landing, Obfw. Friedrich Lindelaub hit a crater and overturned. His aircraft was damaged beyond repair, and Lindelaub suffered injuries to his head and back. The Second Gruppe was ordered to orbit near Cambrai, and landed after thirty minutes to refuel for the next mission.

II/JG 3 scrambled from Schipol at 1320 under orders to climb to maximum altitude and try to get above the escort. As Fw. Polster reached 10,400 meters (34,000 feet), his engine exploded, forcing him to bail out. The rest of the Gruppe returned to base, apparently without making contact.

One wing of B-17s, only sixty aircraft, bombed Münster at 1408. It had been unable to close up with the rest of the Third Bomb Division owing to the weather over England, and had missed the recall signal. At 1420 the First Gruppe scrambled as many fighters from Wevelgem as were serviceable, and the Second Gruppe took off in full strength from Epinoy. The Focke-Wulfs set course for Holland to meet the withdrawing bombers. The small First Gruppe formation failed to make contact with the few remaining bombers, and returned to Wevelgem. The Second Gruppe encountered the lonely wing of unescorted B-17s south of Dordrecht. Major Seifert immediately ordered an attack on the low group, the 94th. After repeated attacks from 12 o'clock and 6 o'clock, four bombers dropped from formation. Three crashed; the fourth disappeared into the undercast in a vertical dive, but the pilot and copilot brought it under control and the bomber returned to base on two engines. Three of the four claims by Seifert's pilots were confirmed.

JG 26 Victory Claims: 11 November 1943

Date	Rank	Name	Unit	Cl #	Aircraft	Place	Time	Opponent	Conf
11-11-43	Obfw.	Glunz	5	44	B-17	SW of Dordrecht	1455	94 BG	yes
11-11-43	Obfw.	Glunz	5		B-17	SW of Dordrecht	1457	94 BG	no
11-11-43	Hptm.	Naumann	7 CO	27	B-17	NNW of Breda	1455	94 BG	yes
11-11-43	Oblt.	Leuschel	8 CO	7	B-17	SW of Numansdorp	1500	94 BG	yes

JG 26 Casualties: 11 November 1943

Date	Rank	Name	Cas	Unit	Aircraft	WNr	Mkgs	Place	Time	Cause	Allied Unit
11-11-43	Fw.	Lindelaub, Friedrich	WIFA	1	Fw 190A-6	550470	wh 7	Wevelgem		landing	n/a
11-11-43	Fw.	Ahrens, Peter	WIA	3	Fw 190A-6	550176	yl 8	5km SW of St Pol		Spitfire	122 Sqd
11-11-43	Uffz.	Spiegel, Arthur	KIA	3	Fw 190A-5	1170	yl 12	11km SE of Hesdin		Spitfire	19 Sqd

13 November

Today's target for the American heavy bombers was Bremen. Bad weather forced the First Bomb Division to abandon the mission; most of the other B-17s and B-24s bombed unidentified "targets of opportunity" through the clouds. The 4th Staffel, flying from Mönchen-Gladbach, is the only unit of the Geschwader known to have taken part in the interception. The Gruppen at Grimbergen and Epinoy were undoubtedly grounded by the weather; I/JG 3 had gotten away from Vendeville, and spent the day flying missions from a Dutch base. No reason for the inactivity of the Third Gruppe is known; possibly the unit was not yet operational after its move to Mönchen-Gladbach.

The 4th Staffel – possibly accompanied by Priller's Stabsschwarm – scrambled at 1330 and met the outbound bomber formations over the Zuider Zee. The American escort force was unusually small, and apparently out of position. I/JG 3 Messerschmitts were already making high, rear passes on the B-17s when Fw. Wiegand arrived at the head of the Adamsonstaffel. Wiegand and his wingman dived on the bombers, zoomed up, and shot down a high cover 355th Fighter Group P-47 from below. A Staffel Focke-Wulf was shot down, but its pilot bailed out without

Pilots of the 4th Staffel at Wevelgem in late 1943. From left: unknown, Fw. Kurt Schmidtke (KIA 7 Jul 44), Fw. Erich Schwarz, unknown, Uffz. Gerd Wiegand, Oblt. Wolfgang Neu (KIA 22 Apr 44), unknown, Obfw. Hermann Schmeinl, Lt. Helmut Menge (KIA 10 Jun 44). *(Hartigs via Petrick)*

injury. Oblt. Neu attacked a 96th Bomb Group B-17, which crashed east of Zwolle. The Staffel was still in the same general area a half hour later when the B-24s of the Second Bomb Division arrived, following the same track. The Liberators' escort was also patchy, and Obfw. Heitmann shot down a 392nd Bomb Group B-24 north of Zwolle. One Focke-Wulf did not make it back to Mönchen-Gladbach, but belly-landed near Antwerp with serious damage; the rest of the Staffel returned to base after a very successful mission.

14 November
RAF Mosquito reconnaissance aircraft had bedeviled the Luftwaffe since late 1941. Their lone missions were flown at such high speed and altitude that they were nearly immune from interception. Two Jagdgruppen had been formed for the express purpose of defeating the Mosquitoes, but had been disbanded as failures. On 17 September, one Mosquito had been tracked all the way to Salzburg and back; eighteen fighters from ten units along its route were scrambled, but none reached it.

This morning it was the turn of the Second Gruppe to make the attempt. Obfw. Addi Glunz, generally considered the most proficient pilot in the Gruppe, was selected to fly the mission, and he chose to fly it alone. The Mosquito had been on the German radar screens for several hours when Glunz took off from Epinoy at 0939. He climbed steadily through thick gray rain clouds, and leveled out at 8500 meters (28,000 feet), 750 meters above the clouds. He recalled later that the sun's glare off the cloud tops in the clear, blue sky gave him the feeling that he was sledding across a blinding white field of snow.

The controller brought Glunz within visual range of the Mosquito – he was above and behind it. Glunz dived and came up beneath the British aircraft, in its blind spot. When he was within range, one press on the firing knob sent fifty cannon shells into it. The Mosquito exploded into a million fragments of plywood, metal, and flesh. Shortly after 1000, Addi Glunz's Focke-Wulf roared across Epinoy, its wings rocking to announce its pilot's 45th victory. The No. 1409 Flight Mosquito had been returning from a weather reconnaissance mission to Stuttgart; its pilot, P/O Frank Clayton, had been on his fifty-third such operation.

Date	Rank	Name	Unit	Cl #	Aircraft	Place	Time	Opponent	Conf
13-11-43	Oblt.	Neu	4 CO	4	B-17	NE of Arnhem (HN)	1215	96 BG	yes
13-11-43	Obfw.	Heitmann	4	8	B-24	Zwolle (FN7-8)	1230	392 BG	yes
13-11-43	Fw.	Wiegand	4	8	P-47	SE of Zwolle (GN)	1223	355 FG	yes
14-11-43	Obfw.	Glunz	5	45	Mosquito	near Lens-SW of Lille	1006	1409 Flt	yes

Ogfr. Norbert Holtz of the 4th Staffel finds a way to beat the transportation shortage – Wevelgem, late 1943. *(Schmidt via Roba)*.

16 November

Bad weather kept the Allied aircraft on the ground. The Luftwaffe bases maintained their daily routine. Fw. Hans Fischer of the 10th Staffel was making a test flight from Mönchen-Gladbach when his Messerschmitt suddenly went out of control 400 meters above the field and crashed, killing Fischer. No reason for the accident was determined.

The 5th and 7th Staffeln transferred from Cambrai-Epinoy to Grevillers, a satellite of Beauvais. They were now seventy miles from the rest of the Second Gruppe, but such dispersion was now necessary on the Kanalfront, when on any day the B-26s could render any airfield unserviceable. At about this time the 4th Staffel sent a detachment of mechanics to Wevelgem, and began dispersing its aircraft to Wevelgem every night. The pilots' quarters were still in Lille, however, and the road trips during the winter nights became very unpleasant. The entire Staffel moved to Wevelgem in late January.

18 November

The 2nd Tactical Air Force was established as the RAF counterpart to the American 9th Air Force. It absorbed No. 2 Group with its medium bombers, together with half of Fighter Command's squadrons. Fighter Command was disbanded; the remaining RAF fighters were assigned to a new home defense command, the Air Defense of Great Britain (ADGB).

20 November

Fw. Hans Oeckel of the 12th Staffel, up on a defensive patrol from Mönchen-Gladbach, ran out of fuel, and had to make a dead-stick landing on Köln-Niehl. His Messerschmitt sustained only minor damage.

23 November

Fw. Polster, still with II/JG 3, was assigned a simple convoy escort to help him recover from his traumatic high-altitude bailout on the 11th. He managed to exhaust the fuel in his short-legged Messerschmitt, and had to force-land west of Amsterdam; fortunately for his career, the damage was minor.

25 November

The 8th Bomber Command remained grounded, but several 8th Fighter Command groups tested the defenses of the Pas de Calais. The first-ever P-47 dive-bombing mission was flown; the 353rd Fighter Group bombed one of the St. Omer airfields, escorted by the 56th Group. The 353rd lost its commanding officer to the airfield Flak, but the experiment was judged a success. At 1305 Major Seifert led the 6th and 8th Staffeln up from Epinoy, and was vectored northwest, not toward the rapidly-withdrawing Thunderbolts, but to a large formation of P-38 Lightnings. This was the 55th Fighter Group, the first P-38 unit in the ETO, flying a sweep of Lille in support of the P-47s. Peter Crump recalls:

> "My testimony about this mission will be exact, since I was flying as an element leader in the Stabsschwarm – exactly for what reason I cannot say. Our twenty Fw 190s climbed to the northwest toward the approaching Lightning formation, which was sighted at the expected coordinates. We still had not reached the enemy's altitude, and it would have been good tactics to have at least banked to one side, until we had gained a more favorable altitude for an attack.
>
> "But Seifert would have none of that. To the surprise and dismay of all of us, he continued climbing right at the Lightnings, which were now about four or five hundred meters above us. They flew right over us without making an attack; thus, we had surprised them.
>
> "Seifert suddenly pulled up to attack the Lightning which was flying at the rear of the formation. The pilot under attack saw what was happening and banked into a dive toward Seifert. They attacked one another *von Schnauze auf Schnauze*. I saw both aircraft take hits, ram each other in the right wing, dive away out of control, and crash.
>
> "No air battle resulted from this encounter. The enemy formation reversed course to the north in a broad curve and flew away. Since this engagement was our first with the Lightning on the Kanalfront, it was suspected that they were simply on a familiarization flight, and they were not looking for combat. At any rate, that is how we explained their behavior at the time."

The Lightning pilot, Lt. Manuel Aldecoa, bailed out, but his parachute streamed, and he was killed. Seifert's body was found still strapped in the wreckage of his plane. Johannes Seifert was a prewar member of JG 26, and in May, 1940, had scored the first First Gruppe victory of the Western campaign. His 439 combat flights had resulted in fifty-four aerial victories; he had been the only pilot in the Geschwader to win the Knight's Cross in 1942.

It is clear from the American records why the P-38 formation turned away. The group commander had been vectored toward another German formation by his controller in England. It is not known why Aldecoa did not warn his unit of the airplanes below them; however, the Americans were now searching elsewhere. The reported aircraft were above the Lightnings in the sun, and difficult to spot. The bogies proved to be Bf 109s. When the American pilots finally saw them, they climbed to the attack, and were credited after the resulting combats with the destruction of two Bf 109s (from I/JG 3, up from Vendeville) and two Fw 190s (from JG 2).

Although one P-38 pilot reported having seen Aldecoa's aircraft in a vertical dive, followed by an (apparently) pursuing Fw 190, the destruction of Seifert's aircraft had not been observed by any of the returning American pilots, and no victory claim was filed. The Americans, looking for the enemy in the sun, never suspected that there were a number of Focke-Wulfs beneath them; the JG 26 pilots, for their part, knew nothing of the presence of other German planes in the area.

Hptm. Wilhelm Gäth was named probationary Kommandeur of the Second Gruppe; Lt. Karl Willius took his place as leader of the 2nd Staffel.

JG 26 Casualties: 16 - 25 November 1943

Date	Rank	Name	Cas	Unit	Aircraft	WNr	Mkgs	Place	Time	Cause	Allied Unit
16-11-43	Fw.	Fischer, Hans	KIFA	10	Bf 109G-6	160633	bk 4	Mönchen-Gladbach	1445	crashed	non-op

26 November

Seven combat wings of B-17s and two of B-24s left the English coast starting at 1000 for another attempt to bomb Bremen through clouds. Two combat wings of B-17s were sent in the other direction, to Paris. The Third Gruppe in Germany apparently saw no action against the Bremen force. Jafü 2 could have sent its fighters in either direction, but chose to intercept the Paris force, which entered and left French airspace between Le Tréport and Dieppe. Secondary raids by several hundred B-26s, Mitchells, Bostons, Spitfires, and Typhoons were for the most part ignored by Jafü 2 and Jafü 3. The First and Second Gruppen, the 4th Staffel, and I/JG 3 were scrambled at 1012. The bombers crossed over Paris a little after 1045, but did not sight their target, and turned back to the northwest without bombing. The escorting 78th Fighter Group had been fending off JG 2 fighters since before Paris, and all of the JG 26 Focke-Wulfs were able to attack the bombers before the P-47s could intervene. Some made an immediate attack from six o'clock low, quickly knocking one Fortress of the low 100th Bomb Group out of formation. Others lined up ahead of the neighboring 94th Bomb Group, peeled off, and made single passes from about two o'clock. Three B-17s crashed north of Paris and Beauvais, claimed by one Second Gruppe and two 4th Staffel pilots – only one of these claims was confirmed, however, and II/JG 2 also claimed three B-17s. Oblt. Leuschel led his 8th Staffel Schwarm in an attack on a damaged bomber, but as he broke away one member of his flight, Oblt. Fritz Falke, disappeared. He crashed in his plane, the victim of the B-17's gunners. Uffz. Franz Vanderveerd of the 3rd Staffel shot down a P-47, as did Obfw. Glunz. Glunz and his wingman then caught up to the straggling 100th Bomb Group B-17 and shot it down.

Six damaged Geschwader Focke-Wulfs had to force-land quickly on various airfields; the rest landed on their home fields, and were informed that after a quick turnaround they would head north to intercept the bombers returning from Bremen.

The 5th Staffel was just leaving Cambrai when the field was bombed by seventy-two B-26s. The Spitfire escort of No. 401 and No. 416 Sqds. (RCAF) shot down two Fw 190s, killing Uffz. Johannes Höhme and Lt. Hans Fischer. Fischer's aircraft hit a

The 4th Staffel Kapitän, Oblt. Wolfgang Neu, is helped down from his Fw 190A-6 "blue 16" (W.Nr. 530755) at Wevelgem in late 1943. Neu was killed in this aircraft on 22 April 1944. *(Hartigs via Petrick)*

Oblt. Neu is congratulated for one of his late-1943 victories by Lt. Hans Hartigs and the Adamson Staffelhund. *(Hartigs via Petrick)*

Oblt. Neu (right) makes a point to Lt. Hartigs and Fw. Schwarz – Wevelgem, late 1943. *(Hartigs via Petrick)*

railway embankment and exploded, killing the attacking Spitfire pilot's wingman. Any success that the other pilots of the Geschwader had against the Bremen force has not been recorded.

JG 26 Victory Claims: 25 - 26 November 1943

Date	Rank	Name	Unit	Cl #	Aircraft	Place	Time	Opponent	Conf
25-11-43	Maj.	Seifert	II CO	57	P-38	near Cuinchy	1321	55 FG	yes

26-11-43	Uffz.	Vandeveerd	3	1	P-47	NW of Paris (TD2)	1100	78 FG	yes
26-11-43	Oblt.	Neu	4 CO	5	B-17	W of Nantes? (GN3?)	1045	94 BG	unk
26-11-43	Obfw.	Heitmann	4	9	B-17	SSE of Creil	1045	94 BG	yes
26-11-43	Obfw.	Glunz	5	46	P-47	Chantilly	1040	78 FG	unk
26-11-43	Obfw.	Glunz	5	47	B-17	near Beauvais	1103	100 BG	yes
26-11-43	Fw.	Zirngibl	8	5	B-17	near Paris	1040	94 BG	unk

JG 26 Casualties: 26 November 1943

Date	Rank	Name	Cas	Unit	Aircraft	WNr	Mkgs	Place	Time	Cause	Allied Unit
26-11-43	Lt.	Fischer, Hans	KIA	5	Fw 190A-6	530769	wh 12	4km W of Cambrai (t/o)		Spitfire	416 Sqd
26-11-43	Uffz.	Höhme, Johannes	KIA	5	Fw 190A-6	530727	wh 1	4km NW of Albert		Spitfire	401 Sqd
26-11-43	Oblt.	Falke, Fritz	KIA	8	Fw 190A-6	530935	bl 7	4km NW of Le Bourget		B-17	

27 November

The Jagdfliegerführer of the German air defenses were renumbered to bring them into conformance with the designations of the new Jagddivisionen. The Jafü for the German Bight in northern Germany became Jafü 2; Jafü Holland-Ruhr became Jafü 3; Jafü 2 became Jafü 4; and Jafü 3 became Jafü 5. Jafü Brittany was not given a number; its fighter strength had by now been reduced to one Gruppe of maritime attack Bf 110s and one Staffel of Fw 190s.

29 November

Six combat wings of B-17s were dispatched to bomb Bremen, although the weather over England and Germany was very bad. Two of the combat wings could not form up owing to icing conditions and abandoned the mission; the rest bombed through solid cloud cover. The Third Gruppe was scrambled from Mönchen-Gladbach and reached the bombers prior to their bomb run. Major Mietusch shot a B-17 from its formation north of Lingen. One of his pilots, Lt. Götz Schmidt, was hit by bomber fire and bailed out with injuries; a second, Lt. Theobald Kraus, force-landed with injuries, and two Messerschmitts were destroyed in dead-stick landings after running out of fuel.

The rest of the Geschwader had exhausted itself while combating a B-26 raid on Chièvres airfield in the morning, and was not used against the B-17s. The Focke-Wulfs were scrambled at 0925 and were ordered to fly to Dunkirk to face the Marauders. The seventy-two B-26s were escorted by only 107 Spitfires, a force small enough to intercept, and air battles soon raged from the Pas de Calais to western Belgium. Only a few First Gruppe Focke-Wulfs reached the B-26s, and they had no luck. An American gunner riddled Uffz. Franz Ruppert's aircraft. When he bailed out, he discovered that his parachute had been holed; he survived his rapid descent, but with severe injuries. A second Focke-Wulf was damaged by the bombers, and its pilot had to force-land on Chièvres during the raid. The five escorting Spitfire squadrons each claimed one Focke-Wulf destroyed. Four in fact crashed, killing Uffz. Johann Scheu, Uffz. Hans-Joachim Thielmann, and Fw. Walter Ullmann, and injuring Uffz. Johann Gulecke. The fifth was also destroyed – Oblt. Sternberg turned it over while trying to crash-land on Lille-Nord. Fw. Crump and Fw. Vogt claimed the only two Spitfires that were lost; both were from No. 412 Sqd. (RCAF). The surviving German pilots were forced to put down on a number of airfields, and saw no more service this day.

JG 26 Casualties: 29 November 1943

Date	Rank	Name	Cas	Unit	Aircraft	WNr	Mkgs	Place	Time	Cause	Allied Unit
29-11-43	Uffz.	Ruppert, Franz	WIA	I St	Fw 190A-6	530745	wh 12	W of Chièvres		B-26	
29-11-43	Uffz.	Gulecke, J-Heinrich	WIA	2	Fw 190A-6	550749	bk 5	f/l Melsbroeck		Spitfire	
29-11-43	Uffz.	Thielmann, H-Joachim	KIA	2	Fw 190A-6	470049	bk 7	6km E of Bruges		Spitfire	
29-11-43	Fw.	Ullrich, Walter	KIA	3	Fw 190A-6	550917	yl 3	Maldegem-Flobecq		Spitfire	

29-11-43	Oblt.	Sternberg, Horst	WIFA 6 CO	Fw 190A-6	470056	bk 6	c/l Lille-Nord a/f		Spitfire
29-11-43	Uffz.	Scheu, Johann	KIA 6	Fw 190A-6	470053	bk 7	3km NW of Passchendaele		Spitfire
29-11-43	Lt.	Kraus, Theobald	WIA 9	Bf 109G-6	440015		nr Ahren		B-17
29-11-43	Lt.	Schmidt, Gottfried	WIA 11	Bf 109G-6/U4	20731	yl 3	Quakenbrück	1500	B-17

30 November

The 8th Bomber Command dispatched 349 B-17s to bomb Solingen, but most of the combat wings had to abandon the mission when clouds reaching to 30,000 feet made it impossible to maintain formation. Hptm. Mietusch's Gruppe scrambled from Mönchen-Gladbach, but the light and unstable Messerschmitts could not stay together in the turbulent stratocumulus, and the pilots were soon either looking for straggling bombers or just trying to get back on the ground. Stabsfw. Wühl claimed a B-17, one of only three that failed to return from the mission. North of Mönchen-Gladbach, Hptm. Mietusch spotted a P-38 that was struggling to get home on one engine, and shot it down. The 20th Fighter Group reported its fighter as having vanished without a trace in the North Sea. Its pilot survived to be taken prisoner, but died of meningitis in POW camp.

Mietusch's pilots had a very rough mission. The 10th Staffel dived into clouds to escape an attack by 78th Fighter Group Thunderbolts, and Uffz. Hans Fieguth was able to make a smooth landing on Rheine with minor injuries. Fw. Ludwig Pötter, however, crashed in his airplane, possibly a victim of the bad weather as well as a P-47. Uffz. Franz Piplitz, who was on his first combat mission, was hit by a B-17 gunner and attempted to make a forced-landing, but misjudged the distance to the ground and crashed. His aircraft "burned for two days, and exploded on the third", according to his casualty report, and Piplitz's remains could only be identified indirectly – he was the only pilot still missing. Obfw. Karl Claar lost the Gruppe formation shortly after takeoff, and was never seen alive again. He probably crashed after becoming disoriented in the clouds; Hptm. Hempel, the Gruppe adjutant, made a point of noting in his casualty report that Claar had had no instrument flight training whatsoever. Ironically, Fw. Wolfgang Polster, who had rejoined the Gruppe after his detached service with II/JG 3, spent the day flying from Mönchen-Gladbach as a passenger in a Go 145, receiving instrument training.

Geschwader personnel moves during November included: the transfer of Uffz.-Fhj. Manfred Derp from the Geschwader; the departure of Obfw. Johann Edmann from the 4th Staffel for instructor duty; and the departure of Obfw. Leopold Eichinger from the 3rd Staffel to serve as a ferry pilot.

Pilots joining the Geschwader from flight training included: Uffz. Wilhelm Düsing, Uffz. Ernst Klumpe, Uffz. Herbert Kolodzie, Lt. Helmut Menge, Fhr. Otto Meyer, Uffz. Herbert Onken, Fw. Günther Schneider, Ofhr. Heinrich Vanderveerd - First Gruppe; Lt. Waldemar Busch, Uffz. Bruno Prüver, Gefr. Alfred Teichmann - Second Gruppe; Uffz. Horst Gewitz, Uffz. Otto Salewski - Third Gruppe.

JG 26 Victory Claims: 29 - 30 November 1943

Date	Rank	Name	Unit	Cl #	Aircraft	Place	Time	Opponent	Conf
29-11-43	Fw.	Crump	6	13	Spitfire	N of Ypres	1005	412 Sqd	yes
29-11-43	Fw.	Vogt	7	18	Spitfire	Coxyde-SW of Ostend	1005	412 Sqd	yes
29-11-43	Hptm.	Mietusch	III CO	51	B-17-HSS	W of Oldenburg (DP-EP)	1430		yes
30-11-43	Hptm.	Mietusch	III CO	52	P-38	North Sea (LN)	1145	20 FG	yes
30-11-43	Stfw.	Wuhl		11	B-17	unknown			yes

JG 26 Casualties: 30 November 1943

Date	Rank	Name	Cas	Unit	Aircraft	WNr	Mkgs	Place	Time	Cause	Allied Unit
30-11-43	Uffz.	Fieguth, Hans-Gerhard	WIA	10	Bf 109G-6	20718	bk 8	near Rheine	1400	P-47	78 FG

30-11-43	Uffz.	Piplitz, Franz	KIA	10	Bf 109G-6	20722	bk 3	Lennep-Ruhr	1245	B-17	
30-11-43	Fw.	Pötter, Ludwig	KIA	10	Bf 109G-6	440009	bk 5	Schwelm-Wuppertal	1230	P-47	78 FG
30-11-43	Obfw.	Claar, Karl-Heinz	KIA	12	Bf 109G-6 /U4	440019	bl 6	NE of Radevornwald	1200	combat	

Fw. Wolfgang Polster of the 11th Staffel is 2nd from the left in this lineup of III/JG 26 and II/JG 3 pilots. Polster spent most of November flying from Schipol with II/JG 3. *(Genth)*

1 December

Heavy activity over England brought all of the Jafü 4 Gruppen to readiness early in the morning. The 8th Bomber Command planned a return trip to Solingen, with an early departure time to take advantage of some rare morning sunshine over England. One hundred and seventy-six 9th Air Force B-26s were ordered to keep the Kanal defenders busy by bombing their airfields, including Lille-Vendeville and Cambrai-Epinoy. The Second Gruppe scrambled with the approach of the medium bombers, but once again the 5th Staffel was caught taking off by Canadian Spitfires. This time it was No. 411 Squadron which did the damage; they downed the Kapitän, Hptm. Hoppe, and his wingman, Fw. Rudi Weyrich, killing both. Obfw. Glunz immediately gained revenge, catching the Spitfires southwest of Arras and downing two of them, including the airplane that had just shot down Hoppe. This was the only German success against the secondary raids, which cratered landing grounds and destroyed six I/JG 3 Bf 109s at Vendeville, but did not put Vendeville or Cambrai out of operation.

The B-17s left the English coast at 1040. The German controllers guessed correctly that this would be a shallow penetration raid, probably to the Ruhr. The Jafü 3 fighters were well-positioned to attack the bombers along their entire route. Jafü 4 sent all of its fighters north in time to attack the incoming bombers. Jafü 3 requested an early takeoff by the Zerstörergruppen in southern Germany. Jafü 5 was also asked for help, and Major Egon Mayer led two JG 2 Gruppen north from Beaumont, timed to attack the bombers on their withdrawal. The result was the most successful defensive mission in over a month, and the destruction of twenty-seven bombers.

Fw. Rudy Weyrich of the 5th Staffel. Weyrich and his Staffel-kapitän, Hptm. Helmut Hoppe, were shot down by No. 411 Sqd. Spitfires while taking off from Cambrai-Epinoy on 1 December. *(Vanoverbeke)*

Cloud cover forced the Third Bomb Division to abandon its mission, while the First Division bombed Solingen and targets of opportunity through solid clouds. The bomber formations became strung out, stretching the available escort past their limit. German formations also found it hard to stay together in the clouds. The Third Gruppe apparently split up early, as Hptm. Mietusch was flying alone when he spotted the P-38s of the 20th Fighter Group, which was escorting the Second Bomb Division's B-24s *en route* to Solingen. Mietusch made a solo bounce on its rear aircraft, which fell into a spin. A P-38 from the adjacent flight turned toward the Bf 109 and opened fire, but Mietusch evaded easily by breaking right and zooming up about one thousand feet (300 meters). He then did a wingover, and came back through the formation, guns blazing. Honor satisfied, he flicked over and dived away, untouched by American fire.

All eight P-47 and P-38 groups filed claims, but the 56th Fighter Group had the hardest time, running into "absolute hell" in the shape of "some awfully rough boys in Focke-Wulfs", in Robert Johnson's words. In the course of driving numerous Fw 190s and Bf 109s away from the bombers, three P-47s were shot down. Two of them were claimed by Oblt. Dippel, Kapitän of the 9th Staffel, and Oblt. Leuschel, Kapitän of the 8th. The RAF Y-intercept operators heard "Rudi" Leuschel warning his pilots to be on their guard against the escorts, "rather in the authoritative manner of the late Wutz Galland."

Two 355th Fighter Group P-47s were shot down, and four 56th Group Thunderbolts made it back to England with heavy damage. At least four German units claimed these P-47s; Major Mayer of JG 2 was credited with three of them.

Four Geschwader pilots were shot down in the vicinity of the bomber stream, but all bailed out successfully. Obfw. Heitmann of the 4th Staffel was the most seriously injured, jamming his spine when landing in his parachute. Six more pilots force-landed with combat damage or out of fuel; one of these men was injured in his landing. Many pilots had to land away from their bases owing to low fuel. The Schlageter pilots pressed their attacks aggressively and persistently. Conditions favored attacks by small formations, always preferred by the Kanal units over the "closed rank" massed charges decreed by Galland and the RLM. Six claims for B-17s were confirmed. Lt. Willius shot his victim out of formation before the bombers had made their initial turn toward Solingen, but most of the bombers downed were singles, caught over Belgium and France on their attempted return flights.

The 2nd Tactical Air Force sent two squadrons of Typhoons to the Arnhem area to cover the withdrawing bombers. They encountered several German fighters returning to their bases, and claimed two destroyed. Uffz. Gerhard Guttmann shot down one of the Typhoons over the Belgian-French border. His claim was never confirmed, although the No. 609 Sqd. pilot survived as a POW, good evidence that the airplane had, in fact, gone down. Guttmann's skirmish proved to be the last of the day for the Geschwader.

Oblt. Johann Aistleitner was recalled early from his tour as an instructor and Staffelkapitän in Jagdgruppe West, and given command of the 5th Staffel.

JG 26 Victory Claims: 1 December 1943

Date	Rank	Name	Unit	Cl #	Aircraft	Place	Time	Opponent	Conf
01-12-43	Oblt.	Beese	1 CO	19	B-17	W of Ostend (LE3)	1330		yes
01-12-43	Lt.	Dietze	1	3	B-17	E of St. Omer (NF1)	1330	384 BG	yes
01-12-43	Lt.	Willius	2 CO	36	B-17	Koblenz (PP)	1146		yes

01-12-43	Oblt.	Neu	4 CO	6	B-17	Steenvoorde(NF7)	1325		yes
01-12-43	Uffz.	Voigt	4	1	B-17	E of St. Omer (NF5-8)	1327	384 BG	yes
01-12-43	Obfw.	Glunz	5	48	Spitfire	SW of Arras	1015	411 Sqd	yes
01-12-43	Obfw.	Glunz	5	49	Spitfire	SW of Arras	1020	411 Sqd	yes
01-12-43	Oblt.	Leuschel	8 CO	8	P-47	SE of Ghent	1320	56 FG	yes
01-12-43	Uffz.	Guttmann	8	1	Typhoon	15km S of Valenciennes	1315	609 Sqd	unk
01-12-43	Hptm.	Mietusch	III CO	53	P-38	Freilingen-Vorneburg (Düren)	1145	20 FG	yes
01-12-43	Oblt.	Dippel	9 CO	18	P-47	Beverlo	1300	56 FG	yes
01-12-43	Lt.	Kempf	11	58	B-17	unknown			yes

JG 26 Casualties: 1 December 1943

Date	Rank	Name	Cas	Unit	Aircraft	WNr	Mkgs	Place	Time	Cause	Allied Unit
01-12-43	Uffz.	Seidl, Norbert	WIFA	2	Fw 190A-5	550450	bk 2	Rengen-Mayen (SE Eifel)		no fuel	n/a
01-12-43	Obfw.	Heitmann, Hans	WIA	4	Fw 190A-6	530741	bl 9	S of Geilenkirchen		P-47	
01-12-43	Hptm.	Hoppe, Helmut	KIA	5 CO	Fw 190A-6	550731	wh 6	Epinoy a/f		Spitfire	411 Sqd
01-12-43	Fw.	Weyrich, Rudi	KIA	5	Fw 190A-6	470055	wh 15	2km S of Moeuvres		Spitfire	411 Sqd
01-12-43	Lt.	Wunschelmeyer, Karl	WIA	12	Bf 109G-6/U4	20711	bl 4	Elsdorf, W of Köln		B-17	
01-12-43	Fw.	Würtz, Wilhelm	WIA	12	Bf 109G-6/U4	15400	bl 8	Warsage, near Visé		combat	

11 December

Persistent rain and sleet over England, France, and the Low Countries reduced flying activity to a minimum. The Allied Combined Chiefs of Staff raised the campaign against the nascent V-weapon sites in France to a top priority for the tactical units, and gave it the code-name Operation Crossbow. All tactical missions this week were recalled owing to the weather.

The 8th Bomber Command sent a large force of B-17s and B-24s to Emden. The raid is noteworthy as the first long-range escort mission for the P-51 Mustang-equipped 354th Fighter Group, which was a unit of the tactical 9th Air Force, as were all of the P-51 groups *en route* to the theater. The 354th would be loaned to the 8th Fighter Command until the latter could get its own Mustang units. The Mustang's range was at least as great as that of the Lightning, which was supposed to solve the problem of long-range support, but was having great difficulty coping with the bad weather and low temperatures at high altitude that were typical in the ETO.

The interception was handled by Jafü 2 and Jafü 3; Jafü 4 made no effort to get its fighters off the ground. The Third Gruppe sortied from Mönchen-Gladbach, but its battles with the bombers and escort over the Dutch province of Groningen were without result. Fw. Polster had to force-land on the north German coast after 105 minutes in the air.

13 December

The 8th Air Force put one thousand fighters and bombers in the air for the first time, and bombed Bremen and Kiel with virtually no opposition from the weather-bound German fighter defenses. Two hundred and eight B-26s bombed Amsterdam-Schipol airport, catching II/JG 3 on the ground and putting the field out of commission. The fifteen remaining Messerschmitts of the Gruppe flew to Volkel on the following day and were placed under the command of III/JG 1.

16 December

Another 8th Air Force raid on Bremen brought the Third Gruppe up from Mönchen-Gladbach despite terrible visibility. Mietusch's unit scored no successes, and was fortunate to lose only one Messerschmitt. Obfw. Heinrich Humburg ran out of fuel and crash-landed, destroying his aircraft and injuring himself.

18 December

As part of the ongoing dispersal program within Jagddivision 4, the First Gruppe began moving today from Grimbergen to Florennes, while the Stab of I/JG 3 left Lille-Vendeville for Denain. The new airfields were farther inland, and could be given earlier warning of incursions by Allied tactical aircraft.

20 December

The 8th Bomber Command flew its third mission to Bremen in eight days. Weather conditions were the best they had been all month; visibility at altitude was greater than ten miles. The Third Gruppe flew a very successful mission, despite the presence of an escort force totaling one P-38 group, one P-51 group, and eight P-47 groups. Details are unfortunately lacking, but Hptm. Mietusch and his men claimed five B-17s near Wilhelmshaven, and sustained no reported losses. All of the claims were later confirmed.

The Focke-Wulf units of the Geschwader were fully occupied by the diversions flown by the 9th Air Force and the 2nd TAF. The Allies overwhelmed the Jafü 4 defenses with raids by 211 B-26s, sixty Mitchells, thirty-seven Bostons, 415 Spitfires, 155 Typhoons, and twenty Hurricanes. The Geschwader brought down only one airplane out of this fleet. The leader of No. 421 Squadron in No. 127 Wing (RCAF) was shot down by Fw. Wiegand, whose 4th Staffel lost Lt. Bernhard Törpisch in the same battle. The Canadians had been battling I/JG 3 Messerschmitts when they were bounced by the two Focke-Wulfs; two of the Bf 109s were shot down.

The Second Gruppe was scrambled three times during the day, but had no successes. Their first mission took off from Grevillers and Epinoy at 1045. The Grevillers fighters were quickly attacked by the Norwegians of No. 132 Wing (ex-North Weald), who shot down two fighters without loss. Uffz. Hermann Butzmann crashed in his plane; Uffz. Gerhard Lissack bailed out with moderate injuries. The second mission of the Gruppe resulted in combat, but no results; the third mission failed to make contact.

JG 26 Victory Claims: 20 December 1943

Date	Rank	Name	Unit	Cl #	Aircraft	Place	Time	Opponent	Conf
20-12-43	Fw.	Wiegand	4	9	Spitfire	SW of Cambrai	1115	421 Sqd	yes
20-12-43	Hptm.	Mietusch	III CO	54	B-17	NW of Wilhelmshaven	1225		yes
20-12-43	Lt.	Reischer	9		B-17	unknown			yes
20-12-43	Uffz.	Seebeck	9		B-17	unknown			yes
20-12-43	Lt.	Kempf	11	59	B-17	unknown			yes
20-12-43	Uffz.	Laub	11	4	B-17	unknown	1156		yes

JG 26 Casualties: 16 - 20 December 1943

Date	Rank	Name	Cas	Unit	Aircraft	WNr	Mkgs	Place	Time	Cause	Allied Unit
16-12-43	Obfw.	Humburg, Heinrich	WIA	9	Bf 109G-6	20702	wh 1	Hoya-Weser		no fuel	n/a
20-12-43	Lt.	Törpisch, Bernhard	KIA	4	Fw 190A-6	530762	bl 11	5km S of Cambrai	1115	Spitfire	421 Sqd
20-12-43	Uffz.	Butzmann, Hermann	KIA	5	Fw 190A-6	470032	wh 8	N of Boursies	1115	Spitfire	331 or 332 Sqd
20-12-43	Uffz.	Lissack, Gerhard	WIA	7	Fw 190A-6	470007	br 11	nr Vitry	1115	Spitfire	331 or 332 Sqd

21 December

Ninth Air Force and 2nd TAF bombers attacked a number of targets in France. The Second Gruppe scrambled from Epinoy and Grevillers at 1120 and formed up in time to make a full-strength attack on the Spitfires of No. 125 Wing as they swept over Cambrai at 1145. Three Spitfires were shot down, claimed by Hptm. Naumann, Oblt. Matoni, and Obfw. Glunz. Uffz. Werner Steinkühler was hit, and crashed in his plane. Ogfr. Leo Przybyl was chased to ground level by the Spitfires. He evaded them, but strikes in his engine caused his canopy to oil over, and he struck a tree. His Focke-

Wulf was totaled, but Przybyl survived with slight injuries. Obfw. Wilhelm Freuwörth force-landed on St. Omer-Arques and overturned on the soft ground, suffering injuries so severe that after his convalescence he did not return to combat duty, but spent the rest of the war in a training unit. The Gruppe was scrambled again later in the afternoon and vectored toward several Typhoon formations, but never found them.

JG 26 Casualties: 21 December 1943

Date	Rank	Name	Cas	Unit	Aircraft	WNr	Mkgs	Place	Time	Cause	Allied Unit
21-12-43	Ogfr.	Przybyl, Leo	WIA	5	Fw 190A-5	1179	wh 7	St. Pirmont		Spitfire	132 or 602 Sqd
21-12-43	Uffz.	Steinkühler, Werner	KIA	6	Fw 190A-6	530738	bk 3	W of Vimy Ridge		Spitfire	132 or 602 Sqd
21-12-43	Obfw.	Freuwörth, Wilhelm	WIA	6	Fw 190A-6	530733	bk 8	St Omer-Arques		Spitfire	132 or 602 Sqd

Obfw. Adolf Glunz in one of his favorite portraits, taken in the cockpit of his Fw 190A-7 "white 9" in the winter of 1943-1944. *(Glunz via Bakker)*

22 December

The 8th Bomber Command sent its B-17s and B-24s to Münster and Osnabrück, despite continued bad visibility over the target areas. The day bomber units were gaining experience with the blind-bombing methods they had picked up from the RAF, even though continuing equipment and personnel failures kept their proficiency level low. The 711 Allied tactical aircraft attacking targets in northern France aroused no response from Jafü 4, which sent parts of the Second Gruppe and I/JG 3 north to refuel at Woensdrecht and intercept the withdrawing bombers. They had no luck at all; one 6th Staffel aircraft was caught in a cross-wind when attempting to land on Leeuwarden and ground-looped, sustaining moderate damage.

The Third Gruppe, under Jafü 3 control, attempted for one hour to get at the bombers, but failed, and was punished severely by the P-47s, losing six Messerschmitts and five pilots. Three probably fell under the gunfire of the 4th Group's Lt. John Godfrey and an impromptu wingman. The 4th Group had the poorest record among the three most experienced P-47 units. The 4th was fiercely loyal to its previous mount, the Spitfire, and the prejudice of its commanders against the Thunderbolt affected their combat tactics – the P-47 was believed to be inferior to German fighters below 20,000 feet (6100 meters), and so the 4th Group's pilots were ordered to stay above this altitude at all times when in the combat zone. As a result the group continued to fly the "detached escorts" it had learned from RAF Fighter Command, and made contact with the Germans very seldom. Godfrey was indignant at his group's lack of aggressiveness, and had already made several unauthorized bounces. On this day he saw two Messerschmitts far below, lining up on the bombers, and called them out. Getting no response, he announced his intent to attack and dived after them. His element leader stayed in formation, but Godfrey was joined by a pilot from another 4th Group squadron. After a violent dogfight in which Godfrey's plane was severely damaged, the two American pilots succeeded in shooting down three Bf 109s under circumstances closely matching the losses of Uffz. Günter Broda, Uffz. Anton Jenner, and Fhj.-Fw. Julius Richter, all of whom crashed between Enschede and Rheine between 1400 and 1410.

Steve Pisanos, a 4th Fighter Group ace, recalls the opinions of that group's commanders and most of its pilots concerning their P-47s:

> "P-47 pilots avoided mixing it up with any German fighters at low altitude, because both the 109 and the 190 could out-maneuver the P-47 at low levels, unless of course you were chasing someone all the way down. We in the 4th perferred to deal with the German fighters at high altitude – bounce the enemy below, then zoom up to altitude again. The P-47 turned out to be a killer aircraft versus both the Me 109 and the Fw 190. The Germans used two maneuvers when bounced by P-47s at altitude, turning and climbing. Some might have dived for a short duration, but that was to build up some speed to zoom up again. Any pilot who attempted to get away from an attacking P-47 by going into a dive in a cloudless sky didn't live long enough to tell his comrades."

Hans Hartigs, a First Gruppe veteran, recalled that the first objective of a Focke-Wulf pilot was always to draw the P-47 down to low altitude, ideally to 3000 meters (10,000 feet). The German pilot would then turn about sharply. The P-47 would overshoot; if its pilot tried to pull up in an equally sharp turn, his plane would lose speed and become vulnerable. The proper maneuver for the P-47 in this situation was to zoom climb and dive back down. Thunderbolt pilots no longer had to avoid turning battles, however. The P-47D of late 1943 was superior to the mid-year P-47C in turn rate, climb rate, and acceleration. The experienced German pilots recognized this without knowing that the technical reasons were engines with greater power, water injection, and paddle-blade propellers. A P-47D could often catch a Fw 190A or a Bf 109G in a high-speed turning chase. According to Hartigs, the proper course of action for the Focke-Wulf pilot was to climb slightly while turning; he would then gain on the P-47 in both altitude and distance. A Messerschmitt pilot, on the other hand, could either slow down and tighten his turn, hoping that the P-47 would stall out, or pull up in a steep climb, which the P-47 could not follow.

Turning combats were rare, however. Fighter pilots gained most of their victories in surprise attacks. The 56th Fighter Group's Lt. Robert Johnson scored such a kill today. Johnson, like John Godfrey an extremely aggressive pilot and something of a disciplinary problem, was escorting the outbound formation when he saw a Fortress pull away from the bomber stream, its pilot intending to abort the mission. He saw two shadows streaking along the cloud tops below; these proved to be Messerschmitts. Johnson and his wingman began stalking the stalkers. The Germans spotted them and turned away; Johnson maintained his course as though he had never seen them. The Bf 109 pilots then reversed course and headed for the bomber. The two Americans dived on them out of the sun; the first burst from Johnson's guns tore into his target's cockpit and killed its pilot, Fw. Karl Trapp of the 12th Staffel.

The fifth Third Gruppe pilot killed today, Uffz. Karl Seebeck, was also shot down on the penetration leg of the bombers' mission. A flight from the 78th Fighter Group, the third of the original 8th Air Force P-47 units, saw five Bf 109s lining up for a head-on attack on the bombers, and went down with all guns blazing to break it up. One Messerschmitt dived into the clouds with its cockpit caved in; it was probably piloted by Uffz. Seebeck, who crashed in his aircraft.

The sixth Third Gruppe aircraft lost was shot down on the bombers' return flight. Lt. Karl-Heinz Kempf of the 11th Staffel had pursued the bombers for an hour waiting for an opportunity to attack. He was then hit by bomber fire, but bailed out successfully, only slightly injured.

The Third Gruppe was credited in the nightly OKW communiqué with shooting down one B-17, but the claim apparently did not get farther than the Geschwader, and was certainly never confirmed. The pilot involved has not been identified.

JG 26 Casualties: 22 December 1943

Date	Rank	Name	Cas	Unit	Aircraft	WNr	Mkgs	Place	Time	Cause	Allied Unit
22-12-43	Uffz.	Broda, Günter	KIA	9	Bf 109G-6	19661	wh 9	W of Hardenberg (NL)	1400	P-47	4 FG
22-12-43	Uffz.	Seebeck, Karl	KIA	9	Bf 109G-6/U4	20712	wh 3	Hellendoorn	1400	P-47	78 FG
22-12-43	Uffz.	Jenner, Anton	KIA	11	Bf 109G-5	110020	yl 2	Rheine-Westfalen	1408	P-47	4 FG
22-12-43	Lt.	Kempf, Karl-Heinz	WIA	11	Bf 109G-6/U4	440012	yl 9	Ems-Weser Canal	1456	B-17	
22-12-43	Fhj-Fw.	Richter, Julius	KIA	11	Bf 109G-6/U4	20723	yl 5	near Rheine-Drierwalde	1408	P-47	4 FG
22-12-43	Fw.	Trapp, Karl	KIA	12	Bf 109G-6/U4	20710	bl 10	Hardenberg-30km W Lingen	1345	P-47	56 FG

Obstlt. Priller in his Fw 190A-6, W.Nr. 530120 – Lille-Nord, winter 1943-44. *(Bundesarchiv-Bildarchiv)*

23 December

Fw. Heinz Münch, an experienced 3rd Staffel pilot, was killed while on a training exercise. His engine failed over Namur, and Münch crashed while attempting a dead-stick landing.

24 December

The remnants of II/JG 3 were withdrawn from Volkel and sent to Rothenburg, near Bremen, to rebuild. During its four months in Jafü 3, the unit had lost twenty-three pilots killed, including two Gruppenkommandeure and two Staffelkapitäne. In contrast, its previous tour on the Eastern Front had lasted fifteen months, and had cost the Gruppe twenty-nine pilots killed or missing; these casualties had included no formation leaders.

28 December

The purpose of the V-1 launching sites was as yet totally unknown to the members of the Allied flying units, but they were a top-priority target, and several methods of attack were tried out during this period. Today a Spitfire squadron attempted to dive-bomb one of the construction sites. The 7th Staffel was scrambled from Grevillers and reached the Spitfires of No. 350 Sqd. (Belgian) as they withdrew at low altitude. Fw. Mayer shot down one of the Spitfires, and damaged a second.

JG 26 Victory Claims: 21 - 28 December 1943

Date	Rank	Name	Unit	Cl #	Aircraft	Place	Time	Opponent	Conf
21-12-43	Obfw.	Glunz	5	50	Spitfire	Vimy Ridge-SW of Douai	1150	132 or 602 Sqd	yes
21-12-43	Oblt.	Matoni	6	8	Spitfire	3km SSW of Boulogne	1208	132 or 602 Sqd	yes
21-12-43	Hptm.	Naumann	7 CO	28	Spitfire	Douai	1151	132 or 602 Sqd	yes
28-12-43	Fw.	Mayer	7	7	Spitfire	Brailly	1607	350 Sqd	yes

30 December

Today's target for the heavy bombers was one the largest chemical complexes in the Third Reich – the I. G. Farben plant at Ludwigshaven, on the upper Rhine. The undercast was solid, but the clouds topped out at 10-12,000 feet (3000-3700 meters), with unlimited visibility above them. These were good conditions for the bombers, which were able to maintain a tight formation, and the escorts, which could keep the bombers in sight while maintaining a close watch below for any German interceptors emerging from the undercast. The 8th Bomber Command planners, who earlier in the year had scrupulously avoided routing their aircraft over the Pas de Calais, now had a new area to avoid, The Netherlands and the Ruhr. They recognized that the German defenses were now strongest in that region, and sent the bombers south from England over the Seine Estuary into France, and then due east to the target. Their strategy worked well, and obviously confused the Luftflotte Reich controllers. Of the 710 bombers dispatched on this full-strength mission, only twenty-three were lost. An estimated 200 sorties were flown by the German defenders, most by the pilots of Jafü 4 and Jafü 5, some of whom flew two or even three sorties.

The Jafü 4 controller – probably Obstlt. Priller, who was once again substituting for Obst. Vieck – ignored the 9th Air Force bombers and kept his fighters on the ground until the heavy bombers began crossing over Beachy Head at 1030. Expecting a raid on Paris, he scrambled the Second Gruppe, the 4th Staffel, and I/JG 3 and sent them south. The bombers crossed the coast at 1045 and made a sharp turn to the left onto an eastward course, bringing them closer to the oncoming Jafü 4 fighters, who climbed into the morning sun and waited for opportunities to strike. While stalking the First Bomb Division stream, Fw. Wiegand inadvertently led the 4th Staffel into the middle of the 353rd Fighter Group; Wiegand quickly shot down one P-47 before escaping. The Americans did not down any Focke-Wulfs, but the Staffel formation was effectively broken up. Fw. Wiegand and Fw. Hager then attacked a straggling 390th Bomb Group B-17. Wiegand left the "kill" to Hager, who thus scored his first confirmed victory. The 353rd broke up the I/JG 3 attack, shooting down two of its Messerschmitts for the loss of another P-47. The Second Gruppe followed the Second Bomb Division for some time, until the rear B-24 wing lost its coverage owing to the

B-17 "Woman's Home Companion" (42-39795) of the 303rd Bomb Group, downed by Fw. Hager (4/JG 26) south of Florennes, Belgium on 30 December. *(Roba)*

B-17G "Sarah Jane" (42-39759) of the 390th Bomb Group, shot down by Fw. Schild (2/JG 26) on 30 December near Vimy in northern France. *(Hallade via Roba)*

Fw-Fhj. Gerd Wiegand of the 4th Staffel attracted the attention of the Propaganda Kompanie photographers, one of whom took this "glamour shot". *(Bundesarchiv-Bildarchiv)*

non-arrival of a P-47 group. The Second Gruppe attacked immediately, along with some fighters from JG 2, but had to break off quickly owing to low fuel. Oblt. Matoni claimed one of the B-24s.

The First and Second Gruppen scrambled at 1250 and headed south to intercept the withdrawing bombers. The First Gruppe reached the Third Bomb Division just as the 56th Fighter Group was breaking off, and was able to make a head-on attack that sent two B-17s to earth before the P-47s returned and scattered the Focke-Wulfs. Uffz. Ewald Schnier was injured, and his aircraft was damaged, but he was able to make a smooth forced landing. The Second Gruppe was willing to wait for an opening, but Fw. Mayer got involved with a P-47, which he claimed to shoot down before making a quick landing on Laon for refueling. He then returned to Grevillers. Uffz. Heinz Wyrich was shot down, probably by a No. 412 Sqd. (RCAF) Spitfire which had ranged all the way to Compiègne, east of Paris. A half hour later Lt. Radener shot down a P-47, and then a B-17 near St. Pol, before the Gruppe headed back to Grevillers.

The 4th Staffel took off from Wevelgem at 1412 and headed for the French coast to look for stragglers. They encountered a flight of three 352nd Fighter Group P-47s that were too low on fuel to stay around and fight. Fw. Wiegand chased one out to sea and shot it down; the other two were downed by the Dunkirk Flak. Fw. Schmidtke then found and shot down a straggling B-17, according to Gerd Wiegand's notes, but the claim was not filed. The day's flying ended with Fw. Mayer's third combat sortie. He scrambled at 1515 and was vectored toward a lone B-17 west of Arras; Mayer quickly shot the crippled bomber down.

JG 26 Victory Claims: 30 December 1943

Date	Rank	Name	Unit	Cl #	Aircraft	Place	Time	Opponent	Conf
30-12-43	Lt.	Willius	2 CO	37	B-17	Soissons (TG)	1343	100 BG	yes
30-12-43	Fw.	Schild	2	2	B-17	Soissons-N of Charleroi (TG)	1343	390 BG	yes
30-12-43	Fw.	Hager R.	4	1	B-17	S of Florennes	1200	303 BG	yes
30-12-43	Fw.	Schmidtke	4		B-17	unknown	1500		no
30-12-43	Fw.	Wiegand	4	10	P-47	S of Florennes	1130	353 FG	yes
30-12-43	Fw.	Wiegand	4	11	P-47	near Dunkirk	1500	352 FG	yes
30-12-43	Oblt.	Matoni	6	9	B-24	15km NW of Soissons	1150		yes
30-12-43	Fw.	Mayer	7	8	P-47	4km N of Soissons	1330		unk
30-12-43	Fw.	Mayer	7	9	B-17	22km NW of Arras	1540		yes
30-12-43	Lt.	Radener	7	7	P-47	12km SE of Beauvais	1400		yes
30-12-43	Lt.	Radener	7	8	B-17	32km WNW of Arras	1436		unk

31 December

The target selection for today's heavy bomber mission was somewhat unusual. One hundred and twenty-five B-17s bombed several factories in Paris, while the other 450 B-17s and B-24s of the 8th Bomber Command crossed the Brittany peninsula and made a broad swing over the Bay of Biscay to attack several airfields on the lower Atlantic French coast from the west. Jafü 5 and Jafü Brittany were better prepared

than the Americans had hoped, and shot down twenty-five bombers; another fifteen were lost to ditchings and accidents. The training units in western France did well. Oblt. Otto Stammberger and Obfw. Xaver Ellenrieder, two long-time Geschwader members now with 2/JGr West at Bergerac, were credited with B-17s. Stotto Stammberger, the Staffelkapitän, had never been cleared for combat duty following his wounding in May, 1943. He was shot down today, as well, and bailed out with new, if minor, injuries. This was his 104th, and last, combat sortie.

Jafü 4 contributed the Second Gruppe to the defense against this raid. Most of its pilots took off at 1020 and flew to Tours, southwest of Paris, to refuel. They took off again at 1405 and attacked the western bomber force as it was recrossing Brittany; Obfw. Glunz shot down one B-17, and Fw. Gomann claimed one of the P-47 escorts, before the German fighters had to put down at Vannes. On the return flight to

Obfw. Xaver Ellenrieder, a long serving First Gruppe pilot, photographed while on duty as an instructor in Biarritz in 1944. *(Ellenrieder)*

Grevillers, the engine of Fw. Mayer's Focke-Wulf seized. He was over some woods and could not make a forced landing, so chose to bail out, but hit the tail of his aircraft and was injured.

Several of the 7th Staffel pilots that had been left behind at Grevillers, mainly newcomers, were ordered to scramble and look for stragglers coming back from the Paris raid. Lt. Vavken found a 96th Bomb Group B-17 crossing the coast and shot it down into the Somme Estuary – the only loss that the Paris bombers sustained.

The 4th Staffel suffered one fatality. Uffz. Ernst Klumpe crashed in his aircraft while ferrying a Fw 190 from Mönchen-Gladbach to Wevelgem. The cause was never determined.

Geschwader personnel moves during December included: the departure of Oblt. Otto Stammberger from the Stab to serve as a Staffelkapitän in Jagdgruppe West; the return of Lt. Georg Kiefner to the First Gruppe from instructor duty; and the return of Uffz. Gerhard Falkner to the 5th Staffel from a ferry unit.

Pilots assigned to the Geschwader during December after completing flight training included: Uffz. Erich Lambertus, Lt. Wilhelm Nink (an ex-infantryman), Uffz. Gerhard Schulz - First Gruppe; Uffz. Walter Enna, Uffz. Paul Gross, Uffz. Paul Jezek, Fw. Edgar Meschkat, Gefr. Wilhelm Peukert, Gefr. Werner Pietruschka - Second Gruppe.

Although the claim-to-loss ratio for the Geschwader in 1943 was about four to one, indicating a high degree of combat efficiency, there were strong signs that the Allies' war of attrition was starting to wear it down. The number of pilots killed in 1943, 158, was more than double that of the previous year, and was equivalent to an annual loss rate of greater than 100%, based on the average number of pilots available for duty. The aircraft inventory had remained at about 50% of authorized strength in December, but only two-thirds of these aircraft were operational. At year's end the entire Geschwader had only sixty-eight operational fighters, nearly all Fw 190A-6s and Bf 109G-6s. The number of pilots "on the books" of the Geschwader was an impressive 185, but only 107 were available for duty; the rest were convalescing, away on leave or detached service, or simply not considered ready for combat missions. The Third Gruppe had only twenty-five pilots on duty out of fifty-four on strength, implying the presence of a large number of inexperienced pilots that Hptm. Mietusch refused to declare operational. This could explain why the Gruppe was sent few, if any, new pilots in December.

Although Galland's plans for expanding the Jagdwaffe had finally been put into effect, they were too little and too late. The Luftwaffe was rapidly losing the war of numbers in the ETO. The Allied fighter force in England already exceeded Germany's total fighter strength on all fronts, and was still growing rapidly. The Americans were now deploying fighters with the range to accompany the bombers to any target in Germany. With the coming of better weather in the spring, the stage would be set for the total defeat of Germany's aerial defenders.

JG 26 Victory Claims: 31 December 1943

Date	Rank	Name	Unit	Cl #	Aircraft	Place	Time	Opponent	Conf
31-12-43	Obfw.	Glunz	5	51	B-17	between Lorient & Auringes	1500		yes
31-12-43	Fw.	Gomann	6	9	P-47	NE of Vire	1414		unk
31-12-43	Lt.	Vavken	7	1	B-17	5km N of Ault	1330	96 BG	yes

JG 26 Casualties: 23 - 31 December 1943

Date	Rank	Name	Cas	Unit	Aircraft	WNr	Mkgs	Place	Time	Cause	Allied Unit
23-12-43	Fw.	Münch, Heinz	KIFA	3	Fw 190A-5	410236	yl 9	Namur-Profondeville	1430	engine	non-op
30-12-43	Uffz.	Schnier, Ewald	WIA	1	Fw 190A-6	530948	wh 6	Hirson		P-47	56 FG
30-12-43	Uffz.	Wyrich, Heinz	WIA	5	Fw 190A-5	1175	wh 16	2km S of Romaine		Spitfire	412 Sqd
31-12-43	Uffz.	Klumpe, Ernst	KIFA	4	Fw 190A-6	530396	bl 5	15km W of Charleroi	1200	crashed	non-op
31-12-43	Fw.	Mayer, Wilhelm	WIFA	7	Fw 190A-6	470005	br 9	Le Fresnes		engine	n/a

Chapter Five

THE AIR WAR IS LOST

January - May 1944

1 January

Gen. Dwight D. Eisenhower had arrived in England from the Mediterranean theater to assume his new position as Supreme Commander for the invasion of Western Europe. He brought with him his air team, several men with whom the general had worked and felt comfortable. Three of them had an important impact on JG 26 and the Jagdwaffe. Air Marshal Arthur Coningham and Air Vice-Marshal Harry Broadhurst took command of the 2nd Tactical Air Force and its fighter component. While in the MTO these two airmen had developed the close air support tactics that would now be used in the ETO for the rest of the war. The 2nd TAF now had a mission, to soften up the invasion coast, and its Spitfire squadrons would soon be relieved of much of their escort responsibility and drop to the deck to seek out the Luftwaffe.

The American air forces in England were reorganized, in part to make room for Eisenhower's people, and in part owing to dissatisfaction in Washington with the pace of the strategic air campaign. LGen. James Doolittle, one of Eisenhower's men, took over the 8th Air Force. He ran it from the former headquarters of the 8th Bomber Command, which was disbanded. Eisenhower made it plain that Allied air superiority was a prerequisite for the successful invasion of the continent. Since the invasion was scheduled for late spring, the air commanders would have to re-order their priorities – and quickly. The Allies could wait no longer for the bomber generals to fulfill their dream of defeating Germany by strategic bombing alone.

In Jimmy Doolittle, Eisenhower had the perfect airman for the task ahead. Doolittle, a reservist, was a brilliant man who had already succeeded in a broad range of aviation endeavors. He was not a bomber general, meaning that he had no loyalty to the theories of strategic bombing. Always a pragmatist, he was quick to discard policies that did not contribute to his immediate goal of defeating the Luftwaffe. The bombers were ordered to fly in weather that previously would have grounded them. Bombing accuracy suffered, and accidents increased, but these concerns were now secondary; the important thing was to keep pressure on the Germans. American escort doctrine soon changed; the fighters were ordered to patrol fixed zones along the bombers' track instead of escorting specific bomber wings. This subtle change in tactics permitted the escort formation leaders to concentrate on finding enemy fighters, rather than the "correct" bomber formation – bomber units which missed rendezvous were left to fend for themselves. At the urging of MGen. Kepner of 8th Fighter Command, Doolittle permitted part of the escort force to range ahead of the bombers – aggressive units such as Hub Zemke's 56th Fighter Group had been doing this for months, without authorization – and ordered that the escort fighters, once their patrol shift was over, were to drop to low altitude, seeking out and destroying German fighters wherever they could be found. This new attitude by the high command, added to further improvements in equipment and total domination in numbers – there were ultimately thirty-three American fighter groups in England – permitted Eisenhower's demand to be fully satisfied by D-Day, 6 June.

2 January

The weather over England was too bad for either the strategic or the tactical bombers to take off. The Geschwader flew its defensive patrols, on one of which Fw. Wiegand intercepted a small flight of No. 349 Sqd. (Belgian) Spitfires that were flying a Rhubarb. Wiegand dropped one of the Spitfires into the Somme Estuary.

While on a surveillance flight from Grevillers to Étaples, the second element of a Schwarm of 5th Staffel Focke-Wulfs collided, killing Uffz. Martin Günther and Uffz. Erwin Hanke.

3 January

The small-scale incursions continued. Uffz. Guttmann of the 8th Staffel shot down a No. 609 Sqd. Typhoon in the day's only encounter over the Pas de Calais.

4 January

The 8th Air Force attacked Kiel and Münster, and the 9th Air Force and the 2nd TAF bombed V-1 sites and airfields, despite poor visibility over the entire Continent. The contributions to the defense by the Geschwader were minor. The Third Gruppe scrambled from Mönchen-Gladbach against the heavies, but failed to make contact. Ofhr. Kemethmüller, on his first flight since his wounding on 17 August, took part in this mission. The First and Second Gruppen flew several missions in search of the medium bombers, but only one combat resulted. Two No. 501 Sqd. Spitfire Vbs were detailed to fly behind and below the Bostons they were escorting in order to photograph the target, Ligescourt. This would have been a suicidal assignment only a year earlier, but encounters with the Luftwaffe were now rare. Lt. Wilhelm Hofmann spotted the pair through a break in the clouds and led his eight 8th Staffel Focke-Wulfs in a quick attack that downed one of the Spitfires.

5 January

The 8th Air Force split its bombers, sending some to Kiel, some to ball-bearing plants in the Ruhr, and some to airfields in western France. The Third Gruppe had no success against the Ruhr force. The First Gruppe was grounded, and the Second Gruppe flew only one successful mission. Lt. Radener led the duty Schwarm up from Grevillers to intercept a lone Fortress that was approaching the airfield at an altitude of 2-3000 meters (6500-10,000 feet). Radener shot it down, and was back on the ground seven minutes after takeoff; uncertainties in the American crash location records make it impossible to identify this B-17.

JG 26 Victory Claims: 2 - 5 January 1944

Date	Rank	Name	Unit	Cl #	Aircraft	Place	Time	Opponent	Conf
02-01-44	Fw.	Wiegand	4	12	Spitfire	Somme Estuary	1630	349 Sqd	yes
03-01-44	Uffz.	Guttmann	8	2	Typhoon	5-10km E of Doullens	1340	609 Sqd	yes
04-01-44	Lt.	Hofmann W.	8	4	Spitfire	near Rue	1610	501 Sqd	yes
05-01-44	Lt.	Radener	7	9	B-17	near Miraumont	1314		yes

7 January

The 8th Air Force paid a full-strength return visit to the I. G. Farben chemical plant at Ludwigshaven. Unlike the 30 December raid, this one was routed east over the Dutch coast, and then southeast to the west of the Ruhr. The Jafü 3 controllers were again confused as to the bombers' destination, and no interceptors reached the bombers until shortly before the bomb run. The bombers' return route took them across France, where today JG 2 and JG 26 were ready, despite the solid cloud cover.

First off the ground was the First Gruppe, which left Florennes at 1210 with orders to move west to Creil, carrying auxiliary tanks. While airborne, Borris's men were vectored toward some Allied aircraft that had been wandering above the undercast for some time. The Allied formation was the new 358th Fighter Group, returning from its first escort mission and totally lost. The commander of one squadron, believing that he was over England and catching a glimpse of an airfield, led his flight down through the clouds. At that moment, Hptm. Borris and his Schwarm attacked them. Three P-47s crashed; the fourth pulled back up into the clouds and returned to tell the tale. The First Gruppe became scattered during this engagement, landed where it could, and played no more part in the day's battles.

The Second Gruppe scrambled at 1245 and was directed south to Paris, where the bomber stream had been located. The Gruppe quickly broke up into Schwärme in the towering clouds, and sought out, first, unprotected bomber groups, and, second, bombers flying in poor or no formation. The Focke-Wulfs shot down three of the total of only five B-17s lost on the mission, following them all the way to the St. Pol area before the Allied fighters intervened. The 4th Fighter Group was returning from an uneventful withdrawal escort when its commander, LCol. Don Blakeslee, sighted twelve Fw 190s lining up for a rear attack on a sloppy B-17 formation. He and his flight dived at top speed, "through a formation of Spitfires", according to one of the wingmen, and shot down three of the Focke-Wulfs before one got on Blakeslee's tail and shot his aircraft full of holes – seventy-one, according to a count made after Blakeslee was able to force-land on Manston. Uffz. Guttmann received a victory credit for Blakeslee's P-47. The Spitfires just mentioned belonged to No. 125 Wing, which also attacked the Focke-Wulfs, claiming 2-0-1 for the cost of one Spitfire which ditched in the Channel, the probable victim of Obfw. Glunz, whose claim for a P-47 was not confirmed. Four Focke-Wulfs went down in these combats. Lt. Rolf Saligman, Lt. Kurt Vavken, and Fhj.-Fw. Hellmuth Wirth were killed, and Uffz. Gerhard Falkner bailed out with mild burns.

JG 26 Victory Claims: 7 January 1944

Date	Rank	Name	Unit	Cl #	Aircraft	Place	Time	Opponent	Conf
07-01-44	Hptm.	Borris	I CO	31	P-47	nr Cousoire		358 FG	yes
07-01-44	Oblt.	Kranefeld	I	2	P-47	nr Cousoire	1230	358 FG	yes
07-01-44	Lt.	Kiefner	1	2	P-47	S of Maubeuge	1230	358 FG	yes
07-01-44	Obfw.	Glunz	5	52	P-47	near Boulogne	1345	4 FG	unk
07-01-44	Oblt.	Hummel	6	1	B-17	10km NW of Abbeville	1327		yes
07-01-44	Uffz.	Guttmann	8	3	P-47	near Doullens	1335	4 FG	yes
07-01-44	Lt.	Hofmann W.	8	5	B-17	2km E of La Calique	1350		yes
07-01-44	Uffz.	Schulwitz	8	2	B-17	1km N of Trois-Marquess	1345		yes

JG 26 Casualties: 2 - 7 January 1944

Date	Rank	Name	Cas	Unit	Aircraft	WNr	Mkgs	Place	Time	Cause	Allied Unit
02-01-44	Uffz.	Günther, Martin	KIFA	5	Fw 190A-5	410238	wh 10	SE of Amiens	1040	collision	n/a
02-01-44	Uffz.	Hanke, Erwin	KIFA	5	Fw 190A-6	550556	wh 1	SE of Amiens	1040	collision	n/a
07-01-44	Uffz.	Falkner, Gerhard	WIA	5	Fw 190A-6	470233	wh 7	SW of Doullens		Spitfire or P-47	125 Wing or 4 FG
07-01-44	Lt.	Saligmann, Rolf	KIA	5	Fw 190A-6	470206	wh 1	E of Doullens		Spitfire or P-47	125 Wing or 4 FG
07-01-44	Fhj.-Fw.	Wirth, Hellmuth	KIA	6	Fw 190A-6	550727	bk 2	SE of Abbeville		Spitfire or P-47	125 Wing or 4 FG
07-01-44	Lt.	Vavken, Kurt	KIA	7	Fw 190A-6	530401	br 7	12km SE of Montreuil		Spitfire or P-47	125 Wing or 4 FG

9 January

The Third Gruppe began a permanent base transfer. The Stab, 9th, and 11th Staffeln moved to Lille-Vendeville, while the 10th and 12th Staffeln went to Denain. The Gruppe exchanged bases with I/JG 3, which moved to Mönchen-Gladbach. The latter Gruppe was to join the rest of JG 3, now in Luftflotte Reich, as a *Höhengruppe*, or high-altitude Gruppe, whose purpose was to shield the bomber-attackers from the escorts. The Third Gruppe is often referred to in the German records as a Höhengruppe or a *leichtes* (light) Gruppe, but its mission orders were generally the same as those of the two Focke-Wulf Gruppen. Although its bases were now in close proximity, JG 26 never went into battle as a single formation; there was never enough time above the Pas de Calais to form up.

10 January

The Kapitän of the 3rd Staffel, Oblt. Heinrich Jessen, was killed while landing on Florennes after a patrol flight. His Focke-Wulf was rammed by that of Fhr. Meyer, who was following him.

Hptm. Wilhelm Gäth became Kommandeur of the Second Gruppe, losing his probationary status. Oblt. Otto Hummel left the 6th Staffel and became Gäth's adjutant. Lt. Herfried Kloimüller replaced Jessen as 3rd Staffel leader, but served for only eleven days, until Fred Heckmann's commission was announced and he took over the job.

11 January

All three 8th Air Force Bomb Divisions took off and assembled, but worsening conditions over the continent forced the recall of all of the Second and most of the Third Division, as well as much of the escort. The B-17s of the First Division made a successful attack on the Fw 190 factory at Oschersleben, but suffered heavily from German fighters in what the after-battle report called "the most intense opposition... since Schweinfurt." Forty-two B-17s failed to return from the mission.

The Third Gruppe was apparently not operational owing to its base move, but the two Focke-Wulf Gruppen were ordered up to intercept the bombers on their return flight, and had very successful missions. Since Obstlt. Priller was again serving as Jafü at St. Pol, his Führungsstaffel, the 4th, left Wevelgem at 0900 to join the rest of the First Gruppe at Florennes. This Gruppe took off at 1222 carrying belly tanks, and flew north. Hptm. Borris led; Fw. Wiegand and his 4th Staffel flew high cover. The cloud deck north of Brussels was solid at 2000 meters (6500 feet). West of Nordhorn, nineteen B-17s, the 306th Bomb Group in its combat box formation, were sighted, entirely without escort. The group had become separated from the rest of its combat wing, further increasing its vulnerability. Wiegand reported that all was clear above, and Borris overtook the bombers, made a broad turn, and lined up ahead of the bombers for a classic head-on attack. According to the leader of the bomber formation, the 30-35 Fw 190s came in on them high from 10:30 to 1:30 o'clock and rolled through the formation, coming back for rear attacks. In seven minutes eight bombers had dropped from the formation, leaving only eleven. Fw. Wiegand led the 4th Staffel down and shot down a B-17 on each of his two attacks. His engine was then hit by defensive fire, and he dived away, his canopy covered in oil. He was preparing to bail out when he caught sight of the ground through the clouds and got his bearings. He was near Deelen, and was able to put his "oily sardine" down on the middle of the field. Uffz. Heinz Voigt of his Staffel bailed out after his aircraft was hit, but was uninjured, and a 2nd Staffel aircraft crash-landed; the losses of the Gruppe thus totaled three aircraft, and no pilots. Of the eight B-17s that were knocked from formation, five crashed west of or in the Zuider Zee; the other three crash-landed back in England. Eight First Gruppe pilots received credit for their destruction; Wiegand's second claim was not filed.

The Second Gruppe scrambled at 1227 and followed the First Gruppe north to the Dutch-German border. Lt. Radener downed a lone P-47, probably a 353rd Fighter Group aircraft that had dropped out of formation with unspecified problems. The bombers, when located, had few escorts around, and the Second Gruppe downed two B-17s, both probably from the 92nd Bomb Group in the scattered 40th Bomb Wing. The Gruppe apparently lost one fighter to engine failure, although the records conflict. Heinz Gomann's story is that he and a wingman landed on Fürstenau to refuel and spent the night in the town. The following morning Gomann lost his wingman on the return flight and was then attacked from the clouds by four Spitfires. He escaped in the

Obstlt. Priller exits his Fw 190A-6 (W.Nr. 530120) while on an inspection trip in early 1944. *(Schrödter)*

clouds, but then lost his orientation, and had to bail out. He returned to Cambrai with his parachute under his arm, and was promptly confined to quarters.

JG 26 Victory Claims: 11 January 1944

Date	Rank	Name	Unit	Cl #	Aircraft	Place	Time	Opponent	Conf
11-01-44	Hptm.	Borris	I CO	32	B-17	Nordhorn-Zuider Zee	1300	306 BG	yes
11-01-44	Oblt.	Kranefeld	I	3	B-17-HSS	unknown	1327	306 BG	yes
11-01-44	Oblt.	Beese	1 CO	20	B-17	Zuider Zee	1300	482 BG	yes
11-01-44	Obfw.	Heckmann	1	59	B-17	Nordhorn-Zuider Zee	1300	306 BG	yes
11-01-44	Lt.	Willius	2 CO	38	B-17	Deventer (GN)	1300	306 BG	yes
11-01-44	Lt.	Triebnig	3	1	B-17	Nordhorn-Zuider Zee	1300	306 BG	yes
11-01-44	Fw.	Vandeveerd	3	2	B-17	Nordhorn	1300	306 BG	yes
11-01-44	Fw.	Wiegand	4		B-17	Nordhorn-Zuider Zee	1300	306 BG	no
11-01-44	Fw.	Wiegand	4	13	B-17	Nordhorn-Zuider Zee	1300	306 BG	yes
11-01-44	Oblt.	Matoni	6	10	B-17	Tubbergen 10km N of Almelo	1330	92 BG	yes
11-01-44	Uffz.	Georgi	7	1	B-17-HSS	E of Lingen	1312	92 BG	yes
11-01-44	Lt.	Radener	7	10	P-47	Backum near Lingen	1315	353 FG	unk
11-01-44	Lt.	Hofmann W.	8	6	B-17-eV	4km NW of Rheine	1318		unk

JG 26 Casualties: 10 - 12 January 1944

Date	Rank	Name	Cas	Unit	Aircraft	WNr	Mkgs	Place	Time	Cause	Allied Unit
10-01-44	Oblt.	Jessen, Heinrich	KIFA	3 CO	Fw 190A-6	470048	wh 2	Florennes a/f		collision	n/a
11-01-44	Uffz.	Voigt, Heinz	no	4	Fw 190A-6	550458	bk 8	Schalkhaar	1315	B-17	
12-01-44	Fw.	Gomann, Heinz	no	6	Fw 190A-6	530931	bk 14	Cambrai-Zwolle		engine	n/a

14 January

The weather over Germany was so bad that the 8th Air Force changed the target for the day to the V-1 sites on the Pas de Calais. Twenty-one sites were bombed by 552 heavy bombers, which were escorted by 645 P-38s, P-47s, and P-51s. Prior to the heavy bomber raid, V-1 sites and other targets in northern France were visited by 844 tactical aircraft. Jafü 4 and Jafü 5 hurled their fighters against this armada, with little success.

The Second and Third Gruppen were scrambled against the medium bomber raids

Members of the 11th and 12th Staffeln, photographed in early 1944. Identifiable pilots are: Fw. Adi Boeckl (tall pilot 11th from left), Uffz. Erich Salewsky (center of seated group) (KIA 14 Jan 1945), Uffz. Otto Salewski (6th from right) (KIA 7 Mar 1945), Uffz. Willibald Malm (3rd from right), Uffz. Willi Dachmann (far right) (KIFA 28 Feb 1945). *(Genth)*

at 1115, and soon found the Spitfires. Hptm. Mietusch led his Gruppe in a bounce of the Northolt Wing over St. Pol, and downed a No. 308 Sqd. (Polish) Spitfire, whose pilot was noted by Mietusch to bail out. Obfw. Kemethmüller and Uffz. Laub also claimed Spitfires, but only one was apparently lost. The Poles in turn shot down and killed Uffz. Hans Hein and Lt. Klaus Reinhardt, one more victory than they claimed. Major Gäth's Second Gruppe headed for the west coast of the Pas de Calais, and reached a B-26 formation before being driven off by the Spitfires of No. 125 Wing. Fw. Mayer received credit for shooting down a B-26, but the American records state that the only two B-26s lost, both from the 322nd Bomb Group, were downed by Flak. Oblt. Matoni probably shot down S/L Colloredo-Mansfeld of No. 132 Squadron, although his loss is also attributed to the Flak. The Spitfires shot down and killed Uffz. Gerhard Maletz.

The Jafü 4 controllers scrambled all three Gruppen as the heavy bombers started crossing the Channel later in the afternoon, but expected a deeper raid, and directed their fighters too far south, where they met only American fighters flying sweeps. Hptm. Johann Aistleitner, the leader of the 5th Staffel, had been visiting his old 1st Staffel comrades at Florennes when the takeoff order came. He joined the First Gruppe on the mission, and was shot down and killed near Montdidier, probably by P-47s of the 4th Fighter Group, although his loss report identifies them as Spitfires. The First Gruppe also lost Uffz. Werner Kaiser, who bailed out near Beauvais but bled to death in his parachute, and made no claims. The Second Gruppe Kommandeur, Major Gäth, was also shot down, probably by the 4th Group, although Spitfires were again given the credit. Gäth bailed out near Soissons with what were described as minor injuries, but was grounded when he returned to the Geschwader, and in March left it for good.

Only the Third Gruppe could claim a success on the afternoon mission. Hptm. Mietusch pulled off a stunt for which he was famous, making a lone bounce on a straggling 356th Fighter Group P-47 from out of the sun, and escaping with a split-S before the Americans could react. Mietusch's Gruppe lost one Messerschmitt, but its pilot escaped injury.

JG 26 Victory Claims: 14 January 1944

Date	Rank	Name	Unit	Cl #	Aircraft	Place	Time	Opponent	Conf
14-01-44	Oblt.	Matoni	6	11	Spitfire	Doullens	1202	132 Sqd	yes
14-01-44	Fw.	Mayer	7	10	B-26	15km WNW of Étaples	1158	322 BG	yes
14-01-44	Major	Mietusch	III CO	55	Spitfire	S of St Omer	1150	308 Sqd	yes
14-01-44	Major	Mietusch	III CO	56	P-47	St Pol	1535	356 FG	yes
14-01-44	Ofhr.	Kemethmüller	9	75	Spitfire	Calais	1200	308 Sqd	yes
14-01-44	Uffz.	Laub	11	5	Spitfire	unknown	1158	308 Sqd	yes

JG 26 Casualties: 14 January 1944

Date	Rank	Name	Cas	Unit	Aircraft	WNr	Mkgs	Place	Time	Cause	Allied Unit
14-01-44	Uffz.	Kaiser, Werner	KIA	3	Fw 190A-6	550241	wh 6	Beauvais		P-47	4 FG
14-01-44	Maj.	Gäth, Wilhelm	WIA	II CO	Fw 190A-6	470009	<< gr 1	Soissons		P-47	4 FG
14-01-44	Hptm.	Aistleitner, Johann	KIA	5 CO	Fw 190A-6	530734	wh 9	Ercheu, 29km NE Montdidier		P-47	4 FG
14-01-44	Uffz.	Maletz, Gerhard	KIA	6		Fw 190A-6	470220	bk 6	nr Abbeville		Spitfire	132 Sqd
14-01-44	Uffz.	Hein, Hans	KIA	11		Bf 109G-6	410577	yl 1	20km E of Hesdin	1200	Spitfire	308 Sqd
14-01-44	Lt.	Reinhardt, Klaus	KIA	11		Bf 109G-6	410677	yl 6	St.Pol-Hesdin-Bellevue	1200	Spitfire	308 Sqd

15 January

Uffz. Philipp Schmelzer of the 1st Staffel was injured while landing at Antwerp on a transfer flight, probably to the ERLA repair factory. He failed to see a taxiing Bf 109, and rammed it. He recalled later with some pride that he was held blameless and was not court-martialed, the usual fate of any pilot who damaged an airplane while not on operations.

Obfw. Addi Glunz was named Hptm. Aistleitner's replacement as leader of the 5th Staffel, the first time the Geschwader staff had named a noncommissioned officer as Staffelführer.

19 January

The Gruppen took advantage of the inactivity across the Channel to schedule a number of training flights in January, but the foul weather that grounded the Allies also took its toll on the Germans. Uffz. Gerhard Schulz of the 3rd Staffel rammed his element leader, Uffz. Kurt Kuhnert, while training in bad weather north of Namur, and both died in their aircraft. Lt. Holger Bruns of the 5th Staffel was also killed on a training flight when his engine caught fire in mid-air.

21 January

At noon, the 9th Air Force sent 119 B-26s with Spitfire escort to attack several V-1 sites. The Third Gruppe had the task of intercepting them, and got into a large fight with Spitfires south of St. Omer. Ofhr. Kemethmüller claimed a Spitfire, but the claim was rejected. Hptm. Staiger claimed two, but these claims were never filed. The Gruppe sustained no losses.

The 8th Air Force dispatched 795 B-17s and B-24s at 1400 to bomb V-1 sites on the Pas de Calais and the Cherbourg peninsula, escorted by 628 USAAF fighters. The weather was so bad that fewer than half the bombers dropped their loads; some combat boxes circled for so long that their escort had to leave them. Hptm. Borris's Gruppe had scrambled from Florennes at 1420, and crossed the Pas de Calais several times dodging fighters and looking for unprotected bombers. Over Poix Borris spotted an unescorted *Pulk* (herd) of B-24s – the 44th Bomb Group – and ordered his fifteen pilots to attack them from the rear. After several stern attacks, five B-24s went down. All crashed near Poix. B-24s, unlike B-17s, rarely managed to stagger back to England with heavy combat damage; victory claim bookkeeping was therefore simple, and the claims of five pilots were, in fact, confirmed.

The Third Gruppe scrambled at 1420 to seek out the heavies, but lost two Messerschmitts and one pilot, and filed no claims. A flight of P-47s from the 353rd

Fighter Group, flying near St. Quentin, came across a Schwarm of Bf 109s beneath them. The Thunderbolt pilots made an undetected bounce from out of the sun. Their leader, Major Walter Beckham, hit the trailing fighter with a short burst of machine gun fire. The Messerschmitt burst into flames. Its pilot, Fw. Hans Oeckel of the 12th Staffel, bailed out quickly, landing safely but suffering from facial burns and a slight concussion. Beckham shifted his sights to the lead fighter, which exploded under the fire of his eight .50s. The pilot of this Messerschmitt, Oblt. Erich Burkert, was killed instantly. Burkert was an experienced pilot, with two victories in seventy-one sorties, and would soon have qualified for promotion to Staffelführer.

The Second Gruppe was also up, but not all of its fighters made contact. Fw. Georgi claimed a P-47 near Poix at 1504; this is the right time, but not the right place, for the day's only P-47 loss, and the lost 56th Fighter Group Thunderbolt may in fact have been downed by a JG 2 pilot.

The 4th Staffel, the Adamsonstaffel, had returned to its independent existence at Wevelgem, and was scrambled alone to face the last raid of the day, which comprised two squadrons of No. 2 Group Mitchells and six Spitfire squadrons. The self-confident Gerd Wiegand took his Focke-Wulfs above the high escort, two squadrons of Spitfire VII high-altitude fighters, and bounced them out of the sun. Fw. Schwarz shot down a No. 616 Sqd. Spitfire in his single pass. Wiegand claimed a second, which did not in fact go down. Chased by the high cover, the Focke-Wulfs continued their dive, burst through the close escort, concentrated their fire on one No. 226 Sqd. Mitchell, damaging it severely, and then dived away to safety. Wiegand and Oblt. Neu both claimed the Mitchell (as a Marauder), but neither claim was confirmed. This was No. 2 Group's only encounter with the Luftwaffe in January.

JG 26 Casualties: 15 - 21 January 1944

Date	Rank	Name	Cas	Unit	Aircraft	WNr	Mkgs	Place	Time	Cause	Allied Unit
15-01-44	Uffz.	Schmelzer, Philipp	WIFA	1	Fw 190A-6	531058	wh 10	Antwerp		landing	non-op
19-01-44	Uffz.	Kuhnert, Kurt	KIFA	3	Fw 190A-6	550738	yl 7	NE of Revin-Namur		collision	non-op
19-01-44	Uffz.	Schulz, Gerhard	KIFA	3	Fw 190A-6	530742	yl 1	NE of Revin-Namur		collision	non-op
19-01-44	Lt.	Bruns, Holger	KIFA	5	Fw 190A-6	470082	wh 3	Givet-Meuse		engine fire	non-op
21-01-44	Oblt.	Burkert, Erich	KIA	9	Bf 109G-6	410675	bl 6	NE of Laon	1445	P-47	353 FG
21-01-44	Fw.	Oeckel, Hans	WIA	12	Bf 109G-6	410723	bl 1	E of Laon-Sissonne	1445	P-47	353 FG

JG 26 Victory Claims: 21 January 1944

Date	Rank	Name	Unit	Cl #	Aircraft	Place	Time	Opponent	Conf
21-01-44	Oblt.	Beese	1 CO	21	B-24	near Poix	1530	44 BG	yes
21-01-44	Oblt.	Beese	1 CO	22	B-24	near Poix	1530	44 BG	yes
21-01-44	Lt.	Altmann	1	1	B-24	near Poix	1530	44 BG	yes
21-01-44	Lt.	Kiefner	1	3	B-24	near Poix	1530	44 BG	yes
21-01-44	Uffz.	Ruppert H.	1	1	B-24	near Poix	1530	44 BG	yes
21-01-44	Oblt.	Neu	4 CO	7	B-26	St. Omer (NE1)		226 Sqd Mitchell	unk
21-01-44	Fw.	Schwarz E.	4	6	Spitfire	Calais area		616 Sqd	yes
21-01-44	Fw.	Wiegand	4	14	Spitfire	Calais area		616 Sqd	yes
21-01-44	Fw.	Wiegand	4	15	B-26	Calais area		226 Sqd Mitchell	unk
21-01-44	Uffz.	Georgi	7	2	P-47	Poix	1504	56 FG	yes
21-01-44	Ofhr.	Kemethmüller	9		Spitfire	S of St Omer	1245		no
21-01-44	Hptm.	Staiger	12 CO	36	Spitfire	E of St Pol			unk
21-01-44	Hptm.	Staiger	12 CO	37	Spitfire	E of Amiens			unk

23 January

The response of the Geschwader to the day's 9th Air Force and 2nd TAF raids was *pro forma*. Fw. Wiegand made the only reported contact, claiming a Boston shot down near Gravelines. The claim was not filed, and no bomber was, in fact, lost.

A Propaganda Kompanie photographer receives instructions from Ofhr. Wolfgang Rose of the 4th Staffel (KIA 27 Jun 44) before being taken aloft in his baggage compartment – Wevelgem, early 1944. *(Bundesarchiv-Bildarchiv)*

24 January

Today's planned 8th Air Force mission to Frankfurt was fouled up completely by assembly problems over England; of the 817 bombers to take off, only fifty-eight completed the mission. The efforts of the Geschwader were also marked by apparent confusion, as Gruppen were scrambled and then recalled or sent to other bases. Part of the First Gruppe wound up at Bonn, while part of the Second Gruppe landed at the First Gruppe base of Florennes. The Third Gruppe had a successful mission from Laon, encountering several 78th Fighter Group P-47s southwest of Brussels and shooting down two, the day's only P-47 losses to fighters. Hptm. Staiger received a victory credit for his, while Ofhr. Kemethmüller was credited with a damaged.

Oblt. Neu and Fw. Wiegand of the Adamsonstaffel took off from Florennes at 1100 and headed north – it is not known who ordered or controlled this sortie. The pair got separated, but Wiegand sighted and shot down a Lightning over the Scheldt Estuary. Lacking a witness, Wiegand did not file a claim, but the 55th Fighter Group P-38 did, in fact, crash south of Terneuzen. At about the same time, Fw. Schmidtke of the Staffel claimed a Fortress over Calais. His claim was not confirmed, but the 95th Bomb Group B-17 did, in fact, crash; it was one of only two B-17s lost in combat this day.

25 January

All of the 9th Air Force B-26s dispatched to bomb V-1 sites were recalled, but several wings of Spitfires completed their missions as sweeps. Part of the Third Gruppe battled some Spitfires near Abbeville, without result. The Second Gruppe scramble was more profitable; Fw. Gomann downed a No. 66 Sqd. Spitfire south of St. Omer.

JG 26 Victory Claims: 23 - 25 January 1944

Date	Rank	Name	Unit	Cl #	Aircraft	Place	Time	Opponent	Conf
23-01-44	Fw.	Wiegand	4		Boston	Gravelines	1600		no
24-01-44	Fw.	Schmidtke	4	1	B-17	Calais		95 BG	unk
24-01-44	Fw.	Wiegand	4		P-38	Scheldt Est	1200	55 FG	no
24-01-44	Ofhr.	Kemethmüller	9		P-47-dam	Brussels	1100	78 FG	dam
24-01-44	Hptm.	Staiger	12 CO	38	P-47	SW of Brussels	1100	78 FG	unk
25-01-44	Fw.	Gomann	6	10	Spitfire	near Montreuil	1005	66 Sqd	yes

28 January

In the absence of bomber raids, the Second Gruppe readiness Staffeln were scrambled from Epinoy and Grevillers against Rhubarbs and Rangers. Two No. 2 Sqd. Mustangs failed to return from their sortie to the Abbeville area. No more information is available from the Allied side, but the two tactical recon planes were downed near Abbeville at 1348 and 1353 by Lt. Hofmann and Fw. Zirngibl of the 8th Staffel.

One hour later three Spitfires were reported behaving in such an insolent fashion that they demanded to be intercepted. They crossed over Lille in line abreast at only 900 meters (3000 feet), one hundred meters below the solid overcast, and turned southwest, passing in turn near the fighter airfields at Valenciennes, Douai, Vitry, and Epinoy. They were readily visible to the Luftwaffe personnel on the bases. The 7th Staffel at Grevillers got the call, and took off to the northeast, led by Fw. Vogt. Knowing the Spitfires' altitude, Vogt climbed just far enough into the cloud to be able to spot the trio beneath. He passed them without sighting them, however, but turned back and finally attacked the Spitfires as they were passing over his own base. Two of the No. 401 Sqd. (RCAF) Spitfires were badly damaged, but made it back to England; their leader was chased up into the cloud and shot down by Fw. Vogt. The pilot, P/O Claude Weaver, attempted to bail out, but was caught on his Spitfire's tail; he died in hospital several hours later. Weaver, an American, had joined the RCAF in early 1941 and had become an ace over Malta at the age of 18. He was the youngest Allied ace of the war; today he had acted his age, and had paid the price.

JG 26 Victory Claims: 28 January 1944

Date	Rank	Name	Unit	Cl #	Aircraft	Place	Time	Opponent	Conf
28-01-44	Fw.	Vogt	7	19	Spitfire	SW of Albert	1537	403 Sqd	yes
28-01-44	Fw.	Mayer	7		Spitfire-dam	nr Grevillers a/f	1540	403 Sqd	dam
28-01-44	Lt.	Hofmann W.	8	7	Mustang	between Abbeville & Berck	1353	2 Sqd	yes
28-01-44	Fw.	Zirngibl	8	6	Mustang	S of Abbeville	1348	2 Sqd	yes

29 January

The heavy bombers attempted another full-strength raid on Frankfurt. This one was judged successful; 803 bombers of the 863 dispatched dropped their loads through the solid undercast. Escort was provided by thirteen groups of P-47s, two groups of P-38s, and one group of P-51s. A new route was tried; the attackers flew southeast along the boundary between Jafü 3 and Jafü 4 (and thus between Luftflotte Reich and Luftflotte 3) and then turned due east to Frankfurt. The two most prominent Jafü 3 units, JG 1 and JG 11, played no role in the defense; it is assumed that they were grounded by the weather. The bombers were intercepted over the target by the south German units, and on both their entry and withdrawal legs by JG 26, with some assistance in the latter stages from JG 2. The Americans lost twenty-nine bombers and fourteen fighters, a large proportion of these to JG 26.

The Geschwader was put on alert at 0830, an hour before the bombers started crossing the English coast. The 4th Staffel and at least part of the Second Gruppe were ordered to Laon-Athies, for better airfield conditions or to put them closer to the bomber stream. It is not known if the Third Gruppe got away from Lille-Vendeville and flew any missions, just that one Bf 109 was destroyed and another was damaged off operations – perhaps on an attempted transfer flight. There are no January victory claims data for the Gruppe as a whole, only information for certain of the pilots.

The bomb divisions crossed the coast at Dunkirk in three separate formations. Their cohesion was soon lost owing to navigational errors and radar problems, and several combat wings had to fly most of the mission without escort. The few intercepting fighters split up into Staffeln to cover a greater area. The 4th Staffel and the First and Second Gruppen scrambled at 1010 and were first vectored east, to Namur. Here they found the Second Bomb Division's B-24s. Some of the Fw 190s began stalking the

Liberators. Part of the First Gruppe flew on. Some reached the Third Bomb Division as it was turning toward Frankfurt at its initial point over Bonn. Hptm. Borris and his men found an entire combat wing without escort, and attacked them until they had to break off to refuel. A few Focke-Wulfs were attacked west of Frankfurt by Lightnings of the 20th Fighter Group, which was responsible for covering the target area. Fhj.-Fw. Günther Schneider of the 3rd Staffel, who was on his first combat mission, was hit by a P-38 and crashed with his plane. Lt. Hans Hartigs then shot down one of the Lightnings. The Gruppe was scattered too badly for any thoughts of second sorties; some pilots had to fly to Strasbourg before finding an airfield through the undercast, and landed after two hours in the air.

The 7th Staffel stayed with the B-24s, and attacked the 44th Bomb Group formation near Trier. Uffz. Kurt Stahnke separated one from its formation, for his first victory; it crashed near Liège. Lt. Waldi Radener claimed a second, but the claim was not filed. As the Staffel continued to stalk the Liberators through the clouds, it was overtaken by some 20th Fighter Group P-38s. The German pilots broke formation and sought cover in the clouds. Uffz. Gerhard Lissack's airplane was hit by a Lightning's fire. The Focke-Wulf pulled up toward the sun, smoking heavily; the American claimed its probable destruction. Lissack later had to bail out. All but one of the other German pilots succeeded in evading the attack. The inexperienced Gefr. Alfred Teichmann was caught flying straight and level by a P-38 pilot who opened fire from dead astern, closing to 75 yards (70 meters). The Fw 190 spun out in flames, and was still spinning when it entered the overcast at 4000 feet (1200 meters). Teichmann and his airplane disappeared without a trace; the wreckage and remains were not found until 1974. Before the mission was over, Gefr. Manfred Talkenburg of the 8th Staffel put down another 20th Fighter Group P-38.

One B-24 combat wing was so far off course that it bombed Ludwigshafen instead of Frankfurt. The 8th Staffel Kapitän, Oblt. Rudi Leuschel, was still with the errant formation, and shot down another 44th Bomb Group Liberator north of Ludwigshafen. Many of the Second Gruppe pilots returned to Epinoy and Grevillers in time to make second sorties, scrambling at about 1220. Fw. Wilhelm Mayer's mission was short. He chased a lost 355th Fighter Group P-47 as it passed by the airfield, shot it down, and landed to top off his fuel and replenish his ammunition. Ten minutes later he and his wingman took off again, looking for more stragglers. He found a B-17, and shot it down also, but this claim was never filed. The rest of the Gruppe scattered across the Pas de Calais looking for targets, and downed a P-47, two B-17s, and a B-24 before quitting for the day. The Fw 190 pilots of the Geschwader claimed seventeen American aircraft destroyed or separated, for the loss of two pilots and six Focke-Wulfs.

JG 26 Victory Claims: 29 January 1944

Date	Rank	Name	Unit	Cl #	Aircraft	Place	Time	Opponent	Conf
29-01-44	Hptm.	Borris	I CO	33	B-17	E of Bonn (NQ-OP)			yes
29-01-44	Oblt.	Kranefeld	I	4	B-17	S of Maubeuge	1245	385 BG	yes
29-01-44	Lt.	Hartigs	2	1	P-38	Saarbrücken-Koblenz (TP-PQ)	1130	20 FG	yes
29-01-44	Lt.	Weide	2	1	B-17	W of Koblenz(PO-PP)			yes
29-01-44	Oblt.	Neu	4 CO	8	B-17	S of Maubeuge		385 BG	yes
29-01-44	Fw.	Wiegand	4		B-17	nr Laon			no
29-01-44	Lt.	Kehl	5		B-24	unknown			unk
29-01-44	Fw.	Gomann	6	11	B-17	8km SSW of Le Cateau	1250	388 BG	yes
29-01-44	Fw.	Gomann	6	12	B-24	W of Calais (in sea)	1348	389 BG	unk
29-01-44	Lt.	Lange F.	6	4	B-17-eV	20km SE of Lille	1300		unk
29-01-44	Oblt.	Matoni	6	12	B-17-HSS	12km SW of Mühlhausen?	1130		unk
29-01-44	Fw.	Mayer	7	11	P-47	10km E of Bapaume	1240	355 FG	yes
29-01-44	Fw.	Mayer	7		B-17	illegible	1320		no
29-01-44	Lt.	Radener	7		B-24-HSS	N of Trier	1125	44 BG	no
29-01-44	Uffz.	Stahnke	7	1	B-24-HSS	NE of Trier	1124	44 BG	yes
29-01-44	Fw.	Vogt	7		P-47	unknown			no

29-01-44	Oblt.	Leuschel	8 CO	9	B-24	Niederflorsheim-Worms		44 BG	yes
29-01-44	Lt.	Hofmann W.	8	8	B-17	2km N of Lutrebois	1330	95 BG	yes
29-01-44	Uffz.	Lindner	8	1	P-47	20km E of Marche	1230	355 FG	yes
29-01-44	Gefr.	Talkenberg	8	1	P-38	Maisborn-Lingenbahn	1150	20 FG	yes
29-01-44	Fw.	Zirngibl	8	7	B-17-HSS	Pferdsfeld-Entempfuhl?	1130		yes

30 January

The 8th Air Force sent 777 bombers to Brunswick, escorted by 635 fighters. Once again the Continent was covered in cloud, and bombs were dropped on the signals of aircraft equipped with British H2S radar. The bombers' track took them across northern Holland on the most direct route to Brunswick. Jafü 3 had the main responsibility for the interception. JG 26 could not repeat its full-scale effort of the previous day, but all three Gruppen sent fighters north at 1030 to assist Jafü 3 in combating the bombers as they returned from Brunswick. The First Gruppe went to Rheine; the Second, to Mönchen-Gladbach; and the Third, to Venlo. The Second Gruppe scrambled at 1230 and reached the B-17 stream as it approached the Zuider Zee. Most of the combat wings were well protected by P-47s. A Thunderbolt pilot fired from long range at Uffz. Karl Bierkamp of the 8th Staffel, who was flying as Lt. Hofmann's wingman. A machine gun shell hit Bierkamp's drop tank, which blew up, killing him. The rest of the Gruppe stayed in contact with the bombers for an hour. Fw. Mayer claimed a P-47, but the claim was not filed; finally, at 1345, Uffz. Schilling downed a straggling B-17.

Jan Schild, a pilot in the Geschwader from 1942 to V-E Day. At the time this photograph was taken in early 1944 he was a Leutnant in the 2nd Staffel. *(Schild)*

The First Gruppe scrambled at 1300 and flew to the Dutch border. Obfw. Lindelaub and Fw. Schwarz each shot down B-17s. Lt. Charlie Willius's 2nd Staffel then ran across some Lightnings. The 20th Fighter Group had responsibility for penetration, target, and withdrawal support of the Third Bomb Division's B-17s. After an hour of intermittent combat, its pilots tormented by erratic engines and frigid cockpits, the Lightning group had split up to return in separate flights. Willius and his eight Fw 190s bounced one of these flights east of Arnhem. After one swift pass, the Focke-Wulfs vanished. Two P-38s, including that of the squadron commander, were last seen spinning into the overcast at 5000 feet. Willius and Fw. Jan Schild, the leader of the second Schwarm, were credited with the victories. Lt. Klaus Kunze was shot down by a P-47 or a P-38, but bailed out with minor injuries.

The few Third Gruppe pilots at Venlo were apparently never scrambled as a unit. Obfw. Kemethmüller and his wingman, Fhj.-Fw. Gottfried Otto, were ordered to take off at 1256 to attack a lone B-17 north of the base. This normally would have been an easy target, but the pair were attacked and split up by a large number of P-47s. Otto did not return to Venlo; his bullet-riddled body was later found, wrapped in his parachute.

JG 26 Victory Claims: 30 January 1944

Date	Rank	Name	Unit	Cl #	Aircraft	Place	Time	Opponent	Conf
30-01-44	Obfw.	Lindelaub	1	5	B-17	unknown			yes
30-01-44	Lt.	Willius	2 CO	39	P-38	3km N of Coesfeld	1330	20 FG	yes
30-01-44	Lt.	Schild	2	3	P-38	SW of Rheine	1330	20 FG	yes
30-01-44	Fw.	Schwarz E.	4	7	B-17	Breda (KK)			yes
30-01-44	Fw.	Mayer	7		P-47	near Geldern	1315		no
30-01-44	Uffz.	Schilling	7	1	B-17	near Geldern	1345		yes

JG 26 Casualties: 29 - 30 January 1944

Date	Rank	Name	Cas	Unit	Aircraft	WNr	Mkgs	Place	Time	Cause	Allied Unit
29-01-44	Fhj-Fw.	Schneider, Gunther	KIA	3	Fw 190A-6	470237	yl 1	near Mainz-Wiesbaden		P-38	20 FG
29-01-44	Uffz.	Lissack, Gerhard	WIA	7	Fw 190A-6	470207	br 5	E of Cochem		P-38	20 FG
29-01-44	Gefr.	Teichmann, Alfred	KIA	7	Fw 190A-6	530749	br 8	SE of Cochem		P-38	20 FG
30-01-44	Lt.	Kunze, Klaus	WIA	2	Fw 190A-6	531061	bk 2	S of Rheine		P-38 or P-47	
30-01-44	Uffz.	Bierkamp, Karl	KIA	8	Fw 190A-6	470045	bl 2	Zuider Zee	1300	P-47	
30-01-44	Fhj-Fw.	Otto, Gottfried	KIA	9	Bf 109G-6	27025	wh 8	Leersum-Woudenberg	1300	P-47	

31 January

Aircraft inventories at month's end showed the Stab and the First Gruppe count to have dropped in January, from four to two and from thirty-eight to thirty-two; nearly all were Fw 190A-6s. The Third Gruppe had received an infusion of Bf 109G-6s; its inventory increased from twenty-six to thirty-five. The Second Gruppe had received thirteen new Fw 190A-7s during the month, and still had eleven of them on the 31st; the total count of Gruppe Fw 190As increased from thirty-two to thirty-eight. Only eighty Fw 190A-7s were built, and they apparently all came west, to JG 2 and JG 26. The A-7 featured a new electrical system, a new gunsight, and heavier armament – the rifle-caliber MG 17 machine guns above the engine were replaced by 12.7 mm MG 131s. Half of the Fw 190A-7s produced were the R2 variant, in which the outer two wing-mounted MG 151 cannon were replaced by 3 cm MK 108s, which had an explosive shell with great destructive capability, and were thus very useful against bombers.

Geschwader personnel moves during January included: the transfer of Hptm. Paul Steindl to the First Gruppe Stab, and his replacement as 11th Staffel leader by Lt. Peter Reischer; the naming of Lt. Karl Kunze of the 2nd Staffel to adjutant of the First Gruppe; the return of Lt. Gottfried Dietze and Obfw. Xaver Ellenrieder to the First Gruppe, and Fw. Horst Schwentick to the Second Gruppe, from training duty; the departure of Fw. Heinrich Heuser for a six-month instructor tour; the transfer of Obfw. Franz Hiller from the 1st Staffel to a factory test unit; the transfer of Uffz. Erich Lambertus from the 2nd Staffel to Sturmstaffel 1; the transfer of Oblt. Baron Konrad von Donner from the Second Gruppe Stab to the Stab of the General der Jagdflieger; and the transfer of Lt. Herfried Kloimüller from the 3rd Staffel to the Ergänzungsgruppe of JG 1.

Pilots assigned to the Geschwader during January after completing flight training included: Uffz. Kurt Hofer, Uffz. Franz Hurtig, Uffz. Robert Marek, Uffz. Gerhard Mohr, Uffz. Ludwig Sattler, Uffz. Erich Schlenker, Gefr. Gerhard Tyczka, Gefr. Hans-Georg Walter - First Gruppe; Uffz. Karl Dehsbesell, Uffz. Edgar Elicker, Uffz. Karl Gathof - Second Gruppe; Gefr. Josef Vogt - Third Gruppe. Hofer was awarded an Iron Cross 2nd Class when he arrived at Lille for shooting down a B-17 while still with his operational training Gruppe, Jagdgruppe Ost.

Germany lost a total of 391 single-engine fighters in January, one-quarter of its strength. Aircraft production was still increasing, but pilots who were killed could not be replaced as easily as aircraft. JG 26 lost twenty pilots in January; fourteen in combat and six in accidents; these included two Staffel leaders. In addition, one Gruppenkommandeur was removed from combat after being wounded.

4 February

Frankfurt was a favorite target for the 8th Air Force during this winter of seemingly incessant bad weather. It was on the Main River, and gave a return on the pathfinder aircraft's H2S radar sufficient to allow it to be located and bombed through the overcast. It had a large number of widely dispersed industrial targets. And last, it was almost within P-47 range, although target support had to be left to the few P-38 and P-51 groups. Frankfurt was the target again today. Fifteen combat wings of B-17s and B-24s were dispatched, escorted by fifteen USAAF fighter groups, plus eight Spitfire squadrons to cover the final stages of the return flight. Radar failures and high crosswinds spoiled the plan. Several combat wings found themselves under fire by the Ruhr Flak. German fighter response was weak – the Luftwaffe was hindered as much by the weather as was the USAAF – and only three bomb groups were subjected to fighter attacks. Two of these attacks were made by the First and Second Gruppen, which accounted for as many as seven of the total of ten bombers lost to fighters.

Only one Staffel was scrambled against the incoming bombers – Lt. Waldi Radener's 7th. His ten fighters were at readiness at Grevillers when word was received that a B-24 had been sighted flying alone in the Amiens area. Radener's men took off at 1144 and quickly located the bomber, a 446th Bomb Group Liberator that had been attempting an early return with equipment problems, and set it ablaze. The Focke-Wulfs were back on the ground by 1203.

The 4th Staffel was scrambled from Wevelgem at 1220 against the withdrawing bombers. The First and Second Gruppen took off at about 1240, and were vectored toward Brussels. Fw. Wiegand led the Adamsonstaffel in a successful attack on the First Bomb Division formation south of Tournai. Wiegand's own target set a large field on fire when it crashed, but his claim was never filed. The First Gruppe made a concentrated attack on the B-17 stream north of Brussels, and shot down two B-17s before the Focke-Wulfs were attacked by 352nd Fighter Group P-47s. Ten or twelve of the Focke-Wulfs formed a defensive circle, but the P-47s, newly equipped with paddle-blade propellers, were able to out-turn them and break up the circle. Lt. Dietze and Fw. Schild were shot down, and bailed out with minor injuries. Dietze was on his first combat mission since returning from instructor duty. The OKW communiqué credited the Gruppe with a third B-17 claim that was not filed and has not been traced.

The Second Gruppe was never able to carry out an attack on the bombers. The Focke-Wulfs were attacked in turn by P-47s, P-38s on their way to England after serving as target escort, and yet another group of P-47s. A 56th Fighter Group pilot shot down Gefr. Werner Pietruschka of the 5th Staffel, who was able to put his aircraft down in a field with only moderate damage to the plane, and slight injuries to himself. Another Thunderbolt pilot shot down and killed Ogfr. Wilhelm Peukert. The Second Gruppe filed no claims, although the nightly OKW communiqué credited them with a victory on this mission.

The Third Gruppe got away from Vendeville late, at 1305, and probably in low strength; its mission was without result. The last Geschwader fighters airborne scattered in search of stragglers. Obfw. Heckmann of the 3rd Staffel found a crippled B-17 east of Rotterdam, and shot the 390th Bomb Group aircraft down at 1430; Heckmann himself must have been on his last drops of fuel.

JG 26 Victory Claims: 4 February 1944

Date	Rank	Name	Unit	Cl #	Aircraft	Place	Time	Opponent	Conf
04-02-44	Lt.	Willius	2 CO	40	B-17	1km E of Cousoire	1350		yes
04-02-44	Obfw.	Heckmann	3 CO	60	B-17	10km ESE of Rotterdam	1430	390 BG	yes
04-02-44	Obfw.	Scheyda	3	16	B-17	3km NE of Brussels	1320		yes
04-02-44	Fw.	Wiegand	4		B-17	S of Tournai	1300		no
04-02-44	Lt.	Radener	7	11	B-24	10km SE of Albert (RF-2)	1200	446 BG	yes

Date	Rank	Name	Cas	Unit	Aircraft	WNr	Mkgs	Place	Time	Cause	Allied Unit
04-02-44	Lt.	Dietze, Gottfried	WIA	1	Fw 190A-6	550517	wh 4	E of Hasselt	1330	P-47	352 FG
04-02-44	Fw.	Schild, Heinrich	WIA	2	Fw 190A-7	642532	bk 14	near Ath	1353	P-47	352 FG
04-02-44	Gefr.	Pietruschka, Werner	WIA	5	Fw 190A-6	470239	wh 8	SE of Dinant	1300	P-47	56 FG
04-02-44	Ogfr.	Peukert, Wilhelm	KIA	6	Fw 190A-6	530413	bk 10	8km SW of Dinant	1300	P-47	56 FG

5 February

The 8th Air Force sent a medium strength raid to bomb some airfields in central France, but were unable to find most of them. Jafü 4 sent all three Gruppen south to assist JG 2, but the effort was futile. No contact was made with the USAAF. Uffz. Lothar Schneider of the 8th Staffel attempted a forced landing in a field northwest of Melun, but turned over. Schneider died of a broken neck.

6 February

The heavy bombers returned to France, with results no better than the previous day. Fewer than one-third of the 642 bombers found targets to bomb. Again the three JG 26 Gruppen were sent to Paris. This time the P-47s were waiting. The Second Gruppe sustained no losses, but only Fw. Hans Prager of the 5th Staffel was able to file a claim, for a P-47, and it was rejected. His target did not, in fact, go down; the 8th Fighter Command lost only one P-47 today, and it was almost certainly shot down by the JG 2 Kommodore, Major Egon Mayer.

Four Third Gruppe Bf 109G-6s were forced down by P-47s of the 56th Fighter Group's 61st Fighter Squadron. The 12th Staffel was caught lining up on the B-17s northeast of Paris, and Obfw. Hans Erbskorn and Uffz. Otto Salewski were hit. Both escaped the Thunderbolts and were able to make smooth belly landings with moderate damage and minor injuries. A few minutes later, Uffz. Rolf Simmank of the 10th Staffel was hit in the same area, and died in his plane.

The fortunes of the First Gruppe were mixed. Lt. Charlie Willius brought his 2nd Staffel Schwarm up through the undercast and made a head-on attack on the low squadron of the 96th Bomb Group, which was in the low position in the 45th Combat Wing formation. Three Focke-Wulfs peeled away early, but Willius barreled on through and hit the low B-17 in the rear vee in the left wing. The gas tank in the wing blew up and the wing fell off. The bomber fell into the undercast; incredibly, one waist gunner survived.

Oblt. Artur Beese, the 1st Staffel Kapitän, was caught by a P-47 south of Paris and shot down. He attempted to bail out, but struck his Focke-Wulf's tail and was killed. Beese, who had scored twenty-two victories in 285 combat sorties, was one of the last of the pre-war Geschwader pilots still flying with the unit. Hptm. Borris named Lt. Leberecht Altmann the interim leader of the 1st Staffel.

JG 26 Casualties: 5 - 6 February 1944

Date	Rank	Name	Cas	Unit	Aircraft	WNr	Mkgs	Place	Time	Cause	Allied Unit
05-02-44	Uffz.	Schneider, Lothar	KIFA	8	Fw 190A-6	470068	bl 2	Melun-Paris		crashed	n/a
06-02-44	Oblt.	Beese, Artur	KIA	1 CO	Fw 190A-6	531060	wh 7	SW of Melun	1130	P-47	
06-02-44	Uffz.	Simmank, Rolf	KIA	10	Bf 109G-6	162031	bk 1	NE of Paris	1125	P-47	56 FG
06-02-44	Obfw.	Erbskorn, Hans	WIA	12	Bf 109G-6	410672	bk 9	Paris	1120	P-47	56 FG
06-02-44	Uffz.	Salewski, Otto	WIA	12	Bf 109G-6	162016	bl 3	Paris-Champs	1112	P-47	56 FG

8 February

The 8th Air Force sent its B-17s back to Frankfurt. As a diversion, the B-24s took off one half hour earlier to hit two V-1 sites. Jafü 4, believing that the B-24s were headed to Paris, once again scrambled all three of its Gruppen and ordered them to fly south. Jafü 5 also directed II/JG 2 and III/JG 2 to Paris. As the B-24s turned east over the Channel toward the Pas de Calais, the two Jafü ordered their fighters back north, but too late to catch the Liberators. The B-17s had now started crossing the French coast, but the bomber formations were already in disarray owing to problems forming up, and got no tighter over the course of the mission. The B-17 groups became so widely scattered that they were fortunate to lose only thirteen aircraft during the day; it helped that the only Jafü 3 unit to get off the ground was JG 1.

The Third Gruppe was unable to avoid the escorts, and never reached the bombers. Uffz. Hubert Schmitz was shot down by P-47s of the 358th Fighter Group, which claimed 2-0-1 Bf 109s. The JG 2 fighters joined the Second Gruppe in attacking the B-17s of the 92nd Bomb Group, which was aborting. Uffz. Guttmann of the 8th Staffel was credited with a final destruction, which was later upgraded to a full victory, and the OKW communiqué announced a second victory for the Gruppe that was not filed. No more unescorted bombers were found, but the First and Second Gruppen had one of their best days against the escorts, claiming seven. In fact, they shot down six of the eight fighters lost to the Luftwaffe; Oberst Walter Oesau of JG 1 got the seventh, and the eighth loss can't be matched up with any known German claim.

One squadron of the 352nd Fighter Group was patrolling the bomber's penetration route when one pilot called out a Fw 190 that was attacking an aborting bomber. As his flight broke away from the rest of its squadron, it was bounced from out of the sun by Hptm. Borris and several of his Focke-Wulfs. Two P-47s went down immediately, the victims of Borris and Obfw. Ellenrieder. As the survivors scattered, one element was attacked by Lt. Radener of the 7th Staffel. He was credited with both of the Thunderbolts in the OKW communiqué, although the claims were never filed. One went down, and the other crash-landed on the English coast.

The three Gruppen landed for refueling. Uffz. Herbert Kolodzie of the 4th Staffel was caught by a wind gust as he was landing on Wevelgem. His Focke-Wulf overturned and was destroyed; Kolodzie suffered minor injuries. The aircraft that could be gotten ready took off to battle the withdrawing bombers. As Oblt. Otto Hummel, the Second Gruppe adjutant, took off with his wingman, Uffz. Manfred Talkenberg, they were attacked by the P-38s of LCol. Robert Montgomery's 20th Fighter Group flight, which had dropped to the deck to look for targets after completing their escort shift. This was a mission profile that had just been authorized that morning. Hummel pulled up; his Focke-Wulf burst into flames, and crashed vertically on the field. Talkenberg escaped into a cloud.

The First Gruppe had the good fortune to encounter a single flight of 354th Fighter Group P-51s that had become separated from the rest of their squadron. Obfw. Heckmann led the attack, which shot down three of the four Mustangs. These were the first examples of the newest USAAF fighter to fall to pilots of the Geschwader. Within a month these long-legged aircraft would be escorting the bombers to the farthest reaches of Germany.

JG 26 Victory Claims: 6 - 8 February 1944

Date	Rank	Name	Unit	Cl #	Aircraft	Place	Time	Opponent	Conf
06-02-44	Lt.	Willius	2 CO	41	B-17	Melun (BF)	1121	96 BG	yes
06-02-44	Fw.	Prager	5	1	P-47	E of Paris	1057		unk
08-02-44	Hptm.	Borris	I CO	34	P-47	E of St. Quentin? (RH-RJ)	1115	352 FG	yes
08-02-44	Ogfr.	Köhn	1	1	P-51	Givet (QK5,7)		354 FG	yes
08-02-44	Obfw.	Heckmann	3 CO	61	P-51	S of Maubeuge (QI8-1)	1245	354 FG	yes
08-02-44	Obfw.	Ellenrieder	3	5	P-47	E of St. Quentin? (RH-SH)	1118	352 FG	yes
08-02-44	Obfw.	Scheyda	3	17	P-51	S of Maubeuge (QI7)	1246	354 FG	yes
08-02-44	Lt.	Radener	7		P-47	N of Laon	1110	352 FG	no
08-02-44	Lt.	Radener	7		P-47	N Laon	1112	352 FG	no
08-02-44	Uffz.	Guttmann	8	4	B-17	Catheux-17km SE of Poix	1115		yes

9 February

Hptm. Johannes Naumann was named acting Kommandeur of the Second Gruppe, to serve until Hptm. Gäth's status had been determined. Lt. Waldemar Radener took Naumann's former position as leader of the 7th Staffel.

11 February

The 8th Air Force mission plan was a near-duplicate of that of the 8th, but was carried out with a smaller force; the Third Bomb Division was given a rest. Once again Jafü 4 and Jafü 5 scrambled their fighters at 0940 and sent them to Paris, only to realize that the B-24s were turning to bomb targets on the Pas de Calais. In the meantime, the B-17s were crossing Belgium, out of range of any Luftflotte 3 fighter. Luftflotte Reich scrambled fifteen Gruppen of fighters, but these could not get past the fifteen American fighter groups to get at the bombers, only five of which went down on the

Oblt. Walter Matoni and Obfw. Adolf Glunz return to Cambrai-Epinoy from a February mission. *(Bundesarchiv-Bildarchiv)*

mission. The bombers kept much better formation than they had on the 8th, but the bombing results were the same – bad.

The Third Gruppe made a quick return to Vendeville and Denain from its fruitless mission to the south. Obfw. Kemethmüller and several other pilots were sent up again at 1040 in pursuit of a single aborting B-17. After an inconclusive battle with twenty P-47s, they returned to base and waited for word on the course of the withdrawing bombers. That course was right toward the Geschwader bases, and all three Gruppen were scrambled at 1300. The fighters could make no headway against the bomber stream itself, and dropped to a lower altitude to wait for stragglers. The first aircraft spotted at low altitude were some withdrawing 20th Fighter Group P-38s. Oblt. Neu of the 4th Staffel shot one of these down near Cambrai. Ten minutes later Fw. Wiegand of the same Staffel shot down two 78th Fighter Group P-47s south of Arras. LCol. Montgomery's 20th Fighter Group flight was seen on the deck near Vitry by Lt. Radener and several Second Gruppe pilots. Montgomery was hoping to repeat his success of the 8th, but all four of his P-38s were shot down, although only two German pilots were awarded victory credits. P-38s were vulnerable to any German fighter if caught at low altitude.

Last came the flak-damaged bombers. Obfw. Scheyda, Obfw. Glunz, and Uffz. Guttmann shot down single B-17s from the 306th, 351st, and 381st Bomb Groups. All three pilots were given full victory credits, although Glunz's claim was originally filed as a final destruction. This would seem to be the only correct way to describe all three of these victories, except that the Flak kept a separate tally of their victories. Only on very rare occasions would the Flak share a claim with the fighters. After a period of indecision, the RLM began confirming claims as final destructions only when they could be paired directly with another pilot's claim for separating the same aircraft from its formation. The Luftflotte 3 fighter units soon began filing all claims for stragglers as full victory claims. As final destructions did not count as victories on the pilots' tally sheets, but only as single points in the point system, this was much better for morale.

Date	Rank	Name	Unit	Cl #	Aircraft	Place	Time	Opponent	Conf
11-02-44	Obfw.	Scheyda	3	18	B-17	Mons (PH7-8)	1337	306 BG	yes
11-02-44	Oblt.	Neu	4 CO	9	P-38	Cambrai (QH1)	1335	20 FG	yes
11-02-44	Fw.	Wiegand	4	16	P-47	S of Arras (QF)	1345	78 FG	yes
11-02-44	Fw.	Wiegand	4	17	P-47	S of Arras (QF)	1346	78 FG	yes
11-02-44	Obfw.	Glunz	5 CO	53	B-17	20km NW of Poix	1405	351 BG	yes
11-02-44	Lt.	Lange F.	6	5	P-38	13km SE of Valenciennes	1347	20 FG	yes
11-02-44	Lt.	Radener	7 CO		P-38	SE of Valenciennes	1350	20 FG	no
11-02-44	Fw.	Mayer	7	12	P-38	Vitry-en-Artois	1345	20 FG	yes
11-02-44	Uffz.	Guttmann	8	5	B-17	24km NE of Beauvais	1355	381 BG	yes
11-02-44	Ofhr.	Kemethmüller	9		B-17-dam	near Douai	1345		dam

13 February

A series of OKL situation maps in the German archives gives a good picture of the true operational strength of the Geschwader during this period. On this date, the Stab, at Lille-Nord, had no serviceable aircraft. The 4th Staffel, also at Lille-Nord, had eight Focke-Wulfs; the rest of the First Gruppe, at Florennes, had eighteen. The 5th and 7th Staffeln, at Grevillers, had eleven Focke-Wulfs; the rest of the Second Gruppe, at Cambrai-Epinoy, had twelve. The 10th and 12th Staffeln, at Denain, had seventeen Messerschmitts; the rest of the Third Gruppe, at Lille-Vendeville, had nineteen. The total operational strength of the Geschwader was eighty-five fighters; its authorized strength was 208.

Weather over most of the Continent was extremely bad, and no near-term improvement was expected. ADGB and 2nd TAF Typhoons flew small Ranger missions to the Pas de Calais. Shortly after noon, Fw. Wiegand's 4th Staffel Schwarm intercepted six No. 198 Sqd. Typhoons near Calais. Wiegand claimed the destruction of one, but it returned to England with only moderate damage.

The 8th Air Force ordered a short-range mission for the afternoon, and the B-17s and B-24s bombed seventeen suspected V-1 sites on the Pas de Calais. Jafü 4 scrambled all three of its Gruppen. The German formations split up in the bad weather, and most pilots failed to make contact with the enemy. A 4th Staffel Schwarm reached the B-17s, but its attack was broken up by a squadron from the 356th Fighter Group. One P-47's gunfire hit the engine of Uffz. Paul Erpenbach's fighter. Erpenbach attempted a forced-landing, but hit a power line, destroying his Focke-Wulf and injuring himself. One Second Gruppe Focke-Wulf was destroyed, but further details are unknown; its pilot was not injured. Ofhr. Kemethmüller of the 9th Staffel was forced to belly-land his Messerschmitt when its propeller's constant-speed mechanism failed.

14 February

The Second Gruppe was scrambled from Epinoy and Grevillers at 1530 to intercept a formation of Spitfires. Only the 7th Staffel made contact. No. 124 Squadron fought off the Focke-Wulfs near Berck-sur-Mer. Fw. Mayer claimed one of the British fighters, but it returned to England with moderate damage; Mayer's claim was not filed. Obfw. Karl Ehret was hit in the combat, and crashed and burned in his aircraft; the Spitfire pilot claimed only a damaged.

16 February

Lt. Joachim Günther and Uffz. Wilhelm Düsing of the 3rd Staffel were making an instrument flight in a Go 145 glider when it crashed near Florennes, injuring both pilots.

JG 26 Casualties: 8 - 16 February 1944

Date	Rank	Name	Cas	Unit	Aircraft	WNr	Mkgs	Place	Time	Cause	Allied Unit
08-02-44	Oblt.	Hummel, Otto	KIA	II St	Fw 190A-7	340296	bk 30	Florennes a/f	1300	P-38	20 FG
08-02-44	Uffz.	Kolodzie, Herbert	WIFA	4	Fw 190A-6	550726	bl 12	Wevelgem		landing	n/a
08-02-44	Uffz.	Schmitz, Hubert	WIA	11	Bf 109G-6	19469	yl 3	NE of Paris	1035	P-47	358 FG

12-02-44	Gefr.	Vogt, Josef	KIFA 11	Bf 109G-6/U4	20720	yl 1	SW of Florennes 1405	crashed	non-op
13-02-44	Uffz.	Erpenbach, Paul	WIA 4	Fw 190A-7	430180	bl 1	SW of Abbeville 1515	P-47	356 FG
14-02-44	Obfw.	Ehret, Karl	KIA 6	Fw 190A-6	550739	br 10	Montreuil-Calais	Spitfire	124 Sqd
16-02-44	Uffz.	Düsing, Wilhelm	WIFA 3	Go 145A-1	2337	GA+OF	near Florennes	crashed	non-op
16-02-44	Lt.	Günther, Joachim	WIFA 3	Go 145A-1	2337	GA+OF	near Florennes	crashed	non-op

A Second Gruppe FW 190A-7 taxies out of its Epinoy hardstand on a rare cloudless February day. *(Bundesarchiv-Bildarchiv)*

17 February

The OKL was preparing a comprehensive plan for the Luftwaffe response to the Allied invasion of the Continent, which was expected in the spring. The two Kanalgeschwader were expected to man the front lines until the arrival of reinforcements. The flying units of JG 2 and JG 26 were to be withdrawn in increments over the next few months for retraining and for restoration to full strength. The 11th Staffel was the first JG 26 unit to be chosen; Obstlt. Priller apparently still considered it his weakest Staffel. Today the Staffel and its six operational Bf 109G-6s withdrew to St. Dizier, where it spent the rest of February in training.

18 February

Snow flurries across northern France made a bombing raid extremely unlikely, and all of the Geschwader flying units but the readiness Staffeln were released from duty. At 1135 the 7th Staffel was ordered to scramble from Grevillers. Aircraft had been detected crossing the Channel at low altitude, and the fact that they were flying in such miserable weather implied that their mission was of some significance to the Allies. The British formation, which consisted of fifteen Mosquitoes escorted by eight No. 174 Sqd. Typhoons, was engaged on Operation Jericho. Their mission was to bomb the prison at Amiens, breaching the walls to aid the escape of captured members of the Resistance. The Focke-Wulfs caught up to the British aircraft as they came off their bombing run. The officer commanding the operation, G/C Charles Pickard, had circled back to observe the results. His Mosquito was hit by Fw. Mayer and crashed next to the prison, killing Pickard and his navigator. The escort kept the Fw 190s away from the rest of the Mosquitoes, but lost one Typhoon to Lt. Radener; a second Typhoon crashed in the Channel on the return flight.

JG 26 Victory Claims: 13 - 18 February 1944

Date	Rank	Name	Unit	Cl #	Aircraft	Place	Time	Opponent	Conf
13-02-44	Fw.	Wiegand	4	18	Typhoon	10km NW of Calais	1240	198 Sqd	yes

14-02-44	Fw.	Mayer	7		Spitfire-prob	Étaples-Berck	1630	124 Sqd	no
18-02-44	Lt.	Radener	7 CO	12	Typhoon	N of Amiens	1205	174 Sqd	yes
18-02-44	Fw.	Mayer	7	13	Mosquito	NE of Amiens	1205	140 Wing	yes
18-02-44	Fw.	Mayer	7		Mosquito-prob	near Amiens	1215	140 Wing	no

19 February

The 8th Air Force needed a week of good weather to carry out Operation Argument, its long-planned knock-out blow to the German aircraft industry. Today the meteorologists detected an extensive high pressure area moving across Germany, and predicted several consecutive days of good weather. The next six days, soon dubbed Big Week, saw the strategic bombing campaign reach a new peak of intensity.

20 February

The 8th Air Force mission for the first day of Operation Argument was the largest and most complex attempted to that time. Sixteen combat wings containing 1003 B-17s and B-24s took off to bomb twelve aircraft factories in central and eastern Germany and western Poland. The smaller Third Bomb Division crossed the English coast at 0900 and took a circuitous route to the easternmost targets. The First and Second Bomb Divisions left England starting at 1045, escorted by all available USAAF fighters, and flew due east across Holland in a single, compact formation two combat wings abreast. It turned southeast when it reached Germany and did not split up until very near its targets in central Germany. The Luftflotte Reich controllers did not want to ignore the eastern force, which was pointed toward Berlin, but the larger force seemed the greater danger. General Schmid and his Jagdkorps I staff apparently could not decide between them. As a result, there was no large-scale interception of the inbound formations, and the fighter attacks on the withdrawing formations were weak and poorly coordinated. The Americans lost only twenty-one bombers and four fighters; the German defenders lost a total of fifty-three single-engine, and twenty-five twin-engine fighters. The day had been a brilliant success for the Allies. Several targets had been severely damaged. Radio intercepts indicated an unprecedented degree of disorganization and confusion on the part of the German fighter controllers. Only 362 sorties were flown by the Jagdwaffe, about half of the number that the Allies had expected.

The day's efforts by the Geschwader were necessarily limited. The First Gruppe scrambled from Florennes at 1125 and flew north, but were too late to catch the bombers. They landed at Deelen to await the return flight. The Second Gruppe had already taken off at 0900 and flown to Laon-Athies, which was a popular assembly airfield, but not near the track of the bombers today. The Gruppe scrambled at 1130 and flew north, but its formation split apart, undoubtedly owing to the weather, and the pilots put down on several airfields; some returned to their home bases. Nothing is known of the activities of the Third Gruppe during the day.

The First and Second Bomb Division B-17s and B-24s were able to re-form their compact defensive formation for the return flight, and all attempts at interception by the First Gruppe were thwarted by the P-47s. Lt. Kiefner damaged one of the Thunderbolts, but no victories were claimed. The widely dispersed Second Gruppe could not even form a battle formation, and was sent up after stragglers. Lt. Friedrich Lange's 6th Staffel Schwarm popped up out of the undercast and sliced through the 91st Bomb Group formation, concentrating their fire on one lagging bomber. The Focke-Wulfs escaped before the bomber's gunners could fire a shot in return. The bomber was hit in three engines, and the pilot ordered the crew to bail out. All landed near the Chièvres airfield, and all but one were captured by Luftwaffe personnel.

Lange's Schwarm joined up with several other Focke-Wulfs and the small force headed east. They saw a combat box of B-17s over the Eifel and attempted to attack it from the rear, but were jumped by 4th Fighter Group P-47s and had to break off; Uffz. Erwin Hell of the 6th Staffel was hit and bailed out with minor injuries. Three more

Focke-Wulfs were damaged, probably in this encounter. In the combat Lt. Lange shot down a 4th Fighter Group P-47, the second victory of the day for him and the second and last for the Geschwader.

21 February

Worsening weather forced the 8th Air Force to reduce the scale of its operations. The bomber crews were briefed to attack a number of airfields in western Germany, but many were forced to bomb targets of opportunity. The bad weather hurt the defensive effort as well, and only 282 sorties were flown by the Jagdwaffe. Thirty-five German fighters were lost, for the destruction of sixteen bombers and six fighters. The Geschwader was not called on to do much. The First and Second Gruppen flew to Rheine and Melsbroek, and operated against bombers straggling during the return flight; nothing is known of the activities of the Third Gruppe. The Second Gruppe scored the only known successes for the Geschwader north of Amsterdam, where Obfw. Glunz and Uffz. Loschinski each shot down a 95th Bomb Group B-17. No losses were sustained by the Geschwader.

JG 26 Victory Claims: 20 - 21 February 1944

Date	Rank	Name	Unit	Cl #	Aircraft	Place	Time	Opponent	Conf
20-02-44	Lt.	Lange F.	6	7	B-17	Ressaix-19km E of Mons	1505	91 BG	yes
20-02-44	Lt.	Lange F.	6	6	P-47	Seraing-6km SW of Liège	1525	4 FG	yes
21-02-44	Obfw.	Glunz	5 CO	54	B-17	6km W of Bergen aan See	1550	95 BG	unk
21-02-44	Uffz.	Loschinski	7	1	B-17	NW of Utrecht	1605	95 BG	yes

22 February

Solid cloud rising to 24,000 feet (7300 meters) over England prevented many heavy bomber formations from assembling, and reduced the size of today's raid on aircraft factories in central Germany. The bombers flew due east from England to their targets. The secondary raid to Denmark was flown by only one group, and was too small to attract the defenders' attention. Jagdkorps I was able to concentrate its fighters against the penetration leg of the mission, which typically was defended by fewer escorts than the target or withdrawal legs. The combat wings were too widely scattered for full coverage by the escorts, and the Jagdflieger took advantage of their opportunities, aggressively attacking both the escorts and the bombers. Forty-one bombers and eleven fighters failed to return to England.

The bombers began crossing the Dutch coast at 1140. The First and Second Gruppen were already flying north; the First Gruppe from Florennes, and the Second Gruppe from Laon-Athies, where it had assembled at 0900. The Third Gruppe probably flew to a Dutch base at this time, but there are no hard data to support this assumption. The First Gruppe made contact with the bombers south of the Zuider Zee, but was driven off by the P-47s, and landed on Venlo at 1320. Although the Gruppe made no claims and sustained no losses, it thinned out the escort for the benefit of the Second Gruppe and II/JG 1, which reached the bomber stream near the Dutch-German border at 1250, found several combat boxes unprotected, and were able to make repeated attacks. The 91st Bomb Group lost five bombers to these attacks; the 384th Bomb Group, four. Addi Glunz, at the head of his 5th Staffel, shot down one B-17 and claimed two others as separations. Uffz. Rudolf Georgi also claimed a separation, and Uffz. Josef Baumann claimed his first victory. That night's OKW communiqué credited the Gruppe with a fourth separation, which was not filed. The Gruppe suffered no losses, and its pilots broke away individually to land at various bases.

All three Gruppen were up versus the withdrawing bombers and escorts. Again the First Gruppe had no claims or losses. Hptm. Staiger of the 12th Staffel claimed a P-47 for his 39th victory and the only known success for the Third Gruppe; the Thunderbolt was probably from the 353rd Fighter Group. The portion of the Second Gruppe that took off from Venlo had a very successful mission. Obfw. Glunz claimed two more B-17s and one P-47 destroyed. Lt. Lange also claimed a Thunderbolt on this mission. B-17 gunners shot down the Focke-Wulf of Ogfr. Leo Przybyl, who bailed out of his flaming aircraft and landed safely near Mönchen-Gladbach. Glunz's claims resulted in four victory credits, his 55th-58th. This was his most successful day of the war.

The fortunes of the rest of the Second Gruppe were mixed. Fw. Wilhelm Mayer of the 7th Staffel had sortied from Athies and flown to Reims, Grevillers, and Florennes without contacting the enemy. A late scramble from Florennes located a P-47 formation near St. Trond. Mayer shot down a Thunderbolt, but did not file the claim; the P-47 was probably a 362nd Fighter Group aircraft, which crashed.

Fw. Peter Crump of the 6th Staffel had an unsuccessful ninety-minute combat sortie after taking off from Athies, trailing the bombers but unable to penetrate the escort screen. He finally broke contact and landed with his last fuel on the Duisberg *Miniplatz* (emergency field), where he had to refuel his Focke-Wulf himself out of fifty-gallon drums, using a hand pump. He then took off for Düsseldorf, the designated assembly airfield for the Gruppe. However, besides Crump, the only Second Gruppe pilots who turned up were his Staffelkapitän, Hptm. Horst Sternberg, and the young Uffz. Paul Gross of the 5th Staffel. The dozen fighters at Düsseldorf, from a number of Geschwader and Gruppen, were ordered to rendezvous with another formation over Venlo. Sternberg ordered Gross and Crump to stick with him.

The Düsseldorf fighters found between thirty and forty Fw 190s and Bf 109s ready to take off from Venlo. After a broad circuit of the field, the hodgepodge formation took up a course to the east under the command of a major, and climbed to attack the withdrawing bomber formations. They had reached 3500 meters (11,000 feet) when the lead Fortress was sighted at 6000 meters (20,000 feet), on the opposite course. The formation leader turned immediately to a parallel course, until the German fighters could reach attack altitude. Sternberg broke away from the formation with his two wingmen and began stalking a badly damaged B-17 that spiraled away from the bomber stream in a broad left turn, trailing thick smoke. He began his attack on the crippled bomber from beneath. Crump saw a dozen Thunderbolts streaming down on their rear. Crump warned Sternberg, raked the leading P-47 with a quick burst, and then dived for his life.

Hptm. Horst Sternberg, Kapitän of the 6th Staffel. (*Vanoverbeke*)

The Thunderbolts were the 4th Fighter Group's 335th Squadron, led by Major George Carpenter. Carpenter opened fire on Sternberg's aircraft from 300 yards (275 meters). Sternberg's violent turns could not shake the P-47, and he finally entered a shallow dive and dived into the ground. Carpenter's wingman attacked the aircraft of Uffz. Gross, who made only gentle maneuvers, permitting the P-47 to keep firing down to a distance of 30-50 yards. Gross bailed out and his parachute opened, but he had been hit by machine gun fire, and died before reaching the ground.

The second element in Carpenter's flight made a quick turn with Crump and then followed him in his dive. They chased him to the deck, but could not close to effective firing range, and broke off the attack. The pursuit was then taken up by three P-47s of the 78th Fighter Group's 83rd Squadron, which had reached the bomber stream a few minutes after the 4th Group. Up until this point, Peter Crump's aircraft had not been hit, and he decided that his best means of escape was to out-climb the heavier Thunderbolts. However, Crump's maneuver allowed two P-47s to close the range. The three aircraft entered a tight circle. The third member of the 78th Group flight, arriving late, did not join the circle, but cut across it, striking Crump's aircraft squarely with a high-deflection burst of machine gun fire. With a single reflexive motion, Crump threw off the canopy, drew up his legs, and climbed out. He pulled his ripcord immediately, and after one swing, hit the frozen ground hard. His only injuries were damaged ligaments in one knee.

Bombing results today were mediocre, and the Americans considered their bomber losses to have been excessive. Eight hundred bombers had been dispatched, but only 430 were credited with combat sorties. However, General Doolittle's war of attrition against the Jagdwaffe reached new levels of success. Forty-eight single-engine, and sixteen twin-engine fighters were lost by the Germans on their 332 defensive sorties.

JG 26 Victory Claims: 22 February 1944

Date	Rank	Name	Unit	Cl #	Aircraft	Place	Time	Opponent	Conf
22-02-44	Obfw.	Glunz	5 CO	55	B-17	7km W of Dorsten	1250	91 or 384 BG	yes
22-02-44	Obfw.	Glunz	5 CO		B-17-HSS	unknown	1255	91 or 384 BG	no
22-02-44	Obfw.	Glunz	5 CO	56	B-17-HSS	12km NE of Wesel	1310	91 or 384 BG	yes
22-02-44	Obfw.	Glunz	5 CO	57	P-47	15km NW of Geilenkirchen	1530	78 FG	yes
22-02-44	Obfw.	Glunz	5 CO	58	B-17	SW of Grevensbroich	1535		yes
22-02-44	Obfw.	Glunz	5 CO		B-17	Geilenkirchen	1540		no
22-02-44	Lt.	Lange F.	6	8	P-47	15km NW of Bruenel	1600		yes
22-02-44	Uffz.	Georgi	7	3	B-17-HSS	Selm-8km N of Luenen	1325	91 or 384 BG	yes
22-02-44	Fw.	Mayer	7		P-47	nr St Trond	1545	362 FG	no
22-02-44	Uffz.	Baumann	8	1	B-17	S of Münster (JQ7)	1305	91 or 384 BG	yes
22-02-44	Hptm.	Staiger	12 CO	39	P-47	Mönchen-Gladbach (MN-LN)	1523	353 FG	yes

JG 26 Casualties: 20 - 22 February 1944

Date	Rank	Name	Cas	Unit	Aircraft	WNr	Mkgs	Place	Time	Cause	Allied Unit
20-02-44	Uffz.	Hell, Erwin	WIA	6	Fw 190A-6	470224	bk 2	Luenebach-Eifel		P-47	4 FG
22-02-44	Uffz.	Gross, Paul	KIA	5	Fw 190A-6	530716	wh 21	nr Wesel-M-Gladbach	1500	P-47	4 FG
22-02-44	Ogfr.	Przybyl, Leo	WIA	5	Fw 190A-5	501238	wh 3	M-Gladbach-Wassenberg		B-17	
22-02-44	Hptm.	Sternberg, Horst	KIA	6 CO	Fw 190A-7	642002	bk 12	Hückelhoven, nr M-Gladbach	1500	P-47	4 FG
22-02-44	Fw.	Crump, Peter	WIA	6	Fw 190A-7	340253	bk 14	Hückelhoven, nr M-Gladbach	1500	P-47	78 FG

24 February

After standing down for one day, the 8th Air Force resumed its offensive with attacks on Schweinfurt, Gotha, and Rostock. Thirteen combat wings of B-17s and B-24s flew the mission. The Third Bomb Division, whose target was on the Baltic Sea, was not escorted, but the rest were protected by nineteen USAAF fighter groups, two of which flew two missions, and eleven RAF fighter squadrons. Total losses were ten fighters and forty-nine bombers. The leading combat wings of the First and Second Bomb Divisions, unaccustomed to clear weather and high winds at altitude, were ahead of schedule for most of the mission, missed most of their escorts, and suffered accordingly.

Lt. Friedrich Lange, Sternberg's successor as 6th Staffel Kapitän. On 2 March Lange was shot down over the Eifel by a 365th Fighter Group P-47. *(Crump)*

Again today the course of the two bomb divisions targeting central Germany was directly east from England across Holland, giving Luftflotte Reich the opportunity to concentrate its fighters early. At 1100, long before the bombers reached the Dutch coast, Jafü 4 scrambled its fighters at Florennes, Athies, Vendeville, and Denain, and sent them northeast. All three JG 26 Gruppen made contact with the leading combat wings over the Dutch-German border. The First Gruppe apparently made a single attack on a B-24 combat wing before the Focke-Wulfs were driven off by the P-47s. Obfw. Ellenrieder claimed to have shot a Liberator out of formation, but the claim was not filed.

The Second and Third Gruppen reached the head of the B-17 column, and found it unescorted. The fighters were able to form up for repeated head-on attacks in the empty air in front of the 40th Combat Wing. Five B-17s went down, three from the 92nd and two from the 306th Bomb Groups; the JG 26 pilots claimed five, plus one separation that was not confirmed. The 78th Fighter Group reached its rendezvous point on schedule and found the leading bombers far to the front, firing green flares. The 83rd Fighter Squadron raced ahead and broke up a Third Gruppe attack. Most of the Messerschmitts tried to dive away, but were caught easily by the Thunderbolts. Fhj.-Fw. Kurt-Heinz Dylewski, Ogfr. Hellmut Greim, Fhr. Burghardt Wölke, and the experienced Oblt. Kurt Wunschelmeyer were all killed.

The rendezvous field today was Rheine. Twelve Schlageter pilots turned up; their senior officer present, Hptm. Borris, took command. After refueling, Borris and his wingman, Uffz. Gerhard Mohr, had just begun their takeoff rolls to intercept the withdrawing bombers when two Thunderbolts roared across the field. Within seconds Mohr's aircraft was reduced to a crumpled, flaming heap, its pilot dead. Fw. Franz Vanderveerd was also hit, and force-landed on the field. Minutes later Borris reported the destruction of one of the Thunderbolts north of Rheine. The victorious P-47, piloted by the 56th Fighter Group's Lt. Fred Christensen, escaped. Christensen claimed one Fw 190 damaged, but it was not confirmed.

The ten remaining Fw 190s circled the field once while forming up. According to a correspondent's report, Borris and his improvised Staffel soon saw a formation of unescorted B-24s north of Frankfurt. Oblt. Matoni (5th Staffel) took on the rear Liberator, while Obfw. Heckmann (3rd Staffel) and Lt. Radener (7th Staffel) attacked the two on the outside of the formation from the rear, firing long bursts. Matoni's Liberator was the first to fall, striking the ground near Rodenrot. A few minutes later, Radener's B-24 crashed northwest of Wetzlar. Lt. Willius and Oblt. Hartigs of the 2nd Staffel each downed a B-24. Four claims for B-24s were confirmed. The American records do not mention an attack on an unbroken B-24 formation after the target had been reached. The German pilots may, in fact, have been after straggling B-24s, of which there were many, and the correspondent may have exhibited a little journalistic license while writing up the major event of the day from a public relations standpoint, the 2000th victory of the Geschwader.

Another member of this formation, Fhr. O. Meyer of the 3rd Staffel, winged a withdrawing 55th Fighter Group P-38, which made it to the coast before being downed by the Watten Flak. Another flight of fighters returning from target support, P-51s from the 357th Fighter Group, spotted the small band of Focke-Wulfs. One Mustang pounced on Oblt. Radener's wingman, Uffz. Gerhard Loschinski, and shot him down. Waldi Radener broke sharply, and then found himself in a turning battle with the Mustang. Radener was out of ammunition, and could only hope that the Mustang pilot would run low on fuel and break off. The American fighter's engine suddenly began spewing smoke; its pilot immediately broke out of the turn and headed northwest. When Radener attempted to form up on it, the pilot half-rolled and bailed out, landing near the Bonn Autobahn. As Radener had no witness, he did not file the claim.

Two more small flights of Geschwader fighters had successful missions. Oblt. Neu and Fw. Wiegand took off from their intermediate field, Wiesbaden, at 1335, and went looking for individual bombers. They found one west of Koblenz, and Wiegand shot it down. They then flew northwest to Aachen, where they ran across a flight of 4th Fighter Group P-47s that had just broken up an attack on a B-24 formation. They claimed three of these, but when the Gruppe intelligence officer decided that the pair had claimed the same plane, Wiegand gave the claim to Neu. This claim was confirmed; Wiegand's claim for the second P-47 was rejected. The 4th Group lost one P-47 in this combat.

The day's last victory went to Fw. Wilhelm Mayer of the 7th Staffel. He had failed to contact the enemy on the early mission of the Second Gruppe from Athies, and had returned to Grevillers. He scrambled at 1517, probably with a wingman, and shot down a straggling 351st Bomb Group B-17 south of Amiens, but not until the bomber's gunners fatally damaged his Focke-Wulf. Mayer bailed out without injury; nine of the bomber's crew bailed out, and six of them evaded capture and eventually returned to England.

When the day's scores were tallied, Walter Matoni's victory, his thirteenth, was judged to be the 2000th for the Geschwader. Such round-number milestones were always cause for recognition in the Wehrmacht. A Staffel command was a suitable reward. Matoni's own 6th Staffel had just received a new Führer, Lt. Lange, as a replacement for Oblt. Sternberg. The next day Matoni was moved to Obfw. Glunz's 5th Staffel and named Kapitän. Glunz transferred to the 6th Staffel as Lange's deputy.

The victory totals for the Geschwader Stab and the three Gruppen were reported in the nightly OKW communiqué. As Luftwaffe air victories remain the subject of controversy, and complete victory lists for the Stab and the Third Gruppe failed to survive the war, these totals are of interest here. They are listed together with minimum and maximum totals compiled from the data presently available, and for which the specifics are known. The minimum comprises just those claims for which a confirmation document is known. The maximum includes these, plus those claims for which confirmation might reasonably have been expected – it often took more than a year for the RLM to confirm a claim. It is apparent that the numbers used by the OKW included "expected" confirmations; it is also apparent that 30-40 Third Gruppe claims for the war up to 24 February, 1944, have not yet been found. Of these, twenty-three are known to be 7th Staffel claims on the Eastern Front.

UNIT	AERIAL VICTORIES		
		Specifics Known	
	OKW Report	Known Confirmed	Maximum Confirmed
Stab/JG 26	117	93	118
I/JG 26	625	542	633
II/JG 26	649	545	656
III/JG 26	609	331	576
TOTAL	2000	1511	1983

The Jagdwaffe lost thirty-nine single-engine and fourteen twin-engine fighters today, a 15.7% loss rate based on the 336 sorties flown. The Americans lost 5.4% of the heavy bombers dispatched, and only 1.3% of the fighters. The war of attrition was clearly going in the Allies' favor.

JG 26 Casualties: 24 February 1944

Date	Rank	Name	Cas	Unit	Aircraft	WNr	Mkgs	Place	Time	Cause	Allied Unit
24-02-44	Uffz.	Mohr, Gerhard	KIA	2	Fw 190A-4	587	bk 2	Rheine a/f		P-47	56 FG
24-02-44	Fw.	Vanderveerd, Franz	WIA	3	Fw 190A-6	530950	yl 9	Rheine a/f		P-47	56 FG
24-02-44	Uffz.	Loschinski, Gerhard	KIA	7	Fw 190A-6	531072	br 12	Ems moor	1300	P-51	357 FG
24-02-44	Ogfr.	Greim, Hellmut	KIA	9	Bf 109G-6	16412	wh 3	Rheine-Lingen		P-47	78 FG
24-02-44	Gefr.	Lienich, Heinz	WIFA	11	Bf 109G-3	16293	yl 2	SSE of St. Dizier	1110	engine	non-op
24-02-44	Fhj-Fw.	Dylewski,Kurt-Heinz	KIA	12	Bf 109G-6	161696	bl 8	Handrup-Stappenberg		P-47	78 FG
24-02-44	Fhr.	Wölke, Burghardt	KIA	12	Bf 109G-6	162025	bl 6	Lengerich-Lingen		P-47	78 FG
24-02-44	Oblt.	Wunschelmeyer, Karl	KIA	12	Bf 109G-6	160778	bl 5	Quakenbrück		P-47	78 FG

JG 26 Victory Claims: 24 February 1944

Date	Rank	Name	Unit	Cl #	Aircraft	Place	Time	Opponent	Conf
24-02-44	Hptm.	Borris	I CO	35	P-47	N of Rheine	1305	56 FG	yes
24-02-44	Lt.	Willius	2 CO	42	B-24	Giessen (OS)	1355		yes
24-02-44	Oblt.	Hartigs	2	2	B-24	W of Koblenz (PP6-9?)	1215		yes
24-02-44	Obfw.	Ellenrieder	3		B-17-HSS	Varrelbusch?	1245		no
24-02-44	Fhr.	Meyer O.	3	1	P-38	S of Bonn (OP5)	1425	55 FG	yes
24-02-44	Oblt.	Neu	4 CO	10	P-47	S of Aachen(ON-OM)	1433	4 FG	yes
24-02-44	Fw.	Wiegand	4	19	B-17	W of Koblenz-Bingen	1410		yes
24-02-44	Fw.	Wiegand	4		P-47	Bingen	1430	4 FG	yes
24-02-44	Oblt.	Matoni	5	13	B-24	Rodenrot Kr. Dillenburg	1355	2000th JG 26	yes
24-02-44	Lt.	Radener	7 CO		B-17-HSS	NW of Ascheberg	1225	92 or	no
24-02-44	Lt.	Radener	7 CO	13	B-24	Asslar-5km NW of Wetzlar	1400	306 BG	yes
24-02-44	Lt.	Radener	7 CO		P-51	NW of Wetzlar-SE of Bonn	1420	357 FG	no
24-02-44	Fw.	Mayer	7	14	B-17	12km S of Amiens	1550	351 BG	unk
24-02-44	Uffz.	Guttmann	8	6	B-17	Rastorf-Lorum Kr Aschberg	1220	92 or 306 BG	yes
24-02-44	Uffz.	Wöge	9		B-17	NE of Lingen (FQ7)	1225	92 or 306 BG	yes
24-02-44	Hptm.	Staiger	12 CO	40	B-17	S of Quakenbrück-Rheine	1220	92 or 306 BG	yes
24-02-44	Uffz.	Böckl	12		B-17	NW of Lingen (FP1)	1230	92 or 306 BG	yes
24-02-44	Oblt.	Wunschelmeyer	12		B-17	Hasselünne	1225	92 or 306 BG	yes

Pilots of the 12th Staffel, photographed in early 1944, probably at Lille-Vendeville. From left: Uffz. Albert 'Adi' Boeckl, Fw. Hans-Joachim Leder (KIA 20 Aug 44), Lt. Hans Oeckel (KIA 17 Jul 44), Fw. Siegfried Göhre (KIA 10 Aug 44), Hptm. Hermann Staiger, Obfw. Alfons Gräve (KIA 20 Mar 44), Uffz. Willi Dachmann (KIFA 28 Feb 45), Uffz. Otto Salewski (KIA 7 Mar 45), and Gefr. Willibald Malm. *(Genth)*

25 February

The 8th Air Force continued its offensive with attacks on Augsburg, Stuttgart, Fürth, and Regensburg. The weather was excellent, and all primary targets were bombed visually. Of 823 bombers dispatched, 670 bombed their briefed targets. To simplify the task for the escort, the three bomb divisions followed a single track, crossing the French coast at Le Tréport. Protection was afforded by twenty groups of USAAF fighters, three of which flew two missions, and twelve squadrons of RAF fighters. Today the absence of a projected headwind increased the bombers' ground speed, resulting in some gaps in coverage that the Luftwaffe fighters took advantage of. Thirty-one bombers and three fighters were lost.

The German controllers expected another large-scale deep-penetration raid, but had no early indications of its route. As a precaution, the Third Gruppe, including even part of the 11th Staffel from St. Dizier, assembled at Laon-Athies and took off at 0940 for Trier.

The bomber stream began crossing the English coast at 1030. The Jafü scrambled the First Gruppe and the 4th Staffel at 1050, but instead of sending them toward the heavies, vectored them north, toward several B-26 formations that were bombing airfields in The Netherlands. The Gruppe was heading for the St. Trond force when it spotted the Venlo Marauders heading west, south of Walcheren. Lt. Willius led his 2nd Staffel in a quick attack that downed two B-26s before the Typhoons of the close escort could react. Obfw. Heitmann shot a third bomber into the North Sea, while Lt. Kiefner damaged his target, but was hit in one wing, and, after his ammunition exploded, put his Focke-Wulf down on Maldegem. Four B-26s, all from the 387th Bomb Group, were shot down.

The Second Gruppe was low in operational fighters, but the 5th and 8th Staffeln assembled early at Laon-Athies and took off at 1130, as the bomber stream passed overhead. The formation was led by the 8th Staffel Kapitän, Hptm. Leuschel, who was under orders to patrol the bomber stream and attack only unescorted combat wings.

Hptm. Mietusch led his Gruppe off from Trier, also at 1130, and headed east and then back west before picking the 40th Combat Wing to attack. The bomber stream was off course slightly to the north and came in range of the Saarbrücken Flak, which opened up on the B-17s at this time, shooting down a 92nd Bomb Group B-17 and disrupting the formation of the low group, the 306th. Mietusch led his Messerschmitts in a head-on attack on the latter group and downed two B-17s on their first pass. The 361st Fighter Group arrived and ended the mass attacks, apparently shooting down one Bf 109 whose pilot bailed out without injury. The rest of the Messerschmitts stayed in the area for another hour as the combat wings passed by, and shot down another three B-17s before returning to Trier for servicing.

Hptm. Leuschel's Focke-Wulfs also headed for Saarbrücken on reports that the escort was light, and upon arrival made a head-on attack on the 96th Bomb Group box that brought down two B-17s. The 4th Fighter Group had just reached the area, and Capt. Don Gentile immediately led the 336th Fighter Squadron in an attack on the Focke-Wulfs, which were attempting to form up for another attack, and shot down Leuschel and Lt. Dietrich Kehl. Leuschel crashed in his plane; Kehl, known as the *Sonnenvogel* or sunbird for his cheerful, serene disposition, even in combat, succeeding in bailing out, but was killed when he struck a power line. Leuschel's wingman, Uffz. Walter Enna, was able to force-land his severely damaged aircraft. Obfw. Joseph Zirngibl evaded these P-47s and attempted to land at Saarbrücken to refuel. While in the landing pattern he was strafed by a P-47 and then hit by the airfield Flak, and crash-landed on the field with injuries.

The 11th Staffel pilots still at St. Dizier carried on with their daily routines. The engine of Gefr. Heinz Lienich's Bf 109G-4 failed while he was on a test flight, and Lienich had to bail out south of the field with injuries.

The First and Third Gruppen and the 6th and 7th Staffeln all scrambled at 1430, and apparently formed a *Gefechtsverband* to attack the withdrawing bomber formations. Shortly after takeoff, Lt. Radener was able to shoot a B-24 from its formation. The combined unit then attacked a B-17 box over Pirmasens, and claimed two separations from formation and one final destruction. Obfw. Glunz, now flying with the 6th Staffel, failed to contact the enemy on this mission, but took off again from Epinoy at 1625 on the report of a straggling B-17. He quickly found it and shot it down, but did not file a claim. The Fortress was probably a 390th Bomb Group aircraft that crashed at Poix.

JG 26 Victory Claims: 25 February 1944

Date	Rank	Name	Unit	Cl #	Aircraft	Place	Time	Opponent	Conf
25-02-44	Lt.	Willius	2 CO	43	B-26	Zeebrugge - N Sea (KF-KG)	1126	387 BG	yes
25-02-44	Lt.	Willius	2 CO	44	B-26	Zeebrugge - N Sea (KG-KF)		387 BG	yes
25-02-44	Obfw.	Heitmann	4	10	B-26	E of Southend -N Sea (KG4-5)	1125	387 BG	yes
25-02-44	Obfw.	Glunz	5 CO		B-17	unknown	1700	390 BG	no
25-02-44	Lt.	Radener	7 CO	14	B-24-HSS	Notweiler-W of Bergzabern	1445		yes
25-02-44	Lt.	Radener	7 CO	15	B-17-eV	Willgartswissen-Pirmasens	1520		yes
25-02-44	Fhr.	Busch W.	8	1	B-17	Alsbach near St. Ingbert	1200	96 BG	unk
25-02-44	Fw.	Zirngibl	8	8	B-17	Saarbrücken	1225	96 BG	yes
25-02-44	Hptm.	Mietusch	III CO	57	B-17	4km SW of Charleville (SK 1-2)	1215	306 BG	yes
25-02-44	Hptm.	Mietusch	III CO	58	B-17-HSS	E of Pirmasens (UQ 3)	1500		yes
25-02-44	Oblt.	Dippel	9 CO	19	B-17-HSS	unknown	1500		unk
25-02-44	Oblt.	Schauder	10 CO	15	B-17	17km SE of Charleville	1145	306 BG	yes
25-02-44	Fw.	Laub	11	6	B-17	10km SE of Longwy	1230		yes
25-02-44	Hptm.	Staiger	12 CO	41	B-17	Birkweiler-Sedan	1300		yes
25-02-44	Uffz.	Böckl	12		B-17	6km N of Rethel	1210		yes

26 February

The return of bad weather over the Continent forced the USAAF to cancel the rest of the raids planned for Operation Argument. The Allies remained on their side of the Channel, and the Luftwaffe counted up the cost of Big Week and began replenishing its stocks for the next campaign. While on a transfer flight to Grevillers with a rebuilt fighter for the 7th Staffel, Uffz. Kurt Stahnke landed at Florennes to refuel. As he took off, the Focke-Wulf's engine seized. Stahnke made an immediate forced-landing, damaging the aircraft and suffering minor injuries.

Contrary to the general American belief at the time, their bombing attacks during Big Week did not cripple the German aviation industry. Another, very real, victory had been won that week, however, even though no single battle with the drama of a Schweinfurt had been fought. Aerial superiority had passed irrevocably to the Allies. The message of Big Week was crystal-clear to the American planners – Allied fighters could dominate the air over any part of Europe, by their mere appearance. The German fighter force suffered no net decrease in numerical strength during the week, and remained a formidable foe. But the era of maximum defensive effort against every American bombing raid was over. The hit-and-run tactics that the Schlageter pilots had found necessary for their personal survival now became the unofficial policy of the entire Jagdwaffe.

27 February

Uffz. Horst Spiess of the 9th Staffel crashed southeast of Lille while on a training flight. He did not bail out, and no cause for the accident was discovered.

JG 26 Casualties: 25 - 27 February 1944

Date	Rank	Name	Cas	Unit	Aircraft	WNr	Mkgs	Place	Time	Cause	Allied Unit
25-02-44	Lt.	Kehl, Dietrich	KIA	5	Fw 190A-7	340336	wh 12	near Metz	1200	P-47	4 FG
25-02-44	Hptm.	Leuschel, Rudolf	KIA	8 CO	Fw 190A-7	340262	bl 11	16km S of Metz	1200	P-47	4 FG
25-02-44	Obfw.	Zirngibl, Joseph	WIA	8	Fw 190A-6	530718	bl 4	Saarbrücken a/f	1250	P-47	
25-02-44	Uffz.	Enna, Walter	no	8	Fw 190A-6			near Metz	1200	P-47	4 FG
26-02-44	Uffz.	Stahnke, Kurt	WIFA	7	Fw 190A-6	470236	br 7	Vendeville a/f		engine	non-op
27-02-44	Uffz.	Spiess, Horst	KIFA	9	Bf 109G-6	27018	wh 11	20km SE of Lille	1620	crashed	non-op

29 February

During February the German fighter force lost 17.9% of its pilot strength. The Reich defenders (Luftflotte Reich plus Luftflotte 3) lost 225 fighter crewmen killed and missing, and 141 wounded. JG 26 lost fifteen pilots killed in action, and a further three in accidents; among the dead were three of its twelve Staffelkapitäne.

Geschwader personnel moves during February included: the transfer of Lt. Johann-Hermann Meier from 3/JG 52 into the 1st Staffel as leader, replacing Lt. Leberecht Altmann, who transferred to the Ergänzungsgruppe of JG 1; the promotion of Lt. Wilhelm Hofmann to leader of the 8th Staffel, replacing Leuschel; the return of Uffz. Werner Schwan to the 1st Staffel after nine months in hospital; the return of Lt. Heinrich Beer to the 3rd Staffel from instructor duty; the arrival of Uffz. Karl Willand in the Geschwader after duty as an instructor, and his assignment to the 8th Staffel; the transfer of Obfw. Hermann Schmeinl to the Stab of the General der Jagdflieger; the transfer of Uffz. Harry Kubon from the Geschwader; and the transfer of Uffz. Horst Gewitz from the 9th Staffel to a ferry unit.

Pilots assigned to the Geschwader during February after completing flight training included: Uffz. Franz Afflerbach, Gefr. Rudolf Franke, Ogfr. Johann Müller, Uffz. Ernst Schande, Uffz. Leopold Schlögl, Uffz. Georg Schwaiger, Uffz. Hans-Werner Winter, Uffz. Heinz Wodarczyk – First Gruppe; Uffz. Heinz Falkenberg, Uffz. Albrecht von Fehr, Fhr. Ulrich-Karsten Frantz, Lt. Hellmut Giebner, Uffz. Friedrich Jacobsen, Uffz. Hans Klees, Uffz. Bernhard Mickmann, Uffz. Josef Peschak, Uffz. Helmut Rektor, Uffz. Waldemar Spiegl, Uffz. Karl Willand, Fhr. Kurt Zippel – Second

Gruppe; Uffz. Karl Frank, Lt. Peter Hauer, Uffz. Rudolf Leinberger, Ofhr. Helmut Lorberg, Uffz. Kurt Rickeit – Third Gruppe.

In addition, Fhj.-Fw. Wolfgang Röhler joined the 6th Staffel after completing fighter transition training. Röhler had won an Iron Cross First Class as a reconnaissance pilot.

2 March

The 8th Air Force returned to Frankfurt. Of the 481 B-17s and B-24s that took off, only 137 were able to locate their assigned target through thick cloud cover. Nine bombers were lost; four of the 589 escort fighters failed to return. Most Luftflotte Reich airfields were socked in, and only two of its Jagdgruppen were able to take off. The Luftflotte 3 fields were clear, and JG 2 and JG 26 operated against both the penetration and withdrawal phases of the bomber mission.

The entire Geschwader scrambled at 1100, just as the leading B-17 wing reached the French coast at Le Tréport and turned east. The Focke-Wulfs and Messerschmitts also flew east, climbing until they were well above the bombers. After the First and Second Gruppen were airborne, they were ordered by Jafü 4 to rendezvous over the Eifel and coordinate their attacks on the rear of the bomber stream. The Second Gruppe decided on a high rear attack, while the First Gruppe flew ahead to attack from the front. As fourteen Fw 190s dived from 8000 meters (27,000 feet) through the rear box of B-17s, 600 meters (2000 feet) below, two squadrons of P-47s from the 365th Fighter Group, a new unit assigned to the tactical 9th Air Force, went after them. Most of the German pilots continued their dives, heading for breaks in the clouds below. The Thunderbolt pilots, confident of their abilities in this, their first air combat, followed the Focke-Wulfs down, and shot down three 6th Staffel aircraft without loss. Lt. Friedrich Lange, the new Staffelkapitän, bailed out at 100 meters (300 feet), but was killed when his parachute did not open. Uffz. Heinrich Berg failed to return; in August his body was found in his aircraft, buried in the mud on the bottom of the Mosel River. Uffz. Georg Meidinger was able to bail out, and survived with wounds.

The First Gruppe lost no aircraft to American fighters, but two of its Fw 190s collided in the clouds while diving to make their attack from 12 o'clock high, killing Uffz. Franz Hurtig and Uffz. Herbert Onken. Lt. Willius continued the pursuit, and eventually downed a B-17 near Wiesbaden. The 365th Fighter Group P-47s continued their escort, periodically breaking into attacks by JG 2 and JG 26 Focke-Wulfs. One more German fighter was shot down before the new Thunderbolt group turned back. This Fw 190 was piloted by the JG 2 Kommodore, Obstlt. Egon Mayer, the originator of the head-on bomber attack and the first Luftwaffe pilot to attain one hundred air victories in the ETO.

The Third Gruppe reached the head of the bomber stream near Koblenz, and made a head-on attack which downed two B-17s. Hptm. Staiger was one of the victors; the other is unknown. Uffz. Heinrich Hering was chased by an American fighter and bailed out with wounds. His casualty report states that the victor was flying a P-38, but there were none in the area; the American pilot was probably from the 4th Fighter Group, which had just been re-equipped with P-51 Mustangs.

The pilots took off again shortly after 1300 to intercept the returning bombers. Obfw. Wilhelm Mayer shot down a 390th Bomb Group B-17 near Abbeville, but took hits in his own cockpit. Obstlt. Priller led the fighters that scrambled from today's assembly airfield, Trier. After Lt. Kiefner downed a B-17 near Arlon, Priller ordered the men to return to their home airfields.

JG 26 Victory Claims: 2 March 1944

Date	Rank	Name	Unit	Cl #	Aircraft	Place	Time	Opponent	Conf
02-03-44	Lt.	Kiefner	1	4	B-17	Arlon (SM2)	1343		yes
02-03-44	Lt.	Willius	2 CO	45	B-17	Wiesbaden(QR2-3)	1208		yes
02-03-44	Obfw.	Mayer	7	15	B-17	24km NE of Abbeville (PD9)	1330	390 BG	yes
02-03-44	Ofhr.	Kemethmüller	9		B-17-dam	unknown	1200		dam
02-03-44	Hptm.	Staiger	12 CO	42	B-17	W of Limburg(PQ-QQ)	1150		yes

Date	Rank	Name	Cas	Unit	Aircraft	WNr	Mkgs	Place	Time	Cause	Allied Unit
02-03-44	Uffz.	Hurtig, Franz	KIA	1	Fw 190A-6	470213	wh 8	Trier-Wittlich	1145	collision	n/a
02-03-44	Uffz.	Onken, Herbert	KIA	3	Fw 190A-6	550915	yl 5	near Trier-Wittlich	1145	collision	n/a
02-03-44	Lt.	Lange, Friedrich	KIA	6 CO	Fw 190A-6	470202	bk 6	Polch-Mayen-Eifel		P-47	365 FG
02-03-44	Uffz.	Berg, Heinrich	KIA	6	Fw 190A-6	530718	bk 4	NE of Cochem	1150	P-47	365 FG
02-03-44	Uffz.	Meidinger, Georg	WIA	6	Fw 190A-7	642001	bk 5	NE of Cochem	1150	P-47	365 FG
02-03-44	Uffz.	Hering, Heinrich	WIA	9	Bf 109G-6	410729	wh 7	Koblenz-Niederzissen	1150	P-38	

3 March

The American air planners were now deliberately choosing targets which would provoke the strongest possible reaction by the German fighter defenses. Today brought the first attempt to bomb Berlin, but the mission had to be aborted owing to the weather. The only unit of the Geschwader to contact the enemy was the 1st Staffel, which was *en route* from Florennes to Metz to meet a He 111 and escort it to Paris.

Obfw. Glunz was named to replace Oblt. Lange as leader of the 6th Staffel.

4 March

Again the weather played havoc with the 8th Air Force's plans to bomb Berlin. Only thirty B-17s reached the target, and five of these were shot down. The 20th Fighter Group attempted to provide withdrawal support, but was unable to find the bombers. A number of its Lightnings had engine problems, and some made it back across the Channel on one engine. The P-38 flown by Lt. Harry Bisher never reached the Channel. Fw. Gerd Wiegand was sitting in the cockpit of his Fw 190 at Wevelgem – despite the bad weather, a Rotte of fighters had been ordered to remain at readiness – when a crippled P-38 whistled overhead on one engine. Wiegand took off immediately and gave chase. The two planes flew in and out of the clouds for several minutes. The Lightning suddenly emerged from the mist, right in front of Wiegand. The German pilot wanted to force the American fighter down in one piece, and so deliberately fired to one side. But the Lightning broke into the attack, and Wiegand shot it down, taking

care not to hit the pilot. The American bailed out at 2000 meters (6500 feet), and Wiegand returned to Wevelgem, landed, and hurried to the crash site. A parachute was floating in the Lys River; Wiegand was told that the pilot had drowned. He had in fact been whisked under cover by Belgian civilians, and eventually made his way back to England *via* the Resistance. Forty years after the war, a Belgian researcher put the two pilots in contact.

The 1st Staffel took off from Le Bourget at 0900 to escort the VIP's He 111 back to Metz. The formation ran into some very bad weather, and Obfw. Friedrich Lindelaub, Lt. Kiefner's wingman, disappeared. The wreckage of his aircraft was later found near Sedan; Lindelaub had crashed into a hill.

Obfw. Friedrich Lindelaub of the 1st Staffel. On 4 March Lindelaub was killed when he crashed into a hill in bad weather. *(Bundesarchiv-Militärarchiv)*

6 March

General Doolittle finally succeeded in putting his bomber force over "Big B", Berlin. Seven hundred and thirty bombers were escorted by 644 fighters from the 8th and 9th US Air Forces and the RAF. Many fighter units flew two missions, boosting the escort sortie total to 943. The bombers' course was directly east from England, over northern Holland, to Berlin, with a few minor course changes to avoid known Flak belts. From the American takeoff, there was little doubt in General Schmid's Jagdkorps I headquarters as to the intended target. As expected, the defenses countered with most of their strength, putting up a total of 528 sorties. Sixty-nine bombers and eleven fighters failed to return to England, the Americans' greatest loss on any raid of the war. However, the bomber loss rate of 10%, while high, was no hindrance to further operations of the same magnitude. The Luftwaffe lost sixty-six fighters, or 12.5% of those scrambled.

The bombers began leaving the English coast at 1000, and were crossing the Zuider Zee by 1130. The Jafü 4 controller squeezed in a quick attack on a formation of B-26s which was raiding Poix. Hptm. Mietusch led his Stabsschwarm and the 9th Staffel up from Vendeville at 1200 and attacked the mediums' escort. Mietusch shot down a No. 3 Sqd. Typhoon. Another Typhoon was damaged; no bombers, and no German fighters, were lost. The Messerschmitts landed on Vitry, an Fw 190 base, and apparently had problems getting serviced; they were not called on to participate in the later mission.

Jafü 4 decided not to send any of its fighters chasing north, but ordered part of the Second Gruppe to scramble and fly east, in case the bombers turned toward Frankfurt or targets in southern Germany. When the bombers maintained their course to the east, the fighters landed at Biblis, near Worms, and waited for the direction of the bombers' return flight to be determined, as did the rest of the First and Second Gruppen, still on their home bases.

The briefed targets were covered in clouds, so the bombers dropped their loads on the Berlin city center at about 1345, and after reassembly, headed back toward England on the reciprocal of their earlier course. Jafü 4 scrambled all of its Focke-Wulfs at 1330. Hptm. Borris and his Gruppe took off from Florennes; Oblt. Matoni led the Second Gruppe fighters that were still on their French bases to Wevelgem, where they met the 4th Staffel; and the rest of the Second Gruppe scrambled from Biblis. The last-named formation apparently never made contact. The other two reached the strung-out bomber stream near Osnabrück at 1430. The bombers were under the protection of the 356th Fighter Group, aided by a few P-38s which were just heading home after their shift as target escort. The Third Bomb Division and Second Bomb Division formations were flying side-by-side, which helped the Fw 190s elude the few P-47s by dodging between the combat boxes. Their attacks downed B-17s from the 94th and 388th Bomb Groups and a 453rd Bomb Group B-24. Obfw. Alfred Heckmann led his 3rd Staffel Schwarm in a bounce on a lone 356th Fighter Group P-47 and shot it down. Hptm. Borris also claimed a P-47, but it reached England, seriously damaged. The P-47s shot down Obfw. Hans Heitmann of the 4th Staffel, who bailed out with a badly injured right arm.

The Focke-Wulf pilots finished their mission by looking for stragglers. Lt. Kiefner shot down a 458th Bomb Group B-24, and Oblt. Matoni polished off a 381st Bomb Group B-17; both bombers had dropped from their formations after being damaged by the Berlin Flak. Heitmann was the only JG 26 casualty on this mission, but Ogfr. Johann Müller of the 4th Staffel was severely injured later in the evening when his Focke-Wulf overturned when landing after a transfer flight.

JG 26 Victory Claims: 4 - 6 March 1944

Date	Rank	Name	Unit	Cl #	Aircraft	Place	Time	Opponent	Conf
04-03-44	Fw.	Wiegand	4	20	P-38	10km S of Courtrai	1525	20 FG	yes
06-03-44	Hptm.	Borris	I CO		P-47	SW of Oldenburg (EQ 3-9)	1435	356 FG	unk

06-03-44	Lt.	Kiefner	1	5	B-24	Almelo (CO5,4)	1500	458 BG	yes
06-03-44	Lt.	Willius	2 CO	46	B-17	N of Koblenz (OP6,2)	1441		yes
06-03-44	Obfw.	Heckmann	3 CO	62	P-47	Almelo (CO5,3)	1447	356 FG	yes
06-03-44	Oblt.	Neu	4 CO	11	B-24	S of Quakenbrück	1445	453 BG	yes
06-03-44	Obfw.	Heitmann	4	11	B-17	NW of Osnabrück	1430	94 BG	yes
06-03-44	Oblt.	Matoni	5 CO	14	B-17	15km E of Jülich	1505	381 BG	yes
06-03-44	Hptm.	Mietusch	III CO	59	Typhoon	5km N of Amiens (QE-RE)	1305	3 Sqd	yes

7 March

The weather over England grounded the heavy bombers, and the few sorties by the medium bombers were ignored by the Jagdwaffe. Two new pilots *en route* to join the Third Gruppe, Uffz. Werner Henske and Gefr. Harry Geiler, collided over Fürth on their transfer flight and were killed.

JG 26 Casualties: 4 - 7 March 1944

Date	Rank	Name	Cas	Unit	Aircraft	WNr	Mkgs	Place	Time	Cause	Allied Unit
04-03-44	Obfw.	Lindelaub, Friedrich	KIFA	1	Fw 190A-7	642979	wh 15	N of Charleville	1415	weather	non-op
06-03-44	Obfw.	Heitmann, Hans	WIA	4	Fw 190A-7	642978	bl 9	Osnabrück-Haste	1430	P-47	356 FG
06-03-44	Ogfr.	Müller, Johann	WIFA	4	Fw 190A-6	551144	bl 5	Vendeville a/f		landing	non-op
07-03-44	Uffz.	Henske, Werner	KIFA	9	Bf 109G-6	162404	wh 16	Fürth-Odenwald	1415	collision	non-op
07-03-44	Gefr.	Geiler, Harry	KIFA	10	Bf 109G-6	162474	BF+VC	Fürth-Odenwald	1415	collision	non-op

8 March

The 8th Air Force returned to Berlin. Favored by cloudless skies, all ten combat wings were ordered to bomb the Erkner ball bearing works. Four hundred and seventy of the 702 bombers dispatched bombed the primary target. Thirty-seven bombers and seventeen fighters were lost.

The early radio traffic from the bomber bases and the good weather led General Schmid to conclude that a deep-penetration raid was in the offing. Jafü 4 was not allowed to repeat its mistake of the 6th; it was asked to send its fighters north at 1000, a full hour before the B-17s started leaving England. The bombers' course was a duplicate of that of the 6th, due east across Holland and northern Germany. The Second and Third Gruppen, plus the 4th Staffel, had landed at Rheine with a total of forty-nine fighters, and were thus much better positioned to contribute to the defense than two days previously. They took off at noon and flew to Steinhuder Lake, a distinctive landmark west of Hannover. Here they rendezvoused with the six Jagdgruppen of JG 1 and JG 11. They succeeded for once in overwhelming the escorts, which on this part of the route were the P-47s of the 56th and 353rd Fighter Groups. The Schlageter fighters formed up ahead of the 45th Combat Wing, which was leading the Third Bomb Division and had already lost cohesiveness owing to early returns. Today the Focke-Wulfs attacked in trail, in closely-spaced strings of ten to twelve aircraft. The B-17 gunners found this confusing; targets were difficult to select, and no JG 26 aircraft was seriously damaged by return fire. Eight 45th Combat Wing B-17s crashed between Steinhuder Lake and Braunschweig, the victims of the Second Gruppe (six claims), Hptm. Mietusch and Hptm. Staiger. The 4th Staffel got into a scuffle with a flight of 56th Fighter Group Thunderbolts. Gerd Wiegand, by now a Fähnrich-Feldwebel or officer candidate, shot down a P-47, but was shot down in turn by another, and suffered injuries that kept him out of combat for three months. Some of the German fighters followed the B-17s to the outskirts of Berlin, where Lt. Hofmann shot down a 363rd Fighter Group P-51 of the target escort, and Hptm. Staiger claimed his second B-17, although the claim was not filed.

Only a few fighters were available to take part in the attack on the withdrawing heavy bombers. Hptm. Borris scrambled from Florennes at 1550 with a dozen Fw 190s and headed north, but crossed the track of a formation of B-26s that had just bombed Sosterberg airfield and decided to attack them instead. The bombers were guarded by

Fw-Fhj. Wiegand with a hand injury suffered on 8 March; his beard marks him as a left-hander. Wiegand is supported by Uffz. Schmidtke. *(G. Schmidt)*

five squadrons of Spitfires. While climbing into position, Borris decided to attack the fighters rather than attempt to penetrate their thick screen. The German bounce, carried out just as the formation crossed the Dutch coast, was successful. One No. 332 Sqd. Spitfire fell under Borris's guns. The Focke-Wulfs then dived away inland to safety.

Hptm. Mietusch did reach the heavy bomber stream, but with only a handful of his Messerschmitts. His first attempt to close with the bombers was fended off by the escort, which shot down Uffz. Emil Kampen, who crashed with his plane. Mietusch and two other pilots made a beam attack on the rear bombers of a combat wing and then rolled away. A flight of P-47s from the 352nd Fighter Group went after the three Messerschmitts. Two got on the tail of Mietusch's wingman. When Mietusch went to his aid, the leader of the P-47 flight was able to damage the German plane with a burst of fire at high deflection. Mietusch broke for the deck, and the Thunderbolt pilot was able to close on him easily, firing down to a range of 100 yards (90 meters). Large pieces flew off of the 109, which was a mass of flames. Mietusch jettisoned his canopy and jumped out. His chute opened immediately, and he landed safely, but with injuries severe enough to keep him in the hospital for the next few weeks. Hptm. Staiger took command of the Gruppe until Mietusch's return.

JG 26 Victory Claims: 8 March 1944

Date	Rank	Name	Unit	Cl #	Aircraft	Place	Time	Opponent	Conf
08-03-44	Hptm.	Borris	I CO	36	Spitfire	E of Utrecht	1650	332 Sqd	yes
08-03-44	Fw.	Wiegand	4	21	P-47	Hunteburg-Zwolle (FR8)	1325	353 FG	yes
08-03-44	Oblt.	Matoni	5 CO	15	B-17	Mittelland Canal (BB3)	1330	388 BG	yes
08-03-44	Oblt.	Matoni	5 CO	16	B-17-HSS	Nienburg-Weser (N of Magdeberg)	1340	452 BG	yes $1/2$
08-03-44	Fw.	Guttmann	5	7	B-17	NE of Helmstedt (GC5)	1400	96 or 388 BG	yes
08-03-44	Fw.	Prager	5	2	B-17	80km NE of Braunschweig	1335	388 BG	yes
08-03-44	Fw.	Vogt	7	20	B-17	16km SW of Gardelegen (GG2)	1330	96 or 388 BG	yes
08-03-44	Fw.	Vogt	7	21	B-17-HSS	15km E of Nienburg (FT3)	1330	452 BG	unk
08-03-44	Lt.	Hofmann W.	8 CO	9	P-51	17km W of Torgau (KF5)	1420	363 FG	yes
08-03-44	Hptm.	Mietusch	III CO	60	B-17-HSS	S of Zwolle-Braunschweig (GB)	1325	381 BG	yes
08-03-44	Hptm.	Staiger	12 CO	43	B-17	N of Hannover		388 BG	unk
08-03-44	Hptm.	Staiger	12 CO	44	B-17	Potsdam			unk

Date	Rank	Name	Cas	Unit	Aircraft	WNr	Mkgs	Place	Time	Cause	Allied Unit
08-03-44	Fhj.-Fw.	Wiegand, Gerd	WIA	4	Fw 190A-6	550718	bl 6	Damme	1325	P-47	56 FG
08-03-44	Maj.	Mietusch, Klaus	WIA	III CO	Bf 109G-6	162032	bk 21	N of Meppen	1600	P-47	352 FG
08-03-44	Uffz.	Kampen, Emil	KIA	9	Bf 109G-6	410743	wh 5	Steinhuder Lake	1500	P-47	352 FG

9 March

The third major raid on Berlin in four days was virtually unopposed by the Jagdwaffe. Only eight bombers failed to return; all of them were lost to antiaircraft fire. Weather conditions played a role in keeping the German fighters on the ground, as did the state of serviceability within the fighter units – JG 26 had only forty-nine fighters ready for operations. The Geschwader flew no combat sorties. Uffz. Walter Enna of the 8th Staffel was killed while transferring a fighter from Frankfurt. Enna apparently got lost, ran out of fuel, and crashed.

12 March

The 9th Staffel flew to St. Dizier for blind flying training, trading places with the 11th Staffel. The pilots of the 11th had by now made themselves unpopular with the townspeople and the base staff. Uffz. Heinz Gehrke, who had reported to the Staffel at St. Dizier directly from operational training, recalls that after several days spent in heavy study the young pilots had decided to relax at a whorehouse in the town. A disturbance ensued; the madam summoned the military police, who turned the airmen out into the street. They marched back to the field, singing loudly. During the next day's noon meal the head of the airfield's permanent staff stood up and announced that because of the events of the previous night they no longer welcomed the company of the Schlageter pilots. The gentlemen of the staff then left the dining hall, leaving the amused pilots to finish their meal alone.

The morning of the Staffel's departure from St. Dizier is one of Heinz Gehrke's happiest memories of the war. According to Gehrke,

> "Obfw. Guhl wanted to make a proper departure. Our Bf 109s stood on the field, ready for takeoff. It was a splendid day with blue skies, cold but clear. Guhl assembled us and the eight of us took off, following his radioed orders. He took us straight up into the blue sky. Leaving splendid white contrails from 5000 meters [16,000 feet] we climbed in a beautiful spiral over the field, higher and higher. Above 10,000 meters [32,000 feet] flying became difficult; the 109s hung in the thin air like ripe grapes. Visibility was perfect. In one direction we could see all the way to England; on the other side the peaks of the Swiss Alps glistened. At 11,000 meters [36,000 feet] we could go no higher, and the order was given, 'all aircraft dive in line astern.' So said, so done. We dived. As we neared the ground, Guhl ordered us to form up in line abreast and charge our guns. Before takeoff he had had the aircraft loaded with practice ammunition; that is, blank rounds. We banked over the city, knifed along the streets (where the personnel at our former quarters waved at us), reassembled outside the city, as ordered, and flew our 109s in a single formation to the garrison headquarters. Then, at the order, 'fire at will', we fired all of our blank ammunition into the air.
>
> "The sight of the officials in the headquarters building fleeing to the air-raid shelter lifted our hearts. Thus we took our departure from St. Dizier, heading for Lille-Vendeville and our first *true* mission."

14 March

Uffz. Paul Thost, a new 9th Staffel pilot, crashed while on a training flight from St. Dizier and was killed. The reason for the crash was not reported.

The 6th Staffel left Cambrai-Epinoy for St. Dizier and the blind-flying course.

15 March

Lt. Johann-Hermann Meier, a Kapitän of the 1st Staffel. Meier claimed seventy-seven victories on the Eastern Front, but died shortly after his transfer to JG 26. *(Roba)*

Obstlt. Priller concluded his latest tour as Jafü 4 at St. Pol, and returned to Lille, where he found the men of his Geschwader in a bad state of mind after a disastrous morning. A small force of B-24s and B-17s had raided Brunswick. Both the First and Second Gruppen were ordered to take off at 1100 and fly to Rheine to await the returning bombers. While taxiing out for takeoff from Florennes, Lt. Johann-Hermann Meier, the 1st Staffel leader, veered to the right and rammed the aircraft of his wingman, Uffz. Hans Ruppert. Both aircraft burst into flames. Ruppert escaped, but Meier was trapped, and burned to death. According to a pilot who witnessed the accident, Meier was "obviously drunk. Ruppert committed no error, but was seriously traumatized, and did not recover prior to his own death on 25 May." Meier had joined the Geschwader from I/JG 51 only two weeks previously. He had gained seventy-seven victories in his 305 missions with the "Mölders" Geschwader, and was awarded a posthumous Knight's Cross. Oblt. Kurt Kranefeld transferred from the First Gruppe Stab to take over the 1st Staffel.

The 7th Staffel failed to receive any warning of Spitfires in the area before taking off for Rheine. While circling the field to form up, they were bounced by No. 401 Sqd. (RCAF), which was escorting some B-26s. Lt. Hans Mayer, Uffz. Kurt Stahnke, and Uffz. Rudolf Georgi were all shot down; only Georgi survived, bailing out with burns. One No. 401 Sqd. Spitfire failed to return from the mission. According to the squadron log, it crashed after its engine failed, but Fw. Böhm of the 7th Staffel was given credit for shooting it down.

The Focke-Wulfs that reached Rheine had only a modest success against the bombers, but did claim two-thirds of all those lost – two out of the three. Lt. Wilhelm Hofmann led his 8th Staffel Schwarm in an attack on the 44th Bomb Group formation shortly after leaving the target, and shot down one B-24. Fw. Willius chased a damaged 392nd Bomb Group B-24 out over the North Sea, and shot it down.

JG 26 Victory Claims: 15 March 1944

Date	Rank	Name	Unit	Cl #	Aircraft	Place	Time	Opponent	Conf
15-03-44	Lt.	Willius	2 CO	47	B-24	E of Norwich - N Sea (FE6?)	1226	392 BG	yes
15-03-44	Fw.	Böhm	7	1	Spitfire	30km NE of Amiens	1054	401 Sqd	yes
15-03-44	Lt.	Hofmann W.	8 CO	10	B-24	NW of Gevelsberg (LP5)	1215	44 BG	yes

JG 26 Casualties: 9 - 15 March 1944

Date	Rank	Name	Cas	Unit	Aircraft	WNr	Mkgs	Place	Time	Cause	Allied Unit
09-03-44	Uffz.	Enna, Walter	KIFA 8		Fw 190A-6	530411	bl 6	S of Paris	1200	no fuel	non-op

Date	Rank	Name		Cl #	Aircraft		Place	Time		
14-03-44	Uffz.	Thost, Paul	KIFA	9	Bf 109G-6	162245 wh 12	SE St Dizier	0905	crashed	non-op
15-03-44	Lt.	Meier, Johann-Herman	KIFA	1 CO	Fw 190A-6	470057 wh 8	Florennes a/f		ground collision	n/a
15-03-44	Uffz.	Georgi, Rudolf	WIA	7	Fw 190A-6	470249 br 12	near Rheine-Colombes		Spitfire	401 Sqd
15-03-44	Lt.	Mayer, Hans	KIA	7	Fw 190A-7	340293 br 2	SW of Bapaume		Spitfire	401 Sqd
15-03-44	Uffz.	Stahnke, Kurt	KIA	7	Fw 190A-6	530399 br 5	nr Rheine-Maurepas		Spitfire	401 Sqd

16 March

The 8th Air Force sent 808 bombers to attack aviation industry targets in southern Germany. The hoped-for break in the weather did not occur, and secondary targets were bombed through solid undercast. Twenty-four bombers, and twelve fighters, failed to return.

The bombers exited the south coast of England at 0930, and the Jafü 4 controller guessed correctly that their course and early departure indicated a deep-penetration raid on south Germany. All three Gruppen were scrambled at 0945 and ordered to form up over Reims. Jafü 5 was asked for help, and scrambled III/JG 2. Jafü 4 ordered the four Gruppen to fly southeast to Nancy-St. Dizier, and the bombers were contacted at 1028. The 56th Fighter Group reached St. Dizier just as the Fw 190s and Bf 109s were forming up in front of the leading B-17 combat wing. The Thunderbolts shot down Lt. Heinrich Beer (3rd Staffel), Uffz. Albrecht von Fehr (6th Staffel), Uffz. Josef Baumann (8th Staffel), and Fhj.-Fw. Kurt Winkel (10th Staffel); all were killed. The surviving German fighters scattered in the clouds and landed at Chaumont, Laon, Reims, or Metz. Hptm. Staiger remained in the St. Dizier area long enough to spot an aborting 445th Bomb Group B-24 and shoot it down.

JG 2 and JG 26 attempted another coordinated attack on the withdrawing bombers; again over St. Dizier, and again with little success. The Third Gruppe found an unescorted B-24 wing, but its attack forced only one 458th Bomb Group aircraft from formation. The Herausschuss was later credited to Lt. Peter Reischer, the 11th Staffel Kapitän. Uffz. Heinz Gehrke retained vivid memories of this, his first combat mission. He found himself behind the crippled bomber and attacked it three times before it finally fell away. He thought it would crash immediately, but the bomber reached the English Channel before ditching. After the attack, Gehrke's Staffel mates, and even his element leader, had disappeared. Gehrke saw some fighters circling in the distance and attempted to join them, only to discover too late that they were Thunderbolts. The 356th Fighter Group P-47 pilots broke around and came after Gehrke. The Messerschmitt pilot was too green to think of anything to do but dive – always a fatal mistake against a P-47. His aircraft was quickly shot to shreds, and he bailed out, hitting the ground with nothing more serious than a strained back.

His comrades attempted to land on St. Dizier, but were spotted in the pattern by some 78th Fighter Group pilots, who quickly dived on the easy targets and shot down one Fw 190 and three Bf 109s. Lt. Klaus Kunze of the First Gruppe Stab was killed; Fhj.-Uffz. Hans-Gerhard Fieguth, Ofhr. Hermann Juhre, and Fw. Werner Kraft, all of the 10th Staffel, bailed out of their Messerschmitts with various degrees of injury.

The Geschwader had one more success to set against the Thunderbolts' toll of five dead and four injured pilots. Lt. Willius claimed a B-17 during the day; the time and location of this claim do not appear to have survived.

JG 26 Victory Claims: 16 March 1944

Date	Rank	Name	Unit	Cl #	Aircraft	Place	Time	Opponent	Conf
16-03-44	Lt.	Willius	2 CO		B-17	unknown			no
16-03-44	Lt.	Reischer	11 CO	8	B-24-HSS	Vitry (BJ2)	1338	458 BG	yes
16-03-44	Uffz.	Gehrke	11		B-24-eV	near Reims		458 BG	yes
16-03-44	Hptm.	Staiger	12 CO	45	B-24	SW of St Dizier-Worms	1210	445 BG	yes

Date	Rank	Name	Cas	Unit	Aircraft	WNr Mkgs	Place	Time	Cause	Allied Unit
16-03-44	Lt.	Kunze, Klaus	KIA	I	Fw 190A-6	550916 gr 3	St. Dizier		P-47	78 FG
16-03-44	Lt.	Beer, Heinrich	KIA	3	Fw 190A-6	470247 br 5	SW of St. Dizier	1100	P-47	56 FG
16-03-44	Uffz.	Fehr, Albrecht von	KIA	6	Fw 190A-6	550437 bk 2	N of St Dizier	1105	P-47	56 FG
16-03-44	Uffz.	Baumann, Josef	KIA	8	Fw 190A-6	550183 bl 7	near Epinoy a/f	0931	P-47	56 FG
16-03-44	Fhj-Fw.	Fieguth, Hans-Gerhard	WIA	10	Bf 109G-6	162030 bk 9	St. Dizier	1420	P-47	78 FG
16-03-44	Ofhr.	Juhre, Hermann	WIA	10	Bf 109G-6	18830 bk 2	St. Dizier	1420	P-47	78 FG
16-03-44	Fw.	Kraft, Werner	WIA	10	Bf 109G-6	161791 bk 10	SE of Vitry-les-Reims	1430	P-47	78 FG
16-03-44	Fhj-Fw.	Winkel, Kurt	KIA	10	Bf 109G-6	161436 bk 5	W of Vitry-les-Reims	1200	P-47	56 FG
16-03-44	Uffz.	Gehrke, Heinz	WIA	11	Bf 109G-6		SE of St. Dizier	1327	P-47	356 FG

17 March

The Second Gruppe was scrambled in early afternoon against a B-26 raid. It was unable to follow the ordered course owing to the weather, and returned to base early, but not until one of its Focke-Wulfs was shot down by the escort. The pilot was not injured.

18 March

The 8th Air Force attempted another attack on aviation industry targets in southern Germany. Forty-three of the 738 bombers dispatched failed to return to England. The First Gruppe took off from Florennes at 1155 and flew to Mannheim-Sandhofen to refuel and await the returning bombers. The Focke-Wulfs scrambled at 1415 and intercepted the B-17 stream near Ulm. Obfw. Erich Scheyda of the 3rd Staffel shot down a 100th Bomb Group aircraft, but Ogfr. Heinz Schulz was shot down by a P-51 and bailed out with severe wounds. After the Gruppe returned to Florennes, Uffz. Johann-Heinrich Gulecke was found to be missing. He disappeared during the mission, probably another victim of the Mustangs.

The Third Gruppe flew a successful mission, although most details are lacking. Hptm. Staiger claimed a B-17 over Colmar. One Messerschmitt was damaged, but no-one was injured.

As part of the preparations for the expected Allied invasion, all Geschwader pilots were to be trained to drop bombs. This was difficult to accomplish under the prevailing circumstances. Gefr. Rudolf Franke and Gefr. Hans Sandoz of the 2nd Staffel were on a practice bombing mission near Namur when they were attacked by P-47s. Sandoz escaped, but Franke was shot down and killed.

20 March

The 8th Air Force targeted southern Germany again, but most of the bombers that completed the mission dropped on Frankfurt. The Third Gruppe took off from Vendeville and Denain and headed for Laon-Athies, their assembly field. Uffz. Karl Frank did not make it. He lost control of his aircraft in the clouds and crashed, dying before flying his first combat mission. After taking off from Athies, the Gruppe was attacked by 356th Fighter Group P-47s, and Obfw. Alfons Gräve was shot down and killed by the American group commander, LCol. Einar Malmstrom. The small Messerschmitt formation stayed airborne but hidden in the clouds until the bulk of the withdrawing bombers and escort had passed. Oblt. Schauder then located a single straggling 401st Bomb Group B-17 near Reims, and after ordering his Staffel to remain alert for fighters, shot it down.

JG 26 Casualties: 18 - 20 March 1944

Date	Rank	Name	Cas	Unit	Aircraft	WNr Mkgs	Place	Time	Cause	Allied Unit
18-03-44	Gefr.	Franke, Rudolf	KIA	2	Fw 190A-6	550903 bk 7	Münster-Achery		P-47	
18-03-44	Uffz.	Gulecke, J-Heinrich	KIA	2	Fw 190A-6	550464 bk 3	Florennes	1436	missing	
18-03-44	Ogfr.	Schulz, Heinz	WIA	3	Fw 190A-6	470080 yl 15	W of Ulm		P-51	
20-03-44	Uffz.	Frank, Karl	KIFA	10	Bf 109G-6	410707 bk 16	15km E of Hirson	1250	crashed	non-op
20-03-44	Obfw.	Gräve, Alfons	KIA	12	Bf 109G-6	27041 bl 2	5km W of Reims	1325	P-47	356 FG

21 March

Obfw. Johann Edmann returned today to the 4th Staffel at Wevelgem after completing his tour as a Jagdgruppe West instructor. He was immediately put on the duty roster. On his first scramble, he was caught by some Mustangs that were flying a sweep, and was shot down and killed.

23 March

Most of the 768 bombardiers taking part in the 8th Air Force's mission to north-central Germany could not find their primary targets, and dropped on targets of opportunity between Brunswick and Osnabrück. Thirty bombers and four fighters were lost. The Third Gruppe moved to Mainz-Finthen to attack the returning bombers; the intermediate airfields of the other two Gruppen are unknown. The First and Second Gruppen made contact with the Third Bomb Division over the southern Netherlands; Lt. Willius and Uffz. Schlögl each shot down a B-17 near Tilburg, but a bomber gunner hit Uffz. Dieter Menz of the 6th Staffel, and he crashed in his plane. The Third Gruppe encountered the escort east of Bochholt, and Uffz. Otto Salewski's Messerschmitt was hit. He bailed out successfully, but was severely injured on landing.

The First Gruppe put up a flight of interceptors in the evening to oppose a B-26 raid on Poix. The propeller control on Lt. Georg Kiefner's Fw 190 failed after an air combat over the coast. He fled at low altitude, pursued by No. 312 Sqd. Spitfires. When he had to pull up to clear a row of poplars near Courtrai, his aircraft was hit. He bailed out immediately, and was taken to the hospital there to have his splinter wounds operated on. After six weeks of convalescent leave, he was back in action in May.

24 March

The 8th Air Force target for today was Schweinfurt, but only sixty B-17s bombed the primary. One hundred and forty-eight B-24s bombed the airfield at St. Dizier, killing two members of the Third Gruppe staff, destroying one Go 145, and damaging one Bf 109. The B-17s received very little attention from the Jagdwaffe, and the only Fortress

"Brown 5", a 7th Staffel Fw 190A-8, taxies out for takeoff with a photographer in the baggage compartment. The fighter has the light-weight drop tank rack common in JG 26 in this period – spring 1944. *(Bundesarchiv-Bildarchiv)*

Oblt. Waldemar Radener, Kapitän of the 7th Staffel, plays "Jägerspiel" (hunters' or fighter pilots' game) for the photographer – spring 1944. *(Bundesarchiv-Bildarchiv)*

lost to the defenses was a 305th Bomb Group aircraft that was downed east of Courtrai by Fw. Robert Hager of the 4th Staffel. Uffz. Richard Vogel of the 10th Staffel turned his Bf 109 over while landing on Charleville after a transfer flight. He was injured, and the airplane was heavily damaged.

25 March

In the day's only Allied raid, 140 B-26s bombed the Hirson railroad yards. Jafü 5 had the primary responsibility for the interception, and scrambled II/JG 2, but also called on Jafü 4, which sent small flights from the Second and Third Gruppen. Oblt. Matoni's Schwarm, which contained pilots from both the 5th and 7th Staffeln, was attacked by a large number of 368th Fighter Group Thunderbolts near Laon; Uffz. Franz Schilling was hit and crashed in his aircraft.

26 March

Five hundred B-17s and B-24s attacked V-1 sites on the Pas de Calais and around Cherbourg. Jafü 4 and Jafü 5 both ordered their fighters inland in anticipation of an attack on Paris. No attempt was made to intercept the bombers after they turned to bomb their coastal targets. Uffz. Anton Geissler of the 11th Staffel crashed and was killed on a transfer flight; no reason was determined.

Hptm. Mietusch received a hard-earned Knight's Cross today, after his 60th victory.

27 March

Eleven Luftwaffe airfields in France were bombed by 701 B-17s and B-24s. II/JG 2 managed to down two B-17s, but JG 26 was unable to get past the escorts. Apparently all three Gruppen (with a total of no more than thirty aircraft) became involved with P-47s of the 359th Fighter Group around Chartres. Hptm. Staiger led four of his fighters in a bounce on one squadron out of the sun, and brought down one Thunderbolt. Lt. Willius and Lt. Reischer also claimed Thunderbolts, but only one P-47 failed to return to England. Fw. Gerhard Guttmann took off late and was shot down easily before contacting his Gruppe.

JG 26 Victory Claims: 18 - 27 March 1944

Date	Rank	Name	Unit	Cl #	Aircraft	Place	Time	Opponent	Conf
18-03-44	Obfw.	Scheyda	3	19	B-17	Ulm (CV4)	1455	100 BG	yes
18-03-44	Hptm.	Staiger	12 CO	46	B-17	Colmar			unk
20-03-44	Oblt.	Schauder	10 CO	16	B-17	W of Reims (TH)	1300	401 BG	yes
23-03-44	Lt.	Willius	2 CO	48	B-17	Tilburg (KL6)	1140	385 BG	yes
23-03-44	Uffz.	Schlögl	3	1	B-17	Tilburg (KL)	1145	96 BG	yes
24-03-44	Fw.	Hager R.	4	2	B-17	E of Courtrai (NH2)	1215	305 BG	yes
27-03-44	Lt.	Willius	2 CO	49	P-47	SE of Dreux (BD1-4)	1424	359 FG	yes
27-03-44	Lt.	Reischer	11 CO	9	P-47	NE of Chartres (BD8)	1427	359 FG	yes
27-03-44	Hptm.	Staiger	12 CO	47	P-47	NE of Chartres (BD)	1435	359 FG	unk

29 March

Three First Gruppe pilots were awarded the German Cross in Gold: Oblt. Artur Beese (posthumously) (twenty-two victories), Obfw. Hans Heitmann (eleven victories), and Fhj.-Fw. Gerhard Wiegand (twenty-one victories).

JG 26 Casualties: 21 - 27 March 1944

Date	Rank	Name	Cas	Unit	Aircraft	WNr	Mkgs	Place	Time	Cause	Allied Unit
21-03-44	Obfw.	Edmann, Johann	KIA	4	Fw 190A-6			unknown		P-51	
23-03-44	Lt.	Kiefner, Georg	WIA	1	Fw 190A-6	530948	wh 11	Menin	1314	Spitfire	312 Sqd
23-03-44	Uffz.	Menz, Dieter	KIA	6	Fw 190A-6	550575	bl 13	N of	1345	B-17	
								s'Hertogenbosch			
23-03-44	Uffz.	Salewski, Otto	WIA	12	Bf 109G-6	161784	bl 14	Helburg-Ruhr		fighter	
24-03-44	Uffz.	Vogel, Richard	WIFA	10	Bf 109G-6	162027	wh 3	Charleville a/f	1215	landing	non-op
25-03-44	Uffz.	Schilling, Franz	KIA	7	Fw 190A-7	340325	br 6	Laon-Charleville		P-47	366 FG
26-03-44	Uffz.	Geissler, Anton	KIFA	11	Bf 109G-4	14987	yl 13	W of Meaux	1655	crashed	non-op
27-03-44	Fw.	Guttmann, Gerhard	KIA	5	Fw 190A-7	643708	wh 11	Chartres		P-47	359 FG

31 March

Today marked the end of the Allied Combined Bomber Offensive. The 8th Air Force would be under General Eisenhower's command until the invasion. The heavy bombers flew missions on twenty-three days during the month, despite continued bad weather, at a cost of 349 aircraft. During March the German fighter force lost 22% of its total pilot strength. The Reich defense force (Luftflotte Reich and Luftflotte 3) lost 229 pilots killed and missing, and 103 wounded. JG 26 lost twenty pilots killed in action, plus seven in accidents; the dead included two Staffelkapitäne. The Jagdwaffe was incapable of replacing its losses of the previous two months during the late-March lull. On 31 March, JG 26, which had an establishment strength of 208 airplanes and pilots, reported fifty-seven aircraft operational out of seventy-three on strength. Of 175 pilots "on the books" of the Geschwader, only seventy-six were available for duty.

Geschwader personnel moves during March included: the transfer of Major Wilhelm Gäth to the Luftwaffe mission in Hungary as fighter liaison officer, and the naming of Hptm. Johannes Naumann as his permanent replacement as Second Gruppe Kommandeur; the transfer of Oblt. Werner Stoll into the Geschwader, and his assignment to the 6th Staffel; the transfer of Lt. Peter Rober, a former transport pilot, into the 6th Staffel from 10/ZG 1; the transfer of Lt. Hermann Müller into the 7th Staffel from 10/ZG 1; the return of Lt. Heinrich Beer to the 3rd Staffel after six months of instructor duty; the return of Obfw. Johann Edmann and Uffz. Karl Weiss to the 4th Staffel from instructor duty; the transfer of Lt. Wolfgang Grimm from the First Gruppe to the Second; the departure of Fw. Wilhelm Mayer for instructor duty; and the transfer of Fhr. Otto Meyer to JG 2 from the 3rd Staffel.

Pilots assigned to the Geschwader during March after completing flight training included: Uffz. Gerhard Corinth, Uffz. Hermann Grad, Uffz. Paul Munack, Lt. Günther Pokorny, Ogfr. Thomas Schwertl, Uffz. Wilhelm Sonnenberg - First Gruppe; Lt. Josef Grimmer, Uffz. Gerhard Langhammer, Uffz. Kurt Petzsch, Oblt. Horst Siemsen, Lt. Siegfried Sy, Fw. Fritz Thiem - Second Gruppe; Uffz. Heinz Gehrke, Gefr. Harry Geiler, Uffz. Werner Henske, Uffz. Robert Röhrig - Third Gruppe.

1 April

The 8th Air Force scheduled a mission to southern Germany, but poor visibility at the time of take-off and high clouds made it very difficult to form up, and only the B-24s continued with the mission; they bombed, among other things, Schiffhausen, a town in Switzerland. The First and Third Gruppen met II/JG 2 over Reims. The combined force attacked a combat wing of B-24s and apparently shot down one 93rd Bomb Group aircraft. Uffz. Boeckl of the 12th Staffel and two JG 2 pilots received credit for it. The engine of Uffz. Kurt Hofer's Focke-Wulf was hit, and he was killed when he attempted a forced landing. The remaining aircraft landed, probably at Laon-Athies, and awaited the return of the bombers.

When the Third Gruppe took off again it located the only unescorted B-24 group, the 448th, which was still off course after bombing Switzerland. Two 11th Staffel pilots, Lt. Reischer and Uffz. Gehrke, shot down Liberators in the Reims-St. Pol area. An hour later the 4th Staffel duty Schwarm was scrambled from Wevelgem and located one last 448th Bomb Group aircraft struggling across the Pas de Calais. Obfw. Schwarz hit it, and claimed its destruction, but the Liberator flew on with one engine before finally settling into the Channel. It stayed together long enough for the crew to escape and climb into the one functioning life raft; eight of the ten-man crew survived forty-four hours in the water before being rescued by a passing fishing boat.

Fw. Wolfgang Polster took seven Third Gruppe pilots to Neubiberg in a Ju 52 on an unusual mission – to pick up new Bf 109s directly from the Messerschmitt production line at Augsburg. The men were immediately commandeered and told to ferry some fighters to the Balkans. A telephone call to Obstlt. Priller got that order canceled, but Polster made fourteen flights in four days in an attempt to locate fighters for his Gruppe.

Several promotions were announced this week. Karl Borris and Klaus Mietusch were promoted to Major. Addi Glunz and Fred Heckmann, who had been leading their Staffeln for some time as Oberfeldwebel (master sergeants), received war-service commissions as Leutnants.

JG 26 Victory Claims: 1 April 1944

Date	Rank	Name	Unit	Cl #	Aircraft	Place	Time	Opponent	Conf
01-04-44	Obfw.	Schwarz E.	4	8	B-24	E of St. Omer (NF7)	1502	448 BG	yes
01-04-44	Lt.	Reischer	11 CO	10	B-24	St Pol (OE7-PE1)	1330	448 BG	yes
01-04-44	Uffz.	Gehrke	11	1	B-24	W of Épernay (UG7)	1352	448 BG	unk
01-04-44	Uffz.	Böckl	12		B-24	NW of Reims	1150	93 BG	yes

A groundcrewman refuels Lt. Kempf's Bf 109G-6 "white 9" at a stop for refuelling at Lille-Nord in late March or early April. *(Bundesarchiv-Bildarchiv)*

4 April

Fw. Polster and his pilots ferried new Bf 109G-6s from Wiesbaden to Vendeville. The aircraft had no weapons or radios. Polster was attacked on the flight by a Spitfire that he mistook for a Dewoitine 520, an ex-French fighter used by Jagdwaffe operational training units. His fighter sustained damage, and Polster was very upset that he was not credited with a combat sortie for this flight.

7 April

The engine of Oblt. Max Groth's Fw 190A-6 caught fire on his transfer flight to join the First Gruppe, and he bailed out with injuries that kept him from reporting for duty for two weeks. Groth was a decorated bomber pilot who had just finished his fighter conversion training. He was also an "unshakeable Nazi", in the words of the Geschwader honors book. Such men were so rare that special notice was taken of them in the Geschwader.

8 April

The B-17s and B-24s that could form up despite the fog covering much of England left the coast at noon to bomb airfields and aircraft industry targets visible beneath the clear skies over north-central Germany. The Jagdwaffe concentrated its attacks on the B-24 wings; at first probably by chance, and later because of their disorganization. Thirty B-24s, four B-17s, and twenty-three escorting fighters were lost.

The Geschwader was not called upon to intercept the incoming bombers; the pilots remained on their bases to await the withdrawal phase. The First and Third Gruppen scrambled at 1415 and flew north to the Zuider Zee; there is no data on the activities of the Second Gruppe at this time.

The Third Gruppe reached the B-24 stream first, and made one pass before the fighters arrived. Fw. Polster damaged one bomber, and then joined up with two other Messerschmitt pilots to attack a pair of P-51s. Polster out-turned one, hit it, and watched it crash in flames south of Vechta. The 355th Fighter Group pilot bailed out and was taken prisoner. The Third Gruppe formation broke up, and the pilots began looking for stragglers. Fw. Walter Gocksch spotted a lone Thunderbolt and shot it down into the Zuider Zee; the 353rd Fighter Group airplane was already damaged, having struck a tree while strafing an airfield.

When the First Gruppe reached the B-24 stream, Oblt. Charlie Willius led an immediate head-on attack on the heavily-escorted lead combat wing, despite orders from the controller to attack the rearmost bombers. The little band of Focke-Wulfs tore through the B-24s and climbed back into the sun. Willius's target, a 44th Bomb Group aircraft, dropped away from the formation in flames. While reforming, the Staffel was hit by a flight of four Thunderbolts from the 361st Fighter Group. Willius and his wingman, Fw. Jan Schild, made a quick Abschwung and headed for the deck. Schild saw a Thunderbolt 150 yards behind Willius's aircraft, firing; pieces were already flying off the Focke-Wulf. Schild evaded the Thunderbolt attacking him and banked toward the one on Willius' tail, giving it a high-deflection burst from the side. The American fighter broke off its attack, trailing smoke. Schild claimed its probable destruction, but the fighter was apparently not severely damaged. Willius's Focke-Wulf was then seen by the Americans to spin into the ground and explode. Schild dived away again, evading another flight of P-47s by flying at low level between the smokestacks and towers of the Ruhr. No German witnessed Willius's crash. His body was not recovered until 1967, buried in his Fw 190 fifteen feet deep in a Dutch polder. Oblt. Willius received a posthumous award of the Knight's Cross for his forty-eight victories, obtained on 371 combat flights. Jan Schild, a mere Feldwebel (staff sergeant), became leader of the 2nd Staffel for operations; Lt. Herbert Weide took over the administrative duties, but lived for only two more days.

The second pair of Thunderbolts in the flight dived through these combatants in

Emil Babenz of the 2nd Staffel. Seen here as a Feldwebel, he was an Oberfeldwebel with 24 victories when killed on 8 April by a 361st Fighter Group P-47. *(Vanoverbeke)*

search of their own targets. One pilot put a burst of .50 caliber machine gun fire into a fighter from 100 yards (90 meters) range, at which the Fw 190 took violent evasive action, split-S'd, and dived vertically away. The American pilot lost sight of it, but claimed its probable destruction. The German fighter did, in fact, continue its terminal dive into the ground, taking *Fähnenjunker-Oberfeldwebel* (senior officer candidate) Emil Babenz to his death. Babenz was one of the most experienced pilots in the Geschwader. He had been an original member of the 11th *Höhen* (high altitude) Staffel in 1942, and had survived its destruction in Tunisia, ultimately returning to JG 26 after serving in the Mediterranean Theater with JG 53. He had been credited with twenty-four victories in 335 combat flights. Charlie Willius was the most aggressive combat leader in the First Gruppe, and Emil Babenz was just regaining his form after his enervating experiences in the Med. These men were, of course, irreplaceable.

Obfw. Erich Scheyda gained a small measure of revenge for the First Gruppe when he chased another 361st Fighter Group Thunderbolt to low altitude and shot it down.

JG 26 Victory Claims: 8 April 1944

Date	Rank	Name	Unit	Cl #	Aircraft	Place	Time	Opponent	Conf
08-04-44	Lt.	Willius	2 CO	50	B-24	near Zwolle (FN)	1518	44 BG	yes
08-04-44	Lt.	Schild	2		P-47	Gelsenkirchen	1600	361 FG	no
08-04-44	Obfw.	Scheyda	3	20	P-47	Lingen (FP)	1520	361 FG	yes
08-04-44	Fw.	Gocksch	10		P-47	S of Assen (EN-EO)	1510	353 FG	yes
08-04-44	Fw.	Polster	11	3	P-51	E of Zwolle (EO-FO)	1515	355 FG	yes

JG 26 Casualties: 1 - 8 April 1944

Date	Rank	Name	Cas	Unit	Aircraft	WNr	Mkgs	Place	Time	Cause	Allied Unit
01-04-44	Uffz.	Hofer, Kurt	KIA	3	Fw 190A-7	340302	yl 8	N of Reims-Pont Faverger		B-24	
07-04-44	Oblt.	Groth, Max	WIFA	1	Fw 190A-6	530918	wh 6	Soissons		engine fire non-op	
08-04-44	Fhj-Ofw.	Babenz, Emil	KIA	2	Fw 190A-6	470046	bk 1	near Bentheim	1545	P-47	361 FG
08-04-44	Oblt.	Willius, Karl	KIA	2 CO	Fw 190A-8	170009	bk 5	near Zwolle-Kamperzeedijk	1545	P-47	361 FG

9 April

The OKL situation map for this date indicates that the 6th and 9th Staffeln had completed their training at St. Dizier and returned to their Gruppen at Cambrai-Epinoy and Lille-Vendeville. Another recent move saw the 5th and 7th Staffeln leave Grevillers for the small field known as Cambrai-Sud, where they were much nearer the rest of the Gruppe.

10 April

In the morning the 8th Air Force began its new top-priority campaign of softening up the invasion coast. The heavy bombers attacked a number of airfields in France. Although two Gruppen of JG 2 attempted to intercept this armada, JG 26 did not. The First Gruppe base of Florennes was one of the targeted airfields. The Gruppe had already begun a permanent move to Vendeville, and casualties were light. One pilot, Uffz. Franz Afflerbach, was killed when a hangar collapsed. Two Gruppe aircraft were destroyed, one Fw 190 and one Bf 108.

In late afternoon the heavy bombers visited some V-1 sites, joined by 9th Air Force medium bombers. The Jafü 4 and Jafü 5 controllers thought at first that the formations over the Channel were heavy bombers headed for Paris, and sent their fighters south. By the time the German fighters had returned to the vicinity of the bombers, their fuel was too low for effective attacks. While on this futile mission Lt. Herbert Weide of the 2nd Staffel, which was now flying from Wevelgem, was shot down by a fighter near Laon and killed. Uffz. Hermann Ayerle of the 12th Staffel caught a single Mosquito flying north of Verdun at only 4000 meters (13,000 feet) altitude and shot it down. If Ayerle's identification was correct, this can only have been a No. 540 Squadron photo-reconnaissance aircraft, which disappeared on a mission to Friedrichshaven.

11 April

Taking advantage of improved weather conditions, the 8th Air Force dispatched 857 bombers to attack aircraft factories in central and eastern Germany. Luftflotte Reich made effective use of its fighter resources, coordinating the attacks of its single-engine and twin-engine fighters and bringing down sixty-four bombers and sixteen escorts. The services of Luftflotte 3 were not requested, and JG 2 and JG 26 spent the day on routine operations. The First Gruppe lost one Focke-Wulf destroyed and five damaged in an airfield strafing attack, whether on Vendeville or Florennes is not stated, and two pilots and aircraft on what should have been a routine transfer flight. Uffz. Heinz Voigt and Uffz. Karl Weiss of the 4th Staffel were caught flying wingtip to wingtip at 1000 feet (300 meters) by a flight of 352nd Fighter Group P-51s on a strafing mission. The American flight leader had just shot down a Ju 52 west of Torgau when he saw the two Focke-Wulfs beneath him. Entering a diving skid, he hit them both with a single high-deflection burst, and watched them crash.

12 April

The 8th Air Force dispatched 455 heavy bombers to bomb Luftwaffe targets in central Germany. Clouds and dense contrails caused severe problems in assembly and rendezvous, and ultimately forced the cancellation of the mission. However, the B-24s of the Second Bomb Division did not turn back until they had reached the German border. The Jafü 4 controller anticipated the direction of the Allied thrust correctly and had assembled three JG 26 and two JG 2 Staffeln over Juvincourt. When the B-24s' exact location was determined, the German fighters were directed to Luxembourg under Oblt. Matoni's command. Matoni found the bombers and a large number of fighters near Liège and began trailing them. When a thin layer of stratus cloud interposed itself between the 445th Bomb Group and its fighter escort, the German fighters attacked from beneath, pumping 20 mm cannon shells into the Liberators' thin bellies. Five bombers went down before the Thunderbolt escorts regained sight of their charges and went to their defense. Matoni and his Second Gruppe pilots claimed two outright victories, seven bombers separated from formation, and one destroyed after separation, but only three claims were confirmed. The JG 2 pilots also claimed three B-24s. Many damaged bombers were able to reach the clouds after leaving their formations and thus escape destruction.

Thunderbolts of the 78th and 366th Fighter Groups chased the Focke-Wulfs in and around the clouds and shot six of them down. Three Second Gruppe pilots, Uffz. Karl

Major Mietusch preparing to taxi out and take off in his "black 22". By this time, most Third Gruppe aircraft were equipped with the Erla-Haube (clear canopy), which markedly improved a Messerschmitt pilot's vision – Lille-Nord, March-April. *(Bundesarchiv-Bildarchiv)*

Gathof, Lt. Wolfgang Grimm, and Uffz. Karl Willand, and one JG 2 pilot were killed; two JG 26 pilots bailed out without injury.

Major Mietusch's Messerschmitts were unable to find an opening in the escort. They suffered no combat losses, but Mietusch hit a bomb crater while landing on his new field at Rouvres-Étain, and his Bf 109 turned over. Mietusch suffered concussion and was sent back to the hospital for another three weeks.

Later in the afternoon, 251 9th Air Force B-26s and A-20s attacked Belgian airfields, including Wevelgem, as well as other targets. Obstlt. Priller's Stabsschwarm scrambled from Lille-Nord, and the 4th Staffel got away from Wevelgem, but their objective was to save their aircraft rather than intercept the bombers. Priller stayed within sight of the field and radioed the pilots when it was safe to return and land, with caution.

JG 26 Victory Claims: 10 - 12 April 1944

Date	Rank	Name	Unit	Cl #	Aircraft	Place	Time	Opponent	Conf
10-04-44	Uffz.	Ayerle	12		Mosquito	N of Verdun (TL6)	1705	540 Sqd	yes
12-04-44	Oblt.	Matoni	5 CO	18	B-24-HSS	SE of Liège	1305	445 BG	yes
12-04-44	Oblt.	Matoni	5 CO	17	B-24-HSS	S of Liège	1328	445 BG	yes
12-04-44	Uffz.	Falkner	5		B-24-eV	SSE of Goesnes- S of Huy	1317	445 BG	no
12-04-44	Uffz.	Falkner	5	1	B-24-HSS	near Liège	1305	445 BG	yes
12-04-44	Uffz.	Wyrich	5		P-47	Liège	1315		no
12-04-44	Lt.	Radener	7 CO	16	B-24-HSS	18km N of Namur (OM-PM)	1310	445 BG	yes
12-04-44	Fw.	Vogt	7	23	B-24-HSS	SW of Liège	1308	445 BG	unk
12-04-44	Fw.	Vogt	7	22	B-24-HSS	near Liège (OL-OM)	1328	445 BG	unk
12-04-44	Lt.	Hofmann W.	8 CO	11	B-24	52km E of Charleville (RL6)	1340	445 BG	yes
12-04-44	Fhr.	Busch W.	8	2	B-24	12km NE of Namur	1338	445 BG	yes
12-04-44	Uffz.	Schulwitz	8	3	B-24-HSS	SW of Liège	1320	445 BG	unk

JG 26 Casualties: 10 - 12 April 1944

Date	Rank	Name	Cas	Unit	Aircraft	WNr	Mkgs	Place	Time	Cause	Allied Unit
10-04-44	Lt.	Weide, Herbert	KIA	2	Fw 190A-6	550459	bk 2	Laon-Couvron		fighter	
10-04-44	Uffz.	Afflerbach, Franz	KIA	3	none			Florennes a/f		bomb	n/a

11-04-44	Uffz.	Voigt, Heinz	KIA	4	Fw 190A-7	170038 bl 4	Neiden-Torgau	1200	P-51	352 FG
11-04-44	Uffz.	Weiss, Karl	KIA	4	Fw 190A-7	170042 bl 7	near Neiden-Torgau	1200	P-51	352 FG
12-04-44	Uffz.	Gathof, Karl	KIA	6	Fw 190A-7	430484 br 1	5km S of Malmedy	1330	P-47	78 or 366 FG
12-04-44	Lt.	Grimm, Wolfgang	KIA	6	Fw 190A-6		Malmedy		P-47	78 or 366 FG
12-04-44	Uffz.	Willand, Karl	KIA	8	Fw 190A-5	2578 bl 2	N of Dinant	1315	P-47	78 FG
12-04-44	Major	Mietusch, Klaus	WIA	III CO	Bf 109G-6	162345 bk 24	Rouvres-Étain	1415	landing	n/a

13 April

The 8th Air Force put 626 bombers into the air, escorted by twenty-four groups of USAAF fighters. Clear weather over Germany, a noon departure, and a straight south-eastern course by the heavy bombers identified their target area as deep central or southern Germany, and the Luftwaffe controllers began concentrating their fighters early. Oblt. Matoni led the Second Gruppe up from Cambrai at 1209 under orders to meet a JG 2 Gruppe over Reims. But Matoni thought the controller had said to fly at *zwo* (2000 meters) while he had actually said *hoch* (high), and assembly over Reims was delayed while the Gruppe climbed from 2000 to 7000 meters (6500 to 23,000 feet). Matoni was then put in charge of the combined formation and ordered to attack three oncoming waves of bombers over Florennes. Matoni split his force and led half in a head-on attack, while the rest attacked from the rear, out of the sun. Warned constantly of American fighters, the Focke-Wulfs then repeated their attacks from the rear, reassembling in the clouds below. After eleven minutes, the pilots were ordered to break away and land at Athies or Juvincourt, but some stayed with the bombers for another twenty minutes and landed at Trier. Second Gruppe pilots filed two claims for separations and one for a final destruction. The escort, 78th Fighter Group Thunderbolts, succeeded in downing two 6th Staffel Fw 190s, killing Uffz. Karl Dehsbesell and severely injuring Oblt. Werner Stoll. The 8th Staffel Kapitän, Lt. Hofmann, shot down one of the P-47s at 1344, just as the last of the Gruppe pilots were leaving the bomber stream.

The Third Gruppe scrambled from their isolated field at Étain, which was between Verdun and Metz, and flew due east, meeting the bomber stream near Kaiserslautern and joining the Second Gruppe for the last of their attacks. Ofhr. Kemethmüller was

A taxiing 9th Staffel Bf 109G-6/U4, "white 11" – Lille-Nord, March-April. *(Bundesarchiv-Bildarchiv)*

A taxiing Third Gruppe Bf 109G-6/U4 – Lille-Nord, March-April. *(Bundesarchiv-Bildarchiv)*

credited with one B-17. Hptm. Staiger also claimed a B-17, and Stabsfw. Guhl claimed a P-47; neither of these two claims was confirmed. The Gruppe then returned to Étain to await the bombers' return. The bombers flew on the reciprocal of their inbound track, and so the interception took place in the same area, between Kaiserslautern and Karlsruhe. They were joined by those Second Gruppe aircraft that had landed at Trier. Only Oblt. Matoni of the latter unit scored, claiming a P-47 that was not confirmed. The Messerschmitt pilots did better; Uffz. Gehrke was credited with a B-17, and Uffz. Kurt Beck and an unnamed pilot teamed up to separate and destroy a second B-17.

Uffz. Boeckl of the 12th Staffel also claimed a B-17, but the time and location are unknown. Uffz. Beck was shot down after his victory, probably by a 56th Fighter Group P-47, and bailed out with slight wounds. Three more Third Gruppe Messerschmitts were shot down during the day, but their pilots escaped injury. Hptm. Staiger caught a 364th Fighter Group P-38 that was lagging behind its formation, and shot it down southeast of Bitburg; the American pilot's remains were not recovered until 1996.

The day's last victory was scored by Obstlt. Priller, who took off at about 1630 with his Stabsschwarm and the Führungsstaffel, the 4th, and operated against stragglers trying to cross the Pas de Calais. A 401st Bomb Group B-17 was located and shot down north of St. Omer at 1710. This was Priller's 96th victory, his first since the Münster raid the previous October. His duties at St. Pol had left him little time for flying.

JG 26 Victory Claims: 13 April 1944

Date	Rank	Name	Unit	Cl #	Aircraft	Place	Time	Opponent	Conf
13-04-44	Obstlt.	Priller	Ge CO	96	B-17	Poperinghe-N of St Omer	1710		yes
13-04-44	Oblt.	Matoni	5 CO	19	B-17-HSS	15km W of Bitburg	1325	303 BG	yes
13-04-44	Oblt.	Matoni	5 CO	20	P-47	32km N of Kaiserslautern	1600		unk
13-04-44	Uffz.	M...hauer?	5		B-17-eV	NW of Trier	1325		no
13-04-44	Fw.	Vogt	7	24	B-17-HSS	near Trier (SO2-5)	1323		no
13-04-44	Lt.	Hofmann W.	8 CO	12	P-47	near Trier	1344	78 FG	yes
13-04-44	Ofhr.	Kemethmüller	9		B-17-dam	NW of Kaiserslautern (SP)	1334		dam
13-04-44	Uffz.	Beck	11	10	B-17-HSS	NE of Karlsruhe	1554		unk
13-04-44	Obfw.	F...t?	11		B-17-eV	NE of Karlsruhe	1554		no
13-04-44	Uffz.	Gehrke	11	2	B-17	Karlsruhe (US 7-9)	1550		yes
13-04-44	Stfw.	Guhl	11	10	P-47	Glanbrücken?	1324		unk
13-04-44	Hptm.	Staiger	12 CO	49	P-38	W of Trier (RN8)	1620	364 FG	yes
13-04-44	Hptm.	Staiger	12 CO	48	B-17F	NW of Kaiserslautern (SP)	1334		unk
13-04-44	Uffz.	Böckl	12	5	B-17	unknown			unk

9th Staffel Bf 109G-6/U4, "white 18" running up its engine. Lt. Dietwin Pape was shot down in this aircraft on 22 June – Lille-Nord, March-April. *(Bundesarchiv-Bildarchiv)*

A springtime inspection of JG 26 by Generalfeldmarschall Erwin Rommel. *(Meyer)*

14 April

The Third Gruppe, once again under the command of Hptm. Staiger, flew today to Pocking, on the German-Austrian border. They had been sent to southern Germany to reinforce Jagddivision 7 in advance of Hitler's birthday on 20 April, when an American attack on München, the Nazi movement's birthplace, was anticipated.

16 April

Ofhr. Kemethmüller scrambled from Pocking, but failed to make contact with any Allied aircraft. Aircraft problems forced him to make a belly landing on Wien-Aspern.

Two 7th Staffel pilots, Oblt. Waldemar Radener and Obfw. Wilhelm Mayer, were awarded the German Cross in Gold, after their sixteenth and fifteenth victories.

17 April

The Third Gruppe transferred from Pocking to München-Neubiberg. Training missions were flown in the afternoon and on the next three days, while waiting for the Americans to put in an appearance over southern Germany.

19 April

The First Gruppe scrambled in the evening to counter a B-26 raid on the railroad yard in Malines, Belgium. Major Borris led an attack on the escort, and he and Oblt. Neu each claimed a Spitfire. Nos. 310 and 312 Squadrons (Czech) each lost a Spitfire on this mission.

The flying elements of the Second Gruppe were now at Cazaux, on the French Riviera. The nominal purpose of the move was to obtain training in attacking ground targets with WGr 21 rockets, but the real reason was to give the pilots a little rest and recuperation in advance of the Allied invasion, which was expected at any time. Fw. Fritz Thiem of the 8th Staffel flew a little low over the Mediterranean, struck the water with his landing gear, and crashed. He drowned in his airplane.

22 April

The 8th Air Force dispatched a raid to the Hamm railroad yards, one of the most important transportation centers in northwestern Germany. The departure time of 1800

Oblt. Wolfgang Neu, 4th Staffel Kapitän. Neu was killed in combat with American fighters on 22 April. *(Hartigs via Petrick)*

was necessitated by the weather, but the lateness of the hour and the bombers' course gave away the probable target area, and General Schmid deployed his forces accordingly. The strength of the escort available for this relatively short-range mission, fourteen fighter groups, proved overwhelming. Had it not been for navigational mistakes, which caused the combat wings to separate, and the return to England after darkness, which gave the Luftwaffe night intruders an unprecedented opportunity to attack the bombers over their English bases, the bombers would have had to face only the Flak. Fifteen bombers and thirteen fighters were lost on the mission; another fifteen bombers were scrapped after crash-landing in England.

The First Gruppe and the semi-independent 4th Staffel were the only JG 26 units called on by Jafü 4. The aircraft at Vendeville and Wevelgem were scrambled at 1708 and flew southeast to meet the 3rd Staffel, which was already at Denain, and had already lost one pilot, Gefr. Gerhard Tyczka, on an early-morning training flight. The purpose for the Gruppe mission is unknown, as the only Allied aircraft in the area were fighters flying sweeps. The 3rd Staffel made a successful attack on one squadron of the 368th Fighter Group which was returning from an early sweep of Bonn. One Schwarm attacked from out of the sun at 7 o'clock high, while the other Schwarm attacked from the rear. Obfw. Ellenrieder claimed two of the Thunderbolts; one crashed south of Aachen, while the second made it back to England and crash-landed on the Manston emergency field. The American squadron claimed 3-0-1 Focke-Wulfs, but no German losses are known. The German pilots landed on Florennes or Bonn-Hangelar and were serviced as quickly as possible for use against the withdrawing bombers.

Probably no more than a dozen fighters made it into the air on second sorties. Hptm. Wolfgang Neu, Kapitän of the 4th Staffel, was killed in combat over the Eifel. Neu, the "old man" of the Geschwader, had overcome a slow start and had become a steady combat leader. His final record was twelve air victories, including seven heavy bombers, gained in 111 combat sorties.

The other fighters crossed Belgium looking for stragglers. Obfw. Waldemar Söffing and Fw. Michael Hecker shot down 392nd and 445th Bomb Group B-24s between Courtrai and the coast. Both bombers were already badly damaged, and the crew of the 445th Bomb Group Liberator had bailed out before it was shot down; the airplane was flying on autopilot. "Vladimir" Söffing had just returned to duty after recovering from a broken neck suffered the previous July. At 2108 the First Gruppe formation leader, identity unknown, was heard by the RAF Y-intercept operators requesting that the Wevelgem landing lights be turned on. He canceled the request at 2112, preferring to land in the dark rather than attract the attention of Allied fighters. Two Gruppe Focke-Wulfs were damaged during the day, possibly during these landing attempts.

Date	Rank	Name	Unit	Cl #	Aircraft	Place	Time	Opponent	Conf
19-04-44	Major	Borris	I CO	37	Spitfire	ENE of Mechelen	1905	310 or 312 Sqd	unk
19-04-44	Oblt.	Neu	4 CO	12	Spitfire	Brussels (NI 3)	1855	310 or 312 Sqd	unk
22-04-44	Obfw.	Söffing	1	11	B-24	E of Courtrai (NH)	2102	445 BG	unk
22-04-44	Fw.	Hecker	2	3	B-24	E of Courtrai (NH)	2103	392 BG	unk
22-04-44	Obfw.	Ellenrieder	3	6	P-47	S of Aachen (ON8)	1826	368 FG	yes
22-04-44	Obfw.	Ellenrieder	3	7	P-47	S of Aachen (ON7-8)	1828	368 FG	yes

JG 26 Casualties: 13 - 22 April 1944

Date	Rank	Name	Cas	Unit	Aircraft	WNr	Mkgs	Place	Time	Cause	Allied Unit
13-04-44	Uffz.	Dehsbesell, Karl	KIA	6	Fw 190A-6	470236	br 7	Trier-Steffeln	1320	P-47	78 FG
13-04-44	Oblt	Stoll, Werner	WIA	6	Fw 190A-7	431150	wh 6	Kaiserslautern		P-47	78 FG
13-04-44	Uffz.	Beck, Kurt	WIA	11	Bf 109G-6	162343	yl 15	NW of Würtemmberg	1330	P-47	56 FG
19-04-44	Fw.	Thiem, Fritz	KIFA	8	Fw 190A-8	170065	bl 2	near Cazaux		hit sea	non-op
22-04-44	Gefr.	Tyczka, Gerhard	KIFA	3	Fw 190A-8	680109	yl 1	Juvincourt-Laon	1312	crashed	non-op
22-04-44	Hptm.	Neu, Wolfgang	KIA	4 CO	Fw 190A-6	530755	bl 16	Katenborn-Eifel		combat	

23 April

The Third Gruppe flew its first combat mission from southern Germany. It scrambled from Neubiberg at 1305, joined up with III/JG 3 over the field, and climbed through the clouds to an altitude of 7000 meters (23,000 feet) near Steyr. Shortly after 1400 they saw two *Pulks* of 15th Air Force heavy bombers south of Vienna, returning to their bases in Italy. The bombers were escorted by the 31st Fighter Group, the first 15th Air Force unit to receive P-51s. The two Messerschmitt Gruppen attacked until their fuel ran low, and then landed on several Austrian airfields. The Third Gruppe claimed two B-17s and one B-24; III/JG 3 claimed the destruction of two B-24s, and the separation of a third. Bomber losses were five B-24s and two B-17s over Austria, and three B-24s and one B-17 on the return flight over Yugoslavia. The newly-commissioned Lt. Heinz Kemethmüller claimed two P-51s; the 31st lost three over Austria. Obfw. Johannes Pauli of the 9th Staffel failed to return from the mission, and was thought to have crashed in the Neusiedler Lake.

JG 26 Victory Claims: 23 April 1944

Date	Rank	Name	Unit	Cl #	Aircraft	Place	Time	Opponent	Conf
23-04-44	Oblt.	Dippel	9 CO	20	B-17	S of W Neustadt (FN9-FO7)	1445	97 or 483 BG	yes
23-04-44	Lt.	Kemethmüller	9		P-51	S of W Neustadt (FO-5)	1422	31 FG	yes
23-04-44	Lt.	Kemethmüller	9	76	P-51	S of Neusiedler Lake	1422	31 FG	yes
23-04-44	Lt.	Reischer	11 CO	11	B-24	E of W Neustadt (EO4)	1410	459 BG	yes
23-04-44	Hptm.	Staiger	12 CO	50	B-17	SE of W Neustadt (EO9-FO3)	1415	97 or 483 BG	yes

24 April

The weather over southern Germany was still clear, and the 8th Air Force sent 754 heavy bombers, escorted by twenty-two fighter groups, to bomb Luftwaffe targets at München, Oberpfaffenhofen, and Friedrichshafen. Resistance in the target area was unexpectedly heavy (at least in part owing to the presence of III/JG 26), and thirty-nine bombers and seventeen fighters failed to return to England. The crews of thirteen B-17s chose to fly to Switzerland for internment.

This was the day that Hptm. Staiger and the Third Gruppe had been waiting for. The Messerschmitts scrambled from Neubiberg at 1240 and climbed toward Ulm, where they met III/JG 3 at 7000 meters (23,000 feet). Staiger led the combined formation toward the position reported by the Jafü 7 controller, who was female, and thus a great novelty to the JG 26 pilots. They found the B-17 stream heavily escorted by P-51s. Staiger led the Bf 109s upsun and stayed there, waiting for the escort to leave. It didn't, but the B-17 formation soon split, and Staiger found that two combat wings had been left unescorted. These contained the 108 Fortresses bound for Oberpfaffenhofen. The German fighters were well positioned, and Staiger quickly led the thirty Bf 109s in a textbook attack from 12 o'clock high. Staiger's own Messerschmitt carried a 30 mm MK 108 cannon in its nose, and he used it to good effect, shooting down three B-17s and forcing two more from their formations, to be shot down by two young pilots in the Gruppe. The German fighters attacked repeatedly, retiring only when they had exhausted their ammunition. The final score for the Gruppe totaled twelve B-17s. Their initial head-on attack succeeded in breaking up the American combat box; thus separated, the B-17s were fairly easy prey. III/JG 3 claimed eleven B-17s. The Oberpfaffenhofen force lost twenty-six of the First Bomb Division's total of twenty-seven losses.

The frantic calls of the bomber pilots soon brought 355th Fighter Group P-51s to the rescue. Third Gruppe pilots shot down two of the Mustangs, and completed the mission without a single loss. III/JG 3 was not as fortunate, claiming the third 355th Fighter Group aircraft to go down, but losing three pilots killed and two injured, and seven of the total of twenty fighters claimed by the 355th Fighter Group this day.

The success of the Third Gruppe over southern Germany was counterbalanced by a poor performance by the Second Gruppe, back on the Kanalfront. The Gruppe had taken to the air at 1100 under the command of Oblt. Radener, and joined two JG 2 formations in an attack on the incoming bomber stream. The RAF Y-intercept service observed that Waldi's transmissions to his men were filled with cautious instructions to "close up" and "look out". No Second Gruppe aircraft was lost in this encounter, but only one pilot, Radener himself, filed a victory claim, and it was rejected. Late in the afternoon a small Second Gruppe formation was vectored toward the bombers' return route, but the German pilots' radio transmissions indicated that they were more interested in avoiding the escort fighters than in locating the bombers. No contact was made with the American formations. The RAF intelligence report commented in supercilious tones on Waldi's problems and the lack of aggressiveness shown by the once-fearsome Kanalgeschwader.

The German fighter pilots were now being treated with open contempt by their own commanders, as well. Reichsmarschall Göring used the term *Jägerschreck* (fear of fighters) to describe the pilots' excessive caution. Adolf Galland's sympathy for his beleaguered fighter pilots seemed to decrease with each passing month, and the outspoken and caustic general now took every opportunity to excoriate them. Pips Priller and his men saw things differently. They had always been fewer in numbers than their opponents across the Channel, but through mid-1943 the Germans' experience, superior equipment, and aggressive tactics had held sway. Now things were different, and they faced the future from a position of qualitative as well as quantitative inferiority. The tactics imposed by Berlin had only made things worse. For long stretches their orders for bomber intercept missions had forbidden the fighter pilots to attack enemy fighters; they were to attack only bombers. As the Allied fighters became more numerous and experienced, the gaps in their escort coverage disappeared. The Jagdwaffe's orders were now impossible to execute; the German defensive strategy was bankrupt. Berlin's response was to exhort its fighter pilots to fight more bravely, compensating for their qualitative and quantitative shortcomings with superior strength of character.

Someone in authority had the common sense to realize that mental toughness could not overcome physical exhaustion, and had ordered the Gruppen of the Kanalgeschwader to be rested. The Second Gruppe had already spent several days in Cazaux, and today the First Gruppe flew south for a brief rest period.

Date	Rank	Name	Unit	Cl #	Aircraft	Place	Time	Opponent	Conf
24-04-44	Oblt.	Radener	7 CO	17	B-17-HSS	NE of St. Dizier	1222		unk
24-04-44	Uffz.	Tamann?	7		P-51	S of Speis...see?	1340		yes
24-04-44	Oblt.	Dippel	9 CO	21	B-17	N of Augsburg	1330		unk
24-04-44	Uffz.	Zeller	9		P-51	Mühldorf-E of München (CF8-9)	1400	355 FG	unk
24-04-44	Oblt.	Schauder	10 CO		B-17	unknown			no
24-04-44	Lt.	Reischer	11 CO	12	B-17	S of Donauwörth (BB6)	1328		yes
24-04-44	Uffz.	Gehrke	11	3	B-17	Donauwörth (BB5-9)	1335		unk
24-04-44	Fw.	Laub	11	7	B-17	S of Donauwörth (BB6-9/BC4-7)	1340		unk
24-04-44	Hptm.	Staiger	12 CO		B-17	Donauwörth (BB7-8)	1330		yes
24-04-44	Hptm.	Staiger	12 CO	51	B-17	Donauwörth (BB7-8)	1330		yes
24-04-44	Hptm.	Staiger	12 CO	54	B-17	S of München (ED 5-6)	1355		yes
24-04-44	Hptm.	Staiger	12 CO	53	B-17-HSS	S of München (ED)	1355		yes
24-04-44	Hptm.	Staiger	12 CO	52	B-17-HSS	S of München (ED)	1355		yes
24-04-44	Uffz.	Ayerle	12		P-51	N of München (CD)	1405	355 FG	unk
24-04-44	Uffz.	Böckl	12		B-17	S of München (ED4-5)	1345		yes
24-04-44	Uffz.	Böckl	12		B-17	N of Murnau (EC7-FC1)	1400		yes
24-04-44	Uffz.	Leder, Joach.	12		B-17-eV	N of Innsbruck (FC7-8)	1410		no
24-04-44	Uffz.	Leder, Joach.	12	1	B-17	S of Donauwörth (BB7-8)	1330		unk
24-04-44	Fhr.	Lorberg	12		B-17-eV	N of Innsbruck (FC6)	1405		no
24-04-44	Fw.	Oeckel	12	2	B-17	S of Donauwörth (BB7-8)	1345		unk

Hptm. Hans-Georg Dippel, Kapitän of the 9th Staffel. Dippel was killed on 8 May when he lost control of his Messerschmitt while stunt flying. *(Hays)*

25 April

Three hundred and fifty-five B-17s were dispatched to bomb airfields in France, and 129 B-24s were sent to bomb the railroad yards in Mannheim. The Second Gruppe put up a small force versus the incoming formations. Uffz. Werner Pietruschka of the 5th Staffel shot down a 458th Bomb Group B-24 near Vitry-le-Francois, but 78th Fighter Group P-47s shot down two 6th Staffel Focke-Wulfs in the same area. One pilot bailed out without injury, but Uffz. Werner Salomo was killed.

The Third Gruppe spent the day reassembling its scattered pilots at Neubiberg. Several had landed on strange airfields after the mission of the 24th, and were enjoying their new surroundings. Uffz. Gehrke suffered slight injuries when force-landing his Bf 109 after its engine failed while he was making a victory pass over the Neubiberg landing ground, and had to answer to Hptm. Staiger.

26 April

The First Gruppe holiday at Cazaux was marred by a sailboat accident which killed two pilots. The new leader of the 1st Staffel, Oblt. Kurt Kranefeld, and one of his pilots, Ofhr. Josef Burglechner, were drowned when their sailboat capsized. Oblt. Groth, an experienced officer but a brand-new fighter pilot, replaced Kranefeld as 1st Staffel leader.

Date	Rank	Name	Cas	Unit	Aircraft	WNr	Mkgs	Place	Time	Cause	Allied Unit
23-04-44	Obfw.	Pauli, Johannes	KIA	9	Bf 109G-6	162249	wh 15	Neusiedler See	1430	missing	
25-04-44	Uffz.	Salomo, Werner	KIA	6	Fw 190A-6			Vitry-le-Francois		P-47	78 FG
25-04-44	Uffz.	Gehrke, Heinz	WIFA	11	Bf 109G-6			München-Neubiberg		engine	non-op
26-04-44	Oblt.	Kranefeld, Kurt	KAC	1 CO	none			Cazaux		drowned	non-op
26-04-44	Ofhr.	Burglechner, Josef	KAC	1	none			Cazaux		drowned	non-op

27 April

The 8th Air Force turned its attention to tactical targets, V-1 sites on the coast and various railroad centers in the interior of France. The Third Gruppe was returning from Neubiberg, and some of these pilots were called on to assist in the interception from Étain. The Messerschmitt pilots had no known successes, and Uffz. Ernst Lessin of the 12th Staffel was shot down by the bomber gunners, crashing in his plane near Reims. Uffz. Heinz Schreiber of the 11th Staffel ran out of fuel near Thionville, and broke a number of bones in his crash-landing.

The attempted interception of the heavy bombers by the Second Gruppe resulted in a vicious battle with Thunderbolts near Reims. Fifteen Second Gruppe Fw 190s attacked the twelve P-47s of the 356th Fighter Group's 360th Squadron, and were then engaged by the American group's 359th Squadron. At some point in the prolonged battle Focke-Wulfs from JG 2 became involved. The 356th, the least successful fighter group in the 8th Air Force, acquitted itself fairly well. The Thunderbolt pilots claimed 4-0-1 Fw 190s, and killed one 5th Staffel pilot, Uffz. Gerhard Falkner, plus the Kommodore of JG 2, Major Kurt Ubben. One JG 2 Focke-Wulf crash-landed on Juvincourt after the battle. Three P-47s were shot down, one each by Oblt. Waldemar Radener, Obfw. Gerhard Vogt, who had transferred temporarily from the 7th to the 5th Staffel, and an 11/JG 2 pilot. Uffz. Helmut Rektor of the 6th Staffel was killed during the day, but the details are unknown; his loss was considered to be non-operational.

Lt. Gottfried Dietze and Uffz. Hans-Georg Becker of the 1st Staffel both returned to active duty at Vendeville after recovering from wounds, and attempted to join the rest of the First Gruppe pilots at Cazaux. The engine of Dietze's Focke-Wulf failed on the transfer flight, and he crash-landed on Denain, destroying his airplane. He was permitted to complete the transfer in another plane.

29 April

Today's 8th Air Force mission was a full-strength effort by 768 bombers against the center of Berlin. Luftflotte Reich put up what was probably the best-coordinated defensive effort of the war, destroying sixty-three bombers and thirteen fighters for the loss of twelve pilots killed and five injured, and twenty-one fighters destroyed.

The role of the Geschwader in the day's defensive success was minor, as it had only the Second Gruppe operational. The Staffeln of the Gruppe were now dispersed among several bases. Fw. Peter Crump had just returned to duty after his February injury. He was transferred from the 6th to the 7th Staffel, and was allowed one familiarization flight from Juvincourt before he was put on the duty roster and scrambled with the rest of the Gruppe to search out bombers straggling behind the formations returning from Berlin. He claimed to have shot down a B-17 south of Reims, but his claim was apparently never filed. Oblt. Radener and Obfw. Vogt were successful, shooting down single Fortresses from the 401st and the 92nd Bomb Groups.

The First Gruppe suffered one loss today. Obfw. Willi Kalitzki crashed fatally while ferrying a repaired aircraft back to the front. The cause of the crash was not reported.

Uffz. Salewsky in informal attire – Etain, late April-early May. *(Genth)*

A 12th Staffel Bf 109G-6 is serviced at Etain in late April or early May. *(Genth)*

JG 26 Victory Claims: 25 - 29 April 1944

Date	Rank	Name	Unit	Cl #	Aircraft	Place	Time	Opponent	Conf
25-04-44	Uffz.	Pietruschka	5	1	B-24	10km ENE of Vitry-le-Francois (AI-BI)	0835	458 BG	unk
27-04-44	Obfw.	Vogt	5	25	P-47	7km S of Soissons	1740	356 FG	yes
27-04-44	Oblt.	Radener	7 CO	18	P-47	SW of Reims	1742	356 FG	yes
29-04-44	Obfw.	Vogt	5	26	B-17	NE of St. Omer (NF4)	1430	92 BG	yes
29-04-44	Oblt.	Radener	7 CO	19	B-17-HSS	5km SE of Roubaix	1335	401 BG	yes
29-04-44	Fw.	Crump	7		B-17	5km S of Reims	1330		no

JG 26 Casualties: 27 - 29 April 1944

Date	Rank	Name	Cas	Unit	Aircraft	WNr	Mkgs	Place	Time	Cause	Allied Unit
27-04-44	Uffz.	Falkner, Gerhard	KIA	5	Fw 190A-8	170007	wh 14	Couvron-Laon a/f		P-47	356 FG
27-04-44	Uffz.	Rektor, Helmut	KIFA	6	Fw 190A-6			unknown		crashed	non-op
27-04-44	Uffz.	Schreiber, Heinz	WIFA	11	Bf 109G-6	163316	yl 13	Lothringen-Thionville	2120	no fuel	n/a
27-04-44	Uffz.	Lessin, Ernst	KIA	12	Bf 109G-6	161772	bl 12	Reims-Cramant	1815	bomber gunner	
29-04-44	Obfw.	Kalitzki, Willi	KIFA	1	Fw 190A-6	530735	wh 12	W of Poitiers		crashed	non-op

30 April

The First Gruppe pilots and key personnel returned from Cazaux. One mechanic coming back from Cazaux by train was killed in a B-17 attack on a train station. The Gruppe was now split up among a number of airfields. The Stab and 1st Staffel were at Lille-Vendeville; the 2nd Staffel, at Wevelgem; the 3rd Staffel, at Denain; and the 4th Staffel, at Lille-Nord.

The 8th Air Force lost 409 bombers, its highest single-month loss of the war. However, the Americans could easily replace their losses. The Germans could not. The wastage of the Jagdwaffe continued at a ruinous pace. Luftflotte Reich lost 38% of its

Uffz. Erich Salewsky of the 12th Staffel (KIA 14 Jan 1945) with his crew chief at Etain in late April or early May. *(Genth)*

fighter pilots; Luftflotte 3 lost 24%. The entire Luftwaffe lost 489 fighter pilots in April, while completing the training of only 396. JG 26 lost sixteen pilots in combat, and a further six in accidents; the dead included two more Staffelkapitäne. Only three replacement pilots are known to have arrived during the month: Lt. Wolfgang Rose went to the First Gruppe; Uffz. Otto Bräsen to the Second, and Uffz. Karl Hennemann to the Third. Other Geschwader personnel moves during April included: the return of Uffz. Horst Gewitz to the 9th Staffel from duty as a ferry pilot; and the return of Uffz. Hans-Georg Becker to the 1st Staffel after recovering from an injury.

1 May

In the morning, 8th Air Force attempted a raid on a number of V-1 sites, but most of the bombers had to abort in the face of bad weather. Later in the day, attacks were made on a number of French railroad yards by individual combat wings. All three Gruppen put up small forces to intercept broken formations. The Third Gruppe mission reported a success. The 355th Fighter Group had just broken up an attack on the Metz raiders by a large number of Luftflotte Reich Bf 109s when six Messerschmitts bounced a flight of the P-51s from out of the sun, shot down one of them, and continued their dive into the clouds below. Oblt. Schauder and Lt. Reischer claimed victories as a result of this attack; only Lt. Reischer's claim was confirmed.

Neither the First nor the Second Gruppen made contact; the engine of Fw. Karl-Heinz Zeschke's Focke-Wulf quit, and Zeschke force-landed in a field with slight injuries but major damage to his aircraft.

2 May

The daily OKL situation map presents an interesting picture. The Geschwader Stab, at Lille-Nord, had two operational Fw 190s. The First Gruppe Stab and 1st Staffel, at Lille-Vendeville, had four. The 2nd and 3rd Staffeln, at Denain, had fourteen; The 4th Staffel, reportedly at Lille-Nord, had three. The Second Gruppe Stab and 8th Staffel, at Cambrai-Epinoy, had four Fw 190s; the 5th and 7th Staffeln, at Cambrai-Süd, had nine, and the 6th Staffel, reportedly still rebuilding at St. Dizier, had no aircraft available for operations. The Third Gruppe Stab and the 10th and 11th Staffeln had eighteen Bf 109s at Rouvres-Étain; the 9th and 12th Staffeln had eighteen at Doncourt. The operational strength of the Geschwader was thus seventy-two, 35% of establishment. Counting back in the aircraft that were not serviceable, there were probably one hundred assigned to the Geschwader.

According to logbook evidence, the 2nd and 4th Staffeln were actually flying from Wevelgem at this time, and the 6th Staffel was in the process of returning to Epinoy from Mons-en-Chauseé. The 4th Staffel is known to have maintained staffs at both Lille-Nord and Wevelgem for the first five months of 1944, but did nearly all of its flying from Wevelgem.

The engine of Fhj.-Uffz. Konrad Benk's 11th Staffel Bf 109G-6 failed while he was on a test flight from Rouvres-Chaumont. Unable to return to the field, Benk attempted to bail out, but his parachute streamed, and he was killed.

4 May

The First and Second Gruppen were scrambled in bad weather to oppose various Allied incursions, but failed to make contact. Lt. Kemethmüller's flight from Wevelgem was his first as leader of the 4th Staffel. The 6th Staffel leader, Lt. Glunz, took off from Mons-en-Chauseé and landed on Cambrai-Epinoy; this was Glunz's first flight since returning from an extended home leave. The 2nd Staffel leader, Fw. Schild, and Lt. Dietze, who had transferred from the 1st Staffel to the 2nd, took off from Wevelgem with the Staffel and landed on Denain, joining the 3rd Staffel.

5 May

Faced with rain over both England and the Continent, the Allies sent over a few medium bombers and a single heavy bomber formation, which made an attack on a V-1 site under the guidance of a Pathfinder bomber with a new radar device. The First and Second Gruppen scrambled and sought out enemy aircraft in the murk. The First Gruppe failed to make contact. Part of the Second Gruppe encountered W/C Johnnie Johnson's new No. 144 Wing (RCAF), which was sweeping across the Pas de Calais in advance of the medium bombers. Johnson caught a glimpse of some Fw 190s below him, and ordered two flights of his fighters to drop into the mist and look for the German planes. The Focke-Wulfs suddenly whipped around and came at the stalking Spitfires head-on. A general dogfight ensued in which Fw. Horst Schwentick and Uffz. Manfred Talkenberg were shot down and killed; one flight leader from No. 441 Squadron disappeared during the battle, and did not return from the mission.

Fw. Crump claimed the Spitfire. He took part in the Second Gruppe mission, but was not involved in the head-on attack. Peter Crump recalls:

> "I had an unexpected encounter with Spitfires, and my belly tank would not drop. Had I not found salvation in a low-lying bank of stratus clouds, often found in this area at this time of year, I would have at least been forced to make my second parachute jump. I was able to escape my attacker, who had certainly perceived my difficulty. Further attempts to drop the damned thing from within the cloud were unsuccessful. A comrade's call for help made me forget my own technical difficulty. I shot from the cloud deck like an arrow, heading for ground level. I would have to avoid any enemy aircraft that were right beneath my nose. However, there were only two aircraft in front of me – the threatened Focke-Wulf and a single attacking Spitfire. At full throttle and emergency boost I took up the pursuit; I ordered the Focke-Wulf to bank sharply to the right, both to allow me to open fire on the attacker and to shorten the distance to my assistance. But no – he sought salvation in flight. What happened next was inevitable. The Focke-Wulf showed a black smoke plume and disappeared below the horizon. In the meantime I had come so close to the Spitfire that he had discovered me. He banked left toward the cloud bank, and took up a north-west course for home, covering his blind angle underneath by rocking to and fro. He looked for me, but did not see me, since as soon as he turned left I had followed him, and was already in his dead angle. I matched his every rocking motion immediately – I was still at minimum altitude. So I remained invisible to him. Soon he stopped these movements, believing himself alone. So he flew on calmly in the direction of the coast, about 200 meters below the stratus deck. I drew ever nearer to him, until I was directly underneath him. After a last reassuring glance behind me I zoomed up and took him under fire. The Spitfire immediately flipped onto its back and headed straight for a sloping field. It crashed into a line of poplar trees, which immediately gave the single dwelling nearby the appearance of a sawmill. I have a clear recollection, because I visited the site from the nearby airfield at Chièvres."

Obfw. Gerhard Vogt of the 7th Staffel was awarded the German Cross in Gold today. His current victory total was twenty-six.

7 May

An early-morning mission to the Liège railroad yards was recalled when the two new B-24 groups involved were unable to form up properly, but not before the First and Second Gruppen were ordered to fly to Laon-Athies to refuel and form a Gefechtsverband. Soon after the combined force had taken off, the 3rd Staffel was attacked by a flight of Spitfires from No. 411 Sqd. (RCAF). The Canadian flight leader shot down two Fw 190s, which were piloted by Ofhr. Erich Scheyda and his wingman, Ogfr. Thomas Schwertl. Both died in their aircraft. Scheyda had been with the Geschwader since August 1941, and had been credited with twenty victories in 188 combat missions. He was awarded a posthumous German Cross in Gold at month's end.

The leader of the 1st Staffel, Oblt. Max Groth, was injured on landing after bailing out of his Focke-Wulf when its engine seized.

JG 26 Casualties: 1 - 7 May 1944

Date	Rank	Name	Cas	Unit	Aircraft	WNr	Mkgs	Place	Time	Cause	Allied Unit
01-05-44	Fw.	Zeschke, Karl-Heinz	WIFA	7	Fw 190A-7	340308	br 9	SW of Charleville		engine	n/a
02-05-44	Fhj-Uffz.	Benk, Konrad	KIFA	11	Bf 109G-6	163141	yl 16	Rouvres-Chaumont a/f	1430	engine	non-op
05-05-44	Fw.	Schwentick, Horst	KIA	5	Fw 190A-8	170116	wh 10	N of Chimay		Spitfire	443 Sqd
05-05-44	Uffz.	Talkenberg, Manfred	KIA	8	Fw 190A-8	170315	bl 6	SW of Mons	0830	Spitfire	441 Sqd
07-05-44	Oblt.	Groth, Max	WIFA	1 CO	Fw 190A-6	550913	wh 6	8km NE of Soissons		engine	n/a
07-05-44	Ofhr.	Scheyda, Erich	KIA	3	Fw 190A-8	730321	yl 1	Athies-Laon		Spitfire	411 Sqd
07-05-44	Ogfr.	Schwertl, Thomas	KIA	3	Fw 190A-8	170401	yl 3	Athies-11km N of Laon		Spitfire	411 Sqd

8 May

Berlin and Brunswick were visited in the morning by nearly 800 heavy bombers. The Geschwader was not used against this force; the mediums and the tactical fighters gave it more than it could handle today. The Allied plan to isolate Normandy by destroying all of the railroad and highway bridges serving the area was put into effect. To avoid pinpointing the invasion area, the bridges around the Pas de Calais were given just as much attention as those surrounding Normandy. The 9th Air Force bombers flew 450 sorties; the 2nd TAF was also up in force. The Jafü 4 controller scrambled all three Gruppen at 0930 and ordered them to rendezvous over Juvincourt with a JG 2 Gruppe. The formations all became involved in their own combats before reaching Juvincourt, and the concentration was never effected. The First Gruppe engaged P-47s near St. Quentin, and Lt. Kemethmüller was credited with shooting one down. North of Soissons the Second Gruppe was bounced from out of the sun by 404th Fighter Group P-47s, which shot down Uffz. Werner Winter. Winter bailed out with slight wounds. Oblt. Radener then shot down one of the Thunderbolts. The Third Gruppe was hit by twenty Mustangs southeast of Metz. Uffz. Adolf Tabbat was shot down; he bailed out safely, suffering slight injuries on landing. Neither the Allied unit involved nor any claims by the Gruppe are known.

In the afternoon the Third Gruppe lost one of its best men in a mindless accident. Hptm. Hans-Georg Dippel was a highly competent but overly confident acrobatic pilot. While flying at low speed on a training flight he pulled up sharply, stalling his Bf 109; he crashed before he could regain control. Dippel had gained nineteen victories in his 272 missions with the Geschwader. He was replaced as leader of the 9th Staffel by Oblt. Viktor Hilgendorff, a 29-year-old pre-war pilot who had recently returned to duty after a crash in 1942 had cost him his right leg. Hilgendorff was noted for his courage and for the vigor with which he expressed his political convictions; he was one of the few outspoken Nazis in the Geschwader.

JG 26 Victory Claims: 1 - 8 May 1944

Date	Rank	Name	Unit	Cl #	Aircraft	Place	Time	Opponent	Conf
01-05-44	Oblt.	Schauder	10 CO	17	P-51	E of Saarbrücken (TP-TQ)	1835	355 FG	unk
01-05-44	Lt.	Reischer	11 CO	13	P-51	E of Saarbrücken (TP9)	1845	355 FG	yes
05-05-44	Fw.	Crump	7	14	Spitfire	15km NE of Mons	0830	441 Sqd	yes
08-05-44	Lt.	Kemethmüller	4 CO	78	P-47	W of Hirson-SE of St Quentin (RH 7-9)	1005		yes
08-05-44	Oblt.	Radener	7 CO	20	P-47	6km N of Soissons (TG-SG)	1032	404 FG	yes

9 May

The 8th Air Force and the Allied Expeditionary Air Force (AEAF), which commanded the 9th US Air Force and the 2nd TAF, began a full-scale bomber and fighter-bomber campaign against the Luftwaffe bases in France and Belgium. The objective was to drive the German air force from the invasion area by D-Day. Airfields attacked this morning by the heavy bombers included Florennes, Juvincourt, Laon-Athies, Lille-Vendeville, and St. Dizier.

The Second Gruppe was led by Lt. Glunz to Florennes at 0630. It refueled and at 0855 took off with the First Gruppe as the B-24s approached. The Gefechtsverband made one attack on a B-24 formation which had just dropped its bombs, and Glunz shot down a bomber from the 466th Bomb Group. Glunz lost his wingman, Lt. Peter Rober, to a bomber gunner. Rober was able to force-land his plane and suffered only slight injuries. The Focke-Wulfs were then attacked by 357th Fighter Group P-51s that were on a supporting sweep. One flight of Mustangs attacked twenty Fw 190s, and the P-51s were quickly boxed in. Lt. Hofmann and Uffz. Norbert Seidl of the 2nd Staffel each downed a Mustang before the turning combat broke up. Seidl was chased to low altitude. His aircraft was hit. He half-rolled and dropped out; his parachute opened immediately, and he hit the ground with only minor injuries.

Addi Glunz's fighters had now been split up beyond reformation, and he went on a lone hunt for targets. He sighted a returning B-24 formation in the distance, and flew toward it from high above and head-on, facing the morning sun. He did not attack immediately. Lt. Herman Neeck, a bombardier in the nose turret of a 453rd Bomb Group B-24, tells the story:

> "I saw the approaching fighter up ahead in the distance. It quickly passed from my view, and I gave the word to the top turret gunner. He must have lost it in the sun, because a few minutes later the entire plane shook as the control wheels flew out of the hands of the pilot and copilot. A burst of cannon fire had cut the control cables. The airplane flipped upside down, showering me with shell casings. The navigator struggled forward without his parachute and opened my turret door, saving my life. Just as I emerged from the turret, the airplane exploded. The next thing I knew, I was hanging in space beneath my parachute."

Five men in the bomber's crew survived, and were quickly taken prisoner. The navigator, Lt. Robert Hall, was found in the wreckage of the plane. After the war Hall was awarded a posthumous Silver Star for his life-saving action, based on Neeck's recommendation.

Some of the First Gruppe fighters stayed together, looking for approachable targets, until their fuel state forced them to break away and look for landing grounds. German aircraft flying individually or in pairs were always vulnerable, and two 1st Staffel pilots, Gefr. Siegfried Machner and Uffz. Ewald Schnier, failed to return to Florennes.

Oblt. Waldemar Radener leads the 7th Staffel in his Fw 190A-7 "brown 4" (W.Nr. 340001) in early May; its rudder shows twenty victory bars. Uffz. Gerhard Langhammer turned this airplane over in a bomb crater while landing on Epinoy on 12 May. This photograph was incorrectly captioned in *JG 26: Top Guns of the Luftwaffe*. With the aid of computer enhancement, it has now been identified and dated accurately. *(Sy)*

Both were lost over the Eifel to 357th Fighter Group Mustangs. Schnier was shot down; Machner hit the ground while attempting an evasive maneuver.

The Third Gruppe at Étain was not near any other Jagdwaffe units, and flew its missions alone. The Gruppe lost one Messerschmitt to a P-51, probably from the 339th Fighter Group, but its pilot escaped injury. Any victory claims by the Third Gruppe remain unknown.

JG 26 Victory Claims: 9 May 1944

Date	Rank	Name	Unit	Cl #	Aircraft	Place	Time	Opponent	Conf
09-05-44	Uffz.	Seidl	2	1	P-51	Antwerp (LK)	0947	357 FG	yes
09-05-44	Lt.	Glunz	6 CO	59	B-24	7km E of Turnhout (LL7)	0951	453 BG	yes
09-05-44	Lt.	Glunz	6 CO	60	B-24	7km SSW of Turnhout (LK9)	0957	466 BG	yes
09-05-44	Lt.	Hofmann W.	8 CO	13	P-51	13km WNW of Turnhout (LK8)	0940	357 FG	yes

JG 26 Casualties: 8 - 9 May 1944

Date	Rank	Name	Cas	Unit	Aircraft	WNr	Mkgs	Place	Time	Cause	Allied Unit
08-05-44	Uffz.	Winter, Werner	WIA	7	Fw 190A-6	470023	br 12	NE of Soissons		P-47	404 FG
08-05-44	Hptm.	Dippel, Hans-Georg	KIFA	9 CO	Bf 109G-6/U4	440714	wh 17	Doncourt	1400	crashed	non-op
08-05-44	Uffz.	Tabbat, Adolf	WIA	10	Bf 109G-6	410757	bk 13	4km SE of Metz	0945	P-51	
09-05-44	Gefr.	Machner, Siegfried	KIA	1	Fw 190A-6	551139	wh 1	Maspelt-Eifel		P-51	354 FG
09-05-44	Uffz.	Schnier, Ewald	KIA	1	Fw 190A-8	680166	wh 3	6km N of Echternach		P-51	354 FG
09-05-44	Uffz.	Seidl, Norbert	WIA	2	Fw 190A-8	680167	bk 1	Burg-Tourhout		P-51	357 FG
09-05-44	Lt.	Rober, Peter	WIA	6	Fw 190A-8	170426	bk 10	nr Keel		B-24	466 BG

10 May

The 8th Air Force attempted to assemble its bombers for another early morning tactical mission, but bad weather forced its cancellation. Some of the AEAF missions were canceled for the same reason. The Jafü 4 and Jafü 5 controllers, taking no chances, moved their more exposed units inland very early in the morning. The First Gruppe flew to Metz at 0640. It was scrambled at 1000 and ordered to rendezvous with some JG 2 aircraft over Reims. They dropped their tanks, but failed to make contact, and flew farther west toward Beauvais, where part of the formation encountered the Spitfires of No. 602 Squadron. Uffz. Leopold Schlögl of the 3rd Staffel shot one of the fighters down; the Gruppe sustained no losses.

The Third Gruppe scramble resulted in no losses, and no known claims. Nothing is known of Second Gruppe activities today, except that Oblt. Walter Matoni received his German Cross in Gold, after twenty air victories.

11 May

The Allied offensive against tactical targets in France and Belgium picked up momentum. The 8th Air Force put up 387 B-24s, escorted by 823 P-38s, P-47s, and P-51s. The 9th Air Force flew 1746 sorties; the 2nd TAF, 781, and the Air Defense of Great Britain (ADGB), 406.

The response of Luftflotte 3 was perhaps eighty fighter sorties, of which only half made contact. The First and Second Gruppen again started the day with a transfer flight inland, to Metz. The Fw 190s were scrambled at 1315 and ordered west to rendezvous south of Reims with the Third Gruppe and some JG 2 aircraft. The Third Gruppe did not show up, for unknown reasons, and the formation was sent farther west, toward Orleans. The JG 2 pilots sighted nothing, but JG 26 made three separate attacks. On the first, Lt. Glunz shot a 44th Bomb Group B-24 from its formation; his claim was not confirmed, but the bomber in fact crashed near Orleans. The Focke-Wulf pilots next sighted the B-24s of the new 96th Combat Wing, which had become so badly disorganized after losing its leader and deputy leader to Flak that it failed to bomb. Lt. Wilhelm Hofmann led his 8th Staffel Schwarm so close to the bombers in their head-on pass that his wingman, Fhr. Waldemar Busch, rammed a 487th Bomb Group B-24, causing it to crash. Busch's propeller was knocked off, but he was able to force-land his aircraft and suffered only slight wounds. Lt. Radener made a successful attack on a B-24 and then accidentally rammed a second; Radener bailed out with minor injuries. Both of these 487th Bomb Group B-24s made it back to England, where the crew of one bailed out.

The 353rd Fighter Group was responsible for escorting these B-24s, but reported only a few contacts with the German pilots, who were "very much on the ball." Most were able to avoid contact with the P-47s by flying into thin clouds. In one of the few combats, Obfw. Waldemar Söffing of the 1st Staffel claimed, and was credited with, two P-47s, but none were lost.

JG 26 Victory Claims: 10 - 11 May 1944

Date	Rank	Name	Unit	Cl #	Aircraft	Place	Time	Opponent	Conf
10-05-44	Uffz.	Schlögl	3	2	Spitfire	W of Amiens-S of Dieppe (RC-RD)	1115	602 Sqd	yes
11-05-44	Obfw.	Söffing	1	12	P-47	Chateaudun (DC)	1420	353 FG	yes
11-05-44	Obfw.	Söffing	1	13	P-47	Chateaudun (DC)	1423	353 FG	yes
11-05-44	Lt.	Glunz	6 CO	61	B-24-HSS	NE of Chateaudun (DC6)	1400	44 BG	unk
11-05-44	Oblt.	Radener	7 CO	21	B-24	44km W of Chartres (CB38)	1400	487 BG	yes
11-05-44	Fhr.	Busch W.	8	3	B-24	38km S of Chartres (ED4-7)	1413	487 BG	yes

12 May

Although the Combined Bomber Offensive had ended on 1 April, the senior American air officer, General Spaatz, obtained permission from General Eisenhower's SHAEF

This antiaircraft gun was improvised by Robert Balloff of the Adamsonstaffel from a salvaged MG151, and was equipped with a Revi reflector gunsight. It was credited with two victories in May. The gunners, Hans Schmidt and Günter Kleeman, were awarded Iron Crosses Second Class. (G. Schmidt)

(Supreme Headquarters, Allied Expeditionary Forces), to continue attacking targets in Germany whenever permitted by the weather. He argued successfully that this would not prevent his bombers from fulfilling their duties in support of the invasion. Today Spaatz ordered Doolittle to begin their long-planned campaign against the German petroleum industry. Eight hundred and eighty-six bombers and 735 escorts were dispatched against six German oil refineries.

The Geschwader was ordered to *Sitzbereitschaft* at 1045, but the Jafü 4 controller ignored both the marauding tactical aircraft and the incoming heavy bombers. The absence of German radio transmissions led the Allied intelligence officers to infer that the fighters had transferred to bases in the Rhineland in complete radio silence, but there is no direct evidence for this. The First Gruppe flew to Metz in mid-afternoon for possible employment against the withdrawing bombers, but was not called on, and flew back north late in the evening. The Second Gruppe remained on its bases for the entire day.

Uffz. Gerhard Langhammer of the 7th Staffel overturned in a bomb crater while landing on Epinoy with a newly-repaired Fw 190A-7, and suffered severe head injuries.

The Third Gruppe flew a successful mission against the B-17s as they withdrew across the Ardennes. Major Mietusch located the badly chewed up 45th Combat Wing, which was in disarray after losing a number of bombers. Lt. Reischer separated a B-17 near St. Vith; a 452nd Bomb Group aircraft crashed in this area. Major Mietusch claimed a separation, and Fw. Walter Kopp a shootdown, near Bastogne. Neither claim was confirmed. Two damaged 452nd Bomb Group Fortresses ditched in the Channel, possibly as a result of this combat. The Gruppe lost one plane and pilot; Uffz. Kurt Rickeit crashed and burned in his Messerschmitt near St. Vith. The Germans gave American fighters the credit, but no fighter combat is known, and Rickeit was probably hit by a bomber gunner.

Oblt. Franz Kunz was given command of the 2nd Staffel. Jan Schild received his commission as a war-service Leutnant and stayed in the Staffel as Kunz's deputy.

13 May
The Allied plan was a repeat of the previous day's. The 8th Air Force attacked oil installations, while the AEAF attacked coastal defenses and V-weapon sites. The First and Second Gruppen transferred to Metz in the morning, flew no missions, and returned to their own bases in late afternoon.

14 May
The Fw 190A's BMW 801 radial engine was never developed into a fully reliable powerplant, and its sudden seizures and fires could threaten the life of even the best of

pilots. Ernst Battmer, the Geschwader technical officer, told of one series of mishaps which took place in May. Obstlt. Priller was attempting to send Major Mietusch's service records to Luftflotte 3 headquarters in Paris, in support of Priller's recommendation for the Oak Leaves, the next decoration above Mietusch's recently-awarded Knight's Cross. Battmer was to take the folder to the JG 2 command post at Creil. As Allied fighters were by this time maintaining a watch on all known Luftflotte 3 airfields, Battmer delayed his takeoff until evening, and then flew an Fw 190 from Lille-Nord to Creil, which took only twenty-five minutes.

After passing on the package to Major Bühligen, the JG 2 Kommodore, Battmer was invited to spend the night. The next morning Battmer received telephoned instructions from the JG 26 operations officer, Hptm. Philipp, to delay his takeoff until noon. After the usual circuit of the field, he turned onto his course at an altitude of only 20 meters (65 feet), also the customary practice.

After a few minutes of flight his engine power dropped, his propeller automatically positioned itself to minimum pitch, and his airspeed decreased, despite full throttle. He was able to avoid a forest in front of him, pull up over a row of short trees, lower the landing gear, and drop in on a hard piece of newly-ploughed field. Shortly before touchdown he shut off the ignition and fuel valve. Battmer telephoned JG 2 from a nearby railroad signal box and requested that they come get him and place a guard on the airplane. Investigation of the engine failure ultimately revealed a plugged fuel filter, apparently caused by Creil's gasoline, which was stored in iron drums which contained sludge.

From Creil that afternoon Battmer reported by telephone to his command post in Lille-Nord and was told that it was not possible to come for him and that he should ferry back a brand-new Fw 190 from Paris-Le Bourget. Battmer reached Le Bourget, selected an aircraft, inspected and preflighted it, and at 2130 finally taxied to the takeoff position, after checking the brakes. He calculated that a compass course of fifteen degrees would bring him to Lille-Nord in twenty minutes.

Once airborne Battmer took up course immediately, again at minimum altitude. After fifteen minutes, while over the mining region of Douai, he heard a loud noise from the engine. Oil streamed over the front and sides of his canopy and blocked his vision. He turned on the fuel spray, which was a canopy washer installed on the Fw 190 because of its tendency to throw oil. He was able to clean off the front pane. He could see small flames licking out from between the cowling panels. The smell of gasoline was strong, so he shut off the fuel spray. Battmer next attempted to open the canopy, but could not, because of his high speed. He thus had to climb in order to decrease his speed without altering the engine settings; the engine was still running, although it was clanging like a blacksmith shop. With effort he was able to open the canopy about four inches, permitting him to catch glimpses of the slag heaps, cable railways, and hoist towers of northern France's mining region. It looked like the Ruhr. Battmer could neither land nor bail out. He flew on at a height of 50 meters (160 feet), his engine pounding and gently burning, trailing smoke, covered in oil. He had lost his exact bearings and awaited his fate. When all of the oil was lost the engine would seize, and he would have to plough straight ahead, unable to see.

About five minutes after the first noise from the engine, Battmer saw an airfield alongside his plane. It was Lille-Vendeville, the base of Major Borris's First Gruppe. Battmer flew straight over the field, made a 180 degree turn, lowered landing gear and flaps, and trimmed for landing. His approach took him straight over the Gruppe command post. He could not see ahead, but spotted the radio mast to his right and flew past the hangars on his left. He cut the throttle and dropped to the ground, hoping that the most recent bomb craters in his chosen landing path had been filled. But Borris was a reliable officer; Battmer trusted him to have kept his field in shape.

The field's boundary markings came nearer. Battmer bounced along, ignition off, fuel off, braking. Finally he stopped. Canopy off, he jumped out and ran away from the airplane. Now for the first time his nerves gave way, and his knees started to shake. The firemen came and took him away. The aircraft crackled but did not burn. The fuselage was covered in oil all the way to the tail; the fire service had seen him coming by his oil plume.

The First Gruppe test group later determined the cause of the engine failure – a broken piston ring had torn an entire cylinder from its mounting. The connecting rod hammered the cylinder against the crankcase until the rod broke. The sheared rod then dug a deep groove in the crankcase. The torn-off fuel injector sprayed fuel on the hot exhaust ducts of the intact cylinders, resulting in the flames visible beneath the cowling panels. Ernst Battmer thanked his lucky stars for his survival, but we can attribute it as well to his flying skill and years of experience.

The Third Gruppe flew to Nancy today for a week of training.

15 May

The Second Gruppe transferred to Mont de Marsan, south of Bordeaux near the Spanish border. The Gruppe was placed under the tactical command of Jafü Brittany. Although the southwestern coast of France was in theory a possible invasion site, this was in reality another rest period. The basis for selecting the Second Gruppe for this plum assignment is unknown.

The Geschwaderstab and the First Gruppe now had the sole responsibility for the defense of that portion of France and Belgium assigned to Jafü 4. At this point the First Gruppe lost the services of its Kommandeur, Major Borris, who left the Geschwader for two and one-half months. His able interim replacement was Hptm. Hermann Staiger, who was in turn replaced as leader of the 12th Staffel by Oblt. Karl-Hermann Schrader.

Despite light Allied air activity, the Gruppe put in a long day, beginning with a pre-dawn reconnaissance mission to the English coast. This was a very unusual assignment for this period of the war, but the OKW was obviously anxious to fill in the gaps left by the conventional photo recon units. The two Focke-Wulf pilots couldn't help much, however, reporting no shipping between Eastbourne and Dover and a large number of barrage balloons over the latter town.

The Fw 190s of the First Gruppe left their three bases at 0905 and flew south to Reims, in anticipation of a heavy bomber raid. But the bombers did not come, and the fighters returned to their home bases. They were not vectored to intercept any of the AEAF formations in the area. Uffz. Philipp Schmelzer's engine failed, and he bailed out with an injured thigh, probably sustained by hitting the aircraft's tail. A flight of Spitfires from No. 403 Sqd. (RCAF) swept across Wevelgem as the 4th Staffel was landing and hit the aircraft of Fw. Erich Schwarz, who force-landed on the field with severe burns. Uffz. Hans Schmidt, a 4th Staffel groundcrewman, shot down one of the Spitfires with a 20mm antiaircraft gun adapted from an Fw 190 machine cannon.

JG 26 Casualties: 11 - 15 May 1944

Date	Rank	Name	Cas	Unit	Aircraft	WNr	Mkgs	Place	Time	Cause	Allied Unit
11-05-44	Oblt.	Radener, Waldemar	WIA	7 CO	Fw 190A-8	680120	br 2	Chateaudun-Bazoches		rammed B-24	487 BG
11-05-44	Fhr.	Busch, Waldemar	WIA	8	Fw 190A-7	340261	bl 1	15km N of Orleans	1345	rammed B-24	487 BG
12-05-44	Uffz.	Langhammer, Gerhard	WIA	FA 7	Fw 190A-7	340001	br 4	Epinoy		landing	non-op
12-05-44	Uffz.	Rickeit, Kurt	KIA	9	Bf 109G-6/U4	440586	wh 6	St. Vith	1545	combat	
15-05-44	Uffz.	Schmelzer, Philipp	WIA	FA 1	Fw 190A-8	170085	wh 11	W of Armentières		engine	non-op
15-05-44	Fw.	Schwarz, Erich	WIA	4	Fw 190A-8	170066	bl 3	Wevelgem		Spitfire	403 Sqd

20 May

Bad weather gave the First Gruppe a few days' respite, while totally frustrating the invasion planners at SHAEF. Today many Allied missions had to be recalled, but the 8th Air Force attacked the Paris airfields, and those AEAF formations that could find targets attacked airfields, coastal defenses and V-weapon installations. Once again Jafü 4 anticipated a deep raid and at 0940 ordered the First Gruppe to fly to Metz with twenty-three Fw 190s, where it was to join the Third Gruppe, which had flown north from Nancy with twenty-two Bf 109s. Having recognized his mistake, the controller sent the First Gruppe back north again at 1024. A portion of the Gruppe flew due north to Maastricht, where it split up upon sight of some *Indianer*. Some of the Focke-Wulfs continued flying straight and level, luring one flight of 355th Fighter Group P-51s away from its squadron. While climbing, the Mustangs were bounced from above and behind by six fighters from the 1st Staffel. Two Mustangs fell in flames, the victims of Obfw. Söffing and Lt. Kiefner. The German fighters continued their dive through the American formation to safety, eventually landing on Venlo. Uffz. Hans Winter was shot down on the final leg of this long flight and bailed out near Mönchen-Gladbach with minor injuries. The German records credit this victory to a P-47, but there is no evidence for any air combat in this area, and Winter could have been a victim of German Flak.

If it was intended to bring the Second Gruppe up to strength while in southwestern France, no improvement was yet apparent. Jafü Brittany reported today that the Gruppe had a strength of only twelve Fw 190s, of which nine were operational.

JG 26 Victory Claims: 12 - 20 May 1944

Date	Rank	Name	Unit	Cl #	Aircraft	Place	Time	Opponent	Conf
12-05-44	Major	Mietusch	III CO	61	B-17-HSS	Bastogne (QM-QL)	1542	452 BG	unk
12-05-44	Fw.	Kopp	10	1	B-17F	Bastogne (QM-QL)	1542	452 BG	unk
12-05-44	Lt.	Reischer	11 CO	12	B-17-HSS	Liège-St Vith (PM2)	1554	452 BG	yes
20-05-44	Lt	Kiefner	1	6	P-51	E of Courtrai (NH)	1050	355 FG	yes
20-05-44	Obfw.	Söffing	1	14	P-51	E of Courtrai (NH)	1050	355 FG	yes

22 May

The Allied Y-intercept report provides a full account of two frustrating missions for the Stab and First Gruppe; the only information from the German side resides in two one-line logbook notations. Obstlt. Priller, his Stabsschwarm, and part of the First Gruppe, probably the 4th Staffel, were scrambled at 1058 on the report of heavy bombers over the Channel. Priller was warned continually of Allied fighters until 1136, when he was turned over to the Jafü 5 controller. The bombers were B-24s *en route* to bomb some V-1 sites, and the fighters were up in ample time to intercept them, but no contact of any kind was made. The rest of the First Gruppe was scrambled at 1720 under orders to rendezvous over Courtrai. This accomplished, the Focke-Wulfs were sent on a full circle over the Pas de Calais without being vectored to any targets. They were ordered to drop their belly tanks at 1832, but still no contact was made, and they landed shortly thereafter.

Uffz. Edgar Elicker of the 6th Staffel was killed in a flying accident from Mont de Marsan.

23 May

The 8th Air Force dispatched a record 1045 heavy bombers against railroad yards in central France and western Germany. The Third Gruppe scrambled twenty-seven Bf 109s from Nancy and reached a B-17 formation near Colmar, but a planned frontal attack was broken off with the approach of the Mustang escort. Uffz. Werner Teichmann of the 9th Staffel was shot down in the resulting combat and crashed in his plane. Obfw. Karl Laub of the 11th Staffel and his brand-new wingman, Uffz. Erhard Tippe, were chased to the deck by eight Mustangs, but evaded six, and were able to out-turn the other two. Laub damaged his quarry, and Tippe's was saved from an equal

Members of the Third Gruppe staff, photographed at Nancy, France, between 14 May and 6 June. From left: Hptm. Bernhard Wollnitz (KIFA 28 Feb 45), Major Mietusch (KIA 17 Sep 44), Oblt. Viktor Hilgendorff (KIA 18 Jul 44), and Lt. Gottfried Schmidt. *(Wollnitz via Poelchau).*

or worse fate when his cannon failed to fire owing to a twisted ammunition belt.

Jafü 4 did not call on the First Gruppe to fly today, but Jafü Brittany did scramble the Second Gruppe from Mont de Marsan to oppose what the Jafü called "lively Allied air activity." The controller was unable, however, to bring any of his Focke-Wulfs into contact with it.

24 May

The 8th Air Force sent 517 B-17s to bomb Berlin, and 400 B-24s to bomb the airfields of JG 2. Four hundred and fifty 9th Air Force B-26s and A-20s bombed other airfields, including Denain, as well as coastal defenses and V-1 sites. The Jafü 4 and Jafü 5 controllers ignored the early B-24 raids entirely, but Jafü 4 scrambled its two Gruppen at 1050 and ordered them to rendezvous over Charleville. They failed to meet, and went their separate ways. The Third Gruppe did not contact the enemy, and landed back on Nancy-Essey at 1250. The First Gruppe flew north, back toward its own bases. Lt. Gottfried Dietze was forced to belly-land on Chièvres when his engine quit. Most of the pilots were credited with combat sorties, but only one significant engagement is known. The seven Fw 190s of the 1st Staffel bounced a flight of 373rd Fighter Group P-47s near Courtrai, and Obfw. Söffing shot one down.

The two Gruppen scrambled again at 1840, the First Gruppe contribution being eighteen Focke-Wulfs, and this time their rendezvous near Charleville was successful. The combined force was ordered to Reims to engage Allied fighters. The Third Gruppe and part of the First soon turned north and engaged some P-47s over the French-Belgian border. Uffz. Leopold Schlögl of the 3rd Staffel was shot down and killed; the victorious P-47 pilot filed no claim, and his unit cannot be identified.

The rest of the First Gruppe formation continued west from Reims until the pilots spotted a small formation of *Indianer* near St. Quentin. They were able to approach them undetected and came in on their rear. The Allied aircraft were a flight of three 339th Fighter Group P-51s escorting a single F-5, the photo recon variant of the P-38. It was following the bombers attacking Soissons in order to take strike photographs. The P-51 pilots saw "fifty Focke-Wulfs" – actually, twelve – diving on their tails and broke into them while the F-5 headed for the nearest cloud. After a prolonged chase, Obfw. Söffing shot one of the P-51s down. When rescued from a Wehrmacht hospital after the invasion, the Mustang pilot claimed two Focke-Wulfs, but none sustained reportable damage. Three Focke-Wulf pilots claimed the F-5. Lt. Kemethmüller gave his share to his wingman, Uffz. Wodarczyk, and claims were then filed for two Lightnings. One claim, that of Oblt. Kunz, was confirmed, but if the F-5 went down, it is not noted in any of the standard American loss records.

The B-26 attack on Denain killed two groundcrewmen and injured four, and destroyed two Fw 190s and one Fi 156.

25 May

The 8th Air Force continued its campaign against airfields, railroad yards, and coastal defenses in France. Nancy-Essey was the target for seventy-five B-17s. The Third Gruppe was scrambled at 0800 as the bombers came near, and strained for altitude as the bombs began falling. The Messerschmitts began an approach on the withdrawing B-17s, but the 356th Fighter Group, which had just finished its close escort assignment, received word of the Messerschmitts from the Allied controller and climbed for the German fighters' altitude, which was 5000 feet above the bombers. One P-47 squadron then made a headlong attack and scattered the Gruppe formation. One pilot shot down Uffz. Kurt Beck and Uffz. Egon Rummler; both men died in their aircraft. A number of the Bf 109s passed through a second P-47 squadron, which joined the chase. Uffz. Adolf Boeckl of the 12th Staffel fired on these P-47s as he tore through them, but hit nothing. Lt. David Thwaites led his flight after Boeckl's Messerschmitt. After making a single turn, which the P-47 followed easily, the inexperienced German pilot entered a straight, level dive, permitting Thwaites to close to 50-100 yards (45-90 meters). The first burst from the Thunderbolt's eight .50's knocked large pieces off the 109, which began smoking heavily. A spray of oil coated Thwaites' windshield; he overshot, and watched Boeckl jettison his canopy and bail out. The Thunderbolts climbed back to rejoin their Group at 18,000 feet. The surviving Messerschmitt pilots made their way back to their field at Nancy singly or in pairs, only to lose two more fighters to 78th Fighter Group Thunderbolts; both of their pilots survived.

Unfortunately for the men of the Third Gruppe, they were only guests on Nancy-Essey. Its defenses and dispersals were far inferior to those on fields maintained by the Geschwader. The Gruppe Stab lost two men killed and one injured in the B-17 attack. The non-operational Bf 109G-6s of the Gruppe had been parked in the open, and eleven were destroyed; another five were damaged.

The First Gruppe fighters on Metz-Frescaty scrambled at 0747, but failed to make contact with the bomber formations. They were followed back to the airfield by some P-47s, two of which proceeded to strafe just as Fw. Hans Ruppert had parked his Focke-Wulf in its revetment and climbed out of its cockpit onto the wing. He was hit in the stomach by a .50 caliber shell, fell off the wing, and bled to death. The men of the emergency crew were apparently afraid to leave their trenches to treat him; according to one pilot, Obfw. Söffing had to be restrained from shooting them with his flare pistol.

JG 26 Victory Claims: 24 - 25 May 1944

Date	Rank	Name	Unit	Cl #	Aircraft	Place	Time	Opponent	Conf
24-05-44	Obfw.	Söffing	1	15	P-47	Roubaix (OG)	1145	373 FG	yes
24-05-44	Obfw.	Söffing	1	16	P-51	St Quentin (RG)	1930	339 FG	yes
24-05-44	Oblt.	Kunz	2 CO	9	P-38	St Quentin (RG)	1924		yes
24-05-44	Uffz.	Wodarczyk	4	1	P-38	Cambrai (QF-QG)	1930		yes
25-05-44	Uffz.	Boeckl	12		P-47	Nancy-Essey a/f- S of Neufchateau	0843	356 FG	yes

Date	Rank	Name	Cas	Unit	Aircraft	WNr	Mkgs	Place	Time	Cause	Allied Unit
20-05-44	Uffz.	Winter, Hans-Werner	WIA	3	Fw 190A-8	170360	yl 9	NW Mönchen-Gladbach		combat	
22-05-44	Uffz.	Elicker, Edgar	KIFA	6	Fw 190A-6			Mont de Marsan		crashed	non-op
23-05-44	Uffz.	Teichmann, Werner	KIA	9	Bf 109G-6/U4	440725	wh 14	SW of Luneville	0930	P-51	
24-05-44	Uffz.	Schlögl, Leopold	KIA	3	Fw 190A-8	170114	yl 4	nr Charleroi	2015	P-47	
25-05-44	Fw.	Ruppert, Hans	KIA	1	Fw 190A-8	170020	wh 5	Metz-Frescaty a/f		P-47	
25-05-44	Uffz.	Rummler, Egon	KIA	10	Bf 109G-6	162701	bk 2	30km NE of Chaumont	0855	P-47	356 FG
25-05-44	Uffz.	Beck, Kurt	KIA	11	Bf 109G-6	162681	yl 4	NE of Chaumont	0915	P-47	356 FG
25-05-44	Uffz.	Boeckl, Albert	WIA	12	Bf 109G-6/U4	440989	bl 18	Roncourt	0850	P-47	356 FG

27 May

The 8th Air Force and the AEAF attacked numerous targets in France and Germany; the USAAF alone flew more than 3000 sorties. The First and Third Gruppen were scrambled several times and vectored to various locations, but the real if unstated goal of these missions was to keep out of the Allies' way. The only serious attempt at an interception came at 1415, when a single Rotte of Fw 190s scrambled from Epinoy to hunt down a single straggling B-17 reported in the area. Both pilots were First Gruppe men who had just happened to find themselves on the Second Gruppe base. A flight of 361st Fighter Group P-51s that was keeping the field under surveillance quickly dived on the pair. Fw. Kurt Schmidtke climbed away and escaped. Fw. Michael Hecker attempted to dive, and was quickly overtaken and shot down, crashing in his plane.

Part of the Second Gruppe flew a mission from Mont de Marsan against medium bombers in the Paris region. The Focke-Wulf pilots returning from the mission reported no contact, but Uffz. Heinz Wyrich of the 5th Staffel failed to return. He reported on the radio that his aircraft had been damaged, and then disappeared. His body was found two days later; he had been shot in the back in his parachute.

JG 26 Casualties: 27 - 29 May 1944

Date	Rank	Name	Cas	Unit	Aircraft	WNr	Mkgs	Place	Time	Cause	Allied Unit
27-05-44	Fw.	Hecker, Michael	KIA	2	Fw 190A-8	170001	bk 7	SE of Armentières	1430	P-51	361 FG
27-05-44	Uffz.	Wyrich, Heinz	KIA	5	Fw 190A-8	730357	wh 4	nr Paris-N of Romilly		combat	
28-05-44	Uffz.	Munack, Paul	KIFA	2	Fw 190A-8	170119	br 5	Mont de Marsan		collision	non-op
28-05-44	Uffz.	Mickmann, Bernhard	KIFA	7	Fw 190A-6	550727	br 1	Mont de Marsan		collision	non-op
29-05-44	Lt.	Hilliger, K-Dietrich	WIA	9	Bf 109G-6	163471	bl 12	Metz-Frescaty a/f	1330	combat	

28 May

The First and Third Gruppen were kept on the ground in spite of the unremitting attacks by the 8th Air Force and the AEAF. Uffz. Bernhard Mickmann and Uffz. Paul Munack collided while on a training flight from Mont de Marsan, and both were killed. Munack was on the rolls of the 2nd Staffel in the First Gruppe, and was probably in the process of transferring to the Second Gruppe.

29 May

The Allied attacks continued unabated. The First Gruppe flew from its northern fields to Metz-Frescaty, but after one brief, ineffective sortie the pilots returned to their bases in the evening. The Third Gruppe attempted to attack one bomber formation as it passed over Metz. One pilot was shot down, but bailed out without injury. The engine of Lt. Dietrich Hilliger's Messerschmitt caught fire, and he bailed out over Metz-

Frescaty with moderate burns.

30 May
In the morning, part of the First Gruppe flew to Trier, and the rest to Denain. The story for the two detachments was the same; no enemy contact, and a return to the north in the evening. The Third Gruppe flew one mission from Nancy-Essey with no contact; the Second Gruppe continued training at Mont de Marsan.

31 May
Luftflotte 3 kept nearly all of its aircraft on the ground. Jafü 4 reported that one thousand Allied aircraft had passed through its area before noon; none were intercepted. The Second Gruppe flew fifty-two sorties in a fruitless search for a Ju 290 missing off Bordeaux. Gefr. Günter Kleeman shot down a Mustang with the Fw 190 MG 151/20 that the 4th Staffel had converted into an antiaircraft gun. Kleeman and Hans Schmidt, who had downed a Spitfire with this weapon on the 15th, were awarded Iron Crosses Second Class.

Geschwader personnel moves during May included: the departure of Uffz. Ludwig Sattler from the 1st Staffel for duty as a ferry pilot; the return of Oblt. Otto Stammberger from his latest stint in hospital and his assignment as First Gruppe adjutant; and the commissioning of Xaver Ellenrieder as a war-service Leutnant.

Three experienced pilots reported to the Geschwader after completing fighter transition training: Fw. Roman Joziak, a member of the Luftwaffe since 1937 whose most recent duty was as a ferry pilot, joined the 8th Staffel. Lt. Wolfgang Marx, another former ferry pilot, joined the 4th Staffel. Ogfr. Helmut Merten, formerly a pilot in KG 4 and SKG 10, joined the 3rd Staffel.

New pilots assigned to the Geschwader during May after completing flight training included: Lt. Hans Bleich, Uffz. Otto Horch, Lt. Werner Lauer, Fw. Günter Muche, Obfw. Ernst Rudolph, Uffz. Josef Wendl, Uffz. Wilhelm Wüst - 1st Gruppe; Uffz. Max Chemnitzer, Lt. Edmund Fischer, Obfw. Erwin Franke, Uffz. Bruno Grolms, Fhr. Martin Hennemann, Uffz.-Fhj. Gerhard Just, Fw. Arthur Paul, Gefr. Heinz Sachse, Uffz. Leopold Speer, Uffz. Josef Ursprung, Uffz. Heinz Worthmann, Lt. Heinz Zedler - Second Gruppe; Lt. Dietrich Hilliger - Third Gruppe. Erwin Franke had been a member of the Luftwaffe since 1935 and had won the Spanish Cross in Silver with Diamonds as a bomber crewman.

The continuing struggle against ever-increasing odds cost the German home defenses 276 fighter pilots and 487 fighters in May. The German fighter arm lost 25% of its pilots, and 50% of its aircraft, during the month. Despite strenuous efforts to build up the Jagdwaffe, the number of fighter pilots on duty had dropped since the beginning of the year from 2395 to 2283. Losses so far in 1944 totaled 2262 pilots, or about 100% of average strength. The mission count of JG 26 decreased in May, probably in anticipation of its projected role as a front-line defender against the forthcoming invasion, and its strength showed an appreciable increase. The Stab reported 2 (2) Fw 190s at Lille-Nord; the First Gruppe had 59 (42) Fw 190s at Lille-Vendeville, Denain, and Wevelgem; the Second Gruppe had 38 (25) Fw 190s at Mont de Marsan and Denain; and the Third Gruppe had 72 (34) Bf 109s at Metz, St. Dizier, and Loupcourt. The number of operational aircraft had increased from seventy-two at the beginning of the month to 103 at the end.

Chapter Six

THE INVASION FRONT

June - August 1944

1 June

Every member of the Geschwader knew that the invasion was imminent. The Allies were expected to come ashore somewhere on the coast of the Pas de Calais, which put JG 26 right on the firing line. The OKL had a long-standing plan to reinforce Luftflotte 3 with fighter units from Germany once the enemy landings began. JG 2 and JG 26 would provide the experienced nucleus for the 5th Jagddivision, which would command the "pure" fighter units under Genmaj. Werner Junck's Jagdkorps II. About half of the new Jagdgruppen would join Genlt. Alfred Buelowius's Fliegerkorps II, a ground-attack command which had established a fully-staffed headquarters in France in advance of the invasion.

The Geschwader was far below its authorized strength in aircraft and pilots, but was in its best shape in months. Obstlt. Priller's Geschwaderstab and the First and Second Gruppen were equipped almost entirely with the Fw 190A-8. An improved Fw 190A-7, it would become the Fw 190 model built in the greatest numbers, 1334 eventually rolling off the production lines. The Fw 190A-8 retained the A-7's powerful armament of four wing-mounted MG 151s and two cowling-mounted MG 131s, although some examples had the outer wing cannon removed to save weight. It had a new radio with homing capabilities and a new 25 gallon fuel tank behind the cockpit. In the R4 variant this fuel tank was replaced by a nitrous oxide tank in a system called GM 1 boost, which increased top speed by as much as 36 mph at altitudes above 8000 meters (26,000 feet). The Fw 190A-8 had the same 1700 HP BMW 801D-2 engine that had powered the Fw 190A-3 in 1942, so the boost was necessary to remain competitive with improved Allied fighters. It raised the fighter's critical altitude from 5500 to 6300 meters (18,000 to 20,700 feet) at which height its maximum speed was 656 km/h (408 mph). At low or medium altitudes the performance of this fighter was comparable to that of the four major Allied types, and its pilots, even the new ones, had a great deal of confidence in their mount.

The Third Gruppe was still flying its old Bf 109G-6 *Beulen* (boils), so named from the bulbous fairings covering the breeches of their cowling-mounted MG 131 machine guns. While still an effective dogfighter, the Bf 109 was showing its age, and lacked the speed necessary to initiate combat or escape from Allied fighters. An experienced pilot could use its ability to climb and turn to regain the advantage if caught by surprise; inexperienced pilots, who were the great majority, were easy targets.

3 June

As the Allies completed their preparations for the invasion, the Germans still had no clue as to its date or location. Rain and mists covering France led to a reduction in the Wehrmacht state of readiness. The First Gruppe kept up its routine of flying from its northern bases to Trier or Metz in the morning, and returning in the evening. The Third Gruppe remained on Nancy-Essey, and was scrambled a few times. Contact was not sought with the enemy.

The Second Gruppe continued training at Mont de Marsan. A pilot was lost today on a routine Rotte training mission. Obfw. Heinz Gloyer was killed in the crash of his Focke-Wulf; the reason for the crash was not reported.

4 June

The Allied air forces continued their blizzard of attacks on tactical objectives in France. In England, the assault craft had been loaded and were on their way to the Normandy beaches when an urgent message from SHAEF was received postponing the D-Day landings one day, from 5 June to 6 June, to take advantage of a predicted improvement in the weather. The convoys put back into port, still unobserved by the Luftwaffe.

In the course of a late-evening scramble from Nancy-Essey, Major Mietusch, concerned that his pilots were losing their edge, sought out a bomber formation near Melun and attempted an attack, despite a swarm of escorts. The Messerschmitts were driven off by P-51s of the 361st Fighter Group, which shot one of them down; the German pilot was uninjured. In return, Mietusch was able to down one of the Mustangs, which he called a Typhoon; its pilot evaded capture and eventually returned to his unit.

6 June

The Geschwader got word of the Normandy invasion via the well-known telephone call to Obstlt. Priller at his Lille-Nord command post. Priller was told that JG 26 was now under the command of the 5th Jagddivision, and that he should begin transferring his Gruppen to bases nearer to the beachhead area. Orders were quickly passed to the nearby First Gruppe and to the Third Gruppe at Nancy-Essey to get their operational fighters airborne and *en route* to the JG 2 airfields at Creil and Cormeilles. His staff was told to load their trucks and head south toward Poix. The First and Third Gruppe truck convoys were already on the road with those units' ground staffs, but were headed in the wrong direction. The First was heading for Reims in anticipation of a permanent base move; the Third was moving southeast to join its flying units at Nancy. Priller had fought the orders for these transfers into the French interior, but had lost. The convoys were located by radio and told to stop. Hptm. Naumann's Second Gruppe pilots had already taken off from Mont de Marsan and Biarritz at 0700 and had reached Vrox, where they awaited further orders. Other than telling the Second Gruppe ground staff to pack up, Priller had none at the moment; the unexpected landing site had upset all the plans. Having done all he could, Priller and his wingman, Uffz. Heinz Wodarczyk, headed for their Focke-Wulfs, which as usual were parked just outside the command post. The first Luftwaffe response to the invasion was underway.

The pair took off into the gray skies at 0800. Priller's only orders to Wodarczyk were to stick close. They headed west at low altitude, spotting Spitfires above them as far east as Abbeville. Near Le Havre the duo climbed into the solid cloud bank. When they emerged, the ships of the largest assault landing in history were spread before their eyes. After a shouted "Good luck!" to Wodarczyk, Priller dived for the beach at 650 kilometers per hour (400 miles per hour). The British soldiers on Sword, the easternmost of the five landing beaches, jumped for cover as the two fighters roared overhead at fifty feet, their machine guns and cannon clattering. The fleet's antiaircraft guns opened fire with every gun that could track them, but the Focke-Wulfs flew through the barrage unscathed. After traversing the beach, the two pilots climbed for the clouds, honor satisfied.

The two Focke-Wulfs landed on Creil, and Priller went to see Major Bühligen, the Kommodore of the Richthofen Geschwader. Bühligen had no more fighters than did Priller. Only one of his Gruppen was immediately available; another was *en route* from Brittany, and the third was in Germany for rebuilding, and had not yet been released to return to France. After several telephone calls to 5th Jagddivision headquarters, Priller got a decision on relocating his Geschwader. The Second Gruppe could continue north to Guyancourt, near Paris. The First and Third Gruppen could stay at

Creil and Cormeilles until the arrival of the rest of the JG 2 aircraft made things too crowded, and would then move south to bases in the Paris region. Priller made arrangements for Bühligen's radiomen to contact his four road convoys, and returned to the business of fighting the Allies.

Although Priller and Wodarczyk may have been the first German pilots to fly over the beachhead, they were by no means the only ones to contact the enemy on this day. Bühligen himself scored the first victory for JG 2, a P-47 over the Orne Estuary, at 1157. I/JG 2 was active over Caen from noon, and III/JG 2 joined in after it arrived at Cormeilles from Brittany. For the day, the Richthofen Geschwader claimed three P-47s, five P-51s, and nine Typhoons, for the loss of nine Fw 190s. The P-51s included an entire flight of four 4th Fighter Group aircraft, bounced while strafing a convoy near Rouen.

After sitting on the ground at Creil and Cormeilles for three hours waiting to be serviced, the First Gruppe began flying small missions, some jointly with I/JG 2. Uffz. Hans-Werner Winter of the 3rd Staffel either got lost or was chased east by Allied fighters, and was shot down and killed by the Abbeville Flak. Fhr. Gerhard Schulwitz was missing for a day after being shot down by naval gunfire, but returned with slight injuries. Fhj.-Uffz. Friedrich Schneider of the 2nd Staffel was also hit by naval gunners, and belly-landed on Beaumont-le-Roger. By late afternoon, the JG 2 armorers had fit some of the Focke-Wulfs with launchers for 21 cm rockets, and Lt. Kemethmüller led his 4th Staffel in the first rocket attack by the Geschwader on land targets; they had been trained for this at Cazaux. The 2nd Staffel leader, Oblt. Kunz, scored the day's only air victory for the Geschwader, downing a Mustang southeast of Caen at 2055. This was probably a 4th Fighter Group P-51 that had aborted from a mission to Dreux with a bad magneto and was attempting to reach the Allied lines to force-land.

The Third Gruppe had reached the JG 2 bases by 0930, but did not begin flying combat missions until nearly noon. It is known that they tangled with Spitfires, claimed no victories, and sustained no losses or damage. The fragile Messerschmitts probably stayed well away from the beachhead.

The Second Gruppe lost one aircraft on its takeoff from Biarritz. Lt. Hans Bleich was caught in Lt. Glunz's propwash and crashed, suffering slight injuries. Those Focke-Wulfs that reached Vrox flew north in two separate formations. One flew directly to its new Paris base, Guyancourt, and had landed by 1115. They did not fly again this day, probably because there was no-one there to service the aircraft. Lt. Glunz led eight aircraft to Cormeilles; while *en route*, Glunz spotted a flight of P-51s attacking ground targets near Rouen and led a bounce. They were spotted, and the Mustangs broke into the attack. One pair boxed in Uffz. Erich Lindner and shot him down. He attempted to bail out, but caught his parachute on the cockpit framing; he pulled it loose in time and fell free, landing with only slight injuries. Glunz holed one Mustang's wing, but was unable to get an advantage, and both sides broke away. After servicing at Cormeilles, Glunz's group reached Guyancourt by 1700.

The OKL in Berlin believed at first that the Normandy landings were only a diversion, and did not order the Luftflotte Reich fighters westward until afternoon. They began arriving at their assigned bases near nightfall, and none played any role in the day's operations. The effort by the 5th Jagddivision totaled 121 combat sorties, all by JG 2 and JG 26; Fliegerkorps II reported fifty-one sorties, all by SG 4. According to one source, the 8th Air Force and the AEAF flew *14,000* combat sorties today; the 56th Fighter Group flew an unprecedented eleven combat missions.

7 June

The three Gruppen and Priller's Geschwaderstab were active from dawn until dusk. Missions were either strafing attacks on infantry *Stützpunkte* (footholds) or *freie Jagden* (free hunts), sweeps in search of Allied aircraft. Pips Priller was in a friendly race to beat Kurt Bühligen to one hundred Western victories. These two pilots and

The "black 1" of Oblt. Franz Kunz, the 2nd Staffel Kapitän, taxies out for takeoff from Boissy-le-Bois. Kunz was one of the last JG 26 Staffelkapitäne to have a "number 1" as his personal aircraft. *(Dietze via Meyer)*

Josef Wurmheller of JG 2 were the only active pilots nearing this number, considered the pinnacle of achievement for a Luftwaffe fighter pilot. At 1350 Priller shot down a P-51 north of Caen, for his 97th victory, and followed it up at 1900 by downing a P-47 near Évreux, for Number 98. But Bühligen shot down two P-47s in late afternoon, for his 100th and 101st victories. Priller had to present him with a victory bouquet.

The First Gruppe claimed two Mustangs and four Thunderbolts during the day; the Third Gruppe, two P-47s. A Second Gruppe pilot claimed one Mustang, and a second was credited to Ogfr. Erwin Mayer, a gunner with the unit Flakkompanie. He was on the road with the Second Gruppe convoy, which was fighting its way north through army traffic and fighter-bomber attacks.

Most of the day's victories cannot be matched up unambiguously with the day's eighteen Mustang and twenty-seven Thunderbolt losses. Fw. Zimmermann of the 8th Staffel almost certainly shot down a No. 129 Sqd. Mustang that was on an early-morning armed recon mission near Argentan. The four Thunderbolts claimed by the First Gruppe definitely belonged to the 362nd Fighter Group's 379th Squadron, which had a flight bounced near Falaise in mid-afternoon and lost two aircraft; the other two P-47s in the flight were badly damaged and force-landed on the first English airfields their pilots saw. Hptm. Staiger and two of his pilots filed four claims for these aircraft; three were confirmed.

Two 1st Staffel pilots, Uffz. Hans-Georg Becker and Uffz. Helmut Hüttig, dropped into the cloud deck during a combat over the beachhead, and never returned to Cormeilles; they were probably shot down by the marauding Allied fighters. Fhj.-Uffz. Friedrich Schneider of the 2nd Staffel, who had belly-landed his Focke-Wulf on Beaumont-le-Roger the previous day, was sent to Paris by truck to get a replacement fighter. While *en route,* his truck overturned, probably as the result of an Allied air attack, and Schneider was killed.

The Third Gruppe took off from Cormeilles for its morning mission, during which two Messerschmitts were shot down without injury to their pilots, and then flew to Paris, where the pilots located and landed on Villacoublay-Nord. This would be their base for the next two and one-half months.

The Second Gruppe pilots were at nearby Guyancourt, where they struggled to service their own aircraft until their own ground crews arrived. Guyancourt and Villacoublay were the region's two best airfields not already occupied by front-line Luftwaffe units. Obstlt. Priller was very fortunate to have gotten them assigned to his

Gruppen. It is not known if the prestige of his unit, or merely his early arrival in the area, did the trick.

Guyancourt and Villacoublay were located among a cluster of small towns south of Versailles. Guyancourt had been built by Caudron in 1930 as a factory airfield. It had four large hangars, which were used until 17 June, when they were destroyed by B-17s, and three hard-packed grass runways. Most maintenance was carried out in the ten solidly-constructed T-hangars, which were just large enough for one Fw 190 to be pushed into tail-first. The aircraft dispersals were well-hidden in nearby woods. The pilots' quarters were in a nearby château; those of the enlisted groundcrewmen, in barracks on the edge of the field.

The Villacoublay complex comprised two separate airfields, separated by a national highway. Villacoublay-Sud, the larger, was formerly an aircraft factory and a research facility for the French Air Force. One row of hangars and buildings was now an important Fw 190 repair and modification center, operated by Junkers. Another row had previously housed a Bréguet factory, which had now moved elsewhere, and underground. Villacoublay-Nord contained a former Morane factory, now used to assemble Fieseler aircraft. Each field had a large, well-drained landing ground and one concrete or asphalt runway. Each had numerous dispersals well-camouflaged in the surrounding woods. Two small war-service landing grounds, Buc and Toussus, were nearby. These served as overflow and emergency landing fields, and as places of refuge when the larger bases were under Allied attack. The 10th and 12th Staffeln spent a lot of time on Buc, and may in fact have been based there in late June and early July.

Across the highway from the Third Gruppe, on Villacoublay-Sud, were the Focke-Wulfs of III/JG 54, which had just arrived from Germany. The Green Heart Gruppe was fortunate to have been assigned such a well-equipped base. The unit's status as an "independent" Gruppe was always anomalous, and Priller's staff handled administrative matters for the unit while it was on the *Invasionsfront* (invasion front), although it was apparently never formally subordinated to JG 26.

By evening there were only six Gruppen of single-engine fighters left in Germany; seventeen Gruppen were in France. At full strength this would have amounted to a force of 1100 aircraft. However, most units were at half strength or less, and owing to the disorganization resulting from the rapid move and the chaotic state of most French airfields, only 278 fighters from the new units were reported operational in the strength return radioed to the RLM. General Galland complained bitterly in his post-war interrogation about the deplorable conditions at most of the new units' fields, many of which lacked dispersals, headquarters buildings, communications equipment, lights, and critical supplies. Luftflotte 3's phlegmatic Feldmarschall Sperrle cited the manpower shortage as justification for neglecting this task, which the OKL had assigned to his command in early 1944 as an integral part of its plan to repel the invasion.

JG 26 Victory Claims: 3 - 7 June 1944

Date	Rank	Name	Unit	Cl #	Aircraft	Place	Time	Opponent	Conf
04-06-44	Major	Mietusch	III CO	62	Typhoon	NW of Romilly	2015	361 FG P-51	yes
06-06-44	Oblt.	Kunz	2 CO	10	P-51	5km SE of Caen (UU5)	2055	4 FG	yes
07-06-44	Obstlt.	Priller	Ge CO	98	P-51	N of Caen (TU7-8)	1350		yes
07-06-44	Obstlt.	Priller	Ge CO	97	P-47	Évreux (UC3-6)	1900		yes
07-06-44	Hptm.	Staiger	I CO	56	P-47	N of Lisieux	1600	362 FG	yes
07-06-44	Hptm.	Staiger	I CO	55	P-47	N of Lisieux	1558	362 FG	yes
07-06-44	Oblt.	Groth	1 CO	1	P-47	Falaise (UA1)	1601	362 FG	yes
07-06-44	Lt.	Söffing	1	17	P-51	W of Rouen (TB5)	0704		yes
07-06-44	Lt.	Söffing	1	18	P-47	Falaise (UA1)	1601	362 FG	yes
07-06-44	Lt.	Günther	3	1	P-51	W of Rouen (TB5)	0705		yes
07-06-44	Ogfr.	Meyer E	6	1	P-51	22km SE of Saumur (HA8)	1915		flak
07-06-44	Fw.	Zimmermann	8	1	Mustang	SE of Caen (UU)	0620	129 Sqd	yes
07-06-44	Obfw.	Humburg	9		P-47	NW of Rouen (SB3)	1045		unk
07-06-44	Lt.	Kempf	9	60	P-47	E of Dreux (AD3)	0851		yes

Date	Rank	Name	Cas	Unit	Aircraft	WNr	Mkgs	Place	Time	Cause	Allied Unit
03-06-44	Obfw.	Gloyer, Heinz	KIFA	6	Fw 190A-8	170421	bk 4	Bidart	1745	crashed	non-op
06-06-44	Uffz.	Winter, Hans-Werner	KIA	3	Fw 190A-8	730466	yl 3	Abbeville		own flak	n/a
06-06-44	Lt.	Bleich, Hans	WIFA	6	Fw 190A-8	170119	bk 5	Biarritz a/f		takeoff	n/a
06-06-44	Fhr.	Schulwitz, Gerhard	no	6	Fw 190A-8	170335	yl 10	Orne Estuary		ship flak	n/a
06-06-44	Uffz.	Lindner, Erich	WIA	7	Fw 190A-8	170383	br 10	St Opportune		P-51	352 FG
07-06-44	Uffz.	Becker, Hans-Georg	KIA	1	Fw 190A-8	730456	wh 5	40km SW of Rouen		combat	
07-06-44	Uffz.	Hüttig, Helmut	KIA	1	Fw 190A-8	680186	wh 2	30km SW of Rouen		combat	
07-06-44	Fhj.-Uffz.	Schneider, Friedrich	KAC	2	none			Beaumont-Paris		truck accident	n/a

8 June

JG 1, JG 3, JG 11, and III/JG 54 had now arrived from Luftflotte Reich and had been assigned to Fliegerkorps II. This bomber command could not yet mount a concerted attack with its new fighter-bombers, many of which were not yet equipped with bomb shackles. Its only experienced fighter-bomber unit, III/SG 4, carried out the only successful bombing mission of the day, a dive-bombing attack on the Orne Canal bridge. Few of the new pilots had ever dropped a bomb, and most were eager to jettison their loads at the approach of Allied fighters.

The 5th Jagddivision had less difficulty absorbing its new units, primarily Bf 109 Jagdgruppen from JG 27 and JG 53. Its fighters flew forty-three missions, totaling 103 Fw 190 and 175 Bf 109 sorties. JG 26 flew a few strafing missions against the invasion shipping, but the principal missions ordered by the Jagddivision were freie Jagden, uncontrolled free hunts for Allied fighters and fighter-bombers.

The First Gruppe flew two missions without claims or losses and then landed on Boissy-le-Bois, which was to be its permanent base. Boissy-le-Bois was a typical war-construction airfield located on farmland between Beauvais and Paris. Its facilities were very modest, but its dispersals were well-concealed, and the field remained undetected by the Allies for several weeks. Signals intercepted by the Allies and surviving reports by various higher commands list several locations for the Gruppe during the first two weeks of the invasion, in part because the advance detachment of the ground staff was on the road, while the rear detachment remained at Lille-Vendeville. The evidence of the pilots' logbooks is clear, however – the pilots and their aircraft settled in at Boissy-le-Bois on this date, and stayed. Two members of the ground staff were wounded today in a P-47 strafing attack on Beauvais, where the convoy had apparently broken its journey. A third groundcrewman was shot accidentally with a pistol, and died the next day.

Obstlt. Priller's headquarters staff was still on the road, and he handled his own communications for a few more days, probably from Buc, near Guyancourt. His staff was apparently traveling with the First Gruppe convoy, and Priller joined them at Chaumont, the town nearest Boissy-le-Bois, when they arrived.

The Second Gruppe was fully operational from Guyancourt, and its fighters flew several missions. While on a freie Jagd, one 5th Staffel pilot, Lt. Helmut Giebner, was shot down and killed by an Allied fighter. A dozen Fw 190s were up at dawn and caught a small flight of No. 168 Sqd. Mustangs on a tactical recon mission. Lt. Vogt and Lt. Hofmann each claimed a victory, but only one Mustang crashed. Lt. Hofmann claimed two P-47s on a mid-afternoon mission to Caen. These claims were not confirmed, and the identity of the Thunderbolts cannot be established.

Major Mietusch's dawn mission from Villacoublay was productive. At 0645 he caught a flight of 371st Fighter Group P-47s attacking ground targets near Le Havre, and he and his wingman Uffz. Zeller shot three of them down, although two claims were not confirmed. At the same time, Lt. Reischer bounced a No. 198 Sqd. Typhoon north of Caen, and shot it down into the Channel, from which its pilot was rescued. The only Gruppe loss was sustained in early afternoon, when Gefr. Heinz Lienich of

A Schwarm of 1st Staffel Focke-Wulfs prepares to take off from Boissy-le-Bois. *(Dietze via Meyer)*

the 11th Staffel was shot down by Spitfires southwest of Caen. He bailed out with only slight injuries.

JG 26 Victory Claims: 8 June 1944

Date	Rank	Name	Unit	Cl #	Aircraft	Place	Time	Opponent	Conf
08-06-44	Lt.	Vogt	5	27	Mustang	N of Caen (UU-TU)	0600	168 Sqd	yes
08-06-44	Lt.	Hofmann W.	8 CO	14	Mustang	NW of Caen (UU1-2)	0605	168 Sqd	yes
08-06-44	Lt.	Hofmann W.	8 CO	15	P-47	20km SE of Caen (UU9)	1650		unk
08-06-44	Lt.	Hofmann W.	8 CO	16	P-47	W of Rouen (SB,TB,SC,TC)	1705		unk
08-06-44	Major	Mietusch	III CO	63	P-47	NE of Le Havre	0640	371 FG	yes
08-06-44	Major	Mietusch	III CO	64	P-47	E of Le Havre (SA-SB)	0645	371 FG	unk
08-06-44	Uffz.	Zeller	III St		P-47	E of Le Havre (SA-SB)	0646	371 FG	unk
08-06-44	Lt.	Reischer	11 CO	15	Typhoon	N of Caen (TU6)	0635	198 Sqd	yes

9 June

Fliegerkorps II was finally ready to mount a full-scale attack on the landing beaches, but the weather proved uncooperative. The fighter-bombers, and their escorts from the 5th Jagddivision, were airborne before dawn, but all had to land early owing to low-lying clouds, haze, and drizzling rain. Fliegerkorps II headquarters complained bitterly over the radio that disruption of land-line communications had made the planning of operations extremely difficult – a message decoded within hours by the ULTRA code-breaking organization. The Germans' dependence on the radio, necessitated by French sabotage of the telephone system, gave the Allies advance notice of every Wehrmacht operation in Normandy, and complete information on unit locations and strength. The AEAF had established its own radio intercept service to pick up and interpret the interair and ground-to-air communications of Luftflotte 3. The German formation commanders had finally begun to use codenames over the radio, rather than their own nicknames, but the experienced RAF intelligence officers soon matched codes with units, and by early July their daily reports included the identity of each Jagdgruppe that they heard in the air. The Allied ULTRA and airborne radio intercept reports can be combined to give a complete picture of almost every Luftwaffe mission on the *Invasionsfront*: its plan, as reflected in the mission orders; its progress while in the air; and its result, as reported to higher headquarters that night. No student of the Luftwaffe can afford to ignore these Allied records, which are far more informative than anything available in the German archives.

The aborted dawn mission cost the First Gruppe one fatality. While landing on Boissy-le-Bois, the Focke-Wulf of Uffz. Erich Schlenker overturned, killing Schlenker. The 1st Staffel Kapitän, Oblt. Max Groth, had to force-land in a field after his engine quit, but he suffered only slight injuries.

The weather over the landing zones improved somewhat in the afternoon, but Fliegerkorps II did not attempt another mission. The three Gruppen of JG 26 each flew one freie Jagd, but found no enemy aircraft; conditions over England were apparently worse than over France. The Jagddivision had no further orders, and Priller himself ordered a late-evening strafing mission. Shortly before sunset, the Kommodore led eleven First Gruppe Focke-Wulfs on their second mission of the day. For unknown reasons they were unable to reach the beachhead. Instead, they headed for the Allied airborne forces' D-Day landing grounds, and destroyed fifteen gliders by gunfire. The gliders had been left undefended, as they were in fact utterly worthless targets. This attack, and the pilots' subsequent "victory" claims, are a sad commentary on the relevance and effectiveness of the German fighter force at this stage of the war.

10 June

The weather showed an improvement, with only intermittent rain showers. Fliegerkorps II was still unable to assemble its fighter-bombers for a mission in strength, and the 5th Jagddivision continued flying strafing missions and sweeps. Lt. Helmut Menge of the 4th Staffel disappeared on an early mission over the beachhead; his fate remains unknown. Uffz. Rudolf Waldherr of the 9th Staffel was hit by American fighters at 1115 near Beauvais and crashed in his airplane. The first success for the Geschwader came in mid-afternoon, when part of the Second Gruppe got involved in a battle north of Argentan between 78th Fighter Group P-47s and Bf 109s. Lt. Hofmann accounted for one of the five Thunderbolts that went down in this battle. The day's last combats took place between the Orne Estuary and Lisieux, and again involved a Thunderbolt unit, this one the 9th Air Force's 365th Fighter Group. An undercast now hid the ground, while cumulus clouds were thick at altitude. Ofhr. Gerhard Dewald of the 9th Staffel popped up out of the low clouds in front of a Thunderbolt that promptly shot him down. Dewald bailed out and dropped back into the undercast, landing with slight injuries. Another 9th Staffel pilot, Lt. Dietwin Pape, and Lt. Glunz of the 6th Staffel went hunting for Thunderbolts within the towering clouds. Pape claimed one of the fighters, and Glunz claimed three; he caught two in a single burst of fire while in a skidding turn. Only one of these four claims was eventually confirmed; the 365th in fact lost two P-47s in these combats in the clouds. Glunz's three air victories in two minutes gained him an interview with a war correspondent.

JG 26 Victory Claims: 10 June 1944

Date	Rank	Name	Unit	Cl #	Aircraft	Place	Time	Opponent	Conf
10-06-44	Lt.	Glunz	6 CO	63	P-47	N of Lisieux (TA-UA)	1758	365 FG	yes
10-06-44	Lt.	Glunz	6 CO	62	P-47	N of Lisieux (TA-UA)	1756	365 FG	unk
10-06-44	Lt.	Glunz	6 CO	64	P-47	N of Lisieux (TA-UA)	1758	365 FG	unk
10-06-44	Lt.	Hofmann W.	8 CO	17	P-47	NW of Lisieux	1428	78 FG	yes
10-06-44	Lt.	Pape	9		P-47	Lisieux (UA1-4)	1758	365 FG	unk

JG 26 Casualties: 8 - 10 June 1944

Date	Rank	Name	Cas	Unit	Aircraft	WNr	Mkgs	Place	Time	Cause	Allied Unit
08-06-44	Lt.	Giebner, Helmut	KIA	5	Fw 190A-8	170625	wh 5	E of Toqueville		fighter	
08-06-44	Gefr.	Lienich, Heinz	WIA	11	Bf 109G-6	162707	yl 15	5km SW of Caen	1315	Spitfire	
09-06-44	Oblt.	Groth, Max	WIA	1 CO	Fw 190A-8	680417	wh 6	Beauvais-Boissy-le-Bois		engine	n/a
09-06-44	Uffz.	Schlenker, Erich	KIFA	2	Fw 190A-8	174007	bk 2	Boissy-le-Bois	0615	landing	n/a
10-06-44	Lt.	Menge, Helmut	KIA	4	Fw 190A-8	730414	bl 10	Orne Estuary	0630	fighter	
10-06-44	Ofhr.	Dewald, Gerhard	WIA	9	Bf 109G-6	412297	wh 22	Orne Estuary	1815	P-47	365 FG
10-06-44	Uffz.	Waldherr, Rudolf	KIA	9	Bf 109G-6	440584	bk 10	E of Beauvais	1115	fighter	

11 June

Fliegerkorps II ordered its Jagdgruppen to finish installing bomb racks on their fighters – a "rest day" was to be taken to accomplish this. But Gen. Buelowius's opportunities, and units, were slipping away. III/SG 4, his only experienced day bomber unit, was down to four serviceable aircraft. I/SKG 10 was under orders to transfer to Fliegerkorps IX, a night bombing command. And ZG 1 was to transfer to Geschwader Bongart, an ad hoc unit thrown together to fight the Resistance in southern France. Luftflotte 3 issued an unhelpful order that *all* fighters were to be fitted with bomb racks; bombing would now be the primary mission for all fighters, and the shooting down of enemy aircraft would be secondary. Events rapidly overtook this wildly unrealistic edict.

The Geschwader was grounded until mid-afternoon by the weather. Allied air activity was greatly reduced for the same reason, and afternoon freie Jagden by the Second and Third Gruppen failed to contact the enemy. Obstlt. Priller, his wingman Uffz. Wodarczyk, and Priller's former Führungsstaffel, the 4th, were vectored to a formation of P-38 Lightnings. These distinctive twin-tailed fighters had been restricted since D-Day to patrolling the shipping lanes, but had now been released to head inland and join in the general attacks on the German defenses. The 55th Fighter Group bombed railroad yards in the Compiègne area. After turning for England, one of the Lightning Group's squadrons received word from their controller of air activity at Beauvais. They turned onto the new course, but as they reached the airfield they were struck by Priller and his dozen Fw 190s. For once the numerical odds were even, and the heavy Lightnings, caught at low altitude, were theoretically at a disadvantage. Priller's target fell away immediately. The sky above Beauvais then became a confusing whirl of aircraft. Two Lightnings, and one Focke-Wulf, crashed. The German fighter was piloted by Lt. Gerd Wiegand. He was hit by a Lightning pilot who took a 70° deflection shot and saw strikes in front of the Focke-Wulf's cockpit and smoke from its engine before he was taken under attack himself, and snap-rolled into a cloud. Wiegand bailed out without injury, but shattered his thigh when landing. He made a full recovery, but never returned to combat; his career in the Adamsonstaffel ended with 106 combat sorties and seventeen confirmed air victories.

Priller and his enthusiastic pilots claimed five certain and one probable victory, and four of the claims were confirmed. I/JG 5 also claimed two P-38s today, but the only Lightning losses to fighters were the two resulting from this 55th Fighter Group combat.

JG 26 Victory Claims: 11 June 1944

Date	Rank	Name	Unit	Cl #	Aircraft	Place	Time	Opponent	Conf
11-06-44	Obstlt.	Priller	Ge CO	99	P-38	NW of Compiègne (SF-TF)	1535	55 FG	yes
11-06-44	Fw.	Schmidtke	4	2	P-38	Beauvais (TE1-4)	1532	55 FG	yes
11-06-44	Lt.	Wiegand	4	22	P-38	Compiègne (TF-SF)	1530	55 FG	yes
11-06-44	Lt.	Wiegand	4	23	P-38	Clermont (TF-SF)	1535	55 FG	yes
11-06-44	Uffz.	Wodarczyk	4	2	P-38	Compiègne (TF)	1538	55 FG	yes
11-06-44	Uffz.	Wodarczyk	4		P-38-prob	Compiègne (SF-TF)	1548	55 FG	prob

12 June

The ULTRA organization decoded three OKL orders to Luftflotte 3 proving that the Luftwaffe defensive plan had collapsed. First, all fighters were to have their bomb racks removed and saved "for future use". Second, Jagdkorps II, the parent organization of the 5th Jagddivision, was to take over all Jagdgruppen now in France, plus the ground-attack unit III/SG 4. Fighters were to be concentrated against the spearheads of Allied attacks, where their principal mission would be to fight off Allied aircraft; ground attacks were to be made with guns only. Third, two Jagdgruppen formerly in Luftflotte Reich, IV/JG 3 and III/JG 11, were to return to Germany immediately – the first to preserve the specialized skills of its pilots as bomber destroyers, and the second because it had already been ground into impotence over Normandy. The next day Fliegerkorps II was disbanded, and Gen. Buelowius and his staff were sent back to Germany. The 5th Jagddivision was now responsible for all of the fighter units in the invasion zone, some twenty Jagdgruppen. This was far more than its control organization, Jafü 5, could handle, and until the other two Jagdfliegerführer in France, Jafü 4 and Jafü Brittany, could pick up some of the load, nearly all fighter missions over the *Invasionsraum* (lodgment area) would have to be conducted as uncontrolled freie Jagden.

At dawn Lt. Wilhelm Hofmann, Obfw. Peter Crump, and their wingmen took off from Guyancourt and headed for the beachhead. A broken cloud layer extended from 1000 to 1500 meters (3,000 to 5,000 feet). The quartet stayed well beneath the clouds, in the ground haze. Southeast of Rouen they came across a pair of climbing Thunderbolts which were beginning an attack on a Bf 109. Approaching out of the dawn haze, with the dark earth behind them, Hofmann and Crump were not seen. Before the American pilots could open fire on the Messerschmitt, Crump fired on one from an angle of 30°; the salvo hit the left side of the P-47's engine and fuselage. The plane immediately burst into flames and dived away to the left. The pilot of the other P-47, surprised in like manner by Hofmann, saved himself by bailing out. The Focke-Wulf pilots completed their mission without further incident. They had had a small part in the 353rd Fighter Group's most disastrous mission of the war.

The Thunderbolt group had taken off from England at 0434 for a bombing mission to the Évreux area. While making ground attacks near Dreux, two squadrons were attacked by several very aggressive Bf 109 Staffeln which dropped from the clouds onto the rear of the P-47 formations. The P-47s were immediately split up into flights and elements. Those that climbed through the clouds found a high cover of Bf 109s waiting to pounce on them. The Thunderbolt pilots stayed in the area, dodging in and out of the clouds, until low fuel forced them to break for base or until they were shot down. The American pilots that got back claimed 6-1-4 Bf 109s, but eight P-47 pilots failed to return.

Lt. Kempf and Fw. Polster led the dawn patrol of the Third Gruppe. They contacted a single P-47 east of the landing zone, and Kempf shot it down. This was possibly one of the 353rd Fighter Group aircraft escaping the struggle over Évreux. The Geschwader continued to fly sweeps for the rest of the day. Most made contact with P-47s, but no claims or losses resulted. The Second Gruppe did suffer one fatality; a groundcrewman committed suicide in his Guyancourt barracks by shooting himself.

13 June

The Allied mission count was down somewhat owing to cloud cover over France. The 5th Jagddivision ordered thirty-two missions; a total of 288 Bf 109 and fifty-six Fw 190 sorties were flown. The Geschwader continued its sweeps and Jabo escorts. The First Gruppe gained a new task, a *Strassenjagd* or road hunt, which was a strafing and/or rocket mortar mission against Allied road traffic. Obstlt. Priller sent an urgent radio message to the 5th Jagddivision requesting 21 cm rocket barrel supports for his Stab and First Gruppe Fw 190s. Lt. Söffing of the 1st Staffel claimed the day's only success, a Mustang near Dreux at 1615. The claim was confirmed, but the details of this combat have not been traced.

Missions over the beachhead cost the Second Gruppe two pilots, for no successes. Oblt. Hermann Müller and Gefr. Hans-Walter Sander disappeared, and were later found to have crashed in their aircraft, probably victims of Allied antiaircraft fire. Another Second Gruppe pilot, Uffz. Werner Winter, overturned after hitting a patch of soft ground in a night landing after a transfer flight. He suffered numerous minor injuries; the Focke-Wulf was repairable.

In late afternoon the Third Gruppe flew an escort mission for another Bf 109 Gruppe which was to make rocket mortar attacks on British armor around Caen. While still

Lt. Waldemar "Vladimir" Söffing, one of the *Draufgängern* (daredevils) of the First Gruppe, photographed when a Feldwebel. *(Bundesarchiv-Militärarchiv)*

sixty miles from the beachhead, the sixty-fighter formation encountered eight P-51s, and broke up. Uffz. Heinz Gehrke of the 11th Staffel lost even his element leader, and had to land alone at Orleans for fuel. Ten minutes after takeoff, he blundered across a squadron of 78th Fighter Group P-47s hunting trains near Orleans. According to the American records, one pilot called out a 109 which he spotted "stooging along on the deck". The American took an awkward deflection shot, and at first thought the Messerschmitt had crashed. He then saw it again, and the chase was on. Firing from 800 yards (730 meters), he closed the range somewhat, but ran out of ammunition. His squadron commander then closed to 150 yards, firing short bursts which caused pieces to fly off the 109. As it caught fire, Gehrke jumped. The airplane then hit a French farmhouse and exploded. A passing army truck saved Gehrke from a mob of pitchfork-waving French peasants. After ten days in hospital to have shell splinters removed from his legs, Heinz Gehrke rejoined his unit, only to be sentenced to three days confinement by his Staffelkapitän, Lt. Peter Reischer, for destroying government property (and probably for leaving the formation.) The sentence was served in a Parisian public toilet that had been converted into a stockade.

JG 26 Victory Claims: 12 - 13 June 1944

Date	Rank	Name	Unit	Cl #	Aircraft	Place	Time	Opponent	Conf
12-06-44	Lt.	Crump	6	15	P-47	15-20km SE of Rouen (TC)	0623	353 FG	unk
12-06-44	Lt.	Hofmann W.	8 CO	18	P-47	40km SE of Rouen	0625	353 FG	yes
12-06-44	Lt.	Kempf	9	61	P-47	Lisieux (UA2)	0614	353 FG	i.O.
13-06-44	Lt.	Söffing	1	19	P-51	Dreux (AC6)	1635		yes

JG 26 Casualties: 11 - 13 June 1944

Date	Rank	Name	Cas	Unit	Aircraft	WNr	Mkgs	Place	Time	Cause	Allied Unit
11-06-44	Lt.	Wiegand, Gerd	WIA	4	Fw 190A-8	170310	bl 6	15km N of Compiègne	1530	P-38	55 FG
13-06-44	Gefr.	Sander, Hans-Walter	KIA	6	Fw 190A-8	170717	bk 1	N of Caen		flak	n/a
13-06-44	Oblt.	Müller, Hermann	KIA	7	Fw 190A-8	730491	br 12	N of Caen		flak	n/a
13-06-44	Uffz.	Winter, Werner	WIA	7	Fw 190A-8	174017	br 8	Étampes		landing	non-op
13-06-44	Uffz.	Gehrke, Heinz	WIA	11	Bf 109G-6	162100	yl 7	Orleans	2130	P-47	78 FG

14 June

The 8th Air Force canceled a scheduled mission to Germany because of bad weather, and in the morning sent 983 B-17s and B-24s to attack Luftwaffe airfields and supply dumps in France. The 9th Air Force dispatched more than 500 B-26s and A-20s to bomb railroad targets south of Paris. All of these bombers were, of course, heavily escorted. American fighters also flew well over one thousand ground-attack sorties.

The effort of the 2nd TAF was on a similar scale.

Jafü 5 responded to the waves of oncoming heavy bombers by sending most of its fighters up on sweeps. Only one formation leader attempted an attack on the bombers in their combat boxes – Klaus Mietusch. His Third Gruppe scrambled from Villacoublay at 0645 to intercept a formation of B-17s that was headed for nearby Le Bourget. Uffz. Joachim Zeller flew as Mietusch's wingman; Fw. Wolfgang "Poldi" Polster and Uffz. Erhard Tippe were the second element in his Stabsschwarm. The eighteen Bf 109s immediately climbed north of Paris to an altitude of about 8000 meters (26,000 feet), and formed a battle line. Major Mietusch spotted a large formation of P-38s flying as high cover to the B-17s, but 2000 meters (6500 feet) below the Messerschmitts. Mietusch lifted his wing and dived, followed by his seventeen fighters in a single string. The leading Bf 109s got to pick out their targets before the P-38 formation broke up, and each member of the Stabsschwarm claimed a Lightning; Lt. Reischer claimed a fifth. While some of his fighters were battling the P-38s, Mietusch and others broke through to the bombers. Mietusch and Lt. Hans Oeckel of the 12th Staffel each shot down a B-17, one each from the 384th and the 401st Bomb Groups. These were the only two Fortresses lost to fighters on the mission.

The Messerschmitts left behind to battle the Lightnings took some punishment. The new pilots, as usual, bore the brunt of it. Lt. Ernst Prüll was shot down and killed on his first mission. Uffz. Bruno Frotzscher, another new pilot, was also killed. Uffz. Tippe, a third *Neuling*, took a single hit in a coolant line, escaped in a cloud, and was able to make a smooth belly landing on cropland outside of Paris. A fourth pilot was shot down, but bailed out without injury. Some Thunderbolts, probably from the 368th Fighter Group, got involved in the last stages of this battle, and Uffz. Stoll chased one to low altitude and shot it down, but his claim was not confirmed. Three of the five Lightning claims of the Gruppe were confirmed, exactly matching the losses of the 55th Fighter Group.

The First Gruppe also flew a successful early-morning sweep, besting the P-51s of the 357th Fighter Group, which was flying a sweep of its own ahead of the bombers. One squadron was bounced by sixteen Fw 190s east of Paris. Lt. Ellenrieder and his wingman, Gefr. Edwin Zubiako, each claimed Mustangs; only Ellenrieder's claim was confirmed. One Mustang was lost; the American pilots claimed 2-0-1 "long nosed Fw 190s", but none of the short-nosed Focke-Wulfs went down. (Allied aircrewmen had been told by their intelligence officers to expect the Fw 190D, and had been reporting them all year; these "long noses" would not enter combat for four more months.)

The Second Gruppe lost two of its newest pilots, and made no claims. Uffz. Bruno Prüver got involved in the big combat with American fighters east of Paris, and was killed in his aircraft; it was his first mission. Fhr. Ulrich-Karsten Frantz had engine problems on the mission, and attempted to force-land on Évreux. He crashed, and his fighter exploded, killing Frantz after his third mission.

JG 26 Victory Claims: 14 June 1944

Date	Rank	Name	Unit	Cl #	Aircraft	Place	Time	Opponent	Conf
14-06-44	Lt.	Ellenrieder	3	8	P-51	E of Paris (AF)	0805	357 FG	yes
14-06-44	Gefr.	Zubiako	3	1	P-51	E of Paris (AF)	0807	357 FG	yes
14-06-44	Major	Mietusch	III CO	65	P-38	NW of Paris (AE1-UE7)	0735	55 FG	yes
14-06-44	Major	Mietusch	III CO	66	B-17	E of Paris (UG-AG)	0800	384 or 401 BG	yes
14-06-44	Uffz.	Zeller	III St		P-38	NW of Paris (AE1-UE7)	0735	55 FG	yes
14-06-44	Lt.	Reischer	11 CO	16	P-38	SW of Évreux (AD3)	0735	55 FG	unk
14-06-44	Fw.	Polster	11	4	P-38	N of Paris (UD9-UE7)	0736	55 FG	unk
14-06-44	Uffz.	Stoll	11		P-47	NE of Chartres (BD2-6)	0740	368 FG	unk
14-06-44	Uffz.	Tippe	11	1	P-38	N of Paris (UD9-UE7)	0730	55 FG	i.O.
14-06-44	Lt.	Oeckel	12	3	B-17	E of Paris (AG)	0807	384 or 401 BG	unk

15 June

The 8th Air Force again attacked tactical targets in France. The 5th Jagddivision ordered 36 missions; a total of 121 Fw 190 and 195 Bf 109 sorties were flown.

Again today, Jafü 5 ordered its fighters aloft at dawn. Again today, JG 26 shot down all of the 8th Air Force bombers that were lost to German aircraft. Obstlt. Priller and Uffz. Wodarczyk had flown to Guyancourt on the 14th, and joined the Second Gruppe on the mission, which was originally to be a sweep west of Caen with all three Gruppen and III/JG 54. The mission was led by Hptm. Matoni of the 6th Staffel. It promised to be a sunny, cloudless day, and the German fighters assembled quickly and were barreling over the Normandy countryside toward the beachhead when ordered to change course. Five *Pulks* of heavy enemy bombers were just then crossing the French coast, flying in the direction of Paris. The German pilots soon spotted them – small, twinkling points of light at an altitude of about 5000 meters (16,000 feet). Matoni and Priller also saw the escort fighters swarming above them, and decided on a swift attack. Priller made an oblique attack on the first box from the side, at the same altitude, and obtained several strikes on a B-17. He then fought off the close escort and attacked a formation of about twenty B-24s from the front. He fired at the Liberator flying the left outboard position in the first vee, and saw strikes in the cockpit and on the two left engines. As he dived away, he saw the Liberator sheer away from the formation, bright flames coming from three engines, and dive.

Priller's Liberator belonged to the 492nd Bomb Group. It headed for the beachhead on two engines. When the propeller governor on a third engine quit, the pilot told the crew to stand by. They were at 2000 meters (7000 feet), and the coast was visible thirty miles away. The navigator signaled, mistakenly, that they were over Allied territory, and bailed out. A moment later the fourth engine quit, prompting all of the remaining crew but the pilot to bail out within fifteen seconds. The pilot then trimmed the plane and jumped out himself. The navigator was captured, but the other nine men landed safely within the Allied lines. Ironically, the navigator's error saved his life; the rest of his crew were killed in the crash of another B-24 less than three weeks later.

Pips Priller's victory was his hundredth. All had been obtained on the Kanalfront. Only a handful of pilots had scored a hundred victories in the West; such a milestone gave the Geschwader reason to celebrate. After Priller landed, he was feted with the customary bouquet. Messages congratulating him on his extraordinary achievement

Obstlt. Priller is presented the traditional flowers after his 100th victory. The pilot to his right is Hptm. Matoni, who led the Second Gruppe on the mission – Guyancourt, 15 June. *(Bundesarchiv-Bildarchiv)*

continued to arrive at his various temporary headquarters – Chaumont, Buc, and Guyancourt – for the next several weeks. At the end of June, he was summoned to Adolf Hitler's headquarters to receive the Swords to his Knight's Cross. He was the second (and last) pilot to be awarded this decoration while a member of JG 26.

The Second Gruppe did not escape the escorts unscathed. Oblt. Radener's 7th Staffel flew high cover, and was attacked by 339th Fighter Group P-51s. Radener shot down a Mustang, but was then shot down himself. He bailed out, but his parachute fouled on his aircraft. He pulled free in time to make a hard landing, suffering injuries that kept him out of combat until the end of the month. Lt. Gerhard Vogt took his place as leader of the 7th Staffel. Radener's Mustang claim was not filed.

Obfw. Alfred Günther of the 6th Staffel was chased away from the battlefield by Mustangs and shot down into a river south of Orleans. His body was found in the 1970s, but was not identified until 1991, and then by his cigarette lighter, which was presented to his widow by a French researcher.

Staiger's and Mietusch's Gruppen each attacked bomber *Pulks* on this mission. Staiger claimed to have shot a B-17 from its formation south of Chartres, but his claim was not confirmed; both B-17s lost today were credited to Flak.

Major Mietusch had selected Uffz. Tippe to fly as his wingman on the mission. The Third Gruppe caught the B-24s of the 392nd Bomb Group without escort, and the Bf 109s were able to make three attacks from the front and the rear of the formation. Mietusch claimed one victory, while Tippe claimed a separation after shooting a second B-24 from its formation. The claims of Mietusch and Tippe matched the group's actual losses. One Liberator went down immediately, while a second badly damaged bomber made it back across the Channel, and crashed on an English emergency field.

The gunners of the 392nd Bomb Group claimed two victories. One Messerschmitt, that of the 9th Staffel Kapitän, Oblt. Victor Hilgendorff, was in fact downed. Hilgendorff was 29 years old, and had been a fighter pilot since 1934. In 1941 he had joined JG 26 to fly as Obstlt. Galland's wingman. As a result of injuries suffered when he was shot down in 1942, Hilgendorff's right leg was amputated above the knee. His left leg had to be pinned from the knee to the foot, as its shin had had a one-inch piece shot from it. After eighteen months in the hospital, and still not fully recovered, Hilgendorff returned to the Geschwader. He was first made the non-flying technical officer of the Third Gruppe, but was able to regain his combat status, and took over the 9th Staffel on 10 May. After his Messerschmitt was hit by B-24 fire, he first snapped off his artificial leg, so he wouldn't lose it. He then jumped out and came to earth by parachute, his leg under his arm. It is reported that a French farmer, seeing the pilot's descent, took to his heels, thinking himself out of his mind. Hilgendorff broke a vertebra during his landing, but was flying missions again one week later.

JG 26 Casualties: 14 - 15 June 1944

Date	Rank	Name	Cas	Unit	Aircraft	WNr	Mkgs	Place	Time	Cause	Allied Unit
14-06-44	Fhr.	Frantz, Ulrich-Karsten	KIFA	5	Fw 190A-8	170609	wh 4	Évreux		engine	n/a
14-06-44	Uffz.	Prüver, Bruno	KIA	7	Fw 190A-8	170716	br 7	SE of Paris-Mary sur Marne		fighter	
14-06-44	Uffz.	Frotzscher, Helmut	KIA	11	Bf 109G-6	440913	yl 18	Meulan-NW of Paris	0730	P-38	55 FG
14-06-44	Lt.	Prüll, Ernst	KIA	12	Bf 109G-6	412682	bl 12	nr Paris	0700	P-38	55 FG
15-06-44	Obfw.	Günther, Alfred	KIA	6	Fw 190A-8	170712	bk 6	S of Orleans	0830	P-51	339 FG
15-06-44	Oblt.	Radener, Waldemar	WIA	7 CO	Fw 190A-8	730934	br 2	Danoy		P-51	339 FG
15-06-44	Oblt.	Hilgendorff, Viktor	WIA	9 CO	Bf 109G-6	410689	wh 6	6km W of Pau	0712	B-24	392 BG

16 June

Jagdkorps II ordered the five Jagdgeschwader and one Schlachtgruppe of Jafü 5 to make concentrated attacks on the British sector of the beachhead from dawn, while the

Lt. Glunz chats with a groundcrewman beside his "black 9"; its rudder displays sixty-two victories – Guyancourt, 15 June. (*Bundesarchiv-Bildarchiv*)

Fw. Erhard Tippe of the 11th Staffel, photographed when a Gefreiter. (*Bundesarchiv-Militärarchiv*)

two fighter units now controlled by Jafü Brittany supported the Army's resistance to the American drive on Cherbourg. The weather disrupted the dawn mission of the Geschwader, and only one pilot made contact with the enemy. Erhard Tippe was now to be Major Mietusch's permanent wingman. His assigned aircraft was not cleared for the mission, however, and by the time Tippe found a replacement, his Gruppe had taken off and disappeared into the pre-dawn darkness. He took off alone, and located and joined a Gruppe from an unknown Jagdgeschwader just as that formation dropped through the cloud deck. The pilots took one look at the huge array of ships through the mass of wires holding down the barrage balloons, and then broke in all directions. To avoid being rammed, Tippe pulled up sharply into the cloud. When he emerged, he was in the midst of six Spitfires. He evaded their fire briefly by entering a tight spiral, but was soon hit and had to bail out. Tippe's promising career ended in a bramble bush. Erhard Tippe recalls:

"Suddenly three Canadian soldiers with machine pistols appeared in front of me. 'Come on, boy!' was how they put it to me, just that simply. As I took off my parachute, I realized that my right shoulder was injured. I could no longer bend my right arm. I crept painfully out of the bushes and was thoroughly searched. My personal articles were taken from me. I then said, in English, 'This cigarette case is a souvenir from my brother. Give it back to me.' They then returned everything but the military items. Finally the three Canadians took me to their command post. A short conversation; then, because of my injury I was taken to a field hospital. There was a great deal of activity. Orderlies brought in a severely wounded soldier on a litter, the cover of which was soaked through with blood. The litter was set down in front of me. Another orderly brought him a cup of tea. The wounded man shook his head firmly and said, 'Give this German prisoner a cup of tea, and a cigarette, too'. I was greatly moved by these words; the insanity of this war between our peoples impressed itself on me. As they carried him off to the operating room, I wished him a speedy recovery."

Erhard Tippe's opponents were from No. 443 Sqd. (RCAF), six of whose Spitfires scrambled from their French airstrip at 0500 to intercept twenty Bf 109s. Tippe's was the only one shot down. He was the only Geschwader pilot taken prisoner in June; that this was a rare occurrence is indicative of the small percentage of the unit's sorties that succeeded in crossing the battle lines.

Tippe was the day's only Geschwader loss; its only victory was gained by Oblt. Schauder, 10th Staffel Kapitän, who shot down a No. 438 Sqd. Typhoon near Lisieux.

Hptm. Josef Wurmheller, the Kommandeur of III/JG 2, scored his 100th air victory on the Western Front today, the last Luftwaffe pilot to do so. His Gruppe intercepted Mustangs in the evening, and Wurmheller's claim was one of four that were confirmed. No American Mustangs were lost today; one 2nd TAF TacR Mustang from No. 2 Squadron was lost in the area of Wurmheller's combat.

Obstlt. Priller was again bending the rules in an attempt to get replacement aircraft. The ULTRA service decoded a transmission in which he ordered his Gruppen to send all pilots without aircraft to Sammelgruppe West (Ferry Group West) at Villacoublay during the daylight hours. Every morning at 0200 the ferry unit was to fly the pilots to the collection depot in eastern France; the pilots were then to fly the new fighters directly to their own units.

JG 26 Victory Claims: 15 - 16 June 1944

Date	Rank	Name	Unit	Cl #	Aircraft	Place	Time	Opponent	Conf
15-06-44	Obstlt.	Priller	Ge CO	100	B-24	W Dreux-SW of Chartres	0710	492 BG	yes
15-06-44	Hptm.	Staiger	I CO	57	B-17-HSS	80km S of Chartres			no
15-06-44	Oblt.	Radener	7 CO		P-51	E of Bonneval		339 FG	no
15-06-44	Major	Mietusch	III CO	67	B-24	SW of Chartres (CB-DC)	0700	392 BG	yes
15-06-44	Uffz.	Tippe	11	2	B-24-HSS	SW of Chartres	0700	392 BG	unk
16-06-44	Oblt.	Schauder	10 CO	18	Typhoon	near Lisieux (UU4-UA6)	1735	438 Sqd	unk

17 June

The 5th Jagddivision planned four concentrated operations south of Bayeux; forty-nine unit missions, 129 Fw 190 and 152 Bf 109 sorties, were flown. The missions of the Geschwader were specified as either freie Jagden or *Jabojagden* (fighter-bomber hunts) in the invasion zone. The Second Gruppe scored all of the victories credited to the Geschwader, but also suffered all of its casualties. Hptm. Matoni and Lt. Prager claimed Mustangs on the dawn mission to Caen. In mid-afternoon, Lt. Hofmann downed a P-47 near St. Lô, and in late afternoon, Uffz. Lissack claimed a Mustang at low altitude near Bayeux. Uffz. Werner Hofmann, Uffz. Hans Klees, Uffz. Hans Worthmann, and Fhj.-Fw. Hans Zimmermann were all shot down near the beachhead by Allied fighters. Their loss reports include no times, so it has not been possible to identify the Allied victors. The only other aircraft lost by the Geschwader was a Third Gruppe Bf 109, but its pilot, Uffz. Ayerle, escaped injury.

Peter Crump of the 6th Staffel received his commission as a war-service Leutnant, after fifteen air victories in 150 western combat sorties.

The ULTRA code-breakers reported the minutes of a Luftwaffe fighter commanders' conference held today. Among the attendees were Major Mietusch and the III/JG 54 Gruppenkommandeur, Hptm. Robert Weiss. Both expressed confidence in their aircraft and pilots, "except for the most recent replacements", but stated that operations over the landing zone should only be attempted with formations containing at least twenty fighters – flights with fewer fighters suffered high losses. They also agreed that the lack of experienced Staffel leaders jeopardized the chances of future success.

Mietusch made some points concerning the Bf 109:

Lt. Hans Prager of the Second Gruppe and III/JG 54, photographed when a Feldwebel. Prager was transferred several times to fill temporary needs, and considered himself a "fireman." (*Bundesarchiv-Militärarchiv*)

1. "The speed differential between Bf 109s and Fw 190s causes problems in mixed formations. In such cases, Bf 109s must be given the better tactical position – i.e., the greater altitude.

2. "Bf 109 operations at low level and in low cloud are to be avoided.

3. "Bf 109s have the best chance of success in dives from above.

4. "The MK 108 3 centimeter nose cannon has proved its worth; the slight adverse affect on flight performance is bearable."

Hptm. Weiss had these comments on the experiences of III/JG 54:

1. "The unit left Germany with eighteen Fw 190s; fourteen were serviceable on arrival.

2. "The Gruppe flew thirteen Jabo operations while in Fliegerkorps II. Aimed bombing was possible only twice. Bombs were jettisoned in every other instance, owing to lack of Jabo training, inadequate or poorly-flown escort, and/or formations that were too small.

3. "Operational strength of the Gruppe has decreased rapidly in the theater."

JG 26 Victory Claims: 17 June 1944

Date	Rank	Name	Unit	Cl #	Aircraft	Place	Time	Opponent	Conf
17-06-44	Hptm.	Matoni	5 CO	21	P-51-prob	Caen (UU6-9)	0638		unk
17-06-44	Lt.	Prager	5	3	P-51	Caen (UU3)	0640		yes
17-06-44	Uffz.	Lissack	7	1	P-51	Bayeux (UT1-2)	1908		yes
17-06-44	Lt.	Hofmann W.	8 CO	19	P-47	St. Lô (US1-5)	1335		yes
17-06-44	Obfw.	Zirngibl	8	9	P-47	St. Lô-Perrier	1337		yes

JG 26 Casualties: 16 - 17 June 1944

Date	Rank	Name	Cas	Unit	Aircraft	WNr	Mkgs	Place	Time	Cause	Allied Unit
16-06-44	Fw.	Tippe, Erhard	POW	11	Bf 109G-6	412351	yl 21	Le Havre	0530	Spitfire	443 Sqd
17-06-44	Uffz.	Hofmann, Werner	KIA	5	Fw 190A-8	730388	wh 3	W of Caen		fighter	
17-06-44	Uffz.	Klees, Hans	KIA	8	Fw 190A-8	730959	bl 2	SE of Avranches		fighter	
17-06-44	Uffz.	Worthmann, Hans	KIA	8	Fw 190A-8	170730	bl 8	SW of Caen		fighter	
17-06-44	Fhj-Fw.	Zimmermann, Hans	KIA	8	Fw 190A-8	170379	bl 7	Vire-SW of Bayeux		fighter	

18 June

Jagdkorps II reported that its fighters flew three hundred sorties, primarily against Allied fighter-bombers around Caen, St. Lô, and farther south. Despite the effort, it could claim only five victories against the enemy Jabos, for three aircraft and one pilot lost. The First Gruppe lost one of the aircraft; its pilot was uninjured. The Second Gruppe accounted for two of the claims. Addi Glunz took Uffz. Lissack, a young 7th Staffel pilot, on a two-airplane evening sweep. They encountered a pair of tactical reconnaissance Mustangs from No. 414 Sqd. (RCAF), and shot them both down. The more experienced of the Geschwader's pilots could best most Allied pilots in single

combat, but such opportunities came rarely. This was Glunz's last flight until early September. During this period he attended a training course for war-service officers. He retained formal command of the 6th Staffel, however, and on the 20th was promoted from Staffelführer to Staffelkapitän.

19 June
Poor weather made this the quietest day over Normandy since the invasion. Jafü 5 and Jafü Brittany reported flying only nine missions, with a total of sixty Bf 109s on road patrol and three on weather recon. JG 26 did not fly.

20 June
Bad weather restricted flying by the Allies, but Jafü 5 and Jafü Brittany were still able to put up 153 Fw 190 and 172 Bf 109 sorties. Pilots of the Geschwader fought a number of small-scale combats with Allied fighters. Fw. Zeschke of the 7th Staffel crash-landed after one of these, but was uninjured. The only major engagement came in late afternoon, and pitted the First

Obstlt. Priller and Major Mietusch engage in a serious conference – Villacoublay, late June. *(Bundesarchiv-Militärarchiv)*

Gruppe against a squadron of P-38s from the 370th Fighter Group. Each unit was conducting a sweep when they met near Évreux. Hptm. Staiger, Lt. Nink, and Lt. Schild each claimed a Lightning, and apparently two of the claims were confirmed; one P-38 was in fact lost. The Lightning pilots claimed one Fw 190, but the claim was later reduced to a damaged.

Despite their isolated successes, the German fighters were totally incapable of any effective challenge to Allied air supremacy. The commanding general of Flakkorps III complained to Generalfeldmarschall Sperrle today about the absence of German fighters over the front. In the words of the chief of staff of Jagdkorps II, "Destructive criticism of the day fighters became increasingly prevalent."

21 June
The 8th Air Force dispatched a major raid to Berlin in the morning, escorted by both 8th Fighter Command and the fighters of the 9th Air Force, which were still based in England. Jagdkorps II underwent a minor reorganization to better utilize the control staffs in France. Some of the new Jagdgruppen from Germany had transferred from Normandy to eastern France to find functioning airfields. The 4th Jagddivision and its Jafü 4, which had controlled only night fighters since the departure of JG 26 on D-Day, picked up all of the fighter units now based east of Paris, a total of two Geschwaderstäbe and seven Jagdgruppen.

JG 26 apparently flew no missions until mid-afternoon, and the first ones failed to contact the enemy. The Second and Third Gruppen were both scrambled in late evening for interceptions under Jafü 5 ground control, a rarity for the period. Lt. Kempf led the Third Gruppe in a successful bounce of Mustangs east of Dreux, and was heard by the Allied radio intercept operators to claim two victories. Two No. 430 Sqd. TacR Mustangs were lost in this area, and were probably Kempf's victims. Kempf filed only one victory claim. The Third Gruppe was apparently attacked by

406th Fighter Group Thunderbolts while returning to Villacoublay. The P-47s shot down two Messerschmitts; one pilot was uninjured, but Obfw. Walter Gocksch was killed in his aircraft.

Two hours later, Hptm. Matoni led the Second Gruppe in an attack on a Lightning formation in the same area. The P-38s belonged to the 474th Fighter Group's 428th Squadron, whose pilots had been called away from a late-evening awards ceremony for a rushed bombing mission against railroad traffic between Paris and Dreux. Apparently no-one was assigned to high cover, because Matoni's bounce caught them in the middle of their bombing runs. One American pilot bailed out with severe burns. The Resistance hid him from the Germans, shuttling him from house to house while he received treatment from a doctor summoned from Paris. The pilot died six days later, and was buried under a French name. Matoni and Oblt. Stoll both filed claims for the downed Lightning. Obfw. Joseph Zirngibl was shot down by the Lightnings; he crash-landed his Focke-Wulf, was unable to

Hptm. Hermann Staiger. An outstanding formation leader, he served as interim Kommandeur of both the Third and First Gruppen before gaining a permanent appointment at the end of July as a Gruppen-kommandeur – unfortunately for JG 26, it was in II/JG 1. (*Vanoverbeke*)

get out of it, and burned to death.

JG 26 Victory Claims: 18 - 21 June 1944

Date	Rank	Name	Unit	Cl #	Aircraft	Place	Time	Opponent	Conf
18-06-44	Lt.	Glunz	6 CO	65	Mustang	Coutances (AT9)	1729	414 Sqd	yes
18-06-44	Uffz.	Lissack	7	2	Mustang	Coutances (A8-9)	1729	414 Sqd	yes
20-06-44	Hptm.	Staiger	I CO	58	P-38	Ch. Thierry-NE of Meaux (UC7-9)	1735	370 FG	yes
20-06-44	Lt.	Schild	2	4	P-38	Évreux	1735	370 FG	yes
20-06-44	Lt.	Nink	3	1	P-38	Chateau Thierry (UG7-9)	1735	370 FG	yes
21-06-44	Hptm.	Matoni	5 CO	22	P-38	W of Paris (AC7-AD9)	2146	474 FG	yes
21-06-44	Oblt.	Stoll	5	1	P-38	W of Paris (AD9)	2147	474 FG	yes
21-06-44	Lt.	Kempf	9	62	Mustang	E of Dreux (AD5)	1937	430 Sqd	i.O.

22 June

After the morning mists cleared away, the skies over France were clear. The Allied ground advance from the eastern side of the beachhead had stalled in the Norman hedgerows, and an all-out effort was called on from the 8th Air Force and the AEAF. The 8th Air Force dispatched 1099 B-17s and B-24s in small formations to attack tactical targets. The 9th Air Force bombers flew 600 sorties, and its fighter-bombers 1200, mostly in support of the American attack on Cherbourg. The Geschwader was up from noon until nightfall on defensive missions against this armada.

The First and Third Gruppen took off at 1310, assembled under Obstlt. Priller's command, and headed for the Invasionsfront on a Jabojagd across the battle lines to Cherbourg. Targets were apparently scarce, and at 1353 Priller announced his intent to strafe ground targets. He was probably joined by the First Gruppe, which completed its mission with no encounters. The Third Gruppe continued west, approached Cherbourg, and turned back. At 1430 the pilots became embroiled with more Jabos than they could handle. Southwest of Caen Lt. Peter Reischer led the eight Bf 109s of his 11th Staffel in a bounce of four P-47s – one flight of the 365th Fighter Group's 386th Squadron. The Germans were spotted, and as the P-47s broke into them, the American cover flight dived on the Messerschmitts from above. The flight leader picked out Reischer's Bf 109, which led the P-47 toward the ground in a series of violent maneuvers. The American pilot blacked out in a low-altitude split-S and lost Reischer. As the American was rejoining his flight, another Messerschmitt crossed his path. A barrel roll brought the P-47 in on the German fighter's tail. A brief chase permitted the American to close to point-blank range. After taking a brief burst of fire, the German pilot zoomed for altitude and bailed out. The P-47 circled the pilot, Uffz. Bruno Schwarz of the 11th Staffel, and then joined up with a flight of P-47s from the 368th Group, another 9th Air Force fighter-bomber unit, which had just concluded its own combat with other Third Gruppe Staffeln.

The rest of Reischer's formation, sandwiched between the two flights of P-47s, fought for their lives. Gefr. Heinz Lienich and Lt. Klaus-Rudolf Meyer were killed, while P-47s were shot down by Fw. Günther Patzke and Uffz. Zeichert. The other two 386th Squadron flights spotted two Bf 109s leaving the area, and engaged them in a turning combat in which the German fighters had the advantage. One P-47 was shot down, apparently by Lt. Reischer, who was later credited with a P-51. Reischer had to crash-land his damaged aircraft a few minutes later.

In the meantime, two squadrons of the 368th Fighter Group had encountered other Third Gruppe fighters west of Vire, and shot down several in small-scale dogfights. Fw. Kurt Franzke was killed, and Lt. Dietwin Pape and Uffz. Willi Dachmann bailed out with wounds after these combats. Uffz. Hans Speichert was chased and caught by Lt. Paul Jasper, whose P-47D-16 was 15-20 mph faster than any other in his squadron owing to his crew chief's initiative in sanding, waxing, and polishing it. Paul Jasper recalls:

> "As the Bf 109 turned away and started a gentle climb, obviously at full power, we pursued in the normal flight position...The Bf 109, having an advantage in initial acceleration, pulled away and then held his lead at about 300 to 400 yards [275-365 meters]. As we passed 10,000 feet [3000 meters], the second stage of his supercharger cut in, and he began to increase the distance.
>
> "I told [my flight leader] that I could catch the Bf 109 and opened the throttle and supercharger all the way. At about 15,000 feet [4600 meters] I was gaining on him steadily and at about 200 yards [180 meters] gave him a short burst, seeing strikes in his right wing root. He flipped over into a split-S and dived. I followed and quickly closed the distance. I fired another burst at him, but then my aircraft was bouncing so violently at that speed (and probably the result of his propwash) that I couldn't see any hits. However, he pulled up into a zoom-climb and I followed. As he lost speed, I was sitting about twenty-five yards behind and below him. I steadied the needle and ball in the center, placed the gun sight in his right wheel well, and pulled the trigger. I could see the flashes of hits in the engine area. His propeller froze, one landing gear came down, and bits and pieces flew over my head, as did his canopy.
>
> "I chopped my throttle, dropped my flaps, and skidded my aircraft sideways to prevent overrunning him and inadvertently getting in front of his guns. I slid up inside his right wing and looked at the pilot. He was young, in white helmet and blue flight suit. As our eyes met, he raised his right hand in a military salute and stood up, bailing out over the tail..."

Lt. Jasper's flight leader ordered him to rejoin the formation, which was flying in close order. The leader attempted a sharp turn; another pilot stalled out and collided with Jasper's airplane. Jasper fought his way out of his aircraft and bailed out with two injured hips; the other American did not get out. The two P-47s crashed very near to Speichert's Bf 109, nineteen miles southwest of St. Lô. Jasper was taken prisoner. Speichert made it back to the Third Gruppe on 27 June, and was then sent on convalescent leave until 7 August. Claims by the two P-47 groups totaled 9-1-4 Bf 109s. According to the 5th Jagddivision war diary, twelve Third Gruppe pilots had failed to return to base or make their whereabouts known by nightfall. Eight of the men had been shot down; the other four had made emergency landings.

The Second Gruppe was scrambled at 1740 to oppose heavy bombers and escorts approaching the Paris region. Lt. Vogt separated a B-17 from its formation east of Paris, while Lt. Hofmann was doing the same to a B-24. Their claims were filed as separations, but were confirmed as full victories. No heavy bomber is known to have been shot down by fighter attack on this mission, but several Third Bomb Division B-17s and B-24s crash-landed on the English coast; Vogt's and Hofmann's targets were probably among these. The Second Gruppe suffered no losses to the heavy bombers or their escort during this interception.

The Richthofen Geschwader suffered a chilling loss today. Hptm. Wurmheller, the III/JG 2 Gruppenkommandeur, collided with his wingman over Alençon and was killed.

The results of the Third Gruppe mission lent credence to Major Mietusch's complaints on the 17th. When the highly proficient Hptm. Staiger was ordered from the Third Gruppe to the First to fill in for Major Borris, Mietusch's Gruppe was left with only three experienced formation leaders – himself, Lt. Reischer, and Oblt. Paul Schauder of the 10th Staffel. The unit was proving unable to best even the enemy's fighter-bombers, which were piloted by young men with as little experience in air-to-air combat as Mietusch's average NCO pilot. Whenever possible, the Messerschmitts were employed as high cover for the faster and more heavily armored Fw 190s. But Mietusch's aircraft proved vulnerable even in this role. Morale in the Gruppe began to drop.

The two Focke-Wulf Gruppen were in better shape. Most of their Staffeln contained at least two experienced officers, and the pilots had a high degree of confidence in their aircraft. The survivors claim today that the Fw 190A could outrun any Allied fighter on the deck, regardless of the official performance figures. The fighter's superb rate of roll gave it a useful maneuver for both attack and escape. And the weight and dispersion of fire of its wing-mounted cannon gave even the most inexperienced pilot a chance to knock down enemy aircraft. The claim to loss ratio of both the First and Second Gruppen remained well over two to one throughout the summer; this was a far better performance than that of the Jagdwaffe as a whole.

JG 26 Victory Claims: 22 June 1944

Date	Rank	Name	Unit	Cl #	Aircraft	Place	Time	Opponent	Conf
22-06-44	Lt.	Vogt	7 CO	28	B-17-HSS	SE-E of Paris	1900		yes
22-06-44	Lt.	Hofmann W.	8 CO	20	B-24-HSS	SE of Paris (BF2-3)	1910	34 BG	yes
22-06-44	Fw.	Patzke	9	1	P-47	S of St. Lô (AS5)	1421	365 FG	i.O.
22-06-44	Uffz.	Zeichert	9		P-51	S of St. Lô (AS5)	1419	365 FG P-47	i.O.
22-06-44	Lt.	Reischer	11 CO	17	P-51	S of Cherbourg (TR6)	1443	365 FG P-47	unk

JG 26 Casualties: 21 - 22 June 1944

Date	Rank	Name	Cas	Unit	Aircraft	WNr	Mkgs	Place	Time	Cause	Allied Unit
21-06-44	Obfw.	Zirngibl, Joseph	KIA	8	Fw 190A-6	530763	bl 11	NE of St. Cyr	2200	P-38	474 FG
21-06-44	Obfw.	Gocksch, Walter	KIA	10	Bf 109G-6	412684	bk 2	SW of Paris- N of Boissy	1940	P-47	406 FG

Date	Rank	Name	Status	Staffel	Aircraft	W.Nr.	Location	Time	Claimant	Unit
22-06-44	Lt.	Pape, Dietwin	WIA	9	Bf 109G-6/U4	440578 wh 18	Charges (NF)	1450	P-47	365 or 368 FG
22-06-44	Uffz.	Speichert, Hans	WIA	9	Bf 109G-6/U4	440667 wh 15	30km SW of St. Lô	1450	P-47	368 FG
22-06-44	Fw.	Franzke, Kurt	KIA	10	Bf 109G-6	165169 bk 1	5km S of Alençon	1445	P-47	365 or 368 FG
22-06-44	Lt.	Reischer, Peter	no	11 CO	Bf 109G-6	440580 yl 2	Alençon	1441	P-47	365 or 368 FG
22-06-44	Lt.	Meyer, Klaus-Rudolph	KIA	11	Bf 109G-6	440712 yl 3	Cherbourg	1430	P-47	365 or 368 FG
22-06-44	Uffz.	Schwarz, Bruno	WIA	11	Bf 109G-6	162101 yl 22	nr Bayeux-Cherbourg	1430	P-47	365 or 368 FG
22-06-44	Gefr.	Lienich, Heinz	KIA	11	Bf 109G-6	163499 yl 16	Cornier-S of Tinche	1500	P-47	365 or 368 FG
22-06-44	Gefr.	Malm, Willibald	WIA	12	none		Buc a/f		air attack	n/a
22-06-44	Uffz.	Dachmann, Willi	WIA	12	Bf 109G-6	163741 bl 20	Cherbourg	1400	P-47	365 or 368 FG

23 June

The 5th Jagddivision scheduled Jabojagd missions for the Geschwader from dawn until dusk. The Second and Third Gruppen were unable to take off for the earliest mission because of the weather conditions, and the First Gruppe was recalled for the same reason. During the noon mission, the First Gruppe fought small battles with Mustangs and Spitfires from Bayeux to Le Havre. Hptm. Staiger claimed one Spitfire; the Gruppe suffered no losses.

Shortly after noon, Hptm. Hans Naumann took his Second Gruppe to Caen to hunt Allied fighter-bombers. The eight Focke-Wulfs encountered two No. 414 Sqd. (RCAF) Mustangs which were scouting the battle lines, and Lt. Vogt and Lt. Hofmann shot them down. One Canadian pilot bailed out within the Allied lines, and the second was able to crash-land with injuries. During the chase Naumann's aircraft was hit by British flak. He was able to re-cross the lines into German-held territory before bailing out from an altitude of 200 meters (650 feet), but he then hit both legs on the tail of his airplane, injuring them severely.

In mid-afternoon, Major Mietusch returned to his private war against the

A Fw 190A-7 of the Geschwader Stabsschwarm is positioned in its revetment – Boissy-le-Bois, 23 June. (*Bundesarchiv-Bildarchiv*)

A well-camouflaged Second Gruppe Fw 190A-8 at Guyancourt. *(Sy)*

Lightnings, and shot down two P-38s of the 55th Fighter Group's 38th Squadron. The Third Gruppe was returning from an unproductive sweep, very low on fuel, when he and his wingman Uffz. Zeller caught the American squadron circling in the vicinity of Villacoublay, and made an immediate attack in order to distract the American pilots and permit his own men to land. Zeller's claim was also confirmed; only two P-38s in fact went down.

The Schlageter pilots' wearying routine continued for the next two months. Whenever the weather permitted flying, they were either on readiness or in the air, from dawn at 0600 to full darkness at 2300. Their main meal was at noon, and was brought to them by truck. A typical meal consisted of potatoes, goulash, and mashed peas, "as much as we wanted", according to Heinz Gehrke. Weather and flight duties permitting, they would then nap under the neighboring trees. They spent the brief nights in tents near their dispersals; the few buildings as yet undamaged by bombs were needed by the ground staff. The grass strips at both Guyancourt and Villacoublay had well-engineered drainage, and few aircraft were lost here in takeoff or landing accidents. Both bases were almost surrounded by woods, as was Boissy-le-Bois, providing excellent camouflage for the aircraft dispersals. The maintenance crews worked around the clock to keep their aircraft serviceable. Fuel and spare parts were in good supply. The major deficiencies were simply in the numbers of planes and pilots.

JG 26 Victory Claims: 23 June 1944

Date	Rank	Name	Unit	Cl #	Aircraft	Place	Time	Opponent	Conf
23-06-44	Hptm.	Staiger	I CO	59	Spitfire	W of Rouen-NE of Bayeux (TA1-2)	1220		yes
23-06-44	Lt.	Vogt	7 CO	29	Mustang	St. Lô (TU7-8)	1308	414 Sqd	yes
23-06-44	Lt.	Hofmann W.	8 CO	21	Mustang	NE of Caen (UU2)	1308	414 Sqd	yes
23-06-44	Major	Mietusch	III CO	68	P-38	E of Chartres (CD-CE)	1358	55 FG	yes
23-06-44	Major	Mietusch	III CO	69	P-38	SE of Chartres (CE)	1400	55 FG	yes
23-06-44	Uffz.	Zeller	III St		P-38	E of Chartres (CD-CE)	1338	55 FG	yes

24 June

The early mission of the First Gruppe was another uncontrolled Jabojagd to the beachhead. Soon after takeoff, Lt. Xaver Ellenrieder's Schwarm sighted a squadron of

approaching P-47s and shadowed them west of Paris before attacking. Ellenrieder downed a 362nd Fighter Group Thunderbolt in the successful bounce.

The Second and Third Gruppen and III/JG 54 were scrambled at 0700 and directed toward a large Allied force headed for Paris. The formations collided between Évreux and Dreux. The Allied aircraft were 2nd TAF Mustangs from Nos. 19 and 65 Squadrons. Four No. 65 Squadron aircraft went down in the subsequent dogfights, claimed by Oblt. Werner Stoll, Lt. Hofmann, and six Green Heart pilots. Hptm. Matoni, who was once again leading most Second Gruppe missions, claimed a Spitfire, but lacked a witness. Uffz. Hermann Ayerle of the 12th Staffel was shot down, and was fired at in his parachute. He was not hit, but his parachute was, and Ayerle was injured in a hard landing after a swift descent. A second Third Gruppe Messerschmitt was shot down, possibly in this combat; its pilot was uninjured. Oblt. Werner Stoll was shot down by "three Thunderbolts", according to his loss report, and bailed out with burns. No P-47 pilot claimed an Fw 190 today, and Stoll was probably another victim of the RAF Mustang pilots, who claimed a total of 7-0-1 Fw 190s and one Bf 109.

The distinctive markings of Obstlt. Priller's Fw 190A-8 "Jutta", exposed briefly before the Gefreiter finish covering them after a flight – Boissy-le-Bois, 23 June. *(Bundesarchiv-Bildarchiv)*

Genlt. Pickert, commander of the Third Flak Division, inspects the First Gruppe. The face of Oblt. Stammberger, third from left, still bears scars from a 1943 crash – Boissy-le-Bois, 23 June. *(Bundesarchiv-Bildarchiv)*

III/JG 54 losses on this mission are not known.

The 8th Air Force B-17s and B-24s flew a number of small, heavily escorted missions to tactical targets in central France, but the Jafü 4 and Jafü 5 controllers kept their fighters away from them. Buc had now been located by the Allies, who bombed it today. One 12th Staffel mechanic was killed, and a second was injured; material losses were insufficient to be listed in the daily report.

The day's last combat came on another scramble by the Second Gruppe against tactical aircraft west of Paris. A squadron of 373rd Fighter Group P-47s had to jettison their bombs when attacked at 2130 by eight Fw 190s. Lts. Hofmann and Vogt again led the Gruppe bounce, which sent one Thunderbolt down in flames. The German flights then split up into Schwärme and out-ran the American fighters. Hofmann and Vogt were both credited with victories, but only the one P-47 was hit. Lt. Kemethmüller claimed a P-47 at this time, but near St. Dizier, far to the east of the known combats.

Lt. Adolf Glunz was awarded the Oak Leaves to his Knight's Cross today. He was now credited with sixty-five air victories.

JG 26 Victory Claims: 24 June 1944

Date	Rank	Name	Unit	Cl #	Aircraft	Place	Time	Opponent	Conf
24-06-44	Lt.	Ellenrieder	3	9	P-47	Rambouillet (BD3)	0727	362 FG	yes
24-06-44	Lt.	Kemethmüller	4 CO	79	P-47	20km NE of St Dizier (DL2-3)	2137		yes
24-06-44	Hptm.	Matoni	5 CO	23	Spitfire	S of Évreux (AC)	0728		unk
24-06-44	Oblt.	Stoll	5	2	Mustang	7km W of Brezolles (BB3)	0730	65 Sqd	yes
24-06-44	Lt.	Vogt	7 CO	30	P-47	W of Dreux (BC1-4)	2133	373 FG	yes
24-06-44	Lt.	Hofmann W.	8 CO	22	Mustang	25km WSW of Dreux (AC5,6,8)	0722	65 Sqd	yes
24-06-44	Lt.	Hofmann W.	8 CO	23	P-47	W of Dreux (BC1-7)	2132	373 FG	yes

25 June

The 8th Air Force repeated its tactics of the previous day, sending small escorted formations of its bombers to attack airfields and communications targets south of the battlefield. The 5th Jagddivision planned to support the defenders of Cherbourg in the morning, and then switch its efforts to the Caen area, where the SS Panzer Korps was holding firm against British attacks – but there were so many Allied aircraft up that few German fighters got anywhere near the Invasionsraum.

The first two missions of the Geschwader were briefed as Jabo hunts, but both became entangled with the heavy bombers and their escorts. The first took off at 0630 and succeeded in reaching a bomber formation, but damaged only a few B-17s. Oblt. Schauder claimed a P-47, but its identity cannot be confirmed. Hptm. Staiger was overheard by the Allies calling for reinforcements, but none arrived. After breaking away to land, the Third Gruppe pilots were heard complaining about enemy aircraft over their own bases. B-24s bombed both Buc and Villacoublay, and destroyed three Third Gruppe Bf 109s.

The second JG 26 mission took off at 1015 and almost reached the Caen area, but was diverted from its hunt for fighter-bombers when a weakly-escorted B-24 formation was sighted. The American escorts arrived in time to break up the attack and scatter the German fighters. Uffz. Wolf-Dietrich Glahn of the 2nd Staffel and his wingman, Uffz. Robert Marek, were departing the area at low level when the pair were taken under attack by Thunderbolts from the 365th Fighter Group, arguably the most aggressive of the 9th Air Force P-47 units in seeking out enemy aircraft. Marek's aircraft was hit, and Glahn saw Marek pull up into a cloud, stall out, and then dive vertically into the ground.

The third mission took off at 1500, and succeeded in reaching the eastern edge of the Invasionsraum, where pilots of the First and Second Gruppen saw several scattered flights of P-38s. That fighting pair from the Second Gruppe, Lt. Hofmann and Lt. Vogt, attacked a straggling P-38, and shot it down; both claimed it, but only one claim was confirmed. Hptm. Staiger also claimed a P-38, possibly the same one, and the only one to go down. The leader of the First Gruppe *Holzaugerotte* ("wooden-eye", or protection element), Oblt. Hans Hartigs, recalls:

"At this time I had a splendid wingman, Oberfähnrich Wolfgang Marx. The boy could fly, but he couldn't stay with me. After each mission I came home alone. It was enough to make one vomit. One time I had had too much, and I threatened to send him back to the *Ergänzungsgruppe* (operational training unit). Flake off once more and the ticket was ready. He was flying with me again today. After a couple of hours at *Sitzbereitschaft* (cockpit readiness), we received the order to take off.

"We sixteen Fockes were vectored perfectly to a Lightning formation 1000 meters [3300 feet] below us. We had obviously been reported to the Lightnings, because they began to climb, but our attack out of the sun was a complete surprise. Two fell away in flames. As my Gruppe climbed away from its attack, the sky was suddenly empty – no more Lightnings or Fockes. As I banked around to find my little brothers, I spotted two Thunderbolts, flying straight and level just above the clouds at 4000 meters [13,000 feet]. The wingman was too far behind – a perfect target. I closed on him and opened fire. His leader, an 'old hare', pulled up immediately. I lost sight of him, and then, just behind me, there appeared a gigantic snout.

"Badly frightened, I sought my salvation in a steep climbing turn. The boy was still there. I shoved the stick forward and to the left; all of the trash in my cockpit whirled around me as I dived for the ground, pulling out just above the trees...I saw an Allied airfield, and raced across it at top speed, hoping that the gunners' late reaction would catch the fighter behind me. But nothing happened. I would have bailed out, but he had not yet opened fire. Was his pepper mill empty? The fighter gradually gained on me, and pulled alongside. Marx! It had been Marx all along! I waved at him and led him back to the field. After landing, he came up to me and said,

"'Congratulations, Herr Oberleutnant, on your victory! That was the craziest mission I have ever flown. How many were there behind us? I never looked around, I was trying so hard to stay with you – and I did it!'"

Uffz. Hermann Grad (4/JG 26) (KIA 26 Dec 44) celebrates his first victory; to his left and right are pilot Uffz. Norbert Holtz and mechanic Uffz. Gottfried Schmidt – Boissy-le-Bois, 25 June. *(Schmidt via Meyer)*

The evening round of heavy bomber attacks was ignored by the German controllers, who were still attempting to get their fighters in position to help the army. The First Gruppe was preparing for a late-evening freie Jagd when a B-24 flew over Boissy-le-Bois only 2-3000 meters (6500-10,000 feet)

Uffz. Grad's victory celebration. From left: Hpfw. Brann (back to camera), Fw. Schmidtke, Uffz. Rüterkamp (parachute rigger), Grad, unknown, Lt. Kemethmüller (back to camera), Uffz. Wurzer (armorer), Oblt. Hartigs, Ogfr. Schmitz (engine mechanic), Ofhr. Rose (in checkered shirt), unknown, Ogfr. Hübler (radio mechanic), unknown. *(Schmidt via Meyer)*

above the ground. Only two engines were turning over. Oblt. Kemethmüller's 4th Staffel was at Sitzbereitschaft, and he and his wingman, Uffz. Hermann Grad, took off immediately. The bomber was quickly caught, and Kemethmüller ordered his wingman to shoot it down. Grad, who had yet to score his first victory, made a careful approach from 11 o'clock high and shot out a third engine. The bomber was from the 489th Bomb Group; it had been flying on two engines since a flak hit over Villacoublay. Its pilot, Lt. J D Coffman, gave the order to bail out, and all ten men exited safely. The two Germans returned to Boissy-le-Bois, where Grad was greeted with a boisterous welcome and a victory bouquet. His crew chief, Gottfried Schmidt, photographed the celebration; several of those photos are reprinted in this book.

The injured members of Lt. Coffman's crew were captured quickly; Coffman and the rest were hidden successfully by the local citizens for over a month until the Resistance took them away to smuggle them through the lines. Only two made it; the rest, Coffman included, were betrayed to the Gestapo and crammed onto the last train out of Paris before it was retaken by the US Army. He was not turned over to the Luftwaffe. Because he had been captured in civilian clothing, the Gestapo transported him to their Buchenwald concentration camp, where he joined 167 other Allied airmen. A list containing their names was smuggled out to a nearby Luftwaffe base. The OKL demanded that the airmen be turned over to the Luftwaffe, and this was done, supposedly within a week of their scheduled execution date. J D Coffman spent the rest of the war in the Luftwaffe POW camp, Stalag Luft III. His daughter has written a book, *Boots from Heaven*, about his wartime experiences.

JG 26 Victory Claims: 25 June 1944

Date	Rank	Name	Unit	Cl #	Aircraft	Place	Time	Opponent	Conf
25-06-44	Hptm.	Staiger	I CO	60	P-38	SW of Rouen (TB)	1530	370 FG	yes
25-06-44	Uffz.	Grad	4	1	B-24	E of Rouen (TD7)	2028	489 BG	yes
25-06-44	Oblt.	Hartigs	4	3	P-47	SW of Rouen (TB)	1535		unk
25-06-44	Lt.	Vogt	7 CO	31	P-38	W of Rouen (TA3-TB1)	1535	370 FG	unk

| 25-06-44 | Lt. | Hofmann W. | 8 CO | 24 | P-38 | W of Rouen (TA3-TB1) | 1530 | 370 FG | yes |
| 25-06-44 | Oblt. | Schauder | 10 CO | 19 | P-47 | S of Lisieux (AA-AB) | 0725 | | i.O. |

26 June

The 8th Air Force was grounded by bad weather over England, as was most of the AEAF, few of whose units had yet transferred to France owing to the narrowness of the beachhead. The 5th Jagddivision repeated its orders of the previous day, and the limited Allied air activity made it possible to carry out the morning missions as planned. The fighter's freie Jagden and road strafing forays across the lines served to demonstrate the existence of the Luftwaffe to the German army, but had to be flown along carefully selected routes to minimize fire from the German Flak gunners, who now assumed all aircraft to be Allied. Only a few Allied fighters were encountered by pilots of the Geschwader before rain clouds covered France and forced the recall of the afternoon missions. Lt. Hans Oeckel of the 12th Staffel claimed a Spitfire near Caen. The claim was not confirmed, and no Spitfire went down, although one returned to base with damage reportedly inflicted by an Fw 190. This Focke-Wulf was probably piloted by Hptm. Emil Lang of III/JG 54, who also claimed a Spitfire today.

27 June

Bad weather continued to hamper 8th Air Force operations, but the tactical fighters of the AEAF were active over the invasion zone for the entire day. The 5th Jagddivision reported 134 Fw 190 and 196 Bf 109 sorties during the day, in thirty-five ordered missions. It is probable that a "mission" in this context represented an effort by one Gruppe; a Gruppe mission thus contained an average of fewer than ten aircraft. The daily report listed a total of 18-2-2 victory claims by the Jagddivision for a loss of nineteen fighters, some of whose pilots were merely late reporting in after landing away from their bases.

Geschwader activities for the day were muted. Oblt. Kemethmüller's logbook documents a new mission for the German fighters – a hunt for the light aircraft used by the Allies to spot for artillery. These airplanes were called *Ariflieger* by the Germans; thus, the mission was an *Ariffiegerjagd*. At least two 5th Jagddivision pilots claimed Ariflieger today. Several combats with Allied fighters are documented in JG 26 logbooks, but there were no claims. One pilot was lost – Ofhr. Wolfgang Rose of the 4th Staffel was hit by P-47s or P-51s and crashed in his airplane. His casualty report gives neither time nor location, and his loss thus cannot be matched up with any Allied claim.

JG 26 Casualties: 23 - 27 June 1944

Date	Rank	Name	Cas	Unit	Aircraft	WNr	Mkgs	Place	Time	Cause	Allied Unit
23-06-44	Hptm.	Naumann, Hans	WIA	II CO	Fw 190A-8	730425	bk 30	SSW of Caen		flak	n/a
24-06-44	Oblt.	Stoll, Werner	WIA	5	Fw 190A-8	170384	wh 9	W of Versailles		P-47	
24-06-44	Uffz.	Ayerle, Hermann	WIA	12	Bf 109G-6	165177	bl 5	St. Andre	0730	Mustang	19 or 65 Sqd
25-06-44	Uffz.	Marek, Robert	KIA	2	Fw 190A-8	170402	bk 6	SSW of Caen	1045	P-47	365 FG
27-06-44	Ofhr.	Rose, Wolfgang	KIA	4	Fw 190A-7	431159	bl 15	E of Ennencourt		fighter	

28 June

Because of the peculiarities of English geography and weather patterns, the 9th Air Force was grounded for most of the day, while the 8th Air Force and the 2nd TAF were able to fly missions. The 5th Jagddivision concentrated all of its efforts on Field Marshal Montgomery's offensive around Caen. The target-rich environment gave the 2nd TAF's three Canadian Spitfire wings the opportunity they had been looking for ever since D-Day. The Canadians claimed a total of 25-1-13 Bf 109s and Fw 190s during the day, scoring every one of the 2nd TAF's victories. The American

Hptm. Johannes Naumann, Second Gruppe Kommandeur. A member of JG 26 since 1939, Naumann was transferred to II/JG 6 after recovering from a 23 June injury. *(Naumann)*

contribution to the day's tally was two Bf 109s and one Fw 190. Allied losses were five Spitfires, one Mustang, and their pilots. The 5th Jagddivision fighters flew 356 sorties, and reported claims for five Spitfires, one Mustang, and two P-47s, and losses of twenty-four Bf 109s and Fw 190s, including late returns. Unfortunately, owing to the intensity and concentration of the action it is impossible to match up the specific combatants.

The Gruppen of JG 26 were up from dawn until dark, as usual. Uffz. Erich Lindner of the 7th Staffel claimed a probable Spitfire, a category that was not recognized by the RLM, which rejected the claim. All of the day's losses were to Spitfires. The 2nd Staffel Kapitän, Oblt. Franz Kunz, was attacked shortly after takeoff, returned, and made a normal landing on Boissy-le-Bois, despite a shell wound in his shoulder. The First Gruppe lost the services of a second pilot, Lt. Martin Koch, who bailed out with severe burns. The Second Gruppe lost Uffz. Gerhard Lissack and Uffz. Waldemar Spiegl, both of whom crashed in their Focke-Wulfs. The Third Gruppe lost three Messerschmitts, but two pilots bailed out safely. The third pilot, Lt. Josef Menze, was injured.

Two 2nd Staffel groundcrewmen present their Kapitän, Oblt. Franz Kunz, with a bouquet and garland after the completion of his 350th combat sortie – Boissy-le-Bois, late June – early July. *(Dietze via Meyer)*

Oblt. Max Groth, the 1st Staffel Kapitän, helps Kunz celebrate his 350th sortie at Boissy-le-Bois. Groth was killed on 5 July, which this photograph dates as late June – early July. *(Dietze via Meyer)*

Hptm. Naumann required hospitalization for the injuries he had suffered on 23 June, and Priller sought a replacement to command the Second Gruppe. He succeeded in obtaining an experienced pilot from the Green Hearts, a man with an outstanding reputation as an aggressive combat leader – Hptm. Emil Lang. The thirty-five year-old Lang was a former Lufthansa pilot and a noted athlete. He had gained 159 victories with JG 54, mostly on the Eastern Front, and wore the Oak Leaves to the Knight's Cross. Priller had to give up an officer in exchange for Lang. He selected the newest officer in the Second Gruppe, Lt. Peter Crump, who had only received his commission on 17 June. Crump moved to the Green Heart side of Villacoublay on 13 July. Lang, a long-time JG 54 Staffelkapitän, was overdue for promotion to Gruppenkommandeur,

A fine shot of a First Gruppe Fw 190A-8 – date and location unknown. *(Ossenkop)*

and was prepared to make the most of his opportunity. His long combat tour had done nothing to sap his energy, and he swiftly made his mark on the Second Gruppe, which already led the Geschwader in victories and victory/loss ratio.

29 June

Again the 5th Jagddivision concentrated its efforts around Caen, where the ground situation was so critical that the unit commanders were ordered to "risk everything to reach the battle area with strong forces." The fighters' primary mission was to be the destruction of Allied fighter-bombers and artillery spotters. The 5th Jagddivision fighters flew 386 sorties, despite the previous day's losses, and claimed thirteen victories for thirteen losses. At least three of the reported losses are known to be simple "late reports" – Fw. Karl-Heinz Zeschke of the Second Gruppe and Lt. Harald Lenz and Obfw. Heinrich Humburg of the Third Gruppe landed away from their bases. The Geschwader flew four joint missions during the day. Nearly all encounters were with Spitfires, which shot down Fw. Günter Muche and Uffz. Walter Richter of the 3rd Staffel and Uffz. Fritz Dobryn of the 4th; all three men died in their aircraft. Two Staffel leaders, Lt. Kemethmüller of the 4th and Lt. Hofmann of the 8th, claimed Spitfires on the early-morning mission. Hofmann's victim was almost certainly from No. 222 Squadron; Kemethmüller's opponent has not been identified.

JG 26 Casualties: 28 - 29 June 1944

Date	Rank	Name	Cas	Unit	Aircraft	WNr	Mkgs	Place	Time	Cause	Allied Unit
28-06-44	Lt.	Koch, Martin	WIA	1	Fw 190A-8	171076	wh 2	Serquigny		Spitfire	
28-06-44	Oblt.	Kunz, Franz	WIA	2 CO	Fw 190A-7	431163	bk 2	Boissy-le-Bois		Spitfire	
28-06-44	Uffz.	Spiegl, Waldemar	KIA	5	Fw 190A-8	170625	wh 5	E of Caen		Spitfire	
28-06-44	Uffz.	Lissack, Gerhard	KIA	7	Fw 190A-8	170915	wh 1	Caen-Emieville		Spitfire	
28-06-44	Lt.	Menze, Josef	WIA	12	Bf 109G-6	165186	bl 10	W of Dreux-l'Aigle	1120	Spitfire	
29-06-44	Fw.	Muche, Günter	KIA	3	Fw 190A-8	170077	yl 7	SW of Caen		Spitfire	
29-06-44	Uffz.	Richter, Walter	KIA	3	Fw 190A-8	171074	yl 1	W of Bernay		Spitfire	
29-06-44	Uffz.	Dobryn, Fritz	KIA	4	Fw 190A-8	170672	bl 9	near Caen		Spitfire	

30 June

Bad weather again played havoc with the assembly of Allied formations over England, reducing the number of Allied fighters over the beachhead. The 5th Jagddivision sent eight combined missions to the front lines. Each was a joint effort of up to twelve Jagdgruppen. Its fighters flew more than five hundred sorties; today was the high mark of Luftwaffe efforts against the invasion. One or more Gruppen of the Geschwader took part in at least five of these combined missions. Most pilots contacted P-38s, P-47s, or Spitfires, and thus carried out their assignments, but serious combats were few. Only one victory was reported; a Spitfire was claimed at 1500 by Uffz. Karl-Heinz Friedrich of the 10th Staffel, but the claim was not confirmed, and no Spitfire loss has been identified. Only one JG 26 pilot, Uffz. Wilhelm Sonnenberg of the 3rd Staffel, was not accounted for by the end of the day, and he turned up later.

There were few transfers from the Geschwader in this month of maximum effort. One move saw Uffz. Friedrich Jacobsen leave the 8th Staffel for a flight test unit. Fw. Karl Hofmann, a former JG 2 pilot whose most recent posting had been as a test pilot, joined the First Gruppe after a brief Fw 190 familiarization course.

New pilots assigned to the Geschwader during June after completing flight training included: Uffz. Erich Burmeister, Ogfr. Hermann Hillebrand, Uffz. Hans Kukla - First Gruppe; Fw. Erich Ahrens, Fw. Walter Hasenclever (a prewar bomber mechanic), Uffz. Helmut Holzinger, Lt. Günter Seyd, Lt. Werner Schramm - Second Gruppe; Uffz. Hans Streufert - Third Gruppe.

By the end of June, Invasionsfront service had cost the Geschwader twenty-eight pilots killed in combat and another three in accidents. One pilot had been taken prisoner, and at least twenty-four had been injured. The wounded included one

Gruppenkommandeur and four Staffelkapitäne. Based on the Luftwaffe strength returns, the three JG 26 Gruppen represented 15% of the fighter strength of Jagdkorps II on this date. The pilots of JG 26 claimed eighty-eight victories between 6 and 30 June; this was over 30% of the 5th Jagddivision victory claims.

A document prepared by an OKL staff officer after a visit to Luftflotte 3 has preserved some telling statistics for the period 6-30 June. Jagdkorps II had twenty single-engine fighter Gruppen in its two Jagddivisionen. Its table of organization strength was 1300 fighters and pilots; actual strength on the evening of 30 June was 233 airplanes and 419 pilots. Victory claims over occupied France and the Low Countries by pilots of single-engine fighters totaled 414, against 458 losses. A total of 998 fighters had reached the invasion front as reinforcements, but almost half had already been destroyed. Single-engine fighters had flown 10,061 sorties on the invasion front, counting pure fighter, fighter-bomber, and reconnaissance missions, against an estimated 120,000-140,000 sorties flown by the Allies. It was the opinion of the Jagdkorps II staff that it was pointless to attack heavy bomber formations, since there was no possibility of destroying enough aircraft to lessen the effect of their bombing attacks. Fighter attacks were now being directed exclusively at enemy fighter-bombers and artillery spotters, as these presented the greatest threat to the Army. The loss rate on combat missions was running 20-30%. Three German fighters were being lost for every Allied fighter loss. Pilots were being lost at the rate of two for one.

JG 26 Victory Claims: 26 - 30 June 1944

Date	Rank	Name	Unit	Cl #	Aircraft	Place	Time	Opponent	Conf
26-06-44	Lt.	Oeckel	12	4	Spitfire	Caen (UT-UU)	1120		unk
28-06-44	Uffz.	Lindner	7	2	Spitfire	Coutances (TT9)	1121		unk
29-06-44	Lt.	Kemethmüller	4 CO	80	Spitfire	N of Caen (TU8)	0840		yes
29-06-44	Lt.	Hofmann W.	8 CO	25	Spitfire	10km SW of Lisieux (UA4)	0848	222 Sqd	yes
30-06-44	Uffz.	Friedrich	10		Spitfire	E of Caen (UU-UA)	1500	441 Sqd	unk

1 July

Bad weather once again hampered the efforts of the 8th Air Force and the AEAF. The 5th Jagddivision ordered five combined missions to the beachhead; one or more JG 26 Gruppen were involved in all five of these. Some missions were recalled because of the weather; the few contacts that were made with Allied aircraft were tentative and unsuccessful.

Genlt. Junck was relieved as commander of Jagdkorps II. His replacement was Genlt. Buelowius, who returned from Germany. Junck was allowed to retire, and joined Kurt Tank's Focke-Wulf staff as a consultant.

2 July

The aircraft based in England were grounded, but those Allied fighter units that had moved to France were active all day over and beyond the invasion zone. The 5th Jagddivision ordered its fighters to fly four combined missions to the Caen area in support of the beleaguered army. All three JG 26 Gruppen took part in the last three missions. The Second Gruppe was not called on for the earliest combined mission, but Lt. Waldemar Busch led a Schwarm up from Guyancourt at 0620 for a weather reconnaissance flight to the invasion zone. A flight of Spitfires from No. 411 Sqd. (RCAF) spotted the four Fw 190s in the poor light of early dawn and in a prolonged dogfight over Lisieux shot down and killed Lt. Crump's wingman, Uffz. Gerhard Kraft. Busch in turn downed one of the Spitfires. Two full-strength missions to the Caen area later in the day resulted in claims for Spitfires destroyed by Lt. Crump and Hptm. Matoni. Two Focke-Wulf pilots, Uffz. Rudolf Oltmanns and Lt. Heinz Zedler, were killed, and one, Lt. Wilhelm Nink, was injured. Nink bailed out with burns and landed in British-held territory, but succeeded in making his way back through the lines and returned to the 3rd Staffel. Nink had started the war as an infantryman, and after service on the Eastern Front had volunteered for pilot training in the Luftwaffe. Ogfr. Günter Suckrow was injured when he bailed out of his 9th Staffel Messerschmitt after its engine failed.

JG 26 Victory Claims: 2 July 1944

Date	Rank	Name	Unit	Cl #	Aircraft	Place	Time	Opponent	Conf
02-07-44	Hptm.	Matoni	5 CO	24	Spitfire	NW of Caen (UT5-6)	2052		yes
02-07-44	Lt.	Crump	6	16	Spitfire	NW of Caen (UT3-UU1)	1558		yes
02-07-44	Fhr.	Busch W.	8	4	Spitfire	10km E of Lisieux (UA5)	0706	411 Sqd	yes

JG 26 Casualties: 2 July 1944

Date	Rank	Name	Cas	Unit	Aircraft	WNr	Mkgs	Place	Time	Cause	Allied Unit
02-07-44	Uffz.	Oltmanns, Rudolf	KIA	1	Fw 190A-8	171080	wh 1	S Aigle-Falaise	2100	Spitfire	453 Sqd
02-07-44	Lt.	Nink, Wilhelm	WIA	3	Fw 190A-8	174032	yl 3	E of Caen		Spitfire	
02-07-44	Uffz.	Kraft, Gerhard	KIA	6	Fw 190A-8	680107	bk 5	Le Mesnil-S of Lisieux	0645	Spitfire	411 Sqd
02-07-44	Lt.	Zedler, Heinz	KIA	8	Fw 190A-8	170333	bl 1	NW of Caen		combat	
02-07-44	Ogfr.	Suckrow, Günter	WIFA	9	Bf 109G-6	162509	wh 10	7km N of Évreux	1540	engine	n/a

4 July

After a day on the ground, both sides returned to the skies over the battlefield today, despite continuing rain. The 5th Jagddivision ordered seven combined missions to the tip of the British offensive southwest of Caen. JG 26 pilots took part in six of these missions, and encountered not only the 2nd TAF, which tended to concentrate very near the front lines, but fighters of the 9th Air Force, which roamed far to the east and south of the US Army's zone of operations in search of targets. The Second Gruppe suffered two fatalities. Lt. Busch failed to return from a mission to Caen in mid-afternoon, probably the victim of a No. 340 Sqd. (Free French) Spitfire. Fhr. Kurt Zippel was shot down by Mustangs, probably of No. 414 Sqd. (RCAF). The Second Gruppe pilots did not score until late evening, when Lt. Prager and Uffz. Pietruschka of the 5th Staffel downed two Spitfires near Caen. These No. 602 Squadron aircraft were probably also attacked by III/JG 54, which claimed two Spitfires at the same place and time.

Major Mietusch's Third Gruppe flew a very successful mid-afternoon mission, claiming four P-38s, one Spitfire, and one P-47 between Évreux and Lisieux for the loss of one Messerschmitt, whose pilot was uninjured. Only one of the P-38 claims was confirmed; the victim was from the 370th Fighter Group, which lost only the one Lightning. The Thunderbolt was probably from the 406th Fighter Group; the Spitfire unit cannot be identified.

JG 26 Victory Claims: 4 July 1944

Date	Rank	Name	Unit	Cl #	Aircraft	Place	Time	Opponent	Conf
04-07-44	Uffz.	Pietruschka	5	2	Spitfire	Caen (UU1-2)	1941	602 Sqd	unk
04-07-44	Lt.	Prager	5	4	Spitfire	Caen (UU1-2)	1946	602 Sqd	yes
04-07-44	Lt.	Prager	5	5	Spitfire	NW Lisieux	2144		no
04-07-44	Major	Mietusch	III CO	70	P-38	W of Évreux (UB)	1450	370 FG	unk
04-07-44	Uffz.	Zeller	III St		P-38	W of Évreux (UB)	1450	370 FG	yes
04-07-44	Lt.	Kempf	9	63	P-47	SW of Évreux (AB1)	1442	406 FG	i.O.
04-07-44	Lt.	Kempf	9	64	Spitfire	SW of Évreux (AB1)	1443		i.O.
04-07-44	Uffz.	Malm	12		P-38	E of Lisieux (UA-UB)	1455	370 FG	unk
04-07-44	Uffz.	Salewski	12		P-38	E of Lisieux (UA-UB)	1455	370 FG	unk

5 July

The American bombers were still grounded in England, but the fighters of the 8th and 9th Air Forces were released to fly armed reconnaissance sweeps south of the landing zone. The 5th Jagddivision ordered sweeps of its own. Nearly five hundred sorties were flown to the critical battle zone around Caen in seven combined missions. JG 26 pilots took part in five of these. They succeeded in avoiding the marauding American aircraft, and engaged in several unsuccessful combats with Spitfires. Oblt. Max Groth, Kapitän of the 1st Staffel, was shot down and killed east of Évreux, and the Focke-Wulf of Lt. Gerhard Vogt, leader of the 7th Staffel, was severely damaged. Vogt destroyed his aircraft, and injured himself, when he hit some power lines in an attempted forced landing. Lt. Georg Kiefner replaced Groth as leader of the 1st Staffel.

ULTRA decoded an order by Reichsmarschall Göring stating that because of the recent high rate of loss of indispensable combat leaders, these men could no longer fly combat missions unless at least the following numbers of aircraft were available: Staffelkapitäne required six aircraft; Gruppenkommandeure, fifteen; and Geschwaderkommodoren, forty-five. Most units on the Invasionsfront were severely constrained by this order.

JG 26 Casualties: 4 - 5 July 1944

Date	Rank	Name	Cas	Unit	Aircraft	WNr	Mkgs	Place	Time	Cause	Allied Unit
04-07-44	Fhr.	Zippel, Kurt	KIA	6	Fw 190A-8	172711	bk 1	Caen-Bayeux		Mustang	414 Sqd
04-07-44	Lt.	Busch, Waldemar	KIA	8	Fw 190A-8	171100	bl 1	Caen-Bayeux	1500	Spitfire	340 Sqd
05-07-44	Oblt.	Groth, Max	KIA	1 CO	Fw 190A-8	731041	wh 4	E of Évreux		Spitfire	
05-07-44	Lt.	Vogt, Gerhard	WIA	7 CO	Fw 190A-8	170661	br 13	Buré-Mêle sur Sarthe		Spitfire	

6 July

The skies over England were clear, and the Americans dispatched 1100 heavy bombers to supplement the mediums' attacks on V-1 sites on the Pas de Calais and on bridges and railroads south of Paris. General Buelowius, a bomber man, modified the standing orders issued previously by Jagdkorps II. Ground-attack missions would again be flown, in addition to hunts for Jabos and Ariflieger. His fighter units did not respond well to the new challenge, and only managed four hundred sorties despite the good

A First Gruppe Fw 190A-8 taxies out of the Boissy-le-Bois woods in June or July. The absence of outer wing guns is worth noting; many JG 26 pilots had them removed to improve speed and maneuverability. *(Dietze via Meyer)*

weather. JG 26 furnished aircraft for six of the eight missions dispatched to the Caen battle zone. Few of the fighters made it that far; most formations were broken up by Allied fighters between Paris and Évreux. Early returns owing to problems with engines, radios, and drop tanks were also a growing problem. The Geschwader neither claimed any victories nor suffered any losses.

7 July

The 8th Air Force returned to its campaign against the synthetic oil industry, leaving France to the attentions of the AEAF. JG 26 fighters took part in five of the six combined missions ordered to the battlefield. The first mission was recalled because of bad weather, but the others successfully engaged fighters or dropped bombs. In one late-morning mission to the Orne River, III/JG 54 was assigned to strafe ground targets while the Second and Third Gruppen flew cover. Spitfires from No. 401 Sqd. (RCAF) attacked the escorts near Lisieux. They claimed two Messerschmitts and one Focke-Wulf. The Messerschmitt pilots were Lt. Josef Menze, who was killed, and Uffz. Bruno Schwarz, who bailed out with severe burns. Uffz. Werner Hoffmann bailed out of his Focke-Wulf with moderate injuries. Lt. Prager was credited with one of the Canadian Spitfires, but none in fact went down. III/JG 54 succeeded in making two strafing passes on ground targets without loss.

The dusk mission reached Caen, found no targets, and was *en route* back to Paris when it was bounced by some P-51s from the 354th Fighter Group's 353rd Squadron. The Mustangs shot down five fighters before escaping unscathed. Losses to the Geschwader in this combat were Fw. Kurt Schmidtke (4th Staffel), who was killed, and Gefr. Friedrich Wissel (12th Staffel), who bailed out with such severe injuries that he was evacuated to Germany.

JG 26 Casualties: 7 July 1944

Date	Rank	Name	Cas	Unit	Aircraft	WNr	Mkgs	Place	Time	Cause	Allied Unit
07-07-44	Fw.	Schmidtke, Kurt	KIA	4	Fw 190A-8	731033	yl 6	6km SE of Nantes	2045	P-51	354 FG
07-07-44	Uffz.	Hoffmann, Werner	WIA	6	Fw 190A-8	731069	bk 2	St. Aubin-N of Caen		Spitfire	401 Sqd
07-07-44	Uffz.	Schwarz, Bruno	WIA	11	Bf 109G-6	163412	yl 1	Évreux	1120	Spitfire	401 Sqd
07-07-44	Lt.	Menze, Josef	KIA	12	Bf 109G-6	163616	bl 1	20km E of Caen	1100	Spitfire	401 Sqd
07-07-44	Gefr.	Wissel, Friedrich	WIA	12	Bf 109G-6	165265	bl 19	W of St Lô	2100	P-51	354 FG

8 July

Despite heavy rain, the AEAF and the 8th Air Force were active over northern France for most of the day. The 5th Jagddivision had planned three concentrated operations, but its aircraft had great difficulty in making rendezvous in the bad weather. The AEAF radio intercept operators heard the German pilots calling out Luftwaffe aircraft as enemy. Pilots of the Geschwader took part in all three of these missions, claimed no victories, and suffered no losses.

9 July

Bad weather continued. The German army still considered Caen to be the most critical portion of the front, despite the American successes farther west. General Buelowius took direct operational control away from the 5th Jagddivision and assigned it to his own Jagdkorps II headquarters. He planned three concentrated operations to the tip of the British penetration, but only one mission took place. The fighters came from eight Jagdgruppen, and assembled northwest of Paris to fly to the beachhead. The Second Gruppe, by pushing its "black men" (ground crews) to the limit, was barely able to report enough Focke-Wulfs operational to permit its new Kommandeur to fly under Göring's new restrictions. Hptm. Lang was the senior pilot airborne, and led the forty fighters to Caen. There were few RAF fighters up, but he spotted some Spitfires from

No. 453 Sqd. (RAAF), and led his entire formation in a bounce. After ten minutes of furious combat, the two sides disengaged. The Australian pilots claimed 2-0-2 Bf 109s and 2-0-3 Fw 190s. None of these fighters was from JG 26, which reported no losses or damage, although the radio intercept operators heard Major Mietusch declare his intention to make a forced landing. The only German claims were filed by Emil Lang himself – for three Spitfires, downed in the space of five minutes. The claims were confirmed, but no Spitfires were in fact lost. Fortunately for the Second Gruppe and the Luftwaffe, Lang's ebullience, energy, and drive manifested themselves in more ways than his exaggerated claims. Morale, and with it the performance of his Gruppe, increased measurably after his arrival.

The Geschwader was overdue for a rest period, but conditions did not permit it. The First Gruppe was given one day off to restore the serviceability of its aircraft. At day's end the Geschwaderstab reported 3 (2) Fw 190s on strength; the First Gruppe, 17 (10) Fw 190s; the Second Gruppe, 12 (7) Fw 190s; and the Third Gruppe, 47 (29) Bf 109s. Lang was effectively grounded again by the low strength of his Gruppe.

10 July
Again the weather hampered the operations of both sides. Jagdkorps II planned three major missions, and executed one. At least eight Jagdgruppen, including the three from JG 26, took part. Ground attacks were dropped from the task list, but Allied fighters were scarce, and several unit leaders ordered their pilots to strafe ground targets. Fw. Roman Joziak of the 8th Staffel failed to return from the mission. He was last seen on his strafing run, and was probably shot down by ground fire. His Staffel leader, Lt. Hofmann, claimed a Spitfire on the mission, but no Spitfires were lost at this time. The engine of Obfw. Heinrich Teilken's Focke-Wulf caught fire, and he attempted a forced landing on Villacoublay. The aircraft was destroyed, and Teilken was severely injured.

Major Mietusch was awarded a pendant to his gold mission clasp for his 400th combat sortie, all as a pilot in the Third Gruppe of JG 26, and flown in all three of Germany's war theaters: the Western, Eastern, and Mediterranean Fronts.

11 July
Jagdkorps II relayed a rare commendatory message to all its units. Panzergruppe West reported that during its recent operation the Luftwaffe was seen over its battle headquarters; this appearance was much appreciated by all. The 86th Armeekorps especially was thrilled and grateful for the support. The available English translation gives no hint of any sarcasm in the German original.

As the rain continued, Jagdkorps II continued attempting to fulfill its mission of screening the Caen area by attacking enemy Jabos and Ariflieger. Two combined missions were flown in the afternoon; JG 26 units took part in both. Few enemy aircraft were encountered. The new leader of the 1st Staffel, Lt. Georg Kiefner, claimed a probable P-51 that was filed as a full victory claim and rejected by the RLM. The Geschwader suffered no losses.

JG 26 Victory Claims: 7 - 11 July 1944

Date	Rank	Name	Unit	Cl #	Aircraft	Place	Time	Opponent	Conf
07-07-44	Lt.	Prager	5	6	Spitfire	Caen (UU3-UA1)	1144	412 Sqd	yes
09-07-44	Hptm.	Lang	II CO	160	Spitfire	Caen (UU-UA)	1319	453 Sqd	yes
09-07-44	Hptm.	Lang	II CO	161	Spitfire	Caen (UU-UA)	1321	453 Sqd	yes
09-07-44	Hptm.	Lang	II CO	162	Spitfire	Caen (UU-UA)	1324	453 Sqd	yes
10-07-44	Lt.	Hofmann W.	8 CO	26	Spitfire	N of Caen (TU7)	1135		yes
11-07-44	Lt.	Kiefner	1 CO	7	P-51	Caen (UU2-TU8)	1950		unk

12 July
There was no change in the weather or in the situation at the front. In the morning, Jagdkorps II took advantage of the scarcity of Allied fighters to order ground attacks.

One Third Gruppe Bf 109 was shot down by ground fire, but its pilot made it back to the German side of the lines without injury. The Germans' two afternoon missions encountered more Allied aircraft. The Second Gruppe reported attacking gliders near Caen, with unknown results. Lt. Kemethmüller led the First Gruppe in a bounce of some P-47s near Évreux, and claimed to have shot down two and damaged a third. The time and location match the account of the 358th Fighter Group's 366th Squadron, which lost one P-47 in the attack. The matter is complicated by the fact that III/JG 54 claimed three P-47s at the same time and place as Kemethmüller. No other suitable engagements between P-47s and Fw 190s are known.

The Second Gruppe received welcome news today. It and four other Jagdgruppen were to cease operations immediately and return to Germany to rest and refit.

13 July

The orders from Jagdkorps II were the same as those of the previous day: ground attacks in the morning, in the expected absence of Allied fighters; and combined patrols over the Caen battlefront in the afternoon in search of fighter-bombers and artillery spotters. The morning mission of the First and Third Gruppen was recalled, as the front could not be found in the low clouds. The mid-afternoon flight to Caen did succeed in locating enemy aircraft. Lt. Kemethmüller's 4th Staffel Schwarm was attacked by the 366th Fighter Group commander's flight. Ogfr. Helmut Merten was shot down and died in his aircraft. Merten was an experienced pilot, but was new to fighters; he had previously piloted bombers in KG 4 and night fighter-bombers in SKG 10. Uffz. Hermann Grad was also hit; he succeeded in bailing out, but suffered several broken bones. Kemethmüller claimed one of the Thunderbolts, but all of the American fighters returned to base.

At about this time, Oblt. Schauder was leading the Third Gruppe in an extended combat with Spitfires from No. 401 Sqd. (RCAF) near Caen; he kept the AEAF radio intercept operators informed of its progress for a full thirty minutes. Both sides disengaged without loss, although the Canadians claimed one Fw 190 damaged and Schauder claimed one Spitfire destroyed.

Lt. Peter Crump reported today to III/JG 54 at Villacoublay-Sud.

JG 26 Victory Claims: 12 - 13 July 1944

Date	Rank	Name	Unit	Cl #	Aircraft	Place	Time	Opponent	Conf
12-07-44	Lt.	Kemethmüller	4 CO	81	P-47	SW of Elbeuf-Quitte beuf (AB6)	1430	358 FG	yes
12-07-44	Lt.	Kemethmüller	4 CO	82	P-47	Conches-W of Danville (AB6-AC7)	1431	358 FG	yes
12-07-44	Lt.	Kemethmüller	4 CO		P-47-dam	SW of Breteuil	1435	358 FG	no
13-07-44	Lt.	Kemethmüller	4 CO	83	P-47	NW of Vernon	1658	366 FG	yes
13-07-44	Oblt.	Schauder	10 CO	20	Spitfire	Lisieux (UA5-8)	1715	401 Sqd	i.O.

14 July

There was no flying in the morning. Jagdkorps II ordered three combined missions to Caen in the afternoon and evening. The First and Third Gruppen took part in the first two of these, but saw combat only on one, attacking two squadrons of the 358th Fighter Group. Major Borris had returned to the Geschwader, but had not yet reclaimed the command of the First Gruppe from Hptm. Staiger. He did fly missions, however, and this afternoon he led the First and Third Gruppen west from Paris on a hunt for American fighter-bombers. Near Alençon they encountered two squadrons of Thunderbolts. Splitting into Schwärme, the Focke-Wulfs dived out of the clouds, made brief firing passes, and zoomed back to safety, carrying out their long-time leader's careful tactics to perfection. They returned to Guyancourt to claim the destruction of five Thunderbolts; one claim was later disallowed. Uffz. Willi Haun of the 9th Staffel was also credited with a victory; four Thunderbolts were in fact shot down. The surviving American pilots claimed six German fighters, and were ultimately credited with two. One of Borris's men, Uffz. Emil Brühan, was shot down; he bailed out and survived. Haun's Messerschmitt was shot down after his victory, and he bailed out with injuries.

JG 26 Victory Claims: 14 July 1944

Date	Rank	Name	Unit	Cl #	Aircraft	Place	Time	Opponent	Conf
14-07-44	Major	Borris	I CO	38	P-47	W of Paris (UB9. UC7,AC1)	1436	358 FG	yes
14-07-44	Lt.	Günther	3	2	P-47	W of Paris (AC)	1438	358 FG	yes
14-07-44	Lt.	Günther	3	3	P-47	W of Paris (AC)	1440	358 FG	unk
14-07-44	Lt.	Kemethmüller	4 CO	84	P-47	St Andre-W of Paris (AC)	1436	358 FG	yes
14-07-44	Oblt.	Hartigs	4	4	P-47	W of Paris (AC)	1440	358 FG	yes
14-07-44	Uffz.	Haun	9		P-47	W of Dreux (AB6-9)	1457	358 FG	i.O.

JG 26 Casualties: 10 - 14 July 1944

Date	Rank	Name	Cas	Unit	Aircraft	WNr	Mkgs	Place	Time	Cause	Allied Unit
10-07-44	Obfw.	Teilken, Heinrich	WIFA	1	Fw 190A-8	170944	wh 6	Villacoublay		engine	n/a
10-07-44	Fw.	Joziak, Roman	KIA	8	Fw 190A-8	731068	bl 14	N of Caen	1115	flak	n/a
13-07-44	Uffz.	Grad, Hermann	WIA	4	Fw 190A-6	530923	bl 15	Bernay	1705	P-47	362 FG
13-07-44	Ogfr.	Merten, Helmut	KIA	4	Fw 190A-8	170319	bl 7	WSW of Bernay-Eure	1705	P-47	362 FG
14-07-44	Uffz.	Brühan, Emil	WIA	1	Fw 190A-7	431175	wh 12	60km W of Paris	1440	P-47	358 FG
14-07-44	Uffz.	Haun, Willi	WIA	9	Bf 109G-6	164957	wh 5	Breteuil	1500	P-47	358 FG

15 July

This morning, Jagdkorps II dispatched its Jagdgruppen to the battle zone in independent Gruppe formations, as the weather made it impossible to assemble a Gefechtsverband. The First and Third Gruppen encountered Spitfires from No. 412 and No. 602 Squadrons near Caen, and claimed three; none were in fact lost. The Spitfire pilots claimed two Focke-Wulfs, and shot down Uffz. Wilhelm Wüst, who was killed. Three combined missions were flown by the German fighters in the afternoon. The noon mission cost the Third Gruppe two Messerschmitts. Uffz. Erich Salewsky and Ofhr. Rudolf Leinberger bailed out of their aircraft with injuries after a battle near Paris. Their opponents are unknown. Neither the RAF nor the USAAF claimed any Messerschmitts today.

JG 26 Casualties: 15 July 1944

Date	Rank	Name	Cas	Unit	Aircraft	WNr	Mkgs	Place	Time	Cause	Allied Unit
15-07-44	Uffz.	Wüst, Wilhelm	KIA	1	Fw 190A-8	170037	wh 8	Caen		Spitfire	
15-07-44	Ofhr.	Leinberger, Rudolf	WIA	11	Bf 109G-6	412928	yl 15	near Paris	1155	combat	
15-07-44	Uffz.	Salewsky, Erich	WIA	12	Bf 109G-6	441476	bl 3	near Paris	1150	combat	

16 July

The continuing British efforts to expand their cramped holdings around Caen were countered by fighters using weapons that had not seen much use since shortly after D-Day. The 21 cm rocket mortar shells used in 1943 to break up bomber formations were now slung once more beneath the wings of First Gruppe Fw 190s, to be employed against Allied armor. The rockets were spectacular but highly inaccurate weapons; the pilots heartily disliked both the rockets and their heavy launch tubes, but they were much less detrimental to their fighters' performance than externally-carried bombs, and the weapon was much more powerful than their 20 mm cannon.

In the morning, the first full-strength mission of the First Gruppe as the Geschwader *Werfergruppe* ([rocket] launcher Gruppe) was recalled because of the weather, and the tubes were removed before the afternoon missions, which were flown as freie Jagden.

The day's only victory was claimed late in the evening by Lt. Kemethmüller, who sighted a lone 373rd Fighter Group P-47 and shot it down.

JG 26 Victory Claims: 15 - 16 July 1944

Date	Rank	Name	Unit	Cl #	Aircraft	Place	Time	Opponent	Conf
15-07-44	Lt.	Kiefner	1 CO	8	Spitfire	Caen (UU1)	0715		yes
15-07-44	Uffz.	Holl	10		Spitfire	S of Caen (UU4)	0710		i.O.
15-07-44	Oblt.	Schmidt G.	11		Spitfire	S of Caen (UU4)	0710		i.O.
16-07-44	Lt.	Kemethmüller	4 CO	85	P-47	25km SW of Rouen (TB3)	2131	373 FG	yes

17 July

General Buelowius issued increasingly complex orders to his fighters, despite their ever-decreasing operational strength. Today's mission orders were decoded by ULTRA and reported to the Allied air commanders. As soon as the weather permitted, a combined mission was to be flown to the British concentrations south and southwest of Caen in two waves. The first wave would consist of JG 2 and JG 3, with the III/JG 2 Gruppenkommandeur in command. His Gruppe was to attack with rockets, while II/JG 2 and JG 3 flew close escort. The second wave would consist of JG 26 and JG 11, with the I/JG 26 Gruppenkommandeur in command. His Gruppe would attack with rockets, escorted by III/JG 26 and JG 11. JG 27 would sweep the target area at X-10 minutes, its objective being to draw the Allied fighters to the west. JG 1 would supply high-altitude protection over the entire battle area. After the mortar attacks, every Jagdgeschwader but JG 27 and JG 1 was to strafe the British concentrations. The assembly point for both waves was to be Dreux.

This beautiful plan was never executed. Four conventional combined missions to the battle zone were flown, each in a strength of three to twelve Jagdgruppen. The Third Gruppe was hammered on two of these missions. Its mid-afternoon sweep of the Caen area ended in a large battle with Allied fighters. At 1640 Major Mietusch claimed one Spitfire from No. 125 Wing, but four of his pilots were shot down. Fw. Heimfried Schmerker and Lt. Hans Oeckel were killed, and Uffz. Hermann Ayerle and Uffz. Karl-Heinz Friedrich were injured.

Uffz. Heinz Gehrke had returned from hospital and was flying his first-ever mission as Mietusch's wingman. This was a position of great honor and great responsibility. Mietusch tended to focus on the task at hand at the expense of good communication. On the trip back to Villacoublay, Gehrke spotted an unknown aircraft to their rear, and warned his Kommandeur. Mietusch acknowledged, but held to his course. A moment later Gehrke recognized the airplane as a Spitfire, yelled again, and broke into the attack. The Spitfire, probably from the sweeping No. 411 Sqd. (RCAF), shot down the leading Messerschmitt, which was still flying straight ahead. Mietusch bailed out, landed with injuries, and did not return to base until the next day. He was sent immediately to a hospital in Germany. Fortunately for Heinz Gehrke, his radioed warnings had been monitored at base, and he was held blameless in the incident. Klaus Mietusch was a high-strung man who from all indications had almost reached his breaking point. His social skills were limited, and he did not mingle with his NCO pilots. He never spoke to Gehrke after he returned from Germany, either to rebuke him or to thank him for his actions this day.

Late that evening the Gruppe again encountered Allied fighters. It was flying near Évreux as part of a large mixed formation when it was attacked from below by seven P-51s of the 354th "Pioneer Mustang" Group's 355th Squadron. The Third Gruppe lost two more pilots, Oblt. Fritz Bracher and Ofhr. Gerhard Dewald, but Mustangs were shot down by two of the Staffelkapitäne, Hptm. Schauder (10th Staffel), who was probably leading the formation, and Oblt. Viktor Hilgendorff (9th Staffel). A new First Gruppe pilot was killed during the day; Lt. Günter Pokorny crashed when his engine quit on a transfer flight.

JG 26 Victory Claims: 17 July 1944

Date	Rank	Name	Unit	Cl #	Aircraft	Place	Time	Opponent	Conf
17-07-44	Major	Mietusch	III CO	71	Spitfire	SW of Caen (UT2-6)	1640	602 Sqd	yes
17-07-44	Oblt.	Hilgendorff	9 CO	2	P-51	NW of Le Perron (AB3-6)	1950	354 FG	i.O.
17-07-44	Obfw.	Humburg	9		P-47	W of Dreux (AB3-6)	1940		i.O.
17-07-44	Oblt.	Schauder	10 CO		P-51	Lisieux		354 FG	no
17-07-44	Uffz.	Tabbat	10		P-51	Dreux (AC9)	1935	354 FG	i.O.

JG 26 Casualties: 17 July 1944

Date	Rank	Name	Cas	Unit	Aircraft	WNr	Mkgs	Place	Time	Cause	Allied Unit
17-07-44	Lt.	Pokorny, Günter	KIFA	3	Fw 190A-8	170720	yl 4	N of Chartres		crashed	non-op
17-07-44	Maj.	Mietusch, Klaus	WIA	III CO	Bf 109G-6/U4	440640	wh 20	Argentan-Alençon	1700	Spitfire	411 Sqd
17-07-44	Ofhr.	Dewald, Gerhard	KIA	9	Bf 109G-6	441633	wh 20	Évreux	1945	P-51	354 FG
17-07-44	Oblt.	Bracher, Fritz	KIA	10	Bf 109G-6	165157	bk 18	Dreux	1925	P-51	354 FG
17-07-44	Uffz.	Friedrich, Karl-Heinz	WIA	10	Bf 109G-6	412538	bk 15	Chartres	1706	Spitfire	411 or 602 Sqd
17-07-44	Uffz.	Ayerle, Hermann	WIA	12	Bf 109G-6	413559	bl 21	Toussous le Noble	1625	Spitfire	411 or 602 Sqd
17-07-44	Lt.	Oeckel, Hans	KIA	12	Bf 109G-6	165193	bl 7	S of Liseux-Alençon	1630	Spitfire	411 or 602 Sqd
17-07-44	Fw.	Schmerker, Heimfried	KIA	12	Bf 109G-6/U4	491851	bl 15	SE of Caen-Alençon	1630	Spitfire	411 or 602 Sqd

18 July

The orders from Jagdkorps II were a repeat of the previous day's, with one exception. Three Jagdgeschwader, not including JG 26, were to prepare to shift their main effort to a new crisis point, the American penetration at St. Lô. The *Schwerpunkt* (main focus) for JG 26 would continue to be Caen. Unconditional radio silence was ordered during all approach flights until the point of contact; the value to the Allies of the German fighter pilots' radio chatter had obviously become apparent. The First and Third Gruppen took part in the day's two combined missions, but only the morning mission made contact with the enemy. The two Gruppen had just formed up with III/JG 54 for the flight to Caen when the 474th Fighter Group's three Lightning squadrons dived on them north of Paris. Three P-38s went down in the subsequent combats, as did Uffz. Josef Wendl of the 1st Staffel, who crashed with his plane. Victory credits were awarded to Lt. Kemethmüller and three Green Heart pilots, including Peter Crump. This was Crump's first victory in his new unit, and his 17th for the war.

The Third Gruppe was split up in this combat, but most pilots resumed their flight to the northwest after breaking free. North of Dreux a flight of four Thunderbolts from the 373rd Fighter Group's 412th Squadron sighted "twenty Me 109s" four thousand feet below them and down-sun, dived immediately, and shot down two out of a flight of six without loss. The survivors were chased back toward Paris, but were let go when the American flight leader ran out of ammunition. The German victims were the one-legged 9th Staffel Kapitän, Oblt. Hilgendorff, and his wingman, Lt. Völmle. Both pilots bailed out; Völmle reached the ground with only minor injuries, but Hilgendorff was shot and killed while hanging from his parachute. This practice was not unusual for American pilots in the summer of 1944, and all German aircrewmen in the west were instructed to free-fall as long as possible after bailing out. Lt. Gottfried "Cognac" Schmidt replaced Hilgendorff as leader of the 9th Staffel.

19 July

Jagdkorps II dispatched five joint missions to the Caen battle zone, still considered the area of greatest danger. Most formations shrank considerably in size before reaching Caen, owing to early returns or Allied fighter attacks on the approach leg of the flight.

In the evening, the First Gruppe flew a successful *Werfereinsatz* against British armor. One pilot was shot down by ground fire, but reached the German lines safely. Fw. Walter Holl of the 10th Staffel was killed when his Messerschmitt spun in while on a non-operational flight.

20 July

Rain kept both sides on the ground until mid-afternoon. The First Gruppe flew a successful Werfereinsatz against British armor to the east of Caen, escorted by the Third Gruppe, which lost an airplane to ground fire. Only a few Spitfires were seen. In the evening Major Borris made an evaluation flight to an auxiliary field known as *Schneisenplatz,* which can be translated literally as "field slashed in the woods." Borris took as his wingman Fw. Heinrich Heuser, who had recently returned from instructor duty. The trip was uneventful.

21 July

Neither Jagdkorps II nor the AEAF were able to fly any missions. Lt. Jan Schild transferred from the 2nd Staffel to the 10th to serve as interim Staffelführer; Oblt. Schauder was filling in for Major Mietusch during the latter's hospital stay.

22 July

The weather prevented Jagdkorps II from mounting any large-scale missions. An order was issued stating that one weather reconnaissance mission would be flown to the front each morning by a pair of experienced pilots. They would report the suitability for operations with a single code word. The duty was to be rotated among the Jagdgeschwader.

Oblt. Wilhelm Hofmann was awarded the German Cross in Gold for his twenty-six air victories, twelve of them scored on the Invasionsfront.

23 July

Weather again prevented offensive operations for most of the day. A late-evening mission to attack the American concentrations around St. Lô was completely unsuccessful. According to the AEAF radio intercept service, it was abandoned owing to "extra-heavy antiaircraft fire."

The unsuccessful attempt on Hitler's life on 20 July began to have repercussions in the combat units. Reichsmarschall Göring, acting in his role as deputy commander-in-chief of the armed forces, ordered the Wehrmacht to drop the military salute in favor of the *deutsche Gruss,* or Nazi salute. Also, the loyalty of his Luftwaffe, widely considered the least Nazified of the armed forces, was now to be monitored by Nazi "leadership officers", or NSFOs, which were to be attached to each unit of Gruppe size or greater.

24 July

Operation Cobra, an all-out air attack in advance of the American First Army's push to break out of the beachhead, was delayed for a day by the heavy bombers' inability to find their targets. They dropped their bombs on nearby tactical targets. Jagdkorps II made no attempt to intercept the heavy bombers, but did send four Jagdgruppen to strafe in the St. Lô area. Most of the German fighters were sent to Caen in the afternoon, and swept the American sector late in the evening. The First and Third Gruppen took part in these missions, but with no known result.

25 July

Operation Cobra began with carpet-bombing attacks by American medium and heavy bombers on the German positions south of the St. Lô-Perrier road. The German defenders were immobilized – many were buried alive or driven insane – and the ground assault began moving forward. General Buelowius attempted to split his forces between Caen and the new target area, and nowhere achieved an effective concentration. Four joint missions were attempted, but all were apparently broken up by American fighters before reaching the front lines. Two Third Gruppe Messerschmitts were shot down, without harm to their pilots. Neither the First nor the Third Gruppe reported any successes.

Back in Germany, Emil Lang began rebuilding the Second Gruppe at Reinsehlen in his typically energetic and unconventional manner. He first sent his best pilots on recruiting visits to the *Ergänzungsgruppen* (advanced training groups). Lt. Gerhard Vogt's first stop was Jagdgruppe Süd, which had relocated from southern France to Hohensalza in eastern Germany. He told the assembled Fw 190 pilot trainees that they would be given the opportunity to volunteer for service in the famous Schlageter Geschwader, in the Gruppe commanded by the renowned Hptm. Emil Lang. Lang was quoted as saying, "Give me several experienced Staffelkapitäne and Schwarmführer, and I will seek out the rest from among the *Nachwuchs* and get results." (Nachwuchs or "new growth" was the term commonly used in Germany for the late-war crop of poorly-trained replacement pilots.) A number of the Nachwuchs stepped forward. Vogt's task was to evaluate the volunteers' flying skills, and take only the best back to Reinsehlen. The first test flight ended in a fatal crash, which brought the evaluation program to a close. All of the surviving volunteers, a total of eight to ten men, were selected, and their orders to join the Second Gruppe at Reinsehlen were soon in hand. Walter Stumpf's logbook indicates that he joined the combat unit after a total of 180 hours of flight training. He had spent fewer than twenty hours at the controls of a fighter aircraft. A typical RAF fighter pilot had 450 hours of flight training before receiving his first operational posting; the average American pilot, 600 hours.

New pilots reported to Reinsehlen over a period of two weeks from Jagdgruppe Süd and other training units, but this day saw the most arrivals. The new recruits for the Second Gruppe included: Lt. Siegfried Benz, Fhr. Maximilian Busch, Ofhr. Otto Fussi, Uffz. Helmut Gross, Gefr. Willi Hanitz, Lt. Robert Heinrichs, Uffz. Johannes Hoffmann, Uffz. Friedhelm Hönig, Uffz. Karl Hött, Uffz. Erhard Jähnig, Ofhr. Klaus Knappmann, Lt. Albrecht Kraus, Uffz. Georg Kreth, Ofhr. Bruno Krüper, Uffz. Ottomar Kruse, Lt. Helmut Lampe, Uffz. Ernst Lampferhoff, Fw. Kurt Müller, Ofhr. Alfred Pfützner, Ogfr. Otto Putschenjack, Uffz. Günther Reuter, Uffz. Adolf Richter, Uffz. Walter Richter, Lt. Hans Rösen, Uffz. Johannes Schlimper, Uffz. Anton Schrettinger, Uffz. Josef Smischek, Uffz. Michael Spiess, Lt. Wolf-Dietmar Stein, Ogfr. Walter Stumpf, Gefr. Willi Tebbe, Fw. Werner Verhöven, Fw. Peter Vogelbacher, Uffz. Rudolf Walter, and Oblt. Walter Wedekind.

Two pilots transferred into the Gruppe from the staff of Jagdgruppe Süd. Oblt. Konrad Bertels had been a member of the Luftwaffe since 1937, originally in ground postings. The Geschwader honors book noted that the strongest attribute of Lt. Hans-Joachim Brede, the second pilot, was that he was a "firm Nazi".

Fw. Helmut Taubert joined the Gruppe after completing a Fw 190 transition course at Jagdgruppe West. A Bf 109 pilot with 105 missions, he had flown in JG 77 in 1941-42, and most recently with a reconnaissance unit.

Of these thirty-eight men, twenty-three were killed and three were taken prisoner while serving with the Second Gruppe.

26 July

Today it was the turn of JG 26 to provide the weather Rotte. Fw. Heinrich Heuser and his wingman were chosen for the duty. Heuser apparently reported that conditions were suitable only for operations with small formations of one to three Gruppen, as that is what was ordered for the entire day. Gruppe formations now frequently contained a dozen or fewer aircraft, which infuriated General Buelowius. Operational strengths had recovered greatly in the recent weather-enforced lull, and he radioed his Kommodoren with orders that every pilot on their duty rosters in the morning should fly at least one mission that day. But he was ignored; most Gruppen kept one Schwarm on the ground at all times, at readiness to defend their own airfields.

A First Gruppe Fw 190A-8 prepares to take off from Boissy-le-Bois in late July, carrying two WGr 21 rocket mortar tubes underwing. *(Matthiesen via Petrick)*

Offensive formations containing twelve or fewer aircraft were ineffective. Many formation leaders felt that this was an insufficient number to attack Allied fighter-bomber formations, which usually contained two flights, or eight aircraft, and avoided contact. The Third Gruppe reported no engagements today; the First Gruppe had two, both with RAF Mustangs. In mid-morning, Oblt. Hans Hartigs of the 4th Staffel downed a Mustang, probably a No. 414 Sqd. (RCAF) photo-recon aircraft, east of Rouen. At 1900, No. 122 Squadron had a massive dogfight southeast of Caen with twenty Fw 190s from I/JG 26 and JG 2. Lt. Ellenrieder shot one Mustang down, but the Gruppe lost Uffz. Herbert Kind, who crashed in flames, and Uffz. Alfred Schuster, who bailed out, landed in a pond, and drowned when be became entangled in his parachute.

JG 26 Casualties: 18 - 26 July 1944

Date	Rank	Name	Cas	Unit	Aircraft	WNr	Mkgs	Place	Time	Cause	Allied Unit
18-07-44	Oblt.	Hilgendorff, Viktor	KIA	9 CO	Bf 109G-6	413482	wh 3	S of Dreux	0952	P-47	373 FG
18-07-44	Lt.	Völmle, Dieter	WIA	9	Bf 109G-6	163186	wh 19	N of Dreux	0950	P-47	373 FG
18-07-44	Uffz.	Wendl, Josef	KIA	1	Fw 190A-8	730467	wh 1	WSW of Nantes	0930	P-38	474 FG
19-07-44	Fw.	Holl, Walter	KIA	10	Bf 109G-6	165146	bk 13	Boucouvillers	1520	crashed	non-op
26-07-44	Uffz.	Kind, Herbert	KIA	2	Fw 190A-6	170056	bk 4	near Nantes	1900	Mustang	122 Sqd
26-07-44	Uffz.	Schuster, Alfred	KIA	3	Fw 190A-8	174101	yl 8	50km S of Rouen		Mustang	122 Sqd

27 July

Few Allied bombers could find their targets owing to a persistent ground haze, but AEAF fighter-bombers swept northern France on armed reconnaissance flights, now their most common mission profile. Jagdkorps II ordered four combined missions to the front lines. Pilots from the First and Third Gruppen participated in all of them. The first mission contained elements of nine Jagdgruppen. It assembled in the Paris area and was proceeding westward by 0657. East of Caen the Third Gruppe, III/JG 54, and possibly a second Fw 190 Gruppe contacted No. 122 Sqd. Mustangs that were on an armed reconnaissance mission. The Mustang pilots reported being attacked by forty Focke-Wulfs and Messerschmitts, and after a prolonged dogfight claimed 4-0-3 Fw 190s for the loss of one Mustang shot down and one badly damaged. Uffz. Wolfgang Polster and Lt. Karl-Dietrich Hilliger of the Third Gruppe claimed Mustangs in this battle, as did the new Green Heart, Lt. Peter Crump. The Third Gruppe suffered no losses.

Lt. Kemethmüller skirmished with Spitfires and P-47s on the morning mission, his 453rd combat sortie of the war, and then left for a month's leave. His First Gruppe failed to score during the day. One of its Focke-Wulfs reported damage from an enemy aircraft. The Third Gruppe chalked up another victory in mid-afternoon, when Uffz. Hennemann shot down a flak-damaged 404th Fighter Group P-47 that was flying alone.

JG 26 Victory Claims: 18 - 27 July 1944

Date	Rank	Name	Unit	Cl #	Aircraft	Place	Time	Opponent	Conf
18-07-44	Lt.	Kemethmüller	4	86	P-38	25km SE of Vernon (AD1)	0930	474 FG	yes
26-07-44	Lt.	Ellenrieder	3	10	Mustang	Verneuil (BB)	1902	122 Sqd	yes
26-07-44	Oblt.	Hartigs	4	5	Mustang	E of Rouen (TD5-6)	1015	414 Sqd	yes
27-07-44	Uffz.	Hennemann	9		P-47	St. Lô (US6-UT4)	1515	404 FG	i.O.
27-07-44	Lt.	Hilliger	9	1	Mustang	Caen (UU3)	0718	122 Sqd	unk
27-07-44	Fw.	Polster	11	5	Mustang	N of Lisieux (UU3)	0715	122 Sqd	i.O.

28 July

The German Army now recognized that its point of greatest danger was west of St. Lô, where the Americans had broken cleanly through the defenses. Jagdkorps II committed to send all of its fighters to this area. The First Gruppe was ordered to transfer to the JG 2 base at Creil at first light, and to fly joint rocket mortar missions with III/JG 2 until further notice. The Gruppe did not go to Creil, however, instead moving to Waldwiese, a small overflow field southwest of Paris. The early mission was postponed until mid-afternoon owing to bad weather. Ten Jagdgruppen attempted to assemble in the Paris area while under constant harassment by Allied fighters. Part of the First Gruppe, escorted by III/JG 54, broke through to St. Lô and made a successful rocket attack on American tank assemblies and truck columns. Lt. Ellenrieder then made the first successful attack by a JG 26 pilot on an Auster, the Luftwaffe name for any light Allied spotter aircraft (Aeronca, Piper, Stinson, and Taylorcraft being those used by the USAAF.)

A second combined mission was attempted late in the evening, but the seven Jagdgruppen involved apparently got no farther west than the Caen-Argentan area. Uffz. Boeckl of the 12th Staffel claimed an RAF Mitchell near Lisieux, but the claim was not confirmed. His opponent may have been a Mitchell, but was more likely a B-26, two of which were lost. III/JG 54 claimed two B-26s in this battle, which was monitored by the AEAF radio intercept service; one of these claims was confirmed.

29 July

Weather again grounded the AEAF units that were still flying from England. Jagdkorps II placed all of its fighters on twenty minutes readiness from 0345. A full-strength sweep of the break-through area southwest of St. Lô was to be flown as early as possible; the intended targets were fighter-bombers and artillery spotters. III/JG 2 was to land at Guyancourt after the first mission and then prepare to fly a joint rocket mortar mission with the First Gruppe, under JG 26 control. Other Jagdgruppen were detailed as close and detached escort for the rocket carriers.

The Jagdkorps II orders were decoded by ULTRA at 2139 on the 28th, and neither of these missions was carried out as planned owing to interference by Allied fighters. Seven Jagdgruppen took part in the early mission, but apparently got no farther west than Évreux. The Third Gruppe encountered No. 65 Sqd. Mustangs on an armed recon mission to Dreux, and shot down one, without loss. Lt. Karl-Dietrich Hilliger and Ogfr. Heinz Nieter both filed claims, but neither was confirmed.

Little is known about the afternoon mission. The First Gruppe did not take part, as Obstlt. Priller was in the process of moving it and his Geschwaderstab to Rambouillet after a search for landing grounds that were neither excessively bomb-damaged nor waterlogged. The 1st and 2nd Staffeln were now flying most of their missions from Schneisenplatz. The 10th and 12th Staffeln had already moved to Toussus from Villacoublay-Nord, to relieve the strain on the latter field.

JG 26 Victory Claims: 28 - 29 July 1944

Date	Rank	Name	Unit	Cl #	Aircraft	Place	Time	Opponent	Conf
28-07-44	Lt.	Ellenrieder	3	11	Auster	Breteuil (AB)	1653		unk
28-07-44	Uffz.	Boeckl	12		Mitchell	Lisieux (UA)	2008		unk
29-07-44	Lt.	Hilliger	9	2	Mustang	S of Soissons (UG7-8)	0715	65 Sqd	unk
29-07-44	Ogfr.	Nieter	10		Mustang	Dreux-Évreux	0715	65 Sqd	unk

30 July

Fw. Polster and his 11th Staffel wingman were picked this morning to fly the Jagdkorps II weather recon mission. They reported that the skies over the battle front were clearing, and two combined missions were ordered to St. Lô in the afternoon and evening. The task today was ground attack, and the First Gruppe flew two successful Werfereinsätze, escorted by the Third Gruppe. The Geschwader suffered no losses.

31 July

The orders from Jagdkorps II were a repeat of those of the previous day, but the crisis around Avranches, where General Patton's newly-activated Third Army was threatening to outflank all of the German forces in Normandy, required an emphasis on anti-air missions rather than ground support. At day's end the Jagdkorps reported that it had successfully prevented the Allied fighters and fighter-bombers from fulfilling their ground-support objectives, but in the process had suffered "not inconsiderable losses." Today's missions by the Geschwader resulted in neither claims nor losses, and there is no evidence that they engaged in any serious combats.

Major Karl Borris resumed full control of the First Gruppe, and Hptm. Hermann Staiger left the Geschwader to take command of II/JG 1. Staiger was overdue for a permanent Gruppenkommandeur posting, but his departure was a severe blow to JG 26; he had developed into one of the best formation leaders in the Jagdwaffe.

Geschwader personnel moves during July included: the return of Oblt. Günther Blömertz from hospital to the Second Gruppe, and his posting as adjutant; the transfer of Lt. Karl Kempf from the 11th Staffel to the 2nd, and the temporary transfer of Lt. Gottfried Dietze and Ogfr. Hermann Hillebrand from the First Gruppe to III/JG 54. Only a few pilots joined the Geschwader in France this month after completing flight training. Two men, Fw. Karl Hofmann and Uffz. Wilhelm Schäfer, are known to have joined the First Gruppe.

JG 26 claimed at least forty-five aerial victories in July, at the cost of twenty pilots killed in combat (including two Staffelkapitäne), one killed in a flying accident, and at least sixteen injured, including two more Kapitäne. Their ratio of victories to losses dropped from June, in large part because they had been forced to fly in ever-smaller formations.

1 August

Jagdkorps II was ordered to keep attacking in the Avranches area, but to shift its emphasis from anti-air to direct attacks on the American tank concentrations and truck convoys. The weather postponed operations until the afternoon, but the First and Third Gruppen then flew two successful missions. The Third Gruppe flew as escort for the

The opposition. Pilots of No. 315 Squadron (Polish), photographed on 1 August. From left: British intelligence officer, P/O Swistun, S/L Horbaczewski (KIA 18 Aug 44), F/O Nowosielski, F/L Cwynar, W/O Jankowski, F/S Bedkowski. *(Nowosielski via Mucha)*

rocket-carrying First, and during both missions the Messerschmitts were able to use cloud cover to bounce and disperse American fighters before they could approach the Focke-Wulfs. The Messerschmitt pilots claimed no victories, but accomplished their task, while suffering no casualties. The evening mission was flown by only ten Fw 190s and thirteen Bf 109s. Fw. Heinz Thiemann of the 2nd Staffel was shot down by ground fire northeast of Avranches and taken prisoner.

2 August

Today's orders, missions, and results were similar to those of the previous day. Aircraft from at least five Jagdgruppen took part in the mid-afternoon mission. The Third Gruppe was able to put up twenty Messerschmitts, and succeeded in driving some P-47s away from the rocket-carriers near St. Malo. Fw. Heuser reported that his rockets exploded a gasoline tanker. III/JG 54 was one of the units taking part in this mission. Peter Crump recalls:

"I was ordered to lead a low-level attack on enemy ground troops in the Invasionsraum as part of a mixed formation of about 25-30 aircraft from the Jagdgeschwader in the greater Paris area. During one of these attacks, at an altitude of about 200-300 meters (650-1000 feet), my wingman, Ofhr. Günter Zilling, was shot down by enemy flak. He appeared to me to take a hit from a heavy shell; his aircraft exploded in a bright fireball, only 40-50 meters (130-160 feet) beside me. With this horrible sight, the limit of my endurance was reached or exceeded – I want to state it plainly. Thus when I was told by Hauptmann Neumann, the Gruppenadjutant – a non-flying officer – shortly after my return to Villacoublay that I was to lead another mission to the Invasionsraum in the next hour, with yet another mixed formation, I completely lost my self-control. Since as a newcomer to III/JG 54 I felt myself discriminated against in favor of the 54th fomation leaders, I was furious, and slammed down the receiver. At that moment nothing mattered to me. I wanted to escape; to see and hear nothing of the war for one or two days.

A camouflaged Second Gruppe Fw 190A-8 sits in its revetment. This photograph was probably taken in Reinsehlen in late July or early August. The new aircraft received by the Gruppe had the spirals painted on their spinners immediately. *(Sy)*

"I was in this state of mind when a short time later the Kommandeur, Hptm. Weiss, entered my room, accompanied by the Gruppe physician, Dr. Busemeyer. Neither had any real understanding of my request – how could anyone at this time avoid seeing or hearing of the war for one or two days? – but the Kommandeur was short and to the point; I was to leave that same day for the Fighter Pilots' Rest Home at Bad Wiessee. Thus it happened that the following day I unexpectedly found myself in the peaceful and beautiful mountains of the Tegernsee."

Peter Crump rejoined III/JG 54 after its withdrawal from the front. His next flight with the unit was on 24 September, from their Oldenburg training base.

The evening mission to the critical battle area was flown by ten First Gruppe rocket-carriers, escorted by eight Third Gruppe Messerschmitts and an unknown number of III/JG 54 Focke-Wulfs. It was carried out in complete radio silence, and was apparently successful.

The Second Gruppe lost a pilot on a training mission from Reinsehlen. Lt. Albrecht Krauss attempted a forced landing after the engine of his Focke-Wulf failed, but the fighter burst into flames and burned Krauss, who died the next day.

3 August

Patton's army had now reached Rennes, and threatened to cut off the entire Brittany peninsula. Jagdkorps II ordered all of its fighters, even the escort Gruppen, to attack road traffic between Avranches and Rennes. The first combined mission took off at 0850 in persistent light rain, which reduced Allied air activity to a minimum. The Third Gruppe was able to put up nineteen fighters for this maximum-strength mission, which was carried out in complete radio silence. Some pilots got lost and did not find the front, but the rest carried out a successful mission in the absence of American fighters. A second mission was flown in mid-afternoon; the First Gruppe rocket-carriers claimed good results on both.

The day's third mission was flown in the evening, in low strength. JG 1 had no serviceable fighters; JG 2 was grounded after a noon B-17 raid left Creil littered with unexploded bombs. The Third Gruppe lost one pilot; Fw. Karl Hennemann was shot down by ground fire while strafing enemy troops northwest of Avranches, and crashed in his plane. Fw. Heuser of the 2nd Staffel was also shot down, but survived. Heinrich Heuser recalls:

"We were flying from a meadow called Schneisenplatz, which was in some woods near Rambouillet, south of Paris. Some of our aircraft, including mine, were equipped with 'stovepipes' under each wing for carrying 21 cm rockets. We took off for this mission at 1850, carrying rockets, and headed for the Invasionsraum at 1500 meters. Many enemy fighters were reported at various altitudes. We were to attack tank concentrations near Avranches. When we reached the target area, we were able to recognize the enemy tanks by large orange-colored triangles on their engine compartments. We dived and fired our rockets. We were then to return to base at minimum altitude. While I was coming off the target at only 50 meters (160 feet) altitude, a four-barrel 20 mm antiaircraft battery opened up on me. My aircraft was hit after a few rounds. The throttle was shot from my left hand, which was severely injured. I pulled up in a steep climb, but another hit set my engine on fire. I jumped from my burning machine at 500 km/hr [300 mph] speed and an altitude of about 180 meters [600 feet]. I pulled my ripcord, and my parachute opened about thirty meters above the ground. I landed in a field beside the main road through Avranches. I was captured immediately by an American soldier carrying a machine pistol. Because of my shot-through hand, he helped me remove my parachute with its attached inflatable boat, as well as my life jacket. I asked him to remove the watch from my swelling wrist and stick it in my trousers pocket, but he collected it for himself. After complaining to an approaching officer, I got my watch back.

"I was carried in a jeep to the next collection station, where the next day my hand was operated on. I must mention that I was treated very correctly in all phases of my capture. Since my flying clothes were soaked through with blood, I lay naked on a cot for three days. On the fourth day I was given prisoner-of-war clothing (a black-dyed American uniform with large white letters 'PW' on arms, legs, and back) and was shipped to England on a landing boat with other wounded German prisoners. We were taken to an American field hospital at Henley, which was guarded and provisioned by English soldiers (one meal per day). There I was operated on a second time. At about the end of August, I was shipped with many other wounded prisoners from Plymouth to Staten Island in a convoy of approximately eighty escorted transport ships. After completing all formalities, we traveled in a Pullman train (only for wounded, with four persons in a compartment, which was arranged for the night with four beds and each night was supplied with new towels) ...to Camp Forrest, Tennessee. On 24 November a mixed medical commission, comprising an American and two Swiss military doctors, visited the camp. They decided to exchange me for a wounded American in German captivity.

"In late December the wounded prisoners to be exchanged were taken to Brooklyn and loaded onto an American hospital ship, which took us to Marseille, France in fourteen days. After the arrival of further 'exchange-ships', we were put on a train of the International Red Cross, which took us to the German border at Constance. The exchange between German and American wounded prisoners of war took place in Constance on 18 January, 1945. I saw no more employment in the war.

"Finally, I must say that I was always treated, personally, medically, and militarily, very correctly and very well."

A 5th Staffel Fw 190A-8 taxies out for takeoff from Reinsehlen during late July or early August. The cable-cantilevered airplane shelter was a common feature on German airfields. (*Genth*)

4 August

Again today Jagdkorps II sent all of its fighters west to strafe and fire rockets at the Americans who were moving south through Avranches and defending against German attacks east of the town. Again today the constant light rain kept the American fighters from finding the Germans. The routine assembly point was now over the Versailles palace, which worked well until ULTRA passed the location on to the AEAF. Two *Werfereinsätze* were flown. The First and Third Gruppen took part in both, and reported no losses. The AEAF radio intercept service reported that eight Jagdgruppen were active, and flew a minimum of 133 sorties. Eleven Third Gruppe pilots took part in the first mission; eight First Gruppe pilots flew the second one.

The Second Gruppe sent a signal from Reinsehlen to General Galland's office that was intercepted and decoded by ULTRA. The Gruppe had sixty-three Fw 190A-8 aircraft, all with FuG 16Z homing radios. Forty-three aircraft were operational; two were suitable for training only. Sixty-eight pilots were present, but only twenty-two were considered ready for combat duty.

5 August

The orders from Jagdkorps II were a repeat of those of the previous day, except that the *Schwerpunkt* (focal point) for the strafing and rocket attacks was moved southeast of Avranches to Fougères, where one of Patton's Third Army corps was now sweeping eastward and threatening to envelop the German armies. The heavy antiaircraft zone around Avranches was to be avoided; the critical road bottleneck had thus been conceded to the Americans. Two combined missions were flown. The First and Third Gruppen participated in both, and suffered no losses. The AEAF radio intercept service reported that the eight active Jagdgruppen flew a minimum of 148 sorties. Thirteen First Gruppe and twenty Third Gruppe pilots flew the first mission, according to warnings radioed to the German Flak units.

6 August

The mission orders from Jagdkorps II were a repeat of the previous day's, but circumstances intervened and prevented their execution. Shortly before noon every fighter unit in the Paris area, Werfergruppen excluded, was scrambled and sent north to intercept a formation of heavy bombers which was reported to have light or nonexistent escort. Twenty-six Third Gruppe Bf 109s took off for the mission. The bombers, when seen, were the answer to every experienced German fighter pilot's prayer – these were not B-17s or B-24s, but RAF night-bombing Lancasters and Halifaxes. The British bombers' light armament and open formations made them very vulnerable to fighter attack, but with the decline of the Jagdwaffe they were now being used occasionally by day. Today 222 had been dispatched to bomb two large V-1 storage depots. I/JG 1 apparently arrived at the bomber stream first, but was driven off by a single squadron of Spitfires. III/JG 26 and III/JG 54 next hit separate parts of the formation, and were able to exhaust their ammunition on the bombers without seeing an Allied fighter. III/JG 1 was last on the scene, and was prevented from making a decisive attack on the cripples by the Spitfires of No. 332 Sqd. (Norwegian), which shot down the two Bf 109s providing high cover for the Gruppe and then dived on the main German formation, dispersing it. Three Lancasters and one Halifax were shot down on the mission, and several damaged bombers were written off after their return to England.

Third Gruppe pilots claimed four Halifaxes and three Lancasters; four of these claims were apparently confirmed. Uffz. Heinz Gehrke's element leader, Fw. Karl Laub, selected a straggling Lancaster flying at 3000 meters [10,000 feet] to attack. The two pilots could see the tail gunner slumped over, dead; the turret was totally destroyed. The Messerschmitts were able to attack from the rear, entirely unmolested. During the attack the bomber crewmen, who had no weapons that could bear on the fighters, threw bundles of window (radar-reflecting aluminum foil) out of their aircraft, in an apparent attempt to distract or defy the German pilots. Gehrke's fire hit the left outboard engine, and the bomber dived away, smoking. As the bomber had previously been damaged, Gehrke was not awarded a full victory credit, but rather one for a "final destruction", but it was nonetheless added to his victory total. His story matches that of the surviving crew of a No. 207 Squadron aircraft in most details; this Lancaster was one which reached England and was then scrapped. Heinz Gehrke believed for decades that this combat was in mid-July, and it was so described in *JG 26: Top Guns of the Luftwaffe*, but the newly-discovered German claims microfilms and a wealth of British data have convinced us of our error.

The returning Jagdkorps II fighter pilots claimed a total of four Lancasters, three Halifaxes, eight B-24s, and one B-17 destroyed, plus two shot from formation. All of these bombers were actually Lancasters and Halifaxes. The excessive claims can be attributed to excitement at finding so many unescorted bombers, and inexperience in attacking them; after two months on the Invasionsfront, there were few experienced RLV pilots left in the Jagdgruppen in France.

Jagdkorps II ordered a ground-attack mission in mid-afternoon, but it was necessarily made in low strength. It did not reach the Avranches area, but was diverted to Mortain and Vire, to soften up the American First Army in advance of an attack by the German Army that was scheduled to begin in the evening. Uffz. Wilhelm Sonnenberg of the 3rd Staffel was shot down on this mission, but was able to reach the German lines before bailing out with severe injuries. His casualty report credits this victory to a Thunderbolt, but no American pilot filed a claim, and he may have been the victim of a No. 131 Sqd. Spitfire.

The day's third fighter mission was made in such weak strength that the pilots were told to attack targets of opportunity. Some were dispersed by Allied fighters, but Lt. Georg Kiefner's 1st Staffel was able to fire its rockets at a concentration of American troops.

Major Mietusch was now back in command of his Third Gruppe. Oblt. Schauder resumed command of the 10th Staffel, displacing Lt. Schild, who transferred to the 12th Staffel.

The Second Gruppe reported from Reinsehlen that it now had sixty-eight pilots available for duty; only one new pilot who had arrived the previous day failed to make the list.

JG 26 Victory Claims: 6 August 1944

Date	Rank	Name	Unit	Cl #	Aircraft	Place	Time	Opponent	Conf
06-08-44	Oblt.	Schmidt G.	9 CO		Halifax	N of Paris (UE7)	1213		i.O.
06-08-44	Gefr.	Deshombes	9		Lancaster	N of Paris (UE5)	1216		unk
06-08-44	Lt.	Kopp	10	2	Halifax	N of Paris (UE7)	1215		i.O.
06-08-44	Uffz.	Gehrke	11	4	Lancaster-eV	Le Bourget-Paris (UE8-9)	1223	207 Sqd	i.O.
06-08-44	Uffz.	Scholtz	11		Lancaster	N of Paris (UE7)	1215		unk
06-08-44	Oblt.	Schrader	12 CO		Halifax	NE of Paris (UE9-UF7)	1210		i.O.
06-08-44	Uffz.	Böckl	12		Halifax	N of Paris (UF7-UE9)	1210		unk

JG 26 Casualties: 1 - 6 August 1944

Date	Rank	Name	Cas	Unit	Aircraft	WNr	Mkgs	Place	Time	Cause	Allied Unit
01-08-44	Fw.	Thiemann, Heinz	POW 2		Fw 190A-8	173029	bk 5	NE of Alençon-Avranches	1930	light flak	n/a
02-08-44	Lt.	Krauss, Albrecht	KIFA 8		Fw 190A-8	731741	bl 11	Reinsehlen a/f		engine	non-op
03-08-44	Fw.	Heuser, Heinrich	POW 2		Fw 190A-8	172719	bk 2	Avranches		light flak	n/a
03-08-44	Fw.	Hennemann, Karl	KIA 9		Bf 109G-6/U4	440668	wh 16	NW of Avranches	1950	light flak	n/a
06-08-44	Uffz.	Sonnenberg, Wilhelm	WIA 3		Fw 190A-8	731082	yl 12	SE of Vire		P-47	

7 August

Hitler ordered his Panzer units in Normandy to attack westward through Mortain to the Atlantic Ocean at Avranches, to cut the American Third Army's single line of supply. Generalfeldmarschall von Kluge, the German commander in France, knew that he was putting his best units' necks into a noose, but orders were orders.

The skies cleared in the morning, which was bad news for the Wehrmacht. Jagdkorps II had to ask its fighter pilots to keep American fighter-bombers away from the advancing German Panzers, in addition to their previously-assigned task of strafing and rocketing the American positions west of Mortain. The fighter forces available were insufficient to succeed at either of these missions. According to the AEAF radio intercepts, the eight Jagdgruppen flew at least 128 sorties during the day.

At 1400 six rocket-carrying First Gruppe Fw 190s and eighteen Third Gruppe Bf 109s flew a combined mission with III/JG 1, III/JG 3, I/JG 5, and III/JG 54. Their orders called for an attack on an American ground column, but the German fighters were set upon and dispersed by several squadrons of 9th Air Force P-47s and P-51s, which claimed a total of 12-0-2 victories. The first sighting was apparently made by eight P-47 pilots from the 368th Fighter Group, who reported the approach of 35+ Messerschmitts carrying bombs (undoubtedly drop tanks) and heading toward the American lines. When the P-47s were spotted, the German fighters jettisoned their loads and began to orbit a large cumulus cloud. The American squadron commander radioed for help, which soon arrived. The P-47s then fell on the Messerschmitts, which in the words of the Americans "did not want to fight. Some hit the deck and started for home; others just milled around as though they didn't know what had happened." Two Third Gruppe pilots were killed in this engagement. Ogfr. Günter Deshombes died in his plane; Gefr. Hans Thran bailed out successfully, but according to ground witnesses, was shot in his parachute by a P-47 pilot while only 20 meters (65 feet) above the ground. A victory claim was filed in Thran's name; it was apparently confirmed, but no P-47s were in fact lost in this battle.

Jagdkorps II attempted another mission late in the evening, with identical results. Fighters from five Jagdgruppen took part. The First Gruppe contributed ten Focke-Wulfs; the Third Gruppe, five Messerschmitts. The small formation got no farther than Évreux when it was diverted to attack two squadrons of P-47s just coming off their bomb runs. The 373rd Fighter Group Thunderbolts were the clear winners in the subsequent dogfights, claiming 2-1-5 Fw 190s and 1-2-1 Bf 109s. Lt. Kiefner downed one of the P-47s, but his 1st Staffel lost Lt. Wolf-Dietrich Glahn, who died in his airplane. Uffz. Karl Hofmann of the 3rd Staffel crash-landed in a field southwest of Paris with severe injuries, and Uffz. Herbert Scholz of the 9th Staffel made a smooth forced landing northwest of Chartres with only minor injuries.

JG 26 Casualties: 7 August 1944

Date	Rank	Name	Cas	Unit	Aircraft	WNr	Mkgs	Place	Time	Cause	Allied Unit
07-08-44	Uffz.	Glahn, Wolf-Dietrich	KIA	1	Fw 190A-8	172736	wh 4	SW of Dreux	1900	P-47	373 FG
07-08-44	Uffz.	Hofmann, Karl	WIA	3	Fw 190A-8	171077	yl 9	S of Paris-Dourdan		P-47	373 FG
07-08-44	Uffz.	Scholz, Herbert	WIA	9	Bf 109G-6	165522	wh 5	NW of Chartres	1940	P-47	373 FG
07-08-44	Uffz.	Thran, Hans	KIA	10	Bf 109G-6	20034	bk 12	Mortain-Le Mans	1510	P-47	368 FG
07-08-44	Ogfr.	Deshombes, Günter	KIA	11	Bf 109G-6	165179	yl 9	E of Avranches	1520	P-47	368 FG

8 August

The mission orders from Jagdkorps II called for support of the ground offensive by attacks on fighter-bombers and artillery spotters near Mortain. The importance of large formations was stressed, but the difficulty of assembly owing to enemy attack and bad weather was acknowledged. Aircraft were to wait ten minutes at the assembly point for late arrivals and then fly the mission. If a minimum of fifty aircraft could not be pulled together for a rocket mortar mission, that mission was to be flown as a freie Jagd. The fighter units based farthest to the west, JG 1 and JG 27, were preparing to move east, as were all of the Luftwaffe personnel based in Brittany.

The day's first mission never left Versailles. P-38s were waiting in the clouds, and Major Mietusch quickly ordered a recall, but had to get past the P-51s that were now orbiting over Villacoublay-Nord. The JG 26 units did not participate in the second mission, which had to be dispatched toward the combat zone as individual Gruppen. By noon the Army was complaining to Luftflotte 3 that since daybreak the presence of American fighter-bombers had prevented any road movements in the battle zone. Sperrle's staff in turn informed Jagdkorps II that fighter protection in the area of the offensive was absolutely necessary.

The third mission took off at 1300 and finally able to assemble six Jagdgruppen, despite the presence in the area of heavy bombers and their escorts. Soon after the formation started west, a single squadron of P-51s was seen, and the First Gruppe formation leader took the opportunity to bounce the Mustangs, the 359th Fighter Group's 368th Squadron, with his ten Fw 190s. In the resulting dogfight, two young Unteroffiziere, Otto Horch and Werner Schwan, claimed their first victories. Uffz. Ernst Schande was shot down and killed, and Uffz. Hans Sandoz crash-landed his fighter west of Versailles with minor wounds.

The Geschwader contributed fourteen fighters to the late-evening mission, which included aircraft from seven Jagdgruppen. Some succeeded in reaching Mortain, where a III/JG 54 pilot shot down a P-38.

The Jagdkorps II evening report was decoded by ULTRA. The sortie total, 244, was of interest, as it was greater than the 170 that the Allies inferred from the radio intercepts, proving that Jagdwaffe radio discipline had improved. Two Jagdkorps II fighters were known lost, and a further ten pilots had not yet reported in. The low loss rate was a strong indication to both sides that the German fighter missions were not being pushed to the limit.

9 August

Jagdkorps II ordered its units to make two full-strength sweeps of the Mortain area during the day. Four Jagdgruppen were to prepare to withdraw to Germany to rest and refit. Four rebuilt Jagdgruppen, including II/JG 26, would be returning to France to replace them. In the short term, JG 26 was to ensure that Guyancourt was ready to accept the Second Gruppe. For the long term, Obstlt. Priller was to make plans to transfer the entire Geschwader to Beauvais-Tillé at short notice.

The early-morning mission contained elements of nine Jagdgruppen, including nine First Gruppe Fw 190s and eleven Third Gruppe Bf 109s. The formation encountered a number of P-47s and P-51s, and apparently failed to reach the battle zone. Paul Ostrzecha (2nd Staffel) and Uffz. Horst Gewitz (9th Staffel) failed to return from the mission. Both were probably the victims of the 373rd Fighter Group's 410th Squadron, which claimed two Fw 190s and 1-0-2 Bf 109s near Alençon at 0930.

The mid-afternoon mission, of identical makeup to the first, failed to get past the marauding Allied fighters to reach the battle zone. The late evening mission was a success in that some of the fighters reached Mortain. The pilots of the Geschwader reported no victories, and the 9th Staffel leader, Oblt. Gottfried Schmidt, force-landed with minor injuries after an air battle southeast of Chartres. His aircraft was then strafed and set on fire by a Mustang. No American pilot claimed this Messerschmitt, which was probably the victim of an RAF fighter.

JG 26 Casualties: 8 - 9 August 1944

Date	Rank	Name	Cas	Unit	Aircraft	WNr	Mkgs	Place	Time	Cause	Allied Unit
08-08-44	Uffz.	Sandoz, Hans	WIA	2	Fw 190A-8	731036	bk 7	W of Paris-N of Houdan	1330	P-51	359 FG
08-08-44	Uffz.	Schande, Ernst	KIA	2	Fw 190A-6	530120	bk 8	E of Dreux	1330	P-51	359 FG
09-08-44	Uffz.	Ostrzecha, Paul	KIA	2	Fw 190A-8	170124	bk 6	Chartres-Orleans		P-47	373 FG
09-08-44	Oblt.	Schmidt, Gottfried	WIA	9 CO	Bf 109G-6	412429	wh 9	30km SSE of Chartres	1810	Mustang	
09-08-44	Uffz.	Gewitz, Horst	KIA	9	Bf 109G-6	440668	wh 16	Chartres-Orleans	1000	P-47	373 FG

10 August

Despite the critical ground situation, Jagdkorps II gave the First Gruppe and III/JG 54 the next two days off to rest and restore their operational strength. The other units were given a repeat of the previous day's orders – attack enemy fighter-bombers and artillery spotters around Mortain. The early mission was apparently flown by the Third Gruppe alone. A dozen Bf 109s took off from Villacoublay-Nord and Toussus at 0900 and flew the mission in complete silence. The Gruppe lost Fw. Siegfried Göhre in a combat with unidentified fighters west of Évreux. The rest of the Messerschmitts were east of Dreux on their return flight when they were bounced by P-51s of the 364th Fighter Group's 384th Squadron. Lt. Harald Lenz crash-landed and was injured by a strafing P-51. Two Mustangs were then lost to antiaircraft fire from one of the many airfields in the area.

Major Mietusch led the two afternoon combined missions. The first, flown as a freie Jagd, got no farther west than Falaise; the Gruppe was attacked while forming up southeast of Paris by Mustangs, which shot down Uffz. Richard Vogel. Vogel bailed out 150 meters above the ground and was severely injured when he struck a tree. The second combined mission was a Werfereinsatz, and apparently made a successful ground attack west of Alençon.

11 August

The daily orders for concentrated missions to attack fighter-bombers and artillery spotters around Mortain showed that Jagdkorps II was totally out of touch with the true situation on the ground. The German offensive had failed, and the army was fleeing eastward. American armor operating on the Germans' open southern flank had already reached Alençon. The Luftwaffe fighters were grounded by fog in the morning, but the 8th Air Force heavy bombers were able to fly, and attacked numerous targets around Paris. Villacoublay was bombed by seventy-six B-17s; Toussus, by forty-five B-24s.

Uffz. Heinz Gehrke's Bf 109G-6 "yellow 1", which survived five or six weeks at the front before its destruction on the ground in a B-17 raid on Villacoublay, probably on 11 August. The aircraft illustrates the markings changes ordered in late June for fighters in France – removal of the yellow paint on the undercowl and rudder, which had been theater markings since 1941, and repainting of the black-green spinner in black, with a white spiral.*(Gehrke)*

The Third Gruppe lost two Bf 109s destroyed and two damaged; one groundcrewman was slightly injured. III/JG 54 reported that its half of Villacoublay would be unserviceable for a day, but that it had lost no aircraft or personnel. The few German fighters to take off during the afternoon were unable to reach the combat zone.

Hptm. Georg-Peter Eder, an experienced western *Kanaljäger* (Channel fighter) and Knight's Cross holder, reported to the Second Gruppe at Reinsehlen. He was assigned to the 6th Staffel as its interim leader, substituting for Lt. Glunz, who was still not on the duty roster.

12 August
The top priority for Jagdkorps II switched back to ground attack. The German defenses in Normandy had broken down completely, and the ground forces were in danger of being encircled west of Falaise and Alençon. All means were to be used to stop the Allied tank columns. The early mission was a successful Werfereinsatz for the First Gruppe, whose pilots claimed hits on tanks and trucks north of Le Mans. The Third Gruppe did not take part, as its new dispersal field, Buc, had just been bombed. Its pilots moved again during the day; some to Biévres, which was nothing more than a cultivated field, and the rest back to Toussus.

The Third Gruppe got five aircraft airborne for the afternoon mission, joining twelve First Gruppe rocket-carriers and elements of four other Jagdgruppen in an attack on vehicles between Chartres and Alençon. Uffz. Fritz Rapsch of the 3rd Staffel disappeared after an encounter with enemy fighters. After firing their rockets, two 1st Staffel fighters were hit by American ground fire. Uffz. Franz Putsch bailed out within the German lines with severe burns. Lt. Georg Kiefner returned to Schneisenplatz with a large hole in the wing of his Fw 190A-8.

At 1100 the pilots of the Second Gruppe received their orders to leave Reinsehlen for the front. By 1200 the aircraft were loaded, but their departure was delayed until late afternoon. Takeoff was in order of Staffeln – Stabsschwarm, 5th, 6th, 7th, 8th Staffel. One Focke-Wulf force-landed on the field with a dead engine. The rest formed up in close formation and headed for Mönchen-Gladbach. Fw. Heinz Gomann broke away near Münster with his engine on fire. He crash-landed at the Handorf Luftwaffe

Lt. Georg Kiefner, Groth's replacement as leader of the 1st Staffel, describes his mission after his "white 5" was hit by antiaircraft fire during a low-level attack on American armor positions west of Paris. Crew chief Fricke examines the damage – Les Mesnuls, 12 August. *(Kiefner)*

base, but had to fight his way out of his burning aircraft himself; the fire service would not leave their bunker. Gomann suffered severe burns, but was once again "fortunate" in that the local hospital had a good burn treatment facility.

When the rest of the Gruppe arrived at Mönchen-Gladbach, they were made to circle the field for some time, until low fuel finally forced them to land in the twilight, which they did without incident. The pilots saw to the servicing of their planes, reported in, and then headed to the pilots' common room. Hauptmann Lang praised his new pilots – "not a single crash". The pilots from the unit stationed on the field greeted them. Supper – fried potatoes, eggs, and milk – was brought in and served by the chief paymaster, to the amazement of the Nachwuchs, who were not yet used to the status awarded a German combat pilot.

JG 26 Casualties: 10 - 12 August 1944

Date	Rank	Name	Cas	Unit	Aircraft	WNr	Mkgs	Place	Time	Cause	Allied Unit
10-08-44	Uffz.	Vogel, Richard	WIA	10	Bf 109G-6	412485	bk 4	SE of Paris-N of Ablis	1330	P-51	
10-08-44	Lt.	Lenz, Harald	WIA	11	Bf 109G-6	163184	yl 18	N of Ablis	0930	P-51	364 FG
10-08-44	Fw.	Göhre, Siegfried	KIA	12	Bf 109G-6	165239	bl 22	W of Breteuil	0845	fighter	
12-08-44	Lt.	Kiefner, Georg	no	1 CO	Fw 190A-8	171079	wh 5	E of Paris		flak	n/a
12-08-44	Uffz.	Putsch, Franz	WIA	1	Fw 190A-8	174111	wh 9	Verneuil		flak	n/a
12-08-44	Uffz.	Rapsch, Fritz	KIA	3	Fw 190A-8	731758	yl 10	E of Alençon (CB)		fighter	

13 August

The Third Gruppe and JG 1 were given the next two days off to rest and restore serviceability. The orders from Jagdkorps II to its other Jagdgruppen were for concentrated sweeps against fighter-bombers, as well as rocket and ground strafing attacks on the American columns between Alençon and Le Mans. A dozen rocket-laden First Gruppe Focke-Wulfs took off at 0730 and flew a successful Werfereinsatz to Le Mans, escorted by fighters from three Jagdgruppen. The 4th Staffel had put up one Schwarm for the mission, and flew at the rear of the formation. The Schwarmführer was Fw. Robert Hager; his wingman was Uffz. Erich Burmeister. Lt. Wolfgang Marx led the second element, with Uffz. Hans Kukla as his wingman. Kukla, who was flying his third combat sortie, was thus the *Holzauge* – the wooden-eye or lookout – for the entire Focke-Wulf formation. Kukla let his guard drop on the return flight, lulled into a sense of security by the Bf 109 high cover. When he finally glanced to the rear, the Messerschmitts had turned into Mustangs, which had dispersed the 109s and were bearing down on Kukla's flight. He shouted a warning, but the flight was at low altitude, and there was no escape. Kukla's aircraft was the first to be hit. He quickly pulled its nose up and bailed out. His parachute opened 20 meters (65 feet) above the ground, and he landed in a farmyard. In return for his parachute, the farmer's wife told him that he was in no-man's land and directed him toward the German lines. He returned to Rambouillet with a facial burn and severe bruises that put him out of action until October.

The Mustang that shot Hans Kukla down was from the 9th Air Force's 363rd Fighter Group. Eight P-51s from its 382nd Squadron took off at about 0700 for a patrol of the Alençon-Le Mans area. The second of the two flights was led by Lt. Lee Webster, and flew at about 9000 feet (2700 meters). Near the end of their patrol, Webster spotted aircraft below, heading east at 4000 feet (1200 meters). His cover flight did not hear Webster's call, so he led his four Mustangs down alone. He identified the bogies as Bf 109s, and saw a dozen more aircraft in front of them, on the deck. The 109s turned into the attack. Webster's first salvo sent one Messerschmitt pilot over the side. The American pilot broke out of his turn and headed for the formation below with his wingman, Lt. George Brooks, who was a new pilot on his fifth mission. The remaining 109s were left to his No. 3 and No. 4. Webster joined the tail end of a formation of about ten Fw 190s. He missed the rear plane with his first burst, but then corrected and scored hits all over the fuselage. The pilot – Hans Kukla – pulled his nose up and bailed out. The next plane in line, that of Lt. Marx, took a full salvo from Brooks's four .50's and entered a "dead man's turn" to the right. Webster had now opened fire on Hager's wingman, Uffz. Burmeister, and saw his plane burst into flames and crash. Fw. Hager succeeded in turning his Focke-Wulf around, but was then hit and crashed to his death. The two Mustang pilots had shot down the entire 4th Staffel Schwarm. Lt. Joachim Günther had turned his Focke-Wulf around on hearing Kukla's cry, and led his 3rd Staffel Schwarm in an attack on the two Mustangs. Both were hit; Brooks took a shell in a coolant line and soon had to bail out. George Brooks' story from this point has eerie parallels with Hans Kukla's – a landing in no-man's land with a severely burned hand, aid from the French peasants – except that Brooks' walk took him in the opposite direction from Kukla. George Brooks and Hans Kukla, now close friends, have walked the site of their battle together, and have located some of the people who helped them.

There was another survivor from the 4th Staffel Schwarm, Erich Burmeister. He too was trapped between the lines, and like Hans Kukla, was carried as missing until he finally made his way back to Rambouillet.

Uffz. Wilhelm Schäfer of the 3rd Staffel was shot down on the morning mission by another flight of 363rd Fighter Group Mustangs, and was killed. The evening mission was flown in very low strength, and very late, but some of its aircraft succeeded in finding the enemy; Lt. Ellenrieder of the 3rd Staffel reported the destruction of two tanks near Le Mans with his rockets.

Jagdkorps II now had to withdraw all of its rocket-carrying aircraft from service, as all had flown more than thirty minutes at emergency power and required engine changes. Reinforcements were on the way; six Jagdgruppen that had been sent back to Germany to reform were *en route* back to the front. Two brand-new Jagdgruppen were also headed to France. II/JG 6 and III/JG 76 were formerly *Zerstörergruppen* (heavy fighter groups), flying Bf 110s in the RLV organization.

Most of the Second Gruppe was back in France before nightfall. Uffz. Adolf Richter was killed when his engine failed on takeoff from Mönchen-Gladbach, but most of the pilots arrived safely at St. Dizier in the morning; the rest were delayed by various deficiencies in their aircraft. Lang waited most of the day at St. Dizier. Lt. Hofmann finally arrived with twelve aircraft, and after refueling the newcomers, the formation took off for Paris. The guide aircraft from the First Gruppe did not wait for the Focke-Wulfs to form up, but headed out immediately. Ogfr. Walter Stumpf found himself last in the formation, but feeling that "the last one is bitten by the dogs", he gave his aircraft full throttle, slowly caught the others, and formed up on Lt. Prager. They remained at low altitude. Soon they spotted the Eiffel Tower – they had reached Paris.

The first report of Indianer came from Hofmann; then Lang, then Prager. Stumpf saw nothing, and thought only of landing. They were now over Guyancourt, which had been the site of his basic flight training earlier that year. The airbase now presented a scene of total destruction. Right beside it was a crude landing ground. All of the Staffeln but the 7th landed there. The 7th Staffel flew past it, to an airfield near Rambouillet. Suddenly they banked, on radioed orders, and prepared to land. Stumpf saw nothing but a ploughed field crossed by power lines. There proved to be a gap in the lines; the fighters landed through the gap. Within a few minutes all of the planes had landed and had been pushed into the woods and covered in brush. The field had not yet been discovered by the Allied fighters. The pilots reported the status of their aircraft to Lt. Vogt, retrieved their gear, and then boarded a wood-powered bus to go to their quarters, which proved to be in a castle.

JG 26 Victory Claims: 7 - 13 August 1944

Date	Rank	Name	Unit	Cl #	Aircraft	Place	Time	Opponent	Conf
07-08-44	Lt.	Kiefner	1 CO	9	P-47	E of Melun (BG4-5)	1925	373 FG	yes
07-08-44	Uffz.	Thran	10	1	P-47	Mortain-SW of Flers (BT)	1510	368 FG	i.O.
08-08-44	Uffz.	Schwan	1	1	P-51	Versailles (AD7-8)	1430	359 FG	yes
08-08-44	Uffz.	Horch	4	1	P-51	Breteuil (AB7-8)	1425	359 FG	yes
13-08-44	Lt.	Günther	3	4	P-51	Alençon (CB2-3)	0811	363 FG	yes

JG 26 Casualties: 13 August 1944

Date	Rank	Name	Cas	Unit	Aircraft	WNr	Mkgs	Place	Time	Cause	Allied Unit
13-08-44	Uffz.	Schäfer, Wilhelm	KIA	3	Fw 190A-8	680837	yl 3	50km W of Boulogne		P-51	363 FG
13-08-44	Uffz.	Burmeister, Erich	MIA	4	Fw 190A-8	680844	bl 10	NE of Le Mans	0825	P-51	363 FG
13-08-44	Fw.	Hager, Robert	KIA	4	Fw 190A-8	172674	<<gr 3	NE of Le Mans	0825	P-51	363 FG
13-08-44	Uffz.	Kukla, Hans	WIA	4	Fw 190A-7	340329	bl 9	NE of Le Mans	0825	P-51	363 FG
13-08-44	Lt.	Marx, Wolfgang	KIA	4	Fw 190A-8	173023	bl 14	NE of Le Mans	0825	P-51	363 FG
13-08-44	Uffz.	Richter, Adolf	KIFA	8	Fw 190A-8	171530	bl 14	M-Gladbach a/f		takeoff	non-op

14 August

Jagdkorps II added a new top-priority mission to its list, defense against air landings and paratroops, which must have given the hard-pressed fighter unit leaders a chuckle. Two concentrated rocket mortar and strafing missions were ordered, but only eighty-seven sorties were flown all day. The time of the first mission was moved up to dawn; even then the fighters were unable to assemble owing to the presence of Allied aircraft. The eight First Gruppe pilots flew their Werfereinsatz without escort, and achieved success; both Lt. Kiefner and Lt. Ellenrieder reported making rocket attacks on trucks and tanks near Le Mans. A second mission was attempted in mid-afternoon, in weaker strength. Only four First Gruppe aircraft took part; its results are unknown. A 3rd

Staffel pilot, Obfw. Ernst Rudolph was injured while crash-landing his airplane after its engine failed.

The rest of Hptm. Lang's aircraft arrived at Guyancourt and Rambouillet. He was under orders from General Buelowius to have his unit operational by the 15th. Hptm. Matoni left the Gruppe to take command of I/JG 11. Lt. Vogt left the 7th Staffel to take command of Matoni's former Staffel, the 5th, and Lt. Prager took over the 7th Staffel as Führer.

15 August

Jagdkorps II called on its experienced units to strafe and mortar American vehicles between Le Mans and Alençon. Eleven First Gruppe rocket-carriers flew the dawn mission, escorted by twenty-one Third Gruppe Messerschmitts. Elements of six other Jagdgruppen took part. The formation had assembled and headed for the battlefield by 0730, but was broken up by the attack of a single squadron of RAF Mustangs, No. 19, which reported bouncing a formation of 80-100 Bf 109s and Fw 190s while on an armed recon mission to Dreux, and claimed 1-0-1 Bf 109s and 0-0-3 Fw 190s, without loss. The damaged Bf 109 was piloted by Fw. Polster, who returned safely to Biévres. The Focke-Wulf was piloted by Lt. Hans Hartigs, who reached the Paris area before having to bail out with minor injuries. The First Gruppe pilots jettisoned their rockets, and all surviving pilots returned to base. Lt. Gottfried Dietze had returned from his temporary duty with III/JG 54, and took part in this mission. He was now in the 4th Staffel, helping to rebuild it after its losses on the 13th.

Emil Lang's Second Gruppe was, by definition, operational, but Jagdkorps II gave him some more breathing space with an order that all new pilots be "especially instructed" about alternative airfields in the Paris area. Lang therefore ordered his Gruppe up at 1130 for a familiarization flight. There were more pilots than serviceable aircraft, and about thirty-four were chosen to fly the mission. Eight 7th Staffel Focke-Wulfs took off from the Rambouillet satellite field and flew to Guyancourt to meet the rest of the Gruppe. The Rambouillet takeoff strip was a field of dry stubble, and the aircraft left a huge dust cloud behind them that hung in the air for at least ten minutes; the field would not be kept hidden from the Allies for long. Walter Stumpf and the other pilots not picked to fly watched from the ground as the Focke-Wulfs disappeared. The men were still standing around smoking an hour later when eight strafing Thunderbolts roared across the field. Just as the American fighters came off their strafing run, the 7th Staffel returned with the rest of the Second Gruppe formation, and Walter Stumpf witnessed his first air combat. The howling and screaming seemed to go on forever, but lasted for perhaps five minutes before the two sides disengaged. Five smoke pillars could be seen surrounding the field. Two came from the wreckage of the aircraft of Oblt. Walter Wedekind and Fw. Kurt Müller; both pilots were killed.

The first successful combat of the Second Gruppe since its return to France resulted in considerable overclaiming. Eight Thunderbolts were claimed. Seven of these were confirmed. One claim was also filed by a First Group pilot; it was not confirmed. Only three P-47s were in fact lost.

Ten First Gruppe Focke-Wulfs and sixteen Third Gruppe Messerschmitts had also taken off at 1130, to attempt the aborted dawn mission again. They apparently reached the front and carried out their ground attacks, and were nearing their bases when the high cover of Messerschmitts was attacked, first by No. 19 Sqd. Mustangs, which had returned to their Dreux hunting grounds, and next by a squadron of P-47s. The First Gruppe Focke-Wulfs reached Rambouillet while the battle with the Second Gruppe was still going on, and joined in; Lt. Fred Heckmann claimed a Mustang, and Uffz. Gerhard Corinth claimed a Thunderbolt. The P-47 squadrons were from the 373rd Fighter Group, whose 411th Squadron claimed four Focke-Wulfs, and lost three P-47s; the 412th Squadron claimed four Messerschmitts, for no losses. One Messerschmitt was piloted by the luckless Heinz Gehrke, who survived a turning battle with a

Uffz. Ritter, Uffz. Gehrke's "erster Wart" (crew chief), and his assistant tend to "Pikus the Tomcat". Personal markings were strongly discouraged in the Third Gruppe, but several pilots had them. According to Heinz Gehrke, "We were following the policy of 'Why the hell not?'" – Villacoublay, summer 1944. *(Gehrke)*

Mustang but was then boxed in and shot down by P-47s. This time he bailed out cleanly, but had the misfortune to land on a railroad embankment. He rolled down the slope and was knocked numb when his head hit a railroad tie, stopping his descent. He was rescued by a squad of engineers who were destroying the tracks. The squad was supposedly the last unit in front of the onrushing American army, which was already in Dreux. Gehrke went with the engineers to Paris, and was grounded for a few days with a bad headache and a stiff neck.

Two aircraft of the Geschwader Stabsschwarm took off in late afternoon, apparently ran out of fuel before reaching Guyancourt, and force-landed on a road east of Rouen. One made a wheels-down landing, and was refueled and flew off the next day. The other made a belly-landing, and was abandoned on the 19th after its critical equipment had been removed. This airplane was Obstlt. Priller's "Jutta", his personal Fw 190A-8 in which he had scored his 100th victory, and undoubtedly the one he had flown on D-Day. The wreckage was examined closely by a French teenager, P. Condadzian, an aviation enthusiast who noted its markings in his diary. Incredibly, the diary has survived, and his notes were used when researching the jacket painting for this book.

Two combined missions were ordered for the evening, but they were flown in very low strength and achieved nothing. There was too much else going on. Jagdkorps II ordered six of its depleted Jagdgruppen, including III/JG 54, to leave for Germany to refit. In late afternoon those elements of JG 26 not necessary for combat flying were ordered to leave at once for new bases at Mons-en-Chausée and Rosières. The pilots helped the support personnel pack up, and went to bed at midnight, the sound of enemy tank engines in their ears. The Third Gruppe mechanics were under especially heavy pressure; of their forty-one aircraft, only ten were operational when the evening report was filed. Of the forty-four pilots on the Gruppe roster, only twenty-four were considered available for duty.

JG 26 Victory Claims: 15 August 1944

Date	Rank	Name	Unit	Cl #	Aircraft	Place	Time	Opponent	Conf
15-08-44	Lt.	Heckmann	3 CO	63	Mustang	SE of Dreux (BC3)	1228	19 Sqd	yes
15-08-44	Uffz.	Corinth	4	1	P-47	Versailles (AD8)	1234	373 FG	unk
15-08-44	Hptm.	Lang	II CO	163	P-47	Rambouillet (AD-BD)	1231	373 FG	yes
15-08-44	Hptm.	Lang	II CO	164	P-47	Rambouillet (AD-BD)	1232	373 FG	yes
15-08-44	Lt.	Vogt	5 CO	32	P-47	Versailles (BD-AD)	1229	373 FG	yes
15-08-44	Lt.	Stein	5	1	P-47	Rambouillet (BD-6)	1230	373 FG	yes
15-08-44	Oblt.	Eder	6	50	P-47	Rambouillet (BD)	1238	373 FG	yes
15-08-44	Oblt.	Eder	6	51	P-47	Rambouillet (BD)	1240	373 FG	yes
15-08-44	Lt.	Prager	7 CO	7	P-47	Rambouillet (BD3-6)	1235	373 FG	unk
15-08-44	Lt.	Hofmann W.	8 CO	27	P-47	Versailles (AC-AD)	1234	373 FG	yes

16 August

Jagdkorps II ordered its remaining fighters to fly two concentrated anti-Jabo missions to the neck of the Falaise-Argentan pocket, through which the German 1st and 7th Armies were pushing to escape while under constant air attack. No German fighter reached the intended operational area. Luftflotte 3 ordered Guyancourt, Villacoublay, Buc and Toussus evacuated and destroyed, and the Geschwader joined the mass exodus from Paris toward the east. Walter Stumpf recalls that the 7th Staffel pilots at Rambouillet were awakened at 0300, taken back to the field, and told to fly all operational aircraft to Guyancourt. The mechanics were working frantically to make as many fighters airworthy as possible. Most pilots took off by flights and elements. Stumpf had to take off alone in foul weather, but found nearby Guyancourt despite his inexperience and made an adequate landing. The airplane he had flown was an oil leaker, and could not be made ready for the longer flight to Mons-en-Chausée that afternoon.

At Guyancourt, Ottomar Kruse's fighter was operational, and he waited eagerly in the ready room. Lt. Hofmann had not chosen him for a mission up to now, but this time there was no choice, and Hofmann assigned Kruse to the No. 4 position in his own Schwarm. The transfer flight to Mons-en-Chausée was to be made as an operational flight, a freie Jagd. After takeoff the Focke-Wulfs climbed to 3500 meters (11,000 feet) and turned to the predetermined course. There was a shouted warning, and Kruse turned to see a flight of Mustangs banking in on his Schwarm from the rear, with him as the first in the line of fire. He never thought to use the radio, as the new pilots had been told to keep their mouths shut. When Kruse could see the leader's gun barrels, he pulled up sharply in a half-loop, passing inverted over the P-51. He had lost speed, and fell in behind the No. 4 Mustang. Another flight was now behind Kruse; this time he dived steeply until the Mustangs had passed, and then zoomed up. A fighter passed across his nose from left to right, at about 300 meters (325 yards) range. Kruse turned right immediately, aimed, fired until he was very close, and then passed above it to the right. The P-51 burst into flames, dived away, and crashed. Kruse then looked around and could see no-one.

Kruse turned to the prearranged course and reached Mons-en-Chausée as the last arrival. He buzzed the field at ground level, rocking his wings as he had seen in the newsreels. At the far end he banked sharply around, and repeated the scene from the other side before landing. After shutting down his machine, he reported to Hofmann, who gave him a dark look. Kruse excitedly told his story, and Hofmann replied calmly that he had seen the crash and would confirm the victory. At supper that night Hptm. Lang cut through Kruse's leather flight jacket with a table knife to attach his Iron Cross Second Class; the jacket now hangs in a north-German museum.

Only eight Mustangs took part in this battle. Their pilots, from the 354th Fighter Group, did not hesitate to attack the "approximately seventy" Fw 190s that they encountered over Rambouillet forest. Two P-51s were shot down. One was the victim of Ottomar Kruse; the other, of Oblt. Konrad Bertels. One Focke-Wulf pilot, Oblt. Horst Siemsen, bailed out, suffering burns.

The Stabsschwarm and the First Gruppe returned to Boissy-le-Bois, east of the Seine. The Third Gruppe headed farther east, to Rosières on the Somme. One 9th Staffel Unteroffizier dropped far behind his formation, which contained ten Bf 109s from the 9th and 11th Staffeln. He then turned his airplane around and headed west. When well past the Allied lines, he half-rolled and bailed out. An anti-Nazi, he had been seeking this opportunity since D-Day, and provided British Air Intelligence with much accurate information about Major Mietusch's Gruppe. Uffz. Heinz Gehrke, who was off operations because of his neck injury, made the trip to Rosières at night, in a former French armored car. He recalled that a number of Bf 109s had to be blown up on the ground at Villacoublay, as there were not enough pilots to fly them.

JG 26 Casualties: 14 - 16 August 1944

Date	Rank	Name	Cas	Unit	Aircraft	WNr	Mkgs	Place	Time	Cause	Allied Unit
14-08-44	Obfw.	Rudolph, Ernst	WIFA	3	Fw 190A-7	643714	yl 11	W of Houdan		engine	n/a
15-08-44	Oblt.	Hartigs, Hans	WIA	4	Fw 190A-8	170710	bl 6	W of "Field 111"- Paris region		Mustang	19 Sqd
15-08-44	Oblt.	Wedekind, Walter	KIA	II St	Fw 190A-8	171786	gr 2	E of Guyancourt	1230	P-47	373 FG
15-08-44	Fw.	Müller, Kurt	KIA	5	Fw 190A-8	731746	wh 5	Rambouillet		P-47	373 FG
15-08-44	Uffz.	Gehrke, Heinz	WIA	11	Bf 109G-6	410688	yl 11	E of Dreux	1230	P-47	373 FG
16-08-44	Oblt.	Siemsen, Horst	WIA	II St	Fw 190A-8	732725	gr 4	Rambouillet	1940	P-51	354 FG
16-08-44	Uffz.	Speichert, Hans	POW	9	Bf 109G-6	440278	wh 20	NW of La Haye du Puits	1720	captured	none

17 August

The Jagdkorps II orders called its relocated fighter units to readiness at 0430, with operations by Geschwader or combined formations to commence as early as possible. Two types of mission were envisaged: anti-Jabo operations in the Falaise-Argentan corridor, and strafing and mortar attacks on the American spearheads nearing Paris. Most Luftwaffe operations today were in small formations. A First Gruppe force took off from Boissy-le-Bois at 0840 and flew a freie Jagd *en route* to Poix, a new base farther to the east. Contact with Mustangs was reported. Another detachment of First Gruppe aircraft took off from Beauvais at 1115 and attacked American assemblies southwest of Paris near Rambouillet. Lt. Kiefner shot down an observation plane, and was then shot down himself by ground fire. He bailed out and landed without injury, made an eight-hour hike into Paris, and caught a ride on an east-bound truck just before the Allies entered the city.

The Second Gruppe component at Mons-en-Chausée took off at 1100, joined some Gruppe fighters that had been made operational at Guyancourt, and flew west to strafe the American tank formations between Chartres and Dreux. Near Rambouillet, Hptm. Eder had a remarkable success. He shot down a Spitfire from very low altitude; it crashed between two M-4 Sherman tanks, destroying them both. Less than a minute later he shot down a second Spitfire, which crashed on a third tank, setting it on fire. Eder filed an *Abschussmeldung* (shoot-down report) for the Spitfires, and a *Panzervernichtungsmeldung* (tank destruction report) for the Shermans, and received confirmations for all. Unfortunately, this episode cannot be confirmed from the Allied side; no record can be found of any Allied fighter of any type being shot down under these circumstances. The two witnesses from Eder's Staffel were both killed in combat on the following day.

Eder was the only successful pilot on this mission, which cost the Gruppe three pilots. Uffz. Bruno Grolms, Lt. Hans Rösen, and Fw. Karl-Heinz Zeschke were all killed by ground fire. The surviving pilots landed on Beauvais or Mons-en-Chausée after the mission. Fhr. Dietrich Schlösser crashed while taking off on a transfer flight, and was killed. Part of the Gruppe took off in mid-afternoon and joined some Third Gruppe Messerschmitts in a hunt for Spitfires reported near Fécamp. Lt. Hofmann sighted them first, and led his Schwarm in a bounce of a dozen No. 1 Squadron aircraft that were on a sweep from England. Hofmann, Uffz. Borreck, and Uffz. Klein were credited with victories; two Spitfires went down. The Focke-Wulfs escaped without damage. The last Second Gruppe fighters on Guyancourt took off later in the afternoon and joined the Gruppe at Mons-en-Chausée.

The Third Gruppe flew freie Jagden while transferring their fighters farther east. By nightfall most of the Gruppe was located at Roye or Warvillers.

The commitment by Jagdkorps II to support the army in its effort to escape the Falaise-Argentan pocket went for the most part unfulfilled. Nearly all of its fighter units were engaged by Allied fighters much farther to the east. Only one Gruppe made a successful attack on Allied fighter-bombers over the Falaise killing zone. It took place today; III/JG 27 bounced a section of No. 183 Sqd. Typhoons, and downed four of them.

JG 26 Victory Claims: 16 - 17 August 1944

Date	Rank	Name	Unit	Cl #	Aircraft	Place	Time	Opponent	Conf
16-08-44	Oblt.	Bertels	II	1	P-51	Rambouillet (AD)	1532	354 FG	yes
16-08-44	Uffz.	Kruse	8	1	P-51	Rambouillet (AD)	1435	354 FG	yes
17-08-44	Lt.	Kiefner	1 CO	10	Auster	Rambouillet (BD4)	1150		yes
17-08-44	Uffz.	Borreck	5	1	Spitfire	NW of Rouen (SB4)	1623	1 Sqd	yes
17-08-44	Oblt.	Eder	6	52	Spitfire	Rambouillet (BC6-BD4)	1153		yes
17-08-44	Oblt.	Eder	6	53	Spitfire	Rambouillet (BC6-BD4)	1153		yes
17-08-44	Lt.	Hofmann W.	8 CO	28	Spitfire	NW of Rouen (SB-SC)	1622	1 Sqd	yes
17-08-44	Uffz.	Klein E.	8	1	Spitfire	NW of Rouen (SB)	1623	1 Sqd	yes

JG 26 Casualties: 17 August 1944

Date	Rank	Name	Cas	Unit	Aircraft	WNr	Mkgs	Place	Time	Cause	Allied Unit
17-08-44	Lt.	Kiefner, Georg	no	1 CO	Fw 190A-8	<		NE of Chartres (BD)	1155	light flak	n/a
17-08-44	Fhr.	Schlösser, Dietrich	KIFA 5		Fw 190A-8	680157	wh 12	Manancourt		takeoff	n/a
17-08-44	Uffz.	Grolms, Bruno	KIA 6		Fw 190A-8	171638	bk 8	Dreux		light flak	n/a
17-08-44	Lt.	Rösen, Hans	KIA 6		Fw 190A-8	170976	bk 1	near Chartres-Dreux		light flak	n/a
17-08-44	Fw.	Zeschke, Karl-Heinz	KIA 7		Fw 190A-8	731740	br 9	Caen		light flak	n/a

18 August

Jagdkorps II ordered its fighters to make concentrated anti-Jabo raids to the Falaise pocket, while screening the Dreux-Chartres area on their inbound flights. The First Gruppe and several others were rested to restore their serviceability. Only the Second and Third Gruppen and I/JG 2 were able to get away from their fields for the morning mission owing to the fog. While still taking off from Beauvais and forming up, the Second Gruppe Focke-Wulfs were bounced by the twelve Mustangs of No. 315 Sqd. (Polish), which were sweeping the area. The Nachwuchs were slaughtered: Lt. Hans-Joachim Brede, Obfw. Erwin Franke, Ogfr. Willi Hanitz, Fw. Walter Hasenclever, Uffz. Helmut Holzinger, Fhj.-Fw. Wolfgang Röhler, Uffz. Anton Schrettinger, and Uffz. Josef Smischek were all killed in their aircraft; none were able to bail out. Fw. Werner Verhöven shot down an unidentified P-38 as he lifted off the runway, and fired at a Mustang before his Focke-Wulf was itself hit. Verhöven crash-landed in a field beside the runway with minor injuries.

Uffz. Alfred Wagner and Uffz. Ottomar Kruse were detailed to be the covering element for the 8th Staffel, and were the last fighters to take off. The air battle could be seen above them to their left. The two Fw 190s made a shallow bank to the left, at full throttle and maximum rate of climb. Three Mustangs tore past them. The pair turned in their direction, and had almost reached firing position when Wagner disappeared beneath Kruse's left wing. Suddenly vulnerable, Kruse pulled up and tipped over his left wing. Rosettes then appeared on the upper surface of his wing; he was being fired at from beneath. He flipped his airplane around again and dived for the ground. When he leveled out at low altitude, he had no idea of what was behind him, so he headed for the airfield and shot past the control tower, about 300 meters (325 yards) from its 20 mm flak emplacement. Seeing its tracers fall behind him, Kruse felt that he was now alone. He cleared a small hill, and found himself in a fog bank. When he emerged, he followed a rail line until he came to a town with a large racetrack. Totally lost, he decided to land on the racetrack. After landing and switching off his engine, he learned from a Labor Service officer bicycling past that he was at Arras.

The Poles claimed sixteen victories, three on behalf of S/L E. Horbaczewski, the leading Polish ace, who failed to return. I/JG 2 was involved in this battle, and lost two Focke-Wulfs. The Second Gruppe lost eight pilots killed, and two wounded. Uffz. Wagner, Kruse's element leader, was hit in the legs, bailed out, and was taken to the hospital at Beauvais, where one of his legs had to be amputated. Their mission disrupted, the surviving pilots landed as soon as the Polish Mustangs had departed. The Gruppe claimed five Mustangs and one P-38, but three of the claims were rejected by the RLM. The only Allied casualty was S/L Horbaczewski.

The 6th Staffel scrambled a small number of fighters at noon to oppose some Thunderbolts, and Lt. Edmund Fischer claimed one of them. Despite the early-morning losses, the Second Gruppe put up another full-strength mission shortly after noon. This time they were able to rendezvous with Major Mietusch and his Third Gruppe before encountering a large formation of Allied fighters, and the results favored the Schlageter pilots. Three P-47s were claimed by the Second Gruppe. One was confirmed, and this 356th Fighter Group aircraft was, in fact lost.

Closer to Dreux, Mietusch led his Messerschmitts in a bounce of a section of 358th Fighter Group P-47s, and downed two, while losing Uffz. Heinrich Hering. Late that evening, Oblt. Jan Schild led eight Bf 109Gs of his 10th Staffel up from Warvillers, which was an improvised landing ground on the edge of a small woods, and headed for the action around Beauvais. They caught a squadron of the 4th Fighter Group strafing ground targets, and shot down three of its P-51s without loss. Schild shot down one, for his 10th victory, and damaged another, which flew off westward at very low altitude, trailing a long black smoke plume. The identities of three of the day's successful Third Gruppe pilots are unknown. Again today, no Geschwader fighter got any farther west than Dreux.

In the meantime, Uffz. Kruse struggled to get back from Arras. Ottomar Kruse recalls:

"The Labor Service guarded the plane while I went to the nearest phone. I gave my exact position and extent of damage to the technical officer, and then could only wait. I had breakfast and went to see the town, famous as a First World War battlefield. A truck from the maintenance platoon arrived that afternoon with two mechanics... The next morning I was awakened while it was still dark... We arrived at the racetrack just as dawn was breaking. The second mechanic, who had remained with the aircraft, said, 'The engine is still warm. Ready for takeoff.' I examined my takeoff run carefully, then clambered into the cockpit. The mechanic helped me fasten my parachute and harness. We started the engine and let it run for a while. Everything seemed OK. I taxied all the way down the racetrack, to the edge of the ploughed field on the other side. I closed the canopy, applied the brakes, and advanced the throttle slowly. I gave it more and more gas, until it began bouncing on its tires. I released the brakes, rolled for a short distance, and gave it full throttle. The Fw 190 did not lift off cleanly, but dragged its tail. The ploughed field came nearer and nearer. The wheels brushed the freshly-turned sod as the plane broke free. I raised the gear and flaps, circled around, and made a short pass at the field, rocking my wings as a brief farewell.

"I followed the short road to Mons at low altitude. It was now full daylight. Visibility was good. I landed on the base, and upon reporting in, learned that Wagner had lost a leg, and was out of the war. I myself had escaped this time with a whole skin."

JG 26 Victory Claims: 18 August 1944

Date	Rank	Name	Unit	Cl #	Aircraft	Place	Time	Opponent	Conf
18-08-44	Uffz.	Borreck	5	2	Mustang	Beauvais (TE1)	0823	315 Sqd	unk
18-08-44	Uffz.	Borreck	5	3	P-47	Beauvais (TE6)	1330	356 FG	unk
18-08-44	Obfw.	Mayer	5	16	Mustang	Beauvais (TE1)	0825	315 Sqd	yes
18-08-44	Obfw.	Mayer	5	17	P-47	Beauvais (TE6)	1329		yes
18-08-44	Lt.	Fischer E.	6	1	P-47	Beauvais (TE)	1240	356 FG	unk
18-08-44	Fw.	Verhöven	6	1	P-38	Beauvais (TD-TE)	0822		yes
18-08-44	Fw.	Verhöven	6	2	Mustang	Beauvais (TD-TE)	0824	315 Sqd	unk
18-08-44	Ofhr.	Scharf	7	1	P-47	Beauvais (TE4-5)	1335	356 FG	unk
18-08-44	Lt.	Hofmann W.	8 CO	29	Mustang	Beauvais (TD1-2)	0822	315 Sqd	yes
18-08-44	Uffz.	Klein E.	8	2	Mustang	Beauvais (TE1)	0823	315 Sqd	unk
18-08-44	Major	Mietusch	III CO	72	P-47	NW of Paris (UD 7-8)	1406	358 FG	yes
18-08-44	Oblt.	Schild	10	5	P-51	SE of Orleans (FE1-9)	1933	4 FG	i.O.

JG 26 Casualties: 18 August 1944

Date	Rank	Name	Cas	Unit	Aircraft	WNr	Mkgs	Place	Time	Cause	Allied Unit
18-08-44	Obfw.	Franke, Erwin	KIA	5	Fw 190A-8	731757	wh 11	Beauvais-Tillé	0830	Mustang	315 Sqd
18-08-44	Ogfr.	Hanitz, Willi	KIA	6	Fw 190A-8	172748	bk 3	E of Amiens	0830	Mustang	315 Sqd
18-08-44	Fhj-Fw.	Röhler, Wolfgang	KIA	6	Fw 190A-8	174104	bk 12	Beauvais-Tillé		Mustang	315 Sqd
18-08-44	Uffz.	Smischek, Josef	KIA	6	Fw 190A-8	170980	bk 10	Beauvais-Tillé		Mustang	315 Sqd
18-08-44	Fw.	Verhöven, Werner	WIA	6	Fw 190A-8	731096	bk 17	Beauvais-Tillé	0830	Mustang	315 Sqd
18-08-44	Lt.	Brede, Hans-Joachim	KIA	7	Fw 190A-8	172993	br 10	Beauvais-Tillé		Mustang	315 Sqd
18-08-44	Fw.	Hasenclever, Walter	KIA	7	Fw 190A-8	174114	br 3	Beauvais-Tillé		Mustang	315 Sqd
18-08-44	Uffz.	Schrettinger, Anton	KIA	7	Fw 190A-8			Beauvais-Tillé		Mustang	315 Sqd
18-08-44	Uffz.	Holzinger, Helmut	KIA	8	Fw 190A-8	731995	bl 2	Chartres		Mustang	315 Sqd
18-08-44	Uffz.	Wagner, Alfred	WIA	8	Fw 190A-8	170986	bl 3	Beauvais-Tillé		Mustang	315 Sqd
18-08-44	Uffz.	Hering, Heinrich	KIA	12	Bf 109G-6/U4	440991	yl 8	Falaise-Argentan	1345	P-47	358 FG

19 August

The American Third Army linked up with the Canadians and Poles near Falaise and closed the pocket on the remnants of the German 7th Army. Jagdkorps II ordered its fighters to fly anti-Jabo missions to the pocket, screening the Chartres-Dreux area on the return flights. Their rendezvous point was moved eastward, to Beauvais. Flakkorps III complained to Luftflotte 3 that Allied air superiority had doubled or even trebled over the past few days, and that Allied Jabos flying at very low levels were preventing movement of cyclists and even individual foot soldiers by day. The German fighters were powerless to intervene, never getting any farther west today than Rouen.

The Geschwader attempted to fly offensive sorties while continuing the transfer of its bases to the east of Paris. At 0900, aircraft from all three Gruppen undertook a combined mission with six other Gruppen. Near Dreux Hptm. Lang led his fighters in a bounce of P-47s from the 406th Fighter Group's 513th Squadron, which were shooting up barges in the Seine River. Lt. Vogt shot down and killed the American squadron leader. Lt. Bob O'Neill shot down Fhj.-Uffz. Otto Horch of the 4th Staffel near Bernay, but Hptm. Lang immediately stitched O'Neill's Thunderbolt with 20 mm fire from the left wing into the cockpit. O'Neill bailed out and was taken prisoner.

Horch bailed out successfully, but while descending was shot and killed by SS troops who mistook him for an Allied pilot. The SS ordered French civilians to bury him in an unmarked grave in an apple orchard. The thirty Bf 109s and Fw 190s remaining in the formation proceeded west, but scattered under the attack of a single squadron of RAF Mustangs, No. 19.

The three Gruppen took part in combined missions at noon and late in the afternoon, but reported no successes. Uffz. Karl Hött of the 6th Staffel participated in the late mission while transferring his fighter from Hancourt to Cambrai-Epinoy. Hött was attacked by three Mustangs; one hit his Focke-Wulf twenty times and set his parachute on fire. Unable to bail out, Hött evaded the fighters and landed on Epinoy with severe burns.

20 August

Jagdkorps II was under pressure to get its fighters to Falaise, despite pouring rain, but was also struggling to fit its new units into the order of battle. Thanks to the efforts of Hptm. Lang, the Second Gruppe was the only rebuilt unit that had returned from Germany at anything like its full authorized strength, and was forced to carry much of the load. The first mission did not get underway until mid-afternoon. All three Gruppen assembled with II/JG 1 near Amiens, and the combined force strafed the Allied spearheads near Rouen. Two Third Gruppe Messerschmitts were shot down by ground fire; Fw. Hans-Joachim Leder was killed, while Uffz. Willibald Malm was able to reach the German lines before bailing out with slight wounds. Hofmann led the Second Gruppe south in a search for enemy air activity, and met another Focke-Wulf Gruppe, I/JG 11, which an old Second Gruppe comrade, Hptm. Walter Matoni, had just led back from Germany after rebuilding. In a conversation monitored by the Allies, Matoni ordered his green Gruppe to fly high cover while he himself flew with Lt. Hofmann.

Hofmann and Matoni were southwest of Paris at 3000 meters [10,000 feet] when they spotted some P-47s tangling with Bf 109s below them and led a bounce. The P-47s consisted of two flights from the 362nd Fighter Group's 378th Squadron; the Bf 109s belonged to II/JG 3 and III/JG 3, which had been on a mission to Falaise, but broke it off to attack the small Thunderbolt formation. Lt. Joe Matte was leading the cover flight, and his diving attack on two III/JG 3 Bf 109s that were closing in on his squadron leader caused them to collide. One Messerschmitt pilot crashed in his airplane, but the other pilot, the formation leader, was able to ride his plane down to a belly-landing. Matte still had a height advantage, and put it to good use by forcing two more Messerschmitts to break into his attacks. One tried to loop, wound up in front of his guns, and blew up, spraying his canopy with blood. Matte was able to close the range on his fourth target after three tight turns; a short burst of fire persuaded the German pilot to bail out. Joe Matte recalls the next few moments:

> "I was climbing back for 'cover'... As I reached 5,000 feet [1500 meters] a 109 overshot me without firing. So I started after him in a slight dive. It was at this time that I spied 20+ Fw 190s coming down from approximately 10,000 feet [3000 meters]. I told my wingman to wait until I gave the signal to 'break'. He was to dive hard left, I would go hard right, and we would meet up at ground level. I continued chasing the 109 and was almost ready to fire when I looked around for my No. 2, and he wasn't in sight. I looked too long, and allowed the 190s to catch me. When I hit 1000 feet, two 190s were firing, one from the left and one from the right. The one on the right hit me in the accessory section; the one on the left hit me in the left wing and tail. They both went under me at the same time, and I can't see how they got past me. The third ship that fired on me shot above, but hit the prop, and came above me, breaking to the left and up. I turned to the right and down, and as I made a 180 degree turn I saw two large explosions on the ground, but I can't claim these to be the two 190s, because I didn't have time to look. I hit for the deck and home, and managed to get away from the Fw 190s."

The two explosions were the crashing P-47s of Matte's wingman, who was killed, and a second pilot who survived and returned to his unit with injuries. Hofmann and Matoni each claimed Thunderbolts in this combat, and their Gruppen suffered no losses. The two JG 3 Gruppen lost a total of six Bf 109s. The 378th Squadron pilots claimed exactly six, four of them by Joe Matte. The Messerschmitt pilots claimed six Thunderbolts, but accounted for no more than one. Hofmann and Matoni, who were leading their formation in its dive, must have been the pilots who attacked the highest P-47s, which were piloted by Matte and his wingman. The wingman, who was on only his third mission, panicked and broke away too soon, obviously not sharply enough, and was shot down by one of the two Focke-Wulfs, which continued diving and then took Matte under attack. Joe Matte has always been puzzled that he was attacked by both Fw 190s at once – this was definitely not standard element leader-and-wingman tactics. But when a Gruppenkommandeur meets a Staffelkapitän in the air and indicates that he wants to join his formation, who flies wing? In this case, neither pilot did.

Joe Matte had done well in his first encounter with the enemy. It was past time for it, in his opinion; he had flown escort missions for 8th Air Force B-24s all spring and had never had an enemy airplane approach his formation. Matte's aggressive attitude and his affection, approaching love, for his airplane were common among 9th Air Force Thunderbolt pilots, who often flew complete tours without encountering a German airplane, but were eager to take advantage of any opportunity for air combat. He recalls that combat tactics were a frequent topic of conversation among his squadron mates. The common opinion was that the Messerschmitt outfits had better aircraft and better pilots than those flying Focke-Wulfs. From the perspective of the P-47 pilot, the flight characteristics of Bf 109s (always called Me 109s) and Fw 190s were similar, but the Fw 190 had a fatal inability to make sharp right turns. The objective of a P-47 pilot dogfighting with a Fw 190 was thus to make the German fighter turn right – a tactic that Matte used with success in his next encounter with Focke-Wulfs, which did not come until November. The P-47 could out-run the Bf 109 and Fw 190 in level flight, and with its paddle-blade propeller could out-turn them in high-speed climbing turns. The P-47D-25, the first model with a bubble canopy, incorporated a two-inch rudder extension allowing it to turn tighter than the German fighters at low speed, as well; the P-47 could now turn around its tail while in a vertical climb, without stalling out. A P-51 was faster than a P-47 in level flight, but the P-47 could pull away in even a slight dive. Joe Matte summed up his feeling for his airplane by stating that if he had 5000 feet of altitude, the enemy couldn't touch him.

At 1900 five Jagdgruppen were ordered to take off on independent missions and screen the German Army's rearward movements across a broad front – from Beauvais to Orleans. The Third Gruppe encountered Spitfires near Lisieux. The Bf 109G-6 of Fhj. Robert Röhrig was hit, and he bailed out with injuries. He was probably shot down by No. 401 Sqd. (RCAF), although the Canadians claimed only two Fw 190s at this time. Lt. Hofmann led a half dozen of his Focke-Wulfs in a bounce of a section of 404th Fighter Group P-47s that were bombing the Seine barges. Hofmann and Lt. Prager each claimed a Thunderbolt; one went down.

The Third Gruppe ground staff was traveling through Paris in a road convoy when one truck was attacked by partisans. The Gruppe adjutant, Hptm. Adolf Hempel, was killed, along with two others; three members of the staff were wounded.

JG 26 Casualties: 19 - 20 August 1944

Date	Rank	Name	Cas	Unit	Aircraft	WNr	Mkgs	Place	Time	Cause	Allied Unit
19-08-44	Fhj.-Uffz.	Horch, Otto	KIA	4	Fw 190A-8	680842	bl 8	Bernay		P-47	406 FG
19-08-44	Uffz.	Hött, Karl	WIA	6	Fw 190A-8	170978	br 2	NE of Amy		Mustang	
20-08-44	Hptm.	Hempel, Adolf	KIA	III St	none			Paris		Maquis	n/a
20-08-44	Fhj.	Röhrig, Robert	WIA	10	Bf 109G-6	441479	bk 10	near Rouen-SE of Lisieux	2025	Spitfire	401 Sqd
20-08-44	Fw.	Leder, Hans-Joachim	KIA	12	Bf 109G-6	165647	bl 14	near Rouen	1530	light flak	
20-08-44	Uffz.	Malm, Willibald	WIA	12	Bf 109G-6	165541	bl 5	near Rouen	1530	light flak	

Pilots of the 11th Staffel take a rest break during a ground movement in France during the summer of 1944. *(Gehrke)*

21 August
The 8th Air Force and the entire AEAF were grounded all day by the weather. Although Jagdkorps II ordered more missions to Falaise, none were carried out. The Jagdgruppen continued their transfer east in short hops, beneath the overcast. Obstlt. Priller's Geschwaderstab was first ordered to Haspres, south of Denain, and then to Valenciennes; the First Gruppe was ordered to fly either to Lambres, near Douai, or to Fresnes, west of Vitry. The Second Gruppe was assembling at Hancourt and one unidentified field; the Third Gruppe, at Rosières and Warvillers.

22 August
The First Gruppe and III/JG 2 spent the previous non-operational day strapping the Werfer barrels back onto the wings of their Focke-Wulfs. This morning they were ordered to mortar and strafe the Allied forces crossing the Seine bridges. Ten Jagdgruppen were assembled for the mission under Hptm. Lang. The undercast was too thick and too low; the formation quickly lost its way, and Lang was able to have the mission recalled. Four more combined missions were attempted during the day; all were in small strength owing to assembly problems in the low cloud, and had little success to report. Shortly after noon, Lt. Fred Heckmann of the 3rd Staffel claimed an Auster northwest of Paris. He was also scrambled during the day to oppose some Allied aircraft approaching Fresnes. One of the members of his flight, Uffz. Hans Sandoz of the 2nd Staffel, was shot down by the airfield Flak. Sandoz was able to bail out, but his parachute streamed, and he was killed.

JG 26 Victory Claims: 19 - 22 August 1944

Date	Rank	Name	Unit	Cl #	Aircraft	Place	Time	Opponent	Conf
19-08-44	Hptm.	Lang	II CO	165	P-47	E of Vernon (UD7)	1024	406 FG	yes
19-08-44	Lt.	Vogt	5 CO	33	P-47	NE of Paris (AF)	1024	406 FG	yes
20-08-44	Lt.	Prager	7 CO	8	P-47	W of Rouen (TB)	2005	404 FG	yes
20-08-44	Lt.	Hofmann W.	8 CO	30	P-47	NW of Paris (AE1)	1602	362 FG	yes

20-08-44	Lt.	Hofmann W.	8 CO	31	P-47	W of Rouen (TB)	2003	404 FG	yes
22-08-44	Lt.	Heckmann	3 CO	64	Auster	NW of Paris (UD8)	1235		yes

23 August

The experienced fighter units of Jagdkorps II were doing a fair job of keeping their operational strengths up during the retreat. The JG 26 Geschwaderstab reported 3 (1) Fw 190s and 4 (1) pilots on strength; the First Gruppe, 31 (15) Fw 190s and 42 (25) pilots; the Second Gruppe, 57 (27) Fw 190s and 53 (32) pilots; and the Third Gruppe, 30 (11) Bf 109s and 28 (22) pilots. The main task was the same as the previous day's: the Werfergruppen, led by the First Gruppe, were to strafe and rocket the Seine bridges and Allied concentrations west of the river. The escort Gruppen were to assemble and proceed independently to the target area, and while there would provide high-altitude area cover for the rocket units. The Second and Third Gruppen were up early on a defensive patrol east of the Seine, but had no known success.

The Werfergruppen were unable to get off the ground, probably owing to the weather, which as usual was bad, and the mission of the escort Gruppen was changed to a Jabojagd. Shortly after noon, eighteen Second Gruppe Fw 190s met five Third Gruppe Bf 109s and aircraft of four other Jagdgruppen over Montdidier, and flew west in search of Allied fighter-bombers. Northeast of Paris, the gaggle of over sixty German fighters was attacked by twenty-four Spitfires of No. 127 Wing, led by their wing commander, Johnnie Johnson. Johnson had taken his aircraft southeast of Paris, and had then swept northward in hopes of catching some Germans unawares. Johnson's bounce did achieve complete surprise, and his first burst of fire exploded an Fw 190's belly tank. The battle then split up into individual dogfights, in which the Spitfires were heavily outnumbered. Johnson downed another 190, but he was then caught up in a Lufbery with six Messerschmitts. For the first time in the war, Johnson's aircraft was hit, but he finally out-climbed his pursuers, of whom only the leader was a decent shot, and returned to his base at Crepon. He was the last man back, and found that his Wing had claimed twelve German fighters while losing three Spitfires. I/JG 11 claimed three Spitfires, and the Second Gruppe claimed the destruction of six in this battle, which cost neither the Second nor the Third Gruppe any casualties. Uffz. Gross also claimed a P-38, which cannot be identified.

The Geschwader suffered only one casualty during the day. Ogfr. Heinz Nieter of the 10th Staffel crashed while taking off for the afternoon mission, destroying his Messerschmitt and injuring himself.

After nightfall Hptm. Lang radioed Obstlt. Priller that his base had no stocks of aviation fuel at all. Ten aircraft had been made operational for the next day's missions, but only by draining all of the fuel from the unserviceable aircraft.

JG 26 Victory Claims: 23 August 1944

Date	Rank	Name	Unit	Cl #	Aircraft	Place	Time	Opponent	Conf
23-08-44	Hptm.	Lang	II CO	166	Spitfire	NE of Paris (UE-UF)	1338	421 or 443 Sqd	yes
23-08-44	Hptm.	Lang	II CO	167	Spitfire	N of Paris (UE)	1340	421 or 443 Sqd	yes
23-08-44	Uffz.	Hanusch	6	1	Spitfire	SW of Creil (UN)	1339	421 or 443 Sqd	yes
23-08-44	Fw.	Müller W. II	6	3	Spitfire	Évreux (UC)	1342	421 or 443 Sqd	yes
23-08-44	Lt.	Prager	7 CO	9	Spitfire	NE of Paris (UE-UF)	1340	421 or 443 Sqd	yes
23-08-44	Lt.	Hofmann W.	8 CO	32	Spitfire	NE of Paris (UF7-8/AF1-2)	1346	421 or 443 Sqd	yes
23-08-44	Uffz.	Gross H.	8	1	P-38	Chartres (RC)	1402		yes

24 August

The task of the German fighters today was to protect the Seine crossings. Bad weather and fuel constraints made this impossible. Only thirty sorties were flown by Jagdkorps II fighters during the entire day. Eight of these were by the First Gruppe, which took off at 0920 for a freie Jagd but was recalled owing to the low ceilings. Gefr. Helmut Jäger of the 2nd Staffel crashed on a test flight and was killed. Gefr. Willi Tebbe of the 5th Staffel was also killed while on a non-operational flight; whether this was a test flight or a transfer is not known. Jagdkorps II ordered the First and Second Gruppen to send trucks to a Luftwaffe fuel depot 100 km east of Cambrai and pick up forty tons of aviation fuel.

JG 26 Casualties: 22 - 24 August 1944

Date	Rank	Name	Cas	Unit	Aircraft	WNr	Mkgs	Place	Time	Cause	Allied Unit
22-08-44	Uffz.	Sandoz, Hans	KIA	2	Fw 190A-8	170912	bk 4	St Cyr-Athies		own flak	n/a
23-08-44	Ogfr.	Nieter, Heinz	WIFA	10	Bf 109G-6	163962	bl 9	Warvillers	1530	takeoff	n/a
24-08-44	Gefr.	Jäger, Helmut	KIFA	2	Fw 190A-8	172665	bk 10	Fresnes a/f		crashed	non-op
24-08-44	Gefr.	Tebbe, Willi	KIFA	5	Fw 190A-8	350168		Cornantes		takeoff	non-op

25 August

The commander of the German garrison surrendered the city of Paris to a Free French armored unit. After the morning fog lifted, the 9th Air Force took advantage of an afternoon of good weather to attempt to knock out the German fighter forces remaining in France. The staff of Jagdkorps II continued to order up the usual missions. Its fighters were grounded all morning, but shortly after 1300, sixty-one JG 26 fighters – twelve from the First Gruppe, thirty-two from the Second, and seventeen from the Third – took to the air, along with elements of at least four other Jagdgruppen. Their orders were to sweep along the fluid front lines and attack Allied fighter bombers and artillery spotters.

The Second Gruppe formation contained flights from all four of its Staffeln, and was led by Hauptmann Lang. They formed up over Mons-en-Chausée and headed west, climbing for their ordered altitude of 3500 meters (11,500 feet). Lt. Hofmann was the first to sight enemy aircraft, and briefly took over the lead, before Lang spotted P-38s, apparently engaged in ground attacks with no high cover. Lang led his entire Gruppe in the attack, which caught the Lightnings in ones and twos at low level. According to Ottomar Kruse, the air was so thick with swirling aircraft that it was hard to pick out a target. When he finally latched onto one, he was startled by tracers coming over his airplane. The firing was from two other Fw 190s, and Kruse made a large circle to let things calm down. Everyone had disappeared when he returned, but after joining a pair of Focke-Wulfs he spotted a pair of P-38s that were leaving the area and shot one down from a tight bank around a cloud, thus gaining a victory in the battle, and his second overall.

The American side of this combat is worth relating. Two dozen 474th Fighter Group P-38s had formed up over their field at 1250 hours, before heading east to attack airfields in the Laon area. Each carried two 500 pound (200 kg) bombs. The 429th Squadron was above and behind the 428th, at 12,000 feet (3700 meters). The Allied controller called the formation leader, and reported 40+ bandits southeast of Rouen. A few minutes later they were spotted and identified as Bf 109s. The two forces turned toward each other; the Bf 109s dropped their tanks and the P-38s jettisoned their bombs. The head-on pass completely dispersed the 429th Squadron, which split up into flights and elements. The 428th engaged the Messerschmitts, following many of them down to the deck. A small formation of Fw 190s also joined the battle at this time. A second, larger force of Fw 190s – the Second Gruppe – was then spotted diving on the 428th Squadron from above, but the P-38 pilots could do nothing but attempt to evade the attackers individually, or at most, in pairs. The leader radioed the recall. Capt. James Austin, a 428th flight leader, had lost his flight and was headed for his base with a wingman. Austin saw a lone Fw 190 and chased it around a large cumulus cloud to the left. His wingman headed right, and never saw Austin again. He did see a "crumpled-wing Fw 190" spinning down, on the basis of which Austin was given a victory credit. It is more likely that this was Austin's aircraft. Austin was trapped in and around the clouds by several Fw 190s and shot down. He bailed out with serious injuries, and was captured, but was found by American forces in an abandoned German hospital and returned to the United States. Based on a close reading of the American encounter and missing aircrew reports, James Austin was shot down by Ottomar Kruse.

After the Americans tallied their scores, the 429th Squadron was credited with 9-5-2 Bf 109s; the 428th, with 9-0-0 Bf 109s and 3-1-0 Fw 190s. 25 August would go down in the 428th Squadron's history as "Black Friday". Eight of the twelve 428th Squadron Lightnings were shot down, as were three from the 429th Squadron. In contrast, the pilots of the Second Gruppe returned to Mons-en-Chausée in a jubilant mood. They had suffered no losses, and filed claims for twelve Lightnings, eight of which were ultimately confirmed by the RLM. Their high spirits were in no way tempered by knowledge of any German losses; Ottomar Kruse, for one, never noticed the presence of the Messerschmitts at all. The first Focke-Wulfs to attack the Lightnings were probably from the First Gruppe, which filed no claims and lost one fighter, whose pilot, Uffz. Ludwig Sattler, bailed out with injuries. The Messerschmitts involved in this battle were from the new day fighter unit III/JG 76, which claimed six P-38s. Their losses in this specific combat are unknown, but the next morning JG 76 reported that its two Gruppen in France had lost twenty-one Bf 109s destroyed and five damaged during the day; three of its pilots were wounded, and eighteen were still missing.

It had been the 474th Group's extreme bad fortune to encounter what was undoubtedly the most effective Fw 190 unit then in France. The story of another combat that day between P-38s and Fw 190s had quite a different ending. II/JG 6 had been one of the few operational fighter units left in the Reich after D-Day, flying Bf 110 Zerstörern as II/ZG 26. The Gruppe had been ordered to France over the strenuous protests of General Galland, and had arrived in France three days previously with forty Fw 190s. Today they took off on their first mission as a single-engine fighter unit, a freie Jagd to the Seine. Once in the air they were vectored to St. Quentin, where P-38s were reported strafing the airfield. The German bounce went well, sending about six P-38s down. The rest of the Lightning formation, which was from the 367th Fighter Group, then arrived, and the odds turned sharply in the Americans' favor. On their return the pilots of the 367th claimed the destruction of 25 Fw 190s, a performance that won the Group the Presidential Unit Citation. Reassessment reduced the final confirmations to 16-1-3. II/JG 6 in fact lost exactly sixteen aircraft, with fourteen pilots killed and three wounded. Its Gruppenkommandeur was relieved, and replaced by the JG 26 veteran, Hptm. Hans Naumann.

Late in the afternoon, Jagdkorps II ordered freie Jagden by six Jagdgruppen, including the Second and Third Gruppen, to the area of Amiens. Ogfr. Walter Stumpf was picked to fly his first combat sortie, and took off from Hancourt at 1838. His aircraft was one of the last to leave the ground, and was attacked by P-51s west of the field, before the Gruppe had fully assembled. He escaped from a dogfight with three P-51s, and landed again at 1910. His Focke-Wulf had taken fifteen hits. The rest of the Gruppe claimed four P-51s, but lost Ofhr. Alfred Pfützner, Lt. Peter Rober, Uffz. Kurt Petzsch, and Uffz. Otto Ursprung. The P-51s belonged to the crack 354th Fighter Group's 355th Squadron, which lost four Mustangs on this mission, but claimed a total of 14-0-3 German fighters.

JG 26 Casualties: 25 August 1944

Date	Rank	Name	Cas	Unit	Aircraft	WNr	Mkgs	Place	Time	Cause	Allied Unit
25-08-44	Uffz.	Sattler, Ludwig	WIA	1	Fw 190A-8	173815	wh 7	Clermont		P-38	474 FG
25-08-44	Ofhr.	Pfützner, Alfred	KIA	5	Fw 190A-8	171632	wh 7	nr Amiens		P-51	354 FG
25-08-44	Lt.	Rober, Peter	KIA	6	Fw 190A-8	731085	bk 1	S of St. Quentin		P-51	354 FG

25-08-44	Uffz.	Petzsch, Kurt		KIA 7	Fw 190A-8	730995 br 5	W of Mons-- en Chausée		P-51	354 FG
25-08-44	Uffz.	Ursprung, Otto		KIA 8	Fw 190A-8	732037 bl 2	Beauvais	1838	P-51	354 FG

JG 26 Victory Claims: 25 August 1944

Date	Rank	Name	Unit	Cl #	Aircraft	Place	Time	Opponent	Conf
25-08-44	Hptm.	Lang	II CO	168	P-38	W of Beauvais (TD)	1343	474 FG	yes
25-08-44	Hptm.	Lang	II CO	169	P-38	E of Vernon (UD)	1345	474 FG	yes
25-08-44	Hptm.	Lang	II CO	170	P-38	W of Beauvais (TD)	1348	474 FG	yes
25-08-44	Lt.	Vogt	5 CO	34	P-38	W of Beauvais (TD)	1345	474 FG	yes
25-08-44	Uffz.	Hoffmann J.	5	1	P-38	W of Beauvais (TE)	1349	474 FG	yes
25-08-44	Uffz.	Just	5	1	P-38	W of Beauvais (TD)	1348	474 FG	unk
25-08-44	Obfw.	Mayer	5	18	P-51	St. Quentin (RG8)	1905	354 FG	unk
25-08-44	Ofhr.	Benz	6	1	P-38	SW of Beauvais (TE4-5)	1342	474 FG	yes
25-08-44	Lt.	Fischer E.	6	2	P-38	Beauvais (TE)	1340	474 FG	unk
25-08-44	Fhr.	Hennemann	6	1	P-38	Creil (TE9)	1350	474 FG	unk
25-08-44	Fhr.	Fischer W.	7	1	P-38	W of Beauvais (TD)	1345	474 FG	unk
25-08-44	Uffz.	Salomon	7	1	P-51	N of Soissons (SG1-5)	1901	354 FG	unk
25-08-44	Lt.	Hofmann W.	8 CO	33	P-38	W of Beauvais (TE1)	1353	474 FG	yes
25-08-44	Lt.	Hofmann W.	8 CO	34	P-51	N of Soissons (SG1-5)	1900	354 FG	yes
25-08-44	Lt.	Hofmann W.	8 CO	35	P-51	N of Soissons (SG1-5)	1904	354 FG	yes
25-08-44	Uffz.	Kruse	8	2	P-38	N of Beauvais (TE)	1355	474 FG	yes

26 August

American fighter pilots encountered very few German fighters today, leading them to conclude that the Jagdwaffe in France had been destroyed. However, according to an ULTRA intercept, Jagdkorps II still had 279 serviceable fighters, which flew about 200 sorties in three combined missions. Most were employed against the 2nd TAF as the RAF fighter-bombers attempted to block the German army from crossing the lower Seine between Rouen and the coast.

The day's first mission got off the ground at 0830, and included seventeen First Gruppe Fw 190s under Major Borris, twenty-eight Second Gruppe Fw 190s under Hptm. Lang, and aircraft from five other Jagdgruppen. The fighters formed up and headed to Rouen below the overcast. Hptm. Lang led his fighters in an attack on Nos. 416 and 421 Sqds. (RCAF), which were strafing the crossing zones. Two Spitfires went down, the victims of Lang and Lt. Vogt, but four Second Gruppe pilots were killed: Uffz. Heinz Falkenberg, Uffz. Joachim Hennig, Lt. Wolf-Dietmar Stein, and Lt. Helmut Lampe. Hennig had only joined the unit from training four days previously; Lang's intention to break his new pilots in slowly was no longer practicable. Major Borris also spotted an isolated formation of Spitfires from No. 602 Squadron. He and his pilots claimed four victories, for the loss of one Fw 190 whose pilot was uninjured. The German claims were overstated; one Spitfire was in fact lost.

A mission to the same area was ordered shortly after noon. Twelve First Gruppe Fw 190s, seventeen Second Gruppe Fw 190s, twenty-three Third Gruppe Bf 109s, and aircraft from five other Jagdgruppen took part. Near Rouen the Focke-Wulf Gruppen made a combined bounce on No. 341 Sqd. (French), and shot down two Spitfires, including that of the squadron leader, Cdt. Schloesing, without loss. Hptm. Lang's victory was his 173rd. Major Mietusch's Messerschmitts caught a squadron of P-47s from the 50th Fighter Group intruding into the 2nd TAF's territory near Rouen. Mietusch led a bounce on the squadron's cover flight, and personally shot down two of the Thunderbolts. In the ensuing dogfight, Lt. Karl-Dietrich Hilliger of the 9th Staffel was shot down and killed.

A third mission was attempted in the evening. Eighteen First Gruppe and thirteen Third Gruppe aircraft took off, but assembly was hampered by the weather, and the mission was cut short. Allied aircraft were sighted, but no contact was initiated.

Date	Rank	Name	Cas	Unit	Aircraft	WNr	Mkgs	Place	Time	Cause	Allied Unit
26-08-44	Lt.	Lampe, Helmut	KIA	5	Fw 190A-8	731748	wh 5	Amiens-Beauvais		Spitfire	416 or 421 Sqd
26-08-44	Lt.	Stein, Wolf-Dietmar	KIA	5	Fw 190A-8	171468	wh 3	Amiens-Beauvais		Spitfire	416 or 421 Sqd
26-08-44	Uffz.	Hennig, Joachim	KIA	6	Fw 190A-8	730969	bk 8	E of Rouen		Spitfire	416 or 421 Sqd
26-08-44	Uffz.	Falkenberg, Heinz	KIA	7	Fw 190A-8	680934	br 1	Rouen-Le Havre		Spitfire	416 or 421 Sqd
26-08-44	Lt.	Hilliger, Karl-Dietrich	KIA	9	Bf 109G-6	410218	wh 2	S of Rouen	1440	P-47	50 FG
26-08-44	Lt.	Kopp, Walter	WIA	10	Bf 109G-6	413492	bk 2	Warvillers a/f	1945	landing	n/a

JG 26 Victory Claims: 26 August 1944

Date	Rank	Name	Unit	Cl #	Aircraft	Place	Time	Opponent	Conf
26-08-44	Major	Borris	I CO	39	Spitfire	Rouen (TC2)	0932	602 Sqd	yes
26-08-44	Lt.	Kiefner	I CO	11	Spitfire	Rouen (TC5)	0933	602 Sqd	yes
26-08-44	Uffz.	Schwan	1	2	Spitfire	Rouen (TC4)	0935	602 Sqd	yes
26-08-44	Lt.	Kempf	2	65	Spitfire	Rouen (TC4)	0933	602 Sqd	yes
26-08-44	Lt.	Günther	3	5	Spitfire	W of Beauvais (TD4)	1428	341 Sqd	yes
26-08-44	Lt.	Kemethmüller	4	87	Spitfire	W of Beauvais (TD4)	1425	341 Sqd	unk
26-08-44	Hptm.	Lang	II CO	171	Spitfire	E of Neufchatel (SD7)	0917	421 Sqd	yes
26-08-44	Hptm.	Lang	II CO	172	Spitfire	Rouen (TC3)	0919	421 Sqd	yes
26-08-44	Hptm.	Lang	II CO	173	Spitfire	E of Rouen (TD1)	1428	341 Sqd	yes
26-08-44	Lt.	Vogt	5 CO	35	Spitfire	E of Neufchatel (SD)	0920	421 Sqd	yes
26-08-44	Major	Mietusch	III CO	73	P-47	Rouen (TC4)	1450	50 FG	yes
26-08-44	Major	Mietusch	III CO	74	P-47	W of Rouen (TB6)	1500	50 FG	yes

27 August

Although the weather was adequate, Jagdkorps II ordered no combined missions, and fewer than fifty sorties were flown. The Third Gruppe did put up sixteen fighters for one mission, but no favorable opportunities for combat presented themselves, and the Messerschmitts stayed in the clouds until cleared to land. The Gruppe was then ordered to take the rest of the day off.

Reichsmarschall Göring apparently felt that his fighter formation leaders were taking advantage of his earlier orders to fly only with large formations, and rescinded them. His new edict required each Staffelkapitän to fly at least one mission on each day that his Staffel flew three times or more. Each Gruppenkommandeur was to fly at least one mission for each two days on operations; each Kommodore, one mission for each three days on operations.

Lang asked that an experienced formation leader from III/JG 54, Lt. Alfred Gross, join him to fly in his Stabsschwarm. The request was granted; Gross arrived from Germany today.

28 August

The German fighter units were once again moving to the east, and only the three Gruppen of JG 26 and II/JG 53 were operational. The pilots of the Geschwader flew eighty-three sorties in low cloud, and reported one success – Lt. Hofmann claimed an Auster. The light planes were not easy targets; Lt. Kemethmüller and Lt. Dietze of the 4th Staffel also engaged one, but were unable to bring it down. Obfw. Rudolf Protze of the same Staffel failed to return from one mission, apparently the victim of fighters. The 7th Staffel Fw 190 flown by Ogfr. Stumpf was damaged slightly by ground fire. Lt. Dieter Völmle of the 10th Staffel was injured when forced to bail out after the engine of his Bf 109G-6 failed.

Four new graduates of the Ergänzungsgruppe, Ofhr. Heinz-William Bartels, Ofhr. Hans-Theobald Bühring, Fhj. Walter Fischer, and Uffz. Karl-Georg Genth, arrived at Rosières in new Bf 109G-14s for duty in the Third Gruppe. Each had 140 flying hours in his logbook. Major Mietusch had already left for his new base, and the rear detachment at Rosières was under the command of Hptm. Lang, who greeted the new arrivals heartily, "like an old comrade", and told them that they would be leaving for Brussels in the morning. Genth, the junior man, would be given the job of ferrying the Gruppe liaison aircraft, a Fieseler Storch. Genth's mild complaint that he had never flown a Storch was parried by Lang's "They fly themselves!", said with a grin.

JG 26 Casualties: 28 August 1944

Date	Rank	Name	Cas	Unit	Aircraft	WNr	Mkgs	Place	Time	Cause	Allied Unit
28-08-44	Obfw.	Protze, Rudolf	KIA	4	Fw 190A-8	170710	bl 1	unknown		combat	
28-08-44	Lt.	Völmle, Dieter	WIFA	10	Bf 109G-6	441848	bk 9	St Quentin-Roupy	2130	engine	n/a

29 August

The morning strength return for the Geschwader was intercepted by the Allied signal intelligence service. The Stab reported having one airplane operational and one pilot on duty; the First Gruppe, fourteen aircraft and thirty-four pilots; the Second Gruppe, twenty-eight aircraft and forty-three pilots; and the Third Gruppe, thirteen aircraft and only fourteen pilots.

The Geschwader flew one morning mission in driving rain and low strength. The task was to shoot down fighter-bombers and artillery spotters. The former were all grounded, but the 5th Staffel's Lt. Vogt succeeded in downing an Auster near Soissons. Two First Gruppe pilots, Lt. Kiefner and Lt. Dietze, reported encountering Austers, but were unable to shoot them down.

The pilots then began packing. In the evening, they flew to airfields in the Brussels area – the Stab to Brussels-Nord, the First Gruppe to Grimbergen, the Second to Melsbroek, and the Third to Evere *via* Chièvres. Signs of the German collapse were everywhere. The airfields had not been prepared for the new arrivals, and lacked fuel and supplies. The Second Gruppe pilots found I/JG 11 and IV/NJG 1 already occupying Melsbroek, but were unable to find alternate fields in the area, and wedged themselves onto the crowded base, which had none of the C3 fuel required by their Focke-Wulfs.

Georg Genth did not get to fly the Storch from Rosières. Another pilot pulled rank on him. Instead, Genth was assigned a Bf 109 that had been shot up while landing and was still without a canopy; its pilot had jettisoned it. Genth was told it was a "special attraction", as no-one had flown such a 109 before. He was careful to fly in the middle of the formation, but no enemy aircraft were seen.

30 August

Only one mission was flown, despite orders from Jagdkorps II for continuous operations. The weather was bad, many units lacked the fuel to fly, and those that did were concerned with evacuating the last of their aircraft from their former French bases. The single mission was put up by Major Borris's First Gruppe. Fourteen Fw 190s flew a freie Jagd to the Scheldt Estuary. Some pilots contacted enemy aircraft among the clouds, and received credit for a combat sortie; others did not.

Georg Genth was today ordered to an abandoned airfield with two other pilots to pick up some Bf 109s. Their driver took them to the field at night, on a secret route through the lines. Only one Messerschmitt was found to be airworthy. Genth spotted an old Fw 190A that was to be destroyed. He had never been in the cockpit of one before, but he persuaded the driver, a qualified Fw 190 mechanic, to check him out in it and clear it for flying. Genth then ferried it back to Evere, while the third pilot returned in the vehicle with the mechanic. Genth recalls that his feat impressed the groundcrewmen, but some of the few experienced pilots in the Gruppe, the "fought-out old hares", were cool to him.

31 August

A Jagdkorps II order stated that missions in support of the Army would normally be flown in Schwärme strength only, owing to bad weather and low stocks of aviation fuel. Units were instructed to keep enough fuel in reserve to facilitate another retrograde move of at least 150 km. The Korps now commanded four Geschwader headquarters: JG 2, JG 26, JG 27, and JG 53. JG 26 controlled its three organic Jagdgruppen; the other three Geschwader commanded units from a number of Jagdgeschwader, as Gruppen shuffled back and forth to Germany for refitting.

Jagdkorps II fighters flew 120 sorties, and despite the new orders, one large combined mission was undertaken. The Geschwader was up in full strength – eighteen aircraft took part from the First Gruppe, thirty-four from the Second Gruppe, and seventeen from the Third Gruppe. The Second and Third Gruppen flew high cover for the First Gruppe, which attacked Allied tanks in the Reims area. The mission was flown as ordered; the only noteworthy incident was the destruction of an Auster on the ground by Ofhr. Friedrich Ramthun of the 1st Staffel. The first Allied fighters were not seen until the return flight, and these were avoided in the clouds.

By the time the Second Gruppe reached Melsbroek, the red fuel warning lights were glowing in every airplane. They had to get down as fast as they could. On a normal airfield they could land side-by-side in Schwärme, but Melsbroek was too small. They dropped into the airfield in single file, spaced a few hundred yards apart. As soon as a Focke-Wulf's nose was pulled up, its pilot became blind straight ahead, so all hoped that those in front of them would keep their speeds up as they touched down, and get out of the way quickly. All thirty-four aircraft landed without incident – something of a minor miracle, in Ottomar Kruse's opinion. This mission proved to be Kruse's longest of the war – 135 minutes in the air.

Geschwader personnel moves during August included: the transfer of Uffz. Hermann Kühn from the 5th Staffel to a ferry unit; the return of Lt. Gottfried Dietze and Ogfr. Hermann Hillebrand from temporary duty with III/JG 54; and the return of Fhj.-Obfw. Wilhelm Mayer to the Second Gruppe from instructor duty.

Fw. Alois Becker and Obfw. Rudolf Protze joined the First Gruppe after Fw 190 conversion training. Becker had flown 253 Stuka missions in StG 77; Protze was an experienced Zerstörer and Stuka pilot. Uffz. Heinz Meiss joined the Second Gruppe from II/JG 11, only six weeks out of flight school.

New pilots assigned to the Geschwader during August after completing flight training included: Uffz. Leo Dombrowa, Ofhr. Wolfgang Franz, Obfw. Anton Freiberger, Lt. Karl-Heinz Ossenkop - First Gruppe; Uffz. Valentin Baier, Uffz. Siegfried Burckhardt, Uffz. Armin Florian, Uffz. Gerhard Hamel, Uffz. Fritz Hanusch, Uffz. Joachim Hennig, Uffz. Edwin Kalbus, Lt. Theodor Kersting, Uffz. Jürgen Kracht, Lt. Bruno Mischkot, Obfw. Wilhelm Müller, Lt. Helmut Wirth - Second Gruppe; Ofhr. Heinz-William Bartels, Ofhr. Hans-Theobald Bühring, Fhj. Walter Fischer, Uffz. Karl-Georg Genth - Third Gruppe.

Forty JG 26 pilots were killed in combat in August, the highest monthly loss so far for the Geschwader. Six were killed in accidents, three were taken prisoner, and more than twenty were injured. At least eighty-five aerial victories were claimed. ULTRA intercepted a message summarizing JG 26 aircraft losses. The Stab lost none on operations, and one to non-operational causes; the First Gruppe, 25 operational/16 non-operational; the Second Gruppe, 31 operational/28 non-operational; the Third Gruppe, 36 operational/35 non-operational.

JG 26 Victory Claims: 28 - 31 August 1944

Date	Rank	Name	Unit	Cl #	Aircraft	Place	Time	Opponent	Conf
28-08-44	Lt.	Hofmann W.	8 CO	36	Auster	Melun (AF9-BF3)	1210		yes
29-08-44	Lt.	Vogt	5 CO	36	Auster	Soissons (TG9)	0940		yes
31-08-44	Ofhr.	Ramthun	1		Auster-ground	Reims (TI5)			no

Chapter Seven

DEFENSE OF THE GERMAN BORDER

September - December 1944

1 September

General Patton's Third Army was sweeping east almost without opposition, and Jagdkorps II assigned its highest priority to ground attacks on the American spearheads. The First Gruppe strapped on its rocket mortar tubes, and the three Gruppen took off from their Belgian fields at noon to locate and attack the Americans between Nancy and Toul. The area was out of range of the Allied tactical fighters, and the Second and Third Gruppen dropped to low altitude to strafe. The 7th Staffel Fw 190A-8 of Uffz. Walter Richter was hit by heavy antiaircraft fire, and Richter bailed out into captivity. Some First Gruppe pilots had to land at Trier for fuel, and were unable to get serviced for a second mission. Those that returned to Grimbergen reloaded and flew a repeat mission to the same area. A 12th Staffel pilot, Gefr. Gerhard Bruckauf, got lost while ferrying a Bf 109G-6 in mid-afternoon, and crashed with the airplane. Second Gruppe aircraft flew a scouting mission to the Pas de Calais late in the evening to check on the progress of the British and the Canadians.

2 September

Jagdkorps II ordered more attacks on the Third Army spearheads, which were now approaching Verdun. But British armor was approaching Brussels, and it was time for the Geschwader to retreat once more, this time to German soil. Many of the Allied tactical air units were themselves changing bases, and enemy air activity was light.

3 September

The Third Gruppe flew a morning armed reconnaissance mission to Mons, and located and strafed Allied armor. One Messerschmitt was shot down, but its pilot reached the German lines without injury. The Geschwader transfer flights began about midday. The Stab and the First Gruppe headed for Krefeld; the Second Gruppe, to Kirchhellen *via* Düsseldorf; and the Third Gruppe, to Mönchen-Gladbach. Most flights were uneventful. Two were intercepted, however, with disastrous consequences.

The 2nd Staffel was the last to take off from Grimbergen, at about 1300. All of the ground staff but the 2nd Staffel groundcrewmen were already on the road, out of touch with higher authority. The weather was ideal: 8-10 kilometers (5-6 miles) visibility, with 8/10 cloud cover at 800 meters (2500 feet). The eight aircraft of the 2nd Staffel took off to the west, made a broad left turn, and headed east at 1500 meters (5000 feet). Lt. Karl-Heinz Ossenkop, who had been with the Gruppe less than two weeks, was the last to take off, as wingman to Uffz. Düsing. Ossenkop's landing gear would not retract, and he and Düsing were still turning south of the field while Ossenkop worked with his gear lever when they saw between six and eight P-51s pass 200 meters (650 feet) overhead, firing at the last Focke-Wulfs in front of them. Ossenkop jerked his aircraft to the left and crossed behind the P-51s, dropped his flaps, and landed quickly. Three kilometers to the east, he could see four crashes, and the P-51s climbing away. Ossenkop taxied directly into a hangar in the 2nd Staffel dispersal area, just ahead of two strafing P-51s, which did not see him. He jumped into a truck with the

Lt. Karl-Heinz Kempf. Kempf, a very popular leader, won the Knight's Cross with JG 54 on the Eastern Front before joining JG 26 in late 1943. He was killed with the 2nd Staffel during the disastrous transfer flight on 3 September, a victim of 55th Fighter Group P-51s. *(Genth)*

Lt. Karl-Heinz Ossenkop. Ossenkop, a trained officer, reported to the 2nd Staffel from flight training in August, and survived the war in that unit. *(Bundesarchiv-Militärarchiv)*

Oberwerkmeister (line chief) and three armed men and headed for the crash sites.

The Luftwaffe men had to force their way past a column of retreating infantrymen, but reached the first site within five minutes. The Focke-Wulf was in flames; ammunition was exploding, and the smells of burning fuel, oil, rubber, and flesh assaulted the men's noses as they circled the plane looking for a way through the smoke. The canopy was off, and the pilot's headless corpse sat burning in the cockpit. The airplane's *Werkenummer* (serial number) was still visible on the tail. The line chief consulted his list, and said, "Herr Leutnant, that is Unteroffizier Büker."

Herbert Büker was beyond help, and the two men returned to the truck and headed for the other sites. The line chief noted the circumstances and location of Büker's crash in his diary. The next pile of smoking wreckage was only 600 meters (2000 feet) away. Belgian civilians beckoned the men into a nearby house. There lay Uffz. Leo Dombrowa; he had been able to bail out of his aircraft, but his leg had been shot through with a .50 caliber machine gun shell. His injury was not life-threatening, but the civilians urged Ossenkop to take Dombrowa away immediately. The Leutnant and the Oberwerkmeister decided to end their search and return to the field. Dombrowa accompanied them in the truck, crying in pain.

Ossenkop's fighter had been jacked up in his absence, and the landing gear found to be functional. Its circuit breaker had been jarred open during Ossenkop's takeoff run, and he hadn't noticed it. Had he been able to raise his gear, he would have been last in the formation, and thus the P-51s' first victim. In his words, "My stupidity and inexperience had saved my life and one Fw 190A-8 for the Luftwaffe."

The Leutnant took off alone, two hours late, and headed east at an altitude of 800 meters (2500 feet), right below the cloud deck. He saw four Thunderbolts, but avoided them by pulling up into the cloud and staying there. After landing on Venlo, an unserviceable field, to get directions, he reached Krefeld, where he had been given up

The frequently-photographed Fw 190A-8 "blue 6" (W.Nr. 175140), abandoned by the 8th Staffel on Melsbroek on 3 September. Its markings have previously been identified as brown, but a painting made on the scene by a Canadian war artist shows them as blue. This aircraft continued its war service after the base was turned over to the USAAF. It had been booby-trapped by burying a 250 kg bomb underneath the nose, and when the aircraft was moved, the bomb detonated, causing American casualties and destroying a number of US aircraft. *(Taylor via Matusiak)*

A second Fw 190A-8 abandoned on Melsbroek was "white 7" (W.Nr. 171568) of the 5th Staffel. *(Taylor via Matusiak)*

for lost. He reported to Major Borris, and learned that the other two missing men were Uffz. Heinz Karch and Lt. Karl-Heinz Kempf. Kempf was a former Green Heart. He had gained sixty-four victories in 445 sorties, and had been awarded the Knight's Cross in 1942 while with JG 54 on the Eastern Front. Kempf was very popular with his men, and was said to consider his primary duty to be the training of young pilots,

Another view of "white 7". The airmen are probably members of No. 439 Sqd. (RCAF), the first Allies to occupy the airfield. *(Taylor via Matusiak)*

at which he was very conscientious. Karl-Heinz Ossenkop can still recall the advice he had gotten from Kempf on his arrival at the front two weeks previously:

> "Don't go off on your own. Check your rear two or three times before opening fire. You'll fly your first missions as my wingman. Stick with me, stick with me and secure my rear! Don't think about aerial successes for the first six weeks. It's more important that you gain experience and bring your ass home. Fly just like me, and you'll survive. If the brothers get me, it'll be during takeoff or landing!"

Kempf was killed while taking off to return to his home town, Krefeld.

The 2nd Staffel was bounced by an 8th Air Force unit, the 55th Fighter Group's 38th Squadron. The 55th had been the first ETO Lightning group, and had fought a number of engagements with JG 26 over the previous months. It had recently re-equipped with P-51 Mustangs. That morning it had escorted heavy bombers to Ludwigshaven. On the return leg, two squadrons broke escort to look for trouble over the Low Countries. Capt. McCauley Clark, a flight leader in the 38th Squadron, spotted activity on the deck from 10,000 feet (3000 meters), called out the bogies, and led his flight down, followed by his squadron commander's flight. The Mustangs' 400 mph (650 km/h) dive to the deck caused their windshields to frost up. They made a broad arc to reduce speed and clear their canopies, and then came in behind the Focke-Wulfs, whose pilots had still not seen them. Capt. Clark was first across the airfield. He hit his target from dead astern, and its pilot bailed out. Clark's flight members then downed two more Fw 190s in flames, and his squadron CO claimed the fourth.

At Melsbroek, Hptm. Lang's airplane had been giving trouble, and the aircraft of his Stab thus took off last, at 1320. According to the casualty reports and Josef Priller's 1956 Geschwader history, they flew in a *Kette* of three airplanes. Lang's two companions were supposedly his long-time wingman, Lt. Alfred Gross, and a promising Nachwuchs, Uffz. Hans-Joachim Borreck. Lang had had problems getting his landing gear up after takeoff, but ten minutes later they were on course at an altitude of 200 meters (650 feet) when Borreck called out Thunderbolts to their rear.

Lang broke upward, to the left; Gross, straight left. Borreck dived, two fighters on his tail. After taking hits in the wing and engine, he broke hard left and somehow avoided his pursuers. He could see little, as his canopy had oiled over, but did spot Lang's aircraft in a vertical dive toward the ground, its gear extended. Borreck made a forced landing at another Belgian field, and caught a ride to Düsseldorf. Gross's report, filed from the hospital, states that he first broke into the attackers and shot one Spitfire down; his claim was not witnessed, and was not confirmed. He saw Lang's 190 diving in flames, and then zoomed upward. Gross's plane was hit by an unseen fighter, and he bailed out, badly injured; he never returned to JG 26.

The accounts of Borreck and Gross are not easily reconciled. Was Emil Lang the victim of a P-47 or a Spitfire? No Thunderbolt unit reported an encounter with Fw 190s today, and the presence of P-47s should probably be rejected as the product of an excited Unteroffizier's imagination. An examination of the American records does, however, yield an excellent match with most, but not all, of the German data. The Mustangs of the 55th Fighter Group's 338th Squadron were flying a few minutes behind the 38th Squadron, at 9000 feet (2700 meters). After the 38th Squadron called out 190s on the deck near Brussels, the commander of the 338th led his own unit down. As he broke out of the cloud layer at 3000 feet (900 meters), he saw "three to six bogies flying a loose formation heading east, balls out on the deck", and started after the Focke-Wulf on the right. Lt. Darrell Cramer, his wingman, took the one on the left, which rolled into a steep left turn and then back to the right. Cramer's speed was much greater than that of the German plane, and he was able to take a high-deflection shot at the Focke-Wulf while he himself was turning right. Cramer broke up and then hard right again, and saw the Fw 190, which was upside down in a steep dive toward the ground. It hit so hard that it generated shock waves along the ground like a rock thrown into a pond of water. The airplane skidded a few yards, shedding bits and pieces, and then blew up in a fireball.

Lt. Cramer's victim was undoubtedly Hptm. Lang. Cramer's CO also claimed a Fw 190, and another was taken under fire by Lt. Herman Schonenberg, who last saw his fighter in a dive at one hundred feet but did not see it crash. This last Focke-Wulf was the one piloted by Uffz. Borreck, who escaped. The present author theorized in *JG 26: Top Guns of the Luftwaffe* that Cramer's squadron CO shot down Lt. Gross. But one inconvenient piece of data does not fit—the Spitfire pilot whom Gross shot down is buried at Geel, Belgium, in a grave marked 3 September, 1944. The pilot, W/O Peter Chattin, was from No. 41 Squadron, an ADGB unit flying Spitfire XIIs on a rare sweep of Belgium. At 1330 its eight Spitfires had attacked three Fw 190s heading east near Tirlemont at 2500 feet (760 meters), probably right above the undercast. After a brief, sharp combat, the Spitfire pilots claimed two Focke-Wulfs, but lost W/O Chattin.

The conflicting stories can be reconciled if it is assumed that there were *two* Ketten of Focke-Wulfs; six fighters, not three. Lang and Borreck were in the leading Kette. From the details in the encounter reports, both Cramer and his CO could have made independent claims for Lang's aircraft; Borreck escaped, in the manner already described. Gross would have been leading the second Kette, a cover flight for the first, flying at a higher altitude. This was the flight bounced by No. 41 Squadron. The Spitfire pilots claimed two Focke-Wulfs, but Gross was obviously an adept pilot, and two pilots may have gotten hits on his twisting plane.

If there were indeed two Ketten, the fiction that there was just one was an early German attempt to rationalize Gross's hospital statement that he was next to Lang when he crashed. It is likely that Gross pulled his Kette up into the cloud deck when the P-51s were seen approaching, and he was too embarrassed to admit that he had thus abandoned his Kommandeur to his fate. Gross's Kette was spotted by the Spitfire pilots shortly thereafter, just above the thin cloud layer.

Borreck reached Düsseldorf locked in the baggage compartment of an Fw 190 from another unit. His dramatic arrival, followed by his announcement of Lang's crash, left the gathered pilots of the Second Gruppe in deep shock. Lang was supposed to be a very lucky pilot. It was said about him that in his entire flying career he had never had an accident. His aircraft had never even been struck by enemy fire. Emil Lang had brought great success to his unit with his superb leadership, and now he was dead, after scoring 173 victories in 403 combat sorties. With this piece of news, the Abbeville Kids' four-year tour of duty in occupied western Europe had come to an end.

JG 26 Casualties: 1 - 3 September 1944

Date	Rank	Name	Cas	Unit	Aircraft	WNr	Mkgs	Place	Time	Cause	Allied Unit
01-09-44	Uffz.	Richter, Walter	POW	7	Fw 190A-8	731767	br 13	Nancy		heavy flak	n/a
01-09-44	Gefr.	Bruckauf, Gerhard	KIFA	12	Bf 109G-6	165806	bl 6	near Siegen	1530	crashed	non-op
03-09-44	Uffz.	Bücker, Herbert	KIA	2	Fw 190A-8	171743	bk 4	E of Brussels	1300	P-51	55 FG
03-09-44	Uffz.	Dombrowa, Leo	WIA	2	Fw 190A-8	680846	bk 1	E of Brussels	1300	P-51	55 FG
03-09-44	Uffz.	Karsch, Heinz	KIA	2	Fw 190A-8	170445	bk 11	14km E of Brussels	1300	P-51	55 FG
03-09-44	Lt.	Kempf, Karl-Heinz	KIA	2	Fw 190A-8	171739	bk 9	Baal	1300	P-51	55 FG
03-09-44	Hptm.	Lang, Emil	KIA	II CO	Fw 190A-8	171240	gr 1	Brussels-N of St Trond	1330	P-51	55 FG
03-09-44	Lt.	Gross, Alfred	WIA	II St	Fw 190A-8	171569	gr 4	Brussels-St Trond	1330	Spitfire	41 Sqd

4 September

The end of the wild retreat of the Wehrmacht across France and Belgium brought the Geschwader to a temporary refuge behind the German border. On their departure from Brussels, the ground echelons found themselves among endless streams of army trucks, barreling past burning vehicles which had been shot up by the Allied Jabos. Nearer the homeland, the German sense of order quickly reasserted itself—Ernst Battmer recalls being asked to produce his passport by the customs officer on duty at the German border. The fighters of Jagdkorps II flew only twenty-two sorties today, owing to base disorganization, low serviceability and low fuel stocks.

Hptm. Eder was named Emil Lang's successor as Kommandeur of the Second Gruppe. Lt. Glunz was once again placed on the Gruppe duty roster, and resumed operational command of the 6th Staffel.

5 September

The advance of the western Allies came to a halt in early September, stopped not by the Wehrmacht but by their own supply problems. The Germans took full advantage of their unanticipated reprieve to re-form their shattered army units and move them into the much-vaunted West Wall, which in reality had been nothing but a hollow shell prior to September. Starting at the mouth of the Scheldt, the defensive line ran roughly along the Belgian-Dutch, Belgian-German, and Luxembourg-German borders before heading south across France, along the Moselle River to Switzerland. The OKL assigned the responsibility for the aerial defense of this entire line to Luftflotte 3. Jagdkorps II commanded the western day fighter units, which were, from north to south, JG 26, JG 27, JG 2, JG 53, and JG 76. Operational strength continued to build; 349 fighters were reported serviceable at first light. But the Jagdkorps was ordered by the Luftflotte to show "economy in the use of fighter units" owing to the shortage of fuel. Operations today were by Gruppen; 133 sorties were flown. The JG 26 Gruppen flew freie Jagden. Their results are unknown.

Jagdkorps II ordered the Third Gruppe to relocate immediately from Mönchen-Gladbach to Bönninghardt. Major Mietusch did not want to move, and sent a radio message arguing that it would take him three weeks. However, the transfer was completed by the 8th.

9 September

Few missions were flown owing to the fuel situation. Uffz. Georg Kreth of the 6th Staffel was shot down today by German Flak, and bailed out with injuries. Operations over the homeland brought the pilots a new adversary – the new prima donnas of the Luftwaffe, the antiaircraft troops. The principal responsibility for the aerial defense of Germany now belonged to the Flak, rather than the fighter arm. A broad free-fire zone extended from Bonn past the Ruhr down both sides of the Rhine River. Free-fire belts also encircled all major cities. Navigation was never the fighter pilots' strong suit, and they frequently found themselves in the Flak gunners' sights. It was an enervating if not enraging experience for the pilots of the Schlageter Geschwader, which had spent years in the operational zone, to return to the homeland only to be taken under fire by their own forces.

The 8th Staffel had a noteworthy experience with the antiaircraft gunners soon after returning to Germany. The few missions flown in early September were usually over the Rhineland, as cover flights for the West Wall construction workers. This mission had started out as just such a freie Jagd. However, Lt. Hofmann's eagle eyes spotted a formation of heavy bombers high above, and he led his Staffel up after them. Ottomar Kruse recalls:

"We climbed to 7800 meters [25,000 feet] over Düren – I didn't like it at all. It was the highest I had ever been, and the controls of my 190 were very, very soft indeed. We could have gone a bit higher, but I don't know how the aircraft would have reacted. All at once I saw a gray ball of smoke behind the plane of my No. 2, Helmut Gross. I had never seen antiaircraft fire, and thought it was his engine – then I saw a second one appear, and called him on the intercom. He couldn't see the smoke. Just then Hofmann called out antiaircraft fire. He ordered us to fire our recognition signals from our flare pistols. Of course I'd forgotten mine. Of the eleven 190s, only five fired their flares. The antiaircraft gunners had our height but not our speed, so we adopted the following tactics – we maintained our direction, increased our speed, dropped our noses slightly, and slid to one side by pushing in the rudder. The gunners were plotting along our longitudinal axis, and their next shots would go to one side. They would correct immediately, but we would be somewhere else. We were then over Düren, flying toward Köln. We were handed from one battery to the next; several thousand shots were fired – the heavy stuff, 10.5's. Hofmann probably called the ground, but no-one took any notice. Also, they could hear his transmissions to us, giving us orders. Just before we reached the bombers, Hofmann said we would have to go down again; something was wrong with his oxygen supply. I was quite thankful for that, because I didn't fancy the idea of attacking B-17s."

11 September

Jagdkorps II was ordered to participate in the largest interception of an 8th Air Force raid since 28 May. Five hundred German fighters were airborne. Most were from Luftflotte Reich, but about 50-70 fighters from the western units took part, including some from the Third Gruppe. Its bomber attack was ineffective, but Lt. Reischer and Lt. Schild claimed Thunderbolts near Maastricht. The Americans reported no P-47 losses. Uffz. Hans Erbskorn of the 10th Staffel crash-landed east of Venlo with slight injuries after his engine failed. Uffz. Heinz Gehrke of the 11th Staffel blew a tire when landing on Bönninghardt after the mission. His Messerschmitt overturned, but Gehrke suffered only minor injuries.

The new JG 26 bases were near the Ruhr, in far western Germany. The Geschwaderstab and the First Gruppe settled in at Krefeld and its nearby satellite field, Krefeld-Linn. Krefeld was a prewar Jagdwaffe airbase with a well-drained grass landing ground and a full allotment of hangars, workshops, and barracks. There were no woods nearby to help hide the aircraft, so full use was made of camouflage netting. Krefeld was a mile west of the Rhine River, which made a sharp bend pointing directly at the field. This was a useful navigational aid for the poorly-trained German fighter pilots, but also benefited the Allied reconnaissance aircraft, which kept a close watch on activities at the field.

Hptm. Eder's Second Gruppe moved east of the Rhine. Its Stab and the 5th and 6th Staffeln occupied the field at Kirchhellen, a typical war-built landing ground with rudimentary facilities. There was only a single hangar, and no barracks, so accommodations were sought in the nearby town. The field was surrounded on all sides by thick woods, which were of great assistance in hiding the Focke-Wulfs from prying Allied eyes. The 7th and 8th Staffeln moved thirty miles north of Kirchhellen, to Coesfeld-Stevede. Construction of the base at Stevede had begun in 1943. It was intended as an intermediate or emergency landing field, and according to residents of the area saw little activity until 1944. The landing ground was simply a meadow, used normally for grazing cattle. It was a small grassy rectangle, 2600 feet long and 650 feet wide (800 x 200 meters). When it rained, the field became soggy, and the pilots had great difficulty getting their planes off the ground. The field's length was barely adequate for lightly-loaded fighters; fortunately during this period the pilots were not required to take off carrying bombs. The dispersals of the two Staffeln were located in the woods. In the beginning, the aircraft were simply parked in small lanes that had been cut between the trees. Revetments were built in mid-October. The ground personnel slept in barracks that had been built earlier for antiaircraft troops covering a nearby dummy airfield; there was also a kitchen and a sick bay. The pilots seldom remained on the field overnight. Their quarters were in Coesfeld, in an old training school.

The 7th Staffel was on the north end of the landing ground, and ordinarily took off from the northeast to the southwest. Landings were made in the reverse direction when possible, so that the Fw 190s could taxi quickly off of the field and be hidden from the Allied Jabos. Oblt. Waldemar Radener returned from injury leave to resume command of the 7th Staffel. Lt. Hans Prager left the Geschwader and joined III/JG 54, which was in training at Oldenburg.

The 8th Staffel was located on the other side of the landing ground, somewhat to its south. While the 7th Staffel had the use of only a small patch of woods, the 8th Staffel was surrounded by an extensive forest. The 8th Staffel used an unusual takeoff technique – they normally took off from the southwest to the northeast, opposite the 7th Staffel, and thus usually with the wind to their backs. This enabled them to keep in the cover of the trees until just prior to takeoff. Lt. Wilhelm Hofmann, the 8th Staffel Kapitän, commanded both Staffeln in the air when they operated jointly.

The Third Gruppe was also split between two airfields. The 11th and 12th Staffeln were based at Bönninghardt, one of the original prewar bases of the Geschwader, while the Gruppenstab and the 9th and 10th Staffeln moved to Coesfeld-Lette. Lette was originally a dispersal field for Stevede. It is not known why Major Mietusch based his Third Gruppe Stab here instead of Bönninghardt, which was much better equipped. Lette had a simple 3900 foot by 600 foot (1200 x 200 meters) grass airstrip. Generally takeoffs were made to the east, and landings to the west. There were no suitable dispersals or revetments for the aircraft. The Messerschmitts were parked in the surrounding woods or simply under single trees. In the beginning, the pilots slept in the neighboring farmhouses, but shortly after their arrival barracks were completed on the field. In contrast to Stevede, which remained undetected by the Allies, the field at Lette was soon seen by reconnaissance aircraft. After Spitfires attacked the field in late October, the Gruppe moved.

JG 26 Casualties: 9 - 11 September 1944

Date	Rank	Name	Cas	Unit	Aircraft	WNr	Mkgs	Place	Time	Cause	Allied Unit
09-09-44	Uffz.	Kreth, Georg	WIA	6	Fw 190A-8	175122		Lackhausen		own flak	n/a
11-09-44	Obfw.	Erbskorn, Hans	WIA	10	Bf 109G-6	165156	bk 5	E of Venlo	1440	engine	n/a
11-09-44	Uffz.	Gehrke, Heinz	WIA	11	Bf 109G-6	441481	yl 20	Bönninghardt a/f	1408	landing	n/a

12 September

The primary task of the western fighter units was now the protection of the civilians and servicemen requisitioned to work on the West Wall fortifications near Aachen, Maastricht, and Metz. Luftflotte 3 issued a directive that operations were to be controlled such that fighter formations contained a minimum of forty aircraft. Jagdkorps II managed four such missions today, and reported "repeated and very hard air battles from bases to the target area." The Third Gruppe took part in one successful mission, joining II/JG 6 in a bounce of the 474th Fighter Group near Düren. The P-38 pilots reported being attacked by 70+ aircraft, and claimed 8-1-9 for the loss of five. Fw. Albert Boeckl of the 12th Staffel claimed one of the Lightnings; the Gruppe suffered no losses.

JG 26 Victory Claims: 3 - 12 September 1944

Date	Rank	Name	Unit	Cl #	Aircraft	Place	Time	Opponent	Conf
03-09-44	Lt.	Gross A.	II St	52	Spitfire	7km E of Tirlemont	1245	41 Sqd	unk
11-09-44	Lt.	Reischer	11 CO	18	P-47	W of Maastricht (NL5-9)	1458		unk
11-09-44	Oblt.	Schild	12	6	P-47	S of Maastricht (NM)	1458		yes
12-09-44	Fw.	Boeckl	12		P-38	W of Bonn (OO1)	1605	474 FG	yes

16 September

The return to the homeland provided the men with one important benefit – the opportunity to meet large numbers of young German women. The 7th and 8th Staffeln located a suitable restaurant in Coesfeld and began planning a party for tonight to consume some of the alcohol they had brought with them from Brussels. Lt. Hofmann instructed his pilots to find female companions for the social; they set out in all directions from the field, and had little trouble finding dates for the big evening. For a reason he no longer remembers, Ottomar Kruse went to the Coesfeld train station. He spotted his dream maiden there, behind the ticket counter. His first approach was rejected, for the sound reason that "Flyers never keep their appointments." Kruse replied, "The only excuse for me not to make it would be if I were shot down." This line did the trick. She turned a little pale, and agreed to meet him at the party.

The western fighters had only one mission assigned to them at this time, cover for the West Wall construction sites, but bad weather as well as low fuel had hampered their efforts for the past several days. Today all units of the Geschwader were in combat for the first time since their return to Germany. All was quiet for most of the day, however. Pilots were airborne only for test and ferry flights; Uffz. Arnim Florian of the 6th Staffel was injured in the crash of a Focke-Wulf he was testing at Düsseldorf.

Shortly after 1700 all three Gruppen received orders to take off immediately on a Jabojagd to Aachen. The mission brought the Third Gruppe only an inconclusive combat with Spitfires. Major Borris reached Aachen with his entire First Gruppe, attacked a formation of P-38s, and claimed four for the loss of one Fw 190, whose pilot escaped injury.

Lt. Hofmann led eleven 7th and 8th Staffeln Focke-Wulfs on the mission. Apparently Hofmann made no effort to join up with any other fighters, but led his unit toward Aachen alone. Uffz. Ottomar Kruse led the cover Rotte; his wingman was Uffz. Erich Klein. The mission was flown at 3500 meters (11,500 feet), Kruse's Rotte 200 meters (600 feet) above the rest. Visibility was clear, with broken cumulus clouds. After 20 minutes, Indianer were called out 500 meters (1600 feet) below; eight Thunderbolts. Hofmann signaled the attack, and dived. Kruse and Klein were in a poor position to attack, and began to circle. Lightnings, and more Thunderbolts, suddenly emerged from around a large cumulus cloud. Kruse dived to assist a Focke-Wulf that was being pursued by Thunderbolts, and was quickly caught up in the whirling melee. His aircraft took hits in the cockpit and engine, which began running away. Kruse decided it was time to get out. After evading the tracers, the procedure was automatic – unlatch the canopy, disconnect the radio helmet, unbuckle the harness, jam the stick hard left with the left hand – Kruse squirted out. He opened his chute – too soon, he quickly decided – and after pulling his lines to fall faster, hit the release disc when he was two meters above the ground. The four harness straps fell away, and he dropped to the ground and quickly disappeared into a ditch. Two Thunderbolts circled overhead, but didn't come down to look for him.

Kruse had never doubted that he was over German-controlled territory, and that he would make it back to Coesfeld for that night's party, but the first civilian he encountered let him know that he was a mile behind the American lines. It was still broad daylight, and he was certain that he had been seen. He invited himself into a farmhouse for some water, was offered coffee and buttered toast, and was soon ordered out by some American soldiers. Ottomar Kruse recalls,

"After surrendering my pistol, I was loaded onto a jeep, between the driver and the corporal. A soldier stood on the right running board, his weapon pointed at me. The second sat behind me, his barrel in my back. The corporal kept his Colt in his hand. Then while it was still daylight they led me at slow speed past American positions. My identity could be guessed from my leather coveralls. Everyone stared; some shouted out. One red-faced soldier drew his hand across his throat and yelled, 'Kill him! Kill him!' I stared straight ahead and took not the slightest notice of my surroundings. The corporal asked whether I had understood. I replied disdainfully that such a thing would never happen in the Wehrmacht. It was unbelievable to me that a downed flyer would be paraded in front of our units for their amusement.

"Later I was placed in a small wooden building that was already full of captured German infantrymen. One sat between the legs of the man behind him, and the one in front did likewise. There were about 150-200 men guarded by a few Amis commanded by a lieutenant. There was no light, and scarcely a word was spoken. My thoughts turned to my comrades and their party and I realized my true situation for the first time. I could have cried from despair... After three days of various interrogations and having been brought to a large open-air compound, I was finally taken to an airfield. There I was loaded under guard into an American twin-engine plane, and was flown to London."

Hofmann's simple bounce proved to be a disaster for the Germans. His intended victims were twelve P-47s of the 50th Fighter Group's 81st Squadron. They jettisoned their bombs, turned into the attack, and after the resulting combat claimed 6-0-2 of the eleven attacking Focke-Wulfs. No P-47 was lost. The P-38s reported by several of the surviving Germans were from the 370th Fighter Group, returning from their engagement with the First Gruppe, in which they claimed five Fw 190s for one loss. The P-47s which Kruse remembers coming down with the P-38s were probably from the 404th Fighter Group, which had claimed 4-0-2 Fw 190s near Aachen a half hour before this battle. None of the American units, all ground attack outfits, lost any aircraft in this engagement with Hofmann's force. It was a very creditable performance for the Americans. None of them were experienced in air combat; the 81st Squadron had only encountered German aircraft four times previously.

Four 7th Staffel pilots, Lt. Theodor Kersting, Ogfr. Hermann Hillebrand, Uffz. Heinz Salomon, and Ofhr. Alfred Scharf, were killed. Uffz. Kruse of the 8th Staffel and Uffz. Jürgen Kracht of the 7th were shot down and taken prisoner. As the final blow, Lt. Hofmann's wingman, Lt. Josef Grimmer, was shot down on the return flight by German light Flak. Grimmer bailed out at low altitude and broke both legs. He never returned to the Geschwader, and thus probably survived the war. If he did, he was the only one of Ottomar Kruse's 8th Staffel comrades to do so.

Date	Rank	Name	Unit	Cl #	Aircraft	Place	Time	Opponent	Conf
16-09-44	Major	Borris	I CO	40	P-38	Bonn (NN8)	1740	370 FG	yes
16-09-44	Lt.	Söffing	1	20	P-38	Bonn (NN8)	1745	370 FG	yes
16-09-44	Fw.	Vandeveerd	3	4	P-38	Bonn (NN8)	1740	370 FG	yes
16-09-44	Lt.	Kemethmüller	4 CO	88	P-38	Monschau-SE of Stolberg (ON2-3)	1741	370 FG	yes

JG 26 Casualties: 16 September 1944

Date	Rank	Name	Cas	Unit	Aircraft	WNr	Mkgs	Place	Time	Cause	Allied Unit
16-09-44	Uffz.	Florian, Armin	WIFA	6	Fw 190A-8	170974	bk 3	Düsseldorf		crashed	non-op
16-09-44	Lt.	Grimmer, Josef	WIA	7	Fw 190A-8	732007	bl 11	near Jülich	1815	own flak	n/a
16-09-44	Ogfr.	Hillebrand, Hermann	KIA	7	Fw 190A-8	172962	br 4	Schinnen	1745	P-47 or P-38	50, 370 or 404 FG
16-09-44	Lt.	Kersting, Theodor	KIA	7	Fw 190A-7	340338	br 9	NW of Vaals	1745	P-47	404 FG
16-09-44	Uffz.	Kracht, Jürgen	POW	7	Fw 190A-8	730513	br 7	E of Vaals	1745	P-47 or P-38	50, 370 or 404 FG
16-09-44	Uffz.	Salomon, Heinz	KIA	7	Fw 190A-8	171667	br 10	NE of Heerlen	1745	P-47 or P-38	50, 370 or 404 FG
16-09-44	Ofhr.	Scharf, Alfred	KIA	7	Fw 190A-8	170978	br 2	Limburg	1745	P-47 or P-38	50, 370 or 404 FG
16-09-44	Uffz.	Kruse, Ottomar	POW	8	Fw 190A-8	171505	bl 13	Nutherveld	1810	P-47	50 FG

17 September

In the early afternoon, Luftflotte 3 headquarters received word of large-scale Allied parachutist and glider landings in The Netherlands. This was the beginning of Operation Market Garden, the Allies' attempt to outflank the Germans' Rhine defenses by a narrow, deep thrust across Holland. The initial German air response appeared to the Allies to be weak and hesitant, reminiscent of their reaction to the D-Day landings in Normandy. However, the Luftwaffe was doing as much as its permanently weakened state allowed. The Luftflotte 3 war diary entry for the date reads:

> "In the morning, 145 aircraft of Jagdkorps II provided cover for civilians working on West Wall defenses in the Aachen-Bitburg area. In the afternoon, six formations (about twenty-five aircraft each) were made ready to attack enemy airborne landings in the Arnhem-Nijmegen area, but only three formations carried out operations in the battle area. The remaining aircraft could not take off owing to the approach of bad weather."

The three formations referred to were the three Gruppen of JG 26, the Jagdgeschwader based the closest to the landing sites. The missions were not successful, as no German fighter reached the transports. All were fended off by the swarms of Allied escort fighters. Fighters of the American 8th Air Force and the British ADGB flew a total of 1037 escort and patrol sorties in support of the operation. The First Gruppe claimed three Spitfires near Nijmegen, for the loss of Uffz. Artur Neumann; the victorious pilots were Oblt. Heckmann, Lt. Kemethmüller, and Uffz. Düsing. The Second Gruppe fought two battles with Mustangs. In mid-afternoon fifteen Focke-Wulfs bounced the 4th Fighter Group's 335th Squadron in the Emmerich-Bocholt area. After a battle ranging from 3000 meters (10,000 feet) to the deck, the American squadron re-formed, less two of its Mustangs, the victims of Lt. Hofmann and Ofhr. Schulwitz. The Americans were credited with downing six Fw 190s, but in fact only two were lost; Uffz. Helmut Gross and Uffz. Johann Holzleitner, both of the 8th Staffel, were killed. Later that evening Second Gruppe pilots claimed three more Mustangs, this time without loss to themselves; these fighters were from the 2nd TAF's No. 19 and No. 65 Squadrons, which lost two aircraft.

The Third Gruppe also fought a battle with Mustangs, with ruinous consequences for itself. In mid-afternoon, Major Mietusch assembled about fifteen Bf 109s of his scattered command and headed for the landing zones, climbing all the way. The weather had taken a turn for the worse, and there was a continuous layer of thin cloud at 5000 meters (16,000 feet). The Germans climbed through it, and then, while above the Dutch-German border, Mietusch spotted a squadron of P-51s below them. He radioed that he was attacking, and dived through the cloud. His first burst of fire destroyed the No. 4 plane of the cover flight. Oblt. Schild hit the No. 2 Mustang's drop tank, and it dived away trailing a solid sheet of flame.

The leader of that P-51 flight, Lt. William Beyer of the 361st Fighter Group's 376th Squadron, looked around just in time to see "about fifteen German fighters closing in with all their guns firing." His wingmen had not been doing their jobs, and had already paid the price. Beyer broke 180 degrees, called out the attack, and tore back through the whole German formation. After another 180, he picked out a Messerschmitt in the center of the formation, and the chase was on. The rest of the German fighters zoomed back up into the clouds and disappeared. Beyer's target first dropped his flaps and chopped his throttle, forcing Beyer to do the same, plus lower his wheels, fishtail, and weave, to slow down enough to keep from overrunning the Messerschmitt and becoming the target himself. The maneuver was repeated three times, and was followed by steep dives and sharp recoveries. The P-51 pilot had to stay behind the Bf 109 at all times, or the German pilot would be able to zoom up and fall in behind him. Beyer did not fire a shot until the two aircraft pulled out from their last dive, just above the ground. The Messerschmitt was hit with Beyer's first burst of fire, and continued its turn until it hit the ground and broke up.

Lt. Beyer's victim was Major Klaus Mietusch. Mietusch was one of the most fascinating individuals in the history of the Geschwader. He was a career officer, had joined the Geschwader in 1938, and was its senior pilot in length of service when he died at age twenty-five. His early combat career was marked by a seemingly endless series of failures and frustrations. A member of the successful 7th Staffel under Müncheberg, he did not come into his own until he succeeded to its command and led it on detached assignment in Russia in 1943. He was the opposite of the typical extroverted, self-confident fighter pilot. He compensated for what he believed to be his lack of ability by an act of will. Mietusch was shot down ten times, and was wounded at least four times. He was said never to have turned down a mission, and had logged 452 combat sorties at the time of his death. His seventy-five victories finally brought the award of the Oak Leaves to his Knight's Cross, two months after his death. His original Knight's Cross had also been inexplicably late; one wonders what this did for his shaky self-confidence.

Priller quotes the following self-assessment, taken from a war correspondent's story on Mietusch:

> "I was a decidedly unskilled, poor fighter pilot, since I could not shoot. Everything happened too fast. When I had the enemy in front of me, everything turned red. The rush of blood clouded my reason, and my cone of fire lay below or above the target, but not on it. My motto became, bore in, until the enemy is as large as a barn door in your sights."

The final words on this introspective fighter pilot are his own comments on combat leadership:

> "When the situation becomes critical, there is usually only one correct reaction out of a hundred possibilities. Then you fight as though in a trance. The lightning swiftness of the necessary reactions does not permit calm deliberation. The situation requires immediate action. You grasp only fragments of the swirling, lightning-swift images. Later you can sometimes remember one thing or another; these are painful recollections if the situation was not grasped properly, and happier if you did the one and only correct thing."

Lt. William R. Beyer of the 361st Fighter Group, the man responsible for downing Klaus Mietusch on 17 September, is debriefed by Capt. Roy E. Webb. *(Gotts)*

JG 26 Victory Claims: 17 September 1944

Date	Rank	Name	Unit	Cl #	Aircraft	Place	Time	Opponent	Conf
17-09-44	Oblt.	Heckmann	3 CO	65	Spitfire	Nijmegen (IN7)	1751		yes
17-09-44	Uffz.	Düsing	3	1	Spitfire	Nijmegen (IN7)	1755		unk
17-09-44	Lt.	Kemethmüller	4 CO	89	Spitfire	Nijmegen-W of Kleve (IN7)	1756		unk
17-09-44	Lt.	Vogt	5 CO	37	Mustang	Bocholt (JN-JO)	1800	19 or 65 Sqd	yes
17-09-44	Uffz.	Borreck	5	4	Mustang	Nijmegen (JN6-JO4)	1801	65 Sqd	unk
17-09-44	Ofhr.	Benz	6	2	Mustang	Krefeld (KO1-4)	1808	19 or 65 Sqd	yes
17-09-44	Lt.	Hofmann W.	8 CO	37	P-51	Emmerich (JO)	1440	4 FG	yes
17-09-44	Ofhr.	Schulwitz	8	4	P-51	Emmerich (JO)	1441	4 FG	yes
17-09-44	Major	Mietusch	III CO	75	P-51	N of M-Gladbach (LN1-7)	1455	361 FG	yes
17-09-44	FjFw.	Zeller	III St		P-51	E of Nijmegen (JN)	1455	361 FG	yes
17-09-44	Oblt.	Schild	12	7	P-51	N of M-Gladbach (LN1)	1458	361 FG	yes

JG 26 Casualties: 17 September 1944

Date	Rank	Name	Cas	Unit	Aircraft	WNr	Mkgs	Place	Time	Cause	Allied Unit
17-09-44	Uffz.	Neumann, Artur	KIA	4	Fw 190A-8	171535	bl 7	Kleve		Spitfire	602 Sqd
17-09-44	Uffz.	Gross, Helmut	KIA	8	Fw 190A-8	171565	bl 5	Hoxfeld-Borken	1438	P-51	4 FG
17-09-44	Uffz.	Holzleitner, Johann	KIA	8	Fw 190A-8	170309	bl 4	Bochholt	1440	P-51	4 FG
17-09-44	Maj.	Mietusch, Klaus	KIA	III CO	Bf 109G-6/U4	441646	bk 25	Rath-Aldekerk	1511	P-51	361 FG

18 September

The Luftwaffe High Command ordered Luftflotte Reich and Luftflotte 3 to give their highest priority to attacking transports and gliders, higher even than defending the Reich against heavy bomber raids. In the morning the weather, that enemy of Allies and Axis alike, took a turn for the worse. This hindered both the Allied efforts to resupply and reinforce the landing zones, and the German attempts to block them. The first Allied resupply mission did not get underway until noon. A total of 193 German fighters, including components from all three JG 26 Gruppen, was scrambled and attempted to reach the aerial convoys, but all were parried by the Allied escorts.

The First and Third Gruppen encountered Spitfires near the landing zone. One of them damaged Lt. Kemethmüller's Focke-Wulf. Kemethmüller made it back to Krefeld-Linn. He does not appear on the list of injured, but did not fly again for a month. Some pilots of the Gruppe strafed ground targets on their return flight. Ofhr. Karl Willi was struck by fire from an antiaircraft battery attached to the American 2nd Armored Division, and he crashed to his death near Maastricht. Lt. Vogt led a dozen Second Gruppe Focke-Wulfs in a bounce of No. 19 Squadron near Eindhoven, and shot one of the RAF Mustangs down.

Jagdkorps II mounted a late-afternoon combined mission, but results were no better than before. JG 26 reported no claims or losses.

Hptm. Paul Schauder was named interim Kommandeur of the Third Gruppe, while General Galland's staff searched the personnel lists for a more senior, and more successful, officer to succeed Klaus Mietusch.

19 September

The weather improved slightly. Jagdkorps II reported that forty-eight fighter-bomber sorties were flown to the Nijmegen area in the morning. In the afternoon, 148 German fighters "engaged in dogfights with enemy fighter formations over the target area. By concentrated effort, air superiority was gained over the landing area between 1715 and 1800 hours." This hard-won "victory" gained the Germans nothing, as they did not reach their targets, the transport formations themselves. The Allied escort comprised 127 ADGB Spitfires and 182 8th Air Force P-51s. Fifty-four of the Mustangs belonged to the 357th Fighter Group, which reached Arnhem in late afternoon to find an eerily-lit purplish-blue sky full of milling British, American, and German warplanes; machine gun strikes on the aircraft flickered like distant fireworks. There was a solid cloud deck at 6000 meters (20,000 feet). Another cloud formation walled off the eastern edge of the drop zone, sharply restricting the combat area. The Mustang pilots waded into the cauldron, and returned to England claiming 20-1-1 Bf 109s and 5-0-0 Fw 190s. Five American pilots were lost, however, including Major Edward Hiro, commander of the 363rd Squadron and formation leader on the mission.

The Geschwader was active over the combat zone all day, and lost only one pilot, Ofhr. Klaus Knappmann of the 6th Staffel, who failed to return from a strafing attack on the airborne troops. Lt. Vogt's 5th Staffel claimed four Mustangs between 1802 and 1804 hours – one by the Kapitän, two by his inseparable companion, Ofhr. Mayer, and one by Uffz. Borreck. Oblt. Schild of the 12th Staffel also claimed a Mustang at this time. JG 26 was responsible for at least four of the 357th Group's losses, and possibly all five. Capt. Bruce McIntyre's flight of three P-51s was separated from its squadron, attacked by a large number of fighters, and shot down, probably by the 5th Staffel. Major Hiro was last seen by his wingman after a combat with Bf 109s. The fifth P-51 lost was bounced by Bf 109s out of the clouds. One of these last two P-51s was probably Schild's victim.

JG 26 Victory Claims: 18 - 19 September 1944

Date	Rank	Name	Unit	Cl #	Aircraft	Place	Time	Opponent	Conf
18-09-44	Lt.	Vogt	5 CO	38	Mustang	Luxembourg (KM)	1325	19 Sqd	yes
19-09-44	Lt.	Vogt	5 CO	39	P-51	Emmerich (JN)	1803	357 FG	yes
19-09-44	Uffz.	Borreck	5	5	P-51	Nijmegen (JN4-6)	1802	357 FG	yes
19-09-44	Obfw.	Mayer	5	19	P-51	Nijmegen (JN5)	1802	357 FG	yes
19-09-44	Obfw.	Mayer	5	20	P-51	Nijmegen (JN5)	1804	357 FG	yes
19-09-44	Oblt.	Schild	12	8	P-51	Emmerich (JN4)	1815	357 FG	yes

21 September

Both sides were grounded by the weather on the 20th. The situation of the British 1st Airborne Division in Arnhem was now desperate, and the long-delayed drop of the Polish 1st Parachute Brigade was ordered, despite the poor weather. Only ninety American fighters, the Thunderbolts of the 56th and 353rd Fighter Groups, could get off their bases for escort and patrol. The 56th Group engaged a large formation of Fw 190s, which fought back aggressively, drawing the combat eastward toward Osnabrück. The Wolfpack claimed 15-0-1 German fighters for the loss of one P-47, but in their absence the twenty-five Fw 190s of the First Gruppe burst from the clouds over s'Hertogenbosch and raked the defenseless transports of the RAF's 38th and 46th Groups. Borris's men claimed seventeen "Douglas transports" before escaping unscathed. The most successful pilot was Oblt. Fred Heckmann, who downed four transports for his 66th-69th victories.

The 353rd Fighter Group's Thunderbolts reached the Nijmegen area in time to break up the attacks on the transports by the Second and Third Gruppen, but not until the Focke-Wulf pilots had downed three of them. The American pilots claimed 3-1-1 Fw 190s and one Bf 109, but lost one P-47 to Lt. Hofmann. The Second Gruppe lost Ofhr. Otto Fussi, who disappeared, and was presumed killed; Fhr. Martin Hennemann, who bailed out with injuries; and Oblt. Werner Stoll, who force-landed with minor injuries. The Third Gruppe lost Ofhr. Günther Patzke, who crashed in his airplane.

Sixteen Stirlings (bombers converted to glider tugs) and thirteen Dakotas (Douglas C-47s) crashed in the Arnhem-Nijmegen area on this mission, out of 114 transports dispatched. Some were undoubtedly shot down by antiaircraft fire, but the actual losses to JG 26 were very close to the twenty claims submitted. This proved to be the only successful attack by the Luftwaffe on what turned out to be the largest aerial assault and resupply operation of the war. As for the luckless Polish force, the main task of its survivors was to cover the return of the remnants of the 1st Airborne Division across the Rhine on the night of 24-25 September.

JG 26 Victory Claims: 21 September 1944

Date	Rank	Name	Unit	Cl #	Aircraft	Place	Time	Opponent	Conf
21-09-44	Obfw.	Teilken	1	2	C-47	Nijmegen (IL-IM)	1717	38 or 46 Gp	yes
21-09-44	Oblt.	Kunz	2 CO	11	C-47	Nijmegen (IL-IM)	1718	38 or 46 Gp	yes
21-09-44	Oblt.	Kunz	2 CO	12	C-47	S,Hertogenbosch (IL9)	1720	38 or 46 Gp	yes
21-09-44	Lt.	Günther	2	6	C-47	Nijmegen (IL-IM)	1717	38 or 46 Gp	yes
21-09-44	Ofhr.	Heindtke	2	1	C-47	W of Arnhem	1723	38 or 46 Gp	yes
21-09-44	Oblt.	Heckmann	3 CO	66	C-47	Nijmegen (IL-IM)	1717	38 or 46 Gp	yes
21-09-44	Oblt.	Heckmann	3 CO	67	C-47	Nijmegen (IL-IM)	1718	38 or 46 Gp	yes
21-09-44	Oblt.	Heckmann	3 CO	68	C-47	W of Arnhem	1719	38 or 46 Gp	yes
21-09-44	Oblt.	Heckmann	3 CO	69	C-47	W of Arnhem	1720	38 or 46 Gp	yes
21-09-44	Uffz.	Herbster	3	1	C-47	W of Arnhem	1720	38 or 46 Gp	yes
21-09-44	Uffz.	Herbster	3	2	C-47	W of Arnhem	1721	38 or 46 Gp	unk
21-09-44	Gefr.	Kohler	3	1	C-47	S,Hertogenbosch (IH)	1722	38 or 46 Gp	unk
21-09-44	Gefr.	Kohler	3	2	C-47	W of Arnhem	1725	38 or 46 Gp	yes
21-09-44	Uffz.	Schulz	3	1	C-47	W of Arnhem	1720	38 or 46 Gp	yes
21-09-44	Uffz.	Schulz	3	2	C-47	W of Arnhem	1723	38 or 46 Gp	yes
21-09-44	Fw.	Vandeveerd	3	5	C-47	Nijmegen (IL-IM)	1718	38 or 46 Gp	yes
21-09-44	Fw.	Vandeveerd	3	6	C-47	Nijmegen (IL-IM)	1719	38 or 46 Gp	yes
21-09-44	Lt.	Vogt	5 CO	40	C-47	Nijmegen (JM)	1717	38 or 46 Gp	yes
21-09-44	Lt.	Glunz	6 CO	66	C-47	Nijmegen (JM)	1718	38 or 46 Gp	yes
21-09-44	Lt.	Hofmann W.	8 CO	38	C-47	Deelen (JM)	1720	38 or 46 Gp	yes
21-09-44	Lt.	Hofmann W.	8 CO	39	P-47	Zwolle (FN)	1733	353 FG	yes

JG 26 Casualties: 18 - 21 September 1944

Date	Rank	Name	Cas	Unit	Aircraft	WNr	Mkgs	Place	Time	Cause	Allied Unit
18-09-44	Ofhr.	Willi, Karl	KIA	4	Fw 190A-8	171539	bl 10	Munstergeleen (NL)		flak	n/a
19-09-44	Ofhr.	Knappmann, Klaus	KIA	6	Fw 190A-8	732050	bk 9	Arnhem area	1800	combat	
21-09-44	Ofhr.	Fussi, Otto	KIA	6	Fw 190A-8	172985	bk 11	Nijmegen	1700	P-47	353 FG

21-09-44	Fhr.	Hennemann, Martin	WIA	6	Fw 190A-8	175116 bk 13	9km W Cleve-Groesbeek		P-47	353 FG
21-09-44	Oblt.	Stoll, Werner	WIA	7	Fw 190A-8	175100 bk 6	5km W of Borken-Ruhr	1710	P-47	353 FG
21-09-44	Ofhr.	Patzke, Günther	KIA	9	Bf 109G-6	780912 wh 2	Groesbeek	1700	P-47	353 FG

22 September

Both sides were grounded all day by the weather. Far behind the battle lines, the Luftwaffe was preparing for what now appeared to be a lengthy battle at the frontiers to the homeland. In Berlin, General of the Fighters Adolf Galland readied plans for *der grosse Schlag* (The Great Blow) against the American 8th Air Force. The Jagdwaffe was to be conserved and built up for use against the heavy bombers in one mighty full-strength mission. Gen. Galland hoped to shoot down 400-500 bombers. This would force a pause in the American bomber offensive of sufficient length to permit Galland's great hope, the jet-powered Me 262, to reach the operational units in large numbers. Somewhat to Galland's surprise, the Luftwaffe High Command expressed no opposition to his plans at this time, and he proceeded to build up a reserve force of seven Jagdgeschwader. Göring's contribution to the defensive effort was another exhortation to his troops. Its re-transmission by Luftflotte 3 was read by the Allies, thanks to ULTRA; in it Göring ordered every effort to be made for the aerial defense of the Reich. He empowered local commands to court-martial suspected cowards on the spot, and if convicted, to execute them by firing squad in front of their assembled comrades.

In a separate "request", Göring proposed his solution to the desperate shortage of combat leaders – fighter Staffeln that were not up to operational requirements were to be taken over temporarily by an experienced Staffel leader from another unit of the Geschwader concerned. It is unclear whether this meant that Staffeln should be combined under the one leader, or that leaders should be transferred temporarily from one Staffel to another. Both expedients were to be tried by the Geschwader in the months ahead.

A less draconian edict by the Reichsmarschall was specific to Luftflotte 3. Only a rather quaint English translation has been located. It states that "The PX privileges of all Luftflotte 3 personnel are to be revoked" because of their cowardly behavior during the retreat from France. It is not known whether this directive reached the combat units. If so, their commanding officers probably filed it away and forgot it. It is undoubtedly true that the conduct of the Luftflotte 3 rear echelon during the withdrawal further poisoned relations between the German Army and Air Force. It is also true that Luftflotte 3 had grown as soft and corpulent as its commander, Generalfeldmarschall Sperrle. In France on D-Day there were 400,000 Luftwaffe personnel – to support 891 aircraft! Sperrle himself was relieved in August and sent home on indefinite leave, which lasted until the end of the war. Luftflotte 3 was downgraded in status today. It was renamed Luftwaffenkommando West (LwKdo West) and subordinated to Luftflotte Reich, but its mission remained unchanged – the aerial defense of the western front.

23 September

The weather over England remained bad. The skies over the Dutch drop zones were relatively clear, however, and a large resupply mission was mounted, escorted by 519 8th Fighter Command fighters and forty 9th Air Force P-38s. Luftflotte Reich responded with two combined missions to Arnhem, totaling 135 fighter sorties. The transports were not reached. Most of the German fighter units were dispersed easily by the Americans, who were engaged in serious combat only twice – once each by the First and Second Gruppe of JG 26. The Third Gruppe was given a rest day; the two Focke-Wulf Gruppen flew a total of fifty-two sorties.

Major Borris led the First Gruppe up from Krefeld at 1430, and flew a freie Jagd in the Goch-Wesel area. Just before the patrol ended, Borris spotted a large formation of

P-51s beneath him and reverted to an old Jagdwaffe trick. One flight of his Fw 190s was sent down through the formation as a decoy; the remainder stayed above to fall on the Americans when they dived after the sacrificial flight. The Mustangs, from the 339th Fighter Group, split up and went after both German formations. A general battle followed, in which the Americans claimed 7-1-1 Focke-Wulfs while losing four Mustangs. Borris's force claimed the four P-51s, while losing Uffz. Albrecht Dantschke, Lt. Wilhelm Nink, and Uffz. Werner Schwan, all of whom crashed with their airplanes.

Two hours later it was the turn of the Second Gruppe to patrol the same area. Over Goch the German pilots caught sight of four P-51s far below them. The Mustangs, a flight from the 352nd Fighter Group's 487th Squadron, were flying straight and level, at an altitude of only 1200 meters (4000 feet), on the return leg of their patrol. The rest of the squadron heard only the single radioed word, "Break!" from the flight leader. The four P-51s and pilots then simply disappeared, the victims of a perfect bounce. It was led by Lt. Vogt, who claimed his 41st and 42nd victims. Ofhr. Mayer scored his 21st victory; Fw. Paul, his first. The only German casualty was Fhr. Maximilian Busch, who collided with a P-51 that had just been shot down and crashed to his death.

24 September

A 3rd Jagddivision Gefechtsverband led by the Kommandeur of III/JG 11, Major Späte, attempted to bomb the Nijmegen pontoon bridges at dawn. After takeoff was delayed for an hour by the weather, the pilots still could not find the bridges. The first Jagdkorps II mission, of sixty-six fighters, was recalled. A late afternoon mission of forty-five fighters, all from the three JG 26 Jagdgruppen, was more successful.

For the first week of Operation Market Garden, the 2nd TAF was hardly to be seen in the skies over the Low Countries. All planning for escort and ground support was done by the AEAF staff in England, and for reasons of their own they chose not to employ the RAF's specialist ground support units. The Typhoons of the 2nd TAF were now making tentative forays into the area. At 1741, Lt. Ellenrieder, who was substituting for Lt. Kemethmüller as leader of the 4th Staffel, shot down the Typhoon of the No. 137 Squadron commander over Goch. Four minutes later, Lt. Dietwin Pape of the 9th Staffel shot down a No. 439 Sqd. Typhoon north of Arnhem. The Geschwader suffered no losses.

JG 26 Victory Claims: 23 - 24 September 1944

Date	Rank	Name	Unit	Cl #	Aircraft	Place	Time	Opponent	Conf
23-09-44	Major	Borris	I CO	41	P-51	Wesel (KP)	1709	339 FG	yes
23-09-44	Oblt.	Heckmann	3 CO	70	P-51	Goch (KN)	1650	339 FG	yes
23-09-44	Fw.	Franz	3	1	P-51	Wesel (KP)	1710	339 FG	yes
23-09-44	Uffz.	Schulz	3	3	P-51	Goch (KN)	1651	339 FG	yes
23-09-44	Lt.	Vogt	5 CO	41	P-51	Goch (KN)	1733	352 FG	yes
23-09-44	Lt.	Vogt	5 CO	42	P-51	Goch (KN)	1735	352 FG	yes
23-09-44	Obfw.	Mayer	5	21	P-51	Goch (KN)	1734	352 FG	yes
23-09-44	Fhr.	Busch W.	6		P-51	Goch (KN)	1735	352 FG	no
23-09-44	Fw.	Paul	6	1	P-51	Goch (KN)	1735	352 FG	yes
24-09-44	Lt.	Ellenrieder	4	12	Typhoon	Goch (KN)	1741	137 Sqd	yes
24-09-44	Lt.	Pape	9		Typhoon	N of Arnhem (HM5-7-8)	1740	439 Sqd	unk

25 September

The weather improved sufficiently for Jagdkorps II to order two large missions against the lower Rhine crossings at Oosterbeek and the Nijmegen bridges. One bomb hit the main Nijmegen bridge, which remained in service. The two 2nd TAF Canadian Spitfire wings were now operational from new bases in Belgium, and had been given the task of protecting the Allies' newly-won bridges at Nijmegen and what was left of the British perimeter around Arnhem. The Spitfires swarmed over the German attackers, claiming 14-0-5 fighters. According to the LwKdo West diary, losses from all causes totaled eighteen aircraft. The Germans claimed ten certain and four probable RAF fighters. Over the entire day, the RAF lost eleven Spitfires to fighters.

The Geschwader played a major, and successful, role in the above combats. Many pilots took part in both missions. The First and Second Gruppen each claimed three Spitfires, and each lost one Fw 190 downed and one damaged, but no pilots. The Focke-Wulfs also made strafing attacks on gliders and ground troops. Uffz. Gerhard Corinth of the 4th Staffel claimed an Auster near Nijmegen, but the claim was not confirmed; the Auster, from No. 662 Squadron, managed to survive the attack. Lt. Edmund Fischer of the 6th Staffel shot down an RAF Mustang near Eindhoven; the fighter was from the ADGB's No. 129 Squadron, which was still making daily sweeps of the landing zones.

The Third Gruppe flew a rare ground-attack mission to Nijmegen in the morning, and the more common anti-Jabo sweep in the afternoon, which cost it two Messerschmitts. One was piloted by Uffz. Hermann Ayerle of the 12th Staffel, who was shot down by Spitfires, bailed out, and was badly banged up when he hit the ground. Ayerle was awarded the Wound Badge in Silver for this, his fourth combat injury of the war. Fhj.-Fw. Joachim Zeller was also downed by Spitfires, and survived his bailout with only slight injuries. Ofhr. Bartels claimed a Spitfire on the mission; this was probably an aircraft of No. 416 Squadron.

The diary entries of LwKdo West establish a framework which helps put the efforts of the Geschwader into perspective. Luftflotte Reich ordered Jagdkorps II to delay the takeoff of its fighters whenever enemy aircraft were known to be in the area. This order greatly reduced the number of cheap victories obtained by Allied fighters over known German airfields, but also effected a net reduction in the number of missions that could be flown. The primary mission of the fighters of LwKdo West was clarified by Reichsmarschall Göring's order that its fighter formations were to be employed solely against Allied fighter-bombers – i.e., on anti-Jabo missions. Ground support operations were to be undertaken only in emergencies, or as an alternative mission if no enemy aircraft were encountered.

JG 26 Victory Claims: 25 September 1944

Date	Rank	Name	Unit	Cl #	Aircraft	Place	Time	Opponent	Conf
25-09-44	Obfw.	Freiberger	1	1	Spitfire	Arnhem (HM5-9)	1739	416 or 441 Sqd	yes
25-09-44	Lt.	Söffing	1	21	Spitfire	Arnhem (HM5-9)	1738	416 or 441 Sqd	yes
25-09-44	Uffz.	Corinth	4	2	Auster	Nijmegen (JM5)		662 Sqd	unk
25-09-44	Lt.	Ellenrieder	4	13	Spitfire	Arnhem (HM5-9)	1739	416 or 441 Sqd	unk
25-09-44	Lt.	Vogt	5 CO	43	Spitfire	Arnhem (JM)	1754	416 or 441 Sqd	yes
25-09-44	Ofhr.	Benz	6	3	Spitfire	Arnhem (LM4-9)	1754	416 or 441 Sqd	yes
25-09-44	Lt.	Fischer E.	6	3	Mustang	Arnhem (LM4-9)	1800	129 Sqd	yes
25-09-44	Fhr.	Fischer W.	7	2	Spitfire	Arnhem (HM9-JM3)	1744	416 or 441 Sqd	unk
25-09-44	Ofhr.	Bartels	11		Spitfire	N of Arnhem (HM8-9)	1735	416 Sqd	yes

JG 26 Casualties: 23 - 25 September 1944

Date	Rank	Name	Cas	Unit	Aircraft	WNr	Mkgs	Place	Time	Cause	Allied Unit
23-09-44	Uffz.	Dantschke, Albrecht	KIA	1	Fw 190A-8	731762	wh 7	Rayen-Neuenkirchen	1545	P-51	339 FG
23-09-44	Uffz.	Schwan, Werner	KIA	1	Fw 190A-8	171731	wh 3	Dehaart-5km ESE of Aalten	1545	P-51	339 FG
23-09-44	Lt.	Nink, Wilhelm	KIA	3	Fw 190A-8	175105	yl 7	Aalten	1545	P-51	339 FG
23-09-44	Fhr.	Busch, Maximilian	KIA	6	Fw 190A-8	171576	bk 12	30km NNW of Wesel	1700	P-51	352 FG
25-09-44	Fhj.-Fw.	Zeller, Joachim	WIA	III St	Bf 109G-6	780851	bk 22	nr Arnhem	1740	Spitfire	
25-09-44	Uffz.	Ayerle, Hermann	WIA	12	Bf 109G-6	165170	bl 9	N of Deelen a/f	1745	Spitfire	

26 September

The 3rd Jagddivision and Jagdkorps II continued their ineffective efforts to attack the air landing zones. JG 26 flew no missions, and the three Gruppen were apparently granted a rest day.

27 September

The fighters of the 3rd Jagddivision and Jagdkorps II fought vainly all day to penetrate the Spitfire screen to the east of the new Allied defense line across southern Holland. Gefechtsverband Späte attempted to bomb the tiny area still held by the British 1st Airborne Division north of the Rhine, but failed. The Jagdkorps II effort totaled 187 sorties in two combined Jabojagd missions. The three JG 26 Gruppen flew the first mission in full strength. Uffz. Erich Burmeister recalls that the First Gruppe formation split up – "turned back", in his words – at the first sight of Spitfires. Burmeister himself scored the only victory for the Gruppe. A Spitfire chasing a Focke-Wulf emerged from a cloud right in front of him, and he hit it with a quick burst of fire before the Spitfire's wingman in turn hit Burmeister, who bailed out north of Kleve. The Spitfires, probably from No. 411 Squadron, shot down and killed Fw. Alois Becker, Uffz. Gerhard Corinth, and Gefr. Lothar Wentzel. Burmeister damaged his target, but it regained its base.

The Second Gruppe encountered a large number of Spitfires between Arnhem and Nijmegen. The Focke-Wulf pilots were credited with downing three of them, but the Allied units cannot be identified. No. 412 Squadron almost certainly downed three Second Gruppe aircraft, killing Uffz. Valentin Baier, Fhr. Werner Fischer, and Flg. Friedrich Sziedat.

The morning mission of the Third Gruppe was a significant event in the career of Uffz. Georg Genth, who was chosen to fly his first combat mission as wingman to his Staffelkapitän, Oblt. Karl-Hermann Schrader. The twenty Bf 109s assembled without incident, and climbed to 3000 meters (10,000 feet) without seeing the enemy. After twenty minutes, someone called out Indianer. A formation of Spitfires, equal in number to the Messerschmitts, was flying within a cloud layer only a hundred meters (300 feet) above them. Genth recalls that radio discipline broke down instantly, and his earphones were filled with wild, almost hysterical yelling. Genth had been playing the role of the wingman to the hilt, weaving constantly to keep Schrader's tail clear. Suddenly, without warning, Schrader pulled up into the cloud layer in a left bank so tight that Genth could not follow. Genth pulled up through the cloud, saw nothing, and dived back out – directly behind a lone Spitfire, only 50 meters (55 yards) in front. Genth panicked momentarily and zoomed back up into the cloud, but came back out to find the Spitfire in the same position. He drew closer and walked a burst of fire from the Spitfire's rear fuselage into its engine. The Unteroffizier then had another anxiety attack, and pulled back on the stick so sharply that he sheared the restraining pins on his landing gear, which dropped. He stayed in the clouds a few minutes, dived to 300 meters (1000 feet), and set course for Bönninghardt. Schrader formed up on him during the short trip back, and informed Genth in pantomime that his gear was down. After landing, Genth was congratulated by Ofhr. Lorberg, who had seen the Spitfire pilot bail out. Lorberg, who was flying as Schrader's No. 3, had stayed behind Genth after Schrader had disappeared, and witnessed his victory, which was never confirmed, although it closely matches the circumstances of a No. 412 Squadron loss. The Gruppe had suffered no losses on this mission, and scored a second victory when Obfw. Heinrich Humburg downed a lone No. 168 Sqd. TacR Mustang.

Georg Genth's high expectations after Emil Lang had welcomed him to the front in late August had quickly been dashed by the attitudes he found in his own Gruppe. He sought out the experienced pilots to get their advice on combat tactics, but none of the officers were willing to tell him anything beyond, "Stick to your Rottenführer at all costs! If you lose him, you are as good as dead!" It was now perfectly clear to Genth that he was expected to sacrifice himself so that his war-weary officers could survive the war. That was not why he had volunteered to become a fighter pilot. He decided to operate independently in combat from then on. He would keep his leader in sight, but maneuver to protect himself while seeking to obtain firing position on enemy aircraft. He practiced skidding maneuvers, which he felt would keep pursuing fighters from drawing the proper lead. Genth befriended an experienced element leader, Uffz. Willibald Malm, who offered to select him as a wingman whenever possible. Malm had the best long-distance vision in the Gruppe, and survived the war without injury. The pair formed a good team – Malm located the enemy, while Genth provided gunnery and tactics. Genth believes today that it was only his willingness to abandon the principles he was taught in training that allowed him to survive eighteen air battles in 1944 and 1945.

The Third Gruppe had by now replaced its Bf 109G-6 Beulen with a new model of the Messerschmitt fighter, the Bf 109G-14, which had a new 1800 horsepower DB 605ASM engine with methanol-water injection as standard equipment, giving it a greater maximum speed than the G-6 at all altitudes – a speed of 680 km/h (408 mph) is quoted at its critical altitude of 7500 meters (24,600 feet). It also featured enlarged main wheels and an extended tail wheel leg, for better ground handling and vision; a clear-vision canopy; and the FuG 16ZY direction-finding radio. These amenities all improved the aircraft's survivability under the poor weather conditions prevalent during the north European autumn and winter, and were greatly appreciated by the pilots. Later, a few Bf 109G-10s were taken on charge. This model had yet another engine, the DB 605DCM, which had an enlarged supercharger, and was intended to be a high-altitude fighter. It also had methanol-water as standard equipment. The G-10 had a service ceiling of 12,500 meters (41,000 feet), and was the fastest Bf 109G of all, with a maximum speed of about 685 km/h (425 mph). Both the G-14 and the G-10 had an armament of one 20 mm cannon and two 13 mm machine guns, all in the nose. This was an effective armament against fighters, which were now the most common aerial targets for the Gruppe.

The FuG 16ZY was standard equipment in all aircraft reaching the Geschwader from the fall of 1944. This remarkably compact device incorporated a receiver, a transmitter, and a direction finding loop, and was intended to aid ground-controlled interceptions. Its transmissions provided the ground control organization with both the range and bearing of the aircraft making them. Its two frequencies also facilitated communications among members of a formation. By the time the FuG 16ZY arrived at the front, bomber interceptions in strength were almost a thing of the past. The FuG 16ZY evolved into a navigational aid, used primarily to provide homing information to lost German pilots. It was to save many lives during the last winter of the war.

Today the Third Gruppe welcomed the arrival of Hptm. Walter Krupinski, Klaus Mietusch's successor as Gruppenkommandeur. Krupinski was a celebrated Eastern fighter who had been awarded the Oak Leaves for his 177 victories, mostly gained in the Soviet Union. He was only 23 years old, and became very popular with the young NCO pilots. Krupinski had been burned on his hands and face while leading II/JG 11 on the Invasionsfront. He was just about ready to return to this unit when he got a call in the hospital from General Galland offering him the new posting. Galland called it a "special honor", since it was Galland's old command, the Gruppe in which he had first gained fame. Krupinski led his first mission this afternoon, and claimed the destruction of a Spitfire, although the victory was apparently never filed in Berlin.

It soon became apparent that Krupinski held the reins of command very loosely. He made no changes in his four Staffeln, but left things to run as they had under Mietusch – and by all the existing evidence this was very chaotically indeed. It is difficult to speak badly of Walter Krupinski, who later had a very successful career in the Bundeswehr, retiring as a Generalleutnant, and who remains a highly regarded figure among the fraternity of German fighter pilots. Krupinski refuses to comment on his six months in JG 26, preferring to dwell on his service in JG 52 on the Eastern Front, and later in JV 44, General Galland's jet unit. It is hard to escape the conclusion that when he arrived at JG 26, Krupinski was as weary of the war as were the pilots in his new command. The decline of the Third Gruppe continued unabated.

The two Focke-Wulf Gruppen achieved little of note on the afternoon mission. Uffz. Erich Klein, Ottomar Kruse's last wingman, was shot down and killed by the Spitfires of No. 412 Squadron, which then pursued the Second Gruppe back to Kirchhellen. Ofhr. Mayer was able to shoot one of the Spitfires down over the airfield. Mayer's is the last Geschwader victory claim known to have been confirmed by the RLM. The lists kept by the First and Second Gruppen and the recently-discovered RLM claims microfilms imply strongly that no later claims had been processed fully by the end of the war. The microfilmed RLM ledger ends on 31 October, 1944. October claims with a good chance of confirmation were logged as "i.O."

JG 26 Victory Claims: 27 September 1944

Date	Rank	Name	Unit	Cl #	Aircraft	Place	Time	Opponent	Conf
27-09-44	Uffz.	Burmeister	4	1	Spitfire	Nijmegen (JN)	1025	411 Sqd	yes
27-09-44	Lt.	Vogt	5 CO	44	Spitfire	Nijmegen (JM)	1041		yes
27-09-44	Obfw.	Mayer	5	22	Spitfire	Kirchhellen (KO6)	1722	412 Sqd	yes
27-09-44	Ofhr.	Benz	6	4	Spitfire	Nijmegen (JM1-3)	1040		yes
27-09-44	Lt.	Fischer E.	6	4	Spitfire	Nijmegen (JM1-2)	1035		yes
27-09-44	Hptm.	Krupinski	III CO	192	Spitfire	unknown	1821		unk
27-09-44	Obfw.	Humburg	9		Mustang	Nijmegen (JM4-5)	1040	168 Sqd	unk
27-09-44	Uffz.	Genth	12	1	Spitfire	Nijmegen (JM6)	1030	412 Sqd	unk

JG 26 Casualties: 27 September 1944

Date	Rank	Name	Cas	Unit	Aircraft	WNr	Mkgs	Place	Time	Cause	Allied Unit
27-09-44	Fw.	Becker, Alois	KIA	1	Fw 190A-8	175127	wh 13	W Emmerich-Spijk		Spitfire	411 Sqd
27-09-44	Uffz.	Burmeister, Erich	WIA	4	Fw 190A-8	680571	bl 3	N of Kleve		Spitfire	411 Sqd
27-09-44	Uffz.	Corinth, Gerhard	KIA	4	Fw 190A-8	175106	bl 2	Rheden-W of Arnhem		Spitfire	411 Sqd
27-09-44	Gefr.	Wentzel, Lothar	KIA	4	Fw 190A-8	173807	bl 9	S of Giesbeek		Spitfire	411 Sqd
27-09-44	Flg.	Sziedat, Friedrich	KIA	5	Fw 190A-8	731765	wh 1	nr Wesel-NW of Emmerich		Spitfire	412 Sqd
27-09-44	Fhr.	Fischer, Werner	KIA	7	Fw 190A-8	731773	br 14	E of Moers		Spitfire	412 Sqd
27-09-44	Uffz.	Baier, Valentin	KIA	8	Fw 190A-8	173014	bl 3	nr Arnhem	1100	Spitfire	412 Sqd
27-09-44	Uffz.	Klein, Erich	KIA	8	Fw 190A-8	680831	bl 7	S of Nijmegen	1750	Spitfire	412 Sqd

29 September

Bad weather stopped operations until the afternoon. Jagdkorps II had a request from the Army to attack specific artillery batteries that were hindering operations behind the new defensive lines in The Netherlands, but only fifty-two fighters took part in the afternoon mission, which was totally ineffective.

30 September

The weather closed in once more, and Jagdkorps II released all of its fighters for a day of maintenance. The operational zone of the Geschwader now ran along the newly-established front line up the lower Maas and Waal Rivers in The Netherlands, and then south along the Dutch-German border. The Jagdwaffe would never again command the air over the battle lines. The German fighter pilots preferred to fight their battles from ambush, seeking out opportunities to pick off isolated Allied aircraft or unwary formations; combat with enemy formations of equal size was frequently avoided. However, when a straight-up engagement was inevitable, the experienced formation leaders of the First and Second Gruppen could often bring the battle to a successful conclusion.

The headquarters of the 3rd Jagddivision left for eastern Germany, giving up all its day fighters and becoming a night fighter command organization. Jagdkorps II did not gain any units from this move, and a week later lost JG 27 to RLV duties with Jagdkorps I. The northern half of the western front would for a time be manned by only two Jagdgeschwader, JG 26 and JG 2.

Geschwader personnel moves during September included the arrival of Uffz. Bruno Krusen and Uffz. Willi Hildebrandt from III/JG 54; Krusen joined the Second Gruppe, and Hildebrandt, who had left the Ergänzungsgruppe only six weeks previously, was assigned to the First. Also, Oblt. Horst Siemsen transferred from the 7th Staffel to the staff of the General der Jagdflieger; and Lt. Gottfried Dietze transferred from the 4th Staffel in the First Gruppe to the 7th Staffel in the Second.

New pilots assigned to the Geschwader during September after completing flight training included: Uffz. Karl Strauss - Geschwader Stab; Uffz. Erich-Joachim Schombel - First Gruppe; Uffz. Johannes Holzleitner, Obfw. Karl-Heinz Knobeloch, Uffz. Heinz Salomon, Ofhr. Alfred Scharf, Flg. Friedrich Sziedat - Second Gruppe; Ofhr. Karl-Manfred Hark - Third Gruppe.

Judged solely by the victory/loss ratio, September was a very successful month for the Geschwader. This ratio was well over two to one, based on a victory total of seventy-three and a loss total of thirty-one (twenty-seven pilots killed in combat, one killed in an accident, and three taken prisoner). However the full effect of the loss of men such as Emil Lang and Klaus Mietusch does not show up on the tally sheet.

2 October

Whenever permitted by the weather, the Geschwader continued its inconclusive but deadly struggle along the Dutch border with the Spitfires of the 2nd TAF. Today the three Gruppen flew two missions, both Jabojagden to the Nijmegen-Arnhem area. Forty-two fighters flew on the first mission, and thirty-five took part in the second. At noon the Second Gruppe sprang a successful trap on No. 401 Sqd. (RCAF). When a section of Spitfires bounced a seemingly unwary flight of Fw 190s north of Nijmegen, the rest of the Gruppe fell on them from above. Spitfires were claimed by Oblt. Glunz, Lt. Hofmann, and Ofhr. Benz; two in fact were lost. Just south of this battle, the First Gruppe encountered a larger force of Spitfires, as many as fifty; victories were claimed by Lt. Günther and Ogfr. Leder, but the RAF unit involved has not been identified, and sustained no losses. The Third Gruppe did not contact the enemy on this mission, and all three Gruppen failed to make contact on the second mission. The day's only casualty was Uffz. Erich Ahrens of the 7th Staffel, who struck his head on his gunsight during a forced landing necessitated by engine failure.

JG 26 Victory Claims: 2 October 1944

Date	Rank	Name	Unit	Cl #	Aircraft	Place	Time	Opponent	Conf
02-10-44	Ogfr.	Leder Jos.	1	1	Spitfire	Arnhem (HM8)	1205		unk
02-10-44	Lt.	Günther	2	7	Spitfire	Nijmegen (JM2-3)	1218		unk
02-10-44	Lt.	Glunz	6 CO	67	Spitfire	S of Nijmegen (JM8-9)	1215	401 Sqd	i.O.
02-10-44	Ofhr.	Benz	6	5	Spitfire	Nijmegen (JM7-8)	1216	401 Sqd	i.O.
02-10-44	Lt.	Hofmann W.	8 CO	40	Spitfire	Cleve-Nijmegen	1210	401 Sqd	i.O.

4 October

The new defensive line in The Netherlands had stabilized, and the Geschwader returned to its mission of protecting the West Wall laborers west of Aachen. The First and Third Gruppen flew a single mid-afternoon mission. The First Gruppe encountered some 48th Fighter Group P-47s near Mönchen-Gladbach, and Lt. Söffing shot one of them down. Uffz. Erich Burmeister was chased all the way to Emmerich by four Thunderbolts. His aircraft was finally hit, and he had to bail out with minor wounds. He was carried as missing for eight days until he finally showed up at Krefeld. As this was Burmeister's second late return in two months, he was court-martialed for cowardice before the enemy. His punishment was extremely mild –

Uffz. Stumpf, Lt. Sy, Lt. Andel, Uffz. Heinz Meiss (KIA 13 Mar 45), and Uffz. Ahrens kill some time in front of the 7th Staffel command post while awaiting a mission assignment – Stevede-Coesfeld, 2 October. *(Stumpf)*

banishment to a ferry unit. Burmeister knew the commander of this unit from his training days, and with the officer's help eventually got back to the front, as a member of JG 51.

The First Gruppe suffered a fatality in a non-operational accident. Uffz. Georg Dieterlen landed too fast after a test flight, overturned, and crushed his skull. He died the next day in the hospital.

5 October

The principal source for the history of any military unit should be that unit's war diaries. In JG 26 these diaries were maintained by the Gruppen. Nearly all of them were destroyed at the end of the war, on orders from above. The only JG 26 unit diaries which have been located belonged to the First Gruppe, and cover Gruppe operations from 5 October 1944 to 7 May 1945. Appropriately enough, the first entry in the First Gruppe diary notes that all operations today were canceled because of bad weather.

6 October

Jagdkorps II fighters flew 135 sorties to the new critical area, the German defenses around Eindhoven. In the afternoon JG 26 and JG 27 were ordered to fly a combined freie Jagd to the Eindhoven area, followed by a patrol of the fortifications under construction west of Aachen. Major Borris was to lead the combined formation; his deputy was to be Oblt. Heckmann. Of the twenty-one First Gruppe Fw 190s which took off from Krefeld, thirteen aborted, including those piloted by Borris and Heckmann. Leadership of the unit thus passed to Lt. Kiefner. His nine Fw 190s contacted ten Spitfires south of Nijmegen, but the resulting combat was inconclusive. Shortly after 1500 the Second Gruppe fought a battle between Eindhoven and Tilburg with fighters it identified as Mustangs. Fw. Helmut Taubert was hit, and crashed in his airplane; Ofhr. Robert Heinrichs and Gefr. Hans-Georg Walter each claimed a Mustang. The Allied fighter unit has not been identified. There were no American P-51s in the area, and the RAF Mustang III squadrons had all returned to England, where they were to serve as long-range escorts for Bomber Command. The Allied fighters may have been 2nd TAF Tempests; the type had just returned to the Continent after a successful stint in southern England as V-1 destroyers. No. 56 Sqd. Tempests did, in fact, claim two Fw 190s in this area at 1530, while sustaining no losses.

JG 26 Casualties: 2 - 6 October 1944

Date	Rank	Name	Cas	Unit	Aircraft	WNr	Mkgs	Place	Time	Cause	Allied Unit
02-10-44	Uffz.	Ahrens, Erich	WIFA	7	Fw 190A-8	731751	br 12	S of Borken		engine	n/a
04-10-44	Uffz.	Burmeister, Erich	WIA	4	Fw 190A-8	680571	bl 3	S of Emmerich		P-47	48 FG
04-10-44	Uffz.	Dieterlen, Georg	KIFA	4	Fw 190A-8	173814	bl 8	Krefeld		landing	non-op
06-10-44	Fw.	Taubert, Helmut	KIA	8	Fw 190A-9	750151	bl 7	NE of Groesbeek	1505	Mustang	

7 October

Jagdkorps II ordered its fighters to patrol the new defensive lines in The Netherlands, aiding the army by attacking fighter-bombers and artillery spotters. The morning weather was too poor for flying, but improved sufficiently in the afternoon for the Geschwader to fly a single joint mission to Arnhem and Nijmegen. Nineteen First Gruppe Fw 190s took off at 1555 under Lt. Heckmann. Twelve were still with him at 1630, when a battle was fought between Kleve and Arnhem with twenty Spitfires. Ofhr. Siegfried Heindtke failed to return; his body was found on the 15th. Fw. Paul Jentzsch was shot down by a Spitfire and crashed in his aircraft. A victory claim was filed in Jentzsch's behalf; owing to the miserable autumn weather, this was the last victory claim by the First Gruppe until 26 November. The Third Gruppe took part in this mission, but reported neither victories nor losses. The Second Gruppe fought with both Spitfires and P-47s, and lost Ofhr. Siegfried Hamel and Obfw. Wilhelm Müller. Uffz. Max Chemnitzer and Fw. Arthur Paul both overturned while landing on the soft soil of Kirchhellen, and were injured. Ofhr. Wilhelm Mayer claimed two Spitfires, his claims were considered suitable for confirmation. Fw. Werner Verhöven claimed one, which was not confirmed.

The Spitfires involved in this battle were from No. 442 Squadron, which claimed 3-0-2 Fw 190s and suffered no losses. The P-47s were probably from the 365th Fighter Group's 388th Squadron, which lost three aircraft when bounced by a small number of German fighters, and then claimed 0-2-3 Fw 190s in the subsequent dogfights. These two squadrons were the only Allied units known to be in the Nijmegen-Kleve area at this time; the identification of all three Second Gruppe victims as Spitfires instead of Thunderbolts is unusual, but not unprecedented.

JG 26 Victory Claims: 4 - 7 October 1944

Date	Rank	Name	Unit	Cl #	Aircraft	Place	Time	Opponent	Conf
04-10-44	Lt.	Söffing	1	22	P-47	Mönchen-Gladbach (LO1)	1615	48 FG	i.O.
06-10-44	Ofhr.	Heinrichs	5	1	P-51	Eindhoven (LM)	1508		i.O.
06-10-44	Gefr.	Walter	5	1	P-51	Eindhoven (LM)	1507		i.O.
07-10-44	Fw.	Jentzsch	4	1	Spitfire	E of Tilburg (KN)	1630		i.O.
07-10-44	Obfw.	Mayer	5	23	Spitfire	Nijmegen (JM2-5)	1630	442 Sqd	i.O.
07-10-44	Obfw.	Mayer	5	24	Spitfire	Nijmegen (JM2-5)	1632	442 Sqd	i.O.
07-10-44	Fw.	Verhöven	6	3	Spitfire	Nijmegen (JM5-6)	1630	442 Sqd	no

JG 26 Casualties: 7 October 1944

Date	Rank	Name	Cas	Unit	Aircraft	WNr	Mkgs	Place	Time	Cause	Allied Unit
07-10-44	Ofhr.	Heindtke, Siegfried	KIA	2	Fw 190A-8	173806	bk 7	nr Arnhem	1640	Spitfire	442 Sqd
07-10-44	Fw.	Jentzsch, Paul	KIA	4	Fw 190A-8	171517	bl 2	SE of Kleve	1640	Spitfire	442 Sqd
07-10-44	Lt.	Hamel, Gerhard	KIA	6	Fw 190A-8	730963	bk 21	Nijmegen-S of Silvolde	1634	Spitfire	442 Sqd
07-10-44	Obfw.	Müller, Wilhelm	KIA	6	Fw 190A-8	171649	bk 14	Nijmegen	1640	Spitfire	442 Sqd
07-10-44	Fw.	Paul, Arthur	WIA	6	Fw 190A-8	732023	bk 1	Stevede		landing	n/a
07-10-44	Fw.	Chemnitzer, Max	WIFA	7	Fw 190A-8	173824	wh 10	Kirchhellen a/f		landing	n/a

Fw. Heinz Gomann of the Second Gruppe looks forward to better times – Stevede, October. *(Stumpf)*

Jagdkorps II told its fighter units to hold themselves ready for an RLV mission. The Geschwader was ordered to form a Gefechtsverband over Münster with two other Jagdgeschwader, but all combat missions were then canceled because of the weather.

The OKW communiqué commended JG 26 for its 300th air victory since D-Day, and its 2500th of the war.

Hptm. Georg-Peter Eder received orders to report to Kommando Nowotny, the first operational Me 262 fighter unit. He was replaced as Second Gruppe Kommandeur by Major Anton "Toni" Hackl. Hackl was a 30-year-old professional officer with a reputation as an aggressive, intelligent, and most important, lucky, pilot and combat commander. He had served on all fronts and arrived at JG 26 credited with 165 victories. He had been awarded the Swords to his Knight's Cross on 13 July 1944, eleven days after Obstlt. Priller's receipt of the same decoration. Hackl was one of only four recipients of this high award to serve in JG 26; the other two were Adolf Galland and Joachim Müncheberg. His leadership style was similar to that of Emil Lang – performance in combat was all that mattered; traditional military courtesies were enforced only to the extent demanded by higher commands. He was just the right commander for the aggressive pilots of the Second Gruppe, which continued to lead the Geschwader in victory claims and victory/loss ratio.

Each of the three Gruppen had by now developed its own distinct personality, a reflection in all cases of that of its most influential Kommandeure. Major Karl Borris, the long-time leader of I/JG 26, was a dour, superstitious, outwardly humorless man – a "typical East Prussian", in the opinion of his pilots. His rigid enforcement of all regulations, including those which restricted the employment of his forces, resulted in lower serviceability rates and fewer missions flown than the Second Gruppe. Borris was considered an excellent combat pilot and air leader, owing in part to what was described by one of his pilots, an officer from the upper class, as "peasant cunning". In combat, the Gruppe had no major failures, but few spectacular successes.

The Third Gruppe in the hands of Major Mietusch had been a sharp, but very brittle, weapon. By October 1944 it had very little edge left. It had never regained its numerical strength in pilots after its casualties of June, 1944. A more serious problem than mere numbers, however, was its shortage of aggressive, successful formation leaders. This lack greatly reduced its combat efficiency. Combat leadership in the Gruppe fell by default to the most experienced enlisted pilots, who were called "old hares" for the erratic, jerky courses traced by their aircraft while in the combat zone. Some of these survivors, such as Obfw. Hermann Guhl and Obfw. Karl Laub, were excellent pilots; Guhl had been a test pilot. These two men had a reputation for caution, and were popular among the Nachwuchs for the concern that they showed for the survival of all of the pilots in their formations.

"Dicke Autos über dem Platz!" (Heavy bombers over the field!) From left: Lt. Andel, Lt. Sy, Uffz. Stumpf, Uffz. Leopold Speer (KIA 1 Jan 45) – Stevede-Coesfeld, October. *(Stumpf via Terbeck)*

9 October

Jagdkorps II informed JG 2, JG 26, and JG 27 of assembly points, radio callsigns, and control arrangements for a joint RLV mission. Flying was then canceled.

Dr. Walter Messerklinger, a flight surgeon on the Geschwader Stab, was taken prisoner by the Allies. Further details are unknown.

11 October

Jagdkorps II still expected that its three northernmost Jagdgeschwader would fly an RLV mission, but LwKdo Reich never issued the orders. A few missions were flown by small formations; Lt. Glunz's 6th Staffel Schwarm contacted four P-51s while on a hunt for fighter-bombers and artillery spotters, but no combat ensued. A sortie by Lt. Dietze of the 7th Staffel ended in a belly-landing on Köln-Butzweilerhof when his engine caught on fire. Uffz. Karl Hött of the 6th Staffel flew area familiarization flights as the last step in his return to duty after recovering from injuries.

12 October

The 8th Air Force was restricted to targets in northwestern Germany by a large weather front covering the rest of the country. Twelve bomber wings were sent to attack four airfields and the Bremen Focke-Wulf plant. It was known from ULTRA that Luftflotte Reich had been planning to use the tactical fighters on Germany's western border on an RLV mission; today's weather conditions were such that these fighters would be the only possible opposition. The American mission planners believed that a small escort force of eleven fighter groups would be sufficient. These would be more than enough.

At 0900 heavy bomber formations were reported over the Zuider Zee. Jagdkorps II was told that its fighters would make up the German defense. Of its three northern Jagdgeschwader, only JG 26 was able to form up; its fifty-seven fighters would be up against 552 bombers and 514 P-47s and P-51s. The First Gruppe war diary reports that by 1020 twenty-two of the unit's pilots were strapped in their Fw 190s' cockpits in their dispersals. At 1028 they took off, and flew toward the northeast, climbing to 6700 meters (22,000 feet). Obstlt. Priller led the formation, which was to join the Second and Third Gruppen over Dümmer Lake. The Allied radio intercept operators listened in fascination as Priller cursed his pilots by name, trying to get them into formation. The units gradually drifted apart; the Second and Third Gruppen pulled ahead of Priller and the First. Over Hannover the First Gruppe was attacked from above by a large force of P-47s and P-51s, and the German fighters were dispersed. After combats ranging down to ground level, the Focke-Wulfs landed where they could. The survivors reported back to Krefeld from four different fields. Three Unteroffizier pilots, Willi Hildebrandt, Erich Kohler, and Erich-Joachim Schombel were never heard from again, and Schombel's body was not found until the following February. The pilots were the victims of Thunderbolts from the 56th and 78th Fighter Groups. No victory claims were filed by the Gruppe. That evening it had twelve Fw 190s operational out of the thirty assigned to the unit.

Obstlt. Priller shot down an isolated P-51 south of Wunstorf for his 101st (and last) victory. Priller's victim was the 357th Fighter Group's Capt. H. T. Pascoe, who was taken prisoner. The identification of Priller's victim is verified by Pascoe's USAAF missing aircrew report, which was compiled after the war and contains a German interrogation document naming Priller as the victor. It was an easy match for the German interrogators to make, because Priller was the only German pilot to claim a victory over Germany. That evening Priller's Stab reported a combat strength of two Fw 190s.

After losing the rest of the Geschwader formation, the Second Gruppe succeeded in locating the bomber stream and an apparently unescorted B-17 combat box. They were just forming up to attack it when they were hit by 364th Fighter Group P-51s. The green German pilots could do nothing but dive away, and were easy prey for the experienced Americans, who shot down five of the Focke-Wulfs. Lt. Edmund Fischer, Ofhr. Robert Heinrichs, Fhr. Martin Hennemann and Uffz. Erhard Meinel died in their aircraft; Ofhr. Werner Schramm bailed out with minor burns. Four of the Mustangs did not return to England. Two were the victims of German Flak, and the other two disappeared without a trace, probably colliding in the clouds. Lt. Glunz stalked the bombers, but was never able to make an attack. He returned to Kirchhellen after 134 minutes in the air. The Gruppe pilots claimed no victories. Their evening report listed fourteen fighters operational out of thirty-nine on strength.

The end result of the Third Gruppe mission was the same. They flew the farthest, to Bremervörde west of Hamburg, before running afoul of the ubiquitous Mustangs and losing five Messerschmitts. Two pilots, Ofhr. Hans-Theobald Bühring and Ogfr. Horst Grimm, were killed. The pilots of two fighters apparently parachuted without injury; the fifth Bf 109 was piloted by Oblt. Jan Schild, who recalls losing his controls after being struck by a single Mustang at an altitude of 11,000 meters [35,000 feet]. He bailed out with severe burns, regained consciousness four days later, and remained in the hospital for two months before returning to the Third Gruppe as a non-flying Staffel leader. No Third Gruppe victories are known. That night eight of its Bf 109s remained operational out of sixteen on strength.

The most noteworthy performance by an American fighter pilot on 12 October was that of Lt. Charles Yeager of the 357th Fighter Group. Yeager had been given the air command of his entire forty-nine plane group formation that day, despite his very junior rank. Although his current victory total was only 1.5, his keen eyesight and obvious tactical sense had attracted favorable attention within the leadership of the 357th. After Yeager had positioned two squadrons of his group on the flanks of the bombers, which had reached Bremen without incident, he led his own squadron, the 363rd, one hundred miles ahead of the stream. He spotted specks fifty miles in the distance, at the P-51s' altitude of 28,000 feet. The Mustang squadron closed rapidly on the bogies. Yeager identified them as twenty-two Bf 109s, circling while awaiting the arrival of the bombers. Yeager, in the lead, closed to within 900 meters (1000 yards) of the last two Messerschmitts, which were lagging behind the formation. Just as he reached firing range, both German pilots half-rolled their planes and jumped out, one behind the other. Both Americans and Germans now dropped their tanks, and a wild melee began. Yeager's encounter report reads:

> "I closed up to the last Jerry and opened fire from 600 yards [550 meters], using the K-14 sight. I observed strikes all over the ship, particularly heavy in the cockpit. He skidded off to the left and was smoking and streaming coolant and went into a slow diving turn to the left. I was closing up on another Me 109, so I did not follow him down. Lt. Stern, flying in Blue Flight, reports this e/a on fire as it passed him and went into a spin. I closed up on the next Me 109 to 100 yards [90 meters], skidded to the right and took a deflection shot of about 10 degrees. I gave it about a three-second burst and the whole fuselage split open and blew up after we passed. Another Me 109 to the right had cut his throttle and was trying to get behind me. I broke to the right and quickly rolled to the left onto his tail. He started pulling it in and I was pulling 6 G's. I got a lead from around 300 yards [275 meters] and gave him a short burst. There were hits on his wings and tail section. He snapped to the right three times and bailed out when he quit snapping at around 18,000 feet [15,000 meters]. I did not black out during this engagement due to the efficiency of the G-suit. Even though I was skidding, I hit the second Me 109 by keeping the bead and range on the e/a. In my estimation the K-14 sight is the biggest improvement in fighter combat equipment up to this date."

Yeager was credited with the two pilots who bailed out before the attack, giving him five victories and the coveted status of ace-in-a-day. This was but the first spectacular accomplishment in Chuck Yeager's long and distinguished aviation career. His report gives full credit to two new pieces of equipment that had further increased the qualitative superiority of the American escort force – the K-14 gyroscopic gunsight and the pressurized G-suit.

The other pilots of Yeager's flight claimed three more 109s. The other two squadrons of his group were shut out, since Yeager didn't vector them to the combat. His rejoinder back in England was, "There just weren't enough... to go around". He had attacked the Third Gruppe formation. Lt. Yeager's last victim, the only one to exhibit a modicum of flying skill, was probably Oblt. Schild.

The Third Gruppe was not finished flying for the day. Hptm. Krupinski flew a mission to the battle front in late afternoon, and claimed the destruction of a Mustang; Uffz. Walter Tepperis was injured while force-landing his Bf 109G-14 after its engine failed on a transfer flight.

If the use of JG 26 on a bomber intercept mission had been meant as a dry run for General Galland's grosse Schlag, it had failed the test. The Allied intelligence report summarized its efforts as follows: "The tactical fighters proved themselves incapable of making an effective assembly and inexperienced in attacking escorted formations. This may be classed as one of the GAF's [German Air Force's] poorer shows."

JG 26 Casualties: 12 October 1944

Date	Rank	Name	Cas	Unit	Aircraft	WNr	Mkgs	Place	Time	Cause	Allied Unit
12-10-44	Uffz.	Hildebrandt, Willi	KIA	2	Fw 190A-8	690142	bk 4	Osnabrück-Hannover	1200	P-47	56 or 78 FG
12-10-44	Uffz.	Schombel, Erich-Joachim	KIA	2	Fw 190A-8	171541	bk 10	Osnabrück-Hannover	1200	P-47	56 or 78 FG
12-10-44	Uffz.	Kohler, Erich	KIA	3	Fw 190A-8	732041	yl 8	E of Hannover	1200	P-47	56 or 78 FG
12-10-44	Ofhr.	Heinrichs, Robert	KIA	5	Fw 190A-9	750125	wh 2	3km SW of Bremervörde	1130	P-51	364 FG
12-10-44	Lt.	Fischer, Edmund	KIA	6	Fw 190A-8	171642	bk 10	Osnabrück-Hannover	1100	P-51	364 FG
12-10-44	Fhr.	Hennemann, Martin	KIA	6	Fw 190A-8	171580	bk 8	Osnabrück-Hannover	1100	P-51	364 FG
12-10-44	Uffz.	Meinel, Erhard	KIA	7	Fw 190A-8	730965	bl 12	W of - Wunstorf	1200	P-51	364 FG

Uffz. Erich Ahrens (POW 1 Jan 45), Uffz. Leopold Speer (KIA 1 Jan 45), Lt. Peter "Pit" Andel, Lt. Siegfried Sy, Lt. Gottfried Dietze, and Uffz. Walter Stumpf return from the 7th Staffel dispersal – Stevede-Coesfeld, October. *(Sundermann)*

12-10-44	Ofhr.	Schramm, Werner	WIA	8	Fw 190A-8	173028 bl 14	near Stade	1227	P-51	364 FG
12-10-44	Ogfr.	Grimm, Horst	KIA	9	Bf 109G-14	461979 wh 1	Bremervörde-Hipstedt	1220	P-51	357 FG
12-10-44	Uffz.	Tepperis, Walter	WIFA	11	Bf 109G-14	462676 yl 1	Merfelder Bruch a/f	1730	engine	non-op
12-10-44	Ofhr.	Bühring, Hans	KIA	12	Bf 109G-14	461538 bl 8	Bremervörde	1215	P-51	357 FG
12-10-44	Oblt.	Schild, Heinrich	WIA	12	Bf 109G-14	781300 wh 6	E of Bremervörde	1230	P-51	357 FG

13 October

The American First Army was closing in on Aachen, the first German city to come under attack by the Allies. Jagdkorps II ordered missions against fighter-bombers and artillery spotters around the new critical point, weather permitting. The First Gruppe was bogged in. The 11th and 12th Staffeln were able to get away from Bönninghardt, but only to transfer to Gross-Reken, which was a war-service field that had seen little service, and was not yet covered in ruts and mud.

Eighteen Second Gruppe Focke-Wulfs were able to fly a successful freie Jagd to Aachen. The Gruppe's major combat was with Lightnings and Thunderbolts from the 474th and 368th Fighter Groups. Uffz. Benno Prantke of the 7th Staffel was shot down and killed by a Thunderbolt. P-47s were downed by Uffz. A. Fritsch and Uffz. Paul Lampferhoff. Lt. Glunz shot down a P-38 in a dogfight and then found himself in a bad spot. His oil pressure suddenly dropped to zero; his engine immediately seized up. Glunz evaded two Thunderbolts by banking sharply and diving into a cloud bank. He was then able to make a clean belly landing in a beet field. The source of his engine trouble was later traced to a broken oil line. This was the closest the lucky Glunz came to losing an aircraft in combat during the entire war.

JG 26 Victory Claims: 12 - 13 October 1944

Date	Rank	Name	Unit	Cl #	Aircraft	Place	Time	Opponent	Conf
12-10-44	Obstlt.	Priller	Ge CO	101	P-51	S of Wunstorf (GT6)	1125	357 FG	i.O.
12-10-44	Hptm.	Krupinski	III CO	193	P-51	unknown	1550		no
13-10-44	Uffz.	Lampferhoff	5	1	P-47	Mönchen-Gladbach (MN)	1504	368 FG	i.O.
13-10-44	Lt.	Glunz	6 CO	68	P-38	Düren (NN9)	1500	474 FG	unk
13-10-44	Uffz.	Fritsch A.	8	1	P-47	W of Düren (NN-NO)	1503	368 FG	unk

III/JG 54 was the first unit to be equipped with the "long-nosed Dora", the inline-engined Fw 190D-9. Training and rebuilding began with the withdrawal of the Gruppe from the Invasionsfront on 15 August, and continued until the unit re-entered combat alongside JG 26 in late December. Fw. Friedrich Ungar, a pilot of 9/JG 54, is seated in "white 2", W.Nr. 210015, in Hesepe in mid-October. *(Ungar)*

Staffelhund Struppi joins Fw. Ungar in the cockpit of "white 2". Struppi survived the war and returned home with Ungar, but died in 1946 of distemper – Hesepe, mid-October. *(Ungar)*

Fähnrich Hans-Joachim Schmauser (KIA 29 Dec 44) joins Staffelhund Struppi on a 500kg bomb – Hesepe, mid-October. *(Ungar)*

14 October

Jagdkorps II notified JG 2 and JG 26 to be ready for an RLV mission in the morning, if called on by Luftflotte Reich. If not, they were to fly an afternoon mission against fighter-bombers and artillery spotters on both sides of Aachen. The latter mission was flown. Twenty-two First Gruppe Fw 190s took off at 1600 and joined twenty-four Second Gruppe aircraft on a mission to Aachen. The Third Gruppe was still changing airfields, and was not given a mission. East of Köln the combined formation was bounced by two squadrons of 474th Fighter Group P-38s. Two First Gruppe Focke-Wulfs were damaged before the German fighters escaped in a cloud layer at 1800 meters (6000 feet). Ofhr. Vanderveerd returned to Krefeld, where he force-landed his airplane without injury to himself. Uffz. Bischoff had to put his plane down on an Autobahn, but he too escaped injury.

15 October

The orders issued by Jagdkorps II were the same as the previous day's: an RLV mission in the morning, if called on by Luftflotte Reich; otherwise, an afternoon mission against fighter-bombers and artillery spotters around Aachen. The Second Gruppe was apparently given the day off. Twenty First Gruppe Focke-Wulfs took off from Krefeld at 1440 under Oblt. Kunz's command, joined ten Third Gruppe Messerschmitts, and swept around Aachen without sighting enemy aircraft. While landing on Krefeld, Ogfr. Josef Leder hit a soft patch of ground and turned over. He fractured his skull, and died the next day.

The Allied air forces underwent two changes today that affected the Geschwader not at all, but do alter the nomenclature used in this history. The Allied Expeditionary Air Force (AEAF) was disbanded; the 9th US Air Force and the RAF's 2nd TAF returned to their national chains of command. The Air Defense of Great Britain (ADGB) reverted to its previous name, RAF Fighter Command, under which it had gained its greatest fame.

Pit Andel runs up his Fw 190A-8 "brown 3" at Stevede. *(Molge)*

16 October

The orders from Jagdkorps II mirrored those of the past few days, but the First Gruppe would stay on the ground for the next four days because of its boggy airfield, and the Third Gruppe was not yet fully operational at Gross-Reken. The Second Gruppe mission to Aachen was flown by one Schwarm of Focke-Wulfs. It was successful; Obfw. Mayer and Ofhr. Benz each claimed an Auster near Düren. One 101st Airborne Division L-4 Grasshopper was shot down in this area by German fighters.

20 October

After struggling for several days, the First Gruppe finally succeeded in moving its aircraft from Krefeld-Linn to Krefeld-Bockum, which was in marginally better condition. The weather today was good, and Jagdkorps II ordered the two Focke-Wulf Gruppen to fly a combined Jabojagd mission to Aachen, while the Third Gruppe patrolled the Geschwader airfields and the army facilities in the rear. The First and Second Gruppen took off at 1455. The last three of the thirteen aircraft leaving Krefeld under Lt. Heckmann's command were bounced by eight P-47s, which did no damage before escaping in the clouds. The Second Gruppe engaged P-47s in combat near Aachen, but no claims or losses resulted.

21 October

The ground fighting had spread over such a wide front to the north and south of Aachen that Jagdkorps II ordered morning sweeps to be flown by independent Schwärme, to cover more ground. A dozen First Gruppe Fw 190s took off from Krefeld at 0945. Oblt. Kunz's Schwarm aborted owing to the weather. Ofhr. Vanderveerd's Schwarm patrolled Venlo. They saw no enemy aircraft, and were harassed by heavy antiaircraft fire. Lt. Ellenrieder's Schwarm patrolled Nijmegen. Ellenrieder shot down an L-4 of the American 320th Field Artillery Battalion, but did not claim the "Auster" because he lacked a witness. His small force then strafed vehicles and troops, until Obfw. Heinrich Teilken was hit by antiaircraft fire and crashed in his plane. Neither the Second nor the Third Gruppen provided any aircraft

for the morning mission, probably owing to the conditions of their airfields.

In the afternoon, the First and Second Gruppen were ordered to fly a combined mission to the front. The First Gruppe formation took off at 1400 under Lt. Heckmann and followed the Second Gruppe fighters toward Wesel. The First Gruppe contacted some P-47s, and sighted a larger formation of P-38s, but no attack order came from the Second Gruppe mission leader, who was probably Oblt. Hofmann. The Lightnings were from the 474th Fighter Group's 429th Squadron. They hit Hofmann's force while the Focke-Wulfs were skirmishing with some P-47s, and shot down Uffz. Artur Fritsch, who died in his plane. Uffz. Hött had to make a belly-landing in his damaged Focke-Wulf, but was uninjured. Oblt. Hofmann was injured slightly by shell fragments, but his Fw 190A-9 was not badly damaged. None of the Focke-Wulf pilots claimed any damage to an American fighter.

Lt. Wilhelm Hofmann, 8th Staffel Kapitän until its disbandment, and then Kapitän of the 5th Staffel. He is shown here after his ground accident on 22 October. Hofmann joined the Second Gruppe in 1942 as an Unteroffizier, and was killed on 26 March 1945, shot down by his own wingman. He was credited with 44 victories in 260 combat flights, and was awarded the Knight's Cross in October. *(Cranston)*

22 October

The weather once again became the airmen's worst enemy. Little combat was seen for the rest of October. Several more missions were flown to the Aachen area, where the Geschwader engaged the 474th Fighter Group's Lightnings in several inconclusive combats. Action over the city itself died down after the 20th, when it became the first German city to fall to the Allies.

Oblt. Hofmann was injured today in a freak ground accident. He was examining a dismounted aircraft machine gun when the bolt closed suddenly, injuring his eye. He retained his sight, but lost the ability to focus the eye. He refused hospitalization, and returned to his unit wearing an eyepatch. Hofmann insisted on flying combat missions, but the job of leading his 8th Staffel in the air was assigned temporarily to Lt. Wilhelm Mayer from the 5th Staffel. Two days after his accident, Oblt. Hofmann was awarded the Knight's Cross, the first such decoration received by a Geschwader pilot since the previous June.

JG 26 Casualties: 13 - 22 October 1944

Date	Rank	Name	Cas	Unit	Aircraft	WNr	Mkgs	Place	Time	Cause	Allied Unit
13-10-44	Uffz.	Prantke, Benno	KIA	7	Fw 190A-8	680553	br 3	Jülich		P-47	368 FG
15-10-44	Ogfr.	Leder, Josef	KIFA	1	Fw 190A-9	205289	wh 7	Krefeld a/f		landing	n/a
21-10-44	Obfw.	Teilken, Heinrich	KIA	1	Fw 190A-9	205249	wh 2	near Wesel		flak	n/a
21-10-44	Uffz.	Fritsch, Artur	KIA	8	Fw 190A-9	750131	bl 1	nr Krefeld-S of Viersen	1430	P-38	474 FG
21-10-44	Oblt.	Hofmann, Wilhelm	WIA	8 CO	Fw 190A-9			S of Viersen	1430	P-38	474 FG
22-10-44	Oblt.	Hofmann, Wilhelm	WAC	8 CO	none			Stevede a/f		machine gun	n/a

Major Anton "Toni" Hackl, Second Gruppe Kommandeur from 8 October until he left JG 26 to take command of JG 300 in late January, 1945. A recipient of the Knight's Cross with Oak Leaves and Swords for his prowess on all combat fronts, Hackl was a popular, intelligent leader who kept his Gruppe performing at a high level. *(Cranston)*

23 October

Jagdkorps II fighters were grounded for several days owing to the weather. The First Gruppe was under orders to transfer to Greven as soon as possible; it did not fly again until the 28th. The Third Gruppe was preparing to move to Plantlünne; its advance detachment was on the site and taking inventory.

26 October

ULTRA decoded a remarkable message to the Third Gruppe from Jagdkorps II. Its major points stated:

1. "The Gruppe is to be brought up to a strength of 70-80 aircraft by delivery to Plantlünne of a further twenty new Bf 109K-4s with DB 605D engines.

2. "If the new airfield proves to be too small, reserve aircraft are to be parked at a nearby field to the rear.

3. "A field workshop is essential at the new base, and is to accompany the Gruppe in any further moves, because:

4. "The serviceability of this Gruppe during the invasion months was the worst in Jagdkorps II."

28 October

This was a rare clear day, and Jagdkorps II ordered three combined missions in support of a Panzer offensive intended to stabilize the lines between Weert and Venlo. JG 2 and JG 26 flew 202 sorties against fighter-bombers and artillery spotters. Many German fighters did not reach the combat zone because of Allied fighter attacks, and others were shot at by German Flak, which brought a complaint by the Jagdkorps headquarters in the evening. The morning mission started out with thirty First Gruppe Focke-Wulfs, led by Major Borris, and elements of all three JG 2 Gruppen. Ten of Borris's pilots turned back early. The JG 2 Gruppen were dispersed by P-47s. The First Gruppe sighted P-47s, but did not engage them in strength; many of its pilots were therefore denied combat sortie credit.

The second mission got off the ground at 1250, and contained aircraft from two JG 2 and two JG 26 Gruppen. The First Gruppe contributed nineteen aircraft, again under Borris. Typhoons were sighted near Venlo, but were not engaged. Major Hackl's thirteen Second Gruppe Focke-Wulfs did attack them. One No. 182 Sqd. Typhoon went down in flames; Major Hackl and Lt. Vogt both claimed victories. Vogt himself was hit by a Typhoon and had to force-land with minor injuries. On the return flight the Gruppe was bounced by No. 412 Sqd. (RCAF) Spitfires, and after a long combat, Obfw. Karl-Heinz Knobeloch's Fw 190A-9 was hit. Knobeloch bailed out very low, and died when his parachute failed to open. During the chase, Uffz. Johannes Hoffmann of the 5th Staffel rammed the Focke-Wulf of his element leader, who landed his airplane unharmed. Hoffmann bailed out with injuries.

The third mission, comprising sixteen Second Gruppe and six Third Gruppe aircraft, took off at 1600. The Focke-Wulfs failed to contact the enemy. The Messerschmitts had not yet formed up when they were struck by No. 412 Squadron, which had refueled and returned to the area of its earlier battle. Lt. Hermann Juhre and Obfw. Hans Erbskorn were killed over their Lette base. Fw. Karl-Heinz Friedrich force-landed, and Oblt. Theobald Kraus bailed out, both with slight injuries. The Bf 109G-14 of Uffz. Heinz Nieter was hit, but he evaded the Spitfires, only to be hit by antiaircraft fire over his own field of Gross-Reken. He crash-landed with moderate injuries. The Canadian Spitfire pilots once again returned to their Belgian base without loss.

JG 26 Casualties: 28 October 1944

Date	Rank	Name	Cas	Unit	Aircraft	WNr	Mkgs	Place	Time	Cause	Allied Unit
28-10-44	Lt.	Vogt, Gerhard	WIA	5 CO	Fw 190A-8	175130	wh 13	Venlo/Orsay	1330	Typhoon	182 Sqd
28-10-44	Uffz.	Hoffmann, Johannes	WIA	5	Fw 190A-9	750118	wh 1	near Wesel		collision	n/a
28-10-44	Obfw.	Knobeloch, Karl-Heinz	KIA	6	Fw 190A-9	750139	bk 1	Krefeld-Ürdingen	1450	Spitfire	412 Sqd
28-10-44	Obfw.	Erbskorn, Hans	KIA	10	Bf 109G-14	462977	bk 9	W of Dülmen-Merfelder Bruch	1549	Spitfire	412 Sqd
28-10-44	Fw.	Friedrich, Karl-Heinz	WIA	10	Bf 109G-14	462701	bk 4	Krefeld-Ürdingen a/f	1600	Spitfire	412 Sqd
28-10-44	Lt.	Juhre, Hermann	KIA	10	Bf 109G-14	464279	bk 8	SW of Münster-Senden	1555	Spitfire	412 Sqd
28-10-44	Oblt.	Kraus, Theobald	WIA	10	Bf 109G-14	462674	bk 11	Senden	1555	Spitfire	412 Sqd
28-10-44	Uffz.	Nieter, Heinz	WIA	10	Bf 109G-14	461509	bk 12	W of Dülmen-Merfelder Bruch	1555	Spitfire	412 Sqd

JG 26 Victory Claims: 16 - 28 October 1944

Date	Rank	Name	Unit	Cl #	Aircraft	Place	Time	Opponent	Conf
16-10-44	Obfw.	Mayer	5	25	Auster	Düren (NN7-8)	1410	101 A/B Div L-4	i.O.
16-10-44	Ofhr.	Benz	6	6	Auster	Düren (NN7-8)	1410	101 A/B Div L-4	i.O.
21-10-44	Lt.	Ellenrieder	4		Auster	unknown	1015	320 F/A Bat L-4	no
28-10-44	Maj.	Hackl	II CO	166	Typhoon	between Venlo and Kempen	1325	182 Sqd	i.O.
28-10-44	Lt.	Vogt	5 CO	45	Typhoon	between Venlo and Kempen	1325	182 Sqd	i.O.

29 October

Jagdkorps II ordered its fighter units to maintain the highest possible state of serviceability so that missions in maximum strength could be flown in support of the ongoing Panzer offensive. However, both JG 2 and JG 26 were held at readiness all morning for possible RLV duty, on orders from Luftflotte Reich. In early afternoon, Lt. Heckmann led twenty-three First Gruppe and an unknown number of Second Gruppe Focke-Wulfs on a freie Jagd to Kleve. The First Gruppe sighted enemy aircraft, but did not engage them; the Second Gruppe did have a scuffle, and suffered damage to one airplane. A little later, thirty First Gruppe aircraft got away from Krefeld on a transfer flight to their new base, but the Second Gruppe could not form up for a second offensive mission owing to the presence of enemy aircraft over their airfields; four airborne Focke-Wulfs were actually recalled.

The Geschwaderstab and the First Gruppe had lost their battle with the mud of Krefeld, and moved seventy miles to the northeast, to a clearing in a forest outside the village of Greven. It was a poor choice. The Dortmund-Ems canal was nearby, and ran in a concrete channel several feet above ground level. The canal was bombed several times by the British, each time causing the inundation of the surrounding countryside. Bedeviled by these unnatural floods and the autumn rains, the men soon found themselves in deeper mud than they had experienced at Krefeld.

30 October

It had not taken long for the 8th Air Force's campaign against the German petroleum industry to take effect. Oil production had been cut to 31% of the monthly average the previous spring. Most fuel now came from tiny benzol plants, which produced synthetic petroleum from coke oven byproducts. Luftwaffenkommando West issued the following orders today:

1. "In view of the current fuel situation, no operation is justified unless weather and the mission prerequisites promise certain success.
2. "Training flights, even within the combat units, are forbidden with immediate effect, unless special quotas of fuel are allotted for special retraining.
3. "All flights except those for operations, transfer, repair testing, or ferrying purposes are forbidden."

31 October

Today it was the turn of the Third Gruppe to move. Plantlünne was 50 kilometers (30 miles) north of Lette. Plantlünne, codenamed *Plantenspeck* (vegetable fat), was a fully-equipped prewar airbase with a large grass landing ground of irregular shape. The long axis was roughly west-east, corresponding to the prevailing wind direction; it was 1400 meters long, with an additional 500 meter overrun. Its width was 850 meters (4500 + 1600 x 2800 feet). The field had been used by an experimental bomber unit earlier in the war. It had both Freya and Würzburg radars, and was defended by at least three flak towers, equipped primarily with light 20 mm guns. Most of the antiaircraft crews were schoolboys from the nearby towns. Instead of conventional hangars, there were covered repair stations. These had concrete foundations, brick or wooden walls, and flat wooden roofs covered with tar and camouflaged with bushes and small trees. The aircraft were parked under trees or in camouflaged tents. All large trees had been cut down to minimize the danger from fire. Sheep from a nearby farm trimmed the grass on the well-drained landing ground. All personnel lived in barracks at the field. The pilots and ground crews of the Third Gruppe settled into these relatively comfortable surroundings for the winter. Their stay was to last for four months.

Geschwader personnel moves during October included: the transfer out of Hptm. Gerhard Philipp, the Geschwader operations officer; the arrival of Uffz. Werner Binge from a ferry unit, and his assignment to the Second Gruppe; the return of Lt. Peter Ahrens to the First Gruppe after eleven months in hospital; the transfer of Fw. Albert Boeckl from the 12th Staffel to Kommando Nowotny; and the arrival of two new pilots, Lt. Peter Andel and Uffz. Erhard Meinel, from training; they were both assigned to the Second Gruppe.

2 November

The 8th Air Force oil offensive reached a crescendo. Eleven hundred B-17s and B-24s bombed oil targets in Germany, escorted by 968 fighters. The First and Second Gruppen were ordered to attack this armada, but could not take off because of the presence of enemy fighters in the area, and aborted the mission. The fighters of Luftflotte Reich flew 490 sorties, but only 305 made contact because of the weather. Seventy German pilots were killed, and another twenty-eight were injured. Only forty American bombers were brought down, some by antiaircraft fire, and sixteen American fighters were lost. The recriminations from Hitler's headquarters over the failure of the Jagdwaffe were even more pointed than usual. Göring made a three and one-half hour speech attributing Germany's problems to the cowardice of his fighter pilots. He had the speech recorded, and sent excerpts to the fighter units for the edification of the pilots and the betterment of their morale.

Jagdkorps II ordered the Second Gruppe to fly a Jabojagd to the Wesel-Lingen area, behind the German lines. They were to be escorted by the First Gruppe. At 1530 twenty-five Focke-Wulfs attempted to take off from Greven under Lt. Heckmann, but nine of them bogged down in the mud. Heckmann's fighters did not make rendezvous, and flew their own Jabojagd mission. They attacked eight Typhoons between Coesfeld and Rheine, but were in turn attacked by six Mustangs, which shot down Uffz. Ludwig Sattler. Sattler bailed out safely. Five of the Fw 190s returned to Greven with damage: two from combat, two from engine problems, and one from a hit by German Flak. No appropriate claims by Mustangs have been located, and the Allied fighters involved in this combat were probably Spitfires from No. 442 Sqd. (RCAF), which claimed two Fw 190s near Coesfeld after 1600.

The Second Gruppe failed to contact the enemy on its mission. The Third Gruppe spent the afternoon transferring aircraft from Coesfeld-Lette and Gross-Reken to Plantlünne, despite the presence over Gross-Reken of Spitfires, which damaged one Messerschmitt. Uffz. Fritz Quitter of the 9th Staffel hit a tree while taking off from Lette, and crashed from an altitude of ten meters (32 feet), suffering severe injuries.

3 November

Only the Second Gruppe made a combat flight today. It was ordered to send a single Schwarm to Hürtgen to hunt for artillery spotters. The mission was unsuccessful.

4 November

In the morning the First Gruppe was ordered to fly a Jabojagd mission to Münster and Rheine. Twenty-one Focke-Wulfs took off from Greven at 0930 under Oblt. Kunz, but thirteen, including that of Lt. Kemethmüller, returned early with engine and other problems. Heinz Kemethmüller, who according to witnesses had not yet sobered up from the previous night, landed long, ground-looped, and turned over in the soft soil of the overrun area. He was taken to the hospital with severe injuries, and on his return to the First Gruppe did not regain his flight status. Kemethmüller ended his combat career with eighty-nine air victories in 463 combat sorties; Lt. Söffing took over the leadership of the 4th Staffel. Uffz. Josef Piesslinger suffered engine failure while on the mission, and crashed into the day-care center at the Mönchen-Gladbach train station, killing himself. The pilots who completed the mission reported no contact with the enemy.

Jagdkorps II ordered a combined Jabojagd mission for mid-afternoon, but apparently only the First Gruppe took part, and it was only able to get eight fighters up from Greven. They reported sighting, but not engaging, enemy fighters, and lost two more fighters when landing; one crashed when its engine failed, and the other ripped off its landing gear in the mud. The Second Gruppe apparently made no flights all day. The Third Gruppe, still attempting to get operational from Plantlünne, lost one Bf 109G and sustained damage to a second while on non-combat flights.

5 November

The First and Second Gruppen flew Jabojagd missions beneath a solid cloud deck at 3000 meters (10,000 feet). No enemy aircraft were seen. The First Gruppe diary complains of Allied radio interference, which prevented the formation leaders from hearing the controller. The 7th and 8th Staffeln left Coesfeld-Stevede and joined the rest of the Second Gruppe on Kirchhellen. Uffz. Hans-Joachim Zutz of the 8th Staffel collided with his element leader, Lt. Bruno Mischkot, while the pair were circling their new field; Mischkot landed safely, but Zutz crashed and burned. The Third Gruppe was still not operational from Plantlünne; one of its Messerschmitts was damaged today on a non-combat flight.

6 November

This morning found the aircraft of the Geschwaderstab and the First Gruppe mired in mud up to their axles, 30-40 cm (12-16 in) deep. They were bogged in, and completely out of action. Jagdkorps II ordered full-strength Jabojagd missions to be flown in support of the ground fighting at Hürtgen and Schmidt, if the weather was suitable;

Lt. Sy, the 7th Staffel mascot Seppe, and Lt. Andel while in training on the Fw 190D-9 at Reinsehlen in late 1944. *(Dietze via Meyer)*

otherwise each Gruppe was to send a single Schwarm to the same area in search of artillery spotters. The latter mission was the one flown. The Third Gruppe flew a mission from Plantlünne. but failed to contact the enemy. The Second Gruppe Schwarm was led by Uffz. Hans-Joachim Borreck, with five victories the most successful of the 1944 Nachwuchs pilots. They failed to find any Grasshoppers, but did sight a small formation of P-47s southwest of Düren at low altitude. Borreck and Uffz. Ernst Lampferhoff teamed up to shoot down one of the P-47s, which was from the 36th Fighter Group's 22nd Squadron. The Focke-Wulfs were then taken under fire by light antiaircraft guns and zoomed for cover in the clouds. Borreck disappeared, and failed to return; he was claimed by the US Army's 555th Antiaircraft Battalion.

JG 26 Casualties: 2 - 6 November 1944

Date	Rank	Name	Cas	Unit	Aircraft	WNr	Mkgs	Place	Time	Cause	Allied Unit
02-11-44	Uffz.	Sattler, Ludwig	no	4	Fw 190A-8			near Coesfeld-Lette	1605	P-51	
02-11-44	Uffz.	Quitter, Fritz	WIFA 9		Bf 109G-14	462729	wh 7	Coesfeld-Lette a/f		takeoff	non-op
04-11-44	Uffz.	Piesslinger, Josef	KIFA	1	Fw 190A-8	171560	wh 4	M-Gladbach Kinderhaus		engine	n/a
04-11-44	Lt.	Kemethmüller, Heinz	WIFA 4 CO		Fw 190A-9	205206	bl 6	Greven a/f	1025	landing	n/a
05-11-44	Uffz.	Zutz, Hans-Joachim	KIFA 8		Fw 190A-8	170989	bl 10	Kirchhellen a/f		collision	non-op
06-11-44	Uffz.	Borreck, Hans-Joachim	KIA	5	Fw 190A-9	750132	wh 8	nr Wahlheim-Aachen	1213	flak	n/a

7 November

The Second and Third Gruppen flew small missions of ca. twelve aircraft apiece to the rear areas in search of enemy fighter-bombers. None were found. Major Hackl's Gruppe was informed that they would be transferring to Reinsehlen, near Hamburg, for re-equipment with Kurt Tank's latest fighter, the inline-engined Fw 190D-9. They would be the second Gruppe to get the fighter. The first, III/JG 54, had gone directly to Oldenburg for reforming and re-equipment with the Fw 190D-9 after their

Lt. Joachim Günther of the 2nd Staffel (KIA 24 Feb 45) receives his Iron Cross from General Stumpff, commander of Luftflotte Reich, at Greven on 8 November. Note the lack of adornment on Stumpff's cap and uniform. *(Schäfer-Günther via G. Schmidt)*

withdrawal from the Invasionsfront in mid-August. The process had proved lengthy, and the Green Heart unit had not yet returned to the combat zone in strength.

8 November

The Third Gruppe flew two Jabojagd missions toward the Schmidt area, which the Army was defending fiercely against the American First Army. Only one formation reached the front, and its successes went unrecorded. Genobst. Stumpff, the commander of Luftflotte Reich, visited the fighter bases today. Lt. Joachim Günther of the 2nd Staffel received his Iron Cross from General Stumpff at Greven.

11 November

The Third Gruppe flew one freie Jagd to the rear areas. Its successes are unknown. One Messerschmitt crashed for a cause not combat-related; its pilot escaped injury.

Second Gruppe pilots began moving to Reinsehlen. Some picked up new Fw 190D-9s at Helmstedt and flew them to the training base.

12 November

General Galland's staff today completed its planning for der grosse Schlag. Its execution awaited only favorable weather and a suitable deep-penetration mission by the 8th Air Force. Jagdkorps I, the principal RLV command unit, was to employ 2000 fighters in eleven Gefechtsverbände. Jagdkorps II was to employ 150 fighters against the bombers as they entered and left Germany. Five hundred fighters were to fly second sorties. One hundred night fighters were to patrol the Swedish and Swiss flanks in search of stragglers. Galland expected to shoot down 4-500 bombers, for the loss of four hundred fighters and 100-150 pilots. The American air offensive would be set back by two or three months, giving German industry time to complete its program of decentralization, and the new Me 262 jet fighter units the opportunity to become operational.

The First Gruppe was ordered to transfer to Fürstenau, 45 kilometers (28 miles) north of Greven. An advance detachment left to prepare the new base, but the Focke-Wulfs were still embedded in the mud. Jagdkorps II reported that its fighters flew no operations today because of the weather.

13 November

Jagdkorps II reported that its fighters flew no operations again today because of the weather. The engine of Lt. Wilhelm Landsberg's Bf 109G-14 failed while he was on a test flight from Plantlünne; he was killed in the crash.

14 November

ULTRA received indications that a number of fighter units were moving west when Jagdkorps II informed these units by radio that future communications would be by land line. This was Allied Intelligence's first hint that a major German operation was being prepared in the west; it would mean the death of der grosse Schlag.

Lt. Andel in the cockpit of a Fw 190D-9 at Reinsehlen. It is not known why Andel was so popular among those members of the Second Gruppe fortunate enough to have film in late 1944. *(Dietze via Meyer)*

17 November

Jagdkorps II had to inform the army units fighting along the German-Dutch border that the weather still did not permit flying. The Third Gruppe reported that it had forty-six aircraft available for operations from Plantlünne. The First Gruppe was still stuck in the Greven mud. Jagdkorps II suggested that Major Borris pick up new aircraft at Fürstenau, leaving his old airplanes at Greven until winter froze the ground. Borris refused to abandon his aircraft, and instead dismantled them. A crew of Italian laborers was drafted to hand-carry the wings and fuselages across the field to the nearest hard-surfaced road. There they were loaded onto trucks and sent on their way to Fürstenau.

19 November

Jagdkorps II ordered the Second and Third Gruppen to fly two missions against fighter-bombers and artillery spotters in the Roermond-Geilenkirchen area. The morning mission cost the lives of two pilots: Oblt. Konrad Bertels, who had just transferred from the First Gruppe into the Second as a prospective Staffelkapitän, and Lt. Hans-Friedrich Wagner of the 12th Staffel. Bertels reported engine trouble and was last seen entering a cloud trailing white smoke; he crashed near Rheine at 0945. Wagner's casualty report credits eight Spitfires with shooting him down, but there were no claims by RAF pilots today. The only suitable claim was by a P-47 pilot of the 365th Fighter Group's 386th Squadron, who at 0945 drove off a pair of Bf 109s that had attacked his flight leader north of Düren, shooting one down.

That afternoon, the Spitfires of No. 412 Sqd. (RCAF) were attacking the bridge at Veen when they were hit by a large number of Fw 190s, led by Lt. Gerhard Vogt and his 5th Staffel. The Staffel claimed four Spitfires, among them Vogt's 46th victory and Ofhr. Wilhelm Mayer's 26th and 27th. Three Spitfires were in fact lost. This was the last full-scale mission for the Second Gruppe in the radial-engine Fw 190A. This evening the last Second Gruppe pilots at Kirchhellen boarded trucks for Reinsehlen, while the Gruppe ground crews proceeded directly to their next projected operational base, Nordhorn-Clausheide.

The base movements of the Focke-Wulf Gruppen left the Third Gruppe temporarily the strongest fighter unit in the area. The pilots' routine at Plantlünne was typical for the last period of the war. Their service day began with sunrise and continued until darkness. After breakfast in the pilots' *Casino*, or common room, they went to their Staffel dispersal. They were informed about weather conditions, and waited there at readiness. The operational aircraft were assigned to the pilots on duty; this late in the war, few pilots had their own aircraft assigned to them.

The Gruppe had received a number of examples of the last version of the Bf 109 to see service, the Bf 109K-4. A top speed of 710 km/h (440 mph) is quoted at its critical altitude of 7500 meters (24,750 feet). This variant was very similar to the G-10, but a number of features that had been introduced in stages were standardized. Among these were an enlarged wooden tail assembly, a retractable tail wheel, and a 30 mm MK 108 or MK 103 nose cannon. The 30 mm cannon were extremely potent weapons, but had a tendency to jam, and apparently all of the K-4s supplied to the Third Gruppe were also equipped with 20 mm guns in the despised underwing tubs. Uffz. Georg Genth's regular aircraft was a G-10, but on occasion he flew a K-4. He preferred the G-10 as a dogfighter, as the K-4's bulky armament sharply reduced its maneuverability. Moreover, at high altitudes, above about 8500 meters (28,000 feet), the K-4 began to float. Genth found that during formation flight at high altitudes it was unnaturally sensitive, and gave him the same signals that most aircraft give shortly before a stall. Formation flight had to conform to the speed of the lead aircraft, and a small change in its speed caused the pilots to start "swimming" in space in the very thin air at high altitudes.

21 November

According to the ULTRA intercepts, the Third Gruppe flew two missions today. Ten fighters served as high-altitude cover for JG 3, which was on an unspecified mission or transfer flight. At noon, thirty-three Gruppe aircraft scrambled to intercept heavy bombers. There is no evidence that they made contact; the unit reported no losses, and any successes are unknown.

ULTRA noted that the headquarters of the 3rd Jagddivision had come west again to command some of the fighter units that were moving into northwestern Germany to take part in an as-yet unspecified offensive operation. IV/JG 54 was now at Münster-Handorf; I/JG 27, at Rheine, II/JG 27, at Hopsten, and III/JG 27, at Hesepe. JG 3, JG 4, and JG 77 were also heading west, but the Luftwaffe's new emphasis on radio security made it impossible to establish their bases.

22 November

Ogfr. Rudolf Geis, a driver in the Third Gruppe Stabskompanie, was killed when his motorcycle hit a tree at 0145. The fighters of Jagdkorps II were grounded for the next two days.

24 November

The Third Gruppe flew thirty sorties in two operations. Both were Jabojagden to the Geilenkirchen area. The Gruppe reported no claims or losses.

Obstlt. Priller and Major Borris reported the arrival of the Geschwaderstab and the First Gruppe at Fürstenau, which was also known as Handrup. Fürstenau was a war-construction base that had until recently seen service only as a decoy field. It had a small, L-shaped, but reasonably well-drained landing ground, and the Gruppe personnel welcomed the opportunity to pass the winter on fairly firm soil. Lodgings were located in nearby villages; the Gruppe ground staff moved into a Catholic girls' school, the Kloster Handrup.

25 November

Major Borris reported that the First Gruppe was now operational from Fürstenau, but in very low strength. Jagdkorps II ordered a freie Jagd in support of the retreating army. Nine Focke-Wulfs took off at 1500. P-47s were contacted southeast of Münster, but no combat resulted. One Gruppe aircraft force-landed after its engine failed. The Third Gruppe flew a similar mission, but apparently failed to make contact. The engine of Uffz. Georg Ritter's new Bf 109K-4 caught fire while he was on the mission, and he bailed out with slight injuries. Two more Messerschmitts crashed on non-operational flights, but their pilots escaped injury.

Major Borris was awarded the Knight's Cross today for his forty-one air victories. The 5th Staffel's Lt. Gerhard Vogt also received the award, for forty-six victories.

26 November

The 8th Air Force dispatched 1137 B-17s and B-24s to bomb petroleum facilities and railroad yards in northwestern and north central Germany. The skies over the

Lt. Andel prepares to take off from Reinsehlen in a Fw 190D-9. He called the plane his "Spitzmaus" (shrew; a derogatory term for a woman in German as well as English).*(Dietze via Meyer)*

Jagdkorps II bases were cloudless, and Luftflotte Reich ordered the western fighter units to participate in the intercept mission. Jagdkorps II ordered up all of its available forces: JG 3, JG 27, and the First and Third Gruppen of JG 26. The fighters were to form a Gefechtsverband led by JG 27. Lt. Ellenrieder led five First Gruppe Fw 190s up from Fürstenau at 1030 and met the Third Gruppe over the base. The Schlageter fighters sighted a bomber formation near Osnabrück, but were driven off by 364th Fighter Group P-51s. Uffz. Hans Streufert of the 10th Staffel crashed in his Messerschmitt, and Gefr. Horst Sengpiel of the 12th Staffel belly-landed in a field near Cloppenburg. Apparently the Mustang flight led by Lt. Jack Gaston was chasing one of these two Messerschmitts when Gaston's wingman pulled ahead to shoot it down. Gaston's tail was left uncovered, and he was promptly shot down by Lt. Ahrens of the 3rd Staffel. The JG 26 formation was well split up; the five First Gruppe aircraft landed on three different airfields. Luftflotte Reich suffered another stinging defeat today. The Americans lost thirty-four bombers and nine fighters. The Germans lost ninety-eight fighters, with fifty-seven pilots killed and thirty injured.

JG 26 Victory Claims: November 1944

Date	Rank	Name	Unit	Cl #	Aircraft	Place	Time	Opponent	Conf
06-11-44	Uffz.	Borreck	5		P-47	Eschweiler	1213	36 FG	no
06-11-44	Uffz.	Lampferhoff	5	2	P-47	Kreuzau SW of Düren (ON3)	1220	36 FG	unk
19-11-44	Uffz.	Lampferhoff	5	3	Spitfire	N of Kirchhellen (KO3)	1408	412 Sqd	unk
19-11-44	Obfw.	Mayer	5	26	Spitfire	N of Kirchhellen (KO3)	1408	412 Sqd	unk
19-11-44	Obfw.	Mayer	5	27	Spitfire	N of Kirchhellen (KO3)	1408	412 Sqd	unk
19-11-44	Lt.	Vogt	5 CO	46	Spitfire	N of Kirchhellen (KO3)	1406	412 Sqd	unk
26-11-44	Lt.	Ahrens	3	10	P-51	Osnabrück	1130	364 FG	unk

JG 26 Casualties: 13 - 26 November 1944

Date	Rank	Name	Cas	Unit	Aircraft	WNr	Mkgs	Place	Time	Cause	Allied Unit
13-11-44	Lt.	Landsberg, Wilhelm	KIFA	12	Bf 109K-4	330368	bl 20	Plantlünne a/f	1603	crashed	non-op
19-11-44	Oblt.	Bertels, Konrad	KIFA	I St	Fw 190A-8		gr 1	Rheine-Bentheim	0945	engine	n/a
19-11-44	Lt.	Wagner, Hans-Friedrich	KIA	12	Bf 109G-14	463112	bl 1	S of Mönchen-Gladbach	0930	P-47	365 FG

25-11-44	Uffz.	Ritter, Georg	WIFA 9	Bf 109K-4	330419 wh 20	Moers	1515	engine	n/a
26-11-44	Uffz.	Streufert, Hans	KIA 10	Bf 109G-14	462794 bk 1	4km SE of Fürstenau	1150	P-51	364 FG
26-11-44	Gefr.	Sengpiel, Horst	WIA 12	Bf 109G-14	461497 bl 2	Löningen-Oldenburg	1139	P-51	364 FG

A long-nosed Dora from the Second Gruppe takes off from Reinsehlen on a training mission in late 1944. (Dietze via Meyer)

27 November

The 8th Air Force attempted to squeeze in another mission to northwestern Germany before the weather closed in once more. Five hundred and eighty B-17s and B-24s bombed three railroad yards before an eastward-moving front covered Germany with cloud. The Geschwader pilots on duty could see the clouds coming in, and were very surprised to receive an order to scramble and rendezvous with the Bf 109s of JG 3 and JG 27 for an attack on the heavy bombers. Oblt. Gottfried Schmidt led fifteen Bf 109s up from Plantlünne at 1105 and met the First Gruppe Fw 190s over Fürstenau. The latter group comprised only four fighters; two others had become stuck on the field. The Third Gruppe had been ordered to fly high cover, and struggled to reach 10,000 meters (32,000 feet), higher than most of the pilots had ever flown. The First Gruppe Schwarm attempted to stay with the Messerschmitts, although their Focke-Wulfs were barely controllable above 9,000 meters (30,000 feet).

Uffz. Georg Genth recalls that the Messerschmitts could not maintain close formation, but lurched around in the sky like so many drunks. The canopy of his Bf 109K-4 iced over, and he could see only straight ahead through the armored glass panel. He cleared a small spot on the left canopy pane by breathing on it, so he could see to the rear. He was at the rear of the formation, and when he saw two P-47s banking on an attack curve he gave a warning and fled for the clouds below, switching on his artificial horizon as he dived. The cloud proved to be thousands of feet thick, and he wound up flying at terminal speed – 750 km/h (470 mph) – in an inverted bank, from which he barely completed recovery after he left the clouds about 500 meters (1600 feet) above the ground. His cowling panels had popped off, and oil lines had burst from the overstraining of his engine, but Genth was able to land on Rheine and get a ride back to Plantlünne. As he stood on the Rheine landing ground, he heard the shrieking engines, and then the crashes, of three airplanes. Two of them were piloted by Fhj.-Uffz. Robert Röhrig and Genth's good friend Ofhr. Helmut Lorberg. These two men were buried so deeply with their aircraft that their remains were not located and identified until 1992. Georg Genth states that he has never been able to strike the ghastly noises from his memory.

It is not known whether Lorberg and Röhrig were shot down or simply lost control in the clouds and were unable to recover before crashing. Four Geschwader fighters are known to have been shot down by P-51s. One pilot escaped injury, and the other three were able to bail out with slight injuries. The injured men were Oblt. Schmidt and Fw. Willi Niedermeyer of the 9th Staffel and Uffz. Emil Brühan of the 1st Staffel.

The 268 American escort fighters ran wild on this fairly short-range mission, claiming 98-4-11 German fighters for the loss of fifteen. Not a single bomber was shot down.

The Second Gruppe had turned over its Fw 190As to the First Gruppe, which today reported its highest aircraft strength to date, sixty-four Fw 190As. This report must have been embarrassing to Major Borris and his maintenance staff, who were having trouble getting six aircraft operational for a mission.

JG 26 Casualties: 27 November 1944

Date	Rank	Name	Cas	Unit	Aircraft	WNr	Mkgs	Place	Time	Cause	Allied Unit
27-11-44	Uffz.	Brühan, Emil	WIA	1	Fw 190A-8	171516	wh 3	Salzbergen-Rheine		P-51	
27-11-44	Oblt.	Schmidt, Gottfried	WIA	9 CO	Bf 109K-4	330372	wh 21	Bad Iburg	1215	P-51	
27-11-44	Fw.	Niedermeyer, Willi	WIA	9	Bf 109G-14	464309	wh 15	Salzbergen	1220	P-51	
27-11-44	Fhj-Uffz	Röhrig, Robert	KIA	10	Bf 109G-14	460514	bk 16	Wettringen near Rheine	1230	P-51	
27-11-44	Ofhr.	Lorberg, Helmut	KIA	12	Bf 109K-4	330152	bl 26	Wettringen near Rheine	1230	P-51	

Lt. Gottfried "Cognac" Schmidt, 9th Staffel Kapitän from July 1944 until the Third Gruppe's dissolution, when he took over the Second Gruppe's 6th Staffel. *(Genth)*

28 November

The First Gruppe was not called on to fly another mission until 2 December, giving it the opportunity to reach a respectable operational strength. Jagdkorps II and the 3rd Jagddivision sent several Gefechtsverbände to the critical areas of Venlo, Geilenkirchen, and Köln. The Third Gruppe contacted the enemy, but made no claims and suffered no casualties; Fw. Wolfgang Polster's Bf 109K-4 was hit by ground fire over Roermund.

30 November

The Geschwader was now attached to the 3rd Jagddivison, which had temporarily severed its ties to Jagdkorps I and was reporting to Jagdkorps II. JG 26 and every other fighter unit on the western front was grounded during this period owing to the weather conditions.

Geschwader personnel moves during November included: the transfer of Lt. Bruno Mischkot from the 8th Staffel to JG 3; the return of Lt. Hans Hartigs to the First Gruppe after recovering from his August wound; and the departure of Lt. Xaver Ellenrieder from the 4th Staffel for a training unit.

New pilots assigned to the Geschwader during November after completing flight training included: Gefr. Reinhard Anselment, Uffz. Wilhelm Jesinger, Uffz. Erwin Kabowski (an ex-Flak gunner), Ogfr. Dieter Krägeloh, Fhj.-Uffz. Kurt Meyer, Uffz. Hans Schöndorf, Uffz. Franz Wehring - First Gruppe; Gefr. Harro Bexen, Ogfr. Günter Boeke, Uffz. Hans-Georg Böhter, Gefr. Reinhold Fehr, Fw. Werner Frass, Ogfr. Volkmar Haarberg, Ofhr. Helmut Heuser, Fw. Alfred Hoppe, Uffz. Franz Körner, Fw. Bernhard Meindl, Uffz. Wilhelm Mittag, Gefr. Werner Molge, Uffz. Benno Prantke, Obfw. Friedrich Roggenkamp (a Wehrmacht member since 1934), Uffz. Wilhelm Schmitz, Uffz. Alfred Stuppan, Ofhr. Johann Spahn - Second Gruppe.

3 December

Good flying weather finally returned to the Western front. Jagdkorps II ordered continuous operations by individual Gruppen and Staffeln to Roermond and Venlo, the new critical sector of the front. Lt. Reischer led the first Third Gruppe mission, taking off from Plantlünne at 0840. Reischer claimed a Spitfire south of Kleve. The Gruppe flew a second mission in early afternoon, but any results went unrecorded. Two of its Messerschmitts were damaged during the day while on operations, but not in combat.

Major Borris himself led the First Gruppe mission. Twenty-seven Fw 190As sortied from Fürstenau at 1100. Four pilots aborted with engine trouble; Ogfr. Richard Walter was injured in his forced landing. Lt. Günther and his Schwarm failed to form up and flew an independent mission to Münster. Günther sighted three Typhoons and shot one of them

Oblt. Peter Reischer, 11th Staffel Kapitän for most of 1944. He committed suicide on 18 December. *(Genth)*

down in flames. The rest of the Gruppe completed their mission as ordered. The pilots sighted two Austers near Linnich and damaged one, and then strafed ground troops, apparently with good effect. The fighters finally ran low on fuel and landed on various fields. One did a headstand on Achmer. Uffz. Hans Schöndorf refueled and returned to Fürstenau, where he overturned, injuring himself and destroying his aircraft. That evening the Gruppe received a rare expression of gratitude in the form of a commendatory signal from Gen. Manteuffel's headquarters.

Ogfr. Karl-Heinz Wagner, a member of the Second Gruppe Stabskompanie, was wounded in a fighter-bomber attack on a train in which he was riding. Wagner was carrying a new radio for the Gruppe.

4 December

Jagdkorps II ordered its fighters to fly freie Jagden to the Düren area, where they were to engage fighter-bombers or strafe ground installations depending on the circumstances. The First Gruppe had strapped rocket tubes onto its Fw 190s, but was not called on to fly a mission. The Third Gruppe flew two missions, a total of 45-50 sorties. The 10th Staffel Bf 109K-4 flown by Lt. Dieter Völmle was hit by ground fire. He made a forced landing near Zülpich. Völmle was injured, and his aircraft was badly damaged. Two more Messerschmitts were damaged during the day while on operations, but not in combat.

5 December

Jagdkorps II was ordered to send JG 2 and JG 26 to support the army fighting along the Roer River west of Aachen, while the rest of its fighters flew an RLV mission against an 8th Air Force raid on Berlin. At 0925 Oblt. Heckmann led twenty-nine Fw 190As up from Fürstenau and headed for the front. South of Linnich a number of P-47s were sighted at an altitude of 2000 meters (6500 feet). Lt. Günther led his Schwarm in a bounce of the Thunderbolts, forcing them to jettison their bombs and downing one fighter in flames. The P-47s were from the 365th Fighter Group, which was engaged in bombing the Roer bridges. One Thunderbolt crashed, but according to the American records it was hit by Flak. As had become typical after a combat, the First Gruppe did not reform, but landed on several airfields. Obfw. Friedrich Buschegger was attempting to reach Fürstenau alone when he was spotted by a pilot of the 4th Fighter Group who was escorting a pair of Aphrodite radio-controlled bombers. Buschegger's fighter was shot up, and he was killed when he crashed attempting to land.

Oberst Hannes Trautloft, Inspector of Day Fighters, was at Fürstenau to give Major Borris his Knight's Cross. While Trautloft was in the command post, radio messages were received describing the American raid on Berlin. Trautloft decided to try his hand at tactical command, and ordered the First Gruppe to take off and attack straggling bombers, although the standing orders from Jagdkorps II forbade its units from taking off while the heavy bombers and their escorts were over northwestern Germany, unless specifically detailed to the RLV force. Only five Focke-Wulfs could be made ready. They took off at 1325, led by Major Borris. Ten minutes later came the report, *Abschuss* (shoot-down). It was the Major. He had caught an isolated B-17 over Lohnerfeld and dispatched it, resulting in the first Geschwader victory over a heavy bomber in months. As always, Karl Borris could be relied upon to carry out his orders to the letter. The bomber, from the 452nd Bomb Group, had been struggling to reach England on one engine. Only one member of its crew succeeded in bailing out after Borris's attack.

The First Gruppe was ordered up in mid-afternoon for another mission to the Roer Valley. Nine Focke-Wulfs took part. Third Gruppe Messerschmitts were met over Fürstenau; the combined force was led by Oblt. Heckmann. The fighters fought with fifty Thunderbolts between Düren and Jülich. Neither side sustained any losses.

Ogfr. Hans Limburg, a Third Gruppe mechanic, was wounded at Greven in a fighter-bomber attack.

JG 26 Victory Claims: 3 - 5 December 1944

Date	Rank	Name	Unit	Cl #	Aircraft	Place	Time	Opponent	Conf
03-12-44	Lt.	Günther	2	8	Typhoon	W of Münster (IP9-KP3)	1210	439 Sqd	unk
03-12-44	Oblt.	Reischer	11 CO	19	Spitfire	S of Kleve (KN9-5)	0925		unk
05-12-44	Major	Borris	I CO	42	B-17	W of Lingen	1335	452 BG	unk
05-12-44	Lt.	Günther	2	9	P-47	Linnich (BN2-3)	1013	365 FG	unk

8 December

After two days of weather-induced inactivity, the Geschwader returned to its principal area of operations between Köln and Aachen, despite heavy rain. Lt. Söffing led the 1st and 4th Staffeln in a morning mission, but failed to contact the enemy. Lt. Reischer's 11th Staffel Messerschmitts did; Uffz. Paul Klingelhöfer was shot down by 368th Fighter Group P-47s and bailed out with minor injuries. The 2nd and 3rd Staffeln were kept on the ground until 1300, when seventeen took off under Major Borris. They joined the Third Gruppe above the clouds covering the base and contacted eighty fighter-bombers, which were flying 2000 meters (6500 feet) above them. Borris ordered his fighters to disperse in the clouds. All returned to Fürstenau safely, but the 1st and 4th Staffeln, which were ordered up to protect the fighters as they landed, lost Fhj.-Gefr. Alfred Reppel, who accidentally contacted the ground, crashed, and burned.

JG 26 Casualties: 3 - 8 December 1944

Date	Rank	Name	Cas	Unit	Aircraft	WNr	Mkgs	Place	Time	Cause	Allied Unit
03-12-44	Uffz.	Schöndorf, Otto	WIFA	1	Fw 190A-8	960465	wh 2	Fürstenau-Handrup		landing	non-op

03-12-44	Ogfr.	Walter, Richard	WIA	4	Fw 190A-8	173867 bl 4	SW of Bremen-Wildeshausen		engine	n/a
04-12-44	Lt.	Völmle, Dieter	WIA	10	Bf 109K-4	330413 bk 8	Zülpich	1605	flak	n/a
05-12-44	Obfw.	Buschegger, Friedrich	KIA	2	Fw 190A-8	732019 bk 11	Maiburg-NW of Fürstenau	1030	P-51	4 FG
08-12-44	Fhj.-Gefr.	Reppel, Alfred	KIFA	1	Fw 190A-8	171573 wh 12	Greven	1400	hit ground	n/a
08-12-44	Uffz.	Klingelhöfer, Paul	WIA	11	Bf 109G-14	464163 yl 16	Hopsten a/f	1012	P-47	368 FG

Lt. Hermann Guhl, last Kapitän of the 11th Staffel. One of the Third Gruppe "old hares", so-called for their cautious tactics and erratic courses in the combat zone, Guhl was a very experienced (and lucky) enlisted pilot who had begun the war as an Oberfeldwebel in I(Jagd)/LG 2 and had seen duty as a test pilot; he accepted a commission in 1945 only under protest. *(Genth)*

Lt. Karl-Hermann Schrader, 12th Staffel Kapitän from May 1944 until its dissolution in March 1945. *(Genth)*

10 December

Jagdkorps II kept its fighters on the ground in the morning, and then ordered operations to the Aachen-Düren area by small formations. The Third Gruppe formation took off from Plantlünne at 1430, contacted P-47s and Spitfires south of Ereklenz, and landed on a number of fields without claims or losses. The First Gruppe formation took off at 1450, led by Oblt. Heckmann. Near Jülich the twenty-six Fw 190s bounced the 373rd Fighter Group's 411th Squadron, forcing the Thunderbolts to jettison their bombs. The American pilots got the upper hand in dogfights ranging from 4000 meters (13,000 feet) to the deck, and shot down three Focke-Wulfs. Gefr. Reinhard Anselment and Fhj.-Gefr. Kurt Meyer crashed with their aircraft. Obfw. Anton Freiberger bailed out with serious burns and two broken legs after he was hit by P-47s and German Flak. He survived until the next April, and then succumbed to his injuries. A fourth pilot crash-landed his aircraft when it ran out of fuel. The rest of the German pilots landed on several airfields. Lt. Söffing claimed a Thunderbolt for the only Gruppe success, although the P-47 made it back to the American lines before crash-landing.

12 December

The First and Third Gruppen were ordered to fly an RLV mission against the heavy bombers in a Gefechtsverband with JG 27. The two JG 26 Gruppen met up over

Fürstenau, but the mission was recalled. The Third Gruppe then flew several sweeps in Schwarm strength, without result; two of its fighters were damaged on operations, but not in combat. Obfw. Paul Weczera of the 4th Staffel bailed out of a Fw 190A-8 when it caught fire on a test flight; Weczera suffered slight injuries.

JG 26 Casualties: 10 - 12 December 1944

Date	Rank	Name	Cas	Unit	Aircraft	WNr	Mkgs	Place	Time	Cause	Allied Unit
10-12-44	Obfw.	Freiberger, Anton	KIA	1	Fw 190A-8	738134	wh 7	Düren-Eschweiler	1545	P-47	373 FG
10-12-44	Fhj-. Gefr	Meyer, Kurt	KIA	2	Fw 190A-8	734021	bk 15	NW of Meppen-Schöningsdorf	1630	P-47	373 FG
10-12-44	Gefr.	Anselment, Reinhard	KIA	4	Fw 190A-9	205280	bl 8	Neurath-Grevenbroich	1545	P-47	373 FG
12-12-44	Obfw.	Weczera, Paul	WIFA	4	Fw 190A-8	738184	bl 1	Emsdetten		engine	non-op

14 December

The thirty-year-old Genmaj. Dietrich Peltz, a bomber commander and a favorite of Adolf Hitler, was now in command of Jagdkorps II. He convened a conference of his fighter commanders in an inn near Altenkirchen, east of Bonn, to plan Unternehmen Bodenplatte (Operation Baseplate), a concentrated attack on the fighter bases of the 2nd TAF and the 9th Air Force by all of the western fighter units. The date of the operation was left open.

The First Gruppe was grounded again today, and the Second Gruppe had not yet returned to the front from Reinsehlen, although inquiries by Jagdkorps II were growing increasingly impatient. None of the western fighter units could get off the ground in the morning because of the rain, but JG 2, JG 4, and III/JG 26 flew a total of one hundred sorties in the afternoon. Twenty-two Third Gruppe Messerschmitts left Plantlünne at 1400 on what was a new mission for them – a patrol of the Me 262 Blitzbomber base at Rheine, to help protect the valuable jets during the vulnerable takeoff and landing stages of their missions. South of Rheine, the formation was attacked from above and behind by eight No. 56 Sqd. Tempests. Gefr. Wolfgang Kraus of the 12th Staffel crashed with his airplane, and was not found until 1951. Uffz. Heinz Gehrke was flying as Obfw. Karl Laub's wingman, and the pair maneuvered sharply in an effort to evade the much faster Tempests. After recovering from a split-S less than 600 meters (2000 feet) above the ground, Gehrke saw a fairing pop loose from Laub's wing and stick up into the airstream, where it was held by a cable. Laub was unable to counter the asymmetric control forces and dived straight into the ground. Gehrke pulled up, was hit, and bailed out for the fourth time in the war. The Spitfires of No. 412 Sqd. (RCAF) joined in the chase, and shot down Uffz. Friedrich Wissel of the 12th Staffel, who was able to bail out with minor wounds. The Allied units suffered no losses in this combat.

16 December

Early in the morning, strong German armored forces attacked the thinly-held American front lines in the Ardennes region of southern Belgium and northern Luxembourg. The "Battle of the Bulge" had begun. Heavy snowstorms prevented much flying by either side on the 16th – which was undoubtedly the way the German Army preferred it. Much of General Galland's precious reserve of fighters had been brought west to support the drive, ending his last opportunity to influence the course of the war.

Two Third Gruppe Schwärme flew sweeps over the Ardennes in an effort to keep fighter-bombers away from the advancing Panzers, but failed to contact any Allied aircraft.

17 December

Genmaj. Peltz ordered his fighters to exert every effort to clear the skies of fighter-bombers and artillery spotters ahead of the advancing 5th and 6th Panzer Armies. The

Uffz. Hans Kukla of the 4th Staffel at Fürstenau in late 1944. Kukla received the abbreviated training course typical of the *Nachwuchs* ("new growth") replacements, but was atypical in that he survived the war, albeit with injuries. *(Kukla)*

First and Third Gruppen took off at 0930 in scattered snow showers. The twenty-six Fw 190As of the First Gruppe were led by Major Borris. It is probable that they were vectored toward the 404th Fighter Group, whose P-47s were *en route* to bomb Bonn-Hangelar, but no contact was made in the swirling snow.

The First Gruppe was ordered to fly another mission in the afternoon. Oblt. Heckmann led the nineteen Fw 190As. Uffz. Hans Kukla led the 4th Staffel contingent, one Schwarm, which was assigned to fly high cover. Over the Eifel Heckmann spotted a small formation of Lightnings strafing ground targets, and attacked. Four of the eight P-38s fell, including three from the American cover flight, which was the target of Kukla's Schwarm. Kukla shot down his first airplane, but had no witness, and so did not bother to file a claim. His wingman, Uffz. Rudolf Delor, was not so bashful, however, and claimed two. Hans Kukla always believed that one of these was his, but it wasn't – only three claims were filed for the four downed P-38s. The third claim was filed by Lt. Joachim Günther of the 2nd Staffel; this was his 10th victory, all scored since D-Day. No Fw 190 was damaged in the encounter. The P-38s belonged to a frequent opponent of the Geschwader, the 474th Fighter Group's 428th Squadron. The four Americans that returned filed claims for 3-3-3 Fw 190s, probably a case of overclaiming by a unit caught in an unfavorable tactical situation, although I/JG 2 may have gotten involved in this battle. The P-38 pilots were ultimately awarded credits of 1-4-1. The Fw 190 pilots landed on Krefeld to refuel, and spent the night there.

The first First Gruppe pilots practiced flying Fw 190D-9s today. Borris's outfit was not afforded the luxury of withdrawing from the front, but had to train in their new equipment while remaining on combat status at Fürstenau. It was planned to re-equip each Staffel of the First Gruppe in turn, to minimize the disruption to operational flying.

For the third time this year, the Second Gruppe had been taken off operations for an extended period to train and refit, while the First and Third Gruppen soldiered on at the front. This could not be a coincidence, but the source and reason for this favored treatment is unknown. Was it believed that the Second Gruppe could benefit more from the down time because it was inherently the strongest Gruppe, or the weakest? Based on the data, the former is more likely, but politics may have played a role. Major Borris and Major Mietusch may have pleaded that it was their patriotic duty to remain at the front.

The Second Gruppe pilots returned to the front and their new base at Nordhorn-Clausheide in seventy-four Fw 190D-9s, their numbers bolstered by twenty brand-new pilots. The pilots' opinions of the "long-nosed Dora", or Dora-9, as it was variously nicknamed, were mixed. The new model was intended to correct the Fw 190's most glaring weakness, its poor high-altitude performance. What came out of Kurt Tank's shop was a compromise. Tank did not like the liquid-cooled Jumo 213A engine, but it was the best choice available. The long in-line engine had to be balanced by a lengthened rear fuselage to maintain the proper center of gravity, making the Fw 190D four feet longer than the Fw 190A. The new airplane lacked the high turn rate and incredible rate of roll of its close-coupled radial-engine predecessor. It was a bit faster, however, with a maximum speed of 680 km/h (422 mph) at 6600 meters (21,650 feet). Its 2240 horsepower with methanol-water injection (MW 50) gave it excellent acceleration in combat situations. It also climbed and dived more rapidly than the Fw 190A, and so proved well suited to the dive-and-zoom ambush tactics favored by the Schlageter pilots. Many of the early models were not equipped with tanks for methanol, which was in very short supply in any event. At low altitude, the top speed and acceleration of these examples were inferior to those of Allied fighters. Hans Hartigs recalled that only one of the first batch of Dora-9s received by the First Gruppe had methanol-water injection, and the rest had a top speed of only 590 km/h (360 mph). The armament of the Fw 190D-9 was much lighter than that of the Fw 190A-8. The planned engine-mounted cannon had not materialized, and the standard D-9 was armed with two 13 mm MG 131 machine guns above the engine and two 20 mm MG 151/20 machine cannon in the wing roots.

The Second Gruppe winter home at Nordhorn-Clausheide (Nordhorn was the town, Clausheide was the airfield) was 34 kilometers (21 miles) southwest of the Geschwaderstab and the First Gruppe at Fürstenau, and had the best facilities of the three Geschwader airfields. It had been built originally in 1928 as a private airfield for the Krupp organization, and had been in constant use since then, first as a civil field, and since 1939 as a Luftwaffe base. Its landing ground was carpeted with heath over sand, and was usable in the worst weather. The field was approximately 1000 meters long by 400 meters wide (3250 x 1300 feet); its long axis was aligned with the prevailing westerly wind. The 5th Staffel dispersal was at the west end of the field; the 6th, 7th, and 8th, at the east end. The 5th served as the alert Staffel. On Gruppe missions the 5th always took off first, from west to east, and made a gentle left turn away from the field. The 6th, 7th, and 8th Staffeln then took off to the west, joining the 5th Staffel over the town of Nordhorn. The Gruppe could be assembled very quickly in the air. There were few permanent revetments for the aircraft, only parking spaces, but these were very well hidden within the dense forest found on three sides of the landing ground. Five flak towers surrounded the field. There were six stone buildings, including a sheep barn used as a hangar. The other buildings were standard wooden huts and barracks. The pilots were quartered in private homes in Nordhorn. This proved very beneficial to morale; the citizens were very supportive of "their" pilots, and a number of romances bloomed. The pilots breakfasted in their quarters before coming to the field in the mornings. Dinner was on the base; supper, in a restaurant in town that was used as a pilots' mess.

JG 26 Victory Claims: 10 - 17 December 1944

Date	Rank	Name	Unit	Cl #	Aircraft	Place	Time	Opponent	Conf
10-12-44	Lt.	Söffing	4 CO	23	P-47	Bonn (NN6,1)	1538	373 FG	unk
17-12-44	Lt.	Günther	2	10	P-38	Aachen (PN3-ON1-2)	1527	474 FG	unk

17-12-44	Uffz.	Delor	4	1	P-38	Aachen (PN-ON)	1525	474 FG	unk
17-12-44	Uffz.	Delor	4	2	P-38	Aachen (PN-ON)	1530	474 FG	unk

18 December

The First Gruppe reported a strength of 52 Fw 190As and 28 Fw 190D-9s, but most of the serviceable Fw 190As were still at Krefeld. Only six aircraft could be made ready for a morning mission, and they failed to contact the enemy. Seventeen Focke-Wulfs took off at 1215 for a Jabojagd to St. Vith. The pilots sighted twelve P-38s, and were then attacked by thirty P-51s from above, but evaded the Americans and headed for Krefeld, landing to report no successes or losses.

The Second Gruppe flew its first mission in its Dora-9s, but failed to contact the enemy. The Third Gruppe flew two missions; the second ended in tragedy. Oblt. Reischer, the leader on both missions, was killed. His casualty report states that he failed to return from a combat mission, but that is not what happened. In the morning, Reischer took off on a full-strength mission, but rather than heading for the Ardennes as ordered, he flew around Lower Saxony for the next hour, never approaching the combat zone. Reischer left for the command post immediately after landing. Soon afterward, Uffz. Gehrke was summoned to the telephone to speak to Hptm. Krupinski. Gehrke had piloted the designated control aircraft, the "locomotive", whose FuG 16ZY transmissions were used by the command post to keep track of the formation's location. Krupinski simply wanted to know if Gehrke had stayed with the formation at all times. Gehrke answered yes. Reischer soon returned to the dispersal, red-faced from what his pilots believed to be a few cognacs, with orders for a second mission. The aircraft were serviced quickly and took off, this time flying southwest to the Ardennes. The pilots sighted Allied fighters, but could not reach a position for an attack, and returned to Plantlünne thirty minutes later. Reischer disappeared in the clouds shortly before the rest of the Gruppe landed, and he was discovered some time later sitting in his plane on the other side of the large Plantlünne landing ground. He was dead – shot in the head with his own pistol. Heinz Gehrke later learned that after the first mission, Reischer had reported that the Gruppe attacked armor around Aachen, and later fought an air battle – which Krupinski knew had not taken place because of the transmissions of Gehrke's FuG 16ZY.

Reischer apparently suffered a total failure of nerve on the morning mission. Such failures were not an uncommon experience in the Geschwader, but this one involved an entire Gruppe. Reischer tried to lie his way out of the situation, and was caught by the evidence of the FuG 16ZY. Walter Krupinski states that he was ordered by Obstlt. Priller to offer Reischer the options of flying an immediate, successful (or fatal) second mission, or standing trial for cowardice in the face of the enemy – the penalty for which was the firing squad. The second mission was inconclusive, and Peter Reischer found and took a third option. The newly-commissioned Lt. Hermann Guhl replaced Reischer as leader of the 11th Staffel.

JG 26 Casualties: 14 - 18 December 1944

Date	Rank	Name	Cas	Unit	Aircraft	WNr	Mkgs	Place	Time	Cause	Allied Unit
14-12-44	Uffz.	Gehrke, Heinz	WIA	11	Bf 109G-14	463111	yl 23	S of Rheine	1430	Tempest	56 Sqd
14-12-44	Obfw.	Laub, Karl	KIA	11	Bf 109K-4	330357	yl 8	NW of Münster-Burgsteinfurt	1445	Tempest	56 Sqd
14-12-44	Gefr.	Kraus, Wolfgang	KIA	12	Bf 109G-14	462983	yl 11	5km NE of-Borghorst	1445	Tempest	56 Sqd
14-12-44	Uffz.	Wiesel, Friedrich	WIA	12	Bf 109K-4	331323	bl 22	W of Dorsten	1435	Spitfire	412 Sqd
18-12-44	Uffz.	Burckhardt, Gottfried	WIA	8	Fw 190D-9	400209	bl 13	Plantlünne a/f	1535	landing	n/a
18-12-44	Oblt.	Reischer, Peter	KIA	11 CO	Bf 109K-4	330386	yl 20	Almelo	1250	combat	

23 December

The entire Geschwader was grounded for four days because of fog, snow, and freezing rain. Today a high-pressure front pushed enough moisture from the skies over the

A gathering of First Gruppe officers at Fürstenau on 20 December. From left: Lt. Waldemar Söffing, unknown, Lt. Joachim Günther, Oblt. Franz Kunz, Oblt. Georg Kiefner, Lt. Hans-Hermann Krieger (POW 24 Dec 44), Lt. Wiedemann (engineer). *(Ossenkop)*

Ardennes to permit aerial activity by both sides. A beautiful sunrise meant a good day for the beleaguered American defenders in the Ardennes. Ninth Air Force B-26s, P-37s, and P-38s soon filled the skies; the 8th Air Force and RAF's Bomber Command mounted hastily-planned operations to bomb transportation targets east of the battle zone. Jagdkorps II split its fighters; some were sent after the heavy bombers, but most were ordered to the Ardennes.

Twenty-three Fw 190As of the 2nd and 3rd Staffeln took off from Fürstenau at 1114. Their orders were to fly to the tip of the Ardennes salient, there to defend the Panzers of Army Group B against attacks by Allied bombers. Their first challenge was to avoid P-47s in the vicinity of the airfield. Six Focke-Wulfs successfully drew off the Thunderbolts, and then sighted an Allied artillery spotter, which was shot down by Lt. Günther. The rest of the German force proceeded to the ordered patrol zone, and attacked a formation of Marauders, claiming the destruction of three. Thunderbolts then arrived, in the form of the 8th Air Force's 56th Fighter Group on a sweep, and treated the Fw 190s very roughly. Four were shot down; their pilots were all initially reported as missing. The bodies of Uffz. Franz Wering and Uffz. Edwin Zubiako were recovered, but Uffz. Hermann Bischoff and Ogfr. Erhard Schmidt remained missing in 1998. By 1200, the pilots of the Gruppe were landing wherever they could; most chose Krefeld. Five aircraft made crash landings, injuring two pilots, Ogfr. Dieter Krägeloh and Lt. Werner Mathony. The Gruppe was released from further operations at noon. The B-26 units cannot be identified. The 9th Bomber Command lost thirty-eight medium bombers today, to what it described as the most furious aerial opposition it ever encountered.

The Second Gruppe flew its first Fw 190D-9 mission. Nineteen of the "long-nosed Doras" left Nordhorn at 1152 and headed southwest toward the Ardennes. They were spotted and attacked by a squadron of 364th Fighter Group P-51s which was flying a sweep in support of the 8th Air Force mission. Fw. Werner Frass was shot down and killed. Lt. Helmut Wirth force-landed without injury, and ran from his airplane just before it exploded. Major Hackl claimed one of the P-51s, which was able to make a forced landing on the Allied side of the lines. Hackl then received word of an unescorted heavy bomber formation near Köln, and led five aircraft in that direction. The bombers soon came into view – a small force of Lancasters and Mosquitoes. The first victim of the fighters' attack was the leading Lancaster; it was followed by five more Lancasters and one Mosquito. Major Hackl and his men filed seven victory claims, exactly matching the RAF losses. Uffz. Karl Hött also claimed a Lancaster, but his claim was not filed. The German fighters were not touched by British return fire.

The RAF mission had gone wrong almost from the start, when two Lancasters collided over the Channel. The attacking force comprised thirty Lancasters and two Mosquitoes from Bomber Command's elite No. 8 (Pathfinder) Group. Their target was the Köln railroad station. It was to have been located and bombed using the Oboe navigation aid, but a sudden clearing of the solid cloud cover necessitated a change in tactics, resulting in a great deal of confusion within the formation. The German fighters hit them on the target run, and destroyed any remaining hope of a successful bombing attack. Five of the Lancasters lost were from No. 582 Squadron; the sixth, from No. 405 Squadron. A No. 105 Sqd. Oboe-equipped Mosquito was downed by Major Hackl. The leader of the attack force, S/L R.A.M. Palmer, was awarded a posthumous Victoria Cross.

The American fighter-bombers had already discovered the new bases of the Geschwader. The Second Gruppe lost two of its new Dora-9s to fighter-bombers, and another two were destroyed in forced-landings after their mission. The Third Gruppe was apparently not called on to fly today. It lost one Messerschmitt in a bombing attack on Plantlünne.

JG 26 Victory Claims: 23 December 1944

Date	Rank	Name	Unit	Cl #	Aircraft	Place	Time	Opponent	Conf
23-12-44	Lt.	Günther	2	11	Auster	Aachen (PN2-3)	1120		unk
23-12-44	Lt.	Ahrens	3	11	B-26	Aachen (PN7)	1130		unk
23-12-44	Fw.	Franz	3	2	B-26	Aachen (PN7)	1130		unk
23-12-44	Maj.	Hackl	II CO	167	P-51	Köln-Bonn	1252	364 FG	unk
23-12-44	Maj.	Hackl	II CO	168	Lancaster	Köln	1254	405 or 582 Sqd	unk
23-12-44	Maj.	Hackl	II CO	169	Mosquito	Köln-Mönchen-Gladbach	1256	105 Sqd	unk
23-12-44	Ofhr.	Seyd	5	1	Lancaster	40km W of Köln	1300	405 or 582 Sqd	unk
23-12-44	Ofhr.	Heuser Helm.	6	1	Lancaster	W of Köln	1300	405 or 582 Sqd	unk
23-12-44	Fw.	Hött	6		Lancaster	near Hengelo	1300	405 or 582 Sqd	no
23-12-44	Oblt.	Radener	7 CO	22	Lancaster	W of Köln	1257	582 Sqd	unk
23-12-44	Oblt.	Radener	7 CO	23	Lancaster	NW of Köln-NNW of Düren	1301	405 or 582 Sqd	unk
23-12-44	Ofhr.	Schulwitz	8	5	Lancaster	Köln-Bonn	1257	582 Sqd	unk

JG 26 Casualties: 23 December 1944

Date	Rank	Name	Cas	Unit	Aircraft	WNr	Mkgs	Place	Time	Cause	Allied Unit
23-12-44	Uffz.	Bischoff, Hermann	KIA	2	Fw 190A-8	171523	bk 16	Nettersheim-St. Vith	1145	P-47	56 FG
23-12-44	Lt.	Mathony, Werner	WIFA	2	Fw 190A-9	750136	bk 6	Krefeld		landing	n/a
23-12-44	Ogfr.	Schmidt, Erhard	KIA	2	Fw 190A-8	171506	bk 3	Münster area		P-47	56 FG
23-12-44	Ogfr.	Krägeloh, Dieter	WIFA	3	Fw 190A-8	738172	yl 13	Rondorf		no fuel	n/a
23-12-44	Uffz.	Wering, Franz	KIA	3	Fw 190A-8	732040	yl 16	W of Düren		P-47	56 FG
23-12-44	Uffz.	Zubiako, Edwin	KIA	3	Fw 190A-8	173822	yl 3	W of Düren-SE of Malmedy	1130	P-47	56 FG
23-12-44	Lt.	Wirth, Helmut	WIA	5	Fw 190D-9	210164	wh 12	near Münster-Buldern		P-51	364 FG
23-12-44	Fw.	Frass, Werner	KIA	8	Fw 190D-9	210168	bl 5	W of Köln	1250	P-51	364 FG

Lt. Peter Crump (center) shows the proper respect for the III/JG 54 Spiess (sergeant major) at Varrelbusch in late 1944. The civilian on the left is a Junkers engineer; next to him is Lt. Theo Nibel. *(Crump)*

24 December

The skies over western Europe dawned clear, permitting the 8th Air Force to mount its largest mission of the war. More than two thousand heavy bombers were escorted by 853 fighters to a number of airfields and communications centers in western Germany. General Peltz was forced to divert his fighters from the Ardennes battlefield to combat this armada.

The first combat mission for the new Fw 190D-9s of the First Gruppe was an attempted interception of the heavy bombers. It was not a success. Eighteen fighters, most from the 1st Staffel, took off from Fürstenau at 1114, led by Oblt. Heckmann. Eight planes aborted immediately. Lt. Günther crash-landed, suffering minor injuries. Uffz. Seidl apparently made off on his own with his Schwarm, and returned claiming one "Auster", actually an American L-5 from the 153rd Liaison Squadron, which crashed. The seven airplanes left in the formation attacked between sixty and eighty B-17s and their fighter escorts northwest of Liège. The German survivors straggled back to Fürstenau after 1600, having made intermediate landings at other fields. They claimed the destruction of one P-38 and damage to one B-17, but three 1st Staffel Dora-9s never returned. Two had suffered engine failure. Both of their pilots made successful forced landings, but behind the Allied lines, resulting in the capture of Uffz. Erwin Kabowski and Lt. Hans Krieger. The third pilot, Uffz. Wilhelm Jesinger, was shot down by a P-38, probably from the 367th Fighter Group, and was still missing in 1998.

The interceptors sent up by the Second Gruppe did not succeed in reaching the bombers, but had some success against the swarming fighter-bombers. Five P-47s were claimed over Liège. They were from the 36th Fighter Group's 53rd Squadron, which lost two aircraft, while claiming four German fighters. Fw. Emil Paul and Uffz. Hans-Georg Walter failed to return from the mission; Walter's body was found in 1986, and Paul was still missing in 1998. Uffz. Franz Körner bailed out with severe injuries that prevented him from returning to the Geschwader. Lt. Siegfried Sy force-landed on Köln-Wahn with combat damage. He left his airplane there and returned to Nordhorn by train. He detoured to Coesfeld to wish his former landlady a merry Christmas – and met Lt. Gottfried Dietze in the town trying to unwind after a traumatic afternoon.

Lt. Siegfried Benz of the 6th Staffel also failed to return from the mission; his fate was unusually tragic. A Luftwaffe eyewitness on the airfield at Düsseldorf saw a single Bf 109 chase two Fw 190D-9s across the field, with the Dora-9s rocking their wings and firing recognition signals. Benz's aircraft crashed on the edge of the field and exploded, while Gottfried Dietze belly-landed on the landing ground. The III/JG 1 Messerschmitt pilot then landed on the field to claim his two "Mustangs" as victories.

The Second Gruppe formation leaders had all taken part in the early mission, and when a second mission was ordered, Fw. Heinz Gomann was the senior pilot on the duty list. He led about fifteen Focke-Wulfs to the north of the Ardennes, where they encountered Spitfires, but the resulting combat was without result. Uffz. Hött claimed a Thunderbolt, but his claim was never filed. While *en route* back to Nordhorn, Gomann and his wingman formed up on Hptm. Steindl from the First Gruppe Stab, who was returning to Fürstenau after an intermediate landing on Krefeld. Gomann had been an instructor at Avignon under Steindl's command, and decided to follow him to Fürstenau to wish him a merry Christmas. Gomann's wingman forgot to lower his landing gear at Fürstenau, and belly-landed. This could have resulted in confinement, but Major Borris was apparently in a forgiving mood. The pilots spent the evening celebrating the season, and then at midnight decided to wish the other units in the area a merry Christmas. Their vehicle managed to collide head-on with the only other truck in the area, which happened to be on a similar mission. The celebrants were taken to the hospital with minor injuries.

Hptm. Krupinski's Third Gruppe was also ordered to intercept the heavy bombers, and led about twenty Bf 109s up from Plantlünne. While the Messerschmitts were forming up at 6000 meters (20,000 feet), a lone P-51 passed right in front of the Gruppe. Krupinski exploded the Mustang with a single burst of fire. The propeller governor on Uffz. Georg Genth's aircraft then malfunctioned, and he aborted the mission. He had to evade some P-47s, was then taken under fire by German Flak, and decided to land on Köln-Butzweilerhof for fuel and servicing. The airfield had just been bombed, and a Fw 190 landing ahead of Genth taxied into a crater. Genth landed between the craters and taxied to the refueling point. The groundcrewmen tinkered with his propeller mechanism and announced that it was fixed. Genth was anxious to leave before dark and get back to Plantlünne for the base Christmas party, and took off despite warnings from the technical officer and the weatherman. He took off into a low-lying cloud, and immediately discovered that the propeller governor had been connected backward, and could not be gotten out of fine pitch. His radiator boiled over, and his engine began overheating. Genth had to drop below the overcast and crash-land his aircraft, which overturned in a farmyard. His life was saved by a woman who pulled him free, not knowing that Genth had forgotten to turn off the ignition, and that the airplane was liable to explode at any moment. He thought that he had come through the crash uninjured, but later found that he had jammed four discs in his spine; these would give him constant problems after the war. Genth was still anxious to get back to Plantlünne, and walked to the local train station. He found a comrade from training days in the waiting room. The two decided not to tempt fate by doing any more traveling, and celebrated Christmas eve in the small town.

JG 26 Victory Claims: 24 December 1944

Date	Rank	Name	Unit	Cl #	Aircraft	Place	Time	Opponent	Conf
24-12-44	Lt.	Kiefner	1 CO	12	P-38	Liège (PL3)	1224	367 FG	unk
24-12-44	Fw.	Seidl	2		Auster	Bastogne (QM2-6)	1130	L-5	unk
24-12-44	Maj.	Hackl	II CO	170	P-47	Liège (PL-PM)	1228	36 FG	unk
24-12-44	Maj.	Hackl	II CO	171	P-47	Liège (PL-PM)	1230	36 FG	unk
24-12-44	Lt.	Vogt	5 CO	47	P-47	Liège (PL-PM)	1228	36 FG	unk
24-12-44	Lt.	Glunz	6 CO	69	P-47	Liège (PL-PM)	1227	36 FG	unk
24-12-44	Lt.	Glunz	6 CO	70	P-47	Liège (PL-PM)	1228	36 FG	unk
24-12-44	Fw.	Hött	6		P-47	N of Liège (OL-OM)	1500		no

Date	Rank	Name	Cas	Unit	Aircraft	WNr	Mkgs	Place	Time	Cause	Allied Unit
24-12-44	Uffz.	Jesinger, Wilhelm	KIA	1	Fw 190D-9	600174	wh 13	SE of Huy	1130	P-38	367 FG
24-12-44	Uffz.	Kabowski, Erwin	POW	1	Fw 190D-9	210912	wh 9	Liège	1130	engine	n/a
24-12-44	Lt.	Krieger, Hans-Hermann	POW	1	Fw 190D-9	600164	wh 10	Liège	1130	engine	n/a
24-12-44	Lt.	Günther, Joachim	WIFA	2	Fw 190A-9	750149	bl 14	SW of Rheine		engine	n/a
24-12-44	Uffz.	Walter, Hans-Georg	KIA	5	Fw 190D-9	210146	wh 1	E of Malmedy		P-47	36 FG
24-12-44	Lt.	Benz, Siegfried	KIA	6	Fw 190D-9	210188	bk 5	near Düren		Bf 109	III/JG 1
24-12-44	Fw.	Paul, Arthur	KIA	6	Fw 190D-9	210114	bk 11	Liège-Bastogne		P-47	36 FG
24-12-44	Uffz.	Körner, Franz	WIA	8	Fw 190D-9	500031	bl 2	Haltern-Dülmen		P-47	36 FG

Oblt. Glunz distributes bottles of egg liqueur to his 6th Staffel pilots after a successful December mission, probably that of the 24th. *(Molge)*

25 December

A heavy morning fog burned off, leaving clear skies. It was apparent by now that the German offensive would never reach its initial objective, the Meuse River. The Allies were building up their forces on the flanks of the salient for a counterattack. Jagdkorps II, while still ordering its fighters to defend the German spearheads, added the requirement that they should also protect the flanks, while attempting to locate the Allied tank forces by armed reconnaissance. After the celebrations of the previous night, the efforts by the Geschwader were largely ineffectual. The First Gruppe reported in the morning that only nine of its Focke-Wulfs were serviceable. The Stab and the 2nd and 3rd Staffeln were taken off operations to train in the Fw 190D-9. The morning mission took off at 1100 – seven Fw 190D-9s, led by Obfw. Schwarz. Two aborted with bad engines; the other five reached Koblenz at an altitude of 1000 meters (3200 feet), and were attacked there by fifteen P-51s. The Focke-Wulfs evaded the Mustangs and returned to base without loss.

Major Hackl led his Second Gruppe and the Third Gruppe in a morning mission, probably in conjunction with that of the First Gruppe. Hackl claimed a Lightning near Wesel, but Fw. Alfred Hoppe of the 7th Staffel was shot down by P-51s and crashed in his plane, and two more pilots were killed, probably by P-51s, after making intermediate landings on Fürstenau: Fw. Bernhard Meindl (6th Staffel) and Uffz. Rupert Sigmund (10th Staffel).

The afternoon mission was another combined one, this time under the leadership of Lt. Glunz. At 1420 fighters of the three Gruppen assembled over Plantlünne at 200 meters and headed for Dinant to search for fighter-bombers and medium bombers. The formation split up, and the Second and Third Gruppen failed to contact the enemy. The five First Gruppe Fw 190D-9s found plenty – an estimated sixty P-47s and 60-80 medium bombers. Lt. Hans Hartigs of the 4th Staffel was able to hit a Thunderbolt by diving on their formation from ahead and then zooming back into the overcast before the rest could pursue. He found solid cloud to hide in at 7500 meters (25,000 feet). The five Dora-9s returned to Fürstenau without damage.

Oblt. Adolf Glunz and Lt. Heinz Kemethmüller engage in a little horseplay at Nordhorn after the return of the Second Gruppe to the front in December. *(Glunz via Bakker)*

III/JG 54 returned to the combat zone, still led by Hptm. Robert Weiss, a member of JG 26 back in its glory days on the Kanalfront. His Gruppe was put under the command of JG 26, and it is thus appropriate to summarize its story in this history. Its new base was near the village of Varrelbusch, 50 kilometers (30 miles) northeast of Fürstenau. Obstlt. Priller welcomed the assembled pilots back to the front today, shaking each man's hand. The unit had been built up to its full strength of sixty-eight Fw 190D-9s. The Staffelkapitäne were all experienced pilots. Oblt. Willi Heilmann led the 9th Staffel; Lt. Peter Crump, the 10th; Lt. Hans Prager, the 11th; and Lt. Hans Dortenmann, the 12th. Most of the other pilots were Nachwuchs, fresh from the training schools.

26 December

The weather today was excellent, with cloudless skies and unlimited visibility. In its daily orders, Jagdkorps II stressed its desire to make concentrated, decisive attacks on low-flying enemy aircraft over the Ardennes combat zone, while simultaneously carrying out tactical reconnaissance; learning the locations of Allied troop concentrations on the flanks of the salient was especially important.

Despite the stated need for concentration, the morning mission of the First Gruppe was an independent one. Oblt. Hartigs led every operational Dora-9, fifteen in all, up from Fürstenau at 1018 and headed for the combat zone. Twelve of them got there. The mission was intended to be a ground-controlled interception, but when Hartigs' FuG 16ZY failed, he changed the mission to a freie Jagd, since he did not trust any other pilot of the formation with command of the unit. Hartigs reached the tip of the Ardennes salient and spotted the leading Panzer units, but saw that they had been abandoned, apparently from lack of fuel and/or ammunition. He had carried out his original instructions as best he could, but had not seen any Allied aircraft. Since his unit was under standing orders not to return from a mission without contacting the enemy, he turned his twelve Focke-Wulfs to the north and began to climb, knowing full well that he would be detected by Allied radar, which would vector fighters to attack the intruders.

Hans Hartigs' wish for combat was soon fulfilled. The Mustangs of the 8th Air Force's 361st Fighter Group had moved from England to France on 23 December to reinforce the air forces available to resist the German push. On this day, the Group's 376th Squadron was flying a sweep near Trier at 5200 meters (17,000 feet) when a dozen Focke-Wulfs crossed its course, two thousand feet below, and then turned and climbed toward them. A general dogfight ensued. Lt. Vanden Heuvel, who was flying as ass-end Charlie, engaged a Fw 190 which was attacking his element leader. He hit the fighter squarely with a 20-degree deflection shot , and it dived into the ground. He zoomed up, looking for more action, and spotted two fighters on the deck. These proved to be an Fw 190 and a pursuing P-51. The latter was piloted by the American formation leader, who was out of ammunition, and asked Vanden Heuvel to take over. The Focke-Wulf was already smoking, and took very little evasive action as the American closed to 180 meters (200 yards). At the first burst of fire, the German fighter half-rolled and its pilot dropped out. George Vanden Heuvel retains an image of the German pilot's "beautiful leather outfit trimmed in white".

That splendidly-dressed pilot was Oblt. Hartigs, wearing his fighter pilot's leather coveralls. He bailed out when his oil pressure dropped and his canopy filmed over with oil. The first thing he saw when he landed was the body of one of his 4th Staffel pilots, Uffz. Hermann Grad, lying on his parachute; he had been shot at close range. Hartigs had no way of knowing the depth of feeling of the American infantry against any and all Germans, as a result of the SS massacres at Malmedy and elsewhere in the Ardennes. He feels today that his clothing may have saved his life. He was wearing no decorations or badges of rank, and feigned confusion when his captors shouted at him. He thus survived the critical first few minutes after his capture, and did not produce his pilot's identity card until he was safely inside an American command post. Hartigs spent his first night of captivity in a pigsty, under the close guard of Belgian resistance fighters.

Two 4th Staffel pilots, Flg. Hans Bergmeier and Uffz. Ludwig Sattler, were killed by the Mustangs. A 1st Staffel pilot, Uffz. Hans Schöndorf, was shot down and taken prisoner. This was Schöndorf's first flight since injuring his hand on 3 December, and thus his first flight in an Fw 190D-9. It was badly out of trim and pulled constantly to the right, but Schöndorf refused to abort the mission, which was his third combat sortie. After the formation was split up by Mustangs, Schöndorf tried to come to the aid of a comrade with an enemy fighter on his tail, but was hit himself, and spun out. He recovered near the ground and headed for the German lines, but was overtaken easily by two P-51s and shot down at low altitude. He landed north of Sedan with severe injuries, was quickly taken prisoner, and was sent to a hospital in England. He was then shipped to a POW camp in Tennessee, and was returned to Germany and discharged in November, 1945.

The Americans were awarded six victory credits for this engagement; the true German losses were five. No Mustangs were lost, although Obfw. Schwarz claimed a certain, and Uffz. Delor a probable victory when they eventually returned to Fürstenau after intermediate landings for fuel. The biggest news the returning pilots had for their comrades was the Mustangs' superiority in speed and acceleration to their Dora-9s, none of which were equipped with methanol injection. The Gruppe was released from further duty for the day. The 2nd and 3rd Staffeln continued training. Fw. Norbert Seidl was burned slightly when his fighter caught fire on a training mission. His airplane was badly damaged when he force-landed on Fürstenau.

There is no evidence that the Second or Third Gruppen flew a morning mission. They both took off for the battle zone in early afternoon. This may have originated as a combined mission, but the formation split up, and many of the pilots failed to make contact with the enemy. Lt. Gerhard Vogt, the 5th Staffel Kapitän, claimed an Auster near Bastogne. The OKW communiqué credited the Third Gruppe with three P-38s, but this battle cannot be traced. Lt. Wolfgang Kühne of the 12th Staffel was shot down and killed between Aachen and Liège by P-51s.

JG 26 Victory Claims: 25 - 26 December 1944

Date	Rank	Name	Unit	Cl #	Aircraft	Place	Time	Opponent	Conf
25-12-44	Oblt.	Hartigs	4	6	P-47-prob	Dinant-Liège	1500		no
25-12-44	Major	Hackl	II CO	172	P-38	Wesel (KO5-7)	1155		unk
26-12-44	Obfw.	Schwarz E.	1	9	P-51	Givet (QU-QL)	1100	361 FG	unk
26-12-44	Uffz.	Delor	4	3	P-51-prob	Dinant (QL-PL)	1100	361 FG	no
26-12-44	Lt.	Vogt	5 CO	48	Auster	Bastogne (near QM)	1415		unk

27 December

The orders from Jagdkorps II took on an increasingly strident tone. The German Army's complaints about the performance of the Luftwaffe over the Ardennes had reached Hitler *via* Albert Speer, who had visited the headquarters of the two army commanders, SS General Sepp Dietrich and General Hasso von Manteuffel. The Army's supply lines east of the battle zone were totally disrupted. Nothing could move during the daytime, either on the lines of communication or in the front lines. In response to the growing complaints, German fighters flew 357 Jabojagd sorties today, and an additional seventy-eight sorties that were classed as ground support. Twenty-eight air victories were claimed, according to the OKW communiqué, but thirty-six pilots were lost or missing, and fourteen were wounded.

The contributions to this effort by JG 26 were minimal. The Second Gruppe flew one mission, but without result. Nothing is known of the activities of the Third Gruppe. The 1st and 4th Staffeln took off at 1400 under Lt. Kiefner's command to fly a combined mission to Bastogne with II/JG 1. Three pilots aborted, and the rest got split up without contacting the enemy. The eight First Gruppe Focke-Wulfs that completed the mission landed on four different fields.

Uffz. Hans Kukla was now the acting leader of the 4th Staffel, although he had flown fewer than a dozen combat missions. Hartigs' loss left the Staffel with no officers on its active roster. The Staffelführer, Lt. Söffing, had run his automobile into a tree shortly before Christmas and had not yet been restored to combat status. Kukla led a 4th Staffel Schwarm on this mission. He made it back to Fürstenau, while Uffz. Franz Weiss and Uffz. Rudolf Delor landed on Krefeld-Linn. As a former First Gruppe base, this was a favorite alternate landing field with the unit's pilots. Hans Kukla recalls what happened next:

"The afternoon grew late and Uffz. Delor wanted to return to Fürstenau as soon as possible – he had brought his bride to Fürstenau – but there was an order prohibiting the younger pilots from taking off after sundown. Since Uffz. Weiss was an experienced pilot, Uffz. Delor requested that he accompany him on the flight to Fürstenau. Weiss finally yielded to his entreaties, but was late in taking off. Weiss unfortunately lost Delor near Rheine, and landed on Fürstenau by himself. After he had reported to me, he asked whether Delor had already landed. That was not the case, and I had no alternative but to tell the Gruppenkommandeur what had happened. Major Borris naturally became enraged, and held Uffz. Weiss responsible. He had me order the Staffel to fall in. After they had assembled, Major Borris came in. He chewed out the Unteroffizier in front of the Staffel, and sentenced him to five days imprisonment. Weiss was immediately taken by truck to the town jail in Fürstenau. Delor had in the meantime overturned while landing at Hopsten, but suffered no injuries other than a stiff neck. He was restricted from flying for a few days, which caused him no problem at all, since his bride was near at hand."

Despite its long absence from the front for training, there were still doubts as to the combat-worthiness of III/JG 54. Today a familiarization flight over the Münster basin was ordered for all four of its Staffeln. Lt. Crump's 10th Staffel served as high cover, at 8000 meters (26,000 feet). Ground control reported the presence of eight Indianer above them. Hptm. Weiss then reversed course unexpectedly, putting Crump's Staffel in a most precarious position, with both the sun and the unseen enemy to its rear. On the turn, and despite Crump's express warning, two of the Nachwuchs dropped back – to be shot down immediately by Tempests which came plummeting down out of the sun. Lt. Crump shot a Tempest off his wingman's tail, and then caught and hit another fighter in a dive. Back at Varrelbusch, it was discovered that Crump was the only pilot to have fired a shot. Eight Tempests had taken on more than sixty of the newest German aircraft in a surprise attack, downing five for the loss of two. There was so much yelling on the radio that Hptm. Weiss had been unable to find Crump's beleaguered Staffel.

The Tempests belonged to No. 486 Sqd. (RNZAF), which claimed 4-1-1 of the Fw 190Ds. III/JG 54 lost five aircraft destroyed and one damaged; three pilots were killed, and two were injured. Only one Tempest was lost; Crump's first target escaped. Both of the Tempests attacked by Crump belonged to F/O Ray Danzey's Green Section, the squadron's top cover flight. It had climbed while the rest of the squadron dived on Weiss's main formation, but was down-sun when caught by Crump's own Schwarm, which was above everyone else. P/O Jack Stafford was leading Danzey's second element. Jack Stafford recalls:

"In the dogfight I ended up with a German fighter on my tail. He was very close; I could see him through his windshield. We went around & around; he couldn't gain deflection on me, but fired at me several times, almost stalling. I could only keep turning; if I straightened up, I was sure he'd get me. We went around for so long that my coolant boiled over owing to the long period at very slow speed. My windshield was covered, and I left a white trail behind me. When the windshield cleared, the German had gone. Within a minute or so, Bev Hall called me; he was dying. Crump said he was the only one to fire his guns, so it must have been him on my tail. He certainly fired at me, and must have thought he had hit me when I left the coolant trail."

Peter Crump had broken off to defend his wingman, who was under attack by F/O Bev Hall, Danzey's wingman. After Crump shot Hall down, both sides disengaged, Danzey by diving at full throttle. This was the Tempest's standard escape maneuver, giving its pilot the option of leveling out at high speed or zooming back up to altitude; both were maneuvers at which the fighter excelled.

The Hawker Tempest was the newest British fighter to reach the front. It was introduced into the 2nd TAF specifically to fill the air superiority role, and was to become one of the most frequent opponents of III/JG 54 and JG 26. It was clearly superior to the Bf 109K and the Fw 190A at the medium and low altitudes where the ground-support war was fought. It was remarkably similar in concept to the Fw 190D-9, and its published performance figures are close to those of the German fighter. Victory in their combats thus tended to go to the better pilot – which meant that the few experienced German pilots did very well in encounters with the British fighters, but the Nachwuchs generally came out the losers. The Tempest's British and Commonwealth pilots were uniformly enthusiastic about the airplane. Ray Danzey made these comments:

"The Tempest was a huge improvement over its predecessor, the Typhoon, owing to its thinner wing and recessed cannon. It was about 50 mph faster. According to Farnborough tests, the Tempest had better dive and zoom characteristics than any German fighter. All parts, including the engine, were mounted on rubber, which made it a much smoother plane than the Typhoon. It was beautiful, powerful, and rugged, and we felt that we could, if necessary, run away from any German plane except the jets."

Date	Rank	Name	Cas		Unit	Aircraft	WNr	Mkgs	Place	Time	Cause	Allied Unit
25-12-44	Fw.	Meindl, Bernhard	KIA	6		Fw 190D-9	500065	bk 18	Fürstenau-Horneburg		P-51	
25-12-44	Fw.	Hoppe, Alfred	KIA	7		Fw 190D-9	400208	br 13	18km W of Dortmund			P-51
25-12-44	Uffz.	Sigmund, Rupert	KIA	10		Bf 109K-4	330418	bk 8	near Fürstenau	1255	P-51	
26-12-44	Uffz.	Schöndorf, Otto	POW	1		Fw 190D-9	600155	wh 15	Carlsbourg	1100	P-51	361 FG
26-12-44	Fw.	Seidl, Norbert	WIFA	2		FW 190D-9	600362	none	Fürstenau		engine	non-op
26-12-44	Flg.	Bergmeier, Hans	KIA	4		Fw 190D-9	210264	bl 12	near Malmedy	1100	P-51	361 FG
26-12-44	Uffz.	Grad, Hermann	KIA	4		Fw 190D-9	210935	bl 13	near Malmedy	1100	P-51	361 FG
26-12-44	Oblt.	Hartigs, Hans	POW	4		Fw 190D-9	210931	bl 10	E of Florenville	1130	P-51	361 FG
26-12-44	Uffz.	Sattler, Ludwig	KIA	4		Fw 190D-9	210945	bl 8	near Malmedy	1100	P-51	361 FG
26-12-44	Lt.	Kühne, Wolfgang	KIA	12		Bf 109K-4	331331	bl 20	Aachen-Liège	1410	P-51	
27-12-44	Uffz.	Delor, Rudolf	WIFA	4		Fw 190D-9	600364	bl 16	Hopsten a/f		landing	non-op

29 December

After a day of weather-imposed inactivity, the fighters of Jagdkorps II flew 211 sorties, most against RAF fighter-bombers in the Army's rear. The Geschwader again saw little action. The First Gruppe stood down to conduct intensive training in their Fw 190D-9s; 120 flights were made. The Second Gruppe flew a mission early in the afternoon, but apparently no pilot made contact with the Allies. The Third Gruppe was up a little later, with similar results. One Messerschmitt was destroyed, and two damaged, while on this mission, but not in combat.

The Green Heart pilots were fully engaged today; this would go down in the history of III/JG 54 as its *schwarze Tag* (black day). Its mission has been documented elsewhere, but the story bears repeating here, as the incorrect versions reported by some of the less reliable Gruppe members continue to be perpetuated. The morning orders called for a mission by successive Staffeln against British fighter-bombers in the area of Osnabrück, Münster, and Rheine. Altitude was specified as 2000 meters (6500 feet). The orders came from Primadonna, the 3rd Jagddivision controller, who would exercise tactical control using the FuG 16ZY. Contrary to the usual German practice, Hptm. Weiss was not allowed to offer any input into the employment of his Gruppe. Specifically, to fly as individual Staffeln was foolish, and the specified approach altitude was well below the normal patrol height of the 2nd TAF's Tempests and Spitfires.

The Staffeln were ordered to take off one hour apart. Lt. Crump's 10th Staffel, still recovering from the 27th, did not take part in the mission. Oblt. Heilmann led his 9th Staffel up from Varrelbusch at about 0900 hours. As the Staffel approached the Rheine area at its ordered altitude, it was hit from above by the Spitfires of No. 411 Sqd. (RCAF), which quickly killed six of the German pilots; others took to their parachutes. The few survivors landed at Varrelbusch one by one, incoherent from shock. As Heilmann was not among the returnees, Hptm. Weiss could not get a consistent story of what had happened. He nonetheless led his Gruppenstab and the 11th Staffel off the ground at the scheduled time of 1000 hours, determined to carry out the mission as ordered. None of Weiss's Schwarm returned. Fw. Fritz Ungar of the 11th Staffel was the only returnee able to shed any light on the fate of his Kommandeur. After shooting down a Typhoon and losing his Schwarm, Ungar joined up with Weiss and two other pilots. North of Rheine, Ungar saw three Spitfires banking to attack. Weiss and his other two pilots broke sharply to the right. Ungar continued flying ahead, rather than put himself in the line of fire. The other three members of the Schwarm were shot down; the victors were the Norwegian pilots of No. 331 Squadron.

The Typhoon shot down by Fw. Ungar belonged to No. 439 Sqd. (RCAF); its Canadian pilot was taken prisoner by the German Army. Ungar reported engaging "Thunderbolts", but these were really Tempests from No. 56 Squadron. Tempests and Thunderbolts, which had similar wing planforms and canopy shapes, were frequently confused by the Germans. The Tempests and Spitfires shot down and killed a total of seven pilots from the Stab and the 11th Staffel.

Back at Varrelbusch, Oblt. Dortenmann and his 12th Staffel were still scheduled to take off at noon. By interviewing the few returnees and listening to the radio transmissions in the command post, Dortenmann formed a picture of the situation – the entire Münster basin was filled up to an altitude of 5000 meters (16,000 feet) with dozens of enemy air formations of all types, primarily Spitfires. Dortenmann made his decision. He led his twelve Dora-9s off the ground, formed up east of the field, and headed for the battle zone in a steady climb, finally leveling off at 6000 meters (20,000 feet). Dortenmann heard the ground controller's order to drop to 2000 meters and attack Thunderbolts and bombers over Münster, but he stayed where he was. West of Osnabrück, he sighted twenty-two Spitfires 1000 meters (3200 feet) below, made a clean bounce, and shot down two fighters. One German pilot was lost, but Oblt. Dortenmann led his remaining eleven planes back to Varrelbusch in formation.

After Dortenmann's return, Obstlt. Priller informed him that the 3rd Jagddivision had ordered him to be court-martialed. Priller advised him to stay calm and keep a low profile, and the next day instructed Dortenmann to take over the administrative command of III/JG 54. Nothing more was heard of a court-martial.

The Green Heart Gruppe lost thirteen pilots killed and two injured, and at least seventeen aircraft destroyed, while claiming six RAF fighters. The Nachwuchs pilots suffered the worst, but the experienced Obfw. Wilhelm Philipp was injured so severely that he never returned to combat. Philipp had joined II/JG 26 in October 1939 and had fought continuously with the Schlageter Geschwader until transferring to the Green Heart unit in 1942. He was a Knight's Cross holder, and left the battlefield with a score of eighty-one victories. The popular Robert Weiss was also a Knight's Cross recipient, with 121 victories. His Oak Leaves were awarded posthumously. Weiss's position as Gruppenkommandeur was not filled for two months. In the opinion of the survivors, III/JG 54 never recovered entirely from his loss.

31 December

By New Year's Eve, the German drive through the Ardennes had been stopped, and the Americans were pressing in on the salient from both sides. Only the youngest and most naive of the German pilots retained any hopes of Germany's ultimate victory. The successful defense of the western borders that autumn had, however, kept alive the men's hopes for a separate peace with the Western Allies. The Geschwader had performed well since its return to Germany, in that its aerial victories had exceeded its losses. At least 134 victories were claimed; the unit lost 75 pilots killed in combat and another seven in accidents. Seven men had been taken prisoner, and at least forty-eight had been injured. Few pilots spent any time thinking of the record or status of the Geschwader, however. The largest unit to which the typical pilot felt loyalty was the Gruppe, and even the successes of his Gruppe were not as important to him as questions of survival – for himself, his Staffel comrades, and his family.

There were few personnel moves affecting the Geschwader during December other than the addition of replacements to replace the casualties. Oblt. Werner Stoll transferred from the 7th Staffel to a flight test unit. Uffz. Werner Binge, Uffz. Josef Hoppe, and Uffz. Günter Warthemann all transferred into the Geschwader from JG 6, and were assigned to the Second Gruppe. New pilots reporting to the Geschwader during December after completing flight training included: Uffz. Karl Fröb, Ogfr. Helmut Lange, Fhj.-Uffz. Gerhard von Plazer, Uffz. Gerhard Reichow, Ofhr. Hinrich Rodartz, Ogfr. Erhard Schmidt, Gefr. Ernst Thuy, Ogfr. Bodo Vogel – First Gruppe; Uffz. Johannes Brumund, Gefr. Hans Götz, Uffz. Karl Horn, Gefr. Willi Kunz, Ogfr. Hubert Lott, Ogfr. Norbert Risky, Ogfr. Joseph Simmer, Gefr. Horst Trautvetter, Uffz. Helmuth Wirtz - Second Gruppe; Uffz. Andreas Effelsberg, Lt. Kurt Fischer, Lt. Gottfried Meyer, Uffz. Günter Pfeiffer - Third Gruppe.

In the morning the three Gruppen and the attached III/JG 54 flew Jabojagd missions in support of the retreating German armies, despite persistent ground fog and freezing mists. Only III/JG 54 made contact; one of its pilots was wounded in an air battle near Limburg. The Second Gruppe lost one fighter on a non-operational flight, but its pilot was uninjured. No missions were ordered for the afternoon.

At 1430 Priller was handed a flimsy bearing the words "*VARUS 1.1.45 - TEUTONICUS*". This was the order to execute *Unternehmen Bodenplatte* (Operation Baseplate), which had been planned at Genlt. Peltz's 14 December Altenkirchen conference. Priller had not known of his Army's planned Ardennes attack at the time, but it was now obvious that the air and ground attacks had been intended to coincide. However, the weather had generally proved unsuitable for large-scale air operations. The ground offensive had stalled, and to revive the plan now seemed somewhat strange, but *Befehl ist Befehl* (Orders are orders.) Of the enabling code words on the flimsy, *VARUS 1.1.45* set the date for the very next day; *TEUTONICUS* authorized the pilots to be informed, and called for extraordinary measures to prepare all possible aircraft for the operation. There was one positive aspect to the timing; an attack on New Year's morning would in all likelihood find the enemy indisposed. Priller summoned his Gruppenkommandeure to a quick conference in his command post at the Fürstenau middle school. Their first task would be to ensure that their pilots' New Year's Eve celebrations were postponed.

Priller's meeting with Borris, Hackl, and Krupinski was brief. Little time was spent discussing their targets for the following day. These were the familiar Brussels airfields of Evere and Grimbergen, both of which had been occupied by the Geschwader four months previously, on its retreat from France. The length of the mission called for the use of 300 liter auxiliary fuel tanks, so no bombs would be carried. The armorers would be busy, however, re-belting ammunition. A large proportion of incendiary shells would be carried. The radio technicians were to remove the FuG 25 IFF sets from all aircraft. In an unprecedented measure, briefing cards were to be prepared for each pilot. These would contain a map showing check points, turning points, and targets. The pilots would write in further details at their own briefings. Every healthy pilot, however inexperienced, was to take part. The mission would be flown by independent Gruppen, in close formation at low altitude. Each Gruppe would be led across the battle lines by pathfinder aircraft, Ju 88 night fighters, which had been standing by on the three fields of the Geschwader.

The course of each Gruppe would be west across the southern tip of the Zuider Zee. After passing Rotterdam, the fighters would turn south in a broad arc and approach Brussels from the north. After the attack they were to return on a reciprocal course; however, the pilots were not to worry too much about this leg of the mission. In case of problems, they were to fly due east to Germany. Every emergency airfield in western Germany was to be alerted to receive them. In addition, check points and the front lines would be indicated by smoke shells and "golden rain" flares. The plan appeared sound. Pips Priller would once again be leading his Schlageter Geschwader in the air, for the first time as a full Oberst – his promotion had already been announced; it was to become effective New Year's Day. There were no questions, and the Gruppenkommandeure were quickly dismissed to return to their own Gruppe command posts.

Major Karl Borris's headquarters was only a short drive away. He and his staff were lodged in the Kloster Handrup, a Catholic convent and girls' school near the Fürstenau airstrip which his First Gruppe shared with Priller's Geschwaderstab. At 1600, as his own pilots gathered, twenty Fw 190D-9s began landing on the small field. These airplanes represented the entire fighting strength of III/JG 54, which had been placed under Borris's command for the operation. The Green Heart unit had been among the few German Jagdgruppen to fly missions today. Lt. Crump's 10th Staffel had sortied in the morning and had made an intermediate landing at Achmer. From there he led six Dora-9s to Fürstenau. The rest of the unit's aircraft were led in from Varrelbusch by Oblt. Dortenmann, whose formation had been recalled. After seeing to their fighters' servicing, the Green Heart pilots joined the assembly at Handrup.

The pilots waited expectantly in one of the convent's classrooms. Borris entered and told his men and the Green Heart pilots of their mission for the next day. Their target would be the aircraft on the field at Grimbergen, which were to be destroyed by strafing in three or four waves. Borris was a man of few words, not given to bombastic speeches, but his emphasis on the overall strength of the mission and the obvious care devoted to its planning made a deep, favorable impression on the pilots. Their route was discussed orally; maps would be given out the next morning. The time of takeoff was not yet fixed, but all pilots were to be in bed by 2200, in anticipation of an early awakening. New Year's Eve celebrations on base or in the town were strictly forbidden. Not mentioned in the briefing was the action they were to take if they were shot down behind enemy lines. Their only hope was quick surrender; their clothing and equipment were totally inadequate for survival on enemy ground in the winter.

In accordance with Luftwaffe procedure, each pilot was then given his specific formation assignment. The 4th Staffel was well up to strength in aircraft, with thirteen Dora-9s. However, Lt. Söffing, the unit's only officer, was off duty from his automobile accident, and Uffz. Hans Kukla's name had been written in as Staffel leader for the mission. Kukla summoned up all of his courage and refused his orders. His combat experience totaled but one dozen missions, and he felt that the responsibility was too great. Major Borris agreed, and designated Obfw. Erich Schwarz of the 3rd Staffel to lead the 4th.

Pressing his luck, Kukla then put in a word for his friend Franz Weiss, who was in jail in Fürstenau. According to Kukla,

> "Major Borris then told me to get a truck and fetch Weiss back to base. I left immediately with an order to release Weiss. The jailer greeted me and told me laconically that I needed to give Weiss the news myself. I thought I would find Weiss in the cells, but I was wrong. Weiss was sitting in the jailer's dining room with his entire family, celebrating New Year's Eve with cake and punch. My friend was not at all pleased that I had come to take him away – nothing this good had happened to him in quite a while. When he was being admitted to the jail, Franz had told the jailer the reason for his punishment. He was then given the best private room in the building, with a splendid bed. He never even saw a jail cell."

One last pilot straggled in at midnight, displaying the effects of New Year's Eve. Lt. Hans Prager, the 11/JG 54 Staffelführer, had aborted the transfer flight of his Gruppe because of a bad engine, and had then drunk in the New Year in the Green Heart Casino. Much to his surprise, he had been fetched from Varrelbusch by auto. Oberst Priller prevented an ugly confrontation with Borris by pulling Prager aside and appointing him to lead the formation's high cover Schwarm.

Flying by the Second Gruppe had ended at noon. Major Hackl returned from Fürstenau in mid-afternoon and passed the word of the forthcoming mission to his four Staffelkapitäne. They in turn reached all of their pilots before they were dismissed at nightfall, and ordered them to refrain from alcohol that evening, to pack their flight bags for a long mission, and to turn in no later than 2200. Since the pilots were quartered in private homes in Nordhorn, enforcement of the order prohibiting alcohol was up to the self-discipline of each individual pilot.

Although the Third Gruppe route and target were the same as those of the Second Gruppe, Hptm. Krupinski's men were to fly an entirely independent mission. Krupinski's New Year's Eve orders to his pilots at Plantlünne were the same as Major Hackl's at Nordhorn – no alcohol, and lights out at 2200.

Shortly after midnight, the last part of the Bodenplatte order was received in the command posts – *Auftrag HERMANN 1.1.45. Zeit: 09.20 Uhr.* All of the targeted airfields were to be hit simultaneously at the designated time of 0920. A more desirable dawn attack was impossible owing to the limited proficiency of the average German pilot; a dawn takeoff was the best attainable compromise. Each Gruppe flying the mission had to calculate backward to arrive at its own schedule. Wake-up calls for most pilots were ordered for 0430-0500. While the pilots slept, the ground crews worked in the snow to prepare the largest force of German fighters ever to take to the air. The Luftwaffe High Command had thrown the dice for the last time. The ultimate fate of the Jagdwaffe would be determined in the morning.

Chapter Eight

GOTTERDÄMMERUNG

January - 8 May 1945

1 January 1945 - Operation Bodenplatte

I/JG 26 and III/JG 54 Attack Grimbergen

0430: The First Gruppe and III/JG 54 pilots received their wakeup calls.

0500: Breakfast was served in the Gruppe common room at the Kloster Handrup.

0530: The pilots were given their maps and listened to the final briefing. The weather prediction was for a cloudless sky, light winds from the southwest, and a temperature of about -5°C. Takeoff would be aided by canister lights alongside the flying strip. Radio silence was mandatory, and close formation flying was stressed. The men were then issued emergency rations, and in the case of the JG 26 pilots, life jackets; there were not enough for the III/JG 54 pilots.

0630: The pilots reached their dispersals by bus. The aircraft had already been pushed to their takeoff positions by the ground crews. Many of the Jumo 213A engines would not start in the cold, and much last-minute juggling of assignments took place.

0813: The two Ju 88 pathfinder aircraft took off.

0814: Oberst Priller and his long-time wingman, Uffz. Wodarczyk, took off. Next came Major Borris. He was followed by twelve aircraft of Oblt. Heckmann's 3rd Staffel, twelve of Oblt. Kunz's 2nd, ten of Lt. Kiefner's 1st, and ten from the 4th, led by Obfw. Schwarz. Seventeen III/JG 54 pilots brought up the rear. To save time, aircraft took off straight down the field as well as across both diagonals.

0830: All but the last few aircraft formed up in the crystal-clear sky over Fürstenau and then dived for the ground, heading for the Zuider Zee at an altitude of about 30 meters (100 feet). The planned formation of three shallow vees could not be maintained, because it was impossible to keep station in the ground mist. The individual Schwärme, which were flying in line abreast formation, kept together, and the Gruppe formation resolved itself into a long, strung-out line of Schwärme.

0835: The last Focke-Wulf got off the ground. Without their own ground crews, the Green Heart pilots had had great difficulty in getting their aircraft ready to fly the mission. They borrowed several aircraft from the First Gruppe, but three III/JG 54 pilots had to stay behind. At least two ferry pilots belonging to Flüg 1 did fly the mission. Oblt. Dortenmann had brought them with him from Varrelbusch, and selected them in preference to his own men because of their greater experience. Lt. Peter Crump's 10/JG 54 was assigned to flak suppression, and its eight aircraft were positioned last in the formation. The leader of his second Schwarm, Lt. Theo Nibel, had trouble starting his engine, and was the last to take off. It took a long time to catch the formation, but Nibel trailed it toward the target without difficulty.

0842: The Zuider Zee was reached; the formation turned to the southwest, toward Rotterdam.

0845: The formation was fired on by German Flak. The fighters were flying over one of the most heavily defended areas on the continent – the V-2 launching sites around The Hague. The Luftwaffe planners had made a serious error. The pilots were accustomed to being fired on by their own Flak, and some even recall being briefed to expect it on this mission, but none suspected the presence of such a heavy concentration of defensive fire. They had no room to maneuver, and barreled onward through the curtain of tracers.

0845: Ogfr. Manfred Niessen of the 3rd Staffel was shot down near Utrecht. He force-landed without injury, and returned to Fürstenau on the 5th.

0846: The Kapitän of the 2nd Staffel, Oblt. Franz Kunz, was hit. He turned back, was forced to bail out, and was taken to a private clinic in Gouda with severe injuries.

0847: Uffz. Gerhard Kroll of 9/JG 54, who was flying an airplane borrowed from the 4th Staffel, was hit near Rotterdam and made an immediate belly landing. The aircraft burst into flames on impact, and Kroll leapt from the sliding aircraft with the left side of his flying suit on fire. He first jumped into a water-filled ditch, but could not break through the ice, so he beat out the flames with one of his flying boots. He then had to run from the Focke-Wulf's exploding ammunition. Kroll was taken to a Rotterdam hospital with severe facial burns, but was released after only two weeks.

0900: The formation had by now been reduced to forty-seven aircraft. Fourteen aircraft returned early to Fürstenau with equipment defects or damage from German Flak; among the early returns was Oblt. Heckmann. The rest made their turn to the south, and were then taken under fire by Allied ships in the Scheldt.

0910: Obfw. Walter Eckert of 11/JG 54 was shot down and killed. Fw. Paul Steinkamp of 12/JG 54 took a shell in the wing root. He pulled up to 1200 meters (4000 feet) to attempt to regain the German lines, but his controls went out. He had to bail out, and was taken prisoner soon after touching the ground.

0912: Obfw. Werner Zech of 11/JG 54 dived to avoid the ground fire and hit a tree, shearing 10 cm (4 inches) off each propeller blade and puncturing his drop tank, which spewed fuel in a white plume. He turned one wing to the sky and flew as tight a circle as he could to throw off the gunners, and took no hits. He leveled out and headed for Germany, but hit a flock of birds, which further damaged his wings and radiator. The aircraft was almost uncontrollable, but Zech was able to reach Twente. The Fw 190D-9 was repaired sufficiently to regain Varrelbusch on the 8th, but was then handed down to a training unit.

0915: Just past the Scheldt, Major Borris sighted a formation of a dozen Spitfires. He later reported that they turned away without attacking, but the Spitfires, which were from No. 308 Sqd. (Polish), brought down between three and five of the airplanes at the rear of his formation. Ogfr. Dieter Krägeloh had only rejoined the 3rd Staffel a few days previously after sustaining a fractured skull in an October crash. He was detailed to fly as Oblt. Heckmann's wingman, but got off the ground late when his engine was slow to start, and simply joined the nearest formation. Soon after crossing the Scheldt he was struck from the rear by a Spitfire's fire. His wooden propeller was splintered, and he had to kill the engine quickly before it shook the fuselage apart. Too low to bail out, Krägeloh plowed into a clearing in an orchard. Several monks pulled him from the wreckage of his plane. He was interrogated in the hospital by British Intelligence personnel who found him too dazed to be of much value. Later he was taken to England, where he made a complete recovery.

0915: Uffz. Heinz Schulz of the 2nd Staffel was brought down by a Spitfire, but his loss was not witnessed by his comrades. He crashed to his death in a Sinaai street. His identity disk was removed as a souvenir, and he was buried as an

The fuselage of Ogfr. Dieter Krägeloh's Fw 190D-9 "yellow 13" (W.Nr. 500093). It came to rest at Waasmunster after Krägeloh was downed by No. 308 Sqd. (Polish) Spitfires during the Bodenplatte mission. *(Vanlaere via Dedecker)*

unknown airman in the Sinaai cemetery, where he lies today. His case has not yet been resolved by the German authorities.

0916: Fw. Paul Drutschmann of 9/JG 54 was also hit by the Polish Spitfires. His Focke-Wulf was first struck in the right wing from the rear. The startled Drutschmann turned his head, and saw a Spitfire aiming directly at him. The German pilot zoomed up to 200 meters (700 feet) and bailed out. His parachute opened just in time to break his landing in an icy river. He, too, was quickly taken prisoner.

0920: The remaining Focke-Wulfs climbed to 2-300 meters (700-1000 feet) on their approach to Grimbergen. They drifted a little to the west of the field, putting it in the glare of the rising sun. Lt. Peter Crump saw that they were about to miss the field entirely, and took the initiative by diving to the attack, followed by the two flights of his Staffel. Highly visible at the takeoff point on the field was a large white diagonal cross, the international symbol for a non-operational airfield. The Thunderbolt unit that the pilots had been briefed to expect was nowhere to be seen.

0922: Crump made his first pass at this moment, according to the British defenders – two minutes later than the ordered time of attack. He strafed a four-engine bomber at the south edge of the field and set it on fire. Then Crump, seeing no sign of any flak that needed suppressing, led his flight in shooting up everything they saw standing around, including trucks, construction equipment, sheds and barracks.

0925: Lt. Theo Nibel had eventually caught up to his Schwarm, and led it across the field on its assigned task of flak suppression. When Nibel pulled up after the third attack, his engine quit. He had only reached an altitude of 100 meters (320 feet), too low to bail out, so he made a quick decision to belly-land his airplane in a freshly turned field. The landing was perfect, giving the Allies their first example of a near-whole Fw 190D-9. Much to the amazement of the RAF examiners, the airplane had not been brought down by gunfire, but by a partridge strike, which knocked a hole several inches in diameter in his fighter's radiator. In POW camp, Theo Nibel was nicknamed *der Rebhuhnjäger* (the partridge hunter).

0930: The defense of the Grimbergen field was provided by three squadrons of the RAF Regiment, which had no armament heavier than Bren guns. The gunners had ample time to study the German pilots' flight patterns, and corrected their aim accordingly. They kept up their fire, and began to hit their targets. Fhr. Hans-Joachim Werner of the 3rd Staffel was making his second pass when his aircraft caught fire, presumably a result of gunfire. He quickly zoomed to an altitude of 200 meters (650 feet), and bailed out without injury.

0930: Lt. Karl-Heinz Ossenkop of the 2nd Staffel was firing blindly into the smoke on his second pass when his aircraft was hit at an altitude of 60 meters (200 feet). It shuddered and dropped to the right. The airplane was nose-heavy, but kept flying well, except for the pull to the right. He trimmed out the nose-heaviness, throttled back, dropped his flaps

Fhr. Hans-Joachim Werner of the 3rd Staffel. Werner crashed on Grimbergen during the Bodenplatte attack and was captured. *(Bundesarchiv-Freiburg)*

to the takeoff position, and headed east, with no rudder control.

0930: Fw. Karl Hartmann of the 4th Staffel, a rookie on his first combat mission, was flying as Ossenkop's wingman. His aircraft was also hit on his second pass, while in thick smoke. He pulled up and bailed out over the field. He succeeded in impressing his captors as a "particularly dim type", and provided them with no information.

0932: Fw. Günther Egli of 11/JG 54 had had one narrow escape before reaching Grimbergen; German Flak near Rotterdam had ignited his auxiliary tank, but he had managed to jettison it successfully. He was now hit by small-arms fire and had to force-land in the middle of the airfield. He told his captors that he was a pilot in the *Einsatzstaffel* (operational Staffel) of JG 104, an advanced training unit, and that the three pilots of the Staffel had volunteered for, and participated in, Bodenplatte. In fact, Egli had been a member of JG 54 since March, 1944, although he had previously served in JG 104 as a student and later as an instructor. Günther Egli freely admitted to this author that he fabricated the JG 104 Einsatzstaffel as a "white lie" to keep from revealing his true unit to his captors.

0935: The ten Focke-Wulfs of the 4th Staffel were apparently the last to reach Grimbergen. It is not known why they had fallen behind III/JG 54. They arrived after the departure of the rest of the attackers, made several quick strafing passes on the hangars, and turned for home.

0937: The German machine cannon fell silent, according to the British records, after an attack of exactly fifteen minutes duration. Major Borris's pilots, facing only Bren gun fire, claim to have made from seven to ten slow firing passes across the field. They noted the presence of four four-engine bombers, one twin-engine bomber, and one Mustang, and claimed the destruction of all – destruction confirmed by British sources. In addition to the above-listed aircraft, twelve trucks, two tankers, and two hangars were set on fire, several hangars were seriously damaged, and one antiaircraft position was silenced.

0940: Willy Sydow of the 2nd Staffel, flying apart from the main formation, was killed by German Flak near Eindhoven.

0955: Lt. Ossenkop approached the first airfield he saw, which proved to be Twente, and made a smooth landing. His rudder was gone; his right elevator was jammed down. The mechanic told him that he had been hit from beneath by the propeller of another fighter. His airplane was repaired that evening, and Ossenkop returned to Fürstenau on the 2nd. Once he learned that Hartmann had bailed out over Grimbergen and was a prisoner, Ossenkop reported that Hart-

Uffz. Heinz Wodarczyk of 4/JG 26. A long-time wingman of his Kommodore, Wodarczyk failed to return from the Bodenplatte mission. *(Bundesarchiv-Freiburg)*

mann had been hit by ground fire at the same time as himself, rather than reveal that Hartmann had rammed his airplane.

1000: Borris's formation returned to Germany on the reciprocal of their outbound course. The aircraft recognition abilities of the German antiaircraft gunners around Rotterdam had not improved in the previous hour, and they once again put the Focke-Wulfs under fire. More German fighters fell. Ogfr. Bodo Vogel of the 2nd Staffel was killed on his first mission. Uffz. Karl Zeidler of the 4th Staffel was injured in a crash landing southwest of Osnabrück; his Flak-damaged aircraft was destroyed. Uffz. Reichow of the 1st Staffel force-landed his plane on Almelo without injury to himself. Some pilots simply disappeared, probably on this leg of the flight. Uffz. Heinz Wodarczyk, who was a member of the 4th Staffel but flew as Priller's wingman; Hptm. Willi Bottländer, Kapitän of 11/JG 54; Lt. Jürgen Ratzlaff of 12/JG 54; and Ogfr. Karl-Heinz Braunert of the 4th Staffel were the unfortunates who fell into the "missing" category after the mission. Other casualties were Uffz. Aloysius van Hooven of 12/JG 54 and two ferry pilots from Flüg 1, Uffz. Altendorf and Fw. Lange, who were killed; and Uffz. Gerhard Thoss of 11/JG 54, who was captured.

1124: The last pilot to reach Fürstenau landed. Pips Priller himself had returned early, without suffering combat damage. Priller had not flown a mission in several months, was unaccustomed to flying the Dora-9, and may have become disoriented when he lost sight of the ground in the mists. According to Peter Crump, the reason the formation initially overflew the target was that Priller's disappearance "had led to a certain confusion at the head of the formation."

1130: Seven 4th Staffel pilots had stayed together, and landed at Quakenbrück, on their last drops of fuel.

1200: Priller had the task of preparing his mission report for General Peltz. Twelve First Gruppe pilots had failed to return from the mission, one-quarter of the forty-eight who had taken off that morning. Four would eventually turn up, but even eight losses were too many against a worthless target such as Grimbergen had proven to be. III/JG 54 had been shredded. Twelve of its seventeen pilots had failed to return – a devastating seventy per cent loss. Ten other aircraft had reached German bases with various degrees of flak damage. The statistics for the rest of the Geschwader, when they became available that afternoon, made the average casualty rate look somewhat better. One hundred and fifty aircraft had taken off under the command of JG 26 – the largest force ever put into the air by the Geschwader. Thirty-two pilots were killed or taken prisoner, for a loss rate of twenty-one per cent.

II/JG 26 Attacks Brussels-Evere

0430: The Second Gruppe orderly went from house to house in Nordhorn and awakened the pilots by ringing on the doorbells.

0500: Fw. Heinz Gomann and five "old hares", who had celebrated New Year's Eve from bar to bar in Nordhorn, arrived at the field with a three-man jazz band.

0600: Breakfast was served in the pilots' mess at the Berning Hotel.

0630: The bus left for Clausheide. When it turned in at the field, fifty Fw 190D-9s were lined up around the field, glistening in the last light of the moon. The mechanics had worked all night to get them ready, and had then taxied them to the landing ground. Several were still being attended to.

0645: The bus did not go to the Staffel readiness shacks as usual, but to the Gruppe command post, where the band was playing both "hot tunes" and sentimental favorites. At the mission briefing the pilots were finally given their orders and the target – Brussels-Evere. They were handed maps marked with the course from the German border to the target. Each pilot was then issued a one-man life raft, a life jacket, and emergency rations. They also took wrist compasses, flare ammunition, and Pervitin stimulant tablets with them.

0730: The pilots went out to the aircraft, to find their props turning over and their brakes applied. The crew chiefs helped buckle them in.

0800: Takeoff was ordered, and the aircraft began to taxi.

0805: The two Ju 88G-6 pathfinders were first off the ground, taking off into the reddish glare of the now-rising sun. The lead aircraft was piloted by Ofhr. Helmut Bunje; the alternate, by Lt. Lothar Hemmerich. Both were experienced night fighter pilots from II/NJG 6. Major Hackl was next up, leading a full Stabsschwarm consisting of Gefr. Mittag, Ofhr. Heuser, and Ogfr. Przybyl. Next came Oblt. Vogt and the 5th Staffel. There followed, in order, Oblt. Hofmann's 8th Staffel, Oblt. Glunz's 6th Staffel, and Oblt. Radener's 7th Staffel. It was intended that each Staffel formation should contain twelve aircraft; two 7th Staffel pilots, Gefr. Götz and Gefr. Kunz, were assigned to Hofmann to make up his dozen.

0829: The last airplane in the formation took off. There had been no problems, although the Schwärme of four aircraft threw up fountains of snow which greatly hampered visibility. The propwash and the presence of 10-15 cm (4-6 inches) of snow on the ground had made things even more difficult. The individual Staffeln made a large circuit around the field and assembled in Gruppe formation, according to their normal procedure. The Ju 88s then led them off on course at an altitude of 50 meters (160 feet).

0845: Gefr. Hans-Karl Götz finally got his engine started. He took off alone and followed the crowd toward The Netherlands. Götz was flying his first combat sortie.

0900: Other fighter formations were visible in the clear early morning air, flying on the same course. The Second Gruppe flight proceeded smoothly, in total radio silence, until the Zuider Zee check point was reached. They were then suddenly engulfed in a wall of flak, which shot down three Focke-Wulfs. Ogfr. Hubert Lott of the 5th Staffel somersaulted from his aircraft. His parachute opened immediately, but he slipped from his harness, and was still turning somersaults as he hit the ground, shortly after his aircraft had smashed into the icy surface of the Zuider Zee. Uffz. Leopold Speer of the 7th Staffel crashed in his aircraft. Fw. Karl Hött bailed out at 200 meters (650 feet), and suffered a serious head injury; he was taken to the Rotterdam hospital. A fourth pilot was seen to continue his flight with one landing gear leg hanging down; he was one of the ones who did not return.

Ogfr. Hubert Lott of the 5th Staffel. A Bodenplatte fatality, Lott was one of many victims of the German flak installations guarding the V-2 installations near Rotterdam.*(Bundesarchiv-Freiburg)*

0915: The formation made its turn at Rotterdam and then proceeded across the Scheldt, still at low altitude. They were taken under fire by Allied ships, which cost the unit one more Focke-Wulf. This was the Gruppenstab aircraft of Ofhr. Helmut Heuser, who was able to make a belly landing on Tholen Island and was taken prisoner.

0920: Over land once more, Hackl's pilots could see Brussels in the distance. Ofhr.

The remains of a Royal Air Force Handley-Page Halifax bomber after the JG 26 attack on Brussels-Evere airfield. *(Clarey)*

Bunje's Ju 88 took a severe antiaircraft hit which injured his radioman. His task accomplished, Bunje turned his plane around and headed back for Nordhorn, where he made a successful landing on one wheel. After one more course change, Hackl's Focke-Wulfs climbed to their attack altitude of 600 meters (2000 feet), dropping their auxiliary tanks as they neared Evere, which, unlike Grimbergen, was a fully operational airfield of the 2nd TAF. The field was the base for the forty Spitfires of No. 127 Wing (RCAF), whose air commander was the famous W/C Johnnie Johnson. The Spitfires were arrayed in a single row along the eastern edge of the field. They were parked close to the perimeter track, as the ground was soft and boggy. The wing had not even bothered to unpack its camouflage netting, since a number of unpainted bombers and transports were parked conspicuously on the other side of the airfield. Among the transports were Prince Bernhard's Beechcraft and a luxurious VIP Dakota. Antiaircraft defense was the responsibility of two squadrons of the RAF Regiment. One had eleven Bofors 40 mm guns, while the other had nothing heavier than the ubiquitous Bren gun.

0920: No. 127 Wing's customary dawn flights had been delayed by the necessity to sand the field's only hard-surfaced runway. A thin layer of ice had formed on it overnight, imperiling takeoffs. Shortly before 0900 two Spitfires from No. 403 Squadron had gotten off on a weather patrol. Their leader radioed back that the runway was safe to use, and a second element of two No. 403 Sqd. Spitfires now took off.

0925: No. 416 Squadron was called to readiness for a twelve-fighter patrol. As their Spitfires crept along the perimeter track, close behind that of F/L Harling, the sound of many aircraft engines was heard. Just as the first flight of Spitfires started down the runway, sixty Focke-Wulfs and Messerschmitts screamed across the field. The Second and Third Gruppen of JG 26 had arrived. Harling made it off the ground, only to be shot down and killed by Oblt. Glunz before reaching combat speed.

0926: Oblt. Hofmann's well-disciplined 8th Staffel split into Schwärme to begin its assigned task of flak suppression; the other German attackers pounced on the numerous ground targets, displaying no vestige of order or plan. The three Spitfires behind Harling burst into flames as their pilots jumped out and ran for their lives. Three Second Gruppe pilots were credited with their destruction – Major Hackl, Lt. Siegfried Sy of the 6th Staffel, and Uffz. Burckhardt, who was a member of the 8th Staffel but was flying as Sy's wingman. After the mission, several pilots from the Third Gruppe put in claims for the same Spitfires.

0930: After a single pass by Hofmann's men, the antiaircraft guns fell silent. According to Johnnie Johnson, they had run out of ammunition. No JG 26 aircraft was shot down over Evere by antiaircraft fire, despite the defenders' claims for three German fighters destroyed. Several Focke-Wulfs were seriously damaged, however, including that of Uffz. Norbert Risky of the 6th Staffel, who turned toward Germany, trailing oily smoke. He flew all-out until his engine quit and a long tongue of flame burst from the cowling. Risky's crash-landing near Zwolle destroyed his aircraft but did him no harm, and he was back in Nordhorn that evening.

0935: Gefr. Werner Molge was a wingman in Lt. Gerhard "Bubi" Schulwitz's 8th Staffel Schwarm, and dived with it to attack the suspected antiaircraft installations. The flight was then released to join in the general attacks. Molge's third attack was made through thick smoke, and on the fourth, visibility was so bad that he almost hit the ground. He then took up a lone course for Nordhorn.

0938: The four No. 403 Sqd. Spitfires in the air returned to Evere and attempted to intervene. They were engaged by the highest Schwärme of Focke-Wulfs and Messerschmitts, which were serving as cover flights. Three of the Spitfire pilots

A burned-out USAAF C-47 that was caught on Brussels-Evere airfield by the JG 26 attack. *(Clarey)*

claimed a total of 3-0-0 Fw 190Ds and 3-1-0 Bf 109s before running out of ammunition and fleeing for their lives. In fact, only one JG 26 aircraft was lost to Allied fighters over Evere. The 6th Staffel Fw 190D of Uffz. Wilhelm Schmitz was seen by ground witnesses to strike a tree after an engagement with fighters. The fighter then hit the ground and burst into flames, with Schmitz trapped inside.

0940: The German pilots continued their attacks on the now-defenseless airfield until, in Hackl's opinion, no undamaged targets remained. Fw. Wülfken of the 1st Staffel had lost his own formation, failed to find Grimbergen, and joined the Second Gruppe in its more profitable operation at Evere, where he flamed two Spitfires on the ground in three low-level

Uffz. Wilhelm Schmitz of the 6th Staffel, shot down over Evere by Spitfires during the Bodenplatte operation. *(Bundesarchiv-Freiburg)*

attacks. Major Hackl flew seven attacks; Oblt. Glunz, nine. Glunz claimed the definite destruction by fire of five aircraft, heavy damage to two, and the destruction of one truck. He was able to shoot up a twin-engine airplane through the open door of a hangar. On his next pass he attempted once again to take the hangar under fire, but it could no longer be seen through the smoke. After all of the British aircraft were either ablaze or masked by the smoke, the German pilots strafed six tanker trucks and the barracks on the northern edge of the field.

They then left Evere as suddenly as they had arrived, leaving behind them a black cloud of smoke that ultimately reached an altitude of 4000 meters (13,000 feet), and was clearly visible from Nordhorn later that morning.

Gefr. Willi Kunz of the 7th Staffel. Kunz's first combat mission was the Bodenplatte operation; he was shot down and killed by German flak. *(Bundesarchiv-Freiburg)*

0940: The first pilot to be lost during the return flight was Gefr. Hans-Karl Götz. He had caught up with the 8th Staffel over Rotterdam and made several strafing attacks on Evere. Soon after leaving the target area his engine burst into flames. Götz bailed out and landed on Gilze-Rijen airfield, where he was immediately taken prisoner. His first mission had proved to be his last. At about this time Uffz. Edwin Kalbus of the 5th Staffel claimed the destruction of a stray Thunderbolt in the air between Brussels and Antwerp; in all probability this was a Tempest, which escaped.

0945: W/C Johnson had observed the attack from a safe position on the ground, and gave it his expert evaluation. He noted in a later report that the German fighters had made their runs in ones and twos, very slowly – seemingly at no more than 150 mph (240 km/h). They wasted their fire on hangars, rather than on more profitable targets. Furthermore, he concluded, their marksmanship was atrocious. As soon as possible, Johnson ordered a strong formation of Spitfires to take to the air to guard against a return attack. He then surveyed the damage. His Wing had lost one pilot and one groundcrewman killed, and nine more enlisted men injured. Despite the spectacular smoke and flames, only eleven of his Spitfires had been destroyed, and another twelve damaged. His unit had come out of the attack incredibly lightly. Across the field, a number of transports and bombers were ablaze; these included both the prince's Beechcraft and the VIP's Dakota.

0950: The Allied shipping in the Scheldt was fully alerted for the returnees and put up a solid curtain of light antiaircraft fire. Two Focke-Wulfs were hit. Uffz. Ernest Lampferhoff of the 5th Staffel pulled his aircraft up to 850 meters (2800 feet) and bailed out, landing on South Beveland. Fw. Erich Ahrens of the 7th Staffel was hit in the radiator, glided across the Scheldt, and made a belly landing on South Beveland. Both pilots were picked up quickly by Canadian troops. At least one pilot, Uffz. Walter Stumpf of the 7th Staffel, still had ammunition, and fired it off at the ships as he passed them.

1015: There was one last gauntlet to be run – the German flak belt between Rotterdam and The Hague. It claimed one victim from the Gruppe, Gefr. Willi Kunz of the 7th Staffel. He attempted a forced landing, but his aircraft overturned on uneven ground, breaking Kunz's neck and killing him instantly. In common with several other Geschwader pilots, Kunz had been on his first combat sortie.

1045: The last of the pilots reaching Nordhorn landed. Eleven pilots were missing;

three of these men would eventually return. The claims of the Schlageter Geschwader for ground victories at Evere were broadcast in the OKW communiqué that evening. These totaled twenty B-17s and B-24s, twenty-four twin-engine aircraft, and sixty fighters, all destroyed by strafing. Major Hackl's report singled out for praise Oblt. Hofmann, for his combat leadership, and Lt. Glunz, for the destruction he had wrought in his nine low-altitude attacks. This had been Addi Glunz's 238th combat sortie, and it proved to be his last. He flew no missions during the rest of January, and in February was taken off flight status. In March he left the Geschwader for training on the Me 262.

1110: Gefr. Werner Molge landed at Bissel on his last drops of fuel. After leaving Evere, he flew alone for about fifteen minutes. He then joined up with four Second Gruppe Focke-Wulfs, but unaccountably lost them again. He overflew Nordhorn, sighted Bissel, and landed after two hours and fifty minutes in the air. He had to be towed in from the landing field by a half-track, as his engine had run dry. Refueling was a problem; the Bf 109 airfield had only low-octane B4 fuel, while he needed C3. He was then forbidden to take off while enemy aircraft were over the Reich.

1700: Molge showed up unexpectedly at the Berning Hotel pilots' mess, where New Year's was being celebrated belatedly, and was greeted heartily by his comrades. They had already given him up for lost; his landing report from Bissel had not been passed along.

III/JG 26 Attacks Brussels-Evere

0430: The pilots were awakened.

0600: The pilots were briefed in the Gruppe command post at Plantlünne. About forty Bf 109K-4s and Bf 109G-14s had been prepared for the mission. The Gruppe had sixty fighters on strength, but there were not enough pilots to fly them all. There is little documented evidence of the activities of this Gruppe today, but it is known that the 12th Staffel was led by its Kapitän, Oblt. Karl-Hermann Schrader; it is assumed that on this maximum-strength mission the other Staffeln were led by their Kapitäne, as well. These were Oblt. Gottfried "Cognac" Schmidt of the 9th Staffel, Hptm. Paul Schauder of the 10th Staffel, and Lt. Hermann Guhl of the 11th Staffel.

0820: The Gruppe began taking off.

0830: Krupinski had planned to assemble the entire Gruppe in a single 360-degree circuit of the field after takeoff. But something went wrong, as Krupinski recalled it, and he wound up following the first pathfinder aircraft, while the rest of the Gruppe flew with the second pathfinder, about a half mile behind. Georg Genth, who flew as Krupinski's wingman today, recalls that this separation was deliberate; Krupinski and Genth were to function as "flak reporters" to give the larger formation to their rear time to alter its course if necessary. Only twenty-nine aircraft flew the mission.

0850: The Gruppe flight path was the same as that of the rest of the Geschwader. The German flak belt west of the Zuider Zee opened fire on Krupinski's formation, and shot down one airplane, that of Oblt. Harald Lenz of the 11th Staffel, who crashed to his death.

0915: The Messerschmitts apparently made it across the Scheldt without further damage. They then hurtled across a Canadian Army encampment at an altitude of ten meters (32 feet), coming under fire by small arms and Bofors anti-aircraft guns. Hptm. Krupinski's aircraft was hit on the hinge of its left cowling panel, which popped open, forcing him to zigzag across the countryside in order to see. He stayed with the formation for a few more minutes, but finally turned back with Uffz. Genth after coming within sight of the Brussels church steeples.

0918: Uffz. Karl-Heinz Berndt, who was flying as Oblt. Schrader's wingman in the 12th Staffel formation, took a hit in the engine from the antiaircraft fire and had to make an immediate belly landing; he was quickly taken prisoner.

0920: The remaining Messerschmitts reached Evere right on schedule. Uffz. Gehrke struck one of the No. 416 Sqd. Spitfires as it was taking off, and watched it smash flaming into the ground. He then strafed two twin-engine aircraft, which he identified as Mosquitoes, and saw them burst into flames.

0925: Uffz. Willibald Malm saw an RAF pilot, possibly F/L Harling, parachuting into the flaming hell on the field. He was tempted to shoot the man to keep him from burning to death, but could not bring himself to open fire.

0935: After nearly fifteen minutes of unopposed strafing attacks, Gehrke and the other Bf 109 pilots joined up in loose formation and headed north on their return flight.

0945: Lt. Gottfried Meyer of the 9th Staffel disappeared without a trace before reaching the German lines. He is still carried as missing, but according to Dutch researchers, Meyer crashed near Vrasene. His airplane exploded on impact, carbonizing his body in the cockpit.

1000: The German Flak belt took its toll. The 12th Staffel Messerschmitt of Gefr. Horst Sengpiel was hit, and he was observed to fly off to the northeast, trailing smoke. Sengpiel was never seen again. Uffz. Walter Tepperis of the 11th Staffel had to belly-land his aircraft on the island of Schouwen. It could not be salvaged, and Tepperis himself did not make it back to Plantlünne for a week. The last casualty was Lt. Rudolf Leinberger of the 11th Staffel, who reached the field at Kirchhellen in his flak-damaged aircraft, overshot the strip, and wound up in the trees. Leinberger's airplane was repairable, and he himself returned to Plantlünne with only minor injuries.

1010: It was an enthusiastic group of pilots who landed back on Plantlünne. Heinz Gehrke recalls buzzing the field while happily and vigorously rocking his wings, signaling his victory at Evere. Only six pilots were missing, and two of these men returned later. Krupinski called a quick meeting of all of his pilots and praised them for their highly successful mission. The Third Gruppe claims for air and ground victories at Evere could not be separated from those of the Second Gruppe, and no serious attempt was made to do so. Heinz Gehrke recalls that the aerial victory claims of the two Gruppen totaled between six and eight; subtracting the five known claims of the Second Gruppe leaves from one to three for the Third Gruppe, of which one was Gehrke's Spitfire. His Spitfire claim was submitted to Berlin, and he was shortly thereafter awarded the Iron Cross First Class, in part for his successful Bodenplatte mission.

The Reckoning

German planning for Operation Bodenplatte was thorough, and nearly flawless. Only the targeting of one non-operational field (Grimbergen), and the inexplicable failure to route the northernmost Jagdgruppen around the known V-2 Flak area marred the

Josef Priller, photographed soon after his promotion to Oberst (colonel) on 1 January. Bodenplatte was Priller's last mission; his final victory total was 101, all scored on the Western Front. *(Genth)*

concept. But the mission lost all of its strategic purpose once the Ardennes ground offensive had been checked, and should have been canceled. Why wasn't it? When asked by this author, Dietrich Peltz replied, "It never entered our heads." *Befehl ist Befehl*, and war is an exercise in illogic.

Bodenplatte weakened the German fighter force past any last hope of rebuilding. It had sacrificed itself in a single grand, insanely futile gesture. Of the nine hundred German fighters that took off at daybreak on New Year's Day, three hundred failed to return to their bases. Pilots made their way back individually over the next few days, but a total of 214 were killed, taken prisoner, or remained missing. Counted among the casualties were nineteen irreplaceable formation leaders – three Kommodoren, six Gruppenkommandeure, and ten Staffelkapitäne.

The planners of Bodenplatte made a real effort to take into account the limited skills of their fighter pilots, but the operation was much too ambitious for that stage of the war, and was doomed from the start. Thirty-three fighter Gruppen and one ground attack Gruppe flew the mission. Their targets were sixteen tactical airfields in the Netherlands, Belgium, and eastern France. Of the thirty-four Gruppen, ten never found their assigned targets at all; their missions were total failures. Nine Gruppen made ineffectual, low-strength attacks on their targets. Two Gruppen, I/JG 26 and III/JG 54, flew missions that must be described as "technical successes" – all went well until their targeted airfield was discovered to be non-operational. Only one-third of the force, or eleven Gruppen, which included II/JG 26 and III/JG 26, made their attacks entirely according to plan – on time, in strength, and with complete surprise, against airfields which contained the desired targets, Allied tactical aircraft. And even in these cases, the German success was much less than it should have been, and much less than the German pilots themselves believed it to have been.

In their embarrassment at having been taken completely by surprise, the Allied air commanders failed to compile a comprehensive list of their losses, but about three hundred RAF and USAAF aircraft were destroyed or damaged beyond repair. Few Allied pilots were lost, however, and all units were back up to strength in aircraft within a week. The effect of the German fighter pilots' self-sacrifice on the course of the war was thus non-existent. An OKL intelligence appreciation concluded that the attack had had no effect on Allied operations other than to move up the takeoff time of their early-morning patrols.

JG 26 Casualties: 1 January 1945

Date	Rank	Name	Cas	Unit	Aircraft	WNr	Mkgs	Place	Time	Cause	Allied Unit
01-01-45	Uffz.	Reichow, Gerhard	no	1	Fw 190D-9			near Almelo		own flak	n/a
01-01-45	Oblt.	Kunz, Franz	WIA	2 CO	Fw 190D-9	210953	bk 1	NE of Rotterdam	0845	own flak	n/a
01-01-45	Uffz.	Schulz, Heinz	KIA	2	Fw 190D-9	400234	bk 11	near Sinaai		Spitfire	308 Sqd
01-01-45	Uffz.	Sydow, Willy	KIA	2	Fw 190D-9	600147	bk 6	5km SW of Eindhoven	0940	own flak	n/a
01-01-45	Ogfr.	Vogel, Bodo	KIA	2	Fw 190D-9	400237	bk 3	Oostkapelle-Walcheren Is.	1030	own flak	n/a
01-01-45	Ogfr.	Krägeloh, Dieter	POW	3	Fw 190D-9	500093	yl 13	St Anna ter Muiden	0915	Spitfire	308 Sqd
01-01-45	Ogfr.	Niessen, Manfred	no	3	Fw 190D-9	400233	yl 5	Blokland near Utrecht	0845	own flak	n/a
01-01-45	Fhr.	Werner, Hans-Joachim	POW	3	Fw 190D-9	600168	yl 8	Grimbergen a/f	0930	a/f flak	n/a
01-01-45	Ogfr.	Braunert, Karl-Heinz	KIA	4	Fw 190D-9/ R11	210955	bl 10	W of Vremde-Antwerp		missing	n/a
01-01-45	Fw.	Hartmann, Karl-Heinz	POW	4	Fw 190D-9	210126	bl 3	Grimbergen a/f	0930	collision	n/a
01-01-45	Uffz.	Wodarczyk, Heinz	KIA	4	Fw 190D-9	210936	none	Wijhe-15km SSE of Zwolle	1000	missing	n/a
01-01-45	Uffz.	Zeidler, Karl-Erich	WIA	4	Fw 190D-9	600170	bl 2	Lengerich	1100	flak	n/a
01-01-45	Uffz.	Lampferhoff, Ernst	POW	5	Fw 190D-9	210193	wh 7	S of Goes	0930	ship flak	n/a
01-01-45	Ogfr.	Lott, Hubert	KIA	5	Fw 190D-9	500102	wh 11	Hellegatspolder (Zuider Zee)	0900	own flak	n/a
01-01-45	Ofhr.	Heuser, Helmut	POW	6	Fw 190D-9	500034	bk 16	Scherpenisse-Tholen Is.	0915	ship flak	n/a

01-01-45	Fw.	Hött, Karl	WIA 6	Fw 190D-9	400207 bk 2	Brielle	0900	own flak	n/a
01-01-45	Uffz.	Risky, Norbert	no 6	Fw 190D-9	bk 12	Zwolle	1010	a/f flak	n/a
01-01-45	Uffz.	Schmitz, Wilhelm	KIA 6	Fw 190D-9	210274 bk 14	Wieze	1000	Spitfire	403 Sqd
01-01-45	Fw.	Ahrens, Erich	POW 7	Fw 190D-9	210186 br 6	Beveland-SW of Goes	0945	ship flak	n/a
01-01-45	Gefr.	Götz, Hans-Karl	POW 7	Fw 190D-9	600161 bl 2	near Molenschot	1000	engine	n/a
01-01-45	Gefr.	Kunz, Willi	KIA 7	Fw 190D-9	500105 bl 1	W of Borger		own flak	n/a
01-01-45	Uffz.	Speer, Leopold	KIA 7	Fw 190D-9	210165 br 5	near Nijkerk (Zuider Zee)	0900	own flak	n/a
01-01-45	Lt.	Meyer, Gottfried	KIA 9	Bf 109K-4	330404 wh 15	near Vrasene	0945	crashed	n/a
01-01-45	Lt.	Leinberger, Rudolf	WIA 11	Bf 109K-4	330354 bk 18	Kirchhellen a/f	0955	own flak	n/a
01-01-45	Oblt.	Lenz, Harald	KIA 11	Bf 109K-4	330385 yl 18	Harderwijk (Zuider Zee)	0850	own flak	n/a
01-01-45	Uffz.	Tepperis, Walter	no 11	Bf 109G-14	413550 bk 8	Schouwen Is.	0945	own flak	n/a
01-01-45	Uffz.	Berndt, Karl-Heinz	POW 12	Bf 109K-4	330426 bl 30	St Martensdijk	0915	flak	n/a
01-01-45	Gefr.	Sengpiel, Horst	KIA 12	Bf 109K-4	330404 wh 15	Scheldt Est	1004	flak	n/a

JG 26 Victory Claims: 1 January 1945

Date	Rank	Name	Unit	Cl #	Aircraft	Place	Time	Opponent	Conf
01-01-45	Major	Hackl	II CO	173	Spitfire	over Brussels	0925	416 Sqd	unk
01-01-45	Uffz.	Kalbus	5	1	P-47	NE of Brussels (ML9)	1004		unk
01-01-45	Oblt.	Glunz	6 CO	71	Spitfire	S of Brussels-Evere a/f	0925	416 Sqd	unk
01-01-45	Lt.	Sy	7	1	Spitfire	S of Brussels-Evere a/f	0925	416 Sqd	unk
01-01-45	Uffz.	Burckhardt G.	8	1	Spitfire	over Brussels	0926	416 Sqd	unk
01-01-45	Uffz.	Gehrke	11	5	Spitfire	Brussels-Evere a/f	0930	416 Sqd	unk

2 January

From now until the end of the war, the pilots of the Geschwader would be ordered into the air on every day, weather and their fuel stocks permitting. Their task would be to provide support for the German armies defending the northern sector of the Western Front against the Canadian First Army, the British Second Army, and the northernmost of the American armies. The Gruppen flew ground-controlled intercept missions and freie Jagden against Allied tactical aircraft; armed reconnaissance missions; strafing and bombing missions; escorts for other units flying ground support missions; and defensive patrols of the airfields of the jet bomber units, to protect their Me 262s and Ar 234s during takeoffs and landings. Never again would JG 26 be ordered to attack American heavy bomber formations. This job was left to the few Fw 190 and Bf 109 Gruppen remaining in the home defense organization, and to the new jet fighter units.

The weather allowed flying on only a few days in early January, this was not one of them. The First Gruppe pilots moved out of their private lodgings and joined the Gruppe ground staff at the girls' school at Handrup, apparently to economize on transportation. Six to eight pilots bunked in each classroom. Luftwaffe servicewomen were also lodged at the school. Borris addressed the fraternization problem by painting a line down the hallway and forbidding his pilots to cross it. However, as one wag put it, the line was invisible after dark.

Lt. Waldemar Söffing replaced Oblt. Kunz as leader of the 2nd Staffel, while retaining his leadership position with the 4th. Although both Staffeln kept their individual identities, the future direction for the Luftwaffe was clear. Many Jagdgruppen now had fewer than one experienced formation leader per Staffel.

4 January

By noon, the weather around the Geschwader bases had cleared to a light ground haze, and the First Gruppe scheduled a training mission. Twenty-three Dora-9s took off from Fürstenau, led by Oblt. Heckmann. The 4th Staffel, which was still being led in the air by Obfw. Schwarz, took off last, and lost the rest of the formation in the haze. Schwarz headed east, toward a reported formation of Allied fighter-bombers near Osnabrück. Uffz. Kukla's engine caught fire, and he bailed out. The rest of Schwarz's small formation was ordered to reverse course and attack a new formation near Rheine. They climbed to 5000 meters (16,000 feet), crossed the Dutch border, and spotted eight

Fw 190D-9s of 7/JG 26 taxiing out for takeoff from their hold position between the trees at Nordhorn-Clausheide in January. *(Stumpf)*

Typhoons beneath them, escorted by from ten to fifteen Spitfires. The German bounce was fended off by the Spitfires, and a turning combat ensued in which the Allied aircraft held the advantage. Three Focke-Wulfs crashed. Uffz. Helmut Findeisen bailed out with severe wounds, and died in hospital two weeks later. Ofhr. Horst Bernhardt and Obfw. Paul Weczera both suffered injuries so severe that they did not return to JG 26. Two more pilots crash-landed on Fürstenau without injury. The Canadian pilots of No. 411 Squadron claimed six victories in this engagement, and suffered no losses. The fifteen aircraft which had stayed with Oblt. Heckmann made no contact, and returned to Fürstenau without incident.

The Second Gruppe ordered up a small formation of aircraft from the 7th and 8th Staffeln. Shortly after takeoff from Nordhorn, apparently while still forming up on the Dutch side of the nearby border, the Focke-Wulfs were hit by the Spitfires of another Canadian squadron, No. 442. The German formation scattered; Uffz. Stumpf went all the way to Oldenburg. The Canadian pilots filed claims for one probable and one damaged German fighter. The latter was the aircraft piloted by Ogfr. Werner Molge, who crash-landed his Dora-9 near his airfield. The Canadian "probable" in fact crashed, carrying Lt. Wilhelm Mayer to his death. Although a member of Gerhard Vogt's 5th Staffel, Mayer had frequently led the 8th Staffel in the air since Wilhelm Hofmann's eye injury, and was flying an 8th Staffel aircraft on this mission. Mayer was one of the most successful pilots in the Gruppe, with twenty-seven victories, and was awarded a posthumous Knight's Cross in March.

At Nordhorn that evening, the Second Gruppe adjutant, Oblt. Günther Blömertz, filled in Mayer's casualty report – an especially painful chore, since the two pilots had joined the Geschwader together back in 1942. Blömertz had been shot down and severely burned in 1943, and after a year's hospitalization had returned to his old Gruppe in a non-flying capacity. It was Blömertz's fate to watch from the ground as his old Abbeville comrades took off and, one by one, failed to return. The sensitive Blömertz brooded on the effect that this latest death would have on Mayer's closest friend, Gerhard Vogt. Vogt and Mayer were inseparable on the ground, and Blömertz felt certain that Vogt would soon join Mayer in death. After the war, Günther Blömertz expunged his feelings of guilt over his own survival by writing a novel, *Dem Himmel am Nächsten*. It was based on his experiences in II/JG 26, and was meant as a tribute to the fallen fighter pilots of his Gruppe. The book, which appeared in English in 1953 as *Heaven Next Stop*, proved quite successful, and was translated into several languages. The casual reader might assume from its first-person narration that the book is an autobiography, but it is not. According to Blömertz himself, it is a historical novel. Although the events depicted in the book all have a basis in fact, they are re-arranged in sequence as a literary device, and individuals are associated with combats in which they did not take part. His book is thus of no value as a factual history, although the thoughts and feelings of the doomed fighter pilots are accurately portrayed.

7 January

The headquarters of the 3rd Jagddivision, to which JG 26 was again reporting, issued orders to its units forbidding all flights over Allied-held territory until the day fighter Geschwader could be restored to full operational readiness. Also, until further notice, operational flights by the Kommodoren were forbidden.

The OKL, desperate for fighter formation leaders, issued instructions that all officers qualified to become Gruppenkommandeure or Staffelkapitäne after brief training were to be sent to the office of the General der Jagdflieger for interviews, as volunteers if possible. The sole criterion for the promotion of NCOs to Staffelkapitäne was a large number of aerial victories. Even Nachwuchs were to be considered, if they had obtained a good score in their few flights.

9 January

The popular Hptm. Peter-Paul Steindl, an Austrian from Pola who had served as a father figure for many of the young pilots, was now flying in the Geschwaderstab. He was killed when his Fw 190D-9 crashed on a test flight.

12 January

The Russians began a major offensive along the Vistula River. Twenty Gruppen of single-engine fighters were sent east from the Western front to bolster the German defenders. These units were the remnants of Galland's one-time strategic reserve, which had been brought west for Unternehmen Bodenplatte. The aerial defense of the skies over Germany's western borders was now left to the same four Geschwader that had had the task the previous autumn. From north to south, these were JG 26, JG 27, JG 2, and JG 53.

13 January

The 3rd Jagddivision ordered its fighters to clear their own areas of responsibility of low-flying aircraft. The Second and Third Gruppen and III/JG 54 flew afternoon Jabojagd missions, but none contacted the enemy. Uffz. Friedrich Kerner of the 10th Staffel aborted the mission when the engine of his Bf 109K-4 caught fire. He belly-landed on Coesfeld, overturned, and was severely injured; Kerner died in hospital on the 16th.

JG 26 Casualties: 4 - 13 January 1945

Date	Rank	Name	Cas	Unit	Aircraft	WNr	Mkgs	Place	Time	Cause	Allied Unit
04-01-45	Uffz.	Findeisen, Helmut	KIA	2	Fw 190D-9	210993	bk 6	near Melle-Osnabrück	1600	Spitfire	411 Sqd
04-01-45	Ofhr.	Bernhardt, Horst	WIA	4	Fw 190D-9	210964	bl 15	near Osnabrück	1600	Spitfire	411 Sqd
04-01-45	Uffz.	Kukla, Hans	no	4	Fw 190D-9			near Osnabrück	1350	engine	n/a
04-01-45	Obfw.	Weczera, Paul	WIA	4	Fw 190D-9	210965	bl 16	near Melle-Osnabrück	1600	Spitfire	411 Sqd
04-01-45	Lt.	Mayer, Wilhelm	KIA	8 CO	Fw 190D-9	500052	bl 16	Lohnerbruch	1400	Spitfire	442 Sqd
04-01-45	Ogfr.	Molge, Werner	no	8	Fw 190D-9		bl 17	1mi E of Nordhorn		Spitfire	442 Sqd
09-01-45	Hptm.	Steindl, Peter-Paul	KIFA	Ge	Fw 190D-9	210983	bl 10	SE of Fürstenau a/f		crashed	non-op
13-01-45	Uffz.	Kerner, Friedrich	KIFA	10	Bf 109K-4	330365	bk 17	E of Coesfeld	1600	engine	n/a

14 January

Jagdkorps II was under heavy pressure to get its fighters back into the air. Heavy ground fog persisted up to 300 meters (1000 feet) this morning, but the skies above were clear. All three JG 26 Gruppen were assigned missions, despite signs of a large heavy bomber raid, which according to the current standing orders was sufficient reason to keep the Geschwader on the ground. But the Army, in retreat in the Ardennes, needed relief from the American fighter-bombers, and so shortly before 1100 the Second and Third Gruppen began taking off, under orders to attack Jabos at St. Vith. At this moment, the van of a massive 8th Air Force bomber formation was crossing the coast at Ostend. Most were *en route* to bomb oil industry targets in central Germany, but the 187 B-17s of the First Air Division were headed for the Rhine bridges at Köln, closely escorted by forty-two P-51s, and preceded by a sweep of sixty-two P-47s. This armada was on a collision course with the small German force of Focke-Wulfs and Messerschmitts. The Second Gruppe was led by Major Hackl, who was flying with Oblt. Hofmann and the 8th Staffel. Hackl was apparently not able to assemble his Gruppe because of the weather, and so ordered them south as a string of independent Staffeln. The 5th was led by Oblt. Vogt; the 6th, by Oblt. Glunz; and the 7th, by Oblt. Radener. Glunz turned back shortly after takeoff, and command of the 6th was assumed by his deputy, Lt. Siegfried Sy.

When about half-way to the assigned patrol zone, the head of the formation was bounced by seven P-47s, the "alert" flight of the 366th Fighter Group, which had been scrambled from Asch, Belgium, on the report of enemy aircraft near Düren. Major Hackl and the 8th Staffel's Fhr. Spahn each shot down a Thunderbolt. No German fighter was lost in this battle, although the surviving P-47 pilots claimed 2-0-2. Their first encounter with the "long-nosed Doras" impressed them. The German fighters had enough speed to keep up with the Thunderbolts without difficulty, and one pilot reported that he had been out-turned at 13,000 feet (4000 meters).

Hackl crossed Aachen, and led his small unit in a shallow left turn west of Köln in the hope of reaching his assigned patrol area. The German formation was being followed by American radar on the Continent, and twenty-five P-51s from the 78th Fighter Group were now released from bomber escort and vectored to meet them. The trailing Staffeln of Hackl's Gruppe, along with the Bf 109s of the Third Gruppe, were spotted three miles southwest of Köln. The twenty fighters appeared to the American pilots to be disorganized, as though they were just in the process of forming up. The Mustangs' attack apparently caught the Germans by surprise. Four Fw 190Ds, three from the 6th Staffel and one from the 7th, went down in the heavily-forested area between St. Vith and Bastogne. The remains of Uffz. Werner Binge were identified in 1986; Uffz. Hans-Georg Böhter, Ogfr. Volkmar Haarberg, and Obfw. Friedrich Roggenkamp were still missing in 1998.

Oblt. Vogt's 5th Staffel formation was broken up by the American attack. Vogt himself attempted to escape in the cloud deck. Ground witnesses southeast of Köln heard gunfire in the clouds, followed by the crash of an aircraft, which proved to be Vogt's. The Knight's Cross recipient had been killed in his cockpit; he thus followed his friend Wilhelm Mayer in death by only ten days, fulfilling Günther Blömertz' prediction. His final record stood at forty-eight victories, gained in 174 combat sorties.

A second 5th Staffel pilot, Uffz. Johannes Hoffmann, escaped to the northeast, but was shot up by four Spitfires. He was unable to find a landing field, and finally force-landed near Minden when he ran out of fuel. He was burned in the crash, but later returned to his unit. Another member of the 5th Staffel, Gefr. Reinhold Feld, a former Me 163 pilot who had recently joined JG 26, fled the combat to the southwest, but at 1245 was shot down west of Frankfurt by German Flak. He was pulled from his burning Dora-9 by two Russian POWs, and was still in the Luftwaffe hospital in Meisenheim when it was captured in March by the Americans. Yet a fourth 5th Staffel pilot, Uffz. Alfred Stuppan, was shot down at this time, and was still carried as missing in 1998.

The battle moved eastward. The swirling fighters dropped to the deck, where combats continued in and out of the thick clouds. Two Third Gruppe Messerschmitts crashed; Fhr. Walter Fischer and Uffz. Erich Salewsky were killed. Lt. Walter Kopp apparently escaped the battle and flew north, but disappeared. His remains were found in the early 1990s near Borghorst, matching a claim by a Tempest pilot of No. 486 Sqd. (RNZAF). A fourth Messerschmitt pilot, Lt. Dietwin Pape of the 9th Staffel, bailed out successfully, and returned to Plantlünne two days later. Hackl led his fighters back into the action, and claimed two P-51s, Hackl's 175th victory and Gefr. Mittag's first. The 8th Staffel got split up in this combat, and one Rotte was pursued back to Köln by P-51s. The American pilots saw one of these two Focke-Wulfs crash-land on Köln-Wahn airfield; its pilot, Uffz. Gottfried Burckhardt, was killed in the crash.

The 78th Group pilots filed claims for 6-0-3 Fw 190s and 6-0-3 Bf 109s. The actual losses by the Geschwader in the Köln area were seven Fw 190s and four Bf 109s, in reasonably close agreement with the American claims. No P-51 was shot down in this battle, although three pilots had to make emergency landings on the Continent.

Back at Fürstenau, the First Gruppe had been at readiness since 1000. Their orders finally came through; they were to fly a defensive patrol of the jet bomber airfields in the Rheine-Hopsten area. Thirty-one Dora-9s took off at 1525, led by Major Borris. Three aborted; shortly thereafter Borris's remaining twenty-eight planes engaged a Spitfire formation of the same size, which was *en route* to its own patrol of the Rheine airfields. Major Borris claimed one Spitfire, for his 43rd victory. Lt. Ossenkop also claimed one, for his first. Uffz. Karl Russ's Focke-Wulf collided with a Spitfire; it was reported that both aircraft crashed in flames. Uffz. Kurt Ullerich was shot down and bailed out, but died when his parachute failed to open. Uffz. Friedrich Worster also bailed out, and survived with injuries. Six Focke-Wulfs were pursued to the Dortmund area, where they landed when low on fuel. Borris carried out his ordered patrol with his last dozen aircraft. His scattered force landed back on Fürstenau between 1545 and 1630 hours.

The Spitfire pilots, who belonged to the 2nd TAF's two Norwegian squadrons, Nos. 331 and 332, claimed the destruction of four German fighters, and lost only one of their number, undoubtedly to Karl-Heinz Ossenkop, who clearly remembers the attack over Ibbenbüren by 30-35 Spitfires. Borris saw them in time, and formed a defensive circle. After one and one-half or two turns, a Spitfire tried to attack the Focke-Wulf ahead of Ossenkop, who opened fire from 200 meters (220 yards) range. The Spitfire dived away to the right, followed by Ossenkop, who closed to 80 meters (90 yards) with full throttle and methanol injection. Ossenkop fired until the Spitfire disappeared beneath his cowling, then saw it dive, trailing black smoke, until it turned on its back and hit the ground, bursting into flames and leaving a long black groove in the white snow. Ossenkop was told later that his victim was a "Polish major"; this is close enough to confirm his identity, considering that the pilot was wearing a dark blue uniform without RAF rank badges and had the non-Nordic name of Detlev.

After five months at the front, Karl-Heinz Ossenkop was now a proficient air fighter. His comments on his aircraft are worth noting:

"The Fw 190D-9 was quickly adopted by the pilots, after some initial reservations. They felt it was equal to or better than the equipment of the opposition. Its serviceability was not so good, owing to the circumstances. I felt that aircraft built at Sorau had the best fit and finish.They could be recognized by their dark green camouflage. I hit 600 km/h [370 mph] in my "own" green aircraft, "black 8", with full power and MW 50 [methanol injection], clean, 20-30 meters [65-100 feet] above the ground.

"Compared with the Fw 190A-8, the Dora-9: 1) with 40-50 more horsepower, had a greater level speed, climb rate, and ceiling, 2) had much better visibility to the rear, owing to its bubble canopy; 3) was much quieter – the Jumo 213A vibrated much less than the BMW 801; 4) handled better in steep climbs and turning, owing probably to its greater shaft horsepower at full throttle; 5) had less torque effect on takeoff or landing; and 6) had slightly greater endurance.

"Compared with the Spitfire, the Dora-9: 1) had greater level, climbing, and diving speeds; and 2) was inferior in turns, especially in steep climbing turns typical of combat.

"Compared with the Tempest, the Dora-9: 1) was better in the climb and in turns; 2) had the same or lower level speed, depending on its fit and finish; and 3) had a lower diving speed.

"Compared with the Thunderbolt, the Dora-9: 1) had a greater level and climbing speed; 2) had a better turning ability; and 3) was inferior past all hope in diving speed."

The Geschwader lost more lives in the bitter fighting today, thirteen, than on any other day of the war, including 1 January, and was again grounded for several days. The Third Gruppe was taken off operations for conversion to the Fw 190D-9. Oblt. Adolf Glunz was no longer on the Second Gruppe duty roster; Lt. Sy took over leadership of the 6th Staffel for operations.

JG 26 Victory Claims: 14 January 1945

Date	Rank	Name	Unit	Cl #	Aircraft	Place	Time	Opponent	Conf
14-01-45	Major	Borris	I CO	43	Spitfire	Ibbenbüren	1545	331 or 332 Sqd	unk
14-01-45	Uffz.	Russ	1	1	Spitfire	Rheine (GQ5)	1545	331 or 332 Sqd	unk
14-01-45	Lt.	Ossenkop	2	1	Spitfire	Ibbenbüren	1545	331 or 332 Sqd	unk
14-01-45	Maj.	Hackl	II CO	174	P-47	E of Liège (near ON)	1205	366 FG	unk
14-01-45	Maj.	Hackl	II CO	175	P-51	Remscheid (near MP-MQ)	1215	78 FG	unk
14-01-45	Gefr.	Mittag	II St	1	P-51	Remscheid (near MP-MQ)	1218	78 FG	unk
14-01-45	Fhr.	Spahn	8	1	P-47	W of Koblenz (near PO-PN)	1210	366 FG	unk

JG 26 Casualties: 14 January 1945

Date	Rank	Name	Cas	Unit	Aircraft	WNr	Mkgs	Place	Time	Cause	Allied Unit
14-01-45	Uffz.	Russ, Karl	KIA	1	Fw 190D-9	210109	wh 6	Ibbenbüren	1545	Spitfire	331 or 332 Sqd
14-01-45	Uffz.	Ullerich, Kurt	KIA	1	Fw 190D-9	210971	wh 10	Lengerich	1545	Spitfire	331 or 332 Sqd
14-01-45	Uffz.	Worster, Friedrich	WIA	1	Fw 190D-9	600179	wh 4	NE of Esch-Ibbenbüren	1545	Spitfire	331 or 332 Sqd
14-01-45	Oblt.	Vogt, Gerhard	KIA	5 CO	Fw 190D-9	210176	wh 13	SE of Köln-Eil	1200	P-51	78 FG
14-01-45	Gefr.	Feld, Reinhold	WIA	5	Fw 190D-9	211005	wh 7	W of Bingen-Rheine	1245	own flak	n/a
14-01-45	Uffz.	Hoffmann, Johannes	WIA	5	Fw 190D-9	400214	wh 3	near Minden	1245	Spitfire	
14-01-45	Uffz.	Stuppan, Alfred	KIA	5	Fw 190D-9	600352	wh 16	near Köln-N of Bonn	1215	combat	
14-01-45	Uffz.	Binge, Werner	KIA	6	Fw 190D-9	600148	bk 11	SE of Bonn	1215	P-51	78 FG
14-01-45	Uffz.	Böhter, Hans-Georg	KIA	6	Fw 190D-9	400242	bk 1	St Vith-Bastogne	1130	P-51	78 FG
14-01-45	Ogfr.	Haarberg, Volkmar	KIA	6	Fw 190D-9	500121	bk 8	St Vith-Bastogne	1130	P-51	78 FG
14-01-45	Obfw.	Roggenkamp, Friedrich	KIA	7	Fw 190D-9	500379	br 7	St. Vith area	1215	P-51	78 FG
14-01-45	Uffz.	Burckhardt, Gottfried	KIA	8	Fw 190D-9	500123	bl 5	Köln-Wahn a/f	1215	P-51	78 FG
14-01-45	Uffz.	Schlimper, Johannes	no	8	Fw 190D-9			Nordhorn a/f		landing	n/a
14-01-45	Lt.	Pape, Dietwin	no	9	Bf 109K-4	330390	wh 21	S of Köln	1201	P-51	78 FG
14-01-45	Lt.	Kopp, Walter	KIA	10	Bf 109K-4	330380	bk 28	W of Koblenz (PO-PP)	1200	Tempest	486 Sqd
14-01-45	Fhr.	Fischer, Walter	KIA	11	Bf 109G-14	462899	yl 3	N of Overath	1145	P-51	78 FG
14-01-45	Uffz.	Salewsky, Erich	KIA	12	Bf 109K-4	330439	bl 29	Uckerath-Bonn	1130	P-51	78 FG

15 January

Several administrative moves were announced. Oblt. Wilhelm Hofmann replaced

Gerhard Vogt as leader of the 5th Staffel, while retaining formal command of the 8th. Lt. Gerhard "Bubi" Schulwitz, his deputy, led the 8th Staffel in the air. Lt. Georg Kiefner, Lt. Waldemar Söffing, and Oblt. Gottfried Schmidt were named Kapitäne of the 1st, 2nd, and 9th Staffeln respectively. They had already been leading these Staffeln, but as Staffelführer.

An anecdote from this period illustrates why Hptm. Krupinski was popular with most of the Third Gruppe enlisted men. Heinz Gehrke recalls:

"We received new aircraft in January – the Dora-9. The first of them arrived at our field in December. Naturally we all wanted to see the bird. I climbed in, had a look at everything, closed the canopy and opened it again, and remarked to the pilots around me, 'This is a first class bird, but hard to bale out of.' For this remark, my

Lt. Kurt Fischer of the 9th Staffel. Fischer was killed on 28 January when the engine of his Fw 190D-9/R11 failed shortly after takeoff. *(Genth)*

Staffelkapitän, Oblt. Reischer, proceeded to rip me up in front of everyone. 'You only think of baling out, etc. etc.' It was most embarassing. Just then a car drove up, and who climbed out? Krupinski! He also wanted to have a look at the new bird. After a careful examination from inside the cockpit, Krupinski opened the canopy and said, 'Reischer, I'll tell you this. It's going to be damned hard to bale out of this thing.' So it goes. As folk wisdom has it, *Haste wat, biste wat. Haste nix, biste nix.* (If you have something, you are something. If you have nothing, you are nothing.)"

17 January
The First Gruppe got its aircraft off the ground for a training mission. According to Lt. Kiefner's logbook, the mission orders were changed in the air to a Jabojagd behind the German lines, but no contact was made with the enemy.

The 3rd Jagddivision issued an order that III/JG 54 was to be considered for all purposes a fourth Gruppe of JG 26.

18 January
Three First Gruppe Fw 190D-9s made a flight today; the sources disagree as to whether it was a patrol flight or a transfer. Two aircraft force-landed owing to darkness; Lt. Peter Ahrens bailed out of the third when its engine caught fire, and landed with mild burns.

20 January
The skies showed signs of clearing, and the First Gruppe was ordered to fly a full-strength mission to cover the jet bomber airfield at Münster-Handorf. Twenty-seven Fw 190Ds took off at 0830 under the leadership of Major Borris. Over Handorf Fw. Walter Kerber's airplane collided with that of Fw. Naeger. Naeger bailed out without injury; Kerber was killed. The Gruppe landed at 1000 without contacting the enemy. The weather closed in again, ending flying for the day.

22 January

The day was cloudless, and the First Gruppe and III/JG 54 flew full-strength morning missions against Jabos in the Rheine-Münster area. The Third Gruppe was off operations to train on the Fw 190D-9, and the Second Gruppe was not called on to fly. Thirty First Gruppe aircraft took off at 1100, led by Major Borris. Six pilots aborted; one was Ofhr. Klaus Wendler, who crash-landed on the field when his engine failed. His fighter overturned, injuring him slightly. The rest of the Gruppe flew the ordered mission. At 1117 they encountered Spitfires near Rheine at 4000 meters (13,000 feet). Ogfr. Lange claimed his first victory, a Spitfire, but that was the only success for the Gruppe. The Spitfires, which were from No. 421 Sqd. (RCAF), shot down four Focke-Wulfs, while claiming five. Fhr. Christian Jensen and Uffz. Günter Kaehler were killed; Uffz. Venners bailed out without injury. The fourth pilot, Uffz. Hans Kukla, was hit from behind in a dogfight. His engine immediately caught fire, and Kukla bailed out with serious burns which kept him in the hospital until the beginning of April. Borris's Gruppe landed at various fields between 1129 and 1152 hours. III/JG 54 was also up, but any successes for this Gruppe are unknown.

JG 26 Casualties: 18 - 22 January 1945

Date	Rank	Name	Cas	Unit	Aircraft	WNr	Mkgs	Place	Time	Cause	Allied Unit
18-01-45	Lt.	Ahrens, Peter	WIFA	3	Fw 190D-9	210939	yl 7	near Meppen		engine	n/a
20-01-45	Fw.	Kerber, Walter	KIFA	2	Fw 190D-9	210940	bk 10	Münster-Handorf a/f	0830	collision	n/a
22-01-45	Uffz.	Kaehler Günter	KIA	1	Fw 190D-9	210281	wh 5	Recke-Osnabrück	1125	Spitfire	421 Sqd
22-01-45	Fhr.	Jensen, Christian	KIA	2	Fw 190D-9	600163	bk 7	SW of Ibbenbüren	1125	Spitfire	421 Sqd
22-01-45	Ofhr.	Wendler, Klaus	WIFA	3	Fw 190D-9	211024	yl 16	Fürstenau a/f		engine	n/a
22-01-45	Uffz.	Kukla, Hans	WIA	4	Fw 190D-9	210943	bl 7	N of Ibbenbüren	1120	Spitfire	421 Sqd

23 January

Today brought the last missions of the month. Once again it was the First Gruppe and III/JG 54 that got the call. In the morning, the First Gruppe was ordered to fly high escort for JG 27 on an anti-Jabo mission to Mönchen-Gladbach. Oblt. Heckmann led twenty Focke-Wulfs up from Fürstenau at 0900. The mission orders had spelled out the route and altitude of each Staffel in detail. Because of its low altitude, the Gruppe was successfully bounced from above by Spitfires, which dived through the German formation at high speed and shot down three Focke-Wulfs. The hard-hit 4th Staffel lost two officers – Lt. Hans Cordt was killed, while Lt. Xaver Ellenrieder, who had just returned to the Gruppe from detached duty with ZG 76, bailed out at 500 meters (1600 feet) and suffered severe head injuries. Uffz. Walter Planz was killed. The enemy fighters were Spitfire XIVs from No. 41 Squadron. The British pilots claimed three Fw 190Ds destroyed, while one of their own aircraft failed to return. This was the first major air combat for the Griffon-engined Spitfire XIV, which had just begun moving to the Continent after employment in England against the V-1 threat. The Spitfire XIV was a most formidable combat aircraft; fortunately for the Germans, only four squadrons saw service with the 2nd TAF. S/L Tony Gaze, who joined No. 41 Squadron in April, had the following comments about his aircraft:

> "The Spit XIV outclassed everything for speed but the Tempest at low level. It outclimbed anything else by at least 1000 ft/min [300 m/min]. It could outrun a Mustang (we had to often, when attacked by them) and outclimb them by 2000 ft/min [600 m/min]. I caught up with both Me 262s and Ar 234s at 10,000 feet [3000 meters], and they were supposed to cruise at 450 mph [724 km/h]."

The combat scattered the First Gruppe. Lt. Kiefner was shot down by German Flak, but bailed out without injury. Oblt. Heckmann led the remnants of his formation back to Fürstenau at 1000. In the meantime III/JG 54 had been battling Tempests and Spitfires near Münster. Several German pilots were lost, including Lt. Crump's wingman, Obfw. Ludwig Goos.

At 1430 orders were received for another mission. The First Gruppe and III/JG 54 were to cover the jet airfield at Handorf between 1600 and 1630 hours. At 1530, the scheduled time of takeoff, only ten First Gruppe aircraft were ready. Major Borris led them off to meet the Green Heart Gruppe. Fifteen minutes into their patrol, contact was made with a dozen Spitfires and eighteen Tempests. For the next thirty minutes, combats took place around Enschede, from 3000 meters (10,000 feet) to ground level. At 1630, according to the Gruppe War Diary, Borris changed the mission to a freie Jagd, the assigned patrol having been completed. This made no difference to his pilots, who were at that moment fighting for their lives. His small force lost only two aircraft. Fw. Harald Wülfken escaped in his damaged aircraft, ran out of fuel, and was killed when his airplane overturned in his attempted dead-stick landing. Lt. Werner Lauer bailed out with minor injuries. III/JG 54 again suffered severely. During the day the Gruppe lost Oblt. Heinz Seiffert, Obfw. Joachim Siekers, and Uffz. Günther Langer killed; another three aircraft were shot down. The victors this afternoon were the Spitfire pilots of No. 421 Sqd.(RCAF), who claimed two of the Fw 190Ds, and the Tempests of No. 122 Wing, which claimed 10-1-7 Fw 190s for the day without loss to themselves, on what proved to be the Tempest wing's most successful day of the war.

JG 26 Casualties: 23 January 1945

Date	Rank	Name	Cas	Unit	Aircraft	WNr	Mkgs	Place	Time	Cause	Allied Unit
23-01-45	Lt.	Kiefner, Georg	no	1	Fw 190D-9	600158	wh 5	near Albachten	0920	own flak	n/a
23-01-45	Lt.	Lauer, Werner	WIA	1	Fw 190D-9	211059	wh 8	W of Gelow?		combat	
23-01-45	Uffz.	Planz, Walter	KIA	1	Fw 190D-9	210153	wh 11	Albachten-W of Münster	0930	Spitfire	41 Sqd XIV
23-01-45	Fw.	Wülfken, Harald	KIA	1	Fw 190D-9	210924	wh 14	W of Fürstenau	1700	no fuel	n/a
23-01-45	Lt.	Cordt, Hans-Helmuth	KIA	4	Fw 190D-9	400605	bl 16	near Leeden-Tecklenburg	0930	Spitfire	41 Sqd XIV
23-01-45	Lt.	Ellenrieder, Xaver	WIA	4	Fw 190D-9	211006	bl 6	Ostbevern	0945	Spitfire	41 Sqd XIV

26 January

As German-held territory shrank, and the strength of the combat units continued to decline, many Luftwaffe higher commands became superfluous. Jagdkorps II was disbanded today. Three Fliegerdivisionen were formed under Luftwaffenkommando West to control all of the Luftwaffe combat units in the west – bomber and reconnaissance units in addition to the day fighters. JG 26 was assigned to the 14th Fliegerdivision, which was responsible for the northern part of the front.

28 January

Oberst Josef "Pips" Priller left Jagdgeschwader 26 today. After five continuous years on the Western Front, his tour of combat duty had finally ended. He had scored 101 aerial victories in 307 combat sorties. He was to become Inspector of Day Fighters (West), a sinecure which would keep him from further combat flying. Priller's successor was Major Franz Götz, who assumed the command on his 32nd birthday. Götz was a prewar NCO pilot who had come up through the ranks, claiming 63 victories in more than 700 combat sorties, mostly on the Eastern Front. His most recent posting was as a Gruppenkommandeur in JG 53. The weather was too bad to permit a proper change-of-command ceremony. Only the First Gruppe could be paraded for Götz at Fürstenau.

On a less pleasant note, Lt. Kurt Fischer of the 9th Staffel was killed when the engine of his fighter quit unexpectedly at an altitude of 800 meters (2600 feet), immediately after taking off from Plantlünne. Fischer could not control the plane, which crashed, trapping him inside. The fully-fueled fighter caught fire, and Fischer shot himself with his pistol before the flames reached the cockpit. According to Third Gruppe folk wisdom, Fischer's death was an example of the "frontier justice" prevalent during the last year of the war. Fischer was thirty-eight years old, and a firm Nazi. He had spent the entire war at a primary flight school, and expected its standards of strict discipline to apply at the front. He insisted that all enlisted men salute him (with the now-standard deutsche Gruss) at each meeting, something that was unheard of in JG 26. Some of the mechanics apparently decided to put an end to this perceived harassment by sabotaging his airplane.

Fischer's fighter was a Fw 190D-9/R11, a variant that was supplied to JG 26 in some numbers. The R11 equipment package turned the Focke-Wulf into a "bad weather" fighter, and comprised a PKS 12 autopilot, a FuG 125 VHF radio beacon receiver, an LGW K23 course indicator, and heated cabin side windows.

29 January

Major Anton Hackl received orders to report to JG 300, as its Kommodore. He replaced Obstlt. Dahl, who took over the job of Inspector of Day Fighters from Obstlt. Gollob. Gollob became the new General der Jagdflieger, replacing Genlt. Galland, who for the present received no posting. Oblt. Waldemar Radener took command of the Second Gruppe; his 7th Staffel command was assumed by Lt. Gottfried Dietze.

31 January

During January the Geschwader lost thirty-one pilots killed in combat, three in accidents, and eight as prisoners. At least fourteen were seriously injured. III/JG 54, which was a fourth JG 26 Gruppe in all but name, lost fifteen pilots killed on only two missions. Until the last weeks of the war, JG 26 would continue to receive ample supplies of Germany's best piston-engine fighter in service, the Fw 190D. However, the Geschwader had no special claim to pilots, and its operational strength, which was limited by the number of pilots available for duty, declined steadily.

The combat proficiency of the Geschwader had declined in direct proportion to the level of skill of its average Nachwuchs pilot. The performance of any combat unit can generally be related directly to its morale and leadership. But the morale of the Geschwader at this point in the war cannot be summarized in simple terms, nor can it be determined merely by interviewing the surviving pilots – each man's opinion is inevitably colored by his own morale at the time. The morale of most of the enlisted pilots who survived the war was surprisingly high at this time – one former Obergefreiter claims to have believed in the *Endsieg* (final victory) until his own home city, Hamburg, fell to the Allies in late April. The pilots were serving in the most glamorous and exciting of the combat arms, and were convinced of their own elite status, although some were too embarrassed to go home on leave during the last year of the war and face the glares of their bombed-out neighbors. The Second Gruppe under Lang, Eder, and Hackl fostered the spirit and individuality of its pilots by reducing formal military discipline to a minimum. They sponsored dances at which a jazz band played; dancing and jazz were both officially forbidden under the state of emergency proclaimed in 1944. Major Borris's First Gruppe, on the other hand, observed all military courtesies with the greatest rigidity – even in POW camp after the war – and this technique seemed to work, as well. The spirits of the III/JG 54 pilots remained fairly high, despite their high losses. The morale in Hptm. Krupinski's Third Gruppe, on the other hand, was very low, if the surviving enlisted pilots can be believed. After Klaus Mietusch's death, Walter Krupinski was the only officer to gain their respect. The breach between commissioned and enlisted pilots has never healed; the few surviving members of the latter group continue to hold reunions to which the officers are not invited.

It is also difficult to generalize about the leadership of the Geschwader during the last six months of the war, and it would be extremely unfair to judge these men. The superstars among the combat pilots had all flamed out. A few Staffelkapitäne, notably

Waldemar Söffing and Wilhelm Hofmann, could act boldly when required by the circumstances, but the operative word for most formation leaders was caution. They knew the rules by which they would be judged, and could be counted on to accomplish enough to stay out of trouble. The better ones could do this while minimizing their own losses.

By 1945, none of the JG 26 Staffelkapitäne were professional officers. All had been promoted from the enlisted ranks, and few had had any form of officers' or formation leaders' training. They had not been promoted because of their abilities as leaders, and these abilities varied widely. Several surviving pilots divide the leaders into two categories: the majority, who tried conscientiously to fulfill the role of combat leader that had been thrust upon them, and the rest, who thought only of their own personal survival. There was a third category, containing those men who still hungered after personal glory and decorations. By the end of January, there was apparently only one man associated with the Geschwader who still fit this description, Hans Dortenmann of 12/JG 54. His skills as a formation leader and combat pilot were so great that most of his pilots forgave him for this quirk, even though it put them at great personal risk.

Geschwader personnel moves during January included: the return of Uffz. Hermann Kühn to the 5th Staffel from a flight school; the return of Lt. Xaver Ellenrieder to the 4th Staffel after a temporary assignment with ZG 76; the transfer of Ofhr. Hinrich Rodartz from the 3rd Staffel to a flight test unit; and the arrival of Lt. Josef Bott, a former Ju 52 pilot, after fighter conversion training, and his assignment to the Second Gruppe. The following flight instructors joined the Geschwader after their schools closed: Lt. Erich Asmus - First Gruppe; Hptm. Friedrich-Wilhelm Fahnert, Lt. Willi Wiese - Second Gruppe; Oblt. Friedrich Burkardt, Fhr. Heinrich Hermann - Third Gruppe. New pilots joining the Geschwader during January after completing flight training included: Fw. Hans Marischka, Uffz. Friedrich Rohrmann, Uffz. Erich Schumacher, and Lt. Alfred Vieweg. All were assigned to the Second Gruppe.

1 February

The weather continued to be unfit for combat flying. On the ground, the American First and Third Armies squeezed out the last of the "Bulge", restoring the battle lines in the Ardennes to their mid-December location. During the few flying hours, the Geschwader pilots made test and training flights. The technical officers attempted to find solutions for the problems that were cropping up in their Dora-9s, but serviceability rates would continue to drop for the rest of the war.

Ernst Battmer, the Geschwader technical officer, finally got his first opportunity to fly an Fw 190D. He remembers it as a short but eventful flight:

> "While I was still circling the field, a cloud of steam burst from the left side of the engine. I banked around for a crash landing, and tried to lower the gear just before setting down. Too late. The aircraft sat down hard on its partially-extended gear and tore a furrow in the ground a half-meter deep. My shoulder harness gave way, and I struck my head on the instrument panel, breaking my nose. The aircraft tore along on its belly, finally coming to a halt.
>
> "Major Borris later told me that my belly landing had been fortunate, since if my gear had been fully extended I would have bogged down in a muddy spot in the field, and would surely have overturned. My engine quit because of the failure of a piston ring and connecting rod. The torn-off rod broke through the coolant chamber and caused the engine to seize owing to loss of coolant. Despite this incident, I still felt that the new Jumo 213 engine was more reliable than the BMW 801."

3 February

Hptm. Krupinski's men attempted to train in their new Fw 190D-9s. This was difficult when the end of their flying-off field was invisible in the freezing rain. Uffz. Heinz

Brünn hit a water puddle while taxiing at high speed, and overturned, suffering slight injuries while seriously damaging his Dora-9. Another Third Gruppe pilot destroyed his aircraft in a crash-landing that was attributed to pilot error.

Hptm. Radener's Second Gruppe also made a few training flights. Uffz. Johannes Schlimper of the 8th Staffel attempted a forced-landing on Clausheide when his canopy iced over, but overshot the runway and destroyed his aircraft. Schlimper was unhurt. On the following day, Oblt. Glunz successfully completed a training flight; it proved to be his last flight of the war.

6 February

Although Jagdkorps II was in the process of disbanding, it was still responsible for the daily activity report covering the northern sector of the front, which stated that eighty-five fighters from JG 26 and JG 27 were up in the afternoon to screen the jet airfields or to hunt artillery spotters. The missions were all without result; one pilot was injured, and three fighters were damaged. III/JG 54 flew a mission against artillery spotters in the Monschau-Eupen area, but failed to make contact. The First Gruppe flew an airfield protection mission, with no more success. Major Borris led twenty-four aircraft up from Fürstenau at 1430, but fourteen either aborted the mission with bad engines or became separated from the formation in the weather. Fw. Herbert Kaiser of the 3rd Staffel was the day's only Jagdkorps II casualty; he attempted a forced landing on Horsten after his engine failed, but destroyed the aircraft and suffered a severe head injury. Borris and his nine remaining pilots reached the Köln area, but then abandoned the mission owing to the approach of bad weather.

7 February

Ogfr. Günther Boeke of the 7th Staffel was killed on a ferry flight from Düsseldorf. The reason for his crash was never established.

JG 26 Casualties: 28 January - 7 February 1945

Date	Rank	Name	Cas	Unit	Aircraft	WNr	Mkgs	Place	Time	Cause	Allied Unit
28-01-45	Lt.	Fischer, Kurt	KIFA 9		Fw 190D-9/ R11	210950	wh 1	Plantlünne a/f	1028	crashed	non-op
03-02-45	Uffz.	Schlimper, Johannes	no	8	Fw 190D-9	600350	none	Nordhorn a/f		landing	non-op
03-02-45	Uffz.	Brünn, Heinz	WIFA 10		Fw 190D-9	500386	bk 4	Plantlünne a/f	0930	takeoff	non-op
06-02-45	Fw.	Kaiser, Herbert	WIFA 3		Fw 190D-9	600348	yl 12	E of Horsten-Schultenort		engine	n/a
07-02-45	Ogfr.	Boeke, Günther	KIFA 7		Fw 190D-9	210105	br 1	Düsseldorf a/f		takeoff	non-op

8 February

The First Canadian Army began Operation Veritable, a major offensive in the Reichswald. Its goal was to clear the territory between the Maas and the Rhine Rivers of German forces.

10 February

Ogfr. Leo Przybyl of the 9th Staffel crash-landed his Fw 190D-9 on Rheine while on a practice flight. The reason was given as pilot error. Przybyl's aircraft was destroyed; his injuries were severe enough to prevent him from returning to the Geschwader.

11 February

Ofhr. Klaus Meixner, a pilot in 12/JG 54, was killed when his Fw 190D-9 crashed while on a transfer flight. The reason was given as a technical failure.

12 February

On his landing approach to Plantlünne from a training mission, Uffz. Paul Klingelhöfer of the 11th Staffel let his airspeed drop too far and stalled. His Focke-

Wulf half-rolled and crashed inverted on the landing ground. Klingelhöfer suffered severe facial injuries from his contact with the frozen ground, and was trapped in the cockpit. According to Georg Genth, the airfield emergency crews had recently been drafted into the infantry and had been replaced by untrained women who refused to approach the bloody pilot. Genth and several groundcrewmen lifted the airplane by hand and rescued Klingelhöfer.

13 February

The First Gruppe and III/JG 54 were ordered to fly a combined mission with JG 27 to hunt low-flying aircraft in the Nijmegen-Kleve area. Lt. Söffing, finally restored to combat status, led twenty-eight aircraft from Fürstenau at 1215. They failed to contact the enemy, and all but two fighters returned to base at 1343, where weather conditions shortly brought flying to an end. Uffz. Karl Loy got lost in the haze, ran out of fuel, and crashed fatally at Bocholt. Ogfr. Niessen also got lost, but made a smooth belly-landing near Lingen.

The Green Heart pilots flew two missions. 9/JG 54 and 10/JG 54 flew the same mission profile as the First Gruppe, but did not accompany them. Uffz. Günther "Peipl" Koch was shot down and killed, apparently by an RAF fighter. In late afternoon fourteen aircraft from 11/JG 54 and 12/JG 54 took off from Babenhausen on a Jabojagd and flew south to the Limburg-Koblenz area. Here they encountered the 36th Fighter Group's 22nd Squadron strafing roads. Obfw. Hans Hegener and Uffz. Hermann Rapke were shot down and killed in a prolonged air battle in which two P-47s also crashed. The dozen surviving Focke-Wulf pilots returned to base claiming eight Thunderbolts, according to the LwKdo West daily report. The victory list for III/JG 54 is incomplete, but it is known that Lt. Prager and Oblt. Dortenmann each claimed two Thunderbolts on this mission.

14 February

The First Gruppe and III/JG 54 were called on for an early protection flight to Rheine, with III/JG 54 as high cover and the First Gruppe as low cover. Major Borris took off at 0745 with his twenty-four Focke-Wulfs. He met the III/JG 54 contingent, which was led by Lt. Crump, and was soon over Rheine. The Schlageter Focke-Wulfs orbited at low altitude, which was not a wise maneuver under the circumstances. Seven No. 41 Sqd. Spitfire XIVs dived through both formations and shot down four Focke-Wulfs. Ogfr. Rudolf Zogboom and Uffz. Oskar Seidenfuss, both of 9/JG 54, were killed; Uffz. Wilhelm Düsing of the 2nd Staffel and Uffz. Helmut Brisch of 10/JG 54 bailed out slightly injured. In return, Lt. Söffing claimed one Spitfire, for his 24th victory. The British pilots claimed one confirmed and two probable victories over the "long noses", and sustained no losses. The Focke-Wulfs fulfilled their mission; under their cover, fifty-three Me 262 Blitzbombers got away from Rheine to bomb Nijmegen, Kleve, and Gennep.

JG 26 Victory Claims: 22 January - 14 February 1945

Date	Rank	Name	Unit	Cl #	Aircraft	Place	Time	Opponent	Conf
22-01-45	Ogfr.	Lange H.	4	1	Spitfire	Rheine-Ibbenbüren	1120	421 Sqd	unk
14-02-45	Lt.	Söffing	2 CO	24	Spitfire XIV	Rheine (GP 5)	0815	41 Sqd	unk

15 February

III/JG 54 finally received a Kommandeur today – Hptm. Rudolf Klemm, who had commanded IV/JG 54 until its recent dissolution. Klemm was no Robert Weiss; he was judged by the cynical Green Heart pilots as aloof on the ground, and overly concerned for his personal security while in the air.

The 8th Staffel was disbanded; its nine surviving pilots were transferred to the other three Staffeln of the Second Gruppe. Oblt. Hofmann, still flying with only one good

eye, took over the leaderless 5th Staffel on a permanent basis. On the 16th, the 4th Staffel was disbanded; its eleven pilots were split up among the rest of the First Gruppe. On the 19th, it was the turn of 12/JG 54; its pilots went to the rest of III/JG 54. The Kapitän of 12/JG 54, Oblt. Dortenmann, took command of 11/JG 54, while the latter unit's Staffelführer, Lt. Prager, moved to 9/JG 54 as deputy to Oblt. Heilmann. The junior members of the ground staffs of these three Staffeln were drafted into the infantry; most were sent to the Luftwaffe field divisions.

Three 2nd Staffel officers relax at Fürstenau in February. From left: Lt. Ossenkop, Lt. Söffing (Kapitän), Oblt. Georg Kittelmann (KIA 25 Feb 45). *(Ossenkop)*

21 February

The Second Gruppe flew its first full-scale mission in more than a month. About twenty Focke-Wulfs took off from Nordhorn at 1515 for a freie Jagd. While in the air, the Gruppe was ordered to intercept a formation of medium bombers. To the pilots' amazement, they reached the Marauders without contacting enemy fighters. One box of 394th Bomb Group B-26s had strayed off course after losing one bomber to flak over its target, the Vlotho railroad bridge. The Focke-Wulfs struck the loose formation east of Arnhem, and brought down three bombers, while seriously damaging four others. Uffz. Walter Stumpf of the 7th Staffel saw the crew bail out of his target. His claim was submitted as a "final destruction" – his first victory. Other claims were filed for five bombers destroyed and one separated from its formation. Unusually, all claims were filed by junior pilots rather than formation leaders, and it has not been possible to determine who led this successful mission, which proved to be the last time that the Geschwader attacked bombers. All of the successful pilots were claiming their first or second victories; in addition to Uffz. Stumpf, they were Lt. Andel, Lt. Wirth, Ofhr. Spahn, Uffz. Just, and Uffz. Krusen. Several Spitfires arrived as the Focke-Wulfs were reforming. One of these was claimed shot down by Uffz. Meiss. The Germans suffered no losses to the Spitfires or to the Marauders, but Uffz. Johannes Brumund of the 6th Staffel was shot down by German Flak while returning to Nordhorn, and crashed to his death.

The First Gruppe was grounded by poor visibility at Fürstenau, and the Third Gruppe was not yet operational on its Fw 190D-9s. In late afternoon, III/JG 54 was assigned another protection flight to Rheine. There they met the Mustang IIIs of Fighter Command's No. 315 Sqd. (Polish). Two Mustangs went down; one of the victors was Oblt. Dortenmann. Lt. Prager claimed a Thunderbolt by collision while returning from Babenhausen to Varrelbusch earlier in the afternoon; the P-47s shot down and killed Obfw. Siegfried Müller, one of the most experienced III/JG 54 pilots.

JG 26 Victory Claims: 21 February 1945

Date	Rank	Name	Unit	Cl #	Aircraft	Place	Time	Opponent	Conf
21-02-45	Uffz.	Just	5	2	B-26	E of Arnhem (near HO-HP)	1601	394 BG	unk

Officers of the First Gruppe, photographed at Füstenau in February. From left: Lt. Günther, Lt. Peter Ahrens (KIFA 4 Mar 45), Oblt. Otto Stammberger (adjutant), Oblt. Fred Heckmann, Major Karl Borris. *(Ossenkop)*

21-02-45	Uffz.	Krusen	5	1	B-26	E of Arnhem (near HO-HP)	1601	394 BG	unk
21-02-45	Ofhr.	Spahn	5	2	B-26-HSS	E of Arnhem (near HO-HP)	1600	394 BG	unk
21-02-45	Lt.	Wirth	5	1	B-26	E of Arnhem (near HO-HP)	1603	394 BG	unk
21-02-45	Lt.	Andel	7	1	B-26	Ahaus (HP4)	1604	394 BG	unk
21-02-45	Lt.	Andel	7	2	B-26	WNW of Ahaus (HO6)	1607	394 BG	unk
21-02-45	Uffz.	Meiss	7	1	Spitfire	E of Arnhem (near HO-HP)	1604		unk
21-02-45	Uffz.	Stumpf	7		B-26-eV	near Ahaus	1603	394 BG	unk

JG 26 Casualties: 10 - 21 February 1945

Date	Rank	Name	Cas	Unit	Aircraft	WNr	Mkgs	Place	Time	Cause	Allied Unit
10-02-45	Ogfr.	Przybyl, Leo	WIFA	5	Fw 190D-9	600136		Plantlünne a/f		takeoff	non-op
12-02-45	Uffz.	Klingelhöfer, Paul	WIFA	11	Fw 190D-9	210169		Plantlünne a/f		landing	non-op
13-02-45	Uffz.	Loy, Karl	KIFA	1	Fw 190D-9	500091	wh 16	Winterswijk, 55km E of Arnhem	1340	no fuel	n/a
13-02-45	Ogfr.	Niessen, Manfred	no	3	Fw 190D-9			N of Lingen		crashed	n/a
14-02-45	Uffz.	Düsing, Wilhelm	WIA	2	Fw 190D-9	400238	bk 12	near Rheine a/f	0815	Spitfire XIV	41 Sqd
21-02-45	Uffz.	Brumund, Johannes	KIFA	6	Fw 190D-9	210139	bk 12	SE of Meppen		own flak	n/a

22 February

The 8th and 9th Air Forces began Operation Clarion, a general assault against the German transportation system. In the absence of effective Luftwaffe defenses, many of the 9th Air Force medium bombers dropped to low level for the first time since May, 1943. After the morning fog lifted from its airfields, the 14th Fliegerdivision split its fighter resources between jet airfield defense and sweeps against fighter-bombers and medium bombers. The First Gruppe orders called for an anti-Marauder mission. Lt. Söffing led twenty-three Focke-Wulfs up from Fürstenau at 1430. Twenty minutes later, fifteen of them contacted six Tempests south of Rheine and attacked immediately; the assigned mission was abandoned. After a prolonged dogfight, Lt.

Söffing shot down his 25th opponent. One Focke-Wulf was shot down by the small formation of No. 3 Sqd. Tempests; Uffz. Franz Weiss bailed out, severely wounded.

III/JG 54 took off from Varrelbusch at 1345 for a Jabojagd, but had barely cleared their field when they were attacked by some 8th Air Force P-51s that were sweeping the area. The Mustangs, from the 364th Fighter Group's 383rd Squadron, shot down Fw. Robert Gasser and Fw. Gustav Westedt, killing both pilots, but lost two of their number to Lt. Prager and Oblt. Dortenmann. Two Focke-Wulfs crash-landed on Oldenburg without injury to their pilots.

The time was near for the Third Gruppe to return to combat in its Fw 190D-9s. This afternoon four Third Gruppe pilots flew a short test hop from Plantlünne, to run-in their Focke-Wulfs' engines. They were spotted by the American leader of the 2nd TAF's No. 274 Squadron, S/L D.C. "Foob" Fairbanks, who led his Tempests in a bounce. Fairbanks quickly shot down Fw. Alfred Girstenbreu, who was killed. Uffz. Gehrke tried to escape in a thin cloud, but popped out the other side and was hit by Fairbanks' fire. Gehrke's engine burst into flames, and he had to bail out. He got caught on his fighter's tail, but finally broke free, and his parachute opened just before he hit the ground, 100 meters (330 feet) from his exploding and burning aircraft. He had suffered second and third degree burns on the face and hands, multiple splinters in both legs, and a shell wound in the left foot, and was in the hospital until November, 1945. In August, three months after the end of the war, he was awarded the Wound Badge in Silver for his five combat injuries.

The Second Gruppe lost its Kommandeur today. Major Hackl asked for Oblt. Waldemar Radener to join him at JG 300 as a Gruppenkommandeur. Radener would receive the Knight's Cross on 12 March for his service in JG 26. The freie Jagd flown in the afternoon by the Gruppe was without result. Only one pilot, Gefr. Werner Molge, received credit for a combat sortie, on what Molge describes as one of his most noteworthy missions, second only to Bodenplatte.

All military service, even in time of war, has its elements of farce. Some veterans think back more on their good times in the service; others more on the bad. When prompted, most pilots recall scenes of heroism and horror. Not the high-spirited Werner Molge; he came up with the following light-hearted account of this mission:

> "The Second Gruppe of Jagdgeschwader 26 had not flown a single mission that morning. The weather was not especially good. The continuous cloud cover at 300 meters [1000 feet] was, however, apparently breaking up slowly, and the usual drizzling rain was also letting up.
>
> "We, the pilots of the 7th Staffel, sat in our lounge chairs in the readiness room, dozing or playing Doppelkopf or Skat. All were apparently calm. But each of us was alert for the crackling of the field loudspeakers of the command post circuit which would announce a mission. And sure enough, the well-known voice of the command post officer, Hptm. Groos, came on the air to announce, 'All Staffeln to take off in thirty minutes to attack low-altitude aircraft. The Gruppe is to assemble above the clouds. The individual Staffeln will, however, assemble beneath the cloud deck.'
>
> "Our leisure-time activities were broken off and we made ready to take off. The Fw 190D-9s had already been checked out for takeoff and warmed up by the mechanics; they sat there with brakes applied. The back parachutes were already in the cockpits. All we had to do was fasten the parachute and seat harnesses, put on the radio gear and plug in the oxygen coupling. Flare pistol and ammunition – all was in its place. We were ready to go.
>
> "Taxiing from the revetments in the forest where the 7th Staffel dispersal was located could only be accomplished with the aid of the mechanics. Taxiing along the lane to the field was also difficult due to its narrowness, since the sandy forest path had been chewed up considerably by the wheels, and was deeply rutted.
>
> "At the edge of the field all was the usual apparent confusion, until the

individual Rotten and Schwärme had sorted themselves out into their Staffel formations. Takeoff was by pairs, pairs following at distances of 150-200 meters [500-650 feet]. That was not entirely without danger, because of the propwash from the preceding aircraft. If one was caught in the wash at the moment of liftoff, he could make an awful mess.

"According to our orders, the Gruppe was to assemble above the thinning cloud cover. The 5th Staffel took off first; it was to be high cover. The 6th and 7th Staffeln took off shortly thereafter and assembled while making a left circuit of the field. The Staffeln then climbed in formation. The individual Schwärme in each Staffel flew close together in bad weather formation until they had broken through the thin cloud deck at 300 meters [1000 feet]. Above the clouds in the glaring sunlight, sunglasses were needed.

"The Staffeln assembled above the clouds into Gruppe formation, and finally headed south, in the direction of the Ruhr. We changed course several times, looking for our 'comrades with a different field post office number' [opponents]. But there was nothing doing. Apparently either our ground control hadn't a clue as to what was going on, or else our formation leader had been unable to make good radio contact with ground control. (My radio couldn't pick up ground control, which transmitted only to the formation leaders.) This was fine with me, as I had enough to do just to keep from losing my bearings. According to my mental navigation we had to be about over Emsland. According to the compass we were at that moment on a northerly course.

"Oddly enough, I was dropping back from my wingman – I was flying as No. 3 in my Schwarm – and had to close up constantly by giving my engine more gas. That was a new experience for me, as I had always held my position well in formation. Finally I noticed that I had already advanced my throttle to full power. A glance at the tachometer showed scarcely 2700 rpm, which startled me. Full power was supposed to be about 3000 rpm. This explained why I was constantly falling behind my wingman.

"I radioed my engine problems to the formation leader, and reported that I was leaving the formation – 'From Brown 7, I have engine problems. I am making Reise-Reise to Gartenzaun.'

"What now? I moved to the side of the formation, which was already pulling away from me, and made a magneto check, which was usually done on the ground during preflight. I switched from magneto setting M.1+2 to M.1 – nothing. Then to M.2 – that was it! The engine cut out. I quickly switched back to M.1+2; the Jumo 213 sprang to life again. I quickly made a split-S over my right wing into a suitable break in the clouds, leveling out without difficulty just below the cloud bank. As soon as I had restored the aircraft to normal flying conditions, I saw in front of me the very thing we had been looking for – a flight of aircraft bearing roundels on their wings. English, probably Tempests. Our fighter control had erred only in their altitude. I was upon them so quickly I didn't even have time to turn the firing lever on the control stick. I instinctively tried to slow down by stepping on the rudder pedals – but an aircraft in flight doesn't brake well that way.

"I burst through the flight of Tempests like greased lightning and now had them behind me, undoubtedly with weapons cocked and ready to fire. Things didn't look so good. There was only one salvation – head straight for the clouds and hide. I had plenty of excess speed. During the moment I had broken through the Tempest flight, I had seen how their formation burst apart in complete surprise. They probably thought twenty Fw 190s were coming along behind me.

"From my relatively secure position in the clouds, I radioed my formation leader, 'From Brown 7. Family of Indianer on Südpol, Caruso 360, Hanni 250-300. I make Reise-Reise to Gartenzaun. Question – Victor?' 'Victor, victor' came over the headset. That was the end of my enemy contact.

"After flying in the clouds for three to four minutes, I cautiously looked out into the pure air. Nothing. I was alone; the Indianer had gone. I recognized the border canal beneath me, and the small city of Frisoythe. I knew where I was from previous flights, and took up a southerly course. A short time later I saw the city of Lingen through the haze; it was not far from our airfield at Nordhorn, along the Ems-Vechte Canal. Upon return, I reported to the command post as usual.

"My mechanic confirmed my burned-out magneto, which kept me out of the soup. 'Bodo' (the command post) had heard my radio report. That made it a Feindflug (combat sortie) for me, since I had made contact with the enemy. My comrades in the Gruppe had only an Einsatzflug (non-contact sortie). They weren't able to find the Tempests. The most important thing to us was that we had all returned safely and without loss."

23 February

The American Ninth Army began Operation Grenade, which was intended to clear the Roer Valley and the Hürtgen Forest prior to a general advance to the Rhine River. The 14th Fliegerdivision planned a variety of missions, but weather conditions were unsuitable for combat flights. Uffz. Andreas Effelsberg of the 9th Staffel was trapped in a rainstorm and attempted an emergency landing on Twente, but overturned and was killed.

Hptm. Paul Schauder of the 10th Staffel was given command of the Second Gruppe. Oblt. Theobald Kraus replaced Schauder as leader of the 10th Staffel; Oblt. Jan Schild, who had not yet returned to flying status after his burns and ankle injury of the previous October, became Kraus's deputy.

24 February

The 14th Fliegerdivision ordered a maximum-strength effort by its fighters against low-flying aircraft in the Linnich-Jülich area, despite mediocre weather. Oblt. Heckmann led twenty-two Dora-9s up from Fürstenau at 0840. The engine of Ogfr. Niessen's aircraft caught fire soon after takeoff, and he crash-landed with slight injuries. Twenty fighters reached the target area, but no enemy aircraft were found. The formation was split up, probably by the weather, and landed on various airfields. Ofhr. Erich Schneider force-landed southwest of Münster with minor injuries after his engine was damaged in an air battle. Lt. Joachim Günther of the 3rd Staffel lost his Schwarm, and was attempting a lone landing on Meppen when he was shot down and killed by Spitfires of No. 332 Sqd. (Norwegian). Günther had been one of the best of the 1943 class of replacement pilots, with eleven victories since D-Day.

III/JG 54 flew a morning mission to Rheine, in which it engaged Spitfires, claiming one without loss. Its afternoon mission was to be a joint one with the First Gruppe, under the leadership of Lt. Söffing. The First Gruppe fighters were still scattered at

Lt. Joachim Günther of the 3rd Staffel. *(Schäfer-Günther via G. Schmidt)*

various fields, and only seven took off from Fürstenau at 1540 for the mission. Söffing aborted with a bad radio, and two other pilots had to abort the mission. The other four lost contact with the III/JG 54 aircraft, and returned early. III/JG 54 completed its mission, battling Typhoons and Spitfires with unknown success. The Green Heart Gruppe lost three Focke-Wulfs during the day. Fw. Erich Lange was shot down and killed near Emsbüren; Fw. Hermann Sinz was injured in a dead-stick landing after running out of fuel.

The Second Gruppe was not given a mission today, and the Third Gruppe was still training. One of the latter unit's most dependable pilots, Fw. Wolfgang Polster of the 11th Staffel, was strafed and wounded by Tempests after landing on Plantlünne. Polster had been preoccupied with instructing his wingman during the landing, and had not seen the approaching fighters. He was the 12th victim of No. 274 Squadron's S/L Foob Fairbanks. Wolfgang Polster's war flying was over; he was credited with five victories during his 108 combat sorties. His determination and sense of duty never wavered during the last year of the war and its bitter aftermath. According to Heinz Gehrke, Polster flew more missions during this period than any other Third Gruppe pilot. His sense of moral rectitude was so pronounced and consistent that for years he refused this author's requests for an interview, stating that any history written this long after events would inevitably be biased in favor of the few survivors. Wolfgang Polster was finally convinced of the value of the effort, and his assistance with this volume is gratefully acknowledged.

JG 26 Casualties: 22 - 24 February 1945

Date	Rank	Name	Cas	Unit	Aircraft	WNr	Mkgs	Place	Time	Cause	Allied Unit
22-02-45	Uffz.	Weiss, Franz	WIA	1	Fw 190D-9	210026 wh	10	near Greven	1450	Tempest	3 Sqd
22-02-45	Uffz.	Gehrke, Heinz	WIA	11	Fw 190D-9	500096 yl	1	Dreierwalde-Hopsten	1745	Tempest	274 Sqd
22-02-45	Fw.	Girstenbreu, Alfred	KIA	12	Fw 190D-9	500418 wh	2	nr Altenrheine	1750	Tempest	274 Sqd
23-02-45	Uffz.	Effelsberg, Andreas	KIFA	9	Fw 190D-9	500402 wh	5	Twente a/f	1322	landing	non-op
24-02-45	Lt.	Günther, Joachim	KIA	3	Fw 190D-9/R11	210941 yl	12	Zutphen		Spitfire	332 Sqd
24-02-45	Ogfr.	Niessen, Manfred	no	3	Fw 190D-9/R11	210951 yl	11	N of Kirchhellen a/f	1000	engine fire n/a	
24-02-45	Ofhr.	Schneider, Erich	WIA	3	Fw 190D-9/R11	210969 yl	10	SW of Münster-Handorf a/f	1000	Tempest	222 Sqd
24-02-45	Fw.	Polster, Wolfgang	WIA	11	Fw 190D-9	500603 yl	10	Plantlünne a/f	0805	Tempest	274 Sqd

25 February

Early in the morning the First Gruppe received orders to attack fighter-bombers supporting the American 9th Army's offensive in the Roer valley. Major Borris led twenty-two Focke-Wulfs up from Fürstenau at 0735. Four aborted; the rest formed up and headed toward Köln. A small force of between six and eight Thunderbolts was spotted making low-level attacks on German ground positions. Two Focke-Wulfs with mechanical problems broke away from the formation before combat was joined. Both were shot down by Allied fighters; Ofhr. Heinrich Vanderveerd was killed, and Uffz. Emil Brühan suffered serious injuries and died a week later. While banking for an attack, Borris's pilots saw a number of Spitfires above them, headed in their direction. Borris ordered an immediate attack on the P-47s, out of the morning sun. Two Thunderbolts were claimed shot down on the initial bounce, one by Lt. Söffing and the other by Oblt. Heckmann. The P-47s fought back, joined by the Spitfires. In a fifteen minute battle, four First Gruppe aircraft were shot down. Oblt. Georg Kittelmann, Hptm. Günther Krause, Ogfr. Helmut Lange, and Uffz. Günter Siegel were all killed. The P-47s belonged to the 36th Fighter Group's 22nd Squadron, whose pilots claimed 2-1-0 Fw 190s and 1-0-1 Bf 109s, while losing only one of their number.

The Spitfire unit involved with the First Gruppe was No. 41 Squadron, whose eight Spitfire XIVs also succeeded in disrupting the takeoff of the Second Gruppe from Nordhorn. Uffz. Josef Bott of the 5th Staffel taxied into a revetment, dived out of his aircraft, and was shot in the arm. The Tempests of No. 486 Sqd. (RNZAF) joined in the strafing attacks; one of its aircraft was hit by flak, and made a smooth belly landing near the airfield. Three Fw 190D-9s were destroyed on the field. The fighters that got off the ground were unable to form up, and landed on several airfields. As Fhj.-Uffz. Gerhard Just approached Köln-Wahn to land, he was shot down and killed by the airfield Flak.

The only Geschwader unit ordered to attempt an afternoon mission was the First Gruppe. Major Borris led fourteen aircraft off the ground at 1305, but his orders were impossible to fulfill in the constant rain and 100 meters (330 feet) visibility, and Borris called off the mission at 1340.

Today the battered Third Gruppe of JG 54, which had lost at least fifty Fw 190D-9s since returning to combat the previous December, officially became part of JG 26, as its Fourth Gruppe. 9/JG 54, with ten pilots commanded by Oblt. Heilmann, became 15/JG 26. 10/JG 54, whose nine pilots were led by Lt. Crump, became 13/JG 26. Oblt. Dortenmann's 11/JG 54 and its twelve pilots became 14/JG 26. The basis for assigning the new Staffel designations is not known, but the identification numbers on every airplane had to be repainted to conform with Luftwaffe requirements for the first, second, and third Staffeln of a Jagdgruppe. The 13th Staffel repainted its black numbers white; the 14th Staffel covered its yellow numbers with black; and the 15th Staffel repainted its white numbers yellow. The new Fourth Gruppe continued to base at Varrelbusch, under the command of Hptm. Klemm.

JG 26 Victory Claims: 22 - 25 February 1945

Date	Rank	Name	Unit	Cl #	Aircraft	Place	Time	Opponent	Conf
22-02-45	Lt.	Söffing	2 CO	25	Tempest	near Rheine (HO)	1500	3 Sqd	unk
25-02-45	Lt.	Söffing	2 CO	26	P-47	Köln	0825	36 FG	unk
25-02-45	Oblt.	Heckmann	3 CO	71	P-47	SE of Köln	0825	36 FG	unk

JG 26 Casualties: 25 February 1945

Date	Rank	Name	Cas	Unit	Aircraft	WNr	Mkgs	Place	Time	Cause	Allied Unit
25-02-45	Uffz.	Brühan, Emil	KIA	1	Fw 190D-9	400241	wh 13	15km N of Münster	0745	combat	
25-02-45	Ogfr.	Lange, Helmut	KIA	1	Fw 190D-9	210992	wh 3	near Köln-Wahn	0825	P-47	36 FG
25-02-45	Oblt.	Kittelmann, Georg	KIA	2	Fw 190D-9	600167	bk 5	Gronau-Rheine	0825	P-47	36 FG
25-02-45	Uffz.	Siegel, Günter	KIA	2	Fw 190D-9	210952	bk 17	Hamm area-Troisdorf	0825	P-47	36 FG
25-02-45	Ofhr.	Vanderveerd, Heinrich	KIA	2	Fw 190D-9	210985	bk 10	Köln area	0745	combat	
25-02-45	Hptm.	Krause, Günther	KIA	3	Fw 190D-9/ R11	600984	yl 9	NE of Köln-Wahn	0825	P-47	36 FG
25-02-45	Lt.	Bott, Josef	WIA	5	Fw 190D-9	600351	wh 17	Nordhorn-Rheine		Spitfire XIV	41 Sqd
25-02-45	Fhj-Uffz.	Just, Gerhard	KIA	5	Fw 190D-9	211008	wh 8	Köln-Wahn a/f		own flak	n/a

26 February

The Geschwader attempted no missions because of the poor weather. The engine of Ogfr. Richard Walter's Fw 190D-9/R11 failed while the 3rd Staffel pilot was landing on Fürstenau after a test flight. The aircraft caught fire in the crash-landing, and Walter was killed.

27 February

Only the First Gruppe was ordered up today, on an unusual dusk mission as escorts for four Fw 190A-8s from NSGr 20, a night attack Gruppe that normally flew its missions individually. Nine Gruppe aircraft took off at 1550. Lt. Kiefner aborted with radio and fuel tank problems, but the other eight followed the attack aircraft to the target area near Mönchen-Gladbach while screening them from attack by eight Thunderbolts that

were hovering above. The mission was completed successfully, and the fighters were back on the ground by 1710.

28 February

The entire Geschwader was ordered to fly a Jabojagd to the area of Mönchen-Gladbach to attack fighter-bombers that were supporting the American advance on that city. The Third Gruppe, flying its first Fw 190D-9 mission, was the first up; Hptm. Krupinski led them off from Plantlünne at about 0730. Shortly after 0800, they were hit at 1500 meters (5000 feet) by S/L Fairbanks and six No. 274 Sqd. Tempests. The Focke-Wulfs proved more than willing to mix it up, and the Allied pilots, badly outnumbered, were soon fighting for their lives. Three German planes crash-landed during the battle. Uffz. Franz Schmidt later died of his injuries, but the other two pilots were uninjured. Two Tempests went down, including that of Fairbanks. Foob Fairbanks was the highest-scoring Tempest pilot of the war, with eleven confirmed victories while flying the type. Both RAF pilots survived as prisoners of war.

Uffz. Willi Dachmann of the 11th Staffel, killed over Plantlünne on 28 February when his Fw 190D-9 collided with that of Hptm. Wollnitz. *(Genth)*

This successful battle, which could have gotten the Third Gruppe off to an excellent start in their new aircraft, had a disastrous conclusion. Two Fw 190Ds collided while in the landing circuit above Plantlünne. Both crashed in flaming balls of fire, which Georg Genth of the 12th Staffel recalls flying over on his own return. The two pilots, Hptm. Bernhard Wollnitz of the Stab flight and his wingman, Uffz. Willi Dachmann, were, of course, killed. The thirty-three-year-old Wollnitz had been a dedicated National Socialist; his service to the Nazi party dated back at least to 1931, when he had joined the Sturmabteilung (SA). He was not a successful air fighter, but was considered one of the best pure pilots in the Gruppe. The accident occurred as Wollnitz was making a tight bank around a farmhouse on the edge of the field; he was showing off for his girlfriend, whom he had brought to Plantlünne and installed in the house. The horrible scene was witnessed by everyone on the base, and set the unit's morale back once again.

Oblt. Theobald Kraus, the 10th Staffel leader, had run out of fuel before reaching Plantlünne and was slightly injured in his subsequent belly landing. One Tempest crash had been reported by ground witnesses. After Kraus returned to base, Krupinski called the pilots together to establish who had shot the Typhoon down. Kraus, Uffz. Genth, and the anti-aircraft gunners all claimed the victory. Genth had attacked his target from a difficult position, passing from right to left in a tight bank, and had seen his fire strike in the wing region; the Tempest flew right through his cone of fire. The shell pattern must have matched up with those on the crashed Tempest, for Genth was credited with the victory within the Gruppe, although of course no confirmation was ever received from Berlin. Since two Tempests failed to return from the mission, it appears that the claims of both Kraus and Genth were valid, and that one of them brought down the top-scoring Tempest pilot. Kraus's victory was his first in over one hundred combat sorties; it is said that this was the first time he had even hit his target.

The First Gruppe put up twenty-one aircraft at 1145, but Major Borris ordered them to return to Fürstenau when they encountered a solid cloud front near Rheine. The Fourth Gruppe got off at the same time as the First, and apparently carried out a patrol of its assigned area, but without making contact. The Second Gruppe was the only unit of the Geschwader to carry out its mid-day mission according to plan. Oblt. Hofmann's 5th Staffel reached the Mönchen-Gladbach area shortly after noon. Hofmann quickly spotted a formation of P-47s, and led a successful attack which resulted in claims for two P-47s destroyed – Hofmann's forty-first victory and Ofhr. Johann Spahn's third. The P-47s were from the 406th Fighter Group, which claimed 1-1-1 Fw 190s in this combat, and lost one Thunderbolt. Uffz. Bruno Krusen of the 5th Staffel was shot down during the battle, and was still carried as missing in 1998.

The weather closed in again, and only the Fourth Gruppe was able to carry out an afternoon mission, which was without result. The other Gruppen were released from duty in mid-afternoon. Georg Genth joined several companions in a Lingen restaurant to get drunk and mourn Willi Dachmann. There were complaints about the noise, and Genth made an insulting comment to a "golden pheasant", a civilian Nazi functionary who was dining out in full uniform with a young woman. When Genth returned to base, he was ordered to report to Hptm. Krupinski immediately. The Nazi had turned him in; Genth had been identified by his unusual nickname, "Schorsch". Before ever joining the Geschwader, Genth had been court-martialed for a minor infraction, with his punishment to be deferred until after the war, and he was expecting the firing squad this time. He assumed, based on Krupinski's consistent use of Nazi terminology in his public expressions, that Krupinski himself was a firm Nazi. But the Kommandeur, after listening to Genth's story, simply returned the folder to the NSFO, the Nazi "morale" officer, without comment. Genth heard no more of the incident.

Other than the transfers resulting from the dissolution of three Staffeln, there were few moves affecting Geschwader personnel in February. Oblt. Peter Hauer was transferred from the 9th Staffel to JG 27 in exchange for Fw. Georg Raith. Uffz. Otto Beckert joined the Second Gruppe from IV/JG 54, which had disbanded. A few new pilots arrived after completing highly-abbreviated flight training courses. These included Uffz. Karl Strauhs, who joined the First Gruppe, and Uffz. Günther Issleib, who joined the Second.

JG 26 Victory Claims: 28 February 1945

Date	Rank	Name	Unit	Cl #	Aircraft	Place	Time	Opponent	Conf
28-02-45	Oblt.	Kraus	10	1	Tempest	Osnabrück	0800	274 Sqd	unk
28-02-45	Uffz.	Genth	12	3	Tempest	Osnabrück	0800	274 Sqd	unk
28-02-45	Oblt.	Hofmann W.	5 CO	41	P-47	near Mönchen-Gladbach	1223	406 FG	unk
28-02-45	Lt.	Schulwitz	5	6	P-47	near Mönchen-Gladbach	1224	406 FG	unk
28-02-45	Ofhr.	Spahn	5	3	P-47	near Mönchen-Gladbach	1225	406 FG	unk

JG 26 Casualties: 26 - 28 February 1945

Date	Rank	Name	Cas	Unit	Aircraft	WNr	Mkgs	Place	Time	Cause	Allied Unit
26-02-45	Ogfr.	Walter, Richard	KIFA	3	Fw 190D-9/ R11	210986	yl 16	Fürstenau a/f		crashed	non-op
28-02-45	Uffz.	Krusen, Bruno	KIA	5	Fw 190D-9			S of Mönchen-Gladbach	1230	P-47	406 FG
28-02-45	Hptm.	Wollnitz, Bernhard	KIFA	III St	Fw 190D-9	600349	gr 3	Plantlünne a/f	0812	collision	n/a
28-02-45	Uffz.	Schmidt, Franz	KIA	9	Fw 190D-9	500601	wh 17	near Lengerich	0810	Tempest	274 Sqd
28-02-45	Oblt.	Kraus, Theobald	WIA	10 CO	Fw 190D-9	400256	bk 16	SE of Gütersloh	0840	no fuel	n/a
28-02-45	Uffz.	Dachmann, Willi	KIFA	11	Fw 190D-9	500568	yl 7	Plantlünne a/f	0812	collision	n/a

1 March

The orders for the Geschwader were the same as those of the past few days – support the German Army in its retreat to the Rhine by attacking American fighter-bombers in the Mönchen-Gladbach area. The four Gruppen were ordered to form a single Gefechtsverband, and sixty-two fighters took off between 0830 and 0845. The combat zone was some distance south of the Geschwader airfields, and reaching it through the curtain of patrolling 2nd TAF aircraft was difficult. The Third Gruppe failed to make an appearance over the battle zone. Part of the Fourth Gruppe got there, but had no luck. Lt. Crump's 13th Staffel reached Mönchen-Gladbach at 0930, and engaged some P-51s, probably from the 363rd Tactical Reconnaissance Group, without loss or apparent success. The 14th Staffel was intercepted by 25-30 Spitfires near Dortmund; Uffz. Günther Rey claimed one of them. Uffz. Otto Friedrich was killed, and the remaining Focke-Wulfs scattered. At least one pilot, Obfw. Fritz Ungar, landed on Ahlhorn.

The other two Gruppen reached the combat zone in strength at about 0930, and both engaged P-47 formations in fierce and prolonged combat. Major Borris had led twenty-four aircraft up from Fürstenau at 0835. He and seven other pilots had to abort because of radio or landing gear difficulties, and the sixteen remaining planes were led south by Oblt. Heckmann. They engaged about forty P-47s and P-51s in and beneath the clouds between Düsseldorf and Köln at altitudes of 500-1000 meters [1500 to 3000 feet]. The Gruppe war diary comments that the Thunderbolt pilots were experienced, and were able to turn with the Focke-Wulfs. The Germans were badly scorched. Five pilots failed to return; all were killed. One was Hans Kukla's former wingman, the newlywed Uffz. Hans Delor; the others were Lt. Hans Bleich, Uffz. Leo Dombrowa, Uffz. Franz Putsch, and Uffz. Karl Zeidler. Only Delor's and Putsch's remains had been found and identified by 1998. The survivors landed on a number of fields, and claimed no victories. Their opponents were the 406th Fighter Group's 512th Squadron, which had jettisoned its bombs when bounced by more than a dozen "very aggressive" fighters. The Thunderbolt pilots claimed 2-0-2 Fw 190s and 2-0-2 Bf 109s, while losing none of their number.

The Second Gruppe freie Jagd had a more favorable result for the Germans. Its three Staffeln left Nordhorn at 0810, and reached the battle zone in good order. *En route*, Oblt. Hofmann and Fw. Chemnitzer each saw and shot down an artillery spotter. Hofmann then saw eight P-47s pulling up from their bomb runs, and led a bounce. Unknown to the German pilots, the Thunderbolts, from the 366th Fighter Group's 389th Squadron, had dropped nothing more lethal than surrender leaflets. The two flights of Thunderbolts were immediately split up into pairs by the attack and the low overcast. The pilots of both sides took quick deflection shots at enemy aircraft as they appeared suddenly from the clouds. Four P-47s were shot down in the battle zone, one pilot bailing out with wounds. A fifth crashed on the return flight, its pilot bailing out without injury. The Thunderbolt pilots claimed 1-0-1 Fw 190s. The American pilots, and their comrades who did not return, apparently did better than they claimed – three Second Gruppe pilots, Fw. Max Chemnitzer, Uffz. Armin Florian, and Fw. Werner Verhöven, were killed in the combat, and Uffz. Josef Hoppe was shot down and taken prisoner. Some of the losses may have been due to American antiaircraft fire, however; at least one Focke-Wulf, that of Uffz. Stumpf, sustained damage from that source. The Gruppe pilots claimed five P-47s destroyed, exactly matching the American losses. The victorious pilots were Oblt. Hofmann, Lt. Sy, Lt. Andel, and Ofhr. Spahn. Two more pilots claimed probables.

The Third Gruppe was grounded in the afternoon for lack of fuel. Several 11th and 12th Staffel pilots were standing around watching B-17s fly overhead. Georg Genth remarked that rather than watch the bombers while stuck on the ground, it would be better to head to Switzerland and sit out the war there. A new replacement pilot, one of the last to arrive, clapped Genth on the shoulder and cried, "You are under arrest!

Give me your weapon and come with me!" Everyone stared in shock – Nazi justice had arrived in the Luftwaffe! Genth followed the Unteroffizier to the office of the NSFO, Major Reiser, who was a good-natured Austrian schoolteacher with no combat experience in the present war. The young pilots had found him easy to manipulate. Genth convinced Reiser that he had spoken only out of frustration at his inability to take off and attack the bombers. Genth was then dismissed. The *Schnüffler* (snooper) was killed a few days later. "No loss to us", was Georg Genth's comment.

JG 26 Victory Claims: 1 March 1945

Date	Rank	Name	Unit	Cl #	Aircraft	Place	Time	Opponent	Conf
01-03-45	Oblt.	Hofmann W.	5 CO	42	Auster	near Mönchen-Gladbach	0932		unk
01-03-45	Oblt.	Hofmann W.	5 CO	43	P-47	near Mönchen-Gladbach	0936	366 FG	unk
01-03-45	Hptm.	Fahnert	5	1	P-47-prob	near Mönchen-Gladbach	0938	366 FG	unk
01-03-45	Ofhr.	Spahn	5	4	P-47	near Mönchen-Gladbach	0935	366 FG	unk
01-03-45	Uffz.	Hanusch	6	2	P-47-prob	near Mönchen-Gladbach	0943	366 FG	unk
01-03-45	Lt.	Sy	6	2	P-47	near Mönchen-Gladbach	0937	366 FG	unk
01-03-45	Lt.	Andel	7	3	P-47	near Mönchen-Gladbach	0936	366 FG	unk
01-03-45	Lt.	Andel	7	4	P-47	near Mönchen-Gladbach	0937	366 FG	unk
01-03-45	Fw.	Chemnitzer	7	1	Auster	near Mönchen-Gladbach	0935		unk
01-03-45	Uffz.	Rey	14	3	Spitfire	Viersen-Mönchen-Gladbach	0941		unk

JG 26 Casualties: 1 March 1945

Date	Rank	Name	Cas	Unit	Aircraft	WNr	Mkgs	Place	Time	Cause	Allied Unit
01-03-45	Lt.	Bleich, Hans	KIA	1	Fw 190D-9	600353	wh 7	Düsseldorf	0915	P-47	406 FG
01-03-45	Uffz.	Putsch, Franz	KIA	1	Fw 190D-9	210920	wh 11	S of Düsseldorf	0915	P-47	406 FG
01-03-45	Uffz.	Zeidler, Karl-Erich	KIA	1	Fw 190D-9/R11	211003	wh 1	Düsseldorf	0915	P-47	406 FG
01-03-45	Uffz.	Dombrowa, Leo	KIA	2	Fw 190D-9	210273	bk 6	Düsseldorf	0915	P-47	406 FG
01-03-45	Uffz.	Delor, Rudolf	KIA	3	Fw 190D-9/R11	211009	yl 16	Düsseldorf	0915	P-47	406 FG
01-03-45	Uffz.	Florian, Armin	KIA	6	Fw 190D-9			Mönchen-Gladbach	0930	P-47	366 FG
01-03-45	Fw.	Verhöven, Werner	KIA	6	Fw 190D-9			Mönchen-Gladbach	0930	P-47	366 FG
01-03-45	Fw.	Chemnitzer, Max	KIA	7	Fw 190D-9			Düsseldorf	0930	P-47	366 FG
01-03-45	Uffz.	Friedrich, Otto	KIA	14	Fw 190D-9	600156	bk 6	Dortmund		Spitfire	

2 March

Twenty-one Third Gruppe Focke-Wulfs took off from Plantlünne at 0822 on a training mission. North of Rheine, the seventeen aircraft still with the formation took on a number of "P-47s, Tempests, and Spitfires" at 3-7000 meters (10-23,000 feet). The Allied fighters might have all been Spitfire XIVs of No. 125 Wing's two squadrons, which were on a patrol of Rheine and had already engaged JG 27 Bf 109s that were in the area to screen Me 262 takeoffs. Uffz. Walter Hähnel of the 10th Staffel was shot down and killed; Third Gruppe pilots as yet unidentified claimed 2-1 Thunderbolts. The losses were possibly Spitfire XIVs of No. 130 Squadron, two of which were downed either by this unit or by JG 27.

The only other Geschwader mission was flown by the Second Gruppe. Nineteen of its aircraft took off from Nordhorn at 1330 on a freie Jagd northwest of Rheine. The fighters were up for seventy-five minutes, and failed to contact the enemy.

4 March

The weather limited the Geschwader to small flights for several days. Lt. Peter Ahrens, a successful 3rd Staffel pilot, was killed at Fürstenau when his engine failed on a test flight. His landing approach was too fast, his airplane overturned, and Ahrens burned to death in his cockpit. Two more First Gruppe pilots made successful belly landings on Fürstenau when their engines failed. Eight Second Gruppe Focke-Wulfs took off at 1330 on a weather reconnaissance mission to Düsseldorf; the mission was broken off when bad weather was encountered too soon. Uffz. Helmut Wirtz of the 6th Staffel was caught near Wesel by P-47s and was shot down and killed.

5 March

Small missions were flown by pilots from three of the Gruppen. Major Borris led eleven fighters up from Fürstenau at 0720 on a Jabojagd to Düsseldorf. The weather forced them back early. No contact was made with the enemy, but they were able to observe and report the status of some of the Rhine bridges to the 14th Fliegerdivision.

Four 7th Staffel Focke-Wulfs were the next up. They left Nordhorn at 1220 to hunt low-flying aircraft to the south. Near Krefeld they found a flight of five artillery spotters; Lt. Dietze and Lt. Andel shot down three of them. The Allied aircraft have not yet been identified, although a formation flight of Grasshoppers was so unusual that it should have left a trace in the records.

The Fourth Gruppe put up four Focke-Wulfs at 1618, under specific orders to hunt artillery spotters between Köln and Bonn. They did not have the luck of the Second Gruppe pilots, and failed to contact the enemy.

6 March

Again today the fighters of the 14th Fliegerdivision were limited to small flights. Lt. Crump led four 13th Staffel Focke-Wulfs up from Varrelbusch at 1140 on a weather reconnaissance mission and a hunt for artillery spotters around Duisburg, but failed to contact the enemy. The Third Gruppe put up Schwärme at 1140 and 1540 on armed reconnaissance missions to the Arnhem area. These also failed to make contact.

7 March

The American First Army's 9th Armored Division captured an intact bridge over the Rhine at Remagen, creating another instant crisis point for the Wehrmacht. Luftwaffenkommando West was unable at short notice to alter the missions of the western day fighters, which were limited by the weather and low fuel supplies, and these were flown as scheduled. The Third was the only JG 26 Gruppe to fly today. Four of its Focke-Wulfs took off at 1330 on a freie Jagd to Emmerich. Fw. Karl-Heinz Friedrich was shot down by what were described as Mustangs, and belly-landed with minor wounds. Shortly thereafter, orders for a full-strength freie Jagd to Enschede were received in the Plantlünne command post. Unfortunately, no experienced formation leader was available, and Obfw. Willi Zester of the 9th Staffel was ordered to lead the mission. Zester was an experienced pilot, but had never before led a formation. Lt. Heinz-William Bartels was the only officer on the flight roster, and he was so green that he was flying as Uffz. Otto Salewski's wingman.

After sitting in their cockpits for some time, seventeen pilots were ordered to take off at 1445. Uffz. Georg Genth was flying as Zester's wingman, which Genth felt was much better than his usual "place of honor" at the rear of the formation. The Focke-Wulfs climbed to an altitude of 3000 meters [10,000 feet], quickly reached Enschede, and determined that the sky was filled with enemy activity – Typhoons were attacking motor convoys, and Spitfires were circling just above the Typhoons. Genth then saw several flights of Tempests below him. This was very dangerous, as the Tempest was superior in performance to the Fw 190D-9 below 5000 meters [16,000 feet]. Genth tried to warn his comrades, but they did not acknowledge his message. He began fiddling with his radio, and when he next looked around, he discovered that he and

Zester were alone. The Tempests had used their superb climbing performance to attack the rear of the formation from beneath.

Six Tempests were now approaching Zester and Genth in their dead angle below. The two German pilots banked in opposite directions, as Genth felt that to follow Zester would have put him right in the Tempests' line of fire. Genth turned on his methanol injection, and his speed increased to about 600 km/h [373 mph]. An oil line feeding his engine broke, and Genth left a long stream of oil behind as he headed for the nearest cloud layer, about two miles away. His engine still ran quietly, but he now had Tempests above, behind, and below him. He began crabbing to the left and right with his rudder, using a trick he had worked out the previous autumn with Willibald Malm. This made the pilot behind him miss, and Genth reached the cloud safely, intending to pull up into a zoom climb and make a head-on pass at the Tempests. But the cloud was too thin; he was seen from beneath, and a Tempest met him when he emerged. The Focke-Wulf was hit; Genth lost elevator control and tried to bail out. The plane was standing on its nose, and Genth's arm struck the fin so hard that the bone broke cleanly through. Genth had to slow down from his estimated 650 km/h [404 mph] and shift his body to open his parachute with the other hand. It had just opened when a V-2 rocket took off from a nearby base, so startling Genth that he was not prepared to hit the ground, which he did with such force that the nerve in his broken arm was severed. Despite the pain, he rejoiced that his war was now over.

Four Focke-Wulfs failed to return to Plantlünne. Obfw. Zester and Uffz. Genth bailed out with injuries, and Lt. Bartels and Uffz. Salewski were killed in their aircraft. The Tempests were up in full force that afternoon. Aircraft from five squadrons took shots at the Third Gruppe Focke-Wulfs. It was probably No. 56 Squadron that made the initial attack; the British pilots claimed the destruction of one Bf 109 and one Fw 190. S/L Mackie of No. 80 Squadron engaged a Focke-Wulf in a prolonged turning battle, in which both aircraft were leaving wingtip contrails at 900 meters (3000 feet). The British pilot finally hit his target, probably Uffz. Salewski, in a desperate, high-deflection burst of fire, and watched it crash and explode. Mackie returned to base wringing wet with sweat, having emerged victorious from the most difficult battle of his career.

Uffz. Genth was shot down by a Greek pilot from No. 3 Squadron, F/L B. M. Vassiliades, who had already had a very successful tour in the 2nd TAF as a Mustang pilot. Vassiliades saw a Focke-Wulf flying alone and began to pursue it. He scored one strike, which caused the German pilot to take violent evasive action in and out of several clouds. The Tempest pilot followed below for nearly ten minutes, and when the aircraft finally emerged, got on its tail and hit it in the cockpit area. The German pilot then jettisoned his canopy and bailed out, landing two miles southeast of Enschede. Pieces of Genth's aircraft were excavated from this crash site forty years later. Vassiliades was to live for only two more weeks after this battle; he was shot down and killed on 21 March by German Flak.

Uffz. Genth's war may have been over, but his adventures were only beginning. Georg Genth recalls,

"The curiosities of this story are still not over, for other events surrounding my bailout and hospital stay were learned from Dutch friends, exactly forty years after they happened! After landing in a marshy meadow I came across a corduroy road and reached firm ground. A German army unit found me and brought me to the Hoeltinghof Inn for my initial treatment. The inn was then the headquarters of Admiral Canaris, who was in charge of the Wehrmacht espionage forces. A shot-down English flyer was hiding not fifty yards away in a farmhouse, waiting to be passed through to his own lines by the resistance fighters! That's how crazy things were at that time. We laughed heartily when the present owner of the Hoeltinghof told me this story."

While Genth was in the hospital a group of Waffen-SS troops burst in, demanding that their blood-type tattoos be surgically removed so that they would not be shot if captured. This reminded Genth of what he had been fighting for, and he decided to prolong his stay in the hospital and be taken prisoner. But the hospital staff did not cooperate, and he was released several weeks later to march back to Plantlünne.

JG 26 Casualties: 2 - 7 March 1945

Date	Rank	Name	Cas	Unit	Aircraft	WNr	Mkgs	Place	Time	Cause	Allied Unit
02-03-45	Uffz.	Hähnel, Walter	KIA	10	Fw 190D-9	400257	bk 10	NW of Ibbenbüren	0800	Spitfire XIV	130 Sqd
04-03-45	Lt.	Ahrens, Peter	KIFA	3	Fw 190D-9/ R11	211011	yl 11	NW of Fürstenau a/f		engine	non-op
04-03-45	Uffz.	Wirtz, Helmuth	KIA	6	Fw 190D-9			Rheinkamp		P-47	
07-03-45	Obfw.	Zester, Willi	WIA	9	Fw 190D-9	601032	wh 18	Drievorden	1530	Tempest	122 Wing
07-03-45	Fw.	Friedrich, Karl-Heinz	WIA	10	Fw 190D-9	500090	bk 9	SW of Oberhausen	1330	P-51	
07-03-45	Uffz.	Salewski, Otto	KIA	10	Fw 190D-9	400247	bk 4	Schüttorf	1528	Tempest	122 Wing
07-03-45	Lt.	Bartels, Heinz-William	KIA	11	Fw 190D-9	210927	yl 18	near Gildehaus	1531	Tempest	122 Wing
07-03-45	Uffz.	Genth, Karl-Georg	WIA	12	Fw 190D-9	500118	yl 15	near Enschede	1538	Tempest	3 Sqd

8 March

Today it was the turn of the First Gruppe to fly. Despite the situation at Remagen, the 14th Fliegerdivision was still focusing on its own part of the front, the northern sector. Lt. Söffing led five aircraft up from Fürstenau at 1600 for an armed reconnaissance of Arnhem. Söffing reached the ordered area, or so he believed, but could see nothing through the solid cloud deck. Ogfr. Günther Dingler turned over when landing at his base, doing serious damage to his Focke-Wulf and injuring himself. Pilot error was recorded as the cause of the accident.

9 March

The Luftwaffe fighters and bombers to the south of the 14th Fliegerdivision zone of operations were attacking the Remagen bridge and the rapidly-expanding bridgehead in full strength. Luftwaffenkommando West ordered the 14th Fliegerdivision to join in the effort. The First Gruppe was chosen to make the first attempt. At 1455 Major Borris led seventeen aircraft up from Fürstenau and headed south. However, a solid cloud front blocked their path, and Borris changed the mission to a Jabojagd in the Rheine area. They contacted a squadron of Typhoons, and damaged one, but could not continue the attack because of the weather. On the return flight, one pilot got lost and had to bail out, while a second crash-landed with a bad engine. Neither pilot was injured.

At 1620 twenty-four Second Gruppe fighters took off from Nordhorn under orders to support the Army at Remagen. They made it as far south as Wesel, which was in front of the advancing American Ninth Army. At 2000 meters (7000 feet) over Wesel, the Gruppe made a head-on attack on a squadron of P-47s. The Second Gruppe had once again encountered part of the 366th Fighter Group; this time it was the 391st Squadron. The German pilots claimed the destruction of four P-47s; the victors were Lt. Andel, Lt. Schulwitz, Uffz. Meiss, and Uffz. Hanusch. Three German pilots failed to return. Lt. Helmut Wirth was killed; Uffz. Hanusch was shot down after his own victory, and bailed out with severe injuries. The third pilot to go down was Uffz. Walter Stumpf of the 7th Staffel, who dived through a cloud and emerged directly in front of three P-47s. The leading Thunderbolt destroyed Stumpf's rudder with its first shot, leaving the airplane uncontrollable. The two trailing P-47s were shot down by Fw 190s which were behind them. Stumpf and one Thunderbolt pilot bailed out and landed next to one another, just behind the German lines.

The returning American pilots reported that their opponents had been "aggressive" – this was worth noting, because many German formations at this stage in the war avoided contact – and filed claims for 6-0-3 Focke-Wulfs. Their own losses amounted to two P-47s which crashed during the combat; one which made a forced landing on an advanced base; and two others which returned with major combat damage.

Fw 190D-9 "yellow 8" (W.Nr. 600375) of the 11th Staffel, abandoned at an airfield near Celle in March. In this photograph it appears to be in good condition except for its smashed wooden propeller, but it was later stripped by souvenir hunters. *(Stafford)*

JG 26 Victory Claims: 5 - 9 March 1945

Date	Rank	Name	Unit	Cl #	Aircraft	Place	Time	Opponent	Conf
05-03-45	Lt.	Dietze	7 CO	4	Auster	near Krefeld	1252		unk
05-03-45	Lt.	Dietze	7 CO	5	Auster	near Krefeld	1255		unk
05-03-45	Lt.	Andel	7	5	Auster	near Krefeld	1252		unk
09-03-45	Lt.	Schulwitz	5	7	P-47	near Wesel	1651	366 FG	unk
09-03-45	Uffz.	Hanusch	6	3	P-47	Wallach near Wesel	1650	366 FG	unk
09-03-45	Lt.	Andel	7	6	P-47	near Wesel	1649	366 FG	unk
09-03-45	Uffz.	Meiss	7	2	P-47	near Wesel	1650	366 FG	unk

10 March

The Fourth Gruppe flew the only 14th Fliegerdivision fighter mission. At 1640 Lt. Crump led four Focke-Wulfs up from Varrelbusch to hunt artillery spotters in the Wesel-Krefeld area. Four Spitfires were engaged, and the probable destruction of one was claimed. One Focke-Wulf was damaged when its landing gear collapsed upon landing back at base.

11 March

The 14th Fliegerdivision was still ordering most of its fighter missions to be flown in Schwarm strength. Forty JG 27 Bf 109s flew combat sorties today, in ten formations, and claimed six Austers for the loss of three Messerschmitts. The Second Gruppe put up eleven Fw 190D-9s in three Schwärme. These flew armed reconnaissance missions to the Rees area, but did not contact the enemy.

12 March

Missions were flown by one Schwarm from each of three Gruppen. Four First Gruppe aircraft took off at 0830 under Lt. Kiefner's command to reconnoiter the Arnhem area. One aborted immediately, and the other three were split up when attacked by Spitfires from above. Kiefner carried out the mission alone. Uffz. Karl Strauhs crashed for unknown reasons while returning to Fürstenau, and was killed.

The Third and Fourth Gruppen each put up a Schwarm at 1515 to fly the same mission. The Fourth Gruppe aircraft completed their task under Lt. Crump's leadership, without loss. The Third Gruppe lost Ofhr. Karl-Manfred Hark east of Arnhem to German Flak.

JG 26 Casualties: 8 - 12 March 1945

Date	Rank	Name	Cas	Unit	Aircraft	WNr	Mkgs	Place	Time	Cause	Allied Unit
08-03-45	Ogfr.	Dingler, Günther	WIFA	3	Fw 190D-9	601036	yl 9	Fürstenau a/f		landing	non-op
09-03-45	Lt.	Wirth, Helmut	KIA	5	Fw 190D-9			Wesel-Vreden	1650	P-47	366 FG
09-03-45	Uffz.	Hanusch, Fritz	WIA	6	Fw 190D-9	210239	bk 3	S of Wesel	1650	P-47	366 FG
09-03-45	Uffz.	Stumpf, Walter	no	7	Fw 190D-9		br 16	Wesel	1700	P-47	366 FG
12-03-45	Uffz.	Strauhs, Karl	KIA	1	Fw 190D-9	210929	wh 12	near Fürstenau	0845	Spitfire	
12-03-45	Obfw.	Hark, Karl-Manfred	KIA	10	Fw 190D-9	600122	bk 7	E of Arnhem	1610	own flak	n/a

13 March

Geschwader fuel inventories had built up to the point that missions could again be flown in full strength, if the weather cooperated. Twenty-four Fourth Gruppe aircraft were the first up, at 1015. A freie Jagd was flown to the Remagen-Bonn area, but failed to contact the enemy. The Gruppe put up a dozen more fighters at 1220 to hunt medium bombers in the Münster area; this mission, too, was unsuccessful.

Twenty-four Third Gruppe aircraft were next off the ground, at 1320. They, too, headed for Münster to search for medium bombers. Fw. Bruno Schwarz crashed for unknown reasons, and was killed. The other pilots found three enemy fighters of undetermined type which were able to split up the German formation and shoot down two Focke-Wulfs. The 10th Staffel leader, Oblt. Theobald Kraus, bailed out with severe wounds. The second German pilot apparently escaped injury.

Sixteen First Gruppe aircraft were close behind; Oblt. Heckmann led them off Fürstenau at 1325. They were also sent to hunt the bombers near Münster, but were recalled at 1415 because of the weather.

Twenty-one Second Gruppe Focke-Wulfs took off at 1615 and flew south, to hunt fighter-bombers over the Remagen bridgehead. They did not get that far, meeting nine No. 130 Sqd. Spitfire XIVs which were on their way to sweep Rheine. Uffz. Heinz Meiss was shot down, and crashed in his aircraft. Uffz. Marischka shot down one of the Spitfires; its pilot bailed out with injuries.

Fifteen First Gruppe aircraft flew the day's last mission, again under Oblt. Heckmann. They were up at 1702 and headed for Remagen, but were recalled at 1740 because the weather was closing in at Fürstenau.

JG 26 Casualties: 13 March 1945

Date	Rank	Name	Cas	Unit	Aircraft	WNr	Mkgs	Place	Time	Cause	Allied Unit
13-03-45	Uffz.	Meiss, Heinz	KIA	7	Fw 190D-9			Unna-Werl	1630	Spitfire XIV	130 Sqd
13-03-45	Oblt.	Kraus, Theobald	WIA	10 CO	Fw 190D-9	500615	bk 18	NE of Greven	1602	fighter	
13-03-45	Fw.	Schwarz, Bruno	KIFA	11	Fw 190D-9	500084	yl 17	near Münster	1400	crashed	n/a
13-03-45	Fw.	Köhler, Arnfried	KIA	13	Fw 190D-9			near Fürstenau		combat	

17 March

The rain that had prevented any operations for several days let up just enough to permit flying by small formations. The Fourth Gruppe put up a Schwarm at 1140 for a weather reconnaissance and a hunt for artillery spotters between Wesel and Düsseldorf. Twelve P-38s were seen above them, but the quartet avoided contact.

A dozen Second Gruppe Focke-Wulfs took off at 1600 for a freie Jagd to the same area. Two pilots, including Uffz. Stumpf, aborted immediately. Lt. Schulwitz led the patrol at very low altitude, beneath the Allied radar, and popped up to make quick attacks whenever observation planes were seen. An L-5 from the 47th Field Artillery

Battalion, attached to the US 5th Armored Division, was shot down northwest of Düsseldorf by the string of German fighters. Schulwitz claimed two Grasshoppers on the mission, and another member of the formation claimed damage to a third. All of the German aircraft returned to Nordhorn safely; Lt. Dietze's aircraft had sustained damage from ground fire.

At 1645 eight Third Gruppe aircraft took off from Plantlünne to hunt medium bombers. Three aborted; the engine of Uffz. Eugen Krümpelmann's Focke-Wulf seized, and he died in the crash. The five remaining fighters were surprised by Spitfires which attacked them out of the clouds over Coesfeld. No claims were made; one German fighter was damaged.

18 March

The skies above a solid cloud deck at 1000 meters (3300 feet) were clear; three of the four Gruppen were able to put up combat formations. At 0935 Fw. Karl Hofmann and his wingman took off from Fürstenau on a weather recon mission to Münster and Düsseldorf. They were attacked by five Spitfires, but were able to escape in the ground haze.

The Fourth Gruppe scrambled twenty fighters from Varrelbusch at 1150 to intercept low-flying aircraft near their base. Near Dümmer Lake they were bounced by P-51s of the 339th Fighter Group's 503rd Squadron, which was sweeping the area. Four 14th Staffel Focke-Wulfs went down. Uffz. Werner Merz and Fhj.-Obfw. Leo Klatt were killed. Fw. Otto Weber was shot down, and bailed out with injuries; Obfw. Werner Zech bailed out as soon as a Mustang reached firing position on his tail, and landed with minor injuries. Capt. Francis Gerard, the pilot chasing Zech, claimed the victory, and was then hit badly by a trailing Focke-Wulf. Gerard considered bailing out, but was able to crash-land at his base; his aircraft was claimed by a Fourth Gruppe pilot. Zech's Fw 190D-9 was excavated in 1996-1997.

In mid-afternoon, the Third and Fourth Gruppen put up a total of eleven Focke-Wulfs to sweep from Wesel to Düsseldorf. Six returned early; the other five completed their mission without contacting Allied aircraft. Five First Gruppe fighters took off at 1654 for a Jabojagd under Oblt. Heckmann. Their patrol of the Krefeld-Wesel area was uneventful.

Oblt. Glunz left the Geschwader for jet training with III/EJG 2. He was caught up in the general chaos, and never got to fly an Me 262. After the war, Addi Glunz was always reluctant to discuss his military experiences, but he did write the following brief summary on the last page of his logbook:

"I was very enthusiastic about flying jets and hoped for an early return to combat duty. But there was to be no more. The great advance of the British and the Americans began. We transferred from Brandenburg to Prague. I had no hope for a satisfactory ending to the war. We then went from Prague to Lechfeld by way of Plattling, and from Lechfeld via Fürstenfeldbruck to Mühldorf. All one could do was flee before the Americans. There was no longer any possibility of flying missions. We obtained food and planned to draw back into the Alps. The Americans approached Mühldorf. We moved again, south of Peterskirchen, and hid in a forest. Reconnaissance showed that to move further into the mountains would be senseless. The Alps were full of troops, primarily SS, and they were confiscating all vehicles. The soldiers were to be made to return to the ground fighting. It was said that the SS was defending the Alps. We wanted no part of that nonsense. We had no desire to be shot dead so that the SS could live a little longer. The SS was ruthless. During the move from Peterskirchen I saw frightful scenes and learned for the first time something of the conditions in the concentration camps."

Date	Rank	Name	Cas	Unit	Aircraft	WNr	Mkgs	Place	Time	Cause	Allied Unit
17-03-45	Uffz.	Krümpelmann, Eugen	KIFA	11	Fw 190D-9	210262	yl 11	Plantlünne a/f	1635	engine	n/a
18-03-45	Fhj-Ofw.	Klatt, Leo	KIA	14	Fw 190D-9			W of Twistringen	1235	P-51	339 FG
18-03-45	Uffz.	Merz, Werner	KIA	14	Fw 190D-9			W of Twistringen	1235	P-51	339 FG
18-03-45	Fw.	Weber, Otto	WIA	14	Fw 190D-9			W of Twistringen	1235	P-51	339 FG
18-03-45	Obfw.	Zech, Werner	WIA	14	Fw 190D-9	211028	bk 8	W of Twistringen	1235	P-51	339 FG

19 March

The skies over northwestern Germany were predicted to be cloudless, with a visibility of 50 kilometers (30 miles), and the Geschwader prepared for a full day of flying once the morning haze burned off. The First Gruppe was first off the ground. Seventeen Focke-Wulfs took off at 0917 on a Jabojagd. Lt. Asmus suffered engine failure, and bailed out without injury. A second pilot aborted, but the rest proceeded to Osnabrück, where they were attacked by 12-18 fighters – Tempests or Thunderbolts, depending on the account. The Gruppe made no claims; one Focke-Wulf was damaged.

Today brought the Geschwader its last large-scale encounters with the 8th Air Force. Nearly seven hundred P-51s swept across the continent in advance of 1200 heavy bombers, which by now had no industrial targets left to attack, and were targeting rail yards and airfields. The 78th Fighter Group was assigned the task of neutralizing the airfields around Osnabrück, which included all of the JG 26 and JG 27 bases. The forty-seven Mustangs reached the area at 1230. The Messerschmitts of IV/JG 27 were up on an airfield protection mission, and were punished severely by the Americans, losing eight pilots killed and four injured. Twelve Bf 109s were destroyed and two more were damaged. The Gruppe claimed one victory.

The Second Gruppe took off into the midst of the action, and engaged P-51s in a dogfight right over Plantlünne airfield. Ofhr. Johann Spahn's ship was hit. Spahn attempted to bail out, but the American pilot kept firing, as he noted in his combat report, and hit Spahn as he fell away from his aircraft; he did not open his parachute. Spahn had flown as Wilhelm Hofmann's wingman since the latter had lost the use of one eye. He had served as Hofmann's "eyes", taking off and landing alongside him to aid Hofmann in judging his distance from the ground. The Gruppe filed no claims.

The Fourth Gruppe was returning from a freie Jagd to Münster, and reached the area in time to join the combats. According to the LwKdo West evening report, the Gruppe claimed eight Mustangs for the loss of Uffz. Renatus Spitz and Fw. Arnfried Köhler. Major Klemm claimed one of the P-51s; Oblt. Dortenmann claimed two; Lt. Prager a fourth; Lt. Crump, a fifth, and Uffz. Hein, a sixth. Peter Crump furnished some details of his combat. While returning to Varrelbusch at low altitude, he spotted a lone Mustang. The American pilot saw him and attempted to flee, but Crump caught him and shot him down easily. The Mustang pilot bailed out successfully, with moderate burns to his neck and head. At Varrelbusch that evening, Crump was able to congratulate him on his survival.

Five 78th Group P-51s were shot down; two pilots were killed, and three were taken prisoner. Hans Dortenmann claimed the 84th Squadron commander, Major Harry Downing, and Peter Crump entertained Lt. Elmer Nieland in the Gefechtsstand. The remaining Mustangs left the area at 1330. This was the group's most successful mission of the war. Victory credits were ultimately awarded for 6-0-6 Fw 190s and 24-0-12 Bf 109s. The only three Luftwaffe Jagdgruppen in the area were II/JG 26, IV/JG 26, and IV/JG 27. Their losses are known to have totaled six destroyed or damaged Fw 190s and fourteen lost or damaged Bf 109s. The high American claims are unusual for this stage of the war, and must be attributed to the excitement and confusion associated with a combat of this scale.

Later in the afternoon, the First and Fourth Gruppen drew the assignment of airfield coverage for the jet base at Handorf. Rather than the expected Tempests and Spitfires, the Focke-Wulfs encountered 8th Air Force P-51s, making their last sweep of the day. At 1630, the fourteen First Gruppe Fw 190D-9s engaged eight Mustangs from the 479th Fighter Group's 434th Squadron, led by their commander, Major Robin Olds. After a brief turning battle, the P-51s broke away, leaving behind them the wreckage of two Focke-Wulfs. Both pilots bailed out, but Fw. Karl Hofmann's parachute failed to open, and Uffz. Wilhelm Düsing hit his head when landing, taking him out of the war. The German pilots were only able to claim damage to one Mustang; Lt. Ramthun got the credit.

According to the First Gruppe claims list, Uffz. Hans Backhaus, a 1st Staffel mechanic, shot down a P-51 near Fürstenau, probably with one of the 20 mm Flak guns improvised by the mechanics from machine cannon salvaged from crashed aircraft.

Oblt. Otto Stammberger, who had served as First Gruppe adjutant since recovering from his wounds, received word today of his promotion to Hauptmann and his selection to the War Academy. He left the Geschwader and joined the staff of the 14th Fliegerdivision to await the beginning of the next class, which was never to convene. Stammberger was assigned to a ground unit, but made his way back to the Geschwader before war's end in order to surrender with it. Oblt. Heinz Kemethmüller replaced him as adjutant.

The Third Gruppe did not fly today, despite perfect conditions, and three of its most successful and experienced noncommissioned pilots, Obfw. Heinrich Humburg, Fw. Adolf Tabbat, and Fhj.-Fw. Joachim Zeller, were informed that they were being transferred to JG 7, the first jet fighter Geschwader.

JG 26 Victory Claims: 13 - 19 March 1945

Date	Rank	Name	Unit	Cl #	Aircraft	Place	Time	Opponent	Conf
13-03-45	Uffz.	Marischka	5	1	Spitfire	Dortmund (KQ9)	1635	130 Sqd	unk
17-03-45	Lt.	Schulwitz	5	8	Auster	NW of Düsseldorf	1630	47 FAB L-5	unk
17-03-45	Lt.	Schulwitz	5	9	Auster	SW of Düsseldorf	1635		unk
19-03-45	Maj.	Klemm	IV CO		P-51	10km NW of Nordhorn (GQ3)	1335	78 FG	unk
19-03-45	Lt.	Crump	13 CO	22	P-51	Varrelbusch	1330	78 FG	unk
19-03-45	Oblt.	Dortenmann	14 CO	29	P-51	Rheine-Lingen (PQ FP6)	1336	78 FG	unk
19-03-45	Oblt.	Dortenmann	14 CO	30	P-51	Rheine-Lingen (PQ FQ4)	1337	78 FG	unk
19-03-45	Uffz.	Hein K.	14	5	P-51	S of Haselünne	1336	78 FG	unk
19-03-45	Lt.	Prager	15	17	P-51	Osnabrück (PQ GR3-6)	1350	78 FG	unk

20 March

The skies were again clear. The Fourth Gruppe was assigned the first mission of the day. Nine Focke-Wulfs took off at 0845 to intercept low-flying aircraft near their airfield. They engaged what were described as thirty Thunderbolts at an altitude of 2-3000 meters (6500-10,000 feet). No victories were claimed, and one German aircraft was destroyed; its unidentified pilot was injured.

Defense of the III/KG 76 airfield at Achmer became a priority assignment for the Geschwader. The unit's Ar 234s had developed into effective attack bombers, and were the best offensive weapons in the Luftwaffe arsenal, far superior to the Me 262 Blitzbomber. Seventeen Fourth Gruppe aircraft took off at 1720 and headed to Achmer. Thirty enemy aircraft – Thunderbolts or Mustangs, depending on the account – were engaged near the field at an altitude of 1000 meters (3300 feet). Oblt. Heilmann claimed a P-51 near Bramsche. Lt. Kurt Siebe of the 15th Staffel failed to return, and was eventually classified as killed in action. The only plausible Allied opponents are the 357th Fighter Group's 363rd Squadron, which at 1800 shot down a Focke-Wulf that tried to join their formation near Dümmer Lake.

The First Gruppe was scheduled to accompany the Fourth to Achmer, but Major Borris kept his fifteen aircraft on the ground owing to the presence of heavy bombers

Canadian mechanics dismantle a 15th Staffel Fw 190D-9 at an airfield near Wilhelmshaven, where it had been abandoned in March. It cannot be seen in this photo, but the aircraft had a Fourth Gruppe "wave" marking in yellow, the 15th Staffel color. *(National Archives of Canada)*

and escorts over the field. They took off thirty minutes late, and failed to make contact before breaking off the mission in order to regain Fürstenau before dark.

21 March

Twenty-seven Focke-Wulfs from the Second and Fourth Gruppen were up at 0650 to cover the return of the Ar 234s to Achmer from their dawn mission. Uffz. Otto Beckert of the 7th Staffel hit a tree near Hopsten and crashed to his death. No enemy aircraft were seen, and the Focke-Wulfs returned to their fields at 0740. The Geschwader was then grounded owing to the presence of heavy bombers overhead. The 8th Air Force made a special effort to take out all of the known jet fighter and bomber bases, attacking Hesepe, Achmer, Hopsten, Essen-Mühlheim, and Rheine.

JG 26 Casualties: 19 - 21 March 1945

Date	Rank	Name	Cas	Unit	Aircraft	WNr	Mkgs	Place	Time	Cause	Allied Unit
19-03-45	Uffz.	Düsing, Wilhelm	WIA	2	Fw 190D-9	210930	bk 15	near Münster-Ostbevern	1620	P-51	479 FG
19-03-45	Fw.	Hofmann, Karl	KIA	2	Fw 190D-9	500044	bk 6	near Rastrup	1620	P-51	479 FG
19-03-45	Ofhr.	Spahn, Johann	KIA	5	Fw 190D-9			near Lingen		P-51	78 FG
19-03-45	Uffz.	Spitz, Renatus	KIA	13	Fw 190D-9			NE of Fürstenau		P-51	78 FG
19-03-45	Fw.	Köhler, Arnfried	KIA	13	Fw 190D-9			near Fürstenau		P-51	78 FG
20-03-45	Lt.	Siebe, Kurt	KIA	15	Fw 190D-9			SE Quakenbrück		P-51	357 FG
21-03-45	Uffz.	Beckert, Otto	KIA	7	Fw 190D-9			10km N of Rheine		combat	

22 March

Dawn broke with a cloudless sky and perfect visibility. The jet fields were unserviceable after the bombing attacks, and JG 26 resumed the task of locating and destroying Allied bombers. A small number of Fourth Gruppe fighters took off before 0800 on a Jabojagd, but failed to find any Allied fighters out so early. The mission was repeated at noon, with no better luck. The Third Gruppe flew a freie Jagd in its own area, but it, too, was unsuccessful.

The First Gruppe stood by at fifteen minutes readiness starting at 0605, but did not receive mission orders until 1539. The Gruppe was to take off immediately and attack a B-26 formation near Rheine. Major Borris led fourteen fighters off the ground, but he soon turned back with a defective radio, passing the lead to Oblt. Heckmann. Heckmann also had radio problems, but continued the mission. Southeast of Dümmer Lake he saw twenty-two P-47s, and soon thereafter a small formation of eight B-26s, escorted by a dozen fighters. Heckmann avoided contact, and led his unit back to Fürstenau; all had landed by 1654. Heckmann's reason for not carrying out his mission, "My pilots were mere boys, and I had no radio" was entered *verbatim* into the Gruppe diary, in an unusual example of candor in an official Wehrmacht document.

The Second Gruppe was also kept on the ground until mid-afternoon, when it was ordered to join the hunt for Marauders near Rheine. Its dozen fighters were caught near Lingen by two squadrons of sweeping Tempests. The British pilots quickly shot down five Focke-Wulfs. Uffz. Günter Issleib, Uffz. Edwin Kalbus, Ogfr. Otto Putschenjack, and Lt. Willi Wiese were killed; Uffz. Günther Warthemann's gunfire hit a Tempest, but he was then hit by another. He bailed out cleanly, but broke a leg on landing, and did not return to the unit. Uffz. Johannes Hoffmann claimed a Tempest, but none in fact were lost. No. 56 Squadron claimed 3-0-1 Fw 190Ds and No. 80 Squadron claimed 2-0-2, in exact agreement with the actual losses of the Gruppe.

JG 26 Casualties: 22 March 1945

Date	Rank	Name	Cas	Unit	Aircraft	WNr	Mkgs	Place	Time	Cause	Allied Unit
22-03-45	Uffz.	Kalbus, Edwin	KIA	5	Fw 190D-9			Lohne-Lingen	1603	Tempest	56 or 80 Sqd
22-03-45	Uffz.	Issleib, Günter	KIA	6	Fw 190D-9			Drope	1603	Tempest	56 or 80 Sqd
22-03-45	Ogfr.	Putschenjack, Otto	KIA	6	Fw 190D-9			Dreierwalde	1603	Tempest	56 or 80 Sqd
22-03-45	Uffz.	Warthemann, Günther	WIA	6	Fw 190D-9		bk 15	Dreierwalde	1603	Tempest	56 or 80 Sqd
22-03-45	Lt.	Wiese, Willi	KIA	6	Fw 190D-9			8km SE of Fürstenau	1605	Tempest	56 or 80 Sqd

24 March

This morning every airfield in northwestern Germany whose location was known to Allied Intelligence was attacked by American heavy bombers. The attacks were in support of Operation Varsity, the assault crossing of the lower Rhine River by the British Second Army and the American Ninth. All four Geschwader airfields were pounded into moonscapes. Fürstenau received 133.5 tons of bombs; Nordhorn, 121.7 tons; Plantlünne, 328.5 tons; and Varrelbusch, 339.2 tons. It is known that no aircraft were destroyed on the ground at either Fürstenau or Nordhorn. The other two airfields, which received double the bomb loads, may have suffered more severely. All personnel worked to fill in narrow takeoff strips. The First Gruppe was the first to report that it was again operational. At noon the Stab and the First Gruppe were ordered to transfer operations to Drope, only seven miles northwest of Fürstenau; the quarters for the men would for now remain in Handrup. The ground staff began packing.

25 March

The Geschwader airfields were all operational by morning, but all auxiliary services had been knocked out by the bombing, and it was time to move on. Field Marshal Montgomery's armies were across the Rhine in force, and only seventy miles from Nordhorn. The Second and Fourth Gruppen received orders to move out this morning. The Third Gruppe, however, received the shocking news that it was to be disbanded, effective immediately. The only Third Gruppe officer to be given a new command was

Oblt. Gottfried "Cognac" Schmidt, a friend of Hptm. Schauder's who took over the 6th Staffel from Lt. Sy. The Third Gruppe aircraft and pilots were split among the three remaining Gruppen; the non-essential ground staff was formed into an airfield defense unit. Hptm. Krupinski and Oblt. Schrader left for the fighter pilots' rest home at Bad Wiessee, where they planned to sit out the rest of the war. The junior pilots got the job of ferrying the Gruppe aircraft to other airfields. Uffz. Otto Bock ran into a crater while landing on Delmenhorst and overturned, suffering minor injuries.

Sy was never given another Staffel command, and remained bitter for the rest of his life over his displacement by a younger man with a victory list no longer than his. Sy was a pre-war veteran of the Wehrmacht who had taken part in the Polish campaign in an engineering company. He did not become a pilot until 1943, and had then joined the Second Gruppe on the Kanalfront. As a professionally trained officer, he was a rarity in the Gruppe, and his advancement should have been rapid, but circumstances such as his Nazi party membership and a mediocre combat record prevented it.

The Second and Fourth Gruppen were to move to Bissel, a ten minute flight northeast of Varrelbusch. The Geschwader's new fields were very much makeshifts, to be used until permanent facilities farther to the rear could be made ready. The Second Gruppe pilots ate breakfast early and were bussed to the field at Clausheide before daylight. Only a narrow takeoff strip had been filled in. The possibility of a taxi accident in a Fw 190D was always great, owing to its lack of vision to the front. Hptm. Schauder ordered the experienced pilots to take off first, to reduce the possibility that an early crash on the field would block it for the rest. Lt. Gerhard Schulwitz of the 5th Staffel was first off the ground, and began to circle the field in a tight bank. Uffz. Hermann Kühn was next to take off, but instead of joining Schulwitz in the circuit he pulled up in a steep climb, apparently to make a dramatic exit, and collided with Schulwitz. The flaming wreckage landed in the woods, five hundred meters from Werner Molge and Heinz Gomann, who were the closest to the crash site. Molge pulled the partially-opened parachute away from Schulwitz's body, and got a view of the smashed corpse that could never be erased from his mind. In 1985, Werner Molge described the location of the crash to an aviation "digger", who found Schulwitz's Iron Cross and his watch, which had stopped at 0557, the time of his crash.

Further takeoffs were prohibited; the airstrip and the 6th Staffel dispersal were covered in fragments of metal and human flesh. The ground crews began to clear the debris from the takeoff strip, while the pilots stood around in a state of shock – "Bubi" Schulwitz had been one of the most popular pilots in the Gruppe. An hour later, takeoffs were resumed. The 6th Staffel took off last. Lt. Sy was in the lead; it was his last day as Staffelführer. He and his pilots made the short flight with no problems, but he noted in his diary that evening that the new field's dispersals, although well camouflaged, were a long way from the edge of the landing ground, which would increase the chances of being surprised from the air while taxiing. The only building on the field was a crude barracks; there was neither a command post nor a ready room for the pilots.

The First Gruppe completed its short transfer hops by 0625, and reported itself operational. Shortly after noon, it received orders to attack fighter-bombers in the area of Kirchhellen. When attempting to take off from the unfamiliar field, Gefr. Ernst Thuy struck a tree, damaging his aircraft. His attempted forced landing ended fatally. Fifteen Focke-Wulfs got off the ground, but several, including that of Major Borris, had to return immediately because of high oil pressure. Eleven were forming up northeast of Drope at 2000 meters (6500 feet) when they were hit from above by Tempests. After a brief dogfight, two Focke-Wulfs crashed. Ogfr. Manfred Niessen bailed out without injury, but Fhr. Heinrich Hermann, who had just joined the First Gruppe from the 10th Staffel that morning and had not yet been assigned to a Staffel, was killed in his aircraft. The Tempest pilots, from No. 222 Squadron, suffered no losses in this battle, and claimed three Fw 190Ds. Five Fourth Gruppe aircraft flew from Drope to Bissel to cover the landings of the First Gruppe, but the Tempests had already gone.

The Second Gruppe joined the Fourth Gruppe on an evening mission from Drope. The 15th Staffel Kapitän, Oblt. Willi Heilmann, led fifteen Focke-Wulfs up at 1740 for a freie Jagd to Bocholt. They encountered enemy fighters whose identity remains a mystery. Fw. Gerhard Kroll, Heilmann's wingman, described them as Tempests. When he first spotted them, they were below, but were outclimbing the German aircraft, and close to overtaking them. Heilmann suddenly dived away in a sharp turn that would have placed Kroll directly in front of the enemy's guns, had he followed. Kroll was left to face three Tempests alone, and was quickly shot down. He bailed out, but only after suffering burns that took him out of the war. Fw. Gerhard Müller-Berneck crash-landed with injuries, and four Focke-Wulfs were destroyed or damaged. Uffz. Pfeiffer of the 5th Staffel claimed a Spitfire in this battle, and Lt. Prager of the 15th Staffel claimed a Thunderbolt; but no Allied unit reported any claims or losses at this time and place.

ULTRA intercepted a message from the 14th Fliegerdivision reporting the results of a poll it had taken of all its pilots, asking them if they would volunteer to transfer to Me 262 jet fighter units. Positive responses were obtained from fifty-eight KG 30 pilots, thirty-six NSGr 20 pilots, forty-nine JG 27 pilots, but only fourteen JG 26 pilots, a good indication of the high morale within the Geschwader, even at this late date. Ironically, ULTRA also intercepted today a message from Fliegerkorps IX (Jagd), General Peltz's new command, stating that it would accept for Me 262 training only pilots who had been awarded the Knight's Cross or the German Cross in Gold.

JG 26 Victory Claims: 20 - 25 March 1945

Date	Rank	Name	Unit	Cl #	Aircraft	Place	Time	Opponent	Conf
20-03-45	Oblt.	Heilmann	15 CO		P-51	near Bramsche	1740	357 FG	unk
22-03-45	Uffz.	Hoffmann J.	5	2	Tempest	near Rheine	1603	56 or 80 Sqd	unk
22-03-45	Uffz.	Warthemann	6		Tempest	near Rheine	1603	56 or 80 Sqd	no
25-03-45	Uffz.	Pfeiffer	5	1	Spitfire	S of Stadtlohn (JO3)	1823		unk
25-03-45	Lt.	Prager	15	18	P-47	NW of Bocholt			unk

JG 26 Casualties: 25 March 1945

Date	Rank	Name	Cas	Unit	Aircraft	WNr	Mkgs	Place	Time	Cause	Allied Unit
25-03-45	Fhr.	Hermann, Heinrich	KIA	I	Fw 190D-9			20km SW of Meppen	1340	Tempest	222 Sqd
25-03-45	Gefr.	Thuy, Ernst	KIFA	3	Fw 190D-9	210203	yl 14	Drope a/f	1320	takeoff	n/a
25-03-45	Uffz.	Kühn, Hermann	KIFA	5	Fw 190D-9			Nordhorn a/f	0557	takeoff collision	non-op
25-03-45	Lt.	Schulwitz, Gerhard	KIFA	5	Fw 190D-9			Nordhorn a/f	0557	takeoff collision	non-op
25-03-45	Uffz.	Bock, Otto	WIFA	11	Fw 190D-9			Delmenhorst a/f		landing	non-op
25-03-45	Fw.	Kroll, Gerhard	WIA	15	Fw 190D-9		yl 15	NW of Bocholt	1500	fighter	
25-03-45	Fw.	Müller-Berneck, Gerhard	WIA	15	Fw 190D-9			near Bocholt		fighter	

26 March

The Geschwader was kept busy at its two new bases. Bissel was found to have virtually no aviation fuel, and while the ground staff scavenged the area, its aircraft had to land on Drope to top off their fuel tanks before beginning their missions. Fifteen First Gruppe aircraft were led off Drope at 0615 by Oblt. Heckmann for a Jabojagd over the front. Three turned back early. A ten-minute battle with a dozen Spitfires near Wesel was without result. At 0800 the Focke-Wulfs had to land on Gütersloh for fuel.

At 1310 four Second Gruppe and eleven Fourth Gruppe fighters landed on Drope to refuel and await orders. The orders that came in were for a combined Jabojagd mission to the Wesel-Bocholt area by the First and Second Gruppen. Four Focke-Wulfs from the First Gruppe and four from the Second took off from Drope at 1500, led by Oblt. Hofmann, the 5th Staffel Kapitän. There was solid cloud cover at 3000 meters (10,000 feet). Visibility below the clouds was restricted to less than a kilometer by the flames and smoke from destroyed Wehrmacht installations. Hofmann's small force encountered a formation of B-26s near Münster, and he led a bounce of the escort, nine Tempests from No. 33 Squadron. Hofmann shot down one of the British fighters, for his 44th victory, but the other planes of the victim's flight got the upper hand in the ensuing dogfight, and shot down three of the four First Gruppe aircraft. Ofhr. Wolfgang Franz and Uffz. Gerhard Reichow were killed; Lt. Wilhelm Blickle bailed out with burns.

Wilhelm Hofmann did not return from this, his 260th mission. The crash of his airplane was not observed in the smoky haze. At Drope, the only First Gruppe pilot to return, Ofhr. Erich Schneider, was arrested for shooting Hofmann down. The next day he stood trial at the headquarters of the 14th Fliegerdivision, but was acquitted. There was apparently no further investigation at that time, but the identity of the miscreant was known to everyone at Bissel. Peter Crump recalls:

> "I was waiting in the Bissel command post, which was used by both the Second and Fourth Gruppen, when Hofmann's *Katschmarek* (wingman) stormed jubilantly into the room, loudly proclaiming his first air victory. Soon afterward an officer pilot came in from the mission and quickly rained on the happy victor's parade. Do you know whom you have shot down? Our Staffelkapitän!'"

Hofmann had been fired on when his aircraft loomed up suddenly through the haze. His body was not found until 2 April. It was in a forest, a half-mile from the wreckage of his aircraft. He had bailed out, but at too low an altitude, and his parachute had not opened. Hofmann was buried in a field grave in the forest. His body was exhumed after the war and buried in a military cemetery, but in the prevailing post-war chaos its identity was lost. Not until 1988 was his identity officially confirmed, and his name could only then be removed from the list of pilots missing in action. Wilhelm Hofmann was the last of the Second Gruppe *Draufgängern* (daredevils). Siegfried Sy claimed that the "Schlageter spirit" disappeared with Hofmann's death.

The eleven Fourth Gruppe aircraft at Drope finally got to fly their mission at 1630, a Jabojagd to Wesel. Lt. Prager claimed a Mustang between Münster and Osnabrück. After completing their sweep, the Focke-Wulfs landed on Bissel.

27 March
The Geschwader was grounded by bad weather and low fuel supplies. The First Gruppe reported that it had only nine fighters operational; the dozen fighters at Gütersloh could not return for lack of fuel.

Wilhelm Hofmann's replacement as Kapitän of the 5th Staffel was Oblt. Alfred Heckmann of the 3rd Staffel. Heckmann had been the most steadfast formation leader in the First Gruppe. He had led more Gruppe missions since the unit's return to Germany than had Major Borris himself. His mature good judgment had frequently enabled the First Gruppe to carry out its ordered missions with a minimum of losses. He was very popular with the younger pilots for his accessibility, and for the fact that he rarely lost a wingman. It is probable that Heckmann's failure to carry out his mission orders on the 22nd had made him expendable to Borris. His steadying influence was much needed in the Second Gruppe just at this time.

28 March
Lt. Kiefner led nine First Gruppe aircraft from Gütersloh back to Drope, encountering enemy aircraft on the way, but the Gruppe was then taken off operations until it could get fuel. Enough aviation gasoline had reached Bissel to permit operations from that

base to resume. Three freie Jagden were flown during the day. Their intended patrol area was the Allied breakout near Wesel, but most German fighters got no farther than the Münster area, which was swarming with Allied fighter-bombers. Oblt. Dortenmann took a dozen Fourth Gruppe aircraft off the ground at 1105. Dortenmann led part of his force in a bounce of No. 56 Sqd. Tempests; one fell, claimed by Dortenmann and Uffz. Hein. Lt. Prager also claimed a Tempest today, probably in this combat, but the claim was apparently not filed. Lt. Crump and his wingman flew off alone. Near Münster, Crump spotted a formation of between ten and twelve P-47s, strafing a freight yard. Crump sent his wingman home, rather than endanger the youngster in a dogfight with superior numbers of enemy aircraft. Crump used the sun and the clouds to sneak undetected into the attackers' circle. He shot one P-47 down and zoomed up into the clouds. According to the American records, Lt. Vern Hendershott of the 406th Fighter Group's 512th Squadron was hit from behind at 3000 feet (900 meters) by Crump's quick bounce and spun out, still carrying his bombs. After two turns, he got out of his P-47, and made a successful parachute descent into the rail yard. His companions were unable to catch the lone Fw 190D, which had disappeared in the cloud layer.

A dozen Second Gruppe aircraft took off from Bissel at 1330 for a freie Jagd, but failed to contact the enemy. The Fourth Gruppe left on another mission at 1607. The sparse data are in conflict, but it appears that the Gruppe lost four pilots. East of Münster at 1645, fifteen Fw 190Ds were bounced by eight Spitfire XIVs of No. 130 Squadron. Uffz. Reinhard Flakowski, Ofhr. Hans-Jürgen Hansen, and Uffz. Harry Kaps were probably shot down by the Spitfires. Kaps was still missing in 1998; the remains of the other two pilots were not conclusively identified until the late 1980s. While making his escape at low altitude, Uffz. Otto Weigl hit a row of oak trees and crashed. Weigl's remains were not found until 1988. The Spitfire pilots claimed 7-1-2 Fw 190Ds on this mission.

JG 26 Casualties: 26 - 28 March 1945

Date	Rank	Name	Cas	Unit	Aircraft	WNr	Mkgs	Place	Time	Cause	Allied Unit
26-03-45	Uffz.	Reichow, Gerhard	KIA	1	Fw 190D-9			Münster-Lengerich	1530	Tempest	33 Sqd
26-3-45	Lt.	Blickle, Wilhelm	WIA	3	Fw 190D-9			Münster-Handorf	1530	Tempest	33 Sqd
26-03-45	Ofhr.	Franz, Wolfgang	KIA	3	Fw 190D-9	210944 yl 1		Lengerich-Münster	1530	Tempest	33 Sqd
26-03-45	Oblt.	Hofmann, Wilhelm	KIA	5 CO	Fw 190D-9			Hasselünne-Flechum	1530	Fw 190D	II/JG 26
28-03-45	Uffz.	Flakowski, Reinhard	KIA	13	Fw 190D-9			Osnabrück-Laer	1630	Spit XIV	130 Sqd
28-03-45	Uffz.	Kaps, Harry	KIA	14	Fw 190D-9			Osnabrück area		Spit XIV	130 Sqd
28-03-45	Ofhr.	Hansen, Hans-Jürgen	KIA	15	Fw 190D-9	400255		Osnabrück-Hardenstetten	1630	Spit XIV	130 Sqd
28-03-45	Uffz.	Weigl, Otto	KIA	13	Fw 190D-9			Vreden	1130	hit tree	n/a

29 March

In the morning, pilots of the Fourth Gruppe flew the last fighters at Varrelbusch the short distance to Bissel, and Uffz. Schumacher ferried the last flyable Second Gruppe Fw 190D-9 from Nordhorn to Bissel. At Nordhorn the last spare parts were loaded onto the few available trucks, and the airfield's fuel inventory – 16,000 gallons of aviation gasoline – was turned over to the retreating German Army. The Second Gruppe had been especially fortunate at Nordhorn in that its source of supplies was the nearby Ems-Vechta Canal rather than the vulnerable railroad. The canal was used only at night. Before dawn, the barges were re-moored in their previous locations and the canal was drained. The Allies never realized that the canal and its barges were operational, and never attacked them.

The Second Gruppe flew one freie Jagd in the afternoon, but failed to contact the enemy. The Fourth Gruppe was not employed. The First Gruppe was grounded because of a solid cloud front to the east of Drope. Oblt. Dortenmann, Oblt.

Heckmann's replacement as Kapitän of the 3rd Staffel, reported in at Drope. Of all the Geschwader officers still flying, Dortenmann was considered the most ambitious and eager for combat, qualities that undoubtedly endeared him to Major Borris. Lt. Hans Prager took over the 14th Staffel from Dortenmann.

30 March

The three Gruppen were active all afternoon against the Allied bridgehead across the Dortmund-Ems Canal near Lüdwighausen. Their primary mission was to strafe traffic crossing the canal. Sixty-two sorties were flown in five or six formations. Lt. Kiefner led nine fighters up from Drope at noon. Three aborted, but the other six carried out their assigned strafing mission. Two Fourth Gruppe Schwärme left Bissel at 1240 with the same assignment. Major Borris led the next First Gruppe formation. It began taking off at 1630, but Allied fighter-bombers were hovering over Drope, and Borris canceled the mission after five fighters got off the ground. The two Gruppen at Bissel got sixteen fighters into the air at 1700. They flew a successful strafing mission in the ordered target area, but Fw. Hans Eisenberg of the 13th Staffel was hit by a No. 402 Sqd. Spitfire, and crashed with fatal injuries. Lt. Kiefner was ordered to lead the day's last mission, a repeat of the one Borris had called off. Nine fighters took off from Drope at 1825, but four of them aborted. Kiefner sighted six Tempests above his five fighters, successfully avoided contact, canceled the mission, and returned to Drope, landing at 1915.

31 March

Aviation fuel had reached the two Geschwader airfields, and no fewer than eighty-four sorties were flown today against the advancing Allied armies. The First Gruppe put up two independent missions at dawn. Oblt. Dortenmann got off the ground at 0545 and led twelve Focke-Wulfs toward the fluid front lines. They shot up a radio post southeast of Ülmen and strafed traffic on the Lüdinghausen-Olfen road, leaving four vehicles in flames. Uffz. Heinrich Herbster was hit by Allied ground fire and bailed out, suffering only mild burns. He fought his way back through the lines, and returned to the Geschwader on 6 April. Dortenmann's fighter was also hit by the Allied fire, but returned to base. The formation was hit by German Flak on the return trip, and lost another aircraft. Fw. Arnold Reuther crashed east of Plantlünne. His aircraft was found in 1997, but no remains were recovered. Fhr. Gerhard von Plazer had to make a belly-landing east of Münster, and Ogfr. Günther Dingler crash-landed on Drope; neither of these pilots was injured.

Lt. Kiefner led six aircraft up from Drope at 0550 on an armed reconnaissance flight to Rheine. Their mission was successful; no enemy ground activity was seen.

Bissel had a good supply of bombs, and the Second Gruppe armorers mounted bomb racks on their fighters, which today flew their first missions as true fighter-bombers. Eight aircraft took off from Bissel at 0545 to bomb the Lüdinghausen-Olfen road. While searching for it in the ground haze, they were attacked by Spitfire XIVs of No. 402 Sqd. (RCAF). The Focke-Wulfs jettisoned their bombs into Dümmer Lake and attempted to escape, but Oblt. Friedrich Burkardt and Fw. Georg Raith of the 5th Staffel were shot down and killed.

Eight more Second Gruppe fighter-bombers took off at 0615. They located the assigned road and dropped 250 kg containers of anti-personnel bombs, without observing the results. They returned to Bissel with no losses.

Seven Fourth Gruppe fighters got away from Bissel at 1150 under orders to strafe the Lüdinghausen-Olfen road. Two aborted, and the other five were engaged in combat with six Tempests, without loss to either side. The fighters could not complete their mission, but had to return to base when their fuel ran low.

The next mission was a joint one. Oblt. Dortenmann escorted Second Gruppe bomb-carriers with fifteen First Gruppe fighters. The mission got underway at 1400. Two First Gruppe fighters aborted, but the mission was apparently successful. One Focke-

Wulf was damaged. On the return flight Dortenmann sighted an Auster artillery spotter, and shot it down. Lt. Crump then led several Fourth Gruppe pilots back to Varrelbusch, which was not yet threatened by the Allied advance. They would fly from there as long as they could, and use up some of that base's inventory of aviation fuel, which would otherwise have to be destroyed.

The day's last mission was an armed reconnaissance flight to the Rheine-Greven area. Major Borris led seven First Gruppe aircraft up from Drope at 1820. The mission was successfully carried out; Borris reported that the roads were now choked with convoys.

Amazingly, a few flight schools remained operational, despite being last on the priority list for aviation fuel, and continued to send half-trained Nachwuchs to the front. Pilots arriving at the Geschwader in March included: Uffz. Günther Bergmann, Uffz. Matthias Cassens, Gefr. Günther Dingler, Uffz. Franz Göttle, Uffz. Albert Hütterer, Fw. Arnold Reuther, Fw. Helmut Walter, Uffz. Max Waschke - First Gruppe; Gefr. Hubert Altmann, Uffz. Rudolf Bellmann, Uffz. Karl-Friedrich Hüber, Uffz. Alfred Langer, Ogfr. Kurt Linzbach, Fw. Otto Wilck - Second Gruppe; Uffz. Reinhard Flakowski, Uffz. Alois Horner, Uffz. Harry Kaps, Uffz. Günter Schitkowsky, Uffz. Wolfgang Schneider, Uffz. Kurt Soeder - Fourth Gruppe. Uffz. Max Krümpelmann reported to the Third Gruppe on the 12th, and was killed on the 17th.

JG 26 Victory Claims: 26 - 31 March 1945

Date	Rank	Name	Unit	Cl #	Aircraft	Place	Time	Opponent	Conf
26-03-45	Oblt.	Hofmann W.	5 CO	44	Tempest	SW of Münster	1532	33 Sqd	unk
26-03-45	Lt.	Prager	15	19	P-51	N of Münster-SW of Osnabrück (HQ)	1646		unk
28-03-45	Lt.	Crump	13 CO	23	P-47	SW of Münster	1150	406 FG	unk
28-03-45	Oblt.	Dortenmann	14 CO	31	Tempest	5km SW Münster (IP3)	1135	56 Sqd	unk
28-03-45	Uffz.	Hein K.	14	6	Tempest	5km SW of Münster (IP3)	1134	56 Sqd	unk
28-03-45	Lt.	Prager	15	20	Tempest	unknown			no
31-03-45	Oblt.	Dortenmann	3 CO	32	Auster	Ludwighausen (JQ8)	1446		unk

JG 26 Casualties: 30 - 31 March 1945

Date	Rank	Name	Cas	Unit	Aircraft	WNr	Mkgs	Place	Time	Cause	Allied Unit
30-03-45	Fw.	Eisenberg, Hans	KIA	13	Fw 190D-9			35km NE of Heilbronn	Spitfire		402 Sqd
31-03-45	Oblt.	Dortenmann, Hans	no	3 CO	Fw 190D-9	210003	yl 1	near Lüdinghausen	0700	flak	n/a
31-03-45	Uffz.	Herbster, Heinrich	WIA	3	Fw 190D-9		yl 10	Lüdinghausen (S of Münster)	0700	flak	n/a
31-03-45	Fw.	Reuther, Arnold	KIA	3	Fw 190D-9			Plantlünne a/f	0700	own flak	n/a
31-03-45	Oblt.	Burkardt, Friedrich	KIA	5	Fw 190D-9			5km E of Bissel	0600	Spitfire	402 Sqd
31-03-45	Fw.	Raith, Georg	KIA	5	Fw 190D-9			7km NE of Bissel	0600	Spitfire	402 Sqd

1 April

The Allies had broken through the thin defenses along the Rhine, and were beginning to surge across Germany with a speed reminiscent of their race across France the previous summer. The most important tasks for the Geschwader were now reconnaissance and Jabo attacks on the Allied columns. Reconnaissance was especially important, because there were no German defensive lines as such. The best the Army could do was block the roads being used by the Allied spearheads. Each of the three Gruppen was called upon to fly two or three combat missions per day. These flights, which generally contained between four and twelve fighters, were known to the pilots as *Himmelfahrtskommandos,* which can be translated loosely as "missions to heaven". There was a slow but steady loss of pilots by the three already-depleted Gruppen.

Lt. Kiefner led a Schwarm up from Drope at 0620 to reconnoiter the highways in the Rheine-Greven area. Kiefner located the leading enemy armor between Greven and Ladbergen, and later in the day the 14th Fliegerdivision authorized awards of Iron Crosses to the four pilots for their successful mission. In the meantime the First Gruppe received orders to pick up some pilots from the Fourth Gruppe and begin ferrying aircraft to Hustedt and Delmenhorst, prospective bases in the rear.

In the afternoon, all three Gruppen received orders to mount Jabo attacks in the area between Rheine and Ibbenbüren. Attacks were to be flown by independent Schwärme. The First Gruppe put up formations at 1700 and 1705. The first, five aircraft under Ofhr. Schneider, evaded two Mustangs and was then split up by antiaircraft fire and failed to make an attack. Schneider's flight returned without loss. The second mission of eight aircraft was led by Lt. Guhl. It made a successful strafing attack on a column of ten trucks despite heavy antiaircraft fire and then returned, also without loss. The Fourth Gruppe mission was led by Lt. Crump. It left Varrelbusch at 1745 and successfully strafed targets around Ibbenbüren, but lost Uffz. Heinz Müller to ground fire. The Second Gruppe took off from Bissel at about 1740 in two independent flights, both from the 7th Staffel. The first, a full Schwarm, bombed and strafed the bridges at Ibbenbüren, and returned safely. The second comprised only two fighters, piloted by Fw. Heinz Gomann and his wingman. Gomann was ordered by Hptm. Schauder to make a two-man attack on the advancing armor, in retaliation, Gomann believed, for Gomann's tart radio comments about Schauder's frequent early returns. The two Focke-Wulfs dropped their bombs, but Gomann's took hits from ground fire, and the pair landed on an air base already abandoned by the Luftwaffe. Gomann's wingman volunteered to switch airplanes; he had decided to wait on the field and surrender to the Allies. Heinz Gomann thus returned to Bissel that evening in a borrowed aircraft. His wingman turned up later; he had had a change of heart, either on his own or with persuasion.

2 April

The First Gruppe was the only unit of the Geschwader to be given mission orders. Three aircraft took off at 0702 to reconnoiter the Rheine-Greven Canal. The mission was completed. All personnel were now packing for the move to their new base, Delmenhorst. At 1540 Oblt. Dortenmann led seventeen aircraft up from Drope to strafe enemy troops advancing in the Rheine-Greven area. After a successful attack, the Fw 190Ds landed at Delmenhorst. The rear detachment cleared Drope at 2000. According to an ULTRA intercept, the base movement involved fifteen officers, 183 NCOs and enlisted personnel, and nineteen Fw 190Ds.

3 April

The American 17th Airborne Division completed its capture of Münster. The Wehrmacht was withdrawing to the east and northeast in some disorder. The Geschwaderstab and the First Gruppe were given a day off operations to settle in at Delmenhorst. The Fourth Gruppe pilots still at Bissel apparently flew to join their comrades at Varrelbusch. There were enough supplies at Bissel to maintain the Second Gruppe, which stayed there for a few more days.

From now until the end of the war, the Second Gruppe specialized in bombing attacks. Apparently only the Fw 190Ds of this Gruppe were equipped with bomb racks, giving the unit additional punch for its Jabo missions. Werner Molge describes the ordnance carried by his Gruppe:

> "We carried either 250 kg or 500 kg high explosive bombs, or droppable containers. The latter held a number of 2 kg fragmentation bomblets. We weren't happy about carrying these things, because it was dangerous to land with them – which happened often, due to engine failure. You couldn't jettison the container in

an emergency, because the small bombs in it all had impact fuses. The regular bombs, on the other hand, had electric fuses that were energized through the release gear, and could thus be jettisoned on 'safe'".

The Gruppe actually received two types of anti-personnel bomb canisters. The AB 250 was the one so disliked by the pilots; it contained 125 2 kg bomblets with impact fuses that could not be disarmed after takeoff. The newer SC 250, on the other hand, contained the same number and size of bombs, but these had electrical fusing, and could be armed and disarmed by the pilot with his regular controls.

The Second Gruppe flew the day's first mission, a reconnaissance of the Rheine-Osnabrück area. Four aircraft took off at 1208, but two turned back immediately. The other pair completed the mission. The Gruppe put up formations of twelve and ten fighters at 1615. The first force completed a freie Jagd to Lingen without incident; two Austers were spotted, but got away. The second, which was ordered to bomb targets in the Lingen area, was attacked by eight Tempests shortly after takeoff. The Focke-Wulfs jettisoned their bombs and escaped without damage, but their mission was scrapped. The Fourth Gruppe put up nine fighters from Varrelbusch at 1753 under orders to strafe roads around Rheine, but the presence of enemy fighter-bombers over their field kept the formation from assembling, and the target area was not reached. Uffz. Günther Rey's aircraft was hit by ground fire, and he had to land at another base; he returned to Varrelbusch on the 5th.

Fw. Heinz Gomann and Uffz. Erwin Böttge, neither of whom was on good terms with the Geschwader brass, received the welcome news that their transfer to JG 7, the jet fighter Geschwader, had been approved. Gomann was the longest-serving pilot in the Second Gruppe. He had gotten off to a very good start in 1942, but had had nothing but bad luck since then, suffering three serious injuries in 1943 and 1944. It was obvious to all that the two men had received their tickets to survival; it was unlikely that their conversion training would be completed before the war's inevitable end. After a night of celebration, the two men started off on foot for Brandenburg-Briest, the JG 7 headquarters.

4 April

This was a very full day for all three Gruppen. The early morning reconnaissance flight by the First Gruppe could not get off the field because of its boggy condition. That evening a court-martial officer came to Delmenhorst from the 14th Fliegerdivision to question Major Borris about this failure, but the Gruppe diary makes no further mention of the investigation. Eleven fighters took off at 1604 under Oblt. Dortenmann for an armed reconnaissance of the area Lingen-Rheine-Nordhorn. The mission was carried out, but Ogfr. Günther Dingler did not return. He was still missing and being sought in the Lingen-Nordhorn area in 1998. This Gruppe flew a late-evening freie Jagd which had more success. Sixteen Focke-Wulfs took off at 1905, led by Lt. Söffing. Seven aborted, but the others jumped a small formation of Allied fighter-bombers near Diepholz, downing two. The victorious pilots were Lt. Söffing and Lt. Ramthun; they claimed Tempests, but their victims were probably Typhoons from No. 438 Squadron (RCAF). Uffz. Fröb claimed an "effective damage" in this combat; parts were seen to fly off his target during his attack. Three Focke-Wulfs force-landed away from the base when they ran low on fuel; the other six landed on Delmenhorst at 2010.

The early mission of the Second Gruppe got away at 0630 without any problems, and successfully bombed and strafed vehicles and troops between Lingen and Nordhorn. The next mission was a full-strength bombing attack on Canadian armor near the former Gruppe base of Nordhorn-Clausheide. Hptm. Schauder led twenty-eight aircraft away from Bissel at 1530. Lt. Sy led the 7th Staffel in place of the ill Lt. Dietze. He flew in Fw. Gomann's old 7th Staffel airplane, on the assumption that as the senior pilot in the Gruppe, Gomann would have insisted on a good one. Soon after takeoff Oblt. Schmidt turned back with a bad engine, and Sy took the 6th Staffel aircraft under his wing as well. No aircraft were seen until Nordhorn was reached. The armor park was spotted, and the Focke-Wulfs dropped their bombs in the middle of the tanks. Sy then turned back for a strafing attack, but he was followed by only three aircraft – his own Schwarm. This time his airplane took hits; minor at first, but a strike in the rudder left him unable to turn, and flying away from his own lines. His engine was then hit solidly, and quit. He was unable to open his canopy to bail out, and rode the airplane down to a rough crash landing in a clearing. The canopy then popped open, and Sy jumped from his plane and sprinted for the nearby trees. This had been his fifth time to be shot down. He did not ignite the explosive charge, as he did not want to give away his position, and he felt that the Allies had all of the Fw 190s that they wanted.

Siegfried Sy jogged and walked through the forest all night, following the North Star. He passed groups of German soldiers waiting to surrender to the first Allied soldier to come along. He followed a north-bound road and reached the border crossing, which was manned by a single guard who was under orders to stay put and who had no means of communication or transport to offer him. Back on German soil, Sy finally reached a German defensive unit – but this proved to be an SS detachment engaged in rounding up deserters. They were firmly convinced that Sy belonged in that category, and offered him the option of joining a tank-hunting unit or facing a firing squad. His pilot's pass, which was supposed to guarantee priority treatment, brought only the retort, "Your Luftwaffe no longer exists!" Sy escaped this nightmare by hiding in a truck belonging to a passing antiaircraft unit. The convoy passed near Bissel, and Lt. Sy was able to report back to Hptm. Schauder in mid-afternoon, to the latter's great surprise.

On the evening of the 4th, the Second Gruppe had flown a third bombing mission to the same area. Werner Molge recalls:

> "The approach flight went well, without opposition if one discounts the machine gun fire coming from the vehicles. The bombs, 250 kg high explosive, were dropped with delayed-action fuses. I flew as No. 2 in a Schwarm, and had my No. 1 right in front of me from the peeloff to the release. I saw No. 1's bomb come free, and then, moving at the same speed as I, fly in front of me for a few seconds. To avoid it, I had to alter my course somewhat before dropping my own bomb, which hit alongside the target. My mistake was that I had begun my dive too soon, with my No. 1 only 50 meters (160 feet) in front of my cockpit. Next we strafed the motor convoy. During our strafing attack the Spitfires arrived, wishing us evil. While pulling up from my last low-level attack, I suddenly saw a Spit fly past at about 60 meters (200 feet), from right above to left below. Startled, I grabbed the stick harder, and undoubtedly the firing lever as well. It was of course switched on, because of the previous ground attack. I saw a few tracers, but nothing more, because a few seconds later I was taken under fire. I dived immediately to treetop height and took up a course for home. A Spit followed me for a while, but could not get a good shot at me because of my extreme low altitude. So it went all the time."

The Fourth Gruppe also flew three missions today, taking off from Varrelbusch at 0630, 0900, and 1345. All were described as armed reconnaissance missions to Münster or Minden, and resulted in no claims or losses.

After Georg Genth was released from the Enschede hospital, he learned of the dissolution of his Third Gruppe and the abandonment of his former base, but was unable to get to Plantlünne to retrieve his personal effects. Genth reached Delmenhorst on foot and was assigned to a barracks. At Delmenhorst men and women triple-bunked in the same rooms, and Genth spent an uncomfortable night; he was propositioned by his bunkmate despite the full cast on his arm. The next morning he went looking for his Third Gruppe comrades, but there were none left. He then asked for, and received, orders to report to the hospital in Naumburg, his home town. The following day he boarded a train, and took his leave of the Geschwader for the last time.

Georg Genth was still in the Naumburg hospital when the city was occupied by the Americans. The hospital was taken over by American military personnel. Genth began trading pistols and war souvenirs with the new hospital staff for the currency of the day, cartons of American cigarettes. A friendly guard told him that the city was to be turned over to the Russians. While Genth was trying to decide how to forge release papers that would let him and his mother settle in the Western Zone, he broke out of the hospital four times to steal radio parts from a Wehrmacht warehouse next door. He hid them in his grandmother's house, and then returned to the hospital unnoticed. The parts would be enough to build a number of small radios, which would be in great demand after the war as inexpensive sources of entertainment. He eventually got his travel papers the easy way, by slipping the responsible German functionary some cigarettes, and headed for Braunschweig with his radio parts, ready to enter the post-war economy.

5 April

All three Gruppen saw action today, despite the disruption associated with yet another round of base moves. The First Gruppe flew three successful missions without contacting an Allied aircraft. At 0645 Lt. Kiefner led four aircraft up from Delmenhorst for a battle reconnaissance and strafing mission beyond the fluid lines between Nordhorn and Osnabrück. The next mission was led by Oblt. Dortenmann, and got underway at 1300. Ten First Gruppe fighters escorted four Second Gruppe bomb-carriers to Hengelo. At 1542 Lt. Söffing led nine fighters on a strafing mission to the roads around Diepholz. The mission was successful, although one fighter was damaged by German Flak. At 1900 the thirteen serviceable Gruppe fighters took off for Celle-Hustedt, their new base. At 2305 the female auxiliaries were ordered to move all the way to Stade, and wait for the rest of the Gruppe to join them there.

The Second Gruppe flew fifty-one sorties in six missions. During a flight in mid-morning, the Focke-Wulfs had to jettison their bombs when attacked by Spitfires from No. 402 Sqd. (RCAF). The German pilots disengaged from the battle without loss; Uffz. Friedrich Rohrmann then got separated and attacked a small formation of No. 350 Sqd. (Belgian) Spitfire XIVs that were strafing roads near Friesoythe. He claimed a probable victory but his target in fact crashed; its pilot was taken prisoner. Rohrmann was then shot down and bailed out with injuries. One afternoon mission was led by Hptm. Schauder. His wingman, Hptm. Friedrich-Wilhelm Fahnert, suddenly broke from formation and dived vertically into Dümmer Lake. His casualty report gave the reason as British antiaircraft fire, but it was widely accepted within the Gruppe that Fahnert had committed suicide; he had been Wilhelm Hofmann's wingman on his final mission. By evening the aircraft of the Gruppe were split between Bissel and Delmenhorst. All took off at about 1900 and flew to Hustedt, which they would share with the Geschwaderstab and the First Gruppe. Lt. Vieweg smelled fuel after taking off and returned to Bissel, where he made a bad landing and wiped out his landing gear. The flight surgeon pulled an unconscious Vieweg from his cockpit; he had been overcome by fumes from a broken fuel line.

The Fourth Gruppe flew a total of eighteen combat sorties between 0910 and 1425, most on armed reconnaissance and strafing missions to Minden and Rinteln. Major Klemm was hit by German Flak while on a recon mission, but returned to base safely. At about 1140 a flight of five fighters under Lt. Prager's command was attacked by No. 402 Sqd. (RCAF) Spitfire XIVs. Ofhr. Günther Schitkowsky and Uffz. Kurt Soeder were shot down and killed; Prager and Fw. Sinz claimed Spitfires, but apparently none went down.

The Fourth Gruppe lost a Staffelkapitän. Oblt. Willi Heilmann failed to return from a mission; other pilots saw him land on the Münster-Handorf airfield, his airplane

The burned-out wreckage of 15th Staffel Fw 190D-9, W.Nr. 210980. It was found by the Canadian Army on the Varrelbusch taxi strip, near a second wrecked Dora; both were possibly involved in a ground collision as the Fourth Gruppe was abandoning the airfield on 5 April. *(National Archives of Canada)*

apparently undamaged. Unfortunately, the field had been captured by the British several days before, a fact that was well-known to Heilmann and the other German pilots. There appears to have been an official cover-up of the circumstances of Heilmann's loss; he was said to have entered a hospital. His 15th Staffel was immediately disbanded, and its pilots were reassigned to the 13th and 14th Staffeln. In his 1951 memoir *Alarm im Westen*, published in the US as *I Fought You From the Skies*, Willi Heilmann claimed that his departure from the war was preceded by a solemn ceremony in which he discharged his entire Staffel to return to their homes. He implies strongly that this took place only days before the end of the war. This part of his story is, of course, nonsense. German veterans draw a sharp distinction between "desertion" and "honorable surrender"; Heilmann's action took place one month too soon to come under the latter category.

The day's problems for the Fourth Gruppe were not yet over. Its pilots were ordered to leave Varrelbusch in mid-afternoon for their new base, Dedelsdorf. Lt. Rudolf Leinberger took off, but returned immediately. While landing, his Focke-Wulf struck a parked aircraft, became airborne, crashed on the field, and burst into flames. The seriously-burned Leinberger was dragged from the blazing wreckage. He was taken to the nearest hospital, and died there. The Geschwader was never notified of his death, and he was apparently buried hurriedly, without identification, when the Allies approached. Wolfgang Polster, an eyewitness to the accident, reported what he knew after the war, but the matter was never cleared up, and Leinberger was still carried as missing in 1998.

JG 26 Victory Claims: 4 - 5 April 1945

Date	Rank	Name	Unit	Cl #	Aircraft	Place	Time	Opponent	Conf
04-04-45	Lt.	Ramthun	1	1	Tempest	6km E of Diepholz	1945	438 Sqd Typhoon	unk
04-04-45	Lt.	Söffing	2 CO	27	Tempest	6km E of Diepholz	1945	438 Sqd Typhoon	unk

04-04-45	Uffz.	Fröb	2	1	Tempest-dam	6km E of Diepholz	1945	438 Sqd Typhoon	no
05-04-45	Uffz.	Rohrmann	5	1	Spitfire-prob	near Hilkenbrook	1127	350 Sqd	unk
05-04-45	Lt.	Prager	14	21	Spitfire	Lingen-Haselünne	1210	402 Sqd	unk
05-04-45	Fw.	Sinz	15		Spitfire	Lingen-Haselünne	1210	402 Sqd	unk

JG 26 Casualties: 1 - 5 April 1945

Date	Rank	Name	Cas	Unit	Aircraft	WNr	Mkgs	Place	Time	Cause	Allied Unit
01-04-45	Uffz.	Müller, Heinz	KIA	13	Fw 190D-9			10km W of Cloppenburg		flak	n/a
04-04-45	Ogfr.	Dingler, Günther	KIA	3	Fw 190D-9			Lingen-Nordhorn	1700	combat	
04-04-45	Lt.	Sy, Siegfried	no	6	Fw 190D-9		br 9	Itterbek	1630	flak	n/a
05-04-45	Hptm.	Fahnert, Friedrich-Wilhelm	KIA	5	Fw 190D-9			Dümmer Lake		flak	n/a
05-04-45	Uffz.	Rohrmann, Friedrich	WIA	5	Fw 190D-9		wh 14	10km W of Friesoythe		Spitfire XIV	350 Sqd
05-04-45	Lt.	Vieweg, Gerd	WIA	7	Fw 190D-9			Bissel a/f	1500	fuel leak	n/a
05-04-45	Maj.	Klemm, Rudolf	no	IV CO	Fw 190D-9		gr 3	near Minden		own flak	n/a
05-04-45	Ofhr.	Schitkowsky, Günter	KIA	13	Fw 190D-9			Haselüne-Huden	1140	Spitfire XIV	402 Sqd
05-04-45	Lt.	Leinberger, Rudolf	KIFA	14	Fw 190D-9			Varrelbusch a/f		landing	n/a
05-04-45	Oblt.	Heilmann, Willi	POW	15 CO	Fw 190D-9			Münster-Handorf a/f		captured	n/a
05-04-45	Uffz.	Söder, Kurt	KIA	15	Fw 190D-9			N of Lingen	1140	Spitfire XIV	402 Sqd

6 April

The previous evening the Geschwaderstab and the First Gruppe had received word that they were moving again, and the advance party was on the road to Stade at 0200. In the morning, rain and a solid overcast kept all Geschwader aircraft on the ground. Twenty-four sorties were flown in the afternoon, in five formations. Their principal task was to make low-level attacks in the Diepholz area. The First Gruppe flew one mission. Lt. Kiefner led five aircraft to Diepholz, and reported a successful reconnaissance, followed by a strafing attack.

The Second Gruppe flew two bombing missions from Hustedt. The first was broken off early; the second was apparently successful. Lt. Sy bypassed Hustedt entirely, leading Bissel's last seven Fw 190Ds directly to Uetersen, north of Hamburg. Sy attempted to prepare the base for the arrival of the rest of the Gruppe. When his men began to arrive, he had difficulty controlling them – the base contained a large number of servicewomen, who had taken over many of the mechanics' jobs on bases behind the front, and who according to Sy were all looking for a good time.

The Fourth Gruppe flew two missions from Dedelsdorf. The first was recalled; results of the second are unknown. Obfw. Ungar force-landed on Hoppe-Schwarmstedt after being hit by ground fire. The Gruppe lost two more pilots. Uffz. Alois Horner and Uffz. Wolfgang Schneider were both shot down by No. 80 Sqd. Tempests west of Stolzenau and bailed out into captivity.

7 April

The three Gruppen flew a total of thirty sorties against the advancing Allied columns. No claims or losses are known. Twenty-three Second Gruppe aircraft reached Uetersen; the rest continued to operate from Hustedt. The First Gruppe transferred to Stade, a major Reichsluftverteidigung airbase on the west bank of the Elbe River, across from Hamburg. The aircraft of the Fourth Gruppe were scattered among several bases. Hptm. Klemm was ordered to find them and send them to Stade.

8 April

As the Geschwader was withdrawing northeast to the Hamburg area, the American spearheads were rolling due east through Hannover on the shortest route to Berlin, while the Canadians and British converged on Bremen. The Focke-Wulfs were thus

The remains of a Second Gruppe Fw 190D abandoned at Hustedt. The airplane was burned as part of the No. 439 Sqd. (RCAF) V-E Day celebrations, resulting in several reprimands. *(Hallford via Fochuk)*

called on to attack targets in two widely divergent areas. The Geschwader flew five bombing and strafing missions, but these totaled only thirty-two sorties. The First Gruppe flew two Schwarm-strength missions to Bremen. The dawn mission turned back owing to solid cloud cover over the target; the afternoon mission turned back because the sky was now cloudless, and too many Allied fighters were seen. The Gruppe then concentrated on getting the last of its aircraft from Hustedt to Stade.

The Second Gruppe flew two bombing missions to Hannover from Hustedt. One Schwarm took off at 1025 and made a successful attack on a truck convoy. As many as twenty aircraft flew the mid-afternoon mission, but they jettisoned their bombs near Hildesheim when attacked by a squadron of American fighters. Ogfr. Harro Bexen was shot down and killed. Two more Focke-Wulfs were downed, but their pilots escaped injury. Their opponents were described as ten Mustangs, but almost certainly they were the P-47s of the 373rd Fighter Group's 410th Squadron, whose pilots claimed a remarkable 12-0-2 Fw 190 "long noses" over the Hildesheim airbase.

9 April

In the morning, the Fourth Gruppe was ordered to prepare to disband at Stade. It was to turn its operational aircraft over to the First and Second Gruppen. The latter two units had left no fewer than thirty-five operational aircraft at Hustedt, and the 14th Fliegerdivision ordered the two Gruppen to send pilots by truck to Hustedt and ferry the planes to Uetersen and Neumünster.

In the afternoon, the Geschwader flew forty-five strafing and bombing sorties to the Hildesheim-Hannover area. Oblt. Dortenmann led nine First Gruppe aircraft up from Stade at 1224 and made what were described in the unit diary as seven or eight strafing runs on a road convoy. The American gunners eventually found the range, and Fw. Herbert Kaiser was shot down and killed. The First and Second Gruppe pilots still at Hustedt flew two combined missions, following one of which Lt. Friedrich Ramthun failed to return. He was shot down by ground fire, but reached Stade on the 11th. Uffz. Werner Hoffmann of the 5th Staffel was shot down and killed near the field at Uetersen by what was described as a Spitfire; no suitable Allied claims can be found.

The Second Gruppe pilots landed on Uetersen after this mission. Luftflotte Reich credited the Geschwader with downing one Thunderbolt and damaging another today. The claimants are unknown, and were probably Fourth Gruppe pilots. By evening the aviation fuel at both Stade and Uetersen was almost gone; the bases had not been stocked in anticipation of the fighters' arrival.

10 April

The Second Gruppe flew the day's only mission for the Geschwader. Lt. Dietze led seven fighters from Uetersen on a sweep of Bremen. Enemy fighters were contacted, but no claims or losses resulted. The rest of the Geschwader was off operations owing to the fuel shortage. There was some confusion as to its next destination. The First Gruppe was ordered to Klein-Kummersfelde, 20 kilometers (12 miles) northeast of Uetersen, but the orders were then rescinded. The Fourth Gruppe actually transferred some of its fighters to Klein-Kummersfelde. The rest of its fighters and personnel were still scattered among Oldenburg, Uetersen, and Dedelsdorf.

11 April

Today it was the turn of the First Gruppe to fly a mission. Lt. Söffing led ten fighters up from Stade to strafe vehicles crossing the Weser River at Bremen. The bridges were found to be clear, and no targets were found on the roads in the Delmenhorst area.

12 April

Enough aviation fuel had reached Stade to permit a full day of operations. The First Gruppe was ordered to attack targets across the Weser as early as possible. Oblt. Dortenmann led twelve Focke-Wulfs up from Stade at 0625. He flew over Bremen at 3500 meters (11,500 feet) and observed many road convoys, but broke off the attack and returned to Stade owing to heavy flak. At 1230 Dortenmann and a dozen fighters took off again into cloudless skies, under orders to reconnoiter the lower Elbe and determine the British positions. A few minutes after takeoff, the right Schwarm reported Indianer. Lt. Ossenkop was an element leader in Lt. Söffing's 2nd Staffel Schwarm, on the left. Karl-Heinz Ossenkop recalls:

> "Eight Tempests were crossing beneath us. We dropped our tanks and dived to the attack. They fired their rockets into the empty sky. A turning combat began. I reached firing position on my target; because of my superior height, I needed little lead. At 100-70 meters [110-75 yards] distance I gave him a short salvo. The Tempest burst into flames, and seconds later, crashed to the ground. The pilot had no chance to get out. I saw several parachutes and smoke plumes, and heard several victory cries over the radio. I next saw Söffing chasing an escaping Tempest at ground level. 'Come with me! We'll catch him!', he shouted. I flew left, Vladimir flew right, but the Tempest pulled away from us at tree-top height, despite our use of full throttle and MW 50 methanol injection."

Dortenmann and his men returned to Stade to claim five victories and one probable, for the loss of Lt. Erich Asmus. No. 33 Squadron lost two Tempests in this battle; a third was written off after its return. The British pilots in their turn claimed the destruction of three Focke-Wulfs.

In the evening, Lt. Dietze led seven Second Gruppe fighter-bombers to Bremen, where bombs were dropped on artillery and supply installations. The Second Gruppe was secure at Uetersen for a few more days, although still low on fuel. The First Gruppe received orders to transfer to Schwerin-Sülte, and ferried twenty Focke-Wulfs to its new base. Sülte was a small, grass-covered sand field at the southern end of a forest. Its landing ground was 120 meters wide by 900 meters long (400 x 3000 feet). Its long direction ran east and west, and its southern side was open. The field was very well camouflaged from the Allies, and also from the German pilots, for whom it was very difficult to locate.

The transfer proved to be Hans Kukla's last flight of the war. Upon his return to the Gruppe after his injury in January, he had found only one pilot whom he knew from his time in Fürstenau – Fhr. Gerhard von Plazer. Von Plazer had a strong premonition that he would not survive the war, and was not very good company. One of Kukla's burned eyelids had not healed properly, and the Gruppe surgeon mercifully ordered him into the hospital. Hans Kukla's war was over; Gerhard von Plazer's would last for one more week.

JG 26 Victory Claims: 12 April 1945

Date	Rank	Name	Unit	Cl #	Aircraft	Place	Time	Opponent	Conf
12-04-45	Lt.	Söffing	2 CO	28	Tempest	15km N of Uelsen	1300	33 Sqd	unk
12-04-45	Lt.	Ossenkop	2	2	Tempest	15km N of Uelsen	1300	33 Sqd	unk
12-04-45	Oblt.	Dortenmann	3 CO	33	Tempest	15km N of Uelsen (DA9)	1253	33 Sqd	unk
12-04-45	Oblt.	Dortenmann	3 CO	34	Tempest	15km N of Uelsen (DA9)	1254	33 Sqd	unk
12-04-45	Lt.	Konrad	3	1	Tempest	15km N of Uelsen	1255	33 Sqd	unk
12-04-45	Ogfr.	Schneider E.	3	1	Tempest-prob	15km N of Uelsen	1255	33 Sqd	no

14 April

The Second Gruppe flew the day's main operation. Fifteen Focke-Wulfs left Uetersen at 0830 and bombed a truck column east of Nienburg from an altitude of 700 meters (2300 feet). Results were not observed. On his return, Lt. Gottfried Dietze entered the hospital to obtain treatment for a chronic illness. His war was over, after his 159th combat sortie. His final tally of air victories was five. Uffz. Georg Kreth rejoined the Gruppe after recovering from injuries suffered the previous September. His tenure would be brief.

Two steady Staffelkapitäne, Lt. Georg Kiefner of the 1st Staffel and Oblt. Alfred Heckmann of the 5th, received orders to join General Galland's "Jet Unit of the Aces", JV 44, at München-Reim. Kiefner had scored a dozen victories in his 140 combat sorties; Heckmann's score was seventy-four, after about 600 sorties. The two men were probably slated to join the jet unit's protection Staffel, which flew Fw 190Ds, but they got no farther than Lechfeld before the war ended. Kiefner was succeeded by Lt. Xaver Ellenrieder, who had not flown since his injury on 23 January.

15 April

The First Gruppe was still grounded for lack of fuel. The Second Gruppe put up nineteen Focke-Wulfs for an armed reconnaissance of the Celle area. Ten Spitfires were encountered. The Gruppe made no claims, and one Focke-Wulf failed to return to Uetersen. Its pilot, Fw. Willi Niedermeyer, was shot down, bailed out and landed in a shallow pond. He had been shot, was too weak to disentangle himself from his shrouds, and drowned in the pond.

16 April

On a bright, cloudless spring day, the Geschwader flew a total of forty-nine sorties to the Celle area. A Second Gruppe Schwarm left Uetersen at dawn; the details of its mission are unknown. The Gruppe also flew a late-evening mission to Celle, and returned to report an effective bombing and strafing attack on motor transport.

The First Gruppe stayed on the ground during a mid-morning attack by four Tempests on the nearby highway. The Gruppe put twenty Focke-Wulfs up in the afternoon for a freie Jagd to Celle. All aircraft but two returned to Sülte reporting no contact; one of the returnees was destroyed in landing. The two pilots who did not return were Uffz. Günther Rey and Fw. Bruno Ostrowitzki. The two former Green Heart pilots had spent the preceding two weeks ferrying aircraft and salvaging equipment from the airfields once occupied by their Gruppe. Oblt. Dortenmann ordered them to accompany him on this mission. Rey had engine problems, and landed on Ludwigslust, a He 162 base, escorted by Ostrowitzki. The pair returned to Sülte the next morning.

Lt. Xaver Ellenrieder was injured on a test flight and was taken off flying status for the last time. His final score was thirteen air victories, obtained in 175 combat sorties.

JG 26 Casualties: 6 - 16 April 1945

Date	Rank	Name	Cas	Unit	Aircraft	WNr	Mkgs	Place	Time	Cause	Allied Unit
06-04-45	Uffz.	Horner, Alois	POW	13	Fw 190D-9			5km W of Stolzenau		Tempest	80 Sqd
06-04-45	Uffz.	Schneider, Wolfgang	POW	14	Fw 190D-9			5km W of Stolzenau		Tempest	80 Sqd
08-04-45	Ogfr.	Bexen, Harro	KIA	5	Fw 190D-9			20km ENE of Hannover		P-47	373 FG
09-04-45	Fw.	Kaiser, Herbert	KIA	3	Fw 190D-9			8km NE Diepholz	1300	flak	n/a
09-04-45	Uffz.	Hoffmann, Werner	KIA	5	Fw 190D-9			Heist-Uetersen		combat	
12-04-45	Lt.	Asmus, Erich	KIA	I St	Fw 190D-9	210069		NNW of Uelsen	1300	Tempest	33 Sqd
15-4-45	Fw.	Niedermeyer, Willi	KIA	5	Fw 190D-9			Winsen-Drebber		fighter	
16-04-45	Lt.	Ellenrieder, Xaver	WIFA	1 CO	Fw 190D-9	401357	wh 3	Sülte a/f	1610	landing	non-op

17 April

The remaining Fourth Gruppe pilots had by now reached Sülte and Uetersen and joined their new units. Lt. Dietrich Preuss was assigned to the Geschwader Stab. Oblt. Karl-Hermann Schrader was put down for the First Gruppe Stab, but this was probably a matter of cleaning up the books; Schrader had apparently left with Krupinski. Nine pilots joined the three Staffeln of the First Gruppe: Ofhr. Heinz Birkner, Uffz. Kurt Hein, Fw. Karwik, Fw. Bruno Ostrowitzki, Uffz. Günther Rey, Uffz. Rolf Sundermeyer, Obfw. Fritz Ungar, Obfw. Werner Zech, and Uffz. E-G. Zessin. Lt. Peter Crump and nine pilots joined the combat Staffeln of the Second Gruppe; the men were Fhr. Bruno Schmidt, Fw. Theodor Fenzl, Fw. Hermann Sinz, Uffz. Helmut Brisch, Uffz. Anton Eyerle, Uffz. Erwin Böttge, Uffz. Paul Klingelhöfer, Uffz. Willibald Malm, and Flg. Heinz Schreiber. Eight more pilots joined the Second Gruppe *Genesendenstaffel* (convalescent Staffel), which contained pilots who were off flying status while recovering from injuries; this was a successful ploy to keep them out of the infantry. These men were: Uffz. Otto Beck, Uffz. Werner Bucher, Fw. Johannes Grüner, Fw. Gerhard Kroll, Uffz. Max Middelstädt, Fw. Gerhard Müller-Berneck, Fw. Wolfgang Polster, and Obfw. Willi Zester. Major Klemm and Lt. Prager had no takers. Klemm was able to get orders to JG 7, but never reached the unit. Prager was ordered to the last of the operational training units, EJG 1. He later headed for JG 7, but failed to arrive. Lt. Crump took command of the 5th Staffel, but was too ill from blood poisoning to fly.

Oblt. Dortenmann led eighteen First Gruppe Focke-Wulfs up from Sülte at 1110 on a mission to Vorsfelde, where they were to attempt to screen an infantry division that was trapped far behind the fluid lines. Uffz. Karl Fröb disappeared shortly after takeoff, never to be seen again. The formation was then struck from above by Spitfires. Lt. Ossenkop, who was flying *ein lahmer Bock* (a lame goat) because his own airplane was unserviceable, was apparently the only German pilot hit. He bailed out with injuries to his shoulder, chest, knee, and foot. The Spitfire pilot circled him and rocked his wings; Ossenkop was glad that he had voted with the majority of the Gruppe to refrain from strafing parachuting Allied pilots in retaliation for the behavior of the Americans.

The rest of the formation proceeded with the mission. South of Lübeck, the Tempests of No. 80 Squadron were met at 2000 meters (6500 feet), and a furious battle ensued, after which the German pilots claimed the destruction of three Tempests. The victorious German pilots were Oblt. Dortenmann, Lt. Söffing, and Ogfr. Böcker. Four Focke-Wulfs were lost, but only one pilot, Uffz. Albert Hütterer was killed. Lt. Konrad and Lt. Blickle bailed out, and Ogfr. Böcker crash-landed, all without injury. The

British squadron claimed 2-0-2 Fw 190s, for the loss of only one pilot and airplane.

Dortenmann's aircraft was damaged by German Flak, and he was being escorted across Lake Schwerin by Fw. Bruno Ostrowitzki and a second pilot when Ostrowitzki misjudged his distance above the mirror-clear lake and flew right into it. A Fw 190D-9 was discovered in the lake in 1990 and was immediately assumed to be Ostrowitzki's; he was the only missing Dora-9 pilot known to have crashed in the lake. But the aircraft was identified as that of Karl Fröb. The reason for Fröb's crash will never be known.

The First Gruppe lost another pilot, Ogfr. Manfred Niessen, on his return trip to Sülte by train after crash-landing his fighter. An RAF fighter strafed the train and killed Niessen.

In mid-afternoon the Second Gruppe flew an armed reconnaissance of the highways south of Hamburg. The formation was shot at by antiaircraft guns, and also attacked by five Spitfire XIVs of No. 350 Sqd. (Belgian). Fw. Hans Marischka disappeared; in 1989 his body was found near Harburg, south of Hamburg.

JG 26 Casualties: 17 April 1945

Date	Rank	Name	Cas	Unit	Aircraft	WNr	Mkgs	Place	Time	Cause	Allied Unit
17-04-45	Fw.	Ostrowitzki, Bruno	KIFA	1	Fw 190D-9			Lake Schwerin		hit water	n/a
17-04-45	Uffz.	Fröb, Karl	KIA	2	Fw 190D-9	210968	bk 8	Lake Schwerin	1130	combat	
17-04-45	Uffz.	Hütterer, Albert	KIA	2	Fw 190D-9			SW of Lübeck	1130	Tempest	80 Sqd
17-04-45	Lt.	Ossenkop, Karl-Heinz	WIA	2	Fw 190D-9			nr Ratzenburg	1130	Spitfire	
17-04-45	Ogfr.	Niessen, Manfred	KIA	3	ground			Grevesmühlen		train strafed	n/a
17-04-45	Fw.	Marischka, Hans	KIA	5	Fw 190D-9			Hamburg-Harburg		Spitfire	350 Sqd

18 April

The First Gruppe stood by at readiness all day to fly airfield protection for a special operation; the mission was finally scrubbed at 2015. Two Second Gruppe Schwärme flew missions to the Soltau-Lüneburg-Uelsen area. The first took off at 1100; the second followed fifty minutes later. Both flew armed reconnaissances of the ordered area, and then bombed and strafed motor transport. Results were not observed in detail. There were no losses.

After a last combing out of the non-combat flying units, seven pilots arrived at the Second Gruppe from the ferry unit Flüg 1: Uffz. Horst Eickhoff, Fw. Herbert Palige, Fw. Arthur Rennack, Fhj.-Uffz. Hubert Reuschel, Obfw. Walter Rother, Fw. Gustav Schmidt, and Obfw. August Stratbücker.

19 April

The Geschwader flew a total of thirty-five sorties. The Second Gruppe flew a dawn mission, and dropped antipersonnel bombs on vehicles found on the Uelsen-Soltau highway. One aircraft was lost, but its pilot was apparently not injured. The Gruppe probably flew a second mission in the afternoon, but it is not documented. The First Gruppe flew a single mission. Oblt. Dortenmann led seventeen aircraft up from Sülte at 1625 with orders to fly an armed reconnaissance of Lüneburg. The formation apparently never reached the assigned area, but returned to base without contacting the enemy. If Dortenmann had an excuse, it was not entered in the Gruppe diary. The rocket that Major Götz sent the Gruppe is entered, but only the exclamation points are legible.

20 April

Oblt. Dortenmann was awarded his Knight's Cross, to the joy and the probable relief of his 3rd Staffel pilots. This was to be the last major decoration received by a member of the Geschwader; Waldemar Söffing was also nominated for the award, but never

Fw 190D-9 "brown 4" (W.Nr. 500647) of the 7th Staffel, abandoned at Hustedt. *(Hampton via Wadman)*

received it. The infrastructure of the Wehrmacht was rapidly disintegrating. The American Ninth Army had already reached the Elbe River northwest of Berlin, and within a few days Germany would be cut in two by the American and Russian armies. The Luftwaffe no longer made a distinction between the Western and Eastern fronts. All air units in the north now came under Genobst. Stumpff's Luftwaffenkommando Reich. JG 26 remained the only day fighter unit in the 14th Fliegerdivision, which became one of the subordinate units within LwKdo Reich.

Hans Dortenmann was not called on to fly, probably in recognition of his decoration, and Major Borris led the only First Gruppe mission. Eleven Focke-Wulfs took off at 1540 on a Jabojagd to Lüneburg. As the unit was forming up north of Sülte, Spitfires were reported attacking the field. Borris led his fighters back, and found about a dozen enemy aircraft. Lt. Söffing shot one down over the airfield, for his 29th victory. Fhr. von Plazer shot down another, for his first victory, but was then shot down himself and killed. The Spitfires were from No. 401 Sqd. (RCAF), which claimed 8-0-3 Bf 109s over a Schwerin airfield at 1600, and lost one airplane and pilot down and a second pilot wounded. The First Gruppe suffered another fatality when Lt. Franz Göttle attempted to land at Wismar after this mission; he was shot down by naval Flak and crashed into Lake Schwerin.

The Second Gruppe had a full and productive day. At dawn, Lt. Sy led a 7th Staffel Schwarm to reconnoiter the Lüneburg Heath, and found an armored column backed up on the main Hannover-Hamburg highway. Sy notified ground control of the choice target and turned back to base. Lt. Schramm's 6th Staffel Schwarm was quickly bombed up, and took off at 0845, after Sy had landed and ordered his own Schwarm to be refueled and loaded with anti-personnel bombs. Eight more Focke-Wulfs were made ready, and Sy led the dozen aircraft off the field at 0900 and headed south, meeting Schramm's formation on its return flight. The British formation could now be located by the smoke plumes. The highway ran straight as an arrow through farmland, and there was no way for the drivers to conceal their vehicles. Werner Molge was on the mission, and recalls making the approach flight at low level to evade the Allied radar, and bypassing the target to one side. At Soltau the fighters pulled up to 500 meters (1640 feet) and reversed course, following the highway north, in order to attack in the direction of their own base. The bombs were armed, and were dropped on the first pass over the vehicles. The fighters then dropped to 10 meters (32 feet) and began their strafing runs perpendicular to the road. They made a firing pass, reversed course, and passed back over the road, firing again. The German pilots proceeded north in this serpentine fashion until they had exhausted their ammunition. The pilots were then ordered by Sy to form up and return to Uetersen, where they received the congratulations of Hptm. Schauder, who had been in conference and unable to fly the mission. Incredibly, only one of Sy's fighters was seriously damaged by ground fire; none of Schramm's four aircraft had even been hit.

Siegfried Sy's own story of this mission was told in this author's *JG 26: Top Guns of the Luftwaffe*. Sy believed that it had taken place on 24 April. Logbooks and Allied radio intercepts, plus Werner Molge's own memory, are in agreement that the correct date was 20 April.

The Second Gruppe flew a mission late in the day that was not as successful. Again the target was the highway north of Soltau, but this time the enemy was ready. Uffz. Erich Schumacher and Uffz. Joseph Simmer were damaged by ground fire and disappeared in the growing darkness. Neither returned to uetersen, and both were still missing in 1998.

After dark, Heinz Gomann landed on Uetersen in a Focke-Wulf, and had a story to tell. After leaving the Geschwader with orders to join JG 7 he had walked to Brandenburg, only to learn that the jets had transferred to München. He broke the trip with a visit to his parents in Berlin, and then got on a train for München, but soon learned that the Red Army's latest breakthrough had cut the railroad line. He returned to Berlin and got his father's chauffeur to drive him and his dog to Güstrow, a nearby Focke-Wulf base, in the family's wood-gas automobile. The pilots were all in the Casino drinking cognac, and Gomann had difficulty persuading anyone that he was actually trying to get back to the front. Borrowing an aircraft was no problem, but he was unable to take off until late afternoon. He reached Hamburg after dark with his dog in his radio compartment. He could not find the field, but the base engineer recognized the sound of the Focke-Wulf's engine and turned on the airfield lights, saving Heinz Gomann, his dog, and one Focke-Wulf for further duty. Uffz. Böttge also failed to reach JG 7. He returned to the Geschwader at about this time, but probably without a dog or an airplane.

To the surprise of Major Götz, five student pilots showed up at Sülte during the day with orders to join a combat unit. One pilot, Gefr. Detlef Bornholdt, was sent to Uetersen to join the Second Gruppe. Uffz. Willi Baumbach, Uffz. Udo Busch, Uffz. Emil Hötz, and Fw. Viktor Karwik remained at Sülte with the First Gruppe.

JG 26 Victory Claims: 17 - 20 April 1945

Date	Rank	Name	Unit	Cl #	Aircraft	Place	Time	Opponent	Conf
17-04-45	Ogfr.	Böcker	1	1	Tempest	SW of Lübeck	1130	80 Sqd	unk
17-04-45	Lt.	Söffing	2 CO	29	Tempest	SW of Lübeck	1130	80 Sqd	unk
17-04-45	Oblt.	Dortenmann	3 CO	35	Tempest	SW of Lübeck	1134	80 Sqd	unk
20-04-45	Lt.	Söffing	2 CO	30	Spitfire	Sülte a/f	1600	401 Sqd	unk
20-04-45	Fhr.	Plazer v.	2	1	Spitfire	Sülte a/f	1600	401 Sqd	unk

JG 26 Casualties: 20 April 1945

Date	Rank	Name	Cas	Unit	Aircraft	WNr	Mkgs	Place	Time	Cause	Allied Unit
20-04-45	Lt.	Göttle, Franz	KIA	1	Fw 190D-9			Wismar a/f	1630	own naval flak	n/a
20-04-45	Fhr.	Plazer, Gerhard von	KIA	2	Fw 190D-9			Sülte a/f	1550	Spitfire	401 Sqd
20-04-45	Uffz.	Schumacher, Erich	KIA	7	Fw 190D-9			near Soltau		flak	n/a
20-04-45	Uffz.	Simmer, Joseph	KIA	7	Fw 190D-9			near Soltau		flak	n/a

21 April

The pilots received orders to repeat the previous day's highway patrols. Lt. Jan Schild led five 1st Staffel fighters up from Sülte at 1050. Schild had replaced the injured Xaver Ellenrieder as Staffelführer; this was Schild's first flight since being wounded the previous October. He encountered such heavy ground fire on the roads around Rothenburg that he abandoned the mission without attacking. Lt. Guhl was the next to try his luck, taking off at 1210 with five fighters from his 2nd Staffel. They were sent after some artillery spotters, but never found them, and used too much fuel in the search to make a ground attack. At 1435 Oblt. Dortenmann took off with nine fighters from the 1st and 3rd Staffeln. His assigned highway was clear of traffic, so he went hunting for Allied fighter-bombers. They were found at 1500 meters (5000 feet) near Buchholz, south of Hamburg; the Focke-Wulf pilots claimed three Spitfires, without loss, but the Allied fighters involved cannot be traced; none were lost.

Late in the evening the Second Gruppe located several British fighters northwest of Perleberg; Hptm. Schauder and Lt. Schramm each claimed a Tempest, probably from No. 3 Squadron, which lost one. One 6th Staffel pilot, Uffz. Georg Kreth, failed to return, and was still missing in 1998. Kreth was shot down northeast of Wismar by a Tempest of No. 486 Sqd. (RNZAF).

Hptm. Schauder decided that two of his new replacements were better suited to be reconnaissance pilots, and sent Fw. Arthur Rennack and Obfw. August Stratbücker to NAGr 6.

JG 26 Victory Claims: 21 April 1945

Date	Rank	Name	Unit	Cl #	Aircraft	Place	Time	Opponent	Conf
21-04-45	Oblt.	Dortenmann	3 CO	36	Spitfire	Buchholz (S of Harburg)	1519		unk
21-04-45	Fw.	Hein K.	3	7	Spitfire	Buchholz (S of Harburg)	1515		unk
21-04-45	Uffz.	Rey	3	4	Spitfire	Buchholz (S of Harburg)	1510		unk
21-04-45	Hptm.	Schauder	II CO	20	Tempest	NW of Perleberg	1910	3 Sqd	unk
21-04-45	Lt.	Schramm	6	1	Tempest	NW of Perleberg	1912	3 Sqd	unk

22 April

The weather soured again, and the First Gruppe was grounded by heavy rains and a solid overcast at 250 meters (800 feet). The Second Gruppe flew at least one mission, an attack by bombs and gunfire on road traffic south of Hamburg. Uffz. Karl Hött's wingman, Uffz. Rudolf Bellmann, was hit by ground fire near Buchholz and crashed to his death.

23 April

The First Gruppe was not assigned a mission today. A 6th Staffel Schwarm flew a dawn bombing mission, but it was unsuccessful. Southwest of Hamburg the Focke-Wulfs jettisoned their bombs when attacked by four Spitfires of No. 403 Sqd. (RCAF). Uffz. Hött's aircraft took four hits, but he got away, claiming effective damage to a Spitfire; the No. 403 Sqd. fighter made a safe belly-landing on the Bremen-Hamburg Autobahn. Hött's wingman today, Fw. Otto Wilck, was not so lucky; he crashed in his aircraft. The Canadians claimed two "long nose" Fw 190s. Wilck's aircraft and remains were located in 1986, in spongy ground too extensive to permit recovery of his body.

24 April

The First Gruppe flew against the Russians for the first time since 1943. Oblt. Dortenmann led seventeen aircraft up from Sülte at 0750 to strafe Soviet truck convoys in their salient at Oranienburg, just north of Berlin. The Focke-Wulfs encountered eight Yak-3 fighters north of Spandau at 2400 meters (8000 feet) and shot

The fin and rudder of "brown 4" at Hustedt. The empennage of this aircraft was a broad-chord, all-metal design intended for the Ta 152 – an example of the chaos and resourcefulness that reigned in the Luftwaffe production plants in 1945. *(Blain via Hampton via Thomas)*

down three, without loss; the victors were Lt. Söffing, Obfw. Schwarz, and Fw. Hein. They then landed at the Rechlin-Lärz experimental station to refuel. They were delayed in taking off by Tempests over Rechlin, but finally arrived back at Sülte at 2040.

Part of the Second Gruppe also flew to Rechlin, but had no successes *en route*, and apparently remained at Rechlin overnight. Uffz. Günter Pfeiffer of the 5th Staffel was killed, either on this day or the next; the records are unclear.

25 April

The American 69th Infantry Division contacted the Red Army at Torgau, on the Elbe River, splitting the remains of the Third Reich into northern and southern sections. Both Gruppen staged through Rechlin and flew missions over Berlin. At 0600 Lt. Söffing led ten aircraft up from Sülte to attack the Russian bridgeheads. Trucks and gun installations were strafed, and Söffing shot a Po-2 artillery spotter into flames. It was on the ground, and no claim was filed. Uffz. Nieter's aircraft was hit by ground fire; he was able to make a forced-landing behind the German lines, but destroyed his aircraft and injured himself. The nine remaining aircraft landed at Rechlin and were placed under the command of Obstlt. Michalski of JG 4. Their first mission was an escort for six Fw 190F Panzerblitze, which were lethal tank-busters mounting R4M rockets underwing. The first effort was recalled, but Söffing's second attempt, by only three aircraft, was successful. Eight Yak-3s were encountered, and Lts. Söffing and Ramthun each downed one of them. It was intended that the Gruppe spend the night at Rechlin, but after Söffing and five of his pilots were scrambled to intercept nine escorted Red Air Force Pe-2s that never showed up, he led the formation back to Sülte.

Eight Second Gruppe aircraft left Uetersen at 0940, battled eight Tempests west of Schwerin without result, and landed on Rechlin-Lärz at 1030. One Schwarm was quickly loaded with 250 kg high-explosive bombs and sent to bomb the bridge over the Havel Canal at Oranienburg. They made a successful attack, but Gefr. Molge found himself unable to keep up with the formation on their return. They met another Second

A haggard Lt. Peter Crump, ill from blood poisoning, photographed in Uetersen in April. Crump ended the war as Kapitän of the 1st Staffel. *(Crump)*

Gruppe Schwarm, whose pilots waggled their wings and pointed below Molge's airplane. Only then did he notice the red warning light on his instrument panel; he had forgotten to arm his bomb, and it had not released. Molge dropped from the formation, armed the bomb, and jettisoned it into Lake Müritz, only to see it skip ashore without exploding. He then returned to Uetersen alone, taking a circuitous route to avoid Allied fighters. His landing ended in a headstand. Hptm. Schauder was not amused, and confined him to quarters for three days.

The other pilots had taken off from Lärz at 1250 and battled a dozen Pe-2s over the Oranienburg salient. The pilots still at uetersen left at 1330 and flew straight to Oranienburg, where they strafed the roads and bridges and battled inconclusively with Yak-9s before landing on Rechlin. The entire formation flew a late-afternoon mission to Berlin that resulted in the only Second Gruppe success over a Red fighter. Lt. Sy claimed an Airacobra, his third victory of the war; it was the 902nd, and last, air victory for the Gruppe.

The Gruppe then returned to Uetersen, where they had a rendezvous to keep – a "birthday party" in the Casino to celebrate the rebirth of all those pilots who had narrowly escaped death, which was most of them. The resourceful administrative officer, Hptm. Groos, had found supplies of cognac, beer, and tobacco. There were plenty of women, in the forms of the female auxiliaries. Dancing was forbidden, and the men of the Gruppe, who were considered interlopers and troublemakers by Uetersen's permanent staff, did not press that particular issue. The party was apparently a smashing success, nonetheless. Siegfried Sy got drunk, but later remembered making a speech while standing on a table, using a chandelier as an ashtray. He could not remember what he said, but it was not enough to get him arrested. In the midst of the festivities, Hptm. Groos appeared and asked for four volunteers for an anti-Auster mission that had been requested by the Army for dawn. Gefr. Molge offered to volunteer if Groos could get him released from confinement, which was done.

JG 26 Victory Claims: 23 - 25 April 1945

Date	Rank	Name	Unit	Cl #	Aircraft	Place	Time	Opponent	Conf
23-04-45	Fw.	Hött	6		Spitfire-dam	near Elsdorf	0615	403 Sqd	no
24-04-45	Obfw.	Schwarz E.	1	10	Yak-3	near Stolpe (N of Spandau)	0820		unk
24-04-45	Lt.	Söffing	2 CO	31	Yak-3	S of Stolpe	0820		unk
24-04-45	Fw.	Hein K.	3	8	Yak-3	N of Spandau	0820		unk
25-04-45	Lt.	Ramthun	1	2	Yak-3	Reinickendorf	1230		unk
25-04-45	Lt.	Söffing	2 CO	32	Yak-3	Reinickendorf	1230		unk
25-04-45	Lt.	Sy	7	3	P-39	E of Oranienburg	1755		unk

Date	Rank	Name	Cas		Unit	Aircraft	WNr	Mkgs	Place	Time	Cause	Allied Unit
21-04-45	Uffz.	Kreth, Georg	KIA	6		Fw 190D-9			NE of Wismar		Tempest	486 Sqd
22-04-45	Uffz.	Bellmann, Rudolf	KIA	6		Fw 190D-9			Buchholz		flak	
23-04-45	Fw.	Wilck, Otto	KIA	6		Fw 190D-9			Elzdorf	0610	Spitfire	403 Sqd
24-04-45	Uffz.	Pfeiffer, Günter	KIA	5		Fw 190D-9			Lünow (DDR)		unknown	
25-04-45	Uffz.	Nieter, Heinz	WIA	1		Fw 190D-9			Hemmingsdorf	0615	flak	n/a

26 April

The day began early for the Geschwader. At 0500 orders for the next move were received. The Stab and the First Gruppe would go to Klein-Kummersfeld; the Second Gruppe, to Neumünster. The ground staffs began packing. The dawn mission for the First Gruppe would be a strafing attack on Oranienburg, followed by further missions from Rechlin-Lärz under the direction of JG 4. Oblt. Dortenmann led fourteen Focke-Wulfs on the mission, but was unable to contact the enemy owing to thick clouds over the battle front.

The Second Gruppe flew two early missions. Gefr. Molge and the other three volunteers were awakened at 0500 for their anti-Auster mission. Hptm. Groos had obtained some genuine coffee, which helped clear their heads from the previous night's festivities. The quartet took off at about 0630 and climbed to 7000 meters (23,000 feet) over Bremen to breathe some pure oxygen and cure their hangovers. Not surprisingly, no Austers were to be found there. The skies over northern Germany were clear, and the pilots could see both the North and the Baltic seas. The quartet dived to look for targets on the roads south of Bremen, spotted two squadrons of Tempests, and streaked back to Uetersen at "720 km/h (447 mph)" (*sic*). After landing, their hangovers promptly returned.

The Second Gruppe put up a conventional ground-attack mission at 0625. The pilots returned to their favorite hunting area south of Hamburg, and made an effective bombing and strafing run on a highway convoy.

It was not until late afternoon that Dortenmann's men at Rechlin were assigned a mission. The dozen Focke-Wulfs were to rendezvous with a dozen Panzerblitze and escort them on a tank-busting mission to Prenzlau. While over Berlin, they were to determine whether the East-West Axis (a large, broad street in the center of Berlin) was usable as a landing strip, or whether the Russians had already taken it under artillery fire. The skies had cleared except over Berlin, which was covered in a pall of smoke. The German formation approached Berlin at 3000 meters (10,000 feet). Almost all of the city was in flames, "an indescribably overwhelming sight", in Fritz Ungar's words. The pilots were able to orient themselves easily, and could see shell bursts on the East-West Axis.

The Focke-Wulfs were now at 4000 meters (13,000 feet), and were chased across the sky by strings of anti-aircraft tracers. This was a novelty to the men of the Geschwader; no British or American rapid-fire antiaircraft gun could reach that altitude. In the target area near Prenzlau, a number of small aircraft approached. They were "swarming like bees", and had to be Russian. Dortenmann led an attack which resulted in claims for four Yaks, and returned to Rechlin to report a successful mission.

JG 26 Victory Claims: 26 April 1945

Date	Rank	Name	Unit	Cl #	Aircraft	Place	Time	Opponent	Conf
26-04-45	Obfw.	Schwarz E.	1	11	Yak-3	SE of Prenzlau	1915		unk
26-04-45	Ofhr.	Birkner	2	1	Yak-3	SE of Prenzlau	1915		unk
26-04-45	Oblt.	Dortenmann	3 CO	37	Yak-9	SE of Prenzlau	1916		unk
26-04-45	Lt.	Blickle	3	1	Yak-3	SE of Prenzlau	1915		unk

27 April

The Geschwader ground staffs spent the day preparing their new bases for operations.

Hptm. Groos divided up the last liquor and tobacco in the Second Gruppe inventory among the men. The pilots remained at Uetersen, and were not given a mission. Dortenmann's pilots at Rechlin waited until late afternoon before receiving an assignment. Nine Focke-Wulfs took off from Rechlin-Lärz at 1720 to fly an armed reconnaissance over Berlin. The group encountered seven Yak-3s at 2000 meters (6500 feet) northeast of Berlin, and Hans Dortenmann shot one down. It was his 38th, and last, air victory, attained in about 150 combat missions. The fighters returned to Rechlin, where they landed at 1840.

There was possibly more to the mission than the First Gruppe clerk entered in that unit's diary. Jan Schild of the 1st Staffel was one of the nine pilots, and his logbook indicates that this was an escort mission. There were ten Fw 190Ds on the flight from Rechlin. Crammed into the tenth were Genobst. Ritter von Greim and the test pilot Hanna Reitsch, making a lunatic odyssey to the Führerbunker. Von Greim dropped away from the formation, and landed at Berlin's Gatow airport, from where the duo continued to the inner city in a trainer. Russian fire hit the small airplane, and nearly severed von Greim's foot, before he could put the craft down on the East-West Axis.

At 2035 Dortenmann sent four aircraft back to Sülte; these could not be cleared for operations without maintenance that was unavailable at Rechlin.

28 April

No combat missions were assigned. The only contact with enemy aircraft came on Oblt. Dortenmann's afternoon flight from Rechlin-Lärz to the new First Gruppe base at Klein-Kummersfeld, when Yak-3s were seen, but not engaged. The First Gruppe rear guard left Sülte at 2100. Hptm. Schauder decided to keep his Second Gruppe operating from Uetersen for one more day.

29 April

At 1230 Lt. Söffing took off from Klein-Kummersfeld with six First Gruppe aircraft to attack the British armor spearheads near Lauenburg. A few minutes later, Lt. Sy led a strengthened armed reconnaissance mission of two Second Gruppe Schwärme up from Uetersen, and also headed for Lauenburg. Both formations were attacked by RAF fighters, and were unable to carry out any ground attacks. The Second Gruppe was manhandled by Tempests, according to the reports, losing Lt. Werner Schramm and Uffz. Johannes Schlimper over what became the Democratic German Republic (East Germany) after the war. Schramm's remains were identified in 1989, but Schlimper was still carried as missing in 1998. Schlimper had been flying as Fw. Hött's wingman, and was the third wingman Karl Hött had lost in a week. The Second Gruppe made no claims.

The First Gruppe was attacked by what were described as Griffon-engine Spitfires. Söffing claimed one, but the unit lost Fw. Helmut Walter. Walter was the last of 757 JG 26 pilots to be killed in the course of the war. His grave was identified incorrectly after the war, and his fate was not clarified on the official records until 1988.

The two RAF fighter formations were actually the Merlin-engine Spitfire IXes of No. 412 Sqd. (RCAF), which attacked the two German formations in succession. They claimed four Fw 190Ds at the correct time and place to be the opponents of the Geschwader, and lost no aircraft.

At 1615 Söffing led seven aircraft in an escort mission for fourteen SG 151 Fw 190F Panzerblitze. SG 151 was the training wing for the *Schlachtflieger* (ground attack units), and had been made operational to combat the armor approaching its base at Lauenburg. The Tempests of No. 486 Squadron had returned to the area after downing four SG 151 Focke-Wulfs and three JG 27 Messerschmitts earlier in the afternoon. Söffing sighted them and attacked, claiming one Tempest for his 34th victory, but was unable to prevent the Tempests from shattering the formation of attack planes. Three SG 151 aircraft went down at this time. Söffing could not reform the attack unit, and led his own Doras back to base. No Tempests went down in this combat.

In the last command shakeup of the war, by which Major Götz hoped to strengthen both Gruppen, Lt. Crump moved from the 5th Staffel in the Second Gruppe to take over the 1st Staffel in the First Gruppe, while Oblt. Schild left the 1st Staffel to take command of the 5th. For whatever reason, the exchange worked; both men began their new assignments with renewed vigor.

30 April

The Second Gruppe moved to Neumünster, which was near the Stab and First Gruppe at Klein-Kummersfeld. The two Gruppen spent the day attempting to attack British armor while avoiding 2nd TAF fighters. Only the dawn mission of the Second Gruppe succeeded in its task. Uffz. Walter Stumpf of the 7th Staffel, who was flying daily and who had become an accomplished Jabo pilot, was promoted to Feldwebel after successfully bombing and strafing enemy troops around Lauenburg. The First Gruppe missions led by Lt. Guhl and Lt. Söffing were broken up by Tempests and Spitfires.

Many of the First Gruppe groundcrewmen had been in the Geschwader since before the war. Major Borris released those veterans who lived nearby and wanted to attempt to reach their homes. Obfw. Hans Backhaus left on a bicycle. He was picked up by American troops, but was soon released. He was carrying an official-looking document bearing the stamp of the president of Prussia and discharging him from the Luftwaffe for a congenital heart condition.

Lt. Ossenkop was released from the hospital and returned to the First Gruppe, but was not cleared for flight duty.

1 May

The Geschwader attempted three combined missions against ground targets near Lauenburg and Schwarzenbeck; a total of fifty-four sorties was flown. The First Gruppe provided the escort force for Second Gruppe bomb-carriers. The first mission got underway at 1030. Dortenmann's pilots attacked several formations of Spitfires and Tempests, but the Second Gruppe was forced to jettison its bombs. Lt. Guhl of the 2nd Staffel claimed the probable destruction of a Spitfire; this was the 817th claim for the First Gruppe, and would prove to be the last Geschwader victory claim. The aircraft of Fw. Walter Napierski was damaged by a Spitfire, and turned over as he was landing from the mission, injuring him. Fw. Ungar was first reported missing, but he had returned early and was elsewhere on the base.

The next mission got underway at 1610. Spitfires were contacted, but the Focke-Wulfs evaded them and proceeded to the target area, which was bombed by the Second Gruppe as ordered. The First Gruppe formation was split up by German flak, and was unable to make a strafing attack.

The last mission got underway shortly after 2000. The First Gruppe fighters were recalled because of weather conditions, but the Second Gruppe proceeded to Schwarzenbeck and dropped its bombs on the armor spearhead.

The Second Gruppe lost its Kommandeur on one of these missions. Hptm. Paul Schauder disappeared from his formation near Lauenburg and was shot down by British antiaircraft fire. He was taken prisoner, injured. Schauder was probably flying one of the two dozen Fw 190D-12s and D-13s that reached the Geschwader in the final days of the war. These models were armed with a machine cannon mounted on the engine and firing through the propeller hub, and two MG 151/20 cannons in the wing roots. There were no cowl weapons. A smooth metal fairing in their former location eliminated the hump which gave the Dora-9 its characteristic broken-nosed look. The central cannon was a 3 cm MK 108 in the D-12, and a MG 151/20 in the D-13. Major Götz and Major Borris are known to have had Fw 190D-13s assigned to them.

At 2100 the Geschwader advance party left Klein-Kummersfeld under the command of Hptm. Causin, the administrative officer, and headed for Flensberg, on the Danish border. There was enough war left for one more base transfer.

Date	Rank	Name	Unit	Cl #	Aircraft	Place	Time	Opponent	Conf
27-04-45	Oblt.	Dortenmann	3 CO	38	Yak-3	NE of Neuruppin-Berlin	1825		unk
29-04-45	Lt.	Söffing	2 CO	33	Spitfire XIV	W of Lauenburg	1250	412 Sqd Spitfire IXe	unk
29-04-45	Lt.	Söffing	2 CO	34	Tempest	S of Ratzeburg-Lübeck	1640	486 Sqd	unk
01-05-45	Lt.	Guhl	2	15	Spitfire-prob	N of Schwarzenbeck	1050		no

JG 26 Casualties: 29 April - 1 May 1945

Date	Rank	Name	Cas	Unit	Aircraft	WNr	Mkgs	Place	Time	Cause	Allied Unit
29-04-45	Fw.	Walter, Helmut	KIA	1	Fw 190D-9			Lauenburg-Elbe	1250	Spitfire	412 Sqd
29-04-45	Uffz.	Schlimper, Johannes	KIA	6	Fw 190D-9			Wittenberge (DDR)		Spitfire	412 Sqd
29-04-45	Lt.	Schramm, Werner	KIA	6	Fw 190D-9			Wittenberge (DDR)		Spitfire	412 Sqd
01-05-45	Fw.	Napierski, Walter	WIA	1	Fw 190D-9	210961	wh 6	near Schwarzenbeck	1110	Spitfire	
01-05-45	Hptm.	Schauder, Paul	POW	II CO	Fw 190D			Lauenburg-Elbe		flak	

2 May

The two Gruppen were active all day. Fw. Hött was up at 0700 and flew an armed reconnaissance mission to Hamburg with a 6th Staffel Schwarm. Motor transport was strafed. Oblt. Schild, the new leader of the 5th Staffel, led a mission to Lauenburg at 1030. He noted in his logbook that his formation made three effective low-level attacks. Oblt. Crump, the new leader of the 1st Staffel, was scrambled at 1255 with nine First Gruppe aircraft to intercept eight Typhoons over Klein-Kummersfeld. Crump damaged one, but took a hit in his engine; the rest of the Typhoons evaded combat in the clouds. Lt. Konrad lost his formation and was shot down by a No. 486 Sqd. (RNZAF) Tempest; he bailed out without injury. His Focke-Wulf was the last combat loss of the First Gruppe; Crump's mission was his 202nd, and last. The Second Gruppe flew another armed recon mission to the Hamburg area in mid-afternoon, without recorded results.

Most of the aircraft were ferried to their new Schleswig bases in late afternoon and evening. The First Gruppe had no fewer than twenty-three flyable Fw 190Ds; all were moved to Flensberg. Some Second Gruppe pilots flew to Husum, where Fw. Stumpf ended his war with a headstand. Oblt. Schild flew one last mission from Neumünster, bombing and destroying an antiaircraft position before returning to base at 2110; this was his 220th, and last, combat sortie.

3 May

A Schwarm of Focke-Wulfs left Husum for an early-morning reconnaissance mission. At 300 meters (1000 feet) the engine of Uffz. Molge's aircraft exploded and his airplane caught fire. Molge landed by parachute, very near the airfield. He was uninjured, and his Focke-Wulf was the last aircraft lost by the Second Gruppe. The cause of the explosion – enemy aircraft, Flak, maintenance defect, or sabotage – was never determined.

Each Gruppe flew one afternoon mission before heavy rains brought flying to an end. Lt. Söffing led eight First Gruppe aircraft on a patrol of the Kiel Canal, which was filled with ships carrying civilians attempting to escape the Russians. No enemy aircraft were seen. Oblt. Schild's transfer flight to Husum was considered an armed reconnaissance mission, but no contact was made with the enemy owing to the rain.

The Luftwaffe bases in Schleswig were now crowded with aircraft and personnel from a number of units. At Leck, twenty miles from Flensberg, a series of events took place that typified conditions in the Luftwaffe and Germany. Two JG 11 pilots, Lt.

Hermann Gern and Fw. Franz Keller, made plans to steal a Bf 108 Taiphun and return to their homes in southern Germany. They talked too much, and a Schnüffler (Snooper) turned them in. The air police were waiting to arrest them as they approached the Taiphun.

4 May

Field Marshal Montgomery succeeded in obtaining a separate peace on his portion of the collapsed front. Generalfeldmarschall Keitel signed a cease-fire for the Wehrmacht forces facing the Western Allies in northern Germany, to go into effect at 0800 on the 5th.

Both Gruppen flew their final missions today, in constant rain. According to Fw. Hött's logbook, he flew a last mission from Neumünster in the morning, engaging eight Tempests and damaging one, and then flew to Husum in the afternoon. Oblt. Schild led a small force away from Husum at 1310 on a freie Jagd, and swept the combat zone without contact. Oblt. Crump led a Schwarm from Flensberg at 1410, but also failed to make

Uffz. Werner Molge of the 7th Staffel relaxes on V-E Day at Husum, the last base of the Second Gruppe. The twenty-year-old Molge, one of the youngest pilots in the Gruppe, was among the few lucky Nachwuchs who survived the war without injury. (Terbeck)

contact. The last combat mission of the Geschwader was a freie Jagd to the area of the Kiel Canal; it was flown by nine aircraft of the First Gruppe, led by Oblt. Dortenmann. When they landed on Flensberg at 1824, the combat history of Jagdgeschwader 26 "Schlageter" had come to a close.

The controversies and confusion of the war's endgame continued, however. At 2350 the new head of the Luftwaffe, Generalfeldmarschall Ritter von Greim, ordered the Geschwader to relocate to Prague at first light. This nonsensical order would have required a flight of several hundred miles over Allied-held territory, and the abandonment of the Geschwader ground echelon. If this move was not possible – it wasn't, as there was no place to refuel – Major Götz was given the option of flying his aircraft to Norway to continue the war against the Bolsheviks.

At Leck, Lt. Gern and Fw. Keller were brought before a court martial, convicted of *Fahnenflucht* (flight before the enemy), and sentenced to death by firing squad. The sentence was to be carried out at 0200 on the 5th, before the cease-fire. The executions were delayed, and several NCO pilots approached Major Anton Hackl, who had been the JG 11 Kommodore since late February, and spoke up for Keller, a veteran member of JG 11 who was known to Hackl. Keller was spared. Gern was a Nachwuchs who had apparently made few friends in the unit. Toni Hackl was no martinet – on the contrary, he had had a reputation in JG 26 as an easy-going commander – but he was unwilling to lift a hand to save Hermann Gern.

5 May

The Geschwader had received valid orders to transfer to Norway. At Flensberg, Major Borris argued successfully with Major Götz that the morning fog prohibited takeoffs. At Husum, the pilots of the Second Gruppe, without a Kommandeur, argued among themselves as to their course of action. About half decided to stay where they were, and surrender to the British when they arrived at Husum. Oblt. Schild, apparently the senior officer present, convinced thirteen other pilots to obey the order. A claim by a German historian that it took a "pistol-waving NSFO" to persuade the pilots to fly the mission is not true, according to two pilots who were there. Jan Schild recalls that the NSFO was a "harmless old reservist" who could not have conceived of treating combat pilots in that manner.

The scene at the takeoff point was chaotic. Two Focke-Wulfs collided while taxiing, blocking the movement of a third. Ogfr. Molge got into a discussion with the mechanic who was buckling him up. The old-timer pointed down the field and said, "You are from Hamburg, aren't you? See that bomb crater? If you taxi into it, your war is over. Otherwise, you'll be marching back from Norway on foot!" According to Molge, something "clicked in his brain" at that point. He said nothing, but started the engine as usual. When he began to taxi, he headed straight for the crater, ignoring the wildly-waving groundcrewmen. He hit the crater head-on. There was a crash; the wooden propeller splintered; a wheel rolled away, and the Focke-Wulf hung at an angle in the crater, suspended by its wings. Molge clambered out of the cockpit muttering, "Blinded by the rising sun." Shortly before his release from POW camp in August he met several members of the Gruppe who had, indeed, marched back to Germany, from Denmark if not from Norway.

Siegfried Sy was one of these men. The ten fighters to get off the ground reached Denmark and landed to refuel. The process took too long for Sy, and he took off with three pilots without waiting for Schild and the other five. Sy had no maps, his compass was inaccurate, and he found the Norwegian coast hidden behind a solid cloud bank. He finally turned around and returned to Aalborg in Denmark.

Oblt. Schild's six fighters took off fifteen minutes after Sy, and reached Norway. Jan Schild recalled his final flight in JG 26:

"On 5 May I received an order on the telephone from our Kommodore, Major Götz, to transfer my pilots and aircraft to Lister (a peninsula on the southern coast of Norway). Based on this order, which if I had not personally known Major Götz and his voice I probably would not have carried out, we filled up our aircraft's tanks at Husum and at 0615 flew to Grove in Denmark, in order to refuel and fly from there to Lister. I had neither a map nor any other kind of navigational aid. I determined our course by questioning a Bf 110 pilot who had flown that same day from Lister to Grove. The approximate flying time in our Fw 190D-9s was 35 minutes. Because of the bad weather – clouds down to 150-200 meters [500-650 feet], rain, visibility between three and five kilometers [2-3 miles], the transfer flight proved to be very dramatic. We flew in bad-weather formation; that is, the aircraft were about 10-15 meters apart, with the lead aircraft (myself) taking care of the navigation. After about thirty minutes flying time, I should have had the Norwegian coast in sight. Even after another two or three minutes, which seemed like an eternity, I could not see land. After informing the formation behind me by radio, I changed course by about 30-35 degrees. Shortly after changing course, I sighted land, and just where it should have been, an airfield at the tip of a peninsula. Lister was a hazardous airfield, surfaced with wooden planks, steel mats, and rubble. All of the aircraft landed safely with the exception of one, which had lost us when we changed course. We parked our aircraft around the edges of the field... You can imagine how we felt, having fought with these weapons for much of a year. Thereafter we experienced the lot of a prisoner of war in Norway."

To avoid the mission, Fw. Gomann went on sick call with the Gruppe adjutant, Lt. Blömertz, and received orders to enter a hospital in Neumünster for an "infectious illness." The pair paid a call on Baroness von Donner at her Schleswig estate – the Baroness was the widow of a Geschwader pilot and a good friend of Adolf Galland –

Fw 190D-9 "black 1" (W.Nr. 210972), photographed at Lister, Norway, after the flight of the Second Gruppe on 5 May. It is carrying a 300-liter drop tank of a new and seldom-illustrated design. *(Moll via Bracken via Fochuk)*

Fw 190D-9 "brown 7" (W.Nr. 601445) as it appeared after landing at Kjevik, Norway, on 5 May. It has been given a heavy overspray of green paint, a fairly common but poorly-documented practice of the Geschwader in the last spring of the war. According to Norwegian sources, the aircraft that reached Norway were destroyed in place in the autumn of 1945 by an RAF air disarmament wing. *(Thomas via Petrick)*

and hid in her lime pit for a few weeks before heading home. Heinz Gomann entered Göttingen University's first post-war class in September; his transition to peacetime went remarkably smoothly.

6 May

Major Borris paraded his men and aircraft, and made a short speech in which he thanked his Gruppe for their sacrifices for "Volk und Vaterland". That evening he turned the Flensberg airfield over to the Royal Air Force, and led his men into a makeshift POW camp near the town.

7 May

The horrors of the war were not yet over for some, despite the armistice. At Leck, Lt. Hermann Gern was executed by a firing squad of ten groundcrewmen, commanded by a staff officer who had spent the entire war behind a desk. Gern was probably the last of the more than 30,000 Wehrmacht personnel executed between 1939 and 1945 for dereliction of duty.

8 May

The Allies declared today to be Victory in Europe Day, V-E Day, after the articles of surrender were signed in Reims. The war was truly over.

The morale of the First Gruppe stayed high, even in POW camp. Fritz Ungar recalls,

A 13th Staffel Fw 190D-9 that survived the war and was taken into custody at Flensburg. Note the white "wave" that denoted this Staffel. The "USA-12" indicates that the airplane had been selected by the USAAF for evaluation, but it is not known to have reached the US. Based on the large swastika and the absence of a Werkenummer on the right side, this airplane is believed to have belonged to the 600### series. *(Kirlin via Fochuk)*

"Even after the armistice, our military discipline remained excellent. It was the same for all the personnel, not just the pilots. In those days we lived in tents in the Marienhölzung, a forest between Flensberg and our airfield. The war was over for

The final resting place of Pips Priller's last Fw 190A-8 "Jutta" – a junk pile on Flensburg in the summer of 1945. Priller's ace of hearts emblem and the tactical marking "black 13" are clearly visible. It is not known whether the Geschwader had kept the airplane as a "hack" after its conversion to Doras or had passed it to another unit. *(Fraser via Thomas)*

P/O Jim Ruse of No. 439 Sqd. (RCAF) poses on Priller's "Jutta" at Flensburg. Note the shell hole in front of the exhaust stacks; exit holes can be seen on the other side of the cowling in a photograph that is not of publishable quality. *(Ruse via Fochuk)*

us and we led a splendid camp life there. Military courtesies were observed, however. There were no problems. I remember that once an Obergefreiter from another unit came through our area. He walked past our Kommandeur, Major Borris, without saluting him. Major Borris asked him if that was customary behavior for soldiers. The stranger laughed, stuck his hands in his pockets, and sauntered off. Our Kommandeur quickly gathered several Obergefreiten together and told them how the strange Obergefreiter had acted. Borris then walked away. Our Obergefreiten beat the stranger severely. His screams could be heard for some distance."

For all but the officers and the Nazi party members, the period of incarceration was brief. For most, the popular late-war saying, "Enjoy the war. The peace will be frightful!" proved untrue. After the men were released to return to their old homes, or to make new ones, several went back to their old bases in northwestern Germany, married women they had met in late 1944 and early 1945, and settled there. The men did what they had to do to survive the bad times of 1945 and 1946, and then took part in the rebuilding of their country.

A "probable" I/JG 26 Fw 190D-9, W.Nr. 601088. Now on display at the US Air Force Museum in the markings of IV (Sturm)/JG 3, it is shown here at NASM's Silver Hill restoration facility before being loaned to the USAF in 1975. Most of the documentation on this aircraft is missing, but according to the NASM curators it was in all probability one of the JG 26 aircraft collected at Flensburg by the USAAF. It is known to have received the Allied "foreign evaluation" number of FE-120. Computer enhancement of a color print reveals that the original tactical number, "8", was overpainted with the same blue-gray paint used to cover the fuselage and tail crosses. The black chevron on top of the already-overpainted "8" was therefore a post-war addition, as was the "wave", and was probably added to the airplane in the USA in the 1950s to enhance its appearance for a long-forgotten air show. *(Lutz)*

GLOSSARIES

1. ABBREVIATIONS

AEAF: Allied Expeditionary Air Force.
ASR: Air-Sea Rescue.
CO: commanding officer.
e/a: enemy aircraft.
ETO: European Theater of Operations.
I F F: Identification - Friend from Foe.
NCO: non-commissioned officer.
POW: prisoner of war.
PRU: photo reconnaissance unit.
RAAF: Royal Australian Air Force.
RAF: Royal Air Force.
RCAF: Royal Canadian Air Force.
RNZAF: Royal New Zealand Air Force.
SAAF: South African Air Force.
TAF: (RAF) Tactical Air Force.
USAAF: US Army Air Force.

2. AVIATION TERMS

(#-#): (destroyed-damaged) aircraft losses.
(#-#-#): (destroyed-probable-damaged) aircraft claims.
Lufbery: a defensive formation in which two or more aircraft follow each other in a circle for mutual protection. Used loosely for any circling combat.
Split-S: a half-roll followed by a dive; results in a reversal of direction and the loss of a great deal of altitude. A common means of breaking off combat.
TacR: tactical reconnaissance.
Vic: a vee-shaped formation of three aircraft.

3. GERMAN TERMS

Abschuss: "shootdown"—an air victory.
Abschussmeldung: victory report.
Abschwung: split-S; a half-roll followed by a dive.
Alarmstart: scramble; a rapid takeoff for an intercept mission.
Ariflieger: a light airplane used to direct artillery fire.
Casino: pilots' mess.
dicke Autos: "fat cars" – Luftwaffe code designation for Allied heavy bombers.
Einsatzstaffel: operational Staffel (of a training unit).
Endausbildungsstaffel: operational training squadron.
endgültige Vernichtung (eV): final destruction; the shootdown of a bomber already separated from its formation.
Ergänzungsgruppe (ErgGr): advanced training group.
Ergänzungsstaffel (ErgSt): advanced training squadron.
Experte: a fighter pilot proficient in aerial combat; the Allied "ace".
Fliegerkorps (FK): air corps – a higher command containing several types of aircraft.
Flugzeugführer: pilot.
freie Jagd (pl. freie Jagden): "free hunt" – a fighter sweep without ground control.
Führer (pl. Führer): leader.
Führungsstaffel: leader's squadron.
Führungsverband: leader's formation.
Gefechtsstand: command post.
Gefechtsverband: battle formation.
General der Jagdflieger (GdJ): General of the Fighter Arm; a staff position in the RLM. Werner Mölders and Adolf Galland were the most prominent holders of the position.
Geschwader: wing (pl. **Geschwader**) – the largest mobile, homogeneous Luftwaffe flying unit.
Geschwadergruppe: wing commodore's group; a fixed but unofficial grouping of two or three Staffeln under the operational command of a Kommodore.
Geschwaderkommodore: wing commodore – usually a Major, Oberstleutnant, or Oberst in rank.
Gruppe (Gr): group (pl. **Gruppen**) – the basic Luftwaffe combat and administrative unit.
Gruppenkommandeur: group commander – usually a Hauptmann, Major, or Oberstleutnant in rank.
Herausschuss (HSS): "shoot-out" – the separation of a bomber from its combat formation.
Höhengruppe: high-altitude group.
Höhenstaffel: high-altitude squadron.
Holzauge: "woodeneye" – a spotter; the last airplane or the top cover unit of a formation.
Invasionsfront: invasion front.
Invasionsraum: invasion lodgment area.
Jabojagd: fighter-bomber hunt.
Jabostaffel: fighter-bomber squadron.
Jäger: originally, a hunter – now, also, a fighter pilot.
Jagdbomber (Jabo): fighter-bomber.

Jagdflieger: fighter pilot(s).

Jagdfliegerführer (Jafü): fighter command/control unit(s) or its commander. The Jafü originated as administrative units, but quickly evolved into operational control units.

Jagdgeschwader (JG): fighter wing, commanding three or four Gruppen. The authorized strength of JG 26 was 208 aircraft after the reorganization of 1 October 1943.

Jagdgruppe (JGr): fighter group, containing three or four Staffeln. The authorized strength of a JG 26 Gruppe was 68 aircraft after 1 October 1943.

Jagdstaffel: fighter squadron, containing twelve or sixteen aircraft (three or four Schwärme of four aircraft).

Jagdvorstoss: fighter strike.

Jagdwaffe: fighter arm or fighter force.

Kanalfront: (English) Channel Front.

Kanalgeschwader: the Geschwader serving on the English Channel (JG 2 and JG 26).

Kanaljäger: fighter pilot(s) based near the Channel.

Kapitän: "captain"; a command position rather than a rank.

Katschmarek: a slang term for wingman – originally a derogatory term for a dim-witted infantry recruit.

Kette: flight of three aircraft.

Kommandeur: "commander"; a command position rather than a rank.

Kommodore: "commodore"; a command position rather than a rank.

Luftflotte (LF): air fleet; corresponded to a numbered American Air Force.

Luftwaffe: "Air Force" – refers to the German Air Force.

Luftwaffen Befehlshaber Mitte (LBH Mitte): the German air defense command in the mid-war period; superseded by Luftflotte Reich.

Nachwuchs: "new growth" – the late-war crop of replacement pilots.

Oberkommando der Luftwaffe (OKL): the Luftwaffe High Command.

Oberkommando der Wehrmacht (OKW): the (German) Armed Forces High Command.

Pulk: "herd" – one or more combat boxes of heavy bombers.

Reich: "empire" – Hitler's Germany was "the Third Reich".

Reichsluftfahrtministerium (RLM): German Air Ministry; Goering's headquarters, it controlled all aspects of German aviation.

Reichsluftverteidigung (RLV): a general term for the German air defenses, including fighter units, antiaircraft units, ground control units, and the civil defense organization.

Rotte: tactical element of two aircraft.

Rottenflieger: wingman; the second man in a Rotte.

Rottenführer: leader of an element of two aircraft.

Schlageter: JG 26's honor title; commemorated Albert Leo Schlageter.

Schlachtflieger: ground-attack aircraft or unit.

Schnellkampfgeschwader (SKG): fast bomber wing (contained Bf 110, Bf 109, or FW 190 fighter-bombers).

Schwarm: flight of four aircraft (pl. **Schwärme**); the basic unit of all Jagdwaffe tactical formations.

Schwarmführer: flight leader.

Schwarzemann: "black man" – groundcrewman, so-called because of their black coveralls.

Sitzbereitschaft: "seated readiness" – cockpit readiness; the highest form of alert, with pilots seated in their cockpits for immediate takeoff.

Stab: staff.

Stabsschwarm: staff flight.

Staffel (St): squadron (pl. **Staffeln**).

Staffelführer: squadron leader (temporary or probationary).

Staffelkapitän: squadron leader – usually a Leutnant, Oberleutnant, or Hauptmann.

Störangriff: see Störungsangriff.

Störingsangriff: harassing attack or nuisance raid.

Strassenjagd: road hunt; a road patrol over enemy territory.

Werfergruppe: (rocket) launcher Gruppe; group equipped with W Gr 21rocket mortar tubes.

Werfereinsatz: rocket mortar mission.

Wehrmacht: armed forces – refers to the German Armed Forces.

Werkenummer (W.Nr.): aircraft serial number.

Vergeltungsangriff: vengeance raid.

Vorkommando: advance unit – comprised selected ground personnel who were sent ahead of a transferring unit to prepare its new base for operations.

Zerstörer: "destroyer" (heavy fighter) – Bf 110 or Me 410 twin-engined fighter.

Zerstörergeschwader (ZG): heavy fighter wing.

Zerstörergruppe (ZGr): heavy fighter group.

APPENDIX I

ORGANIZATION AND STRENGTH 1943 - 1945

Key
A/C Est, On Str, Serv: aircraft establishment, on strength, serviceable
Pilots Est, Pres, Ready, Ltd Duty: pilot establishment, present, ready for duty, available for limited duty only.

Unit	A/C Type	A/C			Pilots			
		Est	On Str	Serv	Est	Pres	Ready	Ltd Duty
1 January 1943								
Stab	Fw 190A-4	4	5	(5)	4	4	2	2
I. Gruppe	Fw 190A-4	40	34	(23)	40	43	27	14
II. Gruppe	Fw 190A-4	40	33	(26)	40	53	28	18
	Bf 109G-4		11	(7)				
*III. Gruppe	Bf 109G-4	40	2	(2)	40	48	35	12
	Bf 109G-1/R2		1	(0)				
	Fw 190A-4		35	(29)				
11. Staffel	Bf 109G-1+G-4	15	12	(8)	15	10	0	10
10.(Jabo) Staffel	Fw 190A-4/U3	15	14	(13)	15	13	12	1
31 March 1943								
Stab	Fw 190A-4+A-5	4	6	(4)	4	5	1	4
I. Gruppe (USSR)	Fw 190A-4+A-5	40	35	(24)	40	48	35	13
II. Gruppe	Fw 190A-4+A-5	40	42	(37)	40	48	31	17
*III. Gruppe	Bf 109G-4	40	4	(38*)	40	40	26	14
	Fw 190A-4+A-5		33					
7. Staffel (USSR)	Fw 190A-4+A-5		13					
11. Staffel	Bf 109G-1+G-3	17	17	(27)	17	11	6	5
	Fw 190A-4		10					
30 June 1943								
Stab	Fw 190A-5+A-6	4	10	(7)	4	4	2	0
I. Gruppe	Fw 190A-4+A-5	52	29	(25)	52	46	31	15
*II. Gruppe	Fw 190A-4, A-5, A-6	68	49	(61*)	68	45	31	6
10. Staffel	Fw 190A-4+A-5		17					
*III. Gruppe	Bf 109G-4+G-6	52	44	(33*)	52	38	25	7
8. Staffel	Fw 190A-4,A-5, A-6	16	11	(8)	16	12	7	2
11. Staffel	Bf 109G-3	16	13	(8)	16	13	7	0
30 September 1943								
Stab	Fw 190A-5+A-6	4	2	(2)	4	4	0	2
*I. Gruppe	Fw 190A-4,A-5, A-6	68	45	(31)	68	67	38	6
*II. Gruppe	Fw 190A-4,A-5, A-6	68	38	(33*)	68	59	36	20
10. Staffel	Fw 190A-5+A-6		7					
*III. Gruppe	Bf 109G-4+G-6	68	38	(34)*	68	65	39	4
11. Staffel	Bf 109G-3		6					
12. Staffel	Bf 109G-4		6					

Unit	A/C Type	A/C			Pilots			
		Est	On Str	Serv	Est	Pres	Ready	Ltd Duty
31 December 1943								
Stab	Fw 190A-4,A-5, A-6	4	4	(3)	4	3	2	0
I. Gruppe	Fw 190A-4,A-5, A-6	68	38	(27)	68	63	42	1
II. Gruppe	Fw 190A-4,A-5, A-6	68	32	(20)	68	65	38	8
III. Gruppe	Bf 109G-4, G-5, G-6	68	26	(18)	68	54	25	29
31 March 1944								
Stab	Fw 190A-6+A-7	4	3	(2)	4	3	2	1
I. Gruppe	Fw 190A-6+A-7	68	19	(15)	68	62	29	3
II. Gruppe	Fw 190A-6+A-7	68	23	(20)	68	59	22	13
III. Gruppe	Bf 109G-6	68	28	(20)	68	51	23	0
30 June 1944								
Stab	Fw 190A-7+A-8	4	3	(1)	4	4	2	0
I. Gruppe	Fw 190A-6,A-7, A-8	68	24	(10)	68	50	39	0
II. Gruppe	Fw 190A-6,A-7, A-8	68	14	(6)	68	43	23	0
III. Gruppe	Bf 109G-6	68	31	(18)	68	55	36	1
30 September 1944								
Stab	Fw 190A-7+A-8	4	2	(2)	4	2	2	0
I. Gruppe	Fw 190A-6,A-7, A-8	68	28	(18)	68	38	23	15
II. Gruppe	Fw 190A-6,A-7, A-8	68	29	(12)	68	49	25	24
III. Gruppe	Bf 109G-6	68	16	(8)	68	41	25	6
31 December 1944								
Stab	Fw 190A-8	4	1	(0)	4	4	1	3
	Fw 190D-9		2	(1)				
I. Gruppe	Fw 190A-8	68	3	(0)	68	52	41	11
	Fw 190D-9		49	(32)				
II. Gruppe	Fw 190D-9	68	39	(32)	68	50	41	6
III. Gruppe	Bf 109G-14	68	14	(7)	68	40	29	6
	Bf 109K-4		29	(13)	68	40	29	6
	Fw 190D-9		1	(1)				
III./JG 54	Fw 190D-9	68	49	(32)	68	51	44	7
9 April 1945								
Stab	Fw 190D-9	4	4	(3)	4	n/a	n/a	n/a
I. Gruppe	Fw 190D-9	52	44	(16)	52	n/a	n/a	n/a
II. Gruppe	Fw 190D-9	52	57	(29)	52	n/a	n/a	n/a
IV. Gruppe	Fw 190D-9	36	35	(15)	36	n/a	n/a	n/a

Notes:

1 Jan 43	III. Gruppe data include 7., 8., 9. Staffeln
31 Mar 43	III. Gruppe data include 7., 8., 9. Staffeln
30 Jun 43	II. Gruppe data include 4., 5., 6., 10. Staffeln
	III. Gruppe data include 7., 9., 12. Staffeln
30 Sep 43:	I. Gruppe data include 1., 2., 3., 8. Staffeln
	II. Gruppe data include 4., 5., 6., 10. Staffeln
	III. Gruppe data include 7., 9., 11., 12. Staffeln

APPENDIX II

UNIT COMMANDERS 1943 – 1945

Geschwader Kommodoren

06 Dec 41 – 1 0 Jan 43	Major Gerhard Schöpfel	transferred
11 Jan 43 – 27 Jan 45	Obst. Josef Priller	transferred
28 Jan 45 – 07 May 45	Major Franz Götz	

First Gruppe Kommandeure

11 Jul 41 – 31 May 43	Major Johannes Seifert	transferred
01 Jun 43 – 22 Jun 43	Major Fritz Losigkeit	transferred
23 Jun 43 – 14 May 44	Hptm. Karl Borris	off operations
15 May 44 – 31 Jul 44	Hptm. Hermann Staiger	interim, transferred
01 Aug 44 – 07 May 45	Major Karl Borris	

Second Gruppe Kommandeure

22 Jul 42 – 02 Jan 43	Hptm. Conny Meyer	transferred
03 Jan 43 – 17 Aug 43	Hptm. Wilhelm-Ferdinand Galland	KIA
18 Aug 43 – 08 Sep 43	Hptm. Johannes Naumann	interim
09 Sep 43 – 25 Nov 43	Obstlt. Johannes Seifert	KIA
26 Nov 43 – 01 Mar 44	Major Wilhelm Gäth	WIA, transferred
02 Mar 44 – 28 Jun 44	Hptm. Johannes Naumann	WIA, transferred
29 Jun 44 – 03 Sep 44	Hptm. Emil Lang	KIA
04 Sep 44 – 08 Oct 44	Hptm. Georg-Peter Eder	transferred
09 Oct 44 – 29 Jan 45	Major Anton Hackl	transferred
30 Jan 45 – 22 Feb 45	Oblt. Waldemar Radener	transferred
23 Feb 45 – 01 May 45	Hptm. Paul Schauder	POW

Third Gruppe Kommandeure

06 Dec 41 - 10 Jan 43	Hptm. Josef Priller	to CO JG 26
11 Jan 43 - 06 Apr 43	Hptm. Fritz Geisshardt	KIA
07 Apr 43 - 13 Jun 43	Hptm. Kurt Ruppert	KIA
15 Jun 43 - 04 Jul 43	Hptm. Rolf Hermichen	interim
05 Jul 43 - 17 Sep 44	Major Klaus Mietusch	KIA
18 Sep 44 - 26 Sep 44	Hptm. Paul Schauder	interim
27 Sep 44 -25 Mar 45	Hptm. Walter Krupinski	transferred

Fourth Gruppe Kommandeur

25 Feb 45 -17 Apr 45	Major Rudolf Klemm	transferred

1st Staffel Kapitäne (First Gruppe)

30 Oct 42 - 05 Jan 43	Oblt. Frans Nels	to III/JG 26
06 Jan 43 - 19 Jun 43	Hptm. Walter Höckner	transferred
20 Jun 43 - 06 Feb 44	Oblt. Artur Beese	KIA
07 Feb 44 - 28 Feb 44	Lt. Leberecht Altmann	interim
29 Feb 44 - 15 Mar 44	Lt. Johann-Hermann Meier	KAC
16 Mar 44 - 26 Apr 44	Oblt. Kurt Kranefeld	KAC
27 Apr 44 - 05 Jul 44	Oblt. Max Groth	KIA
06 Jul 44 - 14 Apr 45	Lt. Georg Kiefner	transferred
15 Apr 45 - 30 Apr 45	Lt. Xaver Ellenrieder	WIFA
01 May 45 - 07 May 45	Oblt. Peter Crump	

2nd Staffel Kapitäne (First Gruppe)

17 Mar 42 - 14 Mar 43	Hptm. Fülbert Zink	KIA
15 Mar 43 - 24 Nov 43	Major Wilhelm Gäth	to CO II/JG 26
25 Nov 43 - 08 Apr 44	Oblt. Karl Willius	KIA
09 Apr 44 - 11 May 44	Lt. Heinrich Schild	interim – to III/JG 26
12 May 44 - 01 Jan 45	Oblt. Franz Kunz	WIA – off operations
02 Jan 45 - 07 May 45	Lt. Waldemar Söffing	

3rd Staffel Kapitäne (First Gruppe)

01 May 42 - 12 Jun 43	Hptm. Rolf Hermichen	to CO III/JG 26
13 Jun 43 - 04 Jul 43	Oblt. Wolfgang Neu	to 4/JG 26
05 Jul 43 - 15 Oct 43	Major Rolf Hermichen	transferred
16 Oct 43 - 10 Jan 44	Oblt. Heinrich Jessen	KIFA
11 Jan 44 - 22 Jan 44	Lt. Herfried Kloimüller	interim
23 Jan 44 - 28 Mar 45	Oblt. Alfred Heckmann	to CO 5/JG 26
29 Mar 45 - 7 May 45	Oblt. Hans Dortenmann	

4th Staffel Kapitäne (Second Gruppe)

20 Dec 42 - 25 Feb 43	Hptm. Kurt Ebersberger	instructor duty
26 Feb 43 - 13 May 43	Oblt. Otto Stammberger	WIA – off operations
14 May 43 -	**renamed 5th Staffel – 01 Oct 43**	
01 Dec 43	Hptm. Helmut Hoppe	KIA
02 Dec 43 - 14 Jan 44	Hptm. Johann Aistleitner	KIA
15 Jan 44 - 24 Feb 44	Obfw. Adolf Glunz	to 6/JG 26
25 Feb 44 - 14 Aug 44	Hptm. Walter Matoni	transferred
15 Aug 44 - 14 Jan 45	Oblt. Gerhard Vogt	KIA
15 Jan 45 - 14 Feb 45	Oblt. Wilhelm Hofmann	interim
15 Feb 45 - 26 Mar 45	Oblt. Wilhelm Hofmann	KIA
29 Mar 45 - 16 Apr 45	Oblt. Alfred Heckmann	transferred
17 Apr 45 - 30 Apr 45	Lt. Peter Crump	to CO 1/JG 26
01 May 45 – 05 May 45	Oblt. Heinrich Schild	

5th Staffel Kapitäne (Second Gruppe)

05 May 42 - 02 Jan 43	Oblt. Wilhelm-Ferdinand Galland	to CO II/JG 26
03 Jan 43 -	**renamed 6th Staffel – 01 Oct 43**	
22 Feb 44	Hptm. Horst Sternberg	KIA
23 Feb 44 - 02 Mar 44	Lt. Friedrich Lange	KIA
03 Mar 44 - 10 Aug 44	Lt. Adolf Glunz	off operations
11 Aug 44 - 03 Sep 44	Hptm. Georg-Peter Eder	interim – to CO II/JG 26
04 Sep 44 - 18 Mar 45	Oblt. Adolf Glunz	transferred
18 Mar 45 - 25 Mar 45	Lt. Siegfried Sy	interim
26 Mar 45 - 05 May 45	Oblt. Gottfried Schmidt	

6th Staffel Kapitäne (Second Gruppe)

21 Sep 42 – 17 Aug 43	Hptm. Johannes Naumann	to CO II/JG 26
18 Aug 43 - 08 Sep 43	Oblt. Waldemar Radener	interim
09 Sep 43 -	**renamed 7th Staffel – 01 Oct 43**	
09 Feb 44	Hptm. Johannes Naumann	to CO II/JG 26
10 Feb 44 - 19 Jun 44	Oblt. Waldemar Radener	WIA
20 Jun 44 - 14 Aug 44	Lt. Gerhard Vogt	interim – to CO 5/JG 26
15 Aug 44 - 08 Sep 44	Lt. Hans Prager	interim – transferred
09 Sep 44 - 30 Jan 45	Oblt. Waldemar Radener	to CO II/JG 26
31 Jan 45 - 14 Apr 45	Lt. Gottfried Dietze	into hospital
15 Apr 45 - 05 May 45	Lt. Siegfried Sy	interim

7th Staffel Kapitäne (Third Gruppe)

18 Sep 41 - 29 Jun 43	Hptm. Klaus Mietusch	to CO III/JG 26
30 Jun 43 - 31 Jul 43	Hptm. Günther Kelch	KIA

04 Aug 43 -	**renamed 9th Staffel – 01 Oct 43**	
08 May 44	Hptm. Hans-Georg Dippel	KIFA
10 May 44 - 18 Jul 44	Oblt. Viktor Hilgendorff	KIA
19 Jul 44 - 25 Mar 45	Oblt. Gottfried Schmidt	to CO 6/JG 26

8th Staffel Kapitäne (Third Gruppe)
10 Nov 41 - 22 Jun 43	Oblt. Karl Borris	to CO I/JG 26
26 Jun 43 -	**renamed 4th Staffel – 01 Oct 43 – into First Gruppe**	
21 Oct 43	Hptm. Kurt Ebersberger	KIA
25 Oct 43 - 22 Apr 44	Hptm. Wolfgang Neu	KIA
23 Apr 44 - 04 Nov 44	Lt. Heinz Kemethmüller	WIFA
05 Nov 44 - 15 Feb 45	Lt. Waldemar Söffing	to CO 2/JG 26

9th Staffel Kapitäne (Third Gruppe)
12 Nov 40 - 06 Apr 43	Hptm. Kurt Ruppert	to CO III/JG 26
07 Apr 43 - 01 May 43	Hptm. Peter-Paul Steindl	to CO 11/JG 26
02 May 43 -	**renamed 10th Staffel – 01 Oct 43**	
22 Feb 45	Hptm. Paul Schauder	to CO II/JG 26
23 Feb 45 - 25 Mar 45	Oblt. Heinrich Schild	to 1/JG 26

10th (Jagdbomber) Staffel Kapitäne
| 20 Dec 42 - 24 Mar 43 | Oblt. Paul Keller | KIA |
| 25 Mar 43 – 15 Apr 43 | Oblt. Erwin Busch | became 14/SKG 10 |

10th Staffel Kapitäne (Second Gruppe)
01 May 43 -	**renamed 8th Staffel – 01 Oct 43**	
25 Feb 44	Hptm. Rudolf Leuschel	KIA
26 Feb 44 - 21 Oct 44	Lt. Wilhelm Hofmann	WAC
22 Oct 44 - 04 Jan 45	Lt. Wilhelm Mayer	interim – KIA
05 Jan 45 - 15 Feb 45	Oblt. Wilhelm Hofmann	to CO 5/JG 26

11th Staffel Kapitäne (Third Gruppe)
10 Dec 42 – 15 Jan 43	Lt. Paul Schauder	to Stab/JG 26
16 Jan 43 - 28 Apr 43	Hptm. Werner Patz	transferred
29 Apr 43 - 19 Jun 43	Oblt. Walter Otte	transferred
20 Jun 43 - 11 Jan 44	Hptm. Peter-Paul Steindl	to Stab I/JG 26
12 Jan 44 - 18 Dec 44	Oblt. Paul Reischer	suicide
19 Dec 44 - 20 Mar 45	Lt. Hermann Guhl	

12th Staffel Kapitäne (Third Gruppe)
11 Apr 43 - 04 Jul 43	Oblt. Erwin Leykauf	transferred
05 Jul 43 - 14 May 44	Hptm. Hermann Staiger	to interim CO I/JG 26
15 May 44 - 25 Mar 45	Oblt. Karl-Hermann Schrader	transferred

13th Staffel Kapitän (Fourth Gruppe)
| 25 Feb 45 - 17 Apr 45 | Lt. Peter Crump | to CO 5/JG 26 |

14th Staffel Kapitäne (Fourth Gruppe)
| 25 Feb 45 - 29 Mar 45 | Oblt. Hans Dortenmann | to CO 3/JG 26 |
| 30 Mar 45 - 17 Apr 45 | Lt. Hans Prager | transferred |

15th Staffel Kapitän (Fourth Gruppe)
| 25 Feb 45 - 05 Apr 45 | Oblt. Wilhelm Heilmann | POW |

APPENDIX III

BASES 1943 – 1945

Geschwader Stab

01 Jan 43 - 02 Aug 43	Lille-Vendeville
02 Aug 43 - 08 Sep 43	Amsterdam-Schipol
08 Sep 43 - 06 Jun 44	Lille-Nord
06 Jun 44 - 20 Jun 44	Poix-Nord
20 Jun 44 - 29 Jul 44	Chaumont-en-Vexin
29 Jul 44 - 16 Aug 44	Rambouillet
16 Aug 44 - 22 Aug 44	Chaumont-en-Vexin
22 Aug 44 - 29 Aug 44	Valenciennes
29 Aug 44 - 03 Sep 44	Brussels-Nord
03 Sep 44 - 29 Oct 44	Krefeld
29 Oct 44 - 24 Nov 44	Greven
24 Nov 44 - 25 Mar 45	Fürstenau
25 Mar 45 - 03 Apr 45	Drope
03 Apr 45 - 05 Apr 45	Delmenhorst
05 Apr 45 - 07 Apr 45	Hustedt
07 Apr 45 - 28 Apr 45	Uetersen
28 Apr 45 - 03 May 45	Klein-Kummersfeld
03 May 45 – 07 May 45	Flensburg

First Gruppe

20 Sep 42 - 22 Jan 43	St. Omer-Wizernes
27 Jan 43 - 02 Feb 43	Heiligenbeil
02 Feb 43 - 14 Mar 43	Rielbitzi
14 Mar 43 - 06 May 43	Dno
06 May 43 - 09 May 43	Rielbitzi
09 May 43 - 13 May 43	Smolensk + Schatalovka
13 May 43 - 20 May 43	Ossinovka
20 May 43 - 06 Jun 43	Orel-West + Schatalovka
07 Jun 43 - 10 Jun 43	Rheine
10 Jun 43 - 23 Jun 43	Poix-Nord
23 Jun 43 - 14 Jul 43	Rheine
14 Jul 43 - 31 Aug 43	Woensdrecht
31 Aug 43 - 18 Dec 43	Grimbergen
18 Dec 43 - 10 Apr 44	Florennes
10 Apr 44 - 27 Apr 44	Lille-Vendeville
27 Apr 44- 01 May 44	Cazaux
1 May 44 - 06 Jun 44	Lille-Vendeville
06 Jun 44 - 08 Jun 44	Cormeilles
08 Jun 44 - 29 Jul 44	Boissy-le-Bois
29 Jul 44 - 16 Aug 44	Rambouillet
16 Aug 44 - 21 Aug 44	Boissy-le-Bois
21 Aug 44 - 29 Aug 44	Vitry-en-Artois
29 Aug 44 - 03 Sep 44	Grimbergen
03 Sep 44 - 29 Oct 44	Krefeld-Linn
29 Oct 44 - 24 Nov 44	Greven
24 Nov 44 - 25 Mar 45	Fürstenau
25 Mar 45 - 02 Apr 45	Drope

02 Apr 45 - 05 Apr 45	Delmenhorst
05 Apr 45 - 07 Apr 45	Hustedt
07 Apr 45 - 13 Apr 45	Stade + Uetersen
13 Apr 45 - 28 Apr 45	Sülte
28 Apr 45 - 02 May 45	Klein-Kummersfeld
02 May 45 - 07 May 45	Flensburg

Second Gruppe

22 Dec 41 - 08 Jan 43	Abbeville-Drucat
08 Jan 43 - 28 Jul 43	Vitry-en-Artois
28 Jul 43 - 06 Aug 43	Deelen
06 Aug 43 - 15 Aug 43	Volkel
15 Aug 43 - 02 Oct 43	Beauvais-Tillé
02 Oct 43 - 17 Mar 44	Cambrai-Epinoy
17 Mar 44 - 17 Apr 44	Cambrai-Sud
17 Apr 44 - 25 Apr 44	Cazaux
25 Apr 44 - 15 May 44	Cambrai-Sud
15 May 44 - 06 Jun 44	Mont-de-Marsan
06 Jun 44 - 13 Jul 44	Guyancourt
13 Jul 44 - 12 Aug 44	Reinsehlen
12 Aug 44 - 16 Aug 44	Guyancourt
16 Aug 44 - 29 Aug 44	Mons-en-Chausée
29 Aug 44 - 03 Sep 44	Melsbroek
03 Sep 44 - 22 Nov 44	Kirchhellen + Coesfeld
22 Nov 44 - 25 Mar 45	Nordhorn
25 Mar 45 - 06 Apr 45	Bissel
06 Apr 45 - 30 Apr 45	Uetersen
30 Apr 45 - 02 May 45	Neumünster
02 May 45 - 05 May 45	Husum

Third Gruppe

07 Apr 42 - 14 May 43	Wevelgem
14 May 43 - 18 May 43	Lille-Nord
18 May 43 - 23 May 43	Wevelgem
23 May 43 - 13 Aug 43	Nordholz
13 Aug 43 - 08 Sep 43	Amsterdam-Schipol
08 Sep 43 - 22 Oct 43	Lille-Vendeville
22 Oct 43 - 13 Nov 43	Bönninghardt
13 Nov 43 - 09 Jan 44	Mönchen-Gladbach
09 Jan 44 - 16 Mar 44	Lille-Vendeville + Denain
16 Mar 44 - 18 Apr 44	Étain
18 Apr 44 - 27 Apr 44	Neubiberg
27 Apr 44 - 14 May	Étain
14 May 44 - 06 Jun 44	Nancy
06 Jun 44 - 07 Jun 44	Cormeilles
07 Jun 44 - 16 Aug 44	Villacoublay-Nord
16 Aug 44 - 29 Aug 44	Rosières
29 Aug 44 - 02 Sep 44	Chièvres
02 Aug 44 - 03 Sep 44	Brussels-Evere
03 Sep 44 - 08 Oct 44	Mönchen-Gladbach
08 Oct 44 - 13 Oct 44	Bönninghardt + Lette
13 Oct 44 - 31 Oct 44	Gross-Reken + Lette
31 Oct 44 - 14 Mar 45	Plantlünne
14 Mar 45 - 25 Mar 45	Delmenhorst – disbanded

Fourth Gruppe

25 Feb 45 - 25 Mar 45	Varrelbusch
25 Mar 45 - 03 Apr 45	Bissel
03 Apr 45 - 05 Apr 45	Varrelbusch
05 Apr 45 - 10 Apr 45	Dedelsdorf

10 Apr 45 - 17 Apr 45   Klein-Kummersfeld – disbanded

7th Staffel (on Eastern Front)

17 Feb 43 - 28 Feb 43	Heiligenbeil
28 Feb 43 - 10 Jul 43	Krasnovardeisk-Gatschina
10 Jul 43 -	returned to III/JG 26 at Nordholz

8th/4th Staffel (in Führungsverband)

07 Apr 42 - 02 Apr 43	Wevelgem (8th Staffel in Third Gruppe)
02 Apr 43 - 08 Sep 43	Lille-Vendeville (into Geschwadergruppe)
08 Sep 43 - 06 Jun 44	Lille-Nord + Wevelgem (4th Staffel from 1 Oct 43)
06 Jun 44 -	joined First Gruppe for operations

10th (Jagdbomber) Staffel

18 Dec 42 -15 Apr 43	St. Omer-Wizernes – became 14/SKG 10

11th (Endausbildungs) Staffel

10 Dec 42 -15 Jun 43	Wevelgem
15 Jun 43 -16 Aug 43	Lille-Vendeville
16 Aug 43 -8 Sep 43	Lille-Nord
8 Sep 43 -	joined Third Gruppe for operations

APPENDIX IV

JG 26 VICTORY CLAIMS 1939 – 1945

The following list contains all JG 26 victory claims presently known in alphabetical order of claimant. "Claim #" is the sequential number of the pilot's claim as documented in the unit at the time or by later research, which has required adjustments in a few instances owing to delays by the German Air Ministry (RLM) in confirming or rejecting claims. Not all Third and Fourth Gruppe claims can be assigned claim numbers, owing to the lack of comprehensive lists for these Gruppen. A blank in this column together with a "no" in the "Conf" column means that the claim was never filed by the unit, but has been established by contemporary evidence such as logbook entries, news releases, or eyewitness testimony. The "Place" column includes the Jagdwaffe map coordinates, where available. The unit of the "Opponent" is the author's best estimate. It should not be inferred that this opposing aircraft was actually destroyed; that judgment is made in most cases in the text of the War Diary. The notations in the Confirmation ("Conf") column are conservative: a "yes" means that the number of the confirmation document issued by the RLM is known; a "no" means that either the claim was not filed or is known to have been rejected by the Geschwader or the RLM; cases whose dispositions are unknown are noted as "unk". A fourth category, "i.O.", is taken directly from the newly-located RLM claims microfilms. The exact meaning of these initials is not known, but it was marked on claims with a good chance of ultimate confirmation, and probably means either in Ordnung (in order) or im Ordner (with the supervisor).

Date	Rank	Name	Unit	Cl #	Aircraft	Place	Time	Opponent	Conf
24-08-40	Uffz.	Adam B.	2	1	Hurricane	W of Dover			unk
06-09-40	Uffz.	Adam B.	2		Hurricane	N of Rye	1020	601 Sqd	unk
17-07-41	Uffz.	Adam H-G.	2	1	Spitfire	S Cassel	2100		yes
17-09-41	Uffz.	Adam H-G.	2	2	Spitfire	NW of Dunkirk	1543		yes
21-09-41	Uffz.	Adam H-G.	2	3	Spitfire	3km NW of Étaples	1635	Tangmere	yes
13-03-42	Fw.	Adam H-G.	2	4	Spitfire	40km SW of Dunkirk	1610	303 Sqd	yes
19-08-42	Fw.	Adam H-G.	2	5	Spitfire	5km NE of Dieppe			unk
16-03-43	Uffz.	Adam III	3	1	LaGG-3	USSR (PQ 18872)			yes
11-10-40	Hptm.	Adolph	II CO	10	Spitfire	Maidstone	1738	41 Sqd	yes
11-10-40	Hptm.	Adolph	II CO	11	Spitfire	Maidstone	1738	41 Sqd	yes
15-10-40	Hptm.	Adolph	II CO	12	Hurricane	London	1410	46 or 501 Sqd	yes
25-10-40	Hptm.	Adolph	II CO	13	Spitfire	Maidstone	1104	603 Sqd	yes
01-11-40	Hptm.	Adolph	II CO	14	Spitfire	Maidstone	1250	74 Sqd	yes
08-11-40	Hptm.	Adolph	II CO	15	Spitfire	Tonbridge	1450	302 or 501 Sqd	yes
17-06-41	Hptm.	Adolph	II CO	16	Hurricane	Boulogne	1950	56 or 242 Sqd	yes
22-06-41	Hptm.	Adolph	II CO	17	Spitfire	Gravelines	1600	609 or 611 Sqd	yes
26-06-41	Hptm.	Adolph	II CO	18	Spitfire	Mardyck	1155		yes
06-07-41	Hptm.	Adolph	II CO	19	Spitfire	Wormhout	1445	74 Sqd	yes
08-07-41	Hptm.	Adolph	II CO	20	Spitfire	Gravelines	1530		yes
23-07-41	Hptm.	Adolph	II CO	21	Blenheim	Ostend	1420	21 Sqd	yes
24-07-41	Hptm.	Adolph	II CO	22	Spitfire	Gravelines	1455		unk
16-08-41	Hptm.	Adolph	II CO	24	Spitfire	20km NW of Boulogne	0930	602 Sqd	yes
16-08-41	Hptm.	Adolph	II CO	23	Spitfire	8km N of Marquise	1930	609 Sqd	unk
11-04-43	Fw.	Ahrens	3	2	LaGG-3	USSR (PQ 18241)			yes
13-05-43	Fw.	Ahrens	3	3	Pe-2	USSR (PQ 35481)			yes
31-05-43	Fw.	Ahrens	3	4	Il-2	USSR (PQ 16362)			yes
25-07-43	Fw.	Ahrens	3	5	Spitfire IX	near Vlissingen (KG9)	1515	122 Sqd	yes
28-07-43	Fw.	Ahrens	3	6	B-17-HSS	near Dordrecht (IL8-KL2)	1207	92 BG	unk
17-08-43	Fw.	Ahrens	3	7	B-17	NW of Antwerp (LJ8)	1131	385 BG	yes
17-08-43	Fw.	Ahrens	3	8	B-17	Oostende (N Antwerp)	1530	381 BG	unk
05-11-43	Fw.	Ahrens	3	9	B-17	Vierlingsbeek (KN4)	1403	92 BG	yes
26-11-44	Lt.	Ahrens	3	10	P-51	Osnabrück	1130	364 FG	unk
23-12-44	Lt.	Ahrens	3	11	B-26	Aachen (PN7)	1130		unk
17-06-41	Lt.	Aistleitner	1	1	Hurricane	NW of Boulogne	1947	56 or 242 Sqd	yes

Date	Rank	Name		No.	Type	Location	Time	Unit	Conf.
08-07-41	Lt.	Aistleitner	1	2	Spitfire	10km NW of Cap Gris Nez	0640		unk
23-07-41	Lt.	Aistleitner	1	3	Spitfire	10km W of Gravelines	1400		yes
21-08-41	Lt.	Aistleitner	1	4	Spitfire	N of Calais	1030		unk
28-02-42	Lt.	Aistleitner	1	5	Spitfire	20km NE of Margate		401 Sqd	unk
26-04-42	Lt.	Aistleitner	1	6	Spitfire	10-15km NW of Cap Blanc Nez	1435	411 Sqd	yes
17-05-42	Lt.	Aistleitner	III St	7	Spitfire	15km NW of Calais	1143	313 Sqd	yes
01-06-42	Lt.	Aistleitner	III St	8	Spitfire	unknown	1351	350 Sqd	yes
01-06-42	Lt.	Aistleitner	III St	9	Spitfire	unknown	1843		yes
29-08-42	Lt.	Aistleitner	III St	10	Spitfire	unknown			unk
03-02-43	Lt.	Aistleitner	8	11	Hudson	NW of Gravelines Ventura	1527	464 Sqd	yes
21-01-44	Lt.	Altmann	1	1	B-24	near Poix	1530	44 BG	yes
21-02-45	Lt.	Andel	7	1	B-26	Ahaus (HP4)	1604	394 BG	unk
21-02-45	Lt.	Andel	7	2	B-26	WNW of Ahaus(HO6)	1607	394 BG	unk
01-03-45	Lt.	Andel	7	3	P-47	near Mönchen-Gladbach	0936	366 FG	unk
01-03-45	Lt.	Andel	7	4	P-47	near Mönchen-Gladbach	0937	366 FG	unk
05-03-45	Lt.	Andel	7	5	Auster	near Krefeld	1252		unk
09-03-45	Lt.	Andel	7	6	P-47	near Wesel	1649	366 FG	unk
10-04-44	Uffz.	Ayerle	12		Mosquito	N of Verdun (TL6)	1705	540 Sqd	yes
24-04-44	Uffz.	Ayerle	12		P-51	N of München (CD)	1405	355 FG	unk
17-04-41	Uffz.	Babenz	3	1	Beaufort	Channel -N of Brest	1800	105 Sqd	yes
28-06-41	Uffz.	Babenz	3	2	Spitfire	W of Lille	0825	303 Sqd	yes
11-07-41	Fw.	Babenz	3	3	Spitfire	10km NW of Gravelines	1630		unk
12-08-41	Fw.	Babenz	3	4	Spitfire	S of Goeree Is.	1320	19 or 152 Sqd	yes
21-08-41	Fw.	Babenz	3	5	Spitfire	SE of Dunkirk	1510		yes
27-08-41	Fw.	Babenz	3	6	Spitfire	W of Gravelines	0810		yes
13-10-41	Fw.	Babenz	3	7	Spitfire	10km E of Dungeness	1443		yes
08-11-41	Fw.	Babenz	3	8	Spitfire	near Montreuil	1229	401 Sqd	yes
12-02-42	Fw.	Babenz	3	9	Spitfire	30km N of Dunkirk	1550		yes
08-03-42	Fw.	Babenz	3	10	Spitfire	SE of Bergues	1721	121 Sqd	no
28-03-42	Fw.	Babenz	3	11	Spitfire	Cap Blanc Nez	1858	457 or 602 Sqd	yes
29-03-42	Fw.	Babenz	3	12	Spitfire	10km SE of Dungeness	1705	401 Sqd	yes
30-04-42	Fw.	Babenz	3	13	Spitfire	2km W of Somme Estuary	1938	129 or 340 Sqd	yes
25-05-42	Fw.	Babenz	1	14	Spitfire	near Nieuport	1140	222 Sqd	yes
29-05-42	Fw.	Babenz	1	15	Spitfire	Channel	0820	72 Sqd	yes
01-06-42	Fw.	Babenz	1	16	Spitfire	PQ 22456	1350	65 or 111 Sqd	yes
02-06-42	Fw.	Babenz	1	17	Spitfire	15km W of Somme Estuary	1105	403 Sqd	yes
30-07-42	Fw.	Babenz	3	18	Spitfire	near Watten			yes
19-08-42	Obfw.	Babenz	11H	19	Spitfire	NE of Dieppe			unk
19-08-42	Obfw.	Babenz	11H	20	Spitfire	NE of Dieppe	0952	411, 485 or 610 Sqd	yes
19-08-42	Obfw.	Babenz	11H	21	Spitfire	NE of Dieppe	1330		yes
28-11-42	Ofhr.	Babenz	11H		P-38	20km W of Mateur	1541		yes
19-03-45	Obfw.	Backhaus	1	1	P-51	Fürstenau			flak
19-08-41	Uffz.	Bartels	1/E	1	Spitfire	unknown			unk
27-08-41	Uffz.	Bartels	1/E	2	Spitfire	unknown			unk
25-09-44	Ofhr.	Bartels	11		Spitfire	N of Arnhem (HM8-9)	1735	416 Sqd	yes
23-07-41	Uffz.	Barthel	5	1	Blenheim	Ostend	1409	21 Sqd	yes
22-02-44	Uffz.	Baumann	8	1	B-17	S of Münster (JQ7)	1305	91 or 384 BG	yes
13-04-44	Uffz.	Beck	11	10	B-17-HSS	NE of Karlsruhe	1554		unk
24-07-41	Lt.	Beese	III St	1	Spitfire	unknown	1438		yes
12-08-41	Lt.	Beese	III St	2	Spitfire	unknown	1150		yes
08-03-42	Lt.	Beese	1	3	Spitfire	near Dunkirk	1715	N Weald	yes
05-05-42	Lt.	Beese	1	4	Spitfire	N of Hazebrouck	1540	122 Sqd	yes
09-05-42	Lt.	Beese	1	5	Spitfire	4km N of Ardres	1340	350 or 457 Sqd	yes
23-09-42	Lt.	Beese	1	6	Spitfire	5km W of Cap Gris Nez			yes
17-02-43	Lt.	Beese	1	7	P-40	USSR (PQ 18463)			yes
21-02-43	Lt.	Beese	1	8	P-40	USSR (PQ 18264)			yes
04-03-43	Lt.	Beese	1	9	Il-2	USSR (PQ 18217)			yes
14-03-43	Lt.	Beese	1	10	Il-2	USSR (PQ 19848)			yes
24-03-43	Lt.	Beese	1	11	Pe-2	USSR (PQ 18574)	0728		yes
03-04-43	Lt.	Beese	1	12	Il-2	USSR (PQ 18251)			unk
14-05-43	Oblt.	Beese	1	13	Pe-2	USSR (PQ 54242)			yes
25-07-43	Oblt.	Beese	1 CO	14	Spitfire	N of Ghent (in sea) (LH5)	1511	165 Sqd	yes
15-08-43	Oblt.	Beese	1 CO	15	P-47	Vlissingen -N Sea (KG9)	1157	453 Sqd Spitfire	yes
17-08-43	Oblt.	Beese	1 CO	16	B-17	near Berendrecht (LI8)	1135		yes
17-08-43	Oblt.	Beese	1 CO	17	B-17	N of Louvain (ML)	1450	385 BG	yes 1/2
07-09-43	Oblt.	Beese	1 CO	18	P-47	W of Rotterdam (IJ9)	1003	4 FG	yes
01-12-43	Oblt.	Beese	1 CO	19	B-17	W of Ostend (LE3)	1330		yes
11-01-44	Oblt.	Beese	1 CO	20	B-17	Zuider Zee	1300	482 BG	yes
21-01-44	Oblt.	Beese	1 CO	21	B-24	near Poix	1530	44 BG	yes
21-01-44	Oblt.	Beese	1 CO	22	B-24	near Poix	1530	44 BG	yes
25-08-44	Ofhr.	Benz	6	1	P-38	SW of Beauvais (TE4-5)	1342	474 FG	yes
17-09-44	Ofhr.	Benz	6	2	Mustang	Krefeld (KO1-4)	1808	19 or 65 Sqd	yes

25-09-44	Ofhr.	Benz	6	3	Spitfire	Arnhem (LM4-9)	1754	416 or 441 Sqd	yes
27-09-44	Ofhr.	Benz	6	4	Spitfire	Nijmegen (JM1-3)	1040		yes
02-10-44	Ofhr.	Benz	6	5	Spitfire	Nijmegen (JM7-8)	1216	401 Sqd	i.O.
16-10-44	Ofhr.	Benz	6	6	Auster	Düren (NN7-8)	1410	101 A/B Div L-4	i.O
11-05-40	Maj.	Berg v.	III CO	1	Curtiss H75	unknown	1745	GC I/4	yes
29-05-40	Maj.	Berg v.	III CO	2	Spitfire	W of Dunkirk	1810	64, 229 or 610 Sqd	yes
31-05-40	Maj.	Berg v.	III CO	3	Hurricane	SW of Dunkirk	1540	213 or 264 Sqd	yes
31-05-40	Maj.	Berg v.	III CO	4	Lysander	unknown	2020		yes
16-08-44	Obl.	Bertels	II St	1	P-51	Rambouillet (AD)	1532	354 FG	yes
11-05-40	Oblt.	Beyer	7 CO	1	Curtiss H75	NE of Antwerp	1730	GC I/4	yes
28-05-40	Oblt.	Beyer	7 CO	2	Hurricane	Ostend	1230	213, 229 or 242 Sqd	yes
31-05-40	Oblt.	Beyer	7 CO	3	Hurricane	Dunkirk	1540	213 or 264 Sqd	yes
25-07-40	Oblt.	Beyer	7 CO	4	Spitfire	S of Dover		54 or 64 Sqd	unk
11-08-40	Oblt.	Beyer	7 CO		balloon	Dover	1130	n/a	no
14-08-40	Oblt.	Beyer	7 CO	5	Spitfire	Dover	1335	65 or 610 Sqd	unk
15-08-40	Oblt.	Beyer	7 CO	6	Spitfire	E of Dover	1230	54 Sqd	unk
15-08-40	Oblt.	Beyer	7 CO	7	Spitfire	Folkestone	1945	54 or 266 Sqd	unk
02-07-41	Hptm.	Bieber	I St	1	Blenheim	S of Maerville	1235	226 Sqd	yes
09-08-41	Lt.	Biedermann	9	2	Spitfire	unknown			unk
14-08-41	Lt.	Biedermann	9	3	Spitfire	unknown	1835	306 or 308 Sqd	yes
10-05-40	Fw.	Biegert	2	1	Koolhoven FK 58	SE of Rotterdam	0625	0 in serv	yes
11-05-40	Fw.	Biegert	2	2	Morane 406	S of Antwerp	1810		yes
27-09-41	Obfw.	Bierwirth	5	1	Spitfire	10km NW of Calais	1540		unk
28-03-42	Obfw.	Bierwirth	5	2	Spitfire	Cap Gris Nez	1900	457 or 602 Sqd	yes
08-04-42	Obfw.	Bierwirth	5	3	Spitfire	8km N of Calais	0815	64 Sqd	yes
05-06-42	Obfw.	Bierwirth	5	4	Spitfire	Somme Estuary	1545	133 or 401 Sqds	unk
31-07-42	Obfw.	Bierwirth	5	5	Spitfire	Somme Estuary	1500	121 or 332 Sqd	yes
19-08-42	Obfw.	Bierwirth	5	6	Spitfire	N of Dieppe	0643	340 Sqd	yes
24-08-42	Obfw.	Bierwirth	5	7	Spitfire	St. Valery en Caux	1730	402 Sqd	unk
27-08-42	Obfw.	Bierwirth	5	8	Spitfire	NE of Rue	1339	350 Sqd	yes
24-03-42	Gefr.	Birke	4	1	Spitfire	S of Hurt	1640	19 Sqd	yes
20-06-42	Uffz.	Birke	4	2	Spitfire	Calais-Marck	1556	118 or 501 Sqd	yes
28-06-42	Uffz.	Birke	4	3	Spitfire	SE of Hastings	2115	611 Sqd	unk
31-07-42	Uffz.	Birke	4	4	Spitfire	W ofBerck-sur-Mer	1504	121 or 332 Sqd	yes
26-04-45	Ofhr.	Birkner	2	1	Yak-3	SE of Prenzlau	1915		unk
26-04-45	Lt.	Blickle	3	1	Yak-3	SE of Prenzlau	1915		unk
18-05-40	Lt.	Blohm	6	1	Morane 405/6	Douai	1630		yes
02-06-40	Lt.	Blohm	6	2	Hurricane	Dunkirk	0920	32 Sqd	yes
03-05-43	Lt.	Blömertz	4	1	Mosquito	80km NNW of Fécamp	1345	540 Sqd	unk
23-09-40	Uffz.	Bluder	4	1	Spitfire	Folkestone	1105		yes
14-05-40	Lt.	Blume	7	1	Hurricane	Brussels	1845	504 Sqd	yes
08-06-40	Lt.	Blume	7	2	Hurricane	Dunkirk			unk
14-06-40	Lt.	Blume	7	3	Battle	Dreux	1740	12 or 103 Sqd	yes
25-07-40	Lt.	Blume	7	4	Spitfire	Dover	1635	54 or 64 Sqd	yes
15-08-40	Lt.	Blume	7	5	Spitfire	E of Dover	1555	64 Sqd	yes
16-08-40	Lt.	Blume	7	6	Spitfire	W of Calais			unk
17-04-45	Ogfr.	Böcker	1	1	Tempest	SW of Lübeck	1130	80 Sqd	unk
24-02-44	Uffz.	Böckl	12		B-17	NW of Lingen (FP1)	1230	92 or 306 BG	yes
25-02-44	Uffz.	Böckl	12		B-17	6km N of Rethel	1210		yes
01-04-44	Uffz.	Böckl	12		B-24	NW of Reims	1150	93 BG	yes
13-04-44	Uffz.	Böckl	12	5	B-17	unknown			unk
24-04-44	Uffz.	Böckl	12		B-17	S of München (ED4-5)	1345		yes
24-04-44	Uffz.	Böckl	12		B-17	N of Murnau (EC7-FC1)	1400		yes
25-05-44	Uffz.	Böckl	12		P-47	Nancy-Essey a/f-S of Neufchateau	0843	356 FG	yes
28-07-44	Uffz.	Böckl	12		Mitchell	Lisieux (UA)	2008		unk
06-08-44	Uffz.	Böckl	12		Halifax	N of Paris(UF7-UE9)	1210		unk
12-09-44	Fw.	Böckl	12		P-38	W of Bonn (OO1)	1605	474 FG	yes
03-09-40	Hptm.	Bode	II CO	1	Spitfire	Margate	1104	603 Sqd	yes
03-09-40	Hptm.	Bode	II CO	2	Spitfire	Margate	1108	603 Sqd	unk
06-09-40	Hptm.	Bode	II CO	3	Spitfire	Redhill	1010	234 Sqd	yes
05-03-43	Lt.	Boer	3	1	Pe-2	USSR (PQ 1836)			yes
15-03-44	Fw.	Böhm	7	1	Spitfire	30km NE of Amiens	1054	401 Sqd	yes
07-08-41	Uffz.	Bohn	3	1	Spitfire	10km SE of Calais	1130	19 or 401 Sqds	yes
07-09-41	Uffz.	Bohn	3	2	Spitfire	10km SE of Boulogne	1720	71 Sqd	yes
04-04-42	Fw.	Bohn	3	3	Spitfire	10km SW ofSt. Omer	1135	303 Sqd	yes
12-04-42	Fw.	Bohn	3	4	Spitfire	5km NE ofSt. Omer	1340	41 Sqd	yes
24-04-42	Fw.	Bohn	3	5	Spitfire	near Calais	1504	72 or 124 Sqd	yes
25-07-42	Uffz.	Börner	9	1	Defiant	N of Dunkirk	1430	277 Sqd	yes
17-08-44	Uffz.	Borreck	5	1	Spitfire	NW of Rouen (SB4)	1623	1 Sqd	yes
18-08-44	Uffz.	Borreck	5	2	Mustang	Beauvais (TE1)	0823	315 Sqd	unk
18-08-44	Uffz.	Borreck	5	3	P-47	Beauvais (TE6)	1330	356 FG	unk
17-09-44	Uffz.	Borreck	5	4	Mustang	Nijmegen(JN6-JO4)	1801	65 Sqd	unk

Date	Rank	Name			Aircraft	Location	Time	Unit	
19-09-44	Uffz.	Borreck	5	5	P-51	Nijmegen (JN4-6)	1802	357 FG	yes
06-11-44	Uffz.	Borreck	5		P-47	Eschweiler	1213	36 FG	no
01-06-40	Lt.	Borris	5	1	Spitfire	Dunkirk	1242		unk
02-06-40	Lt.	Borris	5	2	Spitfire	Dunkirk	0910	66, 266 or 611Sqd	yes
13-08-40	Lt.	Borris	5	3	Hurricane	Maidstone-Detling	1705	56 Sqd	yes
13-08-40	Lt.	Borris	5	4	Hurricane	Maidstone-Detling	1707	56 Sqd	unk
06-09-40	Lt.	Borris	4	5	Hurricane	Folkestone	0955	501 Sqd	unk
25-10-40	Lt.	Borris	4	6	Spitfire	Maidstone	1104	603 Sqd	yes
09-08-41	Lt.	Borris	6	7	Spitfire	Campagne	1830	403 Sqd	yes
20-09-41	Oblt.	Borris	6	8	Spitfire	Mardyck	1657		yes
21-09-41	Oblt.	Borris	6	9	Spitfire	Étaples	1630	315 Sqd	yes
13-03-42	Oblt.	Borris	8 CO	10	Spitfire	unknown	1609	602 Sqd	yes
04-04-42	Oblt.	Borris	8 CO	11	Spitfire	unknown	1140		yes
04-04-42	Oblt.	Borris	8 CO	12	Spitfire	3km N of Sangatte	1146		yes
15-04-42	Oblt.	Borris	8 CO	13	Spitfire	E of Cap Gris Nez	1904	222 Sqd	yes
17-04-42	Oblt.	Borris	8 CO	14	Spitfire	unknown	1614	121Sqd	yes
24-04-42	Oblt.	Borris	8 CO	15	Spitfire	75km WNW of Ostend	1450	122 Sqd	yes
28-04-42	Oblt.	Borris	8 CO	16	Spitfire	S of Gravelines	1134	121, 222 or 317 Sqd	unk
28-04-42	Oblt.	Borris	8 CO	17	Spitfire	unknown	1159	401 Sqd	yes
17-05-42	Oblt.	Borris	8 CO	18	Spitfire	6km NW of Sangatte	1150	64 or 122 Sqd	yes
01-06-42	Oblt.	Borris	8 CO	19	Spitfire	8km N of La Panne	1358	71 or 350 Sqd	unk
30-07-42	Oblt.	Borris	8 CO	20	Spitfire	unknown	1920		yes
19-08-42	Oblt.	Borris	8 CO	21	Spitfire	Dieppe	1015	19 or 121 Sqd	yes
03-02-43	Hptm.	Borris	8 CO		Spitfire	N of Poperinghe	1521	416 Sqd	yes
03-02-43	Hptm.	Borris	8 CO		Spitfire	Poperinghe-Bergues	1521	416 Sqd	yes
07-02-43	Hptm.	Borris	8 CO		Typhoon	Staden	1446	609 Sqd	yes
04-04-43	Hptm.	Borris	8 CO		B-17	Rouen-Dieppe	1440	303 or 305 BG	yes
25-07-43	Hptm.	Borris	I CO	27	Spitfire	N of Ghent (LH9-8)	1504	165 Sqd	yes
25-07-43	Hptm.	Borris	I CO	28	Spitfire	N of Ghent (LH2-1)	1509	165 Sqd	yes
17-08-43	Hptm.	Borris	I CO	29	B-17	10km E of Deest (NL2)	1130	94 BG	yes
19-09-43	Hptm.	Borris	I CO	30	Spitfire	E of Ipswich (N Sea) (HF1)	1252	91 Sqd	yes
07-01-44	Hptm.	Borris	I CO	31	P-47	nr Cousolre		358 FG	yes
11-01-44	Hptm.	Borris	I CO	32	B-17	Nordhorn-Zuider Zee	1300	306 BG	yes
29-01-44	Hptm.	Borris	I CO	33	B-17	E of Bonn (NQ-OP)			yes
08-02-44	Hptm.	Borris	I CO	34	P-47	E of St. Quentin? (RH-RJ)	1115	352 FG	yes
24-02-44	Hptm.	Borris	I CO	35	P-47	N of Rheine	1305	56 FG	yes
06-03-44	Hptm.	Borris	I CO		P-47	SW of Oldenburg (EQ 3-9)	1435	356 FG	unk
08-03-44	Hptm.	Borris	I CO	36	Spitfire	E of Utrecht	1650	332 Sqd	yes
19-04-44	Major	Borris	I CO	37	Spitfire	ENE of Mechelen	1905	310 or 312 Sqd	unk
14-07-44	Major	Borris	I CO	38	P-47	W of Paris (UB9,UC7,AC1)	1436	358 FG	yes
26-08-44	Major	Borris	I CO	39	Spitfire	Rouen (TC2)	0932	602 Sqd	yes
16-09-44	Major	Borris	I CO	40	P-38	Bonn (NN8)	1740	370FG	yes
23-09-44	Major	Borris	I CO	41	P-51	Wesel (KP)	1709	339 FG	yes
05-12-44	Major	Borris	I CO	42	B-17	W of Lingen	1335	452 BG	yes
14-01-45	Major	Borris	I CO	43	Spitfire	Ibbenbüren	1545	331 or 332 Sqd	unk
24-08-40	Uffz.	Braun	6	1	Spitfire	Southend	1645	54 or 65 Sqd	no
11-10-42	Uffz.	Bremer	3	1	Spitfire	15km SSE of Dunkirk	1535	64 Sqd	yes
16-05-40	Uffz.	Brügelmann	8	1	Spitfire	Mureaux	1345		yes
05-12-40	Fw.	Brügelmann	8	2	Hurricane	W of Hastings			unk
12-01-41	Fw.	Brügelmann	8	3	Hurricane	W of Boulogne	1515	242 Sqd	yes
05-09-42	Uffz.	Budde	6	1	Spitfire	W of Cayeux	1132	64 or 340 Sqd	yes
01-01-45	Uffz.	Burckhardt G.	8	1	Spitfire	over Brussels	0926	416 Sqd	unk
17-08-43	Lt.	Burkert E.	7	1	B-17	Eindhoven (LL7)	1142		yes
20-10-43	Lt.	Burkert E.	9	2	B-17	unknown		96 BG	yes
28-05-40	Uffz.	Burkhardt A.	3	1	Spitfire	between Dover & Ostend	1042	616 Sqd	yes
27-09-44	Uffz.	Burmeister	4	1	Spitfire	Nijmegen (JN)	1025	411 Sqd	yes
28-09-39	Lt.	Bürschgens	2	1	Curtiss H75	near Tündorf	1730	GC II/5	unk
09-06-40	Lt.	Bürschgens	7	2	Morane 406	Mantes	1515	GC 1/145	yes
25-07-40	Lt.	Bürschgens	7	3	Spitfire	Dover		54 or 64 Sqd	unk
14-08-40	Lt.	Bürschgens	7	4	Spitfire	Dover	1340	65 or 610 Sqd	yes
15-08-40	Lt.	Bürschgens	7	5	Spitfire	E of Dover	1230	54 Sqd	unk
15-08-40	Lt.	Bürschgens	7	6	Spitfire	E of Dover	1555	64 Sqd	yes
18-08-40	Lt.	Bürschgens	7	7	Hurricane	Canterbury	1405	17 Sqd	yes
18-08-40	Lt.	Bürschgens	7	8	Hurricane	Canterbury	1410	17 Sqd	unk
25-08-40	Lt.	Bürschgens	7	9	Hurricane	Littlestone			unk
01-09-40	Lt.	Bürschgens	7	10	Spitfire	Croydon	1450	72 Sqd	unk
31-05-40	Uffz.	Busch E.	9	1	Hurricane	Dunkirk	1540	213 or 264 Sqd	unk
02-06-40	Uffz.	Busch E.	9	2	Hurricane	unknown	0925	32 Sqd	yes
08-06-40	Uffz.	Busch E.	9	3	Hurricane	NW of Beauvais	1030		yes
08-06-40	Uffz.	Busch E.	9	4	Hurricane	Beauvais	1040		no
04-07-41	Obfw.	Busch E.	9	5	Spitfire	unknown	1505		yes
09-08-41	Obfw.	Busch E.	9	6	Spitfire	unknown	1125	Tangmere	yes
24-02-42	Obfw.	Busch E.	9	7	Spitfire	unknown	1320	92 Sqd	yes

Date	Rank	Name			Type	Location	Time	Unit	Conf.
25-03-42	Obfw.	Busch E.	10J	8	Hurricane	E of Harwich			no
25-02-44	Fhr.	Busch W.	8	1	B-17	Alsbach near St. Ingbert	1200	96 BG	unk
12-04-44	Fhr.	Busch W.	8	2	B-24	12km NE of Namur	1338	445 BG	yes
11-05-44	Fhr.	Busch W.	8	3	B-24	38km S of Chartres (ED4-7)	1413	487 BG	yes
02-07-44	Fhr.	Busch W.	8	4	Spitfire	10km E of Lisieux (UA5)	0706	411 Sqd	yes
23-09-44	Fhr.	Busch W.	6		P-51	Goch (KN)	1735	352 FG	no
13-05-40	Lt.	Butterweck	1	1	Potez 63	Peppel-S of Tilburg	1838	GAO 501	yes
31-07-42	Lt.	Cadenbach	4	1	Spitfire	W ofBerck-sur-Mer	1517	121 or 332 Sqd	yes
17-08-42	Lt.	Cadenbach	4	2	Spitfire	SW of Dieppe	1853	401 or 402 Sqd	yes
28-07-40	Fw.	Carl	9	1	Spitfire	NE of Dover	1525	74 Sqd	yes
14-08-40	Fw.	Carl	9	2	Spitfire	unknown	1230	65 or 610 Sqd	unk
25-08-40	Fw.	Carl	9	3	Spitfire	unknown	1950	610 or 616 Sqd	yes
06-09-40	Fw.	Carl	9	4	Spitfire	unknown	1415		unk
01-03-45	Fw.	Chemnitzer	7	1	Auster	near Mönchen-Gladbach	0935		unk
31-08-40	Lt.	Christennecke	7	1	Spitfire	N of Sevenoaks	1900	222 Sqd	unk
04-07-41	Gefr.	Christof	1	1	Spitfire	W of St. Omer	1458		yes
14-07-41	Uffz.	Christof	1	2	Spitfire	E of Dover	1040		unk
27-11-41	Uffz.	Christof	1	3	Hurricane	15km W of Boulogne	1735	607 Sqd	yes
29-06-42	Uffz.	Christof	1	4	Spitfire	W of Gravelines	1645	222 or 332 Sqd	unk
19-08-42	Uffz.	Christof	1	5	Spitfire	5km NE of Dieppe			unk
14-05-43	Uffz.	Christof	1	6	LaGG-3	USSR (PQ 54331)			yes
03-06-43	Uffz.	Christof	1	7	Pe-2	USSR (PQ 44289)			yes
22-06-43	Fw.	Christof	1	8	Spitfire	Goeree Is.	1032	453 Sqd	yes
30-07-43	Fw.	Christof	1	9	B-17-eV	E of Ghent (MI5-7)	0835	388 BG	yes
15-08-44	Uffz.	Corinth	4	1	P-47	Versailles (AD8)	1234	373 FG	unk
25-09-44	Uffz.	Corinth	4	2	Auster	Nijmegen (JM5)		662 Sqd	unk
27-08-42	Uffz.	Crump	5	1	Spitfire	W of Berck-sur-Mer	1350	350 Sqd	yes
06-12-42	Uffz.	Crump	5	2	Spitfire	15km NW of Calais	1242	122 Sqd	yes
12-12-42	Uffz.	Crump	5		Spitfire	20km N of Dieppe	1130	331 or 412 Sqd	no
23-01-43	Uffz.	Crump	5	3	Mustang	S of Montreuil	1345	168 Sqd	yes
23-01-43	Uffz.	Crump	5	4	Mustang	S of Montreuil	1346	168 Sqd	yes
26-01-43	Uffz.	Crump	5		Spitfire	5km N of Dunkirk	1245	64 or 306 Sqd	no
03-02-43	Uffz.	Crump	5		Spitfire	5km N of Calais	1100	308 Sqd	no
13-02-43	Uffz.	Crump	5		Spitfire	near Watten	1030		no
17-02-43	Uffz.	Crump	5	5	Spitfire	1km W of Guines	1049	124 Sqd	yes
27-02-43	Uffz.	Crump	5	6	Spitfire	50-60km NNW of Dunkirk	1432	403 Sqd	yes
08-03-43	Uffz.	Crump	5		B-24-HSS	N of Rouen	1400	44 BG	no
24-03-43	Uffz.	Crump	5	7	B-17-HSS	10km NNW of Cap Gris Nez	1015	91 Sqd	yes
31-03-43	Uffz.	Crump	5		B-17-HSS	Thames Estuary	1245	305 BG	no
21-04-43	Uffz.	Crump	5	8	Spitfire	2km S of Boismont	1217	610 Sqd	yes
14-05-43	Uffz.	Crump	5		B-17	10km NW of Vlissingen	1330	95 BG	no
18-05-43	Uffz.	Crump	5		Spitfire	6km SE of Dieppe	1500		no
16-06-43	Uffz.	Crump	5		Spitfire	mid-Channel	0700	91 Sqd	no
20-06-43	Uffz.	Crump	5	9	Spitfire	near Vielles les Blequin	1334	403 Sqd	yes
22-06-43	Uffz.	Crump	5		B-17	5km NW of Vlissingen	0930	381 or 384 BG	no
26-06-43	Fw.	Crump	5	10	P-47	15-20km NW of Somme Estuary	1910	56 FG	yes
30-07-43	Fw.	Crump	5		YB-40	near Arnhem	1030		no
09-09-43	Fw.	Crump	5		B-17	Beauvais-Somme	0930		no
11-09-43	Fw.	Crump	5	11	Typhoon	near Haudramont	1841	175 Sqd	yes
03-10-43	Fw.	Crump	6	12	Spitfire	near Noyon	1850	41 Sqd	unk
24-10-43	Fw.	Crump	6		B-26	S of Montdidier	1230		no
29-11-43	Fw.	Crump	6	13	Spitfire	N of Ypres	1005	412 Sqd	yes
29-04-44	Fw.	Crump	7		B-17	5km S of Reims	1330		no
05-05-44	Fw.	Crump	7	14	Spitfire	15km NE of Mons	0830	441 Sqd	yes
12-06-44	Lt.	Crump	6	15	P-47	15-20km SE of Rouen (TC)	0623	353 FG	unk
02-07-44	Lt.	Crump	6	16	Spitfire	NW of Caen (UT3-UU1)	1558		yes
19-03-45	Lt.	Crump	13 CO	22	P-51	Varrelbusch	1330	78 FG	unk
28-03-45	Lt.	Crump	13 CO	23	P-47	SW of Münster	1150	406 FG	unk
17-09-41	Fw.	Cwilinski	2	1	Spitfire	6km SW of Boulogne	1555		yes
21-06-42	Obfw.	Cwilinski	2	2	Spitfire	N of Gravelines	1812		yes
16-05-40	Uffz.	Dahmer	4	1	Morane 406	Tournai	1631		unk
28-05-40	Uffz.	Dahmer	4	2	Spitfire	Thames Estuary	1250		yes
29-05-40	Uffz.	Dahmer	4	3	Spitfire	Dover	1900	64, 229 or 610 Sqd	yes
07-06-40	Uffz.	Dahmer	4	4	Hurricane	Dieppe	1935	43 Sqd	yes
07-06-40	Uffz.	Dahmer	4	5	Hurricane	Dieppe	1940	43 Sqd	unk
31-08-40	Uffz.	Dahmer	6	6	Hurricane	Brentwood	0945	56 Sqd	yes
31-08-40	Uffz.	Dahmer	6	7	Spitfire	Gravesend	1945		unk
24-09-40	Uffz.	Dahmer	6	8	Hurricane	Southend	1055		yes
30-09-40	Uffz.	Dahmer	6	9	Hurricane	Tonbridge	1025	229 Sqd	yes
12-08-40	Oblt.	Dähne	1	1	Spitfire	NE of Goodwin			unk
14-09-40	Oblt.	Dähne	I St	2	Hurricane	SE of Maidstone	1703	253 Sqd	no
17-07-43	Uffz.	David	12		B-17F	W of Helgoland (SO7)	0932	351 BG	yes
17-12-44	Uffz.	Delor	4	1	P-38	Aachen (PN-ON)	1525	474 FG	unk

Date	Rank	Name	Unit	No.	Aircraft	Location	Time	Unit2	Conf
17-12-44	Uffz.	Delor	4	2	P-38	Aachen (PN-ON)	1530	474 FG	unk
26-12-44	Uffz.	Delor	4	3	P-51	Dinant (QL-PL)	1100	361 FG	unk
06-08-44	Gefr.	Deshombes	9		Lancaster	N of Paris (UE5)	1216		unk
21-07-41	Uffz.	Dietze	2	1	Spitfire	SW ofCap Gris Nez	2100	19 Sqd	yes
20-09-41	Uffz.	Dietze	2	2	Spitfire	8km SW of Calais	1700		yes
01-12-43	Lt.	Dietze	1	3	B-17	E of St. Omer (NF1)	1330	384 BG	yes
05-03-45	Lt.	Dietze	7 CO	4	Auster	near Krefeld	1252		unk
05-03-45	Lt.	Dietze	7 CO	5	Auster	near Krefeld	1255		unk
07-07-41	Lt.	Dippel	2	1	Spitfire	Samer	1520		yes
24-07-41	Lt.	Dippel	2	2	Hurricane	15km NW of Calais	1500		yes
19-08-41	Lt.	Dippel	2	3	Spitfire	near Gravelines	1940	111 Sqd	yes
20-09-41	Lt.	Dippel	2	4	Spitfire	6km N of Wissant	1655		yes
15-02-42	Lt.	Dippel	2	5	Spitfire	15km W of Cap Gris Nez	1100	452 Sqd	yes
28-03-42	Lt.	Dippel	2	6	Spitfire	N of Wissant	1845	64 Sqd	yes
04-04-42	Lt.	Dippel	2	7	Spitfire	3km NNW of Cap Blanc Nez	1142	316 Sqd	yes
23-05-42	Lt.	Dippel	2	8	Spitfire	Channel off Folkestone	1205		no
04-12-42	Lt.	Dippel	2	9	Spitfire	Tilques	1445	401 or 402 Sqd	no
17-02-43	Lt.	Dippel	2	10	P-40	USSR (PQ 18433)			yes
23-02-43	Lt.	Dippel	2	11	Il-2	USSR (PQ 18272)			yes
27-02-43	Lt.	Dippel	2	12	Pe-2	USSR (PQ 18394)			yes
05-03-43	Lt.	Dippel	2	13	Il-2	USSR (PQ 18484)			yes
02-06-43	Lt.	Dippel	2	14	P-40	USSR (PQ 62195)			yes
25-06-43	Oblt.	Dippel	2	15	B-17	6km S of Emden (CP8-4)	0908		yes
26-07-43	Oblt.	Dippel	8	16	Spitfire	3km E of Roubaix	1134	317 Sqd	yes
20-10-43	Oblt.	Dippel	9 CO	17	P-47	unknown			yes
01-12-43	Oblt.	Dippel	9 CO	18	P-47	Beverlo	1300	56 FG	yes
25-02-44	Oblt.	Dippel	9 CO	19	B-17-HSS	unknown	1500		unk
23-04-44	Oblt.	Dippel	9 CO	20	B-17	S of W Neustadt (FN9-FO7)	1445	97 or 483 BG	yes
24-04-44	Oblt.	Dippel	9 CO	21	B-17	N of Augsburg	1330		unk
27-08-41	Gefr.	Dirksen	8	1	Spitfire	unknown	0812		yes
27-10-41	Uffz.	Dirksen	8	2	Spitfire	unknown	1325	401 Sqd	yes
27-08-42	Lt.	Donner v.	5	1	Spitfire	8km WNW of Somme Estuary	1341	350 Sqd	yes
13-02-43	Lt.	Donner v.	II St	2	Spitfire	8-10km W of Boulogne	1018		yes
04-05-43	Oblt.	Donner v.	II St	3	B-17	Scheldt Estuary	1548		unk
25-07-42	Uffz.	Dörre	9	1	Spitfire	NW of Dunkirk	1428	416 Sqd	yes
19-08-42	Uffz.	Dörre	9	2	Spitfire	Dieppe	1520		yes
19-11-42	Uffz.	Dörre	9	3	Spitfire	10km N of Zeebrugge	1458	4 FG	unk
23-01-43	Uffz.	Dörre	9	4	B-17	unknown	1420	303 BG	unk
16-02-43	Fw.	Dörre	9	5	B-17	2.5km SW of Pleuradeur	1120		i.O.
12-03-43	Fw.	Dörre	9	6	Spitfire	unknown	1630	4 FG	unk
25-06-43	Fw.	Dörre	9	7	B-17	30-40km NW of Helgoland	0902		yes
28-07-43	Fw.	Dörre	9	8	B-17F	NW of Helgoland (RO1-2)	0915		unk
17-08-43	Fw.	Dörre	9	9	B-17	Genk	1135		yes ¹/₂
19-03-45	Oblt.	Dortenmann	14 CO	29	P-51	Rheine-Lingen(FP6)	1336	78 FG	unk
19-03-45	Oblt.	Dortenmann	14 CO	30	P-51	Rheine-Lingen(FQ4)	1337	78 FG	unk
28-03-45	Oblt.	Dortenmann	14 CO	31	Tempest	5km SW of Münster (IP3)	1135	56 Sqd	unk
31-03-45	Oblt.	Dortenmann	3 CO	32	Auster	Ludwighausen (JQ8)	1446		unk
12-04-45	Oblt.	Dortenmann	3 CO	33	Tempest	15km N of Uelsen (DA9)	1253	33 Sqd	unk
12-04-45	Oblt.	Dortenmann	3 CO	34	Tempest	15km N of Uelsen (DA9)	1254	33 Sqd	unk
17-04-45	Oblt.	Dortenmann	3 CO	35	Tempest	SW of Lübeck (AB4)	1134	80 Sqd	unk
21-04-45	Oblt.	Dortenmann	3 CO	36	Spitfire	Buchholz (S of Harburg)	1519		unk
26-04-45	Oblt.	Dortenmann	3 CO	37	Yak-9	SE of Prenzlau	1916		unk
27-04-45	Oblt.	Dortenmann	3 CO	38	Yak-3	NE of Neuruppin-Berlin	1825		unk
09-03-43	Lt.	Draheim	I St	1	LaGG-3	USSR (PQ 18346)			yes
17-09-44	Uffz.	Düsing	3	1	Spitfire	Nijmegen (IN7)	1755		yes
13-05-40	Hptm.	Ebbighausen	4 CO	1	Fokker T5	Dordrecht	0718	BomVA	yes
13-05-40	Hptm.	Ebbighausen	4 CO	2	Fokker G1	Dordrecht	0720	1-4 JaVA	yes
18-05-40	Hptm.	Ebbighausen	4 CO	3	Morane 406	Douai	1630		yes
24-05-40	Hptm.	Ebbighausen	4 CO	4	Spitfire	Dunkirk	1655	74 Sqd	yes
14-06-40	Hptm.	Ebbighausen	4 CO	5	Defiant	Vernon	1753	12 or 103 Sqd	yes
14-08-40	Hptm.	Ebbighausen	II CO	6	Spitfire	Folkestone	1335	65 or 610 Sqd	unk
15-08-40	Hptm.	Ebbighausen	II CO	7	Spitfire	Dover	1300	54 Sqd	unk
17-05-40	Lt.	Ebeling	8	1	Morane 406	Gramont	1830		yes
28-05-40	Lt.	Ebeling	8	2	Hurricane	NW of Ostend	1225	213, 229 or 242Sqd	yes
31-05-40	Lt.	Ebeling	8	3	Hurricane	Dunkirk	1545	213 or 264 Sqd	yes
09-06-40	Lt.	Ebeling	8	4	Morane 406	Rouen	1530	GC 1/145	yes
13-06-40	Lt.	Ebeling	8	5	Defiant	Paris	1240	142 Sqd	yes
12-08-40	Lt.	Ebeling	8	6	Hurricane	Thames Estuary	1215	151 or 501 Sqd	yes
12-08-40	Lt.	Ebeling	8	7	Hurricane	Thames Estuary	1220	151 or 501 Sqd	yes
12-08-40	Lt.	Ebeling	8	8	Spitfire	SW of Dover	1820	64 Sqd	yes
15-08-40	Lt.	Ebeling	8	9	Spitfire	Folkestone	1240	54 Sqd	unk
15-08-40	Lt.	Ebeling	8	10	Hurricane	Folkestone	1945	151 Sqd	unk
18-08-40	Oblt.	Ebeling	8	11	Spitfire	N London	1845		yes

30-08-40	Oblt.	Ebeling	9 CO	12	Hurricane	S England	1835	253 Sqd	yes
31-08-40	Oblt.	Ebeling	9 CO	13	Hurricane	North Weald	0950	56 Sqd	yes
31-08-40	Oblt.	Ebeling	9 CO	14	Hurricane	NW of Folkestone	1910	85 Sqd	yes
31-08-40	Oblt.	Ebeling	9 CO	15	Hurricane	NW of Folkestone	1920	85 Sqd	yes
06-09-40	Oblt.	Ebeling	9 CO	16	Hurricane	NW of Dover	1105	303 Sqd	yes
07-09-40	Oblt.	Ebeling	9 CO	17	Spitfire	SE of London	1850	603 Sqd	unk
07-09-40	Oblt.	Ebeling	9 CO		Spitfire	SE of London	1850	603 Sqd	unk
18-09-40	Oblt.	Ebeling	9 CO	18	Hurricane	London	1350		unk
15-08-40	Oblt.	Ebersberger	4	1	Spitfire	Tonbridge	1940	54 or 266 Sqd	yes
23-08-40	Oblt.	Ebersberger	4	2	Battle	Boulogne	2015	142 Sqd	yes
01-09-40	Oblt.	Ebersberger	4	3	Spitfire	Dungeness	1440	72 Sqd	yes
06-09-40	Oblt.	Ebersberger	II St	4	Spitfire	Redhill	1010	234 Sqd	yes
14-09-40	Oblt.	Ebersberger	II St	5	Spitfire	Eastchurch	1710	222 Sqd	yes
01-11-40	Oblt.	Ebersberger	4 CO	6	Spitfire	Herne Bay	1535	92 Sqd	yes
05-12-40	Oblt.	Ebersberger	4 CO	7	Hurricane	Rochester	1220	46 Sqd	yes
11-06-41	Oblt.	Ebersberger	4 CO	8	Spitfire	Nieuport	1655	609 Sqd	yes
23-06-41	Oblt.	Ebersberger	4 CO	9	Spitfire	St. Omer	2040		yes
27-06-41	Oblt.	Ebersberger	4 CO	10	Spitfire	Marquise	1659	19 or 266 Sqd	yes
21-08-41	Oblt.	Ebersberger	4 CO	11	Spitfire	Merville	1500	610 Sqd	yes
17-09-41	Oblt.	Ebersberger	4 CO	12	Spitfire	Boulogne	1536		yes
20-09-41	Oblt.	Ebersberger	4 CO	13	Spitfire	Mardyck	1652		yes
27-09-41	Oblt.	Ebersberger	4 CO	14	Spitfire	Gravelines	1539		yes
21-10-41	Oblt.	Ebersberger	4 CO	15	Spitfire	SW of Boulogne	1306		yes
08-11-41	Oblt.	Ebersberger	4 CO	16	Spitfire	N of Dunkirk	1304	Digby or 412 Sqd	yes
08-12-41	Oblt.	Ebersberger	4 CO	17	Spitfire	Boulogne	1302		yes
13-03-42	Oblt.	Ebersberger	4 CO	18	Spitfire	Wimereux	1618	124 Sqd	yes
10-04-42	Oblt.	Ebersberger	4 CO	19	Spitfire	Le Touquet	1742	340 Sqd	yes
24-04-42	Oblt.	Ebersberger	4 CO	20	Spitfire	Le Touquet	1446	234 Sqd	yes
24-04-42	Oblt.	Ebersberger	4 CO	21	Spitfire	Le Touquet	1453	234 Sqd	yes
27-04-42	Oblt.	Ebersberger	4 CO	22	Spitfire	30km NW of Calais	1446	T'mere or 340 Sqd	unk
09-05-42	Oblt.	Ebersberger	4 CO	23	Spitfire	Gravelines	1344	118 or 501 Sqd	yes
20-06-42	Oblt.	Ebersberger	4 CO	24	Spitfire	Calais	1548	118 or 501 Sqd	yes
19-08-42	Oblt.	Ebersberger	4 CO	25	Spitfire	W of Dieppe	1003	31 FG or 130 Sqd	yes
19-08-42	Oblt.	Ebersberger	4 CO	26	Spitfire	NW of Dieppe	1607		yes
24-08-42	Oblt.	Ebersberger	4 CO	27	Spitfire	E of Ourville	1730	402 Sqd	unk
30-07-43	Hptm.	Ebersberger	8 CO	28	B-17	Liège	0828		yes
31-07-43	Hptm.	Ebersberger	8 CO	29	Spitfire	Gravelines	1130	165 Sqd	yes
27-08-43	Hptm.	Ebersberger	8 CO	30	Spitfire	Arras (PF5-6)			yes
11-05-40	Fw.	Eberz	9	1	Curtiss H75	NE of Antwerp	1730	GC I/4	yes
19-05-40	Uffz.	Eberz	9	2	Hurricane	NE of Courtrai			unk
02-06-40	Uffz.	Eberz	9	3	Spitfire	unknown	0925	66, 266 or 611Sqd	yes
15-08-44	Oblt.	Eder	6	50	P-47	Rambouillet (BD)	1238	373 FG	yes
15-08-44	Oblt.	Eder	6	51	P-47	Rambouillet (BD)	1240	373 FG	yes
17-08-44	Oblt.	Eder	6	52	Spitfire	Rambouillet (BC6-BD4)	1153		yes
17-08-44	Oblt.	Eder	6	53	Spitfire	Rambouillet(BC6-BD4)	1153		yes
31-10-42	Fw.	Edmann	8	1	Spitfire	20km W of Calais	1815		unk
29-04-43	Obfw.	Edmann	8		Spitfire	5-10km N of Zeebrugge	1324	56 FG P-47	yes
22-03-41	Uffz.	Ehlen	7	1	Hurricane	N of Malta	1625	261 Sqd	yes
22-03-41	Uffz.	Ehlen	7	2	Hurricane	N of Malta	1627	261 Sqd	yes
22-03-41	Uffz.	Ehlen	7	3	Hurricane	N of Malta	1630	261 Sqd	yes
15-06-41	Uffz.	Ehlen	7	4	Hurricane	Sidi Barrani, Egypt	1655	73 Sqd	unk
29-07-41	Fw.	Ehlen	7	5	Tomahawk	50km E of Bardia,Libya	1747	2 Sqd SAAF	unk
18-09-41	Fw.	Ehlen	7	6	Spitfire	30km NW of Dieppe	1623	452 Sqd	unk
12-04-42	Fw.	Ehlen	7	7	Spitfire	E of Arques	1336	41 Sqd	yes
02-09-43	Fw.	Ehret	6	1	P-47	near Merville	2018	56 FG	yes
22-10-43	Fw.	Ehret	7	2	Spitfire	SW of Beauvais	1033	421 Sqd	unk
01-06-42	Obfw.	Eichinger	3	1	Spitfire	NE of Ostend	1348	65 or 111 Sqd	yes
30-07-42	Obfw.	Eichinger	3	2	Spitfire	4km off St. Omer			yes
14-10-43	Obfw.	Eichinger	3	3	B-17	St. Omer (NE1)	1400		yes
17-06-41	Oblt.	Eickhoff	2	1	Spitfire	NW ofCap Gris Nez	1940		yes
09-07-41	Oblt.	Eickhoff	I St	2	Spitfire	SW of St. Omer	1403		yes
19-07-41	Oblt.	Eickhoff	2 CO	3	Stirling	SE of Bergues	1425	XV Sqd	yes
12-08-41	Oblt.	Eickhoff	2 CO	4	Blenheim	Scheldt Estuary	1255		yes
21-09-41	Oblt.	Eickhoff	2 CO	5	Spitfire	near Bethune	1620	Tangmere	yes
19-06-41	Uffz.	Eierstock	9	1	Spitfire	NW of Cap Gris Nez	1935		no
21-06-41	Uffz.	Eierstock	9	2	Spitfire	unknown	1250		yes
26-03-43	Fw.	Ellenrieder	7	1	LaGG-3	USSR	0915		unk
11-07-43	Obfw.	Ellenrieder	8	2	Typhoon	E of Ghent	1550	198 Sqd	i.O.
08-02-44	Obfw.	Ellenrieder	3	5	P-47	E of St. Quentin? (RH-SH)	1118	352 FG	yes
24-02-44	Obfw.	Ellenrieder	3		B-17-HSS	Varrelbusch?	1245		no
22-04-44	Obfw.	Ellenrieder	3	6	P-47	S of Aachen (ON8)	1826	368 FG	yes
22-04-44	Obfw.	Ellenrieder	3	7	P-47	S of Aachen (ON7-8)	1828	368 FG	yes
14-06-44	Lt.	Ellenrieder	3	8	P-51	E of Paris (AF)	0805	357 FG	yes

Date	Rank	Name	Unit	Claim	Aircraft	Location	Time	Squadron	Conf
24-06-44	Lt.	Ellenrieder	3	9	P-47	Rambouillet (BD3)	0727	362 FG	yes
26-07-44	Lt.	Ellenrieder	3	10	Mustang	Verneuil (BB)	1902	122 Sqd	yes
28-07-44	Lt.	Ellenrieder	3	11	Auster III	Breteuil (AB)	1653		unk
24-09-44	Lt.	Ellenrieder	4	12	Typhoon	Goch (KN)	1741	137 Sqd	yes
25-09-44	Lt.	Ellenrieder	4	13	Spitfire	Arnhem (HM5-9)	1739	416 or 441 Sqd	unk
21-10-44	Lt.	Ellenrieder	4		Auster	unknown	1015	320 F/A Bat L-4	no
13-06-43	Obfw.	Erbskorn	9	1	B-17	18km N of Lütjenburg	0938	95 BG	unk
25-06-43	Obfw.	Erbskorn	9	2	B-17	15-20km NNW of Wangerooge	0903		yes
13-04-44	Obfw.	F...t?	11		B-17-eV	NE of Karlsruhe	1554		no
01-03-45	Hptm.	Fahnert	5	1	P-47	near Mönchen-Gladbach	0938	366 FG	unk
12-04-44	Uffz.	Falkner	5		B-24-eV	SSE of Goesnes-S of Huy	1317	445 BG	no
12-04-44	Uffz.	Falkner	5	1	B-24-HSS	nr Liège	1305	445 BG	yes
21-10-41	Uffz.	Fast	2	1	Spitfire	15km SW of Boulogne	1817	611 Sqd	yes
12-02-42	Uffz.	Fast	2	2	Spitfire	25km NW of Dunkirk	1550	401 Sqd	yes
27-08-42	Uffz.	Fast	2	3	Spitfire	10km E of Watten		71 Sqd	yes
12-10-42	Uffz.	Fast	2	4	Spitfire	8km NNW of Cap Gris Nez			unk
04-03-43	Uffz.	Fast	2	5	Pe-2	USSR (PQ 1986)			yes
08-07-41	Uffz.	Finke	6	1	Spitfire	near Ypres			yes
18-08-44	Lt.	Fischer E.	6	1	P-47	Beauvais (TE)	1240	356 FG	unk
25-08-44	Lt.	Fischer E.	6	2	P-38	Beauvais (TE)	1340	474 FG	unk
25-09-44	Lt.	Fischer E.	6	3	Mustang	Arnhem (LM4-9)	1800	129 Sqd	yes
27-09-44	Lt.	Fischer E.	6	4	Spitfire	Nijmegen (JM1-2)	1035		yes
21-04-43	Lt.	Fischer H.	4	1	Spitfire	N of Port le Grand	1213	610 Sqd	yes
17-12-41	Uffz.	Fischer O.	7	1	Spitfire	near Wevelghem			no
25-08-44	Fhr.	Fischer W.	7	1	P-38	W of Beauvais (TD)	1345	474 FG	unk
25-09-44	Fhr.	Fischer W.	7	2	Spitfire	Arnhem(HM9-JM3)	1744	416 or 441 Sqd	unk
23-09-44	Fw.	Franz	3	1	P-51	Wesel (KP)	1710	339 FG	yes
23-12-44	Fw.	Franz	3	2	B-26	Aachen (PN7)	1130		unk
25-09-44	Obfw.	Freiberger	1	1	Spitfire	Arnhem (HM5-9)	1739	416 or 441 Sqd	yes
24-03-43	Fw.	Freuwörth	5	57	Spitfire	8km E of Dungeness	1017	91 Sqd	unk
25-03-43	Fw.	Freuwörth	5	58	Spitfire	5km S of Dover	1814	609 Sqd Typhoon	yes
30-06-44	Uffz.	Friedrich	10		Spitfire	E of Caen (UU-UA)	1500	441 Sqd	unk
13-10-44	Uffz.	Fritsch A.	8	1	P-47	W of Düren (NN-NO)	1503	368 FG	unk
24-08-42	Fw.	Fritsch P.	5	1	Spitfire	Veules les Roses	1732	402 Sqd	unk
27-02-43	Obfw.	Fritsch P.	5	2	Spitfire	50-60km NNW of Dunkirk	1434	403 Sqd	yes
23-04-43	Obfw.	Fritsch P.	5	3	Mustang	25km W of Somme Estuary	1128	41 Sqd	yes Spitfire
24-06-43	Lt.	Fritsch P.	5	4	Typhoon	NW of Somme Estuary	1445	486 Sqd	yes
04-04-45	Uffz.	Fröb	2	1	Tempest-dam	6km E of Diepholz	1945	438 Sq Typhoon	no
23-09-40	Uffz.	Fröhlich	2	1	Spitfire	Channel	1520		yes
08-07-41	Uffz.	Fröhlich	2	2	Spitfire	NE of Calais	1550		yes
18-07-41	Uffz.	Fröhlich	2	3	Spitfire	NW of Dunkirk	1130		yes
27-07-41	Uffz.	Fröhlich	2	4	Hurricane	near Gravelines	1438		yes
12-02-42	Fw.	Fröhlich	2	5	Beaufort	30km SW of Ostend	1555		unk
15-05-40	Oblt.	Fronhöfer	9	1	Mureaux	unknown	0835		yes
29-05-40	Oblt.	Fronhöfer	9	2	Spitfire	W of Dunkirk	1810	64,229 or 610 Sqd	yes
15-08-40	Oblt.	Fronhöfer	9	3	Hurricane	Folkestone	2020	151 Sqd	yes
14-06-40	Hptm.	Galland A.	III CO	13	Blenheim	22km SE of Vernon-Breval	1715	21 or 40 Sqd	yes
14-06-40	Hptm.	Galland A.	III CO	14	Defiant	10km S of Évreux	1728	12 or 103 Sqd	yes
24-07-40	Hptm.	Galland A.	III CO	15	Spitfire	30km N of Margate	1330	54 Sqd	unk
25-07-40	Hptm.	Galland A.	III CO	16	Spitfire	Dover Harbor	1617	54 Sqd	yes
28-07-40	Hptm.	Galland A.	III CO	17	Spitfire	10km NNE of Dover	1520	74 Sqd	yes
12-08-40	Hptm.	Galland A.	III CO	18	Hurricane	NNW of Margate	1241	501 Sqd	unk
14-08-40	Hptm.	Galland A.	III CO	19	Hurricane	SW of Dover	1330	32 or 615 Sqd	yes
15-08-40	Hptm.	Galland A.	III CO	20	Spitfire	10km E of Dover-Folkestone	1255	54 Sqd	yes
15-08-40	Hptm.	Galland A.	III CO	21	Spitfire	15km SE of Folkestone	1600	64 Sqd	yes
15-08-40	Hptm.	Galland A.	III CO	22	Spitfire	20km SE of Dover-mid-Channel	1607	64 Sqd	yes
25-08-40	Maj.	Galland A.	Ge CO	23	Spitfire	Dungeness-Folkestone	1950	610 or 616 Sqd	unk
28-08-40	Maj.	Galland A.	Ge CO	24	Defiant	Faversham	1000	264 Sqd	unk
31-08-40	Maj.	Galland A.	Ge CO	25	Spitfire	20km SE of Cambridge	0942	19 Sqd	yes
31-08-40	Maj.	Galland A.	Ge CO	26	Spitfire	Gravesend	1850		yes
31-08-40	Maj.	Galland A.	Ge CO	27	Hurricane	Maidstone	1903		yes
01-09-40	Maj.	Galland A.	Ge CO	28	Hurricane	SE edge of London	1455	79 or 85 Sqd	yes
03-09-40	Maj.	Galland A.	Ge CO	29	Hurricane	Chelmsford	1132	257 Sqd	yes
06-09-40	Maj.	Galland A.	Ge CO	30	Hurricane	Tonbridge	1020	601 Sqd	yes
11-09-40	Maj.	Galland A.	Ge CO	31	Hurricane	NW of Dungeness	1620	501 Sqd	yes
14-09-40	Maj.	Galland A.	Ge CO	32	Hurricane	SE edge of London	1703	253 Sqd	yes
15-09-40	Maj.	Galland A.	Ge CO	33	Hurricane	Thames Estuary	1530	310 Sqd	yes
18-09-40	Maj.	Galland A.	Ge CO	34	Hurricane	unknown	1335	46 Sqd	yes
18-09-40	Maj.	Galland A.	Ge CO	35	Hurricane	W of Rochester	1352	46 Sqd	yes

Date	Rank	Name	Unit	No.	Aircraft	Location	Time	Squadron	Conf.
18-09-40	Maj.	Galland A.	Ge CO	36	Hurricane	W of Rochester	1355	46 Sqd	yes
20-09-40	Maj.	Galland A.	Ge CO	37	Spitfire	S of Hornchurch	1205	222 Sqd	yes
21-09-40	Maj.	Galland A.	Ge CO	38	Spitfire	W of Ashford-Canterbury	1925	92 Sqd	yes
23-09-40	Maj.	Galland A.	Ge CO	39	Hurricane	N of Rochester	1045	257 Sqd	yes
23-09-40	Maj.	Galland A.	Ge CO	40	Hurricane	N of Rochester	1045		yes
24-09-40	Maj.	Galland A.	Ge CO	41	Hurricane	Rochester	1000	17 Sqd	yes
30-09-40	Maj.	Galland A.	Ge CO	42	Hurricane	S of Guildford	1805	303 Sqd	yes
08-10-40	Maj.	Galland A.	Ge CO	43	Spitfire	S of Eastchurch	1020	66 Sqd	unk
11-10-40	Maj.	Galland A.	Ge CO	45	Spitfire	SE of Chatham-Ashford	1700	421 Flt	unk
11-10-40	Maj.	Galland A.	Ge CO	44	Hurricane	Dartford-Rochester	1712	253 Sqd	unk
15-10-40	Maj.	Galland A.	Ge CO	46	Spitfire	S of Rochester-Gillingham	1350		yes
26-10-40	Maj.	Galland A.	Ge CO	47	Hurricane	Maidstone-S of London	1730		yes
30-10-40	Maj.	Galland A.	Ge CO	48	Spitfire	E London	1255	222 Sqd	yes
30-10-40	Maj.	Galland A.	Ge CO	49	Spitfire	S of Eastchurch-Maidstone	1730	41 Sqd	yes
30-10-40	Maj.	Galland A.	Ge CO	50	Spitfire	Canterbury-Maidstone	1740	41 Sqd	yes
01-11-40	Maj.	Galland A.	Ge CO	51	Spitfire	W of Ashford	1250	74 Sqd	yes
14-11-40	Obstlt.	Galland A.	Ge CO	52	Spitfire	10km S of Dover	1528	66 or 74 Sqd	yes
15-11-40	Obstlt.	Galland A.	Ge CO	53	Hurricane	near Dover	1415	605 Sqd	yes
17-11-40	Obstlt.	Galland A.	Ge CO	56	Hurricane?	5km E of Detling	1015	257 Sqd	unk
17-11-40	Obstlt.	Galland A.	Ge CO	54	Hurricane	W of Harwich	1020	17 Sqd	unk
17-11-40	Obstlt.	Galland A.	Ge CO	55	Hurricane	20km E of lightship "Sunk"	1020	257 Sqd	yes
27-11-40	Obstlt.	Galland A.	Ge CO		Spitfire	E of Kenley	1707	74 Sqd	no
28-11-40	Obstlt.	Galland A.	Ge CO	57	Hurricane	Dartford	1540	249 Sqd	unk
05-12-40	Obstlt.	Galland A.	Ge CO	58	Spitfire	Dover-Dungeness	1230	64 Sqd	unk
04-04-41	Obstlt.	Galland A.	Ge CO	59	Spitfire	Dover-Canterbury	1750	91 Sqd	yes
15-04-41	Obstlt.	Galland A.	Ge CO	60	Spitfire	30km W of Dover	1750	Wittering W	yes
15-04-41	Obstlt.	Galland A.	Ge CO	61	Spitfire	Dover-Margate	1800	266 Sqd	yes
15-04-41	Obstlt.	Galland A.	Ge CO		Spitfire	S England	1800	266 Sqd	no
13-06-41	Obstlt.	Galland A.	Ge CO	62	Hurricane	5km W of Dover	1315	258 Sqd	unk
13-06-41	Obstlt.	Galland A.	Ge CO	63	Hurricane	10km NE of Ashford	1318	258 Sqd	unk
16-06-41	Obstlt.	Galland A.	Ge CO	64	Hurricane	W Boulogne	1635	258 Sqd	unk
17-06-41	Obstlt.	Galland A.	Ge CO	65	Hurricane	15km W of St. Omer	1938	56 or 242 Sqd	yes
17-06-41	Obstlt.	Galland A.	Ge CO	66	Hurricane	5km SE of Boulogne	1940	56 or 242 Sqd	yes
18-06-41	Obstlt.	Galland A.	Ge CO	67	Spitfire	1km E of Ardres	1818	145 Sqd	yes
21-06-41	Obstlt.	Galland A.	Ge CO	68	Blenheim	S of St Omer near Lumbres	1232	21 Sqd	yes
21-06-41	Obstlt.	Galland A.	Ge CO		Blenheim	Merville	1236	21 Sqd	no
21-06-41	Obstlt.	Galland A.	Ge CO	69	Spitfire	N of Étaples	1637	616 Sqd	unk
02-07-41	Obstlt.	Galland A.	Ge CO	70	Blenheim	Merville	1230	226 Sqd	yes
23-07-41	Obstlt.	Galland A.	Ge CO	71	Spitfire	40km NW of Gravelines	1335		unk
23-07-41	Obstlt.	Galland A.	Ge CO	72	Spitfire	Bruges	2010		yes
23-07-41	Obstlt.	Galland A.	Ge CO	73	Spitfire	Bruges	2015		yes
07-08-41	Obstlt.	Galland A.	Ge CO	74	Spitfire	Lumbres	1123		yes
07-08-41	Obstlt.	Galland A.	Ge CO	75	Spitfire	10km NW ofSt Omer	1740		yes
09-08-41	Obstlt.	Galland A.	Ge CO	76	Spitfire	NW of St. Pol	1132	452 Sqd	yes
09-08-41	Obstlt.	Galland A.	Ge CO		Spitfire	N of Ardres	1741		no
12-08-41	Obstlt.	Galland A.	Ge CO	77	Spitfire	25km W of Vlissingen	1312	19 or 152 Sqd	unk
12-08-41	Obstlt.	Galland A.	Ge CO	78	Blenheim	W Haamstede-Scheldt Estuary	1318		yes
19-08-41	Obstlt.	Galland A.	Ge CO	79	Spitfire	Bergues	1155	452 or 485 Sqd	unk
19-08-41	Obstlt.	Galland A.	Ge CO	80	Spitfire	NW of St Omer	1932	111 Sqd	yes
19-08-41	Obstlt.	Galland A.	Ge CO	81	Hurricane	SE of Gravelines	1945	71 Sqd	yes
04-09-41	Obstlt.	Galland A.	Ge CO	82	Blenheim	N of St. Omer	1719	18 Sqd	yes
07-09-41	Obstlt.	Galland A.	Ge CO	83	Spitfire	20km W of Boulogne	1719	71 Sqd	yes
20-09-41	Obstlt.	Galland A.	Ge CO	84	Spitfire	Bergues-Bourbourg	1645		unk
20-09-41	Obstlt.	Galland A.	Ge CO	85	Spitfire	6km NW of Braye-Dunes	1655		unk
21-09-41	Obstlt.	Galland A.	Ge CO	86	Spitfire	SE of Étaples	1623	Tangmere	yes
21-09-41	Obstlt.	Galland A.	Ge CO	87	Spitfire	S of Dunkirk	1735	111 Sqd	yes
13-10-41	Obstlt.	Galland A.	Ge CO	88	Spitfire	St. Omer	1417		yes
13-10-41	Obstlt.	Galland A.	Ge CO	89	Blenheim	Samer	1427	139 Sqd	yes
21-10-41	Obstlt.	Galland A.	Ge CO	90	Spitfire	W of Samer	1254		yes
21-10-41	Obstlt.	Galland A.	Ge CO	91	Spitfire	6km W of Hardelot	1258		yes
21-10-41	Obstlt.	Galland A.	Ge CO	92	Spitfire	15km W of Boulogne	1816	611 Sqd	yes
27-10-41	Obstlt.	Galland A.	Ge CO	93	Spitfire	S of Dunkirk	1325	401 Sqd	yes
08-11-41	Obstlt.	Galland A.	Ge CO	94	Spitfire	near Montreuil	1258	315 Sqd	yes
08-11-41	Obstlt.	Galland A.	Ge CO	95	Spitfire	10km S of Hazebrouck	1300	302 or 316 Sqd	yes
18-11-41	Obstlt.	Galland A.	Ge CO	96	Spitfire	20km W of Boulogne	1232	602 Sqd	yes
06-07-41	Lt.	Galland P.	8	1	Spitfire	unknown			unk
04-09-41	Lt.	Galland P.	8	2	Spitfire	unknown	1730		yes
17-09-41	Lt.	Galland P.	8	3	Spitfire	unknown		306 Sqd	unk
12-02-42	Lt.	Galland P.	8	4	Swordfish	N of Gravelines	1345	825 Sqd	yes
10-04-42	Lt.	Galland P.	8	5	Spitfire	unknown	1743	313 Sqd	yes
24-04-42	Lt.	Galland P.	8	6	Spitfire	NW of Ostend	1451	122 Sqd	yes
25-04-42	Lt.	Galland P.	8	7	Spitfire	unknown	1640		yes
26-04-42	Lt.	Galland P.	8	8	Spitfire	SE of Calais	1757	306 Sqd	yes
01-05-42	Lt.	Galland P.	8	9	Spitfire	unknown	1932	457, 485 or 602 Sqd	yes

Date	Rank	Name	Unit	No.	Aircraft	Location	Time	Squadron	Conf.
03-05-42	Lt.	Galland P.	8	10	Spitfire	Calais	1600	174 or 303 Sqd	unk
01-06-42	Lt.	Galland P.	8	11	Spitfire	unknown	1346	71 or 350 Sqd	yes
29-06-42	Lt.	Galland P.	8	12	Spitfire	unknown	1655	64 or 350 Sqd	yes
30-07-42	Lt.	Galland P.	8	13	Spitfire	unknown			unk
30-07-42	Lt.	Galland P.	8	14	Spitfire	unknown			unk
19-08-42	Lt.	Galland P.	8	15	Spitfire	Dieppe	1243		yes
27-08-42	Lt.	Galland P.	8	16	Spitfire	unknown			unk
31-10-42	Lt.	Galland P.	8	17	Boston	Dixmuide-Comines	1230	107 Sqd	unk
23-07-41	Oblt.	Galland W-F.	6	1	Spitfire	NW of Hesdin	2050		unk
27-09-41	Oblt.	Galland W-F.	6	2	Spitfire	Boulogne	1535		yes
06-11-41	Oblt.	Galland W-F.	6	3	Spitfire	Calais	1535	452 Sqd	yes
28-03-42	Oblt.	Galland W-F.	6	4	Spitfire	Cap Gris Nez	1850	457 or 602 Sqd	yes
10-04-42	Oblt.	Galland W-F.	6	5	Spitfire	5km W of Étaples	1745	340 Sqd	yes
24-04-42	Oblt.	Galland W-F.	6	6	Spitfire	Cap d'Albert	1454	234 Sqd	yes
01-05-42	Oblt.	Galland W-F.	6	7	Spitfire	Dover	1945	122 or 222 Sqd	yes
05-05-42	Oblt.	Galland W-F.	6	8	Spitfire	Boulogne	1453	41 Sqd	yes
02-06-42	Oblt.	Galland W-F.	5 CO	9	Spitfire	Somme Estuary	0710	64 or 174 Sqd	yes
02-06-42	Oblt.	Galland W-F.	5 CO	10	Spitfire	Somme Estuary	0718	64 or 174 Sqd	yes
20-06-42	Oblt.	Galland W-F.	5 CO	11	Spitfire	Guines	1546	118 or 501 Sqd	yes
31-07-42	Oblt.	Galland W-F.	5 CO	12	Spitfire	WNW of Somme Estuary	1507	121 or 332 Sqd	yes
31-07-42	Oblt.	Galland W-F.	5 CO	13	Spitfire	WNW of Somme Estuary	1508	121 or 332 Sqd	yes
19-08-42	Oblt.	Galland W-F.	5 CO	14	Spitfire	N of Dieppe	0755	242, 331 or 332 Sqd	yes
27-08-42	Oblt.	Galland W-F.	5 CO	15	Spitfire	NW of Somme Estuary	1345	350 Sqd	yes
28-08-42	Oblt.	Galland W-F.	5 CO	16	Spitfire	E of Amiens	1435	401 Sqd	unk
05-09-42	Oblt.	Galland W-F.	5 CO	17	Spitfire	Le Tréport	1135	64 or 340 Sqd	yes
15-10-42	Oblt.	Galland W-F.	5 CO	18	Spitfire	WNW of Fécamp	1634	122 Sqd	yes
04-12-42	Oblt.	Galland W-F.	5 CO	19	Spitfire	20km NW of Boulogne	1455	401 or 402 Sqd	yes
12-12-42	Oblt.	Galland W-F.	5 CO	20	Spitfire	NW of Boulogne	1139	331 or 412 Sqd	yes
31-12-42	Oblt.	Galland W-F.	5 CO	21	Spitfire	NNW of Somme Estuary	1445	306 Sqd	i.O.
09-01-43	Hptm.	Galland W-F.	II CO	22	Spitfire	W of Somme Estuary	1345	340 Sqd	yes
22-01-43	Hptm.	Galland W-F.	II CO	23	Spitfire	WNW of Gravelines	1530	350 Sqd	yes
26-01-43	Hptm.	Galland W-F.	II CO	24	Spitfire	Watten	1252	64 or 306 Sqd	yes
03-02-43	Hptm.	Galland W-F.	II CO	25	Hudson	10km from Fort Philip	1105	21 Sqd Ventura	yes
03-02-43	Hptm.	Galland W-F.	II CO	26	Spitfire	12-15km N of Fort Philip	1112	308 Sqd	yes
03-02-43	Hptm.	Galland W-F.	II CO	27	Spitfire	12-15km N of Dunkirk	1528	416 Sqd	yes
13-02-43	Hptm.	Galland W-F.	II CO	28	Spitfire	6km W of Hardelot	1017	340 Sqd	yes
13-02-43	Hptm.	Galland W-F.	II CO	29	Spitfire	SE of Le Touquet	1220	485 Sqd	yes
15-02-43	Hptm.	Galland W-F.	II CO	30	Spitfire	6-8km SE of Ramsgate	1604		yes
26-02-43	Hptm.	Galland W-F.	II CO	31	Spitfire	10-15km W ofSt. Omer	1035	122 Sqd	yes
08-03-43	Hptm.	Galland W-F.	II CO	32	B-24	Totes?	1404	44 BG	yes
13-03-43	Hptm.	Galland W-F.	II CO	33	Spitfire	Étaples	1535	402 or 403 Sqd	yes
14-03-43	Hptm.	Galland W-F.	II CO	34	Spitfire	10km SW of Boulogne	1755	B Hill Wing	yes
04-04-43	Hptm.	Galland W-F.	II CO	35	Spitfire	SE of Fécamp	1440	315,316 or 403 Sqd	yes
04-04-43	Hptm.	Galland W-F.	II CO	36	B-17	8km E of Fécamp	1445	303 or 305 BG	yes
04-04-43	Hptm.	Galland W-F.	II CO	37	B-17	20-30 km N of Fécamp	1455	303 or 305 BG	unk
05-04-43	Hptm.	Galland W-F.	II CO	38	B-17	S of Antwerp	1525	306 BG	yes
17-04-43	Hptm.	Galland W-F.	II CO	39	Mustang	20km WNW of Somme Estuary	1506	56 Sqd Typhoon	yes
21-04-43	Hptm.	Galland W-F.	II CO	40	Ventura	NE of Somme Est NW of Abbeville	1214	21 Sqd	yes
21-04-43	Hptm.	Galland W-F.	II CO	41	Ventura	10-20km W of Somme Est	1220	21 Sqd	yes
16-06-43	Hptm.	Galland W-F.	II CO	42	Spitfire	between Calais & Dover	0710	91 Sqd	yes
20-06-43	Hptm.	Galland W-F.	II CO	43	Spitfire	NE of Hesdin	1330	403 Sqd	i.O.
22-06-43	Hptm.	Galland W-F.	II CO	44	B-17	10km NW of Vlissingen	0922	381 or 384 BG	yes
22-06-43	Hptm.	Galland W-F.	II CO		B-17-eV	20km NW of Vlissingen	0925	381 or 384 BG	yes
26-06-43	Hptm.	Galland W-F.	II CO	45	P-47	N of Neufchatel	1852	56 FG	yes
26-06-43	Hptm.	Galland W-F.	II CO	46	P-47	10km NW of Dieppe	1904	56 FG	yes
04-07-43	Maj.	Galland W-F.	II CO	47	Spitfire	near Amiens	1737	122 Sqd	yes
09-07-43	Maj.	Galland W-F.	II CO	48	Spitfire	near Boulogne	0816		yes
14-07-43	Maj.	Galland W-F.	II CO	49	P-47	NW of Hesdin	0750	78 FG	unk
14-07-43	Maj.	Galland W-F.	II CO	50	P-47	10-15km W of Étaples	0805	78 FG	yes
15-07-43	Maj.	Galland W-F.	II CO	51	Boston	Somme Estuary	1650	107 Sqd	unk
15-07-43	Maj.	Galland W-F.	II CO	52	P-47	10km NW of Somme Estuary	1655	181 Sqd Typhoon	unk
30-07-43	Maj.	Galland W-F.	II CO	53	B-17	near Apeldoorn	1005	381 BG	yes
12-08-43	Maj.	Galland W-F.	II CO	54	B-17	near Siegburg	0908		unk
09-06-40	Fw.	Gärtner	8	1	Morane 406	unknown	1535	GC 1/145	yes
14-06-40	Fw.	Gärtner	8	2	Defiant	unknown	1750	12 or 103 Sqd	yes
15-08-40	Fw.	Gärtner	8	3	Spitfire	SE of Dover	1240	54 Sqd	unk
06-09-40	Fw.	Gärtner	8	4	Spitfire	unknown	1415		unk
11-09-40	Fw.	Gärtner	8	5	Hurricane	SE of London	1930		yes
07-10-40	Fw.	Gärtner	8	6	Hurricane	unknown	1735		yes
12-04-42	Hptm.	Gäth	Ge St	5	Boston	unknown	1357	107 Sqd	yes
27-04-42	Hptm.	Gäth	Ge St	6	Spitfire	near Wylder	1550	457 or 485 Sqd	yes

Date	Rank	Name		No.	Aircraft	Location	Time	Unit	Conf.
22-05-43	Hptm.	Gäth	2 CO	7	P-39	USSR(PQ 6218/19)			yes
01-06-43	Hptm.	Gäth	2 CO	8	Pe-2	USSR (PQ 35652)			yes
25-06-43	Hptm.	Gäth	2 CO	9	B-17	10km W of Papenburg (DP8)	0908	306 BG	yes
16-02-43	Ogfr.	Gauss	1	1	Il-2	USSR (PQ 18454)			yes
23-02-43	Ogfr.	Gauss	1	2	LaGG-3	USSR (PQ 29773)			yes
16-03-44	Uffz.	Gehrke	11		B-24-eV	near Reims		458 BG	yes
01-04-44	Uffz.	Gehrke	11	1	B-24	W of Épernay (UG7)	1352	448 BG	unk
13-04-44	Uffz.	Gehrke	11	2	B-17	Karlsruhe (US 7-9)	1550		yes
24-04-44	Uffz.	Gehrke	11	3	B-17	Donauwörth (BB5-9)	1335		unk
06-08-44	Uffz.	Gehrke	11	4	Lancaster-eV	Le Bourget-Paris (UE8-9)	1223	207 Sqd	i.O.
01-01-45	Uffz.	Gehrke	11	5	Spitfire	Brussels-Evere a/f	0930	416 Sqd	unk
27-09-44	Uffz.	Genth	12	1	Spitfire	Nijmegen (JM6)	1030	412 Sqd	unk
28-02-45	Uffz.	Genth	12	3	Tempest	Osnabrück	0800	274 Sqd	unk
11-01-44	Uffz.	Georgi	7	1	B-17-HSS	E of Lingen	1312	92 BG	yes
21-01-44	Uffz.	Georgi	7	2	P-47	Poix	1504	56 FG	yes
22-02-44	Uffz.	Georgi	7	3	B-17-HSS	Selm 8km N of Luenen	1325	91 or 384 BG	yes
18-12-39	Uffz.	Gerhardt W.	10N	1	Wellington	25-35km SSW of Helgoland	1435	3 Gp	yes
24-03-42	Obfr.	Gerhardt W.	5	9	Spitfire	Somme Estuary	1638	19 Sqd	yes
04-04-42	Obfw.	Gerhardt W.	5	10	Spitfire	Calais	1140		yes
30-07-42	Obfw.	Gerhardt W.	5	11	Spitfire	Channel Narrows	1932	616 Sqd	yes
31-07-42	Obfw.	Gerhardt W.	5	12	Spitfire	W of Dungeness	1523	121 or 332 Sqd	unk
31-07-42	Obfw.	Gerhardt W.	5	13	Spitfire	SW of Dungeness	1512	121 or 332 Sqd	unk
23-02-43	Uffz.	Glaser	2	1	Il-2	USSR (PQ 18261)			yes
19-03-43	Uffz.	Glaser	2	2	R-2	USSR (PQ 19883)			yes
27-08-41	Uffz.	Glunz	4	6	Spitfire	Bergues	0825		yes
05-11-41	Fw.	Glunz	4	7	Spitfire	Gravelines	1040	611 Sqd	yes
08-11-41	Fw.	Glunz	4	8	Spitfire	15km N of Calais	1308	Digby or 412 Sqd	unk
09-01-42	Fw.	Glunz	4	9	Spitfire	Le Touquet	1536	71 Sqd	yes
12-02-42	Fw.	Glunz	4	10	Spitfire	East of Eu	1708	118 or 234 Sqd	yes
13-03-42	Fw.	Glunz	4	11	Spitfire	mid-Channel-Dungeness	1629	401 Sqd	no
10-04-42	Fw.	Glunz	4	12	Spitfire	Étaples	1743	340 Sqd	yes
14-04-42	Fw.	Glunz	4	13	Spitfire	Calais	1850	317 Sqd	yes
25-04-42	Fw.	Glunz	4	14	Spitfire	Abbeville	1643		yes
17-05-42	Fw.	Glunz	4	15	Spitfire	Ardres	1135	602 Sqd	yes
05-06-42	Fw.	Glunz	4	16	Spitfire	WNW of Ault	1550	133 or 401 Sqds	unk
08-06-42	Fw.	Glunz	4	17	Spitfire	WNW of Dunkirk	1359	H'church or Kenley Wing	yes
28-06-42	Fw.	Glunz	4	18	Spitfire	Hastings	2116	611 Sqd	yes
31-07-42	Fw.	Glunz	4	19	Spitfire	W of Berck-sur-Mer	1501	121 or 332 Sqd	yes
31-07-42	Fw.	Glunz	4	20	Spitfire	W of Berck-sur-Mer	1508	121 or 332 Sqd	unk
19-08-42	Fw.	Glunz	4	21	Spitfire	W of Dieppe	1028	31 FG or 130 Sqd	unk
05-09-42	Fw.	Glunz	4	22	Spitfire	Somme Estuary	1141	64 or 340 Sqd	yes
02-11-42	Fw.	Glunz	4	23	Spitfire	W of Berck-sur-Mer	1657	91 Sqd	yes
03-02-43	Fw.	Glunz	4		Spitfire	N France	1530	416 Sqd	no
17-02-43	Obfw.	Glunz	4	24	Spitfire	Ardres	1045	124 Sqd	yes
26-02-43	Obfw.	Glunz	4	25	Spitfire	W of St. Omer	1037	122 Sqd	yes
08-03-43	Obfw.	Glunz	4	26	Spitfire	Rouen	1406	340 Sqd	unk
14-03-43	Obfw.	Glunz	4	27	Spitfire	2-3km SW of Boulogne	1759	B Hill Wing	yes
28-03-43	Obfw.	Glunz	4	29	Mosquito	S of Lille	1841	105 Sqd	yes
28-03-43	Obfw.	Glunz	4	28	Mosquito	S of Lille	1842	105 Sqd	yes
03-04-43	Obfw.	Glunz	4	30	Spitfire	Le Touquet	1608	416 Sqd	yes
04-04-43	Obfw.	Glunz	4	31	Spitfire	SW of Dieppe	1442	315,316 or 403 Sqd	unk
05-04-43	Obfw.	Glunz	4	32	B-17	N of Scheldt Estuary	1538	306 BG	unk
11-06-43	Obfw.	Glunz	4	33	Spitfire	N of Doullens	1642	611 Sqd	yes
16-06-43	Obfw.	Glunz	4	34	Spitfire	20km NW of Cap Gris Nez	0707	91 Sqd	yes
20-06-43	Obfw.	Glunz	4	35	Spitfire	NE of Etaples	1335	403 Sqd	yes
22-06-43	Obfw.	Glunz	4	36	B-17	Katz - N of Beveland Is	0915	381 BG	yes
26-06-43	Obfw.	Glunz	4	37	P-47	NW of Neufchatel	1854	56 FG	unk
26-06-43	Obfw.	Glunz	4		P-47	NW of Neufchatel	1855	56 FG	no
04-07-43	Obfw.	Glunz	4		Spitfire	unknown	1745		no
12-08-43	Obfw.	Glunz	4	38	B-17-eV	near Hagen	0905		yes
12-08-43	Obfw.	Glunz	4	39	B-17	W of Mönchen-Gladbach	0928		yes
17-08-43	Obfw.	Glunz	4	40	B-17	NW of Schouwen (Hasselt-Antwerp)	1745	305 BG	yes
19-08-43	Obfw.	Glunz	4		B-26-dam	N France	1230	323 BG	no
31-08-43	Obfw.	Glunz	4	41	B-17	Le Tréport	1932	303 BG	yes
03-09-43	Obfw.	Glunz	4	42	B-17	E of Paris	1035	381 or 384 BG	unk
03-10-43	Obfw.	Glunz	5		Spitfire	unknown	1600	341 or 485 Sqd	no
10-10-43	Obfw.	Glunz	5	43	B-17	N of Deelen	1541	100 BG	yes
14-10-43	Obfw.	Glunz	5		P-47	near Budel	1400	353 FG	no
11-11-43	Obfw.	Glunz	5	44	B-17	SW of Dordrecht	1455	94 BG	yes
11-11-43	Obfw.	Glunz	5		B-17	SW of Dordrecht	1457	94 BG	no
14-11-43	Obfw.	Glunz	5	45	Mosquito	near Lens-SW of Lille	1006	1409 Flt	yes

Date	Rank	Name	Unit	No.	Aircraft	Location	Time	Unit claimed	Conf.
26-11-43	Obfw.	Glunz	5	46	P-47	Chantilly	1040	78 FG	unk
26-11-43	Obfw.	Glunz	5	47	B-17	near Beauvais	1103	100 BG	yes
01-12-43	Obfw.	Glunz	5	48	Spitfire	SW of Arras	1015	411 Sqd	yes
01-12-43	Obfw.	Glunz	5	49	Spitfire	SW of Arras	1020	411 Sqd	yes
21-12-43	Obfw.	Glunz	5	50	Spitfire	Vimy Ridge SW of Douai-	1150	132 or 602 Sqd	yes
31-12-43	Obfw.	Glunz	5	51	B-17	between Lorient & Auringes	1500		yes
07-01-44	Obfw.	Glunz	5	52	P-47	near Boulogne	1345	4 FG	unk
11-02-44	Obfw.	Glunz	5 CO	53	B-17	20km NW of Poix	1405	351 BG	yes
21-02-44	Obfw.	Glunz	5 CO	54	B-17	6km W of Bergen aan See	1550	95 BG	unk
22-02-44	Obfw.	Glunz	5 CO	55	B-17	7km W of Dorsten	1250	91 or 384 BG	yes
22-02-44	Obfw.	Glunz	5 CO		B-17-HSS	unknown	1255	91 or 384 BG	no
22-02-44	Obfw.	Glunz	5 CO	56	B-17-HSS	12kn NE of Wesel	1310	91 or 384 BG	yes
22-02-44	Obfw.	Glunz	5 CO	57	P-47	15km NW of Geilenkirchen	1530	78 FG	yes
22-02-44	Obfw.	Glunz	5 CO	58	B-17	SW of Grevensbroich	1535		yes
22-02-44	Obfw.	Glunz	5 CO		B-17	Geilenkirchen	1540		no
25-02-44	Obfw.	Glunz	5 CO		B-17	unknown	1700	390 BG	no
09-05-44	Lt.	Glunz	6 CO	59	B-24	7km E of Turnhout (LL7)	0951	453 BG	yes
09-05-44	Lt.	Glunz	6 CO	60	B-24	7km SSW of Turnhout (LK9)	0957	466 BG	yes
11-05-44	Lt.	Glunz	6 CO	61	B-24-HSS	NE of Chateaudun (DC6)	1400	44 BG	unk
10-06-44	Lt.	Glunz	6 CO	62	P-47	N of Lisieux(TA-UA)	1756	365 FG	unk
10-06-44	Lt.	Glunz	6 CO	63	P-47	N of Lisieux(TA-UA)	1758	365 FG	yes
10-06-44	Lt.	Glunz	6 CO	64	P-47	N of Lisieux(TA-UA)	1758	365 FG	unk
18-06-44	Lt.	Glunz	6 CO	65	Mustang	Coutances (AT9)	1729	414 Sqd	yes
21-09-44	Lt.	Glunz	6 CO	66	C-47	Nijmegen (JM)	1718	38 or 46 Gp	yes
02-10-44	Lt.	Glunz	6 CO	67	Spitfire	S of Nijmegen (JM8-9)	1215	401 Sqd	i.O.
13-10-44	Lt.	Glunz	6 CO	68	P-38	Düren (NN9)	1500	474 FG	unk
24-12-44	Lt.	Glunz	6 CO	69	P-47	Liège (PL-PM)	1227	36 FG	unk
24-12-44	Lt.	Glunz	6 CO	70	P-47	Liège (PL-PM)	1228	36 FG	unk
01-01-45	Oblt.	Glunz	6 CO	71	Spitfire	S of Brussels-Evere a/f	0925	416 Sqd	unk
08-04-44	Fw.	Gocksch	10		P-47	S of Assen (EN-EO)	1510	353 FG	yes
30-07-43	Lt.	Göhringer	I St		B-17-HSS	S of Antwerp (MK3)	0825		yes
12-12-42	Ogfr.	Gomann	5	1	Spitfire	20km NNW of Dieppe	1344	331 or 412 Sqd	yes
05-02-43	Uffz.	Gomann	5	2	Spitfire	8km NNW of Boulogne	1211	611 Sqd	yes
14-05-43	Uffz.	Gomann	5	3	Spitfire	W of Schouwen	1326		yes
13-06-43	Uffz.	Gomann	5	4	P-47	Armentières	1448	78 FG	yes
24-06-43	Uffz.	Gomann	5	5	Spitfire	Calorme sur la Lys	1215	403 Sqd	yes
15-07-43	Uffz.	Gomann	5	6	Spitfire	5km W Berck - Somme	1700	602 Sqd	yes
30-07-43	Uffz.	Gomann	6		B-17-HSS	unknown	1015		no
21-09-43	Uffz.	Gomann	5	7	Spitfire	10-15km NW of Le Tréport	1110		no
24-09-43	Uffz.	Gomann	5	8	Spitfire	SW of Amiens	1215	129 Sqd	yes
31-12-43	Fw.	Gomann	6	9	P-47	NE of Vire	1414		unk
25-01-44	Fw.	Gomann	6	10	Spitfire	near Montreuil	1005	66 Sqd	yes
29-01-44	Fw.	Gomann	6	11	B-17	8km SSW ofLe Cateau	1250	388 BG	yes
29-01-44	Fw.	Gomann	6	12	B-24	W of Calais(in sea)	1348	389 BG	unk
13-10-41	Lt.	Göring	Ge St	1	Blenheim	Hubertus-Samer	1430	139 Sqd	no
06-09-40	Obfw.	Gottlob	6	1	Spitfire	Littlestone	1428	72 Sqd	yes
20-09-40	Obfw.	Gottlob	6	2	Hurricane	London	1215	605 Sqd	yes
23-09-40	Obfw.	Gottlob	6	3	Hurricane	Thames Estuary	1110		yes
05-11-40	Obfw.	Gottlob	6	4	Hurricane	Ramsgate	1225	310 Sqd	yes
16-06-41	Oblt.	Gottlob	1	5	Spitfire	S of Dungeness	1650	74 or 92 Sqd	yes
23-06-41	Oblt.	Gottlob	1	6	Spitfire	NW of Calais	2050		yes
25-06-44	Uffz.	Grad	4	1	B-24	E of Rouen (TD7)	2028	489 BG	yes
02-11-42	Uffz.	Granabetter	6	1	Spitfire	SW of Boulogne	1523	611 Sqd	yes
23-09-40	Oblt.	Grawatsch	6	1	Hurricane	Thames Estuary	1110		yes
15-10-40	Oblt.	Grawatsch	II St	2	Hurricane	London	1412	46 or 501 Sqd	yes
08-07-41	Gefr.	Grebe	1	1	Spitfire	SE of Dunkirk	1540		yes
08-07-41	Gefr.	Grebe	1	2	Spitfire	N of Dunkirk	1545		yes
05-03-43	Lt.	Grimm	3	1	Il-2	USSR (PQ 1864)			yes
07-03-43	Lt.	Grimm	3	2	LaGG-3	USSR (PQ 18543)			yes
03-09-44	Lt.	Gross A.	II St	52	Spitfire	7km E of Tirlemont	1245	41 Sqd	unk
23-08-44	Uffz.	Gross H.	8	1	P-38	Chartres (RC)	1402	474 FG	yes
07-06-44	Oblt.	Groth	1 CO	1	P-47	Falaise (UA1)	1601	362 FG	yes
28-05-40	Lt.	Gruel	3	1	Spitfire	between Dover & Ostend	1043	616 Sqd	yes
25-04-42	Uffz.	Grünlinger	9	1	Spitfire	unknown	1650		yes
04-12-42	Fw.	Grünlinger	III St	2	Spitfire	20km E of Dover	1440	401 or 402 Sqd	yes
09-04-43	Fw.	Grünlinger	Ge		Typhoon	15km NW of Cap Gris Nez	1845	611 Sqd Spitfire	unk
19-08-43	Obfw.	Grünlinger	Ge		B-17	Gilze-Rijen a/f	1900	305 BG	unk
14-05-40	Uffz.	Grzymalla	8	1	Morane 406	unknown			unk
19-05-40	Fw.	Grzymalla	8	2	Potez 63	unknown			unk
31-05-40	Fw.	Grzymalla	8	3	Hurricane	Dunkirk	1545	213 or 264 Sqd	yes
08-08-40	Fw.	Grzymalla	8	4	Hurricane	NE of Margate-Canterbury	1240		yes
12-08-40	Fw.	Grzymalla	8	5	Spitfire	SW of Dover	1830	64 Sqd	yes
11-09-40	Fw.	Grzymalla	8	6	Spitfire	SE of London	1933	66 or 92 Sqd	yes

Date	Rank	Name		No.	Type	Location	Time	Unit	Conf.
18-09-40	Fw.	Grzymalla	8	7	Spitfire	London	1415		yes
13-04-44	Stfw.	Guhl	11	10	P-47	Glanbrücken?	1324		unk
01-05-45	Lt.	Guhl	2	15	Spitfire-prob	N of Schwarzenbeck	1050		no
07-06-44	Lt.	Günther	3	1	P-51	W of Rouen (TB5)	0705		yes
14-07-44	Lt.	Günther	3	2	P-47	W of Paris (AC)	1438	358 FG	yes
14-07-44	Lt.	Günther	3	3	P-47	W of Paris (AC)	1440	358 FG	unk
13-08-44	Lt.	Günther	3	4	P-51	Alençon (CB2-3)	0811	363 FG	yes
26-08-44	Lt.	Günther	3	5	Spitfire	W of Beauvais (TD4)	1428	341 Sqd	yes
21-09-44	Lt.	Günther	2	6	C-47	Nijmegen (IL-IM)	1717	38 or 46 Gp	yes
02-10-44	Lt.	Günther	2	7	Spitfire	Nijmegen (JM2-3)	1218		unk
03-12-44	Lt.	Günther	2	8	Typhoon	W of Münster (IP9-KP3)	1210	439 Sqd	unk
05-12-44	Lt.	Günther	2	9	P-47	Linnich(BN2-3)	1013	365 FG	unk
17-12-44	Lt.	Günther	2	10	P-38	Aachen(PN3-ON1-2)	1527	474 FG	unk
23-12-44	Lt.	Günther	2	11	Auster	Aachen (PN2-3)	1120		unk
01-12-43	Uffz.	Guttmann	8	1	Typhoon	15km S of Valenciennes	1315	609 Sqd	unk
03-01-44	Uffz.	Guttmann	8	2	Typhoon	5-10km E of Doullens	1340	609 Sqd	yes
07-01-44	Uffz.	Guttmann	8	3	P-47	near Doullens	1335	4 FG	yes
08-02-44	Uffz.	Guttmann	8	4	B-17	Catheux 17km SE of Poix	1115		yes
11-02-44	Uffz.	Guttmann	8	5	B-17	24km NE of Beauvais	1355	381 BG	yes
24-02-44	Uffz.	Guttmann	8	6	B-17	Rastorf-Lorum Kr. Aschberg	1220	92 or 306 BG	yes
08-03-44	Fw.	Guttmann	5	7	B-17	NE of Helmstedt (GC5)	1400	96 or 388 BG	yes
28-10-44	Maj.	Hackl	II CO	166	Typhoon	between Venlo & Kempen	1325	182 Sqd	i.O.
23-12-44	Maj.	Hackl	II CO	167	P-51	Köln-Bonn	1252	364 FG	unk
23-12-44	Maj.	Hackl	II CO	168	Lancaster	Köln	1254	405 or 582 Sqd	unk
23-12-44	Maj.	Hackl	II CO	169	Mosquito	Köln-Mönchen Gladbach	1256	105 Sqd	unk
24-12-44	Maj.	Hackl	II CO	170	P-47	Liège (PL-PM)	1228	36 FG	unk
24-12-44	Maj.	Hackl	II CO	171	P-47	Liège (PL-PM)	1230	36 FG	unk
25-12-44	Maj.	Hackl	II CO	172	P-38	Wesel (KO5-7)	1155		unk
01-01-45	Maj.	Hackl	II CO	173	Spitfire	over Brussels	0925	416 Sqd	unk
14-01-45	Maj.	Hackl	II CO	174	P-47	E of Liège(near ON)	1205	366 FG	unk
14-01-45	Maj.	Hackl	II CO	175	P-51	Remscheid (near MP-MQ)	1215	78 FG	unk
16-08-40	Lt.	Hafer	I St	1	Spitfire	S of Gravesend	1325		yes
25-08-40	Lt.	Hafer	I St	2	Hurricane	W of Folkestone			unk
12-08-40	Uffz.	Haferkorn	2	1	Morane 406	Channel Narrows	1225		yes
04-04-43	Uffz.	Hager R.	8		Spitfire	E of Rouen near Blauville	1437	315,316 or 403 Sqd	yes
20-10-43	Fw.	Hager R.	4		Spitfire	Dixmuiden	0945	485 Sqd	unk
30-12-43	Fw.	Hager R.	4	1	B-17	S of Florennes	1200	303 BG	yes
24-03-44	Fw.	Hager R.	4	2	B-17	E of Courtrai (NH2)	1215	305 BG	yes
08-06-42	Ogfr.	Hager V.	7	1	Spitfire	unknown		H'church or Kenley	unk
29-06-42	Ogfr.	Hager V.	7	2	Spitfire	unknown	0450	64 or 350 Sqd	yes
02-10-42	Ogfr.	Hager V.	7	3	Spitfire	unknown	1535	331 Sqd	yes
14-03-43	Lt.	Hahne	4	2	Spitfire	St. Cécile Plage	1758	340 Sqd	yes
29-05-40	Lt.	Haiböck	9	1	Spitfire	W of Dunkirk	1810	64, 229 or 610 Sqd	yes
31-05-40	Lt.	Haiböck	9	2	Spitfire	Dunkirk	1540	609 Sqd	yes
08-06-40	Lt.	Haiböck	9	3	Hurricane	NW of Beauvais	1030		yes
15-08-40	Lt.	Haiböck	9	4	Hurricane	W of Folkestone	2025	151 Sqd	yes
28-08-40	Lt.	Haiböck	III St	5	Defiant	E of Canterbury	1000	264 Sqd	yes
03-09-40	Lt.	Haiböck	III St	6	Spitfire	Rochester	1105		unk
05-12-40	Lt.	Haiböck	III St	7	Hurricane	W of Hastings	1215		yes
17-06-41	Oblt.	Haiböck	III St	8	Spitfire	St. Omer	2000		unk
07-08-41	Oblt.	Haiböck	III St		Spitfire	Hazebrouck-Boulogne	1805		unk
27-09-41	Oblt.	Haiböck	9	9	Spitfire	1km W of Calais	1540		yes
12-04-42	Oblt.	Haiböck	1 CO	10	Spitfire	10km E of Dover	1350	41 Sqd	unk
27-04-42	Oblt.	Haiböck	1 CO	11	Spitfire	N of St. Omer	1214	403 Sqd	unk
27-04-42	Oblt.	Haiböck	1 CO	12	Spitfire	N of St. Omer	1214	403 Sqd	yes
09-05-42	Oblt.	Haiböck	1 CO	13	Spitfire	2km N of Cassel	1340	350 or 457 Sqd	unk
02-06-42	Oblt.	Haiböck	1 CO	14	Spitfire	S of Somme Estuary	1055	403 Sqd	yes
08-11-42	Oblt.	Haiböck	1 CO	15	Spitfire	5km N of Gravelines	1215		yes
04-09-43	Uffz.	Hanke	4	1	Spitfire	near Berck-sur-Mer	1948		yes
23-08-44	Uffz.	Hanusch	6	1	Spitfire	SW of Creil (UN)	1339	421 or 443 Sqd	yes
01-03-45	Uffz.	Hanusch	6	2	P-47	near Mönchen-Gladbach	0943	366 FG	unk
09-03-45	Uffz.	Hanusch	6	3	P-47	Wallach near Wesel	1650	366 FG	unk
03-07-41	Lt.	Harder	2	1	Spitfire	S of Boukerque	1545	266 Sqd	yes
11-07-41	Lt.	Harder	2	2	Spitfire	N of Calais	1623		yes
29-01-44	Lt.	Hartigs	2	1	P-38	Saarbrücken-Koblenz (TP-PQ)	1130	20 FG	yes
24-02-44	Oblt.	Hartigs	2	2	B-24	W of Koblenz (PP6-9?)	1215		yes
25-06-44	Oblt.	Hartigs	4	3	P-47	SW of Rouen (TB)	1535		unk
14-07-44	Oblt.	Hartigs	4	4	P-47	W of Paris (AC)	1440	358 FG	yes
26-07-44	Oblt.	Hartigs	4	5	Mustang	E of Rouen(TD5-6)	1015	414 Sqd	yes
25-12-44	Oblt.	Hartigs	4	6	P-47-prob	Dinant-Liège	1500		no
14-07-44	Uffz.	Haun	9		P-47	W of Dreux(AB6-9)	1457	358 FG	i.O.
17-08-43	Uffz.	Hecker	2	1	B-17	E of Lille (OH6-9)	1500	91 BG	unk

Date	Rank	Name			Aircraft	Location	Time	Unit	
27-09-43	Uffz.	Hecker	2	2	Spitfire	Somme Estuary (RC1)	1206	306 Sqd	yes
22-04-44	Fw.	Hecker	2	3	B-24	E of Courtrai (NH)	2103	392 BG	unk
16-02-43	Obfw.	Heckmann	1	54	Il-2	USSR (PQ 28142)			yes
16-02-43	Obfw.	Heckmann	1	55	Il-2	USSR (PQ 18423)			yes
18-02-43	Obfw.	Heckmann	1	56	Il-2	USSR (PQ 28351)			yes
18-02-43	Obfw.	Heckmann	1	57	Il-2	USSR (PQ 28311)			yes
14-10-43	Obfw.	Heckmann	1	58	B-17	Sedan? (RK7?)	1400		yes
11-01-44	Obfw.	Heckmann	1	59	B-17	Nordhorn-Zuider Zee	1300	306 BG	yes
04-02-44	Obfw.	Heckmann	3 CO	60	B-17	10km ESE of Rotterdam	1430	390 BG	yes
08-02-44	Obfw.	Heckmann	3 CO	61	P-51	S of Maubeuge (QI8-1)	1245	354 FG	yes
06-03-44	Obfw.	Heckmann	3 CO	62	P-47	Almelo (CO5,3)	1447	356 FG	yes
15-08-44	Lt.	Heckmann	3 CO	63	Mustang	SE of Dreux (BC3)	1228	19 Sqd	yes
22-08-44	Lt.	Heckmann	3 CO	64	Auster	NW of Paris (UD8)	1235		yes
17-09-44	Oblt.	Heckmann	3 CO	65	Spitfire	Nijmegen (IN7)	1751		yes
21-09-44	Oblt.	Heckmann	3 CO	66	C-47	Nijmegen (IL-IM)	1717	38 or 46 Gp	yes
21-09-44	Oblt.	Heckmann	3 CO	67	C-47	Nijmegen (IL-IM)	1718	38 or 46 Gp	yes
21-09-44	Oblt.	Heckmann	3 CO	68	C-47	W of Arnhem	1719	38 or 46 Gp	yes
21-09-44	Oblt.	Heckmann	3 CO	69	C-47	W of Arnhem	1720	38 or 46 Gp	yes
23-09-44	Oblt.	Heckmann	3 CO	70	P-51	Goch (KN)	1650	339 FG	yes
25-02-45	Oblt.	Heckmann	3 CO	71	P-47	SE of Köln	0825	36 FG	unk
28-05-40	Fw.	Hegenauer	1	1	Spitfire	between Dover & Ostend			unk
14-04-42	Lt.	Hegenauer	Ge St	2	Spitfire	unknown	1835	403 Sqd	yes
20-03-45	Oblt.	Heilmann	15 CO		P-51	near Bramsche	1740		unk
05-11-43	Uffz.	Hein H.	11	1	P-47	unknown		353 FG	yes
19-03-45	Uffz.	Hein K.	14	5	P-51	S of Haselünne	1336	78 FG	unk
28-03-45	Uffz.	Hein K.	14	6	Tempest	5km SW of Münster (IP3)	1134	56 Sqd	unk
21-04-45	Fw.	Hein K.	3	7	Spitfire	Buchholz (S of Harburg)	1515		unk
24-04-45	Fw.	Hein K.	3	8	Yak-3	N of Spandau	0820		unk
21-09-44	Ofhr.	Heindtke	2	1	C-47	W of Arnhem	1723	38 or 46 Gp	yes
15-07-43	Lt.	Heinemann E.	4	1	Spitfire	5km E of Hesdin	1655	602 Sqd	yes
19-08-43	Lt.	Heinemann E.	4	2	Typhoon	1km SE of Canaples?	1224	182 Sqd	unk
01-11-40	Lt.	Heinemann H.	1	1	Spitfire	Ashford	1250	74 Sqd	yes
06-10-44	Ofhr.	Heinrichs	5	1	P-51	Eindhoven (LM)	1508		i.O.
04-04-42	Obfw.	Heitmann	8	3	Spitfire	3km N of Calais	1145		yes
01-05-42	Obfw.	Heitmann	8	4	Spitfire	unknown	1934	457, 485 or 602 Sqd	yes
05-05-42	Obfw.	Heitmann	8	5	Spitfire	Kemmel	1555	122 Sqd	yes
03-02-43	Obfw.	Heitmann	8		Spitfire	Dunkirk-Calais	1108	308 Sqd	unk
29-04-43	Obfw.	Heitmann	8		P-47	Knokke	1320	56 FG	unk
22-07-43	Obfw.	Heitmann	8	6	Mustang	15-20km N of Coxyde	1337	239 Sqd	yes
22-07-43	Obfw.	Heitmann	8	7	Mustang	25-30km N of Dunkirk	1345	239 Sqd	yes
30-07-43	Obfw.	Heitmann	8		B-17-HSS	SE of Antwerp	0820		unk
17-08-43	Obfw.	Heitmann	8		Typhoon	Lille-Vendeville	1200	182 Sqd	no
20-10-43	Obfw.	Heitmann	4		Spitfire	Dixmuiden	0945	485 Sqd	unk
13-11-43	Obfw.	Heitmann	4	8	B-24	Zwolle (FN7-8)	1230	392 BG	yes
26-11-43	Obfw.	Heitmann	4	9	B-17	SSE of Creil	1045	94 BG	yes
25-02-44	Obfw.	Heitmann	4	10	B-26	E of Southend in N Sea (KG4-5)	1125	387 BG	yes
06-03-44	Obfw.	Heitmann	4	11	B-17	NW Osnabrück	1430	94 BG	yes
16-06-41	Uffz.	Held	1	1	Brewster	SW of Boulogne	1641	601 Sqd Hurricane	yes
27-06-41	Uffz.	Held	1	2	Spitfire	N of Dunkirk	2207		yes
07-07-41	Uffz.	Held	1	3	Spitfire	SW of Boulogne	1058		yes
08-07-41	Uffz.	Held	1	4	Spitfire	Merckeghem	0635		yes
17-09-41	Lt.	Helmholz	2	1	Spitfire	NW of Dunkirk	1540		yes
27-10-41	Lt.	Helmholz	2	2	Spitfire	NW of Watten	1315	401 Sqd	yes
08-03-42	Lt.	Helmholz	2	3	Spitfire	30km NW of Dunkirk	1721	403 Sqd	no
25-08-44	Fhr.	Hennemann	6	1	P-38	Creil (TE9)	1350	474 FG	unk
27-07-44	Uffz.	Hennemann	9		P-47	St Lô (US6-UT4)	1515	404 FG	i.O.
13-05-40	Lt.	Henrici	1	1	Morane 405/6	S of Breda	1050	GC III/3	yes
15-08-40	Oblt.	Henrici	1	2	Spitfire	NW of Calais	1805		yes
29-08-40	Oblt.	Henrici	1	3	Spitfire	Littlestone			unk
31-08-40	Oblt.	Henrici	1	4	Hurricane	Gravesend	1850		yes
01-09-40	Oblt.	Henrici	1	5	Hurricane	S of London	1507	79 or 85 Sqd	yes
01-09-40	Oblt.	Henrici	1	7	Hurricane	S of London		79 or 85 Sqd	unk
15-10-40	Oblt.	Henrici	1 CO	6	Hurricane	S of Gillingham	1355	46 or 501 Sqd	yes
21-09-44	Uffz.	Herbster	3	1	C-47	W of Arnhem	1720	38 or 46 Gp	yes
21-09-44	Uffz.	Herbster	3	2	C-47	W of Arnhem	1721	38 or 46 Gp	unk
04-04-42	Oblt.	Hermichen	7	12	Spitfire	unknown	1135		yes
12-04-42	Oblt.	Hermichen	7	13	Spitfire	3km N of Cassel	1340	313 Sqd	yes
09-05-42	Oblt.	Hermichen	3 CO	14	Spitfire	10km NW of Coxyde	1739	72 Sqd	yes
30-07-42	Oblt.	Hermichen	3 CO	15	Hurricane	Wizernes a/f		174 Sqd	yes
18-08-42	Oblt.	Hermichen	3 CO	16	Spitfire	20km S of Dungeness		602 Sqd	yes
19-08-42	Oblt.	Hermichen	3 CO	17	Spitfire	NE of Dieppe			yes
19-08-42	Oblt.	Hermichen	3 CO	18	Airacobra	near Dieppe			yes

04-12-42	Oblt.	Hermichen	3 CO	19	Spitfire	10km NE of Desvres	1434	401 or 402 Sqd	yes
06-12-42	Oblt.	Hermichen	3 CO	20	Spitfire	15-20km W of Le Tréport	1137		yes
19-12-42	Oblt.	Hermichen	3 CO	21	US fighter	25km ESE of Deal	1414	609 Sqd	yes
18-02-43	Hptm.	Hermichen	3 CO	22	LaGG-3	USSR (PQ 28321)			yes
19-02-43	Hptm.	Hermichen	3 CO	23	Il-2	USSR (PQ 18293)			yes
19-02-43	Hptm.	Hermichen	3 CO	24	Il-2	USSR (PQ 18462)			yes
04-03-43	Hptm.	Hermichen	3 CO	25	Pe-2	USSR (PQ 18242)			yes
05-03-43	Hptm.	Hermichen	3 CO	26	P-40	USSR (PQ 18443)			yes
07-03-43	Hptm.	Hermichen	3 CO	27	Pe-2	USSR (PQ 18551)			yes
07-03-43	Hptm.	Hermichen	3 CO	28	Pe-2	USSR (PQ 18254)			yes
23-03-43	Hptm.	Hermichen	3 CO	29	Yak	USSR (PQ 00412)			yes
28-07-43	Hptm.	Hermichen	3 CO	31	Typhoon	W of Rotterdam (IH1-HH7)	1217	4 FG P-47	unk
30-07-43	Hptm.	Hermichen	3 CO	32	B-17	near Nijmegen (IM3)	1012	379 BG	yes
30-07-43	Hptm.	Hermichen	3 CO	33	P-47	near Dordrecht (IL2-3)	1015	4 FG	unk
12-08-43	Hptm.	Hermichen	3 CO	34	B-17	Mönchen-Gladbach (KN3-6)			yes
15-08-43	Hptm.	Hermichen	3 CO	35	Spitfire	Vlissingen -N Sea (KG7)	1158	453 Sqd	yes
15-03-43	Gefr.	Heuser Hein.	2	1	LaGG-3	USSR (PQ 1827)	1600		yes
01-06-43	Uffz.	Heuser Hein.	2	2	A-20	USSR (PQ 35793)	1445		yes
12-08-43	Uffz.	Heuser Hein.	2	3	B-17	E of Arnhem (HO3)	0900	92 BG	yes
18-08-43	Uffz.	Heuser Hein.	2	4	Spitfire	Dunkirk (ME3)	0000		yes
04-09-43	Uffz.	Heuser Hein.	2		Spitfire	Dunkirk (ME3)	1914	131 Sqd	unk
10-10-43	Uffz.	Heuser Hein.	2	5	B-17	S of Rheine (HQ)	1515		yes
23-12-44	Ofhr.	Heuser Helm.	6	1	Lancaster	W of Köln	1300	405 or 582 Sqd	unk
19-07-41	Lt.	Heyarts	I St	1	Spitfire	N of Dunkirk	1415	72 Sqd	yes
17-07-44	Oblt.	Hilgendorff	9 CO	2	P-51	NW of Le Perron (AB3-6)	1950	354 FG	i.O.
11-05-40	Lt.	Hillecke	II St	1	Curtiss H75	Antwerp	1910	GC I/4	unk
16-05-40	Lt.	Hillecke	II St	2	Curtiss H75	Lille	1650		yes
18-05-40	Lt.	Hillecke	II St	3	Morane 406	Cambrai	1630		yes
24-05-40	Lt.	Hillecke	II St	4	Spitfire	Dunkirk	1655	74 Sqd	yes
29-05-40	Lt.	Hillecke	II St	5	Anson	Channel Narrows	1905	48 or 500 Sqd	unk
02-06-40	Lt.	Hillecke	II St	6	Hurricane	Dunkirk	0920	32 Sqd	yes
07-12-42	Fw.	Hiller	1	1	Spitfire	10km NW of Calais	0835	91 Sqd	yes
27-07-44	Lt.	Hilliger	9	1	Mustang	Caen (UU3)	0718	122 Sqd	unk
29-07-44	Lt.	Hilliger	9	2	Mustang	S of Soissons (UG7-8)	0715	65 Sqd	unk
16-02-43	Hptm.	Höckner	1 CO	40	Il-2	USSR (PQ 18453)			yes
16-02-43	Hptm.	Höckner	1 CO	41	Il-2	USSR (PQ 18422)			yes
18-02-43	Hptm.	Höckner	1 CO	42	Il-2	USSR (PQ 28454)			yes
21-02-43	Hptm.	Höckner	1 CO	43	LaGG-3	USSR (PQ 18294)			yes
21-02-43	Hptm.	Höckner	1 CO	44	P-40	USSR (PQ 18264)			yes
27-02-43	Hptm.	Höckner	1 CO	45	P-40	USSR (PQ 28122)			yes
27-02-43	Hptm.	Höckner	1 CO	46	P-40	USSR (PQ 28311)			yes
05-03-43	Hptm.	Höckner	1 CO	47	P-40	USSR (PQ 18214)			yes
07-03-43	Hptm.	Höckner	1 CO	48	Il-2	USSR (PQ 18352)			yes
07-03-43	Hptm.	Höckner	1 CO	49	Il-2	USSR (PQ 18322)			yes
07-03-43	Hptm.	Höckner	1 CO	50	Il-2	USSR (PQ 18193)			yes
07-03-43	Hptm.	Höckner	1 CO	51	Il-2	USSR (PQ 19573)			yes
07-03-43	Hptm.	Höckner	1 CO	52	P-40	USSR (PQ 19673)			yes
07-03-43	Hptm.	Höckner	1 CO	53	P-40	USSR (PQ 18382)			yes
09-03-43	Hptm.	Höckner	1 CO	54	LaGG-3	USSR (PQ 18471)			yes
24-03-43	Hptm.	Höckner	1 CO	55	Pe-2	USSR (PQ 00261)			yes
05-05-43	Hptm.	Höckner	1 CO	56	Pe-2	USSR (PQ 53124)			yes
18-05-40	Fw.	Hoffmann H.	4	1	Morane 406	Cambrai	1615		yes
29-05-40	Fw.	Hoffmann H.	4	2	Spitfire	Dunkirk	1855	64, 229 or 610 Sqd	yes
03-06-40	Fw.	Hoffmann H.	4	3	Morane 406	Paris	1430	GC I/6	unk
03-09-40	Fw.	Hoffmann H.	4	4	Spitfire	Hockley	1120	603 Sqd	unk
08-11-40	Obfw.	Hoffmann H.	4	5	Spitfire	Tonbridge	1450	302 or 501 Sqd	yes
24-04-42	Obfw.	Hoffmann H.	4	6	Spitfire	Berck-sur-Mer	1445	234 Sqd	yes
29-04-42	Obfw.	Hoffmann H.	4	7	Spitfire	Le Touquet	1608	Northolt or 317 Sqd	yes
25-08-44	Uffz.	Hoffmann J.	5	1	P-38	W of Beauvais (TE)	1349	474 FG	yes
22-03-45	Uffz.	Hoffmann J.	5	2	Tempest	near Rheine	1603	56 or 80 Sqd	unk
11-10-42	Uffz.	Hofmann W.	1	1	Spitfire	5km W of Cassel	1540	64 Sqd	unk
14-05-43	Fw.	Hofmann W.	1	2	LaGG-3	USSR (PQ 41484)			yes
18-10-43	Fw.	Hofmann W.	8	3	Spitfire	near Ardres	1420	132 Sqd	yes
04-01-44	Lt.	Hofmann W.	8	4	Spitfire	near Rue	1610	501 Sqd	yes
07-01-44	Lt.	Hofmann W.	8	5	B-17	2km E of La Calique	1350		yes
11-01-44	Lt.	Hofmann W.	8	6	B-17-eV	4km NW of Rheine	1318		unk
28-01-44	Lt.	Hofmann W.	8	7	Mustang	between Abbeville & Berck	1353	2 Sqd	yes
29-01-44	Lt.	Hofmann W.	8	8	B-17	2km N of Lutrebois	1330	95 BG	yes
08-03-44	Lt.	Hofmann W.	8 CO	9	P-51	17km W of Torgau (KF5)	1420	363 FG	yes
15-03-44	Lt.	Hofmann W.	8 CO	10	B-24	NW of Gevelsberg (LP5)	1215	392 BG	yes
12-04-44	Lt.	Hofmann W.	8 CO	11	B-24	52km E of Charleville (RL6)	1340	445 BG	yes
13-04-44	Lt.	Hofmann W.	8 CO	12	P-47	near Trier	1344	78 FG	yes
09-05-44	Lt.	Hofmann W.	8 CO	13	P-51	13km WNW of Turnhout (LK8)	0940	357 FG	yes
08-06-44	Lt.	Hofmann W.	8 CO	14	Mustang	NW of Caen (UU1-2)	0605	168 Sqd	yes

Date	Rank	Name	Unit	No.	Aircraft	Location	Time	Unit2	Conf.
08-06-44	Lt.	Hofmann W.	8 CO	15	P-47	20km SE of Caen (UU9)	1650		unk
08-06-44	Lt.	Hofmann W.	8 CO	16	P-47	W of Rouen (SB,TB,SC,TC)	1705		unk
10-06-44	Lt.	Hofmann W.	8 CO	17	P-47	NW of Lisieux	1428	78 FG	yes
12-06-44	Lt.	Hofmann W.	8 CO	18	P-47	40km SE of Rouen	0625	353 FG	yes
17-06-44	Lt.	Hofmann W.	8 CO	19	P-47	St. Lô (US1-5)	1335		yes
22-06-44	Lt.	Hofmann W.	8 CO	20	B-24-HSS	SE of Paris(BF2-3)	1910	34 BG	yes
23-06-44	Lt.	Hofmann W.	8 CO	21	Mustang	NE of Caen(UU2)	1308	414 Sqd	yes
24-06-44	Lt.	Hofmann W.	8 CO	22	Mustang	25km WSW of Dreux (AC5,6,8)	0722	65 Sqd	yes
24-06-44	Lt.	Hofmann W.	8 CO	23	P-47	W of Dreux(BC1-7)	2132	373 FG	yes
25-06-44	Lt.	Hofmann W.	8 CO	24	P-38	W of Rouen(TA3-TB1)	1530	370 FG	yes
29-06-44	Lt.	Hofmann W.	8 CO	25	Spitfire	10km SW of Lisieux (UA4)	0848	222 Sqd	yes
10-07-44	Lt.	Hofmann W.	8 CO	26	Spitfire	N of Caen (TU7)	1135		yes
15-08-44	Lt.	Hofmann W.	8 CO	27	P-47	Versailles(AC-AD)	1234	373 FG	yes
17-08-44	Lt.	Hofmann W.	8 CO	28	Spitfire	NW of Rouen(SB-SC)	1622	1 Sqd	yes
18-08-44	Lt.	Hofmann W.	8 CO	29	Mustang	Beauvais (TD1-2)	0822	315 Sqd	yes
20-08-44	Lt.	Hofmann W.	8 CO	30	P-47	NW of Paris (AE1)	1602	362 FG	yes
20-08-44	Lt.	Hofmann W.	8 CO	31	P-47	W of Rouen (TB)	2003	404 FG	yes
23-08-44	Lt.	Hofmann W.	8 CO	32	Spitfire	NE of Paris (UF7-8/AF1-2)	1346	421 or 443 Sqd	yes
25-08-44	Lt.	Hofmann W.	8 CO	33	P-38	W of Beauvais (TE1)	1353	474 FG	yes
25-08-44	Lt.	Hofmann W.	8 CO	34	P-51	N of Soissons (SG1-5)	1900	354 FG	yes
25-08-44	Lt.	Hofmann W.	8 CO	35	P-51	N of Soissons (SG1-5)	1904	354 FG	yes
28-08-44	Lt.	Hofmann W.	8 CO	36	Auster	Melun (AF9-BF3)	1210		yes
17-09-44	Lt.	Hofmann W.	8 CO	37	P-51	Emmerich (JO)	1440	4 FG	yes
21-09-44	Lt.	Hofmann W.	8 CO	38	C-47	Deelen (JM)	1720	38 or 46 Gp	yes
21-09-44	Lt.	Hofmann W.	8 CO	39	P-47	Zwolle (FN)	1733	353 FG	yes
02-10-44	Lt.	Hofmann W.	8 CO	40	Spitfire	Cleve-Nijmegen	1210	401 Sqd	i.O.
28-02-45	Oblt.	Hofmann W.	5 CO	41	P-47	near Mönchen-Gladbach	1223	406 FG	unk
01-03-45	Oblt.	Hofmann W.	5 CO	42	Auster	near Mönchen-Gladbach	0932		unk
01-03-45	Oblt.	Hofmann W.	5 CO	43	P-47	near Mönchen-Gladbach	0936	366 FG	unk
26-03-45	Oblt.	Hofmann W.	5 CO	44	Tempest	SW of Münster	1532	33 Sqd	unk
12-08-40	Uffz.	Högel	3	1	Spitfire	S of Folkestone	0920	610 Sqd	yes
04-04-43	Uffz.	Holl	9		Spitfire	Rouen	1440	315,316 or 403 Sqd	yes
13-06-43	Uffz.	Holl	9		B-17	Königsforde	0924	95 BG	yes
17-07-43	Uffz.	Holl	9		B-17	W of Helgoland (UO2)	0940	351 BG	unk
26-07-43	Uffz.	Holl	9		B-17	N of Leeuwarden (UL5)	1340		unk
28-07-43	Uffz.	Holl	9		B-17F	NW of Helgoland (SO5)	0920		yes
15-07-44	Uffz.	Holl	10		Spitfire	S of Caen (UU4 (AU3-6?))	0710		i.O.
05-07-40	Oblt.	Holtey v.	5	1	Blenheim	Senden	1415		yes
12-08-41	Oblt.	Holtey v.	Ge St	2	Blenheim	S of Vlissingen - in sea	1328		unk
02-10-42	Lt.	Hoppe	6	1	Spitfire	Somme Estuary	1658	401 Sqd	yes
08-11-42	Lt.	Hoppe	6	2	Spitfire	SW of Gravelines	1249	421 Sqd	yes
09-01-43	Lt.	Hoppe	6	3	Spitfire	W of Cayeux	1345	340 Sqd	yes
22-01-43	Lt.	Hoppe	5	4	Spitfire	NW of Gravelines	1515	350 Sqd	unk
13-02-43	Lt.	Hoppe	5	5	Spitfire	5km E of Étaples	1230	485 Sqd	yes
17-02-43	Lt.	Hoppe	5	6	Spitfire	6km SE of Calais	1102	124 Sqd	yes
04-04-43	Lt.	Hoppe	5	7	Spitfire	30km S of Beachy Head	1455	315,316 or 403 Sqd	yes
13-05-43	Lt.	Hoppe	5	8	B-17	S of Amiens	1627	91 BG	yes
31-05-43	Lt.	Hoppe	4 CO	9	Spitfire	10km N of Dunkirk	1753	403 Sqd	yes
16-06-43	Lt.	Hoppe	4 CO	10	Typhoon	mid-Channel	0530	1 Sqd	yes
26-06-43	Lt.	Hoppe	4 CO	11	P-47	Neufchatel	1853	56 FG	yes
26-06-43	Lt.	Hoppe	4 CO	12	P-47	10km NW of Somme Estuary	1910	56 FG	yes
10-07-43	Lt.	Hoppe	4 CO	13	B-17	near Fécamp-W of Rouen	0810	95 BG	i.O.
15-07-43	Lt.	Hoppe	4 CO	14	Spitfire	7-8km S of Berck-sur-Mer	1702	602 Sqd	yes
12-08-43	Lt.	Hoppe	4 CO	15	B-17	S of Eindhoven	0930		unk
17-08-43	Lt.	Hoppe	4 CO	16	Spitfire	S of Antwerp	1800	403 Sqd	unk
19-08-43	Lt.	Hoppe	4 CO	17	Typhoon	15km N of Amiens	1225	182 Sqd	yes
19-08-43	Lt.	Hoppe	4 CO	18	Typhoon	3-5km NW of Blangy?	1231	182 Sqd	unk
03-09-43	Lt.	Hoppe	4 CO	19	B-17	N of Paris	0930	92 BG	yes
04-09-43	Lt.	Hoppe	4 CO	20	Spitfire	near Berck-sur-Mer	1946		yes
11-09-43	Lt.	Hoppe	4 CO	21	Typhoon	S of Aumale-Beauvais	1848	124 Wing	yes
24-09-43	Lt.	Hoppe	4 CO	22	Spitfire	NE of Poix	1217	303 Sqd	yes
03-10-43	Lt.	Hoppe	5 CO	23	Spitfire	unknown	1547	341 or 485 Sqd	unk
03-10-43	Lt.	Hoppe	5 CO	24	Spitfire	10-15km W of Cayeux	1550	341 or 485 Sqd	unk
10-10-43	Lt.	Hoppe	5 CO		B-17	unknown			unk
08-08-44	Uffz.	Horch	4	1	P-51	Breteuil (AB7-8)	1425	359 FG	yes
23-09-40	Gefr.	Hornatscheck	9	1	Spitfire	Thames Estuary	1045	92 Sqd	yes
14-08-40	Oblt.	Hörnig	1	1	Spitfire	Dover	1320	65 or 610 Sqd	yes
28-08-40	Oblt.	Horten	Ge St	1	Defiant	Faversham	1003	264 Sqd	yes
28-08-40	Oblt.	Horten	Ge St	2	Defiant	Faversham	1003	264 Sqd	yes
31-08-40	Oblt.	Horten	Ge St	3	Spitfire	unknown	1900		yes
07-09-40	Oblt.	Horten	Ge St	4	Spitfire	unknown	1855	41 or 222 Sqd	yes
15-09-40	Oblt.	Horten	Ge St	5	Hurricane	Thames Estuary	1530	310 Sqd	yes

Date	Rank	Name	Unit	No.	Aircraft	Location	Time	Sqd	Conf
30-09-40	Oblt.	Horten	Ge St	6	Hurricane	Guildford		303 Sqd	unk
30-09-40	Oblt.	Horten	Ge St	7	Hurricane	Guildford		303 Sqd	unk
23-12-44	Fw.	Hött	6		Lancaster	nr Hengelo(NL)	1300	405 or 582 Sqd	no
24-12-44	Fw.	Hött	6		P-47	N of Liège(OL-OM)	1500		no
23-04-45	Fw.	Hött	6		Spitfire-dam	near Elsdorf	0615	403 Sqd	no
15-08-40	Uffz.	Humburg	9	1	Spitfire	E Dover	1615	64 Sqd	yes
07-06-44	Obfw.	Humburg	9		P-47	NW of Rouen (SB3)	1045		unk
17-07-44	Obfw.	Humburg	9		P-47	W of Dreux (AB3-6)	1940		i.O.
27-09-44	Obfw.	Humburg	9		Mustang	Nijmegen (JM4-5)	1040	168 Sqd	unk
07-01-44	Fw.	Hummel	6	1	B-17	10km NW of Abbeville	1327		yes
07-06-40	Uffz.	Iberle	4	1	Hurricane	20km SE of Dieppe		43 Sqd	unk
12-08-40	Ogfr.	Jäckel E.	2	1	Spitfire	near Margate			unk
23-08-40	Ogfr.	Jäckel E.	2	2	Battle	SW of Boulogne	2020	142 Sqd	yes
16-06-41	Fw.	Jäckel E.	2	3	Spitfire	SE of Dungeness	1830	1 or 91 Sqd	yes
21-06-41	Fw.	Jäckel E.	2	4	Spitfire	W of Boulogne	1630		yes
27-06-41	Fw.	Jäckel E.	2	5	Spitfire	E of Sangatte	2210		yes
18-07-41	Fw.	Jäckel E.	2	6	Stirling	SE of Lille	1140	XV Sqd	yes
25-05-42	Fw.	Jäckel E.	2	7	Spitfire	15km NW of Dunkirk	1145	222 Sqd	unk
02-06-42	Fw.	Jäckel E.	2	8	Spitfire	NW of Crécy	1105	403 Sqd	yes
28-05-40	Uffz.	Jäckel K.	8	1	Hurricane	Ostend	1225	213, 229 or 242Sqd	yes
18-08-40	Fw.	Jäckel K.	8	2	Spitfire	N London	1850		yes
31-08-40	Fw.	Jäckel K.	8	3	Hurricane	unknown	1940		yes
17-06-41	Lt.	Janda	4	1	Hurricane	Cap Gris Nez	1950	56 or 242 Sqd	yes
28-08-42	Lt.	Janda	4	2	Spitfire	S of Amiens	1439	401 Sqd	yes
03-02-43	Fw.	Jauer	7	1	Spitfire	5-7km W of Dunkirk	1112	308 Sqd	i.O.
07-03-43	Fw.	Jauer	7	3	Il-2	6km SSW Peterhof (90254)	1249		yes
07-03-43	Fw.	Jauer	7	4	LaGG-3	4km SSW Peterhof (90263)	1250		yes
07-03-43	Fw.	Jauer	7	5	LaGG-3	8km SW Peterhof (90253)	1252		yes
21-03-43	Fw.	Jauer	7	6	LaGG-3	SSW of Ovzino (00272)	1445		yes
22-03-43	Fw.	Jauer	7	7	Il-2	Krasny-Bor (00414)	1515		yes
26-03-43	Fw.	Jauer	7	8	LaGG-3	2km NW of Krasny-Bor (0041)	0955		yes
01-06-43	Fw.	Jauer	7	9	LaGG-3	5km N Ostrovky (00254)	2109		yes
02-06-43	Fw.	Jauer	7	10	Pe-2	2km W of Lipovo (90113)	1456		yes
08-06-43	Fw.	Jauer	7	11	I-180	2-3km NW of Volkhov (20124)	1558		yes
08-06-43	Fw.	Jauer	7	12	Yak-7	N of Yaksolovo (00252)	2029		yes
18-06-43	Fw.	Jauer	7		P-39	USSR (PQ 20161)	0600		unk
18-06-43	Fw.	Jauer	7		P-39	USSR (PQ 20161)	0605		unk
20-09-41	Uffz.	Jennewein	1/E	1	Spitfire	unknown			unk
20-09-41	Uffz.	Jennewein	1/E	2	Spitfire	unknown			unk
20-09-41	Uffz.	Jennewein	1/E	3	Spitfire	unknown			unk
15-10-41	Uffz.	Jennewein	1/E	4	Spitfire	unknown			unk
15-10-41	Uffz.	Jennewein	1/E	5	Spitfire	unknown			unk
07-10-44	Fw.	Jentzsch	4	1	Spitfire	E of Tilburg (KN)	1630		i.O.
16-02-43	Lt.	Jessen	I St	1	Il-2	15km S of Adler 7			yes
23-02-43	Lt.	Jessen	I St	2	Il-2	USSR (PQ 1843)			yes
28-02-43	Lt.	Jessen	I St	3	Pe-2	USSR (PQ 18354)			yes
28-02-43	Lt.	Jessen	I St	4	MiG-3	USSR (PQ 1835)			yes
14-03-43	Lt.	Jessen	I St	5	LaGG-3	USSR (PQ 1827)			yes
15-03-43	Lt.	Jessen	I St	6	MiG-3	USSR (PQ 19733)			yes
07-03-41	Lt.	Johannsen	7	1	Blenheim	W of Gozo Is.	1215	69 Sqd	yes
16-03-41	Lt.	Johannsen	7		Hurricane	Malta		261 Sqd	no
30-04-41	Lt.	Johannsen	7	2	Hurricane	Valetta, Malta		261 Sqd	unk
01-05-41	Lt.	Johannsen	7	3	Hurricane	W Valetta-Hal Far a/f Malta	0754	261 Sqd	unk
01-05-41	Lt.	Johannsen	7	4	Hurricane	SW Luqa a/f, Malta	1714	261 Sqd	yes
25-05-41	Lt.	Johannsen	7		Hurricane-ground	Takali, Malta	1500	249 Sqd	no
29-07-41	Lt.	Johannsen	7	5	Tomahawk	20km S of Sidi Barrani, Egypt	1750	2 Sqd SAAF	unk
02-08-41	Lt.	Johannsen	7	6	Tomahawk	NW of Mersa Matruh,Egypt	1855	1 Sqd SAAF	unk
21-09-41	Lt.	Johannsen	7	7	Spitfire	20km W of Cap Gris Nez	1620	485 or 602 Sqd	unk
21-10-41	Lt.	Johannsen	7	8	Spitfire	2km S of Boulogne	1300		yes
25-08-44	Uffz.	Just	5	1	P-38	W of Beauvais (TD)	1348	474 FG	unk
21-02-45	Uffz.	Just	5	2	B-26	E of Arnhem (near HO-HP)	1601	394 BG	unk
26-05-42	Uffz.	Jutrzenka v.	1	1	Spitfire	Channel	1010		yes
08-06-42	Uffz.	Jutrzenka v.	1	2	Spitfire	6km NW of Dunkirk	1356		yes
08-07-41	Oblt.	Kahse	1	1	Spitfire	NNW ofCoxyde-Calais	1545		unk
21-07-41	Oblt.	Kahse	1	2	Spitfire	W of Calais	0845		unk
16-02-43	Gefr.	Kaiser	1	1	Il-2	USSR (PQ 18454)			yes
16-02-43	Gefr.	Kaiser	1	2	Il-2	USSR (PQ 18452)			yes
01-01-45	Uffz.	Kalbus	5	1	P-47	NE of Brussels (ML9)	1004		unk
03-02-43	Obfw.	Kalitzki	8	1	Spitfire	N of Gravelines	1535	416 Sqd	yes
21-09-41	Uffz.	Karcher	1	1	Spitfire	10km SW of Boulogne			unk
16-06-43	Lt.	Kehl	4	1	Typhoon	6km SE of Arras	0534	1 Sqd	yes
02-09-43	Lt.	Kehl	II St	2	P-47	near Berck-sur-Mer	2025	56 FG	unk
07-09-43	Lt.	Kehl	4	3	Mustang	near Rosay [?]	1627	168 Sqd	yes

Date	Rank	Name	Unit	No.	Aircraft	Location	Time	Allied Unit	Status
29-01-44	Lt.	Kehl	5		B-24	unknown			unk
03-02-43	Hptm.	Kelch	7	1	Ventura	10-15km NW of Dunkirk	1115	21 Sqd	i.O.
23-07-41	Lt.	Keller	II St	1	Blenheim	Ostend	1425	21 Sqd	yes
27-09-41	Lt.	Keller	II St	2	Spitfire	Watten	1538		yes
13-01-43	Obfw.	Kemethmüller	7	61	B-17	Ypres-Lille	1415	305 BG	yes
03-02-43	Obfw.	Kemethmüller	7	62	Ventura	NW of Dunkirk	1112	21 Sqd	i.O.
21-05-43	Obfw.	Kemethmüller	7	63	Pe-2	Glubkoye Osero	0546		yes
21-05-43	Obfw.	Kemethmüller	7	64	LaGG-3	USSR	0551		yes
21-05-43	Obfw.	Kemethmüller	7	65	I-16	USSR	1021		yes
30-05-43	Obfw.	Kemethmüller	7	66	LaGG-3	Kopena USSR	1355		yes
02-06-43	Obfw.	Kemethmüller	7	67	La-5	2km W of Lipovo (90113)	1455		yes
05-06-43	Obfw.	Kemethmüller	7	68	P-40	Lake Ladoga USSR	1210	240th IAD	yes
08-06-43	Obfw.	Kemethmüller	7	69	Yak-7	10km NW of Volkhov (20123)	1557		yes
18-06-43	Obfw.	Kemethmüller	7	70	Yak-1	Ladoga region USSR	0612		yes
18-06-43	Obfw.	Kemethmüller	7	71	LaGG-3	Volknovstroi	1222		yes
22-06-43	Obfw.	Kemethmüller	7	72	Il-2	Siverskaya a/f USSR	0233	9th ShAD	yes
28-07-43	Obfw.	Kemethmüller	7	73	B-17F	N of Sylt (RP 5)	0916		yes
29-07-43	Obfw.	Kemethmüller	7	74	B-17	15km NE of Schleswig	0930	306 BG	yes
17-08-43	Obfw.	Kemethmüller	7		B-17-eV	S of Woensdrecht	1120	385 BG	no
17-08-43	Obfw.	Kemethmüller	7		B-17	Holland	1120		no
14-01-44	Ofhr.	Kemethmüller	9	75	Spitfire	Calais	1200	308 Sqd	yes
21-01-44	Ofhr.	Kemethmüller	9		Spitfire	S of St Omer	1245		no
24-01-44	Ofhr.	Kemethmüller	9		P-47-dam	Brussels	1100	78 FG	no
11-02-44	Ofhr.	Kemethmüller	9		B-17-dam	near Douai	1345		no
02-03-44	Ofhr.	Kemethmüller	9		B-17-dam	unknown	1200		no
13-04-44	Ofhr.	Kemethmüller	9		B-17-dam	NW Kaiserslautern (SP)	1334		no
23-04-44	Lt.	Kemethmüller	9		P-51	S of Wiener Neustadt (FO-5)	1422	31 FG	yes
23-04-44	Lt.	Kemethmüller	9	76	P-51	S of Neusiedler Lake	1422	31 FG	yes
08-05-44	Lt.	Kemethmüller	4 CO	78	P-47	W of Hirson(RH 7-9)	1005		yes
24-06-44	Lt.	Kemethmüller	4 CO	79	P-47	20km NE ofSt Dizier (DL2-3)	2137		yes
29-06-44	Lt.	Kemethmüller	4 CO	80	Spitfire	N of Caen (TU8)	0840		yes
12-07-44	Lt.	Kemethmüller	4 CO	81	P-47-	SW of Elbeuf-Quittebeuf (AB6)	1430	358 FG	yes
12-07-44	Lt.	Kemethmüller	4 CO	82	P-47	W of Danville (AB6-AC7)	1431	358 FG	yes
12-07-44	Lt.	Kemethmüller	4 CO		P-47-dam	SW of Breteuil (Caen?)	1435	358 FG	dam
13-07-44	Lt.	Kemethmüller	4 CO	83	P-47	NW of Vernon (UU-2,6?)	1658	366 FG	yes
14-07-44	Lt.	Kemethmüller	4 CO	84	P-47	St Andre-W of Paris (AC)	1436	358 FG	yes
16-07-44	Lt.	Kemethmüller	4 CO	85	P-47	25km SW of Rouen (TB3)	2131	373 FG	yes
18-07-44	Lt.	Kemethmüller	4 CO	86	P-38	25km SE of Vernon (AD1)	0930	474 FG	yes
26-08-44	Lt.	Kemethmüller	4 CO	87	Spitfire	W of Beauvais (TD4)	1425	341 Sqd	unk
16-09-44	Lt.	Kemethmüller	4 CO	88	P-38	Monschau-SE of Stolberg (ON2-3)	1741	370FG	yes
17-09-44	Lt.	Kemethmüller	4 CO	89	Spitfire	Nijmegen-W of Cleve (IN7)	1756		unk
01-12-43	Lt.	Kempf	11	58	B-17	unknown			yes
20-12-43	Lt.	Kempf	11	59	B-17	unknown			yes
07-06-44	Lt.	Kempf	9	60	P-47	E of Dreux (AD3)	0851		yes
12-06-44	Lt.	Kempf	9	61	P-47	Lisieux (UA2)	0614	353 FG	i.O.
21-06-44	Lt.	Kempf	9	62	Mustang	E of Dreux (AD5)	1937	430 Sqd	i.O.
04-07-44	Lt.	Kempf	9	63	P-47	SW of Évreux (AB1)	1442	406 FG	i.O.
04-07-44	Lt.	Kempf	9	64	Spitfire	SW of Évreux (AB1)	1443		i.O.
26-08-44	Lt.	Kempf	2	65	Spitfire	Rouen (TC4)	0933	602 Sqd	yes
23-01-43	Lt.	Kestel	9	1	B-17	unknown	1417	303 BG	unk
18-05-43	Lt.	Kestel	9	2	P-47	unknown	1705	4 FG	unk
13-06-43	Lt.	Kestel	9	3	B-17	Schönberg	0931	95 BG	yes
05-03-41	Uffz.	Kestler	7	1	Hurricane	Malta	1730	261 Sqd	no
22-03-41	Uffz.	Kestler	7	2	Hurricane	N of Malta	1631	261 Sqd	yes
30-07-43	Lt.	Kiefner	3		Boston-eV	unknown	0715		no
12-08-43	Lt.	Kiefner	3	1	B-17	N of Ghent (LH5-6)	1030	92 BG	unk
17-08-43	Lt.	Kiefner	3	1	B-17-eV	Woensdrecht	1130	385 BG	no
07-01-44	Lt.	Kiefner	1	2	P-47	S of Maubeuge	1230	358 FG	yes
21-01-44	Lt.	Kiefner	1	3	B-24	near Poix	1530	44 BG	yes
02-03-44	Lt.	Kiefner	1	4	B-17	Arlon (SM2)	1343		yes
06-03-44	Lt.	Kiefner	1	5	B-24	Almelo (CO5,4)	1500	458 BG	yes
20-05-44	Lt	Kiefner	1	6	P-51	E of Courtrai (NH)	1050	355 FG	yes
11-07-44	Lt.	Kiefner	1 CO	7	P-51	Caen (UU2-TU8)	1950		unk
15-07-44	Lt.	Kiefner	1 CO	8	Spitfire	Caen (UU1)	0715		yes
07-08-44	Lt.	Kiefner	1 CO	9	P-47	E of Melun(BG4-5)	1925	373 FG	yes
17-08-44	Lt.	Kiefner	1 CO	10	Auster	Rambouillet (BD4)	1150		yes
26-08-44	Lt.	Kiefner	1 CO	11	Spitfire	Rouen (TC5)	0933	602 Sqd	yes
24-12-44	Lt.	Kiefner	1 CO	12	P-38	Liège (PL3)	1224	367 FG	unk
04-04-42	Obfw.	Kierstein	2	1	Spitfire	N of St. Omer	1135	303 Sqd	yes
29-06-42	Obfw.	Kierstein	2	2	Spitfire	N of Coxyde	1643	222 or 332 Sqd	yes
31-10-42	Obfw.	Kierstein	2	3	Spitfire	5km W of Étaples		453 Sqd	yes
31-05-44	Gefr.	Kleemann	4	1	P-51	Romaneski?	1100		flak
03-06-40	Fw.	Klein	3	1	Curtiss H75	S of Le Bourget	1440	GC I/5	yes

Date	Rank	Name	Unit	No.	Aircraft	Location	Time	Sqd/Gp	Conf.
17-08-44	Uffz.	Klein E.	8	1	Spitfire	NW of Rouen (SB)	1623	1 Sqd	yes
18-08-44	Uffz.	Klein E.	8	2	Mustang	Beauvais (TE1)	0823	315 Sqd	unk
19-03-45	Maj.	Klemm	IV CO		P-51	10 km NW of Nordhorn (GQ3)	1335	78 FG	unk
31-07-42	Uffz.	Klems	I St	1	Spitfire	20km W of Étaples		133 Sqd	yes
08-11-42	Uffz.	Klems	I St	2	Spitfire	5km S of Merville			yes
11-05-40	Hptm.	Knüppel	II CO	1	Curtiss H75	Antwerp	1910	GC I/4	yes
16-05-40	Hptm.	Knüppel	II CO	2	Morane 406	Seclin	1650		yes
18-05-40	Hptm.	Knüppel	II CO	3	Morane 406	Cambrai	1630		yes
30-08-40	Fw.	Koch	5	1	Hurricane	Dungeness	1815	253 Sqd	yes
01-10-40	Fw.	Koch	5	2	Hurricane	Brighton	1530	303 Sqd	yes
29-11-40	Fw.	Koch	5	3	Hurricane	Tonbridge	1350	249 Sqd	yes
08-04-41	Obfw.	Koch	5	4	Blenheim	Ile de Batz-NE of Brest	1325	82 Sqd	yes
07-08-41	Oblt.	Koch	5	5	Spitfire	Guines	1130	19 or 401 Sqds	yes
16-08-41	Oblt.	Koch	5	6	Spitfire	E of Gravelines	0930	602 Sqd	yes
19-08-41	Oblt.	Koch	5	7	Spitfire	Wormhout	1200	403 Sqd	yes
27-09-41	Oblt.	Koch	5	8	Spitfire	Gravelines	1535		yes
08-11-41	Oblt.	Koch	5	9	Spitfire	Hardifort	1305		yes
21-09-44	Gefr.	Kohler	3	1	C-47	Hertogenbosch (IH)	1722	38 or 46 Gp	unk
21-09-44	Gefr.	Kohler	3	2	C-47	W of Arnhem	1725	38 or 46 Gp	yes
08-02-44	Ogfr.	Köhn	1	1	P-51	Givet (QK5,7)		354 FG	yes
12-04-45	Lt.	Konrad	3	1	Tempest	15km N of Uelsen	1255	33 Sqd	unk
12-05-44	Fw.	Kopp	10	1	B-17F	Bastogne (QM-QL)	1542	452 BG	unk
06-08-44	Lt.	Kopp	10	2	Halifax	N of Paris (UE7)	1215		i.O.
21-09-41	Uffz.	Korte	8	1	Spitfire	unknown	1620	485 or 602 Sqd	yes
27-08-41	Obfw.	Koslowski	9	10	Spitfire	unknown	0815		yes
08-12-41	Obfw.	Koslowski	9	11	Spitfire	unknown	1300		yes
09-01-42	Obfw.	Koslowski	9	12	Spitfire	unknown			unk
17-05-40	Lt.	Kosse	6	1	Lysander	Mons	1830	16 Sqd	yes
18-05-40	Lt.	Kosse	6	2	Morane 405/6	Cambrai	1630		yes
01-06-40	Lt.	Kosse	6	3	Hurricane	Dunkirk	1245	43, 145 or 245Sqd	yes
02-06-40	Lt.	Kosse	6	4	Hurricane	Dunkirk	0915	32 Sqd	unk
31-08-40	Lt.	Kosse	5 CO	5	Hurricane	Dungeness	1855		yes
06-09-40	Lt.	Kosse	5 CO	6	Hurricane	Guildford	1010	303 Sqd	unk
09-06-41	Lt.	Kosse	5 CO	7	Blenheim	Channel Narrows	1710	18 Sqd	yes
23-07-41	Lt.	Kosse	5 CO	8	Blenheim	Ostend	1420	21 Sqd	yes
09-08-41	Lt.	Kosse	5 CO	9	Spitfire	St. Omer	1145	Tangmere	yes
04-04-42	Oblt.	Kosse	5 CO	10	Spitfire	NNW of Calais	1145		yes
12-04-42	Oblt.	Kosse	5 CO	11	Spitfire	Calais	1342	316 Sqd	yes
30-11-42	Fw.	Kraft	9	1	Hurricane	W of Brighton			unk
17-08-43	Fw.	Kraft	9		B-17-eV	SE of Turnhout	1145	95 BG	unk
17-05-42	Oblt.	Kranefeld	8	1	Spitfire	unknown	1445		yes
07-01-44	Oblt.	Kranefeld	I St	2	P-47	nr Cousolre	1230	358 FG	yes
11-01-44	Oblt.	Kranefeld	I St	3	B-17-HSS	unknown	1327	306 BG	yes
29-01-44	Oblt.	Kranefeld	I St	4	B-17	S of Maubeuge	1245	385 BG	yes
28-02-45	Oblt.	Kraus	10	1	Tempest	Osnabrück	0800	274 Sqd	unk
01-05-42	Uffz.	Krieg	5	1	Spitfire	Marquise	1945	122 or 222 Sqd	yes
13-05-40	Lt.	Krug	5	1	Spitfire	Waalhaven	0645	66 or 264 Sqd	yes
13-05-40	Lt.	Krug	5	2	Spitfire	Dordrecht	0655	66 or 264 Sqd	yes
19-05-40	Lt.	Krug	5		Hurricane	Lille	2030		unk
01-06-40	Lt.	Krug	5	3	Hurricane	Dunkirk	1235	43, 145 or 245Sqd	unk
02-06-40	Lt.	Krug	5	4	Hurricane	Dunkirk	0935	32 Sqd	unk
12-08-40	Lt.	Krug	4	5	Spitfire	Margate	1225		yes
14-08-40	Lt.	Krug	4	6	Spitfire	Dover	1335	65 or 610 Sqd	unk
15-08-40	Lt.	Krug	4	7	Spitfire	Folkestone	1605	64 Sqd	yes
22-08-40	Lt.	Krug	4	8	Spitfire	Marquise	2015	65 Sqd	unk
23-08-40	Lt.	Krug	4	9	Battle	Boulogne	2025	142 Sqd	yes
27-09-44	Hptm.	Krupinski	III CO	192	Spitfire	unknown	1821		unk
12-10-44	Hptm.	Krupinski	III CO	193	P-51	unknown	1550		no
16-08-44	Uffz.	Kruse	8	1	P-51	Rambouillet (AD)	1435	354 FG	yes
25-08-44	Uffz.	Kruse	8	2	P-38	N of Beauvais (TE)	1355	474 FG	yes
21-02-45	Uffz.	Krusen	5	1	B-26	E of Arnhem (near HO-HP)	1601	394 BG	unk
30-04-42	Fw.	Kruska	6	1	Spitfire	Le Tréport	1930	222 Sqd	yes
19-08-42	Obfw.	Kruska	6	2	Mustang	Forêt de Vron	0845	414 Sqd	yes
14-03-43	Obfw.	Kruska	6	3	Spitfire	5km W of Camiers	1754	B Hill Wing	yes
07-03-41	Obfw.	Kühdorf	7	1	Hurricane	Malta	1220	261 Sqd	yes
22-03-41	Obfw.	Kühdorf	7	2	Hurricane	20km N of Malta	1630	261 Sqd	unk
01-05-41	Obfw.	Kühdorf	7		Hurricane	Luqa a/f, Malta	1720	261 Sqd	no
27-04-42	Obfw.	Kühdorf	7	3	Spitfire	3km NW of Calais	1220	111 Sqd	no
24-05-44	Oblt.	Kunz	2 CO	9	P-38	St Quentin (RG)	1924		yes
06-06-44	Oblt.	Kunz	2 CO	10	P-51	5km SE of Caen (UU5)	2055	4 FG	yes
21-09-44	Oblt.	Kunz	2 CO	11	C-47	Nijmegen (IL-IM)	1718	38 or 46 Gp	yes
21-09-44	Oblt.	Kunz	2 CO	12	C-47	Hertogenbosch (IL9)	1720	38 or 46 Gp	yes
05-03-43	Lt.	Kunze	2	1	Il-2	USSR (PQ 18352)	1236		yes
03-09-40	Uffz.	Küpper	8	1	unknown	unknown	1110		unk

Date	Rank	Name	Unit	No.	Type	Location	Time	Unit claimed	Status
13-10-44	Uffz.	Lampferhoff	5	1	P-47	Mönchen-Gladbach (MN)	1504	368 FG	i.O.
06-11-44	Uffz.	Lampferhoff	5	2	P-47	Kreuzau SW of Düren (ON3)	1220	36 FG	unk
19-11-44	Uffz.	Lampferhoff	5	3	Spitfire	N of Kirchhellen (KO3)	1408	412 Sqd	unk
09-07-44	Hptm.	Lang	II CO	160	Spitfire	Caen (UU-UA)	1319	453 Sqd	yes
09-07-44	Hptm.	Lang	II CO	161	Spitfire	Caen (UU-UA)	1321	453 Sqd	yes
09-07-44	Hptm.	Lang	II CO	162	Spitfire	Caen (UU-UA)	1324	453 Sqd	yes
15-08-44	Hptm.	Lang	II CO	163	P-47	Rambouillet(AD-BD)	1231	373 FG	yes
15-08-44	Hptm.	Lang	II CO	164	P-47	Rambouillet(AD-BD)	1232	373 FG	yes
19-08-44	Hptm.	Lang	II CO	165	P-47	E of Vernon (UD7)	1024	406 FG	yes
23-08-44	Hptm.	Lang	II CO	166	Spitfire	NE of Paris(UE-UF)	1338	421 or 443 Sqd	yes
23-08-44	Hptm.	Lang	II CO	167	Spitfire	N of Paris (UE)	1340	421 or 443 Sqd	yes
25-08-44	Hptm.	Lang	II CO	168	P-38	W of Beauvais (TD)	1343	474 FG	yes
25-08-44	Hptm.	Lang	II CO	169	P-38	E of Vernon (UD)	1345	474 FG	yes
25-08-44	Hptm.	Lang	II CO	170	P-38	W of Beauvais (TD)	1348	474 FG	yes
26-08-44	Hptm.	Lang	II CO	171	Spitfire	E of Neufchatel (SD7)	0917	421 Sqd	yes
26-08-44	Hptm.	Lang	II CO	172	Spitfire	Rouen (TC3)	0919	421 Sqd	yes
26-08-44	Hptm.	Lang	II CO	173	Spitfire	E of Rouen (TD1)	1428	341 Sqd	yes
13-06-43	Lt.	Lange F.	5	1	P-47	St. Jean-Ypres	1450	78 FG	yes
22-06-43	Lt.	Lange F.	5	2	B-17	3km W of Goes	0920	384 BG	yes
15-07-43	Lt.	Lange F.	5	3	Spitfire	Somme Estuary	1657	602 Sqd	yes
29-01-44	Lt.	Lange F.	6	4	B-17-eV	20km SE of Lille	1300		unk
11-02-44	Lt.	Lange F.	6	5	P-38	13km SE of Valenciennes	1347	20 FG	yes
20-02-44	Lt.	Lange F.	6	7	B-17	Ressaix-19km E of Mons	1505	91 BG	yes
20-02-44	Lt.	Lange F.	6	6	P-47	Seraing-6km SW of Liège	1525	4 FG	yes
22-02-44	Lt.	Lange F.	6	8	P-47	15km NW of Bruenel	1600		yes
22-01-45	Ogfr.	Lange H.	4	1	Spitfire	Rheine-Ibbenbüren	1120	421 Sqd	unk
18-10-43	Uffz.	Laub	11	3	P-47	St Pol (PE4-9)	1410	78 FG	yes
20-12-43	Uffz.	Laub	11	4	B-17	unknown	1156		yes
14-01-44	Uffz.	Laub	11	5	Spitfire	unknown	1158	308 Sqd	yes
25-02-44	Fw.	Laub	11	6	B-17	10km SE of Longwy	1230		yes
24-04-44	Fw.	Laub	11	7	B-17	S of Donauwörth (BB6-9/BC4-7)	1340		unk
29-04-41	Obfw.	Laube	7	1	Hurricane	St. Pauls Bay, Malta	1846	261 Sqd	unk
25-05-41	Obfw.	Laube	7		Hurricane-ground	Takali, Malta	1500	249 Sqd	no
03-05-42	Oblt.	Laube	7	2	Spitfire	Calais	1603	174 or 303 Sqd	yes
24-04-44	Uffz.	Leder Joach.	12		B-17-eV	N of Innsbruck (FC7-8)	1410		no
24-04-44	Uffz.	Leder Joach.	12	1	B-17	S of Donauwörth (BB7-8)	1330		unk
02-10-44	Ogfr.	Leder Jos.	1	1	Spitfire	Arnhem (HM8) (KM8?)	1205		unk
12-02-41	Fw.	Leibing	7	1	Hurricane	Malta	1645	261 Sqd	yes
12-02-41	Fw.	Leibing	7	2	Hurricane	Malta	1647	261 Sqd	yes
16-06-41	Fw.	Leibold	3	1	Spitfire	W of Boulogne	1632		yes
18-07-41	Fw.	Leibold	3	2	Spitfire	near St. Pol	1129		yes
23-07-41	Fw.	Leibold	3	3	Spitfire	S of Gravelines	1400		yes
07-09-41	Fw.	Leibold	3	4	Spitfire	20km E of Folkestone	1738	71 Sqd	yes
20-09-41	Fw.	Leibold	3	5	Spitfire	10km NE of Clairmarais	1640		yes
27-09-41	Fw.	Leibold	3	6	Spitfire	SW of Gravelines	1531		yes
24-03-42	Obfw.	Leibold	3	7	Spitfire	between Lille & Ypres	1637	411 Sqd	yes
25-03-42	Obfw.	Leibold	3	8	Spitfire	Boulogne	1810	303 Sqd	yes
01-06-42	Obfw.	Leibold	I St	9	Spitfire	2km N of Zeebrugge	1350	111 Sqd	yes
03-06-42	Obfw.	Leibold	I St	10	Spitfire	20km N ofLe Touquet	1653		yes
12-07-42	Obfw.	Leibold	I St	11	Mosquito	Licques	1435		yes
12-07-43	Uffz.	Leitz	7	1	unknown	unknown	1445		yes
13-07-43	Uffz.	Leitz	7	2	unknown	unknown	1217		yes
09-03-42	Lt.	Leuschel	6	1	Spitfire	15km SW of Boulogne	1640		no
13-05-43	Lt.	Leuschel	10 CO	2	Spitfire	E of Bray	1632	416 Sqd	unk
14-05-43	Oblt.	Leuschel	10 CO	3	P-47	6km N of Ath	1325	78 FG	unk
24-06-43	Oblt.	Leuschel	10 CO	4	Spitfire	SW of Ostend	0904	303 Sqd	unk
04-07-43	Oblt.	Leuschel	10 CO	5	Spitfire	near Berck-sur-Mer	1734	122 Sqd	yes
04-09-43	Oblt.	Leuschel	10 CO	6	Spitfire	SE of Roubaix	0903		unk
11-11-43	Oblt.	Leuschel	8 CO	7	B-17	SW of Numansdorp	1500	94 BG	yes
01-12-43	Oblt.	Leuschel	8 CO	8	P-47	SE of Ghent	1320	56 FG	yes
29-01-44	Oblt.	Leuschel	8 CO	9	B-24	Niederflorsheim-Worms		44 BG	yes
18-02-43	Obfw.	Lindelaub	1	1	Il-2	USSR (PQ 28173)			yes
21-02-43	Obfw.	Lindelaub	1	2	LaGG-3	USSR (PQ 18291)			yes
27-02-43	Obfw.	Lindelaub	1	3	LaGG-3	USSR (PQ 18391)			yes
17-08-43	Obfw.	Lindelaub	1	4	B-17	NW of Maastricht (ML)	1446	92 BG	yes
10-10-43	Obfw.	Lindelaub	1		B-17	unknown			no
30-01-44	Obfw.	Lindelaub	1	5	B-17	unknown			yes
21-08-41	Lt.	Lindemann	7	1	Maryland	W ofSidi Barrani, Egypt	1755	12 or 24 Sqd SAAF	yes
18-09-41	Uffz.	Lindemann	7	2	Spitfire	5km W of Fécamp	1605	452 Sqd	yes
29-01-44	Uffz.	Lindner	8	1	P-47	20km E of Marche	1230	355 FG	yes
28-06-44	Uffz.	Lindner	7	2	Spitfire	Coutances (TT9)	1121		unk
17-06-44	Uffz.	Lissack	7	1	P-51	Bayeux (UT1-2)	1908		yes

Date	Rank	Name	Staffel	No.	Aircraft	Location	Time	Unit	Conf.
18-06-44	Uffz.	Lissack	7	2	Mustang	Coutances (A8-9)	1729	414 Sqd	yes
24-04-44	Fhr.	Lorberg	12		B-17-eV	N of Innsbruck (FC6)	1405		no
21-02-44	Uffz.	Loschinski	7	1	B-17	NW of Utrecht	1605	95 BG	yes
28-05-40	Oblt.	Losigkeit	2 CO	1	Spitfire	between Dover & Ostend			unk
01-06-40	Oblt.	Losigkeit	2 CO	2	Spitfire	near Dunkirk	0640	19, 222 or 616 Sqd	yes
28-08-40	Oblt.	Losigkeit	2 CO	3	Hurricane	N of Folkestone	1005	79 Sqd	yes
30-08-40	Oblt.	Losigkeit	2 CO	4	Spitfire	SE of Littlestone	1930		yes
15-09-40	Oblt.	Losigkeit	2 CO	5	Spitfire	SE of London	1540	92 Sqd	yes
27-05-40	Fw.	Lüders	6	1	Spitfire	Ostend	1632		yes
27-05-40	Fw.	Lüders	6	2	Spitfire	Ostend	1740		yes
31-05-40	Fw.	Lüders	6	3	Hurricane	7km NW of Nieuport	1300	245 Sqd	unk
31-08-40	Fw.	Lüders	6	4	Hurricane	Brentwood	0942	56 Sqd	unk
15-09-40	Fw.	Lüders	6	5	Spitfire	Channel	1600	19 Sqd	yes
13-06-40	Lt.	Ludewig	9	1	Potez 63	unknown	1030	GAO 3/551	yes
12-12-42	Uffz.	Lühs	9	1	B-17	SE of Paris	1235	303 BG	yes
13-04-44	Uffz.	M...hauer?	5		B-17-eV	NW of Trier	1325		no
16-08-41	Obfw.	Mackenstedt	6	1	Spitfire	Gravelines	0925	602 Sqd	yes
08-11-41	Obfw.	Mackenstedt	6	2	Spitfire	Calais	1320	Digby or 412 Sqd	unk
23-11-41	Obfw.	Mackenstedt	6	3	Spitfire	W of Dunkirk	1327	315 sqd	yes
09-03-42	Obfw.	Mackenstedt	6	4	Spitfire	near Drionville	1627		no
03-02-43	Obfw.	Mackenstedt	6	5	Spitfire	10-12km NW of Gravelines	1108	308 Sqd	yes
03-04-43	Obfw.	Mackenstedt	6	6	Mosquito	3km S of Beauvais	2030	139 Sqd	yes
04-07-44	Uffz.	Malm	12		P-38	E of Lisieux(UA-UB)	1455	370 FG	unk
13-03-45	Uffz.	Marischka	5	1	Spitfire-prob	Dortmund (KQ9)	1635	130 Sqd	unk
17-06-41	Obfw.	Martin	8	2	Hurricane	unknown	1945	56 or 242 Sqd	yes
21-06-41	Obfw.	Martin	8	3	Spitfire	unknown	1640		yes
09-07-41	Obfw.	Martin	8	4	Spitfire	St. Omer	1410		yes
20-07-41	Obfw.	Martin	8	5	Tomahawk	W Le Touquet (Channel)	1605		yes
27-08-41	Obfw.	Martin	8	6	Spitfire	unknown	0810		yes
17-09-41	Obfw.	Martin	8	7	Spitfire	Longuenesse	1525	308 Sqd	yes
24-05-40	Fw.	März	5	1	Spitfire	Dunkirk	1650	74 Sqd	yes
02-06-40	Fw.	März	5	2	Spitfire	Dunkirk	0930	66, 266 or 611 Sqd	yes
06-04-41	Obfw.	März	5	3	Anson	Brignogan Plage	1340		yes
21-07-41	Obfw.	März	5	4	Spitfire	W of Lille	0835	602 Sqd	unk
17-06-43	Lt.	Matoni	5	5	Spitfire	10km NW of Zeebrugge	0950	316 Sqd	yes
15-07-43	Lt.	Matoni	5	6	Spitfire	5km SW of Rue	1655	602 Sqd	yes
27-08-43	Oblt.	Matoni	5	7	B-17	3km NW of Dunkirk	1935	351 BG	yes
21-12-43	Oblt.	Matoni	6	8	Spitfire	3km SSW of Boulogne	1208	132 or 602 Sqd	yes
30-12-43	Oblt.	Matoni	6	9	B-24	15km NW of Soissons	1150		yes
11-01-44	Oblt.	Matoni	6	10	B-17	Tubbergen 10km N of Almelo	1330	92 BG	yes
14-01-44	Oblt.	Matoni	6	11	Spitfire	Doullens	1202	132 Sqd	yes
29-01-44	Oblt.	Matoni	6	12	B-17-HSS	12km SW of (Channel) Mühlhausen	1130		unk
24-02-44	Oblt.	Matoni	5	13	B-24	Rodenrot Kr. Dillenburg	1355	2000th JG 26	yes
06-03-44	Oblt.	Matoni	5 CO	14	B-17	15km E of Jülich	1505	381 BG	yes
08-03-44	Oblt.	Matoni	5 CO	15	B-17	Mittelland Canal (BB3)	1330	388 BG	yes
08-03-44	Oblt.	Matoni	5 CO	16	B-17-HSS	Nienburg-Weser (N Magdeberg)	1340	452 BG	yes 1/2
12-04-44	Oblt.	Matoni	5 CO	17	B-24-HSS	S of Liège	1328	445 BG	yes
12-04-44	Oblt.	Matoni	5 CO	18	B-24-HSS	SE of Liège	1305	445 BG	yes
13-04-44	Oblt.	Matoni	5 CO	19	B-17-HSS	15km W of Bitburg	1325	303 BG	yes
13-04-44	Oblt.	Matoni	5 CO	20	P-47	32km N of Kaiserslautern	1600		unk
17-06-44	Hptm.	Matoni	5 CO	21	P-51-prob	Caen (UU6-9)	0638		prob
21-06-44	Hptm.	Matoni	5 CO	22	P-38	W of Paris(AC7-AD9)	2146	474 FG	yes
24-06-44	Hptm.	Matoni	5 CO	23	Spitfire	S of Évreux (AC)	0728		unk
02-07-44	Hptm.	Matoni	5 CO	24	Spitfire	NW of Caen(UT5-6)	2052		yes
21-06-41	Oblt.	Mätzke	4	1	Spitfire	N of Ramsgate	1320	145 Sqd	unk
21-08-41	Oblt.	Mätzke	4	2	Spitfire	Hazebrouck	1455	610 Sqd	yes
31-07-42	Uffz.	Mayer	6		Spitfire	mid-Channel	1520	121 or 332 Sqd	no
26-08-42	Uffz.	Mayer	6		Spitfire	unknown	1600		no
28-08-42	Uffz.	Mayer	6		Spitfire	unknown	1445	401 Sqd	no
06-09-42	Uffz.	Mayer	6		B-17	unknown	1845		no
14-03-43	Uffz.	Mayer	6	1	Spitfire	Somme Estuary	1757	B Hill Wing	yes
04-04-43	Uffz.	Mayer	6		Spitfire	25km NW of Dieppe	1500		no
29-04-43	Uffz.	Mayer	6	2	P-47	30km N of Ostend	1332	56 FG	yes
13-06-43	Fw.	Mayer	6	3	P-47	40-50km NNW of Dunkirk	1454	78 FG	yes
22-06-43	Fw.	Mayer	6	4	B-17-HSS	Antwerp	0916	381 or 384 BG	yes
26-06-43	Fw.	Mayer	6		P-47	20-30km NW of Dieppe	1900	56 FG	no
27-08-43	Fw.	Mayer	6		Spitfire	Lens-Bethune-Arras	2000	341 Sqd	no
02-09-43	Fw.	Mayer	6		P-47	Lille-Merville	2030	56 FG	no
03-09-43	Fw.	Mayer	6	5	B-17	near Melun a/f	0957	381 or 384 BG	unk
03-09-43	Fw.	Mayer	6		P-47	near Creil	1000	56 FG	no

Date	Rank	Name	Unit	No.	Aircraft	Location	Time	Sqd	Conf.
06-09-43	Fw.	Mayer	6	6	B-17-HSS	20km WNW of Cormeilles	1208		unk
28-12-43	Fw.	Mayer	7	7	Spitfire	Brailly	1607	350 Sqd	yes
30-12-43	Fw.	Mayer	7	8	P-47	4km N of Soissons	1330		unk
30-12-43	Fw.	Mayer	7	9	B-17	22km NW of Arras	1540		yes
14-01-44	Fw.	Mayer	7	10	B-26	15km WNW of Étaples	1158	322 BG	yes
28-01-44	Fw.	Mayer	7		Spitfire-dam	near Grevillers a/f	1540	403 Sqd	no
29-01-44	Fw.	Mayer	7	11	P-47	10km E of Bapaume	1240	355 FG	yes
29-01-44	Fw.	Mayer	7		B-17	illegible	1320		no
30-01-44	Fw.	Mayer	7		P-47	near Geldern	1315		no
11-02-44	Fw.	Mayer	7	12	P-38	Vitry-en-Artois	1345	20 FG	yes
14-02-44	Fw.	Mayer	7		Spitfire-prob	Étaples-Berck	1630	124 Sqd	no
18-02-44	Fw.	Mayer	7	13	Mosquito	NE of Amiens	1205	140 Wing	yes
18-02-44	Fw.	Mayer	7		Mosquito-prob	near Amiens	1215		no
22-02-44	Fw.	Mayer	7		P-47	nr St Trond	1545	362 FG	no
24-02-44	Fw.	Mayer	7	14	B-17	12km S of Amiens	1550	351 BG	unk
02-03-44	Obfw.	Mayer	7	15	B-17	24km NE of Abbeville (PD9)	1330	390 BG	yes
18-08-44	Obfw.	Mayer	5	16	Mustang	Beauvais (TE1)	0825	315 Sqd	yes
18-08-44	Obfw.	Mayer	5	17	P-47	Beauvais (TE6)	1329		yes
25-08-44	Obfw.	Mayer	5	18	P-51	St. Quentin (RG8)	1905	354 FG	unk
19-09-44	Obfw.	Mayer	5	19	P-51	Nijmegen (JN5)	1802	357 FG	yes
19-09-44	Obfw.	Mayer	5	20	P-51	Nijmegen (JN5)	1804	357 FG	yes
23-09-44	Obfw.	Mayer	5	21	P-51	Goch (KN)	1734	352 FG	yes
27-09-44	Obfw.	Mayer	5	22	Spitfire	Kirchhellen (KO6)	1722	412 Sqd	yes
07-10-44	Obfw.	Mayer	5	23	Spitfire	Nijmegen (JM2-5)	1630	442 Sqd	i.O.
07-10-44	Obfw.	Mayer	5	24	Spitfire	Nijmegen (JM2-5)	1632	442 Sqd	i.O.
16-10-44	Obfw.	Mayer	5	25	Auster	Düren (NN7-8)	1410	101 A/B Div L-4	i.O.
19-11-44	Obfw.	Mayer	5	26	Spitfire	N of Kirchhellen (KO3)	1406	412 Sqd	unk
19-11-44	Obfw.	Mayer	5	27	Spitfire	N of Kirchhellen (KO3)	1408	412 Sqd	unk
21-02-45	Uffz.	Meiss	7	1	Spitfire	E of Arnhem(near HO-HP)	1604		unk
09-03-45	Uffz.	Meiss	7	2	P-47	near Wesel	1650	366 FG	unk
04-04-41	Obfw.	Menge	3	12	Spitfire	W of Dover	1750	91 Sqd	yes
09-06-41	Obfw.	Menge	3	13	Spitfire	E of Dover	1410	74 Sqd	yes
03-09-40	Oblt.	Meyer	8	1	Spitfire	Thames Estuary	1116		yes
14-07-41	Oblt.	Meyer	8	2	Spitfire	unknown	1020		yes
29-08-41	Oblt.	Meyer	8	3	Spitfire	unknown	0830		yes
18-09-41	Oblt.	Meyer	8	4	Spitfire	unknown	1605		yes
21-10-41	Oblt.	Meyer	8	5	Spitfire	unknown	1255		yes
27-10-41	Oblt.	Meyer	8	6	Spitfire	unknown	1320		yes
07-06-44	Ogfr.	Meyer E.	6	1	P-51	22km SE of Saumur (HA8)	1915		flak
19-08-42	Fw.	Meyer H.	4	1	Spitfire	N of Dieppe	1007	31 FG or 130 Sqd	yes
16-09-42	Fw.	Meyer H.	4	2	Spitfire	Ault	1310	611 Sqd	yes
18-01-43	Fw.	Meyer H.	4	3	Mustang	near Rue	1057	4 Sqd	yes
17-02-43	Fw.	Meyer H.	4	4	Spitfire	NW of St. Omer	1046	124 Sqd	yes
24-06-43	Uffz.	Meyer H.	5		Typhoon	NW of Somme Estuary	1445	486 Sqd	no
31-07-42	Hptm.	Meyer K-H.	II CO	8	Spitfire	W of Somme Estuary	1503	121 or 332 Sqd	yes
05-09-42	Hptm.	Meyer K-H.	II CO	9	Spitfire	15km N of Somme Estuary	1141	64 or 340 Sqd	yes
06-09-42	Hptm.	Meyer K-H.	II CO	10	B-17	NW of Amiens	1855	97 BG	yes
20-12-42	Hptm.	Meyer K-H.	II CO	11	B-17	4-6km SW of Nantes	1211	91 BG	i.O.
24-02-44	Fhr.	Meyer O.	3	1	P-38	S of Bonn (OP5)	1425	55 FG	yes
13-05-40	Fw.	Meyer W.	5	1	Spitfire	Dordrecht	0645	66 or 264 Sqd	yes
18-05-40	Fw.	Meyer W.	5	2	Morane 405/6	Douai	1620		yes
29-05-40	Fw.	Meyer W.	5	3	Anson	Channel Narrows	1905	48 or 500 Sqd	unk
24-08-40	Obfw.	Meyer W.	5	4	Spitfire	Sheerness-Thames	1650	54 or 65 Sqd	yes
15-09-40	Obfw.	Meyer W.	5	5	Spitfire	London	1535	19 Sqd	yes
30-09-40	Obfw.	Meyer W.	5	6	Hurricane	Tonbridge	1026	229 Sqd	yes
05-11-40	Obfw.	Meyer W.	6	7	Hurricane	Canterbury	1240	310 Sqd	yes
24-06-41	Obfw.	Meyer W.	6	8	Spitfire	Calais	2040		yes
08-07-41	Obfw.	Meyer W.	6	9	Spitfire	Hazebrouck	1540	303 Sqd	yes
18-07-41	Obfw.	Meyer W.	6	10	Spitfire	Dunkirk	1220	222 Sqd	yes
09-08-41	Obfw.	Meyer W.	6	11	Spitfire	St. Omer	1125	Tangmere	yes
08-11-41	Obfw.	Meyer W.	6	12	Spitfire	St. Omer	1305		yes
17-04-42	Obfw.	Meyer W.	6	13	Spitfire	Calais	1615	121Sqd	yes
26-07-42	Obfw.	Meyer W.	6	14	Spitfire	W of Boulogne	1330	401 Sqd	unk
26-07-42	Obfw.	Meyer W.	6	15	Spitfire	S of Cap Gris Nez	1338	401 Sqd	yes
19-08-42	Obfw.	Meyer W.	6	16	Spitfire	NE of Dieppe	1216		unk
05-09-42	Obfw.	Meyer W.	6	17	Spitfire	W of Somme Estuary	1132	64 or 340 Sqd	yes
09-10-42	Lt.	Meyer W.	7	18	B-17	unknown	1055	92 BG	yes
06-11-41	Lt.	Michalski	4	1	Spitfire	30km NW of Gravelines	1503	607 Sqd	unk
31-05-40	Lt.	Mietusch	7	1	Hurricane	Dunkirk	1540	213 or 264 Sqd	yes
31-08-40	Oblt.	Mietusch	7	2	Spitfire	Chelmsford	0955	19 Sqd	unk
26-02-41	Oblt.	Mietusch	7	3	Hurricane	10km S of Malta	1417	261 Sqd	yes
22-03-41	Oblt.	Mietusch	7	4	Hurricane	40km N of Malta	1624	261 Sqd	yes
22-03-41	Oblt.	Mietusch	7	5	Hurricane	40km N of Malta	1626	261 Sqd	yes
06-04-41	Oblt.	Mietusch	7	6	Fury	NE Podgerica,	1210	2nd FS	yes

Date	Rank	Name	Unit	No.	Aircraft	Location	Time	Enemy Unit	Conf.
						Yugoslavia		Avia BH 33	
11-04-41	Oblt.	Mietusch	7	7	Hurricane	20km N of Malta	1150	261 Sqd	yes
13-04-41	Oblt.	Mietusch	7	8	Hurricane	4km NE of Kalafrana, Malta	1034	261 Sqd	yes
13-05-41	Oblt.	Mietusch	7	9	Hurricane	2km SW Ta Venezia, Malta	1400	185 Sqd	yes
17-06-41	Oblt.	Mietusch	7	10	Hurricane	SE Sidi Omar, Libya	1030	1 Sqd SAAF	yes
21-08-41	Oblt.	Mietusch	7		Maryland	Gambut, Libya		12 or 24 Sqd SAAF	no
18-09-41	Oblt.	Mietusch	7 CO	11	Spitfire	SE of Le Paradis	1615	452 Sqd	yes
21-09-41	Oblt.	Mietusch	7 CO	12	Spitfire	Berck-sur-Mer	1623	485 or 602 Sqd	yes
21-09-41	Oblt.	Mietusch	7 CO	13	Spitfire	20km WNW of Somme Est	1630	485 or 602 Sqd	unk
08-12-41	Oblt.	Mietusch	7 CO	14	Spitfire	Berck-sur-Mer	1255		yes
12-04-42	Oblt.	Mietusch	7 CO	15	Spitfire	SE of St Omer-E of Arques	1334	71 Sqd	yes
12-04-42	Oblt.	Mietusch	7 CO	16	Spitfire	12km WNW of Dunkirk	1349		yes
30-04-42	Oblt.	Mietusch	7 CO		Spitfire	3km W of Somme Estuary	1930		no
03-05-42	Oblt.	Mietusch	7 CO	17	Spitfire	Calais	1605	174 or 303 Sqd	yes
05-05-42	Oblt.	Mietusch	7 CO	18	Spitfire	3km NW of Poperinghe	1535	122 Sqd	yes
19-08-42	Oblt.	Mietusch	7 CO	19	Spitfire	3km NE of Dieppe	1034	19 or 121 Sqd	unk
19-08-42	Oblt.	Mietusch	7 CO	20	Spitfire	10 km NW of Dieppe	1035	19 or 121 Sqd	unk
27-08-42	Oblt.	Mietusch	7 CO	21	Spitfire	15km SW of Calais	1510		yes
27-08-42	Oblt.	Mietusch	7 CO	22	Spitfire	20km WNW of Cap Gris Nez	1516		yes
22-09-42	Hptm.	Mietusch	7 CO	23	Boston	3km E of Ostend	1315	226 Sqd	yes
09-10-42	Hptm.	Mietusch	7 CO		Stirling-HSS	Lille	1035	301 BG	no
09-10-42	Hptm.	Mietusch	7 CO		B-17	NE of Lille	1045	301 BG	no
13-01-43	Hptm.	Mietusch	7 CO		B-17	Lille	1435	305 BG	no
20-01-43	Hptm.	Mietusch	7 CO	27	Spitfire	4-5km S of Margate	1242	91 Sqd	unk
20-01-43	Hptm.	Mietusch	7 CO	28	Spitfire	Ardres	1312	91 Sqd	unk
22-01-43	Hptm.	Mietusch	7 CO	29	Spitfire	10-15Km of Gravelines	1515		unk
21-05-43	Hptm.	Mietusch	7 CO	30	LaGG-3	N part Lake Chapolovo	0547		unk
21-05-43	Hptm.	Mietusch	7 CO	31	LaGG-3	Koporski Bight near Dolgovo	0535		unk
21-05-43	Hptm.	Mietusch	7 CO	32	Pe-2	Cape Ustinski	0555		unk
21-05-43	Hptm.	Mietusch	7 CO	33	I-153	3-4km S of Lavansaari	1020		unk
27-05-43	Hptm.	Mietusch	7 CO	34	LaGG-3	USSR (PQ 00264)	1331	86th GIAP Yak-7B	unk
30-05-43	Hptm.	Mietusch	7 CO	35	LaGG-3	Lake Ladoga (PQ 11782)	1955		unk
31-05-43	Hptm.	Mietusch	7 CO	36	LaGG-3	USSR (PQ 00243)	1615		unk
17-06-43	Hptm.	Mietusch	7 CO	37	LaGG-3	5km NE of Volkhovstroi	0513	29th GIAP	unk
18-06-43	Hptm.	Mietusch	7 CO	38	LaGG-3	forest near Kinderovo	0612		unk
18-06-43	Hptm.	Mietusch	7 CO	39	LaGG-3	swamp N of Podborovye	0619		unk
18-06-43	Hptm.	Mietusch	7 CO	40	LaGG-3	USSR (PQ 00264)	1715		unk
18-06-43	Hptm.	Mietusch	7 CO	41	LaGG-3	USSR (PQ 00292)	1718		unk
18-06-43	Hptm.	Mietusch	7 CO	42	Yak-7	Lake Ladoga (PQ 10131)	2020		unk
22-06-43	Hptm.	Mietusch	7 CO	43	LaGG-3	USSR (PQ 90134)	1530		unk
22-06-43	Hptm.	Mietusch	7 CO	44	LaGG-3	USSR (PQ 90164)	1533		unk
25-07-43	Hptm.	Mietusch	III CO	45	B-17F	10km N of Hamburg	1702		yes
17-08-43	Hptm.	Mietusch	III CO	46	B-17	SE of Schleiden-Eifel	1520		yes
17-08-43	Hptm.	Mietusch	III CO	47	B-17	S of Lake Laacher (PP5)	1525		yes
19-08-43	Hptm.	Mietusch	III CO	48	B-17	NW of Breda	1923	303 BG	yes
19-09-43	Hptm.	Mietusch	III CO	49	Spitfire	near Poperinghe	1246	41 Sqd	yes
27-09-43	Hptm.	Mietusch	III CO		Spitfire-dam	10-15km SW of Poix	1246	222 Sqd	no
03-10-43	Hptm.	Mietusch	III CO		Spitfire-dam	NE of Beauvais	1825	222 Sqd	no
20-10-43	Hptm.	Mietusch	III CO	50	B-17	Cambrai (PG-QH)	1410	303 BG	yes
29-11-43	Hptm.	Mietusch	III CO	51	B-17-HSS	W of Oldenburg (DP-EP)	1430		yes
30-11-43	Hptm.	Mietusch	III CO	52	P-38	North Sea (LN)	1145	20 FG	yes
01-12-43	Hptm.	Mietusch	III CO	53	P-38	Freilingen-Vorneburg (Düren)	1145	20 FG	yes
20-12-43	Hptm.	Mietusch	III CO	54	B-17	NW of Wilhelmshaven	1225		yes
14-01-44	Major	Mietusch	III CO	55	Spitfire	S of St Omer	1150	308 Sqd	yes
14-01-44	Major	Mietusch	III CO	56	P-47	St Pol	1535	356 FG	yes
25-02-44	Hptm.	Mietusch	III CO	57	B-17	(SK1-2) 4km SW Charleville	1215	306 BG	yes
25-02-44	Hptm.	Mietusch	III CO	58	B-17-HSS	E of Pirmasens (UQ 3)	1500		yes
06-03-44	Hptm.	Mietusch	III CO	59	Typhoon	5km N of Amiens (QE-RE)	1305	3 Sqd	yes
08-03-44	Hptm.	Mietusch	III CO	60	B-17-HSS	(GB) S of Zwolle-Braunschweig	1325	381 BG	yes
12-05-44	Major	Mietusch	III CO	61	B-17-HSS	Bastogne (QM-QL)	1542	452 BG	unk
04-06-44	Major	Mietusch	III CO	62	Typhoon	NW of Romilly	2015	361 FG P-51	yes
08-06-44	Major	Mietusch	III CO	63	P-47	NE of Le Havre	0640	371 FG	yes
08-06-44	Major	Mietusch	III CO	64	P-47	E of Le Havre(SA-SB)	0645	371 FG	unk
14-06-44	Major	Mietusch	III CO	65	P-38	NW of Paris(AE1-UE7)	0735	55 FG	yes
14-06-44	Major	Mietusch	III CO	66	B-17	E of Paris (UG-AG)	0800	384 or 401 BG	yes
15-06-44	Major	Mietusch	III CO	67	B-24	SW of Chartres (CB-DC)	0700	392 BG	yes
23-06-44	Major	Mietusch	III CO	68	P-38	E of Chartres(CD-CE)	1358	55 FG	yes
23-06-44	Major	Mietusch	III CO	69	P-38	SE of Chartres (CE)	1400	55 FG	yes
04-07-44	Major	Mietusch	III CO	70	P-38	W of Évreux (UB)	1450	370 FG	unk
17-07-44	Major	Mietusch	III CO	71	Spitfire	SW of Caen(UT2-6)	1640	602 Sqd	yes
18-08-44	Major	Mietusch	III CO	72	P-47	NW of Paris(UD 7-8)	1406	358 FG	yes
26-08-44	Major	Mietusch	III CO	73	P-47	Rouen (TC4)	1450	50 FG	yes

Date	Rank	Name	Unit	No.	Aircraft	Location	Time	Squadron	Conf.
26-08-44	Major	Mietusch	III CO	74	P-47	W of Rouen (TB6)	1500	50 FG	yes
17-09-44	Major	Mietusch	III CO	75	P-51	N of M-Gladbach (LN1-7)	1455	361 FG	yes
14-01-45	Gefr.	Mittag	II St	1	P-51	Remscheid (near MP-MQ)	1218	78 FG	unk
16-02-41	Uffz.	Mondry	7	1	Hurricane	10km S of Valetta,Malta	1042	261 Sqd	unk
26-02-41	Uffz.	Mondry	7	2	Hurricane	Kalafrana Bay,Malta	1410	261 Sqd	yes
30-06-41	Uffz.	Mondry	7		Hurricane	Libya		1 Sqd SAAF	no
03-06-40	Fw.	Müller W. I	3	1	Curtiss H75	E of Le Bourget	1450	GC I/5	yes
08-06-40	Fw.	Müller W. I	3	3	Spitfire	Amiens	1440		yes
08-06-40	Fw.	Müller W. I	3	2	Spitfire	Beauvais			unk
07-07-40	Fw.	Müller W. I	3	4	Blenheim	N of Unterbach	1250		yes
14-08-40	Fw.	Müller W. I	3	5	Spitfire	S of Dover	1330	65 or 610 Sqd	unk
16-08-40	Fw.	Müller W. I	3	6	Hurricane	N of Tonbridge	1315		yes
24-08-40	Fw.	Müller W. I	3	7	Hurricane	NE of Manston			no
25-08-40	Fw.	Müller W. I	3	9	Spitfire	Dover	1935	610 or 616 Sqd	yes
25-08-40	Fw.	Müller W. I	3	8	Spitfire	Channel		610 or 616 Sqd	unk
29-08-40	Obfw.	Müller W. II	2	10	Spitfire	Dover		603 Sqd	unk
23-08-44	Fw.	Müller W. II	6	3	Spitfire	Évreux (UC)	1342	421 or 443 Sqd	yes
14-05-40	Lt.	Müller-Dühe	7	1	Hurricane	Brussels	1845	504 Sqd	yes
28-05-40	Lt.	Müller-Dühe	7	2	Hurricane	Ostend	1230	213, 229 or 242Sqd	yes
25-07-40	Lt.	Müller-Dühe	7	3	Spitfire	Dover		54 or 64 Sqd	unk
11-08-40	Lt.	Müller-Dühe	7		balloon	Dover	1130	n/a	no
14-08-40	Lt.	Müller-Dühe	7	4	Spitfire	Dover	1335	65 or 610 Sqd	unk
15-08-40	Lt.	Müller-Dühe	7	5	Spitfire	Calais-Marck	1550	64 Sqd	yes
19-02-43	Uffz.	Münch	3	1	Il-2	USSR (PQ 18463)			yes
31-05-43	Uffz.	Münch	3	2	Il-2	USSR (PQ 16334)			yes
30-07-43	Uffz.	Münch	3	3	Spitfire	N of Vlissingen (KH7)	0715	66 Sqd	yes
07-11-39	Lt.	Müncheberg	III St	1	Blenheim	SW of Opladen	1343	57 Sqd	yes
11-05-40	Lt.	Müncheberg	III St	2	Curtiss H75	NNE of Antwerp	1745	GC I/4	yes
14-05-40	Lt.	Müncheberg	III St	3	Hurricane	E of Ath	1845	504 Sqd	yes
15-05-40	Lt.	Müncheberg	III St	4	Hurricane	Overijse	1300	3 Sqd	yes
29-05-40	Lt.	Müncheberg	III St	5	Spitfire	W of Dunkirk	1810	64, 229 or 610 Sqd	yes
31-05-40	Lt.	Müncheberg	III St	6	Lysander	Furnes-Dunkirk	1535		yes
31-05-40	Lt.	Müncheberg	III St	7	Hurricane	SW of Dunkirk	1540	213 or 264 Sqd	yes
31-05-40	Lt.	Müncheberg	III St	8	Hurricane	NE of Dunkirk	1545	213 or 264 Sqd	yes
31-05-40	Lt.	Müncheberg	III St	9	Spitfire	Channel-Dunkirk	2010	609 Sqd	unk
28-07-40	Oblt.	Müncheberg	III St	10	Hurricane	15km NE of Dover	1515	257 Sqd	yes
08-08-40	Oblt.	Müncheberg	III St	11	Spitfire	NE of Margate	1255	65 Sqd	unk
14-08-40	Oblt.	Müncheberg	III St	12	Hurricane	Folkestone-Dover	1329	32 or 615 Sqd	yes
15-08-40	Oblt.	Müncheberg	III St	13	Spitfire	SE of Dover mid-Channel-	1601	64 Sqd	yes
24-08-40	Oblt.	Müncheberg	7 CO	14	Hurricane	Ashford	1222	151 Sqd	yes
31-08-40	Oblt.	Müncheberg	7 CO	15	Hurricane	NW of Braintree	1000	56 Sqd	unk
01-09-40	Oblt.	Müncheberg	7 CO	16	Hurricane	W of Goodhurst	1452	79 or 85 Sqd	yes
06-09-40	Oblt.	Müncheberg	7 CO	17	Hurricane	Dungeness	1028	303 Sqd	yes
07-09-40	Oblt.	Müncheberg	7 CO	18	Spitfire	SE of London	1845	603 Sqd	unk
11-09-40	Oblt.	Müncheberg	7 CO	19	Spitfire	E of Ashford	1925	66 or 92 Sqd	unk
14-09-40	Oblt.	Müncheberg	7 CO	20	Spitfire	S of Maidstone	1705	222 Sqd	unk
17-10-40	Oblt.	Müncheberg	7 CO	21	Bloch 151	S of Faversham	1455		yes
25-10-40	Oblt.	Müncheberg	7 CO	22	Spitfire	Marden	1440	92 Sqd	yes
14-11-40	Oblt.	Müncheberg	7 CO	23	Spitfire	SE of Dover	1532	66 or 74 Sqd	unk
12-02-41	Oblt.	Müncheberg	7 CO	24	Hurricane	S of Sigguvi, Malta	1641	261 Sqd	yes
16-02-41	Oblt.	Müncheberg	7 CO	25	Hurricane	off SW coast Malta	1038	261 Sqd	yes
16-02-41	Oblt.	Müncheberg	7 CO	26	Hurricane	E of Ta Venezia, Malta	1045	261 Sqd	yes
25-02-41	Oblt.	Müncheberg	7 CO	27	Hurricane	E of St Paul's Bay,Malta	1645	261 Sqd	yes
26-02-41	Oblt.	Müncheberg	7 CO	28	Hurricane	S of Krendi, Malta	1406	261 Sqd	yes
26-02-41	Oblt.	Müncheberg	7 CO	29	Hurricane	S of Malta	1410	261 Sqd	yes
02-03-41	Oblt.	Müncheberg	7 CO	30	Hurricane	2km W Marsa Scirocco, Malta	1045	261 Sqd	yes
05-03-41	Gefr.	Müncheberg	7 CO	31	Hurricane	S of Hal Far, Malta	1732	261 Sqd	yes
15-03-41	Oblt.	Müncheberg	7 CO	32	Wellington	10km NW ofGozo Is.	0750	148 Sqd	yes
28-03-41	Oblt.	Müncheberg	7 CO	33	Hurricane	S of Gozo Is.	1720	261 Sqd	yes
06-04-41	Oblt.	Müncheberg	7 CO	34	Fury	NE Podgerica, Yugoslavia	1205	2nd FS Avia BH 33	yes
06-04-41	Oblt.	Müncheberg	7 CO		Fury-ground	Podgerica,Yugoslavia		2nd FS Avia BH 33	no
06-04-41	Oblt.	Müncheberg	7 CO		BreguetX IX	Podgerica, Yugoslavia			no
11-04-41	Oblt.	Müncheberg	7 CO	35	Hurricane	SE E coast of Malta	1131	261 Sqd	yes
11-04-41	Oblt.	Müncheberg	7 CO	36	Hurricane	SE of St Paul's Bay, Malta	1153	261 Sqd	yes
23-04-41	Oblt.	Müncheberg	7 CO	37	Hurricane	SE Hal Far, Malta	1807	261 Sqd	yes
29-04-41	Oblt.	Müncheberg	7 CO	38	Hurricane	St. Paul's Bay, Malta	1847	261 Sqd	yes
01-05-41	Oblt.	Müncheberg	7 CO	39	Hurricane	SE St. Paul's Bay, Malta	0753	261 Sqd	yes
01-05-41	Oblt.	Müncheberg	7 CO	40	Hurricane	SW Ta Venezia, Malta	0755	261 Sqd	unk
01-05-41	Oblt.	Müncheberg	7 CO	41	Hurricane	SW Luqa a/f, Malta	1715	261 Sqd	yes
06-05-41	Oblt.	Müncheberg	7 CO	43	Hurricane	1km SW Hal Far, Malta	1226	261 Sqd	yes
06-05-41	Oblt.	Müncheberg	7 CO	42	Hurricane	NE St Paul's Bay, Malta	1222	261 Sqd	yes

25-05-41	Oblt.	Müncheberg	7 CO		Hurricane	Takali, Malta	1500	249 Sqd	no
25-05-41	Oblt.	Müncheberg	7 CO		Hurricane	Takali, Malta	1500	249 Sqd	no
20-06-41	Oblt.	Müncheberg	7 CO	44	Hurricane	20km E BuqBuq, Egypt	0755		yes
24-06-41	Oblt.	Müncheberg	7 CO	45	Hurricane	Lavyet Ungheila, Libya	0800	6 Sqd	yes
15-07-41	Oblt.	Müncheberg	7 CO	46	Hurricane	SW Ras el Milh, Libya	1840	73 or 229 Sqd	yes
29-07-41	Oblt.	Müncheberg	7 CO	47	Tomahawk	40km E Bardia, Libya	1748	2 Sqd SAAF	yes
29-07-41	Oblt.	Müncheberg	7 CO	48	Tomahawk	40km E Bardia, Libya	1752	2 Sqd SAAF	yes
26-08-41	Oblt.	Müncheberg	7 CO	49	Spitfire	2km N of Gravelines	1930		yes
29-08-41	Oblt.	Müncheberg	7 CO	50	Spitfire	10km NE of Dunkirk	0840		yes
04-09-41	Oblt.	Müncheberg	7 CO	51	Spitfire	Vollezeele	1726		yes
04-09-41	Oblt.	Müncheberg	7 CO	52	Spitfire	Zeggers	1729		yes
07-09-41	Oblt.	Müncheberg	7 CO	53	Spitfire	NW of Montreuil	1722	71 Sqd	yes
16-09-41	Oblt.	Müncheberg	7 CO	54	Spitfire	E of Boulogne	1940	306 or 315 Sqd	yes
18-09-41	Oblt.	Müncheberg	7 CO	55	Hurricane	Yvetot	1606	607 Sqd	yes
18-09-41	Oblt.	Müncheberg	7 CO	56	Spitfire	Ste Helene	1615	452 Sqd	yes
13-10-41	Hptm.	Müncheberg	II CO	57	Spitfire	Samer	1433		yes
08-11-41	Hptm.	Müncheberg	II CO	58	Spitfire	Loon Plage	1307	Digby or 412 Sqd	yes
08-11-41	Hptm.	Müncheberg	II CO	59	Spitfire	NNE of Dunkirk	1315	Digby or 412 Sqd	unk
08-12-41	Hptm.	Müncheberg	II CO	60	Spitfire	W of Boulogne	1417		yes
16-12-41	Hptm.	Müncheberg	II CO	61	Spitfire	NW of Dunkirk	1601	411 Sqd	yes
16-12-41	Hptm.	Müncheberg	II CO	62	Spitfire	N of Gravelines	1604	411 Sqd	yes
13-03-42	Hptm.	Müncheberg	II CO	63	Spitfire	Wirre Effroy	1617	124 Sqd	yes
24-03-42	Hptm.	Müncheberg	II CO	64	Spitfire	NW of Rue-Cambron	1630	412 Sqd	yes
24-03-42	Hptm.	Müncheberg	II CO	65	Spitfire	Cambron	1635	412 Sqd	yes
04-04-42	Hptm.	Müncheberg	II CO	66	Spitfire	W of Calais, in sea	1146		yes
10-04-42	Hptm.	Müncheberg	II CO	67	Spitfire	NW of Étaples,in sea	1750	340 Sqd	yes
25-04-42	Hptm.	Müncheberg	II CO	68	Spitfire	SW of Crécy	1640		yes
25-04-42	Hptm.	Müncheberg	II CO	69	Spitfire	SW of Rue	1643		yes
26-04-42	Hptm.	Müncheberg	II CO	70	Spitfire	WNW of Calais,in sea	1805	485 Sqd	unk
26-04-42	Hptm.	Müncheberg	II CO	71	Spitfire	10km W of Cap Gris Nez	1806	485 Sqd	yes
27-04-42	Hptm.	Müncheberg	II CO	72	Spitfire	NE of Dunkirk	1447	T'mere or 340 Sqd	yes
27-04-42	Hptm.	Müncheberg	II CO	73	Spitfire	N of Mardyck	1606	303 Sqd	yes
29-04-42	Hptm.	Müncheberg	II CO	74	Spitfire	Le Touquet	1604	Northolt or 317 Sqd	yes
30-04-42	Hptm.	Müncheberg	II CO	75	Spitfire	W of Somme Estuary	1936	222 Sqd	yes
01-05-42	Hptm.	Müncheberg	II CO	76	Spitfire	SW of Calais	1931	122 or 222 Sqd	yes
01-05-42	Hptm.	Müncheberg	II CO		Spitfire	5km N of Calais	1940		no
06-05-42	Hptm.	Müncheberg	II CO	77	Spitfire	NW of Cap Gris Nez	1853	303 Sqd	yes
09-05-42	Hptm.	Müncheberg	II CO		Spitfire	15km S of Gravelines	1343	118 or 501 Sqd	no
09-05-42	Hptm.	Müncheberg	II CO		Spitfire	15km S of Gravelines	1344	118 or 501 Sqd	no
17-05-42	Hptm.	Müncheberg	II CO		Spitfire	Guines-St Omer	1735		no
31-05-42	Hptm.	Müncheberg	II CO	78	Spitfire	S of Crécy forest	1937	485 Sqd	yes
31-05-42	Hptm.	Müncheberg	II CO	79	Spitfire	Quend Plage les Pins	1941	302 Sqd	yes
02-06-42	Hptm.	Müncheberg	II CO	80	Spitfire	SW of Abbeville	1101	403 Sqd	yes
02-06-42	Hptm.	Müncheberg	II CO	81	Spitfire	15km W of Étaples	1107	403 Sqd	unk
20-06-42	Hptm.	Müncheberg	II CO	82	Spitfire	S of Ardres	1544	118 or 501 Sqd	yes
20-06-42	Hptm.	Müncheberg	II CO	83	Spitfire	E of Boulogne	1547	118 or 501 Sqd	yes
12-08-40	Lt.	Naumann	9		Spitfire	Folkestone	1820	64 Sqd	no
03-09-40	Lt.	Naumann	9	1	Spitfire	Thames Estuary	1110		unk
21-06-41	Lt.	Naumann	9	2	Hurricane	unknown	1635	1 Sqd	yes
03-07-41	Lt.	Naumann	9	3	Spitfire	unknown	1145		yes
21-08-41	Lt.	Naumann	9	4	Spitfire	unknown	1510		yes
12-02-42	Oblt.	Naumann	9	5	Swordfish	N of Gravelines	1345	825 Sqd	yes
12-02-42	Oblt.	Naumann	9	6	Swordfish	N of Gravelines	1347	825 Sqd	yes
27-04-42	Oblt.	Naumann	9	7	Spitfire	4km N of Calais	1230	65 Sqd	yes
23-05-42	Oblt.	Naumann	9	8	Spitfire	N of Calais	1152	350 Sqd	yes
06-09-42	Oblt.	Naumann	4	9	Spitfire	N of Hellancourt	1854	402 Sqd	yes
13-02-43	Oblt.	Naumann	6 CO	10	Spitfire	NE of Rue	1224	485 Sqd	yes
16-02-43	Oblt.	Naumann	6 CO	11	Spitfire	Bourseville	1728	402 Sqd	yes
08-03-43	Oblt.	Naumann	6 CO	12	B-24	15km SE of Hastings	1408	44 BG	yes
04-04-43	Oblt.	Naumann	6 CO	13	Spitfire	10km SW of Dieppe	1442	315,316 or 403 Sqd	yes
03-05-43	Hptm.	Naumann	6 CO	14	Spitfire	W of Zandvoort	1815		unk
13-05-43	Hptm.	Naumann	6 CO	15	Spitfire	20km NW of Albert	1635	416 Sqd	yes
14-05-43	Hptm.	Naumann	6 CO	16	B-17	Dadizele	1240	351 BG	yes
22-06-43	Hptm.	Naumann	6 CO	17	B-17	W of Antwerp - in sea	0915	384 BG	i.O.
26-07-43	Hptm.	Naumann	6 CO	18	Boston	Vendeville a/f	1116	88 Sqd	yes
30-07-43	Hptm.	Naumann	6 CO	19	B-17	5km SE of Est	1025	91 BG	yes
12-08-43	Hptm.	Naumann	6 CO	20	B-17-HSS	near Hagen	0900		yes
17-08-43	Hptm.	Naumann	6 CO	21	P-47	10km W of Liège	1700	56 FG	yes
19-08-43	Hptm.	Naumann	II CO	22	Spitfire	5km NW of Le Tréport	1832		yes
02-09-43	Hptm.	Naumann	II CO	23	P-47	near Lens	2021	56 FG	unk
11-09-43	Hptm.	Naumann	6 CO	24	Typhoon	near Forges			unk
21-09-43	Hptm.	Naumann	6 CO	25	Mitchell	between Arras & St. Pol	1040	98 Sqd	yes

Date	Rank	Name	Unit	No.	Aircraft	Location	Time	Allied unit	Conf.
14-10-43	Hptm.	Naumann	7 CO	26	B-17	Domburg	1330		yes
11-11-43	Hptm.	Naumann	7 CO	27	B-17	NNW of Breda	1455	94 BG	yes
21-12-43	Hptm.	Naumann	7 CO	28	Spitfire	Douai	1151	132 or 602 Sqd	yes
25-07-43	Oblt.	Nels	III St		B-17	10km SW of Stade	1632		yes
27-05-43	Oblt.	Neu	3	1	LaGG-3	USSR (PQ 5366)			yes
02-06-43	Oblt.	Neu	3	2	LaGG-3	USSR (PQ 62159)			yes
27-09-43	Oblt.	Neu	4	3	Boston	NE of Rouen? (SD-HC?)		387 BG B-26	unk
13-11-43	Oblt.	Neu	4 CO	4	B-17	NE Arnhem (HN)	1215	96 BG	yes
26-11-43	Oblt.	Neu	4 CO	5	B-17	W of Nantes? (GN3?)	1045	94 BG	unk
01-12-43	Oblt.	Neu	4 CO	6	B-17	Steenvoorde (NF7)	1325		yes
21-01-44	Oblt.	Neu	4 CO	7	B-26	St. Omer (NE1)		226 Sqd Mitchell	unk
29-01-44	Oblt.	Neu	4 CO	8	B-17	S of Maubeuge		385 BG	yes
11-02-44	Oblt.	Neu	4 CO	9	P-38	Cambrai (QH1)	1335	20 FG	yes
24-02-44	Oblt.	Neu	4 CO	10	P-47	S of Aachen(ON-OM)	1433	4 FG	yes
06-03-44	Oblt.	Neu	4 CO	11	B-24	S of Quakenbrück	1445	453 BG	yes
19-04-44	Oblt.	Neu	4 CO	12	Spitfire	Brussels (NI 3)	1855	310 or 312 Sqd	unk
17-06-41	Lt.	Neumann E.	9	1	Spitfire	unknown	1952	74 Sqd	yes
07-09-42	Uffz.	Niese	9	1	Spitfire	N of Dunkirk	1109		yes
20-12-42	Uffz.	Niese	9	2	B-17	10km W of Chateaubleau	1253	306 BG	n.O.
11-06-43	Fw.	Niese	9	3	B-17	Grossheide-Norden	1757		yes
13-06-43	Fw.	Niese	9	4	B-17	9km SSE of Kiel	0928	95 BG	yes
29-07-44	Ogfr.	Nieter	10		Mustang	Dreux-Évreux	0715	65 Sqd	unk
20-06-44	Lt.	Nink	3	1	P-38	Chateau Thierry (UG7-9)	1735	370 FG	yes
01-06-40	Fw.	Nischik	6	1	Hurricane	Dunkirk	1240	43, 145 or 245Sqd	unk
10-10-43	Uffz.	Oeckel	12	1	B-17	Netherlands		385 BG	yes
24-04-44	Fw.	Oeckel	12	2	B-17	S of Donauwörth (BB7-8)	1345		unk
14-06-44	Lt.	Oeckel	12	3	B-17	E of Paris (AG)	0807	384 or 401 BG	unk
26-06-44	Lt.	Oeckel	12	4	Spitfire	Caen (UT-UU)	1120		unk
14-06-41	Uffz.	Ömler	9	1	Blenheim	NW of Calais	0725	110 Sqd	yes
06-07-41	Uffz.	Ömler	9	2	Spitfire	unknown			unk
14-01-45	Lt.	Ossenkop	2	1	Spitfire	Ibbenbüren	1545	331 or 332 Sqd	unk
12-04-45	Lt.	Ossenkop	2	2	Tempest	15km N of Uelsen	1300	33 Sqd	unk
06-07-41	Oblt.	Otte	3	1	Spitfire	nr Houthem	1436		yes
07-07-41	Oblt.	Otte	3	2	Spitfire	mid-Channel	1045		yes
18-07-41	Oblt.	Otte	3	3	Blenheim	S Mardyck	1125	21 Sqd	yes
10-08-41	Oblt.	Otte	3	4	Blenheim	2km N of a convoy	1304	226 Sqd	yes
31-05-40	Obfw.	Ötteking	7	1	Hurricane	Dunkirk	1540	213 or 264 Sqd	unk
10-06-44	Lt.	Pape	9		P-47	Lisieux (UA1-4)	1758	365 FG	unk
24-09-44	Lt.	Pape	9		Typhoon	N of Arnhem (HM5-7-8)	1740	439 Sqd	unk
22-06-44	Fw.	Patzke	9	1	P-47	S of St Lô (AS5)	1421	365 FG	i.O.
23-09-44	Fw.	Paul	6	1	P-51	Goch (KN)	1735	352 FG	unk
05-11-40	Fw.	Petersen	6	1	Hurricane	Ramsgate	1225	310 Sqd	unk
25-03-45	Uffz.	Pfeiffer	5	1	Spitfire	S of Stadtlohn(JO3)	1823		unk
27-05-40	Uffz.	Philipp	4	1	Spitfire	Ostend	1730		yes
28-05-40	Uffz.	Philipp	4	2	Spitfire	Channel Narrows	1230		yes
29-05-40	Uffz.	Philipp	4	3	Spitfire	Dover	1845	64, 229 or 610 Sqd	yes
07-06-40	Uffz.	Philipp	4	4	Hurricane	Dieppe	1930	43 Sqd	unk
16-08-40	Fw.	Philipp	4	5	Spitfire	Dover	1406	266 Sqd	unk
22-08-40	Fw.	Philipp	4	6	Spitfire	Dover	2005	65 Sqd	yes
08-11-40	Fw.	Philipp	4	7	Spitfire	Tonbridge	1740	603 Sqd	yes
05-02-41	Fw.	Philipp	4	8	Spitfire	Neufchatel	1415		yes
09-03-42	Fw.	Philipp	4	11	Spitfire	Boulogne	1645		yes
17-05-42	Obfw.	Philipp	4	12	Spitfire	3km NE of Calais	1137	602 Sqd	yes
02-06-42	Obfw.	Philipp	4	13	Spitfire	W of Berck (mid-Channel)	1105	403 Sqd	unk
08-06-42	Obfw.	Philipp	4	14	Spitfire	WNW of Dunkirk	1358	H'church or Kenley	yes
13-07-42	Obfw.	Philipp	4	15	Spitfire	mid-Channel	1510	401 Sqd	yes
26-07-42	Obfw.	Philipp	4	16	Spitfire	English Coast	1347	72 Sqd	yes
31-07-42	Obfw.	Philipp	4	17	Spitfire	W of Berck-sur-Mer	1513	121 or 332 Sqd	yes
17-08-42	Obfw.	Philipp	4	18	Spitfire	W of Dieppe	1906	401 or 402 Sqd	yes
19-08-42	Obfw.	Philipp	4	19	Spitfire	SW of Dieppe	0837	31 FG or 130 Sqd	yes
19-08-42	Obfw.	Philipp	4	20	Spitfire	W of Dieppe	1732		yes
24-08-42	Obfw.	Philipp	4	21	Spitfire	NW of Fécamp	1735	402 Sqd	unk
29-08-42	Obfw.	Philipp	4	22	Mosquito	SE of Hastings	1253	105 Sqd	unk
25-04-44	Uffz.	Pietruschka	5	1	B-24	10km ENE of Vitry-le-Francois (AI-BI)	0835	458 BG	unk
04-07-44	Uffz.	Pietruschka	5	2	Spitfire	Caen (UU1-2)	1941	602 Sqd	unk
29-08-40	Hptm.	Pingel	I CO	11	Spitfire	Dungeness	2006		yes
29-08-40	Hptm.	Pingel	I CO	12	Spitfire	Dungeness	2007		yes
31-08-40	Hptm.	Pingel	I CO	13	Spitfire	S of London			unk
07-09-40	Hptm.	Pingel	I CO	14	Spitfire	Tonbridge	1925	41 or 222 Sqd	yes
14-09-40	Hptm.	Pingel	I CO	15	Hurricane	SE of Maidstone	1650	253 Sqd	yes
28-09-40	Hptm.	Pingel	I CO	16	Hurricane	Maidstone	1440	249 Sqd	yes

Date	Rank	Name	Unit	No.	No.	Type	Location	Time	Sqn	Conf
05-11-40	Hptm.	Pingel	I CO	17		Spitfire	E of Gravesend		19 Sqd	unk
16-06-41	Hptm.	Pingel	I CO	18		Blenheim	SE of Boulogne	1635	59 Sqd	yes
16-06-41	Hptm.	Pingel	I CO	19		Spitfire	S of Dungeness	1652	74 or 92 Sqd	yes
22-06-41	Hptm.	Pingel	I CO	20		Spitfire	W of Dunkirk	1610	609 or 611 Sqd	yes
27-06-41	Hptm.	Pingel	I CO	21		Spitfire	near Roubaix	2143		yes
02-07-41	Hptm.	Pingel	I CO	22		Hurricane	S of Dunkirk	1250		yes
18-08-43	Uffz.	Pittmann	1	1		Spitfire	N of Walcheren (IJ2)		131 Sqd	yes
20-04-45	Fhr.	Planzer v.	2	1		Spitfire	Sülte a/f	1600	401 Sqd	unk
30-07-43	Fw.	Polster	11			Spitfire	Scheldt Estuary	1030		no
10-10-43	Fw.	Polster	11	2		B-17	NW of Münster	1500	385 BG	unk
08-04-44	Fw.	Polster	11	3		P-51	E of Zwolle (EO-FO)	1515	355 FG	yes
14-06-44	Fw.	Polster	11	4		P-38	N of Paris (UD9-UE7)	0736	55 FG	unk
27-07-44	Fw.	Polster	11	5		Mustang	N of Lisieux (UU3)	0715	122 Sqd	i.O.
18-05-40	Oblt.	Pomaska	6	1		Morane 405/6	Cambrai	1620		yes
18-12-39	Uffz.	Portz	10N	1		Wellington	25-35km SSW of Helgoland	1435	3 Gp	unk
06-02-44	Fw.	Prager	5	1		P-47	E of Paris	1057		unk
08-03-44	Fw.	Prager	5	2		B-17	80km NE of Braunschweig	1335	388 BG	yes
17-06-44	Lt.	Prager	5	3		P-51	Caen (UU3)	0640		yes
04-07-44	Lt.	Prager	5	4		Spitfire	Caen (UU1-2)	1946	602 Sqd	yes
04-07-44	Lt.	Prager	5	5		Spitfire	NW Lisieux	2144		no
07-07-44	Lt.	Prager	5	6		Spitfire	Caen (UU3-UA1)	1144	412 Sqd	yes
15-08-44	Lt.	Prager	7 CO	7		P-47	Rambouillet(BD3-6)	1235	373 FG	unk
20-08-44	Lt.	Prager	7 CO	8		P-47	W of Rouen (TB)	2005	404 FG	yes
23-08-44	Lt.	Prager	7 CO	9		Spitfire	NE of Paris (UE-UF)	1340	421 or 443 Sqd	yes
19-03-45	Lt.	Prager	15	17		P-51	Osnabrück(GR3-6)	1350	78 FG	unk
25-03-45	Lt.	Prager	15	18		P-47	NW of Bocholt			unk
26-03-45	Lt.	Prager	15	19		P-51	S of Hengelo(HO)	1646		unk
28-03-45	Lt.	Prager	15	20		Tempest	unknown			unk
05-04-45	Lt.	Prager	14	21		Spitfire	Lingen	1215	402 Sqd	unk
16-06-41	Oblt.	Priller	1 CO	21		Spitfire	W of Boulogne	1635		yes
16-06-41	Oblt.	Priller	1 CO	22		Blenheim	SW of Boulogne	1645	59 Sqd	yes
17-06-41	Oblt.	Priller	1 CO	23		Hurricane	W of Cap Gris Nez	1942	56 or 242 Sqd	yes
21-06-41	Oblt.	Priller	1 CO	24		Spitfire	SW of Ramsgate	1240	603 Sqd	yes
23-06-41	Oblt.	Priller	1 CO	25		Spitfire	S of Somme Estuary	1335		yes
25-06-41	Oblt.	Priller	1 CO	26		Spitfire	W of Gravelines	1300	610 or 616 Sqd	yes
27-06-41	Oblt.	Priller	1 CO	27		Spitfire	SW of Gravelines	2200		yes
30-06-41	Oblt.	Priller	1 CO	28		Spitfire	10km NW of St. Inglevert	1856	603 or 616 Sqd	yes
02-07-41	Oblt.	Priller	1 CO	29		Spitfire	10km W of Lille	1245		yes
04-07-41	Oblt.	Priller	1 CO	30		Spitfire	10km SW ofSt. Omer	1455		yes
05-07-41	Oblt.	Priller	1 CO	31		Spitfire	4km NW of Dunkirk	1340	54 or 616 Sqd	yes
07-07-41	Oblt.	Priller	1 CO	32		Spitfire	3km N of Gravelines	1000	Hornchurch	yes
07-07-41	Oblt.	Priller	1 CO	33		Spitfire	W ofSomme Estuary	1047		yes
08-07-41	Oblt.	Priller	1 CO	34		Spitfire	10km N ofSt. Omer	1530		yes
09-07-41	Oblt.	Priller	1 CO	35		Spitfire	S of Aire-SE of Samer	1400		yes
09-07-41	Oblt.	Priller	1 CO	36		Spitfire	2km S of Calais	1410		yes
10-07-41	Oblt.	Priller	1 CO	37		Spitfire	N of St. Omer	1230		yes
10-07-41	Oblt.	Priller	1 CO	38		Spitfire	5km NW of Boulogne	1240		yes
11-07-41	Oblt.	Priller	1 CO	39		Spitfire	20km W of Calais	1610		yes
14-07-41	Oblt.	Priller	1 CO	40		Spitfire	1km N of Ferques (S of Dunkirk)	1030	72 Sqd	yes
19-07-41	Oblt.	Priller	1 CO	41		Spitfire	5km off Dover	1435	72 Sqd	yes
22-07-41	Oblt.	Priller	1 CO	42		Spitfire	10km NW of Gravelines	1340	308 Sqd	yes
23-07-41	Oblt.	Priller	1 CO	43		Spitfire	15km NW of Gravelines	1405		yes
24-07-41	Oblt.	Priller	1 CO	44		Spitfire	7km NW of Dunkirk	1445		yes
07-08-41	Oblt.	Priller	1 CO	45		Spitfire	5km NW of Calais	1130		yes
07-08-41	Oblt.	Priller	1 CO	46		Spitfire	8km W of Calais	1820		yes
04-09-41	Oblt.	Priller	1 CO	47		Spitfire	NW of Bethune	1730		yes
17-09-41	Oblt.	Priller	1 CO	48		Spitfire	5km S of Calais	1535		yes
18-09-41	Oblt.	Priller	1 CO	49		Spitfire	5km W of Dungeness	1625		yes
01-10-41	Oblt.	Priller	1 CO	50		Spitfire	mid-Channel	1457	91 Sqd	yes
01-10-41	Oblt.	Priller	1 CO	51		Spitfire	W of Boulogne	1535		yes
12-10-41	Hptm.	Priller	1 CO	52		Spitfire	5km E ofBerck-sur-Mer	1325	452 or 602 Sqd	yes
13-10-41	Hptm.	Priller	1 CO	53		Spitfire	15km W of Berck-sur-Mer	1530		yes
21-10-41	Hptm.	Priller	1 CO	54		Spitfire	4km W of Étaples	1255		yes
21-10-41	Hptm.	Priller	1 CO	55		Spitfire	15km NNW of Le Touquet	1305		yes
27-10-41	Hptm.	Priller	1 CO	56		Spitfire	5km N of Watten	1315	401 Sqd	yes
08-11-41	Hptm.	Priller	1 CO	57		Spitfire	N of Bethune	1250	302 or 316 Sqd	yes
08-11-41	Hptm.	Priller	1 CO	58		Spitfire	5km NW of Gravelines	1310	302 or 316 Sqd	unk
03-01-42	Hptm.	Priller	III CO	59		Hurricane	5km NW of Calais	1538		unk
27-03-42	Hptm.	Priller	III CO	60		Spitfire	10km W of Ostend	1640	313 Sqd	yes
28-03-42	Hptm.	Priller	III CO	61		Spitfire	Cap Gris Nez-Blanc Nez	1850	457 or 602 Sqd	yes
04-04-42	Hptm.	Priller	III CO	62		Spitfire	Channel Narrows Calais-Dover	1615	129 Sqd	yes
12-04-42	Hptm.	Priller	III CO	63		Spitfire	N of Gravelines	1345	41 Sqd	yes
12-04-42	Hptm.	Priller	III CO			Spitfire	Boulogne			no
16-04-42	Hptm.	Priller	III CO	64		Spitfire	5km N of Calais	1826	118 or 129 Sqd	yes
25-04-42	Hptm.	Priller	III CO	65		Spitfire	10km W of St. Étienne	1654		yes

Date	Rank	Name	Unit	No.	Type	Location	Time	Unit claimed	Conf.
27-04-42	Hptm.	Priller	III CO	66	Spitfire	S of Ardres	1225	65 Sqd	yes
27-04-42	Hptm.	Priller	III CO	67	Spitfire	15km NW of Gravelines	1230	65 Sqd	unk
28-04-42	Hptm.	Priller	III CO	68	Spitfire	Dunkirk-Gravelines	1200	401 Sqd	yes
01-05-42	Hptm.	Priller	III CO	69	Spitfire	5km N of Calais	1930	457, 485 or 602 Sqd	yes
05-05-42	Hptm.	Priller	III CO	70	Spitfire	11km SW of Ypres	1540	313 Sqd	yes
09-05-42	Hptm.	Priller	III CO	71	Spitfire	3km N of Gravelines	1340	118 or 501 Sqd	yes
17-05-42	Hptm.	Priller	III CO	72	Spitfire	S of Guines-Audembert	1133	313 Sqd	yes
01-06-42	Hptm.	Priller	III CO	73	Spitfire	5km N of Blankenberghe	1345	350 Sqd	yes
22-06-42	Hptm.	Priller	III CO	74	Spitfire	30km N of Gravelines	1210	64 Sqd	unk
15-07-42	Hptm.	Priller	III CO	75	Spitfire	8km NE of Dover	1538	402 Sqd	yes
30-07-42	Hptm.	Priller	III CO		Spitfire	Gravelines	1900		no
21-08-42	Hptm.	Priller	III CO	76	Spitfire	50km N of Gravelines	1110		yes
29-08-42	Hptm.	Priller	III CO	77	Spitfire	15km NW of Cap Gris Nez	1146		unk
09-10-42	Maj.	Priller	III CO	78	B-24	SW of Roubaix-Wevelgem	1035	93 BG	yes
04-12-42	Hptm.	Priller	III CO	79	Spitfire	20km E of Dover	1440	401 or 402 Sqd	yes
06-12-42	Hptm.	Priller	III CO	80	Spitfire	5-6km S of Lille	1210		yes
20-12-42	Maj.	Priller	III CO	81	B-24	Bay of Seine	1201	91 BG	i.O.
20-01-43	Maj.	Priller	Ge CO	82	Spitfire	N of Canterbury	1235	332 Sqd	unk
08-03-43	Maj.	Priller	Ge CO	83	Spitfire	8km NW of St Valery-en-Caux	1415	340 Sqd	unk
05-04-43	Maj.	Priller	Ge CO	84	B-17	20km W of Ostend	1512	306 BG	yes
04-05-43	Maj.	Priller	Ge CO	85	Spitfire	Westerschelde-NW of Antwerp	1842		unk
13-05-43	Maj.	Priller	Ge CO	86	B-17	nr Amplier-5km E of Boulogne	1624	91 BG	unk
13-05-43	Maj.	Priller	Ge CO	87	Spitfire	8km NW of Étaples	1646	416 Sqd	unk
16-05-43	Maj.	Priller	Ge CO	88	P-47	Scheldt Estuary	1312	78 FG	yes
10-06-43	Maj.	Priller	Ge CO	89	Ventura	W of Coxyde	1855		yes
22-06-43	Maj.	Priller	Ge CO	90	B-17	near Terneuzen	0932	381 BG	yes
26-06-43	Maj.	Priller	Ge CO	91	B-17	Dieppe-Le Tréport	1852	384 BG	yes
17-08-43	Obstlt.	Priller	Ge CO	92	B-17	N of Liège (ML7)	1740		yes
19-08-43	Obstlt.	Priller	Ge CO	93	B-17	de Beer Is (Gilze-Rijen a/f)	1900	305 BG	unk
21-09-43	Obstlt.	Priller	Ge CO	94	Mitchell	St. Pol	1045	98 Sqd	unk
20-10-43	Obstlt.	Priller	Ge CO	95	B-17-HSS	SE of Arras-Cambrai	1345	96 BG	unk
13-04-44	Obstlt.	Priller	Ge CO	96	B-17	Poperinghe N of St. Omer-	1710		yes
07-06-44	Obstlt.	Priller	Ge CO	98	P-51	N of Caen (TU7-8)	1350		yes
07-06-44	Obstlt.	Priller	Ge CO	97	P-47	Évreux (UC3-6)	1900		yes
11-06-44	Obstlt.	Priller	Ge CO	99	P-38	NW of Compiègne (SF-TF)	1535	55 FG	yes
15-06-44	Obstlt.	Priller	Ge CO	100	B-24	W Dreux-SW of Chartres	0710	492 BG	yes
12-10-44	Obstlt.	Priller	Ge CO	101	P-51	S of Wunstorf (GT6)	1125	357 FG	i.O.
19-08-42	Lt.	Prym	4	1	Spitfire	Somme Estuary	0817	31 FG or 130 Sqd	yes
13-03-43	Lt.	Radener	4		Spitfire	E of Étaples	1533	402 or 403 Sqd	no
03-05-43	Lt.	Radener	4	1	Spitfire	20km W of Somme Estuary	0650	41 Sqd	yes
14-05-43	Lt.	Radener	4		B-17-HSS	NW of Antwerp	1300	351 BG	unk
22-06-43	Lt.	Radener	4	2	P-47	10-15km NW of Domburg	0934		yes
26-06-43	Lt.	Radener	4	3	P-47	10-12km NNW of Le Tréport	1904	56 FG	yes
04-07-43	Lt.	Radener	4		Spitfire	Berck-sur-Mer	1740		no
26-07-43	Lt.	Radener	6		Spitfire	15km SE of Lille	1125	317 Sqd	no
30-07-43	Lt.	Radener	6	4	P-47	near Arnhem	1020	78 FG	yes
30-07-43	Lt.	Radener	6	5	P-47	3km S of Werkendam	1028	56 FG	yes
27-08-43	Lt.	Radener	6 CO		Spitfire	NW of Dunkirk	1940	341 Sqd	no
03-09-43	Lt.	Radener	6 CO	6	P-47	3km N of Guyancourt	0958	56 FG	unk
06-09-43	Lt.	Radener	6 CO		B-17-HSS	S of Reims	1210		unk
10-10-43	Lt.	Radener	7		B-17-HSS	NE of Münster	1535		unk
14-10-43	Lt.	Radener	7		B-17-HSS	N of Koblenz	1335		no
30-12-43	Lt.	Radener	7	7	P-47	12km SE of Beauvais	1400		yes
30-12-43	Lt.	Radener	7	8	B-17	32km WNW of Arras	1436		unk
05-01-44	Lt.	Radener	7	9	B-17	near Miraumont	1314		yes
11-01-44	Lt.	Radener	7	10	P-47	Backum near Lingen	1315	353 FG	unk
29-01-44	Lt.	Radener	7		B-24-HSS	N of Trier	1125	44 BG	no
04-02-44	Lt.	Radener	7	11	B-24	10km SE of Albert (RF-2)	1200	446 BG	yes
08-02-44	Lt.	Radener	7		P-47	N of Laon	1110	352 FG	no
08-02-44	Lt.	Radener	7		P-47	N of Laon	1112	352 FG	no
11-02-44	Lt.	Radener	7 CO		P-38	SE of Valenciennes	1350	20 FG	no
18-02-44	Lt.	Radener	7 CO	12	Typhoon	N of Amiens	1205	174 Sqd	yes
24-02-44	Lt.	Radener	7 CO		B-17-HSS	NW of Ascheberg	1225	92 or 306 BG	no
24-02-44	Lt.	Radener	7 CO	13	B-24	Asslar 5km NW of Wetzlar	1400		yes

---

Date	Rank	Name	Unit	No.	Aircraft	Location	Time	Unit	Conf.
24-02-44	Lt.	Radener	7 CO		P-51	NW of Wetzlar-SE of Bonn	1420	357 FG	no
25-02-44	Lt.	Radener	7 CO	14	B-24-HSS	Notweiler-W of Bergzabern	1445		yes
25-02-44	Lt.	Radener	7 CO	15	B-17-eV	Willgartswissen-Pirmasens	1520		yes
12-04-44	Lt.	Radener	7 CO	16	B-24-HSS	18km N of Namur (OM-PM)	1310	445 BG	yes
24-04-44	Oblt.	Radener	7 CO	17	B-17-HSS	NE of St. Dizier	1222		unk
27-04-44	Oblt.	Radener	7 CO	18	P-47	SW of Reims	1742	356 FG	yes
29-04-44	Oblt.	Radener	7 CO	19	B-17-HSS	5km SE of Roubaix	1335	401 BG	yes
08-05-44	Oblt.	Radener	7 CO	20	P-47	6km N of Soissons (TG-SG)	1032	404 FG	yes
11-05-44	Oblt.	Radener	7 CO	21	B-24	44km W of Chartres (CB38)	1400	487 BG	yes
15-06-44	Oblt.	Radener	7 CO		P-51	E of Bonneval		339 FG	no
23-12-44	Oblt.	Radener	7 CO	22	Lancaster	W of Köln	1257	582 Sqd	unk
23-12-44	Oblt.	Radener	7 CO	23	Lancaster	NW of Köln-NNW of Düren	1301	405 or 582 Sqd	unk
12-02-42	Oblt.	Ragotzi	8	1	Spitfire	unknown	1620		yes
25-03-42	Oblt.	Ragotzi	10J	2	Hurricane	E of Harwich			no
27-04-42	Lt.	Rahardt	2	1	Spitfire	near Steenvoorde	1555	485 Sqd	yes
26-07-42	Lt.	Rahardt	2	2	Spitfire	10km S of Calais		31 FG	yes
31-08-44	Ofhr.	Ramthun	1		Auster-ground	Reims (TI5)			no
04-04-45	Lt.	Ramthun	1	1	Tempest	6km E of Diepholz	1945	438 Sqd Typhoon	unk
25-04-45	Lt.	Ramthun	1	2	Yak-3	Reinickendorf	1230		unk
12-08-40	Oblt.	Regenauer	2	1	Spitfire	Channel-Folkestone	1220	64 Sqd	no
27-09-43	Lt.	Reischer	7		Spitfire	Poix-Le Tréport	1111	313 Sqd	unk
20-12-43	Lt.	Reischer	9		B-17	unknown			yes
16-03-44	Lt.	Reischer	11 CO	8	B-24-HSS	Vitry (BJ2)	1338	458 BG	yes
27-03-44	Lt.	Reischer	11 CO	9	P-47	NE of Chartres (BD8)	1427	359 FG	yes
01-04-44	Lt.	Reischer	11 CO	10	B-24	St Pol (OE7-PE1)	1330	448 BG	yes
23-04-44	Lt.	Reischer	11 CO	11	B-24	E of W Neustadt (EO4)	1410	459 BG	yes
24-04-44	Lt.	Reischer	11 CO	12	B-17	S of Donauwörth (BB6)	1328		yes
01-05-44	Lt.	Reischer	11 CO	13	P-51	E of Saarbrücken (TP9)	1845	355 FG	yes
12-05-44	Lt.	Reischer	11 CO	14	B-17-HSS	Liège-St Vith (PM2)	1554	452 BG	yes
08-06-44	Lt.	Reischer	11 CO	15	Typhoon	N of Caen (TU6)	0635	198 Sqd	yes
14-06-44	Lt.	Reischer	11 CO	16	P-38	SW of Évreux (AD3)	0735	55 FG	unk
22-06-44	Lt.	Reischer	11 CO	17	P-51	S of Cherbourg (TR6)	1443	365 FG P-47	unk
11-09-44	Lt.	Reischer	11 CO	18	P-47	W of Maastricht (NL5-9)	1458		unk
03-12-44	Oblt.	Reischer	11 CO	19	Spitfire	S of Kleve (KN9-5)	0925		unk
01-03-45	Uffz.	Rey	14	3	Spitfire	Viersen-M-Gladbach	0941		unk
21-04-45	Uffz.	Rey	3	4	Spitfire	Buchholz (S of Harburg)	1510		unk
24-07-41	Gefr.	Richter H.	Ge St	1	Spitfire	unknown	1950		yes
09-08-41	Uffz.	Richter H.	Ge St		Spitfire	N of Dunkirk	1130	452 Sqd	no
10-08-41	Uffz.	Richter H.	Ge St	2	Spitfire	NW of Gravelines	1305		yes
07-11-41	Uffz.	Richter H.	Ge St	3	Spitfire	2km N of Étaples	1510	72 Sqd	yes
28-05-40	Uffz.	Richter J.	2		Spitfire	between Dover & Ostend			unk
17-05-40	Lt.	Ripke	8	1	Morane 406	unknown			unk
18-08-40	Lt.	Ripke	8	2	Hurricane	unknown	1635		yes
09-09-40	Lt.	Ripke	8	3	Spitfire	Thames Estuary	1820	92 Sqd	yes
13-05-40	Lt.	Roch	5	3	Spitfire	Dordrecht	0645	66 or 264 Sqd	yes
13-05-40	Lt.	Roch	5	2	Spitfire	Rotterdam	0650	66 or 264 Sqd	yes
13-05-40	Lt.	Roch	5	1	Spitfire	Rotterdam	0705	66 or 264 Sqd	yes
18-05-40	Lt.	Roch	5	4	Morane 405/6	Cambrai	1620		yes
16-08-40	Lt.	Roch	II St	5	Spitfire	Dover	1355	266 Sqd	yes
05-04-45	Uffz.	Rohrmann	5	1	Spitfire-prob	near Hilkenbrook	1127	350 Sqd	unk
18-05-40	Oblt.	Roos	4	1	Morane 406	Douai	1620		yes
18-05-40	Fw.	Roth	4	1	Hurricane	Tournai	1635		yes
19-05-40	Fw.	Roth	4	2	Hurricane	Tournai	2040		yes
29-05-40	Fw.	Roth	4	3	Spitfire	Dunkirk	1850	64, 229 or 610 Sqd	yes
01-06-40	Fw.	Roth	4	4	Hurricane	Dunkirk	1250	43, 145 or 245Sqd	yes
01-09-40	Fw.	Roth	4	5	Spitfire	Cranbrook	1450	72 Sqd	yes
03-09-40	Fw.	Roth	4	6	Hurricane	Wickford	1125	257 Sqd	yes
07-10-40	Fw.	Roth	4	7	Spitfire	Tenterden	1120	603 Sqd	yes
08-11-40	Obfw.	Roth	4	9	Spitfire	Tonbridge	1135	615 Sqd	unk
08-11-40	Obfw.	Roth	4	8	Spitfire	Dover	1450	302 or 501 Sqd	yes
24-06-41	Obfw.	Roth	4	10	Spitfire	Gravelines	2055		unk
21-08-41	Obfw.	Roth	4	11	Spitfire	Capelle	1458	610 Sqd	yes
18-09-41	Obfw.	Roth	4	12	Blenheim	Ostend	1115	88 Sqd	yes
06-11-41	Obfw.	Roth	4	13	Spitfire	Dunkirk	1455	303 Sqd	yes
09-05-42	Obfw.	Roth	4	14	Spitfire	Le Touquet	1355	118 or 501 Sqd	yes
02-06-42	Obfw.	Roth	4	15	Spitfire	mid-Channel	1104	403 Sqd	yes
19-08-42	Obfw.	Roth	4	16	Spitfire	NE of Dieppe	1752		yes
06-09-42	Obfw.	Roth	4	17	B-17	NW of Le Tréport	1906	92 BG	yes
08-03-43	Obfw.	Roth	4	18	B-24	Barentin?	1405	44 BG	yes
12-08-43	Obfw.	Roth	4	19	B-17	near Köln-Ostheim	0910		yes

Date	Rank	Name		No.	Aircraft	Location	Time	Unit	Conf.
14-10-43	Obfw.	Roth	5	20	B-17	SW of Bonn	1403	305 BG	yes
21-01-44	Uffz.	Ruppert H.	1	1	B-24	near Poix	1530	44 BG	yes
28-05-40	Lt.	Ruppert K.	3	1	Spitfire	between Dover & Ostend			unk
12-08-40	Lt.	Ruppert K.	3	2	Spitfire	S of Folkestone	0915	610 Sqd	yes
24-08-40	Oblt.	Ruppert K.	3	3	Hurricane	NE of Dover	1605	32 Sqd	yes
25-08-40	Oblt.	Ruppert K.	3	4	Spitfire	S of Calais	1950	616 Sqd	yes
14-09-40	Oblt.	Ruppert K.	3	5	Hurricane	NE of Dover	1623	253 Sqd	yes
14-11-40	Oblt.	Ruppert K.	9 CO	6	Spitfire	S of Dover	1523	66 or 74 Sqd	yes
12-08-41	Oblt.	Ruppert K.	9 CO	7	Blenheim	20km NW of Walcheren	1320		unk
21-08-41	Oblt.	Ruppert K.	9 CO	8	Spitfire	unknown	1025		yes
27-08-41	Oblt.	Ruppert K.	9 CO	9	Spitfire	unknown	0820		yes
04-09-41	Oblt.	Ruppert K.	9 CO	10	Spitfire	Hesdin-Licques	1743		unk
28-02-42	Oblt.	Ruppert K.	9 CO	11	Spitfire	N of Calais	1437	316 Sqd	yes
04-04-42	Oblt.	Ruppert K.	9 CO	12	Spitfire	unknown	1139		yes
12-04-42	Oblt.	Ruppert K.	9 CO	13	Spitfire	unknown	1446		yes
25-04-42	Oblt.	Ruppert K.	9 CO	14	Spitfire	unknown	1637		yes
25-07-42	Oblt.	Ruppert K.	9 CO	15	Spitfire	W of Dunkirk	1431	416 Sqd	yes
19-08-42	Oblt.	Ruppert K.	9 CO	16	Spitfire	Dieppe	1240		yes
19-08-42	Oblt.	Ruppert K.	9 CO	17	Spitfire	Dieppe	1500		yes
19-08-42	Oblt.	Ruppert K.	9 CO	18	Spitfire	Dieppe	1738		yes
09-10-42	Oblt.	Ruppert K.	9 CO	19	B-17-HSS	unknown	1040	306 BG	unk
13-02-43	Hptm.	Ruppert K.	9 CO	20	Spitfire	5-10km S of Mer de Glinau	1106		i.O.
05-04-43	Hptm.	Ruppert K.	9 CO	21	B-17	N of Ghent	1522	306 BG	yes
14-01-45	Uffz.	Russ	1	1	Spitfire	Rheine (GQ5)	1545	331 or 332 Sqd	unk
28-08-40	Lt.	Rysavy	2	1	Hurricane	S of Faversham		79 Sqd	unk
29-08-40	Lt.	Rysavy	2	2	Hurricane	W of Dover	1937	85 Sqd	yes
18-04-41	Oblt.	Rysavy	2	3	Blenheim	70km W ofIle de Sein	0948	53 Sqd	yes
16-06-41	Oblt.	Rysavy	2 CO	4	Spitfire	S of Hythe	1820	1 or 91 Sqd	yes
17-06-41	Oblt.	Rysavy	2 CO	5	Hurricane	NW of Cap Gris Nez	1952	56 or 242 Sqd	yes
21-06-41	Oblt.	Rysavy	2 CO	6	Spitfire	N of Boulogne	1631		unk
25-06-41	Oblt.	Rysavy	2 CO	7	Spitfire	S of Dunkirk	1240	610 or 616 Sqd	yes
25-06-41	Oblt.	Rysavy	2 CO	8	Spitfire	SW of Dunkirk	1256	610 or 616 Sqd	yes
04-07-44	Uffz.	Salewski	12		P-38	E of Lisieux(UA-UB)	1455	370 FG	unk
25-08-44	Uffz.	Salomon	7	1	P-51	N of Soissons (SG1-5)	1901	354 FG	unk
30-07-43	Flg.	Sander	10	1	B-17-HSS	St. Trond	0930	96 BG	unk
12-08-43	Gefr.	Sandoz	2	1	B-17	Essen (KP2)			yes
18-08-44	Ofhr.	Scharf	7	1	P-47	Beauvais (TE4-5)	1335	356 FG	unk
08-07-41	Lt.	Schauder	3	1	Spitfire	8km NE of Gravelines	1550		yes
18-07-41	Lt.	Schauder	3	2	Blenheim	near Gravelines	1128	21 Sqd	yes
09-08-41	Lt.	Schauder	3	3	Spitfire	15km N of Gravelines	1756		yes
10-08-41	Lt.	Schauder	3	4	Blenheim	8km N of a convoy	1306	226 Sqd	yes
19-08-41	Lt.	Schauder	3	5	Spitfire	NE of Gravelines	1941	111 Sqd	yes
21-09-41	Lt.	Schauder	3	6	Spitfire	E of Hazebrouck	1730	111 Sqd	yes
03-10-41	Lt.	Schauder	3	7	Spitfire	20km NW of Dunkirk	1550	92 Sqd	yes
13-10-41	Lt.	Schauder	3	8	Spitfire	W of St. Omer	1430		yes
13-10-41	Lt.	Schauder	3	9	Spitfire	10km W of Étaples	1535		yes
08-03-42	Lt.	Schauder	3	10	Spitfire	2km W of Bergues	1723	121 Sqd	yes
17-05-42	Lt.	Schauder	3	11	Spitfire	N of Desvres	1132	64 or 122 Sqd	yes
14-05-43	Oblt.	Schauder	9 CO	12	Spitfire V	Bruges-W of Stalhille	1245	611 Sqd	unk
29-07-43	Oblt.	Schauder	9 CO	13	B-17	Schleswig (UQ4)	0925	306 BG	yes
23-09-43	Oblt.	Schauder	9 CO	14	Spitfire	unknown	1710	308 Sqd	no
25-02-44	Oblt.	Schauder	10 CO	15	B-17	17km SE of Charleville	1145	306 BG	yes
20-03-44	Oblt.	Schauder	10 CO	16	B-17	W of Reims (TH)	1300	401 BG	yes
24-04-44	Oblt.	Schauder	10 CO		B-17	unknown			no
01-05-44	Oblt.	Schauder	10 CO	17	P-51	E of Saarbrücken (TP-TQ)	1835	355 FG	unk
16-06-44	Oblt.	Schauder	10 CO	18	Typhoon	near Lisieux (UU4-UA6)	1735	438 Sqd	unk
25-06-44	Oblt.	Schauder	10 CO	19	P-47	S of Lisieux(AA-AB)	0725		i.O.
13-07-44	Oblt.	Schauder	10 CO	20	Spitfire	Lisieux (UA5-8)	1715	401 Sqd	i.O.
17-07-44	Oblt.	Schauder	10 CO		P-51	Lisieux		354 FG	no
21-04-45	Hptm.	Schauder	II CO	21	Tempest	NW of Perleberg	1910	3 Sqd	unk
08-06-40	Lt.	Schauff	8	1	Hurricane	unknown			unk
08-09-40	Gefr.	Scheidt	1	1	Blenheim	Channel		153 Sqd	unk
15-10-40	Uffz.	Scheidt	1	2	Spitfire	Maidstone	1125	92 Sqd	yes
15-10-40	Uffz.	Scheidt	1	3	Hurricane	S of Gillingham		46 or 501 Sqd	unk
28-05-43	Fw.	Schellknecht	3	1	CurtissO-52	USSR (PQ 07583)			yes
14-08-41	Lt.	Schenk	6	1	Spitfire	Loon Plage	1830	306 or 308 Sqd	yes
10-10-43	Uffz.	Scheu	6		B-17	unknown			no
08-06-42	Uffz.	Scheyda	3	1	Spitfire	N of Hazebrouck	1345		yes
19-08-42	Uffz.	Scheyda	3	2	Spitfire	25km W of Dieppe			yes
13-01-43	Uffz.	Scheyda	3	3	B-17	Lô (N of Lille)	1430	305 BG	yes
18-02-43	Uffz.	Scheyda	3	4	Il-2	USSR (PQ 28354)			yes
05-03-43	Fw.	Scheyda	3	5	Il-2	USSR (PQ 1864)			yes
05-03-43	Fw.	Scheyda	3	6	Il-2	USSR (PQ 1838)			yes
05-03-43	Fw.	Scheyda	3	7	Il-2	USSR(PQ 1837/38)			yes

Date	Rank	Name	Unit	No.	Type	Location	Time	Unit	Conf.
05-03-43	Fw.	Scheyda	3	8	Pe-2	USSR (PQ 1836)			yes
17-03-43	Fw.	Scheyda	3	9	Yak-1	USSR (PQ 1844)			yes
18-03-43	Fw.	Scheyda	3	10	Yak-7	USSR (PQ 18275)			yes
18-03-43	Fw.	Scheyda	3	11	Il-2	USSR (PQ 19847)			yes
04-04-43	Fw.	Scheyda	3	12	Yak-4	USSR (PQ 08624)			yes
12-08-43	Fw.	Scheyda	3	13	B-17	N Sea–Walcheren (IH7)		91 BG	unk
06-09-43	Fw.	Scheyda	3	14	B-17	6km NE of Chamont (TE3)	1300		yes
06-09-43	Fw.	Scheyda	3	15	B-17	unknown			unk
04-02-44	Obfw.	Scheyda	3	16	B-17	3km NE of Brussels	1320		yes
08-02-44	Obfw.	Scheyda	3	17	P-51	S of Maubeuge (QI7)	1246	354 FG	yes
11-02-44	Obfw.	Scheyda	3	18	B-17	Mons (PH7-8)	1337	306 BG	yes
18-03-44	Obfw.	Scheyda	3	19	B-17	Ulm (CV4)	1455	100 BG	yes
08-04-44	Obfw.	Scheyda	3	20	P-47	Lingen (FP)	1520	361 FG	yes
07-09-41	Uffz.	Schick	1	1	Spitfire	mid-Channel		71 Sqd	unk
30-09-40	Uffz.	Schieffer	5	1	Hurricane	Tonbridge	1025	229 Sqd	yes
05-12-40	Uffz.	Schieffer	5	2	Spitfire	Chatham	1245	64 Sqd	yes
31-08-40	Obfw.	Schiffbauer	3	1	Spitfire	Chatham			unk
13-11-40	Obfw.	Schiffbauer	3	2	Hurricane	S of Folkestone	1200	249 Sqd	unk
20-08-42	Uffz.	Schild	2		Hurricane	over Channel			no
20-08-42	Uffz.	Schild	2		Hurricane	over Channel			no
20-08-42	Uffz.	Schild	2		Stirling	over Channel			no
25-06-43	Uffz.	Schild	2		B-17	Norden	0915		no
17-07-43	Uffz.	Schild	2		B-17-HSS	unknown	1100		no
28-07-43	Uffz.	Schild	2		B-17	NW of Hertogenbosch	1015		no
28-07-43	Uffz.	Schild	2		P-47	NW of Hertogenbosch	1015		no
12-08-43	Uffz.	Schild	2	1	B-17	Essen (KO8)	0900		yes
14-10-43	Uffz.	Schild	2		B-17-HSS	E of Antwerp	1400		unk
30-12-43	Fw.	Schild	2	2	B-17	Soissons-N of Charleroi (TG)	1343	390 BG	yes
30-01-44	Lt.	Schild	2	3	P-38	SW of Rheine	1330	20 FG	yes
08-04-44	Lt.	Schild	2		P-47	Gelsenkirchen	1600	361 FG	no
20-06-44	Lt.	Schild	2	4	P-38	Évreux	1735	370 FG	yes
18-08-44	Oblt.	Schild	10	5	P-51	SE of Orleans (FE1-9)	1933	4 FG	i.O.
11-09-44	Oblt.	Schild	12	6	P-47	S Maastricht (NM)	1458		yes
17-09-44	Oblt.	Schild	12	7	P-51	N of M-Gladbach (LN1)	1458	361 FG	yes
19-09-44	Oblt.	Schild	12	8	P-51	Emmerich (JN4)	1815	357 FG	yes
30-01-44	Uffz.	Schilling	7	1	B-17	near Geldern	1345		yes
23-03-44	Uffz.	Schlögl	3	1	B-17	Tilburg (KL)	1145	96 BG	yes
10-05-44	Uffz.	Schlögl	3	2	Spitfire	W of Amiens-S of Dieppe (RC-RD)	1115	602 Sqd	yes
22-07-41	Oblt.	Schmid	Ge St	10	Spitfire	unknown	1900		yes
23-07-41	Oblt.	Schmid	Ge St	11	Spitfire	Bruges	2015		yes
03-08-41	Oblt.	Schmid	Ge St	12	Spitfire	unknown	1832		yes
07-08-41	Oblt.	Schmid	Ge St	13	Spitfire	Campagne	1120		unk
07-08-41	Oblt.	Schmid	Ge St	14	Spitfire	SW of Calais	1130	19 or 401 Sqds	yes
07-08-41	Oblt.	Schmid	Ge St	15	Spitfire	St. Omer-Ardres	1743		yes
09-08-41	Oblt.	Schmid	Ge St	16	Spitfire	10km E of St. Omer	1125	452 Sqd	yes
09-08-41	Oblt.	Schmid	Ge St	17	Spitfire	near Gravelines	1744		yes
09-08-41	Oblt.	Schmid	Ge St	18	Spitfire	near Gravelines	1745		yes
10-08-41	Oblt.	Schmid	Ge St	19	Hurricane	N of Gravelines	1300	242 Sqd	yes
10-08-41	Oblt.	Schmid	Ge St	20	Hurricane	N of Gravelines	1301	242 Sqd	yes
10-08-41	Oblt.	Schmid	Ge St	21	Spitfire	N of Gravelines	1303		unk
12-08-41	Oblt.	Schmid	Ge St	22	Spitfire	NW of Vlissingen in sea-	1322	19 or 152 Sqd	unk
19-08-41	Oblt.	Schmid	Ge St	23	Blenheim	NW of Dunkirk	1225	18 Sqd	unk
19-08-41	Oblt.	Schmid	Ge St	24	Spitfire	E of St. Omer	1955	222 Sqd	yes
26-08-41	Hptm.	Schmid	8 CO	25	Blenheim	unknown	1940		yes
27-08-41	Hptm.	Schmid	8 CO	26	Spitfire	25km N of Calais	0830		unk
04-09-41	Hptm.	Schmid	8 CO	27	Spitfire	unknown	1720		yes
04-09-41	Hptm.	Schmid	8 CO	28	Spitfire	unknown	1735		yes
04-09-41	Hptm.	Schmid	8 CO	29	Spitfire	unknown	1750		yes
07-09-41	Hptm.	Schmid	8 CO	30	Spitfire	unknown	1720	71 Sqd	yes
18-09-41	Hptm.	Schmid	8 CO	31	Spitfire	unknown	1600		yes
20-09-41	Hptm.	Schmid	8 CO	32	Spitfire	unknown	1645		yes
21-09-41	Hptm.	Schmid	8 CO	33	Spitfire	unknown	1610	485 or 602 Sqd	yes
21-09-41	Hptm.	Schmid	8 CO	34	Spitfire	unknown	1615	485 or 602 Sqd	yes
27-09-41	Hptm.	Schmid	8 CO	35	Spitfire	unknown	1523		yes
27-09-41	Hptm.	Schmid	8 CO	36	Spitfire	unknown	1535		yes
27-09-41	Hptm.	Schmid	8 CO	37	Blenheim	unknown	1550		yes
01-10-41	Hptm.	Schmid	8 CO	38	Spitfire	Dover	1737		yes
02-10-41	Hptm.	Schmid	8 CO	39	Spitfire	unknown	1842		yes
03-10-41	Hptm.	Schmid	8 CO	40	Spitfire	20km N of Ostend	1552	54 Sqd	yes
13-10-41	Hptm.	Schmid	8 CO	41	Spitfire	unknown	1435		yes
13-10-41	Hptm.	Schmid	8 CO	42	Spitfire	unknown			unk
21-10-41	Hptm.	Schmid	8 CO	43	Spitfire	unknown	1300		yes

Date	Rank	Name	Unit	No.	Aircraft	Location	Time	Squadron	Conf.
27-10-41	Hptm.	Schmid	8 CO	44	Spitfire	Calais	1505		yes
06-11-41	Hptm.	Schmid	8 CO	45	Spitfire	10km N of Calais	1548	452 Sqd	unk
15-07-44	Oblt.	Schmidt G.	11		Spitfire	Caen (UU4)	0710		i.O.
06-08-44	Oblt.	Schmidt G.	9 CO		Halifax	N of Paris (UE7)	1213		i.O.
15-05-44	Uffz.	Schmidt H.	4	1	Spitfire	Courtrai (NG7-8)		403 Sqd	flak
11-06-41	Lt.	Schmidt J.	3	1	Hurricane	mid-Channel	1325	258 Sqd	yes
25-06-41	Lt.	Schmidt J.	3	2	Spitfire	10km N of Dunkirk	1645		yes
27-10-41	Lt.	Schmidt J.	3	3	Spitfire	20km NE of St. Omer	1305	401 Sqd	yes
25-04-42	Oblt.	Schmidt J.	3	4	Tomahawk	5km W of Le Touquet	1640		yes
26-04-42	Oblt.	Schmidt J.	3	5	Tomahawk	5km N of Cap Blanc Nez	1755		yes
30-04-42	Oblt.	Schmidt J.	3	6	Spitfire	S of Somme Estuary	1936	129 or 340 Sqd	yes
25-05-42	Oblt.	Schmidt J.	3	7	Spitfire	near Nieuport	1150	222 Sqd	yes
01-06-42	Oblt.	Schmidt J.	3	8	Spitfire	NE of Ostend	1348	65 Sqd	yes
01-06-42	Oblt.	Schmidt J.	3	9	Spitfire	NW of Ostend	1351	65 Sqd	yes
30-07-42	Oblt.	Schmidt J.	11H CO	10	Spitfire	15km W of Boulogne		616 Sqd	yes
19-08-42	Oblt.	Schmidt J.	11H CO	11	Spitfire	W of Dieppe			yes
19-08-42	Oblt.	Schmidt J.	11H CO	12	Spitfire	near Dieppe			unk
30-12-43	Fw.	Schmidtke	4		B-17	unknown	1500		no
24-01-44	Fw.	Schmidtke	4	1	B-17	Calais		95 BG	unk
11-06-44	Fw.	Schmidtke	4	2	P-38	Beauvais (TE1-4)	1532	55 FG	yes
12-04-45	Ogfr.	Schneider E.	3	1	Tempest-prob	15km N of Uelsen	1300	33 Sqd	unk
18-05-40	Lt.	Schneider W.	5	1	Curtiss H75	Douai	1635		yes
28-05-40	Lt.	Schneider W.	5	2	Hurricane	Channel Narrows	1233	213, 229 or 242Sqd	yes
31-08-40	Oblt.	Schneider W.	6 CO	3	Hurricane	London	1900		yes
06-09-40	Oblt.	Schneider W.	6 CO	4	Spitfire	Littlestone	1425	72 Sqd	yes
06-09-40	Oblt.	Schneider W.	6 CO	5	Spitfire	Littlestone	1429	72 Sqd	yes
23-09-40	Oblt.	Schneider W.	6 CO	6	Hurricane	Margate	1100		yes
23-09-40	Oblt.	Schneider W.	6 CO	7	Hurricane	Thames Estuary	1110		yes
28-09-40	Oblt.	Schneider W.	6 CO	8	Spitfire	Canterbury	1135	603 Sqd	yes
30-09-40	Oblt.	Schneider W.	6 CO	9	Hurricane	Tonbridge	1025	229 Sqd	yes
01-10-40	Oblt.	Schneider W.	6 CO	10	Hurricane	Horsham	1535	303 Sqd	unk
05-11-40	Oblt.	Schneider W.	6 CO	11	Hurricane	Canterbury	1240	310 Sqd	yes
09-06-41	Oblt.	Schneider W.	6 CO	12	Wellington	Knokke	1745	9 Sqd	yes
25-06-41	Oblt.	Schneider W.	6 CO	13	Spitfire	Dunkirk	1640		yes
02-07-41	Oblt.	Schneider W.	6 CO	14	Spitfire	Mardyck	1255		yes
07-08-41	Oblt.	Schneider W.	6 CO	15	Spitfire	Deal	0830		yes
07-08-41	Oblt.	Schneider W.	6 CO	16	Hurricane	Gravelines	1805		yes
14-08-41	Oblt.	Schneider W.	6 CO	17	Spitfire	Dunkirk	1837	306 or 308 Sqd	yes
21-09-41	Oblt.	Schneider W.	6 CO	18	Spitfire	Boulogne	1630	315 Sqd	yes
21-09-41	Oblt.	Schneider W.	6 CO	19	Spitfire	Desvres	1635	315 Sqd	yes
23-11-41	Oblt.	Schneider W.	6 CO	20	Spitfire	W of Dunkirk	1327	315 sqd	yes
06-12-42	Uffz.	Schnell	3	1	B-24	35km W of Étaples	1144	44 BG	yes
07-12-42	Uffz.	Schnell	3	2	Spitfire	4-6km N of Berck	1715		yes
23-12-42	Uffz.	Schnell	3	3	Vanguard	2km E of Dover	1120	609 Sqd	yes
13-06-43	Ogfr.	Schöhl	8		Spitfire	20km N of Dunkirk	0955	65 Sqd	unk
06-08-44	Uffz.	Scholtz	11		Lancaster	N of Paris (UE7)	1215		unk
26-06-43	Fw.	Scholz	5	2	P-47	20km N of Neufchatel	1900	56 FG	yes
19-05-40	Oblt.	Schöpfel	9 CO	1	Hurricane	NE of Courtrai			unk
29-05-40	Oblt.	Schöpfel	9 CO	2	Spitfire	W of Dunkirk	1810	64, 229 or 610Sqd	yes
31-05-40	Oblt.	Schöpfel	9 CO	3	Spitfire	Dunkirk	1540	609 Sqd	unk
02-06-40	Oblt.	Schöpfel	9 CO	4	Spitfire	unknown	0925	66, 266 or 611Sqd	unk
08-08-40	Oblt.	Schöpfel	9 CO	6	Spitfire	W of Canterbury	1234	65 Sqd	yes
08-08-40	Oblt.	Schöpfel	9 CO	5	Hampden	S of Ramsgate	1235	600 Sqd	yes
11-08-40	Oblt.	Schöpfel	9 CO		balloon	S England	1130	n/a	no
12-08-40	Oblt.	Schöpfel	9 CO	7	Spitfire	Folkestone	1230	151 or 501 Sqd	unk
14-08-40	Oblt.	Schöpfel	9 CO	8	Hurricane	Folkestone-Dover	1330	32 or 615 Sqd	unk
18-08-40	Oblt.	Schöpfel	9 CO	9	Hurricane	Canterbury	1355	501 Sqd	yes
18-08-40	Oblt.	Schöpfel	9 CO	10	Hurricane	Canterbury	1355	501 Sqd	yes
18-08-40	Oblt.	Schöpfel	9 CO	11	Hurricane	Canterbury	1356	501 Sqd	yes
18-08-40	Oblt.	Schöpfel	9 CO	12	Hurricane	Canterbury	1356	501 Sqd	yes
22-08-40	Oblt.	Schöpfel	III CO	13	Spitfire	SE of Dover	2025	65 Sqd	yes
28-08-40	Hptm.	Schöpfel	III CO	14	Defiant	E of Canterbury	1010	264 Sqd	yes
31-08-40	Hptm.	Schöpfel	III CO	15	Spitfire	Braintree	1000	56 Sqd	yes
01-09-40	Hptm.	Schöpfel	III CO	16	Spitfire	London	1500	72 Sqd	yes
06-09-40	Hptm.	Schöpfel	III CO		Hurricane	Dungeness	1030	303 Sqd	no
07-09-40	Hptm.	Schöpfel	III CO	17	Spitfire	London	1845	603 Sqd	yes
09-09-40	Hptm.	Schöpfel	III CO	18	Spitfire	Thames Estuary	1805	92 Sqd	yes
09-09-40	Hptm.	Schöpfel	III CO	19	Spitfire	Thames Estuary	1807	92 Sqd	yes
09-09-40	Hptm.	Schöpfel	III CO	20	Spitfire	Thames Estuary	1811	92 Sqd	yes
11-09-40	Hptm.	Schöpfel	III CO		Blenheim	unknown	1730	235 Sqd	no
29-10-40	Hptm.	Schöpfel	III CO	21	Hurricane	unknown	1745	257 Sqd	yes
01-11-40	Hptm.	Schöpfel	III CO	22	Spitfire	Herne Bay	1535	92 Sqd	yes
17-06-41	Hptm.	Schöpfel	III CO	23	Hurricane	unknown	1940	56 or 242 Sqd	yes

23-06-41	Hptm.	Schöpfel	III CO	24	Blenheim	N France	2030	107 Sqd	yes
27-06-41	Hptm.	Schöpfel	III CO	25	Hurricane	unknown	1705		yes
28-06-41	Hptm.	Schöpfel	III CO	26	Spitfire	Audruicq	0850	306 Sqd	yes
02-07-41	Hptm.	Schöpfel	III CO	27	Spitfire	S of Lillers	1250		yes
11-07-41	Hptm.	Schöpfel	III CO	28	Spitfire	unknown	1455		yes
07-08-41	Hptm.	Schöpfel	III CO	30	Spitfire	SW of Dunkirk	1800		yes
07-08-41	Hptm.	Schöpfel	III CO	29	Spitfire	unknown	1140	19 or 401 Sqd	yes
09-08-41	Hptm.	Schöpfel	III CO	31	Spitfire	E of Marquise	1145	616 Sqd	yes
09-08-41	Hptm.	Schöpfel	III CO	32	Spitfire	unknown	1759		yes
21-08-41	Hptm.	Schöpfel	III CO	33	Spitfire	unknown	1018		yes
21-09-41	Hptm.	Schöpfel	III CO	34	Spitfire	unknown	1630	485 or 602 Sqd	yes
27-09-41	Hptm.	Schöpfel	III CO	35	Spitfire	unknown	1530		yes
27-11-41	Hptm.	Schöpfel	III CO	36	Hurricane	5km W of Boulogne	1730	607 Sqd	yes
24-03-42	Maj.	Schöpfel	Ge CO	37	Spitfire	N France		411 Sqd	no
28-03-42	Maj.	Schöpfel	Ge CO	38	Spitfire	unknown	1830	64 Sqd	yes
14-04-42	Maj.	Schöpfel	Ge CO	39	Spitfire	unknown	1833	403 Sqd	yes
01-06-42	Maj.	Schöpfel	Ge CO	40	Spitfire	unknown	1355	65 or 111 Sqd	yes
19-08-42	Maj.	Schöpfel	Ge CO	41	Spitfire	off Dieppe	1631	501 Sqd	yes
19-08-42	Maj.	Schöpfel	Ge CO	42	Spitfire	off Dieppe	1830	222 Sqd	yes
08-11-42	Maj.	Schöpfel	Ge CO	43	B-17	unknown			unk
08-11-42	Maj.	Schöpfel	Ge CO	44	B-17	unknown			unk
06-12-42	Maj.	Schöpfel	Ge CO	45	B-17	unknown		305 BG	unk
20-12-42	Maj.	Schöpfel	Ge CO		B-17	unknown			no
29-12-41	Lt.	Schrader	3	1	Spitfire	80km N of Ostend	1554		yes
06-08-44	Oblt.	Schrader	12 CO		Halifax	NE of Paris(UE9-UF7)	1210		i.O.
21-04-45	Lt.	Schramm	6	1	Tempest	NW of Perleberg	1912	3 Sqd	unk
24-06-43	Uffz.	Schulwitz	10	1	Spitfire	St. Pierre Capelle	0905	303 Sqd	yes
07-01-44	Uffz.	Schulwitz	8	2	B-17	1km N of Trois-Marquess	1345		yes
12-04-44	Uffz.	Schulwitz	8	3	B-24-HSS	SW of Liège	1320	445 BG	unk
17-09-44	Ofhr.	Schulwitz	8	4	P-51	Emmerich (JO)	1441	4 FG	yes
23-12-44	Ofhr.	Schulwitz	8	5	Lancaster	Köln-Bonn	1257	582 Sqd	unk
28-02-45	Lt.	Schulwitz	5	6	P-47	near Mönchen-Gladbach	1224	406 FG	unk
09-03-45	Lt.	Schulwitz	5	7	P-47	near Wesel	1651	366 FG	unk
17-03-45	Lt.	Schulwitz	5	8	Auster	NW of Düsseldorf	1630	47 FAB L-5	unk
17-03-45	Lt.	Schulwitz	5	9	Auster	SW of Düsseldorf	1635		unk
21-09-44	Uffz.	Schulz	3	1	C-47	W of Arnhem	1720	38 or 46 Gp	yes
21-09-44	Uffz.	Schulz	3	2	C-47	W of Arnhem	1723	38 or 46 Gp	yes
23-09-44	Uffz.	Schulz	3	3	P-51	Goch (KN)	1651	339 FG	yes
08-08-44	Uffz.	Schwan	1	1	P-51	Versailles (AD7-8)	1430	359 FG	yes
26-08-44	Uffz.	Schwan	1	2	Spitfire	Rouen (TC4)	0935	602 Sqd	yes
12-12-42	Uffz.	Schwarz E.	9	1	B-17	50km S of Paris	1215	303 BG	yes
16-02-43	Uffz.	Schwarz E.	9	2	B-17	6-10km W of Ploermel	1125		i.O.
26-07-43	Uffz.	Schwarz E.	8	3	Spitfire	Lille-Nord a/f	1130	317 Sqd	yes
19-08-43	Uffz.	Schwarz E.	8	4	B-17-eV	unknown		388 BG	no
08-09-43	Fw.	Schwarz E.	8	5	Spitfire	NW of Menin	1026	302 Sqd	unk
21-01-44	Fw.	Schwarz E.	4	6	Spitfire	Calais area		616 Sqd	yes
30-01-44	Fw.	Schwarz E.	4	7	B-17	Breda (KK)			yes
01-04-44	Obfw.	Schwarz E.	4	8	B-24	E of St. Omer (NF7)	1502	448 BG	yes
26-12-44	Obfw.	Schwarz E.	1	9	P-51	Givet (QU-QL)	1100	361 FG	unk
24-04-45	Obfw.	Schwarz E.	1	10	Yak-3	near Stolpe (N of Spandau)	0820		unk
26-04-45	Obfw.	Schwarz E.	1	11	Yak-3	SE of Prenzlau	1915		unk
17-06-43	Uffz.	Schwarz P.	6	1	Spitfire	10km SW ofSt. Omer	1556	421 Sqd	yes
07-05-43	Fw.	Schwentick	2	1	Il-2	USSR (PQ 1981)			yes
20-12-43	Uffz.	Seebeck	9		B-17	unknown			yes
14-08-41	Oblt.	Seegatz	4	14	Spitfire	Audruicq	1545	41 or 616 Sqd	yes
29-08-41	Oblt.	Seegatz	4	15	Spitfire	Nieuport	0834	72 Sqd	yes
21-10-41	Oblt.	Seegatz	4	16	Spitfire	Boulogne	1310		yes
09-05-44	Uffz.	Seidl	2	1	P-51	Antwerp (LK)	0947	357 FG	yes
24-12-44	Fw.	Seidl	2	2	Auster	Bastogne (QM2-6)	1130	124 L Sqd L-5	unk
10-05-40	Oblt.	Seifert	3 CO	1	Fokker D21	Rotterdam	1015	2-1 JaVA	yes
28-05-40	Oblt.	Seifert	3 CO	2	Spitfire	between Dover & Ostend			unk
08-06-40	Oblt.	Seifert	3 CO	3	Battle	N of Beauvais		103 Sqd	unk
09-06-40	Oblt.	Seifert	3 CO	4	Potez 63	near Rouen			yes
20-09-40	Hptm.	Seifert	3 CO	5	Hurricane	Thames Estuary	1225	253 Sqd	yes
20-09-40	Hptm.	Seifert	3 CO	6	Hurricane	Maidstone	1237	253 Sqd	yes
05-11-40	Hptm.	Seifert	3 CO	7	Hurricane	Thames Estuary	1715	242 Sqd	yes
13-11-40	Hptm.	Seifert	3 CO	8	Hurricane	S of Folkestone	1200	249 Sqd	yes
11-06-41	Hptm.	Seifert	3 CO	9	Hurricane	mid-Channel	1330	258 Sqd	yes
23-06-41	Hptm.	Seifert	3 CO	10	Spitfire	near Samer	1350		yes
04-07-41	Hptm.	Seifert	3 CO	11	Spitfire	N of Bethune	1520		unk
11-07-41	Hptm.	Seifert	I CO	12	Spitfire	E of Wimereux	1505		yes
14-07-41	Hptm.	Seifert	I CO	13	Spitfire	S of Dunkirk	1030		yes
21-07-41	Hptm.	Seifert	I CO	14	Spitfire	SW of Ypres	0825		yes
21-07-41	Hptm.	Seifert	I CO	15	Stirling	Channel	0840	XV Sqd	yes
07-08-41	Hptm.	Seifert	I CO	16	Spitfire	near Gravelines	1125		unk

Date	Rank	Name	Unit	Claim	Type	Location	Time	Squadron	Confirmed
12-08-41	Hptm.	Seifert	I CO	17	Blenheim	SE of Vlissingen	1300		yes
19-08-41	Hptm.	Seifert	I CO	18	Spitfire	near Gravelines	1145	452 or 485 Sqd	unk
19-08-41	Hptm.	Seifert	I CO	19	Spitfire	near Cassel	1940	111 Sqd	yes
17-09-41	Hptm.	Seifert	I CO	20	Spitfire	N of Hazebrouck	1530		yes
03-10-41	Hptm.	Seifert	I CO	21	Spitfire	20km NW of Ostend	1547	92 Sqd	yes
12-10-41	Hptm.	Seifert	I CO	22	Spitfire	Berck-sur-Mer	1320	452 or 602 Sqd	yes
08-11-41	Hptm.	Seifert	I CO	23	Spitfire	NW of Dunkirk	1305	308 Sqd	yes
08-12-41	Hptm.	Seifert	I CO	24	Spitfire	near Le Touquet	1320		yes
13-03-42	Hptm.	Seifert	I CO	25	Spitfire	SW of Dunkirk	1615	303 Sqd	no
24-03-42	Hptm.	Seifert	I CO	26	Spitfire	12km W of Boulogne	1710	411 Sqd	yes
04-04-42	Hptm.	Seifert	I CO	27	Spitfire	S of Gravelines	1140	317 Sqd	yes
12-04-42	Hptm.	Seifert	I CO	28	Spitfire	between Boulogne & St. Omer	1335	41 Sqd	yes
24-04-42	Hptm.	Seifert	I CO	29	Spitfire	near Calais	1502	72 or 124 Sqd	yes
25-04-42	Hptm.	Seifert	I CO	30	Spitfire	10km W of Berck-sur-Mer	1640		yes
27-04-42	Hptm.	Seifert	I CO	31	Boston	near Bourbourg	1550	107 Sqd	yes
28-04-42	Hptm.	Seifert	I CO	32	Spitfire	3km W of Gravelines	1135	121, 222 or 317 Sqd	yes
05-05-42	Hptm.	Seifert	I CO	33	Spitfire	Ballieul	1540	122 Sqd	yes
17-05-42	Hptm.	Seifert	I CO	34	Spitfire	2km NW of Wissant	1140	64 or 122 Sqd	yes
01-06-42	Hptm.	Seifert	I CO	35	Spitfire	15km NNW of Ostend	1345	111 Sqd	no
02-06-42	Hptm.	Seifert	I CO	36	Spitfire	5km S of St. Valery	1125	403 Sqd	yes
30-07-42	Hptm.	Seifert	I CO	37	Spitfire	Boulogne			yes
30-07-42	Hptm.	Seifert	I CO	38	Spitfire	near Dungeness			unk
30-07-42	Hptm.	Seifert	I CO	39	Spitfire	NW of St. Omer			yes
31-07-42	Hptm.	Seifert	I CO	40	Spitfire	20km W of Berck-sur-Mer		133 Sqd	yes
19-08-42	Hptm.	Seifert	I CO	41	Spitfire	7km W of Dieppe			unk
04-12-42	Maj.	Seifert	I CO	42	Spitfire	near Calais	1452	401 or 402 Sqd	yes
16-02-43	Maj.	Seifert	I CO	43	Il-2	8km SE of Adler 7			yes
23-02-43	Maj.	Seifert	I CO	44	Il-2	USSR (PQ 1843)			yes
28-02-43	Maj.	Seifert	I CO	45	P-39	USSR (PQ 18412)			yes
28-02-43	Maj.	Seifert	I CO	46	LaGG-3	USSR (PQ 1835)			yes
05-03-43	Maj.	Seifert	I CO	47	Pe-2	USSR (PQ 1822)			yes
05-03-43	Maj.	Seifert	I CO	48	Il-2	USSR (PQ 1816)			yes
05-03-43	Maj.	Seifert	I CO	49	Il-2	USSR (PQ 1824)			yes
14-03-43	Maj.	Seifert	I CO	50	Pe-2	USSR (PQ 18282)			yes
16-03-43	Maj.	Seifert	I CO	51	Il-2	USSR (PQ 18211)			yes
12-05-43	Maj.	Seifert	I CO	52	Il-2	USSR (PQ 36612)			yes
13-05-43	Maj.	Seifert	I CO	53	MiG-3	USSR(PQ 4556/64)			yes
23-09-43	Maj.	Seifert	II CO	54	Spitfire	Le Fresne	1710	308 Sqd	yes
10-10-43	Maj.	Seifert	II CO	55	B-17	NE of Rheine	1530		yes
14-10-43	Maj.	Seifert	II CO	56	B-17	edge of Maastricht	1332	305 BG	yes
25-11-43	Maj.	Seifert	II CO	57	P-38	near Cuinchy	1321	55 FG	yes
08-11-42	Lt.	Seifert G.	9	1	B-17	unknown	1224	306 BG	unk
23-12-44	Ofhr.	Seyd	5	1	Lancaster	40km W of Köln	1300	405 or 582 Sqd	unk
05-04-45	Fw.	Sinz	15		Spitfire	Lingen-Haselünne	1210	402 Sqd	unk
16-02-43	Fw.	Söffing	1	1	Il-2	USSR (PQ 18464)			yes
16-02-43	Fw.	Söffing	1	2	Il-2	USSR (PQ 18461)			yes
17-02-43	Fw.	Söffing	1	3	P-40	USSR (PQ 10461)			yes
20-02-43	Fw.	Söffing	1	4	Il-2	USSR (PQ 18214)			yes
23-02-43	Fw.	Söffing	1	5	LaGG-3	USSR (PQ 29772)			yes
27-02-43	Fw.	Söffing	1	6	P-39	USSR (PQ 18382)			yes
05-03-43	Obfw.	Söffing	1	7	LaGG-3	USSR (PQ 18251)			yes
18-03-43	Obfw.	Söffing	1	8	Il-2	USSR (PQ 19763)			yes
24-03-43	Obfw.	Söffing	1	9	Pe-2	USSR (PQ 00412)			yes
14-05-43	Obfw.	Söffing	1	10	LaGG-3	USSR (PQ 54312)			yes
22-04-44	Obfw.	Söffing	1	11	B-24	E of Courtrai (NH)	2102	445 BG	unk
11-05-44	Obfw.	Söffing	1	12	P-47	Chateaudun (DC)	1420	353 FG	yes
11-05-44	Obfw.	Söffing	1	13	P-47	Chateaudun (DC)	1423	353 FG	yes
20-05-44	Obfw.	Söffing	1	14	P-51	E of Courtrai (NH)	1050	355 FG	yes
24-05-44	Obfw.	Söffing	1	15	P-47	Roubaix (OG)	1145	373 FG	yes
24-05-44	Obfw.	Söffing	1	16	P-51	St Quentin (RG)	1930	339 FG	yes
07-06-44	Lt.	Söffing	1	17	P-51	W of Rouen (TB5)	0704		yes
07-06-44	Lt.	Söffing	1	18	P-47	Falaise (UA1)	1601	362 FG	yes
13-06-44	Lt.	Söffing	1	19	P-51	W of Paris (AC6)	1635		yes
16-09-44	Lt.	Söffing	1	20	P-38	Bonn (NN8)	1745	370FG	yes
25-09-44	Lt.	Söffing	1	21	Spitfire	Arnhem (HM5-9)	1738	416 or 441 Sqd	yes
04-10-44	Lt.	Söffing	1	22	P-47	Mönchen-Gladbach (LO1)	1615	48 FG	i.O.
10-12-44	Lt.	Söffing	4 CO	23	P-47	Bonn (NN6,1)	1538	373 FG	unk
14-02-45	Lt.	Söffing	2 CO	24	Spitfire	Rheine (GP 5)	0815	41 Sqd	unk
22-02-45	Lt.	Söffing	2 CO	25	Tempest	near Rheine (HO)	1500	3 Sqd	unk
25-02-45	Lt.	Söffing	2 CO	26	P-47	Köln	0825	36 FG	unk
04-04-45	Lt.	Söffing	2 CO	27	Tempest	6km E of Diepholz	1945	438 Sqd Typhoon	unk
12-04-45	Lt.	Söffing	2 CO	28	Tempest	15km N of Uelsen	1300	33 Sqd	unk
17-04-45	Lt.	Söffing	2 CO	29	Tempest	SW of Lübeck(AB4)	1130	80 Sqd	unk
20-04-45	Lt.	Söffing	2 CO	30	Spitfire	Sülte a/f	1600	401 Sqd	unk

Date	Rank	Name	Unit	No.	Type	Location	Time	Unit2	Conf.
24-04-45	Lt.	Söffing	2 CO	31	Yak-3	S of Stolpe	0820		unk
25-04-45	Lt.	Söffing	2 CO	32	Yak-3	Reinickendorf	1230		unk
29-04-45	Lt.	Söffing	2 CO	33	Spitfire XIV	W of Lauenburg	1250	412 Sqd	unk
								Spitfire IXe	
29-04-45	Lt.	Söffing	2 CO	34	Tempest	S of Ratzeburg-Lübeck	1640	486 Sqd	unk
14-01-45	Fhr.	Spahn	8	1	P-47	W of Koblenz (near PO-PN)	1210	366 FG	unk
21-02-45	Ofhr.	Spahn	5	2	B-26-HSS	E of Arnhem (near HO-HP)	1600	394 BG	unk
28-02-45	Ofhr.	Spahn	5	3	P-47	near Mönchen-Gladbach	1225	406 FG	unk
01-03-45	Ofhr.	Spahn	5	4	P-47	near Mönchen-Gladbach	0935	366 FG	unk
10-05-40	Lt.	Sprick	8	1	Fokker T5	Breda		BomVA	
11-05-40	Lt.	Sprick	8	2	Curtiss H75	unknown	1930	GC I/4	yes
17-05-40	Lt.	Sprick	8	3	Morane 406	unknown	1830		yes
02-06-40	Lt.	Sprick	8	4	Spitfire	unknown	0925	66, 266 or	yes
								611Sqd	
06-06-40	Lt.	Sprick	8	5	Bloch 152	unknown			unk
06-06-40	Lt.	Sprick	8	6	Bloch 152	unknown			unk
06-06-40	Lt.	Sprick	8	7	Bloch 152	unknown			unk
13-06-40	Lt.	Sprick	8	8	Defiant	unknown	1239	142 Sqd	yes
14-06-40	Lt.	Sprick	8	9	Hurricane	unknown	1750		yes
12-08-40	Oblt.	Sprick	8 CO	10	Hurricane	Thames Estuary-NW of	1220	151 or 501 Sqd	yes
						Margate			
15-08-40	Oblt.	Sprick	8 CO	11	Spitfire	Dover-NW of Boulogne	1258	54 Sqd	yes
18-08-40	Oblt.	Sprick	8 CO	12	Hurricane	Canterbury	1350	17 Sqd	yes
24-08-40	Oblt.	Sprick	8 CO	13	Hurricane	Ashford	1220	151 Sqd	yes
31-08-40	Oblt.	Sprick	8 CO	14	Hurricane	Folkestone	1905	85 Sqd	yes
31-08-40	Oblt.	Sprick	8 CO	15	Hurricane	Folkestone	1915	85 Sqd	yes
01-09-40	Oblt.	Sprick	8 CO	16	Hurricane	London	1505	79 or 85 Sqd	yes
03-09-40	Oblt.	Sprick	8 CO	17	Spitfire	Rochester-Thames Estuary	1110		yes
17-09-40	Oblt.	Sprick	8 CO	18	Spitfire	Gravesend	1635		yes
23-09-40	Oblt.	Sprick	8 CO	19	Spitfire	Thames Estuary	1035	92 Sqd	yes
28-09-40	Oblt.	Sprick	8 CO	20	Hurricane	Canterbury	1130	501 Sqd	unk
15-10-40	Oblt.	Sprick	8 CO	21	Spitfire	unknown	1345		yes
17-11-40	Oblt.	Sprick	8 CO	22	Spitfire	E of Harwich	1022		yes
27-11-40	Oblt.	Sprick	8 CO	23	Spitfire	Deal	0925	421 Flt	unk
16-06-41	Oblt.	Sprick	8 CO	24	Spitfire	Dungeness-Étaples	1635		unk
17-06-41	Oblt.	Sprick	8 CO	25	Hurricane	unknown	1942	56 or 242 Sqd	yes
17-06-41	Oblt.	Sprick	8 CO	26	Hurricane	unknown	1958	56 or 242 Sqd	yes
18-06-41	Oblt.	Sprick	8 CO	27	Spitfire	unknown	1820	145 Sqd	yes
21-06-41	Oblt.	Sprick	8 CO	28	Hurricane	unknown	1642	1 Sqd	yes
21-06-41	Oblt.	Sprick	8 CO	29	Spitfire	unknown	1655		yes
22-06-41	Oblt.	Sprick	8 CO	30	Spitfire	unknown	1620	609 or 611 Sqd	yes
24-06-41	Oblt.	Sprick	8 CO	31	Spitfire	unknown	2058		yes
29-01-44	Uffz.	Stahnke	7	1	B-24-HSS	NE of Trier	1124	44 BG	yes
17-07-43	Hptm.	Staiger	12 CO	27	B-17F	German Bight(SP 1)	0928	351 BG	unk
25-07-43	Hptm.	Staiger	12 CO	28	B-17F	N of Weser Estuary (BB 4-2)	1650		yes
26-07-43	Hptm.	Staiger	12 CO	29	B-17F	Weser Estuary (CS 9-2)	1154		yes
29-07-43	Hptm.	Staiger	12 CO	30	B-17	Kiel (TQ)	0940	306 BG	yes
29-07-43	Hptm.	Staiger	12 CO	31	B-17	Kiel	0940	306 BG	yes
17-08-43	Hptm.	Staiger	12 CO	32	B-17	W of Pesch (NW of Aachen)	1520		yes
03-10-43	Hptm.	Staiger	12 CO	33	Spitfire	Beauvais		222 Sqd	unk
10-10-43	Hptm.	Staiger	12 CO	34	B-17	W of Münster		385 BG	yes
05-11-43	Hptm.	Staiger	12 CO	35	B-17	Dortmund		388 BG	yes
21-01-44	Hptm.	Staiger	12 CO	36	Spitfire	E of St Pol			unk
21-01-44	Hptm.	Staiger	12 CO	37	Spitfire	E of Amiens			unk
24-01-44	Hptm.	Staiger	12 CO	38	P-47	SW of Brussels	1100	78 FG	unk
22-02-44	Hptm.	Staiger	12 CO	39	P-47	M-Gladbach(MN-LN)	1523	353 FG	yes
24-02-44	Hptm.	Staiger	12 CO	40	B-17	S Quakenbrück-Rheine	1220	92 or 306 BG	yes
25-02-44	Hptm.	Staiger	12 CO	41	B-17	Birkweiler-Sedan	1300		yes
02-03-44	Hptm.	Staiger	12 CO	42	B-17	W of Limburg(PQ-QQ)	1150		yes
08-03-44	Hptm.	Staiger	12 CO	43	B-17	N of Hannover		388 BG	unk
08-03-44	Hptm.	Staiger	12 CO	44	B-17	Potsdam			unk
16-03-44	Hptm.	Staiger	12 CO	45	B-24	SW of St Dizier-Worms	1210	445 BG	yes
18-03-44	Hptm.	Staiger	12 CO	46	B-17	Colmar			unk
27-03-44	Hptm.	Staiger	12 CO	47	P-47	NE of Chartres (BD)	1435	359 FG	unk
13-04-44	Hptm.	Staiger	12 CO	49	P-38	W of Trier (RN8)	1620	364 FG	yes
13-04-44	Hptm.	Staiger	12 CO	48	B-17F	NW Kaiserslautern (SP)	1334		unk
23-04-44	Hptm.	Staiger	12 CO	50	B-17	SE of W Neustadt (EO9-FO3)	1415	97 or 483 BG	yes
24-04-44	Hptm.	Staiger	12 CO		B-17	Donauwörth(BB7-8)	1330		yes
24-04-44	Hptm.	Staiger	12 CO	51	B-17	Donauwörth(BB7-8)	1330		yes
24-04-44	Hptm.	Staiger	12 CO	52	B-17-HSS	S of München(ED)	1355		yes
24-04-44	Hptm.	Staiger	12 CO	53	B-17-HSS	S of München(ED)	1355		yes
24-04-44	Hptm.	Staiger	12 CO	54	B-17	S of München(ED 5-6)	1355		yes
07-06-44	Hptm.	Staiger	I CO	55	P-47	N of Lisieux	1558	362 FG	yes
07-06-44	Hptm.	Staiger	I CO	56	P-47	N of Lisieux	1600	362 FG	yes
15-06-44	Hptm.	Staiger	I CO	57	B-17-HSS	80km S of Chartres			no

Date	Rank	Name	Unit	No.	Type	Location	Time	Unit	Conf.
20-06-44	Hptm.	Staiger	I CO	58	P-38	Ch. Thierry-NE of Meaux (UC7-9)	1735	370 FG	yes
23-06-44	Hptm.	Staiger	I CO	59	Spitfire	W of Rouen-NE of Bayeux (TA1-2)	1220		yes
25-06-44	Hptm.	Staiger	I CO	60	P-38	SW of Rouen (TB)	1530	370 FG	yes
19-08-42	Lt.	Stammberger	9	1	Spitfire	2km N of Dieppe	1457		yes
02-10-42	Lt.	Stammberger	9		Spitfire	E of Deal	1540	331 Sqd	no
09-10-42	Lt.	Stammberger	9	2	B-17	E of Vendeville	1045	306 BG	yes
20-12-42	Lt.	Stammberger	9	3	B-17	5km NW of Meaux	1305	306 BG	n.O.
16-02-43	Lt.	Stammberger	9		B-17-HSS	St Nazaire	1120		no
31-03-43	Oblt.	Stammberger	4 CO	4	B-24	100km NW of Ostend	1248	93 BG	unk
05-04-43	Oblt.	Stammberger	4 CO	5	B-17	N Antwerp-Dintelnoord	1535	306 BG	yes
08-04-43	Oblt.	Stammberger	4 CO	6	Spitfire	5km S of Dieppe	1855	332 Sqd	yes
21-04-43	Oblt.	Stammberger	4 CO		Ventura	N of Abbeville	1220	21 Sqd	no
07-05-43	Lt.	Staschen	2	1	Il-2	USSR (PQ 1976)			yes
15-08-44	Lt.	Stein	5	1	P-47	Rambouillet(BD-6)	1230	373 FG	yes
13-06-43	Uffz.	Steinberg	9	1	B-17	12km NNE of Lake Selenter	0936	95 BG	yes
26-07-43	Uffz.	Steinberg	9	2	B-17	W of Helgoland (UP 5-2)	1340		unk
17-08-43	Uffz.	Steinberg	9	3	B-17-HSS	500m W of Montzen	1144		yes 1/2
11-10-42	Hptm.	Steindl	I St	1	Spitfire	5km E of Dunkirk	1535	64 Sqd	yes
11-04-43	Hptm.	Steindl	9		Mosquito	Destelbergen near Ghent-	2036	139 Sqd	yes
20-10-43	Hptm.	Steindl	11	10	B-17	crashed Mons (PG-PH)	1411	303 BG	yes
18-12-39	Oblt.	Steinhoff	10N CO	1	Wellington	25-35km SSW of Helgoland	1430	37 Sqd	yes
18-12-39	Oblt.	Steinhoff	10N CO	2	Wellington	25-35km SSW of Helgoland	1435	3 Gp	yes
26-06-41	Lt.	Sternberg	5	1	Spitfire	Dunkirk	1150		yes
16-08-41	Lt.	Sternberg	5	2	Spitfire	Dunkirk	0928	602 Sqd	yes
19-08-41	Lt.	Sternberg	5	3	Spitfire	N of Dunkirk	1944	308 or 315 Sqd	yes
21-08-41	Lt.	Sternberg	5	4	Spitfire	Wormhout	1030		yes
13-03-42	Lt.	Sternberg	5	5	Spitfire	mid-Channel	1621	401 Sqd	no
12-04-42	Lt.	Sternberg	5	6	Spitfire	St. Mariakerke	1345		yes
30-04-42	Lt.	Sternberg	5	7	Spitfire	15km NW of Somme Estuary	1942	222 Sqd	unk
09-05-42	Lt.	Sternberg	5	8	Spitfire	W of Calais	1346	118 or 501 Sqd	yes
02-06-42	Lt.	Sternberg	5	9	Spitfire	between Berck & Hastings	0725	64 or 174 Sqd	unk
17-08-42	Lt.	Sternberg	5	10	Spitfire	SW of Eastbourne	1910	401 or 402 Sqd	yes
03-02-43	Lt.	Sternberg	5 CO	11	Spitfire	7km NE of Calais	1110	308 Sqd	yes
13-02-43	Lt.	Sternberg	5 CO	12	Spitfire	NE of Watten	1025		yes
04-04-43	Oblt.	Sternberg	5 CO	13	Spitfire	NW of Rouen	1442	315,316 or 403 Sqd	yes
21-04-43	Oblt.	Sternberg	5 CO	14	Ventura	Acheux	1216	21 Sqd	yes
14-05-43	Oblt.	Sternberg	5 CO	15	B-17	Scheldt Estuary	1315	95 BG	yes
28-05-43	Oblt.	Sternberg	5 CO	16	Spitfire	Bergues	1752	315 Sqd	yes
31-05-43	Oblt.	Sternberg	5 CO	17	Spitfire	1km N of Ostend	1750	403 Sqd	yes
16-06-43	Oblt.	Sternberg	5 CO	18	Spitfire	10km SE of Dover	0706	91 Sqd	yes
17-06-43	Oblt.	Sternberg	5 CO	19	Spitfire	5km SW of Hazebrouck	1545	421 Sqd	yes
06-09-43	Oblt.	Sternberg	5 CO	20	B-17-HSS	30km NW of Paris	1218		unk
10-10-43	Oblt.	Sternberg	5 CO	22	B-17	Haaksbergen-Almelo	1218	390 BG	yes
14-06-44	Uffz.	Stoll	11		P-47	NE of Chartres (BD2-6)	0740	368 FG	unk
21-06-44	Oblt.	Stoll	5	1	P-38	W of Paris (AD9)	2147	474 FG	yes
24-06-44	Oblt.	Stoll	5	2	Mustang	7km W of Brezolles (BB3)	0730	65 Sqd	yes
02-10-42	Uffz.	Stoller	2	1	P-38	near Calais	1625	1 FG	yes
13-05-40	Fw.	Stolz	5	1	Defiant	Dordrecht	0700	264 Sqd	yes
24-08-42	Lt.	Strasen	5	1	Spitfire	E of Fécamp	1745	402 Sqd	unk
05-09-42	Lt.	Strasen	5	2	Spitfire	Le Tréport	1132	64 or 340 Sqd	yes
24-07-40	Fw.	Straub	7	1	Spitfire	N of Margate	1330	54 Sqd	unk
21-02-45	Uffz.	Stumpf	7		B-26-eV	near Ahaus	1603	394 BG	unk
11-06-43	Uffz.	Stutt	III St		B-17	N of Wilhelmshaven	1752		yes
01-01-45	Lt.	Sy	7	1	Spitfire	S of Brussels-Evere a/f	0925	416 Sqd	unk
01-03-45	Lt.	Sy	6	2	P-47	near Mönchen-Gladbach	0937	366 FG	unk
25-04-45	Lt.	Sy	7	3	P-39	E of Oranienburg	1755		unk
18-12-39	Fw.	Szuggar W.	10N	1	Wellington	25-35km SSW of Helgoland	1430	3 Gp	unk
17-07-44	Uffz.	Tabbat	10		P-51	Dreux (AC9)	1935	354 FG	i.O.
29-01-44	Gefr.	Talkenberg	8	1	P-38	Maisborn-Lingenbahn	1150	20 FG	yes
24-04-44	Uffz.	Tamann?	7		P-51	S of Speis...see?	1340		yes
21-09-44	Obfw.	Teilken	1	2	C-47	Nijmegen (IL-IM)	1717	38 or 46 Gp	yes
22-11-41	Lt.	Thorn	7	1	Spitfire	unknown	1652	401 Sqd	yes
07-08-44	Uffz.	Thran	10	1	P-47	Mortain-SW of Flers (BT)	1510	368 FG	i.O.
14-06-44	Uffz.	Tippe	11	1	P-38	N of Paris(UD9-UE7)	0730	55 FG	i.O.
15-06-44	Uffz.	Tippe	11	2	B-24-HSS	SW of Chartres	0700	392 BG	unk
11-01-44	Lt.	Triebnig	3	1	B-17	Nordhorn-Zuider Zee	1300	306 BG	yes
13-03-42	Obfw.	Ufer	4	1	Spitfire	Wirre Effroy	1615	124 Sqd	yes
04-04-42	Obfw.	Ufer	4	2	Spitfire	SE of Calais	1143		yes
30-04-42	Obfw.	Ufer	4	3	Spitfire	St. Valery	1937	222 Sqd	yes
06-07-41	Lt.	Uiberacker G.	1	1	Spitfire	NW of Dunkirk	1455		yes
21-09-41	Lt.	Uiberacker G.	1	2	Spitfire	8km SW of Gravelines	1630	Tangmere	yes

Date	Rank	Name			Aircraft	Location	Time	Squadron	Conf.
08-11-41	Lt.	Uiberacker G.	1	3	Spitfire	E of Somme Estuary	1225	401 Sqd	yes
12-02-42	Lt.	Uiberacker G.	1	4	Hurricane	50km SW of Vlissingen	1600	607 Sqd	yes
08-04-42	Lt.	Uiberacker G.	1	5	Spitfire	5km SE of Dover-Channel	0835		unk
31-07-42	Lt.	Uiberacker G.	1	6	Tomahawk	5km W of Somme Estuary		133 Sqd	yes
04-12-42	Lt.	Uiberacker G.	1	7	Spitfire	5km E of Boulogne	1447	401 or 402 Sqd	yes
31-05-40	Lt.	Ulenberg	2	1	Spitfire	near Dunkirk			unk
08-06-40	Lt.	Ulenberg	2	2	Spitfire	S of Auraines			unk
08-06-40	Lt.	Ulenberg	2	3	Battle	N of Beauvais	1450	103 Sqd	yes
06-09-40	Lt.	Ulenberg	2	4	Hurricane	SW of Tonbridge	1025	601 Sqd	yes
28-09-40	Lt.	Ulenberg	2	5	Spitfire	Ashford	1445		yes
10-04-41	Lt.	Ulenberg	2	6	Spitfire	Plouescat	1925	1 PRU	yes
10-04-41	Lt.	Ulenberg	2	7	Spitfire	N Ile d'Ouessant-W of Brest	0922	1 PRU	yes
25-05-41	Lt.	Ulenberg	2	8	Spitfire	60km N of Brest	0901	1 PRU	yes
16-06-41	Lt.	Ulenberg	2	9	Spitfire	S of Folkestone	1732	54Sqd	yes
02-07-41	Lt.	Ulenberg	2	10	Spitfire	E of Boukerque	1250		yes
05-07-41	Lt.	Ulenberg	2 CO	11	Spitfire	St. Herberthoab	1325	54 or 616 Sqd	unk
06-07-41	Lt.	Ulenberg	2 CO	13	Spitfire	NW of Dunkirk	1425		yes
06-07-41	Lt.	Ulenberg	2 CO	12	Spitfire	S of Socx	1448		unk
09-07-41	Lt.	Ulenberg	2 CO	14	Spitfire	10km N of Étaples	1415		yes
11-07-41	Lt.	Ulenberg	2 CO	15	Spitfire	W of Cap Gris Nez	1520		yes
11-07-41	Lt.	Ulenberg	2 CO	16	Spitfire	SE of Dunkirk	1620		yes
09-06-43	Fw.	Ullrich	3	1	B-17	unknown			unk
16-06-41	Lt.	Unzeitig	1	1	Spitfire	NW of Boulogne	1637		yes
05-07-41	Lt.	Unzeitig	1	2	Spitfire	W of Dunkirk	1340	54 or 616 Sqd	yes
07-07-41	Lt.	Unzeitig	1	3	Spitfire	SW of Boulogne	1056		yes
10-07-41	Lt.	Unzeitig	1	4	Spitfire	N of Cap Gris Nez	1243		yes
14-08-41	Lt.	Unzeitig	1	5	Spitfire	mid-Channel-N of Gravelines	1840	306 or 308 Sqd	unk
21-08-41	Lt.	Unzeitig	1	6	Spitfire	10km S of Boulogne	1520		yes
17-09-41	Lt.	Unzeitig	1	7	Spitfire	5km S of Gravelines	1540		yes
21-09-41	Lt.	Unzeitig	1	8	Spitfire	20km E of Étaples			unk
01-10-41	Lt.	Unzeitig	1	9	Spitfire	mid-Channel	1459	91 Sqd	yes
28-03-42	Lt.	Unzeitig	III St	10	Spitfire	Cap Gris Nez	1855	457 or 602 Sqd	yes
26-11-43	Uffz.	Vandeveerd	3	1	P-47	NW of Paris (TD2)	1100	78 FG	yes
11-01-44	Fw.	Vandeveerd	3	2	B-17	Nordhorn	1300	306 BG	yes
16-09-44	Fw.	Vandeveerd	3	4	P-38	Bonn (NN8)	1740	370FG	yes
21-09-44	Fw.	Vandeveerd	3	5	C-47	Nijmegen (IL-IM)	1718	38 or 46 Gp	yes
21-09-44	Fw.	Vandeveerd	3	6	C-47	Nijmegen (IL-IM)	1719	38 or 46 Gp	yes
31-12-43	Lt.	Vavken	7	1	B-17	5km N of Ault	1330	96 BG	yes
18-08-44	Fw.	Verhöven	6	1	P-38	Beauvais (TD-TE)	0822		yes
18-08-44	Fw.	Verhöven	6	2	Mustang	Beauvais (TD-TE)	0824	315 Sqd	unk
07-10-44	Fw.	Verhöven	6	3	Spitfire	Nijmegen (JM5-6)	1630	442 Sqd	yes
28-05-40	Fw.	Vielhaber	2		Spitfire	between Dover & Ostend			unk
06-11-41	Ogfr.	Vogt	6	1	Spitfire	Calais	1540	452 Sqd	yes
23-11-41	Ogfr.	Vogt	6	2	Spitfire	W of Dunkirk	1328	315 sqd	yes
04-04-42	Uffz.	Vogt	6	3	Spitfire	Watten	1140		yes
01-05-42	Uffz.	Vogt	6	4	Spitfire	Dover	1946	122 or 222 Sqd	yes
08-06-42	Uffz.	Vogt	6	5	Spitfire	Dunkirk	1403	H'church or Kenley Wing	yes
26-07-42	Uffz.	Vogt	6	6	Spitfire	W of Le Touquet	1328	401 Sqd	unk
17-08-42	Uffz.	Vogt	6	7	Spitfire	NNW of Fécamp	1852	401 or 402 Sqd	yes
27-08-42	Uffz.	Vogt	6	8	Spitfire	W of Somme Estuary	1343	111 Sqd	yes
02-11-42	Uffz.	Vogt	6	9	Spitfire	SW of Boulogne	1524	611 Sqd	unk
08-11-42	Uffz.	Vogt	6	10	Spitfire	Calais-Marck road	1251	421 Sqd	yes
06-12-42	Uffz.	Vogt	6	11	Spitfire	10km W of Dieppe	0836	91 Sqd	yes
22-06-43	Fw.	Vogt	6	12	B-17	10km W of Dunkirk	1141	381 or 384 BG	yes
26-07-43	Fw.	Vogt	6	13	Spitfire	Mouscron	1126	504 Sqd	yes
04-09-43	Fw.	Vogt	6	14	Spitfire	S of Le Tréport	1030	66 Sqd	yes
04-09-43	Fw.	Vogt	6	15	Spitfire	W ofBerck-sur-Mer	1955	129 Sqd	yes
27-09-43	Fw.	Vogt	6	16	Spitfire	15km SE of Fécamp	1852	129 Sqd	unk
29-11-43	Fw.	Vogt	7	18	Spitfire	Coxyde-SW of Ostend	1005	412 Sqd	yes
28-01-44	Fw.	Vogt	7	19	Spitfire	SW of Albert	1537	403 Sqd	yes
29-01-44	Fw.	Vogt	7		P-47	unknown			unk
08-03-44	Fw.	Vogt	7	20	B-17	16km SW of Gardelegen (GG2)	1330	96 or 388 BG	yes
08-03-44	Fw.	Vogt	7	21	B-17-HSS	15km E of Nienburg (FT3)	1330	452 BG	unk
12-04-44	Fw.	Vogt	7	22	B-24-HSS	near Liège(OL-OM)	1328	445 BG	unk
12-04-44	Fw.	Vogt	7	23	B-24-HSS	SW of Liège	1308	445 BG	unk
13-04-44	Fw.	Vogt	7	24	B-17-HSS	near Trier (SO2-5)	1323		no
27-04-44	Obfw.	Vogt	5	25	P-47	7km S of Soissons	1740	356 FG	yes
29-04-44	Obfw.	Vogt	5	26	B-17	NE of St. Omer (NF4)	1430	92 BG	yes
08-06-44	Lt.	Vogt	5	27	Mustang	N of Caen(UU-TU)	0600	168 Sqd	yes
22-06-44	Lt.	Vogt	7 CO	28	B-17-HSS	SE-E of Paris	1900		yes
23-06-44	Lt.	Vogt	7 CO	29	Mustang	St. Lô (TU7-8)	1308	414 Sqd	yes
24-06-44	Lt.	Vogt	7 CO	30	P-47	W of Dreux(BC1-4)	2133	373 FG	yes
25-06-44	Lt.	Vogt	7 CO	31	P-38	W of Roue(TA3-TB1)	1535	370 FG	unk
15-08-44	Lt.	Vogt	5 CO	32	P-47	Versailles(BD-AD)	1229	373 FG	yes

Date	Rank	Name	Unit	No.	Aircraft	Location	Time	Unit claimed	Conf.
19-08-44	Lt.	Vogt	5 CO	33	P-47	NE of Paris (AF)	1024	406 FG	yes
25-08-44	Lt.	Vogt	5 CO	34	P-38	W of Beauvais (TD)	1345	474 FG	yes
26-08-44	Lt.	Vogt	5 CO	35	Spitfire	E of Neufchatel (SD)	0920	421 Sqd	yes
29-08-44	Lt.	Vogt	5 CO	36	Auster	Soissons (TG9)	0940		yes
17-09-44	Lt.	Vogt	5 CO	37	Mustang	Bocholt (JN-JO)	1800	19 or 65 Sqd	yes
18-09-44	Lt.	Vogt	5 CO	38	Mustang	Luxembourg (KM)	1325	19 Sqd	yes
19-09-44	Lt.	Vogt	5 CO	39	P-51	Emmerich (JN)	1803	357 FG	yes
21-09-44	Lt.	Vogt	5 CO	40	C-47	Nijmegen (JM)	1717	38 or 46 Gp	yes
23-09-44	Lt.	Vogt	5 CO	41	P-51	Goch (KN)	1733	352 FG	yes
23-09-44	Lt.	Vogt	5 CO	42	P-51	Goch (KN)	1735	352 FG	yes
25-09-44	Lt.	Vogt	5 CO	43	Spitfire	Arnhem (JM)	1754	416 or 441 Sqd	yes
27-09-44	Lt.	Vogt	5 CO	44	Spitfire	Nijmegen (JM)	1041		yes
28-10-44	Lt.	Vogt	5 CO	45	Typhoon	between Venlo & Kempen	1325	182 Sqd	i.O.
19-11-44	Lt.	Vogt	5 CO	46	Spitfire	N of Kirchhellen (KO3)	1406	412 Sqd	unk
24-12-44	Lt.	Vogt	5 CO	47	P-47	Liège (PL-PM)	1228	36 FG	unk
26-12-44	Lt.	Vogt	5 CO	48	Auster	Bastogne(near QM)	1415		unk
20-10-43	Uffz.	Voigt	4		Spitfire	Dixmuiden	0945	485 Sqd	unk
01-12-43	Uffz.	Voigt	4	1	B-17	E of St. Omer (NF5-8)	1327	384 BG	yes
22-04-41	Uffz.	Wagner	7	1	Hurricane	25km SE of Kalafrana,Malta	1620	261 Sqd	yes
29-07-41	Uffz.	Wagner	7	2	Tomahawk	Libya			no
06-10-44	Gefr.	Walter	5	1	P-51	Eindhoven (LM)	1507		i.O.
22-03-45	Uffz.	Warthemann	6		Tempest	near Rheine	1603	56 or 80 Sqd	no
04-09-41	Uffz.	Weber	8	1	Spitfire	unknown	1725		yes
22-11-41	Fw.	Weber	8	2	Spitfire	Calais-Deal	1655	401 Sqd	yes
29-01-44	Lt.	Weide	2	1	B-17	W of Koblenz(PO-PP)			yes
21-09-41	Lt.	Weiss	6	1	Spitfire	Étaples-5km NW of Berck	1625	315 Sqd	unk
09-03-42	Lt.	Weiss	6	2	Spitfire	4km W of Boulogne	1640		yes
31-05-42	Oblt.	Weiss	6	3	Spitfire	Abbeville	1940	485 Sqd	yes
13-05-40	Uffz.	Wemhöner	5	1	Spitfire	Dordrecht	0646	66 or 264 Sqd	yes
19-05-40	Uffz.	Wemhöner	5	2	Curtiss H75	Roubaix	1740		yes
01-06-40	Uffz.	Wemhöner	5	3	Hurricane	Dunkirk	1240	43, 145 or 245Sqd	unk
01-06-40	Uffz.	Wemhöner	5	4	Hurricane	Dunkirk	1248	43, 145 or 245Sqd	yes
14-05-40	Oblt.	Wendt	8 CO	1	Morane 406	unknown	1825		yes
23-07-41	Lt.	Wenzel	1	1	Spitfire	WNW ofFort Philippe	1405		yes
06-12-42	Lt.	Wenzel	6	2	Spitfire	8km W of Dieppe	0835	91 Sqd	yes
14-05-40	Lt.	Westphal	III St	1	Hurricane	E of Ath		504 Sqd	unk
15-08-40	Oblt.	Westphal	III St	2	Spitfire	SE of Dover			no
11-09-40	Oblt.	Westphal	III St	3	Spitfire	unknown			no
11-09-40	Oblt.	Westphal	III St	4	Hurricane	unknown			no
25-10-40	Oblt.	Westphal	7	5	Spitfire	S of Sevenoaks Maidstone-	1110	603 Sqd	yes
09-06-41	Oblt.	Westphal	8	6	Spitfire	Dover	1412	91 Sqd	yes
16-06-41	Oblt.	Westphal	8	7	Spitfire	Boulogne-Étaples	1625		unk
16-06-41	Oblt.	Westphal	8	8	Hurricane	40 km W Boulogne	1700	258 Sqd	unk
17-06-41	Oblt.	Westphal	8	9	Spitfire	N of Étaples	1940	74 Sqd	yes
17-06-41	Oblt.	Westphal	8	10	Spitfire	unknown	1945	74 Sqd	yes
22-06-41	Oblt.	Westphal	8	11	Spitfire	unknown	1610	609 or 611 Sqd	yes
01-06-42	Oblt.	Westphal	7	12	Spitfire	20km N of Dunkirk	1355	71 or 350 Sqd	yes
04-09-43	Fw.	Weyrich	4	1	Spitfire	mid-Channel	1950		unk
30-07-43	Uffz.	Wiegand	8		B-17	W of Eupen	0820	379 BG	no
03-09-43	Uffz.	Wiegand	8	1	Ventura	Gravelines	1430	21 Sqd	yes
05-09-43	Uffz.	Wiegand	8	2	Spitfire	near Dunkirk	0930	129 Sqd	yes
08-09-43	Uffz.	Wiegand	8	3	Mustang	near Dunkirk	1500	414 Sqd	yes
09-09-43	Uffz.	Wiegand	8	4	Spitfire	St. Pol	1600	122 Sqd	yes
19-09-43	Uffz.	Wiegand	8	5	Spitfire V	near Brugge	1300	411 Sqd	yes
03-10-43	Fw.	Wiegand	4		Spitfire	near Dieppe	1830	421 Sqd	no
05-10-43	Fw.	Wiegand	4	6	Typhoon	NW of Courtrai (MF)	1100	3 Sqd	no
10-10-43	Fw.	Wiegand	4	7	B-17	E of Arnhem (HO1)	1510	95 BG	yes
20-10-43	Fw.	Wiegand	4		Spitfire	Dixmuiden	0945	485 Sqd	unk
13-11-43	Fw.	Wiegand	4	8	P-47	SE of Zwolle (GN)	1223	355 FG	yes
20-12-43	Fw.	Wiegand	4	9	Spitfire	SW of Cambrai	1115	421 Sqd	yes
30-12-43	Fw.	Wiegand	4	10	P-47	S of Florennes	1130	353 FG	yes
30-12-43	Fw.	Wiegand	4	11	P-47	near Dunkirk	1500	352 FG	yes
02-01-44	Fw.	Wiegand	4	12	Spitfire	Somme Estuary	1630	349 Sqd	yes
11-01-44	Fw.	Wiegand	4		B-17	Nordhorn-Zuider Zee	1300	306 BG	no
11-01-44	Fw.	Wiegand	4	13	B-17	Nordhorn-Zuider Zee	1300	306 BG	yes
21-01-44	Fw.	Wiegand	4	14	Spitfire	Calais area		616 Sqd	yes
21-01-44	Fw.	Wiegand	4	15	B-26	Calais area		226 Sqd Mitchell	unk
23-01-44	Fw.	Wiegand	4		Boston	Gravelines	1600		no
24-01-44	Fw.	Wiegand	4		P-38	Scheldt Estuary	1200	55 FG	no
29-01-44	Fw.	Wiegand	4		B-17	near Laon			no
04-02-44	Fw.	Wiegand	4		B-17	S of Tournai	1300		no
11-02-44	Fw.	Wiegand	4	16	P-47	S of Arras (QF)	1345	78 FG	yes

11-02-44	Fw.	Wiegand	4	17	P-47	S of Arras (QF)	1346	78 FG	yes
13-02-44	Fw.	Wiegand	4	18	Typhoon	10km NW of Calais	1240	198 Sqd	yes
24-02-44	Fw.	Wiegand	4	19	B-17	W of Koblenz-Bingen	1410		yes
24-02-44	Fw.	Wiegand	4		P-47	Bingen	1430	4 FG	no
04-03-44	Fw.	Wiegand	4	20	P-38	10km S of Courtrai	1525	20 FG	yes
08-03-44	Fw.	Wiegand	4	21	P-47	Hunteburg-Zwolle (FR8)	1325	353 FG	yes
11-06-44	Lt.	Wiegand	4	22	P-38	Compiègne(TF-SF)	1530	55 FG	yes
11-06-44	Lt.	Wiegand	4	23	P-38	Clermont (TF-SF)	1535	55 FG	yes
13-03-43	Lt.	Wiegmann	6	1	Spitfire	5km E ofBerck-sur-Mer	1531	402 or 403 Sqd	yes
18-12-39	Uffz.	Wilke	10N	1	Wellington	25-35km SSW of Helgoland	1435	3 Gp	unk
08-12-41	Fw.	Willius	3	13	Spitfire	10km W of Boulogne	1515		yes
10-04-42	Fw.	Willius	3	14	Spitfire	NE of Calais	1740	313 Sqd	yes
12-04-42	Fw.	Willius	3	15	Spitfire	2-3km S of Bourbourg	1345	41 Sqd	yes
24-04-42	Fw.	Willius	3	16	Spitfire	near Calais	1502	72 or 124 Sqd	yes
27-04-42	Fw.	Willius	3	17	Spitfire	15km NW of Dunkirk	1602	457 or 485 Sqd	unk
17-05-42	Fw.	Willius	3	18	Spitfire	3km S of Calais	1140	64 or 122 Sqd	yes
23-05-42	Fw.	Willius	3	19	Spitfire	10km N of Calais	1200	350 Sqd	yes
08-06-42	Fw.	Willius	3	20	Spitfire	5km SW of Arques	1340		yes
18-08-42	Fw.	Willius	3	21	Spitfire	10km W of Cap Gris Nez		602 Sqd	yes
19-08-42	Fw.	Willius	3	22	Spitfire	4km NE of Dieppe			unk
11-12-42	Fw.	Willius	3	23	Defiant	2-3km E of Dungeness	1215	277 Sqd	no
12-12-42	Fw.	Willius	3	24	Spitfire	15km S of Simmereux	1143	350 Sqd	no
11-04-43	Fw.	Willius	3	25	LaGG-4	USSR (PQ 1835)			yes
13-05-43	Fw.	Willius	3	26	Pe-2	USSR (PQ 35431)			yes
13-05-43	Fw.	Willius	3	27	Pe-2	USSR (PQ 35431)			yes
13-05-43	Fw.	Willius	3	28	Pe-2	USSR (PQ 35462)			yes
13-05-43	Fw.	Willius	3	29	MiG-3	USSR (PQ 4555)			yes
27-05-43	Fw.	Willius	3	30	LaGG-3	USSR (PQ 5362)			yes
28-05-43	Fw.	Willius	3	31	LaGG-3	USSR (PQ 63253)			yes
02-06-43	Fw.	Willius	3	32	LaGG-3	USSR (PQ 62189)			yes
02-06-43	Fw.	Willius	3	33	LaGG-3	USSR (PQ 62194)			yes
30-07-43	Fw.	Willius	2	34	Boston	NW of Antwerp (LI1)	0705	386 BG B-26	yes
18-08-43	Lt.	Willius	2	35	Spitfire	Ipswich (N Sea) (HD8-1)	1907		yes
04-09-43	Lt.	Willius	2		Spitfire	near Dunkirk (ME8-1)	1914	131 Sqd	no
01-12-43	Lt.	Willius	2 CO	36	B-17	Koblenz (PP)	1146		yes
30-12-43	Lt.	Willius	2 CO	37	B-17	Soissons (TG)	1343	100 BG	yes
11-01-44	Lt.	Willius	2 CO	38	B-17	Deventer (GN)	1300	306 BG	yes
30-01-44	Lt.	Willius	2 CO	39	P-38	3km N of Coesfeld	1330	20 FG	yes
04-02-44	Lt.	Willius	2 CO	40	B-17	1km E of Cousolre	1350		yes
06-02-44	Lt.	Willius	2 CO	41	B-17	Melun (BF)	1121	96 BG	yes
24-02-44	Lt.	Willius	2 CO	42	B-24	Giessen (OS)	1355		yes
25-02-44	Lt.	Willius	2 CO	43	B-26	Zeebrugge-N Sea (KF-KG)	1126	387 BG	yes
25-02-44	Lt.	Willius	2 CO	44	B-26	Zeebrugge-N Sea (KG-FK)		387 BG	yes
02-03-44	Lt.	Willius	2 CO	45	B-17	Wiesbaden(QR2-3)	1208		yes
06-03-44	Lt.	Willius	2 CO	46	B-17	N of Koblenz (OP6,2)	1441		yes
15-03-44	Lt.	Willius	2 CO	47	B-24	E of Norwich-N Sea (FE6?)	1226	392 BG	yes
16-03-44	Lt.	Willius	2 CO		B-17	unknown			no
23-03-44	Lt.	Willius	2 CO	48	B-17	Tilburg (KL6)	1140	385 BG	yes
27-03-44	Lt.	Willius	2 CO	49	P-47	SE of Dreux(BD1-4)	1424	359 FG	yes
08-04-44	Lt.	Willius	2 CO	50	B-24	near Zwolle (FN)	1518	44 BG	yes
14-03-43	Lt.	Wilms	1	1	Il-2	USSR (PQ 19849)			yes
14-03-43	Lt.	Wilms	1	2	Il-2	USSR (PQ 19867)			yes
21-02-45	Lt.	Wirth	5	1	B-26	E of Arnhem (near HO-HP)	1603	394 BG	unk
12-08-41	Lt.	Witzel	I St	13	Spitfire	NW of Ijzendijke	1255	19 or 152 Sqd	unk
12-08-41	Lt.	Witzel	I St	14	Spitfire	Groede-30km NW of W'Capelle	1256	19 or 152 Sqd	yes
24-05-44	Uffz.	Wodarczyk	4	1	P-38	Cambrai (QF-QG)	1930		yes
11-06-44	Uffz.	Wodarczyk	4	2	P-38	Compiègne (TF)	1538	55 FG	yes
11-06-44	Uffz.	Wodarczyk	4		P-38-prob	Compiègne(SF-TF)	1548	55 FG	no
24-02-44	Uffz.	Wöge	9		B-17	NE of Lingen (FQ7)	1225	92 or 306 BG	yes
01-06-40	Uffz.	Wolf	3	1	Spitfire	near Dunkirk	0636	19, 222 or 616 Sqd	yes
30-11-43	Stfw.	Wuhl	11		B-17	unknown			yes
24-02-44	Oblt.	Wunschel-meyer	12		B-17	Hasselünne	1225	92 or 306 BG	yes
17-08-43	Fw.	Würtz	12		B-17	Ridder [Ridderkerk NL?]	1545		yes
04-09-43	Gefr.	Wyrich	4	1	Spitfire	mid-Channel	1028	165 Sqd	yes
14-10-43	Gefr.	Wyrich	5	2	P-47	WNW of Weert	1337	353 FG	unk
12-04-44	Uffz.	Wyrich	5		P-47	Liège	1315		no
22-06-44	Uffz.	Zeichert	9		P-51	S of St Lô (AS5)	1419	365 FG P-47	i.O.
24-04-44	Uffz.	Zeller	9		P-51	Mühldorf-E of München (CF8-9)	1400	355 FG	unk
08-06-44	Uffz.	Zeller	III St		P-47	E of Le Havre(SA-SB)	0646	371 FG	unk
14-06-44	Uffz.	Zeller	III St		P-38	NW of Paris(AE1-UE7)	0735	55 FG	yes
23-06-44	Uffz.	Zeller	III St		P-38	E of Chartres(CD-CE)	1338	55 FG	yes
04-07-44	Uffz.	Zeller	III St		P-38	W of Évreux (UB)	1450	370 FG	yes

Date	Rank	Name	Unit	No.	Type	Location	Time	Unit claimed	Conf.
17-09-44	FjFw.	Zeller	III St		P-51	E of Nijmegen (JN)	1455	361 FG	yes
17-08-43	Fw.	Zeschke	6	1	B-17	St. Trond-in Channel	1735		yes
07-06-44	Fw.	Zimmermann	8	1	Mustang	SE of Caen (UU)	0620	129 Sqd	yes
27-04-42	Oblt.	Zink	2 CO	18	Spitfire	near Watten	1220	71 Sqd	yes
30-04-42	Oblt.	Zink	2 CO	19	Spitfire	8km W of Somme Estuary	1940	129 or 340 Sqd	yes
01-06-42	Oblt.	Zink	2 CO	20	Spitfire	6km NE of Dunkirk	1355	65 or 111 Sqd	yes
29-06-42	Oblt.	Zink	2 CO	21	Spitfire	15km NNW of Dunkirk	1648	222 or 332 Sqd	yes
30-07-42	Oblt.	Zink	2 CO	22	Spitfire	15km NW of Boulogne			yes
31-07-42	Oblt.	Zink	2 CO	23	Spitfire	15km W of Authie Estuary		133 Sqd	yes
19-08-42	Oblt.	Zink	2 CO	24	Spitfire	3km NW of Dieppe			yes
19-08-42	Oblt.	Zink	2 CO	25	Spitfire	20km NNE of Dieppe			yes
19-08-42	Oblt.	Zink	2 CO	26	Mustang	15km SW of Dieppe			yes
27-08-42	Oblt.	Zink	2 CO	27	Spitfire	8km NE of Calais		71 Sqd	yes
02-10-42	Oblt.	Zink	2 CO	28	Airacobra	10km NW of Cap Blanc Nez	1540	4 FG	unk
08-11-42	Oblt.	Zink	2 CO	29	Spitfire	10km SE of Dover			yes
12-12-42	Oblt.	Zink	2 CO	30	Spitfire	near Marquise	1135	350 Sqd	yes
20-01-43	Oblt.	Zink	2 CO	31	Spitfire	25km NW of Boulogne	1312	332 Sqd	unk
03-02-43	Oblt.	Zink	2 CO	32	Spitfire	7km SW of Gravelines	1105	308 Sqd	yes
03-02-43	Oblt.	Zink	2 CO	33	Spitfire	N of Cassel	1057	308 Sqd	unk
27-02-43	Oblt.	Zink	2 CO	34	LaGG-3	USSR (PQ 1846)			yes
28-02-43	Oblt.	Zink	2 CO	35	P-39	USSR (PQ 2834)			yes
03-03-43	Hptm.	Zink	2 CO	36	Pe-2	USSR (PQ 1865)			yes
15-12-42	Uffz.	Zirngibl	1	1	Buffalo	2km E of Dover	1557	609 Sqd	yes
14-03-43	Fw.	Zirngibl	3	2	Il-2	USSR (PQ 1988)			yes
15-03-43	Fw.	Zirngibl	3	3	LaGG-3	USSR (PQ 18274)			yes
31-05-43	Fw.	Zirngibl	3	4	SP-2?	USSR (PQ 26854)			yes
26-11-43	Fw.	Zirngibl	8	5	B-17?	near Paris	1040	94 BG	unk
28-01-44	Fw.	Zirngibl	8	6	Mustang	S of Abbeville	1348	2 Sqd	yes
29-01-44	Fw.	Zirngibl	8	7	B-17-HSS	Pferdsfeld-Entempfuhl?	1130		yes
25-02-44	Fw.	Zirngibl	8	8	B-17	Saarbrücken	1225	96 BG	yes
17-06-44	Obfw.	Zirngibl	8	9	P-47	St. Lô-Periers	1337		yes
14-06-44	Gefr.	Zubiako	3	1	P-51	E of Paris (AF)	0807	357 FG	yes
14-08-41		4. Staffel	4	1	Spitfire	Ardres	1550	41 or 616 Sqd	yes
20-12-42		4. Staffel	4	2	B-17	20km W of Dieppe	1350	303 BG	yes
10-05-40		5. Staffel	5	1	Fokker D21	Amsterdam	0620	1-2 JaVA	yes
11-05-40		6. Staffel	6	1	Curtiss H75	Antwerp	1910	GC I/4	yes
17-09-41		6. Staffel	6	2	Spitfire	Boulogne-Dungeness	1905		yes
13-07-42		6. Staffel	6	3	Spitfire	S of Berck-sur-Mer	1455	602 Sqd	yes
07-03-41		7. Staffel	7	1	Sunderland	near Malta		228 Sqd	no
27-04-41		7. Staffel	7	2	Sunderland-water	Kalafrana Bay, Malta		228 Sqd	no
10-05-41		7. Staffel	7	3	Sunderland-water	Kalafrana Bay, Malta		10 Sqd RAAF	no
22-08-42		I. Flak Unit	I	1	Spitfire	E of Arques			flak
29-07-40		II. Flak Unit	II	1	Battle	Marquise	0410		flak
06-11-41		II. Flak Unit	II	2	Spitfire	Coxyde		607 Sqd	flak
13-07-42		II. Stab	II St	3	Spitfire	S of Berck-sur-Mer	1455	602 Sqd	yes
16-02-43		II. Stab	II St	4	Spitfire	8km NW of Abbeville	1735	402 Sqd	yes
10-05-40		III. Gr + 8. St	III		unknown	unknown	0600		yes
10-05-40		III. Gr + 8. St	III		unknown	unknown	0600		yes
10-05-40		III. Gr + 8. St	III		unknown	unknown	0600		yes
10-05-40		III. Gruppe	III		unknown	unknown	0600		yes
18-06-41		III. Gruppe	III		Spitfire	NW of Cap Gris Nez	1835	609 Sqd	unk
12-08-41		III. Stab	III St	1	Spitfire	unknown	2003	485 Sqd	yes

APPENDIX V

JG 26 CASUALTIES: 1939-1945

This list includes all pilot casualties (killed, missing, taken prisoner, wounded) presently known. Aircraft losses in which the pilot escaped injury are listed in only a few special cases. Abbreviations used in the "Cas" column are: KIA = killed in action; KIFA = killed in a flying accident; KAC = killed in a non-flying accident; WIA = wounded in action; WIFA = wounded in a flying accident; WAC = wounded in a non-flying accident; POW = prisoner of war; MIA = missing in action. The date is written in European style: i.e., day first, month second, year third. The time is 24-hour military time.

Date	Rank	Name	Cas	Unit	Aircraft	WNr	Mkgs	Place	Time	Cause	Allied Unit
18-10-42	Ogfr.	Abel, Hans	KIA	7	Fw 190A-4	7052	wh 8	Dover-Ramsgate	1820	ship flak	n/a
17-06-41	Fw.	Adam, Bernhard	KIA	2	Bf 109E-7			Channel-Boulogne		Hurricane	
20-12-42	Lt.	Adam Heinz-Günther	KIA	1	Fw 190A-4	730	wh 5	Abbeville a/f		landing	n/a
18-09-41	Hptm.	Adolph, Walter	KIA	II CO	Fw 190A-1	28	<<+	30km NW of Ostend	1120	Spitfire	41 Sqd
10-04-44	Uffz.	Afflerbach, Franz	KIA	3	none			Florennes a/f		bomb	n/a
02-10-44	Uffz.	Ahrens, Erich	WIFA	7	Fw 190A-8	731751	br 12	S of Borken		engine	n/a
01-01-45	Fw.	Ahrens, Erich	POW	7	Fw 190D-9	210186	br 6	Beveland-SW of Goes	0945	ship flak	n/a
11-11-43	Fw.	Ahrens, Peter	WIA	3	Fw 190A-6	550176	yl 8	5km SW of St Pol		Spitfire	122 Sqd
18-01-45	Lt.	Ahrens, Peter	WIFA	3	Fw 190D-9	210939	yl 7	near Meppen		engine	n/a
04-03-45	Lt.	Ahrens, Peter	KIFA	3	Fw 190D-9/R11	211011	yl 11	NW of Fürstenau a/f	1300	engine	non-op
14-01-44	Hptm.	Aistleitner, Johann	KIA	5 CO	Fw 190A-6	530734	wh 9	Ercheu			4 FG
19-08-43	Lt.	Altmann, Leberecht	WIA	1	Fw 190A-5	1091	wh 4	Epen-W of Breda	1930	P-47	56 FG
10-12-44	Gefr.	Anselment, Reinhard	KIA	4	Fw 190A-9	205280	bl 8	Neurath-Grevenbroich	1545	P-47	373 FG
22-10-40	Fw.	Arp, Heinrich	KIA	2	Bf 109E-4	1124	bk 10	S of Littlestone Channel-	1730	Hurricane	257 Sqd
12-04-45	Lt.	Asmus, Erich	KIA	I St	Fw 190D-9	210069		15km NNW of Uelsen	1300	Tempest	33 Sqd
24-06-44	Uffz.	Ayerle, Hermann	WIA	12	Bf 109G-6	165177	bl 5	St. Andre	0730	Mustang	19 or 65 Sqd
17-07-44	Uffz.	Ayerle, Hermann	WIA	12	Bf 109G-6	413559	bl 21	Toussous le Noble	1625	Spitfire	411 or 602 Sqd
25-09-44	Uffz.	Ayerle, Hermann	WIA	12	Bf 109G-6	165170	bl 9	N of Deelen a/f	1745	Spitfire	
08-04-44	Fhj-Ofw.	Babenz, Emil	KIA	2	Fw 190A-6	470046	bk 1	near Bentheim	1545	P-47	361 FG
14-05-43	Uffz.	Backeberg, Heinz	KIA	5	Fw 190A-4	677	bk 30	E of Ghent-Scheldt Est	1315	B-17	
09-04-43	Lt.	Backhaus, Otto-August	KIA	10J	Fw 190A-5	7290	bk 12 +bomb	NW of Cap Gris Nez		Spitfire	611 Sqd
27-09-43	Uffz.	Bäder, Alfred	KIA	9	Bf 109G-6	140019	yl 12	Beauvais	1155	Spitfire	
27-09-44	Uffz.	Baier, Valentin	KIA	8	Fw 190A-8	173014	bl 3	near Arnhem	1100	Spitfire	412 Sqd
14-09-43	Uffz.	Bannischka, Helmut	KIA	7	Bf 109G-6	18867	wh 6	Wijnnendale	1835	Spitfire	N Weald Wing
07-03-45	Lt.	Bartels,Heinz-Wilhelm	KIA	11	Fw 190D-9	210127	yl 18	near Gildehaus	1531	Tempest	122 Wing
24-07-40	Oblt.	Bartels, Werner	POW	III St	Bf 109E-1	6296	<l+l	Margate	1400	Spitfire	54 or 65 Sqd
23-07-41	Uffz.	Barthel, Alfred	WIA	5	Bf 109E-7	4954		Maningham		Spitfire	
11-08-42	Fw.	Barthel, Alfred	WIFA	5	Fw 190A-2	5412		Epinoy a/f		takeoff	n/a
20-01-43	Fw.	Barthel, Alfred	KIA	5	Fw 190A-4	2460	bk 5	Channel	1245	Spitfire	340 Sqd
16-03-44	Uffz.	Baumann, Josef	KIA	8	Fw 190A-6	550183	bl 7	near Epinoy a/f	0931	P-47	56 FG
20-06-43	Fw.	Bäumener, Helmut	WIA	3	Fw 190A			near Vendeville		Spitfire	421 Sqd
08-09-43	Fw.	Bäumener, Helmut	WIA	3	Fw 190A-5	2688		W of Cambrai - f/l Vendeville		Spitfire	
04-10-42	Uffz.	Baumgartner,Karl	WIFA	10J	Fw 190A–3/U3	248		S of Campaigne		engine	n/a
13-04-44	Uffz.	Beck, Kurt	WIA	11	Bf 109G-6	162343	yl 15	NW-Würtemberg Ettingen	1330	P-47	56 FG
25-05-44	Uffz.	Beck, Kurt	KIA	11	Bf 109G-6	162681	yl 4	NE of Chaumont	0915	P-47	356 FG
27-09-44	Fw.	Becker, Alois	KIA	1	Fw 190A-8	175127	wh 13	W of Spijk-Emmerich		Spitfire	411 Sqd
17-08-43	Uffz.	Becker,Hans-Georg	WIA	1	Fw 190A-4	620	bk 11	Liège-b/l Venlo		B-17	
07-06-44	Uffz.	Becker, Hans-Georg	KIA	1	Fw 190A-8	730456	wh 5	40km SW of Rouen		combat	
21-03-45	Uffz.	Beckert, Otto	KIA	7	Fw 190D-9			10km N of Rheine		combat	

Date	Rank	Name	Fate		Aircraft	WNr	Code	Location	Time	Cause	Unit
16-03-44	Lt.	Beer, Heinrich	KIA	3	Fw 190A-6	470247	br 5	SW of St. Dizier	1100	P-47	56 FG
01-06-40	Uffz.	Beese, Artur	POW	9	Bf 109E-3			Lille		Morane 406	
24-08-40	Fw.	Beese, Artur	no	9	Bf 109E-4		yl 11	St. Inglevert		fighter	
08-09-43	Oblt.	Beese, Artur	WIA	1 CO	Fw 190A-5	550474	wh 2	W of Cambrai		Spitfire	
06-02-44	Oblt.	Beese, Artur	KIA	1 CO	Fw 190A-6	531060	wh 7	SW of Melun	1130	P-47	
24-03-42	Oblt.	Behrens, Otto	WIA	6 CO	Fw 190A-1	10	br 5	near Le Tréport		Spitfire	129 Sqd
20-12-41	Gefr.	Beilstein, Hans	KIFA	1/E	Bf 109E-7	6355		Dongen NW of Tilburg	0950	crashed	non-op
22-04-45	Uffz.	Bellmann, Rudolf	KIA	6	Fw 190D-9			Buchholz		flak	n/a
02-05-44	Fhj-Uffz.	Benk, Konrad	KIFA	11	Bf 109G-6	163141	yl 16	Rouvres Chaumont a/f-	1430	engine	n/a
24-12-44	Lt.	Benz, Siegfried	KIA	6	Fw 190D-9	210188	bk 5	near Düren		Bf 109	III/JG 1
02-03-44	Uffz.	Berg, Heinrich	KIA	6	Fw 190A-6	530718	bk 4	NE of Cochem	1150	P-47	365 FG
19-08-42	Uffz.	Berg, Heinrich von	KIA	10J	Fw 190A-3/U3	2240		4km N of Hesdin		Spitfire	
06-09-43	Uffz.	Berger, Walter	KIA	6	Fw 190A-5	7306	br 8	12km NE of Poix		Spitfire	
26-12-44	Flg.	Bergmeier, Hans	KIA	4	Fw 190D-9	210264	bl 12	near Malmedy	1100	P-51	361 FG
01-01-45	Uffz.	Berndt, Karl-Heinz	POW	12	Bf 109K-4	330426	bl 30	St Martensdijk	0915	flak	n/a
04-01-45	Ofhr.	Bernhardt, Horst	WIA	4	Fw 190D-9	210964	bl 15	near Osnabrück	1600	Spitfire	411 Sqd
19-11-44	Oblt.	Bertels, Konrad	KIFA	I St	Fw 190A-8		gr 1	Rheine-Bentheim	0945	engine	n/a
08-04-45	Ogfr.	Bexen, Harro	KIA	5	Fw 190D-9			20km ENE Hannover		P-47	373 FG
28-08-40	Oblt.	Beyer, Georg	POW	Ge St	Bf 109E-4	2743		S of Canterbury	1100	fighter	501 Sqd
14-05-43	Obfw.	Beyer, Siegfried	WIA	6	Fw 190A-4	7038	br 17	Wevelgem a/f	1230	P-47	4 or 78 FG
03-07-41	Hptm.	Bieber, Rudolf	KIA	I St	Bf 109F-2	7686		St. Omer		Spitfire	609 Sqd
17-09-41	Oblt.	Biedermann, Erwin	KIA	9	Fw 190F-4	7217	yl 2	NW of Calais	1910	Spitfire	
28-05-40	Fw.	Biegert, Ernst	KIA	2	Bf 109E-1			St Pol-NW of Calais		Spitfire	
06-09-40	Gefr.	Bieker, Karl	KIA	7	Bf 109E-1	3578		Channel-S of London	1020	Spitfire	234 Sqd
30-01-44	Uffz.	Bierkamp, Karl	KIA	8	Fw 190A-6	470045	bl 2	Zuider Zee	1300	P-47	
27-08-42	Obfw.	Bierwirth, Heinrich	WIA	5	Fw 190A-3	353	bk 11	Somme Estuary		Spitfire	350 Sqd
27-11-42	Obfw.	Bierwirth, Heinrich	KIA	5	Fw 190A-4	2400	bk 5	Rye-Folkestone	1640	RR explosion	n/a
14-01-45	Uffz.	Binge, Werner	KIA	6	Fw 190D-9	600148	bk 11	SE of Bonn	1215	P-51	78 FG
31-07-42	Uffz.	Birke, Gerhard	WIA	4	Fw 190A-2	5411	wh 5	20km SW of Berck		Spitfire	
17-05-43	Uffz.	Birke, Gerhard	KIFA	4	Fw 190A-5	2636	wh 3	Vitry a/f	2030	ground collision	non-op
04-04-43	Ogfr.	Birn, Jürgen	KIA	4/54	Bf 109G-4	19369	wh 16	St Denis-Rouen	1440	B-17	
23-12-44	Uffz.	Bischoff, Hermann	KIA	2	Fw 190A-8	171523	bk 16	Nettersheim St. Vith-	1145	P-47	56 FG
08-12-41	Uffz.	Bleefe, Joachim	WIFA	I St	Bf 109F-4	8348		Arques		hit ground	n/a
06-06-44	Lt.	Bleich, Hans	WIFA	6	Fw 190A-8	170119	bk 5	Biarritz a/f		takeoff	n/a
01-03-45	Lt.	Bleich, Hans	KIA	1	Fw 190D-9	600353	wh 7	Düsseldorf	0915	P-47	406 FG
26-03-45	Lt.	Blickle, Wilhelm	WIA	3	Fw 190D-9			Münster-Handorf	1530	Tempest	33 Sqd
19-06-40	Lt.	Blohm, Peter	KIA	6	Bf 109E-3			SW of Chateauroux		flak	n/a
24-06-43	Lt.	Blömertz, Günther	WIA	4	Fw 190A-4	5640	wh 8	Ichtegem NE Torhout	1000	P-47	78 FG
01-10-40	Uffz.	Bluder, Hans	KIA	4	Bf 109E-1	1180		Balmer Down-Brighton	1530	Hurricane	303 Sqd
18-08-40	Lt.	Blume, Walter	POW	7	Bf 109E-4		wh 13	Barnham, nr Canterbury	1830	Hurricane	32 Sqd
13-06-43	Obfw.	Böcher,Karl-Heinz	WIA	10/54	Fw 190A-4	2415	wh 15	near Furnes	0930	P-47	56 FG
01-07-43	Uffz.	Bock, Arnulf	KIA	5	Fw 190A-5	7299	br 2	Hazebrouck		Spitfire	331 Sqd
17-09-40	Uffz.	Bock, Heinz	POW	7	Bf 109E-1	6294	wh 2	Camber, nr Rye	1730	engine	n/a
25-03-45	Uffz.	Bock, Otto	WIFA	11	Fw 190D-9			Delmenhorst a/f		landing	non-op
20-11-43	Uffz.	Boeckl, Albert	WIA	12	Bf 109G			Köln		no fuel	n/a
25-05-44	Uffz.	Boeckl, Albert	WIA	12	Bf 109G-6/U4	440989	bl 18	Roncourt	0850	P-47	356 FG
07-02-45	Ogfr.	Boeke, Günther	KIFA	7	Fw 190D-9	210105	br 1	Düsseldorf a/f		takeoff	non-op
12-03-43	Fw.	Boesch, Emil	KIA	10J	Fw 190A-5	829	bk 12+ bomb	10km N of Dunkirk	0829	Typhoon	609 Sqd
25-04-42	Fw.	Bohn, Kurt	KIA	3	Fw 190A-2	5231	yl 5	N of Dunkirk		Spitfire	
14-01-45	Uffz.	Böhter,Hans-Georg	KIA	6	Fw 190D-9	400242	bk 1	St Vith-Bastogne	1130	P-51	78 FG
23-08-43	Obfw.	Borounick, Erich	KIA	10	Fw 190A-5	7223	bl 12	6km E of Févent-Artois		Spitfire	Kenley Wing
06-11-44	Uffz.	Borreck,Hans-Joachim	KIA	5	Fw 190A-9	750132	wh 8	near Wahlheim Aachen-	1213	flak	n/a
13-05-40	Lt.	Borris, Karl	WIA	5	Bf 109E-3			near Dordrecht	0700	Defiant	264 Sqd
14-05-43	Hptm.	Borris, Karl	WIA	8 CO	Fw 190A-5	7326	bk 19	Izegem, NE Wevelgem	1235	B-17	
25-02-45	Lt.	Bott, Josef	WIA	5	Fw 190D-9	600351	wh 17	Clausheide Rheine-		Spitfire XIV	41 Sqd
26-03-40	Uffz.	Boy, Bruno	KIFA	8	Bf 109E			Essen-Mülheim		collision	n/a
17-04-44	Oblt.	Bracher, Fritz	KIA	10	Bf 109G-6	165157	bk 18	Dreux	1925	P-51	354 FG
07-09-40	Uffz.	Braun, Ernst	POW	6	Bf 109E-4	735		off Dover	1900	fighter	
19-08-41	Gefr.	Braun, Reinhardt	KIA	5	Bf 109E-7	3729		Poperinghe-Steenvoorde	1400	Spitfire	
05-11-40	Fw.	Braun, Walter	POW	9	Bf 109E-1/B	3259	yl 11	N Dungeness-Wittersham	1500	collision	n/a
26-06-40	Gefr.	Braune, Heinz	KIFA	2	Bf 109E-1			Lyon		engine	n/a
01-01-45	Ogfr.	Braunert, Karl-Heinz	KIA	4	Fw 190D-9/R11	210955	bl 10	W of Vremde Antwerp-		missing	n/a
18-08-44	Lt.	Brede, Hans-Joachim	KIA	7	Fw 190A-8	172993	br 10	Beauvais-Tillé		Mustang	315 Sqd
15-01-43	Uffz.	Bremer, Herbert	KIA	3	Fw 190A-4	2382	yl 5	off Rye	1710	flak	n/a
22-12-43	Uffz.	Broda, Günter	KIA	9	Bf 109G-6	19661	wh 9	W of Hardenberg (NL)	1400	P-47	4 FG
01-09-44	Gefr.	Bruckauf, Gerhard	KIFA	12	Bf 109G-6	165806	bl 6	near Siegen	1530	crashed	non-op
19-05-40	Lt.	Brucks, Helmut	POW	9	Bf 109E-3			NE of Courtrai		Hurricane	
31-05-40	Uffz.	Brügelmann, Helmut	WIA	8	Bf 109E-1			Dunkirk		Hurricane	213 or 264 Sqd
15-01-41	Fw.	Brügelmann, Helmut	KIFA	8	Bf 109E-4	3728		E of St Valery	1130	crashed	n/a
14-07-44	Uffz.	Brühan, Emil	WIA	1	Fw 190A-7	431175	wh 12	60km W of Paris	1440	P-47	358 FG
27-11-44	Uffz.	Brühan, Emil	WIA	1	Fw 190A-8	171516	wh 3	Salzbergen-Rheine		P-51	

Date	Rank	Name	Fate		Aircraft	WNr	Code	Location	Time	Cause	Unit
25-02-45	Uffz.	Brühan, Emil	KIA	1	Fw 190D-9	400241	wh 13	15km N of Münster	0745	combat	
15-02-43	Uffz.	Bruhn, Karl	KIA	7	Fw 190A-4	5728	wh 6	15km NW of Dunkirk	1546	Spitfire	331 or 332 Sqd
21-02-45	Uffz.	Brumund, Johannes	KIFA	6	Fw 190D-9	210139	bk 12	SE of Meppen		own flak	
03-02-45	Uffz.	Brünn, Heinz	WIFA	10	Fw 190D-9	500386	bk 4	Plantlünne a/f	0930	takeoff taxi	non-op
05-11-43	Ofhr.	Bruns, Holger	WIFA	5	Fw 190A-6	530922	wh 14	Deinze-15km SW of Ghent	1445	engine	n/a
19-01-44	Lt.	Bruns, Holger	KIFA	5	Fw 190A-6	470082	wh 3	Givet-Meuse		engine fire	non-op
20-01-43	Uffz.	Budde, Heinz	POW	6	Bf 109G-4	16102	br 7	E of Dover	1300	Typhoon	609 Sqd
12-10-44	Ofhr.	Bühring, Hans-Theobald	KIA	12	Bf 109G-14	461538	bl 8	Bremervörde	1215	P-51	357 FG
03-09-44	Uffz.	Büker, Herbert	KIA	2	Fw 190A-8	171743	bk 4	E of Brussels	1300	P-51	55 FG
18-12-44	Uffz.	Burckhardt, Gottfried	WIFA	8	Fw 190D-9	400209	bl 13	Plantlünne a/f	1535	landing	n/a
14-01-45	Uffz.	Burckhardt, Gottfried	KIA	8	Fw 190D-9	500123	bl 5	Köln-Wahn a/f	1215	P-51	78 FG
20-10-43	Uffz.	Bürger, Walter	KIA	5	Fw 190A-6	530732	wh 10	Krinkelt near Elsenborn		P-47	78 FG
26-04-44	Ofhr.	Burglechner, Josef	KAC	1	none			Cazaux		drowned	non-op
31-03-45	Oblt.	Burkardt, Friedrich	KIA	5	Fw 190D-9			5km E of Bissel	0600	Spitfire	402 Sqd
21-01-44	Oblt.	Burkert, Erich	KIA	9	Bf 109G-6	410675	bl 6	Chivres-en-Laonnais	1445	P-47	353 FG
08-06-40	Fw.	Burkhardt, Alfred	POW	3	Bf 109E-3			SW of Beauvais		Morane	GC I/2 406
13-08-44	Uffz.	Burmeister, Erich	MIA	4	Fw 190A-8	680844	bl 10	NE of Le Mans	0825	P-51	363 FG
27-09-44	Uffz.	Burmeister, Erich	WIA	4	Fw 190A-8	680571	bl 3	N of Kleve		Spitfire	411 Sqd
04-10-44	Uffz.	Burmeister, Erich	WIA	4	Fw 190A-8	680571	bl 3	S of Emmerich		P-47	48 FG
28-09-39	Lt.	Bürschgens, Josef	WIA	2	Bf 109E		rd 5	SW of Perl	1730	Curtiss H75	GC II/5
11-08-40	Lt.	Bürschgens, Josef	no	7	Bf 109E-1	4095	wh 7	Calais-Caffiers	1130	Spitfire	74 Sqd
01-09-40	Lt.	Bürschgens, Josef	POW	7	Bf 109E-1	3892	wh 11	Wittersham-Rye	1503	Bf 110	
23-09-44	Fhr.	Busch, Maximilian	KIA	6	Fw 190A-8	171576	bk 12	30km NNW of Wesel-Apeldoorn	1700	P-51	352 FG
11-05-44	Fhr.	Busch, Waldemar	WIA	8	Fw 190A-7	340261	bl 1	15km N of Orleans	1345	rammed B-24	487 BG
04-07-44	Lt.	Busch, Waldemar	KIA	8	Fw 190A-8	171100	bl 1	Caen-Bayeux	1500	Spitfire	340 Sqd
05-12-44	Obfw.	Buschegger, Friedrich	KIA	2	Fw 190A-8	732019	bk 11	Maiburg-NW of Fürstenau	1030	P-51	4 FG
12-08-40	Oblt.	Butterweck, Friedrich	KIA	1	Bf 109E-1			Elham-SE of Ashford	0930	Spitfire	610 Sqd
05-02-43	Uffz.	Büttner, Herbert	KIA	10J	Fw 190A-4	2435	bk 1+ bomb	SE of Hastings		Typhoon	609 Sqd
20-12-43	Uffz.	Butzmann, Hermann	KIA	5	Fw 190A-6	470032	wh 8	N of Boursies	1115	Spitfire	331 or 332 Sqd
30-11-42	Lt.	Cadenbach, Wilhelm	KIA	4	Fw 190A-4	5648	wh 1	SW of Portland		ship flak	n/a
30-09-40	Fw.	Carl, Konrad	WIA	9	Bf 109E-4	3891		S of London	1830	Spitfire	
21-06-41	Uffz.	Carmeinke, Heinz	KIA	8	Bf 109F-2	6733	bk 7	W of Le Touquet	1640	Hurricane	
07-10-44	Fw.	Chemnitzer, Max	WIFA	7	Fw 190A-8	173824	wh 10	Kirchhellen a/f		landing	n/a
01-03-45	Fw.	Chemnitzer, Max	KIA	7	Fw 190D-9			Düsseldorf	0930	P-47	366 FG
06-09-40	Oblt.	Christinnecke, Hans	POW	7	Bf 109E-4	2781		Hothfield-Ashford	1020	Spitfire	234 Sqd
30-07-43	Fw.	Christof, Ernst	KIA	1	Fw 190A-4	5616	wh 9	W Burgh-Haamstede	0835	P-47	4 FG
30-11-43	Obfw.	Claar, Karl-Heinz	KIA	12	Bf 109G-6/U4	440019	bl 6	NE of Radevornwald	1100	combat	
02-09-41	Uffz.	Contzen, Herbert	no	E	Bf 109E-7	3633		Scheldt near Oostkapelle		engine	non-op
27-04-42	Uffz.	Contzen, Herbert	KIFA	9	Fw 190A-1	86	yl 10	3km W of Bergues		crashed	n/a
23-01-45	Lt.	Cordt, Hans-Helmuth	KIA	4	Fw 190D-9	400605	bl 16	near Leeden Tecklenburg-	0930	Spitfire XIV	41 Sqd
19-09-42	Fw.	Corinth, Gerhard	KIFA	9	Fw 190A-4	5620		NW of Moorsele a/f		crashed	n/a
27-09-44	Uffz.	Corinth, Gerhard	KIA	4	Fw 190A-8	175106	bl 2	Rheden-W of Arnhem		Spitfire	411 Sqd
15-04-42	Oblt.	Crull, Karl-August	KIA	2	Fw 190A-2	2063		Moringhem-St. Omer		Spitfire	121 Sqd
22-06-43	Fw.	Crump, Peter	WIA	5	Fw 190A-4	793	bk 6	Scheldt Estuary	0930	P-47	
22-02-44	Fw.	Crump, Peter	WIA	6	Fw 190A-7	340253	bk 14	Hückelhoven	1500	P-47	78 FG
04-04-42	Uffz.	Cubillus, Erich	WIFA	1	Fw 190A-1	100		St Omer		engine	n/a
13-04-42	Uffz.	Cubillus, Erich	KIA	1	Fw 190A-2	5229		near Marquise		Spitfire	602 Sqd
19-08-42	Obfw.	Czwilinski, Paul	KIA	2	Fw 190A-4	5396	bk 10	Dieppe harbor	1120	Spitfire	
22-06-44	Uffz.	Dachmann, Willi	WIA	12	Bf 109G-6	163741	bl 20	Cherbourg	1400	P-47	365 or 368 FG
28-02-45	Uffz.	Dachmann, Willi	KIFA	11	Fw 190D-9	500568	yl 7	Plantlünne a/f	0812	collision	n/a
14-09-40	Oblt.	Dähne, Kurt	KIA	1 St	Bf 109E-1	5813	<+	Teynham, Kent	1705	Hurricane	253 Sqd
03-04-43	Uffz.	Damm, Heinrich	KIA	4	Fw 190A-4	732	wh 11	St. Omer-Le Touquet	1630	Spitfire	403 or 416 Sqd
31-05-43	Fw.	Danneberg, Hans	KIA	4	Fw 190A-5	7305	wh 10	sea 10km N of Ostend	1640	Spitfire	403 Sqd
23-09-44	Uffz.	Dantschke, Albrecht	KIA	1	Fw 190A-8	731762	wh 7	Rayen-Neuenkirchen	1545	P-51	339 FG
18-09-43	Fw.	David, Rudolf	WIA	12	Bf 109G-4	19374	bl 4	SE of Pont Audemer	1900	Typhoon	
13-04-44	Uffz.	Dehsbesell, Kurt	KIA	6	Fw 190A-6	470236	br 7	Wael-Steffeln	1320	P-47	78 FG
27-12-44	Uffz.	Delor, Rudolf	WIFA	4	Fw 190D-9	600364	bl 16	Hopsten a/f		landing	non-op
01-03-45	Uffz.	Delor, Rudolf	KIA	3	Fw 190D-9/R11	211009	yl 16	Düsseldorf	0915	P-47	406 FG
07-08-44	Ogfr.	Deshombes, Günter	KIA	11	Bf 109G-6	165179	yl 9	E of Avranches	1520	P-47	368 FG
02-06-41	Oblt.	Dethloff, Hans-Heinz	KIFA	2/E	Bf 109E-4	932		SW of Cognac a/f	1100	landing	non-op
07-07-41	Fw.	Deuse, Erwin	KIFA	4	Bf 109E-7	6480		Loppern, S of Bruges	0925	engine	n/a
10-06-44	Ofhr.	Dewald, Gerhard	WIA	9	Bf 109G-6	412297	wh 22	Orne Estuary	1815	P-47	365 FG
17-07-44	Ofhr.	Dewald, Gerhard	KIA	9	Bf 109G-6	441633	wh 20	Évreux	1945	P-51	354 FG
04-10-44	Uffz.	Dieterlen, Georg	KIFA	4	Fw 190A-8	173814	bl 8	Krefeld		landing	non-op
16-06-41	Gefr.	Dietz, Karl	KIA	1	Bf 109E-7	3817		Marquise-Samer		Spitfire	
07-09-41	Uffz.	Dietze, Gottfried	no	2	Bf 109F-4	7190	bk 7	near Lumbres	1745	crashed	non-op
27-09-41	Uffz.	Dietze, Gottfried	WIA	2	Bf 109F-4	8365	bk 5	Clairmarais	1540	combat	
31-05-42	Fw.	Dietze, Gottfried	WIFA	1	Fw 190A-2	5295		Arques a/f	1957	cockpit fire	n/a

Date	Rank	Name	Status		Aircraft	WNr	Markings	Location	Time	Cause	Unit
04-02-44	Lt.	Dietze, Gottfried	WIA	1	Fw 190A-6	550517	wh 4	E of Hasselt	1330	P-47	352 FG
02-01-41	Fw.	Dietze, Rudolf	KIFA	1/E	Bf 109E-1	3613		Cognac		crashed	non-op
08-03-45	Ogfr.	Dingler, Günther	WIFA	3	Fw 190D-9	601036	yl 9	Fürstenau a/f		landing	non-op
04-04-45	Ogfr.	Dingler, Günther	KIA	3	Fw 190D-9			Lingen-Nordhorn	1700	combat	
17-08-43	Oblt.	Dippel, Hans-Georg	no	9	Bf 109G-6	18833		WSW of Koblenz	1200	B-17	96 BG
08-05-44	Hptm.	Dippel, Hans-Georg	KIFA	9 CO	Bf 109G-6/U4	440714	wh 17	Doncourt	1400	crashed	non-op
21-09-43	Fw.	Dirksen, Hans	KIA	8	Fw 190A-5	1345	bk 11	8km NW of Albert		Spitfire	331 Sqd
29-06-44	Uffz.	Dobryn, Fritz	KIA	4	Fw 190A-8	170672	bl 9	near Caen		Spitfire	
03-09-44	Uffz.	Dombrowa, Leo	WIA	2	Fw 190A-8	680846	bk 1	E of Brussels	1300	P-51	55 FG
01-03-45	Uffz.	Dombrowa, Leo	KIA	2	Fw 190D-9	210273	bk 6	Düsseldorf	0915	P-47	406 FG
17-09-41	Oblt.	Dominikus, Karl	WIA	I St	Bf 109F-4	7225		Bois de Boulogne		Spitfire	
08-06-40	Lt.	Dörr, Hermann	KIA	7	Bf 109E-3			Neufchatel	0930	Morane 406	
08-09-43	Fw.	Dörre, Edgar	KIA	9	Bf 109G-6	18829	yl 5	Lens	1600	Spitfire	
24-04-45	Oblt.	Dortenmann, Hans	no	3 CO	Fw 190D-9	210003	yl 1	Lüdinghausen		flak	non-op
13-02-42	Uffz.	Dovnar, Alfred	KIFA	8	Fw 190A-1	57		Calais-Pihen	1430	takeoff	n/a
21-09-43	Lt.	Draheim, Manfred	KIA	1	Fw 190A-5	7315	bk 8	8km NW of Albert		Spitfire	331 Sqd
16-02-44	Uffz.	Düsing, Wilhelm	WIFA	3	Go 145A-1	2337	GA+OF	near Florennes		crashed	non-op
14-02-45	Uffz.	Düsing, Wilhelm	WIA	2	Fw 190D-9	400238	bk 12	near Rheine a/f	0815	Spitfire XIV	41 Sqd
19-03-45	Uffz.	Düsing, Wilhelm	WIA	2	Fw 190D-9	210930	bk 15	near Münster-Ostbevern	1620	P-51	479 FG
24-02-44	Fhj.-Fw.-	Dylewski, Kurt-Heinz	KIA	12	Bf 109G-6	161696	bl 8	Handrup-Stappenberg		P-47	78 FG
21-09-41	Lt.	Dzialas, Ulrich	KIA	8	Bf 109F-4	7161		S of Boulogne	1615	Spitfire	71,111, 222 Sqd
19-05-40	Hptm.	Ebbighausen, Karl	WIA	4 CO	Bf 109E-3			E of Lille	2005	Hurricane	253 Sqd
16-08-40	Hptm.	Ebbighausen, Karl	KIA	II CO	Bf 109E-4			10km SE of Dover	1400	Spitfire	266 Sqd
31-08-40	Oblt.	Ebeling, Heinz	no	9 CO	Bf 109E-4	3712	yl 3	Channel		fighter	56 Sqd
05-11-40	Oblt.	Ebeling, Heinz	POW	9 CO	Bf 109E-4/B	3740	yl 3	Smittings near Wittersham	1500	collision	n/a
07-10-42	Oblt.	Ebersberger, Kurt	WIFA	4 CO	Fw 190A-4	5646		Ligescourt		engine	n/a
24-10-43	Hptm.	Ebersberger, Kurt	KIA	4 CO	Fw 190A-6	550440	bl 1	3km S of Hesdin		Spitfire	400 Sqd
03-04-43	Uffz.	Ebert, Fritz	KIA	10J	Fw 190A-5	835		Eastbourne		Spitfire	Northolt Wing
						+bomb					
25-07-40	Fw.	Eberz, Bernhard	KIA	9	Bf 109E-1			S of Dover	1730	Hurricane	
20-10-43	Fw.	Eckhardt, Konrad	KIA	9	Bf 109G-6	20480	wh 4	Leuze near Ath	1410	P-47	78 FG
24-04-45	Uffz.	Eckhoff, Horst	WIA	5	Fw 190D-9		wh 12	Uetersen a/f		Tempest	
22-06-43	Obfw.	Edmann, Johann	WIA	8	Fw 190A-5	7313	bk 16	2km S of Woensdrecht	0930	B-17	
21-03-44	Obfw.	Edmann, Johann	KIA	4	Fw 190A-6			unknown		P-51	
23-02-45	Uffz.	Effelsberg, Andreas	KIFA	9	Fw 190D-9	500402	wh 5	Twente a/f	1322	landing	non-op
29-04-42	Lt.	Ehlen, Karl-Heinz	KIFA	7	Fw 190A-2	5215	wh 10	SW of Merckeghem	1600	collision	n/a
03-05-43	Fw.	Ehret, Karl	WIA	6	Fw 190A-4	717	br 9	Rue, S of Berck		Spitfire	416 Sqd
14-02-44	Obfw.	Ehret, Karl	KIA	6	Fw 190A-6	550739	br 10	Montreuil-Calais		Spitfire	124 Sqd
03-09-42	Obfw.	Eichinger, Leopold	WIFA	3	Fw 190A-3	7007		Wizernes a/f		ground collision	n/a
25-10-40	Oblt.	Eichstädt, Kurt	KIA	5	Bf 109E-4	3724	bk 12	Church St Farm, Sussex	1050	Spitfire	66 Sqd
15-04-42	Gefr.	Eickelmann, Alfred	KIA	1	Fw 190A-2	5233	wh 7	Cap Gris Nez		Spitfire	121 Sqd
25-06-41	Fw.	Eierstock, Bartholomaeus	KIA	9	Bf 109F-2	12664		Dunkirk	1245	Spitfire	
30-03-45	Fw.	Eisenberg, Hans	KIA	13	Fw 190D-9			35km NE of Heilbronn		Spitfire XIV	402 Sqd
22-05-44	Uffz.	Elicker, Edgar	KIFA	6	Fw 190A-6			Mont de Marsan		crashed	non-op
23-01-45	Lt.	Ellenrieder, Xaver	WIA	4	Fw 190D-9	211006	bl 6	Ostbevern	0945	Spitfire XIV	41 Sqd
16-04-45	Lt.	Ellenrieder, Xaver	WIFA	1 CO	Fw 190D-9	401357	wh 3	Sülte a/f	1610	landing	non-op
25-02-44	Uffz.	Enna, Walter	no	8	Fw 190A-6			near Metz	1200	P-47	4 FG
09-03-44	Uffz.	Enna, Walter	KIFA	8	Fw 190A-6	530411	bl 6	S of Paris	1200	no fuel	non-op
06-02-44	Obfw.	Erbskorn, Hans	WIA	12	Bf 109G-6	410672	bk 9	Paris	1120	P-47	56 FG
11-09-44	Obfw.	Erbskorn, Hans	WIFA	10	Bf 109G-6	165156	bk 5	E of Venlo	1440	engine	n/a
28-10-44	Obfw.	Erbskorn, Hans	KIA	10	Bf 109G-14	462977	bk 9	W of Dülmen-Merfelder Bruch	1549	Spitfire	412 Sqd
13-02-44	Uffz.	Erpenbach, Paul	WIA	4	Fw 190A-7	430180	bl 1	SW of Abbeville Gamaches	1515	P-47	356 FG
06-12-42	Ogfr.	Eschke, Erich	KIA	1	Fw 190A-4	683	wh 6	NW of Ault		B-24	44 BG
27-11-41	Lt.	Eyler, Theodor	WIFA	III St	Fw 190A-1	79		Cocquelles		crashed	n/a
04-04-43	Fw.	Fackler, Karl	KIA	6	Fw 190A-4	2392	br 12	Channel Narrows		missing	
05-04-45	Hptm.	Fahnert, F-Wilhelm	KIA	5	Fw 190D-9			Dümmer Lake		flak	n/a
18-12-39	Oblt.	Fahrmann	KIA	10N	Bf 109E			North Sea		RAF bomber	
26-11-43	Oblt.	Falke, Fritz	KIA	8	Fw 190A-6	530935	bl 7	4km NW of Le Bourget	1045	B-17	
26-08-44	Uffz.	Falkenberg, Heinz	KIA	7	Fw 190A-8	680934	br 1	Rouen-Le Havre		Spitfire	416 or 421 Sqd
19-04-43	Uffz.	Falkner, Gerhard	WIFA	4	Fw 190A-4	5694	wh 5	Vitry-en-Artois a/f		landing	n/a
30-07-43	Uffz.	Falkner, Gerhard	WIA	4	Fw 190A-5	410257	wh 10	16km N of Almelo		no fuel	n/a
07-01-44	Uffz.	Falkner, Gerhard	WIA	5	Fw 190A-6	470233	wh 7	SW of Doullens		Spitfire or P-47	125 W or 4 FG
27-04-44	Uffz.	Falkner, Gerhard	KIA	5	Fw 190A-8	170007	wh 14	Couvron-Laon a/f		P-47	356 FG
07-03-43	Uffz.	Fast, Hans-Joachim	KIFA	2	Fw 190A-5	2550	bk 7	Rielbitzi a/f		takeoff	n/a
16-03-44	Uffz.	Fehr, Albrecht von	KIA	6	Fw 190A-6	550437	bk 2	N of St. Dizier	1105	P-47	56 FG
14-01-45	Gefr.	Feld, Reinhold	WIA	5	Fw 190D-9	211005	wh 7	W of Bingen-Rheine	1245	own flak	n/a
27-06-41	Uffz.	Fiedrich, Otto	KIA	4	Bf 109E-7	4183	wh 10	St. Omer		Spitfire	
30-11-43	Uffz.	Fieguth, Hans-Gerhard	WIA	10	Bf 109G-6	20718	bk 8	near Rheine	1400	P-47	78 FG
16-03-44	Fhj-Fw.	Fieguth, Hans-Gerhard	WIA	10	Bf 109G-6	162030	bk 9	St. Dizier	1420	P-47	78 FG
04-01-45	Uffz.	Findeisen, Helmut	KIA	2	Fw 190D-9	210993	bk 6	near Melle-Osnabrück	1600	Spitfire	411 Sqd

08-07-41	Uffz.	Finke, Karl	KIA	6	Bf 109E-7	3711	bk 6	Kemmel, S of Ypres		Spitfire	
12-10-44	Lt.	Fischer, Edmund	KIA	6	Fw 190A-8	171642	bk 10	Osnabrück Hannover-	1100	P-51	364 FG
26-11-43	Lt.	Fischer, Hans I	KIA	5	Fw 190A-6	530769	wh 12	4km W of Cambrai (t/o)	1215	Spitfire	416 Sqd
16-11-43	Fw.	Fischer, Hans II	KIFA	10	Bf 109G-6	160633	bk 4	Mönchen-Gladbach	1445	crashed	non-op
28-01-45	Lt.	Fischer, Kurt	KIFA	9	Fw 190D-9/R11	210950	wh 1	Plantlünne a/f	1028	crashed	non-op
20-05-42	Uffz.	Fischer, Oswald	POW	10J	Bf 109F-4/R1	7232	wh 11 +bomb	Beachy Head	1205	ship flak	n/a
14-01-45	Fhr.	Fischer, Walter	KIA	11	Bf 109G-14	462899	yl 3	N of Overath	1145	P-51	78 FG
27-09-44	Fhr.	Fischer, Werner	KIA	7	Fw 190A-8	731773	br 14	E of Moers		Spitfire	412 Sqd
03-11-43	Fw.	Fischer, Willi	WIA	12	Bf 109G-6/U4	19641	bk 1	Stevensbeek		P-47	56 FG
28-03-45	Uffz.	Flakowski, Reinhard	KIA	13	Fw 190D-9			Osnabrück-Laer	1630	Spitfire XIV	130 Sqd
01-08-42	Lt.	Flock, Arnd	KIA	10J	Fw 190A-2/U3	5253	wh 5	S of Newhaven	1050	Spitfire	412 Sqd
16-09-44		Florian, Armin	WIFA	6	Fw 190A-8	170974	bk 3	Düsseldorf		crashed	non-op
01-03-45	Uffz.	Florian, Armin	KIA	6	Fw 190D-9			Mönchen-Gladbach	0930	P-47	366 FG
20-03-44	Uffz.	Frank, Karl	KIFA	10	Bf 109G-6	410707	bk 16	15km E of Hirson	1250	crashed	non-op
13-05-40	Fw.	Frank, Max	WIA	1	Bf 109E-3			near Breda	0830	Morane 406	GC III/3
18-08-44	Obfw.	Franke, Erwin	KIA	5	Fw 190A-8	731757	wh 11	near Beauvais a/f	0830	Mustang	315 Sqd
18-03-44	Gefr.	Franke, Rudolf	KIA	2	Fw 190A-6	550903	bk 7	Münster-Achery		P-47	
14-06-44	Fhr.	Frantz, Ulrich -Karsten	KIFA	5	Fw 190A-8	170609	wh 4	Évreux Ulrich-Karsten		engine	n/a
26-03-45	Ofhr.	Franz, Wolfgang	KIA	3	Fw 190D-9	210944	yl 1	Lengerich-Münster	1530	Tempest	33 Sqd
22-06-44	Fw.	Franzke, Kurt	KIA	10	Bf 109G-6	165169	bk 1	5km S of Alencon	1445	P-47	365 or 368 FG
23-12-44	Fw.	Frass, Werner	KIA	8	Fw 190D-9	210168	bl 5	W of Köln	1250	P-51	364 FG
10-12-44	Obfw.	Freiberger, Anton	KIA	1	Fw 190A-8	738134	wh 7	Düren-Eschweiler	1545	P-47	373 FG
17-06-43	Uffz.	Freitag, Günther	KIA	8	Fw 190A-5	7308	bk 9	Stennvoorde, E of Cassel		Spitfire	Kenley Wing
24-10-43	Obfw.	Freuwörth, Wilhelm	WIA	6	Fw 190A-6	530733	bk 8	S of Montdidier		Spitfire	N Weald Wing
21-12-43	Obfw.	Freuwörth, Wilhelm	WIFA	6	Fw 190A-6	530733	bk 8	St Omer-Arques		Spitfire	132 or 602 Sqd
28-06-41	Uffz.	Friedrich, Hans	no	3	Bf 109E-7	970		Calais		Spitfire	
20-10-43	Uffz.	Friedrich, Hermann	WIA	11	Bf 109G-3	16300	yl 2	Harchies near Mons	1415	P-47	78 FG
10-02-43	Fw.	Friedrich, Karl	KIA	11/54	Bf 109G-4	16103	rd 10	N of Cap Blanc Nez	1715	Typhoon	609 Sqd
17-07-44	Uffz.	Friedrich, Karl-Heinz	WIA	10	Bf 109G-6	412538	bk 15	Chartres	1706	Spitfire	411 or 602 Sqd
28-10-44	Fw.	Friedrich, Karl-Heinz	WIA	10	Bf 109G-14	462701	bk 4	Krefeld-Ürdingen a/f	1600	Spitfire	412 Sqd
07-03-45	Fw.	Friedrich, Karl-Heinz	WIA	10	Fw 190D-9	500090	bk 9	SW Königsrath-Oberhausen	1330	P-51	
07-07-43	Uffz.	Friedrich, Kurt	KIFA	5	Fw 190A-4	2393	bk 2	S of Arras-Grévillers		crashed	non-op
01-03-45	Uffz.	Friedrich, Otto	KIA	14	Fw 190D-9	600156	bk 6	Dortmund		Spitfire	
21-10-44	Uffz.	Fritsch, Artur	KIA	8	Fw 190A-9	750131	bl 1	nr Krefeld-S of Viersen	1430	P-38	474 FG
06-07-43	Lt.	Fritsch, Paul	KIA	5	Fw 190A-4	2436	bk 7	8km W of Somme Est	2000	Spitfire	303 Sqd
17-08-43	Uffz.	Fritzlehner, Fritz	KIA	12	Bf 109G-6	16494	bl 16	near Hasselt	1210	B-17	385 or 100 BG
17-04-45	Uffz.	Fröb, Karl	KIA	2	Fw 190D-9	210968	bk 8	Lake Schwerin	1130	combat	
09-10-40	Uffz.	Fröhlich, Hans-Jürgen	WIA	2	Bf 109E-1	6264		Sandgate, NW of Calais			Blenheim
17-11-41	Fw.	Fröhlich, Hans-Jürgen	WIFA	2	Bf 109F-4	7227		Clairmarais		takeoff	n/a
24-04-42	Fw.	Fröhlich, Hans-Jürgen	KIA	10J	Bf 109F-4/R1	7196		Folkestone		flak	n/a
31-08-40	Oblt.	Fronhöfer, Willy	POW	9	Bf 109E-4	1184	yl 10	Ulcombe London	1945	Spitfire	54 Sqd
14-06-44	Uffz.	Frotzscher, Helmut	KIA	11	Bf 109G-6	440913	yl 18	Meulan NW of Paris-	0730	P-38	55 FG
05-11-40	Lt.	Füschel, Kurt	KAC	6	none			Göttingen	0830	none	n/a
21-09-44	Ofhr.	Fussi, Otto	KIA	6	Fw 190A-8	172985	bk 11	Nijmegen	1700	P-47	353 FG
21-06-41	Obstlt.	Galland, Adolf	WIA	Ge CO	Bf 109F-2	6713	<-+	Billebrune	1637	Spitfire	145 Sqd
21-06-41	Obstlt.	Galland, Adolf	no	Ge CO	Bf 109F-2	5776	<-+	c/l Calais-Marck	1236	Spitfire	303 Sqd
02-07-41	Obstlt.	Galland, Adolf	WIA	Ge CO	Bf 109F-2			unknown		Spitfire	
31-10-42	Lt.	Galland, Paul	KIA	8	Fw 190A-4	2402	bk 1	20km W of Calais	1815	Spitfire	91 Sqd
17-08-43	Maj.	Galland, Wilhelm-Ferdinand	KIA	II CO	Fw 190A-5	530125	<<+	nr Liège-5km W Maastricht	1700	P-47	56 FG
19-06-40	Uffz.	Ganster, Josef	KIA	6	Bf 109E-3			Chateauroux		hit lines	n/a
21-08-41	Fw.	Garbe, Adolf	KIA	6	Bf 109F-2	5783		Boulogne-Desvres		fighter	
25-10-40	Obfw.	Gärtner, Josef	POW	8	Bf 109E-4	5815	bk 7	Yalding, Kent	1430	Spitfire	222 Sqd
16-09-43	Uffz.	Gasser, Franz	KIA	4	Fw 190A-5	530730	wh 13	Cormeilles		Spitfire	91 Sqd
14-01-44	Maj.	Gäth, Wilhelm	WIA	II CO	Fw 190A-6	470009	<< gr 1	Soissons		P-47	4 FG
12-04-44	Uffz.	Gathof, Karl	KIA	6	Fw 190A-7	430484	br 1	5km S of Malmedy	1330	P-47	78 or 366 FG
07-12-42	Ogfr.	Gauss, Horst	WIFA	1	Fw 190A-4	7042		8km E of Berck		no fuel	n/a
15-08-43	Ogfr.	Gauss, Horst	KIA	1	Fw 190A-5	5977	wh 4	10km W of Vlissingen	1210	Spitfire	453 Sqd
10-04-42	Uffz.	Gaykow, Karl-Heinz	WIFA	10J	Bf 109F-4/R1	8353	wh 6	Arques a/f		defect	n/a
21-06-41	Lt.	Geburtig, Hans-Joachim	WIA	8	Bf 109F-2	5521		Samer	1640	Spitfire	
30-07-42	Oblt.	Geburtig, Hans-Joachim	POW	10J U3	Fw 190A-3/CO	7003	bk 1	off Littlehampton		ship flak	n/a
16-03-44	Uffz.	Gehrke, Heinz	WIA	11	Bf 109G-6			SE of St. Dizier	1327	P-47	356 FG
25-04-44	Uffz.	Gehrke, Heinz	WIFA	11	Bf 109G-6			München-Neubiberg		engine	non-op
13-06-44	Uffz.	Gehrke, Heinz	WIA	11	Bf 109G-6	162100	yl 7	Orleans	2130	P-47	78 FG
15-08-44	Uffz.	Gehrke, Heinz	WIA	11	Bf 109G-6	410688	yl 11	E of Dreux	1230	P-47	373 FG
11-09-44	Uffz.	Gehrke, Heinz	WIFA	11	Bf 109G-6	441481	yl 20	Bönninghardt a/f	1408	landing	n/a
14-12-44	Uffz.	Gehrke, Heinz	WIA	11	Bf 109G-14	463111	yl 23	S of Rheine	1430	Tempest	56 Sqd
22-02-45	Uffz.	Gehrke, Heinz	WIA	11	Fw 190D-9	500096	yl 1	Dreierwalde-Hopsten	1745	Tempest	274 Sqd

Date	Rank	Name	Fate	No.	Aircraft	WNr	Code	Location	Time	Cause	Unit
07-03-44	Gefr.	Geiler, Harry	KIFA	10	Bf 109G-6	162474	BF+VC	Fürth-Odenwald	1415	collision	non-op
05-04-43	Hptm.	Geisshardt, Fritz	KIA	III CO	Fw 190A-4	7051	-P	St. Denis-Westrem	1515	B-17	
26-03-44	Uffz.	Geissler, Anton	KIFA	11	Bf 109G-4	14987	yl 13	W of Meaux	1655	crashed	non-op
07-03-45	Uffz.	Genth, Karl-Georg	WIA	12	Fw 190D-9	500118	yl 15	near Enschede	1538	Tempest	3 Sqd
15-03-44	Uffz.	Georgi, Rudolf	WIA	7	Fw 190A-6	470249	br 12	near Rheine-Colombes		Spitfire	401 Sqd
08-04-42	Obfw.	Gerhardt, Werner	WIA	5	Fw 190A-1	94	bk 8	St Omer		Spitfire	
19-08-42	Obfw.	Gerhardt, Werner	KIA	5	Fw 190A-3	538	bk 3	Dieppe area		missing	
01-06-40	Oblt.	Germeroth, Rudolf	WIA	3	Bf 109E			N of Dunkirk		Spitfire	19,222, 616 Sqd
09-08-44	Uffz.	Gewitz, Horst	KIA	9	Bf 109G-6	440668	wh 16	Chartres-Orleans	1000	P-47	373 FG
08-06-44	Lt.	Giebner, Helmut	KIA	5	Fw 190A-8	170625	wh 5	E of Toqueville		fighter	
22-02-45	Fw.	Girstenbreu, Alfred	KIA	12	Fw 190D-9	500418	wh 2	near Altenrheine	1750	Tempest	274 Sqd
07-08-44	Uffz.	Glahn, Wolf-Dietrich	KIA	1	Fw 190A-8	172736	wh 4	SW of Dreux	1900	P-47	373 FG
03-01-43	Uffz.	Glaser, Otto	WIFA	2	Fw 190A-4	648		Arques		engine	non-op
15-04-43	Uffz.	Gläser, Rudolf	no	11/54	Fw 190A-4	7050		Chièvres		engine	non-op
22-06-41	Lt.	Glasmacher, Hans	KIA	2	Bf 109E-7	6219		near Clairmairais a/f		Spitfire	
21-07-41	Ogfr.	Gleixner, Heinrich	KIA	4	Bf 109E-7	6512		NW of Lille		Spitfire	71 Sqd
03-06-44	Obfw.	Gloyer, Heinz	KIFA	6	Fw 190A-8	170421	bk 4	Bidart	1745	crashed	non-op
02-04-42	Lt.	Göcke, Elmar	WIA	9	Fw 190A-1			20km S of Cap Gris Nez		Spitfire	
02-10-42	Oblt.	Göcke, Elmar	KIA	4	Fw 190A-2	5411	wh 5	NW of Amiens		B-17	
21-06-44	Obfw.	Gocksch, Walter	KIA	10	Bf 109G-6	412684	bk 2	SW of Paris N of Poissy	1940	P-47	406 FG
10-08-44	Fw.	Göhre, Siegfried	KIA	12	Bf 109G-6	165239	bl 22	W of Breteuil	0845	fighter	
19-08-42	Fw.	Golub, August	KIA	9	Fw 190A-2	5298	yl 6	NW of Dieppe	1500	Spitfire	
27-02-43	Uffz.	Gomann, Heinz	WIA	5	Fw 190A-4	2455	bk 12	Calais	1430	Spitfire	402 or 403 Sqd
17-08-43	Uffz.	Gomann, Heinz	WIA	5	Fw 190A-5	1243	bk 22	10km NE Hasselt-c/l St Trond		P-47	56 FG
12-01-44	Fw.	Gomann, Heinz	WIFA	6	Fw 190A-6	530931	bk 14	Cambrai-Zwolle		engine	n/a
03-09-41	Ogfr.	Göppner, Helmut	KIFA	2/E	Bf 109E-4	1544		Channel N Goeree Is.		hit water	non-op
22-12-41	Obfw.	Görbig, Kurt	KIFA	6	Fw 190A-1	33	bk 1	E of Boulogne	1400	weather	non-op
30-08-41	Lt.	Göring, Peter	WIFA	E	Bf 109E-7	3787		Hazebrouck		crashed	non-op
13-10-41	Lt.	Göring, Peter	KIA	Ge St	Bf 109F-4	8288		SE of Boulogne-Hubersent	1430	Blenheim	
06-06-42	Fw.	Görtz, Otto	KIA	10J	Bf 109F-4/R1	8532	wh 2	S of Bournemouth		flak	n/a
20-04-45	Lt.	Göttle, Franz	KIA	1	Fw 190D-9			Wismar a/f	1630	own naval flak	n/a
25-06-41	Oblt.	Gottlob, Heinrich	WIA	1	Bf 109E-7	7690		Hardinghem	2105	Spitfire	145 Sqd
01-01-45	Gefr.	Götz, Hans-Karl	POW	7	Fw 190D-9	600161	bl 2	near Molenschot	1000	engine	n/a
13-07-44	Uffz.	Grad, Hermann	WIA	4	Fw 190A-6	530923	bl 15	Bernay	1705	P-47	362 FG
26-12-44	Uffz.	Grad, Hermann	KIA	4	Fw 190D-9	210935	bl 13	near Malmedy	1100	P-51	361 FG
13-06-43	Obfw.	Grams, Willi	KIFA	8	Fw 190A-5	1222	bk 1	Vendeville a/f		landing	n/a
02-11-42	Uffz.	Granabetter, Georg	KIA	6	Fw 190A-4	656	br 3	Somme Est-W of Boulogne		Spitfire	611 Sqd
20-03-44	Obfw.	Gräve, Alfons	KIA	12	Bf 109G-6	27041	bl 2	5km W of Reims	1325	P-47	356 FG
28-06-41	Oblt.	Grawatsch, Harald	WIA	II St	Bf 109E-7	6487		SE of St Omer		Spitfire	
19-07-41	Uffz.	Grebe, Ulrich	KIFA	1	Bf 109F-4	8364		Watten-St Omer		engine	n/a
29-06-42	Lt.	Greffinius, Georg	KIA	2	Fw 190A-1	23	bk 8	N of Dunkirk		Spitfire	
24-02-44	Ogfr.	Greim, Hellmut	KIA	9	Bf 109G-6	16412	wh 3	Rheine-Lingen		P-47	78 FG
21-06-41	Lt.	Gries, Heinz	KIA	8	Bf 109F-2	6732		near Etaples Camiers	1642	Spitfire	
12-10-44	Ogfr.	Grimm, Horst	KIA	9	Bf 109G-14	461979	wh 1	Bremervörde Hipstedt	1220	P-51	357 FG
12-04-44	Lt.	Grimm, Wolfgang	KIA	6	Fw 190A-6			Malmedy		P-47	78 or 366 FG
16-09-44	Lt.	Grimmer, Josef	WIA	7	Fw 190A-8	732007	bl 11	near Jülich	1815	own flak	n/a
13-03-42	Uffz.	Grohmann, Otto	no	9	Fw 190A-2	5213		Abbeville a/f		takeoff	n/a
09-04-42	Uffz.	Grohmann, Otto	KIFA	9	Fw 190A-2	2121	yl 2	N of Moorsele	1804	crashed	n/a
17-08-44	Uffz.	Grolms, Bruno	KIA	6	Fw 190A-8	171638	bk 8	Dreux		light flak	n/a
03-09-44	Lt.	Gross, Alfred	WIA	II St	Fw 190A-8	171569	gr 4	Brussels St Trond	1330	Spitfire	41 Sqd
17-09-44	Uffz.	Gross, Helmut	KIA	8	Fw 190A-8	171565	bl 5	Hoxfeld-Borken	1438	P-51	4 FG
22-02-44	Uffz.	Gross, Paul	KIA	5	Fw 190A-6	530716	wh 21	nr Wesel M-Gladbach	1500	P-47	4 FG
24-07-43	Uffz.	Grossler, Kurt	KIFA	2	Fw 190A-5	410248	bk 6	N Sea E of Ipswich	2036	hit water	n/a
07-04-44	Oblt.	Groth, Max	WIFA	1	Fw 190A-6	530918	wh 6	Soissons		engine fire	non-op
07-05-44	Oblt.	Groth, Max	WIFA	1 CO	Fw 190A-6	550913	wh 6	8km NE of Soissons		engine	n/a
09-06-44	Oblt.	Groth, Max	WIA	1 CO	Fw 190A-8	680417	wh 6	Beauvais-Boissy-le-Bois		engine	n/a
05-07-44	Oblt.	Groth, Max	KIA	1 CO	Fw 190A-8	731041	wh 4	E of Évreux		Spitfire	
01-06-40	Lt.	Gruel, Siegfried	KIA	3	Bf 109E-1			Dunkirk-Pervyse		Spitfire	19, 222, 616 Sqd
20-03-45	Uffz.	Grüner, Johann	WIFA	14	Fw 190D-9			unknown		engine	non-op
27-03-42	Uffz.	Grünlinger, Walter	no	III St	Fw 190A-1	70		Coquelles a/f		engine/combat	
04-09-43	Obfw.	Grünlinger, Walter	KIA	Ge St	Fw 190A-5	7287	bk B-	W of Norrent-Fontes		Spitfire	127 Wing
19-08-43	Lt.	Grupe, Werner	WIA	12	Bf 109G-4	19373	bl 3	Breda	2030	P-47	56 or 78 FG
20-10-43	Lt.	Grupe, Werner	WIA	12	Bf 109G-4	19791	bl 14	6km SW of Hirson	1350	B-17	
23-09-40	Obfw.	Grzymalla, Gerhard	POW	8	Bf 109E-4	5817	bk 9	Biddenden S of London	1045	Spitfire	92 Sqd
29-11-43	Uffz.	Gulecke, J-Heinrich	WIA	2	Fw 190A-6	550749	bk 5	f/l Melsbroek		Spitfire	
18-03-44	Uffz.	Gulecke, J-Heinrich	KIA	2	Fw 190A-6	550464	bk 3	Florennes	1436	missing	

Date	Rank	Name	Fate		Aircraft	WerkNr	Marking	Location	Time	Opponent	Unit
24-06-43	Obfw.	Günther, Alfred	WIA	5	Fw 190A-4	598	bk 11	S of St. Omer		Spitfire	403 Sqd
04-09-43	Obfw.	Günther, Alfred	WIA	5	Fw 190A-5	1234	bk 8	5km N of Berck		Spitfire	
24-09-43	Obfw.	Günther, Alfred	WIFA	5	Fw 190A-5	530728	bk 4	17km W of Amiens		engine	n/a
15-06-44	Obfw.	Günther, Alfred	KIA	6	Fw 190A-8	170712	bk 6	S of Orleans	0830	P-51	339 FG
16-02-44	Lt.	Günther, Joachim	WIFA	3	Go 145A-1	2337	GA+OF	near Florennes		crashed	non-op
24-12-44	Lt.	Günther, Joachim	WIFA	2	Fw 190A-9	750149	bl 14	SW of Rheine		engine	n/a
24-02-45	Lt.	Günther, Joachim	KIA	3	Fw 190D-9/R11	210941	yl 12	Zutphen		Spitfire	332 Sqd
19-08-43	Uffz.	Günther, Martin	WIA	4	Fw 190A-5	2405	wh 2	2.5km NE of Amiens		Spitfire	
02-01-44	Uffz.	Günther, Martin	KIFA	5	Fw 190A-5	410238	wh 10	SE of Amiens	1040	collision	n/a
03-09-43	Uffz.	Guttmann, Gerhard	WIA	10	Fw 190A-5	410258	bl 18	Melun f/l Villaroche-		B-17	
27-03-44	Fw.	Guttmann, Gerhard	KIA	5	Fw 190A-7	643708	wh 11	Chartres		P-47	359 FG
14-01-45	Ogfr.	Haarberg, Volkmar	KIA	6	Fw 190D-9	500121	bk 8	St Vith-Bastogne	1130	P-51	78 FG
17-08-43	Uffz.	Hadraba, Karl	KIA	10	Fw 190A-5	410001	bl 17	NW of Hesdin-Lille	1155	Spitfire	341 Sqd
31-08-40	Oblt.	Hafer, Ludwig	KIA	I St	Bf 109E-1	4806		Rainham, nr Dungeness	1345	Spitfire	603 Sqd
23-08-40	Uffz.	Haferkorn, Gottfried	KIA	2	Bf 109E-1			W of Boulogne		collision	
20-01-43	Uffz.	Hager, Robert	WIA	8	Fw 190A-4	7102	bk 4	Calais-Marck a/f	1328	landing	n/a
04-04-43	Uffz.	Hager, Robert	WIA	8	Fw 190A-4	2391	bk 11	2km SE of Rouen	1350	B-17	
13-08-44	Fw.	Hager, Robert	KIA	4	Fw 190A-8	172674	<<gr 3	NE of Le Mans	0825	P-51	363 FG
09-10-42	Uffz.	Hager, Viktor	KIA	7	Fw 190A-4	7043	wh 2	Chemin de Mesnine	1120	B-17	
14-03-43	Lt.	Hahne, Ernst	KIA	4	Fw 190A-4	653	wh 4	near Boulogne St Cecile	1758	Spitfire	340 Sqd
02-03-45	Uffz.	Hähnel, Walter	KIA	10	Fw 190D-9	400257	bk 10	NW Ibbenbüren	0800	Spitfire XIV	130 Sqd
26-07-42	Oblt.	Haiböck, Josef	WIA	1 CO	Fw 190A-3			N of Calais		Spitfire	
07-10-44	Lt.	Hamel, Gerhard	KIA	6	Fw 190A-8	730963	bk 21	Nijmegen S of Silvolde	1634	Spitfire	442 Sqd
22-12-41	Gefr.	Hämmerle, Eduard	KIFA	6	Fw 190A-1	91		near Samer	1400	weather	non-op
10-07-41	Uffz.	Hammon, Erich	KIA	2	Bf 109E-7	3855	bk 7	Channel Narrows		fighter	
18-08-44	Ogfr.	Hanitz, Willi	KIA	6	Fw 190A-8	172748	bk 3	E of Amiens	0830	Mustang	315 Sqd
20-06-43	Uffz.	Hanke, Erwin	no	4	Fw 190A-4	2372	wh 14	SE of Capelle	1330	Spitfire	421 Sqd
06-09-43	Uffz.	Hanke, Erwin	WIA	4	Fw 190A-5	7321	wh 9	Romilly-sur Seine		no fuel	n/a
02-01-44	Uffz.	Hanke, Erwin	KIFA	5	Fw 190A-6	550556	wh 1	SE of Amiens	1040	collision	n/a
09-04-43	Uffz.	Hanse, Günter	KIFA	Um/54	Fw 190A-5	7251		in sea		crashed	non-op
28-03-45	Ofhr.	Hansen, Hans-Jürgen	KIA	15	Fw 190D-9	400255		Osnabrück-Hardenstetten	1630	Spitfire XIV	130 Sqd
09-03-45	Uffz.	Hanusch, Fritz	WIA	6	Fw 190D-9	210239	bk 3	S of Wesel	1650	P-47	366 FG
12-03-45	Obfw.	Hark, Karl-Manfred	KIA	10	Fw 190D-9	600122	bk 7	E of Arnhem	1610	own flak	n/a
15-08-44	Oblt.	Hartigs, Hans	WIA	4	Fw 190A-8	170710	bl 6	W of "Field 111"-Paris		Mustang	19 Sqd
26-12-44	Oblt.	Hartigs, Hans	POW	4	Fw 190D-9	210931	bl 10	E of Florenville	1130	P-51	361 FG
01-01-45	Fw.	Hartmann,Karl-Heinz	POW	4	Fw 190D-9	210126	bl 3	Grimbergen a/f	0930	collision	n/a
18-08-44	Fw.	Hasenclever, Walter	KIA	7	Fw 190A-8	174114	br 3	Beauvais-Tillé		Mustang	315 Sqd
14-07-44	Uffz.	Haun, Willi	WIA	9	Bf 109G-6	164957	wh 5	Breteuil	1500	P-47	358 FG
31-08-43	Lt.	Heck, Gert	KIA	10	Fw 190A-5	7213	bl 6	S of Lille		Spitfire	
30-07-42	Oblt.	Heck, Herbert	KIA	2	Fw 190A-2	5303		Verlincthun		Spitfire	
09-04-43	Uffz.	Heck, Karl	KIA	10J	Fw 190A-5	831	bk 14 +bomb	Channel-S of Folkestone		Typhoon	609 Sqd
27-05-44	Fw.	Hecker, Michael	KIA	2	Fw 190A-8	170001	bk 7	SE of Armentières	1430	P-51	361 FG
21-06-41	Fw.	Hegenauer, Bruno	no	Ge St	Bf 109F-2			near St Omer	1240	Spitfire	303 Sqd
17-05-40	Obfw.	Heidenpeter, Heinz	POW	4	Bf 109E-3			W of Douai		Hurricane	
05-04-45	Oblt.	Heilmann, Willi	POW	15 CO	Fw 190D-9			Münster Handorf a/f		captured	n/a
14-01-44	Uffz.	Hein, Hans	KIA	11	Bf 109G-6	410577	yl 1	20km E of Hesdin	1200	Spitfire	308 Sqd
07-10-44	Ofhr.	Heindtke, Siegfried	KIA	2	Fw 190A-8	173806	bk 7	near Arnhem	1640	Spitfire	442 Sqd
17-05-43	Lt.	Heinemann, Ernst	WIFA	4	Fw 190A-4	2394		Vitry a/f collision	2030	ground	non-op
04-09-43	Lt.	Heinemann, Ernst	KIA	4	Fw 190A-5	530414	wh 11	near Berck-sur-Mer		Spitfire	
05-12-40	Lt.	Heinemann, Hans	KIA	1	Bf 109E-7	5968	wh 4	SE of Dover in Channel	1215	Spitfire	74 or 92 Sqd
03-04-43	Lt.	Heinemeyer, Hans-Joachim	WIFA	11/54	Fw 190A-4	5606		Merville		engine	non-op
01-07-43	Lt.	Heinemeyer, Hans-Joachim	KIA	11	Bf 109G-3	16254	rd 18	5km NE of Hesdin		Spitfire	403 Sqd
12-10-44	Ofhr.	Heinrichs, Robert	KIA	5	Fw 190A-9	750125	wh 2	SW of Bremervörde	1130	P-51	364 FG
01-12-43	Obfw.	Heitmann, Hans	WIA	4	Fw 190A-5	530741	bl 9	S of Geilenkirchen		P-47	
06-03-44	Obfw.	Heitmann, Hans	WIA	4	Fw 190A-7	642978	bl 9	Osnabrück-Haste	1430	P-47	356 FG
08-07-41	Uffz.	Held, Albrecht	KIA	1	Bf 109F-2	9157		8km N of St. Omer		wing failed	n/a
20-02-44	Uffz.	Hell, Erwin	WIA	6	Fw 190A-6	470224	bk 2	Luenebach-Eifel		P-47	4 FG
07-06-42	Lt.	Helmholz, Gottfried	KIFA	2	Fw 190A-2	2119		Arques a/f		crashed	n/a
20-08-44	Hptm.	Hempel, Adolf	KAC	III St	none			Paris		Maquis	n/a
03-08-44	Fw.	Hennemann, Karl	KIA	9	Bf 109G-6/U4	440668	wh 16	NW of Avranches	1950	light flak	n/a
21-09-44	Fhr.	Hennemann, Martin	WIA	6	Fw 190A-8	175116	bk 13	9km W Kleve Groesbeek		P-47	353 FG
12-10-44	Fhr.	Hennemann, Martin	KIA	6	Fw 190A-8	171580	bk 8	Osnabrück Hannover	1100	P-51	364 FG
26-08-44	Uffz.	Hennig, Joachim	KIA	6	Fw 190A-8	730969	bk 8	E of Rouen		Spitfire	416 or 421 Sqd
17-11-40	Oblt.	Henrici, Eberhard	KIA	1 CO	Bf 109E-7	5967		20km E Harwich	1016	Hurricane	257 Sqd
07-03-44	Uffz.	Henske, Werner	KIFA	9	Bf 109G-6	162404	wh 16	Fürth-Odenwald	1415	collision	non-op
31-03-45	Uffz.	Herbster, Heinrich	WIA	3	Fw 190D-9		yl 10	Lüdingshausen (S of Münster)	0700	flak	n/a
13-08-43	Uffz.	Hering, Heinrich	WIFA	9	Bf 109G-4	19213	wh 14	Nordholz	0638	engine	non-op
02-03-44	Uffz.	Hering, Heinrich	WIA	9	Bf 109G-6	410729	wh 7	Koblenz-Niederzissen	1150	P-38	

Date	Rank	Name	Fate		Aircraft	Werk Nr	Markings	Location	Time	Cause	Unit
18-08-44	Uffz.	Hering, Heinrich	KIA	12	Bf 109G-6/U4	440991	yl 8	Falaise-Argentan	1345	P-47	358 FG
25-03-45	Fhr.	Hermann, Heinrich	KIA	I St	Fw 190D-9			20km SW of Meppen	1340	Tempest	222 Sqd
11-05-40	Fw.	Herzog, Gerhard	POW	2	Bf 109E-3			SW of Antwerp		Morane + flak	
29-08-41	Uffz.	Hetzel, Werner	KIA	4	Bf 109E-7	6463		NE of Hazebrouck		fighter	
03-08-44	Fw.	Heuser, Heinrich	POW	2	Fw 190A-8	172719	bk 2	Avranches		light flak	n/a
01-01-45	Ofhr.	Heuser, Helmut	POW	6	Fw 190D-9	500034	bk 16	Scherpenisse Tholen Is.		0915	ship flak	n/a
16-08-41	Lt.	Heyarts, Josef	KIA	I St	Bf 109F-4	8368		Le Touquet NE of Wissant	1930	Spitfire	
31-08-40	Uffz.	Heyer, Werner	KIA	6	Bf 109E-4	5393		Canterbury		Bf 110?	
03-04-43	Uffz.	Hiess, Hans	KIA	6	Fw 190A-4	2440	br 5	Neuville	1630	Spitfire	Kenley Wing
12-10-44	Uffz.	Hildebrandt, Willi	KIA	2	Fw 190A-8	690142	bk 4	Osnabrück Hannover	1200	P-47	56 or 78 FG
08-06-42	Lt.	Hilgendorff, Viktor	WIA	Ge St	Fw 190A-2	453	bk VH-	near Arques a/f	1345	Spitfire	121 Sqd
15-06-44	Oblt.	Hilgendorff, Viktor	WIA	9 CO	Bf 109G-6	410689	wh 6	6km W of Pau	0712	B-24	392 BG
18-07-44	Oblt.	Hilgendorff, Viktor	KIA	9 CO	Bf 109G-6	413482	wh 3	S of Dreux	0952	P-47	373 FG
16-09-44	Ogfr.	Hillebrand, Hermann	KIA	7	Fw 190A-8	172962	br 4	Schinnen	1745	P-47 or P-38	50, 370,404 FG
26-06-40	Lt.	Hilleke, Otto-Heinrich	KIA	II St	Bf 109E-1			Waltrop SE of Haltern		Blenheim	
29-05-44	Lt.	Hilliger, Karl-Dietrich	WIA	9	Bf 109G-6	163471	bl 12	Metz-Frescaty a/f	1330	combat	
26-08-44	Lt.	Hilliger, Karl-Dietrich	KIA	9	Bf 109G-6	410218	wh 2	S of Rouen	1440	P-47	50 FG
21-08-42	Lt.	Hoch, Hermann	no	I St	Fw 190A-2	5260		Wizernes		crashed	n/a
20-01-43	Lt.	Hoch, Hermann	POW	10J	Fw 190A-4	2409	bk 2 +bomb	Seaford-Surrey	1345	light flak	
01-04-44	Uffz.	Hofer, Kurt	KIA	3	Fw 190A-7	340302	yl 8	N of Reims-Pont Faverger		B-24	
06-12-41	Obfw.	Hoffmann, Hermann	WIFA	5	Fw 190A-1	50		Coxyde		crashed	n/a
17-08-43	Obfw.	Hoffmann, Hermann	KIA	11	Bf 109G-3	20225	rd 7	10km NW of Fruges	1205	Spitfire	485 Sqd
28-10-44	Uffz.	Hoffmann, Johannes	WIA	5	Fw 190A-9	750118	wh 1	near Wesel		collision	n/a
14-01-45	Uffz.	Hoffmann, Johannes	WIA	5	Fw 190D-9	400214	wh 3	near Minden	1245	Spitfire	
03-09-43	Uffz.	Hoffmann, Werner	WIFA	5	Fw 190A-4	5658	bk 6	Creil		engine	n/a
07-07-44	Uffz.	Hoffmann, Werner	WIA	6	Fw 190A-8	731069	bk 2	St. Aubin N of Caen		Spitfire	401 Sqd
09-04-45	Uffz.	Hoffmann, Werner	KIA	5	Fw 190D-9			Heist-Uetersen		combat	
09-05-42	Uffz.	Hofmann, Herbert	KIA	1	Fw 190A-1	49		N of Cassel	1345	Spitfire	
07-08-44	Uffz.	Hofmann, Karl	WIA	3	Fw 190A-8	171077	yl 9	S of Paris Dourdan		P-47	373 FG
19-03-45	Fw.	Hofmann, Karl	KIA	2	Fw 190D-9	500044	bk 6	near Rastrup	1620	P-51	479 FG
17-06-44	Uffz.	Hofmann, Werner	KIA	5	Fw 190A-8	730388	wh 3	W of Caen		fighter	
09-12-42	Uffz.	Hofmann, Wilhelm	WIFA	1	Fw 190A-4	5617		5km N of Watten		engine	n/a
21-10-44	Oblt.	Hofmann, Wilhelm	WIA	8 CO	Fw 190A-9			S of Viersen	1430	P-38	474 FG
22-10-44	Oblt.	Hofmann, Wilhelm	WAC	8 CO	none			Stevede a/f gun		machine	n/a
26-03-45	Oblt.	Hofmann, Wilhelm	KIA	5 CO	Fw 190D-9			Hasselünne-Flechum	1530	Fw 190D	II/JG 26
26-11-43	Uffz.	Höhme, Johannes	KIA	5	Fw 190A-6	530727	wh 1	4km NW of Albert	1220	Spitfire	401 Sqd
17-10-41	Uffz.	Holbach, Josef	KIFA	1/E	Bf 109E-7	5866		Vlaardingen Rotterdam	1755	engine	non-op
19-07-44	Fw.	Holl, Walter	KIA	10	Bf 109G-6	165146	bk 13	Boucouvillers	1520	crashed	non-op
11-05-40	Oblt.	Holtey, Hubertus von	WIA	5 CO	Bf 109E			S of Zuider Zee		flak	n/a
07-06-43	Ogfr.	Holtz, Norbert	WIFA	8	Fw 190A-4	5730	bk 4	Deinze-Nazareth	1100	engine	n/a
06-09-40	Gefr.	Holzapfel, Peter	KIA	7	Bf 109E-1	3877	wh 5	17km W Ashford	1020	Spitfire	234 Sqd
14-08-41	Uffz.	Holzenkämpfer, Heinrich	KIA	8	Bf 109F-4	7101		St. Omer SE of Wisques	1815	Spitfire	
18-08-44	Uffz.	Holzinger, Helmut	KIA	8	Fw 190A-8	731995	bl 2	Chartres		Mustang	315 Sqd
17-09-44	Uffz.	Holzleitner, Johann	KIA	8	Fw 190A-8	170309	bl 4	Bochholt	1440	P-51	4 FG
25-12-44	Fw.	Hoppe, Alfred	KIA	7	Fw 190D-9	400208	br 13	18km W of Dortmund		P-51	
01-12-43	Hptm.	Hoppe, Helmut	KIA	5 CO	Fw 190A-6	550731	wh 6	Epinoy a/f		Spitfire	411 Sqd
19-08-44	Fhj-Uffz.	Horch, Otto	KIA	4	Fw 190A-8	680842	bl 8	Bernay		P-47	406 FG
30-09-40	Gefr.	Hornatschek, Helmut	KIA	9	Bf 109E-1	4820		Tiller Hill nr Canterbury	1800		66 Sqd
06-04-45	Uffz.	Horner, Alois	POW	13	Fw 190D-9			5km W of Stolzenau		flak+Tempest	80 Sqd
21-08-42	Uffz.	Horner, Karl	WIFA	9	Fw 190A-2	5408	yl 8	Moorsele		engine	n/a
19-08-44	Uffz.	Hött, Karl	WIA	6	Fw 190A-8	170978	br 2	NE of Amy		Mustang	
01-01-45	Fw.	Hött, Karl	WIA	6	Fw 190D-9	400207	bk 2	Brielle	0900	own flak	n/a
16-12-43	Obfw.	Humburg, Heinrich	WIA	9	Bf 109G-6	20702	wh 1	Hoya-Weser		no fuel	n/a
24-09-43	Lt.	Hummel, Otto	WIA	5	Fw 190A-5	530729	bk 2	Beauvais		Spitfire	
08-02-44	Oblt.	Hummel, Otto	KIA	II St	Fw 190A-7	340296	bk 30	Florennes a/f	1300	P-38	20 FG
02-03-44	Uffz.	Hurtig, Franz	KIA	1	Fw 190A-6	470213	wh 8	Trier-Wittlich	1145	collision	n/a
31-05-40	Lt.	Hütter-Walleck,	KIA	7	Bf 109E-1			Dunkirk		Hurricane	213 or 264 Sqd
17-04-45	Uffz.	Hütterer, Albert	KIA	2	Fw 190D-9			SW of Lübeck	1130	Tempest	80 Sqd
07-06-44	Uffz.	Hüttig, Helmut	KIA	1	Fw 190A-8	680186	wh 2	30km SW of Rouen		combat	
16-06-41	Lt.	Hüttner, Gustav	KIA	8	Bf 109F-2	8125		E of Montreuil Calais	1630	Spitfire	
07-06-40	Uffz.	Iberle, Rudolf	KIA	4	Bf 109E-3	1541	wh 13	SE of Dieppe		Hurricane	43 Sqd
23-01-43	Uffz.	Immervoll, Alfred	KIA	10J	Fw 190A-4	5636	-+-	Beachy Head Hailsham	1050	lightt flak	
13-01-43	Uffz.	Irlinger, Johann	KIA	5	Bf 109G-4	16119	bk 4	near Abbeville		Fw 190	II/JG 26
22-03-45	Uffz.	Issleib, Günter	KIA	6	Fw 190D-9			Drope	1603	Tempest	56 or 80 Sqd
30-08-40	Uffz.	Jäckel, Ernst	WIA	2	Bf 109E-1	3650		6km NW of Cap Gris Nez		unknown	
29-10-40	Obfw.	Jäckel, Konrad	POW	8	Bf 109E-4	3794	bk 1	Tillingham, Essex	1815	Hurricane	17 Sqd
24-08-44	Gefr.	Jäger, Helmut	KIFA	2	Fw 190A-8	172665	bk 10	Fresnes a/f		crashed	non-op
03-09-43	Oblt.	Janda, Ernst	KIA	8	Fw 190A-5	7234	bk 18	SE of Paris		P-47	56 FG
06-04-43	Ogfr.	Janning, Karl-Heinz	KIFA	3	Fw 190A-4	2485	yl 4	Dno a/f		crashed	non-op
15-11-40	Lt.	Jaros, Otto	POW	3	Bf 109E-1/B	6353	yl 9	Horndon, Essex	1433	Hurricane	605 Sqd

Date	Rank	Name	Fate		Aircraft	W.Nr.	Code	Location	Time	Cause	Unit
18-06-43	Fw.	Jauer, Erich	POW	7	Fw 190A-5	2551	wh 6	nr Schluesselburg a/f	0600	P-39	
22-12-43	Uffz.	Jenner, Anton	KIA	11	Bf 109G-5	110020	yl 2	Rheine Westfalen	1408	P-47	4 FG
22-01-45	Fhr.	Jensen, Christian	KIA	2	Fw 190D-9	600163	bk 7	SW of Ibbenbüren	1125	Spitfire	421 Sqd
07-10-44	Fw.	Jentzsch, Paul	KIA	4	Fw 190A-8	171517	bl 2	SE of Kleve	1640	Spitfire	442 Sqd
24-12-44	Uffz.	Jesinger, Wilhelm	KIA	1	Fw 190D-9	600174	wh 13	Liège	1130	P-38	367 FG
10-01-44	Oblt.	Jessen, Heinrich	KIFA	3 CO	Fw 190A-6	470048	wh 2	Florennes a/f		collision	n/a
28-03-42	Lt.	Johannsen, Hans	KIA	7	Fw 190A-1	75		SW of Audembert a/f		Spitfire	
06-09-43	Fw.	Jörg, Adolf	KIA	6	Fw 190A-5	7300	br 3	Molins		Spitfire	
10-07-44	Fw.	Joziak, Roman	KIA	8	Fw 190A-8	731068	bl 14	N of Caen	1115	flak	n/a
16-03-44	Ofhr.	Juhre, Hermann	WIA	10	Bf 109G-6	18830	bk 2	St. Dizier	1420	P-47	78 FG
28-10-44	Lt.	Juhre, Hermann	KIA	10	Bf 109G-14	464279	bk 8	SW of Münster Senden-	1555	Spitfire	412 Sqd
25-02-45	Fhj Uffz.	Just, Gerhard	KIA	5	Fw 190D-9	211008	wh 8	Köln-Wahn a/f		own flak	n/a
02-09-42	Uffz.	Jutzrenka,POW Konrad von	1	Fw 190A-4		7039	wh 11	off Beachy Head	1155	Spitfire	401 Sqd
24-12-44	Uffz.	Kabowski, Erwin	POW	1	Fw 190D-9	210912	wh 9	Liège	1130	engine	n/a
11-10-42	Uffz.	Käferle, Karl	WIFA	7	Fw 190A-4	5631	wh 6	Wevelgem	1517	ground collision	n/a
22-01-45	Uffz.	Kaeler, Günter	KIA	1	Fw 190D-9	210281	wh 5	Recke Osnabrück	1125	Spitfire	421 Sqd
14-06-41	Oblt.	Kahse	no	1	Bf 109E-7	4105	wh 5	in Channel	0830	Spitfire	603 Sqd
16-05-43	Uffz.	Kaiser, Friedrich	KIA	6	Fw 190A-4	2399	br 4	Zaffelare N of Ghent	1300	bomber	
17-02-43	Gefr.	Kaiser, Helmut	WIA	1	Fw 190A-5	1098	wh 4	near Salutsche		Yak-3	
06-02-45	Fw.	Kaiser, Herbert	WIFA	3	Fw 190D-9	600348	yl 12	E of Horsten-Schultenort		engine	n/a
09-04-45	Fw.	Kaiser, Herbert	KIA	3	Fw 190D-9			8km NE Diepholz	1300	flak	n/a
30-07-43	Uffz.	Kaiser, Werner	WIA	3	Fw 190A-5	5895	yl 9	25km S 0f Breda	0706	B-26	
14-01-44	Uffz.	Kaiser, Werner	KIA	3	Fw 190A-6	550241	wh 6	Beauvais		P-47	4 FG
22-03-45	Uffz.	Kalbus, Edwin	KIA	5	Fw 190D-9			Lohne-Lingen	1603	Tempest	56 or 80 Sqd
12-03-42	Fw.	Kalitzki, Willi	no	8	Fw 190A-1	60		Ostend		engine	n/a
14-05-43	Obfw.	Kalitzki, Willi	WIA	8	Fw 190A-5	7297	wh 12	Woensdrecht	1235	B-17	
29-04-44	Obfw.	Kalitzki, Willi	KIFA	1	Fw 190A-6	530735	wh 12	W of Poitiers		crashed	non-op
28-11-40	Fw.	Kaminsky, Wolfgang	KIA	1	Bf 109E-4	3755	bk 13	10km NE of Dungeness	1710	Spitfire	19 Sqd
08-03-44	Uffz.	Kampen, Emil	KIA	9	Bf 109G-6	410743	wh 5	Steinhuder Lake	1500	P-47	352 FG
28-03-45	Lt.	Kaps, Harry	KIA	14	Fw 190D-9			Osnabrück area		Spitfire XIV	130 Sqd
23-08-43	Lt.	Karl, Gerhard	KIA	9	Bf 109G-4	20442	yl 15	6km NW of Gorinchem	1650	Spitfire	
03-09-44	Uffz.	Karsch, Heinz	KIA	2	Fw 190A-8	170445	bk 11	14km E of Brussels	1300	P-51	55 FG
26-08-42	Obfw.	Kassa, Werner	KIA	10J	Fw 190A-2/U3	2080	bk 13	Eastbourne	0934	light flak	n/a
17-08-43	Lt.	Kehl, Dietrich	no	5	Bf 109G-6	15923		Antwerp		no fuel	n/a
25-02-44	Lt.	Kehl, Dietrich	KIA	5	Fw 190A-7	340336	wh 12	near Metz	1200	P-47	4 FG
04-07-41	Lt.	Kehrhahn, Joachim	KIA	3	Bf 109F-2	6476		NE of St. Pol		fighter	
31-07-43	Hptm.	Kelch, Günther	KIFA	7 CO	Bf 109G-4	19358	wh 15	Neuwerk Knechtsiel	2140	crashed	non-op
24-03-43	Oblt.	Keller, Paul	KIA	10J CO	Fw 190A-5	2787	bk 7 +bomb	Ashford		own bomb	n/a
01-06-40	Lt.	Keller,Paul	WIA	6	Bf 109E-1			Dunkirk-Calais		Hurricane	43,145, 245 Sqd
14-08-40	Uffz.	Kemen, Gerhard	POW	1	Bf 109E-1	4827	wh 8	Coldred-W of Dover	1345	Hurricane	32 Sqd
04-02-43	Obfw.	Kemethmüller, Heinz	WIA	7	Fw 190A-4	2438	wh 5	N of Merville	1302	Spitfire	331 Sqd
17-08-43	Obfw.	Kemethmüller, Heinz	WIA	7	Bf 109G-4	19216	wh 6	Leopoldsburg	1128	P-47	353 FG
04-11-44	Lt.	Kemethmüller, Heinz	WIFA	4 CO	Fw 190A-9	205206	bl 6	Greven a/f	1025	landing	n/a
15-02-43	Uffz.	Kemper, Johannes	KIA	7	Fw 190A-4	2434	wh 8	15km NW of Dunkirk	1550	Spitfire	331 or 332 Sqd
22-12-43	Lt.	Kempf, Karl-Heinz	WIA	11	Bf 109G-6/U4	440012	yl 9	Ems-Weser Canal	1456	B-17	
03-09-44	Lt.	Kempf, Karl-Heinz	KIA	2	Fw 190A-8	171739	bk 9	Baal, NW of Aachot	1300	P-51	55 FG
20-01-45	Fw.	Kerber, Walter	KIFA	2	Fw 190D-9	210940	bk 10	Fürstenau a/f	0830	collision	n/a
08-11-41	Uffz.	Kern, Karl-Heinz	KIA	4	Fw 190A-1	21		Dunkirk Vlamerhinghe	1245	Spitfire	317 Sqd
13-01-45	Uffz.	Kerner, Friedrich	KIFA	10	Bf 109K-4	330365	bk 17	E of Coesfeld	1600	engine	n/a
16-09-44	Lt.	Kersting, Theodor	KIA	7	Fw 190A-7	340338	br 9	NW of Vaals	1745	P-47	404 FG
29-04-42	Lt.	Kessler, Fritz	KIFA	7	Fw 190A-1	74	wh 3	Wulverdinghe	1600	collision	n/a
25-06-43	Lt.	Kestel, Melchior	KIA	9	Bf 109G-6	15423	yl 4	North Sea		missing	
17-08-43	Lt.	Kiefner, Georg	WIA	3	Fw 190A-4	2386	yl 2	30km S of Antwerp	1455	Spitfire	303 Sqd
23-03-44	Lt.	Kiefner, Georg	WIA	1	Fw 190A-6	530948	wh 11	Menin	1314	Spitfire	312 Sqd
12-08-44	Lt.	Kiefner, Georg	no	1 CO	Fw 190A-8	171079	wh 5	E of Paris		flak	n/a
17-08-44	Lt.	Kiefner, Georg	no	1 CO	Fw 190A-8		<	NE of Chartres (BD)	1155	light flak	n/a
23-01-45	Lt.	Kiefner, Georg	no	1	Fw 190D-9	600158	wh 5	near Albachten	0920	own flak	n/a
30-09-40	Hptm.	Kienzle, Walter	POW	Ge St	Bf 109E-4/N	5818		Rochester North Chapel	1805	Hurricane	303 Sqd
08-11-42	Fw.	Kierstein, Paul	WIFA	2	Fw 190A-3	2174		Arques		engine	n/a
20-01-43	Obfw.	Kierstein, Paul	KIA	2	Fw 190A-4	2375	bk 7	Dungeness	1245	Spitfire	B Hill Wing
28-07-43	Uffz.	Kind, Herbert	WIA	2	Fw 190A-5	410008	bk 11	Asperen N of Herwijnen		B-17	
09-09-43	Uffz.	Kind, Herbert	WIA	2	Fw 190A-4	2366		Coyecques-fl St Omer		Spitfire	
26-07-44	Uffz.	Kind, Herbert	KIA	2	Fw 190A-6	170056	bk 4	near Nantes	1900	Mustang	122 Sqd
07-09-43	Lt.	Kipping, Peter	KIFA	5	Fw 190A-4	7054	bk 14	Beauvais a/f		crashed	non-op
25-06-43	Lt.	Kirschenlohr, Gerd	KIFA	12/54	Bf 109G-6	15459	bl 9	Weser Estuary	1025	hit sea	n/a
03-11-43	Uffz.	Kirschner, Horst	KIA	9	Bf 109G			20km W of Haarlem	1605	Spitfire	132 Sqd
25-02-45	Oblt.	Kittelmann, Georg	KIA	2	Fw 190D-9	600167	bk 5	Gronau-Rheine	0825	P-47	36 FG
11-06-40	Lt.	Klammer, Karl	KIFA	6	Kl 35			Bois Jean a/f		wing failed	n/a
31-08-40	Fw.	Klar, Martin	POW	7	Bf 109E-1	3464		Allington E of London	1930	Hurricane	85 Sqd
18-03-45	Fhj-Ofw.	Klatt, Leo	KIA	14	Fw 190D-9			W of Twistringen	1235	P-51	339 FG
17-06-44	Uffz.	Klees, Hans	KIA	8	Fw 190A-8	730959	bl 2	SE of Avranches		fighter	

Date	Rank	Name	Status	Unit	Aircraft	W.Nr	Marking	Location	Time	Enemy	Squadron
20-04-43	Uffz.	Kleffner, Erich	KIA	5	Fw 190A-4	7108	bk 4	NNW of Dieppe	1930	Spitfire	315 Sqd
27-09-44	Uffz.	Klein, Erich	KIA	8	Fw 190A-8	680831	bl 7	S of Nijmegen	1750	Spitfire	412 Sqd
14-07-41	Gefr.	Kleinecke, Robert	KIA	9	Bf 109F-2	6735	yl 3	Marquise	1005	RAF ftr	
05-04-45	Maj.	Klemm, Rudolf	no	IV CO	Fw 190D-9		gr 3	near Minden		own flak	n/a
08-12-44	Uffz.	Klingelhöfer, Paul	WIA	11	Bf 109G-14	464163	yl 16	Hopsten a/f	1012	P-47	368 FG
12-02-45	Uffz.	Klingelhöfer, Paul	WIFA	11	Fw 190D-9	210169		Plantlünne a/f		landing	non-op
31-12-43	Uffz.	Klumpe, Ernst	KIFA	4	Fw 190A-6	530396	bl 5	Anderlues-15km W Charleroi	1200	crashed	non-op
19-09-44	Ofhr.	Knappmann, Klaus	KIA	6	Fw 190A-8	732050	bk 9	Arnhem area	1800	combat	
21-06-41	Gefr.	Knees, Christian	KIA	9	Bf 109F-2			near Desvres	1230	Spitfire	
17-02-43	Uffz.	Kniess, Friedrich	KIA	3	Fw 190A-5	2546	yl 5	near Lake Ilmen (PQ 19713)		hit ground	n/a
22-11-41	Fw.	Knobeloch, Karl-Heinz	WIFA	6	Fw 190A-1	41	br 2	Bruges-Ostend		crashed	n/a
28-10-44	Obfw.	Knobeloch, Karl-Heinz	KIA	6	Fw 190A-9	750139	bk 1	Krefeld Ürdingen	1450	Spitfire	412 Sqd
03-07-43	Uffz.	Knobloch, Bruno	KIFA	11	Bf 109G-3	16264	rd 3	near Lille Vendeville		crashed	non-op
19-05-40	Hptm.	Knüppel, Herwig	KIA	II CO	Bf 109E-3	1542		near Lille-Valenciennes	2005	Hurricane	253 Sqd
27-12-40	Gefr.	Koch, Dietrich	KIA	9	Bf 109E-1	4911	yl 6	W of Le Tréport	1345	Blenheim	59 Sqd
29-03-43	Uffz.	Koch, Joachim	KIA	10J	Fw 190A-5	2576	bk 4 +bomb	Brighton	1215	Spitfire	610 Sqd
28-06-44	Lt.	Koch, Martin	WIA	1	Fw 190A-8	171076	wh 2	Serquigny		Spitfire	
19-03-45	Fw.	Köhler, Arnfried	KIA	13	Fw 190D-9			6km ESE of Fürstenau		P-51	78 FG
12-10-44	Uffz.	Kohler, Erich	KIA	3	Fw 190A-8	732041	yl 8	E of Hannover	1200	P-47	56 or 78 FG
08-02-44	Uffz.	Kolodzie, Herbert	WIFA	4	Fw 190A-6	550726	bl 12	Wevelgem		landing	n/a
26-08-44	Lt.	Kopp, Walter	WIA	10	Bf 109G-6	413492	bk 2	Warvillers a/f	1945	landing	n/a
14-01-45	Lt.	Kopp, Walter	KIA	10	Bf 109K-4	330380	bk 28	W of Koblenz (PO-PP)	1200	Tempest	486 Sqd
24-12-44	Uffz.	Körner, Franz	WIA	8	Fw 190D-9	500031	bl 2	Haltern-Dülmen		P-47	36 FG
21-10-41	Uffz.	Korte, Werner	KIA	8	Bf 109F-4	7252		Dannes, near Camiers	1310	Spitfire	
07-03-41	Gefr.	Korthaus	WIFA	5	Bf 109E-7	3711	bk 6	Detmold		crashed	n/a
12-02-42	Obfw.	Koslowski, Eduard	KIA	9	Fw 190A-2	2068	yl 1	N of Calais	1330	Spitfire	72 Sqd
16-09-44	Uffz.	Kracht, Jürgen	POW	7	Fw 190A-8	730513	br 7	E of Vaals	1745	P-47 or P-38	50, 370, 404 FG
02-07-44	Uffz.	Kraft, Gerhard	KIA	6	Fw 190A-8	680107	bk 5	Le Mesnil S of Lisieux	0645	Spitfire	411 Sqd
30-11-42	Fw.	Kraft, Werner	WIFA	9	Fw 190A-4	675		NW of Le Havre		engine	n/a
17-08-43	Fw.	Kraft, Werner	WIA	9	Bf 109G-6	19466	yl 11	near Waterloo-Hasselt	1130	B-17	385 or 100 BG
16-03-44	Fw.	Kraft, Werner	WIA	10	Bf 109G-6	161791	bk 10	SE of Vitry-les-Reims	1430	P-47	78 FG
23-12-44	Ogfr.	Krägeloh, Dieter	WIFA	3	Fw 190A-8	738172	yl 13	Rondorf		no fuel	n/a
01-01-45	Ogfr.	Krägeloh, Dieter	POW	3	Fw 190D-9	500093	yl 13	St Anna ter Muiden	0915	Spitfire	308 Sqd
23-07-41	Ogfr.	Krämer, Ernst	KIA	9	Bf 109F-2	8847		Radinghem	2030	Spitfire	
14-08-41	Lt.	Kranefeld, Kurt	WAC	8	none			Lille		vehicle	n/a
16-07-43	Oblt.	Kranefeld, Kurt	WIFA	I St	Fw 190A-5	410261	gr 2	Zandvoort, 3km W of Haarlem		engine	n/a
26-04-44	Oblt.	Kranefeld, Kurt	KAC	1 CO	none			Cazaux		drowned	non-op
20-10-43	Uffz.	Kratzel, Anton	KIA	2	Fw 190A-5	5894	bk 8	Chimay NW of Cambrai	1400	B-17	
29-11-43	Lt.	Kraus, Theobald	WIA	9	Bf 109G-6	440015		near Ahren		B-17	
28-10-44	Oblt.	Kraus, Theobald	WIA	10	Bf 109G-14	462674	bk 11	Senden	1555	Spitfire	412 Sqd
28-02-45	Oblt.	Kraus, Theobald	WIA	10 CO	Fw 190D-9	400256	bk 16	SE of Gütersloh	0840	no fuel	n/a
13-03-45	Oblt.	Kraus, Theobald	WIA	10 CO	Fw 190D-9	500615	bk 18	NE of Greven	1602	fighter	
14-12-44	Gefr.	Kraus, Wolfgang	KIA	12	Bf 109G-14	462983	yl 11	5km NE of Borghorst	1445	Tempest	56 Sqd
25-02-45	Hptm.	Krause, Günther	KIA	3	Fw 190D-9/R11	600984	yl 9	NE of Köln-Wahn	0825	P-47	36 FG
02-08-44	Lt.	Krauss, Albrecht	KIFA	8	Fw 190A-8	731741	bl 11	Reinsehlen a/f		engine	non-op
09-09-44	Uffz.	Kreth, Georg	WIA	6	Fw 190A-8	175122		Lackhausen		own flak	n/a
21-04-45	Uffz.	Kreth, Georg	KIA	6	Fw 190D-9			NE of Wismar		Tempest	486 Sqd
13-09-43	Uffz.	Kretschmer, Horst	KIFA	1	Fw 190A-5	410222		Hazebrouck		engine	non-op
15-07-43	Uffz.	Krieg, Heinrich	WIA	5	Fw 190A-4	789	bk 4	NW of Abbeville	1700	Spitfire	602 Sqd
27-08-43	Uffz.	Krieg, Heinrich	KIA	5	Fw 190A-4	2379	bk 5	nr Merville-2km S St Venant		Spitfire	
19-08-41	Ogfr.	Krieger, Alois	KIA	2	Bf 109F-4	8363		Channel		fighter	
24-12-44	Lt.	Krieger, Hans-Hermann	POW	1	Fw 190D-9	600164	wh 10	Liège	1130	engine	n/a
25-03-45	Fw.	Kroll, Gerhard	WIA	15	Fw 190D-9		yl 15	NW of Bocholt	1500	fighter	
07-09-40	Oblt.	Krug, Hans	POW	4 CO	Bf 109E-4/B	5385	wh 12	Pluckley, Kent	1900	fighter	
17-03-45	Uffz.	Krümpelmann, Eugen	KIFA	11	Fw 190D-9	210262	yl 11	Plantlünne a/f	1635	engine	n/a
16-09-44	Uffz.	Kruse, Ottomar	POW	8	Fw 190A-8	171505	bl 13	Nutherveld	1810	P-47	50 FG
28-02-45	Uffz.	Krusen, Bruno	KIA	5	Fw 190D-9			S of Mönchen-Gladbach	1230	P-47	406 FG
09-04-43	Obfw.	Kruska, Kurt	KIA	6	Fw 190A-4	5668	br 11	NW of Boulogne		Spitfire	611 Sqd
14-07-43	Uffz.	Kubon, Harry	WIA	5	Fw 190A-4	7046	bk 4	Somme Est-E of Amiens		P-47	78 FG
11-12-42	Uffz.	Kühn, Bruno	KIA	3	Fw 190A-4	7028	yl 10	Fiennes, N of Hardinghen		Spitfire	401 Sqd
25-03-45	Uffz.	Kühn, Hermann	KIFA	5	Fw 190D-9			Nordhorn a/f	0557	takeoff collision	non-op
26-12-44	Lt.	Kühne, Wolfgang	KIA	12	Bf 109K-4	331331	bl 20	Aachen-Liège	1410	P-51	
19-01-44	Uffz.	Kuhnert, Kurt	KIFA	3	Fw 190A-6	550738	yl 7	NE of Revin-Namur		collision	non-op
13-08-44	Uffz.	Kukla, Hans	WIA	4	Fw 190A-7	340329	bl 9	NE of Le Mans	0825	P-51	363 FG
04-01-45	Uffz.	Kukla, Hans	no	4	Fw 190D-9			near Osnabrück	1350	engine	n/a

Date	Rank	Name	Fate		Aircraft	W.Nr.	Marking	Location	Time	Cause	Unit
22-01-45	Uffz.	Kukla, Hans	WIA	4	Fw 190D-9	210943	bl 7	N of Ibbenbüren	1120	Spitfire	421 Sqd
20-01-43	Lt.	Kümmerling, Hans	KIA	8	Fw 190A-4	7037	bk 8	3km W of Cap Gris Nez	0915	Typhoon	609 Sqd
28-06-44	Oblt.	Kunz, Franz	WIA	2 CO	Fw 190A-7	431163	bk 2	Boissy-le-Bois		Spitfire	
01-01-45	Oblt.	Kunz, Franz	WIA	2 CO	Fw 190D-9	210953	bk 1	NE Rotterdam-Polsbroek	0845	own flak	n/a
01-01-45	Gefr.	Kunz, Willi	KIA	7	Fw 190D-9	500105	bl 1	W of Borger		own flak	n/a
30-01-44	Lt.	Kunze, Klaus	WIA	2	Fw 190A-6	531061	bk 2	S of Rheine		P-38 or P-47	
16-03-44	Lt.	Kunze, Klaus	KIA	1 St	Fw 190A-6	550916	gr 3	St. Dizier		P-47	78 FG
23-09-40	Fw.	Küpper, Arnold	POW	8	Bf 109E-4	3735	bk 4	Isle of Grain S of-London	1055	Spitfire	92 Sqd
26-08-44	Lt.	Lampe, Helmut	KIA	5	Fw 190A-8	731748	wh 5	Amiens Beauvais		Spitfire	416 or 421 Sqd
01-01-45	Uffz.	Lampferhoff, Ernst	POW	5	Fw 190D-9	210193	wh 7	S of Goes	0930	ship flak	n/a
13-11-44	Lt.	Landsberg, Wilhelm	KIFA	12	Bf 109K-4	330368	bl 20	Plantlünne a/f	1603	crashed	non-op
03-09-44	Hptm.	Lang, Emil	KIA	II CO	Fw 190A-8	171240	gr 1	Brussels N of St Trond	1330	P-51	55 FG
17-08-43	Lt.	Lange, Friedrich	WIA	5	Fw 190A-5	710006	bk 10	Eindhoven 2km SW Oerle	1805	B-17	
02-03-44	Lt.	Lange, Friedrich	KIA	6 CO	Fw 190A-6	470202	bk 6	Polch-Mayen Eifel-		P-47	365 FG
25-02-45	Ogfr.	Lange, Helmut	KIA	1	Fw 190D-9	210992	wh 3	near Köln-Wahn	0825	P-47	36 FG
06-04-45	Uffz.	Langer, Alfred	WIFA	7	Fw 190D-9			Hamburg Fuhlsbüttel a/f		landing	non-op
12-05-44	Uffz.	Langhammer, Gerhard	WIFA	7	Fw 190A-7	340001	br 4	Epinoy near Werkendam		landing	non-op
13-05-40	Gefr.	Langner, Günther	KIA	1	Bf 109E					RAF ftr	264 or 66 Sqd
03-11-43	Fw.	Latka, Wilhelm	KIA	12	Bf 109G-6/U4	20706	bl 3	LBH Mitte	1450	P-47	56 FG
14-12-44	Obfw.	Laub, Karl	KIA	11	Bf 109K-4	330357	yl 8	NW of Münster-Burgsteinfurt	1445	Tempest	56 Sqd
23-01-45	Lt.	Lauer, Werner	WIA	1	Fw 190D-9	211059	wh 8	W of Gelow?		combat	
03-10-43	Uffz.	Leder, Hans-Joachim	WIA	12	Bf 109G-6	20783	bl 6	5km NW of Noyon	1835	Spitfire	341 or 485 Sqd
20-08-44	Fw.	Leder, Hans-Joachim	KIA	12	Bf 109G-6	165647	bl 14	near Rouen	1530	light flak	n/a
15-10-44	Ogfr.	Leder, Josef	KIFA	1	Fw 190A-9	205289	wh 7	Krefeld a/f		landing	n/a
28-03-42	Obfw.	Leibold, Erwin	WIA	I St	Fw 190A-2	5205		Marquise		Spitfire	
26-07-42	Obfw.	Leibold, Erwin	KIA	I St	Fw 190A-2	5228		off Arques		Spitfire	91 Sqd
16-05-43	Uffz.	Leicht, Hermann	KIA	4/54	Bf 109G-4	19210	wh 11-	N of Philipine		combat	
15-07-44	Ofhr.	Leinberger, Rudolf	WIA	11	Bf 109G-6	412928	yl 15	near Paris	1155	combat	
01-01-45	Lt.	Leinberger, Rudolf	WIA	11	Bf 109K-4	330354	bk 18	Kirchhellen a/f	0955	own flak	n/a
05-04-45	Lt.	Leinberger, Rudolf	KIFA	14	Fw 190D-9			Varrelbusch a/f		landing	n/a
05-06-40	Uffz.	Leisse, Paul	KIA	4	Bf 109E-3		wh 9	Le Touquet Chièvres		Curtiss H75	
28-07-43	Uffz.	Leitz, Emil	KIFA	7	Bf 109G-4	19349	wh 4	Nordholz-Ostfriesland a/f	0838	takeoff	n/a
03-05-43	Uffz.	Lentz, Ludwig	KIFA	11/54	Bf 109G-3	16275	rd 7	NW of Wevelgem a/f	1347	takeoff	n/a
10-08-44	Lt.	Lenz, Harald	WIA	11	Bf 109G-6	163184	yl 18	N of Ablis	0930	P-51	364 FG
01-01-45	Oblt.	Lenz, Harald	KIA	11	Bf 109K-4	330385	yl 18	Harderwijk (Zuider Zee)	0850	own flak	n/a
27-04-44	Uffz.	Lessin, Ernst	KIA	12	Bf 109G-6	161772	bl 12	Reims-Cramant	1815	bomber gunner	
02-10-42	Lt.	Leuschel, Rudolf	WIA	6	Fw 190A-4	7057	br 3	near Cambrai		Spitfire+landing	
25-02-44	Hptm.	Leuschel, Rudolf	KIA	8 CO	Fw 190A-7	340262	bl 11	16km S of Arlon	1200	P-47	4 FG
14-05-43	Oblt.	Leykauf, Erwin	no	12/54 CO	Bf 109G-6		outline 11+	Wevelgem a/f	1230	taxi	n/a
31-08-40	Uffz.	Liebeck, Horst	POW	7	Bf 109E-1	6309		Stansted-London	1840	Spitfire	54 Sqd
12-08-41	Fw.	Liebherr, Georg	KIFA	2/E	Bf 109E-4	839		Dixmuiden Wevelgem		engine	non-op
24-02-44	Gefr.	Lienich, Heinz	WIFA	11	Bf 109G-3	16293	yl 2	SSE of St. Dizier	1110	engine	non-op
08-06-44	Gefr.	Lienich, Heinz	WIA	11	Bf 109G-6	162707	yl 15	5km SW of Caen	1315	Spitfire	
22-06-44	Gefr.	Lienich, Heinz	KIA	11	Bf 109G-6	163499	yl 16	Cornier-S of Tinche	1500	P-47	365 or 368 FG
27-08-42	Uffz.	Lindelaub, Friedrich	WIA	1	Fw 190A-2	5220	wh 7	Ardres		Spitfire	71 Sqd
11-11-43	Fw.	Lindelaub, Friedrich	WIFA	1	Fw 190A-6	550470	wh 7	Wevelgem		landing	n/a
04-03-44	Obfw.	Lindelaub, Friedrich	KIA	1	Fw 190A-7	642979	wh 15	N of Charleville	1415	weather	non-op
12-12-40	Fw.	Lindemann, Rudolf	POW	7	Bf 109E-4	3708	bk 2	Abbey Farm, Kent	1310	Hurricane	229 Sqd
08-11-41	Oblt.	Lindemann, Theo	WIA	II St	Fw 190A-1	52	<	S of Dunkirk	1310	Spitfire	317 Sqd
06-06-44	Lt.	Lindner, Erich	WIA	7	Fw 190A-8	170383	br 10	St Opportune		P-51	352 FG
21-10-41	Gefr.	Linecker, Alois	KIFA	1/E	Bf 109E-7	916		Maldegem	1530	takeoff	non-op
20-12-43	Uffz.	Lissack, Gerhard	WIA	7	Fw 190A-6	470007	br 11	near Vitry	1115	Spitfire	331 or 332 Sqd
29-01-44	Uffz.	Lissack, Gerhard	WIA	7	Fw 190A-6	470207	br 5	S of Cochem		P-38	20 FG
28-06-44	Uffz.	Lissack, Gerhard	KIA	7	Fw 190A-8	170915	wh 1	Caen-Emieville		Spitfire	
26-03-42	Lt.	Löhr, Alois	KIFA	6	Fw 190A-1	72		near Abbeville-Hautvillers		engine	n/a
13-05-43	Uffz.	Lonsdorfer, Werner	KIA	6	Fw 190A-4	2433	br 13	near St. Omer		Spitfire	
27-11-44	Ofhr.	Lorberg, Helmut	KIA	12	Bf 109K-4	330152	bl 26	Wettringen near Rheine	1230	P-51	
07-06-40	Obfw.	Lorenz, Friedrich	KIA	5	Bf 109E-3			Bois Jean a/fMontreuil		Hurricane	43 Sqd
25-03-43	Lt.	Lörzer, Hans-Günther	WIA	6	Fw 190A-4	7077	br 7	Arras		Spitfire	64 Sqd
03-10-43	Lt.	Lörzer, Hans-Günther	WIA	7	Fw 190A-5	530726	br 8	WNW of Abbeville		combat	222 Sqd
24-02-44	Uffz.	Loschinski, Gerhard	KIA	7	Fw 190A-6	531072	br 12	Ems moor	1300	P-51	357 FG
01-01-45	Ogfr.	Lott, Hubert	KIA	5	Fw 190D-9	500102	wh 11	Hellegatspolder (Zuider Zee)	0900	own flak	n/a
13-02-45	Uffz.	Loy, Karl	KIFA	1	Fw 190D-9	500091	wh 16	Winterswijk	1340	no fuel	n/a
07-08-41	Lt.	Luckhardt, Heinz	WIA	8	Bf 109F-4			30km SE of Guines	1130	unknown	

Date	Rank	Name	Fate	Unit	Aircraft	WkNr	Marking	Location	Time	Cause	Sqd
12-04-42	Lt.	Luckhardt, Heinz	KIA	Ge St	Fw 190A-2	5217		Calais-Wizernes	1335	Spitfire	303 Sqd
21-06-41	Obfw.	Lüders, Franz	POW	6	Bf 109E-7	6497	br 2	SE of Ramsgate	1330	Spitfire	145 or 616 Sqd
10-05-40	Lt.	Ludewig, Wolfgang	WIA	9	Bf 109E-1			SW of The Hague		flak	n/a
25-06-43	Uffz.	Lühs, Walter	KIA	9	Bf 109G-6	15428	yl 13	North Sea		missing	
16-05-41	Fw.	Lyhs, Heinrich	KIFA	9	Bf 109F-2	8106		St. Brieuc a/f	1930	landing	n/a
09-05-44	Gefr.	Machner, Siegfried	KIA	1	Fw 190A-6	551139	wh 1	Maspelt-Eifel		P-51	354 FG
24-04-42	Obfw.	Mackenstedt,	WIA	6	Fw 190A-3	254	br 4	Abbeville Wilhelm		Spitfire	485 Sqd
30-07-43	Obfw.	Mackenstedt,	KIA	6	Fw 190A-5	7311	br 6	Doerinchem Wilhelm		B-17	
14-01-44	Uffz.	Maletz, Gerhard	KIA	6	Fw 190A-6	470220	bk 6	near Abbeville		Spitfire	132 Sqd
22-06-44	Gefr.	Malm, Willibald	WIA	12	none			Buc a/f		air attack	
20-08-44	Uffz.	Malm, Willibald	WIA	12	Bf 109G-6	165541	bl 5	near Rouen	1530	light flak	n/a
25-06-44	Uffz.	Marek, Robert	KIA	2	Fw 190A-8	170402	bk 6	SSW of Caen	1045	P-47	365 FG
17-04-45	Fw.	Marischka, Hans	KIA	5	Fw 190D-9			Hamburg Harburg		Spitfire	350 Sqd
20-01-43	Uffz.	Marquardt, Heinz	POW	6	Bf 109G-4	16113	br 12	E of Ramsgate	1300	Typhoon	609 Sqd
17-09-41	Obfw.	Martin, Max	WIA	8	Bf 109F-4	7122	bk 3	St. Omer	1545	Spitfire collision	308 Sqd
13-08-44	Lt.	Marx, Wolfgang	KIA	4	Fw 190A-8	173023	bl 14	NE of Le Mans	0825	P-51	363 FG
23-12-44	Lt.	Mathony, Werner	WIFA	2	Fw 190A-9	750136	bk 6	Krefeld		landing	n/a
31-08-43	Oblt.	Matoni, Walter	WIA	II St	Fw 190A-5	530118	bk 1	Montdidier		B-17	
07-10-43	Lt.	Matthiesen, Johannes	KIA	1	Fw 190A-4	617	wh 5	Wielsbeke	0741	Typhoon	198 Sqd
15-04-43	Oblt.	Matuschka, Siegfried	KIA	4/54 CO	Bf 109G-4	19222		near St. Inglevert		Spitfire	
20-01-43	Lt.	Mayer, Hans	WIA	6	Bf 109G-4	16121	br 6	Ramsgate	1300	Typhoon	609 Sqd
10-03-43	Lt.	Mayer, Hans	WIA	6	Fw 190A-4	7059	br 6	Arras		Spitfire	B Hill Wing
10-10-43	Lt.	Mayer, Hans	WIA	8	Fw 190A-6	530770	bl 7	Enschede Twente a/f	1530	P-47	
15-03-44	Lt.	Mayer, Hans	KIA	7	Fw 190A-7	340293	br 2	SW of Bapaume		Spitfire	401 Sqd
30-07-43	Fw.	Mayer, Wilhelm	WIA	6	Fw 190A-5	7222	br 4	Netterden		B-17	
31-12-43	Fw.	Mayer, Wilhelm	WIFA	7	Fw 190A-6	470005	br 9	Le Fresnes		engine	n/a
04-01-45	Lt.	Mayer, Wilhelm	KIA	8 CO	Fw 190D-9	500052	bl 16	Lohnerbruch	1400	Spitfire	442 Sqd
02-03-44	Uffz.	Meidinger, Georg	WIA	6	Fw 190A-7	642001	bk 5	NE of Cochem	1150	P-47	365 FG
15-03-44	Lt.	Meier, Johann-Hermann	KIFA	1 CO	Fw 190A-6	470057	wh 8	Florennes a/f		ground collision	n/a
13-03-45	Uffz.	Meiss, Heinz	KIA	7	Fw 190D-9			Unna-Werl	1630	Spitfire XIV	130 Sqd
25-12-44	Fw.	Meindl, Bernhard	KIA	6	Fw 190D-9	500065	bk 18	Fürstenau Horneburg-		P-51	
12-10-44	Uffz.	Meinel, Erhard	KIA	7	Fw 190A-8	730965	bl 12	W of Wunstorf	1200	P-51	364 FG
11-06-43	Uffz.	Meissner, Anton	WIA	4/54	Bf 109G-4	19368	wh 14-	Wilhelmshaven		B-17	
10-05-41	Uffz.	Melzer, Hermann	KIFA	8	Bf 109F-2			W of Warnemünde	0830	takeoff	non-op
10-06-44	Lt.	Menge, Helmut	KIA	4	Fw 190A-8	730414	bl 10	Orne Estuary	0630	fighter	
05-12-40	Obfw.	Menge, Robert	WIA	3	Bf 109E-4	6324		Folkestone	1215	Spitfire	74 or 92 Sqd
14-06-41	Lt.	Menge, Robert	KIA	3	Bf 109E-7	6490		S of Marquise		Spitfire	92 Sqd
19-08-43	Fw.	Mensing, Wilhelm	WIA	7	Bf 109G-4	19783	wh 3	s'Hertogen-bosch-Waspik	1930	B-17	
23-03-44	Uffz.	Menz, Dieter	KIA	6	Fw 190A-6	550575	bl 13	N s'Hertogen bosch-	1345	B-17	
28-06-44	Lt.	Menze, Josef	WIA	12	Bf 109G-6	165186	bl 10	W of Dreux-l'Aigle	1120	Spitfire	
07-07-44	Lt.	Menze, Josef	KIA	12	Bf 109G-6	163616	bl 1	20km E of Caen	1100	Spitfire	401 Sqd
13-07-44	Ogfr.	Merten, Helmut	KIA	4	Fw 190A-8	170319	bl 7	WSW of Bernay-Eure	1705	P-47	362 FG
18-03-45	Uffz.	Merz, Werner	KIA	14	Fw 190D-9			W of Twistringen	1235	P-51	339 FG
17-07-43	Uffz.	Meyer, Alex	WIFA	12	Bf 109G-6	15450		Weser Estuary		engine	n/a
20-10-43	Uffz.	Meyer, Alex	KIA	12	Bf 109G-6	18837	bl 1	N Hirson-6km NE of Chimay	1350	B-17	
01-01-45	Lt.	Meyer, Gottfried	KIA	9	Bf 109K-4	330404	wh 15	near Vrasene	0945	crashed	n/a
24-06-43	Uffz.	Meyer, Hans	KIA	5	Fw 190A-4	2404	bk 18	10km W of Somme Est	1450	Typhoon	486 Sqd
13-03-43	Obfw.	Meyer, Hermann	KIA	4	Fw 190A-4	5615	wh 12	SE of Le Tréport		Spitfire	403 Sqd
19-08-43	Oblt.	Meyer, Johannes	KIA	10	Fw 190A-5	2620	bl 4	25km E of Amiens		fighter	
22-06-44	Lt.	Meyer,KIA		11	Bf 109G-6	440712	yl 3	Cherbourg Klaus-Rudolph	1430	P-47	365 or 368 FG
10-12-44	Fhj-Gefr	Meyer, Kurt	KIA	2	Fw 190A-8	734021	bk 15	W of Meppen-Schöningsdorf	1630	P-47	373 FG
21-08-41	Obfw.	Meyer, Walter	WIFA	6	Fw 190A-1	2	br 2	Moorseele		engine	n/a
11-10-42	Lt.	Meyer, Walter	KIFA	7	Fw 190A-4	660	wh 5	Wevelgem	1517	ground collision	n/a
03-04-43	Uffz.	Meyere, Albert	KIA	5	Fw 190A-5	1159	bk 5	Channel Narrows	1630	Spitfire	403 or 416 Sqd
10-04-42	Lt.	Michalski, Werner	KIA	4	Fw 190A-1	67	wh 5	Abbeville Drucat a/f-	1745	Spitfire	
31-08-43	Hptm.	Michel, Wilhelm	WIA	8	none			Lille-Nord a/f		strafed	
28-05-44	Uffz.	Mickmann, Bernhard	KIFA	7	Fw 190A-6	550727	br 1	Mont de Marsan		collision	non-op
08-06-40	Lt.	Mietusch, Klaus	POW	7	Bf 109E-1	2746		Neufchatel	1030	Hurricane	
20-03-43	Hptm.	Mietusch, Klaus	WIA	7 CO	Fw 190A-4	7147		Gatschina a/f		engine	n/a
08-03-44	Maj.	Mietusch, Klaus	WIA	III CO	Bf 109G-6	162032	bk 21	N of Meppen	1600	P-47	352 FG
12-04-44	Maj.	Mietusch, Klaus	WIA	III CO	Bf 109G-6	162345	bk 24	Rouvres-Étain	1415	landing	n/a
17-07-44	Maj.	Mietusch, Klaus	WIA	III CO	Bf 109G-6/U4	440640	wh 20	ArgentanAlençon	1700	Spitfire	411 Sqd
17-09-44	Maj.	Mietusch, Klaus	KIA	III CO	Bf 109G-6/U4	441646	bk 25	Rath-Aldekerk	1511	P-51	361 FG
24-02-44	Uffz.	Mohr, Gerhard	KIA	2	Fw 190A-4	587	bk 2	Rheine a/f		P-47	56 FG
04-01-45	Ogfr.	Molge, Werner	no	8	Fw 190D-9		bl 17	1mi E of Nordhorn		Spitfire	442 Sqd

Date	Rank	Name	Fate	Unit	Aircraft	WkNr	Markings	Location	Time	Cause	Sqd
05-04-42	Fw.	Mondry, Georg	WIFA	7	Fw 190A-1	84	wh 8	Gravelines		engine	n/a
31-05-43	Lt.	Mondry, Georg	KIA	5	Fw 190A-5	7303	bk 14	sea nr Ostend	1640	Spitfire	403 or 421 Sqd
19-08-43	Fw.	Mössner, Werner	WIA	9	Bf 109G-6	16394	yl 12	Waalwijk N of Breda-	1900	B-17	
29-06-44	Fw.	Muche, Günter	KIA	3	Fw 190A-8	170077	yl 7	SW of Caen		Spitfire	
19-11-42	Uffz.	Müller, Heinz	KIA	9	Fw 190A-4	5623	yl 4	SW Flushing-	1600	Spitfire	4 FG
								10km N Zeebrugge			
01-04-45	Uffz.	Müller, Heinz	KIA	13	Fw 190D-9			10km W of Cloppenburg		flak	n/a
04-01-43	Fw.	Müller, Herbert	KIA	10J	Fw 190A-4	2439	bk 4 +bomb	Winchelsea	1400	hit cable	n/a
13-06-44	Oblt.	Müller, Hermann	KIA	7	Fw 190A-8	730491	br 12	N of Caen		flak	n/a
06-03-44	Ogfr.	Müller, Johann	WIFA	4	Fw 190A-6	551144	bl 5	Vendeville a/f		landing	non-op
19-12-42	Oblt.	Müller, Kurt	KIA	10J CO	Fw 190A-4	712	wh 9	ENE of Deal	1512	flak+ Typhoon	609 Sqd
15-08-44	Fw.	Müller, Kurt	KIA	5	Fw 190A-8	731746	wh 5	Rambouillet		P-47	373 FG
19-01-43	Uffz.	Müller, Leo	no	4	Bf 109G-4	16125		Abbeville Drucat a/f-		aborted t/o	no FF
26-05-43	Uffz.	Müller, Leo	WIFA	4	Fw 190A-4	2395	wh 7	Merville a/f-West		engine	n/a
05-10-40	Gefr.	Müller, Otto-Günther	KIFA	5	Bf 109E-4	5384		Marquise-West		wing failed	n/a
29-07-43	Uffz.	Müller, Walter	KIA	11	Bf 109G-6	20307	rd 3	SW of Merville		Spitfire	331 Sqd
07-11-40	Obfw.	Müller, Wilhelm	KIA	3	Bf 109E-4	677	yl 1	N of Margate	1420	Hurricane	249 Sqd
07-10-44	Obfw.	Müller, Wilhelm	KIA	6	Fw 190A-8	171649	bk 14	Nijmegen	1640	Spitfire	442 Sqd
25-03-45	Fw.	Müller-Berneck,Gerhard	WIA	15	Fw 190D-9			near Bocholt		fighter	
18-08-40	Lt.	Müller-Dühe, Gerhard	KIA	7	Bf 109E-1			Chilham, ne Canterbury	1830	Hurricane	32 Sqd
27-02-43	Lt.	Müller-Göbs, Karl	KIA	5	Fw 190A-4	7063	bk 9	60km NW of Dunkirk	1430	Spitfire	402 or 403Sqd
28-05-44	Uffz.	Munack, Paul	KIFA	2	Fw 190A-8	170119	br 5	Mont de Marsan		collision	non-op
23-12-43	Fw.	Münch, Heinz	KIFA	3	Fw 190A-5	410236	yl 9	Namur-Profondeville	1430	engine	non-op
07-12-42	Ogfr.	Muskatewitz, Willi	KIA	1	Fw 190A-4	5609	wh 7	Friston, Sussex	1250	hit hill	n/a
01-05-45	Fw.	Napierski, Walter	WIA	1	Fw 190D-9	210961	wh 6	near Schwarzenbeck	1110	Spitfire	
22-06-43	Hptm.	Naumann, Hans	WIA	6 CO	Fw 190A-5	7300	br 3	near Antwerp	1000	P-47	
23-06-44	Hptm.	Naumann, Hans	WIA	II CO	Fw 190A-8	730425	bk 30	SSW of Caen		flak	n/a
10-12-40	Lt.	Nels, Franz	WIFA	1/E	Bf 109E-7	5611		Hochgraben		landing	non-op
23-08-42	Lt.	Neu, Wolfgang	WIFA	3	Fw 190A-2	2126		Wizernes a/f		crashed	n/a
09-01-43	Oblt.	Neu, Wolfgang	WIA	3	Fw 190A-4	5642		near Marquise		Spitfire	
22-04-44	Hptm.	Neu, Wolfgang	KIA	4 CO	Fw 190A-6	530755	bl 16	Katenborn-Eifel		combat	
17-09-44	Uffz.	Neumann, Artur	KIA	4	Fw 190A-8	171535	bl 7	Kleve		Spitfire	602 Sqd
24-06-41	Lt.	Neumann, Erdmann	KIA	9	Bf 109F-2			S of Gravelines Audruicq	2040	Spitfire	
02-11-43	Uffz.	Ney, Robert	KIA	6	Fw 190A-6	530711	bk 5	Albert, SW of Bapaume	1250	Mustang	414 Sqd
27-11-44	Fw.	Niedermeyer, Willi	WIA	9	Bf 109G-14	464309	wh 15	Salzbergen	1220	P-51	
15-04-45	Fw.	Niedermeyer, Willi	KIA	5	Fw 190D-9			Winsen-Drebber		Spitfire	80 Sqd
27-06-41	Gefr.	Niese, Alfred	no	E	Bf 109E-7	1132		Haamstede		takeoff	non-op
25-06-43	Fw.	Niese, Alfred	KIA	9	Bf 109G-6	15419	yl 3	North Sea		missing	
17-10-42	Fw.	Niesel, Karl	KIA	10J	Fw 190A-4	2403	bk 14+ <bomb	S of Hastings	1430	Typhoon	486 Sqd
01-01-45	Ogfr.	Niessen, Manfred	no	3	Fw 190D-9	400233	yl 5	Blokland near Utrecht	0845	own flak	n/a
13-02-45	Ogfr.	Niessen, Manfred	no	3	Fw 190D-9			N of Lingen		crashed	n/a
24-02-45	Ogfr.	Niessen, Manfred	no	3	Fw 190D-9/R11	210951	yl 11	N of Kirchhellen a/f	1000	engine fire	n/a
17-04-45	Ogfr.	Niessen, Manfred	KIA	3	ground			Grevesmühlen		train strafed	
23-08-44	Ogfr.	Nieter, Heinz	WIFA	10	Bf 109G-6	163962	bl 9	Warvillers	1530	takeoff	non-op
28-10-44	Uffz.	Nieter, Heinz	WIA	10	Bf 109G-14	461509	bk 12	W of Dülmen- Merfelder Bruch	1555	Spitfire	412 Sqd
25-04-45	Uffz.	Nieter, Heinz	WIA	1	Fw 190D-9			Hemmingsdorf	0615	flak	n/a
02-07-44	Lt.	Nink, Wilhelm	WIA	3	Fw 190A-8	174032	yl 3	E of Caen		Spitfire	
23-09-44	Lt.	Nink, Wilhelm	KIA	3	Fw 190A-8	175105	yl 7	Aalten	1545	P-51	339 FG
12-10-41	Fw.	Nischik, Ernst	no	E	Bf 109F-2	5738		Moorseele		crashed	non-op
24-07-40	Hptm.	Noack, Erich	KIA	II CO	Bf 109E-1			Dover-Marquise-Ost	1300	Spitfire	
10-10-43	Uffz.	Oeckel, Hans	WIA	12	Bf 109G-6	19645		Woerendonk		B-17	
21-01-44	Fw.	Oeckel, Hans	WIA	12	Bf 109G-6	410723	bl 1	E of Laon-Sissonne	1445	P-47	353 FG
17-07-44	Lt.	Oeckel, Hans	KIA	12	Bf 109G-6	165193	bl 7	S Liseux Alençon-	1630	Spitfire	411 or 602 Sqd
08-08-40	Oblt.	Oehm, Willy	KIA	8	Bf 109E-4			E of Margate	1315	Spitfire	64 Sqd
22-09-41	Uffz.	Ohlmann, Hans	no	E	Bf 109E-7	4069		Brugge		engine	non-op
28-09-43	Uffz.	Oltmanns, Rudolf	WIFA	1	Fw 190A-5	470051		Grimbergen a/f		landing	non-op
02-07-44	Uffz.	Oltmanns, Rudolf	KIA	1	Fw 190A-8	171080	wh 1	S Aigle-Falaise	2100	Spitfire	453 Sqd
17-07-41	Uffz.	Ömler, Gerhard	KIA	9	Bf 109F-2	12858	yl 5	10km W of Le Touquet	1850	own flak	n/a
02-03-44	Uffz.	Onken, Herbert	KIA	3	Fw 190A-6	550915	yl 5	near Trier Wittlich-	1145	collision	n/a
17-04-45	Lt.	Ossenkop, Karl-Heinz	WIA	2	Fw 190D-9			near Ratzenburg	1130	Spitfire	
14-05-43	Lt.	Ostrowitski, Gerhard	WIA	12/54	none			Wevelgem	1230	bomb	n/a
17-04-45	Fw.	Ostrowitzki, Bruno	KIFA	1	Fw 190D-9			Lake Schwerin		crashed	n/a
09-08-44	Uffz.	Ostrzecha, Paul	KIA	2	Fw 190A-8	170124	bk 6	Chartres-Orleans		P-47	373 FG
21-06-41	Uffz.	Otto, Ewald	POW	6	Bf 109E-7	6462	br 13	SE of Ramsgate	1400	Spitfire	74 Sqd
14-08-43	Fw.	Otto, Gottfried	WIFA	9	Bf 109G-4	19790		Enghien		engine	non-op
30-01-44	Fhj.	Otto, Gottfried	KIA	9	Bf 109G-6	27025	wh 8	Leersum-Woudenberg	1300	P-47	
15-11-40	Oblt.	Otto, Hans	WIFA	1/E	Bf 109E-7	1442	bk 13	Grand Fort Philippe		collision	non-op
22-06-44	Lt.	Pape, Dietwin	WIA	9	Bf 109G-6/U4	440578	wh 18	Charges? (F)	1450	P-47	365 or 368 FG
14-01-45	Lt.	Pape, Dietwin	no	9	Bf 109K-4	330390	wh 21	S of Köln	1201	P-51	78 FG
21-09-44	Ofhr.	Patzke, Günther	KIA	9	Bf 109G-6	780912	wh 2	Groesbeek	1700	P-47	353 FG

Date	Rank	Name	Fate	No.	Aircraft	Werknr	Markings	Location	Time	Enemy	Unit
07-10-44	Fw.	Paul, Arthur	WIA	6	Fw 190A-8	732023	bk 1	Stevede		landing	n/a
24-12-44	Fw.	Paul, Arthur	KIA	6	Fw 190D-9	210114	bk 11	Liège-Bastogne		P-47	36 FG
23-04-44	Obfw.	Pauli, Johannes	KIA	9	Bf 109G-6	162249	wh 15	Lake Neusiedler	1430	missing	
05-11-43	Uffz.	Pautner, Robert	WIA	9	Bf 109G-6	15408	wh 12	near Buer Gelsenkirchen	1415	P-47	353 FG
30-09-40	Uffz.	Perez, Horst	POW	4	Bf 109E-4/N	1190	wh 4	Eastbourne	1830	Spitfire	92 Sqd
20-01-43	Uffz.	Peters, Helmut	KIA	6	Bf 109G-4	16094	br 14	f/l Ardres	1330	Spitfire	122 Sqd
08-11-40	Fw.	Petersen, Ortwin	WIA	6	Bf 109E-4	2770		Croydon	1450	Hurricane	501 Sqd
24-04-42	Lt.	Petersen, Ortwin	KIA	6	Fw 190A-3	5325	br 2	Berck-sur-Mer Le Biez		Spitfire	485 Sqd
25-08-44	Uffz.	Petzsch, Kurt	KIA	7	Fw 190A-8	730995	br 5	W of Mons-en-Chausée		P-51	354 FG
04-02-44	Ogfr.	Peukert, Wilhelm	KIA	6	Fw 190A-6	530413	bk 10	8km SW of Dinant	1300	P-47	56 FG
24-04-45	Uffz.	Pfeiffer, Günter	KIA	5	Fw 190D-9			Lünow (DDR)		unknown	
25-08-44	Ofhr.	Pfützner, Alfred	KIA	5	Fw 190A-8	171632	wh 7	near Amiens		P-51	354 FG
07-06-40	Uffz.	Philipp, Wilhelm	WIA	4	Bf 109E-3			Dieppe		Hurricane	43 Sqd
31-05-40	Oblt.	Pielmeyer, Kurt	KIA	I St	Bf 109E-3			near Ostend St Georges		Hurricane	17 or 145 Sqd
04-11-44	Uffz.	Piesslinger, Josef	KIFA	1	Fw 190A-8	171560	wh 4	M-Gladbach Kinderhaus		engine	n/a
04-02-44	Gefr.	Pietruschka, Werner	WIA	5	Fw 190A-6	470239	wh 8	SE of Dinant	1300	P-47	56 FG
12-02-42	Fw.	Pilkenroth, Heinrich	KIA	3	Bf 109F-4	13007	wh 3	Dunkirk-Ostend	1530	Spitfire	401 Sqd
28-09-40	Hptm.	Pingel, Rolf	WIA	I CO	Bf 109E-4	3756		off Hastings in Channel	1500	Hurricane	238 Sqd
10-07-41	Hptm.	Pingel, Rolf	POW	I CO	Bf 109F-2	12764	<<+	Dover	1440	Stirling+ Spitfire	7 + 306 Sqd
30-11-43	Uffz.	Piplitz, Franz	KIA	10	Bf 109G-6	20722	bk 3	Lennep-Ruhr	1245	B-17	
24-04-42	Uffz.	Pistor, Georg	KIFA	7	Fw 190A-1	80	wh 9	Marke, S of Courtrai	1645	crashed	n/a
22-10-43	Uffz.	Pittmann, Helmut	KIFA	1	Fw 190A-4/R1	5555	wh 3	5km N of Antwerp		hit church	n/a
23-01-45	Uffz.	Planz, Walter	KIA	1	Fw 190D-9	210153	wh 11	Albachten-W of Münster	0930	Spitfire XIV	41 Sqd
20-04-45	Fhr.	Plazer, Gerhard von	KIA	2	Fw 190D-9			Sülte a/f	1550	Spitfire	401 Sqd
17-07-44	Lt.	Pokorny, Günter	KIFA	3	Fw 190A-8	170720	yl 4	N of Chartres		crashed	non-op
21-08-43	Uffz.	Polster, Wolfgang	WIFA	11	Bf 109G-3	16277	rd 16	SW of Lille-Wavrin		engine	non-op
24-02-45	Fw.	Polster, Wolfgang	WIA	11	Fw 190D-9	500603	yl 10	Plantlünne a/f	0805	strafed	274 Sqd
01-06-40	Hptm.	Pomaska, Alfred	KIA	6 CO	Bf 109E-3			Dunkirk		Hurricane	43,145, 245 Sqd
30-11-43	Fw.	Pötter, Ludwig	KIA	10	Bf 109G-6	440009	bk 5	Schwelm- Wupperta	1230	P-47	78 FG
13-10-44	Uffz.	Prantke, Benno	KIA	7	Fw 190A-8	680553	br 3	Jülich		P-47	368 FG
05-03-43	Fw.	Preeg, Karl	KIA	I St	Fw 190A-4	7141	<llgr 3	S Staraya Russa (PQ 1836)	1302	fighter	
09-07-43	Uffz.	Pritze, Hans	KIA	7	Fw 190A-5	1308	wh 5	Schluesselburg a/f	1626	P-39	
28-08-44	Obfw.	Protze, Rudolf	KIA	4	Fw 190A-8	170710	bl 1	unknown		combat	
14-06-44	Lt.	Prüll, Ernst	KIA	12	Bf 109G-6	412682	bl 12	SE of Paris-	0700	P-38	55 FG
14-06-44	Uffz.	Prüver, Bruno	KIA	7	Fw 190A-8	170716	br 7	SE of Paris-Mary sur Marne		fighter	
30-11-42	Lt.	Prym, Roland	KIA	4	Fw 190A-4	727	wh 10	SW of Portland		ship flak	n/a
21-12-43	Ogfr.	Przybyl, Leo	WIA	5	Fw 190A-5	1179	wh 7	St. Pirmont		Spitfire	331 or 332 Sqd
22-02-44	Ogfr.	Przybyl, Leo	WIA	5	Fw 190A-5	501238	wh 3	M-Gladbach Wassenberg		B-17	
10-02-45	Ogfr.	Przybyl, Leo	WIFA	5	Fw 190D-9	600136		Plantlünne a/f		takeoff	non-op
12-08-44	Uffz.	Putsch, Franz	WIA	1	Fw 190A-8	174111	wh 9	Verneuil		flak	n/a
01-03-45	Uffz.	Putsch, Franz	KIA	1	Fw 190D-9	210920	wh 11	S of Düsseldorf	0915	P-47	406 FG
22-03-45	Ogfr.	Putschenjack, Otto	KIA	6	Fw 190D-9			Dreierwalde	1603	Tempest	56 or 80 Sqd
15-09-43	Fw.	Püttmann, Hans	WIA	3	Fw 190A-5	410234	bk 15	Beauvais		engine	n/a
02-11-44	Uffz.	Quitter, Fritz	WIFA	9	Bf 109G-14	462729	wh 7	Coesfeld-Lette a/f		takeoff	non-op
11-05-44	Oblt.	Radener, Waldemar	WIA	7 CO	Fw 190A-8	680120	br 2	Chateaudun Bazoches-		rammed B-24	487 BG
15-06-44	Oblt.	Radener, Waldemar	WIA	7 CO	Fw 190A-8	730934	br 2	Danoy		P-51	339 FG
21-10-41	Lt.	Ragotzi, Hans	WIA	8	Bf 109F-4	7102		E of St. Omer	1320	Spitfire	
09-06-42	Oblt.	Ragotzi, Hans	KIA	10J	Bf 109F-4/R1	8344	wh 7	50 km W of Somme Est	2120	Spitfire	
19-07-41	Lt.	Rahardt, Heinz	WIA	2	Bf 109F-4	8346		Courtrai Beselaere-	1330	Spitfire	609 Sqd
18-08-42	Lt.	Rahardt, Heinz	KIA	2	Fw 190A-3	5421	bk 4	Cap Gris Nez	1500	Spitfire	133 Sqd
31-03-45	Fw.	Raith, Georg	KIA	5	Fw 190D-9			7km NE of Bissel	0600	Spitfire	402 Sqd
12-08-44	Uffz.	Rapsch, Heinz	KIA	3	Fw 190A-8	731758	yl 10	E of Alençon (CB)		fighter	
02-10-42	Fw.	Rau, Günther	WIA	3	Fw 190A-4	668		Aire		Spitfire	4 FG
18-03-43	Fw.	Rau, Günther	KIA	3	Fw 190A-5	2589	yl 10	near Rielbitzi a/f	1630	missing	
30-05-43	Lt.	Reck, Horst	KIA	7	Fw 190A-4	5802	wh 8	W of Cape Ustje		Finn I-153	
08-04-41	Lt.	Reeh, Horst	KIA	5	Bf 109E-7	2754		N of Morlaix	1353	Blenheim	82 Sqd
12-08-40	Oblt.	Regenauer, Hans-Werner	POW	2	Bf 109E-4			Folkestone	1220	Spitfire	64 Sqd
04-04-41	Lt.	Reiche, Heinz	WIFA	5	Bf 109E-7	5970		Étaples		crashed	n/a
10-07-41	Lt.	Reiche, Heinz	WIA	5	Bf 109E-7	6459		Guines		Spitfire	
09-05-42	Lt.	Reiche, Heinz	KIA	5	Fw 190A-2	5234	bk 7	Eperlecques Watten-		Spitfire	
01-01-45	Uffz.	Reichow, Gerhard	no	1	Fw 190D-9			near Almelo		own flak	n/a
26-03-45	Uffz.	Reichow, Gerhard	KIA	1	Fw 190D-9			Münster-Lengerich	1530	Tempest	33 Sqd
08-06-40	Lt.	Reimer, Walter	KIA	2	Bf 109E-3			9km SE of Amiens		Spitfire	
07-10-43	Lt.	Reinhardt, Klaus	WAC	11	none			Vendeville a/f	1030	accident	non-op
14-01-44	Lt.	Reinhardt, Klaus	KIA	11	Bf 109G-6	410677	yl 6	St. Pol-Hesdin Bellevue-	1200	Spitfire	308 Sqd
22-06-44	Lt.	Reischer, Peter	no	11 CO	Bf 109G-6	440580	yl 2	Alençon	1441	P-47	365 or 368 FG
18-12-44	Oblt.	Reischer, Peter	KIA	11 CO	Bf 109K-4	330386	yl 20	Almelo	1250	combat	
27-04-44	Uffz.	Rektor, Helmut	KIFA	6	Fw 190A-6			unknown		crashed	non-op

Date	Rank	Name	Fate		Aircraft	WNr	Code	Location	Time	E/A	Unit
08-12-44	Fhj Gefr-	Reppel, Alfred	KIFA	1	Fw 190A-8	171573	wh 12	Greven	1400	hit ground	non-op
31-03-45	Fw.	Reuther, Arnold	KIA	3	Fw 190D-9			E of Plantlünne a/f	0700	own flak	n/a
13-08-44	Uffz.	Richter, Adolf	KIFA	8	Fw 190A-8	171530	bl 14	M-Gladbach a/f		takeoff	non-op
15-11-40	Fhr.	Richter, Heinz	KIFA	1/E	Bf 109E-4	1150	bk 4	Channel off Dunkirk		collision	non-op
07-11-41	Uffz.	Richter, Heinz	KIA	Ge St	Bf 109F-4	7166		SE of Desvres Calais	1455	Spitfire	72 Sqd
14-10-43	Uffz.	Richter, Horst	KIA	3	Fw 190A-4	5807	yl 9	Geilenkirchen		B-17	
31-05-40	Uffz.	Richter, Josef	KIA	2	Bf 109E-1			Wuelpes Dunkirk-		Hurricane	17 or 145 Sqd
22-12-43	Fhj-	Richter, Julius	KIA	11	Bf 109G-6/U4	20723	yl 5	nr Rheine Drierwalde	1408	P-47	4 FG
29-06-44	Uffz.	Richter, Walter	KIA	3	Fw 190A-8	171074	yl 1	W of Bernay		Spitfire	
01-09-44	Uffz.	Richter, Walter	POW	7	Fw 190A-8	731767	br 13	Nancy		heavy flak	n/a
12-05-44	Uffz.	Rickeit, Kurt	KIA	9	Bf 109G-6/U4	440586	wh 6	St. Vith	1545	combat	
19-08-42	Uffz.	Rieder, Hans	KIA	5	Fw 190A-2	2120	bk 9	St Valéry-en-Caux	1100	Spitfire	
10-04-42	Fw.	Rieger, Paul	KIA	5	Fw 190A-1	37	bk 2	Berck-sur-Mer	1745	Spitfire	
08-06-40	Lt.	Ripke, Hermann	WIA	8	Bf 109E-1			Amiens		Curtiss H75	
25-10-40	Lt.	Ripke, Hermann	KIA	8	Bf 109E-4	3795	bk 2	Sevenoaks, Kent	1440	Spitfire	92 Sqd
01-01-45	Uffz.	Risky, Norbert	no	6	Fw 190D-9		bk 12	Zwolle	1010	a/f flak	n/a
25-11-44	Uffz.	Ritter, Georg	WIFA	9	Bf 109K-4	330419	wh 20	Moers	1515	engine	n/a
09-05-44	Lt.	Rober, Peter	WIA	6	Fw 190A-8	170426	bk 10	near Keel		B-24	466 BG
25-08-44	Lt.	Rober, Peter	KIA	6	Fw 190A-8	731085	bk 1	S of St. Quentin		P-51	354 FG
03-09-40	Oblt.	Roch, Eckardt	KIA	II St	Bf 109E-4	823		Margate	1135	Spitfire	603 Sqd
14-01-45	Obfw.	Roggenkamp, Friedrich	KIA	7	Fw 190D-9	500379	br 7	St. Vith area	1215	P-51	78 FG
18-08-44	Fhj-Fw.	Röhler, Wolfgang	KIA	6	Fw 190A-8	174104	bk 12	Beauvais		Mustang	315 Sqd
20-08-44	Fhj.	Röhrig, Robert	WIA	10	Bf 109G-6	441479	bk 10	near Rouen SE of Lisieux	2025	Spitfire	401 Sqd
27-11-44	Fhj-Uffz	Röhrig, Robert	KIA	10	Bf 109G-14	460514	bk 16	Wettringen near Rheine	1230	P-51	
05-04-45	Uffz.	Rohrmann, Friedrich	WIA	5	Fw 190D-9		wh 14	10kmW of Friesoythe		Spitfire XIV	350 Sqd
27-06-44	Ofhr.	Rose, Wolfgang	KIA	4	Fw 190A-7	431159	bl 15	E of Ennencourt		fighter	
17-08-44	Lt.	Rösen, Hans	KIA	6	Fw 190A-8	170976	bk 1	near Chartres Dreux		light flak	n/a
24-03-42	Lt.	Rosenblath, Georg	KIA	4	Fw 190A-1	11		Cambron	1630	Spitfire	412 Sqd
20-10-43	Uffz.	Rösner, Raimund	KIA	4	Fw 190A-6	530574	bl 3	NE of Chimay	1400	P-47	355 FG
09-01-43	Uffz.	Roth, Ludwig	KIA	5	Fw 190A-4	2406	< bk 3	near Abbeville-Drucat a/f		Spitfire	
03-06-40	Fw.	Roth, Willi	POW	4	Bf 109E-3			40km N of Paris		Bloch 152	
14-08-44	Obfw.	Rudolph, Ernst	WIFA	3	Fw 190A-7	643714	yl 11	W of Houdan		engine	n/a
21-05-40	Uffz.	Rudolph, Hans-Dieter	WIA	7	Bf 109E			W of Lille		flak	n/a
17-09-41	Lt.	Ruhdel, Wolfgang	KIA	3	Bf 109F-4	8284		Hazebrouck-Lille	1600	Spitfire	
25-05-44	Uffz.	Rummler, Egon	KIA	10	Bf 109G-6	162701	bk 2	30km NE of Chaumont	0855	P-47	356 FG
29-11-43	Uffz.	Ruppert, Franz	WIA	I St	Fw 190A-6	530745	wh 12	W of Chièvres		B-26	
25-05-44	Fw.	Ruppert, Hans	KIA	1	Fw 190A-8	170020	wh 5	Metz-Frescaty a/f		P-47	
13-06-43	Hptm.	Ruppert, Kurt	KIA	III CO	Bf 109G-6	16425	<<+I	Münster	0930	B-17	
14-05-43	Lt.	Rüskamp, Hans-Jürgen	KIA	5	Fw 190A-5	7320	bk 6	St. Niklaas, SW of Antwerp	1315	P-47	4 FG
14-01-45	Uffz.	Russ, Karl	KIA	1	Fw 190D-9	210109	wh 6	Ibbenbüren	1545	Spitfire	331 or 332 Sqd
11-01-43	Uffz.	Rybosch, Friedrich	WIFA	4	Fw 190A-4	2301	wh 7	Beaumont le Roger a/f		crashed	non-op
02-07-41	Oblt.	Rysavy, Martin	KIA	2 CO	Bf 109E-7	3213		E of Calais		own flak	n/a
06-02-44	Uffz.	Salewski, Otto	WIA	12	Bf 109G-6	162016	bl 3	Paris-Champs	1112	P-47	56 FG
23-03-44	Uffz.	Salewski, Otto	WIA	12	Bf 109G-6	161784	bl 14	Helburg-Ruhr		fighter	
07-03-45	Uffz.	Salewski, Otto	KIA	10	Fw 190D-9	400247	bk 4	Schüttorf	1528	Tempest	122 Wing
15-07-44	Uffz.	Salewsky, Erich	WIA	12	Bf 109G-6	441476	bl 3	near Paris	1150	combat	
14-01-45	Uffz.	Salewsky, Erich	KIA	12	Bf 109K-4	330439	bl 29	Uckerath-Bonn	1130	P-51	78 FG
07-01-44	Lt.	Saligmann, Rolf	KIA	5	Fw 190A-6	470206	wh 1	E of Doullens		Spitfire or P-47	125 W or 4 FG
25-04-44	Uffz.	Salomo, Werner	KIA	6	Fw 190A-6			Vitry-le-François		P-47	78 FG
19-08-43	Uffz.	Salomon, Heinz	WIFA	10	Fw 190A-4	794	br 16	Melderslo near Horst	1530	no fuel	n/a
16-09-44	Uffz.	Salomon, Heinz	KIA	7	Fw 190A-8	171667	br 10	NE of Heerlen	1745	P-47 or P-38	50 ,370, 404 FG
15-09-43	Flg.	Sander, Hans-Walter	WIA	10	Fw 190A-5	710009	bl 11	18km E of Beauvais		B-17	
13-06-44	Gefr.	Sander, Hans-Walter	KIA	6	Fw 190A-8	170717	bk 1	N of Caen		flak	n/a
27-09-43	Gefr.	Sandoz, Hans	WIA	2	Fw 190A-5	550720	bk 4	E of Rouen		Spitfire	
08-08-44	Uffz.	Sandoz, Hans	WIA	2	Fw 190A-8	731036	bk 7	W of Paris N of Houdan	1330	P-51	359 FG
22-08-44	Uffz.	Sandoz, Hans	KIA	2	Fw 190A-8	170912	bk 4	St. Cyr-Athies		own flak	n/a
25-08-44	Uffz.	Sattler, Ludwig	WIA	1	Fw 190A-8	173815	wh 7	Clermont		P-38	474 FG
02-11-44	Uffz.	Sattler, Ludwig	no	4	Fw 190A-8			near Coesfeld Lette	1605	P-51	
26-12-44	Uffz.	Sattler, Ludwig	KIA	4	Fw 190D-9	210945	bl 8	near Malmedy	1100	P-51	361 FG
13-08-44	Uffz.	Schäfer, Wilhelm	KIA	3	Fw 190A-8	680837	yl 3	50km W of Boulogne		P-51	363 FG
05-09-41	Gefr.	Schäfer, Wolfgang	no	E	Bf 109E-7	913		Moorseele		collision	non-op
10-10-42	Uffz.	Schammert, Werner	POW	10J	Fw 190A-3/U3	420	bk 7	W of Margate	0855	flak	n/a
08-08-44	Uffz.	Schande, Ernst	KIA	2	Fw 190A-6	530120	bk 8	E of Dreux	1330	P-51	359 FG
16-09-44	Ofhr.	Scharf, Alfred	KIA	7	Fw 190A-8	170978	br 2	Limburg	1745	P-47 or P-38	50, 370, 404 FG
14-05-43	Lt.	Schauder, Paul	WIA	9	Bf 109G-6	16448	yl 8	near Stalhille	1245	Spitfire	611 Sqd
01-05-45	Hptm.	Schauder, Paul	POW	II CO	Fw 190D			near Lauenburg-Elbe		flak	n/a
24-07-40	Lt.	Schauff, Josef	KIA	8	Bf 109E-4			NW of Margate	1405	Spitfire	54 or 65 Sqd
05-11-40	Lt.	Scheidt, Erhardt	POW	1	Bf 109E-1	1374	wh 12	Birchington, Kent	1745	Spitfire	19 or 242 Sqd

Date	Rank	Name	Status	No.	Aircraft	WerkNr	Mark	Location	Time	Cause	Unit
02-06-43	Fw.	Schellknecht,	KIA	3	Fw 190A-5	7365	yl 8	N of Kursk (PQ 62158)		engine	n/a
29-08-41	Lt.	Schenk, Heinz	KIA	6	Fw 190A-1	8		S Dunkirk		own flak	n/a
29-11-43	Uffz.	Scheu, Johann	KIA	6	Fw 190A-6	470053	bk 7	3km NW of Passchendale		Spitfire	
07-05-44	Ofhr.	Scheyda, Erich	KIA	3	Fw 190A-8	730321	yl 1	Athies-Laon		Spitfire	411 Sqd
19-07-42	Fw.	Schick, Erich	KIA	1	Fw 190A-2	5336		N of Dunkirk		Spitfire	71 Sqd
08-04-41	Fw.	Schieffer, Karl	no	5	Bf 109E-7	6500		near Brest		Blenheim	82 Sqd
02-06-42	Fw.	Schieffer, Karl	KIA	5	Fw 190A-2	2117	bk 7	W of Berck-sur-Mer	1100	Spitfire	
15-11-40	Lt.	Schiffbauer, Robert	POW	3	Bf 109E-4/B	1250	yl 2	Eastchurch a/f	1435	Hurricane	605 Sqd
14-10-43	Uffz.	Schild, Heinrich	WIA	2	Fw 190A-5	1348		near Antwerp	1430	P-47	353 FG
04-02-44	Fw.	Schild, Heinrich	WIA	2	Fw 190A-7	642532	bk 14	near Ath	1353	P-47	352 FG
12-10-44	Oblt.	Schild, Heinrich	WIA	12	Bf 109G-14	781300	wh 6	E of Bremervörde	1230	P-51	357 FG
02-09-43	Uffz.	Schilling, Franz	WIFA	6	Fw 190A-4	702		Crillon		no fuel	n/a
25-03-44	Uffz.	Schilling, Franz	KIA	7	Fw 190A-7	340325	br 6	Laon-Charleville		P-47	366 FG
22-11-41	Fw.	Schinabeck, Ignaz	KIA	1	Bf 109F-4	7321		Pihen		Spitfire	
05-04-45	Ofhr.	Schitkowsky, Günter	KIA	13	Fw 190D-9			Hasselünne-Huden	1140	Spitfire XIV	402 Sqd
09-08-41	Uffz.	Schlager, Albert	KIA	3	Bf 109F-4	8350		Aire-Hazebrouck	1130	Spitfire	
09-06-44	Uffz.	Schlenker, Erich	KIFA	2	Fw 190A-8	174007	bk 2	Boissy-le-Bois	0615	landing	n/a
07-06-41	Uffz.	Schlichting	WIFA	2	Bf 109E-7	6509		Brest		engine	n/a
14-01-45	Uffz.	Schlimper, Johannes	no	8	Fw 190D-9			Nordhorn a/f		landing	n/a
03-02-45	Uffz.	Schlimper, Johannes	no	8	Fw 190D-9	600350	none	Nordhorn a/f		landing	non-op
29-04-45	Uffz.	Schlimper, Johannes	KIA	6	Fw 190D-9			Wittenberge (DDR)		Spitfire	412 Sqd
24-05-44	Uffz.	Schlögl, Leopold	KIA	3	Fw 190A-8	170114	yl 4	near Charleroi	2015	P-47	
17-08-44	Fhr.	Schlösser, Dietrich	KIFA	5	Fw 190A-8	680157	wh 12	Manancourt		takeoff	n/a
12-08-43	Uffz.	Schmelzer, Philipp	WIA	1	Fw 190A-5	7367	bk 1	SE of Antwerp		B-17	
15-11-44	Uffz.	Schmelzer, Philipp	WIFA	1	Fw 190A-6	531058	wh 10	Antwerp		landing	non-op
15-05-44	Uffz.	Schmelzer, Philipp	WIFA	1	Fw 190A-8	170085	wh 11	W of Armentières		engine	non-op
17-07-44	Fw.	Schmerker, Heimfried	KIA	12	Bf 109G-6/U4	491851	bl 15	SE Caen Alençon	1630	Spitfire	411 or 602 Sqd
22-12-41	Uffz.	Schmeykal, Karl-Heinz	KIFA	6	Fw 190A-1	22		near Samer	1400	weather	non-op
06-11-41	Hptm.	Schmid, Johannes	KIA	8 CO	Bf 109F-4	7211	bk 1	NW of Calais	1557	hit water	n/a
23-12-44	Ogfr.	Schmidt, Erhard	KIA	2	Fw 190A-8	171506	bk 3	Münster area	1230	P-47	56 FG
28-02-45	Uffz.	Schmidt, Franz	KIA	9	Fw 190D-9	500601	wh 17	near Lengerich	0810	Tempest	274 Sqd
26-06-43	Lt.	Schmidt, Gottfried	WIA	11	Bf 109G-3	16253		near Dieppe		P-47	4 FG
29-11-43	Lt.	Schmidt, Gottfried	WIA	11	Bf 109G-6/U4	20731	yl 3	Quakenbrück	1500	B-17	
09-08-44	Oblt.	Schmidt, Gottfried	WIA	9 CO	Bf 109G-6	412429	wh 9	30km SSE of Chartres	1810	Mustang	
27-11-44	Oblt.	Schmidt, Gottfried	WIA	9 CO	Bf 109K-4	330372	wh 21	Bad Iburg	1215	P-51	
28-06-41	Lt.	Schmidt, Johannes	WIA	3	Bf 109E-7	7689		Samer-Le Touquet		Spitfire	
19-08-42	Oblt.	Schmidt, Johannes	KIA	11H CO	Bf 109G-1	14058		10km N of Dieppe		Spitfire	
03-09-43	Lt.	Schmidt, Karl-Heinz	KIA	4	Fw 190A-4	667	wh 10	Champenoux		B-17	
01-11-40	Uffz.	Schmidt, Otto	KIFA	1/E	Bf 109E-1	3659		St Omer-Calais		crashed	non-op
17-08-43	Uffz.	Schmidtke, Günther	KIA	1	Fw 190A-5	410002	wh 5	Koblenz a/f		landing	n/a
07-07-44	Fw.	Schmidtke, Kurt	KIA	4	Fw 190A-8	731033	yl 6	6km SE of Nantes	2045	P-51	354 FG
08-02-44	Uffz.	Schmitz, Hubert	WIA	11	Bf 109G-6	19469	yl 3	NE of Paris	1035	P-47	358 FG
01-01-45	Uffz.	Schmitz, Wilhelm	KIA	6	Fw 190D-9	210274	bk 14	Wieze	1000	Spitfire	403 Sqd
24-02-45	Ofhr.	Schneider, Erich	WIA	3	Fw 190D-9/R11	210969	yl 10	SW of Münster-Handorf a/f	1000	Tempest	222 Sqd
07-06-44	Fhj-Uffz.	Schneider, Friedrich	KAC	2	none			Beaumont-Paris		truck accident	n/a
29-01-44	Fhj-	Schneider, Günther	KIA	3	Fw 190A-6	470237	yl 1	near Mainz Wiesbaden		P-38	20 FG
24-01-42	Lt.	Schneider, Hans	WIFA	II St	Kl 35B-1	4169		Berck-sur-Mer a/f		engine	n/a
05-02-44	Uffz.	Schneider, Lothar	KIFA	8	Fw 190A-6	470068	bl 2	Melun-Paris		crashed	n/a
22-12-41	Oblt.	Schneider, Walter	KIFA	6 CO	Fw 190A-2	217		Steenvoorde	1400	weather	non-op
06-04-45	Uffz.	Schneider, Wolfgang	POW	14	Fw190D-9			5km W of Stolzenau		Tempest	80 Sqd
17-02-43	Uffz.	Schnell, Heinrich	KIA	3	Fw 190A-5	1099	yl 11	SE Lake Ilmen (PQ 1823)		flak	n/a
30-12-43	Uffz.	Schnier, Ewald	WIA	1	Fw 190A-6	530948	wh 6	Hirson		P-47	56 FG
09-05-44	Uffz.	Schnier, Ewald	KIA	1	Fw 190A-8	680166	wh 3	6km N of Echternach		P-51	354 FG
14-04-42	Uffz.	Schöbel, Willy	KIA	4	Fw 190A-1	9	wh 16	near Hardinghem	1845	Spitfire	124 or 457 Sqd
26-07-43	Uffz.	Schöhl, Horst-Günther	WIA	8	none			Vendeville	1130	Boston	88 Sqd
04-09-43	Uffz.	Schöhl, Horst-Günther	WIA	8	Fw 190A-5	530440	bk 3	Rollegem S of Courtrai		Spitfire	403 Sqd
03-09-43	Uffz.	Scholz, Erwin	KIFA	6	Fw 190A-4	684		Creil		landing	n/a
07-08-44	Uffz.	Scholz, Herbert	WIA	9	Bf 109G-6	165522	wh 5	NW of Chartres	1940	P-47	373 FG
02-10-43	Fw.	Scholz, Walter	WIA	6	Fw 190A-5	550186	bk 6	Epinoy a/f		landing	non-op
12-10-44	Uffz.	Schombel, Erich-Joachim	KIA	2	Fw 190A-8	171541	bk 10	Osnabrück Hannover	1200	P-47	56 or 78 FG
03-12-44	Uffz.	Schöndorf, Otto	WIFA	1	Fw 190A-8	960465	wh 2	Fürstenau Handrup		landing	non-op
26-12-44	Uffz.	Schöndorf, Otto	POW	1	Fw 190D-9	600155	wh 15	Carlsbourg	1100	P-51	361 FG
14-06-41	Lt.	Schrader, Karl	WIA	3	Bf 109E-7	3758		Marquise Audembert		Spitfire	92 Sqd
12-10-44	Ofhr.	Schramm, Werner	WIA	8	Fw 190A-8	173028	bl 14	near Stade	1227	P-51	364 FG
29-04-45	Lt.	Schramm, Werner	KIA	6	Fw 190D-9			Wittenberge (DDR)		Spitfire	412 Sqd
27-04-44	Uffz.	Schreiber, Heinz	WIFA	11	Bf 109G-6	163316	yl 13	Lothringen Thionville	2120	no fuel	n/a
18-08-44	Uffz.	Schrettinger, Anton	KIA	7	Fw 190A-8			Beauvais		Mustang	315 Sqd
17-07-43	Uffz.	Schrickel, Alfred	KIA	12	Bf 109G-4	19367	bl 2	North Sea		missing	
13-07-41	Obfw.	Schrödel, Hans	no	E	Bf 109E-4	1549		Desselgem		collision	non-op
16-05-40	Uffz.	Schröpfer, Martin	POW	9	Bf 109E-1			NE of Brussels		Hurricane	
02-09-39	Uffz.	Schuhbauer, Josef	KIFA	2	Bf 109E			Köln-Ostheim		engine	non-op
06-06-44	Fhr.	Schulwitz, Gerhard	no	6	Fw 190A-8	170335	yl 10	Orne Estuary		ship flak	n/a

Date	Rank	Name	Status	Unit	Aircraft	W.Nr.	Markings	Location	Time	Cause	Enemy unit
25-03-45	Lt.	Schulwitz, Gerhard	KIFA	5	Fw 190D-9			Nordhorn a/f	0557	takeoff collision	non-op
19-01-44	Uffz.	Schulz, Gerhard	KIFA	3	Fw 190A-6	530742	yl 1	NE of Revin-Namur		collision	non-op
18-03-44	Ogfr.	Schulz, Heinz	WIA	3	Fw 190A-6	470080	yl 15	W of Ulm		P-51	
01-01-45	Uffz.	Schulz, Heinz	KIA	2	Fw 190D-9	400234	bk 11	near Sinaai		Spitfire	308 Sqd
20-04-45	Uffz.	Schumacher, Erich	KIA	7	Fw 190D-9			near Soltau		flak	n/a
28-09-40	Fw.	Schür, Fritz	KIA	3	Bf 109E-1	6273		Channel- SE of Dover	1145	Spitfire	603 or 605 Sqd
26-07-44	Uffz.	Schuster, Alfred	KIA	3	Fw 190A-8	174101	yl 8	SW of Conches		Mustang	122 Sqd
19-08-41	Fw.	Schwaiger, Franz	KIA	5	Bf 109E-7	6520		N of Steenvoorde	1400	Spitfire	
06-04-43	Uffz.	Schwan, Werner	WIA	1	Fw 190A-4	7146		Dno a/f		landing	n/a
23-09-44	Uffz.	Schwan, Werner	KIA	1	Fw 190A-8	171731	wh 3	Dehaart-5km ESE of Aalten	1545	P-51	339 FG
14-04-42	Uffz.	Schwardt, Hermann	KIA	6	Fw 190A-1	30	br 2	St Omer-Pihen	1845	Spitfire	124 or 457 Sqd
22-06-44	Uffz.	Schwarz, Bruno	WIA	11	Bf 109G-6	162101	yl 22	near Bayeux Cherbourg	1430	P-47	365 or 368 FG
07-07-44	Uffz.	Schwarz, Bruno	WIA	11	Bf 109G-6	163412	yl 1	Évreux	1120	Spitfire	401 Sqd
13-03-45	Fw.	Schwarz, Bruno	KIFA	11	Fw 190D-9	500084	yl 17	near Münster	1400	crashed	n/a
15-05-44	Fw.	Schwarz, Erich	WIA	4	Fw 190A-8	170066	bl 3	Wevelgem		Spitfire	403 Sqd
15-07-43	Uffz.	Schwarz, Paul	KIFA	6	Fw 190A-5	7310	br 5	Ligescourt a/f	1800	engine	n/a
05-05-44	Fw.	Schwentick, Horst	KIA	5	Fw 190A-8	170116	wh 10	N of Chimay		Spitfire	443 Sqd
07-05-44	Ogfr.	Schwertl, Thomas	KIA	3	Fw 190A-8	170401	yl 3	Athies 11km N of Laon		Spitfire	411 Sqd
22-12-43	Uffz.	Seebeck, Karl	KIA	9	Bf 109G-6/U4	20712	wh 3	Hellendoorn	1400	P-47	78 FG
03-06-42	Lt.	Segler, Ulrich	KIFA	9	Fw 190A-2	343	yl 6	Izegem, N of Courtrai	1550	crashed	n/a
01-12-43	Uffz.	Seidl, Norbert	WIFA	2	Fw 190A-5	550450	bk 2	Rengen-Mayen– (SE Eifel)		no fuel	n/a
09-05-44	Uffz.	Seidl, Norbert	WIA	2	Fw 190A-8	680167	bk 1	Burg-Tourhout		P-51	357 FG
26-12-44	Fw.	Seidl, Norbert	WIFA	2	Fw 190D-9	600362	none	Fürstenau		engine	non-op
04-02-43	Lt.	Seifert, Gerhard	KIA	III St	Fw 190A-4	5725	<gr2+l	2km W of Bailleul	1230	Spitfire	331 Sqd
09-06-40	Oblt.	Seifert, Johannes	WIA	3 CO	Bf 109E			NE of Beauvais		unknown	
25-11-43	Obstlt.	Seifert, Johannes	KIA	II CO	Fw 190A-6	470006	<<+	nr Bethune- 5km S of Estaires	1321	P-38 - coll	55 FG
26-11-44	Gefr.	Sengpiel, Horst	WIA	12	Bf 109G-14	461497	bl 2	Löningen-Oldenburg	1139	P-51	364 FG
01-01-45	Gefr.	Sengpiel, Horst	KIA	12	Bf 109K-4	330404	wh 15	Scheldt Est	1004	flak	n/a
20-03-45	Lt.	Siebe, Kurt	KIA	15	Fw 190D-9			6km SE of Quakenbrück		P-51	357 FG
10-10-39	Uffz.	Siebeck, Fritz	KIFA	1	Bf 109E			Albringhausen		no fuel	n/a
25-02-45	Uffz.	Siegel, Günter	KIA	2	Fw 190D-9	210952	bk 17	Hamm area Troisdorf	0825	P-47	36 FG
09-01-42	Uffz.	Sieker, Josef	KIA	4	Fw 190A-1	76		N of Le Touquet	1540	Spitfire	71 Sqd
30-04-42	Oblt.	Sieling, Wilfried	KIA	Ge St	Fw 190A-2	202	bk He-	S of Gravelines	1025	Spitfire	
16-08-44	Uffz.	Siemsen, Horst	WIA	II St	Fw 190A-8	732725	gr 4	Rambouillet	1940	P-51	354 FG
25-12-44	Uffz.	Sigmund, Rupert	KIA	10	Bf 109K-4	330418	bk 8	near Fürstenau	1255	P-51	
06-02-44	Uffz.	Simmank, Rolf	KIA	10	Bf 109G-6	162031	bk 1	NE of Paris	1125	P-47	56 FG
20-04-45	Uffz.	Simmer, Joseph	KIA	7	Fw 190D-9			near Soltau		flak	n/a
18-08-44	Uffz.	Smischek, Josef	KIA	6	Fw 190A-8	170980	bk 10	Beauvais		Mustang	315 Sqd
05-04-45	Uffz.	Soeder, Kurt	KIA	15	Fw 190D-9			N of Lingen	1140	Spitfire XIV	402 Sqd
02-09-42	Fw.	Söffing, Waldemar	no	1	Fw 190A-4	5598		Samer		Spitfire	401 Sqd
10-03-43	Obfw.	Söffing, Waldemar	WIFA	1	Fw 190A-5	840	wh 7	Podzpotsche, S of Staraya Russa		engine	n/a
28-07-43	Obfw.	Söffing, Waldemar	WIA	1	Fw 190A-5	7375	wh 3	10km W of Dordrecht	1210	B-17	
06-08-44	Uffz.	Sonnenberg, Wilhelm	WIA	3	Fw 190A-8	731082	yl 12	SE of Vire		P-47	
19-03-45	Ofhr.	Spahn, Johann	KIA	5	Fw 190D-9			near Lingen		P-51	78 FG
13-05-40	Uffz.	Speck, Hermann	KIA	1	Bf 109E-1			Tilburg, N of Breda	0830	Morane 406	GC III/3
01-01-45	Uffz.	Speer, Leopold	KIA	7	Fw 190D-9	210165	br 5	near Nijkerk (Zuider Zee)	0900	own flak	n/a
22-06-44	Uffz.	Speichert, Hans	WIA	9	Bf 109G-6/U4	440667	wh 15	30km SW of St. Lô	1450	P-47	368 FG
16-08-44	Uffz.	Speichert, Hans	POW	9	Bf 109G-6	440278	wh 20	NW of La Haye du Puits	1720	captured	none
11-11-43	Uffz.	Spiegel, Arthur	KIA	3	Fw 190A-5	1170	yl 12	11km SE of Hesdin		Spitfire	19 Sqd
28-06-44	Uffz.	Spiegl, Waldemar	KIA	5	Fw 190A-8	170625	wh 5	E of Caen		Spitfire	
09-04-43	Lt.	Spieler, Eugen	KIA	8	Fw 190A-4	5612	bk 3	15km W of Boulogne	1815	Typhoon	1 Sqd
27-02-44	Uffz.	Spiess, Horst	KIFA	9	Bf 109G-6	27018	wh 11	20km SE of Lille	1620	crashed	non-op
23-09-41	Uffz.	Spindler, Arthur	no	E	Bf 109E-7	6319		Wevelgem		engine	non-op
19-03-45	Uffz.	Spitz, Renatus	KIA	13	Fw 190D-9			NE of Fürstenau		P-51	78 FG
14-06-40	Lt.	Sprick, Gustav "Micky"	WIA	8	Bf 109E-1			S of Évreux		flak+FAF Ftr	
28-06-41	Oblt.	Sprick, Gustav "Micky"	KIA	8 CO	Bf 109F-2	5743	bk 4	Gravelines St. Omer	0848	wing failed combat	n/a
30-07-43	Lt.	Sprinz, Heinrich	KIA	2	Fw 190A-4	5578	bk 6	1km W Woensdrecht a/f	0710	B-26	386 BG
24-02-43	Ogfr.	Stahl, Berthold	WIFA	11/54	Bf 109G-1	14087		Merville		engine	non-op
26-02-44	Uffz.	Stahnke, Kurt	WIFA	7	Fw 190A-6	470236	br 7	Vendeville a/f		engine	non-op
15-03-44	Uffz.	Stahnke, Kurt	KIA	7	Fw 190A-6	530399	br 5	near Rheine Maurepas		Spitfire	401 Sqd
10-10-43	Hptm.	Staiger, Hermann	WIA	12 CO	Fw 190G-6	15920	bl 2	near Dorsten	1530	B-17	
13-05-43	Oblt.	Stammberger, Otto	WIA	4 CO	Fw 190A-5	739	wh 9	near St. Omer	1230	Spitfire	331 Sqd
12-02-42	Obfw.	Starke, Henri	KIA	9	Fw 190A-1	89	yl 4	W of Boulogne	1320	unknown	72 Sqd
13-05-43	Lt.	Staschen, Arno	KIA	2	Fw 190A-5	1100	bk 7	E of Smolensk		shot after f/l no fuel	n/a
12-02-42	Uffz.	Stavenhagen, Günther	KIA	9	Fw 190A-1	42	yl 12	N of Calais	1330	Spitfire	72 Sqd

Date	Rank	Fate	Unit	Aircraft	W.Nr	Markings	Location	Time	Cause	Unit
26-08-44	Lt.	Stein, Wolf-Dietmar	KIA	5	Fw 190A-8	171468	wh 3	Amiens Beauvais		Spitfire	416 or 421 Sqd
04-10-43	Uffz.	Steinberg, Günther	KIFA	10	Bf 109G-6	20457	bk 13	St. Trond a/f	1253	takeoff	non-op
03-11-43	Hptm.	Steindl, Peter-Paul	WIA	11 CO	Bf 109G-6/U4	19421	yl 6	E Friesland Holtgast	1400	P-47	56 FG
09-01-45	Hptm.	Steindl, Peter-Paul	KIFA	Ge St	Fw 190D-9	210983	bl 10	SE of Fürstenau a/f		crashed	non-op
21-12-43	Uffz.	Steinkühler, Werner	KIA	6	Fw 190A-6	530738	bk 3	W of Vimy Ridge		Spitfire	132 or 602 Sqd
11-03-43	Fw.	Stern, Artur	KIA	III/54	Bf 109G-4	14886		near Lille		air collision	n/a
17-06-43	Oblt.	Sternberg, Horst	WIA	5 CO	Fw 190A-5	7359	bk 12	W of Hazebrouck	1545	Spitfire	Kenley Wing
29-11-43	Oblt.	Sternberg, Horst	WIFA	6 CO	Fw 190A-6	470056	bk 6	c/l Lille-Nord a/f		Spitfire	
22-02-44	Hptm.	Sternberg, Horst	KIA	6 CO	Fw 190A-7	642002	bk 12	Hückelshoven	1500	P-47	4 FG
13-04-44	Oblt.	Stoll, Werner	WIA	6	Fw 190A-7	431150	wh 6	Kaiserslautern		P-47	78 FG
24-06-44	Oblt.	Stoll, Werner	WIA	5	Fw 190A-8	170384	wh 9	W of Versailles		P-47	
21-09-44	Oblt.	Stoll, Werner	WIA	7	Fw 190A-8	175100	bk 6	5km W of Borken-Ruhr	1710	P-47	353 FG
12-08-42	Uffz.	Stoller, Hans-Joachim	WIFA	2	Fw 190A-2	5306		Mardyck a/f		engine	n/a
02-10-42	Uffz.	Stoller, Hans-Joachim	WIA	2	Fw 190A-4	2371	bk 5	Bollezeele		Spitfire	4 FG
09-08-43	Uffz.	Stoller, Hans-Joachim	KIA	8	Fw 190A-4	5613	bk 11	7km NE of Calais	1930	Spitfire	331 Sqd
16-05-40	Fw.	Stolz, Erwin	KIA	5	Bf 109E-1			E of Lille		Hurricane	
28-08-40	Fw.	Straub, Karl	POW	7	Bf 109E-4	1353	wh 13	Goodnestone, Kent	1030	fighter	501 Sqd
12-03-45	Uffz.	Strauhs, Karl	KIA	1	Fw 190D-9	210929	wh 12	near Fürstenau	0845	Spitfire	
26-11-44	Uffz.	Streufert, Hans	KIA	10	Bf 109G-14	462794	bk 1	4km SE of Fürstenau	1150	P-51	364 FG
09-03-45	Uffz.	Stumpf, Walter	no	7	Fw 190D-9			Wesel	1700	P-47	366 FG
14-01-45	Uffz.	Stuppan, Alfred	KIA	5	Fw 190D-9	600352	wh 16	near Köln N of Bonn	1215	combat	
05-11-43	Uffz.	Stutt, Rudolf	KIA	III St	Bf 109G-6/R2	27148	<+ gr 3	near Wesel Voerde	1325	P-47	353 FG
02-09-41	Uffz.	Sucker, Karl	KIA	2/E	Bf 109E-7	6145		NE of Ostend	1200	combat	452 Sqd
02-07-44	Ogfr.	Suckrow, Günter	WIFA	9	Bf 109G-6	162509	wh 10	7km N of Évreux	1540	engine	n/a
04-04-45	Lt.	Sy, Siegfried	no	6	Fw 190D-9			Itterbek	1630	flak	n/a
01-01-45	Uffz.	Sydow, Willy	KIA	2	Fw 190D-9	600147	bk 6	5km SW of Eindhoven	0940	own flak	n/a
27-09-44	Flg.	Sziedat, Friedrich	KIA	5	Fw 190A-8	731765	wh 1	nr Wesel-NW of Emmerich		Spitfire	412 Sqd
08-05-44	Uffz.	Tabbat, Adolf	WIA	10	Bf 109G-6	410757	bk 13	4km SE of Metz	0945	P-51	
05-05-44	Uffz.	Talkenberg, Manfred	KIA	8	Fw 190A-8	170315	bl 6	20km SW of Mons	0830	Spitfire	441 Sqd
06-10-44	Fw.	Taubert, Helmut	KIA	8	Fw 190A-9	750151	bl 7	NW of Groesbeek	1505	Mustang	
21-01-43	Uffz.	Taufmann, Wolfgang	KIA	4	Fw 190A-4	692	wh 4	SW of Calais		Typhoon	609 Sqd
24-08-44	Gefr.	Tebbe, Willi	KIFA	5	Fw 190A-8	350168		Cornantes		takeoff	n/a
29-01-44	Gefr.	Teichmann, Alfred	KIA	7	Fw 190A-6	530749	br 8	SE of Cochem		P-38	20 FG
23-05-44	Uffz.	Teichmann, Heinrich	KIA	9	Bf 109G-6/U4	440725	wh 14	SW Luneville St. Remy	0930	P-51	
10-07-44	Obfw.	Teilken, Heinrich	WIFA	1	Bf 109G-6	170944	wh 6	Villacoublay		engine	n/a
21-10-44	Obfw.	Teilken, Heinrich	KIA	1	Fw 190A-9	205249	wh 2	near Wesel		flak	n/a
12-10-44	Uffz.	Tepperis, Walter	WIFA	11	Bf 109G-14	462676	yl 1	Merfelder Bruch a/f	1730	engine	non-op
01-01-45	Uffz.	Tepperis, Walter	no	11	Bf 109G-14	413550	bk 8	Schouwen Is.	0945	own flak	n/a
29-11-43	Uffz.	Thielmann, Hans-Joachim	KIA	2	Fw 190A-6	470049	bk 7	6km E of Bruges		Spitfire	
19-04-44	Fw.	Thiem, Fritz	KIFA	8	Fw 190A-8	170065	bl 2	near Cazaux		hit sea	non-op
01-08-44	Fw.	Thiemann, Heinz	POW	2	Fw 190A-8	173029	bk 5	NE of Alençon-Avranches	1930	light flak	n/a
26-02-43	Lt.	Thiessen, Hermann	KIA	8	Fw 190A-4	674	bk 6	SW of Cap Gris Nez	0855	Typhoon	609 Sqd
08-12-41	Lt.	Thorn, Walter	KIA	7	Fw 190A-1	88	wh 4	S of Montreuil	1255	Spitfire	603 Sqd
14-03-44	Uffz.	Thost, Paul	KIFA	9	Bf 109G-6	162245	wh 12	10km SE of Dizier	0905	crashed	non-op
07-08-44	Uffz.	Thran, Hans	KIA	10	Bf 109G-6	20034	bk 12	Mortain Le Mans	1510	P-47	368 FG
25-03-45	Gefr.	Thuy, Ernst	KIFA	3	Fw 190D-9	210203	yl 14	Drope a/f	1320	takeoff	n/a
16-06-44	Fw.	Tippe, Erhard	POW	11	Bf 109G-6	412351	yl 21	Le Havre	0530	Spitfire	443 Sqd
19-09-43	Lt.	Todt, Ernst	KIA	III St	Fw 190A-6	16386	<- gr 1	nr Poperingen	1245	Spitfire	41 Sqd
30-10-40	Uffz.	Töpfer, Kurt	KIA	7	Bf 109E-4	5242	wh 8	Marden, Kent	1300	Spitfire	41 Sqd
20-12-43	Lt.	Törpisch, Bernhard	KIA	4	Fw 190A-6	530762	bl 11	5km S of Cambrai	1115	Spitfire	421 Sqd
20-05-43	Uffz.	Trapp, Karl	no	12	Bf 109G-6	19657		Étaples		no fuel	n/a
22-12-43	Fw.	Trapp, Karl	KIA	12	Bf 109G-6/U4	20710	bl 10	Hardenberg-30km W Lingen	1345	P-47	56 FG
29-08-40	Obfw.	Treuburg, Hubert Graf von	KIA	1	Bf 109E-4	1181		Channel- S of Folkestone		Spitfire	
28-07-43	Lt.	Triebnig, Otto	WIA	3	Fw 190A-5	410237	yl 9	NE of Breda	1230	P-47	4 FG
22-12-41	Fw.	Tripschu, Karl	KIFA	6	Fw 190A-1	6		Hermelinghen Boulogne	1400	weather	non-op
22-04-44	Gefr.	Tyczka, Gerhard	KIFA	3	Fw 190A-8	680109	yl 1	Juvincourt-Laon	1312	crashed	non-op
08-03-42	Ogfr.	Übel, Albert	KIA	2	Bf 109F-4	8342	bk 9	E of Dunkirk		Spitfire	
13-07-42	Obfw.	Ufer, Helmut	KIA	4	Fw 190A-1	36	wh 5	W of Abbeville		Spitfire	
22-04-41	Fhr.	Uiberacker, Friedrich Graf v	WIA	1	Bf 109E-7	4147		Ligescourt		Hurricane	303 Sqd
28-06-41	Ofhr.	Uiberacker, Friedrich Graf v	WIA	1	Bf 109E-7	3776		St. Omer-Wizernes		Spitfire	
06-12-42	Lt.	Uiberacker, Friedrich Graf v	WIA	1	Fw 190A-4	5607	wh 7	W of Etaples		B-17	
12-07-41	Lt.	Ulenberg, Horst	KIA	2 CO	Bf 109E-7	3739		Coquelles		Spitfire	
14-01-45	Uffz.	Ullerich, Kurt	KIA	1	Fw 190D-9	210971	wh 10	Lengerich	1545	Spitfire	331 or 332 Sqd
23-08-43	Gefr.	Ullmann, Helmuth	KIA	10	Fw 190A-5	7380	bl 3	3km NE of Frévent-Artois		Spitfire	Kenley Wing
29-11-43	Fw.	Ullrich, Walter	KIA	3	Fw 190A-6	550917	yl 3	Maldegem Flobecq		Spitfire	
12-04-42	Lt.	Unzeitig, Robert	KIA	III St	Fw 190A-2	214	<+l	N of Watten	1345	Spitfire	
25-08-44	Uffz.	Ursprung, Otto	KIA	8	Fw 190A-8	732037	bl 2	Beauvais	1838	P-51	354 FG
24-02-44	Fw.	Vanderveerd, Franz	WIA	3	Fw 190A-6	530950	yl 9	Rheine a/f		P-47	56 FG

548

25-02-45	Ofhr.	Vanderveerd, Heinrich	KIA	2	Fw 190D-9	210985	bk 10	Södenhorst	0745	combat	
07-01-44	Lt.	Vavken, Kurt	KIA	7	Fw 190A-6	530401	br 7	12km SE of Montreuil		Spitfire or P-47	125 W or 4 FG
18-08-44	Fw.	Verhöven, Werner	WIA	6	Fw 190A-8	731096	bk 17	Beauvais	0830	Mustang	315 Sqd
01-03-45	Fw.	Verhöven, Werner	KIA	6	Fw 190D-9			Mönchen Gladbach	0930	P-47	366 FG
13-07-41	Obfw.	Vierling, Willy	no	E	Bf 109E-4	5047		Desselghem		collision	non-op
19-08-41	Obfw.	Vierling, Willy	KIA	6	Bf 109E-7	4215		N of Cassel		Spitfire	
05-04-45	Lt.	Vieweg, Gerd	WIA	7	Fw 190D-9			Bissel a/f	1500	fuel leak	n/a
01-01-45	Ogfr.	Vogel, Bodo	KIA	2	Fw 190D-9	400237	bk 3	Oostkapelle-Walcheren Is.	1030	own flak	n/a
24-03-44	Uffz.	Vogel, Richard	WIFA	10	Bf 109G-6	162027	wh 3	Charleville a/f	1215	landing	non-op
10-08-44	Uffz.	Vogel, Richard	WIA	10	Bf 109G-6	412485	bk 4	SE of Paris N of Ablis	1330	P-51	
24-03-42	Uffz.	Vogt, Gerhard	WIA	6	Fw 190A-1	13	br 13	Abbeville		Spitfire	411 Sqd
02-02-43	Uffz.	Vogt, Gerhard	WIA	6	Bf 109G-4	16129	br 10	W of Ypres		Spitfire	331 Sqd
30-07-43	Fw.	Vogt, Gerhard	WIA	6	Fw 190A-5	410006	br 13	NE of Duisburg		B-17	
03-09-43	Fw.	Vogt, Gerhard	WIA	6	Fw 190A-4	2456	br 11	Romilly sur-Seine		B-17+P-47	56 FG
05-07-44	Lt.	Vogt, Gerhard	WIA	7 CO	Fw 190A-8	170661	br 13	Buré-Mêle sur Sarthe		Spitfire	
28-10-44	Lt.	Vogt, Gerhard	WIA	5 CO	Fw 190A-8	175130	wh 13	Venlo-Orsay	1330	Typhoon	182 Sqd
14-01-45	Oblt.	Vogt, Gerhard	KIA	5 CO	Fw 190D-9	210176	wh 13	SE of Köln-Eil	1200	P-51	78 FG
12-02-44	Gefr.	Vogt, Josef	KIFA	11	Bf 109G-6/U4	20720	yl 1	SW of Florennes	1405	crashed	non-op
01-07-43	Uffz.	Vohwinkel, Paul	KIA	6	Fw 190A-5	7307	br 3	NE of Hazebrouck		Spitfire	331 Sqd
11-01-44	Uffz.	Voigt, Heinz	no	4	Fw 190A-6	550458	bk 8	Schalkhaar	1315	B-17	
11-04-44	Uffz.	Voigt, Heinz	KIA	4	Fw 190A-7	170038	bl 4	Neiden-Torgau	1200	P-51	352 FG
29-07-43	Lt.	Völmle, Dieter	WIA	III St	Bf 109G-6	13153	< bl 2	20km NE of Kiel	0915	B-17	
18-07-44	Lt.	Völmle, Dieter	WIA	9	Bf 109G-6	163186	wh 19	N of Dreux	0950	P-47	373 FG
28-08-44	Lt.	Völmle, Dieter	WIFA	10	Bf 109G-6	441848	bk 9	St Quentin Roupy	2130	engine	n/a
04-12-44	Lt.	Völmle, Dieter	WIA	10	Bf 109K-4	330413	bk 8	Zülpich	1605	flak	n/a
18-08-44	Uffz.	Wagner, Alfred	WIA	8	Fw 190A-8	170986	bl 3	Beauvais		Mustang	315 Sqd
01-09-42	Obfw.	Wagner, Friedrich	KIA	10J	Fw 190A-2/U3	5315	bk 4	Cap Gris Nez-Dungeness		flak	n/a
19-11-44	Lt.	Wagner, Hans-Friedrich	KIA	12	Bf 109G-14	463112	bl 1	S of Mönchen-Gladbach	0930	P-47	365 FG
10-06-44	Uffz.	Waldherr, Rudolf	KIA	9	Bf 109G-6	440584	bk 10	E of Beauvais	1115	fighter	
24-12-44	Uffz.	Walter, Hans-Georg	KIA	5	Fw 190D-9	210146	wh 1	E of Malmedy		P-47	36 FG
14-08-41	Uffz.	Wälter, Heinrich	WIA	III St	Bf 109F-4	7126		St Omer		Spitfire	Northolt Wing
28-01-43	Uffz.	Wälter, Heinrich	KIA	8	Fw 190A-4	5622	bk 2	Dadizele-Beselaere	1108	Whirlwind	137 Sqd
29-04-45	Fw.	Walter, Helmut	KIA	1	Fw 190D-9			Lauenburg-Elbe	1250	Spitfire	412 Sqd
03-12-44	Ogfr.	Walter, Richard	WIFA	4	Fw 190A-8	173867	bl 4	SW of Bremen-Wildeshausen		engine	n/a
26-02-45	Ogfr.	Walter, Richard	KIFA	3	Fw 190D-9/R11	210986	yl 16	Fürstenau a/f		crashed	non-op
02-10-41	Fw.	Walther, Helmut	WIFA	5	Kl 35B-1	1636		Halluin		crashed	n/a
22-03-45	Uffz.	Warthemann, Günther	WIA	6	Fw 190D-9		bk 15	Dreierwalde	1603	Tempest	56 or 80 Sqd
08-03-42	Fw.	Weber, Gottfried	KIA	8	Fw 190A-1	92	bk 10	20km N of Calais	1730	Spitfire	
18-03-45	Fw.	Weber, Otto	WIA	14	Fw 190D-9			W of Twistringen	1235	P-51	339 FG
12-08-42	Fw.	Weczera, Paul	WIFA	2	Fw 190A-2	2054		near Ostend		engine	n/a
12-12-44	Obfw.	Weczera, Paul	WIFA	4	Fw 190A-8	738184	bl 1	Emsdetten		engine	non-op
04-01-45	Obfw.	Weczera, Paul	WIA	4	Fw 190D-9	210965	bl 16	near Melle Osnabrück	1600	Spitfire	411 Sqd
15-08-44	Uffz.	Wedekind, Walter	KIA	II St	Fw 190A-8	171786	gr 2	E of Guyancourt	1230	P-47	373 FG
18-05-43	Obfw.	Wefes, Heinrich	KIA	4/54	Bf 109G-4	19246	wh 6	Ghistelles, nr Ostend	1705	P-47	4 FG
10-04-44	Lt.	Weide, Herbert	KIA	2	Fw 190A-6	550459	bk 2	Laon-Couvron		fighter	
28-03-45	Uffz.	Weigl, Otto	KIA	13	Fw 190D-9			Vreden	1130	hit tree	n/a
22-02-45	Uffz.	Weiss, Franz	WIA	1	Fw 190D-9	210026	wh 10	near Greven	1450	Tempest	3 Sqd
03-02-43	Uffz.	Weiss, Karl	WIA	8	Fw 190A-4	785	bk 9	SW of Bergues	1535	Spitfire	416 Sqd
11-04-44	Uffz.	Weiss, Karl	KIA	4	Fw 190A-7	170042	bl 7	near Neiden Torgau	1200	P-51	352 FG
13-08-40	Uffz.	Wemhöhner, Hans	POW	5	Bf 109E-1			14km E of Brighton	1715	Spitfire	65 Sqd
18-07-44	Uffz.	Wendl, Josef	KIA	1	Fw 190A-8	730467	wh 1	WSW of Nantes-W Paris	0930	P-38	474 FG
22-01-45	Ofhr.	Wendler, Klaus	WIFA	3	Fw 190D-9	211024	yl 16	Fürstenau a/f		engine	n/a
27-09-44	Gefr.	Wentzel, Lothar	KIA	4	Fw 190A-8	173807	bl 9	S of Giesbeek		Spitfire	411 Sqd
02-07-41	Lt.	Wenzel, Kurt-Erich	WIFA	1	Bf 109F-2	12853		St. Omer		engine	n/a
20-01-43	Lt.	Wenzel, Kurt-Erich	KIA	6	Bf 109G-4	16141	br 11	Thames Estuary	1300	Typhoon	609 Sqd
23-12-44	Uffz.	Wering, Franz	KIA	3	Fw 190A-8	732040	yl 16	W of Düren		P-47	56 FG
12-08-43	Lt.	Wermbter, Hans-Joachim	KIA	8	Fw 190A-5	1329	bk 2	27km NNE of Hasselt	0845	P-47	56 FG
01-01-45	Fhr.	Werner, Hans-Joachim	POW	3	Fw 190D-9	600168	yl 8	Grimbergen a/f	0930	a/f flak	n/a
03-03-43	Lt.	Westermair, Alois	KIFA	7	Fw 190A-4	5750	bk 10	Tossno	1100	crashed	non-op
01-07-43	Uffz.	Westhauser, Albert	KIA	11	Bf 109G-3	16290	rd 14	8km NE of Hesdin		Spitfire	403 Sqd
14-08-41	Oblt.	Westphal, Hans-Jürgen	WAC	8 CO	none			Lille		vehicle	n/a
01-12-43	Fw.	Weyrich, Rudi	KIA	5	Fw 190A-6	470055	wh 15	2km S of Mouevres		Spitfire	411 Sqd
04-11-42	Uffz.	Wiegand, Gerd	WIFA	8	Fw 190A-4	682	bk 4	St. Omer	1300	engine	n/a
30-07-43	Uffz.	Wiegand, Gerd	WIA	8	Fw 190A-5	410252		near Tongeren	0835	B-17	
08-03-44	Fhj-Fw.	Wiegand, Gerd	WIA	4	Fw 190A-6	550718	bl 6	Damme	1325	P-47	56 FG
11-06-44	Lt.	Wiegand, Gerd	WIA	4	Fw 190A-8	170310	bl 6	15km N Compiègne	1530	P-38	55 FG
22-03-45	Lt.	Wiese, Willi	KIA	6	Fw 190D-9			8km SE of Fürstenau	1605	Tempest	56 or 80 Sqd

Date	Rank	Name	Fate		Aircraft	W.Nr	Markings	Location	Time	Enemy	Unit
14-12-44	Uffz.	Wiesel, Friedrich	WIA	12	Bf 109K-4	331323	bl 22	W of Dorsten	1435	Spitfire	412 Sqd
23-04-45	Fw.	Wilck, Otto	KIA	6	Fw 190D-9			Elzdorf	0610	Spitfire	403 Sqd
26-02-43	Uffz.	Wilkemeier, Erich	KIA	III/54	Bf 109G-4	16153		near Boulogne		combat	
12-04-44	Uffz.	Willand, Karl	KIA	8	Fw 190A-5	2578	bl 2	N of Dinant	1315	P-47	78 FG
18-09-44	Ofhr.	Willi, Karl	KIA	4	Fw 190A-8	171539	bl 10	Munstergeleen		flak	n/a
27-03-42	Fw.	Willius, Karl	WIA	3	Fw 190A-2	2083		near Ardres		engine+combat	
08-04-44	Oblt.	Willius, Karl	KIA	2 CO	Fw 190A-8	170009	bk 5	nr Zwolle Kamperzeedijk	1545	P-47	361 FG
16-03-44	Fhj-Fw.	Winkel, Kurt	KIA	10	Bf 109G-6	161436	bk 5	W of Vitry-les-Reims-	1200	P-47	56 FG
19-08-42	Oblt.	Winkelmann	no	II St	Fw 190A-3	2557	<<	unknown		ldg gear	n/a
20-05-44	Uffz.	Winter, Hans-Werner	WIA	3	Fw 190A-8	170360	yl 9	NW of M-Gladbach		combat	
06-06-44	Uffz.	Winter, Hans-Werner	KIA	3	Fw 190A-8	730466	yl 3	Abbeville		own flak	n/a
09-04-43	Uffz.	Winter, Horst-Günther	KIFA	5	Fw 190A-4	7042	bk 4	near Arras		crashed	non-op
08-05-44	Uffz.	Winter, Werner	WIA	7	Fw 190A-6	470023	br 12	NE of Soissons		P-47	404 FG
13-06-44	Uffz.	Winter, Werner	WIFA	7	Fw 190A-6	174017	br 8	Étampes		landing	non-op
07-01-44	Fhj-Fw.	Wirth, Hellmuth	KIA	6	Fw 190A-6	550727	bk 2	SE of Abbeville		Spitfire or P-47	125 W or 4 FG
23-12-44	Lt.	Wirth, Helmut	WIA	5	Fw 190D-9	210164	wh 12	near Münster Buldern		P-51	364 FG
09-03-45	Lt.	Wirth, Helmut	KIA	5	Fw 190D-9			Wesel-Vreden	1650	P-47	366 FG
04-03-45	Uffz.	Wirtz, Helmuth	KIA	6	Fw 190D-9			Rheinkamp		P-47	
07-07-44	Gefr.	Wissel, Friedrich	WIA	12	Bf 109G-6	165265	bl 19	W of St Lô	2100	P-51	354 FG
12-08-41	Uffz.	Witzel, Hans-Karl	WIA	I St	Bf 109F-4	8345		Scheldt Estuary	1255	Blenheim	
17-09-41	Lt.	Witzel, Hans-Karl	KIA	I St	Bf 109F-4	8339		W of Bergues-Nord	1600	Spitfire	
01-01-45	Uffz.	Wodarczyk, Heinz	KIA	4	Fw 190D-9	210936	none	Wijhe-15km SSE of Zwolle	1000	missing	n/a
18-06-40	Uffz.	Wolf, Heinz	WAC	3	none			Sezanne		vehicle	n/a
28-11-40	Uffz.	Wolf, Heinz	POW	2	Bf 109E-4	1289	rd 2	Udimore, Sussex	1710	Spitfire	19 Sqd
20-10-43	Lt.	Wölfert, Hans	KIA	7	Fw 190A-6	530927	br 12	Monschau-Eifel		combat	
18-10-43	Fhr.	Wölke, Burghardt	WIA	11	Bf 109G-6	26063		Bethune		Spitfire	132 Sqd
24-02-44	Fhr.	Wölke, Burghardt	KIA	12	Bf 109G-6	162025	bl 6	Lengerich Lingen		P-47	78 FG
28-02-45	Hptm.	Wollnitz, Bernhard	KIFA	III St	Fw 190D-9	600349	gr 3	Plantlünne a/f	0812	collision	n/a
14-01-45	Uffz.	Worster, Friedrich	WIA	1	Fw 190D-9	600179	wh 4	NE of Esch-Ibbenbüren	1545	Spitfire	331 or 332 Sqd
17-06-44	Uffz.	Worthmann, Hans	KIA	8	Fw 190A-8	170730	bl 8	SW of Caen		fighter	
23-01-45	Fw.	Wülfken, Harald	KIA	1	Fw 190D-9	210924	wh 14	10km W of Fürstenau	1700	no fuel	n/a
21-12-42	Lt.	Wunder, Winfried	KIFA	7	Fw 190A-4	2437	wh 6	near Courtrai		crashed	n/a
01-12-43	Lt.	Wunschelmeyer, Karl	WIA	12	Bf 109G-6/U4	20711	bl 4	Elsdorf, W of Köln		B-17	
24-02-44	Oblt.	Wunschelmeyer, Karl	KIA	12	Bf 109G-6	160778	bl 5	Quakenbrück		P-47	78 FG
01-12-43	Fw.	Würtz, Wilhelm	WIA	12	Bf 109G-6/U4	15400	bl 8	Warsage, near Visé		combat	
15-07-44	Uffz.	Wüst, Wilhelm	KIA	1	Fw 190A-8	170037	wh 8	Caen		Spitfire	
30-12-43	Uffz.	Wyrich, Heinz	WIA	5	Fw 190A-5	1175	wh 16	2km S of Romaine		Spitfire	412 Sqd
27-05-44	Uffz.	Wyrich, Heinz	KIA	5	Fw 190A-8	730357	wh 4	nr Paris N of Romilly		combat	
27-08-41	Ogfr.	Zach, Otto	no	E	Bf 109E-4	2767		Middelburg		crashed	non-op
15-08-43	Uffz.	Zandanell, Erich	WIFA	8	Fw 190A-4	792	bk 4	16km SW of Lille		Spitfire	332 Sqd
18-03-45	Obfw.	Zech, Werner	WIA	14	Fw 190D-9	211028	bk 8	W of Twistringen	1235	P-51	339 FG
02-07-44	Lt.	Zedler, Heinz	KIA	8	Fw 190A-8	170333	bl 1	NW of Caen		combat	
01-01-45	Uffz.	Zeidler, Karl-Erich	WIA	4	Fw 190D-9	600170	bl 2	Lengerich	1100	flak	n/a
01-03-45	Uffz.	Zeidler, Karl-Erich	KIA	1	Fw 190D-9/R11	211003	wh 1	Düsseldorf	0915	P-47	406 FG
25-09-44	Fhj-Fw.	Zeller, Joachim	WIA	III St	Bf 109G-6	780851	bk 22	near Arnhem	1740	Spitfire	
13-06-43	Ogfr.	Zenker, Heinrich	KIA	10/54	Fw 190A-4	795	wh 4	SE of Furnes	0930	P-47	56 FG
29-04-43	Fw.	Zens, Franz	WIFA	5	Fw 190A-4	5663	bk 12	SW of Amiens- N of Poix		lost control	n/a
01-05-44	Fw.	Zeschke, Karl-Heinz	WIFA	7	Fw 190A-7	340308	br 9	SW of Charleville		engine	n/a
17-08-44	Fw.	Zeschke, Karl-Heinz	KIA	7	Fw 190A-8	731740	br 9	Caen		light flak	n/a
07-03-45	Obfw.	Zester, Willi	WIA	9	Fw 190D-9	601032	wh 18	Drievorden	1530	Tempest	122 Wing
30-09-40	Gefr.	Ziemens, Helmut	KIA	7	Bf 109E-4	3645		Channel-London	1800	Spitfire	
17-06-44	Fhj-Fw.	Zimmermann, Hans	KIA	8	Fw 190A-8	170379	bl 7	Vire-SW of Bayeux		fighter	
03-10-39	Fw.	Zimmermann, Herbert	POW	10N	Ar 68	1907		W of Bunde		no fuel	non-op
05-03-43	Hptm.	Zink, Fülbert	no	2 CO	Fw 190A-4	7173		S of Shvinochovo		combat	
14-03-43	Hptm.	Zink, Fülbert	KIA	2 CO	Fw 190A-4	7176	bk 13	E of Werschinskojec	1130	missing	
04-07-44	Fhr.	Zippel, Kurt	KIA	6	Fw 190A-8	172711	bk 1	Caen-Bayeux		Mustang	414 Sqd
25-02-44	Obfw.	Zirngibl, Joseph	WIA	8	Fw 190A-6	530718	bl 4	Saarbrücken a/f	1250	P-47	
21-06-44	Obfw.	Zirngibl, Joseph	KIA	8	Fw 190A-6	530763	bl 11	NE of St. Cyr	2200	P-38	474 FG
23-12-44	Uffz.	Zubaiko, Edwin	KIA	3	Fw 190A-8	173822	yl 3	W of Düren- SE of Malmedy	1130	P-47	56 FG
05-11-44	Uffz.	Zutz, Hans-Joachim	KIFA	8	Fw 190A-8	170989	bl 10	Kirchhellen a/f		collision	non-op

SOURCES

GENERAL

The principal archives consulted, and their file designations, are:
Bundesarchiv-Militärarchiv, Freiburg, Germany (BA-MA): (RL ##/###)
Public Records Office, Kew, England: (AIR ##/###)
ULTRA transcripts: (ULTRA group ## message ####)
USAF Historical Research Agency, Maxwell AFB, AL: (HRA ###.####)

The following primary sources are referenced in passim:
Abschusskladde des I./JG 26 [I/JG 26 victory list]. (RL 10/260)
Abschusskladde des II/JG 26 [II/JG 26 victory list]. (RL 10/261)
Deutsche Dienststelle (WAST), Berlin. [German personnel bureau records – include circumstances of loss for fatalities]. (Files are presently closed to private researchers; abstracted for me by A. Abendroth.)
JG 26 Ehrenbücher [biographies of JG 26 fatalities]. (RL 10/265-275)
Luftwaffen-Personalamt L.P. (A)5(V) Abschüsse-Tagebücher [RLM daily victory claim worksheets]. (microfilm obtained from BA-MA)
Ob.d.L. Gen. Q. Gen. 6. Abt. Flugzeugunfälle und Verluste bei den Verbänden (täglich) [OKL daily aircraft loss lists]. (microfilm obtained from the Imperial War Museum)
USAAF: USAFHRA documents –
Bombardment squadron histories: HRA SQ-BOMB-###(HI).
Bombardment group histories: HRA GP-###-HI (BOMB).
Fighter squadron histories (contain some encounter reports):
HRA SQ-FTR – ###(HI).
Fighter group histories: HRA GP-###-HI (FTR).
8AF Mission Folders (frequently include radio intercept summaries, RAF Fighter Command operational summaries): HRA 520.332.
Missing Aircrew Reports (MACRs) – US National Archives, Suitland MD; 8AF crash sites summarized (from MACRs) in Andrews & Adams, *The Mighty Eighth Combat Chronology.*
Air Victories: Olynyk, *USAAF (European Theater) Credits for the Destruction of Enemy Aircraft in Air-to-Air Combat in World War 2.*

Josef Priller's *JG 26: Geschichte eines Jagdgeschwaders* is referenced in passim for Geschwader and Gruppe organization and base locations, taken from maps drawn by Alfred Iwanek, a Geschwader clerk. Iwanek's source material cannot be found in the BA-MA files.
Data for Geschwader victory claims not in the BA-MA records are taken from:
1. logbooks and interviews.
2. a copy of Priller's claims list prepared in the Geschwader (supplied by De Meester).
3. a copy of Dortenmann's claims list prepared in the Geschwader (supplied by Poelchau).
4. files of Bock and other German researchers, whose original sources are primarily unpublished contemporary records and logbooks.
Data for JG 1, JG 3, and JG 11 are taken from Prien's histories of these units (see reference list).

CHAPTER 1: THE LAST PAUSE

Abschussmeldungen (victory reports): Jauer.
Airfield descriptions: Crump, HRA 512.277.
Biographies (Knight's Cross holders): Obermaier, *Die Ritterkreuzträger der Luftwaffe*

1939-1945 Band 1: Jagdflieger; Renner, *Wilhelm-Ferdinand Galland.*
Crash sites: Bakker, De Decker, Nootenboom, Roba, Vervoort.
Diaries: Jauer.
Interviews: Blömertz, Crump, Galland, Gomann, Heuser, Leykauf, Polster, Stammberger.
Jabo raids on England: Collier, *The Defense of the United Kingdom*; Ramsey, *The Blitz*
    Then & Now; Goss archives, British civil defense document in HRA 512.6741;
    RAF AI(1)K POW interrogation reports in HRA 512.619B; A. Galland's post-raid
    evaluations in HRA K113.007.
Logbooks: Crump, Dietze, Ellenrieder, Glunz, Gomann, Heuser, Kemethmüller,
    Mayer, Polster, Priller (RL 10/262), Stammberger.
Private archives: Abendroth, Bakker, Bock, Kitchens, Koreman, Perry, Roba,
    Vanoverbeke, Vervoort.
RAF Luftwaffe radio intercept files: AIR 22/497-498
Royal Air Force: Bowyer, *Two Group R.A.F.*; Brown, *Canadian Wing Commanders*;
    Godefroy, *Lucky 13* (Fw 190 vs Spitfire IX flight comparison); Richards & Saunders,
    Royal Air Force 1939-1945 Vol. II: The Fight Avails; Shores, *Aces High*;
    Thomas & Shores,*The Typhoon & Tempest Story*; published RAF pilot memoirs
    and squadron histories.
Logbooks: Hugo Armstrong (via McAulay), Dick Due (*via* McAulay), J. E. Johnson.
No. 11 Group operations records: AIR 25/194.
No. 12 Group operations records: AIR 25/220.
No. 403 Squadron ORB (*via* Sarkar).
Private archives: Foreman, Goss, Guest, Mucha, Olynyk, Roba, Sortehaug,
    Vanoverbeke, Vervoort.
RAF evader interviews: AIR 40/259.
RLV organization: Schmid interrogation: HRA K113.107.
USAAF: Craven & Cate, *The Army Air Forces in World War II: Vol. II, Europe: Torch to*
    Pointblank; Freeman, Mighty Eighth War Diary; Hammel, *Air War Europa*;
    published pilot memoirs and unit histories.
Crash sites: Bakker, De Decker, De Meester, Hey, Nootenboom, Roba, Vervoort.
Interviews: Pisanos, Seelos, Zemke.
Private archives: Hess.

CHAPTER 2: THE EASTERN FRONT

Abschussmeldungen (victory reports): Jauer.
Airfield descriptions: Trautloft, Held, & Bob, *Die Grünherzjäger.*
Diaries: Jauer.
Interviews: Heuser, Schild.
Logbooks: Ellenrieder, Heuser, Kemethmüller, Klems, Schild.
Private archives: Bergström, Fahey, Roba.
Soviet Air Force: Hardesty, *Red Phoenix*; Wagner, *The Soviet Air Force in World War II.*
    Private archives: Bergström, Mikhailov.
Theater information: Ziemke, *Stalingrad to Berlin.*

CHAPTER 3: BLOCKING THE TIDE

Abschussmeldungen: W-F. Galland (quoted from Renner).
Airfield descriptions: Crump, HRA 512.277, van den Nieuwendijk, van Loo.
Biographies (Knight's Cross holders): *Obermaier, Die Ritterkreuzträger der Luftwaffe*
1939-1945 Band 1: Jagdflieger; Renner, *Wilhelm-Ferdinand Galland.*
Crash sites: Bakker, De Decker, Leclerq, Nootenboom, Roba, van den Broucke,
    van Loo, Vervoort.
Diary: Wiegand.
Interviews: Blömertz, Crump, Ellenrieder, Gomann, Glunz, Heuser, Kiefner,
    Leykauf, Naumann, Polster, Schild, Wiegand.
Logbooks: Crump, Dietze, Ellenrieder, Glunz, Gomann, Heuser, Kemethmüller,
    Kiefner, Mayer, Polster, Priller (RL 10/262), Schild.
OKW communiqués: Piekalkiewicz, *Luftkrieg 1939-1945.*
POW Interrogations: ADI(K) 210A/1944, in HRA 512.619B-19.
Private archives: Abendroth, Bakker, Bock, I. De Jong, Kitchens, Koreman, Perry,

Roba, van den Nieuwendijk, van Loo, Vanoverbeke, Vervoort.
RAF Luftwaffe radio intercept files: AIR 22/498-499.
Royal Air Force: Bowyer, *Two Group R.A.F.*; Brown, *Canadian Wing Commanders;*
Richards & Saunders, *Royal Air Force 1939-1945 Vol. II: The Fight Avails;*
Shores, *Aces High*; Thomas & Shores, *The Typhoon & Tempest Story*; published
RAF pilot memoirs and squadron histories.
Interview: Gaze.
Logbooks: Due (*via* McAulay), Gaze, J. E. Johnson.
No. 11 Group operations records: AIR 25/194.
No. 12 Group operations records: AIR 25/220.
No. 403 Squadron ORB (*via* Sarkar).
Private archives: Foreman, Goss, Guest, Mucha, Olynyk, Roba, Sortehaug,
Vanoverbeke, Vervoort.
RAF evader interviews: AIR 40/259.
USAAF: Craven & Cate, *The Army Air Forces in World War II: Vol. II, Europe: Torch to
Pointblank;* Freeman, *Mighty Eighth War Diary;* Hammel, *Air War Europa;*
published pilot memoirs and unit histories.
Crash sites: Bakker, De Decker, De Meester, Hey, Nootenboom, Roba, Vervoort.
Interviews: Binnebose, Burford, Zemke.
Private archives: Hess, Olynyk.
XII Fliegerkorps daily reports (victory accounting, equipment evaluation, etc.)
(August 1943 only): RL 8/88.
17 Aug 43 – Middlebrook, *The Schweinfurt-Regensburg Mission.*

CHAPTER 4: THE WAR OF ATTRITION

Airfield descriptions: HRA 512.277.
Biographies (Knight's Cross holders): Obermaier, *Die Ritterkreuzträger der Luftwaffe
1939-1945 Band 1: Jagdflieger.*
Crash sites: Bakker, De Decker, A. De Jong, Leclerq, Nootenboom, Roba,
van den Broucke, van Loo, Vervoort.
Diary: Wiegand.
Interviews: Crump, Galland, Glunz, Gomann, Heuser, Kiefner, Naumann, Polster,
Schild, Wiegand.
Jafü 4 and Höhere Jafü West daily reports: RL 8/233 (September, 1943 only).
Jagdkorps I Kriegsgeschichte: HRA K113.408-2. (September-December 1943).
Kampfanweisung für die Jagd- und Zerstörerverbände in der Luftverteidigung
(Combat Instructions for Fighter and Heavy Fighter Units in the Air Defense): RL10/291.
Logbooks: Crump, Dietze, Glunz, Heuser, Kiefner, Mayer, Polster, Schild.
October air defense reorganization: A. Galland, *Die Reichsluftverteidigung im Jahre 1943:*
HRA K113.312-2 v4.
OKW communiqués: Piekalkiewicz, *Luftkrieg 1939-1945.*
Private archives: Abendroth, Bakker, Bock, Hawkins, Kitchens, Koreman, Mombeek,
Perry, Roba, van den Nieuwendijk, van Loo, Vanoverbeke, Vervoort.
RAF Luftwaffe radio intercept files: AIR 22/499-500.
Royal Air Force: Bowyer, *Two Group R.A.F.*; Brown, *Canadian Wing Commanders;*
Richards & Saunders, *Royal Air Force 1939-1945 Vol. II: The Fight Avails;*
Shores, *Aces High*; Thomas & Shores, *The Typhoon & Tempest Story;*
published RAF pilot memoirs and squadron histories.
Interview: Gaze.
Logbooks: Due (*via* McAulay), Gaze, J. E. Johnson.
No. 11 Group operations records: AIR 25/194.
No. 403 Squadron ORB (*via* Sarkar).
Private archives: Foreman, Goss, Guest, Mucha, Olynyk, Price, Roba,
Sortehaug, Thomas, Vanoverbeke, Vervoort.
RAF evader interviews: AIR 40/259.
USAAF: Craven & Cate, *The Army Air Forces in World War II: Vol. II, Europe:
Torch to Pointblank*; Freeman, *Mighty Eighth War Diary;* Hammel, *Air War Europa;*
published pilot memoirs and unit histories.
Crash sites: Bakker, De Decker, De Meester, Hey, Nootenboom, Roba, van Loo, Vervoort.

Interviews: G. Brown, Patterson, Truluck, Zemke.
Private archives: Deatrick, Hawkins, Hess, Olynyk.
10 Oct 43: Hawkins, *Münster.*

CHAPTER 5: THE AIR WAR IS LOST

Biographies (Knight's Cross holders): Obermaier, *Die Ritterkreuzträger der Luftwaffe 1939-1945 Band 1: Jagdflieger.*
Crash sites: Bakker, De Decker, A. De Jong, Girbig, Leclercq, Manrho, Nootenboom, Roba, Spies, van den Broucke, van Loo, Vervoort.
Daily Luftwaffe aircraft loss totals: RL 2/III/853 *et seq.*
Diary: Wiegand.
Interviews: Battmer, Crump, Galland, Gehrke, Glunz, Gomann, Kiefner, Polster, Schild, Spies, Wiegand.
Jagdkorps I Kriegsgeschichte: HRA K113.408-2. (January-May 1944).
Logbooks: Crump, Dietze, Ellenrieder, Glunz, Kemethmüller, Kiefner, Mayer, Polster, Schild.
OKW communiqués: Abendroth; Piekalkiewicz, *Luftkrieg 1939-1945.*
POW interrogations, cell wiretaps: HRA 512.6061C
Private archives: Abendroth, Bakker, Bock, De Decker, Kitchens, Koreman, Manrho, Mombeek, Perry, Roba, Spies, van den Nieuwendijk, van den Broucke, van Loo, Vanoverbeke, Vervoort.
RAF Luftwaffe radio intercept files: AIR 22/500.
Royal Air Force: Bowyer, *Two Group R.A.F.;* Brown, *Canadian Wing Commanders;* Saunders, *Royal Air Force 1939-1945 Vol. III – The Fight is Won;* Shores, *Aces High;* Shores, *2nd Tactical AirForce;* Thomas & Shores, *The Typhoon & Tempest Story ;* published RAF pilot memoirs and squadron histories.
Interviews: Gaze, R. Smith.
Logbooks: Danzey, Gaze, R. Smith.
No. 11 Group operations records: AIR 25/195.
Private archives: Foreman, Goss, Guest, Mucha, Olynyk, Palmer, Price, Roba, Sarkar, Thomas, Vanoverbeke, Vervoort.
RAF evader interviews: AIR 40/259.
ULTRA intercepts: KV 3500-9700 (various).
USAAF: Craven & Cate, *The Army Air Forces in World War II: Vol. III, Europe: Argument to V-E Day;* Freeman, *Mighty Eighth War Diary;* Hammel, *Air War Europa;* published pilot memoirs and unit histories.
Crash sites: Bakker, De Decker, De Meester, Hey, Koreman, Nootenboom, Roba, van Loo, Vervoort.
Interviews: Bryan, Carpenter, Klibbe, Neeck, Pisanos, Truluck, Zemke.
Private archives: Gray, Hess, Olynyk, Rowe.
20 Feb 44: USSTAF *Post-Hostilities Interrogations,* HRA 519.601A.
04 Mar 44: van den Broucke, *Quand des avions s'abattaient...*
06 Mar 44: Ethell & Price, *Target Berlin – Mission 250: 6 March 1944.*
22 Apr 44: McLachlan, *Night of the Intruders.*
29 Apr 44: van den Broucke, *Quand des avions s'abattaient...*
12 May 44: Girbig, *Mit Kurs auf Leuna.*

CHAPTER 6: THE INVASION FRONT

Abschussmeldungen: Eder.
AEAF Luftwaffe radio intercept files: AIR 22/501-502.
Airfield attacks: Gundeloch, *The Effects of Allied Air Attacks on GAF Bases,* HRA K113.107-185.
Airfield descriptions: Couderchon, Crump, HRA 512.277, Kiefner, Polster, Schild, Schmidt.
Air operations over the invasion front (BAM translations of three RLM documents): HRA 512.621 VII/19,31,32.
Biographies (Knight's Cross holders): Obermaier, *Die Ritterkreuzträger der Luftwaffe 1939-1945 Band 1: Jagdflieger.*
Crash sites: Bakker, Baudru, Chuinard, Leclercq, Manrho, Nootenboom, Roba.
Daily Luftwaffe aircraft loss totals: RL 2/III/853 et seq.
Diaries: Prager, Wiegand.

Jagddivision 5 Kriegstagebuch: HRA K113.408-2 (June 1944 only).
Jagdkorps II Befehle (Daily Orders): RL 8/170.
Interviews: Ayerle, Burmeister, Crump, Galland, Gehrke, Genth, Glunz, Gomann,
  Hartigs, Heuser, Kiefner, Kruse, Kukla, Ossenkop, Polster, Schild, Schmidt, Stumpf,
  Tippe, Wiegand.
Logbooks: Crump, Dietze, Ellenrieder, Glunz, Heuser, Hött, Kemethmüller, Kiefner,
  Polster, Schild, Stumpf.
OKW communiqués: Abendroth; Piekalkiewicz, *Luftkrieg 1939-1945.*
POW interrogations, cell wiretaps: HRA 512.6061C, HRA 512.619B.
Private archives: Abendroth, Baudru, Bock, Chuinard, Howard, Kitchens, Manrho, Molge,
  Mombeek, Perry, Roba.
Royal Air Force: Brown, *Canadian Wing Commanders;* Foreman, *Over the Beaches*
  (June only); Saunders, *Royal Air Force 1939-1945 Vol. III – The Fight is Won;*
  Shores, *Aces High;* Shores, *2nd Tactical AirForce;* Thomas & Shores, *The Typhoon &*
  Tempest Story; published RAF pilot memoirs and squadron histories.
Interviews: Gaze, Nowosielski, R. Smith.
Logbooks: Gaze, R. Smith.
Private archives: Foreman, Guest, Haycock, Mucha, Olynyk, Roba, Thomas.
ULTRA intercepts: KV 6600-9999, XL 0001-8900 (various).
Unit and Commander movements: Schmid, *The Air War in the West: Vols. 5 & 10,*
  HRA K113.107.
USAAF: Craven & Cate, *The Army Air Forces in World War II: Vol. III, Europe:*
  Argument to V-E Day; Freeman, *Mighty Eighth War Diary;* Hammel, *Air War Europa;*
  published pilot memoirs and unit histories.
Crash sites: Chuinard, O'Neill.
Interviews: Brooks, Capron, Jasper, Matte, O'Neill, L. Smith.
Private archives: Hess, Olynyk.
25 Jun 44: Howard & Lavandier, *Boots from Heaven.*
13 Aug 44: Brooks, *Sunflower Wild.*

CHAPTER 7: DEFENSE OF THE GERMAN BORDER

AEAF Luftwaffe radio intercept files: AIR 22/502.
Airfield attacks: Gundeloch, *The Effects of Allied Air Attacks on GAF Bases,*
  HRA K113.107-185.
Airfield descriptions: Eickhoff, Genth, HRA 512.277A, Poelchau, Schmidt, Terbeck.
Ardennes campaign: Parker, *To Win the Winter Sky: Air War over the Ardennes, 1944-1945.*
Biographies (Knight's Cross holders): Obermaier, *Die Ritterkreuzträger der Luftwaffe*
  1939-1945 Band 1: Jagdflieger.
Crash sites: Bakker, A. De Jong, Eickhoff, Manrho, Mol, Oeltjebruns, Poelchau, Pütz.
Daily Luftwaffe aircraft loss totals: RL 2/III/853 *et seq.*
I./JG 26 Kriegstagebuch Nr. 21 (from 5 Oct 44): RL 10/258.
Interviews: Ayerle, Burmeister, Crump, Galland, Gehrke, Genth, Glunz, Gomann, Hartigs,
  Kiefner, Krupinski, Kruse, Kukla, Molge, Ossenkop, Polster, Schild, Schmidt, Schöndorf,
  Stumpf, Sy, Ungar.
Jagddivision 3 Anlagen: RL 8/186.
Jagdkorps II Befehle (Daily Orders): RL 8/170.
Logbooks: Crump, Dietze, Ellenrieder, Glunz, Hött, Kemethmüller, Kiefner, Polster, Schild,
  Stumpf, Ungar.
Luftflotte 3 Kriegstagebuch (September, 1944 only): HRA 512.621 VII/19.
OKW communiqués: Abendroth; Piekalkiewicz, *Luftkrieg 1939-1945.*
POW interrogations, cell wiretaps: HRA 512.6061C, HRA 512.619B.
Private archives: Abendroth, Bock, Kitchens, Manrho, Molge, Mombeek, Perry, Pütz, Roba.
Royal Air Force: Brown, *Canadian Wing Commanders;* Saunders, *Royal Air Force*
  1939-1945 Vol. III – The Fight is Won; Shores, Aces High; Shores, *2nd Tactical AirForce;*
  Thomas & Shores, *The Typhoon & Tempest Story;* published RAF pilot memoirs and
  squadron histories.
Interviews: Danzey, R. Smith, Stafford.
Logbooks: Danzey, R. Smith.
Private archives: Foreman, Guest, Olynyk, Owen, Roba.

ULTRA intercepts: XL 8700-9999, HP 0001-9999, BT 0001-0930 (various).
Unit and Commander movements: Schmid, *The Air War in the West: Vols. 5 & 10,*
  HRA K113.107.
USAAF: Army Air Forces, *Airborne Assault on Holland;* Craven & Cate, *The Army Air
  Forces in World War II: Vol. III, Europe: Argument to V-E Day;* Freeman, *Mighty Eighth
  War Diary;* Hammel, *Air War Europa;* published pilot memoirs and unit histories.
    Interviews: Beyer, Clark, Cramer, Schonenberg, Vanden Heuvel, Yeager.
    Private archives: Hess, Olynyk.

CHAPTER 8: GOTTERDÄMMERUNG

Airfield descriptions: Eickhoff, Genth, HRA 512.277A, Ossenkop, Poelchau, Schmidt.
Ardennes campaign: Parker, *To Win the Winter Sky: Air War over the Ardennes, 1944-1945.*
Biographies (Knight's Cross holders): *Obermaier, Die Ritterkreuzträger der Luftwaffe
  1939-1945 Band 1: Jagdflieger.*
Crash sites: De Decker, A. De Jong, Eickhoff, Manrho, Mol, Poelchau, Pütz.
Daily Luftwaffe aircraft loss totals: RL 2/III/853 *et seq.*
Diaries & Leistenbücher: Backhaus, Nibel, Prager, Sy.
I./JG 26 Kriegstagebuch Nr. 21 (5 Oct 44-4 Apr 45): RL 10/258.
I./JG 26 Kriegstagebuch Nr. 22 (4 Apr 45-8 May 45): RL 10/259.
Interviews: Ayerle, Battmer, Blömertz, Burmeister, Crump, Egli, Galland, Gehrke, Genth,
  Glunz, Gomann, Hartmann, Kiefner, Kroll, Krupinski, Kukla, Molge, Ossenkop, Peltz,
  Polster, Rey, Schild, Schmidt, Stumpf, Sy, Tepperis, Ungar.
Jagdkorps II Befehle (Daily Orders): RL 8/170.
Logbooks: Crump, Dietze, Ellenrieder, Glunz, Hött, Kiefner, Polster, Schild, Stumpf, Ungar.
OKL Führungsstab Ic Fremde West evaluation of Bodenplatte:
  AIR 20/9941(BAM translation).
OKL Tagesmeldungen – Ic West (Feb-Mar 45): RL 2 II/390, AIR 20/7891 (BAM translation);
  (Apr 45): RL 2 II/391.
POW interrogations, cell wiretaps: HRA 512.6061C, HRA 512.619B.
Private archives: Abendroth, Bock, De Decker, Kitchens, Manrho, Molge, Mombeek, Perry,
  Pütz, Roba.
RAF Luftwaffe radio intercept files: 2TAF: AIR 22/503, 40/2371-2373;
  KLAMS (Mar-Apr 45): HRA 512.6061; 382nd WU (Mar-Apr 45): AIR 40-2367.
Royal Air Force: Brown, *Canadian Wing Commanders;* Saunders, *Royal Air Force 1939-1945
  Vol. III – The Fight is Won;* Shores, *Aces High;* Shores, *2nd Tactical Air Force;* Thomas &
  Shores, *The Typhoon & Tempest Story;* published RAF pilot memoirs and squadron
  histories.
    Interviews: Danzey, Gaze, R. Smith.
    Logbooks: Danzey, Gaze, R. Smith.
    Private archives: Foreman, Guest, Olynyk, Owen, Roba.
ULTRA intercepts: BT 800-9999, KO 0001-1938 (various).
Unit and Commander movements: Schmid, *The Air War in the West: Vols. 5 & 10,*
  HRA K113.107.
USAAF: Craven & Cate, *The Army Air Forces in World War II: Vol. III,* Europe:
  Argument to V-E Day; Freeman, *Mighty Eighth War Diary;* Hammel, *Air War Europa;*
  published pilot memoirs and unit histories.
    Private archives: Fry, Hess, Olynyk, Tiedeman.
1 Jan 45: Franks, *Battle of the Airfields;* Girbig, *Start im Morgengrauen.*

APPENDICES

1.   **ORGANIZATION AND STRENGTH:** HRA 137.306-14, OKL maps in RL 40/226
et seq., supplemented by data from Abendroth and Bock archives.

2.   **COMMANDERS: RL 10/264,** supplemented by data from personnel records.

3.   **BASES:** A. Iwanek maps in Priller, *JG 26: Geschichte eines Jagdgeschwaders;*
OKL maps in RL 40/226 *et seq.*

BIBLIOGRAPHY

Aders, G. *History of the German Night Fighter Force 1917-1945*. Jane's (London), 1978.

Anderson, C.E. *To Fly and Fight: Memoirs of a Triple Ace*. St. Martin's Press (New York), 1990.

Andrews, P.M. & Adams, W. H. *The Mighty Eighth Combat Chronology: Heavy Bomber and Fighter Activities 1942-1945*. Eighth Air Force Memorial Museum Foundation (Warrenton, VA), 1997.

Anonymous. *Ultra & the History of the USSAFE vs the GAF*. Univ. Pubs. of America (Frederick, MD), 1980.

Anonymous. ULTRA – *Main Series of Signals Conveying Intelligence to Allied Commands*. Clearwater (New York), ca. 1988 [104 microfilm rolls].

Army Air Forces, *Airborne Assault on Holland: Wings at War Series No. 4*. Arno Press (New York), 1980 (reprint).

Barbas, B. *Planes of the Luftwaffe Fighter Aces Vols. 1 & 2*. Kookaburra (Melbourne), 1985.

Bashow, D.L. *All the Fine Young Eagles: In the Cockpit with Canada's Second World War Fighter Aces*. Stoddart (Toronto), 1996.

Beaman, J. *Messerschmitt Bf 109 in Action Part 2*. Squadron/Signal (Carrollton, TX), 1983.

Bekker, C. *The Luftwaffe War Diaries*. Doubleday (New York), 1964.

Bendiner, E. *The Fall of Fortresses*. G.P. Putnam's (New York), 1980.

Bennett, R. *Ultra in the West*. Chas Scribner's Sons (New York), 1979.

Bishop, C. *Fortresses of the Big Triangle First*. East Anglia Books (Bishops Stortford, UK), 1986.

Bledsoe, M. Thunderbolt – *Memoirs of a World War II Fighter Pilot*. Van Nostrand (New York), 1982.

Blömertz, G. *Heaven Next Stop*. Wm. Kimber (London), 1953.

Blue, A. *The Fortunes of War*. Aero Publishers (Fallbrook, CA), 1967.

Bowman, M. *Fields of Little America*. Wensum (Norwich, UK), 1977.

Bowman, M. *Castles in the Air*. Patrick Stephens (Wellingborough, UK), 1984.

Bowyer, M.J.F. *Two Group R.A.F. – A Complete History, 1936-1945*. Faber & Faber (London), 1974.

Brooks, G.J. *Sunflower Wild*. Privately published (Huntington, WV), 1993.

Brown, G. & Lavigne, M. *Canadian Wing Commanders of Fighter Command in World War II*. Battleline Books (Langley, BC, Canada), 1984.

Caldwell, D.L. *JG 26: Top Guns of the Luftwaffe*. Orion (New York), 1991.

Caldwell, D.L. *JG 26: Photographic History of the Luftwaffe's Top Guns*. Motorbooks (Osceola, WI), 1994.

Caldwell, D.L. *The JG 26 War Diary Volume One: 1939-1942*. Grub Street (London), 1996.

Campbell, J. *Focke Wulf FW 190 in Action*. Squadron/Signal (Carrollton, TX), 1975.

Carson, L. *Pursue & Destroy*. Sentry (Granada Hills, CA), 1978.

Clostermann, P. *The Big Show*. Ballantine (New York), 1951 (reprint).

Collier, B. *The Defense of the United Kingdom*. HMSO (London), 1957.

Comer, J. *Combat Crew*. Wm. Morrow (New York), ca. 1985.

Cooper, M. *The German Air Force 1933-1945*. Jane's (London), 1981.

Craven, W. & Cate, J. *The Army Air Forces in World War II: Vol. II, Europe: Torch to Pointblank*. U. Chicago Press (Chicago), 1949.

Craven, W. & Cate, J. *The Army Air Forces in World War II – Vol. III, Europe: Argument to V-E Day*. U. Chicago Press (Chicago), 1951.

Crosby, H. H. *A Wing and a Prayer: The "Bloody 100th" Bomb Group of the U. S. Eighth Air Force in Action over Europe in World War II*. HarperCollins (New York), 1993.

Davies, A. *The 56th Fighter Group in World War II*. Infantry Journal Press (Washington), 1948.

Dezarrois, A. *The Mouchotte Diaries, 1940-1943*. Staples Press (London), 1956.

Ethell, J. & Price, A. *Target Berlin – Mission 250: 6 March 1944*. Jane's (London), 1981.

Farnol, L. *To the Limit of Their Endurance*. Sunflower Univ. Press (Manhattan, KS), 1944 (reprint).

Foreman, J. *Over the Beaches: The Air War over Normandy and Europe 1st-30th June 1944.* Air Research (Walton-on-Thames, UK), 1994.

Franks, N. *The Battle of the Airfields – 1st January 1945.* Grub Street (London), 1994.

Frappé, J-B. & Lorant, J-Y. *Le Focke-Wulf 190.* Éditions Larivière (Paris), 1995.

Freeman, R. *The Mighty Eighth.* Doubleday (New York), 1970.

Freeman, R. *Mustang at War.* Doubleday (New York), 1974.

Freeman, R. *B-17 Fortress at War.* Chas. Scribner's Sons (New York), 1977.

Freeman, R. *Thunderbolt – A Documentary History of the Republic P-47.* Chas. Scribner's Sons (New York), 1978.

Freeman, R. *Mighty Eighth War Diary.* Jane's (London), 1981.

Freeman, R. *Mighty Eighth War Manual.* Jane's (London), 1984.

Freeman, R. *The Hub – Fighter Leader.* Airlife (Shrewsbury, UK), 1988.

Fry, G. *Eagles over Duxford: The 78th Fighter Group in World War II.* Phalanx (St. Paul, MN), 1991.

Fry, G. & Ethell, J. *Escort to Berlin.* Arco (New York), 1980.

Gabreski, F. & Molesworth, C. *Gabby: A Fighter Pilot's Life.* Orion Books (New York), 1991.

Galland, A. *The First and the Last.* Methuen (London), 1955.

Gianneschi, D. *Mogins Maulers: The 362nd Fighter Group History of World War II.* Privately published (Chicago), 1981.

Girbig, W. *Im Anflug auf die Reichshauptstadt.* Motorbuch (Stuttgart), 1975.

Girbig, W. *Six Months to Oblivion.* Hippocrene (New York), 1975.

Girbig, W. *Mit Kurs auf Leuna.* Motorbuch (Stuttgart), 1980.

Girbig, W. *Vermisst.* Motorbuch (Stuttgart), 1986.

Godefroy, H. *Lucky 13.* Stoddart (Toronto), 1987 (reprint).

Godfrey, J. *The Look of Eagles.* Ballentine (New York), 1958 (reprint).

Gomann, H. *Und über uns der Himmel: Fliegergeschichten vom JG 26.* Kurt Vowinckel (Berg am See, Germany), 1996.

Goodson, J. *Tumult in the Clouds.* St Martin's (New York), 1983.

Green, W. *Augsburg Eagle.* Doubleday (New York), 1971.

Green, W. *Warplanes of the Third Reich.* Doubleday (New York), 1972.

Groh, R. *The Dynamite Gang.* Aero Publishers(Fallbrook, CA), 1983.

Hall, G. *One Thousand Destroyed.* Morgan Aviation Books (Dallas), 1946 (reprint).

Hammel, E. *Air War Europa: America's Air War against Germany in Europe and North Africa 1942-1945.* Pacifica Press (Pacifica, CA), 1994.

Hardesty, V. *Red Phoenix.* Arms & Armour Press (London), 1982.

Harry, G.P., ed. *339th Fighter Group.* Turner Publishing (Paducah, KY), 1991.

Hastings, M. *Bomber Command.* The Dial Press (New York), 1979.

Havelaar, M. & Hess, W. *The Ragged Irregulars of Bassingbourn: The 91st Bombardment Group in World War II.* Schiffer (Altglen, PA), 1995.

Hawkins, I. *Münster – The Way It Was.* Robinson Typographics (Anaheim, CA), 1984.

Hawkins, I. *Courage*Honor*Victory: A First Person History of the 95th Bomb Group (H).* Privately published (Bellevue, WA), 1987.

Heilmann, W. *I Fought You from the Skies.* Award Books (New York), 1951 (reprint).

Held, W. & Trautloft, H. *Die Gruenherzjaeger.* Podzun-Pallas-Verlag (Friedberg, Germany), 1985.

Held, W. *Adolf Galland: Ein Fliegerleben in Krieg und Frieden.* Podzun-Pallas (Friedberg, Germany), 1983.

Hess, W. *P-47 Thunderbolt at War.* Doubleday (New York), 1976.

Hess, W. *Zemke's Wolfpack: The 56th Fighter Group in World War II.* Motorbooks (Osceola, WI), 1992.

Hitchcock, T. *Gustav: Messerschmitt 109G Parts 1 & 2.* Monogram (Boylston, MA), 1977.

Hoseason, J. *The Thousand Day Battle.* Gillingham (Lowestoft, UK), 1979.

Howard, J. L. & Lavandier, O. *Boots from Heaven.* Cross Cultural Publications (Notre Dame, IN), 1994.

Hunt, L. *Twenty-One Squadrons: The History of the Royal Auxiliary Air Force 1925-1957.* Crécy Books (Somerton, UK), 1992 (reprint).

Huntzinger, E.J. *The 388th at War.* Privately published (San Angelo, TX), 1979.

Johnson, C. *History of the Hell Hawks.* Southcoast Typesetting (Anaheim, CA), 1975.

Johnson, J. *Wing Leader.* Ballentine (New York), 1956 (reprint).

Johnson, J. *Full Circle: The Tactics of Air Fighting 1914-1964.* Ballentine (New York), 1964.

Johnson, R. & Caidin, M. *Thunderbolt.* Ballentine (New York), 1958 (reprint).

Joiner, O.W., ed. *The History of the 364th Fighter Group.* Privately published (Marceline,

MO), 1991.

Knocke, H. *I Flew for the Führer*. Henry Holt (New York), 1953.

Kurowski, F. *Der Luftkrieg über Deutschland*. Wilhelm Heyne (München), 1977.

Lallemant, R. *Rendezvous with Fate*. Macdonald (London), 1964.

McAulay, L. *Six Aces: Australian Fighter Pilots 1939-1945*. Banner Books (Melbourne), 1991.

McLachlan, I. *Night of the Intruders: First-Hand Accounts Chronicling the Slaughter of Homeward Bound USAAF Mission 311*. Patrick Stephens (Sparkford, UK), 1994.

McIntosh, D. *High Blue Battle*. Stoddart (Toronto), 1990.

Marshall, B. *Angels, Bulldogs & Dragons*. Champlin Fighter Museum (Mesa, AZ), 1985.

Middlebrook, M. *The Battle of Hamburg: Allied Bomber Forces against a German City in 1943*. Chas. Scribner's Sons (New York), 1980.

Middlebrook, M. *The Schweinfurt-Regensburg Mission*. Chas Scribner's Sons (New York), 1983.

Miller, K. D. *Escort: the 356th Fighter Group on Operations over Europe 1943-1945*. Academy (Fort Wayne, IN), 1985.

Miller, K. D. *Jigger, Tinplate and Redcross: The 359th Fighter Group in World War II*. Academy (Fort Wayne, IN), 1987.

Miller, K. D. *Seven Months over Europe: The 363rd Fighter Group in World War II*. Privately published (Hicksville, OH), 1989.

Mitcham, S. *Men of the Luftwaffe*. Presidio (Novato, CA), 1988.

Murray, W. *Luftwaffe*. Nautical & Aviation (Baltimore, MD) 1985.

Nauroth, H. *Die deutsche Luftwaffe vom Nordkap bis Tobruk 1939-1945*. Pozun-Pallas (Friedberg, Germany), ca. 1980.

Nowarra, H. *Die Bomber Kommen*. Pallas (Friedberg), 1978.

Nowarra, H. *Die 109*. Motorbuch (Stuttgart), 1979.

Nowarra, H. *Focke Wulf FW 190 – Ta 152*. Motorbuch (Stuttgart), 1987.

Obermaier, E. *Die Ritterkreuztraeger der Luftwaffe 1939-1945: Band 1: Jagdflieger*. Dieter Hoffman (Mainz), 1966.

Olmsted, M. *The Yoxford Boys*. Aero Publishers (Fallbrook, CA), 1971.

Olmsted, M. *The 357th over Europe*. Phalanx (St. Paul, MN), 1994.

Olynyk, F. *USAAF (European Theater) Credits for the Destruction of Enemy Aircraft in Air-to-Air Combat in World War 2*. Privately published (Aurora, OH), 1987.

Olynyk, F. *RAF 400 Series Squadrons Credits for the Destruction of Enemy Aircraft in Air-to-Air Combat in World War 2*. Privately published (Aurora, OH), 1989.

Olynyk, F. *RAF 300 Series Squadrons Credits for the Destruction of Enemy Aircraft in Air-to-Air Combat in World War 2*. Privately published (Aurora, OH), 1990.

Oxspring, B. *Spitfire Command*. Grafton (London), 1987 (reprint).

Parker, D. S. *To Win the Winter Sky: Air War over the Ardennes, 1944-1945*. Combined Books (Conshohocken, PA), 1994.

Peaslee, B. *Heritage of Valor*. J. B. Lippincott (New York), 1964.

Piekalkiewicz, J. *Luftkrieg 1939-1945*. Wilhelm Heyne (München), 1978.

Powell, R.H., ed. *The 'Bluenosed Bastards' of Bodney*. Privately published (Dallas, TX), 1990.

Price, A. *Battle over the Reich*. Ian Allen (London), 1973.

Price, A. *World War II Fighter Conflict*. Macdonald and Jane's (London), 1975.

Price, A. *The Bomber in World War II*. Chas. Scribner's Sons (New York), 1976.

Price, A. *Luftwaffe Handbook*. Chas. Scribner's Sons (New York), 1977.

Price, A. *Focke Wulf 190 at War*. Ian Allen (London), 1977.

Prien, J. & Rodeike, P. *Messerschmitt Bf 109F, G, & K Series: An Illustrated Study*. Schiffer (Atglen, PA), 1993.

Prien, J. & Rodeike, P. *Jagdgeschwader 1 und 11: Einsatz in der Reichsverteidigung von 1939 bis 1945: Teile 1-3*. Struve (Eutin, Germany), 1993.

Prien, J. & Stemmer, G. *Messerschmitt Bf 109 im Einsatz bei Stab und I./ Jagdgeschwader 3: 1938-1945*. Struve (Eutin, Germany), 1996.

Prien, J. & Stemmer, G. *Messerschmitt Bf 109 im Einsatz bei der II./Jagdgeschwader 3: 1940-1945*. Struve (Eutin, Germany), 1996.

Prien, J. & Stemmer, G. *Messerschmitt Bf 109 im Einsatz bei der III/Jagdgeschwader 3: 1938-1945*. Struve (Eutin, Germany), 1996.

Priller, J. *JG 26: Geschichte eines Jagdgeschwaders*. Kurt Vowinckel (Heidelberg), 1956.

Pütz, R. *Duel in de wolken: De luchtoorlog in de gevarendriehoek Roermond-Luik-Aken*. Van Soeren (Amsterdam), 1994.

Ramsey, W. (ed.) *The Blitz Then & Now Vols. I-III*. Battle of Britain Prints (London), 1990.

Rawlings, J. *Fighter Squadrons of the Royal Air Force and Their Aircraft*. Macdonald and

---

Jane's (London), 1969.

Renner, W. *Wilhelm-Ferdinand Galland.* Hans Arens Verlag (Berlin), 1943.

Richards, D. & Saunders, H. *Royal Air Force 1939-1945 Vol. II: The Fight Avails.* HMSO (London), 1975.

Ries, K. *Luftwaffe Embleme 1935-1945.* Dieter Hoffmann (Mainz), 1976.

Ring, H. & Girbig, W. *Jagdgeschwader 27.* Motorbuch (Stuttgart), 1971.

Rust, K. *The Ninth Air Force in World War II.* Aero Publishers (Fallbrook, CA), 1967.

Rust, K. *Eighth Air Force Story.* Historical Aviation Album (Temple City, CA), 1978.

Rust, K. *Ninth Air Force Story.* Historical Aviation Album (Temple City, CA), 1982.

Rust, K. & Hess, W. *The Slybird Group.* Aero Publishers (Fallbrook, CA), 1968.

Ryan, C. *The Longest Day.* Simon & Schuster (New York), 1959.

Ryan, C. *A Bridge Too Far.* Simon & Schuster (New York), 1974.

Salisbury, H. *The 900 Days.* Harper & Row (New York), 1969.

Sarkar, D. *Through Peril to the Stars: RAF Pilots Who Failed to Return 1939-1945.* Ramrod (Malvern, Worcs, UK), 1993.

Sarkar, D. *A Few of the Many: Air War 1939-1945 – A Kaleidoscope of Memories.* Ramrod (Malvern, Worcs, UK), 1995.

Saunders, H. *Royal Air Force 1939-1945 Vol. III – The Fight is Won.* HMSO (London), 1975.

Scott, D. *Typhoon Pilot.* Arrow Books (London), 1987 (reprint).

Sharp, C. & Bowyer, M.J.F. *Mosquito.* Faber & Faber (London), 1967.

Shores, C. *Second Tactical Air Force.* Osprey (Reading, UK), 1970.

Shores, C. & Williams, C. *Aces High: A Tribute to the Most Notable Fighter Pilots of the British and Commonwealth Forces in WWII.* Grub Street (London), 1994.

Skawran, P. *Ikaros.* Luftfahrt-Verlag W. Zuerl (Steinebach, Germany), 1969.

Sims, E. *American Aces.* Ballentine (New York), 1958 (reprint).

Sims, E. *The Greatest Aces.* Ballentine (New York), 1967 (reprint).

Sims, E. *The Aces Talk.* Ballentine (New York), 1972 (reprint).

Sloan, J.S. *The Route as Briefed.* Argus Press (Cleveland), 1946.

Smith, D.O. *Screaming Eagle: Memoirs of a B-17 Group Commander.* Dell (New York), 1990.

Smith, J. & Gallaspy, J. *Luftwaffe Camouflage & Markings Vols. 2 & 3.* Kookaburra (Melbourne), 1976.

Smith, J. & Creek, E. *Fw 190D.* Monogram (Boylston, MA), 1986.

Steiner, E. *King's Cliffe.* Privately published (no location), 1947 (1983 reprint).

Steinko, J. *The Geyser Gang: The 428th Fighter Squadron in World War II.* ROMA Association (Minneapolis, MN), 1986.

Strong, R.A. *First over Germany: A History of the 306th Bombardmant Group.* Privately published (Charlotte, NC), 1990.

Swanborough, G. & Green, W. *The Focke-Wulf Fw 190.* Arco (New York), 1976.

Thom, W. *The Brotherhood of Courage.* Privately published (New York), 1986.

Thomas, C. & Shores, C. *The Typhoon & Tempest Story.* Arms & Armour (London), 1988.

Trautloft, H., Held, W. & Bob, E. *Die Grünherzjäger.* Podzun-Pallas-Verlag (Friedberg), 1985.

Vanackere, E. *von Flugplatz tot Airport: de geschiedenis van het vliegeld Bissegem-Wevelgem.* Privately published (Kortrijk, Belgium), 1991.

van den Broucke, D. *Quand des avions s'abattaient...* Imprim'Tout Editions (Mouscron, Belgium), ca. 1990.

Vanoverbeke, L. *Moorsele: één dorp, twee vliegvelden.* Privately published (Kortirjk, Belgium), 1993.

Varian, H.L. *The Bloody Hundredth: Missions and Memories of a World War II Bomb Group.* Privately published (no location given), 1979.

Vickers, R. *The Liberators from Wendling.* Aerospace Historian (Manhattan, KS), 1977.

Wagner, R., ed. *The Soviet Air Force in World War II: The Official History.* Doubleday (Garden City, NY), 1973.

Williams, M. *U.S. Army in World War II: Chronology 1941-1945.* GPO (Washington, DC), 1958.

Wood, T. & Gunston, B. *Hitler's Luftwaffe.* Salamander (London), 1977.

Wooldridge, J.de L., *Low Attack: The Story of Two Mosquito Squadrons 1940-43;* Crécy Books (Bodmin, UK), 1993 (reprint).

Wykeham, P. *Fighter Command.* Putnam (London), 1960.

Yeager, C. & Janos, L. *Yeager.* Bantam Books (New York), 1985.

Ziemke, E. *Stalingrad to Berlin.* GPO (Washington, DC), 1966.

Zijlstra, G. *Diary of an Air War.* Vantage Press (New York), 1977.

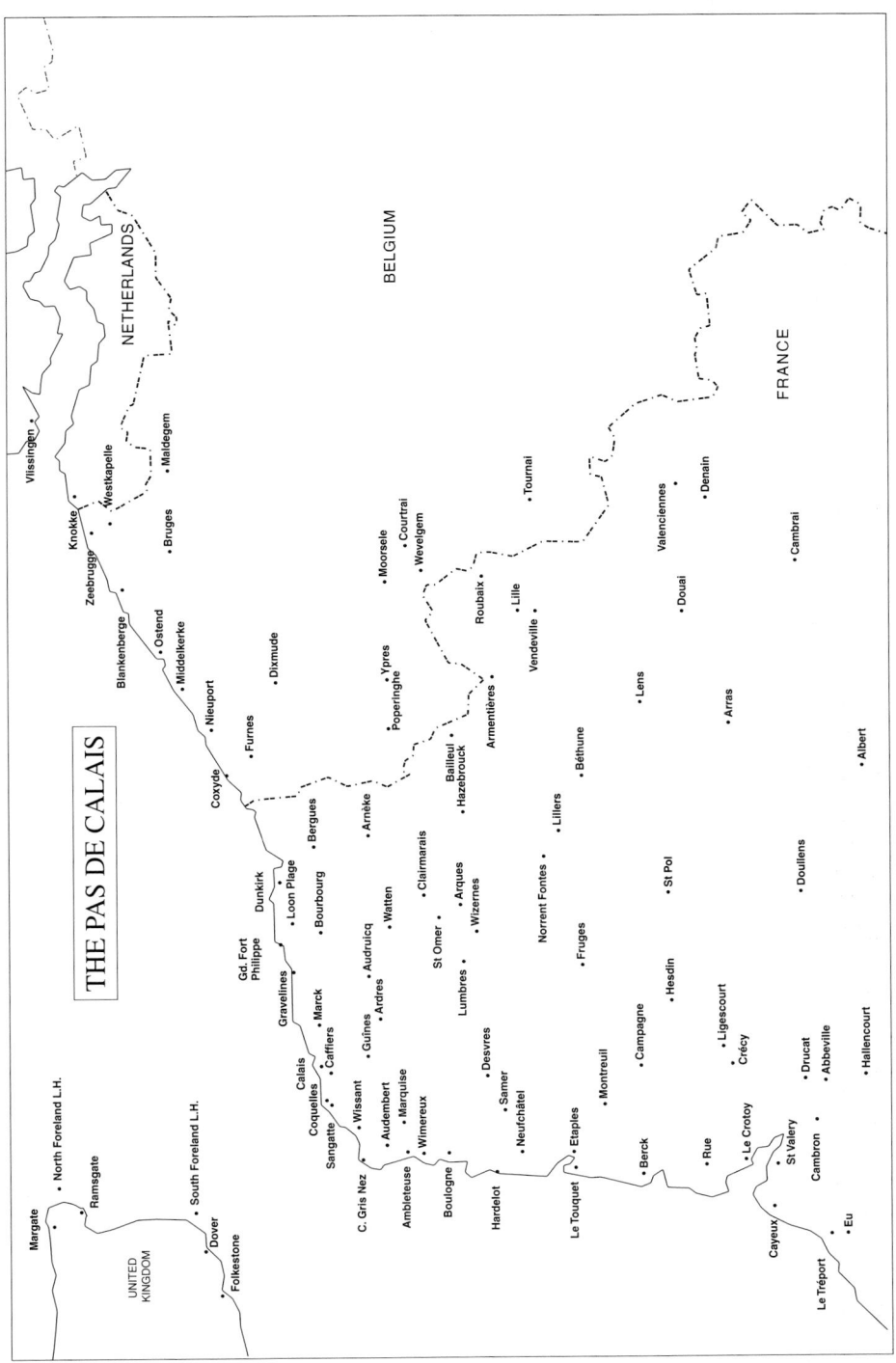

THE PAS DE CALAIS

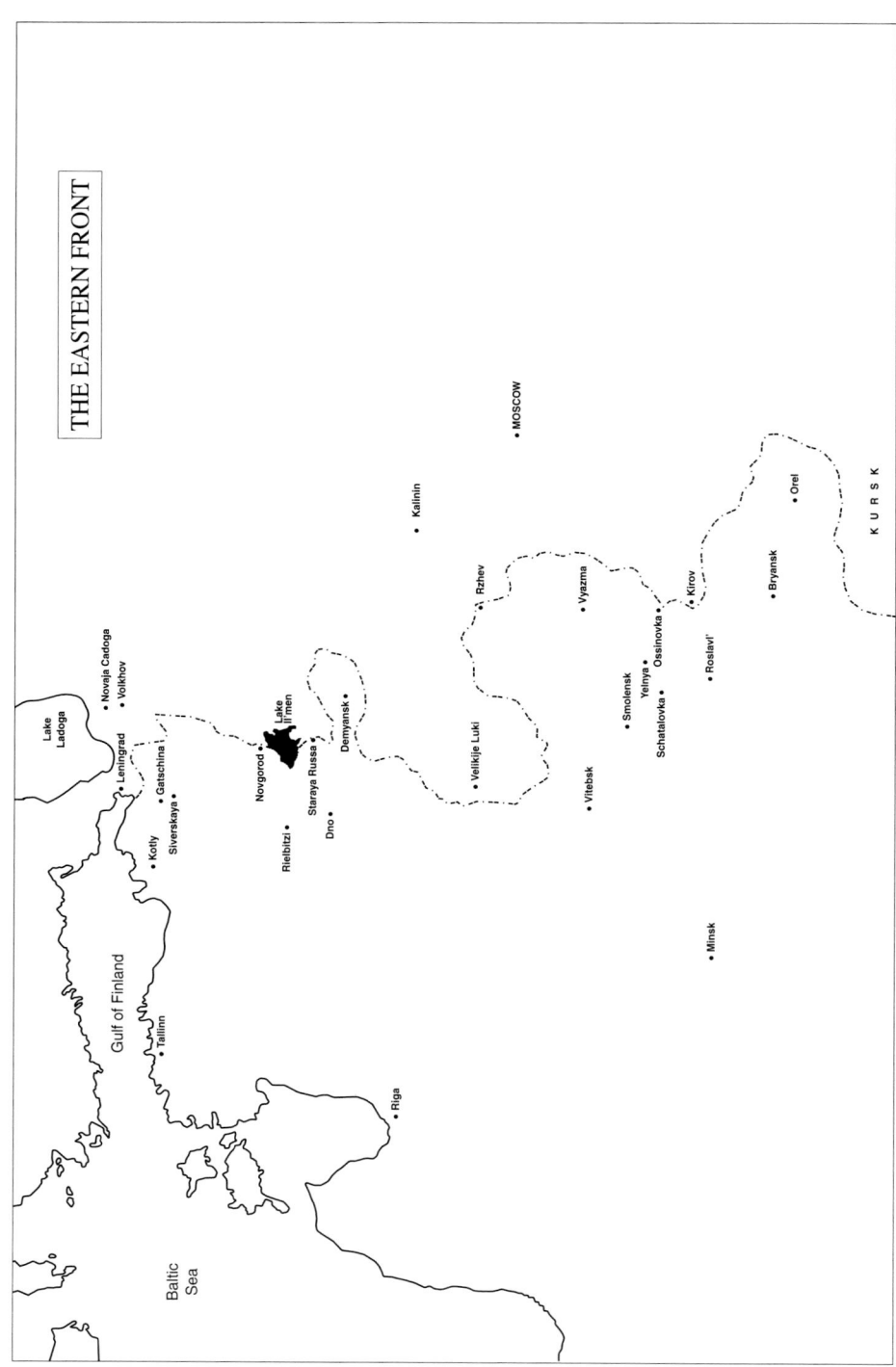

THE EASTERN FRONT

Lake Ladoga

Novaja Cadoga •
• Volkhov

Lake Il'men

Gulf of Finland

• Tallinn

Baltic Sea

• Riga

• Leningrad
Gatschina •
• Kotly
Siverskaya •

Novgorod •
Staraya Russa •
Rielbitzi •
Dno •
Demyansk •

• Kalinin

• MOSCOW

• Rzhev

• Velikije Luki

• Vyazma

• Vitebsk

• Smolensk
Yelnya •
Schatalovka •
Ossinovka •
• Kirov
• Roslavl'

• Bryansk

• Orel

K U R S K

• Minsk

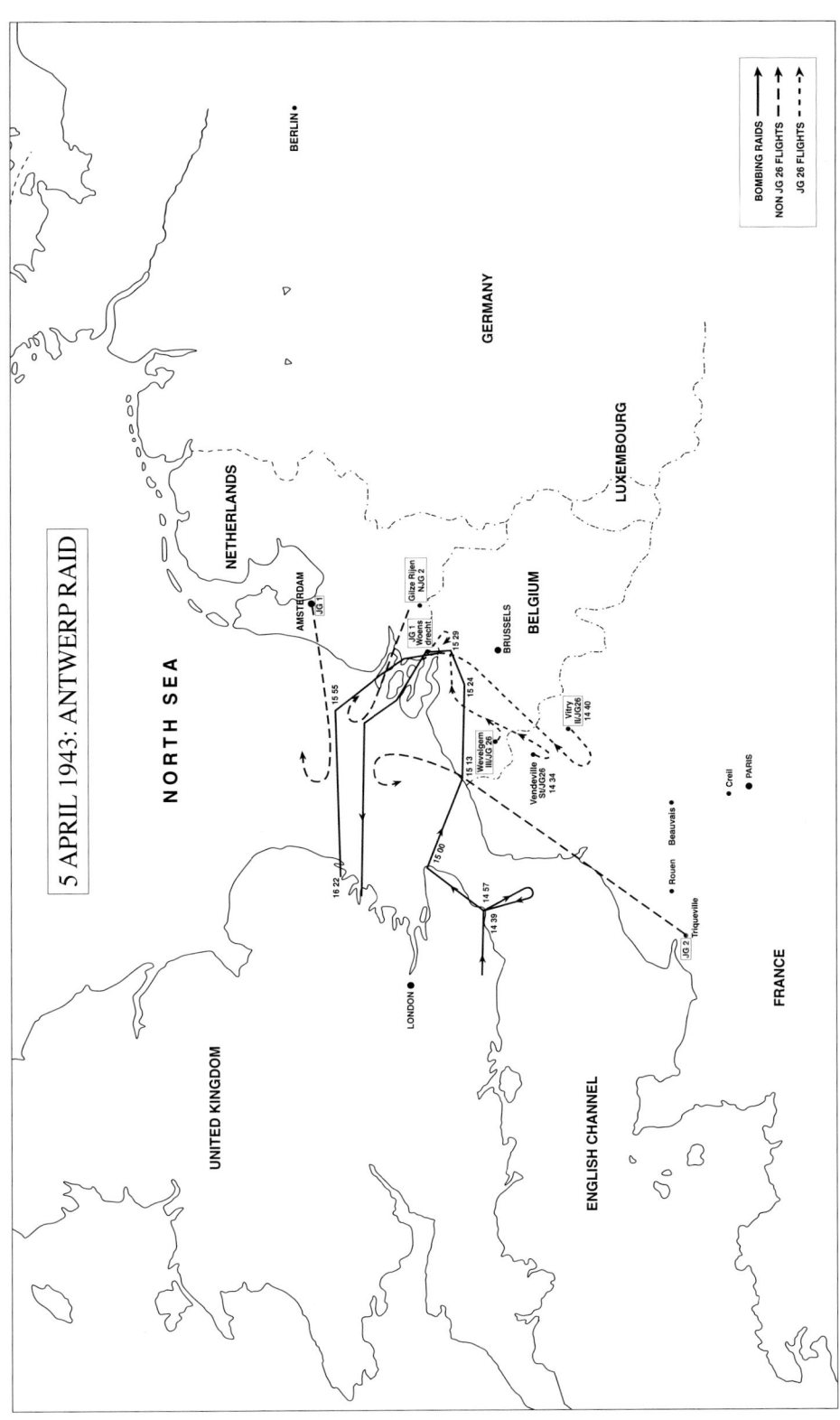

5 APRIL 1943: ANTWERP RAID

NORTH SEA

BERLIN •

GERMANY

NETHERLANDS

AMSTERDAM •
JG 1

LUXEMBOURG

Gilze Rijen
NJG 2

JG 1
Woens drecht

15 55

15 29

BRUSSELS •

BELGIUM

15 24

Vitry
III./JG26
14 40

Wevelgem
III./JG 26

15 13

Vendeville
StG26
14 34

16 22

15 00

14 57

14 39

• Creil

• PARIS

• Rouen

Beauvais •

Triqueville

JG 2

FRANCE

LONDON •

UNITED KINGDOM

ENGLISH CHANNEL

BOMBING RAIDS
NON JG 26 FLIGHTS
JG 26 FLIGHTS

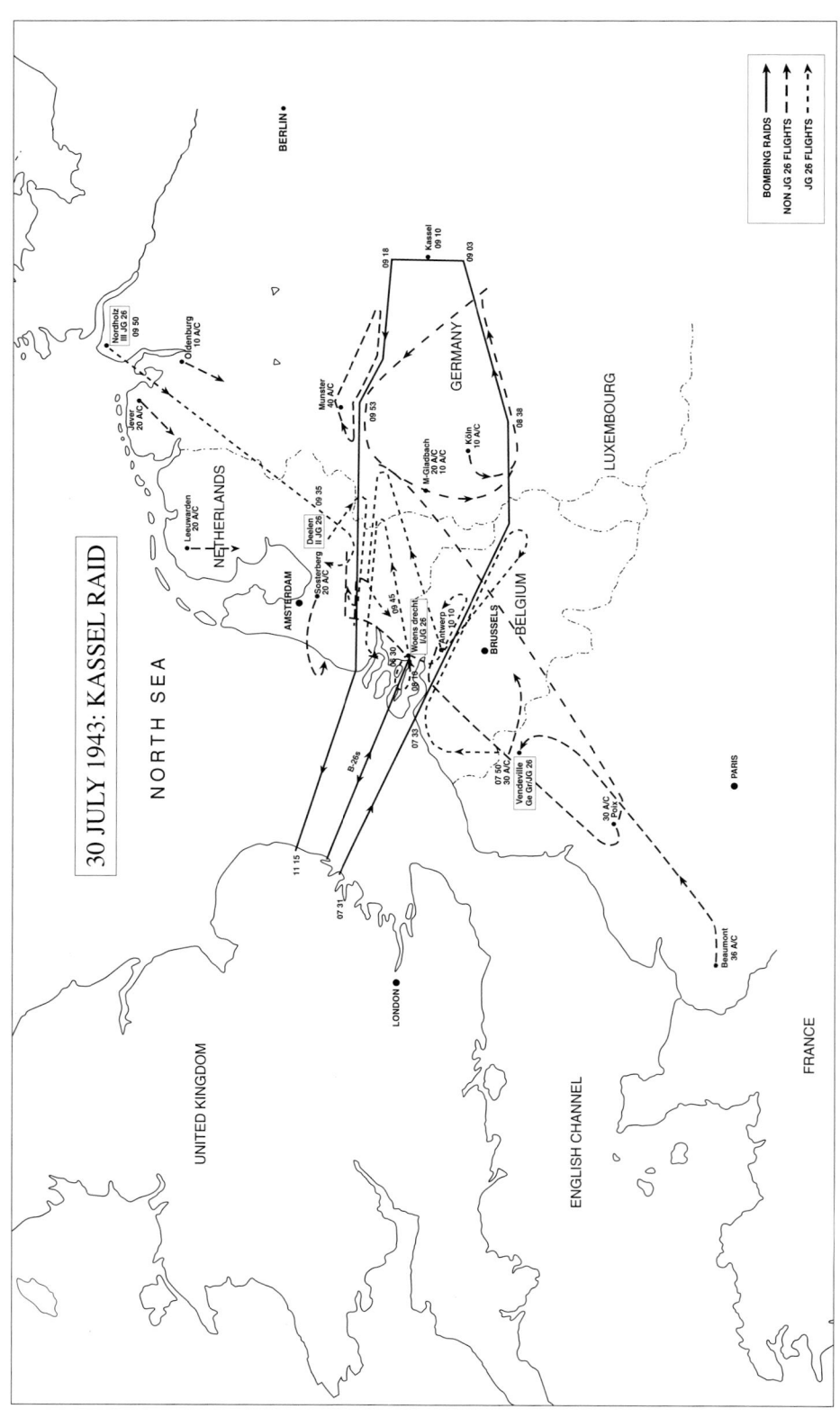

30 JULY 1943: KASSEL RAID

BOMBING RAIDS
NON JG 26 FLIGHTS
JG 26 FLIGHTS

BERLIN

GERMANY

Kassel 09 10

09 18

09 03

Munster 40 A/C

09 53

Köln 10 A/C

08 38

M-Gladbach 20 A/C

LUXEMBOURG

Northolz III/JG 26 09 50

Oldenburg 10 A/C

Jever 20 A/C

Leeuwarden 20 A/C

NETHERLANDS

09 35

Deelen III/JG 26

Soesterberg 20 A/C

09 45

AMSTERDAM

Woens drecht, I/JG 26

Antwerp I/JG 26 10 10

BRUSSELS

BELGIUM

08 15

07 33

07 50 30 A/C

Vendeville Ge Gr/JG 26

30 A/C Poix

PARIS

B-26s

NORTH SEA

11 15

07 31

Beaumont 36 A/C

LONDON

UNITED KINGDOM

ENGLISH CHANNEL

FRANCE

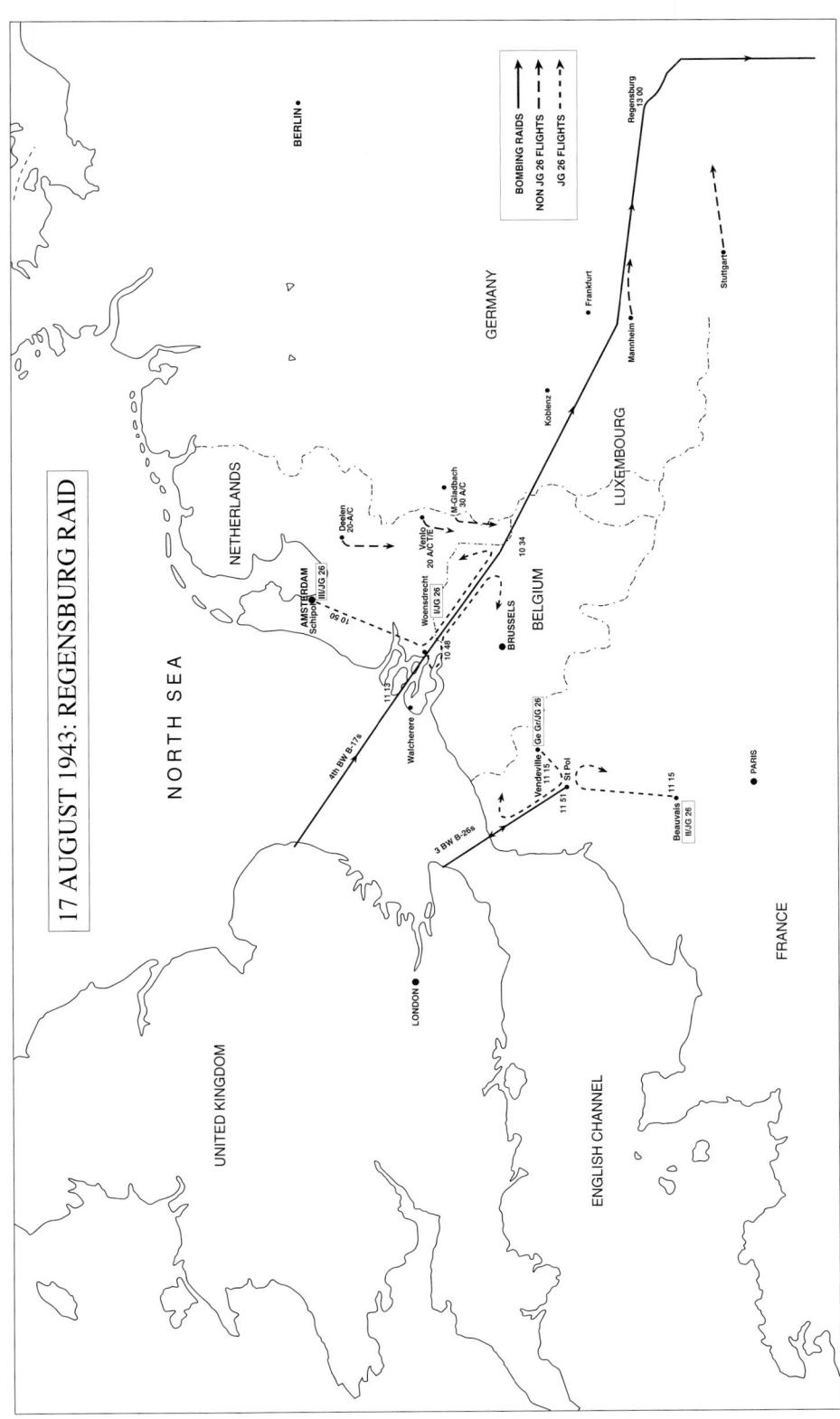

17 AUGUST 1943: REGENSBURG RAID

NORTH SEA

UNITED KINGDOM

LONDON ●

ENGLISH CHANNEL

FRANCE

NETHERLANDS

BERLIN ●

AMSTERDAM
Schipol
III/JG 26

10 58

Woensdrecht
I/JG 26
10 48

Walcherere

11 15

4th BW B-17s

3 BW B-26s

Deelen
20 A/C

Venlo
20 A/C THE

M-Gladbach
30 A/C

Vendeville
St Pol
11 51

Ge Gr/JG 26
11 5

11 51

Beauvais
11 15

III/JG 26

PARIS ●

BRUSSELS ●

BELGIUM

10 34

GERMANY

Koblenz ●

Frankfurt ●

Mannheim ●

LUXEMBOURG

Stuttgart ●

Regensburg
13 00

BOMBING RAIDS
NON JG 26 FLIGHTS
JG 26 FLIGHTS

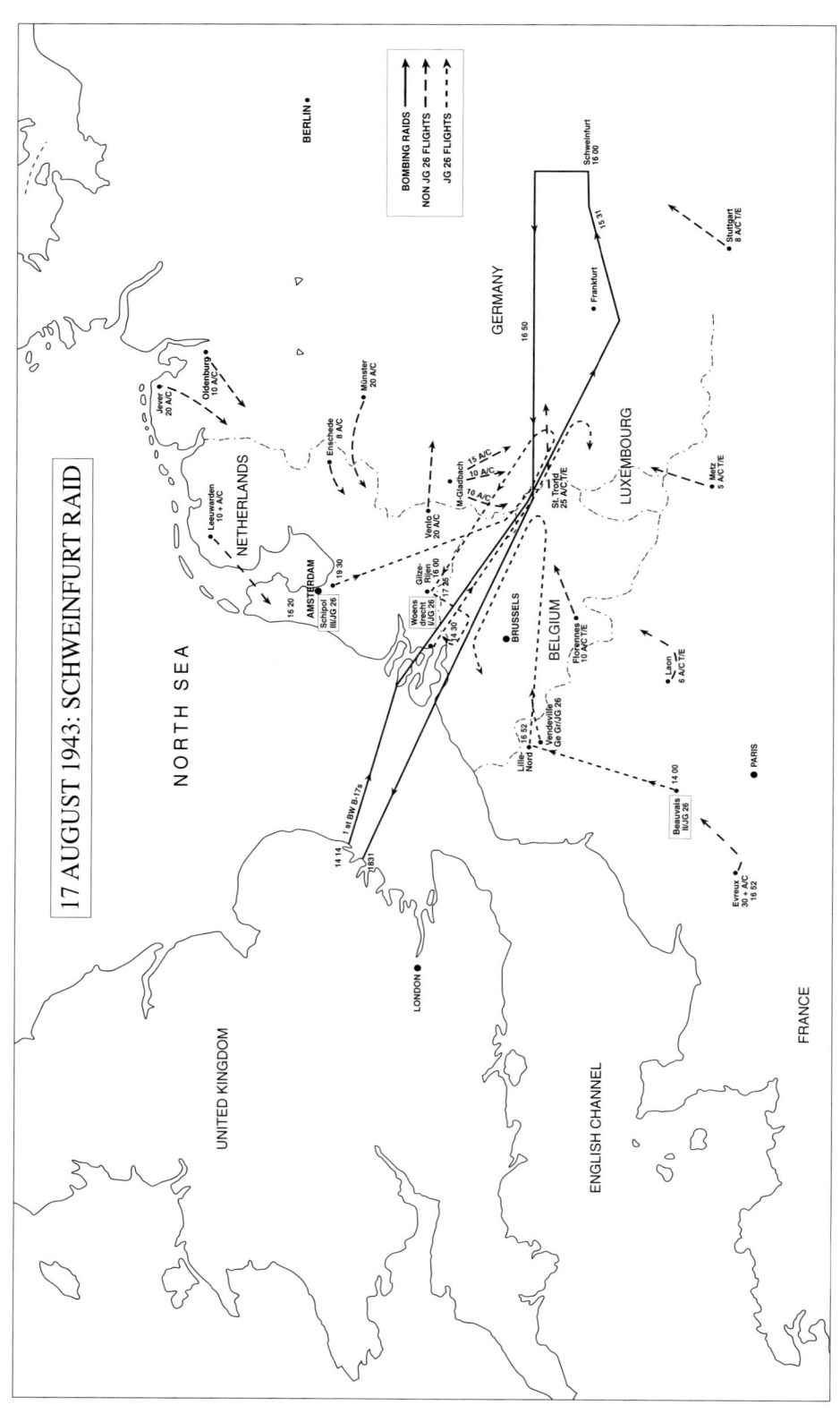

17 AUGUST 1943: SCHWEINFURT RAID

NORTH SEA

UNITED KINGDOM

LONDON •

ENGLISH CHANNEL

FRANCE

NETHERLANDS

BELGIUM

GERMANY

LUXEMBOURG

• BERLIN

BOMBING RAIDS
NON JG 26 FLIGHTS
JG 26 FLIGHTS

Schweinfurt
16 00

15 31

16 50

• Frankfurt

Stuttgart
8 A/C T/E

Metz
5 A/C T/E

St. Trond
25 A/C T/E

Florennes
10 A/C T/E

Laon
6 A/C T/E

• PARIS

Beauvais
III/JG 26
14 00

Evreux
30 + A/C
16 52

Lille-
Nord

Vendeville
Ge Gr/JG 26
16 52

Vlissingen

Woens
drecht
III/JG 26
14 30

Gilze-
Rijen
16 00
17 35

AMSTERDAM
19 30
Schiphol
III/JG 26
16 20

Venlo
20 A/C

M-Gladbach

15 A/C
10 A/C
10 A/C

Enschede
8 A/C

Münster
20 A/C

Oldenburg
10 A/C

Jever
20 A/C

Leeuwarden
10 + A/C

BRUSSELS

I BI BW B-17s
14 14
16 51

566

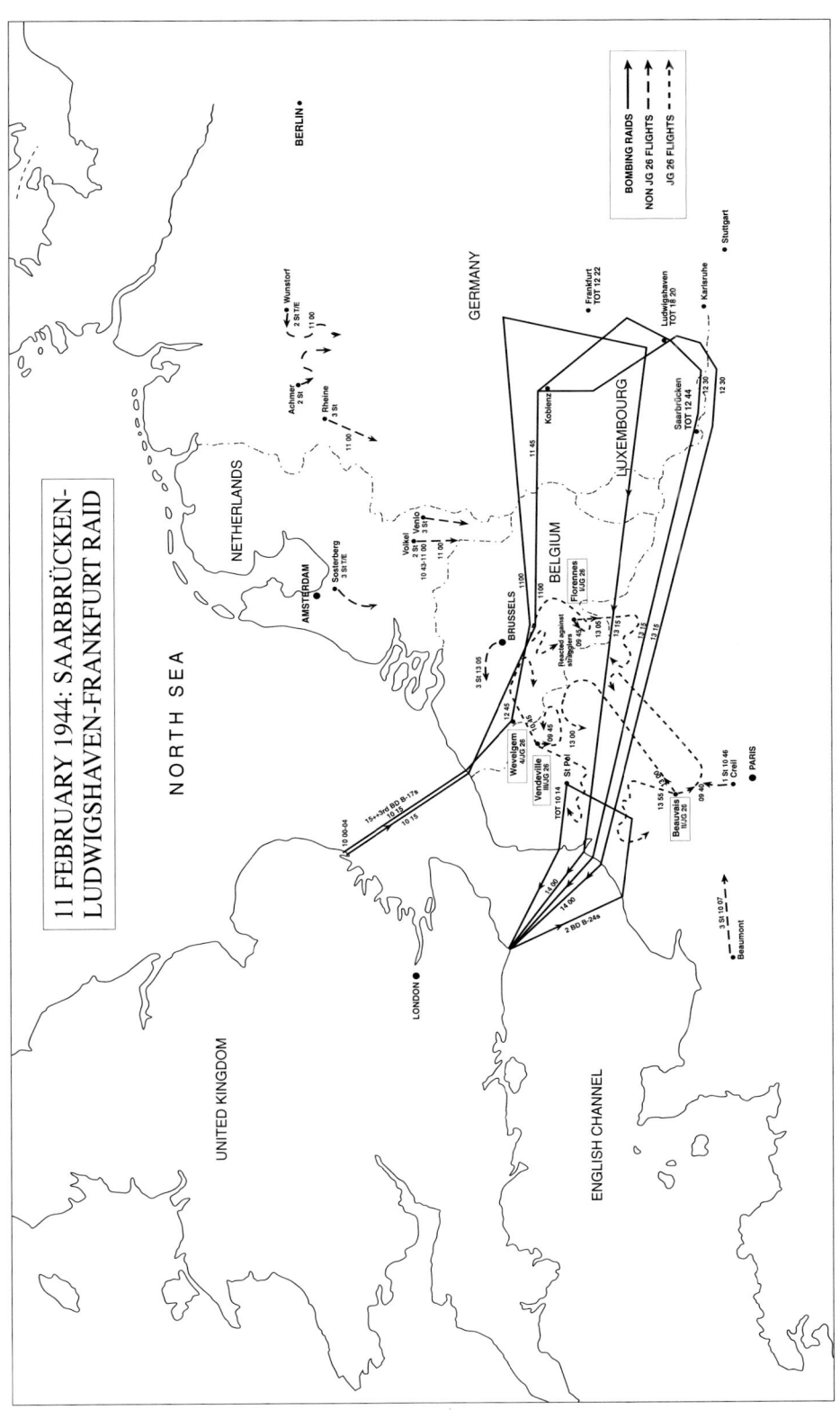

11 FEBRUARY 1944: SAARBRÜCKEN-LUDWIGSHAVEN-FRANKFURT RAID

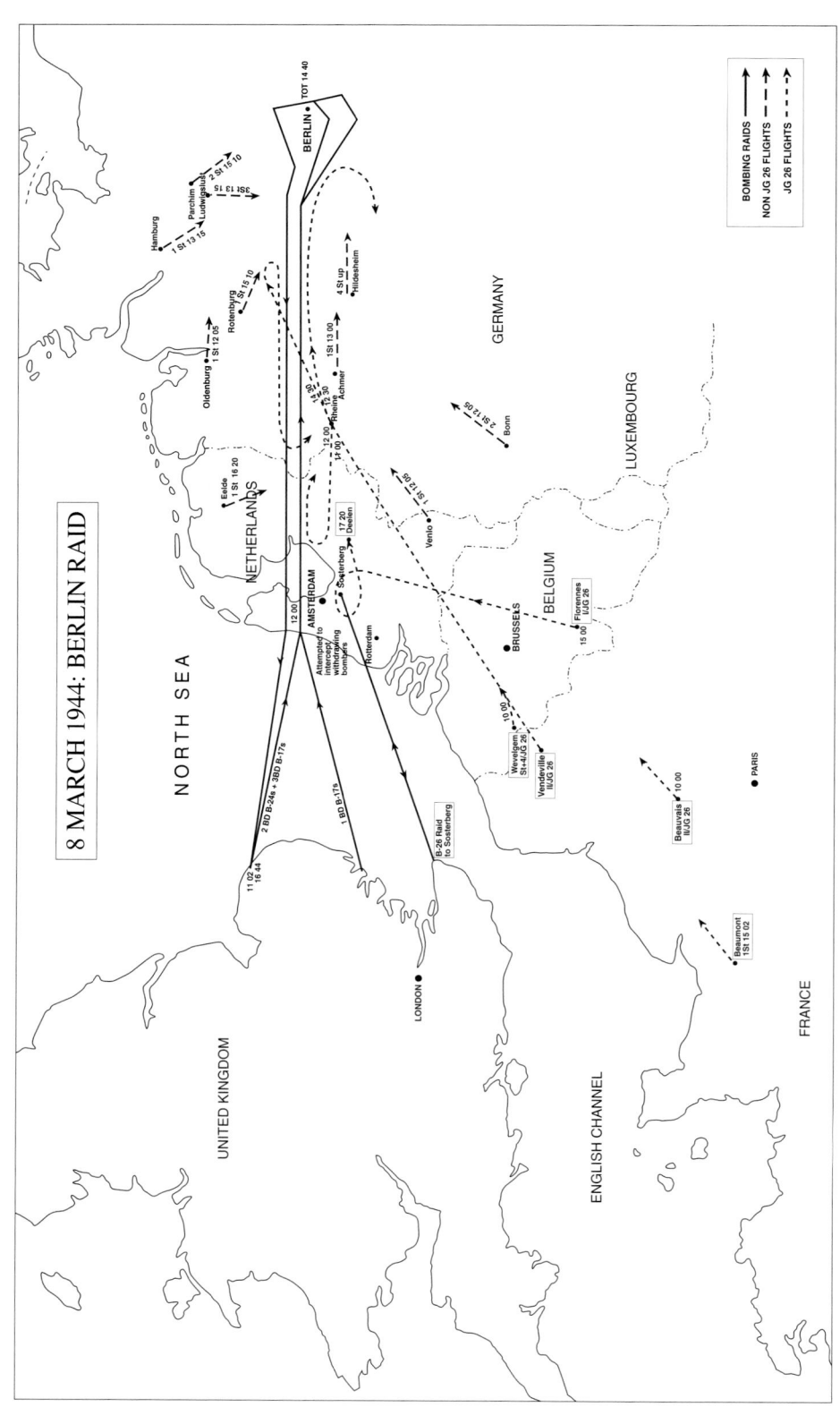

8 MARCH 1944: BERLIN RAID

BOMBING RAIDS
NON JG 26 FLIGHTS
JG 26 FLIGHTS

NORTH SEA

UNITED KINGDOM

LONDON

ENGLISH CHANNEL

FRANCE

NETHERLANDS

GERMANY

BELGIUM

LUXEMBOURG

BERLIN TOT 14 40

Hamburg

Parchim 3St 15 10
Ludwigslust
1 St 13 15 3St 13 15

Rotenburg St 15 10

Oldenburg 1 St 12 05

4 St up Hildesheim

1St 13 00
Rheine Achmer
1 30
12 00
14 00

Eelde 1 St 16 20

Bonn 50 21 IS 2

Venlo 1 St 12 05

AMSTERDAM 12 00

Soesterberg 17 20
Deelen

Attempted to
intercept
withdrawing
bombers

Rotterdam

BRUSSELS

Florennes
II/JG 26 15 00

Wevelgem
St-4/JG 26 10 00

Vendeville
II/JG 26

PARIS

Beauvais 10 00
II/JG 26

Beaumont
1St 15 02

2 BD B-24s • 3BD B-17s

1 BD B-17s

11 02 16 44

B-26 Raid
to Soesterberg

568

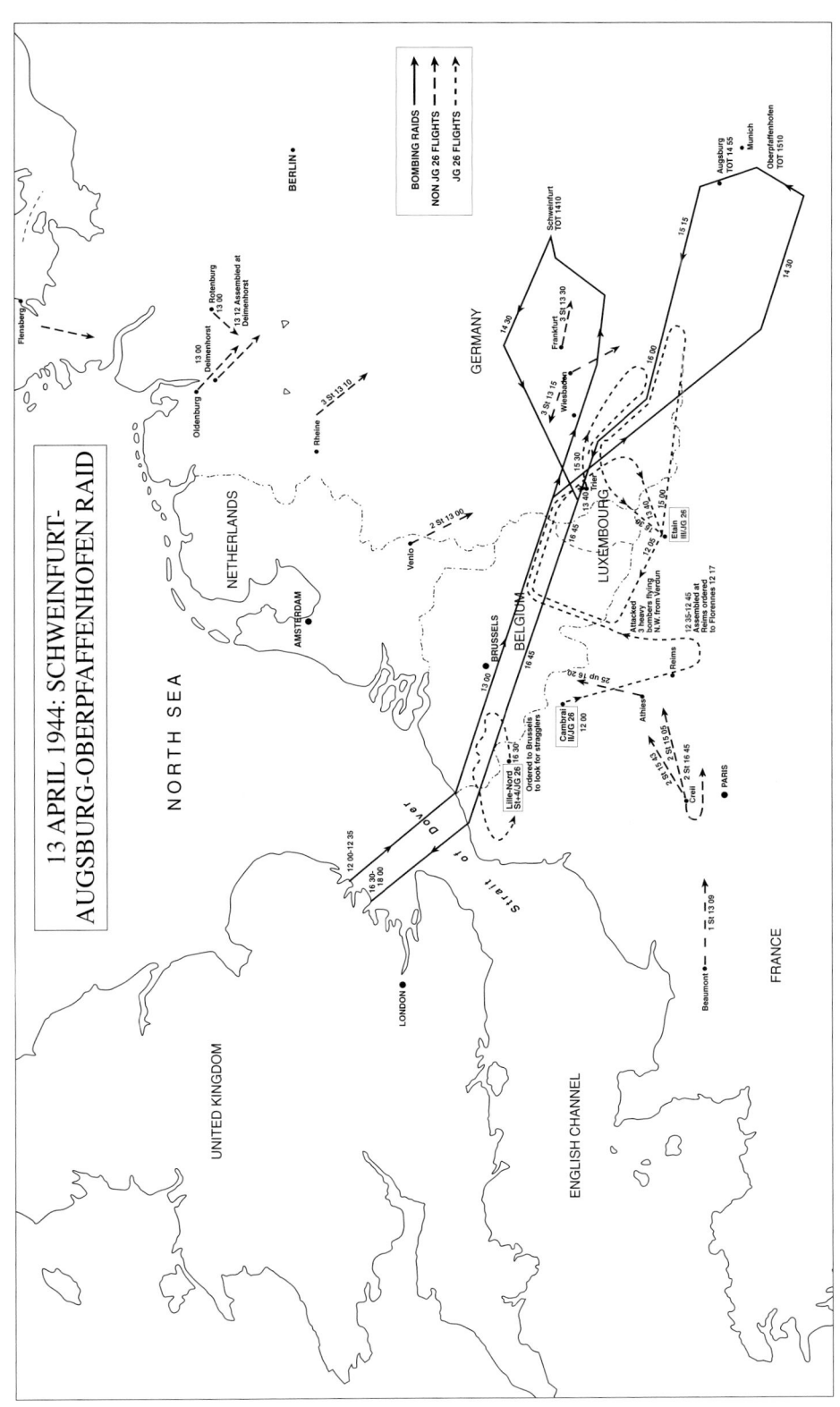

13 APRIL 1944: SCHWEINFURT-AUGSBURG-OBERPFAFFENHOFEN RAID

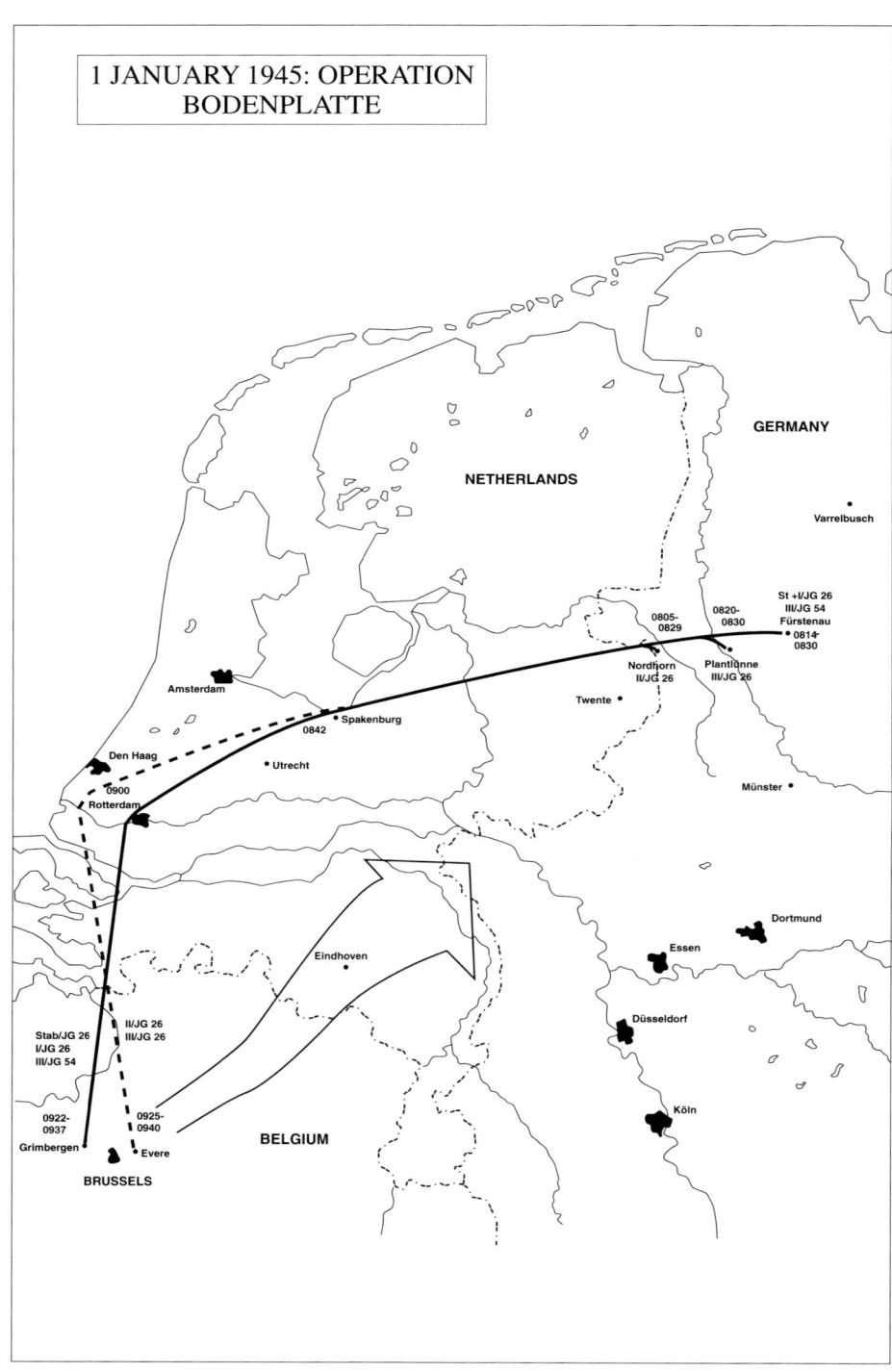

1 JANUARY 1945: OPERATION BODENPLATTE

GERMANY

Varrelbusch

NETHERLANDS

St +I/JG 26
III/JG 54
Fürstenau
0814-
0830

0805-
0829

0820-
0830

Nordhorn
II/JG 26

Plantlünne
III/JG 26

Amsterdam

Twente

Spakenburg
0842

Den Haag

Utrecht

Münster

0900

Rotterdam

Dortmund

Essen

Eindhoven

Düsseldorf

Stab/JG 26
I/JG 26
III/JG 54

II/JG 26
III/JG 26

Köln

0922-
0937

0925-
0940

Grimbergen

Evere

BELGIUM

BRUSSELS

INDEX

Personnel

Axis
NB: Tables of JG 26 claims and casualties are not indexed.

Adam, Fw. H-G., 74
Afflerbach, Uffz. Franz, 223, 239
Ahrens, Fw. Erich, 295, 360, 361, 367, 412
Ahrens, Lt. Peter, 78, 82, 124, 137, 173, 175, 374, 380, 422, 430, 440
Aistleitner, Hptm. Johann, 23, 113, 159, 184, 200, 201, 490
Altendorf, Uffz., 407
Altmann, Lt. Leberecht, 142, 209, 223, 455, 489
Andel, Lt. Peter "Pit", 361, 364, 367, 370, 374, 376, 378, 380, 429, 438, 440, 442
Anselment, Gefr. Reinhard, 382, 385
Asmus, Lt. Erich, 426, 446, 463
Ayerle, Uffz. Hermann, 239, 280, 288, 303, 356
Babenz, Fhj.-Ofw. Emil, 159, 238
Backeberg, Uffz. Heinz, 52, 58
Backhaus, Uffz. Hans, 447, 474
Backhaus, Lt. Otto-August, 31, 45
Bäder, Uffz. Alfred, 159
Baier, Lt. Valentin, 338, 357
Balloff, Uffz. Robert, 257
Bannischka, Uffz. Helmut, 146, 155
Bartels, Lt. Heinz-William, 336, 338, 356, 440, 441
Barthel, Fw. Alfred, 16, 17, 18
Battmer, Fliegerstabsingenieur Ernst, 258, 344, 426
Baumann, Uffz. Josef, 172, 215, 231
Baumbach, Uffz. Willi, 468
Bäumener, Fw. Helmut, 37, 73, 145, 153
Beck, Uffz. Kurt, 242, 262
Beck, Uffz. Otto, 465
Becker, Fw. Alois, 338, 357
Becker, Uffz. Hans-Georg, 131, 135, 249, 251, 268
Beckert, Uffz. Otto, 437, 448
Beer, Lt. Heinrich, 159, 223, 231
Beese, Oblt. Artur, 76, 103, 135, 152, 153, 209, 235, 489
Bellmann, Uffz. Rudolf, 455, 469
Benk, Fhj.-Uffz. Konrad, 251
Benz, Lt. Siegfried, 306, 360, 370, 393
Berg, Uffz. Heinrich, 146, 224
Berger, Uffz. Walter, 131, 152
Bergmann, Uffz. Günther, 455
Bergmeier, Flg. Hans, 396
Berndt, Uffz. Karl-Heinz, 414
Bernhardt, Ofhr. Horst, 417
Bertels, Oblt. Konrad, 306, 325, 378
Bexen, Gefr. Harro, 382, 462
Beyer, Obfw. Siegfried, 58
Bierkamp, Uffz. Karl, 172, 206
Binge, Uffz. Werner, 374, 400, 419
Birke, Uffz. Gerhard, 60
Birkner, Ofhr. Heinz, 465
Birn, Ogfr. Jürgen, 42
Bischoff, Uffz. Hermann, 369, 390
Bleich, Lt. Hans, 264, 267, 438
Blickle, Lt. Wilhelm, 452, 465
Blömert, Lt. Günther, 40, 52, 107, 309, 417, 419, 477
Böcher, Obfw. Karl-Heinz, 99
Bock, Uffz. Arnulf, 113
Bock, Uffz. Otto, 450
Böcker, Ogfr. 465
Boeckl, Uffz. Albert "Adi", 200, 221, 235, 243, 262, 308, 347, 374
Boeke, Ogfr. Günter, 382, 427
Böhm, Fw., 230
Böhter, Uffz. Hans-Georg, 382, 419
Bornholdt, Gefr. Detlef, 468
Borounick, Obfw. Erich, 143
Borreck, Uffz. Hans-Joachim, 326, 342, 343, 352, 376
Borris, Maj. Karl, 23, 25, 41, 42, 58, 89, 107, 124, 130, 132, 135, 137, 154, 156, 196, 198, 201, 205, 209, 210, 218, 226, 227, 236, 244, 258, 259, 285, 301, 305, 309, 335, 337, 341, 347, 353, 354, 361, 362, 372, 378, 379, 382, 383, 384, 387, 388, 393, 397, 401, 402, 403, 404, 406, 407, 416, 420, 422, 423, 424, 425, 426, 427, 438, 434, 435, 437, 438, 440, 442, 447, 449, 450, 452, 454, 455, 457, 467, 474, 476, 480, 481, 489, 491
Bösch, Fw. Emil, 35
Bott, Lt. Josef, 426, 434
Böttge, Uffz. Erwin, 457, 465, 468
Bottländer, Hptm. Willi, 407
Bracher, Oblt. Fritz, 303
Brändle, Maj. Kurt, 173
Brann, Hpfw., 291
Bräsen, Uffz. Otto, 251
Braunert, Ogfr. Karl-Heinz, 407
Brede, Lt. Hans-Joachim, 306, 326
Bremer, Uffz. Herbert, 13

Brisch, Uffz. Helmut, 428, 465
Broda, Uffz. Günter, 131, 188
Bruckauf, Gefr. Gerhard, 339
Brühan, Uffz. Emil, 302, 381, 434
Bruhn, Uffz. Karl, 28
Brumund, Uffz. Johannes, 400, 429
Brünn, Uffz. Heinz, 427
Bruns, Lt. Holger, 159, 172, 174, 201
Bucher, Uffz. Werner, 465
Budde, Uffz. Heinz, 16
Buelowius, Genlt. Alfred, 265, 273, 274, 296, 298, 299, 303, 305, 306, 322
Bühligen, Major Kurt, 258, 266, 267
Bühring, Ofhr. Hans-Theobald, 336, 338, 365
Büker, Uffz. Herbert, 340
Bunje, Ofhr. Helmut, 408, 410
Burger, Fw. Peter, 159
Bürger, Uffz. Walter, 51, 59, 113, 169
Burglechner, Ofhr. Josef, 172, 248
Burckhardt, Uffz. Siegfried, 338, 410, 420
Burkardt, Oblt. Friedrich, 426, 454
Burkert, Oblt. Erich, 94, 168, 202
Burmeister, Uffz. Erich, 295, 320, 357, 360
Busch, Oblt. Erwin, 13, 38, 491
Busch, Fhr. Maximilian, 306, 355
Busch, Uffz. Udo, 468
Busch, Lt. Waldemar, 182, 256, 296, 297
Buschegger, Obfw. Friedrich, 384
Busemeyer, Dr., Karl, 311
Büttner, Uffz. Herbert, 24, 25
Butzmann, Uffz. Hermann, 113, 145, 186
Cassens, Uffz. Matthias, 455
Chemnitzer, Fw. Max, 264, 362, 438
Christof, Fw. Ernst, 85, 104, 128, 129
Claar, Obfw. Karl-Heinz, 146, 182
Cordt, Lt. Hans, 423
Corinth, Uffz. Gerhard, 235, 322, 356, 357
Crump, Oblt. Peter, 12, 13, 18, 20, 25, 31, 32, 38, 40, 48, 52, 57, 60, 97, 101, 103, 104, 128, 153, 154, 161, 168, 169, 171, 172, 178, 181, 216, 249, 252, 274, 280, 294, 296, 301, 304, 308, 310, 311, 392, 395, 398, 399, 401, 403, 405, 407, 424, 428, 435, 438, 440, 443, 444, 446, 452, 453, 455, 456, 465, 471, 474, 475, 476, 489, 490, 491
Dachmann, Uffz. Willi, 200, 221, 436, 437
Dahl, Obstlt. Walther, 425
Damm, Uffz. Heinrich, 41
Danneberg, Fw. Hans, 63
Dantschke, Uffz. Albrecht, 355
David, Fw. Rudolf, 119, 155
Dehsbesell, Uffz. Karl, 207, 241
Delor, Uffz. Rudolf, 387, 396, 397, 438
Derp, Fhj. Manfred, 182
Deshombes, Ogfr. Günter, 315
Deterra, Oblt., 47
Dewald, Ofhr. Gerhard, 272, 303
Dieterlen, Uffz. Georg, 361
Dietrich, General Sepp, 397
Dietze, Lt. Gottfried, 33, 130, 207, 208, 249, 252, 261, 309, 322, 336, 337, 338, 360, 364, 367, 393, 425, 440, 445, 457, 463, 464, 490
Dingler, Ogfr. Günther, 442, 454, 455, 457
Dippel, Hptm. Hans-Georg, 69, 77, 80, 109, 130, 135, 168, 184, 248, 253, 491
Dirksen, Fw. Hans, 130, 157
Dobryn, Uffz. Fritz, 295
Dombrowa, Uffz. Leo, 338, 340, 438
Donner, Baronin Konrad von, 478
Donner, Oblt. Baron Konrad von, 40, 53, 138, 207
Dörre, Fw. Edgar, 29, 35, 153
Dortenmann, Oblt. Hans, 395, 399, 400, 401, 403, 426, 428, 429, 431, 435, 446, 453, 454, 456, 457, 459, 462, 463, 464, 465, 466, 467, 469, 472, 473, 474, 476, 490, 491
Draheim, Lt. Manfred, 13, 157
Drutschmann, Fw. Paul, 405
Düsing, Uffz. Wilhelm, 182, 212, 339, 349, 428, 447
Dylewski, Fhj. Fw. Kurt-Heinz, 218
Ebersberger, Hptm. Kurt, 25, 33, 107, 109, 130, 144, 171, 490, 491
Ebert, Uffz. Fritz, 41
Ecker, Uffz., 77
Eckert, Obfw. Walter, 404
Eckhardt, Fw. Konrad, 168
Eder, Hptm. Georg-Peter, 34, 39, 318, 325, 326, 344, 346, 362, 425, 489, 490
Edmann, Obfw. Johann, 104, 105, 182, 233, 235
Effelsberg, Uffz. Andreas, 400, 433
Egli, Fw. Günther, 406
Ehret, Obfw. Karl, 53, 147, 170, 212
Eichinger, Obfw. Leopold, 13, 130, 166, 182
Eickhoff, Oblt. Christian, 21
Eickhoff, Uffz. Horst, 466
Eisenberg, Fw. Hans, 454
Elicker, Uffz. Edgar, 207, 260

Ellenrieder, Lt. Xaver, 48, 50, 59, 60, 62, 86, 87, 88, 89, 96, 98, 116, 120, 134, 145, 192, 207, 210, 218, 245, 264, 276, 287, 307, 308, 320, 321, 355, 370, 380, 382, 423, 426, 464, 465, 469, 489
Enna, Uffz. Walter, 193, 222, 229
Erbskorn, Obfw. Hans, 209, 345, 373
Erpenbach, Uffz. Paul, 212
Eyerle, Uffz. Anton, 465
Fackler, Fw. Karl, 42
Fahnert, Hptm. Friedrich-Wilhelm, 426, 459
Falke, Oblt. Fritz, 159, 179
Falkenberg, Uffz. Heinz, 223, 335
Falkner, Uffz. Gerhard, 22, 48, 159, 193, 197, 249
Fast, Uffz. Hans-Joachim, 71, 72
Fehr, Uffz. Albrecht von, 223, 231, 382
Feld, Gefr. Reinhold, 419
Fenzl, Fw. Theodor, 465
Fieguth, Fhj.-Fw. Hans-Gerhard, 182, 231
Findeisen, Uffz. Helmut, 417
Fischer, Lt. Edmund, 264, 327, 356, 365
Fischer, Lt. Hans, 47, 48, 63, 179
Fischer, Fw. Hans, 172, 177
Fischer, Lt. Kurt, 400, 422, 424, 425
Fischer, Fhj. Walter, 336, 338, 420
Fischer, Fhr. Werner, 159, 357
Fischer, Fw. Willi, 173
Flakowski, Uffz. Reinhard, 453, 455
Florian, Uffz. Armin, 338, 347, 438
Frank, Uffz. Karl, 224, 232
Franke, Obfw. Erwin, 326
Franke, Gefr. Rudolf, 223, 232, 264
Frantz, Fhr. Ulrich-Karsten, 223, 276
Franz, Ofhr. Wolfgang, 338, 452
Franzke, Fw. Kurt, 284
Frass, Fw. Werner, 382, 390
Freiberger, Obfw. Anton, 338, 385
Freitag, Uffz. Günther, 102
Freuwörth, Obfw. Wilhelm, 33, 38, 171, 187
Fricke, Uffz., 319
Friedrich, Uffz. Hermann, 168
Friedrich, Fw. Karl-Heinz, 295, 303, 373, 440
Friedrich, Fw. Karl, 26
Friedrich, Fw. Kurt, 116
Friedrich, Uffz. Otto, 438
Fritsch, Uffz. Artur, 367, 371
Fritsch, Lt. Paul, 32, 49, 109, 115
Fritzlehner, Uffz. Fritz, 47, 135, 141
Fröb, Uffz. Karl, 400, 457, 465, 466
Frotzscher, Uffz. Bruno, 276
Fussi, Ofhr. Otto, 306, 353
Galland, Genlt. Adolf, 8, 9, 11, 17, 39, 44, 130, 144, 149, 154, 164, 184, 193, 247, 269, 278, 313, 334, 352, 354, 358, 359, 362, 366, 377, 386, 418, 425, 464, 478
Galland, Maj. Wilhelm-Ferdinand "Wutz", 8, 11, 12, 17, 18, 20, 21, 22, 23, 25, 27, 28, 29, 31, 34, 36, 37, 40, 41, 42, 43, 47, 48, 50, 54, 57, 61, 97,100, 101, 102, 103, 104, 105, 106, 107, 110, 116, 117, 118, 128, 132, 138, 139, 143, 489, 490
Gasser, Uffz. Franz, 113, 155, 431
Gäth, Maj. Wilhelm, 35, 37, 48, 73, 81, 83, 84, 178, 198, 200, 211, 235, 489, 490
Gathof, Uffz. Karl, 22, 207, 240
Gehrke, Uffz. Heinz, 229, 231, 235, 236, 242, 248, 275, 287, 303, 314, 318, 322, 323, 325, 345, 386, 389, 414, 422, 431, 434
Geiler, Gefr. Harry, 227, 235
Geisshardt, Hptm. Fritz, 12, 24, 39, 42, 43, 44, 45, 489
Geissler, Uffz. Anton, 234
Genth, Uffz. Karl-Georg, 183, 200, 336, 337, 338, 357, 379, 381, 393, 413, 428, 436, 437, 438, 440, 441, 458, 459
Georgi, Uffz. Rudolf, 131, 202, 215, 230
Gern, Lt. Hermann, 476, 480
Gewitz, Uffz. Horst, 182, 223, 251, 317
Giebner, Lt. Helmut, 223, 270
Girstenbreu, Fw. Alfred, 431
Glahn, Uffz. Wolf-Dietrich, 130, 159, 289, 316
Glaser, Uffz. Otto, 75
Gloyer, Obfw. Heinz, 266
Glunz, Oblt. Adolf "Addi", 14, 24, 31, 33, 39, 41, 43, 56, 60, 62, 99, 101, 103, 106, 114, 138, 141, 144, 145, 146, 166, 176, 179, 183, 186, 187, 192, 197, 201, 211, 215, 216, 219, 222, 225, 236, 252, 254, 256, 267, 272, 279, 281, 289, 318, 344, 360, 364, 365, 367, 394, 395, 408, 410, 411, 413, 419, 421, 427, 445, 490
Gocksch, Obfw. Walter, 237, 283
Gödecker, Uffz., 105
Göhre, Fw. Siegfried, 317
Gollob, Obstlt. Gordon, 425
Gomann, Fw. Heinz, 18, 20, 21, 22, 24, 25, 29, 32, 51, 53, 57, 97, 100, 108, 138, 157, 158, 164, 192, 198, 203, 319, 362, 393, 408, 450, 456, 457, 468, 477

Goos, Obfw. Ludwig, 424
Göring, Reichsmarschall Hermann, 19, 54, 149,
  247, 298, 299, 305, 336, 354, 356, 374
Göttle, Lt. Franz, 455, 467
Götz , Maj. Franz, 86, 400, 408, 412, 424, 466, 468,
  474, 476, 477
Grabmann, Oberst Walter, 134, 137, 142, 160,
  166
Grad, Uffz. Hermann, 235, 290, 291, 301, 396
Grams, Obfw. Willi, 99
Gräve, Obfw. Alons, 232
Greim, Ogfr. Helmut, 218
Greim, Generalfeldmarschall Ritter von, 473
Grimm, Lt. Wolfgang, 40, 235, 240, 365
Grimmer, Lt. Josef , 235, 348
Grollius, Uffz., 96
Grolms, Uffz. Bruno, 264, 326
Groos, Hptm., 471, 472
Gross, Lt. Alfred, 336, 342, 343
Gross, Uffz. Helmut, 306, 332, 345, 349
Gross, Uffz. Paul, 193, 216
Grossler, Uffz. Kurt, 120
Groth, Oblt. Max, 237, 248, 253, 272, 294, 298,
  319, 489
Grüner, Uffz. Johann, 465
Grünlinger, Obfw. Walter, 22, 142, 151
Grupe, Lt. Werner, 142, 168
Guhl, Lt. Hermann, 229, 242, 363, 385, 389, 413,
  456, 469, 474, 491
Gulecke, Uffz. Johann-Heinrich, 131, 181, 232
Günther, Obfw. Alfred, 33, 108, 151, 158, 278
Günther, Lt. Joachim, 159, 212, 320, 360, 377, 383,
  387, 390, 392, 430, 433
Günther, Uffz. Martin, 113, 196
Guttmann, Fw. Gerhard, 148, 184, 196, 197, 210,
  211, 234
Haarberg, Ogfr. Volkmar, 382, 419
Hackl, Maj. Anton "Toni", 362, 372, 376, 390, 391,
  394, 401, 402, 408, 409, 410, 411, 413, 419, 420,
  425, 431, 476, 489
Hadraba, Uffz. Karl, 136, 141
Hager, Uffz. Robert, 16, 42, 190, 234, 320
Hahn, Maj. "Assi", 68
Hahne, Lt. Ernst, 37
Hähnel, Uffz. Walter, 439
Hamel, Lt. Gerhard, 338, 362
Hanitz, Ogfr. Willi, 306, 326
Hanke, Uffz. Erwin, 40, 103, 152, 196
Hansen, Ofhr. Hans-Jürgen, 453
Hanusch, Uffz. Fritz, 338, 442
Hark, Ofhr. Karl-Manfred, 360, 444
Hartigs, Oblt. Hans, 131, 180, 188, 205, 218, 290,
  291, 307, 322, 382, 388, 394, 395, 396, 397
Hartmann, Fw. Karl-Heinz, 406, 407
Hasenclever, Fw. Walter, 295, 326
Hauer, Oblt. Peter, 224, 437
Haun, Uffz. Willi, 301
Heck, Lt. Gert, 131, 145
Heck, Uffz. Karl, 45
Hecker, Fw. Michael, 22, 66, 82, 159, 245, 263
Heckmann, Oblt. Alfred "Fred", 9, 11, 66, 70, 130,
  166, 198, 208, 210, 218, 226, 236, 322, 331, 349,
  353, 361, 362, 370, 371, 373, 374, 383, 384, 385,
  387, 392, 403, 404, 416, 423, 430, 433, 434, 438,
  444, 445, 449, 451, 452, 454, 464, 490
Hegener, Obfw. Hans, 428
Heilmann, Oblt. Wilhelm "Willi", 395, 399, 429,
  435, 447, 451, 459, 491
Hein, Uffz. Hans, 51, 173, 200
Hein, Uffz. Kurt, 446, 453, 465, 470
Heindtke, Ofhr. Siegfried, 362
Heinemann, Lt. Ernst, 51, 60, 151
Heinemeyer, Lt. Hans-Joachim, 113
Heinrichs, Ofhr. Robert, 306, 361, 365
Heitmann, Ofhr. Hans, 50, 59, 113, 120, 136, 176,
  184, 221, 226, 235
Hell, Uffz. Erwin, 172, 214
Hemmerich, Lt. Lothar, 408
Hempel, Hptm. Adolf, 330
Hennemann, Fw. Karl, 251, 308, 312
Hennemann, Fhr. Martin, 264, 353, 365
Hennig, Uffz. Joachim, 335, 338
Henske, Uffz. Werner, 227, 235
Herbster, Uffz. Heinrich, 454
Hering, Uffz. Heinrich, 131, 132, 224
Hering, Uffz. Joachim, 327
Hermann, Fhr. Heinrich, 426, 450
Hermichen, Maj. Rolf, 66, 96, 101, 114, 125, 128,
  135, 167, 489, 490
Heuser, Fw. Heinrich, 15, 25, 27, 28, 69, 70, 74, 75,
  76, 77, 78, 79, 80, 81, 84, 132, 140, 151, 207,
  305, 306, 310, 312
Heuser, Ofhr. Walter, 382, 408, 409
Hiess, Uffz. Hans, 41
Hildebrandt, Uffz. Willi, 360, 365
Hilgendorff, Oblt. Viktor, 253, 261, 278, 303, 304,
  491
Hillebrand, Ogfr. Hermann, 295, 309, 338, 348
Hiller, Obfw. Franz, 22, 159, 207
Hilliger, Lt. Karl-Dietrich, 263, 264, 308, 309, 335

Hitler, Adolf, 44, 68, 149, 244, 278, 305, 315, 374,
  386, 397
Hoch, Lt. Hermann, 13, 16
Hoeckner, Hptm. Walter, 9, 11, 66, 72, 80, 103, 489
Hofer, Uffz. Kurt, 207, 235
Hoffmann, Uffz. Johannes, 306, 372, 419, 449
Hoffmann, Obfw. Hermann, 136
Hoffmann, Uffz. Werner, 131, 148, 299, 462
Hofmann, Fw. Karl, 309, 316, 445, 447
Hofmann, Uffz. Werner, 280
Hofmann, Oblt. Wilhelm, 76, 159, 167, 196, 204,
  206, 223, 227, 230, 241, 254, 256, 270, 272, 274,
  285, 286, 288, 289, 290, 295, 300, 305, 321, 324,
  326, 329, 330, 333, 336, 345, 346, 347, 348, 349,
  353, 360, 371, 408, 410, 413, 417, 419, 421, 426,
  428, 437, 438, 446, 452, 459, 490, 491
Hohagen, Hptm. Erich, 28, 97
Höhme, Uffz. Johannes, 131, 179
Holl, Fw. Walter, 119, 305
Holtz, Ogfr. Norbert, 98, 177, 290
Holzinger, Uffz. Helmut, 295, 326
Holzleitner, Uffz. Johann, 349, 360
Hönig, Uffz. Friedhelm, 306
Hoppe, Fw. Alfred, 382, 394
Hoppe, Hptm. Helmut, 56, 63, 101, 116, 138, 141,
  148, 154, 158, 171, 183, 184, 490
Hoppe, Uffz. Josef, 400, 438
Horch, Fhj.-Uffz. Otto, 264, 316, 328
Horn, Uffz. Karl, 400
Horner, Uffz. Alois, 455, 461
Hött, Fw. Karl, 306, 329, 364, 371, 391, 393, 409,
  469, 473, 475, 476
Hötz, Uffz. Emil, 468
Hüber, Uffz. Karl-Friedrich, 455
Hübler, Ogfr., 291
Humburg, Obfw. Heinrich, 185, 295, 357, 447
Hummel, Oblt. Otto, 37, 40, 158, 198, 210
Hurtig, Uffz. Franz, 207, 224
Hütterer, Uffz. Albert, 455, 465
Hüttig, Uffz. Helmut, 146, 268
Immervoll, Uffz. Alfred, 20
Irlinger, Uffz. Johann, 12
Issleib, Uffz. Günter, 437, 449
Jacobsen, Uffz. Friedrich, 223, 295
Jäger, Gefr. Helmut, 333
Jähnig, Uffz. Erhard, 306
Janda, Oblt. Ernst, 37, 145, 148, 149
Janning, Ogfr. Karl-Heinz, 78
Jauer, Fw. Erich, 23, 26, 86, 87, 88, 92, 93, 94, 96
Jenner, Uffz. Anton, 22, 188
Jensen, Fhr. Christian, 423
Jentzsch, Fw. Paul, 362
Jeschonnek, Genobst. Hans, 140
Jesinger, Uffz. Wilhelm, 382, 392
Jessen, Oblt. Heinrich, 66, 69, 70, 74, 75, 82, 167,
  198, 490
Jezek, Uffz. Paul, 193
Jörg, Fw. Adolf, 131, 152
Joziak, Fw. Roman, 264, 300
Juhre, Lt. Hermann, 231, 373
Junck, Genlt. Werner, 7, 265, 296
Just, Fhj.-Uffz. Gerhard, 264, 429, 435
Kaase, Uffz., 74, 77
Kabowski, Uffz. Erwin, 382, 392
Kaehler, Uffz. Günter, 423
Kaiser, Uffz. Friedrich, 59
Kaiser, Gefr. Helmut, 67
Kaiser, Fw. Herbert, 427, 492
Kaiser, Uffz. Werner, 83, 128, 200
Kalbus, Uffz. Edwin, 338, 412, 449
Kalitzki, Obfw. Willi, 58, 249
Kampen, Uffz. Emil, 228
Kaps, Uffz. Harry, 453, 455
Karl, Lt. Gerhard, 143
Karwik, Fw. Viktor, 465, 468
Kehl, Lt. Dietrich, 37, 101, 117, 147, 152, 222
Keitel, Generalfeldmarschall, 476
Kelch, Hptm. Günther, 22, 26, 86, 87, 88, 91, 94,
  96, 130, 490
Keller, Fw. Franz, 476
Keller, Oblt. Paul, 38, 491
Kemethmüller, Lt. Heinz, 11, 12, 22, 23, 24, 26, 87,
  89, 90, 91, 92, 93, 94, 95, 96, 114, 135, 136, 196,
  200, 201, 203, 206, 211, 212, 241, 244, 246, 252,
  253, 262, 267, 289, 291, 292, 295, 301, 303, 304,
  308, 336, 349, 352, 355, 375, 447, 491
Kemper, Uffz. Johannes, 28
Kempf, Lt. Karl-Heinz, 63, 188, 236, 274, 282, 309,
  340, 341, 342
Kerber, Fw. Walter, 422
Kerner, Uffz. Friedrich, 418
Kersting, Lt. Theodor, 338, 348
Kestel, Lt. Melchior, 61, 112
Kiefner, Lt. Georg, 119, 131, 132, 136, 137, 170,
  193, 214, 221, 224, 225, 226, 233, 298, 300,
  314, 316, 319, 321, 325, 337, 361, 390, 397, 403,
  422, 423, 435, 443, 452, 454, 456, 459, 461, 464,
  489
Kierstein, Obfw. Paul, 15, 16
Kind, Uffz. Herbert, 125, 131, 154, 307

Kipping, Lt. Peter, 131, 152
Kirschenlohr, Lt. Gerd, 110
Kirschner, Uffz. Horst, 113, 172, 173
Kittelmann, Oblt. Georg, 429, 434
Klatt, Fhj.-Obfw. Leo, 445
Kleeman, Gefr. Günter, 257, 264
Klees, Uffz. Hans, 223, 280
Kleffner, Uffz. Erich, 48
Klein, Uffz. Erich, 326, 347, 359
Klemm, Maj. Rudolf, 57, 428, 435, 446, 459, 461,
  465, 489
Klems, Uffz. Heinz-Günther, 69, 82, 172
Klinghöfer, Uffz. Paul, 384, 427, 465
Kloimüller, Lt. Herfried, 172, 198, 207, 490
Klumpe, Uffz. Ernst, 182, 193
Knappmann, Ofhr. Klaus, 306, 352
Kneiss, Uffz. Friedrich, 67
Knobeloch, Obfw. Karl-Heinz, 360, 372
Knobloch, Uffz. Bruno, 114
Koch, Uffz. Günther "Peipl", 428
Koch, Uffz. Joachim, 39
Koch, Lt. Martin, 293
Kohler, Uffz. Erich, 365
Köhler, Fw. Arnfried, 446
Kolodzie, Uffz. Herbert, 182, 210
Konrad, Lt., 465, 475
Kopp, Lt. Walter, 257, 420
Körner, Uffz. Franz, 382, 392
Kracht, Uffz. Jürgen, 338, 348
Kraft, Uffz. Gerhard, 296
Kraft, Fw. Werner, 135, 231
Krägeloh, Ogfr. Dieter, 382, 390, 404, 405
Kranefeld, Oblt. Kurt, 119, 130, 230, 248, 489
Kratzel, Uffz. Anton, 13, 22, 159, 168
Kraus, Lt. Albrecht, 306, 311
Kraus, Oblt. Theobald, 181, 373, 433, 436, 444
Kraus, Gefr. Wolfgang, 386
Krause, Hptm. Günther, 434
Kreth, Uffz. Georg, 306, 344, 464, 469
Kretschmer, Uffz. Horst, 146, 155
Krieg, Uffz. Heinrich, 118, 144
Krieger, Lt. Hans-Hermann, 390, 392
Kroll, Fw. Gerhard, 404, 451, 465
Krümpelmann, Uffz. Eugen, 445, 455
Krüper, Ofhr. Bruno, 306
Krupinski, Maj. Walter, 336, 366, 389, 393, 401,
  402, 413, 414, 422, 425, 426, 436, 437, 450, 465,
  489
Kruse, Uffz. Ottomar, 306, 324, 325, 327, 333, 334,
  338, 345, 347, 348, 359
Krusen, Uffz. Bruno, 360, 429, 437
Kruska, Obfw. Kurt, 45
Kubon, Uffz. Harry, 113, 118, 223
Küchler, Generalfeldmarschall von, 68
Kühn, Uffz. Hermann, 159, 338, 426, 450
Kühne, Lt. Wolfgang, 159, 397
Kuhnert, Uffz. Kurt, 113, 201
Kukla, Uffz. Hans, 295, 320, 387, 397, 402, 416,
  423, 438, 464
Kümmerling, Lt. Hans, 15
Kunz, Oblt. Franz, 77, 257, 267, 268, 293, 294,
  369, 370, 375, 390, 403, 404, 416, 490
Kunz, Gefr. Willi, 400, 408, 412
Kunze, Lt. Klaus, 206, 207, 231
Lambertus, Uffz. Erich, 193, 207
Lampe, Lt. Helmut, 306, 335
Lampferhoff, Uffz. Ernst, 306, 367, 376, 412
Landsberg, Lt. Wilhelm, 377
Lang, Hptm. Emil "Bulle", 292, 294, 299, 300, 306,
  319, 321, 322, 325, 328, 329, 331, 332, 333, 335,
  336, 337, 342, 343, 344, 357, 360, 362, 425, 489
Lange, Fw., 407
Lange, Fw. Erich, 414
Lange, Lt. Friedrich, 98, 101, 138, 172, 214, 216,
  218, 219, 224, 225, 490
Lange, Ogfr. Helmut, 400, 423
Langer, Uffz. Alfred, 455
Langer, Uffz. Günther, 424
Langhammer, Uffz. Gerhard, 235, 255, 257
Laub, Obfw. Karl, 59, 167, 200, 260, 314, 363, 386
Lauer, Lt. Werner, 264, 424
Leder, Fw. Hans-Joachim, 161, 221, 329
Leder, Ogfr. Josef, 360, 369
Lederer, Maj. Werner, 33, 172
Leicht, Uffz. Hermann, 59
Leinberger, Uffz. Rudolf, 224, 302, 414, 460
Leitz, Uffz. Emil, 117, 125
Lentz, Uffz. Ludwig, 52
Lenz, Oblt. Harald, 295, 317, 413
Lessin, Uffz. Ernst, 249
Leuschel, Hptm. Rudolf "Rudi", 51, 57, 107, 150,
  151, 179, 184, 205, 221, 222, 223, 491
Leykauf, Oblt. Erwin, 44, 57, 58, 114, 491
Lienich, Gefr. Heinz, 220, 270, 284
Limburg, Ogfr. Hans, 384
Lindelaub, Obfw. Friedrich, 22, 175, 206, 225
Lindner, Uffz. Erich, 267, 293
Linzbach, Ogfr. Kurt, 455
Lissack, Uffz. Gerhard, 159, 186, 205, 280, 281,
  293

Lonsdorfer, Uffz. Werner, 56
Lorberg, Ofhr. Helmut, 224, 357, 381
Lörzer, Lt. Hans-Günther, 38, 161
Loschinski, Uffz. Gerhard, 159, 215, 219
Losigkeit, Maj. Fritz, 83, 85, 489
Lott, Ogfr. Hubert, 400, 409
Loy, Uffz. Karl, 428
Machner, Gefr. Siegfried, 172, 254
Mackenstedt, Obfw. Wilhelm, 41, 128
Maletz, Uffz. Gerhard, 131, 200
Malm, Uffz. Willibald, 200, 221, 329, 358, 414,
    441, 465
Manteuffel, General Hasso von, 383, 397
Marek, Uffz. Robert, 207, 289
Marischka, Fw. Hans, 426, 444, 466
Marquardt, Uffz. Heinz, 16
Marx, Lt. Wolfgang, 264, 290, 320
Mathony, Lt. Werner, 390
Matoni, Oblt. Walter, 33, 102, 144, 145, 186, 191,
    200, 211, 218, 219, 226, 234, 239, 241, 242, 256,
    277, 280, 283, 288, 296, 322, 329, 330, 490
Matthiesen, Lt. Johannes, 113, 162, 163
Matuschka, Oblt. Siegfried, 39, 46
Mayer, Obstlt. Egon, 26, 27, 111, 112, 149, 183,
    184, 209
Mayer, Ogfr. Erwin, 268
Mayer, Lt. Hans, 16, 34, 165, 230
Mayer, Lt. Wilhelm, 12, 23, 39, 50, 61, 63, 98, 101,
    104, 105, 128, 144, 189, 191, 192, 193, 200, 205,
    206, 212, 213, 216, 219, 224, 234, 338, 352,
    355, 359, 362, 370, 371, 378, 417, 419, 491
Meidinger, Uffz. Georg, 224
Meier, Lt. Johann-Hermann, 223, 230, 489
Meindl, Fw. Bernhard, 382, 394
Meinel, Uffz. Erhard, 365, 374
Meiss, Uffz. Hans, 361, 429, 442, 444
Meissner, Uffz. Anton, 99
Meixner, Ofhr. Klaus, 427
Menge, Lt. Helmut, 176, 182, 272
Mensing, Fw. Wilhelm, 142
Menz, Uffz. Dieter, 233
Menze, Lt. Josef, 113, 293, 299
Merten, Ogfr. Helmut, 264, 301
Merz, Uffz. Werner, 445
Meschkat, Fw. Edgar, 193
Messerklinger, Dr. Walter, 364
Meyer, Uffz. Albert, 41
Meyer, Uffz. Alex, 119, 168
Meyer, Lt. Gottfried, 400, 414
Meyer, Uffz. Hans, 20, 108, 109
Meyer, Obfw. Hermann, 14, 36
Meyer, Oblt. Johannes, 131, 141
Meyer, Hptm. K-H. "Conny", 7, 8, 489
Meyer, Lt. Klaus-Rudolf, 284
Meyer, Fhj.-Gefr. Kurt, 382, 385
Meyer, Fhr. Otto, 182, 198, 219, 235
Meyer, Lt. Walter, 14
Michalski, Obstlt. Gerhard, 470
Mickmann, Uffz. Bernhard, 223, 263
Middelstädt, Uffz. Max, 465
Mietusch, Maj. Klaus, 11, 16, 26, 86, 87, 88, 90, 91,
    94, 95, 96, 114, 130, 135, 137, 142, 156, 159,
    161, 168, 181, 182, 184, 185, 186, 193, 200, 221,
    226, 227, 228, 234, 236, 241, 257, 258, 261, 266,
    270, 276, 278, 279, 280, 282, 285, 286, 297, 300,
    303, 305, 314, 344, 345, 347, 305, 336, 344,
    346, 349, 350, 351, 352, 358, 360, 362, 388, 425,
    489, 490
Mischkot, Lt. Bruno, 338, 375, 382
Mittag, Uffz. Wilhelm, 382, 408, 420
Mohr, Uffz. Gerhard, 207, 218
Molge, Uffz. Werner, 382, 410, 413, 417, 431, 450,
    456, 458, 467, 468, 470, 471, 472, 475, 476, 477
Mondry, Lt. Georg, 63
Mössner, Fw. Werner, 142
Muche, Fw. Günter, 264, 295
Müller, Uffz. Heinz, 456
Müller, Fw. Herbert, 9
Müller, Oblt. Hermann, 235, 274
Müller, Ogfr. Johann, 223, 226
Müller, Fw. Kurt, 306, 322
Müller, Uffz. Leo, 14, 62
Müller, Obfw. Siegfried, 429
Müller, Uffz. Walter, 126, 127
Müller, Obfw. Wilhelm, 338, 362
Müller-Berneck, Fw. Gerhard, 451, 465
Müller-Göbs, Lt. Karl, 32
Munack, Uffz. Paul, 235, 263
Münch, Fw. Heinz, 189
Müncheberg, Maj. Joachim, 37, 350, 362
Naeger, Fw., 422
Napierski, Fw. Walter, 474
Naumann, Hptm. Johannes "Hans", 17, 28, 48, 52,
    57, 104, 122, 123, 124, 126, 128, 138, 140, 141,
    143, 145, 147, 154, 157, 186, 211, 235, 266, 286,
    293, 294, 334, 489, 490
Nels, Oblt. Franz, 9, 489
Neu, Hptm. Wolfgang, 10, 83, 101, 113, 159, 171,
    176, 179, 180, 202, 203, 211, 219, 244, 245, 490,
    491

Neumann, Uffz. Artur, 310, 349
Ney, Uffz. Robert, 159, 172
Nibel, Lt. Theo, 392, 403, 405
Niedermeyer, Fw. Willi, 381, 464
Niessen, Ogfr. Manfred, 404, 428, 433, 450, 466
Nieter, Uffz. Heinz, 309, 332, 373, 470
Nink, Lt. Wilhelm, 193, 282, 296, 355
Oeckel, Lt. Hans, 165, 177, 202, 221, 276, 292, 303
Oesau, Obst. Walter, 29, 42, 210
Oltmanns, Uffz. Rudolf, 113, 159, 296
Onken, Uffz. Herbert, 182, 224
Ossenkop, Lt. Karl-Heinz, 338, 339, 340, 342, 406,
    407, 420, 429, 463, 465, 474
Ostrowitzki, Fw. Bruno, 464, 465, 466
Ostrzecha, Uffz. Paul, 317
Otte, Oblt. Walter, 51, 103, 491
Otto, Fhj.-Fw. Gottfried, 47, 89, 206
Palige, Fw. Herbert, 466
Pape, Lt. Dietwin, 243, 272, 284, 355, 420
Patz, Hptm. Werner, 13, 51, 491
Patzke, Ofhr. Günther, 26, 284, 353
Paul, Fw. Arthur, 264, 355, 362, 392
Pauli, Obfw. Johannes, 246
Pautner, Uffz. Robert, 173, 174
Peltz, Genmaj. Dietrich, 46, 386, 392, 401, 407,
    415, 451
Peschak, Uffz. Josef, 223
Peters, Uffz. Helmut, 16
Pietruschka, Uffz. Werner, 193, 208, 248, 297
Petzsch, Uffz. Kurt, 235, 334
Peukert, Ogfr. Wilhelm, 193, 208
Pfeiffer, Uffz. Günter, 400, 451, 470
Pfützner, Ofhr. Alfred, 306, 334
Philipp, Hptm. Gerhard, 22, 258, 374
Philipp, Obstlt. Hans, 59, 86, 87
Philipp, Obfw. Wilhelm, 400
Pickert, Genlt., 288
Piesslinger, Uffz. Josef, 375
Piplitz, Uffz. Franz, 172, 182
Pittmann, Fw. Hans, 131, 155
Pittmann, Uffz. Helmut, 131, 140, 171
Planz, Uffz. Walter, 423
Plazer, Fhr. Gerhard von, 400, 454, 464, 467
Pleese, Fw., 71, 77, 80
Pokorny, Lt. Günter, 235, 303
Polster, Fw. Walter "Poldi", 18, 26, 33, 128, 143,
    152, 167, 172, 175, 177, 182, 183, 185, 236, 237,
    274, 276, 308, 309, 322, 382, 434, 460, 465
Pötter, Fw. Ludwig, 146, 182
Prager, Lt. Hans, 209, 280, 281, 297, 299, 321, 322,
    330, 346, 395, 402, 428, 429, 431, 446, 451, 452,
    453, 454, 459, 465, 490, 491
Prantke, Uffz. Benno, 367, 382
Preeg, Fw. Karl, 71
Preuss, Lt. Dietrich, 465
Priller, Obst. Josef "Pips", 7, 8, 9, 11, 12, 16, 22,
    23, 24, 25, 27, 28, 33, 34, 35, 39, 41, 42, 43, 44,
    48, 49, 52, 53, 54, 55, 56, 59, 61, 63, 95, 96, 98,
    104, 106, 110, 112, 114, 126, 131, 132, 133, 138,
    139, 142, 145, 151, 153, 157, 160, 161, 168, 175,
    189, 190, 198, 199, 213, 224, 230, 236, 240, 243,
    247, 256, 265, 266, 267, 268, 269, 270, 272,
    273, 274, 277, 280, 282, 283, 288, 294, 309, 317,
    323, 331, 332, 342, 350, 364, 365, 379, 389,
    395, 400, 401, 402, 403, 407, 414, 424, 479, 480,
    489
Pritze, Uffz. Hans, 26, 94, 96
Protze, Obfw. Rudolf, 336, 338
Prüll, Lt. Ernst, 276
Prüver, Uffz. Bruno, 465
Przybyl, Ogfr. Leo, 146, 186, 216, 408, 427
Putsch, Uffz. Franz, 319, 438
Putschenjack, Ogfr. Otto, 306, 449
Quaet-Faslem, Maj. Klaus, 171
Quitter, Uffz. Fritz, 375
Radener, Oblt. Waldemar "Waldi", 33, 52, 104, 128,
    140, 144, 148, 154, 191, 196, 198, 205, 208, 210,
    211, 213, 218, 219, 222, 234, 244, 247, 249, 253,
    255, 256, 278, 346, 408, 419, 425, 427, 431, 489,
    490
Raith, Fw. Georg, 437, 454
Ramthun, Lt. Friedrich, 338, 447, 457, 462, 470
Rapke, Uffz. Hermann, 428
Rapsch, Uffz. Fritz, 172, 319
Ratzlaff, Lt. Jürgen, 407
Rau, Fw. Günther, 74
Reck, Lt. Horst, 91
Reichow, Uffz. Gerhard, 400, 407, 452
Reinhardt, Lt. Klaus, 131, 200
Reischer, Oblt. Peter, 159, 207, 231, 234, 236, 251,
    257, 270, 275, 276, 284, 285, 345, 383, 384, 389,
    422, 491
Reiser, Maj., 439
Reitsch, Hanna, 473
Rektor, Uffz. Helmut, 223, 249
Rennack, Fw. Arthur, 466, 469
Reppel, Fhj.-Gefr. Alfred, 384
Reuschel, Fhj.-Uffz. Hubert, 466
Reuter, Uffz. Günther, 306
Reuther, Fw. Arnold, 454, 455

Rey, Uffz. Günther, 438, 457, 464, 465
Richter, Uffz. Adolf, 306, 321
Richter, Uffz. Horst, 113,166
Richter, Fhj.-Fw. Julius, 159, 188
Richter, Uffz. Walter, 295, 339
Rickeit, Uffz. Kurt, 224, 257
Risky, Uffz. Norbert, 400, 410
Ritter, Uffz., 323
Ritter, Uffz. Georg, 379
Rober, Lt. Peter, 235, 254, 334
Rodartz, Ofhr. Hinrich, 400, 426
Roggenkamp, Obfw. Friedrich, 382, 419
Röhler, Fhj.-Fw. Wolfgang, 224, 326
Röhrig, Fhj.-Uffz. Robert, 235, 330, 381
Rohrmann, Uffz. Friedrich, 426, 459
Rommel, Generalfeldmarschall Erwin, 244
Rose, Ofhr. Wolfgang, 203, 251, 291, 292
Rösen, Lt. Hans, 306, 326
Rösner, Uffz. Raimund, 164, 168, 170
Roth, Uffz. Ludwig, 10
Roth, Obfw. Willi, 54, 59, 113, 166
Rother, Obfw. Walter, 466
Rudolph, Obfw. Ernst, 264, 322
Rummler, Uffz. Egon, 262
Ruppert, Fw. Hans, 22, 66, 230, 262
Ruppert, Uffz. Franz, 181
Ruppert, Hptm. Kurt, 33, 43, 44, 95, 99, 100, 489,
    491
Rüskamp, Lt. Hans-Jürgen, 58
Russ, Uffz. Karl, 420
Rüterkamp, Uffz., 291
Rybosch, Uffz. Friedrich, 11
Sachse, Gefr. Heinz, 264
Salewski, Uffz. Otto, 182, 200, 209, 221, 233, 440,
    441
Salewsky, Uffz. Erich, 200, 250, 251, 302, 420
Saligman, Lt. Rolf, 197
Salomo, Uffz. Werner, 248
Salomon, Uffz. Heinz, 348, 360
Sander, Gefr. Hans-Walter, 47, 51, 63, 155, 274
Sandoz, Uffz. Hans, 131, 159, 232, 316, 331
Sattler, Uffz. Ludwig, 207, 264, 334, 375, 396
Schäfer, Uffz. Wilhelm, 309, 320
Schande, Uffz. Ernst, 223, 316
Scharf, Ofhr. Alfred, 348, 360
Schauder, Hptm. Paul, 13, 57, 59, 157, 232, 251,
    280, 285, 289, 301, 303, 305, 314, 352, 413, 433,
    450, 456, 457, 458, 459, 468, 469, 471, 473, 474,
    489, 491
Schellknecht, Fw. Bernhard, 83, 85
Scheu, Uffz. Johann, 131, 181
Scheyda, Ofhr. Erich, 12, 74, 75, 77, 132, 152, 211,
    232, 238, 253
Schild, Oblt. Heinrich "Jan", 66, 72, 76, 77, 78, 79,
    80, 83, 84, 110, 114, 120, 124, 162, 166, 191,
    206, 208, 237, 252, 257, 282, 305, 314, 327, 345,
    350, 352, 365, 366, 433, 469, 473, 474, 475, 476,
    477, 490, 491
Schilling, Uffz. Franz, 160, 266, 234
Schitkowsky, Ofhr. Günter, 455, 459
Schlenker, Uffz. Erich, 207, 272
Schlimper, Uffz. Johannes, 306, 427, 473
Schlögl, Uffz. Leopold, 223, 233, 256, 261
Schlösser, Fhr. Dietrich, 326
Schmauser, Fhr. Hans-Joachim, 369
Schmeinl, Obfw. Hermann, 13, 159, 172, 176, 223
Schmelzer, Uffz. Philipp, 131, 132, 201, 259
Schmerker, Fw. Heimfried, 303
Schmid, Genlt. Josef "Beppo", 160, 214, 226, 227,
    245
Schmidt, Fhr. Bruno, 465
Schmidt, Ogfr. Erhard, 390, 400
Schmidt, Uffz. Franz, 436
Schmidt, Oblt. Gottfried "Götz" ("Cognac"), 110,
    181, 261, 304, 317, 381, 382, 413, 422, 450, 458,
    490, 491
Schmidt, Uffz. Gottfried, 290, 291
Schmidt, Fw. Gustav, 466
Schmidt, Uffz. Hans, 257, 259, 264
Schmidt, Lt. Karl-Heinz, 47, 148
Schmidtke, Uffz. Günther, 137, 146
Schmidtke, Fw. Kurt, 113, 176, 192, 203, 228, 263,
    291, 299
Schmitz, Ogfr., 210
Schmitz, Uffz. Wilhelm, 281, 382, 411
Schneider, Ofhr. Erich, 453, 452, 456
Schneider, Fhj.-Uffz. Friedrich, 146, 267, 268
Schneider, Fhj.-Fw. Günther, 182, 205
Schneider, Uffz. Lothar, 209
Schneider, Uffz. Wolfgang, 455, 461
Schnell, Uffz. Heinrich, 67
Schnier, Uffz. Ewald, 146, 191, 254
Schöhl, Uffz. Horst-Günther, 99, 102, 124, 151
Scholz, Uffz. Erwin, 131, 148
Scholz, Uffz. Herbert, 316
Scholz, Fw. Walter, 40, 161
Schombel, Uffz. Erich-Joachiim, 360, 365
Schöndorf, Uffz. Hans, 382, 383, 396
Schönrock, Uffz., 110
Schöpfel, Maj. Gerhard "Gerd", 7, 9, 489

Schrader, Oblt. Karl-Hermann, 259, 357, 385, 413, 414, 450, 465, 491
Schramm, Lt. Werner, 295, 365, 467, 469, 473
Schreiber, Flg. Heinz, 465
Schreiber, Uffz. Heinz, 172, 249
Schrettinger, Uffz. Anton, 306, 326
Schrickel, Uffz. Alfred, 119
Schrödter, Hptm. Dr.-Ing. Rolf, 65, 72
Schulwitz, Lt. Gerhard "Bubi", 59, 107, 267, 349, 410, 422, 442, 444, 450
Schulz, Uffz. Gerhard, 193, 201
Schulz, Uffz. Heinz, 232, 404
Schumacher, Uffz. Erich, 426, 453, 468
Schuster, Uffz. Alfred, 307
Schwaiger, Uffz. Georg, 223
Schwan, Uffz. Werner, 37, 78, 223, 316, 355
Schwarz, Bruno, 159, 284, 299, 444
Schwarz, Obfw. Erich, 29, 59, 113, 142, 153, 176, 180, 202, 206, 236, 259, 394, 396, 402, 403, 416, 470
Schwarz, Uffz. Paul, 109, 118
Schwentick, Fw. Horst, 77, 80, 145, 207, 252
Schwertl, Ogfr. Thomas, 235, 253
Seebeck, Uffz. Karl, 22, 37, 87, 188
Seidenfuss, Uffz. Oskar, 428
Seidl, Fw. Norbert, 146, 254, 392, 396
Seifert, Obstlt. Johannes, 7, 11, 24, 25, 66, 69, 70, 71, 72, 74, 81, 82, 84, 106, 154, 157, 166, 175, 178, 489
Seifert, Lt. Gerhard, 24, 83
Seiffert, Oblt. Heinz, 489
Sengpiel, Gefr. Horst, 380, 414
Setz, Hptm. Heinrich, 36
Seyd, Lt. Günter, 295
Siebe, Lt. Kurt, 447
Siegel, Uffz. Günter, 434
Siekers, Obfw. Joachim, 424
Siemsen, Oblt. Horst, 235, 325, 360
Sigmund, Uffz. Rupert, 394
Simmank, Uffz. Rolf, 209
Simmer, Ogfr. Joseph, 400, 468
Sinz, Fw. Hermann, 434, 459, 465
Smischek, Uffz. Josef, 306, 326
Soeder, Uffz. Kurt, 455, 459
Söffing, Lt. Waldemar "Vladimir", 72, 75, 125, 245, 256, 260, 261, 262, 274, 275, 360, 375, 384, 385, 390, 397, 402, 416, 422, 426, 428, 429, 430, 433, 434, 442, 457, 459, 463, 465, 466, 467, 470, 473, 474, 475, 490, 491
Sonnenberg, Uffz. Wilhelm, 235, 295, 314
Spahn, Ofhr. Johann, 382, 419, 429, 437, 438, 446
Späte, Maj. Wolfgang, 355, 357
Speer, Albert, 397
Speer, Uffz. Leopold, 264, 364, 367, 409
Speichert, Uffz. Hans, 284, 285
Sperrle, Generalfeldmarschall Hugo von, 7, 48, 49, 61, 110, 160, 165, 269, 282, 316, 354
Spiegel, Uffz. Arthur, 174
Spiegl, Uffz. Waldemar, 223, 293
Spieler, Lt. Eugen, 45
Spiess, Uffz. Horst, 223
Spiess, Uffz. Michael, 306
Spitz, Uffz. Renatus 446
Sprinz, Lt. Heinrich, 84, 113, 127
Stahnke, Uffz. Kurt, 172, 205, 223, 230
Staiger, Hptm. Hermann, 115, 119, 122, 161, 165, 171, 174, 201, 203, 215, 221, 224, 227, 228, 231, 232, 234, 242, 244, 246, 248, 259, 268, 278, 282, 283, 285, 286, 289, 290, 301, 309, 489, 491
Stammberger, Oblt. Otto "Stotto", 19, 28, 33, 40, 44, 47, 48, 49, 50, 54, 55, 56, 159, 192, 193, 264, 288, 430, 447, 490
Staschen, Lt. Arno, 77, 80, 81, 85
Stein, Lt. Wolf-Dietmar, 306, 335
Steinberg, Uffz. Günther, 162
Steindl, Hptm. Peter-Paul, 33, 44, 46, 59, 103, 168, 173, 207, 393, 418, 491
Steinkamp, Fw. Paul, 404
Steinkühler, Uffz. Werner, 146, 186
Sternberg, Hptm. Horst, 9, 20, 31, 48, 57, 63, 101, 102, 120, 171, 181, 216, 218, 219, 490
Stoll, Oblt. Werner, 235, 241, 276, 283, 288, 353, 400
Stoller, Uffz. Hans-Joachim, 131
Stosberg, Lt. Siegfried, 31
Stratbücker, Obfw. August, 466, 469
Strauhs, Uffz. Karl, 437, 443
Strauss, Uffz. Karl, 360
Streufert, Uffz. Hans, 295, 380
Stumpf, Fw. Walter, 306, 321, 322, 324, 334, 336, 361, 364, 367, 412, 417, 429, 438, 442, 444, 474, 475
Stumpff, Genobst. Hans-Jürgen, 160, 377, 467
Stuppan, Uffz. Alfred, 382, 419
Stutt, Uffz. Rudolf, 22, 37, 173
Suckrow, Ogfr. Günter, 297
Sundermeyer, Uffz. Rolf, 406
Sy, Lt. Siegfried, 235, 361, 364, 367, 376, 392, 410, 419, 421, 438, 450, 457, 458, 461, 467, 468, 471, 477, 490

Sydow, Uffz. Willy, 407
Sziedat, Flg. Friedrich, 357, 360
Tabbat, Uffz. Adolf, 253, 447
Talkenberg, Uffz. Manfred, 210, 252
Tank, Kurt, 296, 376, 388
Taubert, Fw. Helmut, 306, 361
Taufmann, Uffz. Wolfgang, 18
Tebbe, Gefr. Willi, 306, 333
Teichmann, Gefr. Alfred, 182, 205
Teichmann, Uffz. Werner, 260
Teilken, Obfw. Heinrich, 300, 370
Tepperis, Uffz. Walter, 366, 414
Thielmann, Uffz. Hans-Joachim, 113, 181
Thiem, Fw. Fritz, 235
Thiemann, Fw. Heinz, 310
Thiessen, Lt. Hermann, 31
Thoss, Uffz. Gerhard, 407
Thost, Ufz. Paul, 229
Thran, Uffz. Hans, 315
Thuy, Gefr. Ernst, 400, 450
Tippe, Fw. Erhard, 260, 276, 278, 279, 280
Todt, Lt. Ernst, 40, 88, 93, 130, 156
Törpisch, Lt. Bernhard, 172, 186
Trapp, Fw. Lt. 87, 61, 188
Trautloft, Obstlt. Hannes, 29, 384
Trautvetter, Gefr. Horst, 400
Triebnig, Lt. Otto, 37, 125
Tyczka, Gefr. Gerhard, 207, 245
Ubben, Maj. Kurt, 249
Ullerich, Uffz. Kurt, 420
Ullmann, Gefr. Hellmuth, 143, 181
Ullrich, Fw. Walter, 37, 70
Ungar, Obfw. Fritz, 368, 399, 438, 461, 465, 472, 474, 481
Ursprung, Uffz. Otto, 264, 334
Vanderveerd, Fw. Franz, 179, 218, 369
Vanderveerd, Ofhr. Heinrich, 182, 370, 434
Van Hooven, Uffz. Aloysius, 407
Vavken, Lt. Kurt, 159, 193, 197
Venners, Uffz., 423
Vieck, Obst., 7, 113, 126, 144, 150, 160, 190
Vieweg, Lt. Alfred, 426, 459
Vogel, Ogfr. Bodo, 400, 407
Vogel, Uffz. Richard, 169, 234, 317
Vogelbacher, Fw. Peter, 306
Vogt, Oblt. Gerhard, 22, 104, 128, 148, 150, 159, 181, 204, 207, 249, 253, 270, 278, 285, 286, 289, 290, 298, 306, 321, 322, 328, 335, 337, 352, 355, 372, 378, 379, 395, 396, 408, 417, 419, 422, 490
Vohwinkel, Uffz. Paul, 113
Voigt, Uffz. Heinz, 159, 162, 198, 239
Völmle, Lt. Dieter, 125, 304, 336, 383
Wagner, Uffz. Alfred, 327
Wagner, Lt. Hans-Friedrich, 378
Wagner, Ogfr. Karl-Heinz, 383
Waldherr, Uffz. Rudolf, 272
Walter, Uffz. Hans-Georg, 207, 361, 392
Walter, Fw. Helmut, 455, 473
Walter, Ogfr. Richard, 383, 435
Walter, Uffz. Rudolf, 306
Wälter, Uffz. Heinrich, 21
Warthemann, Uffz. Günter, 400, 449
Waschke, Uffz. Max, 455
Weber, Fw. Otto, 445
Weczera, Obfw. Paul, 386, 417
Wedekind, Oblt. Walter, 306, 322
Wefes, Obfw. Heinrich, 61
Wehring, Uffz. Franz, 382
Weide, Lt. Herbert, 159, 237, 239
Weigl, Uffz. Otto, 453
Weiss, Uffz. Franz, 397, 402, 431
Weiss, Uffz. Karl, 23, 130, 235, 239
Weiss, Hptm. Robert, 280, 281, 311, 395, 398, 399, 400, 428
Wendl, Uffz. Josef, 264, 304
Wendler, Ofhr. Klaus, 423
Wentzel, Gefr. Lothar, 357
Wenzel, Lt. Kurt-Erich, 16
Wering, Uffz. Franz, 390
Wermbter, Lt. Hans-Joachim, 132
Werner, Fw. Hans-Joachim, 406
Westedt, Fw. Gustav, 431
Westermair, Lt. Alois, 86
Westhauser, Uffz. Albert, 113
Weyrich, Fw. Rudolf "Rudy", 131, 183, 184
Wiedemann, Lt., 310
Wiegand, Lt. Gerd, 105, 128, 148, 151, 153, 154, 156, 161, 162, 164, 165, 168, 171, 175, 176, 186, 190, 191, 192, 196, 198, 202, 203, 208, 211, 212, 219, 225, 227, 228, 235, 273
Wiese, Lt. Willi, 426, 449
Wilck, Fw. Otto, 455, 469
Willi, Ofhr. Karl, 352
Willand, Uffz. Karl, 223, 240
Willius, Oblt. Karl "Charlie", 13, 76, 78, 81, 83, 127, 140, 145, 151, 178, 184, 206, 209, 218, 221, 224, 230, 231, 233, 234, 237, 238, 490
Winkel, Fhj.-Fw. Kurt, 231
Winter, Uffz. Hans-Werner, 223, 260, 267

Winter, Uffz. Werner, 253, 274
Wirth, Fhj.-Fw. Hellmuth, 197
Wirth, Lt. Helmut, 338, 390, 429, 442
Wirtz, Uffz. Helmuth, 400
Wissel, Uffz. Friedrich, 299, 386
Wodarczyk, Uffz. Heinz, 223, 262, 266, 267, 273, 277, 403, 407
Wöge, Uffz., 26, 92, 94
Wölfert, Lt. Hans, 131, 169, 170
Wölke, Fhr. Burghardt, 131, 167, 218
Wollnitz, Hptm. Bernhard, 261, 436
Worster, Uffz. Friedrich, 420
Worthmann, Uffz. Hans, 264, 280
Wühl, Stabsfw., 182
Wülfken, Fw. Harald, 411, 424
Wunschelmeyer, Oblt. Kurt, 218
Wurmheller, Hptm. Josef, 268, 280, 285
Würtz, Fw. Wilhelm, 47
Wurzer, Uffz., 291
Wüst, Uffz. Wilhelm, 264, 302
Wyrich, Uffz. Heinz, 150, 166, 191, 263
Zandanell, Uffz. Erich, 131, 133
Zech, Obfw. Werner, 404, 445, 465
Zedler, Lt. Heinz, 264, 296
Zeichert, Uffz., 223
Zeidler, Uffz. Karl, 407, 438
Zeller, Fhj.-Fw. Joachim, 270, 276, 287, 356, 447
Zenker, Ogfr. Heinrich, 99
Zeschke, Fw.Karl-Heinz, 138, 159, 251, 282, 295, 326
Zessin, Uffz. E-G., 465
Zester, Obfw. Willi, 440, 441, 465
Zilling, Ofhr. Günter, 310
Zimmermann, Fhj.-Fw. Hans, 268, 280
Zink, Hptm. Filbert, 16, 22, 37, 70, 71, 73, 81, 490
Zippel, Fhr. Kurt, 223, 297
Zirngibl, Obfw. Josef, 74, 130, 204, 222, 283
Zogboom, Ogfr. Rudolf, 428
Zubiako, Uffz. Edwin, 276, 390
Zutz, Uffz. Hans-Joachim, 375

Allied

Aldecoa, Lt. Manuel, 178
Archer, S/L P.L.I., 102
Armstrong, S/L Hugo, 16, 25
Austin, Capt. James, 333
Bader, W/C Douglas, 103
Baldwin, F/O J. R., 16
Beckham, Maj. Walter, 165, 202
Bedkowski, F/S, 310
Beyer, Lt. William R., 350, 351
Birksted, Maj. Kaj, 135
Bisher, Lt. Harry, 225
Blakeslee, LCol. Don, 197
Blatchford, W/C Peter "Cowboy", 52
Broadhurst, Air Vice-Marshal Harry, 195
Brooks, Lt. George, 320
Burford, Lt. Ed, 138
Carpenter, Maj. George, 216
Chattin, W/O Peter, 343
Christensen, Lt. Fred, 218
Clark, Capt. McCauley, 342
Clayton, P/O Frank, 176
Coffman, Lt. J D, 291
Colloredo-Mansfeld, S/L Franz, 200
Condadzian, P., 323
Coningham, Air Marshal Arthur, 195
Cramer, Lt. Darrell, 343
Cwynar, F/L, 310
Danzey, F/O Ray, 108, 398
DeGenero, Lt. August, 118
Detlev-Simonsen, Lt. J.P., 420
Doolittle, LGen. James "Jimmy", 195, 217, 226, 257
Downing, Maj. Harry, 446
Due, F/S Richard, 46
Eisenhower, Gen. Dwight D. "Ike", 195, 235, 256
Fairbanks, S/L D.C. "Foob", 431, 434, 436
Gaston, Lt. Jack, 380
Gaze, S/L Tony, 150, 423
Gentile, Capt. Don, 222
Gerard, Capt. Francis, 445
Godefroy, P/O Hugh, 10, 11
Godfrey, Lt. John, 187, 188
Gorbachevsky, Capt. Aleksander, 94
Grant, S/L F. E., 151
Hall, F/O Bev, 398
Hall, Lt. Robert, 254
Harling, F/L David, 410, 414
Hesselyn, F/L R. B., 161
Hiro, Major Edward, 352
Horbaczewski, S/L Eugeniusz, 310, 327
Hunter, MGen. Frank "Monk", 145
Ingle, W/C Alex, 154
Ista, Lt. Leroy, 174
Jankowski, W/O, 310
Jasper, Lt. Paul, 284
Johnson, W/C J. E. "Johnnie", 27, 41, 63, 102, 112, 118, 132, 143, 151, 252, 332, 410, 412

Johnson, Lt. Robert S., 99, 111, 129, 165, 184, 188
Kempner, MGen. William, 145
Kingaby, S/L Don, 16
Khoroshkov, Sub-Lt. A. P., 91
Kostenko, Gen.-Maj. F. A., 68
MacDonald, F/L Harry, 108, 122
Mackie, S/L Evan "Rosie", 441
Malmstrom, LCol. Einar, 232
Matte, Lt. Joe, 329
McCollom, Maj. Loren, 135
McIntyre, Capt. Bruce, 352
McNair, S/L Robert "Buck", 103, 161
Mehre, Maj. Helge, 113
Milne, W/C Richard, 16, 34, 37
Montgomery, Field Marshal Bernard, 292, 449, 476
Montgomery, LCol. Robert, 210, 211
Moreau, S/L, 10
Mouchotte, Cdt. René, 144
Musgrave, F/O B. L., 21
Nankivell, F/L P., 25
Neeck, Lt. Herman, 254
Nieland, Lt. Elmer, 446
Nowosielski, F/O, 310
Olds, Maj. Robin, 447
O'Neill, Lt. Bob, 328
Palmer, Lt. R.A.M., 391
Pascoe, Capt. H. T., 365
Patton, Gen. George, 309, 311, 313, 339
Peterson, Col. Arman, 113
Pickard, G/C Charles, 213
Pisanos, Lt. Steve, 188
Rankin, W/C James "Jamie", 10
Ruse, P/O Jim, 480
Schilling, Maj. David, 165
Schloesing, Cdt., 27, 335
Schonenberg, Lt. Herman, 343
Scott, S/L Desmond, 109
Seelos, Lt. Robert, 43
Spaatz, Gen. Carl "Tooey", 256
Stafford, P/O Jack, 398
Stern, Lt., John, 366
Swistun, P/O, 310
Thwaites, Lt. David, 262
Vanden Heuvel, Lt. George, 396
Vassiliades, F/L B. M., 441
Weaver, P/O Claude, 204
Webb, Capt. Roy E., 351
Webster, Lt. Lee, 320
Yeager, Lt. Charles "Chuck", 365, 366
Zemke, Col. Hubert "Hub", 99, 138, 147, 195

Air Units

German
NB: JG 26 appears throughout the book, and is
therefore not indexed specifically.

Luftflotte 1, 65, 91, 92
Luftflotte 3, 7, 15, 30, 48, 52, 96, 117, 131, 145,
148, 160, 173, 204, 211, 223, 224, 235, 239, 251,
256, 258, 264, 265, 269, 271, 273, 296, 316, 324,
328, 344, 347, 349, 351, 354
Luftflotte 6, 81, 84
Luftflotte Reich, 160, 190, 197, 204, 211, 214, 218,
223, 224, 235, 239, 249, 250, 251, 267, 270, 273,
345, 351, 354, 356, 364, 369, 373, 374, 377, 380,
463
Luftwaffen Befehlshaber Mitte, 109, 131
LwKdo Reich, 364, 467
LwKdo West, 354, 355, 356, 428, 446
Flakkorps III, 282, 328
Fliegerkorps II, 265, 267, 270, 271, 272, 273, 274,
281
Fliegerkorps IX, 273
Fliegerkorps IX (Jagd), 451
Jagdkorps I, 145, 160, 214, 215, 226, 360, 377, 382
Jagdkorps II, 160, 265, 273, 278, 281, 282, 296,
298, 299, 300, 301, 302, 304, 305, 307, 308, 309,
311, 313, 314, 315, 316, 317, 318, 319, 320, 321,
322, 323, 324, 325, 326, 328, 329, 331, 332, 333,
334, 335, 336, 337, 338, 339, 344, 345, 347, 349,
352, 355, 356, 357, 359, 360, 361, 362, 364, 367,
369, 370, 372, 373, 374, 375, 377, 378, 379, 380,
382, 383, 384, 385, 386, 390, 394, 395, 397, 399,
419, 424, 427
3rd Flakdivision, 288
14th Fliegerdivision, 424, 430, 433, 440, 442, 443,
447, 451, 452, 456, 457, 462, 467
3rd Jagddivision, 357, 359, 379, 382, 399, 400, 418,
422
4th Jagddivision, 160
5th Jagddivision, 265, 267, 270, 271, 272, 273, 274,
285, 286, 289, 292, 295, 296, 297, 298, 299
Jafü 2, 7, 10, 13, 26, 27, 28, 29, 30, 31, 33, 34, 35,
41, 46, 55, 59, 60, 61, 62, 63, 97, 101, 109, 110,
112, 114, 116, 117, 118, 121, 122, 124, 125, 127,
128, 136, 137, 141, 143, 144, 145, 147, 148, 150,
152, 155, 156, 157, 158, 160, 161, 162, 163, 174,
179, 181, 185
Jafü 3, 7, 13, 19, 28, 30, 34, 35, 37, 42, 46, 59, 63,

101, 109, 110, 112, 114, 116, 125, 128, 134, 141,
144, 145, 147, 148, 152, 155, 156, 157, 160, 161,
179, 181, 183, 185, 187, 189, 196, 204, 206, 210
Jafü 4, 181, 183, 185, 186, 187, 190, 192, 199, 200,
204, 209, 211, 212, 218, 224, 226, 227, 230, 231,
234, 239, 245, 253, 256, 257, 259, 260, 261, 264,
274, 282, 289
Jafü 5, 181, 183, 190, 192, 199, 209, 211, 231, 234,
239, 256, 260, 261, 274, 276, 277, 278, 282, 289
Jafü Brittany, 7, 9, 26, 51, 63, 112, 114, 181, 192,
259, 260, 261, 274, 279, 282
Jafü German Bight, 119, 125, 131
Jafü Holland-Ruhr, 13, 37, 54, 61, 104, 106, 116,
119, 121, 122, 125, 127, 131, 134, 136, 144, 145,
160, 163, 166, 167, 181
EJG 1, 465
III/EJG 2, 445
ErprKdo 25, 172
Flüg 1, 407
JG 1, 37, 39, 41, 57, 61, 62, 116, 124, 129, 142,
164, 166, 204, 207, 210, 223, 227, 270, 312, 316,
319
I/JG 1, 83, 98, 113, 136, 164, 167, 314
2/JG 1, 46
II/JG 1, 33, 42, 43, 47, 52, 54, 59, 60, 62, 102, 103,
104, 110, 112, 117, 121, 135, 137, 215, 283, 309,
329, 397
III/JG 1, 99, 104, 121, 139, 142, 166, 185, 314,
315, 393
JG 2, 7, 8, 15, 16, 17, 28, 29, 33, 39, 42, 46, 47, 51,
56, 63, 111, 112, 113, 114, 129, 130, 134, 148,
149, 158, 167, 169, 178, 179, 183, 184, 191, 196,
202, 204, 207, 209, 210, 213, 224, 231, 235, 239,
240, 241, 247, 249, 253, 256, 258, 261, 265, 266,
267, 268, 295, 303, 308, 312, 338, 344, 360, 364,
369, 372, 373, 383, 386, 418
I/JG 2, 20, 23, 25, 29, 42, 43, 47, 59, 101, 109,
111, 117, 144, 157, 267, 326, 327, 387
2/JG 2, 21
II/JG 2, 7, 47, 98, 110, 111, 114, 115, 117, 120,
128, 131, 133, 134, 141, 143, 144, 150, 156, 157,
161, 170, 179, 209, 234, 235, 303
III/JG 2, 8, 10, 19, 26, 27, 29, 33, 60, 111, 112,
155, 157, 170, 209, 231, 267, 280, 285, 303, 308,
331
7/JG 2, 19, 26, 27,28
11/JG 2, 12, 249
12/JG 2, 34, 35, 39
10(Jabo)/JG 2, 15, 35
JG 3, 11, 54, 270, 303, 330, 379, 380, 381, 382
I/JG 3, 104, 116, 136, 142, 166, 171, 172, 173,
175, 178, 179, 183, 186, 187, 190, 197
2/JG 3, 54
II/JG 3, 153, 161, 163, 164, 172, 173, 175, 177,
182, 183, 185, 189, 329
III/JG 3, 136, 137, 246, 247, 315, 329
IV(Sturm)/JG 3, 273, 480
JG 4, 379, 386, 470, 472
I/JG 5, 273, 315
10/JG 5, 40
JG 6, 400
II/JG 6, 293, 321, 334, 347
JG 7, 447, 457, 465, 468
JG 11, 41, 47, 62, 116, 121, 124, 125, 129, 204,
227, 270, 303, 475, 476
I/JG 11, 322, 329, 332, 337
II/JG 11, 338, 358
III/JG 11, 273, 355
JG 27, 270, 303, 316, 338, 344, 360, 361, 364, 380,
381, 385, 418, 423, 427, 428, 437, 439, 443, 446,
451, 473
I/JG 27, 8, 30, 34, 35, 37, 46, 47, 56, 59, 60, 97,
98, 131, 379
2/JG 27, 37, 52
3/JG 27, 34, 98, 110, 115, 117, 120, 128, 131
II/JG 27, 12, 379
III/JG 27, 326, 379
IV/JG 27, 446
JG 51, 70, 85, 115, 361
I/JG 51, 230
JG 52, 359
2/JG 52, 33
3/JG 52, 223
JG 53, 159, 238, 270, 338, 344, 418, 424
II/JG 53, 336
JG 54, 9, 11, 33, 39, 65, 67, 86, 89, 97, 294, 340,
341
I/JG 54, 65, 76, 86, 89
2/JG 54, 44, 51, 52, 57, 62, 86
II/JG 54, 29, 66, 68, 70
4/JG 54, 11, 29, 39, 42, 46, 51, 52, 59, 61, 62,
99, 114
III/JG 54, 11, 27, 30, 31, 34, 35, 38, 39, 47, 57,
59, 62, 65, 66, 104, 106, 114, 116, 121, 124, 126,
132, 269, 270, 278, 287, 301, 289, 198, 132
301, 304, 307, 308, 309, 310, 311, 314, 315, 316,
317, 318, 322, 323, 336, 338, 360, 368, 376,
392, 395, 397, 398, 399, 400, 401, 403, 406, 408,
415, 418, 422, 423, 424, 425, 427, 428, 429, 431,
433, 435

7/JG 54, 31, 63
9/JG 54, 368, 399, 404, 405, 428, 429, 435
10/JG 54, 44, 51, 52, 62, 398, 399, 428, 435
11/JG 54, 29, 37, 44, 51, 52, 56, 59, 62, 63, 87,
97, 399, 402, 404, 406, 407, 428, 429, 435
12/JG 54, 44, 47, 51, 52, 57, 62, 399, 404, 407,
426, 427, 428, 429
IV/JG 54, 62, 114, 130, 159, 379, 428, 437
10(Jabo)/JG 54, 29, 30, 35, 38, 39, 41, 45
JG 76, 321, 334, 344
III/JG 76, 321, 334
JG 77, 12, 37, 306, 379
I/JG 77, 12
JG 104, 406
JG 105, 42
JG 300, 372, 425, 431
JG Bongart, 273
JGr 50, 172
JGr Ost, 33, 70, 159, 207
3/JGr Ost, 37
JGr Süd, 306
JV 44, 359, 364
KG 4, 264, 301
KG 30, 451
III/KG 76, 447
Kdo Nowotny, 362, 374
I(Jagd)/LG 2, 385
NAGr 6, 469
2/NAGr 13, 29
IV/NJG 1, 337
NSGr 20, 435, 451
SamGr West, 280
SG 4, 267
III/SG 4, 270, 273
SG 151, 473
SKG 10, 45, 63, 97, 264, 301
I/SKG 10, 273
14/SKG 10, 45
StG 77, 338
ZG 1, 273
II/ZG 26, 334
ZG 76, 423, 426

RAF
No. 2 Group, 7, 39, 42, 46, 47, 48, 63, 98, 102, 103,
104, 118, 121, 124, 126, 157, 159, 161, 177, 202
No. 8 (Pathfinder) Group, 391
No. 10 Group, 118, 121, 122
No. 12 Group, 52, 121
No. 124 Wing, 154
No. 125 Wing, 186, 197, 200, 303, 439
No. 127 Airfield, 132
No. 132 Wing, 143, 151, 158, 161, 170, 186, 332,
410
No. 132 Wing, 186
No. 144 Wing, 252
Biggin Hill Wing, 16, 25, 34, 37, 53, 144
Digby Wing, 173
Hawkinge Wing, 169
Hornchurch Wing, 22, 103, 112, 113, 168
Kenley Wing, 23, 31, 36, 41, 42, 53, 54, 63, 97,
101, 102, 103, 108, 112, 113, 115, 118, 132
North Weald Wing, 24, 28, 45, 102, 113, 155, 186
Northolt Wing, 22, 23, 42, 53, 63, 107, 115, 200
Spitfire IX Wing, 126

Allied Squadrons
No. 1, 101, 326
No. 2, 204, 280
No. 3, 113, 162, 226, 441, 469
No. 4, 14
No. 19, 116, 174, 288, 322, 329, 352
No. 21, 22, 29, 48
No. 33, 452, 463
No. 41, 49, 52, 343, 423, 428, 434
No. 56, 47, 362, 386, 441, 449, 453
No. 64, 20, 38
No. 65, 99, 288, 309, 349
No. 66, 128, 150, 203
No. 80, 441, 449, 461, 465
No. 91, 16, 38, 101, 155, 156
No. 105, 391
No. 107, 118
No. 122, 16, 31, 154, 174, 307, 308, 424
No. 124, 29, 212
No. 129, 131, 158, 268, 356
No. 130, 439, 453
No. 131, 151, 314
No. 132, 167, 200
No. 137, 21, 355
No. 165, 130, 150
No. 168, 20, 152, 270, 357
No. 174, 213
No. 175, 154
No. 182, 141, 372
No. 183, 326
No. 198, 116, 162, 163, 212, 270
No. 207, 314
No. 222, 159, 161, 295, 450
No. 226, 202

No. 239, 120
No. 274, 431, 434, 436
No. 302, 153
No. 303, 107, 115, 137, 158
No. 306, 20, 159
No. 308, 22, 23, 157, 200, 404, 405
No. 310, 244
No. 312, 233, 244
No. 313, 159
No. 315, 48, 310, 326, 429
No. 316, 102, 116
No. 331, 22, 24, 55, 126, 127, 131, 171, 399, 420
No. 332, 16, 118, 133, 171, 228, 314, 420, 423
No. 340, 10, 16, 17, 27, 37, 297
No. 341, 136, 141, 144, 161, 335
No. 349, 196
No. 350, 18, 189, 459, 466
No. 400, 171
No. 401, 179, 204, 230, 299, 301, 330, 360, 467
No. 402, 36, 159, 454, 459
No. 403, 31, 32, 36, 41, 63, 103, 108, 113, 138, 151, 259, 410, 469
No. 405, 391
No. 411, 156, 183, 184, 253, 296, 303, 357, 399
No. 412, 181, 191, 302, 357, 359, 372, 378, 386, 473
No. 414, 153, 172, 281, 286, 297, 307
No. 416, 23, 41, 108, 179, 335, 356, 410, 414
No. 421, 102, 103, 161, 170, 186, 335, 423, 424
No. 430, 282
No. 438, 280, 457
No. 439, 342, 355, 399, 462, 480
No. 441, 252
No. 442, 362, 375
No. 443, 279, 280
No. 453, 104, 133, 300
No. 464, 23
No. 485, 27, 118, 131, 136, 161, 168
No. 486, 108, 398, 420, 435, 469, 473, 475
No. 487, 52
No. 501, 196
No. 540, 52, 239
No. 582, 391
No. 602, 118, 256, 335
No. 609, 15, 16, 18, 24, 26, 28, 31, 35, 38, 45, 184, 196
No. 610, 27, 39, 49
No. 611, 16, 24, 25, 37, 46, 57, 98
No. 616, 202
No. 662, 356
No. 1409 Flight, 176

Soviet Air Force
13th Air Army, 86
14th Air Army, 86
1st GIAK, 68
240th IAD, 92
9th ShAD, 95
29th GIAP, 94
86th GIAP, 91, 92
156th IAP, 91

USAAF
First BD, 163, 164, 166, 168, 173, 174, 175, 190, 208, 214, 217, 247
Second BD, 164, 176, 184, 190, 204, 214, 217, 226, 239
Third BD, 163, 164, 165, 168, 173, 174, 175, 184, 191, 205, 206, 211, 214, 217, 226, 227, 233
1st BW, 56, 57, 100, 124, 132, 134, 148, 151
3rd BW, 57
4th BW, 56, 57, 100, 112, 124, 132, 134, 135, 148, 152
14th CBW, 164
40th CBW, 198, 218, 222
45th CBW, 209, 227, 257
96th CBW, 256
44th BG, 28, 34, 201, 205, 230, 237, 256
91st BG, 56, 214, 215
92nd BG, 124, 128, 148, 173, 198, 210, 222, 230, 249
93rd BG, 34, 40, 235
94th BG, 175, 179, 226
95th BG, 57, 100, 116, 164, 203, 215
96th BG, 168, 176, 193, 209, 222
100th BG, 164, 179, 232
303rd BG, 19, 54, 145, 168, 190
305th BG, 12, 29, 40, 138, 166, 234
306th BG, 29, 43, 198, 211, 218, 222
322nd BG, 60, 200
351st BG, 57, 144, 211, 219
381st BG, 104, 138, 211, 226
384th BG, 104, 110, 215, 276
385th BG, 135
386th BG, 127
387th BG, 159, 221
388th BG, 174, 226
390th BG, 164, 190, 191, 208, 222, 224
392nd BG, 176, 245, 278
394th BG, 429

401st BG, 232, 243, 249, 276
445th BG, 231, 239, 245
446th BG, 208
448th BG, 236
452nd BG, 257, 384
453rd BG, 226, 254
458th BG, 226, 231, 248
466th BG, 254
487th BG, 256
489th BG, 291
492nd BG, 277
4th FG, 7, 13, 18, 34, 45, 47, 61, 110, 117, 124, 125, 128, 129, 134, 137, 152, 173, 187, 188, 197, 200, 214, 216, 219, 222, 224, 267, 327, 349, 384
334th FS, 61
335th FS, 216, 349
336th FS, 222
20th FG, 182, 184, 205, 206, 210, 211, 225
31st FG, 246
36th FG, 376, 392, 428, 434
22nd FS, 376, 428, 434
53rd FS, 299, 392
48th FG, 360
50th FG, 335, 348
81st FS, 348
55th FG, 170, 178, 203, 219, 273, 276, 287, 340, 342, 343
38th FS, 287, 342
338th FS, 343
56th FG, 45, 99, 107, 111, 126, 128, 129, 132, 134, 136, 138, 139, 142, 148, 149, 164, 165, 173, 178, 184, 188, 191, 195, 202, 208, 209, 218, 226, 227, 231, 243, 267, 353, 365, 390
61st FS, 209
78th FG, 45, 57, 59, 100, 107, 113, 117, 118, 128, 129, 137, 167, 168, 169, 170, 179, 182, 188, 203, 211, 217, 218, 231, 239, 241, 248, 262, 272, 275, 365, 419, 420, 446
83rd FS, 218
84th FS, 446
339th FG, 255, 261, 278, 355, 445
503rd FS, 445
352nd FG, 164, 191, 208, 210, 228, 239, 355
487th FS, 355
353rd FG, 134, 135, 136, 138, 165, 166, 173, 174, 178, 190, 198, 201, 216, 227, 237, 256, 274, 353
354th FG, 185, 210, 299, 303, 325, 334
353rd FS, 299
355th FS, 303, 334
355th FG, 164, 168, 175, 184, 205, 237, 247, 251, 260
356th FG, 200, 212, 226, 231, 232, 249, 262, 327
357th FG, 219, 254, 255, 276, 352, 365, 447
363rd FS, 352, 365, 447
358th FG, 196, 210, 301, 327
366th FS, 301
359th FG, 234, 316
368th FS, 316
361st FG, 222, 237, 238, 263, 266, 350, 351, 396
376th FS, 350, 396
362nd FG, 216, 268, 288, 329
378th FS, 329, 330
379th FS, 268
363rd FG, 227, 320
364th FG, 243, 317, 365, 380, 390, 431
383rd FS, 431
384th FS, 317
365th FG, 218, 224, 272, 284, 289, 362, 378, 383
386th FS, 284, 378
388th FS, 362
366th FG, 239, 301, 419, 438, 442
389th FS, 438
391st FS, 442
367th FG, 334, 392
368th FG, 234, 245, 276, 284, 315, 367, 384
370th FG, 282, 297, 348
371st FG, 270
373rd FG, 261, 289, 303, 304, 316, 317, 322, 385, 462
410th FS, 317, 462
411th FS, 322, 385
412th FS, 304, 322
404th FG, 253, 308, 330, 348, 387
406th FG, 283, 297, 328, 437, 438, 453
512th FS, 438, 453
513th FS, 328
474th FG, 283, 304, 333, 334, 347, 367, 369, 371, 387
428th FS, 283, 333, 334, 387
429th FS, 333, 334, 371
479th FG, 447
434th FS, 447
153rd LS, 392
363rd TRG, 438

Code Names for Military Operations
Operation Argument, 214, 223
Operation Bodenplatte (Baseplate), 386, 401, 418
Operation Büffel, 70, 75
Operation Carmen, 84

Operation Clarion, 430
Operation Cobra, 305
Operation Grenade, 433
Operation Jericho, 213
Operation Market Garden, 349, 355
Operation Starkey, 132, 148, 153
Operation Varsity, 449
Operation Veritable, 427
Operation Zitadelle, 81, 84, 85

German Army Units
Army Group B, 390
1st Army, 324
7th Army, 324, 328
86th Armeekorps, 300

Allied Army Units
American First Army, 305, 314, 367, 377, 426, 440
American Third Army, 315, 328, 426
American Ninth Army, 433, 442, 449, 467
American 17th A/B Div, 456
American 101st A/B Div, 370
American 2nd ADiv, 352
American 5th ADiv, 445
American 9th ADiv, 440
American 69th IDiv, 470
American 47th FABat, 445
American 320th FABat, 370
American 555th AAABat, 376
British Second Army, 416, 449
British 1st A/B Div, 353, 357
Canadian First Army, 416, 427
Polish 1st Para Brigade, 353